MW00812299

2014 North America

Coins & Prices

A GUIDE TO U.S., CANADIAN AND MEXICAN COINS

23RD EDITION

David C. Harper, Editor

Harry Miller, George Cuhaj & Thomas Michael, Market Analysts

The World's Best-Selling Coin Books

Copyright ©2013 F+W Media, Inc.

All rights reserved. No portion of this publication may be reproduced or transmitted in any form or by any means, electronic or mechanical, including photocopy, recording, or any information storage and retrieval system, without permission in writing from the publisher, except by a reviewer who may quote brief passages in a critical article or review to be printed in a magazine or newspaper, or electronically transmitted on radio, television, or the Internet.

Published by

Krause Publications, a division of F+W Media, Inc.
700 East State Street • Iola, WI 54990-0001
715-445-2214 • 888-457-2873
www.krausebooks.com

To order books or other products call toll-free 1-800-258-0929
or visit us online at www.shopnumismaster.com

ISSN 1935-0562
ISBN-13: 978-1-4402-3799-7
ISBN-10: 1-4402-3799-9

Cover Design by Jana Tappa
Designed by Sandi Carpenter
Edited by George Cuhaj

Printed in the United States of America

Contents

1

"A Small Beginning"
The U.S. Mint grew from a modest start

By Robert R. Van Ryzin

It was a "small beginning" but a significant one. In July 1792, a site for the new U.S. Mint not yet having been secured, 1,500 silver half dismes were struck on a small screw press nestled in the cellar of a Philadelphia building owned by sawmaker John Harper. Though some have since categorized these early emissions of the fledgling U.S. Mint as patterns, it is clear that first President George Washington – who is said to have deposited the silver from which the coins were struck – considered this small batch of half dismes the first official U.S. coins.

It is true that this limited coinage, the first since passage of the act establishing the Mint on April 2, 1792, pales by comparison to modern U.S. Mint presses. Today's machines can churn out up to 750 coins a minute, striking as many as four coins at a time and boasting yearly mintages in the billions. But it is also true that these first small pieces – struck from silver and stamped with a plump Liberty on the obverse and a scrawny eagle in flight on the reverse – have tremendous historical importance.

For within what Washington would declare in his 1792 address to Congress as a "small beginning" were the seeds of a monetary system that has lasted more than 200 years and has become the study and admiration of many.

Before the U.S. Mint

Collectors today can trace much of the nation's development and learn of its struggles and growth through its coinage: from a cumbersome system first proposed by Robert Morris, a Revolutionary War financier and first superintendent of finance, to the refinements tendered by Thomas Jefferson and Alexander Hamilton, which firmly placed the nation on an easily understood decimal system of coinage.

At first there was little coinage in circulation, except for foreign coins that arrived through trade or in the purses of the first settlers. Despite a dire need for coinage in the Colonies, Great Britain considered it a royal right and granted franchises sparingly. Much of the Colonial economy, therefore, revolved around barter, with food staples, crops, and goods serving as currency. Indian wampum or bead money also was used, first in the fur trade and later as a form of money for Colonial use.

Copper pieces were produced around 1616 for the Sommer Islands (now Bermuda), but coinage within the American Colonies apparently didn't begin until 1652, when John Hull struck silver threepence, sixpence and shillings under authority of the General Court of Massachusetts. This coinage continued, with design changes (willow, oak and pine trees), through 1682. Most of the coins were dated 1652, apparently to avoid problems with England.

In 1658 Cecil Calvert, second Lord Baltimore, commissioned coins to be struck in England for use in Maryland. Other authorized and unauthorized coinages – including those of Mark Newby, John Holt, William Wood, and Dr. Samuel Higley – all became part of the landscape of circulating coins. In the 1780s this hodgepodge of coinage was augmented by influxes of counterfeit British halfpenny coins and various state coinages.

In terms of the latter, the Articles of Confederation had granted individual states the right to produce copper coins. Many states found this to be appealing, and merchants in the mid-1780s traded copper coins of Vermont, Connecticut, Massachusetts, New Jersey, and New York. Not all were legal issues; various entrepreneurs used this as an invitation to strike imitation state coppers and British halfpence. Mutilated and worn foreign coins also circulated in abundance. Included among these were coins of Portugal, Great Britain and France, with the large majority of the silver arriving from Spain.

The accounting system used by the states was derived from the British system of pounds, shillings and pence. Each state was allowed to set its own rates at which foreign gold and silver coins would trade in relation to the British pound.

In 1782 Robert Morris, newly named superintendent of finance, was appointed to head a committee to determine the values and weights of the gold and silver coins in circulation. Asked simply to draw up a table of values, Morris took the opportunity to propose the establishment of a federal mint. In his Jan. 15, 1782, report (largely prepared by his assistant, Gouverneur Morris), Morris noted that the exchange rates between the states were complicated.

He observed that a farmer in New Hampshire would be hard-pressed if asked to determine the value of a bushel of wheat in South Carolina. Morris recorded that an amount of wheat worth four shillings in his home state of New Hampshire would be worth 21 shillings and eightpence under the accounting system used in South Carolina.

Robert Morris devised a complicated plan for a national coinage based on a common denominator of 1,440.

Morris claimed these difficulties plagued not only farmers, but that "they are perplexing to most Men and troublesome to all." Morris further pressed for the adoption of an American coin to solve the problems of the need for small change and debased foreign coinages in circulation.

In essence, what he was advocating was a monometallic system based on silver. He said that gold and silver had fluctuated throughout history. Because these fluctuations resulted in the more valuable metal leaving the country, any nation that adopted a bimetallic coinage was doomed to have its gold or silver coins disappear from circulation.

Gouverneur Morris calculated the rate at which the Spanish dollar traded to the British pound in the various states. Leaving out South Carolina, because it threw off his calculations, Gouverneur Morris arrived at a common denominator of 1,440. Robert Morris, therefore, recommended a unit of value of 1/1,440, equivalent to a quarter grain of silver. He suggested the striking of a silver 100-unit coin, or cent; a silver 500-unit coin, or quint; a silver 1,000-unit coin, or mark; and two copper coins, one of eight units and the other of five units.

On Feb. 21, 1782, the Grand Committee of Congress approved the proposal and directed Morris to press forward and report with a plan to establish a mint. Morris had already done so. Apparently feeling confident that Congress would like his coinage ideas, Morris (as shown by his diary) began efforts at the physical establishment prior to his January 1782 report. He had already engaged Benjamin Dudley to acquire necessary equipment for the mint and hoped to have sample coins available to submit with his original report to Congress.

Things went awry, however.

By Dec. 12, 1782, 10 months after Congress had approved his plan, Morris still could not show any samples of his coins. He was forced, ironically, to suggest that Congress draw up a table of rates for foreign coins to be used until his report was ready. It was not until April 2, 1783, that Morris was able to note in his diary that the first of his pattern coins were being struck.

"I sent for Mr. Dudley who delivered me a piece of Silver Coin," he wrote, "being the first that has been struck as an American Coin."

He also recorded that he had urged Dudley to go ahead with production of the silver patterns.

It wasn't until April 23, 1783, that Morris was able to send his Nova Constellatio patterns to Congress and suggest that he was ready to report on establishing a mint. Apparently nothing came of Morris' efforts. Several committees looked into the matter, but nothing was accomplished. Dudley was eventually discharged as Morris' hopes dimmed.

Thomas Jefferson was the next to offer a major plan. Jefferson liked the idea of a decimal system of coinage, but disliked Morris' basic unit of value. As chairman of the Currency Committee, Jefferson reviewed Morris' plan and formulated his own ideas.

To test public reaction, Jefferson gave his "Notes on Coinage" to The Providence Gazette, and Country Journal, which published his plan in its July 24, 1784, issue. Jefferson disagreed with Morris' suggestion for a 1/1,440 unit of value and instead proposed a decimal coinage based on the dollar, with the lowest unit of account being the mil, or 1/1,000.

"The most easy ratio of multiplication and division is that by ten," Jefferson wrote. "Every one knows the facility of Decimal Arithmetic."

Jefferson argued that although Morris' unit would have eliminated the unwanted fraction that occurred when merchants converted British farthings to dollars, this was of little significance. After all, the original idea of establishing a mint was to get rid of foreign currencies.

Morris' unit, Jefferson said, was too cumbersome for use in normal business transactions. According to Jefferson, under Morris' plan a horse valued at 80 Spanish dollars would require a notation of six figures and would be shown as 115,200 units.

Jefferson' coinage plan suggested the striking of a dollar, or unit; half dollar, or five-tenths; a double tenth, or fifth of a dollar, equivalent to a pistereen; a tenth, equivalent to a Spanish bit; and a one-fifth copper coin, relating to the British farthing. He also wanted a gold coin of $10, corresponding to the British double guinea; and a copper one-hundredth coin, relating to the British halfpence.

In reference to his coinage denominations, Jefferson said, it was important that the coins "coincide in value with some of the known coins so nearly, that the people may by quick reference in the mind, estimate their value."

Thomas Jefferson proposed that the United States adopt a decimal system of coinage.

More than a year, however, passed without any further action on his plan or that proposed by Morris. In a letter to William Grayson, a member of the Continental Congress, Washington expressed concern for the establishment of a national coinage system, terming it "indispensably necessary." Washington also complained of the coinage in circulation: "A man must travel with a pair of scales in his pocket, or run the risk of receiving gold at one-fourth less than it counts."

A plan at last

On May 13, 1785, the 13-member Grand Committee, to whom Jefferson's plan had been submitted, filed its report, generally favoring Jefferson's coinage system. The committee did, however, make slight alterations, including the elimination of the gold $10 coin, the addition of a gold $5 coin, and the dropping of Jefferson's double tenth, which it replaced with a quarter dollar. The committee also added a coin equal to 1/200th of a dollar (half cent). On July 6, 1785, Congress unanimously approved the Grand Committee's plan. It failed, however, to set a standard weight for the silver dollar or to order plans drawn up for a mint.

These two factors led to new proposals.

On April 8, 1786, the Board of Treasury, which had been reinstated after Morris' resignation as superintendent of finance two years prior, tendered three distinct coinage proposals based on varying weights and bimetallic ratios for the silver dollar. The first of these three plans (the one passed by Congress on Aug. 8, 1786) required the silver dollar to contain 375.64 grains of pure silver. The board's proposal varied from earlier coinage plans in that it advocated a higher bimetallic ratio of 15.256-to-1 and differing charges to depositors for coining of gold and silver. It called for minting of gold $5 and $10 coins, and silver denominations of the dime, double dime, half dollar, and dollar. In copper were a cent and half cent. The proposal came during the peak of state coinages and influxes of debased coppers, which, as the board reported, were being "Imported into or manufactured in the Several States."

Concerned over the need to control state coinages and foreign coppers, the board suggested that, within nine months of passage of its proposal, the legal-tender status of all foreign coppers be repealed and that values be set at which the state coppers would circulate. The board obviously expected immediate action and ordered a supply of copper that was being stored in Boston to be brought to New York in the hope that it might soon be coined. Their hopes, however, rested on the positive and quick action of Congress, something that hadn't occurred with the other proposals and would not occur this time.

Opposition to the mint was beginning to surface. Several members of Congress expressed their belief that the supply of foreign gold and silver coins in circulation was sufficient to preclude any need for a mint. They also argued that the problem with debased coppers could be solved by contracting with private individuals to strike the nation's cents and half cents.

Several proposals were offered for a contract coinage. On April 21, 1787, the board accepted a proposal by James Jarvis to strike 300 tons of copper coin at the federal standard. Jarvis, however, delivered slightly less than 9,000 pounds of his contract. The contract was voided the following year for his failure to meet scheduled delivery times, but helped to delay further action on a mint. Concerted action on a coinage system and a mint would wait until the formation of the new government.

Alexander Hamilton, named in September 1789 to head the new Treasury, offered three different methods by which the new nation could achieve economic stability, including the funding of the national debt, establishment of the Bank of North America, and the founding of the U.S. Mint. On Jan. 21, 1791, Hamilton submitted to Congress a "Report on the Establishment of a Mint." It was compiled through his study of European economic theories and the earlier works of Morris and Jefferson, along with the 1786 report of the Board of Treasury.

Hamilton agreed with Jefferson that the dollar seemed to be best suited to serve as the basic unit, but believed it necessary to establish a proper weight and fineness for the new coin. To do so, Hamilton had several Spanish coins assayed to determine the fine weight of the Spanish dollar. He also watched the rate at which Spanish dollars traded for fine gold (24 3/4 grains per dollar) on the world market.

From his assays and observations he determined that the Spanish dollar contained 371 grains of silver. He then multiplied 24 3/4 by 15 (the gold value of silver times his suggested bimetallic ratio) and arrived at 371 1/4 as the proper fine silver weight for the new silver dollar.

In regard to his findings, Hamilton admitted that Morris had made similar assays and had arrived at a weight of 373 grains for the Spanish dollar. Hamilton attributed the discrepancy to the differing equipment used in making the assays. He failed, however, to observe that silver coins were traded in the world market at actual weight rather than the weight at time of issue. The Spanish dollar contained 376 grains of pure silver when new, 4 3/4 grains more than Hamilton's proposed silver dollar.

Hamilton also wanted a bimetallic ratio of 15-to-1, in contrast to the Board of Treasury's 15.6-to-1 ratio. Hamilton said his ratio was closer to Great Britain's, which would be important for trade, and Holland's, which would be important for repaying loans from that country.

His report suggested the striking of a gold $10; gold dollar; silver dollar; silver tenth, or disme; and copper one-hundredth and half-hundredth. Hamilton felt the last of these, the half cent, was necessary because it would enable merchants to lower their prices, which would help the poor.

Congress passed the act establishing the U.S. Mint in April 1792. It reinstated several coin denominations left out by Hamilton and dropped his gold dollar. In gold, the act authorized at $10 coin, or "eagle"; a $5 coin, or "half eagle"; and a $2.50 coin, or "quarter eagle." In silver were to be a dollar, half dollar, quarter dollar, disme, and half disme, and in copper a cent and half cent.

Though it established a sound system of U.S. coinage, the act failed to address the problem of foreign coins in circulation. It was amended in February 1793 to cancel their legal-tender status within three years of the Mint's opening.

Coinage begins

Coinage totals at the first mint were understandably low. Skilled coiners, assayers and others who could handle the mint's daily operations were in short supply in the United States. Also in want were adequate equipment and supplies of metal for coinage. Much of the former had to be built or imported. Much of the latter was also imported or salvaged from various domestic sources, including previously struck tokens and coins, and scrap metal.

Coinage began in earnest in 1793 with the striking of half cents and cents at the new mint located at Seventh Street between Market and Arch streets in Philadelphia. Silver coinage followed in 1794, with half dimes, half dollars and dollars. Gold coinage did not begin until 1795 with the minting of the first $5 and $10 coins. Silver dimes and quarters and gold $2.50 coins did not appear until 1796.

Production at the first U.S. mint, in Philadelphia, was minuscule by today's standards.

Under the bimetallic system of coinage by which gold and silver served as equal representations of the unit of value, much of the success and failure of the nation's coinage to enter and remain in circulation revolved around the supply and valuation of precious metals. One need only to gain a cursory knowledge of such movements to understand what role precious metals played in development of U.S. coinage. That role, to a large extent, determined why some coins today are rare and why some passed down from generation to generation are still plentiful and of lower value to collectors.

From the Mint's beginning, slight miscalculations in the proper weight for the silver dollar and a proper bimetallic ratio led gold and silver to disappear from circulation. The U.S. silver dollar traded at par with Spanish and Mexican dollars, but because the U.S. coin was lighter, it was doomed to export.

A depositor at the first mint could make a profit at the mint's expense by sending the coins to the West Indies. There they could be traded at par for the heavier Spanish or Mexican eight reales, which were then shipped back to the United States for recoinage. As a result, few early silver dollars entered domestic circulation; most failed to escape the melting pots.

Gold fared no better. Calculations of the bimetallic ratio by which silver traded for gold on the world market were also askew at first and were always subject to fluctuations. Gold coins either disappeared quickly after minting or never entered circulation, languishing in bank vaults. These problems led President Jefferson to halt coinage of the gold $10 and silver dollar.

The gold $10 reappeared in 1838 at a new, lower-weight standard. The silver dollar, not coined for circulation since 1803, returned in 1836 with a limited mintage. Full-scale coinage waited until 1840.

Nor was the coinage of copper an easy matter for the first mint. Severe shortages of the metal led the Mint to explore various avenues of obtaining sufficient supplies for striking cents and half cents.

Witness, for example, the half-cent issues of 1795 and 1797 struck over privately issued tokens of the New York firm of Talbot, Allum & Lee because of a shortage of copper for the federal issue. Rising copper prices and continued shortages forced the Mint to lower the cent's weight from 208 grains to 168 grains in 1795.

By that same year Congress had begun to investigate the Mint. Complaints about high costs and low production had been raised. Suggestions that a contract coinage might be more suitable for the new nation surfaced again, despite bad experiences with previous attempts.

The Mint survived this and another investigation, but the problems of fluctuating metal supplies continued to plague the nation. In 1798, because of the coinage shortage, the legal-tender status of foreign coins was restored. Several more extensions were given during the 1800s, ending with the withdrawal of legal-tender status for Spanish coins in 1857.

In the 1830s great influxes of silver from foreign mints raised the value of gold in relation to silver, which made it necessary for the Mint to lower the standard weight of all gold coins in 1834. It also led to the melting of great numbers of gold coins of the old specifications.

By the 1850s discovery of gold in California had again made silver the dearer metal. All silver quickly disappeared from circulation. Congress reacted in 1853 by lowering the weight of the silver half dime, dime, quarter, and half dollar, hoping to keep silver in circulation. A new gold coin of $20 value was introduced to absorb a great amount of the gold from Western mines.

Not long after, silver was discovered in Nevada. By the mid-1870s the various mines that made up what was known as the Comstock Lode (after its colorful early proprietor, Henry P. Comstock) had hit the mother lode. Large supplies of silver from the Comstock, combined with European demonetization, caused a severe drop in its value, which continued through the close of the 19th century.

It was believed that the introduction of a heavier, 420-grain silver dollar in 1873, known as the Trade dollar, would create a market for much of the Comstock silver, bolster its price, and at the same time wrest control from Great Britain of lucrative trade with the Orient. It didn't. Large numbers of Trade dollars eventually flooded back into the United States, where they were, ironically, accepted only at a discount to the lesser-weight Morgan dollars.

The latter had been introduced in 1878 as a panacea to the severe economic problems following the Civil War. Those who proudly carried the banner of free silver contended that by taking the rich output of the Comstock mines and turning it into silver dollars, a cheaper, more plentiful form of money would become available. In its wake, they believed, would be a much needed economic recovery.

The Free Silver Movement gained its greatest support during the late 19th century when William Jennings Bryan attempted to gain the White House on a plank largely based on restoration of the free and unlimited coinage of the standard 412.5-grain silver dollar. He failed. Silver failed. Shortly thereafter the United States officially adopted a gold standard.

Silver continued to be a primary coinage metal until 1964, when rising prices led the Mint to remove it from the dime and quarter. Mintage of the silver dollar had ended in 1935. The half dollar continued to be coined through 1970 with a 40-percent-silver composition. It, too, was then debased.

Gold coinage ended in 1933 and exists today only in commemorative issues and American Eagle bullion coins with fictive face values. A clad composition of copper and nickel is now the primary coinage metal. Even the cent is no longer all copper; a copper-coated zinc composition has been used since 1982.

Precious-metal supplies were also linked to the opening of additional mints, which served the parent facility in Philadelphia. The impact of gold discoveries in the 1820s in the southern Appalachian Mountains was directly tied to the construction of branch mints in Dahlonega, Ga., and Charlotte, N.C., in 1838. These new mints struck only gold coins. New Orleans also became the site of a branch mint in the same year as Dahlonega and Charlotte. It took in some of the outflow of gold from Southern mines, but also struck silver coins.

Discovery of gold in California in the late 1840s created a gold rush, and from it sprang a great western migration. Private issues of gold coinage, often of debased quality, were prevalent, and the cost of shipping the metal eastward for coinage at Philadelphia was high. A call for an official branch mint was soon heard and heeded in 1852 with the authorization of the San Francisco Mint, which began taking deposits in 1854.

The discovery of silver in the Comstock Lode led to yet another mint. Located only a short distance via Virginia & Truckee Railroad from the fabulous Comstock Lode, the Carson City mint began receiving bullion in early 1870.

Denver, also located in a mineral-rich region, became the site of an assay office in 1863 when the government purchased the Clark, Gruber & Co. private mint. It became a U.S. branch mint in 1906. In addition to the Denver and Philadelphia mints, San Francisco and a facility in West Point, N.Y., continue to serve as U.S. mints, but the others have left behind a rich legacy.

The collector taking a more extended journey into the history of U.S. coinage can find plenty of interesting tales – some as tall as the day is long and others factually based – all of which are part of the rich and ever-changing panoply of U.S. coinage history. There are stories of denominations that failed, great discoveries, great rarities, great collectors, and, for those with an artistic bent, a rich field of pattern coins to be explored and a wealth of much-heralded designs by famous sculptors such as Augustus Saint-Gaudens, Adolph Weinman, James Earle Fraser, and others.

For those who are drawn to the hobby by the allure of age-old relics of days gone by, or by coins handed down through the family, or even by dreams of great wealth, coin collecting has much to offer. The history of the U.S. Mint, with its small but ever so important beginning, is the starting point.

2

The Grading Factor
How to classify a coin's condition

By Arlyn G. Sieber

Grading is one of the most important factors in buying and selling coins as collectibles. Unfortunately, it's also one of the most controversial. Since the early days of coin collecting in the United States, buying through the mail has been a convenient way for collectors to acquire coins. As a result, there has always been a need in numismatics for a concise way to classify the amount of wear on a coin and its condition in general.

A look back

In September 1888, Dr. George Heath, a physician in Monroe, Mich., published a four-page pamphlet titled *The American Numismatist*. Publication of subsequent issues led to the founding of the American Numismatic Association, and *The Numismatist*, as it's known today, is the association's official journal. Heath's first issues were largely devoted to selling world coins from his collection. There were no formal grades listed with the coins and their prices, but the following statement by Heath indicates that condition was a consideration for early collectors:

"The coins are in above average condition," Heath wrote, "and so confident am I that they will give satisfaction, that I agree to refund the money in any unsatisfactory sales on the return of the coins."

As coin collecting became more popular and The Numismatist started accepting paid advertising from others, grading became more formal. The February 1892 issue listed seven "classes" for the condition of coins (from worst to best): mutilated, poor, fair, good, fine, uncirculated, and proof. Through the years, the hobby has struggled with developing a grading system that would be accepted by all and could apply to all coins. The hobby's growth was accompanied by a desire for more grades, or classifications, to more precisely define a coin's condition. The desire for more precision, however, was at odds with the basic concept of grading: to provide a concise method for classifying a coin's condition.

For example, even the conservatively few classifications of 1892 included fudge factors.

"To give flexibility to this classification," *The Numismatist* said, "such modification of fine, good and fair, as 'extremely,' 'very,' 'almost,' etc., are used to express slight variations from the general condition."

The debate over grading continued for decades in *The Numismatist*. A number of articles and letters prodded the ANA to write grading guidelines and endorse them as the association's official standards. Some submitted specific suggestions for terminology and accompanying standards for each grade. But grading remained a process of "instinct" gained through years of collecting or dealing experience.

A formal grading guide in book form finally appeared in 1958, but it was the work of two individuals rather than the ANA. *A Guide to the Grading of United States Coins* by Martin R. Brown and John W. Dunn was a breakthrough in the great grading debate. Now collectors had a reference that gave them specific guidelines for specific coins and could be studied and restudied at home.

The first editions of Brown and Dunn carried text only, no illustrations. For the fourth edition, in 1964, publication was assumed by Whitman Publishing Co. of Racine, Wis., and line drawings were added to illustrate the text.

The fourth edition listed six principal categories for circulated coins (from worst to best): good, very good, fine, very fine, extremely fine, and about uncirculated. But again, the desire for more precise categories were evidenced. In the book's introduction, Brown and Dunn wrote, "Dealers will sometimes advertise coins that are graded G-VG, VG-F, F-VF, VF-XF. Or the description may be ABT. G. or VG plus, etc. This means that the coin in question more than meets minimum standards for the lower grade but is not quite good enough for the higher grade."

When the fifth edition appeared, in 1969, the "New B & D Grading System" was introduced. The six principal categories for circulated coins were still intact, but variances within those categories were now designated by up to four letters: "A," "B," "C" or "D." For example, an EF-A coin was "almost about uncirculated." An EF-B was "normal extra fine" within the B & D standards. EF-C had a "normal extra fine" obverse, but the reverse was "obviously not as nice as obverse due to poor strike or excessive wear." EF-D had a "normal extra fine" reverse but a problem obverse.

But that wasn't the end. Brown and Dunn further listed 29 problem points that could appear on a coin – from No. 1 for an "edge bump" to No. 29 for "attempted re-engraving outside of the Mint." The number could be followed by the letter "O" or "R" to designate whether the problem appeared on the obverse or reverse and a Roman numeral corresponding to a clock face to designate where the problem appears on the obverse or reverse. For example, a coin described as "VG-B-9-O-X" would grade "VG-B"; the "9" designated a "single rim nick"; the "O" indicated the nick was on the obverse; and the "X" indicated it appeared at the 10 o'clock position, or upper left, of the obverse.

The authors' goal was noble – to create the perfect grading system. They again, however, fell victim to the age-old grading-system problem: Precision comes at the expense of brevity. Dealer Kurt Krueger wrote in the January 1976 issue of *The Numismatist*, "Under the new B & D system, the numismatist must contend with a minimum of 43,152 different grading combinations! Accuracy is apparent, but simplicity has been lost." As a result, the "New B & D Grading System" never caught on in the marketplace.

The 1970s saw two important grading guides make their debut. The first was *Photograde* by James F. Ruddy. As the title implies, Ruddy uses photographs instead of line drawings to show how coins look in the various circulated grades. Simplicity is also a virtue of Ruddy's book. Only seven circulated grades are listed (about good, good, very good, fine, very fine, extremely fine, and about uncirculated), and the designations stop there.

In 1977 the longtime call for the ANA to issue grading standards was met with the release of *The Official A.N.A. Grading Standards for United States Coins*. Like Brown and Dunn, the first edition of the ANA grading guide used line drawings to illustrate coins in various states of wear. But instead of using adjectival descriptions, the ANA guide adopted a numerical system for designating grades.

The numerical designations were based on a system used by Dr. William H. Sheldon in his book *Early American Cents*, first published in 1949. He used a scale of 1 to 70 to designate the grades of large cents.

"On this scale," Sheldon wrote, "1 means that the coin is identifiable and not mutilated – no more than that. A 70-coin is one in flawless Mint State, exactly as it left the dies, with perfect mint color and without a blemish or nick." (Sheldon's scale also had its pragmatic side. At the time, a No. 2 large cent was worth about twice a No. 1 coin; a No. 4 was worth about twice a No. 2, and so on up the scale.)

With the first edition of its grading guide, the ANA adopted the 70-point scale for grading all U.S. coins. It designated 10 categories of circulated grades: AG-3, G-4, VG-8, F-12, VF-20, VF-30, EF-40, EF-45, AU-50, and AU-55. The third edition, released in 1987, replaced the line drawings with photographs, and another circulated grade was added: AU-58. A fourth edition was released in 1991.

Grading circulated U.S. coins

Dealers today generally use either the ANA guide or Photograde when grading circulated coins for their inventories. (Brown and Dunn is now out of print.) Many local coin shops sell both books. Advertisers in *Numismatic News*, *Coins* magazine, and *Coin Prices* must indicate which standards they are using in grading their coins. If the standards are not listed, they must conform to ANA standards.

Following are some general guidelines, accompanied by photos, for grading circulated U.S. coins. Grading even circulated pieces can be subjective, particularly when attempting to draw the fine line between, for example, AU-55 and AU-58. Two longtime collectors or dealers can disagree in such a case.

But by studying some combination of the following guidelines, the ANA guide, and Photograde, and by looking at a lot of coins at shops and shows, collectors can gain enough grading knowledge to buy circulated coins confidently from dealers and other collectors. The more you study, the more knowledge and confidence you will gain. When you decide which series of coins you want to collect, focus on the guidelines for that particular series. Read them, reread them, and then refer back to them again and again.

AU-50

AU-50 (about uncirculated): Just a slight trace of wear, result of brief exposure

Indian cent   Lincoln cent

Buffalo nickel   Jefferson nickel

Mercury dime

Standing Liberty quarter

Washington quarter

Walking Liberty half dollar

Morgan dollar

Barber coins

to circulation or light rubbing from mishandling, may be evident on elevated design areas. These imperfections may appear as scratches or dull spots, along with bag marks or edge nicks. At least half of the original mint luster generally is still evident.

XF-40

Indian cent

Lincoln cent

Buffalo nickel

Jefferson nickel

Mercury dime

Standing Liberty quarter

Washington quarter   *Walking Liberty half dollar*

Morgan dollar   *Barber coins*

XF-40 (extremely fine): The coin must show only slight evidence of wear on the highest points of the design, particularly in the hair lines of the portrait on the obverse. The same may be said for the eagle's feathers and wreath leaves on the reverse of most U.S. coins. A trace of mint luster may still show in protected areas of the coin's surface.

VF-20

Indian cent

Lincoln cent

Buffalo nickel

Jefferson nickel

Mercury dime

Standing Liberty quarter

Washington quarter

Walking Liberty half dollar

Morgan dollar

Barber coins

VF-20 (very fine): The coin will show light wear at the fine points in the design, though they may remain sharp overall. Although the details may be slightly smoothed, all lettering and major features must remain sharp.

Indian cent: All letters in "Liberty" are complete but worn. Headdress shows considerable flatness, with flat spots on the tips of the feathers.

Lincoln cent: Hair, cheek, jaw, and bow-tie details will be worn but clearly separated, and wheat stalks on the reverse will be full with no weak spots.

Buffalo nickel: High spots on hair braid and cheek will be flat but show some detail, and a full horn will remain on the buffalo.

Jefferson nickel: Well over half of the major hair detail will remain, and the pillars on Monticello will remain well defined, with the triangular roof partially visible.

Mercury dime: Hair braid will show some detail, and three-quarters of the detail will remain in the feathers. The two diagonal bands on the fasces will show completely but will be worn smooth at the middle, with the vertical lines sharp.

Standing Liberty quarter: Rounded contour of Liberty's right leg will be flattened, as will the high point of the shield.

Washington quarter: There will be considerable wear on the hair curls, with feathers on the right and left of the eagle's breast showing clearly.

Walking Liberty half dollar: All lines of the skirt will show but will be worn on the high points. Over half the feathers on the eagle will show.

Morgan dollar: Two-thirds of the hair lines from the forehead to the ear must show. Ear should be well defined. Feathers on the eagle's breast may be worn smooth.

Barber coins: All seven letters of "Liberty" on the headband must stand out sharply. Head wreath will be well outlined from top to bottom.

F-12

Indian cent

Lincoln cent

Buffalo nickel

Jefferson nickel

Mercury dime

Standing Liberty quarter

Washington quarter

Walking Liberty half dollar

Morgan dollar

Barber coins

F-12 (fine): Coins show evidence of moderate to considerable but generally even wear on all high points, though all elements of the design and lettering remain bold. Where the word "Liberty" appears in a headband, it must be fully visible. On 20th century coins, the rim must be fully raised and sharp.

VG-8

Indian cent

Lincoln cent

Buffalo nickel

Jefferson nickel

Mercury dime

Standing Liberty quarter

Washington quarter

Walking Liberty half dollar

Morgan dollar

Barber coins

VG-8 (very good): The coin will show considerable wear, with most detail points worn nearly smooth. Where the word "Liberty" appears in a headband, at least three letters must show. On 20th century coins, the rim will start to merge with the lettering.

G-4

Indian cent

Lincoln cent

Buffalo nickel

Jefferson nickel

Mercury dime

Standing Liberty quarter

Washington quarter   *Walking Liberty half dollar*

Morgan dollar   *Barber coins*

G-4 (good): Only the basic design remains distinguishable in outline form, with all points of detail worn smooth. The word "Liberty" has disappeared, and the rims are almost merging with the lettering.

About good or fair: The coin will be identifiable by date and mint but otherwise badly worn, with only parts of the lettering showing. Such coins are of value only as fillers in a collection until a better example of the date and mintmark can be obtained. The only exceptions would be rare coins

Collectors have a variety of grading services from which to choose. This set of Arkansas half dollars that appeared in an Early American History Auctions sale used two of the services.

Grading uncirculated U.S. coins

The subjectivity of grading and the trend toward more classifications becomes more acute when venturing into uncirculated, or mint-state, coins. A minute difference between one or two grade points can mean a difference in value of hundreds or even thousands of dollars. In addition, the standards are more difficult to articulate in writing and illustrate through drawings or photographs. Thus, the possibilities for differences of opinion on one or two grade points increase in uncirculated coins.

Back in Dr. George Heath's day and continuing through the 1960s, a coin was either uncirculated or it wasn't. Little distinction was made between uncirculated coins of varying condition, largely because there was little if any difference in value. When *Numismatic News* introduced its value guide in 1962 (the forerunner of today's *Coin Market* section in the *News*), it listed only one grade of uncirculated for Morgan dollars.

But as collectible coins increased in value and buyers of uncirculated coins became more picky, distinctions within uncirculated grade started to surface. In 1975 *Numismatic News* still listed only one uncirculated grade in *Coin Market*, but added this note: "Uncirculated and proof specimens in especially choice condition will also command proportionately higher premiums than these listed."

The first edition of the ANA guide listed two grades of uncirculated, MS-60 and MS-65, in addition to the theoretical but non-existent MS-70 (a flawless coin). MS-60 was described as "typical uncirculated" and MS-65 as "choice uncirculated." *Numismatic News* adopted both designations for *Coin Market*. In 1981, when the second edition of the ANA grading guide was released, MS-67 and MS-63 were added. In 1985 *Numismatic News* started listing six grades of uncirculated for Morgan dollars: MS-60, MS-63, MS-65, MS-65+, and MS-63 prooflike.

Then in 1986, a new entity appeared that changed the nature of grading and trading uncirculated coins ever since. A group of dealers led by David Hall of Newport Beach, Calif., formed the Professional Coin Grading Service. For a fee, collectors could submit a coin through an authorized PCGS dealer and receive a professional opinion of its grade.

The concept was not new; the ANA had operated an authentication service since 1972 and a grading service since 1979. A collector or dealer could submit a coin directly to the service and receive a certificate giving the service's opinion on authenticity and grade. The grading service was the source of near constant debate among dealers and ANA officials. Dealers charged that ANA graders were too young and inexperienced, and that their grading was inconsistent.

Grading stability was a problem throughout the coin business in the early 1980s, not just with the ANA service. Standards among uncirculated grades would tighten during a bear market and loosen during a bull market. As a result, a coin graded MS-65 in a bull market may have commanded only MS-63 during a bear market.

PCGS created several innovations in the grading business in response to these problems:

1. Coins could be submitted through PCGS-authorized dealers only.

2. Each coin would be graded by at least three members of a panel of "top graders," all prominent dealers in the business. (Since then, however, PCGS does not allow its graders to also deal in coins.)

3. After grading, the coin would be encapsulated in an inert, hard-plastic holder with a serial number and the grade indicated on the holder.

4. PCGS-member dealers pledged to make a market in PCGS-graded coins and honor the grades assigned.

5. In one of the most far-reaching moves, PCGS said it would use all 11 increments of uncirculated on the 70-point numerical scale: MS-60, MS-61, MS-62, MS-63, MS-64, MS-65, MS-66, MS-67, MS-68, MS-69, and MS-70.

The evolution of more uncirculated grades had reached another milestone.

Purists bemoaned the entombment of classic coins in the plastic holders and denounced the 11 uncirculated grades as implausible. Nevertheless, PCGS was an immediate commercial success. The plastic holders were nicknamed "slabs," and dealers couldn't get coins through the system fast enough.

In subsequent years, a number of similar services have appeared. Among them, one of the original PCGS "top graders," John Albanese, left PCGS to found the Numismatic Guaranty Corp (NGC). The ANA grading service succumbed to "slab mania" and introduced its own encapsulated product.

There now are numerous other reputable private third-party grading services. PCGS and NGC are the oldest and remain the leaders. In 1990 the ANA sold its grading service to a private company. It operates under the ANACS acronym.

How should a collector approach the buying and grading of uncirculated coins? Collecting uncirculated coins worth thousands of dollars implies a higher level of numismatic expertise by the buyer. Those buyers without that level of expertise should cut their teeth on more inexpensive coins, just as today's experienced collectors did. Inexperienced collectors can start toward that level by studying the guidelines for mint-state coins in the ANA grading guide and looking at lots of coins at shows and shops.

Study the condition and eye appeal of a coin and compare it to other coins of the same series. Then compare prices. Do the more expensive coins look better? If so, why? Start to make your own judgments concerning relationships between condition and value.

According to numismatic legend, a collector walked up to a crusty old dealer at a show one time and asked the dealer to grade a coin the collector had with him. The dealer looked at the coin and said, "I grade it a hundred dollars." Such is the bottom line to coin grading.

Grading U.S. proof coins

Because proof coins are struck by a special process using polished blanks, they receive their own grading designation. A coin does not start out being a proof and then become mint state if it becomes worn. Once a proof coin, always a proof coin.

In the ANA system, proof grades use the same numbers as circulated and uncirculated grades, and the amount of wear on the coin corresponds to those grades. But the number is preceded by the word "proof." For example, Proof-65, Proof-55, Proof-45, and so on. In addition, the ANA says a proof coin with many marks, scratches or other defects should be called an "impaired proof."

Grading world coins

The state of grading non-U.S. issues is similar to U.S. coin grading before Brown and Dunn. There is no detailed, illustrated guide that covers the enormous scope and variety of world coins; collectors and dealers rely on their experience in the field and knowledge of the marketplace.

The *Standard Catalog of World Coins* gives the following guidelines for grading world coins, which apply to the Canadian and Mexican value listings in this book:

In grading world coins, there are two elements to look for: (1) overall wear and (2) loss of design details, such as strands of hair, feathers on eagles, designs on coats of arms, and so on. Grade each coin by the weaker of the two sides. Age, rarity or type of coin should not be considered in grading.

Grade by the amount of overall wear and loss of detail evident in the main design on each side. On coins with a moderately small design element that is prone to early wear, grade by that design alone.

In the marketplace, adjectival grades are still used for Mexican coins. The numerical system for Canadian coins is now commonplace:

Uncirculated, MS-60: No visible signs of wear or handling, even under a 30X microscope. Bag marks may be present.

Almost uncirculated, AU-50: All detail will be visible. There will be wear on only the highest points of the coin. There will often be half or more of the original mint luster present.

Extremely fine, XF-40: About 95 percent of the original detail will be visible. Or, on a coin with a design that has no inner detail to wear down, there will be light wear over nearly the entire coin. If a small design is used as the grading area, about 90 percent of the original detail will be visible. This latter rule stems from the logic that a smaller amount of detail needs to be present because a small area is being used to grade the whole coin.

Very fine, VF-20: About 75 percent of the original detail will be visible. Or, on a coin with no inner detail, there will be moderate wear over the entire coin. Corners of letters and numbers may be weak. A small grading area will have about 60 percent of the original detail.

Fine, F-12: About 50 percent of the original detail will be visible. Or, on a coin with no inner detail, there will be fairly heavy wear over the entire coin. Sides of letters will be weak. A typically uncleaned coin will often appear dirty or dull. A small grading area will have just under 50 percent of the original detail.

Very good, VG-8: About 25 percent of the original detail will be visible. There will be heavy wear on the entire coin.

Good, G-4: Design will be clearly outlined but with substantial wear. Some of the larger detail may be visible. The rim may have a few weak spots of wear.

About good, AG-3: Typically only a silhouette of a large design will be visible. The rim will be worn down into the letters, if any.

Where to write for more information

American Numismatic Association: 818 N. Cascade Ave., Colorado Springs, CO 80903-3279.

Independent Coin Grading Co.: 7901 E. Belleview Ave., Suite 50, Englewood, CO 80111.

Numismatic Guaranty Corp: P.O. Box 4776, Sarasota, FL 34230.

NTC (Numistrust Corp.): 2500 N. Military Trail, Suite 210, Boca Raton, FL 33431.

Professional Coin Grading Service: P.O. Box 9458, Newport Beach, CA 92658.

Sovereign Entities Grading Service: 401 Chestnut St., Suite 103, Chattanooga, TN 37402-4924.

Visit the Krause Publications website
www.numismaster.com

3

Get a Map
How to organize a collection

By David C. Harper

Do you have a jar full of old coins? Did a favorite relative give you a few silver dollars over the years? Or did you just come across something unusual that you set aside?

All three circumstances make good beginnings for collecting coins. It may surprise you, but this is how just about everybody starts in the hobby. It is a rare collector who decides to start down the hobby road without first having come into a few coins one way or another.

What these random groupings lack is organization. It is organization that makes a collection. But think about it another way: Organization is the map that tells you where you can go in coin collecting and how you can get there.

Have you ever been at a large fair or a huge office building and seen the maps that say "you are here"? Did you ever consider that, over time, thousands of other people have stood on the same spot? This is true in numismatics also. Figuratively, you are standing on the same spot on which the writers of this book stood at some point in their lives.

At a fair, the map helps you consider various ways of seeing all the sights. In coin collecting, too, there are different ways to organize a collection. The method you choose helps you see the hobby sights you want to see.

It should be something that suits you. Remember, do what you want to do. See what you want to see. But don't be afraid to make a mistake; there aren't any. Just as one can easily retrace steps at a fair, one can turn around and head in another direction in the coin-collecting hobby. Besides, when you start off for any given point, often you see something along the way that was unplanned but more interesting. That's numismatics.

There are two major ways to organize a collection: by type, and by date and mintmark. These approaches work in basically the same fashion for coins of the

United States, Canada and Mexico. Naturally, there are differences. But to establish the concepts, let's focus first on U.S. coins.

United States

Let's take collecting by type first. Look at your jar of coins, or take the change out of your pocket. You find Abraham Lincoln and the Lincoln Memorial on most cents and four commemorative reverse designs in 2009. You find Thomas Jefferson and his home, Monticello, on most nickels, but special reverse designs were produced in 2004 and 2005 and a new obverse began in 2006. Franklin D. Roosevelt and a torch share the dime. George Washington and an eagle (or since 1999, designs honoring states and the District of Columbia and territories) appear on the quarter. John F. Kennedy and the presidential seal are featured on the half dollar. Sacagawea paired with an eagle or a woman planting and Presidents paired with the Statue of Liberty are on dollars.

Each design is called a "type." If you took one of each and put them in a holder, you would have a type set of recent coins.

With just these six denominations, you can study various metallic compositions. You can evaluate their states of preservation and assign a grade to each. You can learn about the artists who designed the coins, and you can learn of the times in which these designs were created.

As you might have guessed, many different coin types have been used in the United States over the years. You may remember seeing some of them circulating. These designs reflect the hopes and aspirations of people over time. Putting all of them together forms a wonderful numismatic mosaic of American history.

George Washington did not mandate that his image appear on the quarter. Quite the contrary. He would have been horrified. When he was president, he headed off those individuals in Congress who thought the leader of the country should have his image on its coins. Washington said it smacked of monarchy and would have none of it.

Almost a century and a half later, during the bicentennial of Washington's birth in 1932, a nation searching for its roots during troubled economic times decided that it needed his portrait on its coins as a reminder of his great accomplishments and as reassurance that this nation was the same place it had been in more prosperous days.

In its broadest definition, collecting coins by type requires that you obtain an example of every design that was struck by the U.S. Mint since it was founded in 1792. That's a tall order. You would be looking for denominations like the half cent, two-cent piece, three-cent piece, and 20-cent piece, which have not been produced in more than a century. You would be looking for gold coins ranging in face value from $1 to $50 and current bullion coins.

But even more important than odd-sounding denominations or high face values is the question of rarity. Some of the pieces in this multi-century type set are rare and expensive. That's why type collectors often divide the challenge into more digestible units.

Type collecting can be divided into 18th, 19th, 20th and 21st century units. The 21st century set is rapidly growing. Starting type collectors can focus on 20th century coin designs, which are easily obtainable. The fun and satisfaction of putting the 20th century set together then creates the momentum to continue backward in time.

In the process of putting a 20th century type set together, one is also learning how to grade, learning hobby jargon, and discovering how to obtain coins from dealers, the U.S. Mint, and other collectors. All of this knowledge is then refined as the collector increases the challenge to himself.

This book is designed to help. How many dollar types were struck in the 20th century? Turn to the U.S. price-guide section and check it out. We see the Morgan dollar, Peace dollar, Eisenhower dollar, and Anthony dollar. Hobbyists could also add the Ike dollar with the Bicentennial design of 1976 and the silver American Eagle bullion coin struck since 1986. One can also find out their approximate retail prices from the listings.

The beauty of type collecting is that one can choose the most inexpensive example of each type. There is no need to select a 1903-O Morgan when the 1921 will do just as well. With the 20th century type set, hobbyists can dodge some truly big-league prices.

As a collector's hobby confidence grows, he can tailor goals to fit his desires. He can take the road less traveled if that is what suits him. Type sets can be divided by denomination. You can choose more than two centuries of one-cent coins. You can take just obsolete denominations or copper, silver or gold denominations.

You can even collect by size. Perhaps you would like to collect all coin types larger than 30 millimeters or all coins smaller than 20 millimeters. Many find this freedom of choice stimulating.

Type collecting has proven itself to be enduringly popular over the years. It provides a maximum amount of design variety while allowing collectors to set their own level of challenge.

The second popular method of collecting is by date and mintmark. What this means, quite simply, is that a collector picks a given type – Jefferson nickels, for example – and then goes after an example of every year, every mintmark, and every type of manufacture that was used with the Jefferson design.

Looking at this method of collecting brings up the subject of mintmarks. The "U.S. Mint" is about as specific as most non-collectors get in describing the government agency that provides everyday coins. Behind that label are the various production facilities that actually do the work.

In the more than two centuries of U.S. coinage, there have been eight such facilities. Four are still in operation. Those eight in alphabetical order are Carson City, Nev., which used a "CC" mintmark to identify its work; Charlotte, N.C. ("C"); Dahlonega, Ga. ("D"); Denver (also uses a "D," but it opened long after the Dahlonega Mint closed, so there was never any confusion); New Orleans ("O"); Philadelphia (because it was the primary mint, it used no mintmark for much of its history, but currently uses a "P"); San Francisco ("S"); and West Point, N.Y. ("W").

A basic type set of 20th century dollar coins would consist of (from top) a Morgan type, Peace type, Eisenhower type and Anthony type.

A person contemplating the collecting of Jefferson nickels by date and mint-mark will find that three mints produced them: San Francisco, Denver and Philadel-phia. Because the first two are branch mints serving smaller populations, their output has tended over time to be smaller than that of Philadelphia. This fact, repeated in other series, has helped give mintmarks quite an allure to collectors. It provides one of the major attractions in collecting coins by date and mintmark.

The key date for Jeffersons is the 1950-D when using mintages as a guide. In that year, production was just 2.6 million pieces. Because collectors of the time were aware of the coin's low mintage, many examples were saved. As a result, prices are reasonable.

The Depression-era 1939-D comes in as the most valuable regular-issue Jefferson nickel despite a mintage of 3.5 million – almost 1 million more than the 1950-D. The reason: Fewer were saved for later generations of coin collectors.

Date and mintmark collecting teaches hobbyists to use mintage figures as a

Jefferson nickels have been produced at the (from top) Philadephia, Denver and San Francisco Mints. Note the Denver and San Francisco mintmarks to the right of Monticello.

The wartime nickels of 1942-1945 marked the first time a "P" mintmark, for Philadelphia, was used.

guide but to take them with a grain of salt. Rarity, after all, is determined by the number of surviving coins, not the number initially created.

The Jefferson series is a good one to collect by date and mintmark, because the mintmarks have moved around, grown in size, and expanded in number.

When the series was first introduced, the Jefferson nickel was produced at the three mints previously mentioned. In 1942, because of a diversion of certain metals to wartime use, the coin's alloy of 75 percent copper and 25 percent nickel was changed. The new alloy was 35 percent silver, 56 percent copper, and 9 percent manganese.

To denote the change, the mintmarks were moved and greatly enlarged. The pre-1942 mintmarks were small and located to the right of Monticello; the wartime mintmarks were enlarged and placed over the dome. What's more, for the first time in American history, the Philadelphia Mint used a mintmark ("P").

The war's end restored the alloy and mintmarks to their previous status. The "P" disappeared. This lasted until the 1960s, when a national coin shortage saw all mintmarks removed for three years (1965-1967) and then returned, but in a different location. Mintmarks were placed on the obverse, to the right of Jefferson's portrait near the date in 1968. In 1980 the "P" came back in a smaller form and is still used.

Another consideration arises with date and mintmark collecting: Should the hobbyist include proof coins in the set? This can be argued both ways. Suffice to say that anyone who has the desire to add proof coins to the set will have a larger one. It is not necessary nor is it discouraged.

Some of the first proof coins to carry mintmarks were Jefferson nickels. When proof coins were made in 1968 after lapsing from 1965 to 1967, production occurred at San Francisco instead of Philadelphia. The "S" mintmark was placed on the proof coins of that year, including the Jefferson nickel, to denote the change. Since that time, mintmarks used on proof examples of various denominations have included the "P," "D," "S," and "W."

For all of the mintmark history that is embodied in the Jefferson series, prices are reasonable. For a first attempt at collecting coins by date and mintmark, it provides excellent background for going on to the more expensive and difficult types. After all, if you are ever going to get used to the proper handling of a coin, it is far better to experiment on a low-cost coin than a high-value rarity.

In 1968 the mintmarks reappeared on U.S. coins and production of proof coins resumed, this time at the San Francisco Mint. On the nickels, the mintmark moved from the reverse to the obverse below the date.

As one progresses in date and mintmark collecting and type collecting, it is important to remember that all of the coins should be of similar states of preservation. Sets look slapdash if one coin is VG and another is MS-65 and still another is VF. Take a look at the prices of all the coins in the series before you get too far, figure out what you can afford, and then stick to that grade or range of grades.

Sure, there is a time-honored practice of filling a spot with any old example until a better one comes along. That is how we got the term "filler." But if you get a few placeholders, don't stop there. By assembling a set of uniform quality, you end up with a more aesthetically pleasing collection.

The date and mintmark method used to be the overwhelmingly dominant form of collecting. It still has many adherents. Give it a try if you think it sounds right for you.

Before we leave the discussion of collecting U.S. coins, it should be pointed out that the two major methods of organizing a collection are simply guidelines. They are not hard-and-fast rules that must be followed without questions. Collecting should be satisfying to the hobbyist. It should never be just one more item in the daily grind. Take the elements of these collecting approaches that you like or invent your own.

It should also be pointed out that U.S. coinage history does not start with 1792, nor do all of the coins struck since that time conform precisely to the two major organizational approaches. But these two areas are good places to start.

There are coins and tokens from the American Colonial period (1607-1776) that are just as fascinating and collectible as regular U.S. Mint issues. There are federal issues struck before the Mint was actually established. See the Colonial price-guide section in this book.

There are special coins called commemoratives, which have been struck by the U.S. Mint since 1892 to celebrate some aspect of American history or a contemporary event. They are not intended for circulation. There was a long interruption between 1954 and 1982, but currently annual commemoratives are being offered for sale directly to collectors by the Mint.

Collecting commemoratives has always been considered something separate from collecting regular U.S. coinage. It is, however, organized the same way. Commemoratives can be collected by date and mintmark or by type.

Current commemoratives can be purchased from the U.S. Mint. Check the U.S.

Mint Web site at www.usmint.gov. Hobbyists who order from the U.S. Mint's Web site receive notices of product availability by e-mail. Hobbyists will get the various solicitations for not only commemoratives, but regular proof sets and mint sets and proof American Eagle bullion coins. Buying coins from the Mint can be considered a hobby pursuit in its own right. Some collectors let the Mint organize their holdings for them. They buy complete sets and put them away. They never buy anything from anywhere else.

Admittedly, this is a passive form of collecting, but there are individuals around the world who enjoy collecting at this level without ever really going any deeper. They like acquiring every new issue as it comes off the Mint's presses.

Once done, there is a certain knowledge that one has all the examples of the current year. Obviously, too, collectors by date and mintmark of the current types would have to buy the new coins each year, but, of course, they do not stop there.

Varieties and errors make up another area. Under this heading come the coins the Mint did not intend to make. There are all kinds of errors. Many of them are inexpensive. Check out the U.S. Minting Varieties and Errors section in the price guide. If you want to pursue it further, there are specialty books that deal with the topic in more detail.

Canada

Starting point for the national coinage of Canada is popularly fixed at 1858. In that year a large cent was first produced for use in Upper and Lower Canada (Ontario and Quebec). These prices were intended to supplant local copper coinage, which in turn had been attempts to give various regions a medium of exchange.

What was circulating in Canada at the time was a hodgepodge of world issues. The large cent predates a unified national government by nine years, but it is considered the beginning of national issues nevertheless.

There are many similarities between the United States and Canada and their respective monetary systems. Both continent-sized nations thought in terms of taming the frontier, new settlements, and growth. Both came to use the dollar as the unit of account because of the pervasiveness of the Spanish milled dollar in trade. For each, the dollar divides into 100 cents.

However, Canada had a far longer colonial history. Many of its residents resisted the tide that carried the United States to independence and worked to preserve their loyalties to the British crown. As a result, Canada was firmly a part of the British Empire. So even today with its constitution (the British North America Act transferred from Westminster to Ottawa in 1982), parliamentary democracy, and a national consciousness perhaps best symbolized by the maple leaf, Canada retains a loyalty to the crown in the person of Queen Elizabeth II of the United Kingdom. Canada is a member of the British Commonwealth of Nations.

The effect of this on coins is obvious. Current issues carry the queen's effigy. How Canada got its coins in the past was also influenced. The fledgling U.S. government set about creating its own mint as one of its earliest goals, despite that

Canadian coins
have depicted (from
top) Queen Victoria,
King Edward VII,
King George V,
King George VI and
Queen Elizabeth II.

better-quality pieces could be purchased abroad at lower cost. Canada found that ties to mints located in England were logical and comfortable.

The Royal Canadian Mint was not established until 1908, when it was called the Ottawa branch of the British Royal Mint, and it was not given its present name until 1931. Both events are within living memory. Canadian coins, therefore, have a unique mixture of qualities. They are tantalizingly familiar to U.S. citizens yet distinctly different.

The coinage of a monarchy brings its own logic to the organization of a collection. Type collecting is delineated by the monarch. United Canada has had six. The first was Queen Victoria, whose image appeared on those large cents of 1858. Her reign began in 1837 and lasted until 1901.

She was followed by Edward VII, 1901-1910; George V, 1910-1936; Edward VIII, 1936; George VI, 1936-1952; and Queen Elizabeth II, 1952-present. All but Edward VIII had coins struck for circulation in Canada. The collectible monarchs, therefore, number five, but the longer reigns inspired changes of portraits over time to show the aging process at work. Legends also changed. When George VI ceased being emperor of India, Canada's coins were modified to recognize the change.

Like U.S. coins, sizes and alloys were altered to meet new demands placed on the coinage. However, the separateness of each nation might best be summed up this way: Though the United States abolished its large cent in 1857, Canada's was just getting under way in 1858. The United States put an end to the silver dollar in 1935, the very year Canada finally got its series going.

And Canada, the nickel-mining giant, used a small-sized silver five-cent coin until 1921, almost 50 years after the half dime was abolished in the United States. But whereas the Civil War was the major cause of the emergence of modern U.S. coinage as specified by the Coinage Act of 1873, World War I influenced the alterations that made Canada's coins what they are today.

It might be assumed that change in the monarch also signaled a change in the reverse designs of the various denominations. A check of the Canadian price guide section shows this is not necessarily the case. Current designs paired with Queen Elizabeth II basically date back to the beginning of her father's reign. The familiar maple-leaf cent, beaver five-cent piece, schooner 10-cent, caribou 25-cent, and coat-of-arms 50-cent have been running for more than 50 years. Significant changes were made to the 50-cent coin in 1959, but the reverse design remains the coat of arms.

So where does that leave type collectors? It puts them in a situation similar to categorizing the various eagles on U.S. coins. They can be universalists and accept the broadest definitions of type, or they can narrow the bands to whatever degree suits them best.

By checking the price-guide section, date and mintmark collectors will quickly note that their method of organization more or less turns into collecting by date. Though currently there are three mints in Canada – Hull, Quebec; Ottawa, Ontario; and Winnipeg, Manitoba – they don't use mintmarks. Historically, few mintmarks were employed.

Ottawa used a "C" on gold sovereigns of 1908-1919 and on some exported colonial issues. The private Heaton Mint in Birmingham, England, used an "H" on coins it supplied to Canada from 1871 to 1907.

But the coins supplied to Canada by the British Royal Mint and later by its Ottawa branch did not carry any identifying mark. Collectors who confine their activities to the more recent issues need never think about a mintmark.

It would be easy to slant a presentation on Canadian issues to stress similarities or differences to U.S. issues. One should remember that the monetary structures of each evolved independently, but each was always having an impact on the other.

Common events, such as World War II, had a similar impact. For example, the Canadian five-cent coin changed in much the same way as the U.S. nickel. In Canada, nickel was removed and replaced first by a tombac (brass) alloy and then by chromium-plated steel. Peace brought with it a return to the prewar composition.

To see an example of differences between the United States and Canada, take the Canadian approach to the worldwide trend of removing silver from coinage. Canada made its move in 1968, three years after the United States. Instead of choosing a copper-nickel alloy as a substitute for silver, Canada looked to its own vast natural resources and employed pure nickel.

Canada also seems more comfortable with its coinage than the United States. Whereas the United States often feared confusion and counterfeiting from making the least little changes in its coins, Canada has long embraced coinage to communicate national events, celebrations and culture. Its silver-dollar series actually began as a celebration of George V's 25 years on the throne.

Succeeding years saw additional commemorative $1 designs interspersed with the regular Voyageur design. When the centennial of national confederation was observed in 1967, all of the denominations were altered for one year. The United States only reluctantly tried out the idea on three of its denominations for the nation's Bicentennial.

Ultimately, Canada began an annual commemorative dollar series in 1971. It issued coins for the 1976 Montreal Olympic Games and again in 1988 for the Calgary Olympic Games. Bullion coins were created to market its gold, silver and platinum output. A commemorative series of gold $100 coins was also undertaken. Canada, too, issues special proof, prooflike and specimen sets, similar to the United States.

Hobbyists who would like to be informed of new issues should write Royal Canadian Mint, P.O. Box 457, Station A, Ontario K1A 8V5, Canada. The mint also maintains special toll-free lines. In the United States, hobbyists may telephone the Royal Canadian Mint at 1-800-268-6468. In Canada, the number is 1-800-267-1871. You can get on the mailing list by using these numbers and you can buy currently available coins. (See Chapter 6 for Web information.)

When collecting Canada, another thing to remember is the importance varieties play in the nation's various series. Certainly, a type collector has no need to dwell on this information, but the date and mintmark collector may puzzle over the many extra identifying abbreviations in the price guide for certain coins. These varieties

Like the U.S. Mint, the Royal Canadian Mint offers sets of coins in a variety of finishes to the collector market.

should not be confused with the U.S. variety-and-error category.

Here the varieties are not mistakes; they are deliberately created and issued variations of the standard design. We see Voyageur dollars on which the number of water lines changes. Other dollars count the number of beads.

These differences are minor. Though they were deliberately done to meet varying mint needs, they were not intended to be set apart in the public mind. The hobby, however, likes to look at things under a microscope.

Some varieties were indeed intended to be deliberately and noticeably different. An example of this occurs with 1947-dated issues. A maple leaf was placed on the 1947-dated cent through 50-cent issues. This indicated the coin was struck after George VI lost his title of emperor of India, as proclaimed in the Latin legend, but that the design had not yet been altered to reflect this. All of these varieties are considered integral parts of the Canadian series, and they are listed as such.

Do not construe any of this to mean there is no collecting of varieties and errors of the type common in the United States. There is. Collecting Royal Canadian Mint mistakes is just as active, just as interesting, and just as rewarding. After all, mint errors are universal. The methods of manufacture are the same. So the mistakes can be classified in the same manner.

Canada's numismatic listings also include items from various provinces issued before they were part of the confederation. The largest portion of this section is devoted to Newfoundland, because it retained a separate status far longer than the other provinces – until 1949, in fact.

Advice given to collectors of U.S. coins also applies to collectors of Canadian coins: Do what interests you. Do what you can afford. Create sets of uniform grade.

The rules of rarity transcend national boundaries. The only thing to keep in mind is the relative size of the collecting population. Because Canada has only a tenth of the U.S. population, it stands to reason that the number of collectors in that nation is but a fraction of the U.S. number. A mintage that seems to indicate scarcity for U.S. coin, therefore, could indicate something quite common in Canada. Don't forget that mintage is just a guide. The same factors that caused loss of available specimens or preserved unusually large quantities were at work in Canada, too.

Mexico

Coinage produced in Mexico dates to the establishment of a mint in Mexico City in 1536, more than 250 years before a federal mint was set up in the United States and more than 300 years before Canada circulated its own coins. The output of those extra centuries alone would make organizing a Mexican coin collection more challenging than a collection of U.S. or Canadian coins. But there are numerous other factors involved.

You say you like the kings and queens on Canada's coins? Mexico has kings, too – nearly 300 years' worth, plus a couple of emperors. You say the ideals of liberty embodied by the great men and women on U.S. coins is more your cup of tea? Mexico's coins also feature men and women committed to liberty.

In addition, Mexico is the crossroads of civilizations and empires. The great pyramid-building society of southern Mexico and Central America met its end at the hands of the Spanish conquistadors led initially by Hernando Cortez. The great Aztec empire was looted and overturned in 1519-1521 in the name of Spain.

The great natural resources of the area then supported successive Spanish kings in their grand dreams of dominating Europe. Through the doors of the Mexico City Mint and later facilities scattered about the country passed legendary quantities of silver. Even today the country ranks at the top of the list of silver producers.

But while Spain could dominate Mexico for a long time, the basic ideals of liberty and human dignity eventually motivated the people to throw off the foreign yoke. Unfortunately, victory was often neither complete nor wisely led. And in more recent years, the scourge of inflation had exacted a high toll on the currency itself. The numismatic consequences of a long history punctuated by periods of turmoil are an abundance of denominations, metals and types.

It is tempting for a would-be collector of Mexican coins to forget about anything that happened in the country prior to its monetary reform of 1905. By starting at that point, a hobbyist can happily overlook anything other than a decimal monetary system in which 100 centavos equal 1 peso. That system is as modern as any. The coins' striking quality is high. Legends are easy to read and understand, and the variety of issues is wide but not overwhelming.

There always is a certain logic to begin the collecting of any country with recent issues. The costs of learning are minimized, and as one becomes comfortable, a level of confidence can be built up sufficient to prompt diving further into the past.

The issues of 1905 to date also more easily fit into the mold of type collecting and collecting by date and mintmark. To take type collecting, for example, let's look at the peso. In 1905 it was a silver-dollar-sized coin with a silver-dollar-sized quantity of bullion in it, 0.786 ounces. In 1918 it was reduced to 0.4663 ounces; in 1920, 0.3856 ounces; in 1947, 0.2250 ounces; 1950, 0.1285 ounces; 1957, 0.0514 ounces; and in 1970 silver was eliminated completely in favor of a copper-nickel alloy.

At almost every one of those steps, the design changed, too. After sinking to 3,300 to the U.S. dollar, monetary reform dropped three zeroes in 1993. The new

One thousand of these equaled one new peso as 1993 began.

peso, equal to 1,000 old ones, is now about 14 to the U.S. dollar.

By beginning with 1905, a date and mintmark collector misses out on issues of the various branch mints that were located around the country. Regular issues were all struck in Mexico City. Yearly output was reasonably regular for the various denominations, so date sets are extensive.

There have been rumblings since the early 1980s that Mexico would abandon the peso because of its greatly reduced value. The government, however, has been working hard to retain it since the monetary reform. So far it has succeeded.

One thing the government cannot do, however, is turn the clock back to a time when the fractional denominations of 1, 2, 5, 10, 20, 25, and 50 centavos were relatively high face values. However, it is stimulating to assemble sets because they offer a range of rarities. They are neither so expensive that it would prevent a collector from acquiring them at some point, but neither are they so common that you can walk into a shop, write a check, and come away with all of the 20th century sets complete. Check out the price guide section and see.

Gold in the post-1905 era is basically so much bullion. There are some scarcer pieces and some strikingly beautiful designs, such as the Centenario, a gold 50-peso coin containing 1.2 ounces of bullion. It was first struck in 1921 to mark 100 years of independence. Because Mexico actively restruck its gold coins, however, it is virtually impossible to tell an original issue from the newer version.

The result is a retail price structure based on metallic content. Gold, however, does not conjure up the images that silver does. Silver is the magic word for Mexico. That, of course, means the peso.

The modern Mexico City Mint also strikes commemoratives and collector sets from time to time. These are generally marketed to collectors through private firms, details of which are published in hobby newspapers like World Coin News. Mexico, like the United States and Canada, also issues gold and silver bullion coins.

These also are marketed through arrangements with private firms. Interestingly, Mexico's many gold-coin restrikes were the bullion coins of their day. They had the advantage of ready identification, and they were legally tradable according to gold-coin regulations that existed in the United States from 1933 through 1974.

It is appropriate that we conclude discussion of the modern period on the concept of bullion, because bullion is at the root of Mexico's numismatic history. That is a period to which we now turn.

Mexico also strikes commemorative coins for the collector market. They are available through private firms in the United States.

When Cortez toppled the Aztec Empire, for a time the wealth returning to Spain was merely that taken by the victors from the vanquished. But the business of permanently administering a vast area in the name of the Spanish king, exploiting its natural resources, and funneling the proceeds to Spain quite soon involved the establishment of a mint in Mexico City. This was undertaken in 1536, just 15 years after the end of Aztec dominion.

At first, the authorized coins were low denominations: silver quarter, half, 1, 2, 3, and 4 reales, and copper 2 and 4 maravedis. To understand their face values and how they related to each other, let's take the common reference point of a silver dollar. The silver dollar is 8 reales, and you might recognize the nickname for the denomination of "piece of eight" from pirate lore. The eighth part, the silver real, was divided into 34 copper maravedis. That means the 8 reales was worth 272 copper maravedis.

The copper coinage was hated and soon abolished, not to reappear until 1814. The silver coins were fine as far as they went. When the mines of Mexico began producing undreamed of quantities of metal, however, it was the 8 reales that took center stage. This occurred after 1572. The piece of eight became the standard form for shipping silver back to Spain.

Mexico City's output was prodigious. Minting standards were crude. All denominations produced are called "cobs," because they are basically little more than irregular-looking lumps of metal on which bits and pieces of design can be seen. The only constant was weight, fineness, and the appearance of assayer's initials (which guaranteed the weight and fineness). Not showing those initials was cause for severe punishment.

Designs showed the arms of the monarch on one side, a cross on the other, appropriate legends, and an indication of denomination. The period of cob issues lasted until 1732. Rulers of the period start with Charles and Johanna, 1516-1556; Philip II, 1556-1598; Philip III, 1598-1621; Philip IV, 1621-1665; Charles II, 1665-1700; Philip V, 1700-1724 and 1724-1746; and Luis I, 1724.

Modern mint machinery began turning out coins in 1732. Quality was similar to today. The arms design was continued. It was not until 1772 that the monarch's portrait began appearing. The honor of this numismatic debut belongs to Charles III. Kings of this period are Ferdinand VI, 1746-1759; Charles III, 1760-1788; Charles IV, 1788-1808; and Ferdinand VII, 1808-1821. The Standard Catalog of Mexican Coins by Colin R. Bruce II and Dr. George W. Vogt is recommended to those who want to study this period in greater depth.

The revolutionary period begins in 1810, when a parish priest, Miguel Hidalgo y Costilla, issued the call for independence. The first attempts to achieve this were violently suppressed. Hidalgo was executed, but independence did come in 1821.

With revolt against central authority came a dispersal of the right to strike coins. Mexico City continued as the major facility, but other operations began. The list of these over the next century is lengthy. Mintmarks and assayer initials proliferated.

The old colonial coinage standard survived the period. The 8 reales and its parts carried on. A slight reduction in bullion content had been ordered by the king in 1760, but otherwise things continued as they were. Gold was coined during the colonial period beginning in 1679 based on an 8-escudo piece, which divided into eighths just like the 8 reales. Gold, however, was not as important as silver.

Mexico's first emperor came shortly after independence. He was a leader in the struggle that set Mexico free from Spain. Augustin de Iturbide, originally an officer in the service of Spain, was proclaimed emperor in 1822. He abdicated in 1823 and was executed in 1824.

The second emperor had a reign almost as short as the first. Maximilian I, emperor only because he had a French army to secure the throne, reigned from 1863 to 1867. He was shot by a firing squad when the French left.

He is remembered numismatically because he decided to decimalize the coinage. The centavo and peso were born. Soon afterward, the republic was re-established. Further monetary changes were minor thereafter until 1905.

Collectors focusing on Mexico can devote much time to the study of the quasi-official issues of rebels during the periods of instability. They can look at hacienda tokens, which were issued by large farms or ranches that employed hundreds or thousands of people. Or they can pick whichever period in Mexico's history that fascinates them most. Whatever collectors of Mexico eventually settle on, they will find it rewarding.

Where to write for more information:

World Coin News: 700 E. State St., Iola, WI 54990.

4

American Eagles Fly High
Coins a hit with collectors, investors alike

By David C. Harper

Gold has been the stuff of dreams since King Midas. Large silver coins capture the imagination. You don't have to be a collector to appreciate either metal. When you combine dreams of wealth with collector appeal you arrive at the current conception of gold and silver American Eagle coins. While they are not exactly all things to all people, they definitely are two aspects to the appeal of these coins.

American Eagles are bullion coins. A "bullion coin" is a coin with a design that is widely recognized as containing a known quantity of precious metal in convenient troy weights and standard purity called fineness. To distinguish it in legal terms from a medal or a bar, bullion coins are recognized by the issuing government as legal tender and have face values. It is this face value, or denomination, that makes the object a coin rather than a medal. It also endows it with the full recognition and backing of the issuing government. In the case of the American Eagles, this face value has no relationship to the present metallic value of the coin. This is because face values are unchanging and the price of the metal in each coin changes in trading every business day. That is the nature of bullion and bullion trading. Combine the legal-tender status of a coin with the bullion aspect of the precious metal market and you get a "bullion coin."

What makes a coin qualify for the term of bullion coin is the fact that it contains an even troy weight, starting with 1 troy ounce, or convenient fractions like half ounce, quarter ounce and tenth ounce.

The need for a convenient troy weight bullion coin was first recognized in 1967 by South Africa, then the world's top miner of gold bullion. At that time the existing gold coin supply was a hodgepodge of many historical issues with the British sovereign, American $20 gold piece, Austrian 100 coronas and Mexican 50 pesos the most widely traded gold coins.

But there was a problem. The international gold market quoted the price of gold by the troy ounce, which was fixed by international agreement at $35 a troy ounce. None of the commonly traded coins contained an even troy ounce weight. To determine the gold value of each coin was like doing your math homework. The sovereign contains 0.2355 ounce of gold. Multiply that by $35. You get $8.2425 worth of gold. If you happened to own 67 of them, you would have to further multiply $8.2425 by 67 to determine the value of your holdings. In this case, it would be $552.2475. This was before personal computers. These calculations had to be done by hand. Ugh.

The weight of the U.S. $20 gold coin, also called a double eagle, was close to a troy ounce, but close doesn't cut it when determining value. The weight of 0.9675 troy ounces still has to be multiplied by the price of an ounce to determine the value of the coin. This also is true of the .9802 troy ounce weight of the 100 coronas and the 1.2056 ounce weight of the 50 pesos. Further complicating this was the fact that Austria and Mexico were supplying the bullion market with additional coins all carrying dates from the past. In Austria's case the new coins continued to have a 1915 date and Mexico's was 1947. The United States was not striking any new coins and the bulk of the supply of Great Britain's sovereigns were struck before 1914, although some new sovereigns with current dates were struck from time to time.

If you think this is confusing, it was, but gold buyers could put up with it because the price of gold did not change. It had been set by the United States in 1934 and enshrined in the international Bretton Woods treaty of 1944. The United States promised to supply enough gold to the market to keep that price point fixed. Until 1968 it worked, but then the free market was opened up in London and gold began to change value on a daily basis. New coin value calculations became a daily requirement around the world.

South Africa recognized a market need and created the Krugerrand in 1967. The weight of the gold in it was 1 troy ounce. If the price of gold ended trading on a given day at $35.27, well then, that's what the value of the Krugerrand was as well. The need for math was greatly reduced. It was a market winner. Mintages rose from 40,000 in the first year to 211,018 by 1970. By 1973 mintage was 859,000. In 1974 mintage skyrocketed to 3,203,000 pieces. South Africa dominated the market for new gold coins.

The United States began to notice in 1974 when for the first time since 1933 it became legal for Americans to own gold. For 41 years wedding rings and tooth fillings were the only legal avenues for owning gold for average Americans. Krugerrands flooded the country. Because South Africa practiced racial segregation called apartheid, there were soon calls to ban the importation of Krugerrands until that government's policy changed. In 1985 the ban went into effect.

This opened the possibility of the United States taking over the market for gold bullion coins. Production began for both gold and silver American Eagles.

At left is the enhanced uncirculated 2013 silver American Eagle. At right is a gold American Eagle.

Both were wildly popular in the first few years. Investors bought the regular issues and collectors bought proof versions. However, whereas South Africa rode the wave of rising metals prices throughout the 1970s, helping fuel demand for its coins, the years after 1986 saw gold and silver prices slip. Gold was around $425 an ounce when the Eagles were introduced and silver was $5.75. More than 13 years later at the end of 1999, gold was $288.50 and silver was $5.41. Even though the United States took over the market, the market had shrunk and mintages fell.

The decline in precious metals prices proved not to be all bad. Some collectors got used to the idea of obtaining bullion coins as collectibles rather than solely on the basis of bullion content. They got into the habit of building sets of the coins. Collectors enjoyed huge profits on the coins they faithfully acquired when precious metals skyrocked, with gold rising to nearly $1,900 an ounce and silver nearly $50 an ounce by 2011. Soon more investors were attracted to the market.

Mintages exploded with higher precious metals, especially for the silver American Eagle. Mintages of the silver American Eagle rose from 8 million to 10 million a year in the early years of the 21st century and then decisively exceeded the 1987 record mintage of 11,442,335 in 2008 when 19,583,500 were made. Mintages kept going higher. In 2009, 28,766,500 were made. In 2010, output reached 34,662,500. A new record of 39,868,500 was set in 2011. Output then backed off some in 2012 to 33,742,500. Gold's upward mintage trajectory while dramatic merely returned annual output levels to what occurred in the first few years of American Eagle production in the 1980s, but then paying as much as $1,900 for a 1-ounce coin might make that understandable. A silver 1-ounce coin is much more affordable for both collectors and investors.

What will the future bring for the American Eagle bullion coin series? The newest trend in the series are special collector issues. Since 2006 the U.S. Mint has created reverse proofs (design elements are mirror-like while the empty fields are frosted as opposed to the standard proof where design elements like Miss Liberty are frosted and the empty fields are mirror-like). The U.S. Mint has also created mintmarked burnished uncirculated coins and is expanding the number of mintmarks being regularly used. The latest arrival was the enhanced uncirculated silver American Eagle, which alternated frosted finish with polished finish in the stripes of Miss Liberty's skirt. Other design elements will have the usual heavy frosted finish and the field will be lightly frosted rather than mirror-like. The question as this edition goes to press is whether enhanced uncirculated coins will become popular with collectors.

Clearly the fluctuating level of collector and investor interest in American Eagle bullion coins will alternately emphasize the influence of one or the other, but long-term support from both kinds of buyers should keep the gold and silver American Eagle bullion coins as the most popular bullion coins in the world.

Introduction to Pricing

The following value guide is divided into six sections:
1. U.S. minting varieties and errors.
2. Colonial coins, issued prior to the establishment of the United States
3. U.S. issues of 1792.
4. U.S. issues of 1793-present.
5. Canadian coins.
6. Mexican coins.

Value listings

Values listed in the following price guide are average retail prices. These are the approximate prices collectors can expect to pay when purchasing coins from dealers. They are not offers to buy or sell. The pricing section should be considered a guide only; actual selling prices will vary.

The values were compiled by Krause Publications' independent staff of market analysts. They derived the values listed by monitoring auction results, business on electronic dealer trading networks, and business at major shows, and in consultation with a panel of dealers. For rare coins, when only a few specimens of a particular date and mintmark are known, a confirmed transaction may occur only once every several years. In those instances, the most recent auction result is listed.

Grading

Values are listed for coins in various states of preservation, or grades. Standards used in determining grades for U.S. coins are those set by the American Numismatic Association. See Chapter 2 for more on grading.

Dates and mintmarks

The dates listed are the individual dates that appear on each coin. The letter that follows the date is the mintmark and indicates where the coin was struck: "C" — Charlotte, N.C. (1838-1861); "CC" — Carson City, Nev. (1870-1893); "D" — Dahlonega, Ga. (1838-1861), and Denver (1906-present); "O" New Orleans (1838-1909); "P" — Philadelphia (1793-present); "S" San Francisco (1854-present); and "W" — West Point, N.Y. (1984-present). Coins without mintmarks were struck at Philadelphia.

A slash mark in a date indicates an overdate. This means a new date was engraved on a die over an old date. For example, if the date is listed as "1899/8," an 1898 die had a 9 engraved over the last 8 in the date. Portions of the old numeral are still visible on the coin.

A slash mark in a mintmark listing indicates an overmintmark (example: "1922-P/D"). The same process as above occurred, but this time a new mintmark was engraved over an old.

See the "U.S. Minting Varieties and Errors" section for more information on overdates and overmintmarks.

Price charts

Pricing data for the selected charts in the U.S. section were taken from the January issues of *Coin Prices* for the years indicated.

Mexican coin mintages

Quantities minted of each date are indicated when that information is available.

Precious-metal content

Throughout this book precious-metal content is indicated in troy ounces. One troy ounce equals 480 grains, or 31.103 grams.

Abbreviations

AGW. Actual gold weight.

APW. Actual platinum weight.

ASW. Actual silver weight.

BV. Bullion value. This indicates the coin's current value is based on the amount of its precious-metal content and the current price for that metal.

Est. Indicates the exact mintage is not known and the figure listed is an estimate.

G. Grams.

Inc. Abv. Indicates the mintage for the date and mintmark listed is included in the previous listing.

KM#. Indicates "Krause-Mishler number." This sequential cataloging numbering system originated with the *Standard Catalog of World Coins* and provides collectors with a means for identifying coins.

Leg. Legend.

Mkt value. Market value.

MM. Millimeters.

Obv. Obverse.

P/L. Indicates "prooflike," a type of finish used on some Canadian coins.

Rev. Reverse.

Spec. Indicates "specimen," a type of finish used on some Canadian coins.

U.S. Minting Varieties and Errors

Introduction

By Alan Herbert

The P.D.S. cataloging system used here to list minting varieties was originally compiled by Alan Herbert in 1971. PDS stands for the three main divisions of the minting process, "planchet," "die" and "striking." Two more divisions cover collectible modifications after the strike, as well as non-collectible alterations, counterfeits and damaged coins.

This listing includes 445 classes, each a distinct part of the minting process or from a specific non-mint change in the coin. Classes from like causes are grouped together. The PDS system applies to coins of the world, but is based on U.S. coinage with added classes for certain foreign minting practices.

Price ranges are based on a U.S. coin in MS-60 grade (uncirculated.) The ranges may be applied in general to foreign coins of similar size or value although collector values are not usually as high as for U.S. coins. Prices are only a guide as the ultimate price is determined by a willing buyer and seller.

To define minting varieties, "A coin which exhibits a variation of any kind from the normal, as a result of any portion of the minting process, whether at the planchet stage, as a result of a change or modification of the die, or during the striking process. It includes those classes considered to be intentional changes, as well as those caused by normal wear and tear on the dies or other minting equipment and classes deemed to be "errors."

The three causes are represented as follows:
1. (I) = Intentional Changes
2. (W) = Wear and Tear
3. (E) = Errors
Note: A class may show more than one cause and could be listed as (IWE).

Rarity level

The rarity ratings are based on the following scale:
1 - Very Common. Ranges from every coin struck down to 1,000,000.
2 - Common. From 1,000,000 down to 100,000.
3 - Scarce. From 100,000 down to 10,000.
4 - Very Scarce. From 10,000 down to 1,000.
5 - Rare. From 1,000 down to 100.
6 - Very Rare. From 100 down to 10.
7 - Extremely Rare. From 10 down to 1.

Unknown: If there is no confirmed report of a piece fitting a particular class, it is listed as Unknown. Reports of finds by readers would be appreciated in order to update future presentations.

An Unknown does not mean that your piece automatically is very valuable. Even a Rarity 7 piece, extremely rare, even unique, may have a very low collector value because of a lack of demand or interest in that particular class.

Classes, definitions and price ranges are based on material previously offered in Alan Herbert's book, The Official Price Guide to Minting Varieties and Errors and in Coin Prices Magazine.

Pricing information has also been provided by John A. Wexler and Ken Potter, with special pricing and technical advice from Del Romines.

Also recommended is the Cherrypicker's Guide to Rare Die Varieties by Bill Fivaz and J.T. Stanton. Check your favorite coin shop, numismatic library or book seller for availability of the latest edition.

For help with your coin questions, to report significant new finds and for authentication of your minting varieties, include a loose first class stamp and write to Alan Herbert, 700 E. State St., Iola, WI 54990-0001. Don't include any numismatic material until you have received specific mailing instructions from me.

Quick check index

If you have a coin and are not sure where to look for the possible variety:

If your coin shows doubling, first check V-B-I.

Then try II-A, II-B, II-C, II-I (4 & 5), III-J, III-L, or IV-C.

If part of the coin is missing, check III-B, III-C, or III-D.

If there is a raised line of coin metal, check II-D, II-G.

If there is a raised area of coin metal, check II-E, II-F, or III-F.

If the coin is out of round, and too thin, check III-G.

If coin appears to be the wrong metal, check III-A, III-E, III-F-3 and III-G.

If the die appears to have been damaged, check II-E, II-G. (Damage to the coin itself usually is not a minting variety.)

If the coin shows incomplete or missing design, check II-A, II-E, III-B-3, III-B-5 or III-D.

If only part of the planchet was struck, check III-M.

If something was struck into the coin, check III-J and III-K.

If something has happened to the edge of the coin, check II-D-6, II-E-10, III-I, III-M and III-O.

If your coin shows other than the normal design, check II-A or II-C.

If a layer of the coin metal is missing, or a clad layer is missing, check III-B and III-D.

If you have an unstruck blank, or planchet, check I-G.

If your coin may be a restrike, check IV-C.

If your coin has a counterstamp, countermark, additional engraving or apparent official modifications, check
     IV-B and V-A-8.

Do not depend on the naked eye to examine your coins. Use a magnifying lens whenever possible, as circulation damage, wear and alterations frequently can be mistaken for legitimate minting varieties.

Division I: planchet varieties

The first division of the PDS System includes those minting varieties that occur in the manufacture of the planchet upon which the coins will ultimately be struck and includes classes resulting from faulty metallurgy, mechanical damage, faulty processing, or equipment or human malfunction prior to the actual coin striking.

Planchet alloy mix (I-A)

This section includes those classes pertaining to mixing and processing the various metals which will be used to make a coin alloy.

I-A-1 Improper Alloy Mix (WE), Rarity Level: 3-4 . . . . Values: $5 to $10

I-A-2 Slag Inclusion Planchet (WE), Rarity Level: 5-6. . . . . Values: $25 up

Damaged and defective planchets (I-B)

To be a class in this section the blank, or planchet, must for some reason not meet the normal standards or must have been damaged in processing. The classes cover the areas of defects in the melting, rolling, punching and processing of the planchets up to the point where they are sent to the coin presses to be struck.

I-B-1 Defective Planchet (WE), Rarity Level: 6 . . . . .Values: $25 up
I-B-2 Mechanically Damaged Planchet (WE), Rarity Level: – . . . . Values: No Value
(See values for the coin struck on a mechanically damaged planchet.)
I-B-3 Rolled Thin Planchet (WE), Rarity Level: 6 - *(Less rare on half cents of 1795, 1797 and restrikes of 1831-52.)* . . . . .Values: $10 up
I-B-4 Rolled Thick Planchet (WE), Rarity Level: 7 - *(Less rare in Colonial copper coins. Notable examples occur on the restrike half cents of 1840-52.)* . . . . .Values: $125 up
I-B-5 Tapered Planchet (WE), Rarity Level: 7 . . . . .Values: $25 up
I-B-6 Partially Unplated Planchet (WE), Rarity Level: 6. . . . . .Values: $15 up
I-B-7 Unplated Planchet (WE), Rarity Level: 6-7. . . . . .Values: $50 up
I-B-8 Bubbled Plating Planchet (WE), Rarity Level: 1 . . . . Values: No Value
I-B-9 Included Gas Bubble Planchet (WE), Rarity Level: 6-7. . . . . .Values: $50 up
I-B-10 Partially Unclad Planchet (WE), Rarity Level: 6 . . . . .Values: $20 up
I-B-11 Unclad Planchet (WE), Rarity Level: 6-7 . . . . .Values: $50 up
I-B-12 Undersize Planchet (WE), Rarity Level: 7. . . . . .Values: $250 up
I-B-13 Oversize Planchet (WE), Rarity Level: 7 . . . . .Values: $250 up
I-B-14 Improperly Prepared Proof Planchet (WE), Rarity Level: 7. .Values: $100 up
I-B-15 Improperly Annealed Planchet (WE), Rarity Level: - . . . . Values: No Value
I-B-16 Faulty Upset Edge Planchet (WE), Rarity Level: 5-6. . . . . .Values: $10 up
I-B-17 Rolled-In Metal Planchet (WE), Rarity Level: 6-7. . . . . .Values: $50 up
I-B-18 Weld Area Planchet (WE), Rarity Level: Unknown .Values: No Value Established
(See values for the coins struck on weld area planchets.)
I-B-19 Strike Clip Planchet (WE), Rarity Level: 7 . . . . .Values: $150 up
I-B-20 Unpunched Center-Hole Planchet (WE), Rarity Level: 5-7. Values: $5 and up
I-B-21 Incompletely Punched Center-Hole Planchet (WE), Rarity Level: 6-7. . . . . .Values: $15 up
I-B-22 Uncentered Center-Hole Planchet (WE), Rarity Level: 6-7. . . . . Values: $10 up
I-B-23 Multiple Punched Center-Hole Planchet (WE), Rarity Level: 7. . . . . .Values: $35 up
I-B-24 Unintended Center-Hole Planchet (WE), Rarity Level: Unknown . . . . .Values: -
I-B-25 Wrong Size or Shape Center-Hole Planchet (IWE), Rarity Level: 5-7. . . . . .Values: $10 up

Clipped planchets (I-C)

Clipped blanks, or planchets, occur when the strip of coin metal fails to move forward between successive strokes of the gang punch to clear the previously punched holes, in the same manner as a cookie cutter overlapping a previously cut hole in the dough. The size of the clip is a function of the amount of overlap of the next punch.

The overlapping round punches produce a missing arc with curve matching the outside circumference of the blanking punch. Straight clips occur when the punch overlaps the beginning or end of a strip which has had the end sheared or sawed off. Ragged clips occur in the same manner when the ends of the strip have been left as they were rolled out.

The term "clip" as used here should not be confused with the practice of clipping or shaving small pieces of metal from a bullion coin after it is in circulation.

I-C-1 Disc Clip Planchet (WE), Rarity Level: 3-5 . . . . .Values: $5 up
I-C-2 Curved Clip Planchet - (To 5%) (WE), Rarity Level: 5-6 . . . . .Values: $5 up
I-C-3 Curved Clip Planchet - (6 to 10%) (WE), Rarity Level: 6. . . . . .Values: $10 up
I-C-4 Curved Clip Planchet - (11 to 25%) (WE), Rarity Level: 5-6. . . . . Values: $15 up
I-C-5 Curved Clip Planchet - (26 to 60%) (WE), Rarity Level: 6-7. . . . . Values: $25 up
I-C-6 Double Curved Clip Planchet (WE), Rarity Level: 6. . . . . .Values: $10 up
I-C-7 Triple Curved Clip Planchet (WE), Rarity Level: 5-6 . . . . .Values: $25 up
I-C-8 Multiple Curved Clip Planchet (WE), Rarity Level: 6-7 . . . . .Values: $35 up
I-C-9 Overlapping Curved Clipped Planchet (WE), Rarity Level: 6-7 . . . . .Values: $50 up
I-C-10 Incompletely Punched Curved Clip Planchet (WE), Rarity Level: 6 . . . . .Values: $35 up
I-C-11 Oval Curved Clip Planchet (WE), Rarity Level: 6-7 . . . . .Values: $50 up
I-C-12 Crescent Clip Planchet - (61% or more) (WE), Rarity Level: 7 . . . . .Values: $200 up

I-C-13 Straight Clip Planchet (WE), Rarity Level: 6. . . . . .Values: $30 up
I-C-14 Incompletely Sheared Straight Clip Planchet (WE), Rarity Level: 6 . . . . .Values: $50 up
I-C-15 Ragged Clip Planchet (WE), Rarity Level: 6-7 . . . . .Values: $35 up
I-C-16 Outside Corner Clip Planchet (E), Rarity Level: - . . . . Values: No Value
I-C-17 Inside Corner Clip Planchet (E), Rarity Level: - . . . . Values: No Value
I-C-18 Irregularly Clipped Planchet (E) Rarity Level: - . . . . .Values: Value not established
I-C-19 Incompletely Punched Scalloped or Multi-Sided Planchet (E), Rarity Level: 7 . . . . .Values: $25 up

Laminated, split, or broken planchet (I-D)

For a variety of reasons the coin metal may split into thin layers (delaminate) and either split completely off the coin, or be retained. Common causes are included gas or alloy mix problems. Lamination cracks usually enter the surface of the planchet at a very shallow angle or are at right angles to the edge. The resulting layers differ from slag in that they appear as normal metal.

Lamination cracks and missing metal of any size below a split planchet are too common in the 35 percent silver 1942-1945 nickels to be collectible or have any significant value.

I-D-1 Small Lamination Crack Planchet (W), Rarity Level: 4-5 . . . . .Values: $1 up
I-D-2 Large Lamination Crack Planchet (W), Rarity Level: 3-4 . . . . .Values: $5 up
I-D-3 Split Planchet (W), Rarity Level: 5-6 . . . . .Values: $15 up
I-D-4 Hinged Split Planchet (W), Rarity Level: 6-7 . . . . .Values: $75 up
I-D-5 Clad Planchet With a Clad Layer Missing (W), Rarity Level: 5-6 .Values: $35 up
I-D-6 Clad Planchet With Both Clad Layers Missing (W), Rarity Level: 6-7 . . . . .Values: $75 up
I-D-7 Separated Clad Layer (W), Rarity Level: 5 . . . . .Values: $25 up
I-D-8 Broken Planchet (WE), Rarity Level: 3-4 . . . . .Values: $5 up

Wrong stock planchet (I-E)

The following classes cover those cases where the wrong coin metal stock was run through the blanking press, making blanks of the correct diameter, but of the wrong thickness, alloy or metal or a combination of the wrong thickness and the wrong metal.

I-E-1 Half Cent Stock Planchet (IE), Rarity Level: Unknown . . . . .Values: No Value Established
I-E-2 Cent Stock Planchet (IE), Rarity Level: Unknown . . . . .Values: No Value Established
I-E-3 Two Cent Stock Planchet (E), Rarity Level: Unknown .Values: No Value Established
I-E-4 Three Cent Silver Stock Planchet (E), Rarity Level: Unknown. . . . . .Values: No Value Established
I-E-5 Three Cent Nickel Stock Planchet (E), Rarity Level: Unknown . . . . .Values: No Value Established
I-E-6 Half Dime Stock Planchet (E), Rarity Level: Unknown . . . . .Values: No Value Established
I-E-7 Dime Stock Planchet (E), Rarity Level: 7 . . . . .Values: $200 up
I-E-8 Twenty Cent Stock Planchet (E), Rarity Level: Unknown. . . . . .Values: No Value Established
I-E-9 Quarter Stock Planchet (E), Rarity Level: Unknown . . . . .Values: No Value Established
I-E-10 Half Dollar Stock Planchet (E), Rarity Level: Unknown. . . . . .Values: No Value Established
I-E-11 Dollar Stock Planchet (E), Rarity Level: 7. . . . . .Values: $300 up
I-E-12 Token or Medal Stock Planchet (E), Rarity Level: Unknown . . . . .Values: No Value Established
I-E-13 Wrong Thickness Spoiled Planchet (IWE), Rarity Level: Unknown. . . . . . . .Values: No Value Established
I-E-14 Correct Thickness Spoiled Planchet (IWE), Rarity Level: Unknown . . . . . . .Values: No Value Established
I-E-15 Cut Down Struck Token Planchet (IWE), Rarity Level: Unknown . . . . .Values: No Value Established
I-E-16 Experimental or Pattern Stock Planchet (IE), Rarity Level: Unknown . . . . . .Values: No Value Established
I-E-17 Proof Stock Planchet (IE), Rarity Level: Unknown . . . . .Values: No Value Established
I-E-18 Adjusted Specification Stock Planchet (IE), Rarity Level: 7. .Values: $25 up
I-E-19 Trial Strike Stock Planchet (IE), Rarity Level: Unknown . . . . .Values: No Value Established
I-E-20 U.S. Punched Foreign Stock Planchet (E), Rarity Level: 7 . . . . Values: $75 up
I-E-21 Foreign Punched Foreign Stock Planchet (E), Rarity Level: 7. . . . . .Values: $75 up
I-E-22 Non-Standard Coin Alloy Planchet (IE), Rarity Level: 7 . . . . Values: Unknown

Extra metal on a blank, or planchet (I-F)

True extra metal is only added to the blank during the blanking operation. This occurs as metal is scraped off the sides of the blanks as they are driven down through the thimble, or lower die in the blanking press. The metal is eventually picked up by a blank passing through, welded to it by the heat of friction.

A second form of extra metal has been moved to this section, the sintered coating planchet, the metal deposited on the planchet in the form of dust during the annealing operation.

I-F-1 Extra Metal on a Type 1 Blank (W), Rarity Level: 7 . . . . .Values: $50 up
I-F-2 Extra Metal on a Type 2 Planchet (W), Rarity Level: 6-7 . . . . .Values: $75 up
I-F-3 Sintered Coating Planchet (W), Rarity Level: 7 . . . . .Values: $75 up

Normal or abnormal planchets (I-G)

This section consists of the two principal forms – the blank as it comes from the blanking press – and in the form of a planchet after it has passed through the upsetting mill. It also includes a class for purchased planchets and one for planchets produced by the mint.

I-G-1 Type I Blank (IWE), Rarity Level: 3-5 . . . . .Values: $2 up
I-G-2 Type II Planchet (IWE), Rarity Level: 3-4 . . . . .Values: 50 up
I-G-3 Purchased Planchet (I), Rarity Level: 1 . . . . Values: No Value
I-G-4 Mint Made Planchet (I), Rarity Level: 1 . . . . Values: No Value
I-G-5 Adjustment-Marked Planchet (I), Rarity Level: Unknown . . . . .Values: No Value
I-G-6 Hardness Test-Marked Planchet (I), Rarity Level: - .Values: No Value Established
Note: There are no classes between I-G-6 and I-G-23
I-G-23 Proof Planchet (IE), Rarity Level: 6-7 . . . . .Values: $1 up

Coin metal strip (I-H)

When the coin metal strip passes through the blanking press it goes directly to a chopper. This cuts the remaining web into small pieces to be sent back to the melting furnace. Pieces of the web or the chopped up web may escape into the hands of collectors.

I-H-1 Punched Coin Metal Strip (IWE), Rarity Level: 4-6 . . . . Values: $5 up,
depending on size, denomination and number of holes showing
I-H-2 Chopped Coin Metal Strip (IE), Rarity Level: 3-5 . . . . .Values: $5 up

The die varieties

Division II

Die varieties may be unique to a given die, but will repeat for the full life of the die unless a further change occurs. Anything that happens to the die will affect the appearance of the struck coin. This includes all the steps of the die making:

- Cutting a die blank from a tool steel bar.
- Making the design.
- Transferring it to a model.
- Transferring it to the master die or hub.
- The hubbing process of making the die.
- Punching in the mintmark.
- Heat treating of the die.

The completed dies are also subject to damage in numerous forms, plus wear and tear during the striking process and repair work done with abrasives. All of these factors can affect how the struck coin looks.

Engraving varieties (II-A)

In all cases in this section where a master die, or master hub is affected by the class, the class will affect all the working hubs and all working dies descending from it.

Identification as being on a master die or hub depends on it being traced to two or more of the working hubs descended from the same master tools.

II-A-1 Overdate (IE), Rarity Level: 1-7 . . . . Values: $1 up
II-A-2 Doubled Date (IE), Rarity Level: 1-7 . . . . Values: $1 up
II-A-3 Small Date (IE), Rarity Level: 2-5 . . . . Values: $1 up
II-A-4 Large Date (IE), Rarity Level: 2-5 . . . . Values: $1 up
II-A-5 Small Over Large Date (IE), Rarity Level: 4-6 . . . . Values: $15 up
II-A-6 Large Over Small Date (IE), Rarity Level: 3-5 . . . . Values: $10 up
II-A-7 Blundered Date (E), Rarity Level: 6-7 . . . . Values: $50 up
II-A-8 Corrected Blundered Date (IE), Rarity Level: 3-5. . . . . Values: $5 up
II-A-9 Wrong Font Date Digit (IE), Rarity Level: 5-6 . . . . Values: Minimal
II-A-10 Worn, Broken or Damaged Punch (IWE), Rarity Level: 5-6. Values: $5 up
II-A-11 Expedient Punch (IWE), Rarity Level: 5-6 . . . . Values: $10 up
II-A-12 Blundered Digit (E), Rarity Level: 4-5 . . . . Values: $50 up
II-A-13 Corrected Blundered Digit (IE), Rarity Level: 3-6 . . . . Values: $10 up
II-A-14 Doubled Digit (IWE), Rarity Level: 2-6 . . . . Values: $2 up
II-A-15 Wrong Style or Font Letter or Digit (IE), Rarity Level: 3-5. Values: Minimal
II-A-16 One Style or Font Over Another (IE), Rarity Level: 4-6 . . . . Values: $10 up
II-A-17 Letter Over Digit (E), Rarity Level: 6-7 . . . . Values: $25 up
II-A-18 Digit Over Letter (E), Rarity Level: 6-7 . . . . Values: $25 up
II-A-19 Omitted Letter or Digit (IWE), Rarity Level: 4-6. . . . . Values: $5 up
II-A-20 Blundered Letter (E), Rarity Level: 6-7 . . . . Values: $50 up
II-A-21 Corrected Blundered Letter (IE), Rarity Level: 1-3. . . . . Values: $10 up
II-A-22 Doubled Letter (IWE), Rarity Level: 2-6. . . . . Values: $2 up
II-A-23 Blundered Design Element (IE), Rarity Level: 6-7 . . . . Values: $50 up
II-A-24 Corrected Blundered Design Element (IE), Rarity Level: 3-5. . . . . Values: $10 up
II-A-25 Large Over Small Design Element (IE), Rarity Level: 4-6 . . . . Values: $2 up
II-A-26 Omitted Design Element (IWE), Rarity Level: 5-7 . . . . Values: $10 up
II-A-27 Doubled Design Element (IWE), Rarity Level: 2-6. . . . . Values: $2 up
II-A-28 One Design Element Over Another (IE), Rarity Level: 3-6 . . . . Values: $5 up
II-A-29 Reducing Lathe Doubling (WE), Rarity Level: 6-7. . . . . Values: $50 up
II-A-30 Extra Design Element (IE), Rarity Level: 3-5 . . . . Values: $10 up
II-A-31 Modified Design (IWE), Rarity Level: 1-5 . . . . Values: No Value up
II-A-32 Normal Design (I), Rarity Level: 1. . . . . Values: No Extra Value
II-A-33 Design Mistake (IE), Rarity Level: 2-6. . . . . Values: $1 up
II-A-34 Defective Die Design (IWE), Rarity Level: 1. . . . . Values: No Value
II-A-35 Pattern (I), Rarity Level: 6-7 . . . . Values: $100 up
II-A-36 Trial Design (I), Rarity Level: 5-7 . . . . Values: $100 up
II-A-37 Omitted Designer's Initial (IWE), Rarity Level: 3-7 . . . . Values: $1 up
II-A-38 Layout Mark (IE), Rarity Level: 5-7 . . . . Values: Minimal
II-A-39 Abnormal Reeding (IWE), Rarity Level: 2-5. . . . . Values: $1 up
II-A-40 Modified Die or Hub (IWE), Rarity Level: 1-5 . . . . Values: No Value up
II-A-41 Numbered Die (I), Rarity Level: 3-5 . . . . Values: $5 up
II-A-42 Plugged Die (IW), Rarity Level: 5-6 . . . . Values: Minimal
II-A-43 Cancelled Die (IE), Rarity Level: 3-6. . . . . Values: No Value up
II-A-44 Hardness Test Marked Die (IE), Rarity Level: 7 . . . . Values: $100 up
II-A-45 Coin Simulation (IE), Rarity Level: 6-7 . . . . Values: $100 up, but may be illegal to own
II-A-46 Punching Mistake (IE), Rarity Level: 2-6. . . . . Values: $1 up
II-A-47 Small Over Large Design (IE), Rarity Level: 4-6 . . . . Values: $5 up
II-A-48 Doubled Punch (IE), Rarity Level: 5-7. . . . . Values: $5 up
II-A-49 Mint Display Sample (I) Rarity Level: 7. . . . . Values not established
II-A-50 Center Dot, Stud or Circle (IE) Rarity Level: 7, much more common on early cents. . Values not established

Hub doubling varieties (II-B)

Rotated hub doubling   *Hub break*

This section includes eight classes of hub doubling. Each class is from a different cause, described by the title of the class. At the latest count over 2,500 doubled dies have been reported in the U.S. coinage, the most famous being examples of the 1955, 1969-S and 1972 cent dies.

II-B-I Rotated Hub Doubling (WE), Rarity Level: 3-6. . . . . .Values: $1 up
II-B-II Distorted Hub Doubling (WE), Rarity Level: 3-6 . . . . .Values: $1 up
II-B-III Design Hub Doubling (IWE), Rarity Level: 3-6. . . . . Values: $1 up to five figure amounts
II-B-IV Offset Hub Doubling (WE), Rarity Level: 4-6 . . . . .Values: $15 up
II-B-V Pivoted Hub Doubling (WE), Rarity Level: 3-6 . . . . .Values: $10 up
II-B-VI Distended Hub Doubling (WE), Rarity Level: 2-5. . . . . .Values: $1 up
II-B-VII Modified Hub Doubling (IWE), Rarity Level: 2-5 . . . . .Values: $1 up
II-B-VIII Tilted Hub Doubling (WE), Rarity Level: 4-6 . . . . .Values: $5 up

Mintmark varieties (II-C)

Double   *Triple*

Mintmarks are punched into U.S. coin dies by hand (Up to 1985 for proof coins, to 1990 for cents and nickels and 1991 for other denominations). Variations resulting from mistakes in the punching are listed in this section. Unless exceptionally mispunched, values are usually estimated at 150 percent of numismatic value. Slightly tilted or displaced mintmarks have no value.

II-C-1 Doubled Mintmark (IE), Rarity Level: 2-6 . . . . Values: 50 cents up
II-C-2 Separated Doubled Mintmark (IE), Rarity Level: 5-6. . . . . .Values: $15 up
II-C-3 Over Mintmark (IE), Rarity Level: 3-6 . . . . .Values: $2 up
II-C-4 Tripled Mintmark (IE), Rarity Level: 3-5 . . . . .Values: 50 up
II-C-5 Quadrupled Mintmark (IE), Rarity Level: 4-6 . . . . .Values: $1 up
II-C-6 Small Mintmark (IE), Rarity Level: 2-5 . . . . Values: No Extra Value up
II-C-7 Large Mintmark (IE), Rarity Level: 2-5 . . . . Values: No Extra Value up
II-C-8 Large Over Small Mintmark (IE), Rarity Level: 2-5 . . . . .Values: $2 up
II-C-9 Small Over Large Mintmark (IE), Rarity Level: 3-6 . . . . .Values: $5 up
II-C-10 Broken Mintmark Punch (W), Rarity Level: 5-6 . . . . .Values: $5 up
II-C-11 Omitted Mintmark (IWE), Rarity Level: 4-7. . . . . .Values: $125 up
II-C-12 Tilted Mintmark (IE), Rarity Level: 5-7 . . . . .Values: $5 up
II-C-13 Blundered Mintmark (E), Rarity Level: 4-6 . . . . .Values: $5 up

II-C-14 Corrected Horizontal Mintmark (IE), Rarity Level: 4-6 . . . . Values: $5 up
II-C-15 Corrected Upside Down Mintmark (IE), Rarity Level: 4-6 . . . . Values: $5 up
II-C-16 Displaced Mintmark (IE), Rarity Level: 4-6 . . . . Values: $5 to $10
II-C-17 Modified Mintmark (IWE), Rarity Level: 1-4 . . . . Values: No Extra Value up
II-C-18 Normal Mintmark (I), Rarity Level: 1 . . . . Values: No Extra Value
II-C-19 Doubled Mintmark Punch (I), Rarity Level: 6-7 . . . . Values: No Extra Value up
II-C-20 Upside Down Mintmark (E) Rarity Level 6-7 . . . . Values: $5 up
II-C-21 Horizontal Mintmark (E) Rarity Level 6-7 . . . . Values: $5 up
II-C-22 Wrong Mintmark (E) Rarity Level 6-7 . . . . Values $15 up
(Example has a D mintmark in the date, but was used at Philadelphia.)

Die, collar and hub cracks (II-D)

Die cracks

Cracks in the surface of the die allow coin metal to be forced into the crack during the strike, resulting in raised irregular lines of coin metal above the normal surface of the coin. These are one of the commonest forms of die damage and wear, making them easily collectible.

Collar cracks and hub cracks are added to this section because the causes and effects are similar or closely associated.

Die cracks, collar cracks and hub cracks are the result of wear and tear on the tools, with intentional use assumed for all classes.

II-D-1 Die Crack (W), Rarity Level: 1-3 . . . . Values: 10 to $1, $25 up on a proof coin
with a rarity level of 6-7
II-D-2 Multiple Die Cracks (W), Rarity Level: 1-3 . . . . Values: 25 cents to $2
II-D-3 Head-To-Rim Die Crack (Lincoln Cent) (W), Rarity Level: 2-6 . . Values: 25 to $10 for multiple die cracks
II-D-4 Split Die (W), Rarity Level: 5-6 . . . . Values: $10 up
II-D-5 Rim-To-Rim Die Crack (W), Rarity Level: 2-5 . . . . Values: $1 up
II-D-6 Collar Crack (W), Rarity Level: 4-6 . . . . Values: $10 up
II-D-7 Hub Crack (W), Rarity Level: 3-5 . . . . Values: $1-$2

Small die break II-E-2

Clogged letter II-E-1

Major die break, date missing, II-E-5

Rim die break II-E-4

Die breaks (II-E)

Breaks in the surface of the die allow coin metal to squeeze into the resulting holes, causing raised irregular areas above the normal surface of the coin. Die chips and small die breaks are nearly as common as the die cracks, but major die breaks, which extend in from the edge of the coin, are quite rare on the larger coins.

If the broken piece of the die is retained, the resulting design will be above or below the level of the rest of the surface.

II-E-1 Die Chip (W), Rarity Level: 1-2 . . . . Values: 10 to $1
II-E-2 Small Die Break (W), Rarity Level: 1-3 . . . . Values: 10 to $2
II-E-3 Large Die Break (W), Rarity Level: 3-5 . . . . Values: $1 to $50 and up
II-E-4 Rim Die Break (W), Rarity Level: 2-3 . . . . Values: 25 cents to $5
II-E-5 Major Die Break (WE), Rarity Level: 3-6 . . . . Values: $5 to $100 and up
II-E-6 Retained Broken Die (W), Rarity Level: 3-5 . . . . Values: $1 to $10 and up
II-E-7 Retained Broken Center of the Die (W), Rarity Level: 6-7 . . . . Values: $100 up
II-E-8 Laminated Die (W), Rarity Level: 3-5 . . . . Values: 10 cents to $5
II-E-9 Chipped Chrome Plating (W), Rarity Level: 4-5 . . . . Values: $10 to $25 on proofs
II-E-10 Collar Break (W), Rarity Level: 4-6 . . . . Values: $5 to $25 and up
II-E-11 Broken Letter or Digit on an Edge Die (W), Rarity Level: 4-6 . . . . Values: Minimal.
II-E-12 "Bar" Die Break (W), Rarity Level: 3-5 . . . . Values: 25 to $20
II-E-13 Hub Break (W), Rarity Level: 4-6 . . . . Values: 50 to $10 and up

"BIE" varieties (II-F)

A series of small die breaks or die chips in the letters of "LIBERTY" mostly on the wheat-reverse Lincoln cent are actively collected. The name results from the resemblance to an "I" between the "B" and "E" on many of the dies, but they are found between all of the letters in different cases. Well over 1,500 dies are known and cataloged. Numerous more recent examples are known.

II-F-1 ILI Die Variety (W), Rarity Level: 4-5 . . . . Values: 25 cents to $10
II-F-2 LII Die Variety (W), Rarity Level: 3-5 . . . . Values: 50 cents to $15
II-F-3 IIB Die Variety (W), Rarity Level: 3-5 . . . . Values: 50 cents to $15
II-F-4 BIE Die Variety (W), Rarity Level: 3-5 . . . . Values: $1 to $20
II-F-5 EIR Die Variety (W), Rarity Level: 3-5 . . . . Values: 50 to $15
II-F-6 RIT Die Variety (W), Rarity Level: 4-5 . . . . Values: $2 to $25
II-F-7 TIY Die Variety (W), Rarity Level: 4-5 . . . . Values: $5 to $30
II-F-8 TYI Die Variety (W), Rarity Level: 4-5 . . . . Values: $2 to $25

Worn and damaged dies, collars and hubs (II-G)

Many dies are continued deliberately in service after they have been damaged, dented, clashed or show design transfer, since none of these classes actually affect anything but the appearance of the coin. The root cause is wear, but intent or mistakes may enter the picture.

II-G-1 Dented Die, Collar or Hub (IWE), Rarity Level: 3-5 . . . . Values: 25 to $5
II-G-2 Damaged Die, Collar or Hub (IWE), Rarity Level: 3-5 . . . . Values: 25 to $5
II-G-3 Worn Die, Collar or Hub (IWE), Rarity Level: 2-3 . . . . Values: No Extra Value to Minimal Value
II-G-4 Pitted or Rusted Die, Collar or Hub (IWE), Rarity Level: 3-4 . . . . Values: No Extra Value, marker only
II-G-5 Heavy Die Clash (IWE), Rarity Level: 4-5 . . . . Values: $1 to $10 and up
II-G-6 Heavy Collar Clash (IWE), Rarity Level: 3-4 . . . . Values: $1 to $5 and up
II-G-7 Heavy Design Transfer (IWE), Rarity Level: 3-4 . . . . Values: 10 cents to $1

Die progressions (II-H)

The progression section consists of three classes. These are useful as cataloging tools for many different die varieties, but especially the die cracks and die breaks which may enlarge, lengthen or increase in number.

II-H-1 Progression (W), Rarity Level: 3-5 . . . . Values: $1 up

II-H-2 Die Substitution (IW), Rarity Level: 2-4 . . . . .Values: No Extra Value to Minimal Value
II-H-3 Die Repeat (I), Rarity Level: 2-4 . . . . .Values: No Extra Value to Minimal Value

Die scratches, polished and abraded dies (II-I)

This section consists of those classes having to do with the use of an abrasive in some form to intentionally polish proof dies, or repair the circulating die surface. Several classes that previously were referred to as "polished" now are listed as "abraded."

II-I-1 Die Scratch (IW), Rarity Level: 1-2 . . . . .Values: No Extra Value to 10 cents to 25 cents, as a marker
II-I-2 Polished (proof) Die (IW), Rarity Level: 1. . . . . .Values: No Extra Value
II-I-3 Abraded (Circulation) Die (IW), Rarity Level: 1-2. . . . . .Values: No Extra Value up to $10
II-I-4 Inside Abraded Die Doubling (IW), Rarity Level: 1-3 . . . . Values: No Extra Value to $1
II-I-5 Outside Abraded Die Doubling (IW), Rarity Level: 1-3. . . . . Values: No Extra Value to $1
II-I-6 Lathe Marks (IW), Rarity Level: 5-7 . . . . .Values: No Extra Value, marker only

Striking varieties
Division III

Once the dies are made and the planchets have been prepared, they are struck by a pair of dies and become a coin. In this division, we list the misstrikes resulting from human or mechanical malfunction in the striking process. These are one-of-a-kind varieties, but there may be many similar coins that fall in a given class.

Multiples and combinations of classes must be considered on a case by case basis. The first several sections match the planchet sections indicated in the title.

Struck on defective alloy mix planchets (III-A)

This section includes those classes of coins struck on planchets that were made from a defective alloy.

III-A-1 Struck on an Improper Alloy Mix Planchet (IE), Rarity Level: 2-3 . . . . Values: 10 cents to $2
III-A-2 Struck on a Planchet With Slag Inclusions(IE), Rarity Level: 5-6 . . . . .Values: $10 up

Struck on damaged, defective or abnormal planchet (III-B)

Struck on a defective planchet III-B-1   *Struck on a tapered planchet III-B-5*

Coins get struck on many strange objects. The more common, of course, are planchets that have been damaged in some way in the production process. In most of the classes in this section, intent is at least presumed, if not specifically listed as a cause.

III-B-1 Struck on a Defective Planchet (IWE), Rarity Level: 4-6. . . . . .Values: $5 to $10 and up
III-B-2 Struck on a Mechanically Damaged Planchet (IWE), Rarity Level: 5-6. . . . . . .Values: $10 to $20 and up
III-B-3 Struck on a Rolled Thin Planchet (IWE), Rarity Level: 5-6 . . . . .Values: $2 to $5 and up
III-B-4 Struck on a Rolled Thick Planchet (IWE), Rarity Level: 5-6 . . . . .Values: $35 to $50 and up
III-B-5 Struck on a Tapered Planchet (WE), Rarity Level: 4-6 . . . . .Values: $2 to $5 and up
III-B-6 Struck on a Partially Unplated Planchet (WE), Rarity Level: 5 . . . . .Values: $10 up
III-B-7 Struck on an Unplated Planchet (WE), Rarity Level: 6-7 . . . . .Values: $100 up
III-B-8 Struck on a Bubbled Plating Planchet (IWE), Rarity Level: 1 . . . . .Values: No Value
III-B-9 Struck on an Included Gas Bubble Planchet (WE), Rarity Level: 5-6 . . . . .Values: $5 up
III-B-10 Struck on a Partially Unclad Planchet (WE), Rarity Level: 5-6 . . . . .Values: $5 up

III-B-11 Struck on an Unclad Planchet (WE), Rarity Level: 4-5 . . . . .Values: $5 and up
III-B-12 Struck on an Undersize Planchet (WE), Rarity Level: 4-6 . . . . .Values: Minimal
III-B-13 Struck on an Oversize Planchet (WE), Rarity Level: 6-7 . . . . Values: Minimal
III-B-14 Struck on an Improperly Prepared Proof Planchet (IWE), Rarity Level: 3-5 . . . . .Values: $5 up
III-B-15 Struck on an Improperly Annealed Planchet (IWE), Rarity Level: 4-5 . . . . .Values: $5 up
III-B-16 Struck on a Faulty Upset Edge Planchet (IWE), Rarity Level: 4-5 . . . . .Values: $1 to $2
III-B-17 Struck on a Rolled In Metal Planchet (WE), Rarity Level: 4-6 . . . . .Values: $2 up
III-B-18 Struck on a Weld Area Planchet (WE), Rarity Level: 6 . . . . .Values: $25 to $50
III-B-19 Struck on a Strike Clip Planchet (W), Rarity Level: 6-7 . . . . .Values: $25 up
III-B-20 Struck on an Unpunched Center Hole Planchet (WE), Rarity Level: 4-6 . . . . Values: $1 and up
III-B-21 Struck on an Incompletely Punched Center Hole Planchet (WE), Rarity Level: 6-7 . . . . . .Values: $5 up
III-B-22 Struck on an Uncentered Center Hole Planchet (WE), Rarity Level: 6-7 . . . . .Values: $10 up
III-B-23 Struck on a Multiple Punched Center Hole Planchet (WE), Rarity Level: 7 . . . . .Values: $25 up
III-B-24 Struck on an Unintended Center Hole Planchet (WE), Rarity Level: 6-7 . . . . Values: $25 and up
III-B-25 Struck on a Wrong Size or Shape Center Hole Planchet (WE), Rarity Level: 5-7 . . . . . . .Values: $5 up
III-B-26 Struck on Scrap Coin Metal (E), Rarity Level: 4-6 . . . . .Values: $10 up
III-B-27 Struck on Junk Non Coin Metal (E), Rarity Level: 4-6 . . . . .Values: $15 up
III-B-28 Struck on a False Planchet (E), Rarity Level: 3-5 . . . . .Values: $35 up
III-B-29 Struck on Bonded Planchets (E), Rarity Level: 6-7 . . . . .Values: $50 up

Struck on a clipped planchet (III-C)

Ragged edge clip III-C-15

Multiple clip III-C-8   *Incomplete curved clip III-C-10*

Coins struck on clipped blanks, or planchets, exhibit the same missing areas as they did before striking, modified by the metal flow from the strike which rounds the edges and tends to move metal into the missing areas. Values for blanks will run higher than planchets with similar clips.

III-C-1 Struck on a Disc Clip Planchet (WE), Rarity Level: 4-5 . . . . Values: $1 on regular coins,
    $20 and up for clad coins
III-C-2 Struck on a Curved Clip Planchet - to 5% (WE), Rarity Level: 3-5 . . . . Values: 50 cents up
III-C-3 Struck on a Curved Clip Planchet - (6 to 10%) (WE), Rarity Level: 4-5 . . . . .Values: $1 up
III-C-4 Struck on a Curved Clip Planchet - (11 to 25%) (WE), Rarity Level: 4-5 . . . . .Values: $2 up
III-C-5 Struck on a Curved Clip Planchet - (26 to 60%) (WE), Rarity Level: 4-6 . . . . .Values: $10 up
III-C-6 Struck on a Double Curved Clip Planchet (WE), Rarity Level: 3-4 .Values: $2 up
III-C-7 Struck on a Triple Curved Clip Planchet (WE), Rarity Level: 4-5 . . . . .Values: $5 up
III-C-8 Struck on a Multiple Curved Clip Planchet (WE), Rarity Level: 4-6 . . . . .Values: $5 up
III-C-9 Struck on an Overlapping Curved Clipped Planchet (WE), Rarity Level: 5-6 . . . . .Values: $15 up
III-C-10 Struck on an Incomplete Curved Clip Planchet (WE), Rarity Level: 4-5 . . . . .Values: $10 up
III-C-11 Struck on an Oval Clip Planchet (WE), Rarity Level: 5-6 . . . . .Values: $20 up
III-C-12 Struck on a Crescent Clip Planchet - (61% or more) (WE), Rarity Level: 6-7 . . . . .Values: $100 up
III-C-13 Struck on a Straight Clip Planchet (E), Rarity Level: 4-6 . . . . .Values: $10 up

III-C-14 Struck on an Incomplete Straight Clip Planchet (WE), Rarity Level: 5-6 . . . . .Values: $20 up
III-C-15 Struck on a Ragged Clip Planchet (E), Rarity Level: 4-6 . . . . .Values: $15 up
III-C-16 Struck on an Outside Corner Clip Planchet (E), Rarity Level: 7 . . . . .Values: $100 up
III-C-17 Struck on an Inside Corner Clip Planchet (E), Rarity Level: Unknown outside mint. . . . . .Values:
III-C-18 Struck on an Irregularly Clipped Planchet (E), Rarity Level: 6-7 . . . . Values: $20 up.
III-C-19 Struck on an Incompletely Punched Scalloped or Multi-Sided Planchet (E), Rarity Level: 7
. . . . .Values: $20 up.

Struck on a laminated, split or broken planchet (III-D)

Lamination crack III-D-1   *Layer peeled off III-D-2*   *Split planchet III-D-3*

This section has to do with the splitting, cracking or breaking of a coin parallel to the faces of the coin, or at least very nearly parallel, or breaks at right angles to the faces of the coin.

Lamination cracks and missing metal of any size below a split planchet are too common in the 35-percent silver 1942-1945 nickels to be collectible or have any significant value.

III-D-1 Struck on a Small Lamination Crack Planchet (W), Rarity Level: 3-4. . . . . .Values: 10 up
III-D-2 Struck on a Large Lamination Crack Planchet (W), Rarity Level: 3-6. . . . . .Values: $1 up
III-D-3 Struck on a Split Planchet (W), Rarity Level: 4-6. . . . . .Values: $5 up
III-D-4 Struck on a Hinged Split Planchet (W), Rarity Level: 5-6. . . . . .Values: $35 up
III-D-5 Struck on a Planchet With a Clad Layer Missing (W), Rarity Level: 4-5. . . . . .Values: $15 up
III-D-6 Struck on a Planchet With Both Clad Layers Missing (W), Rarity Level: 4-5 . . . . .Values: $25 up
III-D-7 Struck on a Separated Clad Layer or Lamination (W), Rarity Level: 6-7. . . . . .Values: $75 up
III-D-8 Struck on a Broken Planchet Before the Strike (W), Rarity Level: 3-5 . . . . .Values: $10 up
III-D-9 Broken Coin During or After the Strike (W), Rarity Level: 4-6 .Values: $20 up
III-D-10 Struck Coin Fragment Split or Broken During or After the Strike (W), Rarity Level: 3-5. . .Values: $5 up
III-D-11 Reedless Coin Broken During or After the Strike (W), Rarity Level: Unknown . . . . .Values: -

Struck on wrong stock planchets (III-E)

Quarter on dime stock
III-E-7 (lower coin edge)

These classes cover those cases where the wrong stock was run through the blanking press, making planchets of the correct diameter, but of the wrong thickness, alloy or metal or a combination of incorrect thickness and metal.

III-E-1 Struck on a Half Cent-Stock Planchet (IE), Rarity Level: Unknown. . . . . . . .Values: No Value Established
III-E-2 Struck on a Cent-Stock Planchet (IE), Rarity Level: Unknown . . . . .Values: No Value Established
III-E-3 Struck on a Two-Cent-Stock Planchet (E), Rarity Level: Unknown . . . . .Values: -
III-E-4 Struck on a Three-Cent-Silver Stock Planchet (E), Rarity Level: Unknown . . . . .Values: -
III-E-5 Struck on a Three-Cent-Nickel Stock Planchet (E), Rarity Level: Unknown . . . . .Values: -
III-E-6 Struck on a Half Dime-Stock Planchet (E), Rarity Level: Unknown. .Values: -
III-E-7 Struck on a Dime-Stock Planchet (E), Rarity Level: 5-6 . . . . .Values: $20 up

III-E-8 Struck on a Twenty-Cent-Stock Planchet (E), Rarity Level: Unknown.....................Values: -
III-E-9 Struck on a Quarter-Stock Planchet (E), Rarity Level: 6 ....Values: $50 up
III-E-10 Struck on a Half Dollar-Stock Planchet (E), Rarity Level: 6-7....................Values: $100 up
III-E-11 Struck on a Dollar-Stock Planchet (E), Rarity Level: 6-7 ....Values: $300 up
III-E-12 Struck on a Token/Medal-Stock Planchet (E), Rarity Level: 7...........Values: No Value Established
III-E-13 Struck on a Wrong Thickness Spoiled Planchet (IWE), Rarity Level: 7...............Values: $50 up
III-E-14 Struck on a Correct Thickness Spoiled Planchet (IWE), Rarity Level: Unknown. Values: No Value Established
III-E-15 Struck on a Cut Down Struck Token (IWE), Rarity Level: 6-7......................Values: $50 up
III-E-16 Struck on an Experimental or Pattern-Stock Planchet (IE), Rarity Level: 7 ....Values: $50 up
III-E-17 Struck on a Proof-Stock Planchet (IE), Rarity Level: 7 ....Values: $100 up
III-E-18 Struck on an Adjusted Specification-Stock Planchet (IE), Rarity Level: 3-7. Values: No Value to $5 and up
III-E-19 Struck on a Trial Strike-Stock Planchet (IE), Rarity Level: Unknown......Values: No Value Established
III-E-20 U.S. Coin Struck on a Foreign-Stock Planchet. (E), Rarity Level: 5 ....Values: $35 up
III-E-21 Foreign Coin Struck on a Foreign-Stock Planchet (E), Rarity Level: 5-6 ....Values: $25 up
III-E-22 Struck on a Non-Standard Coin Alloy (IE), Rarity Level: 4-7 ....Values: $20 up

Extra metal (III-F)

Extra metal on a
struck coin (III-F-2)

Sintered coating III-F-3

The term "extra metal" for the purpose of this section includes both extra metal added to the blank during the blanking operation and metal powder added to the planchet during the annealing operation.

III-F-1 Struck on a Type 1 Blank With Extra Metal (W), Rarity Level: Unknown...................Values: -
III-F-2 Struck on a Type 2 Planchet With Extra Metal (W), Rarity Level: 4-5 ....Values: $10 up
III-F-3 Struck on a Sintered Coating Planchet (W), Rarity Level: 6-7 ....Values: $35 up

Struck on normal or abnormal blanks, or planchets (III-G)

Half on dime
planchet III-G-10

Cent on dime
planchet III-G-10

Half on quarter
planchet III-G-10

This section includes coins struck on either a blank, as it comes from the blanking press, or as a planchet that has passed through the upsetting mill. Added to this section are those planchets that are normal until they are struck by the wrong dies. These differ from the wrong stock planchets because the wrong stock planchets are already a variety before they are struck.

III-G-1 Struck on a Type 1 Blank (IWE), Rarity Level: 4-6 ....Values: $10 up
III-G-2 Struck on a Type 2 Planchet (I), Rarity Level: 1 ....Values: No Extra Value
III-G-3 Struck on a Purchased Planchet (I), Rarity Level: 1 ....Values: No Extra Value
III-G-4 Struck on a Mint-Made Planchet (I), Rarity Level: 1 ....Values: No Extra Value
III-G-5 Struck on an Adjustment-Marked Planchet (I), Rarity Level: 4-7 .... Values: Minimal, and may
reduce value of coin in some cases
III-G-6 Struck on a Hardness Test-Marked Planchet (I), Rarity Level: 6-7..................Values: $10 up

III-G-7 Wrong Planchet or Metal on a Half Cent Planchet (IE), Rarity Level: 5-7. . . . . .Values: $100 up
III-G-8 Wrong Planchet or Metal on a Cent Planchet (IE), Rarity Level: 3-6 . . . . .Values: $25 up
III-G-9 Wrong Planchet or Metal on a Nickel Planchet (E), Rarity Level: 4-6. . . . . .Values: $35 up
III-G-10 Wrong Planchet or Metal on a Dime Planchet (E), Rarity Level: 4-6 . . . . .Values: $50 up
III-G-11 Wrong Planchet or Metal on a Quarter Planchet (E), Rarity Level: 4-6. . . . . .Values: $100 up
III-G-12 Wrong Planchet or Metal on a Half Dollar Planchet (E), Rarity Level: 6-7 . . . . .Values: $500 up
III-G-13 Wrong Planchet or Metal on a Dollar Planchet (E), Rarity Level: 7 . . . . .Values: $500 up
III-G-14 Wrong Planchet or Metal on a Gold Planchet (E), Rarity Level: 7 . . . . .Values: $1000 up
III-G-15 Struck on a Wrong Series Planchet (IE), Rarity Level: 6-7. .Values: $1500 up
III-G-16 U.S. Coin Struck on a Foreign Planchet (E), Rarity Level: 5-7. . . . . .Values: $35 up
III-G-17 Foreign Coin Struck on a U.S. Planchet (E), Rarity Level: 6-7. . . . . .Values: $50 up
III-G-18 Foreign Coin Struck on a Wrong Foreign Planchet (E), Rarity Level: 6-7 . . . . .Values: $50 up
III-G-19 Struck on a Medal Planchet (E), Rarity Level: 6-7 . . . . .Values: $100 up
III-G-20 Medal Struck on a Coin Planchet (IE), Rarity Level: 3-5 . . . . .Values: $10 up
III-G-21 Struck on an Official Sample Planchet (IE), Rarity Level: Unknown . . . . . .Values: No Value Established
III-G-22 Struck Intentionally on a Wrong Planchet (I), Rarity Level: 6-7 . . Values: Mainly struck as Presentation
Pieces, full numismatic value
III-G-23 Non-Proof Struck on a Proof Planchet (IE), Rarity Level: 6-7 . . . . .Values: $500 up

Struck on coin metal strip (III-H)

Pieces of the coin metal strip do manage at times to escape into the coin press.

III-H-1 (See I-H-1 Punched Coin Metal Strip), Rarity Level: Impossible. . . . . .Values: -
III-H-2 Struck on Chopped Coin Metal Strip (E), Rarity Level: 6-7 . . . . .Values: $25 up

Die adjustment strikes (III-I)

As the dies are set up and adjusted in the coin press, variations in the strike occur
until the dies are properly set. Test strikes are normally scrapped, but on occasion
reach circulation.

III-I-1 Die Adjustment Strike (IE), Rarity Level: 5-6. . . . . .Values: $35 up
III-I-2 Edge Strike (E), Rarity Level: 5-6 . . . . .Values: $10 to $20 and up
III-I-3 Weak Strike (W), Rarity Level: 1 . . . . .Values: No Extra Value
III-I-4 Strong Strike (IWE), Rarity Level: 1. . . . . .Values: No value except for the premium
that might be paid for a well struck coin
III-I-5 Jam Strike (IE), Rarity Level: 7 . . . . .Values: $50 up
III-I-6 Trial Piece Strike (I), Rarity Level: 6-7. . . . . .Values: $100 up
III-I-7 Edge-Die Adjustment Strike (I), Rarity Level: 5-7 . . . . .Values: $5 up
III-I-8 Uniface Strike (I), Rarity Level 7 . . . . .Values: $50 up

Indented, brockage and counter-brockage strikes (III-J)

Indented strike   Counter-brockage strike   Capped die strike
III-J-1   III-J-11   III-J-15

Indented and uniface strikes involve an extra unstruck planchet between one of
the dies and the planchet being struck. Brockage strikes involve a struck coin between
one of the dies and the planchet and a counter-brockage requires a brockage coin
between one of the dies and the planchet.

A cap, or capped die strike results when a coin sticks to the die and is squeezed
around it in the shape of a bottle cap.

III-J-1 Indented Strike (W), Rarity Level: 3-6. . . . . .Values: $5 up
III-J-2 Uniface Strike (W), Rarity Level: 3-5 . . . . .Values: $15 up
III-J-3 Indented Strike By a Smaller Planchet (WE), Rarity Level: 5-7 . . . . .Values: $100 up

III-J-4 Indented Second Strike (W), Rarity Level: 3-5 . . . . Values: $10 up, about the same as a regular double strike of comparable size
III-J-5 Partial Brockage Strike (W), Rarity Level: 3-6. . . . . Values: $15 up
III-J-6 Full Brockage Strike (W), Rarity Level: 3-6. . . . . Values: $5 up
III-J-7 Brockage Strike of a Smaller Coin (WE), Rarity Level: 6-7 . . . . Values: $200 up
III-J-8 Brockage Strike of a Struck Coin Fragment (WE), Rarity Level: 4-6 . . . . Values: $5 up
III-J-9 Brockage Second Strike (WE), Rarity Level: 3-5. . . . . Values: $5 up
III-J-10 Partial Counter-Brockage Strike (WE), Rarity Level: 3-5. . . . . Values: $10 up
III-J-11 Full Counter-Brockage Strike (WE), Rarity Level: 5-7. . . . . Values: $100 up
III-J-12 Counter-Brockage Second Strike (WE), Rarity Level: 4-6 . . . . Values: $10 up
III-J-13 Full Brockage-Counter-Brockage Strike (WE), Rarity Level: 6-7. . . . . Values: $150 up
III-J-14 Multiple Brockage or Counter-Brockage Strike (WE), Rarity Level: 5-7 . . . . Values: $100 up
III-J-15 Capped Die Strike (WE), Rarity Level: 6-7 . . . . Values: $500 up
III-J-16 Reversed Capped Die Strike (WE), Rarity Level: 7 . . . . Values: $1,000 up

Struck through abnormal objects (III-K)

Struck through cloth III-K-1   *Struck through a filled die III-K-4*   *Struck through a dropped filling III-K-5*

This section covers most of the objects or materials that might come between the planchet and the die and be struck into the surface of the coin. Unless noted, the materials - even the soft ones - are driven into the surface of the coin.

III-K-1 Struck Through Cloth (IWE), Rarity Level: 3-6. . . . . Values: $35 up
III-K-2 Struck Through Wire (IWE), Rarity Level: 3-6 . . . . Values: $5 up
III-K-3 Struck Through Thread (IWE), Rarity Level: 3-6. . . . . Values: $5 up
III-K-4 Struck Through Dirt-and-Grease-Filled Die (IWE), Rarity Level: 1-4
. . . . Values: 10 cents to 25 cents up, but no value on a worn or circulated coin
III-K-5 Struck Through a Dropped Filling (IWE), Rarity Level: 5-6 . . . . Values: $10 up
III-K-6 Struck Through Wrong Metal Fragments (IWE), Rarity Level: 4-6 . . . . Values: $1 up
III-K-7 Struck Through an Unstruck Planchet Fragment (IWE), Rarity Level: 3-5 . . . . Values: $1 up
III-K-8 Struck Through a Rim Burr (IWE), Rarity Level: 3-5. . . . . Values: $1 to $2 and up
III-K-9 Struck Through plit-Off Reeding (IWE), Rarity Level: 5-6. . . . . Values: $25 up
III-K-10 Struck Through a Feed Finger (IWE), Rarity Level: 5-7 . . . . Values: $25 to $50 and up
III-K-11 Struck Through Miscellaneous Objects (IWE), Rarity Level: 4-6 . . . . Values: $1 up
III-K-12 Struck Through Progression (IWE), Rarity Level: 4-6 . . . . Values: $1 up
Note: Some 1987 through 1994 quarters are found without mintmarks, classed as III-K-4, a Filled Die. Values depend on market conditions. Filled dies have value ONLY on current, uncirculated grade coins.

Double strikes (III-L)

Only coins that receive two or more strikes by the die pair fall in this section and are identified by the fact that both sides of the coin are affected. Unless some object interferes, an equal area of both sides of the coin will be equally doubled.

The exception is the second strike with a loose die, which will double only one side of a coin, but is a rare form usually occurring only on proofs. A similar effect is flat field doubling from die chatter.

III-L-1 Close Centered Double Strike (WE), Rarity Level: 4-6 . . . . Values: $15 up
III-L-2 Rotated Second Strike Over a Centered First Strike (WE), Rarity Level: 4-6 . . . . Values: $15 up
III-L-3 Off-Center Second Strike Over a Centered First Strike (WE), Rarity Level: 4-6. . . . . Values: $15 up

Off-center second strike over centered first strike III-L-3

Non-overlapping double strike III-L-8

Multiple strike III-L-16

Chain strike III-L-10

III-L-4 Off-Center Second Strike Over an Off-Center First Strike (WE), Rarity Level: 4-6. . . . . . . .Values: $10 up
III-L-5 Off-Center Second Strike Over a Broadstrike (WE), Rarity Level: 5-6. . . . . .Values: $20 up
III-L-6 Centered Second Strike Over an Off-Center First Strike (WE), Rarity Level: 5-6. . . . . . . .Values: $50 up
III-L-7 Obverse Struck Over Reverse (WE), Rarity Level: 5-6. . . . . .Values: $25 up
III-L-8 Nonoverlapping Double Strike (WE), Rarity Level: 5-6. . . . . .Values: $20 up
III-L-9 Struck Over a Different Denomination or Series (WE), Rarity Level: 6 . . . . Values: $300 and up
III-L-10 Chain Strike (WE), Rarity Level: 6 . . . . . Values: $300 up for the pair of coins that were struck together
III-L-11 Second-Strike Doubling From a Loose Die (W), Rarity Level: 6-7 . . . . .Values: $200 up
III-L-12 Second-Strike Doubling From a Loose Screw Press Die (W), Rarity Level: 5-6 . . . . . Values: $100 up
III-L-13 Second Strike on an Edge Strike (WE), Rarity Level: 5-6 . . . . .Values: $20 up
III-L-14 Folded Planchet Strike (WE), Rarity Level: 5-7. . . . . .Values: $100 up
III-L-15 Triple Strike (WE), Rarity Level: 6-7. . . . . .Values: $100 up
III-L-16 Multiple Strike (WE), Rarity Level: 6-7. . . . . .Values: $200 up
III-L-17 U.S. Coin Struck Over a Struck Foreign Coin (WE), Rarity Level: 6-7 . . . . .Values: $300 up
III-L-18 Foreign Coin Struck Over a Struck U.S. Coin (WE), Rarity Level: 6-7 . . . . .Values: $400 up
III-L-19 Foreign Coin Struck Over a Struck Foreign Coin (WE), Rarity Level: 7 . . . . .Values: $500 up
III-L-20 Double Strike on Scrap or Junk (E), Rarity Level: 6 . . . . .Values: $50 up
III-L-21 Struck on a Struck Token or Medal (E), Rarity Level: 5-6 . . . . .Values: $100 up
III-L-22 Double-Struck Edge Motto or Design (E), Rarity Level: 6-7 .Values: $200 up
III-L-23 One Edge Motto or Design Struck Over Another (E), Rarity Level: 7. . . . . .Values: $300 up
III-L-24 Flat Field Doubling (W), Rarity Level: 2-3 . . . . .Values: $1 to $5
III-L-25 Territorial Struck over Struck U.S. Coin: (I) Rarity Level: 6-7 .Values: $200 up
III-L-26 Pattern Struck over Struck U.S. Coin: (I) Rarity Level: 6-7 . . . . .Values: $200 up
III-L-27 Pattern Struck over Struck Pattern:(I) Rarity Level 6-7 . . . . .Values: $200 up
III-L-28 Pattern Struck Over Foreign Coin:(I) Rarity Level 6-7 . . . . Values - $200 up

Collar striking varieties (III-M)

The collar is often referred to as the "Third Die," and is involved in a number of forms of misstrikes. The collar normally rises around the planchet, preventing it from squeezing sideways between the dies and at the same time forming the reeding on reeded coins.

If the collar is out of position or tilted, a partial collar strike results; if completely missing, it causes a broadstrike; if the planchet is not entirely between the dies, an off-center strike.

Flanged partial collar III-M-1

*Struck off center
10 to 30 percent III-M-7*

*Struck off center
31 to 70 percent III-M-8*

*Struck off center
71 percent or more
III-M-9*

III-M-1 Flanged Partial Collar Strike (WE), Rarity Level: 5-6. . . . . .Values: $20 up
III-M-2 Reversed Flanged Partial Collar Strike (WE), Rarity Level: 6-7 . . . . .Values: $35 up
III-M-3 Tilted Partial Collar Strike (WE), Rarity Level: 5-6 . . . . .Values: $20 up
III-M-4 Centered Broadstrike (WE), Rarity Level: 5-6 . . . . .Values: $5 up
III-M-5 Uncentered Broadstrike (WE), Rarity Level: 5 . . . . .Values: $3 up
III-M-6 Reversed Broadstrike (WE), Rarity Level: 6 . . . . .Values: $10 up
III-M-7 Struck Off-Center 10-30% (W), Rarity Level: 3-6 . . . . .Values: $3 up
III-M-8 Struck Off-Center 31-70% (W), Rarity Level: 4-6 . . . . .Values: $5 up
III-M-9 Struck Off-Center 71% or More (W), Rarity Level: 3-5 . . . . .Values: $2 up
III-M-10 Rotated Multi-sided Planchet Strike (W), Rarity Level: 5-6 . . . . .Values: $10 up
III-M-11 Wire Edge Strike (IWE), Rarity Level: 1-2 . . . . .Values: No Extra Value
III-M-12 Struck With the Collar Too High (WE), Rarity Level: 6-7. . . . . .Values: $20 up
III-M-13 Off-Center Slide Strike (W), Rarity Level: 3-6 . . . . .Values: $4 up

Misaligned and rotated (die) strike varieties (III-N)

Misaligned die III-N-1

Normal rotation

90 degrees

180 degrees

One (rarely both) of the dies may be Offset Misaligned, off to one side, or may be tilted (Vertically Misaligned). One die may either have been installed so that it is turned in relation to the other die, or may turn in the holder, or the shank may break allowing the die face to rotate in relation to the opposing die.

Vertical misaligned dies are rarely found, and, like rotated dies, find only limited collector interest. Ninety- and 180-degree rotations are the most popular. Rotations of 14 degrees or less have no value. The 1989-D Congress dollar is found with a nearly

180-degree rotated reverse, currently retailing for around $2,000. Only about 30 have been reported to date.

III-N-1 Offset Die Misalignment Strike (WE), Rarity Level: 3-5 . . . . .Values: $2 up
III-N-2 Vertical Die Misalignment Strike (WE), Rarity Level: 4-6. . . . . .Values: $1 up
III-N-3 Rotated Die Strike - 15 to 45 Degrees (IWE), Rarity Level: 4-6 .Values: $2 up
III-N-4 Rotated Die Strike - 46 to 135 Degrees (IWE), Rarity Level: 5-6 . . . . .Values: $10 up
III-N-5 Rotated Die Strike - 136 to 180 Degrees (IWE), Rarity Level: 5-6 . . . . .Values: $25 up

Lettered and design edge strike varieties (III-O)

Overlapping edge letters III-O-1

Early U.S. coins and a number of foreign coins have either lettered edges or designs on the edge of the coin. Malfunctions of the application of the motto or design to the edge fall in this section.

III-O-1 Overlapping Edge Motto or Design (WE), Rarity Level: 3-4. . . . . .Values: $5 to $10 and up
III-O-2 Wrong Edge Motto or Design (WE), Rarity Level: 5-6-7 . . . . .Values: $50 up
III-O-3 Missing Edge Motto, Design or Security Edge (IWE), Rarity Level: 5-6-7 . . . . .Values: $50 up
III-O-4 Jammed Edge Die Strike (W), Rarity Level: 6. . . . . .Values: $10 up
III-O-5 Misplaced Segment of an Edge Die (E), Rarity Level: 4-7 . . . . .Values: $25 up
III-O-6 Reeded Edge Struck Over a Lettered Edge (IE), Rarity Level: 3-6. . . . . Values: No Extra Value up

Defective strikes and mismatched dies (III-P)

The final section of the Striking Division covers coins that are not properly struck for reasons other than those in previous classes, such as coins struck with mismatched (muled) dies. The mismatched die varieties must be taken on a case by case basis, while the other classes presently have little collector demand or premium.

III-P-1 Defective Strike (WE), Rarity Level: 1. . . . . .Values: No Extra Value
III-P-2 Mismatched Die Strike (E), Rarity Level: 4-7 . . . . .Values: $25 up
III-P-3 Single-Strike Proof (WE), Rarity Level: 4-5 . . . . .Values: Minimal
III-P-4 Single Die-Proof Strike (IE), Rarity Level: 5-6 . . . . .Values: $100 up
III-P-5 Reversed Die Strike (I), Rarity Level: 4-5 . . . . .Values: No Extra Value to Minimal

Official Mint modifications
Division IV

Several mint-produced varieties occur after the coin has been struck, resulting in the addition of the fourth division to my PDS System. Since most of these coins are either unique or are special varieties, each one must be taken on a case by case basis. All classes listed here are by definition intentional.

I have not listed values as the coins falling in these classes, which are sold through regular numismatic channels, are cataloged with the regular issues or are covered in specialized catalogs in their particular area.

Matte proofs (IV-A)

Matte proofs IV-A-1

Matte proofs as a section include several of the forms of proof coins that have the striking characteristics of a mirror proof but have been treated AFTER striking to give them a grainy, non-reflective surface.

IV-A-1 Matte Proof (I), Rarity Level: 3-5 . . . . Values: Normal Numismatic Value
IV-A-2 Matte Proof on One Side (I), Rarity Level: 7 . . . . Values: Normal Numismatic Value
IV-A-3 Sandblast Proof (I), Rarity Level: 4-6 . . . . Values: Normal Numismatic Value

Additional engraving (IV-B)

Counterstamp IV-B-3

This section includes any added markings that are placed on the struck coin and struck coins that later were cut into pieces for various purposes. The warning is repeated: Anything done to a coin after the strike is extremely difficult t o authenticate and is much easier to fake than a die struck coin.

IV-B-1 Counterstamp and Countermark (I), Rarity Level: 3-6 . . . . Values: Normal Numismatic Value
IV-B-2 Perforated and Cut Coins (I), Rarity Level: 4-6 . . . . Values: Normal Numismatic Value

Restrikes (IV-C)

Restrike with new dies IV-C-7

Restrikes cover a complicated mixture of official use of dies from a variety of sources. Whether or not some were officially sanctioned is always a problem for the collector.

IV-C-1) Restrike on the Same Denomination Planchet (I), Rarity Level: 4-6. . .Values: Normal Numismatic Value

IV-C-2 Restrike on a Different Denomination or Series Planchet (I), Rarity Level: 4-6
. . . . .Values: Normal Numismatic Value

IV-C-3 Restrike on a Foreign Coin (I), Rarity Level: 6-7 . . . . .Values: Normal Numismatic Value

IV-C-4 Restrike on a Token or Medal (I), Rarity Level: 5-6 . . . . .Values: Normal Numismatic Value

IV-C-5 Restruck With the Original Dies (I), Rarity Level: 4-6 . . . . .Values: Normal Numismatic Value

IV-C-6 Restruck With Mismatched Dies (I), Rarity Level: 4-6 . . . . .Values: Normal Numismatic Value

IV-C-7 Copy Strike With New Dies (I), Rarity Level: 3-5 . . . . .Values: Normal Numismatic Value

IV-C-8 Fantasy Strike (I), Rarity Level: 4-6 . . . . .Values: Normal Numismatic Value

After strike modifications

Division V

This division includes both modifications that have value to collectors – and those that don't. I needed a couple of divisions to cover other things that happen to coins to aid in cataloging them. This avoids the false conclusion that an unlisted coin is quite rare, when the exact opposite is more likely to be the case.

Collectible modifications after strike (V-A)

Mint modification V-A-8

This section includes those classes having to do with deliberate modifications of the coin done with a specific purpose or intent that makes them of some value to collectors. Quite often these pieces were made specifically to sell to collectors, or at least to the public, under the guise of being collectible.

V-A-1 Screw Thaler, Rarity Level: 5-6 . . . . Values: Normal Numismatic Value
V-A-2 Love Token, Rarity Level: 3-6 . . . . Values: $10 up
V-A-3 Satirical or Primitive Engraving, Rarity Level: 6-7 . . . . Values: $5 up
V-A-4 Elongated Coin, Rarity Level: 2-7 . . . . Values: 50 cents to $1 and up
V-A-5 Coin Jewelry, Rarity Level: 2-5 . . . . Values: $1 up
V-A-6 Novelty Coin, Rarity Level: 1-3 . . . . Values: No Value up to $5 to $10
V-A-7 Toning, Rarity Level: 3-6 . . . . Values: No value up, depending on coloration. Easily faked
V-A-8 Mint Modification, Rarity Level: 4-7 . . . . Values: $5 up. Easily faked
V-A-9 Mint Packaging Mistake, Rarity Level: 5-7 . . . . Values: Nominal $1. Very easily faked

Alterations and damage after the strike (V-B)

Machine doubling damage V-B-1

This section includes those changes in a coin that have no collector value. In most cases, their effect on the coin is to reduce or entirely eliminate any collector value - and in the case of counterfeits they are actually illegal to even own.

V -B-1 Machine Doubling Damage: *NOTE: Machine doubling damage is defined as: "Damage to a coin after the strike, due to die bounce or chatter or die displacement, showing on the struck coin as scrapes on the sides of the design elements, with portions of the coin metal in the relief elements either displaced sideways or downward, depending on the direction of movement of the loose die."* Machine doubling damage, or MDD, is by far the most common form of doubling found on almost any coin in the world. Rarity Level: 0 . . . . Values: Reduces the coin's value
V-B-2 Accidental or Deliberate Damage, Rarity Level: 0 . . . . Values: Reduces the coin's value
V-B-3 Test Cut or Mark, Rarity Level: 0 . . . . Values: Reduces value of coin to face or bullion value
V-B-4 Alteration, Rarity Level: 0 . . . . Values: Reduces value to face or bullion value
V-B-5 Whizzing, Rarity Level: 0 . . . . . . Values: Reduces value sharply and may reduce it to face or bullion value
V-B-6 Counterfeit, Copy, Facsimile, Forgery or Fake, Rarity Level: 0 . . Values: No Value and may be illegal to own
V-B-7 Planchet Deterioration. Very common on copper-plated zinc cents. Rarity level: 0 . . . . . Values: No Value

COLONIAL COINAGE

MARYLAND
Lord Baltimore

PENNY (DENARIUM)

KM# 1 • Copper • Obv. Legend: CAECILIVS Dns TERRAE MARIAE

Date	Good	VG	Fine	VF	XF
(1659) 9 known	—	— 65,000	120,000	200,000

Note: Stack's Auction 5-04, Proof realized $241,500

4 PENCE (GROAT)

KM# 2 • Silver ASW • **Obv:** Large bust **Obv. Legend:** CAECILIVS Dns TERRAE MARIAE **Rev:** Large shield

Date	AG	Good	VG	Fine	VF	XF
(1659)	1,250	1,950	3,500	6,250	13,500	22,000

KM# 3 • Silver ASW • **Obv:** Small bust **Obv. Legend:** CAECILIVS Dns TERRAE MARIAE **Rev:** Small shield

Date	AG	Good	VG	Fine	VF	XF
(1659) unique	—	—	—	—	—	—

Note: Norweb $26,400

6 PENCE

KM# 4 • Silver ASW • **Obv:** Small bust **Obv. Legend:** CAECILIVS Dns TERRAE MARIAE **Note:** Known in two other rare small-bust varieties and two rare large-bust varieties.

Date	AG	Good	VG	Fine	VF	XF
(1659)	850	1,400	2,400	5,000	9,500	15,000

SHILLING

KM# 6 • Silver ASW • **Obv. Legend:** CAECILIVS Dns TERRAE MARIAE **Note:** Varieties exist; one is very rare.

Date	AG	Good	VG	Fine	VF	XF	Unc
(1659)	1,100	1,850	3,250	6,000	13,500	20,000	—

MASSACHUSETTS
New England

3 PENCE

KM# 1 • Silver ASW • **Obv:** NE **Rev:** III

Date	AG	Good	VG	Fine	VF	XF
(1652) Unique	—	—	—	—	—	—

Note: Massachusetts Historical Society specimen

6 PENCE

KM# 2 • Silver ASW • **Obv:** NE **Rev:** VI

Date	Good	VG	Fine	VF	XF
(1652) 8 known	28,000	60,000	115,000	225,000	—

Note: Garrett $75,000

SHILLING

KM# 3 • Silver ASW • **Obv:** NE **Rev:** XII

Date	AG	Good	VG	Fine	VF	XF
(1652)	—	37,500	75,000	150,000	250,000	—

US COLONIAL AMERICA

Oak Tree

2 PENCE

KM# 7 • Silver ASW • **Note:** Small 2 and large 2 varieites exist

Date	AG	Good	VG	Fine	VF	XF	Unc
1662	—	500	900	2,000	3,850	6,500	15,000

3 PENCE

KM# 8 • Silver ASW • **Note:** Two types of legends.

Date	AG	Good	VG	Fine	VF	XF	Unc
1652	350	650	1,250	3,000	6,500	12,000	—

6 PENCE

KM# 9 • Silver ASW • **Note:** Three types of legends.

Date	AG	Good	VG	Fine	VF	XF	Unc
1652	400	900	1,350	3,500	8,000	17,500	35,000

SHILLING

KM# 10 • Silver ASW • **Note:** Two types of legends.

Date	AG	Good	VG	Fine	VF	XF	Unc
1652	375	750	1,250	3,000	6,000	11,500	27,500

Pine Tree

3 PENCE

KM# 11 • Silver ASW • **Obv:** Tree without berries

Date	AG	Good	VG	Fine	VF	XF	Unc
1652	250	500	750	1,650	3,250	6,500	18,500

KM# 12 • Silver ASW • **Obv:** Tree with berries

Date	AG	Good	VG	Fine	VF	XF	Unc
1652	250	500	750	1,650	3,500	6,750	19,500

6 PENCE

KM# 13 • Silver ASW • **Obv:** Tree without berries; "spiney tree"

Date	AG	Good	VG	Fine	VF	XF	Unc
1652	400	700	1,400	2,000	4,000	7,000	22,000

KM# 14 • Silver ASW • **Obv:** Tree with berries

Date	AG	Good	VG	Fine	VF	XF	Unc
1652	300	600	1,000	1,850	3,750	6,500	20,000

SHILLING

KM# 15 • Silver ASW • **Note:** Large planchet. Many varieties exist; some are very rare.

Date	AG	Good	VG	Fine	VF	XF	Unc
1652	375	700	1,100	2,200	4,500	7,750	22,500

KM# 16 • Silver ASW • **Note:** Small planchet; large dies. All examples are thought to be contemporary fabrications.

Date	AG	Good	VG	Fine	VF	XF	Unc
1652	—	—	—	—	—	—	—

US COLONIAL AMERICA

KM# 17 • Silver ASW • **Note:** Small planchet; small dies. Many varieties exist; some are very rare.

Date	AG	Good	VG	Fine	VF	XF	Unc
1652	285	550	850	1,750	3,750	7,250	25,000

Willow Tree

3 PENCE

KM# 4 • Silver ASW •

Date	AG	Good	VG	Fine	VF	XF
1652 3 known	—	—	—	—	—	—

6 PENCE

KM# 5 • Silver ASW •

Date	AG	Good	VG	Fine	VF	XF
1652 14 known	9,500	18,500	30,000	60,000	135,000	225,000

SHILLING

KM# 6 • Silver ASW •

Date	AG	Good	VG	Fine	VF	XF
1652	10,000	20,000	35,000	85,000	165,000	250,000

NEW JERSEY
St. Patrick or Mark Newby

FARTHING

KM# 1 • Copper • Obv. Legend: FLOREAT REX **Rev. Legend:** QUIESCAT PLEBS

Date	AG	Good	VG	Fine	VF	XF	Unc
(1682)	70.00	125	285	775	2,750	6,500	—

Note: One very rare variety is known with reverse legend: QUIESAT PLEBS

KM# 1a • Silver ASW • **Obv. Legend:** FLOREAT REX **Rev. Legend:** QUIESCAT PLEBS

Date	AG	Good	VG	Fine	VF	XF
(1682)	800	1,750	2,750	5,500	9,500	17,500

HALFPENNY

KM# 2 • Copper • Obv. Legend: FLOREAT REX **Rev. Legend:** ECCE GREX

Date	AG	Good	VG	Fine	VF	XF	Unc
(1682)	180	365	850	1,650	4,000	12,500	—

EARLY AMERICAN TOKENS
American Plantations

1/24 REAL

KM# Tn5.1 • Tin • Obv. Legend: ET HIB REX

Date	AG	Good	VG	Fine	VF	XF	Unc
(1688)	125	200	300	450	850	2,000	—

US COLONIAL AMERICA

KM# Tn5.3 • Tin • Rev: Horizontal 4

Date	AG	Good	VG	Fine	VF	XF	Unc
(1688)	275	400	900	1,750	4,250	6,750	—

KM# Tn5.4 • Tin • Obv. Legend: ET HB REX

Date	AG	Good	VG	Fine	VF	XF	Unc
(1688)	—	250	450	850	1,900	3,250	11,500

KM# Tn6 • Tin • Rev: Arms of Scotland left, Ireland right

Date	AG	Good	VG	Fine	VF	XF	Unc
(1688)	450	750	1,250	2,150	5,000	7,750	—

KM# Tn5.2 • Tin • Obv: Rider's head left of "B" in legend **Note:** Restrikes made in 1828 from two obverse dies.

Date	AG	Good	VG	Fine	VF	XF	Unc
(1828)	75.00	110	175	275	500	1,000	—

Elephant

KM# Tn1.1 • 15.5500 g., Copper • Note: Thick planchet.

Date	AG	Good	VG	Fine	VF	XF	Unc
(1664)	125	200	300	550	1,000	1,750	4,500

KM# Tn1.2 • Copper • Note: Thin planchet.

Date	AG	Good	VG	Fine	VF	XF	Unc
(1664)	175	300	500	900	3,000	5,500	12,500

KM# Tn2 • Copper • Rev: Diagonals tie shield

Date	AG	Good	VG	Fine	VF	XF	Unc
(1664)	250	450	650	2,250	7,000	11,500	35,000

KM# Tn3 • Copper • Rev: Sword right side of shield

Date	AG	Good	VG	Fine	VF	XF
(1664) 3 known	—	—	—	25,000	—
Note: Norweb $1,320

KM# Tn4 • Copper • Rev. Legend: LON DON

Date	AG	Good	VG	Fine	VF	XF	Unc
(1684)	340	650	1,000	2,250	4,250	8,000	20,000

KM# Tn7 • Copper • Rev. Legend: NEW ENGLAND

Date	Good	VG	Fine	VF	XF
(1694) 2 known	—	55,000	85,000	110,000	160,000
Note: Norweb $25,300

KM# Tn8.1 • Copper • Rev. Legend: CAROLINA (PROPRIETORS)

Date	AG	Good	VG	Fine	VF	XF
(1694) 5 known	—	—	4,750	7,500	15,000	25,000
Note: Norweb $35,200

KM# Tn8.2 • Copper • Rev. Legend: CAROLINA (PROPRIETORS, O over E)

Date	AG	Good	VG	Fine	VF	XF
1694	1,300	2,500	4,500	7,000	12,500	20,000
Note: Norweb $17,600

Gloucester

KM# Tn15 • Copper • Obv. Legend: GLOVCESTER COVRTHOVSE VIRGINIA **Rev. Legend:** RIGHAVLT DAWSON.ANNO.DOM.1714.

Date	AG	Good	VG	Fine	VF	XF
(1714) 2 known	—	—	—	—	—	—
Note: Garrett $36,000

Hibernia-Voce Populi

FARTHING

KM# Tn21.1 • Copper • Note: Large letters

Date	AG	Good	VG	Fine	VF	XF	Unc
1760	145	250	375	750	1,850	3,500	11,500

KM# Tn21.2 • Copper • Note: Small letters

Date	AG	Good	VG	Fine	VF	XF
1760	—	—	3,250	6,500	25,000	60,000
Note: Norweb $5,940.

HALFPENNY

KM# Tn22 • Copper •

Date	AG	Good	VG	Fine	VF	XF	Unc
1700 Extremely rare	—	—	—	—	—	—	—

Note: Date is in error; ex-Roper $575. Norweb $577.50. Stack's Americana, VF, $2,900

1760	40.00	75.00	145	185	365	675	2,500
1760	50.00	80.00	135	195	425	775	3,500

Note: legend VOOE POPULI

1760 P below bust	65.00	120	200	375	750	1,750	8,250
1760 P in front of bust	55.00	110	180	325	650	1,450	6,500

Higley or Granby

KM# Tn16 • Copper • Obv. Legend: CONNECTICVT Rev. Legend: THE VALVE OF THREE PENCE

Date	AG	Good	VG	Fine	VF	XF
1737	—	10,000	18,500	40,000	85,000	—

Note: Garrett $16,000

KM# Tn17 • Copper • Obv. Legend: THE VALVE OF THREE PENCE Rev. Legend: I AM GOOD COPPER

Date	Good	VG	Fine	VF	XF
1737 2 known	11,000	20,000	42,500	87,500	—

Note: ex-Norweb $6,875

KM# Tn18.1 • Copper • Obv. Legend: VALUE ME AS YOU PLEASE Rev. Legend: I AM GOOD COPPER

Date	AG	Good	VG	Fine	VF	XF
1737	6,500	10,000	18,500	42,000	87,500	—

KM# Tn18.2 • Copper • Obv. Legend: VALVE.ME.AS.YOU.PLEASE. Rev. Legend: I AM GOOD COPPER.

Date	AG	Good	VG	Fine	VF	XF
1737 3 known	—	—	—	—	—	275,000

KM# Tn19 • Copper • Rev: Broad axe

Date	Good	VG	Fine	VF	XF
(1737)	10,000	20,000	45,000	125,000	—

Note: Garrett $45,000

1739 5 known	—	—	—	—	—

Note: Eliasberg $12,650. Oechsner $9,900. Steinberg (holed) $4,400.

KM# Tn20 • Copper • Obv. Legend: THE WHEELE GOES ROUND Rev: J CUT MY WAY THROUGH

Date	AG	Good	VG	Fine	VF	XF
(1737) unique	—	—	—	150,000	—	—

Note: Roper $60,500

New Yorke

KM# Tn9 • **Brass** • **Obv. Legend:**
NEW.YORK.IN.AMERICA

Date	AG	Good	VG	Fine	VF	XF
1700	1,800	3,750	7,250	17,500	28,000	60,000

KM# Tn9a • **White Metal** • **Obv. Legend:**
NEW.YORK.IN.AMERICA

Date	AG	Good	VG	Fine	VF	XF
1700 4 known	—	—	7,750	22,500	32,500	75,000

Pitt

FARTHING

KM# Tn23 • **Copper** •

Date	AG	Good	VG	Fine	VF	XF
1766	—	3,750	7,000	11,500	28,500	42,500

HALFPENNY

KM# Tn24 • **Copper** •

Date	AG	Good	VG	Fine	VF	XF	Unc
1766	145	275	450	750	1,650	3,000	9,500

KM# Tn24a • **Silver Plated Copper** •

Date	AG	Good	VG	Fine	VF	XF	Unc
1766	—	—	—	—	2,250	5,000	12,500

ROYAL PATENT COINAGE

Hibernia

FARTHING

KM# 20 • **Copper** • **Note:** Pattern.

Date	AG	Good	VG	Fine	VF	XF	Unc
1722	135	250	400	600	1,250	3,250	11,500

KM# 24 • **Copper** • **Obv:** 1722 obverse **Obv. Legend:** …D:G:REX.

Date	AG	Good	VG	Fine	VF	XF	Unc
1723	20.00	75.00	120	170	300	550	1,250

KM# 25 • **Copper** • **Obv. Legend:** DEI • GRATIA • REX •

Date	AG	Good	VG	Fine	VF	XF	Unc
1723	25.00	45.00	60.00	180	300	550	950
1724	—	90.00	125	225	700	1,750	4,250

KM# 25a • **Silver** ASW •

Date	AG	Good	VG	Fine	VF	XF	Unc
1723	—	—	1,600	2,250	4,200	6,500	12,000

HALFPENNY

KM# 21 • **Copper** • **Obv:** Bust right **Obv. Legend:** GEORGIUS • DEI • GRATIA • REX • **Rev:** Harp left, head left **Rev. Legend:** • HIBERNIA • 1722 •

Date	AG	Good	VG	Fine	VF	XF	Unc
1722	50.00	90.00	110	160	325	700	1,750

US COLONIAL AMERICA

KM# 22 • Copper • Obv: Bust right **Obv. Legend:** GEORGIVS D: G: REX **Rev:** Harp left, head right **Rev. Legend:** • HIBERNIÆ • **Note:** "Rocks Reverse" pattern.

Date	AG	Good	VG	Fine	VF	XF	Unc
1722	—	—	—	5,000	7,500	12,500	—

KM# 23.1 • Copper • Rev: Harp right

Date	AG	Good	VG	Fine	VF	XF	Unc
1722	35.00	60.00	80.00	120	285	600	1,750
Note: 850							
1723	20.00	35.00	45.00	75.00	190	285	850
1723/22	35.00	60.00	80.00	150	400	850	2,500
1724	25.00	50.00	90.00	160	400	850	2,500

KM# 23.2 • Copper • Obv: DEII error in legend

Date	AG	Good	VG	Fine	VF	XF	Unc
1722	75.00	125	160	325	750	1,500	3,000

KM# 26 • Copper • Rev: Large head **Note:** Rare. Generally mint state only. Probably a pattern.

Date	AG	Good	VG	Fine	VF	XF	Unc
1723	—	—	—	—	—	—	—

KM# 27 • Copper • Rev: Continuous legend over head

Date	AG	Good	VG	Fine	VF	XF	Unc
1724	45.00	80.00	150	300	900	1,850	4,500

Rosa Americana

HALFPENNY

KM# 1 • Copper • Obv. Legend: D • G • REX •

Date	AG	Good	VG	Fine	VF	XF	Unc
1722	20.00	50.00	140	250	525	1,050	4,000

KM# 2 • Copper • Obv: Uncrowned rose **Obv. Legend:** ... • DEI • GRATIA • REX • **Note:** Several varieties exist.

Date	AG	Good	VG	Fine	VF	XF	Unc
1722	50.00	90.00	135	250	450	975	3,500
1723	385	700	850	1,750	3,600	—	—

KM# 3 • Copper • Rev. Legend: VTILE DVLCI

Date	AG	Good	VG	Fine	VF	XF	Unc
1722	250	450	850	2,200	3,800	7,500	—

KM# 9 • Copper • Rev: Crowned rose

Date	AG	Good	VG	Fine	VF	XF	Unc
1723	45.00	85.00	110	165	425	1,100	4,500

PENNY

KM# 4 • Copper • Rev. Legend: UTILE DULCI **Note:** Several varieties exist.

Date	AG	Good	VG	Fine	VF	XF	Unc
1722	60.00	100.00	135	240	450	950	3,750

KM# 5 • Copper • Note: Several varieties exist. Also known in two rare pattern types with long hair ribbons, one with V's for U's on the obverse.

Date	AG	Good	VG	Fine	VF	XF	Unc
1722	18.00	35.00	150	275	750	1,450	6,000

US COLONIAL AMERICA

KM# 10 • Copper • Note: Several varieties exist.

Date	AG	Good	VG	Fine	VF	XF	Unc
1723	40.00	75.00	110	175	425	900	3,600

KM# 12 • Copper • Note: Pattern.

Date	AG	Good	VG	Fine	VF	XF
1724 2 known	—	—	—	—	—	—

KM# 13 • Copper • Rev. Legend: ROSA: SINE: SPINA •

Date	AG	Good	VG	Fine	VF	XF
(1724) 5 known	—	—	—	—	—	—

Note: Stack's Bowers 5-05, VF ralized $21,850; Norweb $2,035

KM# 14 • Copper • Obv: George II **Note:** Pattern.

Date	AG	Good	VG	Fine	VF	XF
1727 2 known	—	—	—	—	—	—

2 PENCE

KM# 6 • Copper • Rev: Motto with scroll

Date	AG	Good	VG	Fine	VF	XF	Unc
(1722)	80.00	150	200	425	750	1,650	7,000

KM# 7 • Copper • Rev: Motto without scroll

Date	AG	Good	VG	Fine	VF	XF
(1722) 3 known	—	—	—	—	—	—

KM# 8.1 • Copper • Obv. Legend: ...REX • **Rev:** Dated

Date	AG	Good	VG	Fine	VF	XF	Unc
1722	70.00	125	175	275	750	1,500	5,500

KM# 8.2 • Copper • Obv. Legend: ...REX

Date	AG	Good	VG	Fine	VF	XF	Unc
1722	70.00	125	175	275	775	1,600	6,000

KM# 11 • Copper • Obv: No stop after REX **Rev:** Stop after 1723 **Note:** Several varieties exist.

Date	AG	Good	VG	Fine	VF	XF	Unc
1723	65.00	125	175	300	550	1,200	3,500

KM# 15 • Copper • Note: Pattern. Two varieties exist; both extremely rare.

Date	AG	Good	VG	Fine	VF	XF	Unc
1724	—	—	—	—	—	—	—

Note: Stack's Bowers 5-05 choice AU realized $25,300. Ex-Garrett $5,775. Stack's Americana, XF, $10,925

US COLONIAL AMERICA

KM# 16 • **Copper** • **Obv:** Bust left **Rev:** Crowned rose **Note:** Pattern.

Date	AG	Good	VG	Fine	VF	XF
1733 4 known	—	—	—	—	—	—

Note: Stacks-Bowers 5-05, Gem Proof realized $63,250; Norweb $19,800

Virginia Halfpenny

KM# Tn25.1 • **Copper** • **Rev:** Small 7s in date.
Note: Struck on Irish halfpenny planchets.

Date	Good	VG	Fine	VF	XF	Unc	Proof
1773	—	—	—	—	—	—	—22,000

KM# Tn25.2 • **Copper** • **Obv. Legend:** GEORGIVS •... **Rev:** Varieties with 7 or 8 strings in harp

Date	AG	Good	VG	Fine	VF	XF	Unc
1773	30.00	50.00	70.00	110	235	425	1,000

KM# Tn25.3 • **Copper** • **Obv. Legend:** GEORGIVS... **Rev:** Varieties with 6, 7 or 8 strings in harp

Date	AG	Good	VG	Fine	VF	XF	Unc
1773	35.00	60.00	75.00	135	275	525	1,350

KM# Tn25.4 • **Copper** • **Obv. Legend:** GEORGIVS... **Rev:** 8 harp strings, dot on cross

Date	AG	Good	VG	Fine	VF	XF	Unc
1773	—	—	—	—	—	—	—

Note: ex-Steinberg $2,600

KM# Tn26 • **Silver** ASW • **Note:** So-called "shilling" silver proofs.

Date	AG	Good	VG	Fine	VF	XF
1774 6 known	—	—	—	—	—	—

Note: Garrett $23,000

REVOLUTIONARY COINAGE
Continental "Dollar"

KM# EA1 • **Pewter** • **Obv. Legend:** CURRENCY.

Date	Good	VG	Fine	VF	XF	Unc
1776	7,500	9,350	12,000	21,000	32,500	70,000

KM# EA2 • **Pewter** • **Obv. Legend:** CURRENCY, EG FECIT.

Date	Good	VG	Fine	VF	XF	Unc
1776	8,000	10,500	13,500	25,000	37,500	80,000

KM# EA2a • **Silver** ASW • **Obv. Legend:** CURRENCY, EG FECIT.

Date	Good	VG	Fine	VF	XF	Unc
1776 2 known	—	—	300,000	450,000	—	—

KM# EA3 • **Pewter** • **Obv. Legend:** CURRENCEY

Date	Good	VG	Fine	VF	XF	Unc
1776 extremely rare	—	—	—	—	150,000	—

KM# EA4 • **Pewter** • **Obv. Legend:** CURRENCY. **Rev:** Floral cross.

Date	Good	VG	Fine	VF	XF	Unc
1776 3 recorded	—	—	—	—	400,000	—

Note: Norweb $50,600. Johnson $25,300

KM# EA5 • Pewter • Obv. Legend: CURENCY.

Date	Good	VG	Fine	VF	XF	Unc
1776	7,500	9,500	12,000	22,500	33,500	75,000

KM# EA5a • Brass • Obv. Legend:
CURENCY. **Note:** Two varieties exist.

Date	Good	VG	Fine	VF	XF	Unc
1776	22,500	28,500	40,000	75,000	135,000	—

KM# EA5b • Silver ASW • Obv. Legend:
CURENCY.

Date	Good	VG	Fine	VF	XF	Unc
1776						
2 known	—	—	285,000	425,000	—	—

Note: Stacks-Bowers 5-05, VF realized $345,000; Romano
$99,000

STATE COINAGE
CONNECTICUT

KM# 1 • Copper • Obv: Bust facing right.

Date	AG	Good	VG	Fine	VF	XF
1785	35.00	55.00	90.00	200	650	1,750

KM# 2 • Copper • Obv: "African head."

Date	AG	Good	VG	Fine	VF	XF
1785	55.00	85.00	150	600	1,500	3,800

KM# 3.1 • Copper • Obv: Mailed bust facing left.

Date	AG	Good	VG	Fine	VF	XF
1785	125	220	375	750	1,800	3,850
1786	30.00	50.00	90.00	175	500	1,400
1787	30.00	50.00	85.00	160	450	1,350
1788	30.00	50.00	80.00	160	435	1,150

KM# 3.3 • Copper • Obv: Perfect date. **Rev.
Legend:** IN DE ET.

Date	AG	Good	VG	Fine	VF	XF
1787	50.00	80.00	125	350	750	1,850

KM# 3.4 • Copper • Obv. Legend: CONNLC.

Date	AG	Good	VG	Fine	VF	XF
1788	44.00	65.00	130	265	700	2,150

KM# 4 • Copper • Obv: Small mailed bust facing
left. **Rev. Legend:** ETLIB INDE.

Date	AG	Good	VG	Fine	VF	XF
1786	45.00	90.00	175	400	1,100	2,750

KM# 5 • Copper • Obv: Small mailed bust facing
right. **Rev. Legend:** INDE ET LIB.

Date	AG	Good	VG	Fine	VF	XF
1786	60.00	100.00	175	450	2,000	4,250

KM# 6 • Copper • Obv: Large mailed bust
facing right.

Date	AG	Good	VG	Fine	VF	XF
1786	55.00	90.00	160	400	1,750	3,750

US COLONIAL AMERICA

KM# 7 • Copper • Obv: "Hercules head."

Date	AG	Good	VG	Fine	VF	XF
1786	60.00	110	220	600	2,500	5,800

KM# 8.1 • Copper • Obv: Draped bust.

Date	AG	Good	VG	Fine	VF	XF
1786	50.00	100.00	200	500	1,250	2,850

KM# 8.2 • Copper • Obv: Draped bust. Note: Many varieties.

Date	AG	Good	VG	Fine	VF	XF
1787	28.00	42.00	70.00	115	325	775

KM# 8.3 • Copper • Obv. Legend: AUCIORI.

Date	AG	Good	VG	Fine	VF	XF
1787	30.00	55.00	90.00	175	450	1,100

KM# 8.4 • Copper • Obv. Legend: AUCTOPI.

Date	AG	Good	VG	Fine	VF	XF
1787	35.00	65.00	110	200	650	1,650

KM# 8.5 • Copper • Obv. Legend: AUCTOBI.

Date	AG	Good	VG	Fine	VF	XF
1787	35.00	65.00	110	200	625	1,550

KM# 8.6 • Copper • Obv. Legend: CONNFC.

Date	AG	Good	VG	Fine	VF	XF
1787	32.00	60.00	95.00	185	525	1,100

KM# 8.7 • Copper • Obv. Legend: CONNLC.

Date	AG	Good	VG	Fine	VF	XF
1787	60.00	90.00	180	375	950	3,000

KM# 8.8 • Copper • Rev. Legend: FNDE.

Date	AG	Good	VG	Fine	VF	XF
1787	35.00	55.00	85.00	175	525	1,650

KM# 8.9 • Copper • Rev. Legend: ETLIR.

Date	AG	Good	VG	Fine	VF	XF
1787	32.00	50.00	75.00	160	475	1,275

KM# 8.10 • Copper • Rev. Legend: ETIIB.

Date	AG	Good	VG	Fine	VF	XF
1787	35.00	50.00	75.00	160	485	1,300

KM# 9 • Copper • Obv: Small head. Rev. Legend: ETLIB INDE.

Date	AG	Good	VG	Fine	VF	XF
1787	65.00	110	180	425	1,750	4,300

KM# 10 • Copper • Obv: Small head. Rev. Legend: INDE ET LIB.

Date	AG	Good	VG	Fine	VF	XF
1787	75.00	135	200	525	2,300	4,600

KM# 11 • Copper • Obv: Medium bust. Note: Two reverse legend types exist.

Date	AG	Good	VG	Fine	VF	XF
1787	60.00	90.00	150	400	1,750	3,450

KM# 12 • Copper • Obv: "Muttonhead" variety. Note: Extremely rare with legend INDE ET LIB.

Date	AG	Good	VG	Fine	VF	XF
1787	60.00	90.00	175	575	2,550	5,200

KM# 13 • Copper • Obv: "Laughing head"

Date	AG	Good	VG	Fine	VF	XF
1787	35.00	60.00	120	240	650	1,800

KM# 14 • Copper • Obv: "Horned head"

Date	AG	Good	VG	Fine	VF	XF
1787	30.00	50.00	80.00	165	450	1,200

KM# 15 • Copper • Rev. Legend: IND ET LIB

Date	AG	Good	VG	Fine	VF	XF
1787/8	100.00	150	250	750	2,000	5,000
1787/1887	85.00	150	225	600	1,750	4,750

KM# 16 • Copper • Obv. Legend: CONNECT. **Rev. Legend:** INDE ET LIB. **Note:** Two additional scarce reverse legend types exist.

Date	AG	Good	VG	Fine	VF	XF
1787	35.00	50.00	120	240	675	1,750

KM# 22.1 • Copper • Obv: Draped bust facing left. **Rev. Legend:** INDE ET LIB.

Date	AG	Good	VG	Fine	VF	XF
1788	49.50	75.00	140	325	750	1,800

KM# 22.2 • Copper • Rev. Legend: INDLET LIB.

Date	AG	Good	VG	Fine	VF	XF
1788	60.00	90.00	195	425	875	1,950

KM# 22.3 • Copper • Obv. Legend: CONNEC. **Rev. Legend:** INDE ET LIB.

Date	AG	Good	VG	Fine	VF	XF
1788	58.00	85.00	190	400	875	1,850

KM# 22.4 • Copper • Obv. Legend: CONNEC. **Rev. Legend:** INDL ET LIB.

Date	AG	Good	VG	Fine	VF	XF
1788	58.00	85.00	190	400	925	2,250

KM# 20 • Copper • Obv: Mailed bust facing right.

Date	AG	Good	VG	Fine	VF	XF
1788	28.00	45.00	90.00	200	650	1,650

KM# 21 • Copper • Obv: Small mailed bust facing right.

Date	AG	Good	VG	Fine	VF	XF
1788	850	1,650	3,750	5,500	12,500	22,500

MASSACHUSETTS

HALFPENNY

KM# 17 • Copper •

Date	Good	VG	Fine	VF	XF	Unc
1776 unique	—	—	200,000	—	—	—

Note: Garrett $40,000

PENNY

KM# 18 • Copper •

Date	Good	VG	Fine	VF	XF	Unc
1776 unique	—	—	—	—	—	—

US COLONIAL AMERICA

HALF CENT

KM# 19 • Copper • Note: Varieties exist; some are rare.

Date	AG	Good	VG	Fine	VF	XF	Unc
1787	60.00	90.00	140	225	575	1,000	3,250
1788	70.00	115	175	275	600	1,100	3,500

CENT

KM# 20.1 • Copper • Rev: Arrows in right talon

Date	Good	VG	Fine	VF	XF	Unc
1787 7 known	9,000	22,500	45,000	—	—	350,000

Note: Ex-Bushnell-Brand $8,800. Garrett $5,500

KM# 20.2 • Copper • Rev: Arrows in left talon

Date	AG	Good	VG	Fine	VF	XF	Unc
1787	60.00	90.00	165	240	650	1,350	6,800

KM# 20.3 • Copper • Rev: "Horned eagle" die break

Date	AG	Good	VG	Fine	VF	XF	Unc
1787	70.00	110	190	275	775	1,550	7,750

KM# 20.4 • Copper • Rev: Without period after Massachusetts

Date	AG	Good	VG	Fine	VF	XF	Unc
1788	70.00	105	190	260	675	1,600	6,250

KM# 20.5 • Copper • Rev: Period after Massachusetts, normal S's

Date	AG	Good	VG	Fine	VF	XF	Unc
1788	60.00	90.00	170	235	600	1,350	5,750

KM# 20.6 • Copper • Rev: Period after Massachusetts, S's like 8's

Date	AG	Good	VG	Fine	VF	XF	Unc
1788	50.00	75.00	135	200	575	1,250	5,400

NEW HAMPSHIRE

KM# 1 • Copper •

Date	AG	Good	VG	Fine	VF	XF
1776 extremely rare	—	—	—	—	—	—

Note: Garrett $13,000

US COLONIAL AMERICA

NEW JERSEY

KM# 8 • Copper • Obv: Date below draw bar.

Date	AG	Good	VG	Fine	VF	XF
1786 extremely rare	—	—	—	75,000	135,000	—

Note: Garrett $52,000

KM# 9 • Copper • Obv: Large horse head, date below plow, no coulter on plow.

Date	AG	Good	VG	Fine	VF	XF	Unc
1786	450	850	1,500	3,000	8,500	22,500	—

KM# 10 • Copper • Rev: Narrow shield, straight beam.

Date	AG	Good	VG	Fine	VF	XF	Unc
1786	38.00	60.00	140	210	550	1,350	—

KM# 11.1 • Copper • Rev: Wide shield, curved beam. **Note:** Varieties exist.

Date	AG	Good	VG	Fine	VF	XF	Unc
1786	45.00	75.00	150	225	600	2,000	—

KM# 11.2 • Copper • Obv: Bridle variety (die break). **Note:** Reverse varieties exist.

Date	AG	Good	VG	Fine	VF	XF	Unc
1786	45.00	70.00	145	235	650	2,400	—

KM# 12.1 • Copper • Rev: Plain shield. **Note:** Small planchet. Varieties exist.

Date	AG	Good	VG	Fine	VF	XF	Unc
1787	35.00	55.00	110	200	500	950	—

KM# 12.2 • Copper • Rev: Shield heavily outlined. **Note:** Small planchet.

Date	AG	Good	VG	Fine	VF	XF	Unc
1787	38.00	60.00	120	215	550	1,150	—

KM# 13 • Copper • Obv: "Serpent head."

Date	AG	Good	VG	Fine	VF	XF	Unc
1787	55.00	85.00	200	375	1,650	4,200	—

KM# 14 • Copper • Rev: Plain shield. **Note:** Large planchet. Varieties exist.

Date	AG	Good	VG	Fine	VF	XF	Unc
1787	45.00	60.00	135	240	750	1,650	—

KM# 15 • Copper • Rev. Legend: PLURIBS.

Date	AG	Good	VG	Fine	VF	XF	Unc
1787	85.00	150	275	500	1,500	3,250	—

US COLONIAL AMERICA

US COLONIAL AMERICA

KM# 16 • Copper • Obv: Horse's head facing right. **Note:** Varieties exist.

Date	AG	Good	VG	Fine	VF	XF	Unc
1788	42.00	60.00	115	190	700	1,275	—

KM# 17 • Copper • Rev: Fox before legend. **Note:** Varieties exist.

Date	AG	Good	VG	Fine	VF	XF	Unc
1788	75.00	145	295	575	2,150	4,750	—

KM# 18 • Copper • Obv: Horse's head facing left. **Note:** Varieties exist.

Date	AG	Good	VG	Fine	VF	XF	Unc
1788	235	425	900	1,650	4,800	13,000	—

NEW YORK

KM# 1 • Copper • Obv: Bust right **Obv. Legend:** NON VI VIRTUTE VICI. **Rev. Legend:** NEO-EBORACENSIS

Date	AG	Good	VG	Fine	VF	XF
1786	3,250	5,000	7,500	15,000	35,000	—

KM# 2 • Copper • Obv: Eagle on globe facing right. **Obv. Legend:** EXCELSIOR **Rev. Legend:** E. PLURIBUS UNUM

Date	AG	Good	VG	Fine	VF	XF
1787	1,400	2,250	3,850	7,000	17,500	33,500

KM# 3 • Copper • Obv: Eagle on globe facing left. **Obv. Legend:** EXCELSIOR **Rev. Legend:** E. PLURIBUS UNUM

Date	AG	Good	VG	Fine	VF	XF
1787	1,250	2,000	3,500	6,500	16,500	32,000

KM# 4 • Copper • Obv. Legend: EXCELSIOR **Rev:** Large eagle, arrows in right talon. **Rev. Legend:** E. PLURIBUS UNUM

Date	Good	VG	Fine	VF	XF
1787	4,500	9,000	16,500	35,000	55,000

Note: Norweb $18,700

KM# 5 • Copper • Obv: George Clinton. **Rev. Legend:** EXCELSIOR

Date	AG	Good	VG	Fine	VF	XF
1787	5,000	9,000	15,500	35,000	75,000	185,000

KM# 6 • Copper • Obv: Indian. **Obv. Legend:** LIBERNATUS LIBERTATEM DEFENDO **Rev:** New York arms. **Rev. Legend:** EXCELSIOR

Date	AG	Good	VG	Fine	VF	XF
1787	4,500	7,500	12,500	30,000	65,000	160,000

KM# 7 • Copper • Obv: Indian. **Obv. Legend:** LIBERNATUS LIBERTATEM DEFENDO **Rev:** Eagle on globe. **Rev. Legend:** NEO EBORACUS EXCELSIOR

Date	AG	Good	VG	Fine	VF	XF
1787	6,500	11,500	17,500	37,500	75,000	145,000

KM# 8 • Copper • Obv: Indian. **Rev:** George III.

Date		AG	Good	VG	Fine	VF	XF
1787	3 Known	—	—	—75,000	—	—	—

KM# 9 • Copper • Obv: Bust right **Obv. Legend:** NOVA EBORAC. **Rev:** Figure seated right. **Rev. Legend:** VIRT.ET.LIB.

Date	AG	Good	VG	Fine	VF	XF	Unc
1787	75.00	115	220	360	1,150	2,700	—

KM# 10 • Copper • Obv: Bust right **Obv. Legend:** NOVA EBORAC **Rev:** Figure seated left. **Rev. Legend:** VIRT.ET.LIB.

Date	AG	Good	VG	Fine	VF	XF	Unc
1787	60.00	100.00	200	325	825	1,750	—

KM# 11 • Copper • Obv: Small head, star above. **Obv. Legend:** NOVA EBORAC. **Rev:** Figure seated left **Rev. Legend:** VIRT.ET.LIB.

Date	AG	Good	VG	Fine	VF	XF	Unc
1787	2,450	3,750	5,500	9,500	22,500	—	—

KM# 12 • Copper • Obv: Large head, two quatrefoils left. **Obv. Legend:** NOVA EBORAC. **Rev:** Figure seated left **Rev. Legend:** VIRT.ET.LIB.

Date	AG	Good	VG	Fine	VF	XF	Unc
1787	350	600	1,250	2,500	7,750	15,000	—

Machin's Mill

KM# 13 • Copper • Note: Crude, lightweight imitations of the British Halfpenny were struck at Machin's Mill in large quantities bearing the obverse legends: GEORGIVS II REX, GEORGIVS III REX, and GEORGIUS III REX, with the BRITANNIA reverse. There are many different mulings. Plain crosses in the shield of Britannia are noticeable on high grade pieces, unlike common British made imitations, which usually have outlined crosses in the shield. Some Machin's Mill varieties are very rare.

Date	AG	Good	VG	Fine	VF	XF
(1747-1788)	40.00	75.00	145	325	800	2,250

Note: Prices are for most common within date ranges. Examples are dated: 1747, 1771, 1772, 1774, 1775, 1776, 1777, 1778, 1784, 1785, 1786, 1787 and 1788. Other dates may exist

VERMONT

KM# 1 • Copper • Rev. Legend: IMMUNE COLUMBIA

Date	AG	Good	VG	Fine	VF	XF
(1785)	4,000	6,000	9,500	13,750	35,000	—

US COLONIAL AMERICA

US COLONIAL AMERICA

KM# 2 • Copper • Obv: Sun rising over field with plow **Obv. Legend:** VERMONTIS. RES. PUBLICA. **Rev:** Eye, with rays and stars **Rev. Legend:** QUARTA. DECIMA. STELLA.

Date	AG	Good	VG	Fine	VF	XF
1785	140	300	750	1,650	5,250	12,500

KM# 3 • Copper • Obv: Sun rising over field with plow **Obv. Legend:** VERMONTS. RES. PUBLICA. **Rev:** Eye, with rays and stars **Rev. Legend:** QUARTA. DECIMA. STELLA.

Date	AG	Good	VG	Fine	VF	XF
1785	150	285	600	1,250	3,150	7,500

KM# 4 • Copper • Obv: Sun rising over field with plow **Obv. Legend:** VERMONTENSIUM.RES.PUBLICA **Rev:** Eye, with pointed rays and stars **Rev. Legend:** QUARTA. DECIMA. STELLA.

Date	AG	Good	VG	Fine	VF	XF
1786	140	235	425	775	2,000	4,400

KM# 5 • Copper • Obv: "Baby head." **Obv. Legend:** AUCTORI: VERMON: **Rev:** Seated figure left **Rev. Legend:** ET:LIB: INDE

Date	AG	Good	VG	Fine	VF	XF
1786	200	350	650	1,750	4,800	12,500

KM# 6 • Copper • Obv: Bust facing left. **Obv. Legend:** VERMON: AUCTORI: **Rev:** Seated figure left **Rev. Legend:** INDE ETLIB

Date	AG	Good	VG	Fine	VF	XF
1786	115	175	350	825	2,850	5,000
1787 extremely rare	—	4,500	10,000	22,500	42,500	—

KM# 7 • Copper • Obv: Bust facing right. **Obv. Legend:** VERMON. AUCTORI. **Rev:** Seated figure left **Rev. Legend:** INDE ETLIB **Note:** Varieties exist.

Date	AG	Good	VG	Fine	VF	XF	Unc
1787	70.00	150	260	575	1,450	3,000	—

KM# 8 • Copper • Obv: Bust right **Obv. Legend:** VERMON AUCTORI **Rev:** Seated figure left **Note:** Britannia mule.

Date	AG	Good	VG	Fine	VF	XF	Unc
1787	65.00	120	170	300	700	1,650	—

KM# 9.2 • Copper • Obv: Bust right. "C" backward in AUCTORI. **Rev:** Seated figure left

Date	AG	Good	VG	Fine	VF	XF
1788 extremely rare	—	4,200	7,000	17,500	38,000	—

Note: Stack's Americana, Fine, $9,775

KM# 10 • Copper • Obv: Bust right **Rev:** Seated figure left **Rev. Legend:** .ET LIB. .INDE.

Date	AG	Good	VG	Fine	VF	XF
1788	200	325	675	1,450	4,750	13,500

KM# 11 • Copper • Obv: Bust right **Rev:** Seated figure left **Note:** George III Rex mule.

Date	AG	Good	VG	Fine	VF	XF
1788	325	575	950	5,000	12,500	12,000

KM# 9.1 • Copper • Obv. Legend: VERMON. AUCTORI. **Rev:** Seated figure left **Rev. Legend:** INDE . ET LIB. **Note:** Varieties exist.

Date	AG	Good	VG	Fine	VF	XF
1788	65.00	125	200	450	950	2,250

EARLY AMERICAN TOKENS

Albany Church "Penny"

KM# Tn54.1 • Copper • Obv: Without "D" above church. **Note:** Uniface.

Date	AG	Good	VG	Fine	VF	XF
5 known	—	—	10,000	25,000	45,000	75,000

KM# Tn54.2 • Copper • Obv: With "D" above church. **Note:** Uniface.

Date	AG	Good	VG	Fine	VF	XF
rare	—	—	9,000	22,500	42,500	67,500

Auctori Plebis

KM# Tn50 • Copper • Obv: Bust left **Obv. Legend:** AUCTORI: PLEBIS: **Rev:** Seated figure left **Rev. Legend:** INDEP: ET. LIBER

Date	AG	Good	VG	Fine	VF	XF	Unc
1787	—	100.00	165	340	700	1,650	15,000

Bar "Cent"

KM# Tn49 • Copper • Obv: USA monogram **Rev:** Horizontal bars

Date	Good	VG	Fine	VF	XF	Unc
(1785)	1,400	1,750	3,100	6,250	9,500	27,500

Castorland "Half Dollar"

KM# Tn87.1 • Silver ASW • Obv. Legend: FRANCO.AMERICANA COLONIA **Edge:** Reeded.

Date	AG	Good	VG	Fine	VF	XF	Unc
1796	—	—	—	—	—	4,500	13,500

US COLONIAL AMERICA

US COLONIAL AMERICA

KM# Tn87.1a • Copper • Obv. Legend:
FRANCO.AMERICANA COLONIA **Edge:** Reeded.

Date	Good	VG	Fine	VF	XF	Unc
1796 3 known	—	—	—	—	3,500	—

KM# Tn87.1b • Brass • Obv. Legend:
FRANCO.AMERICANA COLONIA **Edge:** Reeded.

Date	Good	VG	Fine	VF	XF	Unc
1796	—	—	—	—	225	650

KM# Tn87.2 • Copper • Obv. Legend:
FRANCO.AMERICANA COLONIA **Edge:** Plain.
Note: Thin planchet.

Date	Good	VG	Fine	VF	XF	Unc
1796 unique	—	—	—	—	—	—

KM# Tn87.3 • Silver ASW **• Obv. Legend:**
FRANCO.AMERICANA COLONIA **Edge:** Reeded.
Note: Thin planchet. Restrike.

Date	Good	VG	Fine	VF	XF	Unc	Proof
1796	—	—	—	—	—	1,250	—

KM# Tn87.4 • Silver ASW **• Obv. Legend:**
FRANCO.AMERICANA COLONIA **Edge:** Lettered.
Edge Lettering: ARGENT. **Note:** Thin planchet.
Restrike.

Date	Good	VG	Fine	VF	XF	Unc	Proof
1796	—	—	—	—	—	150	—

KM# Tn87.3a • Copper • Obv. Legend:
FRANCO.AMERICANA COLONIA **Edge:** Reeded.
Note: Thin planchet. Restrike.

Date	Good	VG	Fine	VF	XF	Unc	Proof
1796	—	—	—	—	—	350	—

KM# Tn87.5 • Copper • Obv. Legend:
FRANCO.AMERICANA COLONIA **Edge:** Lettered.
Edge Lettering: CUIVRE. **Note:** Thin planchet.
Restrike.

Date	Good	VG	Fine	VF	XF	Unc	Proof
1796	—	—	—	—	—	—100.00	—

Chalmers

3 PENCE

KM# Tn45 • Silver ASW **•**

Date	AG	Good	VG	Fine	VF	XF
1783	650	1,150	2,200	4,250	9,500	17,500

6 PENCE

KM# Tn46.1 • Silver ASW **• Rev:** Small date

Date	AG	Good	VG	Fine	VF	XF
1783	900	1,650	2,750	6,750	16,500	28,500

KM# Tn46.2 • Silver ASW **• Rev:** Large date

Date	AG	Good	VG	Fine	VF	XF
1783	775	1,450	2,250	6,000	14,500	27,500

SHILLING

KM# Tn47.1 • Silver ASW **• Rev:** Birds with
long worm

Date	AG	Good	VG	Fine	VF	XF
1783	450	775	1,350	2,750	6,000	11,500

KM# Tn47.2 • Silver ASW **• Rev:** Birds with
short worm

Date	AG	Good	VG	Fine	VF	XF
1783	450	750	1,250	2,350	5,500	11,000

KM# Tn48 • Silver ASW **• Rev:** Rings and stars

Date	AG	Good	VG	Fine	VF	XF
1783 4 known	—	—	—	—	200,000	—

Note: Garrett $75,000

Copper Company of Upper Canada

HALFPENNY

KM# Tn86 • Copper • Obv. Legend: BRITISH
SETTLEMENT KENTUCKY

Date	Good	VG	Fine	VF	XF	Unc	Proof
1796	—	—	—	—	—	—	—10,000

Franklin Press

KM# Tn73 • Copper • Obv: Printing press **Obv. Legend:** SIC ORITUR DOCTRINA SURGETQUE LIBERTAS **Edge:** Plain.

Date	AG	Good	VG	Fine	VF	XF	Unc
1794	30.00	75.00	110	150	285	450	1,350

Kentucky Token

KM# Tn70.1 • Copper • Obv. Legend: UNANIMITY IS THE STRENGTH OF SOCIETY **Rev. Legend:** E. PLURIBUS UNUM **Edge:** Plain. **Note:** 1793 date is circa.

Date	AG	Good	VG	Fine	VF	XF	Unc
(1793)	12.00	25.00	40.00	150	200	375	1,210

KM# Tn70.2 • Copper • Obv. Legend: UNANIMITY IS THE STRENGTH OF SOCIETY **Rev. Legend:** E. PLURIBUS UNUM **Edge:** Engrailed.

Date	AG	Good	VG	Fine	VF	XF	Unc
(1793)	35.00	75.00	125	200	500	950	3,400

KM# Tn70.3 • Copper • Obv. Legend: UNANIMITY IS THE STRENGTH OF SOCIETY **Rev. Legend:** E. PLURIBUS UNUM **Edge:** Lettered. **Edge Lettering:** PAYABLE AT BEDWORTH.

Date	AG	Good	VG	Fine	VF	XF
(1793) unique	—	—	—	—	—	1,980

KM# Tn70.4 • Copper • Obv. Legend: UNANIMITY IS THE STRENGTH OF SOCIETY **Rev. Legend:** E. PLURIBUS UNUM **Edge:** Lettered. **Edge Lettering:** PAYABLE AT LANCASTER.

Date	AG	Good	VG	Fine	VF	XF	Unc
(1793)	14.00	28.00	45.00	65.00	225	400	1,250

KM# Tn70.5 • Copper • Obv. Legend: UNANIMITY IS THE STRENGTH OF SOCIETY **Rev. Legend:** E. PLURIBUS UNUM **Edge:** Lettered. **Edge Lettering:** PAYABLE AT I.FIELDING.

Date	AG	Good	VG	Fine	VF	XF
(1793) unique	—	—	—	—	—	—

KM# Tn70.6 • Copper • Obv. Legend: UNANIMITY IS THE STRENGTH OF SOCIETY **Rev. Legend:** E. PLURIBUS UNUM **Edge:** Lettered. **Edge Lettering:** PAYABLE AT W. PARKERS.

Date	AG	Good	VG	Fine	VF	XF
(1793) unique	—	—	—	—	20,000	—

KM# Tn70.7 • Copper • Obv. Legend: UNANIMITY IS THE STRENGTH OF SOCIETY **Rev. Legend:** E. PLURIBUS UNUM **Edge:** Ornamented branch with two leaves.

Date	AG	Good	VG	Fine	VF	XF
(1793) unique	—	—	—	—	—	—

Mott Token

KM# Tn52.1 • Copper • Obv: Clock **Rev:** Eagle with shield **Note:** Thin planchet.

Date	AG	Good	VG	Fine	VF	XF	Unc
1789	50.00	80.00	150	300	550	1,200	1,750

KM# Tn52.2 • Copper • Obv: Clock **Rev:** Eagle with shield **Note:** Thick planchet. Weight generally about 170 grams.

Date	AG	Good	VG	Fine	VF	XF	Unc
1789	60.00	95.00	175	325	525	100.00	—

KM# Tn52.3 • Copper • Obv: Clock **Rev:** Eagle with shield **Edge:** Fully engrailed. **Note:** Specimens struck with perfect dies are scarcer and generally command higher prices.

Date	AG	Good	VG	Fine	VF	XF	Unc
1789	90.00	160	325	450	700	1,750	4,800

Myddelton Token

KM# Tn85 • Copper • Obv. Legend: BRITISH SETTLEMENT KENTUCKY **Rev. Legend:** PAYABLE BY P.P.P.MYDDELTON.

Date	Good	VG	Fine	VF	XF	Unc	Proof
1796	—	—	—	—	—	—	37,500

KM# Tn85a • Silver ASW •

Date	Good	VG	Fine	VF	XF	Unc	Proof
1796	—	—	—	—	—	—	28,000

US COLONIAL AMERICA

New York Theatre

KM# Tn90 • Copper • Obv: Theater building **Obv. Legend:** THE.THEATRE.AT.NEW.YORK. AMERICA **Rev:** Ships at sea, viewed from dock **Rev. Legend:** MAY.COMMERCE.FLOURISH **Note:** 1796 date is circa.

Date	Good	VG	Fine	VF	XF	Unc
1796	—	—	—	7,500	10,000	26,500

North American

HALFPENNY

KM# Tn30 • Copper • Obv: Seated figure left, with harp **Obv. Legend:** NORTH AMERICAN TOKEN **Rev:** Ship **Rev. Legend:** COMMERCE

Date	AG	Good	VG	Fine	VF	XF	Unc
1781	32.00	50.00	70.00	140	300	750	3,250

Rhode Island Ship

KM# Tn27a • Brass • Obv: Without wreath below ship.

Date	AG	Good	VG	Fine	VF	XF	Unc
1779	—	—	325	550	1,000	2,000	7,500

KM# Tn27b • Pewter • Obv: Without wreath below ship.

Date	AG	Good	VG	Fine	VF	XF	Unc
1779	—	—	—	—	5,000	8,500	18,500

KM# Tn28a • Brass • Obv: Wreath below ship.

Date	AG	Good	VG	Fine	VF	XF	Unc
1779	—	—	—	675	1,100	2,100	7,750

KM# Tn28b • Pewter • Obv: Wreath below ship.

Date	AG	Good	VG	Fine	VF	XF	Unc
1779	—	—	—	—	5,500	9,000	20,000

KM# Tn29 • Brass • Obv: VLUGTENDE below ship

Date	AG	Good	VG	Fine	VF	XF
1779 unique	—	—	—	—	—	35,000

Note: Garrett $16,000

Standish Barry

3 PENCE

KM# Tn55 • Silver ASW **• Obv:** Bust left **Obv. Legend:** BALTIMORE • TOWN • JULY • 4 • 90 **• Rev:** Denomination **Rev. Legend:** STANDISH BARRY •

Date	AG	Good	VG	Fine	VF	XF	Unc
1790	—	—	15,000	23,500	55,000	—	—

Talbot, Allum & Lee

CENT

KM# Tn71.1 • Copper • Rev: NEW YORK above ship **Edge:** Lettered. **Edge Lettering:** PAYABLE AT THE STORE OF

Date	AG	Good	VG	Fine	VF	XF	Unc
1794	32.00	50.00	85.00	165	275	550	2,000

KM# Tn71.2 • Copper • Rev: NEW YORK above ship **Edge:** Plain. **Note:** Size of ampersand varies on obverse and reverse dies.

Date	AG	Good	VG	Fine	VF	XF
1794 4 known	—	—	—	—	10,000	24,000

KM# Tn72.1 • Copper • Rev: Without NEW YORK above ship **Edge:** Lettered. **Edge Lettering:** PAYABLE AT THE STORE OF

Date	AG	Good	VG	Fine	VF	XF	Unc
1794	200	375	600	1,250	3,750	7,500	22,000

KM# Tn72.2 • Copper • Edge: Lettered. **Edge Lettering:** WE PROMISE TO PAY THE BEARER ONE CENT.

Date	AG	Good	VG	Fine	VF	XF	Unc
1795	30.00	50.00	75.00	135	250	400	1,200

KM# Tn72.3 • Copper • Edge: Lettered. **Edge Lettering:** CURRENT EVERYWHERE.

Date	Good	VG	Fine	VF	XF	Unc
1795 unique	—	—	—	—	—	—

KM# Tn72.4 • Copper • Edge: Olive leaf.

Date	Good	VG	Fine	VF	XF	Unc
1795 unique	—	—	—	15,000	—	

Note: Norweb $4,400

KM# Tn72.5 • Copper • Edge: Plain.

Date	Good	VG	Fine	VF	XF	Unc
1795 plain edge; 2 known	—	—	—	—	—	—
1795 Lettered edge; unique	—	—	—	15,000	—	

Note: Edge: Cambridge Bedford Huntington.X.X.; Norweb, $3,960

Washington Pieces

KM# Tn35 • Copper • Obv. Legend: GEORGIVS TRIUMPHO.

Date	AG	Good	VG	Fine	VF	XF	Unc
1783	—	95.00	135	285	650	1,150	—

KM# Tn36 • Copper • Obv: Large military bust. **Note:** Varieties exist.

Date	AG	Good	VG	Fine	VF	XF	Unc
1783	—	—	50.00	90.00	185	450	2,600

KM# Tn37.1 • Copper • Obv: Small military bust. **Edge:** Plain.

Date	AG	Good	VG	Fine	VF	XF	Unc
1783	—	—	70.00	95.00	220	525	3,800

Note: One proof example is known. Value: $25,000

KM# Tn37.2 • Copper • Obv: Small military bust. **Edge:** Engrailed.

Date	AG	Good	VG	Fine	VF	XF	Unc
1783	—	75.00	110	150	300	750	4,250

KM# Tn38.1 • Copper • Obv: Draped bust, no button on drapery, small letter.

Date	AG	Good	VG	Fine	VF	XF	Unc
1783	—	40.00	60.00	95.00	185	400	2,250

KM# Tn38.2 • Copper • Obv: Draped bust, button on drapery, large letter.

Date	AG	Good	VG	Fine	VF	XF	Unc
1783	—	85.00	110	150	325	625	4,500

KM# Tn38.4 • Copper • Edge: Engrailed. **Note:** Restrike.

Date	Good	VG	Fine	VF	XF	Unc	Proof
1783	—	—	—	—	—	—	800

KM# Tn38.4a • Copper • Note: Bronzed. Restrike.

Date	Good	VG	Fine	VF	XF	Unc	Proof
1783	—	—	—	—	—	—	

KM# Tn83.3 • Copper • Obv: Large modern lettering. **Edge:** Plain. **Note:** Restrike.

Date	Good	VG	Fine	VF	XF	Unc	Proof
1783	—	—	—	—	—	—	950

KM# Tn83.4b • Silver ASW • Note: Restrike.

Date	Good	VG	Fine	VF	XF	Unc	Proof
1783	—	—	—	—	—	—	1,750

US COLONIAL AMERICA

KM# Tn83.4c • Gold AGW • **Note:** Restrike.

Date	AG	Good	VG	Fine	VF	XF
1783 2 known	—	—	—	—	—	—

KM# Tn60.1 • Copper • Obv. Legend:
WASHINGTON PRESIDENT. **Edge:** Plain.

Date	AG	Good	VG	Fine	VF	XF
1792	850	1,450	3,000	7,500	18,500	—

Note: Steinberg $12,650. Garrett $15,500

KM# Tn60.2 • Copper • Obv. Legend:
WASHINGTON PRESIDENT. **Edge:** Lettered.
Edge Lettering: UNITED STATES OF AMERICA.

Date	AG	Good	VG	Fine	VF	XF	Unc
1792	—	—	—	—	—	—	—

KM# Tn77.1 • Copper • Obv. Legend: LIBERTY
AND SECURITY. **Edge:** Lettered. **Note:** "Penny."

Date	AG	Good	VG	Fine	VF	XF	Unc
(1795)	70.00	110	165	300	500	850	3,500

KM# Tn77.2 • Copper • Edge: Plain. **Note:**
"Penny."

Date	AG	Good	VG	Fine	VF	XF
(1795) extremely rare	—	—	—	—	—	—

KM# Tn77.3 • Copper • Note: "Penny." Engine-
turned borders.

Date	Good	VG	Fine	VF	XF	Unc
(1795) 12 known	275	450	650	1,250	2,400	7,500

KM# Tn78 • Copper • Note: Similar to
"Halfpenny" with date on reverse.

Date	Good	VG	Fine	VF	XF	Unc
1795 very rare	—	—	—	—	—	—

Note: Roper $6,600

KM# Tn61.1 • Copper • Obv. Legend: BORN
VIRGINIA. **Note:** Varieties exist.

Date	AG	Good	VG	Fine	VF	XF	Unc
(1792)	500	1,000	2,000	4,000	7,500	12,000	—

KM# Tn61.2 • Silver ASW • **Edge:** Lettered.
Edge Lettering: UNITED STATES OF AMERICA.

Date	AG	Good	VG	Fine	VF	XF
(1792) 2 known	—	—	—	—	—	—

KM# Tn61.1a • Silver ASW • **Edge:** Plain.

Date	AG	Good	VG	Fine	VF	XF
(1792) 4 known	—	—	—	—	—	200,000

Note: Roper $16,500

KM# Tn62 • Silver ASW • **Rev:** Heraldic eagle.
1792 half dollar. **Note:** Mule.

Date	AG	Good	VG	Fine	VF	XF
(1792) 3 known	—	—	—	—	50,000	75,000

HALFPENNY

KM# Tn56 • Copper • Obv. Legend:
LIVERPOOL HALFPENNY

Date	AG	Good	VG	Fine	VF	XF	Unc
1791	40.00	70.00	1,000	125	300	550	3,250

KM# Tn66.1 • Copper • Rev: Ship **Edge:**
Lettered.

Date	AG	Good	VG	Fine	VF	XF	Unc
1793	25.00	45.00	85.00	225	450	825	3,500

US COLONIAL AMERICA

KM# Tn66.2 • Copper • Rev: Ship **Edge:** Plain.

Date	Good	VG	Fine	VF	XF	Unc
1793 5 known	—	—	—15,000	—	—	

KM# Tn75.1 • Copper • Obv: Large coat buttons **Rev:** Grate **Edge:** Reeded.

Date	AG	Good	VG	Fine	VF	XF	Unc
1795	—	—	70.00	110	200	400	900

KM# Tn75.2 • Copper • Rev: Grate **Edge:** Lettered.

Date	AG	Good	VG	Fine	VF	XF	Unc
1795	90.00	140	210	275	400	800	2,800

KM# Tn75.3 • Copper • Obv: Small coat buttons **Rev:** Grate **Edge:** Reeded.

Date	AG	Good	VG	Fine	VF	XF	Unc
1795	50.00	75.00	120	190	275	585	2,650

KM# Tn76.1 • Copper • Obv. Legend: LIBERTY AND SECURITY. **Edge:** Plain.

Date	AG	Good	VG	Fine	VF	XF	Unc
1795	18.00	35.00	60.00	160	350	700	3,250

KM# Tn76.2 • Copper • Edge: Lettered. **Edge Lettering:** PAYABLE AT LONDON ...

Date	AG	Good	VG	Fine	VF	XF	Unc
1795	40.00	65.00	90.00	140	300	650	3,000

KM# Tn76.3 • Copper • Edge: Lettered. **Edge Lettering:** BIRMINGHAM ...

Date	AG	Good	VG	Fine	VF	XF	Unc
1795	55.00	85.00	125	175	350	800	3,600

KM# Tn76.4 • Copper • Edge: Lettered. **Edge Lettering:** AN ASYLUM ...

Date	AG	Good	VG	Fine	VF	XF	Unc
1795	18.00	35.00	60.00	275	600	1,600	6,500

KM# Tn76.5 • Copper • Edge: Lettered. **Edge Lettering:** PAYABLE AT LIVERPOOL ...

Date	Good	VG	Fine	VF	XF	Unc
1795 unique	—	—	—	—	—	

KM# Tn76.6 • Copper • Edge: Lettered. **Edge Lettering:** PAYABLE AT LONDON-LIVERPOOL.

Date	Good	VG	Fine	VF	XF	Unc
1795 unique	—	—	—	—	—	

KM# Tn81.1 • Copper • Rev. Legend: NORTH WALES **Edge:** Plain.

Date	AG	Good	VG	Fine	VF	XF	Unc
(ca.1795)	60.00	110	175	265	625	1,750	—

KM# Tn82 • Copper • Rev: Four stars at bottom **Rev. Legend:** NORTH WALES

Date	AG	Good	VG	Fine	VF	XF	Unc
(1795)	1,250	2,250	4,750	7,750	21,500	—	—

KM# Tn81.2 • Copper • Rev. Legend: NORTH WALES **Edge:** Lettered.

Date	AG	Good	VG	Fine	VF	XF	Unc
(1795)	350	550	1,150	1,750	5,500	9,500	—

CENT

KM# Tn39 • Copper • Obv: Draped Bust left **Obv. Legend:** WASHINGTON & INDEPENDENCE **Rev:** Denomination in wreath **Rev. Legend:** UNITY STATES OF AMERICA

Date	AG	Good	VG	Fine	VF	XF	Unc
1783	30.00	50.00	70.00	10.00	265	550	2,250

KM# Tn40 • Copper • Note: Double head.

Date	AG	Good	VG	Fine	VF	XF	Unc
(1783)	25.00	45.00	60.00	95.00	250	500	2,750

US COLONIAL AMERICA

KM# Tn41 • Copper • Obv: "Ugly head." **Note:** 3 known in copper, 1 in white metal.

Date	AG	Good	VG	Fine	VF	XF
1784	—	120,000				

Note: Roper $14,850

KM# Tn57 • Copper • Obv: Military bust left **Obv. Legend:** WASHINGTON PRESIDENT. **Rev:** Small eagle

Date	AG	Good	VG	Fine	VF	XF	Unc
1791	—	—	350	500	725	1,000	4,250

KM# Tn58 • Copper • Obv: Military bust left **Obv. Legend:** WASHINGTON PRESIDENT **Rev:** Large eagle

Date	AG	Good	VG	Fine	VF	XF	Unc
1791	—	200	325	485	650	900	3,200

KM# Tn65 • Copper • Obv: "Roman" head **Obv. Legend:** WASHINGTON PRESIDENT.

Date	AG	Good	VG	Fine	VF	XF	Unc
1792	—	—	—	—	—	—	—

HALF DOLLAR

KM# Tn59.1 • Copper • Edge: Lettered. **Edge Lettering:** UNITED STATES OF AMERICA

Date	AG	Good	VG	Fine	VF	XF
1792 2 known	—	—	—	—	—	75,000

Note: Roper $2,860. Benson, EF, $48,300

KM# Tn59.2 • Copper • Edge: Plain.

Date		Good	VG	Fine	VF	XF
1792 3 known		—	—	—	125,000	200,000

KM# Tn59.1a • Silver ASW • **Edge:** Lettered. **Edge Lettering:** UNITED STATES OF AMERICA

Date	AG	Good	VG	Fine	VF	XF
1792 rare	—	—	—	—	40,000	65,000

Note: Roper $35,200

KM# Tn59.2a • Silver ASW • **Edge:** Plain.

Date	AG	Good	VG	Fine	VF	XF	Unc
1792 rare	—	—	—	—	—	—	—

KM# Tn59.1b • Gold AGW • **Edge:** Lettered. **Edge Lettering:** UNITED STATES OF AMERICA

Date	AG	Good	VG	Fine	VF	XF
1792 unique	—	—	—	—	—	—

KM# Tn63.1 • Silver ASW • **Rev:** Small eagle **Edge:** Plain.

Date	AG	Good	VG	Fine	VF	XF
1792	—	—	—	—	200,000	300,000

KM# Tn63.2 • Silver ASW • **Edge:** Ornamented, circles and squares.

Date		VG	Fine	VF	XF	Unc
1792 5 known		—	—	100,000	175,000	400,000

KM# Tn63.1a • Copper • Edge: Plain.

Date	Good	VG	Fine	VF	XF	Unc
1792	4,000	6,500	12,500	32,000	65,000	—

Note: Garrett $32,000

KM# Tn63.3 • Silver ASW • **Edge:** Two olive leaves.

Date	Good	VG	Fine	VF	XF	Unc
1792 unique	—	—	—	—	—	—

KM# Tn64 • Silver ASW • **Rev:** Large heraldic eagle

Date	Good	VG	Fine	VF	XF
1792 unique	—	—	—	100,000	—

Note: Garrett $16,500

EARLY AMERICAN PATTERNS
Confederatio

KM# EA22 • Copper • Obv: Standing figure with bow & arrow **Obv. Legend:** INIMICA TYRANNIS • AMERICANA • **Rev:** Small circle of stars **Rev. Legend:** • CONFEDERATIO •

Date	AG	Good	VG	Fine	VF	XF	Unc
1785	—	—	—	—	50,000	95,000	—

KM# EA23 • Copper • Obv: Standing figure with bow & arrow **Obv. Legend:** INIMICA TYRANNIS • AMERICANA • **Rev:** Large circle of stars **Rev. Legend:** • CONFEDERATIO • **Note:** The Confederatio dies were struck in combination with

13 other dies of the period. All surviving examples of these combinations are extremely rare.

Date	AG	Good	VG	Fine	VF	XF
extremely rare	—	—	—	—	50,000	100,000

Immune Columbia

KM# EA20 • Copper • Obv: George III **Obv. Legend:** GEORGIVS III • REX • **Rev. Legend:** IMMUNE COLUMBIA •

Date	AG	Good	VG	Fine	VF	XF	Unc
1785	3,500	5,250	7,750	11,500	22,500	—	—

KM# EA21 • Copper • Obv: Head right **Obv. Legend:** VERMON AUCTORI **Rev. Legend:** IMMUNE COLUMBIA •

Date	AG	Good	VG	Fine	VF	XF	Unc
1785	—	6,000	9,500	12,500	35,000	—	—

KM# EA17a • Silver ASW • **Obv. Legend:** IMMUNE COLUMBIA • **Rev:** Eye, with pointed rays & stars **Rev. Legend:** NOVA CONSTELLATIO

Date	AG	Good	VG	Fine	VF	XF	Unc
1785	—	—	—	—	45,000	75,000	—

KM# EA19a • Gold AGW • **Obv. Legend:** IMMUNE COLUMBIA • **Rev:** Blunt rays **Rev. Legend:** NOVA CONSTELLATIO •

Date	Good	VG	Fine	VF	XF	Unc
1785 unique	—	—	—	—	—	—

Note: In the Smithsonian Collection

KM# EA17 • Copper • Obv. Legend: IMMUNE COLUMBIA. **Rev:** Eye, with pointed rays & stars **Rev. Legend:** NOVA • CONSTELLATIO

Date	AG	Good	VG	Fine	VF	XF	Unc
1785	—	—	—	—	25,000	45,000	—

KM# EA18 • Copper • Obv. Legend: IMMUNE COLUMBIA • **Rev:** Eye, with pointed rays & stars.

Extra star in reverse legend **Rev. Legend:** NOVA •
CONSTELLATIO *

Date	AG	Good	VG	Fine	VF	XF
1785	—	—	—	—	25,000	45,000

Note: Caldwell $4,675

KM# EA19 • Copper • Obv. Legend: IMMUNE
COLUMBIA • **Rev:** Blunt rays **Rev. Legend:** NOVA
CONSTELATIO

Date	AG	Good	VG	Fine	VF	XF
1785 2 known	—	—	—	—	—	120,000

Note: Norweb $22,000

KM# EA28 • Copper • Obv. Legend: IMMUNIS
COLUMBIA **Rev:** Eagle **Rev. Legend:** * E *
PLURIBUS * UNUM *

Date	Good	VG	Fine	VF	XF
1786 3 known	—	—	—	50,000	90,000

KM# EA24 • Copper • Obv: Washington **Rev:**
Stars in rayed circle **Rev. Legend:** •
CONFEDERATIO •

Date	Good	VG	Fine	VF	XF
1786 3 known	—	—	—	60,000	—

Note: Garrett $50,000. Steinberg $12,650

KM# EA25 • Copper • Obv: Eagle, raw shield
Obv. Legend: * E • PLURIBUS UNUM • **Rev:**
Shield **Rev. Legend:** * E * PLURIBUS * UNUM *

Date	AG	Good	VG	Fine	VF	XF
1786 unique	—	—	—	—	—	—

Note: Garrett $37,500

KM# EA26 • Copper • Obv: Washington **Obv.
Legend:** GEN • WASHINGTON • **Rev:** Eagle

Date	AG	Good	VG	Fine	VF	XF
1786 2 known	—	—	—	—	—	—

KM# EA27 • Copper • Obv. Legend: IMMUNIS
COLUMBIA • **Rev:** Shield **Rev. Legend:** * E *
PLURIBUS * UNUM *

Date	AG	Good	VG	Fine	VF	XF
1786						
extremely rare	—	—	—	—	40,000	60,000

Note: Rescigno, AU, $33,000. Steinberg, VF, $11,000

Nova Constellatio

KM# EA6.1 • Copper • Obv: Pointed rays **Obv.
Legend:** NOVA • CONSTELLATIO • **Rev:** Small
"U•S"

Date	AG	Good	VG	Fine	VF	XF	Unc
1783	50.00	70.00	100.00	225	440	950	3,750

KM# EA6.2 • Copper • Obv: Pointed rays **Obv.
Legend:** NOVA • CONSTELLATIO • **Rev:** Large "US"

Date	AG	Good	VG	Fine	VF	XF	Unc
1783	55.00	75.00	110	250	600	1,400	7,000

KM# EA7 • Copper • Obv: Blunt rays **Obv.
Legend:** NOVA • CONSTELATIO •

Date	AG	Good	VG	Fine	VF	XF	Unc
1783	50.00	75.00	110	250	575	1,350	5,000

US COLONIAL AMERICA

KM# EA8 • Copper • Obv: Blunt rays **Obv. Legend:** NOVA • CONSTELATIO •

Date	AG	Good	VG	Fine	VF	XF	Unc
1785	50.00	75.00	110	260	650	1,550	6,500

KM# EA9 • Copper • Obv: Pointed rays **Obv. Legend:** NOVA • CONSTELLATIO •

Date	AG	Good	VG	Fine	VF	XF	Unc
1785	—	— 100.00	225	450	1,000	3,600

KM# EA10 • Copper • Note: Contemporary circulating counterfeit. Similar to previously listed coin.

Date	AG	Good	VG	Fine	VF	XF
1786 extremely rare	—	—	—	—	—	—

5 UNITS

KM# EA12 • Copper • Obv: Eye, with pointed rays & stars **Obv. Legend:** NOVA CONSTELLATIO **Rev. Legend:** • LIBERTAS • JUSTITIA •

Date	AG	Good	VG	Fine	VF	XF
1783 unique	—	—	—	—	—	—

100 (BIT)

KM# EA13.1 • Silver ASW **• Obv:** Eye, with pointed rays & stars **Obv. Legend:** NOVA

CONSTELLATIO **Rev. Legend:** • LIBERTAS • JUSTITIA • **Edge:** Leaf.

Date	AG	Good	VG	Fine	VF	XF
1783 2 known	—	—	—	—	—	—

Note: Garrett $97,500. Stack's auction, May 1991, $72,500

KM# EA13.2 • Silver ASW **• Obv:** Eye, with pointed rays & stars **Obv. Legend:** NOVA CONSTELLATIO **Rev. Legend:** • LIBERTAS • JUSTITIA • **Edge:** Plain

Date	AG	Good	VG	Fine	VF	XF
1783 unique	—	—	—	—	—	—

500 (QUINT)

KM# EA14 • Silver ASW **• Obv:** Eye with pointed rays & stars **Obv. Legend:** NOVA CONSTELLATIO **Rev. Legend:** • LIBERTAS • JUSTITIA •

Date	AG	Good	VG	Fine	VF	XF
1783 unique	—	—	—	—	—	250,000

Note: Garrett $165,000

KM# EA15 • Silver ASW **• Obv:** Eye, with rays & stars, no legend **Rev. Legend:** • LIBERTAS • JUSTITIA •

Date	AG	Good	VG	Fine	VF	XF
1783 unique	—	—	—	— 75,000	—

Note: Garrett $55,000

1000 (MARK)

KM# EA16 • Silver ASW **• Obv:** Eye, with pointed rays & stars **Obv. Legend:** NOVA CONSTELLATIO **Rev. Legend:** • LIBERTAS • JUSTITIA •

US COLONIAL AMERICA

Date	AG	Good	VG	Fine	VF	XF
1783 unique	—	—	—	—	—	350,000

Note: Garrett $190,000

EARLY FEDERAL COINAGE

Brasher

KM# Tn51.1 • Gold AGW • **Obv:** Sunrise over mountains. **Rev:** Displayed eagle with shield on breast, EB counterstamp on wing.

Date	AG	Good	VG	Fine	VF	XF
1787 6 known	—	—	—	—	—	—

Note: Heritage FUN Sale, January 2005, AU-55, $2.415 million.

KM# Tn51.2 • Gold AGW • **Obv:** Sun rise over mountains **Rev:** Displayed eagle with sheild on breast. EB counterstamp on breast.

Date	AG	Good	VG	Fine	VF	XF
1787 unique	—	—	—	—	—	—

Note: Heritage FUN Sale, January 2005, XF-45, $2.99 million. Foreign gold coins with the EB counterstamp exist. These are valued at over $5,000, with many much higher.

Fugio "Cent"

KM# EA30.1 • Copper • Obv: Club rays, round ends.

Date	AG	Good	VG	Fine	VF	XF	Unc
1787	225	325	450	950	2,000	3,850	—

KM# EA30.2 • Copper • Obv: Club rays, concave ends.

Date	AG	Good	VG	Fine	VF	XF	Unc
1787	1,500	2,500	4,500	9000	27,500	—	—

KM# EA30.3 • Copper • Obv. Legend: FUCIO.

Date	AG	Good	VG	Fine	VF	XF
1787	—	2,000	3,000	7,000	25,000	35,000

KM# EA31.1 • Copper • Obv: Pointed rays. **Rev:** UNITED above, STATES below.

Date	AG	Good	VG	Fine	VF	XF
1787	600	950	1,500	3,250	80,000	11,500

KM# EA31.2 • Copper • Rev: UNITED STATES at sides of ring.

Date	AG	Good	VG	Fine	VF	XF	Unc
1787	110	175	275	550	900	1,800	3,500

KM# EA31.3 • Copper • Rev: STATES UNITED at sides of ring.

Date	AG	Good	VG	Fine	VF	XF	Unc
1787	110	190	275	550	850	1,650	3,500

KM# EA31.4 • Copper • Rev: Eight-pointed stars on ring.

Date	AG	Good	VG	Fine	VF	XF	Unc
1787	150	285	475	700	1,250	2,750	9,000

KM# EA31.5 • Copper • Rev: Raised rims on ring, large lettering in center.

Date	AG	Good	VG	Fine	VF	XF	Unc
1787	185	325	550	950	2,750	6,000	18,500

KM# EA32.1 • Copper • Obv: No cinquefoils, cross after date. **Obv. Legend:** UNITED STATES.

Date	AG	Good	VG	Fine	VF	XF	Unc
1787	300	485	750	1,450	3,850	6,700	—

KM# EA32.2 • Copper • Obv: No cinquefoils, cross after date. **Obv. Legend:** STATES UNITED.

Date	AG	Good	VG	Fine	VF	XF	Unc
1787	175	350	750	1,500	4,000	7,200	—

KM# EA32.3 • Copper • Obv: No cinquefoils, cross after date. **Rev:** Raised rims on ring.

Date	AG	Good	VG	Fine	VF	XF	Unc
1787	—	—	—	—	27,500	—	—

KM# EA33 • Copper • Obv: No cinquefoils, cross after date. **Rev:** With rays. **Rev. Legend:** AMERICAN CONGRESS.

Date		VG	Fine	VF	XF
1787 extremely rare		—	—	225,000	300,000

Note: Norweb $63,800

KM# EA34 • Brass • Note: New Haven restrike.

Date	AG	Good	VG	Fine	VF	XF	Unc
1787	—	—	—	—	—	450	1,000

KM# EA34a • Copper • Note: New Haven restrike.

Date	AG	Good	VG	Fine	VF	XF	Unc
1787	—	—	—	—	450	750	1,000

KM# EA34b • Silver ASW **• Note:** New Haven restrike.

Date	Good	VG	Fine	VF	XF	Unc
1787(ca.1858)	—	—	—	—	2,750	4,000

KM# EA34c • Gold AGW **• Note:** New Haven restrike.

Date	AG	Good	VG	Fine	VF	XF
1787(ca.1858) 2 known	—	—	—	—	—	—

Note: Norweb (holed) $1,430

ISSUES OF 1792

CENT

KM# PnE1 • Bi-Metallic, Silver center in Copper ring •

Date	Good	VG	Fine	VF	XF
1792 14 known	—	—	185,000	325,000	475,000

Note: Norweb, MS-60, $143,000; Heritage 4-12; MS61 $1.15 million

KM# PnF1 • Copper • Note: No silver center.

Date	Good	VG	Fine	VF	XF
1792 9 known	—	—	250,000	500,000	750,000

Note: Norweb, EF-40, $35,200; Benson, VG-10, $57,500

KM# PnG1 • Copper • Edge: Plain **Note:** Commonly called "Birch cent."

Date	AG	Good	VG	Fine	VF	XF
1792 unique	—	—	—	—	—	650,000

KM# PnH1 • Copper • Obv: One star in edge legend **Note:** Commonly called "Birch cent."

Date	AG	Good	VG	Fine	VF	XF
1792 2 known	—	—	—	—	—	600,000

Note: Norweb, EF-40, $59,400

KM# PnI1 • Copper • Obv: Two stars in edge legend **Note:** Commonly called "Birch cent."

Date	Good	VG	Fine	VF	XF
1792 8 known	—	—	200,000	400,000	550,000

Note: Hawn, strong VF, $57,750

KM# PnJ1 • White Metal • Rev: "G.W.Pt." below wreath tie **Note:** Commonly called "Birch cent."

Date	AG	Good	VG	Fine	VF	XF
1792 unique	—	—	—	—	—	—

Note: Garrett, $90,000

US COLONIAL AMERICA

HALF DISME

KM# 5 • Silver ASW •

Date	AG	VG	Fine	VF	XF	Unc
1792	25,000	35,000	55,000	90,000	125,000	450,000

KM# PnA1 • Copper •

Date	AG	Good	VG	Fine	VF	XF
1792 unique	—	—	—	—	—	—

Note: Heritage Auction, 4-06, 5p-67 realized $1,322,500

DISME

KM# PnB1 • Silver ASW •

Date	Good	VG	Fine	VF	XF
1792 3 known	—	—	—	700,000	1,000,000

Note: Norweb, EF-40, $28,600

KM# PnC1 • Copper • Edge: Reeded

Date	VG	Fine	VF	XF	Unc
1792 14 known	—	—	150,000	250,000	500,000

Note: Hawn, VF, $30,800; Benson, EF-45, $109,250

KM# PnD1 • Copper • Edge: Plain

Date	Good	VG	Fine	VF	XF
1792 2 known	—	—	—	450,000	750,000

Note: Garrett, $45,000

QUARTER

KM# PnK1 • Copper • Edge: Reeded **Note:** Commonly called "Wright quarter."

Date	AG	Good	VG	Fine	VF	XF
1792 2 known	—	—	—	—	—	—

KM# PnL1 • White Metal • Edge: Plain **Note:** Commonly called "Wright quarter."

Date	AG	Good	VG	Fine	VF	XF
1792 4 known	—	—	—	—	175,000	—

Note: Norweb, VF-30 to EF-40, $28,600

KM# PnM1 • White Metal • Note: Commonly called "Wright quarter."

Date	AG	Good	VG	Fine	VF	XF
1792 die trial	—	—	—	—	—	—

Note: Garrett, $12,000

UNITED STATES

CIRCULATION COINAGE

HALF CENT

Liberty Cap Half Cent

Head facing left obverse

KM# 10 • 6.7400 g., **Copper**, 22 mm. • **Designer:** Henry Voigt

Date	Mintage	G-4	VG-8	F-12	VF-20	XF-40	MS-60
1793	35,334	3,250	5,350	8,500	15,000	27,000	61,000

Head facing right obverse

KM# 14 • **Copper**, 6.74 g. (1794-95) and 5.44 g. (1795-97), 23.5 mm. • **Designer:** Robert Scot (1794) and John Smith Gardner (1795) **Notes:** The "lettered edge" varieties have TWO HUNDRED FOR A DOLLAR inscribed around the edge. The "pole" varieties have a pole upon which the cap is hanging, resting on Liberty's shoulder. The "punctuated date" varieties have a comma after the 1 in the date. The 1797 "1 above 1" variety has a second 1 above the 1 in the date.

Date	Mintage	G-4	VG-8	F-12	VF-20	XF-40	MS-60
1794 Normal Relief Head	81,600	440	650	975	1,675	3,750	17,000
1794 High Relief Head	Inc. above	—	—	—	—	—	—
1795 lettered edge, pole	25,600	450	700	950	1,500	4,550	17,500
1795 plain edge, no pole	109,000	375	475	800	1,400	3,500	16,000
1795 lettered edge, punctuated date	Inc. above	475	700	1,000	1,600	3,750	50,000
1795 plain edge, punctuated date	Inc. above	350	450	750	1,500	3,000	57,500
1796 pole	5,090	16,000	50,000	53,500	30,000	35,000	—
1796 no pole	1,390	27,000	35,500	47,500	90,000	—	—
1797 plain edge	119,215	400	575	950	1,900	6,000	57,500
1797 lettered edge	Inc. above	1,700	5,700	4,000	8,000	55,000	—
1797 1 above 1	Inc. above	375	475	950	1,600	3,550	50,000
1797 gripped edge	Inc. above	16,000	37,500	48,000	60,000	70,000	—

Draped Bust Half Cent

Draped bust right, date at angle below obverse
Value within thin wreath reverse

Stemless   Stems

KM# 33 • 5.4400 g., **Copper**, 23.5 mm. • **Obv. Legend** LIBERTY **Rev. Legend:** UNITED STATES OF AMERICA **Designer:** Robert Scot **Notes:** The wreath on the reverse was redesigned slightly in 1802, resulting in "reverse of 1800" and "reverse of 1802" varieties. The "stems" varieties have stems extending from the wreath above and on both sides of the fraction on the reverse. On the 1804 "crosslet 4" variety, a serif appears at the far right of the crossbar on the 4 in the date. The "spiked chin" variety appears to have a spike extending from Liberty's chin, the result of a damaged die. Varieties of the 1805 strikes are distinguished by the size of the 5 in the date. Varieties of the 1806 strikes are distinguished by the size of the 6 in the date.

HALF CENT

Date	Mintage	G-4	VG-8	F-12	VF-20	XF-40	MS-60
1800	211,530	65.00	90.00	125	205	500	5,500
1802/0 rev. 1800	14,366	15,000	55,000	30,000	—	—	—
1802/0 rev. 1802	Inc. above	800	1,400	5,750	6,500	17,000	—
1803	97,900	75.00	95.00	105	575	950	7,000
1804 plain 4, stemless wreath	1,055,312	60.00	80.00	90.00	170	550	1,400
1804 plain 4, stems	Inc. above	60.00	90.00	155	550	1,500	15,000
1804 crosslet 4, stemless	Inc. above	65.00	90.00	100.00	195	550	1,350
1804 crosslet 4, stems	Inc. above	62.00	90.00	125	215	300	1,500
1804 spiked chin	Inc. above	75.00	105	155	215	355	1,500
1805 small 5, stemless	814,464	65.00	90.00	105	195	400	3,500
1805 small 5, stems	Inc. above	800	1,500	5,400	4,500	8,000	—
1805 large 5, stems	Inc. above	65.00	85.00	100.00	180	400	3,000
1806 small 6, stems	356,000	500	355	600	1,000	5,750	—
1806 small 6, stemless	Inc. above	65.00	85.00	100.00	215	535	1,350
1806 large 6, stems	Inc. above	65.00	85.00	100.00	215	550	1,500
1807	476,000	65.00	95.00	155	220	300	1,400
1808/7	400,000	300	400	600	1,500	6,000	57,500
1808	Inc. above	65.00	85.00	105	215	350	5,000

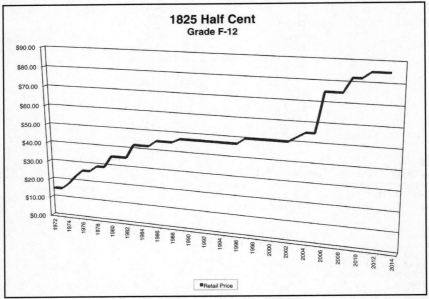

1825 Half Cent
Grade F-12

Classic Head Half Cent

Classic head left, flanked by stars, date below obverse
Value within wreath reverse

KM# 41 • 5.4400 g., Copper, 23.5 mm. • Rev. Legend: UNITED STATES OF AMERICA **Designer:** John Reich **Notes:** Restrikes listed were produced privately in the mid-1800s. The 1831 restrikes have two varieties with different sized berries in the wreath on the reverse. The 1828 strikes have either 12 or 13 stars on the obverse.

Date	Mintage	G-4	VG-8	F-12	VF-20	XF-40	MS-60
1809/6	1,154,572	60.00	80.00	110	150	515	1,000
1809	Inc. above	59.00	78.00	90.00	110	515	800
1809 circle in 0	—	66.00	93.00	90.00	150	550	5,100
1810	215,000	66.00	103	150	500	600	3,550
1811 Close Date	63,140	255	375	750	1,800	4,000	—

Date	Mintage	G-4	VG-8	F-12	VF-20	XF-40	MS-60
1811 Wide Date Inc. Above	—	290	725	1,550	2,550	4,750	—
1811 restrike, reverse of 1802, uncirculated	—	—	—	—	—	—	57,500
1825	63,000	56.00	73.00	85.00	110	500	950
1826	234,000	51.00	68.00	82.00	90.00	500	750
1828 13 stars	606,000	51.00	68.00	75.00	85.00	95.00	225
1828 12 stars	Inc. above	61.00	78.00	125	175	550	850
1829	487,000	51.00	71.00	82.00	100.00	150	500
1831 original	2,200	—	—	—	—	65,000	—
1831 1st restrike, lg. berries, reverse of 1836	—	—	—	—	—	—	6,500
1831 2nd restrike, sm. berries, reverse of 1840, proof	—	—	—	—	—	—	55,000
1832	154,000	51.00	68.00	75.00	85.00	95.00	225
1833	120,000	51.00	68.00	75.00	85.00	95.00	225
1834	141,000	51.00	68.00	75.00	85.00	95.00	225
1835	398,000	51.00	68.00	75.00	85.00	95.00	225
1836 original, proof	—	—	—	—	—	—	6,000
1836 restrike, reverse of 1840, proof	—	—	—	—	—	—	50,000

Braided Hair Half Cent

Head left, braided hair, within circle of stars, date below obverse
Value within wreath reverse

KM# 70 • 5.4400 g., **Copper**, 23 mm. • **Rev. Legend:** UNITED STATES OF AMERICA **Designer:** Christian Gobrecht **Notes:** 1840-1849 and 1852 strikes, both originals and restrikes, are known in proof only; mintages are unknown. The small-date varieties of 1849, both originals and restrikes are known in proof only. The restrikes were produced clandestinely by Philadelphia Mint personnel in the mid-1800s.

Date	Mintage	G-4	VG-8	F-12	VF-20	XF-40	MS-60	Prf-60
1840 original	—	—	—	—	—	3,000	—	3,250
1840 1st restrike	—	—	—	—	—	3,000	—	3,250
1840 2nd restrike	—	—	—	—	—	3,000	—	5,500
1841 original	—	—	—	—	—	3,000	—	3,250
1841 1st restrike	—	—	—	—	—	3,000	—	3,250
1841 2nd restrike	—	—	—	—	—	3,000	—	6,000
1842 original	—	—	—	—	—	3,000	—	3,250
1842 1st restrike	—	—	—	—	—	3,000	—	3,250
1842 2nd restrike	—	—	—	—	—	3,000	—	6,000
1843 original	—	—	—	—	—	3,000	—	3,250
1843 1st restrike	—	—	—	—	—	3,000	—	3,250
1843 2nd restrike	—	—	—	—	—	3,000	—	6,500
1844 original	—	—	—	—	—	3,000	—	3,250
1844 1st restrike	—	—	—	—	—	3,000	—	3,250
1844 2nd restrike	—	—	—	—	—	3,000	—	6,000
1845 original	—	—	—	—	—	3,000	—	6,000
1845 1st restrike	—	—	—	—	—	3,000	—	3,250
1845 2nd restrike	—	—	—	—	—	3,000	—	6,000
1846 original	—	—	—	—	—	3,000	—	3,250
1846 1st restrike	—	—	—	—	—	3,000	—	3,250
1846 2nd restrike	—	—	—	—	—	3,000	—	6,000
1847 original	—	—	—	—	—	3,000	—	3,250
1847 1st restrike	—	—	—	—	—	5,500	—	3,250
1847 2nd restrike	—	—	—	—	—	3,000	—	6,000
1848 original	—	—	—	—	—	3,000	—	6,000
1848 1st restrike	—	—	—	—	—	3,000	—	3,250
1848 2nd restrike	—	—	—	—	—	3,000	—	6,000
1849 original, small date	—	—	—	—	—	3,000	—	3,250
1849 1st restrike small date	—	—	—	—	—	3,000	—	3,250
1849 large date	39,864	58.00	76.00	82.00	92.00	110	300	—
1850	39,812	58.00	76.00	82.00	92.00	110	340	—
1851	147,672	54.00	71.00	77.00	84.00	96.00	195	—
1852 original	—	15,000	55,000	30,000	35,000	40,000	—	90,000
1852 1st restrike	—	1,000	1,500	1,850	2,600	3,000	—	5,000
1852 2nd restrike	—	1,000	1,500	1,850	2,600	3,000	—	7,000
1853	129,694	54.00	71.00	77.00	84.00	96.00	195	—
1854	55,358	54.00	71.00	77.00	84.00	96.00	195	—
1855	56,500	54.00	71.00	77.00	84.00	96.00	195	3,250
1856	40,430	54.00	71.00	77.00	84.00	96.00	195	3,250
1857	35,180	59.00	78.00	87.00	102	126	270	3,250

HALF CENT

CENT

Flowing Hair Cent
Chain reverse

KM# 11 • 13.4800 g., Copper, 26-27 mm. • Designer: Henry Voigt

Date	Mintage	G-4	VG-8	F-12	VF-20	XF-40	MS-60
1793 "AMERI"	36,103	9,950	14,750	25,500	45,500	96,000	245,000
1793 "AMERICA"	Inc. above	6,950	10,500	17,750	36,500	71,500	140,000
1793 periods after "LIBERTY"	Inc. above	7,850	12,250	19,850	38,500	73,500	147,000

Flowing Hair Cent
Wreath reverse

KM# 12 • 13.4800 g., Copper, 26-28 mm. • Designer: Henry Voigt

Date	Mintage	G-4	VG-8	F-12	VF-20	XF-40	MS-60
1793 vine and bars edge	63,353	2,900	3,500	7,000	12,000	22,500	48,500
1793 lettered edge	Inc. above	3,200	4,200	8,100	14,000	25,500	56,000
1793 strawberry leaf; 4 known	—	350,000	550,000	875,000	—	—	—

Liberty Cap Cent

KM# 13 • Copper, 13.48 g. (1793-95) and 10.89 g. (1795-96), 29 mm. • Designer: Joseph Wright (1793-1795) and John Smith Gardner (1795-1796) **Notes:** The heavier pieces were struck on a thicker planchet. The Liberty design on the obverse was revised slightly in 1794, but the 1793 design was used on some 1794 strikes. A 1795 "lettered edge" variety has ONE HUNDRED FOR A DOLLAR and a leaf inscribed on the edge.

Date	Mintage	G-4	VG-8	F-12	VF-20	XF-40	MS-60
1793 cap	11,056	5,500	12,500	23,500	45,000	98,500	—
1794 NO FRACTION BAR	Inc. above	500	800	1,350	3,000	8,000	40,000
1794 head '93	918,521	1,550	2,600	4,250	9,850	21,500	85,000
1794 head '94	Inc. above	445	650	1,025	2,175	4,500	16,500
1794 head '95	Inc. above	525	715	1,090	2,525	5,000	20,000
1794 starred rev.	Inc. above	13,500	23,500	44,500	115,000	275,000	—
1795 Lettered Edge	Inc. above	510	650	1,200	3,200	4,500	16,500
1795 plain edge	501,500	370	550	875	1,525	3,800	12,500
1795 reeded edge	Inc. above	350,000	700,000	—	—	—	—
1795 Jefferson head plain edge	Inc. above	24,500	49,500	95,000	150,000	—	—
1795 Jefferson head lettered edge	Inc. above	75,000	95,000	155,000	250,000	—	—

Liberty Cap Cent

KM# 13a • 10.8900 g., **Copper**, 29 mm. • **Designer:** Joseph Wright (1793-1795) and John Smith Gardner (1795-1796)

Date	Mintage	G-4	VG-8	F-12	VF-20	XF-40	MS-60
1795 lettered edge, "One Cent" high in wreath	37,000	440	675	925	1,925	4,800	15,000
1796	109,825	420	550	1,475	3,850	9,500	36,500

Draped Bust Cent

Draped bust right, date at angle below obverse
Value within wreath reverse

Stemless   Stems

KM# 22 • 10.9800 g., **Copper**, 29 mm. • **Obv. Legend** LIBERTY **Rev. Legend:** UNITED STATES OF AMERICA **Designer:** Robert Scot **Notes:** The 1801 "3 errors" variety has the fraction on the reverse reading "1/000," has only one stem extending from the wreath above and on both sides of the fraction on the reverse, and UNITED in UNITED STATES OF AMERICA appears as "linited."

Date	Mintage	G-4	VG-8	F-12	VF-20	XF-40	MS-60
1796 Rev. of 1794	363,375	300	450	1,050	2,800	6,850	36,500
1796 Rev. of 1795	Inc. above	260	375	850	3,250	9,500	11,000
1796 Rev. of 1797	Inc. above	240	350	1,050	2,150	4,250	75,000
1796 Liberty error	Inc. above	450	850	1,800	5,500	13,500	38,500
1797 reverse of 1795 plain edge	897,510	165	300	600	3,450	5,500	—
1797 reverse of 1795 gripped edge	Inc. above	185	425	850	1,450	4,750	—
1797 stems	Inc. above	165	325	450	1,275	2,650	9,000
1797 stemless	Inc. above	300	495	750	1,850	4,750	38,500
1798/7	1,841,745	200	325	650	2,100	5,100	22,000
1798 reverse of 1796	Inc. above	150	250	600	1,750	3,600	9,500
1798 1st hair style	Inc. above	90.00	130	325	800	4,450	9,850
1798 2nd hair style	Inc. above	85.00	125	310	750	2,850	8,000
1799	42,540	2,750	4,650	11,500	24,500	85,000	650,000
1799/98	Inc. above	2,600	4,300	11,000	34,000	110,000	—
1800	2,822,175	100.00	165	375	1,850	3,000	12,500
1800/798	Inc. above	85.00	225	550	1,550	4,000	—
1800/79	Inc. above	80.00	200	375	1,500	3,300	16,500
1801	1,362,837	75.00	100.00	250	700	1,725	7,750
1801 3 errors	Inc. above	225	500	1,150	2,400	6,850	35,000
1801 1/000	Inc. above	80.00	175	475	1,350	2,650	9,850
1801 100/000	Inc. above	150	325	850	1,650	4,200	12,500
1802	3,435,100	65.00	100.00	250	485	1,200	4,500
1802 stemless	Inc. above	68.00	95.00	200	465	1,500	5,000
1802 fraction 1/000	Inc. above	80.00	135	325	700	1,750	7,500
1803 small date, small fraction	2,471,353	65.00	100.00	225	375	900	32,500
1803 small date, large fraction	Inc. above	65.00	100.00	225	385	950	3,350
1803 large date, small fraction	Inc. above	4,600	11,500	14,500	42,000	75,000	—
1803 large date, large fraction	Inc. above	80.00	135	450	1,550	3,150	—
1803 1/100 over 1/1000	—	95.00	165	360	900	2,600	10,000
1803 Stemless wreath	—	80.00	150	350	650	2,100	6,950
1804	96,500	1,650	2,650	4,000	8,950	16,500	80,000
1804 Restrike of 1860	—	—	—	650	750	875	1,750
1805	941,116	60.00	90.00	245	375	1,300	4,650
1806	348,000	70.00	110	305	550	1,775	7,500
1807 small fraction	727,221	65.00	100.00	265	575	2,200	4,600

CENT

CENT

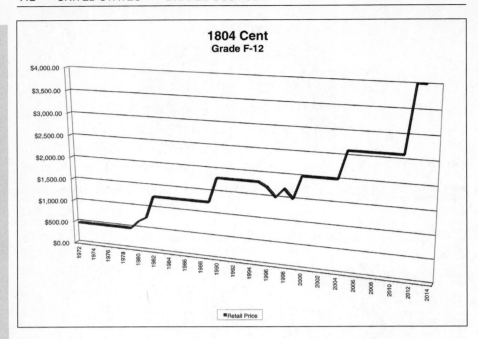

1804 Cent
Grade F-12

Date	Mintage	G-4	VG-8	F-12	VF-20	XF-40	MS-60
1807 large fraction	Inc. above	65.00	100.00	225	460	1,100	3,150
1807/6 large 7/6	Inc. above	65.00	175	225	575	1,400	—
1807/6 small 7/6	Inc. above	1,900	4,250	9,500	24,500	49,500	—
1807 Comet Variety	Inc. above	95.00	175	345	1,100	3,200	16,500

Classic Head Cent

Classic head left, flanked by stars, date below obverse
Value within wreath reverse

KM# 39 • 10.8900 g., Copper, 29 mm. • Rev. Legend: UNITED STATES OF AMERICA Designer: John Reich

Date	Mintage	G-4	VG-8	F-12	VF-20	XF-40	MS-60
1808	1,109,000	106	160	440	700	1,850	9,500
1809	222,867	135	285	450	1,050	3,350	13,500
1810/09	1,458,500	90.00	160	420	675	1,850	10,500
1810	Inc. above	75.00	110	320	675	1,550	9,500
1811/10	218,025	175	300	700	1,950	4,650	60,000
1811	Inc. above	110	225	575	1,300	3,350	11,000
1812 small date	1,075,500	75.00	115	345	650	1,650	8,000
1812 large date	—	75.00	115	345	660	1,700	8,500
1813	418,000	60.00	175	400	800	1,950	9,000
1814 Plain 4	357,830	75.00	120	305	675	1,450	5,750
1814 Crosslet 4	Inc. above	75.00	115	295	650	1,350	5,600

Coronet Cent

Coronet head left, within circle of stars, date below obverse
Value within wreath reverse

KM# 45 • 10.8900 g., **Copper**, 28-29 mm. • **Rev. Legend:** UNITED STATES OF AMERICA **Designer:** Robert Scot

Date	Mintage	G-4	VG-8	F-12	VF-20	XF-40	MS-60
1816	2,820,982	31.00	42.00	60.00	117	245	1,350
1817 13 obverse stars	3,948,400	29.00	33.00	44.00	74.00	155	650
1817 15 obverse stars	Inc. above	35.00	56.00	90.00	225	675	2,650
1818	3,167,000	29.00	35.00	42.00	74.00	150	450
1819 Large date, 9/8	2,671,000	—	—	—	—	—	—
1819	—	31.00	38.00	46.00	116	315	1,000
1819/8	—	—	—	—	—	—	—
1819 Large date	Inc. above	29.00	33.00	42.00	78.00	183	600
1819 Small date	Inc. above	30.00	35.00	45.00	82.00	203	675
1820 Large date, 20/19	4,407,550	31.00	38.00	50.00	88.00	250	950
1820 Large date	—	33.00	39.00	60.00	117	335	1,600
1820 Small date	—	29.00	36.00	46.00	78.00	188	450
1821	389,000	45.00	72.00	200	525	1,375	7,500
1822	2,072,339	31.00	45.00	45.00	150	365	1,500
1823 Included in 1824 mintage	—	90.00	200	450	1,350	3,950	30,000
1823/22 Included in 1824 mintage	—	80.00	165	425	975	3,250	—
1823 Restrike	—	600	650	700	800	900	1,850
1824	1,262,000	31.00	35.00	46.00	210	450	1,950
1824/22	Inc. above	40.00	49.00	110	440	1,000	5,500
1825	1,461,100	30.00	35.00	45.00	125	400	2,150
1826	1,517,425	30.00	35.00	45.00	87.00	265	950
1826/25	Inc. above	40.00	55.00	95.00	275	1,200	4,250
1827	2,357,732	29.00	33.00	42.00	92.00	260	800
1828 Large date	2,260,624	29.00	33.00	44.00	87.00	225	900
1828 Small date	—	32.00	37.00	49.00	110	265	1,650
1829 Large letters	1,414,500	29.00	33.00	40.00	93.00	208	1,100
1829 Medium letters	Inc. above	32.00	45.00	90.00	275	675	5,250
1830 Large letters	1,711,500	25.00	29.00	36.00	70.00	188	650
1830 Medium letters	Inc. above	45.00	90.00	265	650	1,650	7,500
1831 Large letters	3,359,260	25.00	31.00	36.00	70.00	193	500
1831 Medium letters	—	29.00	34.00	41.00	76.00	225	950
1832 Large letters	2,362,000	25.00	31.00	36.00	70.00	158	525
1832 Medium letters	—	27.00	32.00	39.00	74.00	178	850
1833	2,739,000	25.00	31.00	36.00	70.00	158	475
1834 Large 8, stars and letters	1,855,100	75.00	120	145	250	625	2,350
1834 Large 8 & stars, medium letters	Inc. above	190	275	600	1,100	3,250	6,200
1834 Large 8, small stars, medium letters	Inc. above	25.00	29.00	36.00	70.00	158	650
1834 Small 8 & stars	Inc. above	25.00	29.00	36.00	70.00	145	750
1835 Large 8 & stars	3,878,400	25.00	31.00	39.00	74.00	168	1,000
1835 Small 8 & stars	—	25.00	29.00	36.00	70.00	158	650
1835 Head '36	—	25.00	31.00	39.00	74.00	158	550
1836	2,111,000	25.00	29.00	36.00	70.00	125	290
1837 Plain hair cords, medium letters	5,558,300	25.00	29.00	36.00	70.00	125	290
1837 Plain hair cords, small letters	Inc. above	25.00	31.00	39.00	74.00	133	485
1837 Head '38	Inc. above	25.00	31.00	39.00	74.00	125	250
1838	6,370,200	25.00	29.00	36.00	70.00	125	250
1839 Head '38, beaded hair cords	3,128,661	29.00	33.00	40.00	74.00	130	450
1839/36 Plain hair cords	Inc. above	300	600	1,250	2,450	6,800	75,000
1839 Silly head	Inc. above	35.00	40.00	50.00	90.00	165	900
1839 Booby head	Inc. above	34.00	38.00	47.00	85.00	153	875

CENT

Braided Hair Cent
Head left, braided hair, within circle of stars, date below obverse
Value within wreath reverse

KM# 67 • 10.8900 g., **Copper**, 27.5 mm. • **Rev. Legend:** UNITED STATES OF AMERICA **Designer:** Christian Gobrecht **Notes:** 1840 and 1842 strikes are known with both small and large dates, with little difference in value. A slightly larger Liberty head and larger reverse lettering were used beginning in 1843.

Date	Mintage	G-4	VG-8	F-12	VF-20	XF-40	MS-60
1839 Petite Head	3,128,661	29.00	33.00	47.00	62.50	100.00	825
1840 Large date	2,462,700	25.00	28.00	36.00	51.50	80.00	1,250
1840 Small date	Inc. above	30.00	35.00	42.00	53.50	90.00	550
1840 Small date over large 18	Inc. above	40.00	50.00	75.00	125	210	1,150
1841	1,597,367	25.00	28.00	36.00	51.50	79.00	450
1842 Small date	2,383,390	25.00	28.00	36.00	51.50	69.00	400
1842 Large date	Inc. above	28.00	32.00	42.00	57.50	100.00	365
1843 Petite Head, small date	2,425,342	25.00	28.00	35.00	51.50	69.00	360
1843 Petite Head, (rev '44)	Inc. above	27.00	30.00	37.00	51.50	79.00	550
1843 Mature Head	—	28.00	32.00	50.00	140	260	600
1844	2,398,752	25.00	28.00	36.00	51.50	69.00	375
1844/81	Inc. above	40.00	60.00	80.00	100.00	225	1,900
1845	3,894,804	25.00	28.00	33.00	51.50	69.00	300
1846 Small date	4,120,800	23.00	27.00	31.00	51.50	69.00	225
1846 MD	Inc. above	25.00	28.00	35.00	53.50	72.00	375
1846 TD	Inc. above	36.00	45.00	80.00	125	260	1,650
1847	6,183,669	23.00	27.00	31.00	47.50	65.00	250
1847/7	Inc. above	37.00	50.00	90.00	150	385	1,350
1848	6,415,799	25.00	28.00	33.00	47.50	61.00	185
1849	4,178,500	25.00	28.00	33.00	47.50	61.00	225
1850	4,426,844	25.00	28.00	33.00	39.50	61.00	195
1851	9,889,707	23.00	26.00	31.00	37.50	59.00	165
1851/81	Inc. above	36.00	45.00	60.00	90.00	175	700
1852	5,063,094	23.00	26.00	31.00	37.50	59.00	165
1853	6,641,131	23.00	26.00	31.00	37.50	59.00	165

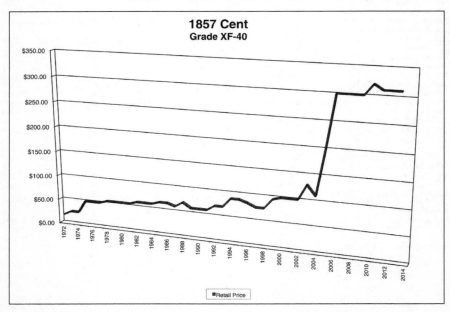

1857 Cent
Grade XF-40

Date	Mintage	G-4	VG-8	F-12	VF-20	XF-40	MS-60
1854	4,236,156	23.00	26.00	31.00	37.50	59.00	165
1855 Slanted 5's	1,574,829	43.00	56.00	65.00	74.50	95.00	215
1855 Upright 5's	Inc. above	23.00	26.00	33.00	37.50	59.00	165
1855 Slanted 5's Knob on Ear	Inc. above	27.00	34.00	46.00	70.00	99.00	450
1856 Slanted 5	2,690,463	23.00	26.00	31.00	37.50	59.00	165
1856 Upright 5	Inc. above	30.00	40.00	52.00	63.50	80.00	220
1857 Large date	333,456	90.00	125	175	235	310	600
1857 Small date	Inc. above	75.00	100.00	160	195	265	550

Flying Eagle Cent

Flying eagle above date obverse
Value within wreath reverse

   Large letters — AM touch at bottom

 Small letters — Space between AM

KM# 85 • 4.6700 g., **Copper-Nickel**, 19 mm. • **Obv. Legend** UNITED STATES OF AMERICA **Designer:** James B. Longacre **Notes:** On the large-letter variety of 1858, the "A" and "M" in AMERICA are connected at their bases; on the small-letter variety, the two letters are separated.

Date	Mintage	G-4	VG-8	F-12	VF-20	XF-40	AU-50	MS-60	MS-65	Prf-65
1856	Est. 2,500	6,250	7,250	9,000	10,750	12,850	13,500	16,500	65,000	28,500
1857	17,450,000	27.50	39.00	40.00	47.00	140	210	425	3,500	29,000
1858/7	Inc. below	65.00	92.50	175	380	760	1,500	3,300	60,000	—
1858 large letters	24,600,000	28.00	41.00	43.50	56.00	160	230	445	3,850	24,500
1858 small letters	Inc. above	27.50	39.00	42.00	47.00	140	210	425	3,650	30,000

Indian Head Cent

Indian head with headdress left above date obverse
Value within wreath reverse

KM# 87 • 4.6700 g., **Copper-Nickel**, 19 mm. • **Obv. Legend** UNITED STATES OF AMERICA **Designer:** James B. Longacre

Date	Mintage	G-4	VG-8	F-12	VF-20	XF-40	AU-50	MS-60	MS-65	Prf-65
1859	36,400,000	13.00	16.00	22.50	48.00	100.00	175	230	3,650	5,200

Indian Head Cent

Indian head with headdress left above date obverse
Value within wreath, shield above reverse

KM# 90 • 4.6700 g., **Copper-Nickel**, 19 mm. • **Obv. Legend** UNITED STATES OF AMERICA **Designer:** James B. Longacre

Date	Mintage	G-4	VG-8	F-12	VF-20	XF-40	AU-50	MS-60	MS-65	Prf-65
1860 Rounded Bust	20,566,000	11.00	15.00	22.00	46.00	68.00	110	190	965	3,600
1860	1,000	—	—	—	—	—	—	—	—	—
1860 Pointed Bust	Inc. above	20.00	30.00	42.00	60.00	100.00	160	300	6,000	—
1861	10,100,000	23.00	30.00	42.00	58.00	95.00	160	180	975	7,250
1862	28,075,000	11.50	11.50	12.50	15.00	28.00	60.00	80.00	1,050	2,350
1863	49,840,000	9.00	9.25	11.00	12.50	25.00	58.00	75.00	1,050	3,100
1864	13,740,000	20.00	28.50	35.00	72.00	125	175	220	1,400	3,200

CENT

Indian Head Cent

Indian head with headdress left above date obverse
Value within wreath, shield above reverse

1864 "L"

KM# 90a • 3.1100 g., **Bronze**, 19 mm. • **Obv. Legend** UNITED STATES OF AMERICA **Designer:** James B. Longacre **Notes:** The 1864 "L" variety has the designer's initial in Liberty's hair to the right of her neck.

Date	Mintage	G-4	VG-8	F-12	VF-20	XF-40	AU-50	MS-60	MS-65	Prf-65
1864	39,233,714	12.50	20.00	25.00	45.00	70.00	80.00	110	335	10,500
1864 L pointed bust	Inc. above	52.50	72.50	139	185	275	325	410	1,700	200,000
1865 plain 5	35,429,286	13.00	14.50	20.00	25.00	45.00	60.00	90.00	485	6,750
1865 fancy 5	Inc. above	12.50	14.00	18.50	23.00	40.00	55.00	85.00	465	—
1866	9,826,500	52.00	66.00	80.00	115	195	240	280	1,350	4,500
1867	9,821,000	52.00	72.00	110	120	195	240	285	1,350	6,100
1867/1867	Inc. above	65.00	85.00	130	190	275	385	565	1,950	—
1868	10,266,500	38.50	50.00	77.00	120	180	245	265	985	5,750
1869/9	6,420,000	190	375	525	750	865	1,000	1,250	2,350	—
1869	Inc. above	90.00	125	230	335	450	560	625	1,750	3,100
1870	5,275,000	62.00	118	225	285	410	510	600	1,400	2,650
1871	3,929,500	88.00	125	280	310	420	510	610	2,400	2,500
1872	4,042,000	110	180	345	425	625	750	840	3,850	4,250
1873 closed 3	11,676,500	30.00	52.00	95.00	135	235	300	400	2,850	2,950
1873 open 3	Inc. above	21.00	34.00	65.00	82.00	175	215	250	1,300	—
1873 Double Liberty die 1	Inc. above	275	450	950	1,500	2,400	4,250	7,500	—	—
1873 Double Liberty die 2	Inc. above	—	—	450	900	1,650	2,800	4,500	—	—
1874	14,187,500	15.00	22.50	46.00	65.00	112	150	225	700	2,850
1875	13,528,000	16.50	29.00	56.00	72.00	120	165	215	800	8,500
1876	7,944,000	30.00	39.50	74.00	130	230	295	325	975	2,600
1877	852,500	985	1,190	1,600	2,050	2,650	3,000	3,450	13,000	12,500
1878	5,799,850	27.00	35.00	68.00	135	245	290	350	875	1,375
1879	16,231,200	7.00	10.00	16.50	33.00	75.00	90.00	100.00	365	1,250
1880	38,964,955	3.50	5.50	6.50	11.00	28.00	48.00	66.00	360	1,250
1881	39,211,575	3.50	4.25	6.50	8.00	22.00	30.00	43.00	325	1,250
1882	38,581,100	3.50	4.25	5.00	10.00	22.00	30.00	40.00	325	1,450
1883	45,589,109	3.00	4.00	4.50	7.50	17.50	30.00	42.00	325	1,600
1884	23,261,742	3.50	4.50	7.00	12.50	29.00	40.00	60.00	460	1,250
1885	11,765,384	6.75	8.00	12.00	27.00	62.00	82.00	105	625	1,500

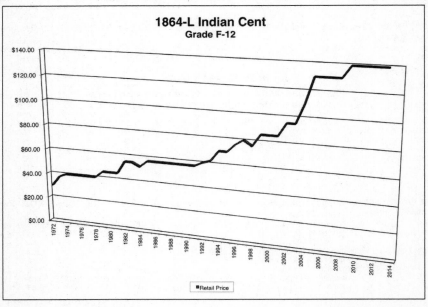

1864-L Indian Cent
Grade F-12

Date	Mintage	G-4	VG-8	F-12	VF-20	XF-40	AU-50	MS-60	MS-65	Prf-65
1886 Type 1 obverse	17,654,290	3.75	6.60	19.75	56.00	148	170	190	1,250	2,650
1886 Type 2 obverse	Inc. above	7.00	10.00	35.00	90.00	200	250	325	2,500	7,500
1887	45,226,483	2.50	3.00	4.00	7.00	19.00	28.00	50.00	400	6,200
1888	37,494,414	2.75	3.25	5.00	8.00	21.00	28.00	48.00	900	5,400
1889	48,869,361	2.25	2.75	3.50	6.00	12.00	26.00	40.00	400	1,900
1890	57,182,854	2.10	2.50	3.00	5.50	10.00	23.00	37.50	400	1,800
1891	47,072,350	2.25	2.75	3.25	5.50	13.00	23.00	37.00	400	2,150
1892	37,649,832	2.40	3.25	4.40	6.00	18.50	25.00	35.00	400	1,325
1893	46,642,195	2.10	2.75	3.25	5.50	10.00	22.00	30.00	340	1,250
1894	16,752,132	5.00	6.00	13.00	20.00	50.00	65.00	85.00	375	1,350
1894/94	Inc. above	24.00	34.00	80.00	150	275	440	800	8,000	—
1895	38,343,636	2.10	2.40	3.50	4.50	11.00	22.00	32.00	200	1,275
1896	39,057,293	1.95	2.50	3.25	4.75	13.00	26.00	34.00	225	1,900
1897	50,466,330	1.95	2.40	2.75	4.00	10.00	22.00	34.00	195	1,600
1898	49,823,079	1.95	2.40	2.75	4.00	10.00	22.00	34.00	195	1,275
1899	53,600,031	1.95	2.20	2.60	4.00	10.00	22.00	34.00	165	1,275
1900	66,833,764	1.95	2.20	2.50	4.00	12.00	23.00	34.00	175	1,275
1901	79,611,143	1.85	2.20	2.50	4.00	11.00	22.00	33.00	165	1,275
1902	87,376,722	1.85	2.20	2.50	4.00	10.00	22.00	32.00	165	1,325
1903	85,094,493	1.85	2.20	2.50	4.00	10.00	21.00	32.00	165	1,275
1904	61,328,015	1.75	2.20	2.50	4.00	10.00	21.00	32.00	165	1,275
1905	80,719,163	1.75	2.20	2.50	3.50	9.00	20.00	32.00	165	1,350
1906	96,022,255	1.75	2.20	2.50	3.50	9.00	21.00	32.00	165	1,275
1907	108,138,618	1.75	2.20	2.50	3.50	8.50	20.00	32.00	165	1,950
1908	32,327,987	1.75	2.30	2.50	3.50	9.00	20.00	32.00	165	1,275
1908S	1,115,000	79.00	84.00	110	127.5	170	190	275	700	—
1909	14,370,645	11.00	13.50	14.00	15.50	19.00	30.00	38.00	155	1,275
1909S	309,000	485	500	535	600	750	800	1,125	2,250	—

Lincoln Cent
Wheat Ears reverse

KM# 132 • 3.1100 g., **Bronze**, 19 mm. • **Designer:** Victor D. Brenner **Notes:** The 1909 "VDB" varieties have the designer's initials inscribed at the 6 o'clock position on the reverse. The initials were removed until 1918, when they were restored on the obverse • MS60 and MS63 prices are for brown coins and MS65 prices are for coins that are at least 90% original red.

Date	Mintage	G-4	VG-8	F-12	VF-20	XF-40	AU-50	MS-60	MS-65	Prf-65
1909 VDB	27,995,000	12.50	13.00	13.25	13.50	14.00	16.50	24.00	50.00	2,750
1909 VDB Doubled Die Obverse	Inc. above	—	—	55.00	75.00	100.00	120	200	1,500	—
1909S VDB	484,000	750	935	1,000	1,175	1,450	1,575	1,825	4,150	—
1909	72,702,618	3.65	3.50	4.35	4.75	5.50	12.50	14.50	85.00	625
1909S	1,825,000	105	110	122	165	245	265	340	750	—
1909S/S S over horizontal S	Inc. above	115	135	148	200	275	290	365	850	—
1910	146,801,218	.50	.60	.75	1.00	4.25	10.00	17.50	120	610
1910S	6,045,000	16.50	21.00	21.00	28.00	47.50	72.00	98.00	425	—
1911	101,177,787	.45	.60	1.60	2.35	6.75	11.00	18.50	175	525
1911D	12,672,000	4.75	5.75	9.00	22.50	50.00	75.00	90.00	750	—
1911S	4,026,000	49.00	53.00	55.00	59.00	75.00	105	175	1,100	—
1912	68,153,060	1.60	1.75	2.35	5.50	13.50	26.00	33.00	235	625
1912D	10,411,000	6.50	9.25	10.00	26.00	70.00	110	165	800	—
1912S	4,431,000	24.00	26.00	29.00	42.00	78.00	118	175	1,250	—
1913	76,532,352	.80	1.00	1.45	3.25	18.50	28.50	34.50	240	625
1913D	15,804,000	2.75	3.25	3.60	11.00	49.00	62.00	105	875	—
1913S	6,101,000	13.50	16.50	21.00	31.00	57.00	110	195	2,100	—
1914	75,238,432	.60	.95	2.10	6.00	18.50	40.00	52.00	240	625
1914D	1,193,000	205	235	320	450	945	1,500	2,100	9,500	—
1914S	4,137,000	25.00	27.50	30.00	40.00	85.00	175	310	3,250	—
1915	29,092,120	2.25	2.90	4.00	18.00	60.00	70.00	82.00	375	625
1915D	22,050,000	2.25	2.85	4.50	6.85	24.00	44.00	72.00	350	—
1915S	4,833,000	21.00	24.50	28.50	32.00	70.00	96.00	190	2,600	—
1916	131,833,677	.45	.55	.85	2.40	8.00	14.50	19.00	135	650
1916D	35,956,000	1.35	2.00	3.10	6.50	17.50	38.00	88.00	850	—
1916S	22,510,000	1.65	3.25	4.40	9.50	27.50	48.00	105	1,100	—
1917	196,429,785	.30	.40	.55	1.85	4.75	14.50	18.50	150	—
1917 Doubled Die Obverse	Inc. above	175	225	2.75	350	1,350	2,000	3,200	15,000	—
1917D	55,120,000	1.00	1.50	2.85	5.00	36.50	44.00	72.00	850	—
1917S	32,620,000	.55	.90	1.40	2.60	11.50	26.00	74.00	1,350	—
1918	288,104,634	.30	.40	.50	1.00	4.40	10.00	13.50	185	—
1918D	47,830,000	.95	1.45	2.45	5.50	15.50	36.00	76.00	1,200	—

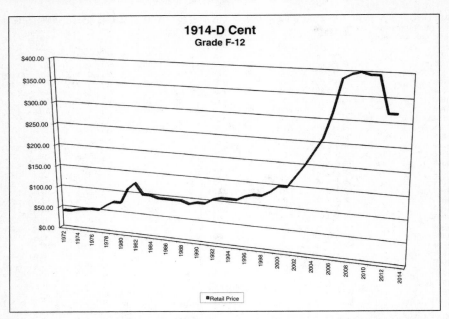

1914-D Cent
Grade F-12

■Retail Price

Date	Mintage	G-4	VG-8	F-12	VF-20	XF-40	AU-50	MS-60	MS-65	Prf-65
1918S	34,680,000	.40	.90	1.45	3.65	11.00	33.00	70.00	1,750	—
1919	392,021,000	.30	.40	.50	.80	1.60	5.75	8.00	85.00	—
1919D	57,154,000	.80	1.20	1.60	4.85	12.75	35.00	60.00	775	—
1919S	139,760,000	.40	.60	1.50	2.45	5.75	17.50	48.00	1,175	—
1920	310,165,000	.25	.35	.75	1.25	2.80	7.50	15.50	225	—
1920D	49,280,000	1.00	1.65	2.90	6.85	18.50	37.00	70.00	650	—
1920S	46,220,000	.60	.80	1.50	2.75	13.00	34.50	105	2,150	—
1921	39,157,000	.55	.80	1.15	3.00	10.75	22.50	42.00	175	—
1921S	15,274,000	1.50	2.00	3.50	6.25	36.50	68.00	110	1,100	—
1922D	7,160,000	23.50	24.50	25.50	27.00	37.50	75.00	105	475	—
1922D Weak Rev	Inc. above	22.00	23.00	24.00	25.50	34.00	65.00	95.00	400	—
1922D Weak D	Inc. above	30.00	44.00	48.00	60.00	135	190	285	7,500	—
1922 No D Die 2 Strong Rev	Inc. above	700	775	975	1,175	2,450	4,750	10,500	85,000	—
1922 No D Die 3 Weak Rev	Inc. above	275	325	375	475	950	3,000	8,500	45,000	—
1923	74,723,000	.40	.60	.85	1.50	5.75	10.50	13.50	160	—
1923S	8,700,000	5.85	7.00	8.50	12.50	42.00	105	190	2,850	—
1924	75,178,000	.25	.45	1.00	1.25	5.25	11.00	17.50	120	—
1924D	2,520,000	37.50	45.00	50.00	62.00	118	170	255	1,800	—
1924S	11,696,000	1.25	1.50	2.75	5.35	34.50	68.00	110	2,350	—
1925	139,949,000	.25	.35	.45	.70	3.00	6.50	9.50	65.00	—
1925D	22,580,000	1.00	1.65	3.10	6.25	15.50	30.00	62.00	625	—
1925S	26,380,000	.80	1.20	1.85	2.75	11.75	31.50	85.00	3,650	—
1926	157,088,000	.25	.35	.45	.60	1.65	5.25	7.50	70.00	—
1926D	28,020,000	1.50	1.70	3.40	5.25	15.50	34.00	82.00	800	—
1926S	4,550,000	9.00	10.00	11.75	16.50	35.00	72.00	140	5,500	—
1927	144,440,000	.20	.25	.35	.60	1.60	5.25	7.50	60.00	—
1927D	27,170,000	1.15	1.70	2.25	3.35	7.50	25.00	60.00	525	—
1927S	14,276,000	1.40	1.85	2.65	5.25	14.50	42.00	65.00	2,550	—
1928	134,116,000	.20	.25	.35	.60	1.45	4.00	7.50	82.00	—
1928D	31,170,000	.90	1.40	2.15	3.65	6.75	19.00	37.50	300	—
1928S Small S	17,266,000	1.00	1.65	2.60	4.00	9.50	31.00	71.50	800	—
1928S Large S	Inc. above	1.65	2.85	4.25	7.50	16.50	55.00	135	1,250	—
1929	185,262,000	.20	.25	.35	.55	2.75	5.25	7.00	55.00	—
1929D	41,730,000	.50	1.00	1.40	2.75	5.85	13.50	25.00	145	—
1929S	50,148,000	.60	1.10	1.85	2.80	6.75	14.75	20.00	100.00	—
1930	157,415,000	.20	.25	.35	.60	1.25	2.75	4.00	45.00	—
1930D	40,100,000	.25	.35	.60	.90	2.00	5.50	11.00	55.00	—
1930S	24,286,000	.25	.35	.55	.80	1.50	6.50	9.50	48.00	—
1931	19,396,000	.65	.75	1.10	2.00	4.00	9.50	19.00	85.00	—
1931D	4,480,000	5.00	5.85	6.50	8.00	13.00	33.50	48.50	375	—
1931S	866,000	105	110	125	125	138	150	160	350	—
1932	9,062,000	1.60	1.95	2.85	3.50	6.75	13.00	17.50	65.00	—
1932D	10,500,000	1.50	1.90	2.50	2.85	4.15	11.00	18.50	65.00	—
1933	14,360,000	1.50	1.80	2.65	2.85	6.50	11.50	16.50	65.00	—
1933D	6,200,000	3.50	4.25	5.65	7.50	13.50	19.00	24.00	60.00	—

CENT

Date	Mintage	G-4	VG-8	F-12	VF-20	XF-40	AU-50	MS-60	MS-65	Prf-65
1934	219,080,000	.15	.25	.30	.45	1.25	4.00	9.00	25.00	—
1934D	28,446,000	.35	.50	.80	1.25	5.50	9.00	20.00	30.00	—
1935	245,338,000	.15	.20	.25	.40	.90	1.50	5.00	20.00	—
1935D	47,000,000	.20	.30	.40	.55	.95	2.50	5.50	20.00	—
1935S	38,702,000	.25	.35	.60	1.75	3.00	5.00	11.00	44.00	—
1936 (Proof in Satin Finish)	309,637,569	.15	.20	.30	.40	.85	1.40	1.90	10.00	600
1936 Brilliant Proof	Inc. above	—	—	—	—	—	—	—	—	800
1936 DDO	Inc. above	—	—	25.00	50.00	80.00	125	175	1,000	—
1936D	40,620,000	.20	.30	.40	.55	.90	1.50	4.00	15.00	—
1936S	29,130,000	.20	.30	.45	.60	1.50	2.25	5.00	18.00	—
1937	309,179,320	.15	.20	.30	.40	.50	.75	1.75	13.50	110
1937D	50,430,000	.20	.30	.40	.60	.80	1.20	2.65	15.00	—
1937S	34,500,000	.20	.30	.40	.55	.90	1.25	2.75	16.50	—
1938	156,696,734	.15	.20	.30	.40	.50	1.20	2.25	18.00	90.00
1938D	20,010,000	.20	.30	.45	.60	1.00	1.50	3.50	20.00	—
1938S	15,180,000	.30	.40	.50	.70	1.00	1.75	3.00	15.00	—
1939	316,479,520	.15	.20	.30	.40	.45	.75	1.00	16.00	60.00
1939D	15,160,000	.35	.45	.50	.60	.95	1.75	3.00	18.00	—
1939S	52,070,000	.30	.40	.50	.60	.80	1.20	2.50	16.00	—
1940	586,825,872	.10	.20	.30	.35	.45	.75	1.00	12.00	65.00
1940D	81,390,000	.20	.30	.40	.55	.75	1.10	2.00	11.00	—
1940S	112,940,000	.20	.30	.40	.55	.70	1.25	2.50	12.50	—
1941	887,039,100	.10	.20	.30	.35	.45	.60	1.25	10.00	60.00
1941 Doubled Die Obv	Inc. above	35.00	50.00	70.00	80.00	95.00	135	200	1,000	—
1941D	128,700,000	.20	.30	.40	.55	.90	1.35	2.20	12.50	—
1941S	92,360,000	.20	.30	.40	.55	.95	1.75	2.50	15.00	—
1942	657,828,600	.10	.20	.30	.35	.40	.55	.85	11.00	65.00
1942D	206,698,000	.20	.25	.30	.35	.45	.60	1.00	12.00	—
1942S	85,590,000	.25	.35	.45	.85	1.25	2.50	5.00	18.00	—
1943 Copper	—	—	—	35,000	42,000	45,000	80,000	155,000	—	—
1943S Copper	—	—	—	125,000	150,000	185,000	275,000	—	—	—

KM# 132a • 2.7000 g., **Zinc Coated Steel**, 19 mm. • **Designer:** Victor D. Brenner

Date	Mintage	G-4	VG-8	F-12	VF-20	XF-40	AU-50	MS-60	MS-65	Prf-65
1943	684,628,670	.20	.30	.35	.45	.60	.85	1.25	18.00	—
1943D	217,660,000	.35	.40	.45	.50	.70	1.00	1.50	—	—
1943D/D RPM	Inc. above	30.00	38.00	50.00	65.00	90.00	125	200	—	—
1943S	191,550,000	.40	.45	.50	.65	.90	1.40	4.00	28.00	—

Lincoln Cent
Wheat Ears reverse

KM# A132 • 3.1100 g., **Brass**, 19 mm. • **Designer:** Victor D. Brenner **Notes:** KM#132 design and composition resumed • MS60 prices are for brown coins and MS65 prices are for coins that are at least 90% original red.

Date	Mintage	XF-40	MS-65	Prf-65	Date	Mintage	XF-40	MS-65	Prf-65
1944	1,435,400,000	.30	8.00	—	1951	295,633,500	.40	16.50	62.00
1944D	430,578,000	.40	14.00	—	1951D	625,355,000	.30	8.50	—
1944D/S Type 1	Inc. above	220	3,750	—	1951S	136,010,000	.40	9.00	—
1944D/S Type 2	Inc. above	175	1,600	—	1952	186,856,980	.40	16.00	36.00
1944S	282,760,000	.35	8.00	—	1952D	746,130,000	.30	8.50	—
1945	1,040,515,000	.40	13.50	—	1952S	137,800,004	.60	12.00	—
1945D	226,268,000	.40	8.00	—	1953	256,883,800	.25	18.00	37.00
1945S	181,770,000	.40	7.50	—	1953D	700,515,000	.25	8.50	—
1946	991,655,000	.25	13.50	—	1953S	181,835,000	.40	8.00	—
1946D	315,690,000	.30	10.00	—	1954	71,873,350	.25	20.00	19.00
1946S	198,100,000	.30	13.50	—	1954D	251,552,500	.25	8.50	—
1946S/D	—	70.00	650	—	1954S	96,190,000	.25	10.00	—
1947	190,555,000	.45	18.50	—	1955	330,958,000	.25	9.00	14.00
1947D	194,750,000	.35	7.50	—	1955 Doubled Die	Inc. above	1,900	37,500	—
1947S	99,000,000	.35	8.00	—	**Note:** The 1955 "doubled die" has distinct doubling of the				
1948	317,570,000	.35	18.50	—	date and lettering on the obverse.				
1948D	172,637,000	.40	12.00	—	1955D	563,257,500	.20	8.00	—
1948S	81,735,000	.40	12.00	—	1955S	44,610,000	.35	7.50	—
1949	217,775,000	.40	18.00	—	1956	421,414,384	.20	12.00	5.00
1949D	153,132,000	.40	15.00	—	1956D	1,098,201,100	.20	7.00	—
1949S	64,290,000	.50	10.00	—	1957	283,787,952	.20	7.50	4.00
1950	272,686,386	.35	16.50	65.00	1957D	1,051,342,000	.20	6.00	—
1950D	334,950,000	.35	12.50	—	1958	253,400,652	.20	9.00	6.50
1950S	118,505,000	.30	9.00	—	1958D	800,953,300	.20	7.00	—

Lincoln Cent
Lincoln Memorial reverse

| Small date | Large date | Small date | Large date |

KM# 201 • 3.1100 g., **Brass**, 19 mm. • **Rev. Designer:** Frank Gasparro **Notes:** MS60 prices are for brown coins and MS65 prices are for coins that are at least 90% original red. The dates were modified in 1960, 1970 and 1982, resulting in large-date and small-date varieties for those years. The 1972 "doubled die" shows doubling of IN GOD WE TRUST. The 1979-S and 1981-S Type II proofs have a clearer mint mark than the Type I proofs of those years. Some 1982 cents have the predominantly copper composition; others have the predominantly zinc composition. They can be distinguished by weight.

Date	Mintage	XF-40	MS-65	Prf-65
1959	610,864,291	—	15.00	10.00
1959D	1,279,760,000	—	12.00	—
1960 small date, low 9	588,096,602	1.85	12.00	16.00
1960 large date, high 9	Inc. above	—	8.00	7.50
1960D small date, low 9	1,580,884,000	—	10.00	—
1960D large date, high 9	Inc. above	—	8.00	—
1960D/D small over large date	Inc. above	—	300	—
1961	756,373,244	—	8.50	9.00
1961D	1,753,266,700	—	18.00	—
1962	609,263,019	—	8.00	8.00
1962D	1,793,148,400	—	14.00	—
1963	757,185,645	—	10.00	6.00
1963D	1,774,020,400	—	12.00	—
1964	2,652,525,762	—	8.50	6.00
1964D	3,799,071,500	—	10.00	—
1965	1,497,224,900	—	10.00	—
1965 SMS	Inc. above	—	7.50	—
1966	2,188,147,783	—	10.00	—
1966 SMS	Inc. above	—	8.00	—
1967	3,048,667,100	—	12.00	—
1967 SMS	Inc. above	—	8.00	—
1968	1,707,880,970	—	12.00	—
1968D	2,886,269,600	—	12.50	—
1968S	261,311,510	—	10.00	4.50
1969	1,136,910,000	—	7.00	—
1969D	4,002,832,200	—	10.00	—
1969S	547,309,631	—	15.00	5.50
1969S Doubled Die Obverse	Inc. above	10,000	125,000	100,000
1970	1,898,315,000	—	8.00	—
1970D	2,891,438,900	—	6.00	—
1970S small date, level 7	Inc. above	30.00	65.00	60.00
1970S large date, low 7	Inc. above	—	15.00	5.00
1970S Doubled Die Obverse	Inc. above	—	20,000	15,000
1971	1,919,490,000	—	20.00	—
1971D	2,911,045,600	—	6.50	—
1971S	528,354,192	—	7.50	5.50
1971S Doubled Die Obverse	Inc. above	—	—	400
1972	2,933,255,000	—	6.00	—
1972 Doubled Die Obverse	Inc. above	290	785	—
1972D	2,665,071,400	—	12.00	—
1972S	380,200,104	—	26.50	5.50
1973	3,728,245,000	—	8.00	—
1973D	3,549,576,588	—	11.00	—
1973S	319,937,634	—	10.00	5.50
1974	4,232,140,523	—	12.00	—
1974D	4,235,098,000	—	9.00	—
1974S	412,039,228	—	12.00	5.00
1975	5,451,476,142	—	8.00	—
1975D	4,505,245,300	—	13.50	—
1975S	2,845,450	—	—	5.00
1976	4,674,292,426	—	14.00	—
1976D	4,221,592,455	—	16.00	—
1976S	4,149,730	—	—	6.00
1977	4,469,930,000	—	16.00	—
1977D	4,149,062,300	—	16.00	—
1977S	3,251,152	—	—	5.00
1978	5,558,605,000	—	16.00	—
1978D	4,280,233,400	—	14.00	—
1978S	3,127,781	—	—	5.00
1979	6,018,515,000	—	12.00	—
1979D	4,139,357,254	—	8.00	—
1979S type I, proof	3,677,175	—	—	5.00
1979S type II, proof	Inc. above	—	—	10.00
1980	7,414,705,000	—	6.50	—
1980D	5,140,098,660	—	12.00	—
1980S	3,554,806	—	—	5.00
1981	7,491,750,000	—	8.50	—
1981D	5,373,235,677	—	9.00	—
1981S type I, proof	4,063,083	—	—	5.00
1981S type II, proof	Inc. above	—	—	42.00
1982 large date	10,712,525,000	—	7.00	—
1982 small date	Inc. above	—	9.00	—
1982D large date	6,012,979,368	—	7.50	—
1982S	3,857,479	—	—	5.00

Lincoln Cent
Lincoln Memorial reverse

KM# 201a • 2.5000 g., **Copper Plated Zinc**, 19 mm. • **Notes:** MS60 prices are for brown coins and MS65 prices are for coins that are at least 90% original red.

Date	Mintage	XF-40	MS-65	Prf-65
1982 large date	—	—	6.00	—
1982 small date	—	—	9.00	—
1982D large date	—	—	8.00	—
1982D small date	—	—	6.00	—

Lincoln Cent
Lincoln Memorial reverse

KM# 201b • **Copper Plated Zinc**, 19 mm. •
Notes: MS60 prices are for brown coins and MS65 prices are for coins that are at least 90% original red.

Date	Mintage	XF-40	MS-65	Prf-65
1983	7,752,355,000	—	7.00	—
1983 Doubled Die	Inc. above	135	450	—
1983D	6,467,199,428	—	5.50	—
1983S	3,279,126	—	—	3.50
1984	8,151,079,000	—	7.50	—
1984 Doubled Die	Inc. above	100.00	325	—
1984D	5,569,238,906	—	6.50	—
1984S	3,065,110	—	—	3.50
1985	5,648,489,887	—	4.50	—
1985D	5,287,399,926	—	4.50	—
1985S	3,362,821	—	—	3.50
1986	4,491,395,493	—	5.00	—
1986D	4,442,866,698	—	8.00	—
1986S	3,010,497	—	—	3.50
1987	4,682,466,931	—	7.50	—
1987D	4,879,389,514	—	5.50	—
1987S	4,227,728	—	—	3.50
1988	6,092,810,000	—	10.00	—
1988D	5,253,740,443	—	6.00	—
1988S	3,262,948	—	—	3.50
1989	7,261,535,000	—	6.50	—
1989D	5,345,467,111	—	6.50	—
1989S	3,220,194	—	—	5.00
1990	6,851,765,000	—	5.00	—
1990D	4,922,894,533	—	5.50	—
1990S	3,299,559	—	—	3.50
1990 no S, Proof only	Inc. above	—	—	4,650
1991	5,165,940,000	—	6.50	—
1991D	4,158,442,076	—	5.50	—
1991S	2,867,787	—	—	3.50
1992	4,648,905,000	—	5.50	—
1992D	4,448,673,300	—	5.50	—
1992D Close AM, Proof Reverse Die	Inc. above	—	—	—
1992S	4,176,560	—	—	3.50
1993	5,684,705,000	—	5.00	—
1993D	6,426,650,571	—	4.50	—
1993S	3,394,792	—	—	3.50
1994	6,500,850,000	—	6.00	—
1994D	7,131,765,000	—	4.50	—
1994S	3,269,923	—	—	3.50
1995	6,411,440,000	—	5.00	—
1995 Doubled Die Obverse	Inc. above	20.00	60.00	—
1995D	7,128,560,000	—	4.50	—
1995S	2,707,481	—	—	3.50
1996	6,612,465,000	—	4.50	—
1996D	6,510,795,000	—	4.50	—
1996S	2,915,212	—	—	3.50
1997	4,622,800,000	—	3.00	—
1997D	4,576,555,000	—	3.50	—
1997S	2,796,678	—	—	4.00
1998	5,032,155,000	—	3.00	—
1998 Wide AM, reverse from proof die	Inc. above	—	110	—
1998D	5,255,353,500	—	3.00	—
1998S	2,957,286	—	—	4.00
1999	5,237,600,000	—	3.00	—

Date	Mintage	XF-40	MS-65	Prf-65
1999 Wide AM, reverse from proof die	Inc. above	—	450	—
1999D	6,360,065,000	—	3.00	—
1999S	3,362,462	—	—	3.50
2000 Wide AM, reverse from proof die	Inc. above	—	45.00	—
2000	5,503,200,000	—	3.00	—
2000D	8,774,220,000	—	3.00	—
2000S	4,063,361	—	—	3.50
2001	4,959,600,000	—	3.00	—
2001D	5,374,990,000	—	3.00	—
2001S	3,099,096	—	—	3.50
2002	3,260,800,000	—	3.00	—
2002S	3,157,739	—	—	3.50
2002D	4,028,055,000	—	3.00	—
2003	3,300,000,000	—	3.50	—
2003D	3,548,000,000	—	3.50	—
2003S	3,116,590	—	—	3.50
2004	3,379,600,000	—	3.50	—
2004D	3,456,400,000	—	3.50	—
2004S	2,992,069	—	—	3.50
2005	3,935,600,000	—	2.50	—
2005 Satin Finish	Inc. above	—	4.00	—
2005D	3,764,450,000	—	2.50	—
2005D Satin Finish	Inc. above	—	4.00	—
2005S	3,273,000	—	—	3.50
2006	4,290,000,000	—	2.00	—
2006 Satin Finish	Inc. above	—	4.00	—
2006D	3,944,000,000	—	2.50	—
2006 Satin Finish	Inc. above	—	4.00	—
2006S	2,923,105	—	—	3.50
2007	—	—	2.00	—
2007 Satin Finish	—	—	4.00	—
2007D	—	—	2.00	—
2007 Satin Finish	—	—	4.00	—
2007S	—	—	—	3.50
2008	—	—	2.25	—
2008 Satin Finish	—	—	4.00	—
2008D	—	—	2.25	—
2008 Satin Finish	—	—	4.00	—
2008S	—	—	—	4.50

Lincoln Bicentennial
Bust right obverse   Log cabin reverse

KM# 441 • 2.5000 g., **Copper Plated Zinc**, 19 mm. • **Rev. Designer:** Richard Masters and James Licaretz

Date	Mintage	XF-40	MS-65	Prf-65
2009P	284,400,000	—	1.50	—
2009D	350,400,000	—	1.50	—

KM# 441a • 3.3100 g., **Brass** • **Rev. Designer:** Richard Masters and James Licaretz

Date	Mintage	XF-40	MS-65	Prf-65
2009S	—	—	—	4.00

Lincoln seated on log reverse

KM# 442 • 2.5000 g., **Copper Plated Zinc**, 19 mm. • **Rev. Designer:** Charles Vickers

Date	Mintage	XF-40	MS-65	Prf-65
2009P	376,000,000	—	1.50	—
2009D	363,600,000	—	1.50	—

KM# 442a • 3.1100 g., **Brass**, 19 mm. • **Rev. Designer:** Charles Vickers

Date	Mintage	XF-40	MS-65	Prf-65
2009S	—	—	—	4.00

Lincoln standing before Illinois Statehouse reverse

KM# 443 • 2.5000 g., **Copper Plated Zinc**, 19 mm. • **Rev. Designer:** Joel Ishowitz and Don Everhart

Date	Mintage	XF-40	MS-65	Prf-65
2009P	316,000,000	—	1.50	—
2009D	336,000,000	—	1.50	—

KM# 443a • 3.1100 g., **Brass**, 19 mm. • **Rev. Designer:** Joel Iskowitz and Don Everhart

Date	Mintage	XF-40	MS-65	Prf-65
2009S	—	—	—	4.00

Capitol Building reverse

KM# 444 • 2.5000 g., **Copper Plated Zinc** • **Rev. Designer:** Susan Gamble and Joseph Menna

Date	Mintage	XF-40	MS-65	Prf-65
2009P	129,600,000	—	1.50	—
2009D	198,000,000	—	1.50	—

KM# 444a • 3.1100 g., **Brass**, 19 mm. • **Rev. Designer:** Susan Ganmble and Joseph Menna

Date	Mintage	XF-40	MS-65	Prf-65
2009S	—	—	—	4.00

Lincoln - Shield Reverse
Lincoln bust right obverse   Shield reverse

KM# 468 • 2.5000 g., **Copper Plated Zinc**, 19 mm. • **Obv. Designer:** Victor D. Brenner **Rev. Designer:** Lyndall Bass and Joseph Menna

Date	Mintage	XF-40	MS-65	Prf-65
2010P	—	—	1.50	—
2010D	—	—	1.50	—
2010S	—	—	—	4.00
2011P	—	—	1.50	—
2011D	—	—	1.50	—
2011S	—	—	—	4.00
2012P	—	—	1.50	—
2012D	—	—	1.50	—
2012S	—	—	—	4.00
2013P	—	—	1.50	—
2013D	—	—	1.50	—
2013S	—	—	—	4.00

2 CENTS

Shield in front of crossed arrows, banner above, date below obverse
Value within wheat wreath reverse

Small motto   Large motto

KM# 94 • 6.2200 g., **Copper-Tin-Zinc**, 23 mm. • **Rev. Legend:** UNITED STATES OF AMERICA **Designer:** James B. Longacre **Notes:** The motto IN GOD WE TRUST was modified in 1864, resulting in small-motto and large-motto varieties for that year.

Date	Mintage	G-4	VG-8	F-12	VF-20	XF-40	AU-50	MS-60	MS-65	Prf-65
1864 small motto	19,847,500	140	210	285	425	650	725	1,125	3,000	45,000
1864 large motto	Inc. above	16.50	18.50	20.00	27.50	42.50	72.00	88.00	375	1,100
1865 fancy 5	13,640,000	16.50	18.50	20.00	27.50	42.50	72.00	88.00	375	—
1865 plain 5	Inc. above	16.50	18.50	21.00	29.00	45.00	75.00	92.00	400	650
1866	3,177,000	17.00	20.00	21.50	29.00	46.00	77.00	98.00	395	650
1867	2,938,750	18.00	21.00	36.00	46.00	60.00	96.00	125	395	650
1867 double die obverse	Inc. above	—	80.00	165	250	350	500	650	4,750	—
1868	2,803,750	18.00	22.00	37.50	47.50	65.00	105	135	465	650
1869	1,546,000	20.00	23.00	40.00	50.00	79.00	125	165	550	650
1869 repunched 18	Inc. above	35.00	45.00	75.00	150	325	550	—	—	—
1869/8 die crack	Inc. above	150	185	375	435	650	900	—	—	—

Date	Mintage	G-4	VG-8	F-12	VF-20	XF-40	AU-50	MS-60	MS-65	Prf-65
1870	861,250	31.00	42.00	60.00	82.00	135	190	280	550	650
1871	721,250	43.50	49.00	70.00	110	150	215	285	650	650
1872	65,000	400	550	700	900	1,200	1,800	3,150	5,500	650
1873 closed 3 proof only	Est. 600	1,250	1,400	1,535	1,650	1,750	2,000	—	—	3,850
1873 open 3 proof only	Est. 500	1,275	1,400	1,575	1,700	1,875	2,150	—	—	4,200

SILVER 3 CENTS

Silver 3 Cents - Type 1

Shield within star, no outlines in star obverse
Roman numeral in designed C, within circle of stars reverse

KM# 75 • 0.8000 g., 0.7500 **Silver**, 0.0193 oz. ASW, 14 mm. • **Obv. Legend** UNITED STATES OF AMERICA **Designer:** James B. Longacre

Date	Mintage	G-4	VG-8	F-12	VF-20	XF-40	AU-50	MS-60	MS-65	Prf-65
1851	5,447,400	32.00	48.50	51.00	58.50	68.00	145	180	825	—
1851O	720,000	38.50	58.50	61.00	95.00	160	275	500	3,100	—
1852	18,663,500	32.00	48.50	51.00	58.50	68.00	145	180	825	—
1853	11,400,000	32.00	48.50	51.00	58.50	68.00	145	180	825	—

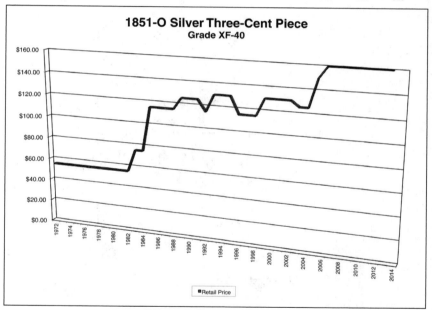

1851-O Silver Three-Cent Piece
Grade XF-40

Silver 3 Cents - Type 2

Shield within star, three outlines in star obverse
Roman numeral in designed C, within circle of stars reverse

KM# 80 • 0.7500 g., 0.9000 **Silver**, 0.0217 oz. ASW, 14 mm. • **Obv. Legend** UNITED STATES OF AMERICA **Designer:** James B. Longacre

Date	Mintage	G-4	VG-8	F-12	VF-20	XF-40	AU-50	MS-60	MS-65	Prf-65
1854	671,000	32.00	48.50	51.00	59.50	112	205	340	2,700	33,500
1855	139,000	44.00	57.50	75.00	125	200	325	520	7,400	15,000

SILVER 3 CENTS

SILVER 3 CENTS

Date	Mintage	G-4	VG-8	F-12	VF-20	XF-40	AU-50	MS-60	MS-65	Prf-65
1856	1,458,000	34.00	50.50	54.00	67.00	119.5	205	260	3,250	15,500
1857	1,042,000	34.00	50.50	54.00	67.00	112	223	285	2,375	13,500
1858	1,604,000	33.00	49.50	52.00	62.00	122	205	230	2,350	6,400

Silver 3 Cents - Type 3
Shield within star, two outlines in star obverse
Roman numeral in designed C, within circle of stars reverse

KM# 88 • 0.7500 g., 0.9000 **Silver**, 0.0217 oz. ASW, 14 mm. • **Obv. Legend** UNITED STATES OF AMERICA **Designer:** James B. Longacre

Date	Mintage	G-4	VG-8	F-12	VF-20	XF-40	AU-50	MS-60	MS-65	Prf-65
1859	365,000	40.00	53.50	56.00	64.00	87.00	160	195	975	2,150
1860	287,000	40.00	53.50	56.00	64.00	83.00	160	195	1,050	4,000
1861	498,000	40.00	53.50	56.00	64.00	83.00	160	195	1,050	1,800
1862	343,550	46.00	55.50	58.00	66.00	88.00	180	235	935	1,400
1862/1	Inc. above	43.00	57.50	62.00	71.00	94.00	177	210	865	—
1863	21,460	375	420	450	485	520	725	825	2,250	1,350
1863/62 proof only; Rare	Inc. above	—	—	—	—	—	—	—	—	5,400
1864	12,470	375	420	450	485	520	725	850	1,675	1,350
1865	8,500	475	525	550	620	665	700	875	1,650	1,350
1866	22,725	375	420	450	485	520	675	775	1,950	1,325
1867	4,625	475	525	575	625	675	725	850	2,750	1,300
1868	4,100	475	535	585	640	690	750	875	5,750	1,400
1869	5,100	475	535	585	640	690	750	875	2,450	1,400
1869/68 proof only; Rare	Inc. above	—	—	—	—	—	—	—	—	—
1870	4,000	450	460	525	600	665	750	950	5,650	1,350
1871	4,360	440	450	535	625	670	710	835	1,800	1,450
1872	1,950	465	485	550	645	690	750	875	5,500	1,350
1873 proof only	600	—	—	—	—	950	1,050	—	—	2,950

NICKEL 3 CENTS
Coronet head left, date below obverse
Roman numeral value within wreath reverse

KM# 95 • 1.9400 g., **Copper-Nickel**, 17.9 mm. • **Obv. Legend** UNITED STATES OF AMERICA **Designer:** James B. Longacre

Date	Mintage	G-4	VG-8	F-12	VF-20	XF-40	AU-50	MS-60	MS-65	Prf-65
1865	11,382,000	15.50	16.50	17.50	22.50	37.50	60.00	100.00	550	6,500
1866	4,801,000	15.50	16.50	17.50	22.50	37.50	60.00	100.00	550	1,725
1867	3,915,000	15.50	16.50	17.50	22.50	37.50	60.00	100.00	670	1,575
1868	3,252,000	15.50	16.50	17.50	22.50	37.50	60.00	100.00	550	1,450
1869	1,604,000	16.50	17.50	19.50	25.50	40.50	61.00	120	730	1,050
1870	1,335,000	17.50	18.50	20.50	26.50	41.50	62.00	135	725	2,250
1871	604,000	17.50	19.00	22.50	27.50	42.50	64.00	155	740	1,200
1872	862,000	19.00	22.50	24.50	29.00	43.50	68.00	175	995	910
1873 Cl 3	1,173,000	16.50	18.50	22.50	25.50	40.50	62.00	145	1,050	1,125
1873 Op 3	Inc. above	16.50	18.50	22.50	26.00	41.50	68.00	180	4,500	—
1874	790,000	17.50	20.50	22.50	27.50	42.50	66.00	160	950	950
1875	228,000	19.00	22.50	27.50	30.50	45.50	82.00	190	750	1,500
1876	162,000	20.50	23.50	26.50	34.50	49.50	97.00	225	1,290	1,025
1877 proof	Est. 900	1,100	1,150	1,175	1,250	1,275	1,350	—	—	3,750
1878 proof	2,350	615	645	720	770	795	830	—	—	1,200
1879	41,200	70.00	80.00	96.00	110	122	180	320	750	690
1880	24,955	100.00	115	130	165	185	235	375	730	700
1881	1,080,575	15.50	16.50	19.00	23.50	39.50	60.00	100.00	585	680
1882	25,300	130	150	180	225	300	325	425	1,025	700
1883	10,609	200	225	265	305	375	425	480	4,850	690
1884	5,642	400	445	550	600	645	730	800	6,250	700
1885	4,790	470	520	645	700	745	775	900	12,000	720
1886 proof	4,290	320	330	345	385	385	420	—	—	715
1887/6 proof	7,961	350	390	415	450	460	515	—	—	940

Date	Mintage	G-4	VG-8	F-12	VF-20	XF-40	AU-50	MS-60	MS-65	Prf-65
1887	Inc. above	305	355	395	440	455	500	540	1,200	1,125
1888	41,083	54.00	63.00	70.00	80.00	100.00	170	315	650	690
1889	21,561	90.00	115	145	180	230	260	320	775	690

HALF DIME

Flowing Hair Half Dime

KM# 15 • 1.3500 g., 0.8920 **Silver**, 0.0387 oz. ASW, 16.5 mm. • **Designer:** Robert Scot

Date	Mintage	G-4	VG-8	F-12	VF-20	XF-40	MS-60
1794	86,416	1,325	1,625	2,150	3,125	7,325	19,000
1795	Inc. above	1,050	1,350	1,875	2,900	5,800	13,000

Draped Bust Half Dime
Draped bust right obverse
Small eagle reverse

KM# 23 • 1.3500 g., 0.8920 **Silver**, 0.0387 oz. ASW, 16.5 mm. • **Designer:** Robert Scot

Date	Mintage	G-4	VG-8	F-12	VF-20	XF-40	MS-60
1796	10,230	1,435	1,550	3,150	4,850	8,650	17,550
1796 LIKERTY	Inc. above	1,485	1,600	3,200	4,900	8,700	17,600
Note: In 1796 the word LIBERTY was spelled LIKERTY on a die.							
1796/5	Inc. above	1,555	1,700	3,300	5,000	8,800	17,700
1797 13 stars	44,527	2,100	2,650	4,250	5,950	9,750	30,750
1797 15 stars	Inc. above	1,385	1,500	3,100	4,800	8,600	17,500
1797 16 stars	Inc. above	1,535	1,750	3,350	5,050	8,850	17,750

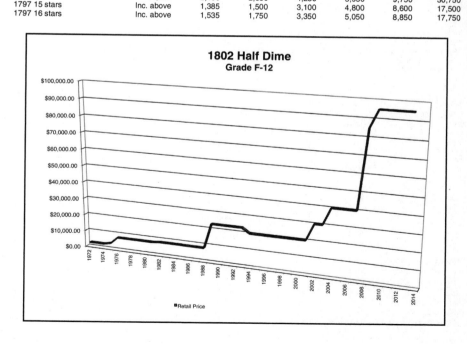

1802 Half Dime
Grade F-12

Draped Bust Half Dime

Draped bust right, flanked by stars, date at angle below obverse
Heraldic eagle reverse

KM# 34 • 1.3500 g., 0.8920 **Silver**, 0.0387 oz. ASW, 16.5 mm. • **Obv. Legend** LIBERTY **Rev. Legend:** UNITED STATES OF AMERICA **Designer:** Robert Scot

Date	Mintage	G-4	VG-8	F-12	VF-20	XF-40	MS-60
1800	24,000	1,000	1,250	1,875	2,550	6,500	13,500
1800 LIBEKTY	Inc. above	1,000	1,250	1,875	2,550	7,000	15,050
1801	33,910	1,225	1,500	2,125	2,800	6,750	17,750
1802	3,060	44,500	65,000	95,000	135,000	300,000	—
1803 Large 8	37,850	1,100	1,375	2,000	2,675	6,625	13,625
1803 Small 8	Inc. above	1,325	1,625	2,250	2,925	6,875	15,850
1805	15,600	1,225	1,525	2,350	3,025	9,900	31,000

Liberty Cap Half Dime

Classic head left, flanked by stars, date below obverse
Eagle with arrows in talons, banner above reverse

KM# 47 • 1.3500 g., 0.8920 **Silver**, 0.0387 oz. ASW, 15.5 mm. • **Rev. Legend:** UNITED STATES OF AMERICA **Designer:** William Kneass

Date	Mintage	G-4	VG-8	F-12	VF-20	XF-40	AU-50	MS-60	MS-65
1829	1,230,000	60.00	75.00	85.00	148	190	275	365	2,750
1830	1,240,000	52.50	67.50	75.00	118	160	225	350	2,600
1831	1,242,700	52.50	67.50	75.00	118	160	225	350	2,600
1832	965,000	52.50	67.50	75.00	118	160	225	350	2,600
1833	1,370,000	52.50	67.50	75.00	118	160	225	350	2,600
1834	1,480,000	52.50	67.50	75.00	118	160	225	350	2,600
1835 large date and 5C.	2,760,000	52.50	75.00	87.00	133	175	245	350	2,600
1835 large date, small 5C.	Inc. above	52.50	67.50	75.00	118	160	225	410	3,800
1835 small date, large 5C.	Inc. above	52.50	67.50	75.00	118	160	225	375	3,500
1835 small date and 5C.	Inc. above	52.50	67.50	75.00	118	160	225	350	2,600
1836 large 5C.	1,900,000	52.50	67.50	75.00	118	160	225	350	2,600
1836 small 5C.	Inc. above	54.50	70.50	79.00	128	172	237	362	3,100
1837 large 5C.	2,276,000	52.50	67.50	83.00	136	175	245	395	3,800
1837 small 5C.	Inc. above	59.50	77.50	90.00	148	240	465	950	11,000

Seated Liberty Half Dime

Seated Liberty, no stars around border, date below obverse
Value within wreath reverse

KM# 60 • 1.3400 g., 0.9000 **Silver**, 0.0388 oz. ASW, 15.5 mm. • **Rev. Legend:** UNITED STATES OF AMERICA **Designer:** Christian Gobrecht **Notes:** A design modification in 1837 resulted in small-date and large-date varieties for that year.

Date	Mintage	G-4	VG-8	F-12	VF-20	XF-40	AU-50	MS-60	MS-65
1837 small date	Inc. above	35.00	46.50	75.00	135	220	495	750	4,450
1837 large date	Inc. above	39.00	49.50	82.00	150	235	445	620	3,650
1838O	70,000	110	130	250	475	975	1,450	2,500	29,500

HALF DIME

Seated Liberty Half Dime
Seated Liberty, stars around top 1/2 of border, date below obverse
Value within wreath reverse

KM# 62.1 • 1.3400 g., 0.9000 **Silver**, 0.0388 oz. ASW, 15.5 mm. • **Rev. Legend:** UNITED STATES OF AMERICA **Designer:** Christian Gobrecht **Notes:** The two varieties of 1838 are distinguished by the size of the stars on the obverse. The 1839-O with reverse of 1838-O was struck from rusted reverse dies. The result is a bumpy surface on this variety's reverse.

Date	Mintage	G-4	VG-8	F-12	VF-20	XF-40	AU-50	MS-60	MS-65
1838 large stars	2,255,000	22.50	25.50	29.00	36.00	88.00	198	265	2,475
1838 small stars	Inc. above	26.50	31.50	46.00	115	189	299	595	3,950
1839	1,069,150	23.50	26.50	30.00	37.00	93.00	203	265	2,000
1839O	1,034,039	27.50	30.50	34.00	41.00	88.00	198	715	6,850
1839O reverse 1838O	Inc. above	500	700	1,200	1,750	3,000	—	—	—
1840	1,344,085	24.50	27.50	31.00	38.00	80.00	190	255	2,275
1840O	935,000	29.50	32.50	38.00	48.00	138	368	1,235	—

Seated Liberty Half Dime
Seated Liberty, stars around top 1/2 of border, date below obverse

KM# 62.2 • 1.3400 g., 0.9000 **Silver**, 0.0388 oz. ASW, 15.5 mm. • **Rev. Legend:** UNITED STATES OF AMERICA **Designer:** Christian Gobrecht **Notes:** In 1840 drapery was added to Liberty's left elbow. Varieties for the 1848 Philadelphia strikes are distinguished by the size of the numerals in the date.

Date	Mintage	G-4	VG-8	F-12	VF-20	XF-40	AU-50	MS-60	MS-65
1840	Inc. above	21.50	18.00	75.00	135	210	350	490	3,850
1840O	Inc. above	52.50	60.00	115	225	650	1,350	6,500	—
1841	1,150,000	18.50	21.50	23.50	31.00	60.50	127	180	1,325
1841O	815,000	21.50	24.50	30.00	50.00	125	300	650	6,750
1842	815,000	18.50	21.50	23.50	28.00	57.50	127	175	1,750
1842O	350,000	39.50	45.00	75.00	225	550	1,050	2,250	16,500
1843	1,165,000	18.50	21.50	23.50	28.00	57.50	122	175	1,365
1844	430,000	20.50	24.50	26.50	34.00	60.50	127	180	1,150
1844O	220,000	80.00	110	210	600	1,300	2,650	5,400	27,500
1845	1,564,000	18.50	21.50	23.50	35.00	60.50	122	175	1,150
1845/1845	Inc. above	20.50	24.50	26.50	38.00	85.00	132	190	1,200
1846	27,000	410	550	850	1,250	2,475	3,600	11,500	—
1847	1,274,000	18.50	21.50	23.50	28.00	57.50	127	175	1,150
1848 medium date	668,000	20.50	24.50	26.50	34.00	67.50	137	215	3,150
1848 large date	Inc. above	24.00	28.00	48.00	65.00	145	275	635	4,250
1848O	600,000	21.50	25.50	33.00	62.00	135	265	450	2,350
1849/8	1,309,000	28.50	35.00	47.50	67.50	140	250	785	2,950
1849/6	Inc. above	24.00	26.00	30.00	56.50	110	200	425	2,800
1849	Inc. above	20.50	18.50	27.50	52.50	67.50	137	190	1,825
1849O	140,000	29.00	40.00	95.00	225	540	1,100	2,350	—
1850	955,000	20.50	24.50	26.50	34.00	62.50	127	190	1,300
1850O	690,000	21.50	24.50	35.00	65.00	125	280	685	4,450
1851	781,000	17.50	21.50	23.50	28.00	59.90	122	175	1,350
1851O	860,000	20.50	24.50	26.50	41.50	110	220	500	4,350
1852	1,000,500	17.50	21.50	23.50	28.00	59.50	122	175	1,150
1852O	260,000	26.50	44.50	79.00	135	275	475	885	11,500
1853	135,000	40.00	60.00	90.00	175	300	525	850	2,850
1853O	160,000	285	325	450	850	1,800	3,500	6,450	27,500

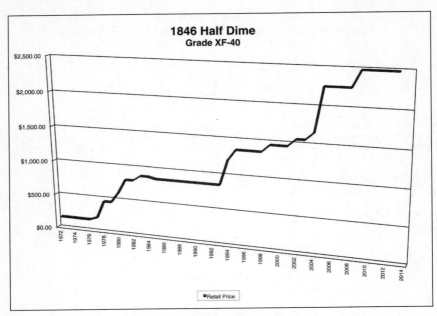

1846 Half Dime
Grade XF-40

Seated Liberty Half Dime

Seated Liberty, stars around top 1/2 of border, arrows at date obverse
Value within wreath reverse

KM# 76 • 1.2400 g., 0.9000 **Silver**, 0.0359 oz. ASW • **Rev. Legend:** UNITED STATES OF AMERICA
Designer: Christian Gobrecht

Date	Mintage	G-4	VG-8	F-12	VF-20	XF-40	AU-50	MS-60	MS-65	Prf-65
1853	13,210,020	17.75	21.50	22.50	28.00	58.00	135	195	1,410	—
1853O	2,200,000	20.75	29.50	30.50	36.00	66.00	143	310	3,260	—
1854	5,740,000	17.75	21.50	24.50	30.00	60.00	137	205	1,410	15,000
1854O	1,560,000	18.75	22.50	32.50	38.00	88.00	165	235	3,560	—
1855	1,750,000	18.75	22.50	24.50	30.00	60.00	137	200	1,810	15,000
1855O	600,000	22.75	27.50	38.50	54.00	140	220	540	4,260	—

Seated Liberty Half Dime

Seated Liberty, stars around top 1/2 of border, date below obverse
Value within wreath reverse

KM# A62.2 • 1.2400 g., 0.9000 **Silver**, 0.0359 oz. ASW • **Rev. Legend:** UNITED STATES OF AMERICA
Designer: Christian Gobrecht **Notes:** On the 1858/inverted date variety, the date was engraved into the die
upside down and then re-engraved right side up. Another 1858 variety has the date doubled.

Date	Mintage	G-4	VG-8	F-12	VF-20	XF-40	AU-50	MS-60	MS-65	Prf-65
1856	4,880,000	17.50	21.00	23.00	27.00	52.50	115	175	1,200	15,000
1856O	1,100,000	18.50	22.00	26.00	28.00	97.50	260	470	2,150	—
1857	7,280,000	17.50	21.00	23.00	27.00	52.50	115	175	1,050	5,600
1857O	1,380,000	18.50	22.00	24.00	28.00	62.50	185	320	1,750	—
1858	3,500,000	17.50	21.00	23.00	27.00	52.50	115	175	1,150	5,500
1858 inverted date	Inc. above	30.00	43.50	62.50	100.00	225	300	675	3,950	—

Date	Mintage	G-4	VG-8	F-12	VF-20	XF-40	AU-50	MS-60	MS-65	Prf-65
1858 double date	Inc. above	45.00	60.00	90.00	175	285	425	800	—	—
1858O	1,660,000	18.50	22.00	24.00	28.00	71.50	137	245	1,650	—
1859	340,000	19.50	23.00	25.00	29.00	54.50	117	225	1,350	4,000
1859O	560,000	20.50	24.00	26.00	42.00	128.5	200	285	1,850	—

Seated Liberty Half Dime

Seated Liberty, date below obverse
Value within wreath reverse

KM# 91 • 1.2400 g., 0.9000 **Silver**, 0.0359 oz. ASW • **Obv. Legend** UNITED STATES OF AMERICA
Designer: Christian Gobrecht

Date	Mintage	G-4	VG-8	F-12	VF-20	XF-40	AU-50	MS-60	MS-65	Prf-65
1860	799,000	17.00	20.00	23.00	26.00	47.00	77.00	155	825	1,550
1860O	1,060,000	18.00	20.00	23.00	29.00	49.00	79.00	180	1,175	—
1861	3,361,000	17.00	20.00	22.00	25.00	45.00	75.00	155	825	1,600
1861/0	Inc. above	26.00	32.50	59.00	125	260	435	560	3,650	—
1862	1,492,550	21.00	25.00	34.00	44.00	64.00	94.00	164	825	1,550
1863	18,460	200	250	300	400	485	550	800	1,375	1,550
1863S	100,000	35.00	45.00	70.00	95.00	165	300	750	3,450	—
1864	48,470	375	475	575	750	950	1,100	1,375	2,350	1,600
1864S	90,000	60.00	75.00	115	175	250	450	785	3,750	—
1865	13,500	375	475	575	750	950	1,100	1,350	1,950	1,550
1865S	120,000	30.00	40.00	60.00	85.00	145	375	975	5,450	—
1866	10,725	350	475	550	700	875	1,000	1,225	2,375	1,550
1866S	120,000	30.00	40.00	60.00	85.00	145	285	485	5,000	—
1867	8,625	550	650	775	900	1,100	1,200	1,375	2,350	1,550
1867S	120,000	30.00	40.00	60.00	85.00	150	325	850	3,850	—
1868	89,200	60.00	90.00	190	225	300	425	625	2,400	1,550
1868S	280,000	21.00	25.00	35.00	42.00	59.00	125	335	3,250	—
1869	208,600	21.00	25.00	35.00	42.00	59.00	135	210	1,175	1,560
1869S	230,000	19.00	24.00	30.00	35.00	55.00	125	320	4,150	—
1870	536,600	19.00	24.00	30.00	35.00	55.00	125	195	775	1,550
1870S unique	—	—	—	—	—	—	—	—	—	—

Note: 1870S, Superior Galleries, July 1986, brilliant uncirculated, $253,000.

Date	Mintage	G-4	VG-8	F-12	VF-20	XF-40	AU-50	MS-60	MS-65	Prf-65
1871	1,873,960	17.00	20.00	22.00	25.00	45.00	75.00	145	775	1,550
1871S	161,000	26.00	30.00	45.00	60.00	90.00	175	320	2,225	—
1872	2,947,950	17.00	20.00	22.00	25.00	45.00	75.00	145	775	1,550
1872S mint mark in wreath	837,000	17.00	20.00	22.00	25.00	45.00	75.00	145	775	—
1872S mint mark below wreath	Inc. above	18.00	21.00	24.00	27.00	47.00	80.00	145	775	—
1873	712,600	17.00	20.00	22.00	25.00	45.00	75.00	145	1,175	1,550
1873S	324,000	21.00	25.00	30.00	42.00	62.00	90.00	160	775	—

5 CENTS

Shield Nickel

Draped garland above shield, date below obverse
Value within center of rays between stars reverse

KM# 96 • 5.0000 g., **Copper-Nickel**, 20.5 mm. • **Obv. Legend** IN GOD WE TRUST **Rev. Legend:**
UNITED STATES OF AMERICA **Designer:** James B. Longacre

Date	Mintage	G-4	VG-8	F-12	VF-20	XF-40	AU-50	MS-60	MS-65	Prf-65
1866	14,742,500	29.00	38.00	55.00	80.00	150	250	280	2,050	3,450
1867	2,019,000	37.00	45.50	63.50	90.00	180	280	330	3,850	75,000

Shield Nickel
Draped garland above shield, date below obverse
Value within circle of stars reverse

KM# 97 • 5.0000 g., **Copper-Nickel** • **Obv. Legend** IN GOD WE TRUST **Rev. Legend:** UNITED STATES OF AMERICA

Date	Mintage	G-4	VG-8	F-12	VF-20	XF-40	AU-50	MS-60	MS-65	Prf-65
1867	28,890,500	18.50	28.00	30.00	37.50	64.00	115	150	825	2,500
1868 Rev'67	28,817,000	18.50	28.00	30.00	37.50	64.00	115	150	675	1,325
1868 Rev'68	Inc. above	22.00	34.00	36.00	45.00	77.00	144	188	—	—
Note: Star points to center of A in STATES.										
1869	16,395,000	18.50	28.00	30.00	37.50	64.00	115	150	700	900
1870	4,806,000	27.00	35.00	54.00	69.00	100.00	150	210	1,600	1,060
1871	561,000	72.00	95.00	140	210	310	365	415	2,100	910
1872	6,036,000	39.00	48.00	85.00	96.00	135	180	235	1,350	715
1873 Open 3	4,550,000	29.00	39.00	54.00	68.00	80.00	135	230	1,950	—
1873 Closed 3	Inc. above	36.00	48.00	70.00	100.00	150	220	350	3,250	715
1874	3,538,000	31.00	45.00	74.00	94.00	120	165	245	1,400	800
1875	2,097,000	46.00	62.00	90.00	125	170	230	290	1,500	1,500
1876	2,530,000	40.00	54.00	84.00	125	165	200	255	1,350	825
1877 proof	Est. 900	—	—	—	2,100	2,150	2,300	—	—	4,850
1878 proof	2,350	—	—	—	1,100	1,250	1,450	—	—	2,100
1879	29,100	390	485	625	660	720	800	970	1,900	750
1879/8	Inc. above	—	—	—	—	—	—	—	—	825
1880	19,995	500	575	700	850	1,275	1,700	3,250	47,500	730
1881	72,375	260	340	430	500	600	675	735	1,800	700
1882	11,476,600	18.50	28.00	30.00	37.50	64.00	115	150	635	645
Note: Many exist with excess metal at numeral 2 & 3 these should not be confused with the following overdate.										
1883	1,456,919	18.50	28.00	32.00	39.50	67.00	135	160	750	645
Note: Many exist with excess metal at numeral 2 & 3 these should not be confused with the following overdate.										
1883/2	Inc. above	220	300	535	850	1,250	1,750	2,000	3,750	—

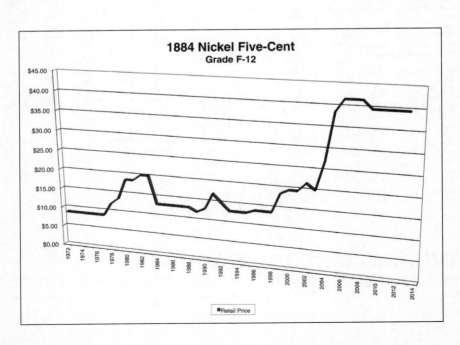

1884 Nickel Five-Cent
Grade F-12

Liberty Nickel

Liberty head left, within circle of stars, date below obverse
Roman numeral value within wreath, without CENTS below reverse

KM# 111 • 5.0000 g., **Copper-Nickel**, 21.2 mm. • **Rev. Legend:** UNITED STATES OF AMERICA
Designer: Charles E. Barber

Date	Mintage	G-4	VG-8	F-12	VF-20	XF-40	AU-50	MS-60	MS-65	Prf-65
1883	5,479,519	7.00	7.75	8.50	8.75	9.25	12.00	25.50	215	1,075

Liberty Nickel

Liberty head left, within circle of stars, date below obverse
Roman numeral value within wreath, CENTS below reverse

KM# 112 • 5.0000 g., **Copper-Nickel**, 21.2 mm. • **Rev. Legend:** UNITED STATES OF AMERICA

Date	Mintage	G-4	VG-8	F-12	VF-20	XF-40	AU-50	MS-60	MS-65	Prf-65
1883	16,032,983	19.00	29.50	39.50	55.00	85.00	120	160	625	610
1884	11,273,942	22.50	33.50	39.50	59.00	92.00	135	190	1,675	610
1885	1,476,490	585	635	875	1,050	1,350	1,650	1,950	8,650	3,150
1886	3,330,290	285	335	400	500	685	850	1,950	7,250	1,950
1887	15,263,652	16.00	25.00	31.00	44.00	78.00	115	150	1,025	585
1888	10,720,483	28.00	44.00	68.00	130	185	250	295	1,500	585
1889	15,881,361	14.50	19.50	30.00	52.50	77.00	125	155	850	585
1890	16,259,272	10.50	20.50	26.00	39.50	68.50	115	165	1,365	585
1891	16,834,350	5.75	11.00	22.00	37.50	60.00	120	160	1,050	585
1892	11,699,642	6.50	11.00	22.50	39.00	65.00	120	165	1,300	585
1893	13,370,195	5.50	11.00	24.00	37.50	60.00	120	155	1,050	585
1894	5,413,132	16.50	31.00	98.00	165	230	295	350	1,500	585
1895	9,979,884	5.75	7.50	24.00	45.00	66.00	120	145	2,200	585
1896	8,842,920	9.00	21.00	41.50	68.50	98.00	150	205	1,950	585
1897	20,428,735	3.25	4.50	12.50	27.50	46.00	69.50	95.00	925	585
1898	12,532,087	2.15	4.25	11.00	23.50	40.00	68.50	130	1,025	585
1899	26,029,031	1.80	3.00	8.50	19.50	34.00	62.50	89.00	560	585
1900	27,255,995	1.60	2.50	8.50	19.00	34.00	69.50	84.00	650	585
1901	26,480,213	1.60	2.50	7.00	14.50	34.00	65.00	100.00	550	585
1902	31,480,579	1.60	2.50	4.00	15.00	32.00	65.00	102	550	585
1903	28,006,725	1.80	2.50	4.75	14.50	32.00	60.00	77.00	500	585
1904	21,404,984	1.60	2.40	4.75	11.50	30.00	65.00	96.00	500	585
1905	29,827,276	1.60	2.40	4.00	12.00	30.00	65.00	96.00	550	585
1906	38,613,725	1.80	2.40	4.00	11.50	30.00	65.00	96.00	650	585
1907	39,214,800	1.50	2.20	4.00	12.00	30.00	65.00	96.00	1,000	585
1908	22,686,177	1.80	2.20	4.00	12.00	30.00	68.00	104	1,100	585
1909	11,590,526	2.50	2.80	4.35	13.00	33.00	80.00	112	1,075	585
1910	30,169,353	1.50	1.85	4.00	10.00	30.00	52.00	62.00	550	585
1911	39,559,372	1.50	1.85	4.00	10.00	30.00	52.00	62.00	500	585
1912	26,236,714	1.50	1.85	4.00	10.00	30.00	52.00	62.00	570	585
1912D	8,474,000	2.75	3.60	11.50	38.00	70.00	170	280	2,200	—
1912S	238,000	165	190	220	480	810	1,300	1,475	5,900	—
1913 5 known	—	—	—	—	—	—	—	—	—	—

Note: 1913, Heritage Sale, January 2010, Proof-64 (Olsen), $3,737,500. Private treaty, 2007, (Eliasburg) Proof-66 $5 million.

Buffalo Nickel

American Bison standing on a mound reverse

KM# 133 • 5.0000 g., **Copper-Nickel**, 21.2 mm. • **Designer:** James Earle Fraser

Date	Mintage	G-4	VG-8	F-12	VF-20	XF-40	AU-50	MS-60	MS-65	Prf-65
1913	30,993,520	8.00	14.50	15.00	16.00	19.00	25.00	32.50	190	3,150
1913D	5,337,000	16.00	19.50	21.00	25.00	35.00	57.00	62.50	310	—
1913S	2,105,000	43.00	47.00	50.00	60.00	75.00	100.00	125	690	—

Buffalo Nickel

American Bison standing on a line reverse

1937D 3-legged   1918/17D

KM# 134 • 5.0000 g., **Copper-Nickel**, 21.2 mm. • **Designer:** James Earle Fraser **Notes:** In 1913 the reverse design was modified so the ground under the buffalo was represented as a line rather than a mound. On the 1937D 3-legged variety, the buffalo's right front leg is missing, the result of a damaged die.

Date	Mintage	G-4	VG-8	F-12	VF-20	XF-40	AU-50	MS-60	MS-65	Prf-65
1913	29,858,700	8.00	12.00	13.00	14.00	19.00	25.00	34.00	355	2,500
1913D	4,156,000	125	155	180	190	265	275	285	1,450	—
1913S	1,209,000	350	400	420	430	575	675	885	3,850	—
1914	20,665,738	18.00	21.00	22.00	23.00	27.50	37.50	47.00	420	2,250
1914/3	Inc. above	150	300	425	525	700	1,050	2,850	30,000	—
1914D	3,912,000	90.00	132	165	200	335	390	475	1,600	—
1914/3D	Inc. above	115	225	335	450	625	900	3,500	—	—
1914S	3,470,000	26.00	37.50	45.00	62.50	90.00	145	165	22,350	—
1914/3S	Inc. above	250	500	750	1,000	1,450	2,260	4,300	—	—
1915	20,987,270	6.25	7.00	7.75	11.00	21.50	38.50	50.00	325	2,100
1915D	7,569,500	21.50	31.00	41.50	66.00	115	150	235	2,250	—
1915S	1,505,000	47.00	74.00	105	185	326	490	625	3,150	—
1916	63,498,066	5.50	6.40	7.00	8.00	13.50	24.00	43.50	315	3,250
1916 2 Feathers	Inc. above	35.00	—	45.00	—	—	—	—	150	—
1916/16	Inc. above	1,800	3,650	7,150	10,850	16,500	34,500	49,500	375,000	—
1916D	13,333,000	15.00	26.50	29.00	38.50	82.50	110	165	2,250	—
1916S	11,860,000	11.00	13.50	26.00	35.00	75.00	125	185	2,300	—
1917	51,424,029	7.50	8.00	8.75	10.00	16.00	32.50	59.00	535	—
1917 2 Feathers	Inc. above	40.00	—	50.00	—	—	—	—	165	—
1917D	9,910,800	26.00	31.00	55.00	80.00	135	255	345	3,250	—
1917S	4,193,000	23.00	42.00	80.00	110	180	285	395	4,850	—
1917S 2 Feathers	Inc. above	50.00	—	95.00	—	—	—	—	315	—
1918	32,086,314	5.25	6.75	8.00	15.00	31.00	48.50	105	1,550	—
1918/17D	8,362,314	1,000	1,475	2,600	4,950	7,950	10,750	36,500	350,000	—
1918D	Inc. above	22.50	39.00	66.00	135	226	330	430	4,650	—
1918 2 Feathers	Inc. above	50.00	—	95.00	—	—	—	—	315	—
1918S	4,882,000	14.00	27.50	55.00	100.00	175	300	495	25,500	—
1919	60,868,000	2.60	3.50	3.90	7.00	16.00	32.00	58.00	535	—
1919D	8,006,000	15.50	31.00	66.00	115	235	335	570	6,850	—
1919S	7,521,000	8.00	26.00	50.00	110	225	360	540	24,000	—
1920	63,093,000	1.50	2.75	3.25	8.00	16.00	30.00	59.00	700	—
1920D	9,418,000	8.50	19.00	35.00	125	275	340	575	6,850	—
1920S	9,689,000	4.50	12.75	30.00	100.00	260	300	525	25,500	—
1921	10,663,000	4.00	6.25	8.50	25.00	53.50	73.00	125	800	—
1921S	1,557,000	64.00	100.00	180	400	825	1,150	1,575	7,350	—
1923	35,715,000	1.70	3.25	4.25	7.00	14.00	37.50	59.00	575	—
1923S	6,142,000	8.00	11.00	27.00	125	275	335	625	11,500	—
1924	21,620,000	1.25	2.40	4.50	10.00	19.00	41.00	73.50	850	—
1924D	5,258,000	8.00	12.00	30.00	90.00	215	315	375	4,950	—
1924S	1,437,000	16.50	32.00	96.00	455	1,100	1,700	2,300	12,850	—
1925	35,565,100	2.50	3.00	3.75	8.50	16.50	32.00	42.00	490	—
1925D	4,450,000	10.00	26.00	38.00	80.00	160	240	375	5,650	—

5 CENTS

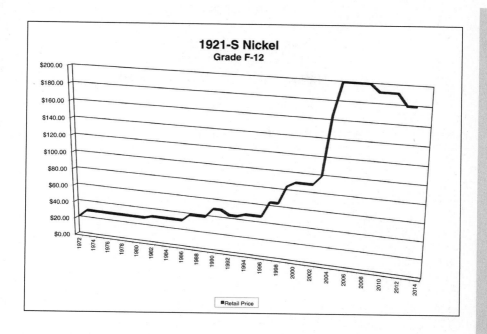

5 CENTS

Date	Mintage	G-4	VG-8	F-12	VF-20	XF-40	AU-50	MS-60	MS-65	Prf-65
1925S	6,256,000	4.50	9.00	17.50	77.50	170	250	425	28,500	—
1926	44,693,000	1.50	2.00	2.80	5.40	11.50	26.00	31.50	235	—
1926D	5,638,000	10.00	17.50	28.50	100.00	170	295	335	5,850	—
1926S	970,000	20.00	42.00	100.00	345	850	2,450	4,950	125,000	—
1927	37,981,000	1.40	1.75	2.50	4.50	12.50	26.00	35.00	290	—
1927D	5,730,000	3.00	6.00	7.00	27.50	75.00	115	155	7,950	—
1927S	3,430,000	2.00	3.00	6.00	31.00	80.00	160	490	18,500	—
1928	23,411,000	1.40	1.75	2.50	4.50	12.50	25.00	32.50	310	—
1928D	6,436,000	1.90	2.50	3.75	16.00	40.00	46.50	53.00	685	—
1928S	6,936,000	1.75	2.35	3.00	12.00	27.50	105	225	4,750	—
1929	36,446,000	1.40	1.75	2.50	4.50	13.00	21.00	35.00	325	—
1929D	8,370,000	1.50	1.85	3.00	6.75	32.50	42.50	60.00	1,850	—
1929S	7,754,000	1.50	1.85	2.25	4.00	12.50	25.00	49.50	485	—
1930	22,849,000	1.40	1.75	2.50	4.50	12.00	21.00	32.50	235	—
1930S	5,435,000	1.50	2.00	3.00	4.50	16.00	37.50	65.00	480	—
1931S	1,200,000	15.00	16.00	17.00	19.00	31.00	46.00	59.00	300	—
1934	20,213,003	1.40	1.75	2.50	4.50	11.00	19.00	47.50	355	—
1934D	7,480,000	2.00	3.00	4.75	9.60	22.00	50.00	79.50	800	—
1935	58,264,000	1.25	1.60	2.25	3.00	4.00	11.00	20.00	145	—
1935 Double Die Rev.	Inc. above	50.00	75.00	125	250	675	1,800	4,000	75,000	—
1935D	12,092,000	1.60	2.50	3.00	9.00	26.00	48.00	72.00	415	—
1935S	10,300,000	1.35	1.75	2.50	3.50	4.50	17.50	48.50	250	—
1936	119,001,420	1.25	1.60	2.25	3.00	4.00	6.75	14.50	105	1,650
1936 Brilliant	Inc. above	—	—	—	—	—	—	—	—	2,450
1936D	24,814,000	1.35	1.75	2.75	4.00	5.35	11.50	33.50	118	—
1936D 3-1/2 leg	Inc. above	750	1,250	2,000	3,500	6,000	10,500	17,500	—	—
1936D/S	Inc. above	1.35	—	10.00	16.00	25.00	—	—	—	—
1936S	14,930,000	1.35	1.75	2.50	3.50	4.50	11.00	33.50	115	—
1937	79,485,769	1.25	1.60	2.25	3.00	4.00	6.75	14.50	69.00	2,100
1937D	17,826,000	1.35	1.75	2.50	3.50	4.50	9.00	29.00	73.00	—
1937D 3-legged	Inc. above	535	660	725	775	965	1,225	2,375	37,000	—
1937S	5,635,000	1.35	1.75	2.50	3.50	4.50	10.00	27.50	72.00	—
1938D	7,020,000	3.50	3.75	3.90	4.00	4.50	8.00	26.00	66.00	—
1938D/D	Inc. above	4.00	4.50	6.00	8.00	10.00	17.00	32.00	125	—
1938D/S	Inc. above	4.50	6.75	9.00	12.50	19.00	32.50	50.00	185	—

Jefferson Nickel

Monticello, mintmark to right side reverse

KM# 192 • 5.0000 g., **Copper-Nickel**, 21.2 mm. • **Designer:** Felix Schlag **Notes:** Some 1939 strikes have doubling of the word MONTICELLO on the reverse.

Date	Mintage	VG-8	F-12	VF-20	XF-40	MS-60	MS-65	-65FS	Prf-65
1938	19,515,365	.50	.75	1.00	2.25	7.50	18.00	125	—
1938D	5,376,000	1.00	1.25	1.50	2.00	4.00	15.00	95.00	—
1938S	4,105,000	1.75	2.00	2.50	3.00	5.25	12.00	165	—
1939 T I, wavy steps, Rev. of 1939	120,627,535	—	—	—	—	3.00	30.00	300	70.00
1939 T II, even steps, Rev. of 1940	Inc. above	—	.20	.25	.30	4.00	45.00	50.00	130
1939 doubled MONTICELLO T II	Inc. above	40.00	60.00	90.00	165	300	1,250	2,000	—
1939D T IT I, wavy steps, Rev. of 1939	3,514,000	—	—	10.00	17.50	75.00	160	275	—
1939D T IIT II, even steps, Rev. of 1940	Inc. above	4.00	5.00	8.00	14.00	55.00	105	400	—
1939S T IT I, wavy steps, Rev. of 1939	6,630,000	.45	.60	1.50	4.00	17.00	45.00	250	—
1939S T IIT II, even steps, Rev. of 1940	Inc. above	—	—	—	5.00	24.00	250	275	—
1940	176,499,158	—	—	—	.25	1.00	12.00	60.00	125
1940D	43,540,000	—	.20	.30	.40	1.50	2.75	25.00	—
1940S	39,690,000	.25	.40	.50	1.25	4.50	20.00	55.00	—
1941	203,283,720	—	—	—	.20	.75	20.00	55.00	—
1941D	53,432,000	—	.20	.30	.50	2.25	7.50	25.00	—
1941S	43,445,000	.25	.40	.50	1.35	5.00	14.00	60.00	—
1942	49,818,600	—	—	—	.40	5.00	22.00	75.00	—
1942D	13,938,000	1.00	1.75	3.00	5.00	38.00	65.00	85.00	—
1942D D over horizontal D	Inc. above	35.00	60.00	100.00	165	750	10,000	25,000	—

Note: Fully Struck Full Step nickels command higher prices. Bright, Fully Struck coins command even higher prices. 1938 thru 1989 - 5 Full Steps. 1990 to date - 6 Full Steps. Without bag marks or nicks on steps.

Jefferson Nickel

Monticello, mint mark above reverse

1943/2P

KM# 192a • 0.3500 **Copper-Silver-Manganese**, 21.2 mm. • **Designer:** Felix Schlag **Notes:** War-time composition nickels have the mint mark above MONTICELLO on the reverse.

Date	Mintage	VG-8	F-12	VF-20	XF-40	MS-60	MS-65	-65FS	Prf-65
1942P	57,900,600	1.87	1.93	2.13	2.00	9.00	20.00	75.00	150
1942S	32,900,000	1.87	1.93	2.13	2.45	8.00	19.00	170	—
1943P	271,165,000	1.87	1.93	2.13	2.00	5.00	20.00	40.00	—
1943P	Inc. above	—	—	32.00	54.00	125	575	1,100	—
1943/2P	Inc. above	35.00	50.00	75.00	110	300	775	1,000	—
1943D	15,294,000	2.12	2.18	2.38	2.05	4.00	18.00	40.00	—
1943S	104,060,000	1.87	1.93	2.13	2.15	6.75	18.50	48.00	—
1944P	119,150,000	1.87	1.93	2.13	2.15	10.00	28.00	75.00	—
1944D	32,309,000	1.92	1.98	2.18	2.25	10.00	22.50	65.00	—
1944S	21,640,000	1.92	1.98	2.18	2.15	8.50	20.00	185	—
1945P	119,408,100	1.87	1.93	2.13	2.15	6.00	28.00	120	—
1945D	37,158,000	1.97	2.03	2.28	2.30	5.50	20.00	40.00	—
1945S	58,939,000	1.87	1.93	2.13	2.15	5.00	18.00	250	—

Note: Fully Struck Full Step nickels command higher prices. Bright, Fully Struck coins command even higher prices. 1938 thru 1989 - 5 Full Steps. 1990 to date - 6 Full Steps. Without bag marks or nicks on steps.

5 CENTS

Jefferson Nickel

Pre-war design resumed reverse

KM# A192 • 5.0000 g., **Copper-Nickel**, 21.2 mm.
• **Designer:** Felix Schlag **Edge Desc:** Plain

Date	Mintage	XF-40	MS-65	Prf-65
1946	161,116,000	.25	200	—
1946D	45,292,200	.35	28.00	—
1946D/D	Inc. above	—	2,000	—
1946S	13,560,000	.40	90.00	—
1947	95,000,000	.25	35.00	—
1947D	37,822,000	.30	35.00	—
1947S	24,720,000	.25	70.00	—
1948	89,348,000	.25	165	—
1948D	44,734,000	.35	30.00	—
1948S	11,300,000	.50	60.00	—
1949	60,652,000	.30	2,000	—
1949D	36,498,000	.40	50.00	—
1949D/S	Inc. above	65.00	1,500	—
1949S	9,716,000	.90	375	—
1950	9,847,386	.75	175	75.00
1950D	2,630,030	10.00	65.00	—
1951	28,609,500	.50	375	70.00
1951D	20,460,000	.50	95.00	—
1951S	7,776,000	1.10	275	—
1952	64,069,980	.25	1,250	42.00
1952D	30,638,000	.45	175	—
1952S	20,572,000	.25	450	—
1953	46,772,800	.25	3,000	45.00
1953D	59,878,600	.25	275	—
1953S	19,210,900	.25	20,000	—
1954	47,917,350	—	400	20.00
1954D	117,136,560	—	1,000	—
1954S	29,384,000	.20	6,000	—
1954S/D	Inc. above	20.00	—	—
1955	8,266,200	.45	750	13.50
1955D	74,464,100	—	5,000	—
1955D/S	Inc. above	25.00	—	—
1956	35,885,384	—	60.00	3.00
1956D	67,222,940	—	750	—
1957	39,655,952	—	150	2.50
1957D	136,828,900	—	135	—
1958	17,963,652	.20	900	8.00
1958D	168,249,120	—	35.00	—

Note: Fully Struck Full Step nickels command higher prices. Bright, Fully Struck coins command even higher prices. 1938 thru 1989 - 5 Full Steps. 1990 to date - 6 Full Steps. Without bag marks or nicks on steps.

Date	Mintage	XF-40	MS-65	Prf-65
1959	28,397,291	—	65.00	1.40
1959D	160,738,240	—	250	—
1960	57,107,602	—	2,500	1.25
1960D	192,582,180	—	—	—
1961	76,668,244	—	3,500	1.00
1961D	229,342,760	—	25,000	—
1962	100,602,019	—	75.00	1.00
1962D	280,195,720	—	10,000	—
1963	178,851,645	—	200	1.00
1963D	276,829,460	—	7,500	—
1964	1,028,622,762	—	350	1.00
1964D	1,787,297,160	—	750	—
1965	136,131,380	—	4,500	—
1965SMS	2,360,000	—	25.00	—
1966	156,208,283	—	3,250	—
1966SMS	2,261,583	—	25.00	—
1967	107,325,800	—	—	—
1967SMS	1,863,344	—	25.00	—
1968 none minted	—	—	—	—
1968D	91,227,880	—	—	—
1968S	103,437,510	—	900	0.75
1969 none minted	—	—	—	—

Date	Mintage	XF-40	MS-65	Prf-65
1969D	202,807,500	—	—	—
1969S	123,099,631	—	—	0.75
1970 none minted	—	—	—	—
1970D	515,485,380	—	5,000	—
1970S	241,464,814	—	500	0.75
1971	106,884,000	—	20.00	—
1971D	316,144,800	—	7.50	—
1971S	3,220,733	—	—	1.00
1972	202,036,000	—	35.00	—
1972D	351,694,600	—	60.00	—
1972S	3,260,996	—	—	1.00
1973	384,396,000	—	7.00	—
1973D	261,405,000	—	40.00	—
1973S	2,760,339	—	—	0.75
1974	601,752,000	—	125	—
1974D	277,373,000	—	30.00	—
1974S	2,612,568	—	—	0.75
1975	181,772,000	—	50.00	—
1975D	401,875,300	—	60.00	—
1975S	2,845,450	—	—	0.75
1976	367,124,000	—	300	—
1976D	563,964,147	—	50.00	—
1976S	4,149,730	—	—	0.75
1977	585,376,000	—	225	—
1977D	297,313,460	—	60.00	—
1977S	3,251,152	—	—	0.75
1978	391,308,000	—	225	—
1978D	313,092,780	—	7.00	—
1978S	3,127,781	—	—	0.75
1979	463,188,000	—	300	—
1979D	325,867,672	—	35.00	—
1979S type I, proof	3,677,175	—	—	0.75
1979S type II, proof	Inc. above	—	—	2.00
1980P	593,004,000	—	75.00	—
1980D	502,323,448	—	45.00	—
1980S	3,554,806	—	—	0.75
1981P	657,504,000	—	750	—
1981D	364,801,843	—	75.00	—
1981S type I, proof	4,063,083	—	—	2.00
1981S type II, proof	Inc. above	—	—	2.50
1982P	292,355,000	—	12.50	—
1982D	373,726,544	—	3.50	—
1982S	3,857,479	—	—	3.50
1983P	561,615,000	—	4.00	—
1983D	536,726,276	—	2.50	—
1983S	3,279,126	—	—	4.00
1984P	746,769,000	—	3.00	—
1984D	517,675,146	—	.85	—
1984S	3,065,110	—	—	5.00
1985P	647,114,962	—	.75	—
1985D	459,747,446	—	.75	—
1985S	3,362,821	—	—	4.00
1986P	536,883,483	—	1.00	—
1986D	361,819,140	—	2.00	—
1986S	3,010,497	—	—	7.00
1987P	371,499,481	—	.75	—
1987D	410,590,604	—	.75	—
1987S	4,227,728	—	—	3.50
1988P	771,360,000	—	.75	—
1988D	663,771,652	—	.75	—
1988S	3,262,948	—	—	6.50
1989P	898,812,000	—	.75	—
1989D	570,842,474	—	.75	—
1989S	3,220,194	—	—	5.50
1990P	661,636,000	—	.75	—
1990D	663,938,503	—	.75	—
1990S	3,299,559	—	—	5.50
1991P	614,104,000	—	.75	—
1991D	436,496,678	—	.75	—
1991S	2,867,787	—	—	5.00
1992P	399,552,000	—	2.00	—
1992D	450,565,113	—	.75	—
1992S	4,176,560	—	—	4.00
1993P	412,076,000	—	.75	—
1993D	406,084,135	—	.75	—
1993S	3,394,792	—	—	4.50
1994P	722,160,000	—	.75	—

5 CENTS

5 CENTS

Date	Mintage	XF-40	MS-65	Prf-65
1994P Special Uncirculed matte finish	167,703	—	—	58.00
1994D	715,762,110	—	.75	—
1994S	3,269,923	—	—	4.00
1995P	774,156,000	—	.75	—
1995D	888,112,000	—	.85	—
1995S	2,707,481	—	—	4.00
1996P	829,332,000	—	.75	—
1996D	817,736,000	—	.75	—
1996S	2,915,212	—	—	4.00
1997P	470,972,000	—	.75	—
1997P Special Uncirculated matte finish	25,000	—	—	160
1997D	466,640,000	—	2.00	—
1997S	1,975,000	—	—	5.00
1998P	688,272,000	—	.80	—
1998D	635,360,000	—	.80	—
1998S	2,957,286	—	—	4.50
1999P	1,212,000,000	—	.80	—
1999D	1,066,720,000	—	.80	—
1999S	3,362,462	—	—	3.50
2000P	846,240,000	—	.80	—
2000D	1,509,520,000	—	.80	—
2000S	4,063,361	—	—	2.00
2001P	675,704,000	—	.50	—
2001D	627,680,000	—	.50	—
2001S	3,099,096	—	—	4.00
2002P	539,280,000	—	.50	—
2002D	691,200,000	—	.50	—
2002S	3,157,739	—	—	2.00
2003P	441,840,000	—	.50	—
2003D	383,040,000	—	.50	—
2003S	3,116,590	—	—	2.00

Jefferson - Westward Expansion - Lewis & Clark Bicentennial

Jefferson era peace medal design: two clasped hands, pipe and hatchet reverse

KM# 360 • 5.0000 g., **Copper-Nickel**, 21.2 mm. •
Obv. Designer: Felix Schlag **Rev. Designer:** Norman E. Nemeth

Date	Mintage	MS-65	Prf-65
2004P	361,440,000	1.50	—
2004D	372,000,000	1.50	—
2004S	—	—	10.00

Lewis and Clark's Keelboat reverse

KM# 361 • 5.0000 g., **Copper-Nickel**, 21.2 mm. •
Obv. Designer: Felix Schlag **Rev. Designer:** Al Maletsky

Date	Mintage	MS-65	Prf-65
2004P	366,720,000	1.50	—
2004D	344,880,000	1.50	—
2004S	—	—	10.00

Thomas Jefferson large profile right obverse   American Bison right reverse

KM# 368 • 5.0000 g., **Copper-Nickel**, 21.2 mm. •
Obv. Designer: Joe Fitzgerald and Don Everhart II
Rev. Designer: Jamie Franki and Norman E. Nemeth

Date	Mintage	MS-65	Prf-65
2005P	448,320,000	1.50	—
2005D	487,680,000	1.50	—
2005S	—	—	6.50

Jefferson, large profile obverse Pacific coastline reverse

KM# 369 • 5.0000 g., **Copper-Nickel**, 21.2 mm. •
Obv. Designer: Joe Fitzgerald and Don Everhart
Rev. Designer: Joe Fitzgerald and Donna Weaver

Date	Mintage	MS-65	Prf-65
2005P	394,080,000	1.25	—
2005D	411,120,000	1.25	—
2005S	—	—	5.50

Jefferson large facing portrait - Enhanced Monticello Reverse

Jefferson head facing obverse Monticello, enhanced design reverse

KM# 381 • 5.0000 g., **Copper-Nickel**, 21.2 mm. •
Obv. Designer: Jamie N. Franki and Donna Weaver **Rev. Designer:** Felix Schlag and John Mercanti

Date	Mintage	MS-65	Prf-65
2006P	693,120,000	2.50	—
2006P Satin finish	—	4.00	—
2006D	809,280,000	2.50	—
2006D Satin finish	—	4.00	—
2006S	—	—	5.00
2007P	—	2.50	—
2007P Satin finish	—	4.00	—
2007D	—	2.50	—
2007D Satin finish	—	4.00	—
2007S	—	—	4.00
2008P	—	2.50	—
2008P Satin finish	—	4.00	—
2008D	—	2.50	—
2008D Satin finish	—	4.00	—
2008S	—	—	4.00

Date	Mintage	MS-65	Prf-65	Date	Mintage	MS-65	Prf-65
2009P	—	2.50	—	2011P	—	2.50	—
2009P Satin finish	—	4.00	—	2011D	—	2.50	—
2009D	—	2.50	—	2011S	—	—	3.00
2009D Satin finish	—	4.00	—	2012P	—	2.50	—
2009S	—	—	3.00	2012D	—	2.50	—
2010P	—	2.50	—	2012S	—	—	3.00
2010P Satin finish	—	4.00	—	2013P	—	2.50	—
2010D	—	2.50	—	2013D	—	2.50	—
2010D Satin finish	—	4.00	—	2013S	—	—	3.00
2010S	—	—	3.00				

DIME

Draped Bust Dime

Draped bust right obverse   Small eagle reverse

KM# 24 • 2.7000 g., 0.8920 **Silver**, 0.0774 oz. ASW, 19 mm. • **Designer:** Robert Scot

Date	Mintage	G-4	VG-8	F-12	VF-20	XF-40	MS-60
1796	22,135	2,850	3,600	5,500	7,000	12,350	24,500
1797 13 stars	25,261	3,100	3,950	6,050	8,000	13,150	70,000
1797 16 stars	Inc. above	3,000	3,850	5,800	7,150	13,650	36,500

Draped Bust Dime

Draped bust right obverse   Heraldic eagle reverse

KM# 31 • 2.7000 g., 0.8920 **Silver**, 0.0774 oz. ASW, 19 mm. • **Obv. Legend** LIBERTY **Rev. Legend:** UNITED STATES OF AMERICA **Designer:** Robert Scot **Notes:** The 1805 strikes have either 4 or 5 berries on the olive branch held by the eagle.

Date	Mintage	G-4	VG-8	F-12	VF-20	XF-40	MS-60
1798 large 8	27,550	725	1,250	1,550	2,100	3,625	8,850
1798 small 8	Inc. above	975	1,450	2,350	3,250	6,000	53,500
1798/97 13 stars	Inc. above	2,150	3,850	5,650	8,850	13,850	59,000
1798/97 16 stars	Inc. above	775	1,125	1,800	2,650	4,600	10,500

Note: The 1798 overdates have either 13 or 16 stars under the clouds on the reverse; Varieties of the regular 1798 strikes are distinguished by the size of the 8 in the date

Date	Mintage	G-4	VG-8	F-12	VF-20	XF-40	MS-60
1800	21,760	700	1,075	1,400	2,700	4,350	37,500
1801	34,640	750	1,150	1,650	3,100	6,250	49,500
1802	10,975	1,750	2,650	3,500	4,750	10,000	37,500
1803	33,040	675	1,150	1,900	2,750	5,900	49,500
1804 13 stars	8,265	2,650	4,450	10,500	19,000	41,500	—
1804 14 stars	Inc. above	4,850	6,500	12,500	24,500	46,500	—
1805 5 berries	Inc. above	625	1,000	1,400	2,100	3,700	9,100
1805 4 berries	120,780	615	920	1,225	1,650	2,950	7,350
1807	165,000	575	900	1,200	1,650	2,950	6,850

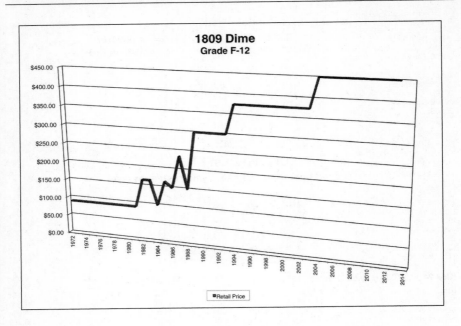

1809 Dime
Grade F-12

Liberty Cap Dime

Draped bust left, flanked by stars, date below obverse
Eagle with arrows in talons, banner above, value below reverse

KM# 42 • 2.7000 g., 0.8920 **Silver**, 0.0774 oz. ASW, 18.8 mm. • **Rev. Legend:** UNITED STATES OF
AMERICA **Designer:** John Reich **Notes:** The 1820 varieties are distinguished by the size of the 0 in the date.
The 1823 overdates have either large E's or small E's in UNITED STATES OF AMERICA on the reverse.

Date	Mintage	G-4	VG-8	F-12	VF-20	XF-40	AU-50	MS-60	MS-65
1809	51,065	140	220	450	700	1,500	2,850	4,500	24,500
1811/9	65,180	110	175	275	650	1,350	2,000	4,000	33,500
1814 small date	421,500	60.00	80.00	145	300	650	1,250	2,000	19,500
1814 large date	Inc. above	43.00	52.00	75.00	135	435	670	1,175	15,000
1814 STATESOF	Inc. above	70.00	88.00	160	335	750	1,400	2,350	24,500
1820 large O	942,587	42.00	50.00	71.00	122	430	665	1,160	12,750
1820 small O	Inc. above	43.00	52.00	75.00	137	450	750	1,425	15,250
1820 STATESOF	Inc. above	43.00	52.00	75.00	135	435	670	1,175	14,500
1821 large date	1,186,512	42.00	50.00	71.00	122	430	665	1,160	12,750
1821 small date	Inc. above	43.00	52.00	75.00	137	450	750	1,425	17,000
1822	100,000	1,000	1,850	3,250	4,500	6,250	7,850	13,500	70,000
1823/22 large E's	440,000	42.00	50.00	71.00	130	450	685	1,210	14,850
1823/22 small E's	Inc. above	42.00	50.00	71.00	130	450	685	1,210	13,600
1824/22	—	50.00	80.00	145	300	650	1,250	2,000	19,500
1825	510,000	39.00	46.00	65.00	112	410	625	1,100	12,850
1827	1,215,000	39.00	46.00	65.00	112	410	625	1,100	12,500
1827/7	Inc. above	250	—	—	750	1,100	1,500	—	—
1828 large date	125,000	70.00	110	175	375	750	1,250	2,850	6,850

Liberty Cap Dime

Draped bust left, flanked by stars, date below obverse
Eagle with arrows in talons, banner above, value below reverse

KM# 48 • **Silver**, 18.5 mm. • **Rev. Legend:** UNITED STATES OF AMERICA **Designer:** John Reich
Notes: The three varieties of 1829 strikes and two varieties of 1830 strikes are distinguished by the size of
"10C." on the reverse. On the 1833 "high 3" variety, the last 3 in the date is higher thatn the first 3. The two
varieties of the 1834 strikes are distinguished by the size of the 4 in the date.

Date	Mintage	G-4	VG-8	F-12	VF-20	XF-40	AU-50	MS-60	MS-65
1828 small date	Inc. above	40.00	48.00	80.00	155	425	625	1,250	12,500
1829 very large 10C.	770,000	60.00	75.00	120	235	550	800	1,500	—
1829 large 10C.	Inc. above	54.00	65.00	110	200	400	600	1,150	9,250
1829 medium 10C.	Inc. above	36.00	42.00	54.00	85.00	255	375	775	6,850
1829 small 10C.	Inc. above	36.00	42.00	56.00	90.00	270	395	795	7,050
1829 curl base 2	Inc. above	7,750	10,500	16,500	27,500	38,500	44,000	—	—
1830 large 10C.	510,000	36.00	42.00	56.00	85.00	255	375	775	6,850
1830 small 10C.	Inc. above	36.00	42.00	54.00	90.00	270	400	825	8,850
1830/29	Inc. above	52.00	75.00	120	220	430	750	1,500	—
1831	771,350	36.00	42.00	54.00	85.00	255	375	775	6,850
1832	522,500	36.00	42.00	54.00	85.00	255	375	775	6,850
1833	485,000	36.00	42.00	54.00	85.00	260	390	790	6,850
1833 last 3 high	Inc. above	36.00	42.00	54.00	85.00	260	390	820	9,350
1834 small 4	635,000	36.00	42.00	54.00	85.00	255	375	775	7,000
1834 large 4	Inc. above	36.00	42.00	54.00	85.00	255	375	775	6,850
1835	1,410,000	36.00	42.00	54.00	85.00	255	375	775	6,850
1836	1,190,000	36.00	42.00	54.00	85.00	255	375	775	6,850
1837	1,042,000	36.00	42.00	56.00	90.00	270	395	795	7,000

Seated Liberty Dime

Seated Liberty, date below obverse
Value within wreath reverse

KM# 61 • 2.6700 g., 0.9000 **Silver**, 0.0773 oz. ASW, 17.9 mm. • **Rev. Legend:** UNITED STATES OF
AMERICA **Designer:** Christian Gobrecht

Date	Mintage	G-4	VG-8	F-12	VF-20	XF-40	AU-50	MS-60	MS-65
1837 flat top	Inc. above	44.00	58.00	110	285	515	700	1,050	6,500
1837 curly top	Inc. above	40.00	52.00	95.00	250	465	750	1,000	6,500
1838O	406,034	47.50	70.00	125	375	725	1,250	3,500	21,000

Seated Liberty Dime

Seated Liberty, stars around top 1/2 of border, date below obverse
Value within wreath reverse

No drapery at elbow

KM# 63.1 • 2.6700 g., 0.9000 **Silver**, 0.0773 oz. ASW, 17.9 mm. • **Obv. Designer:** Christian Gobrecht
Rev. Legend: UNITED STATES OF AMERICA **Notes:** The 1839-O with reverse of 1838-O variety was
struck from rusted dies, it has a bumpy reverse surface.

Date	Mintage	G-4	VG-8	F-12	VF-20	XF-40	AU-50	MS-60	MS-65
1838 small stars	1,992,500	27.00	38.00	55.00	85.00	175	400	625	—
1838 large stars	Inc. above	22.00	25.50	34.50	45.00	135	260	375	8,500
1838 partial drapery	Inc. above	35.00	50.00	85.00	150	225	350	550	—
1839	1,053,115	19.00	23.50	28.50	40.00	125	245	315	3,000

DIME

Date	Mintage	G-4	VG-8	F-12	VF-20	XF-40	AU-50	MS-60	MS-65
1839O	1,323,000	23.50	30.00	47.00	140	150	280	650	6,000
1839O reverse 1838O	Inc. above	165	225	375	550	1,150	—	—	—
1840	1,358,580	19.00	24.50	28.50	40.00	125	245	315	4,000
1840O	1,175,000	23.00	28.50	36.50	60.00	165	325	2,750	6,500

Seated Liberty Dime

Seated Liberty, stars around top 1/2 of border, date below obverse
Value within wreath reverse

Drapery at elbow

KM# 63.2 • 2.6700 g., 0.9000 **Silver**, 0.0773 oz. ASW, 17.9 mm. • **Rev. Legend:** UNITED STATES OF AMERICA **Designer:** Christian Gobrecht **Notes:** Drapery added to Liberty's left elbow

Date	Mintage	G-4	VG-8	F-12	VF-20	XF-40	AU-50	MS-60	MS-65
1840	Inc. above	32.00	50.00	90.00	175	300	400	2,400	—
1841	1,622,500	17.50	20.00	22.50	29.00	50.00	150	310	2,700
1841O	2,007,500	23.50	28.50	33.00	41.50	90.00	250	1,500	5,000
1841O large O	Inc. above	600	900	1,200	2,500	—	—	—	—
1842	1,887,500	16.50	18.00	22.00	28.50	47.00	150	280	2,700
1842O	2,020,000	25.00	30.00	37.50	75.00	225	1,350	2,900	—
1843	1,370,000	16.50	18.00	22.00	28.50	47.00	150	280	3,000
1843/1843	Inc. above	16.00	18.50	22.50	30.00	75.00	200	295	—
1843O	150,000	50.00	75.00	135	300	1,100	3,450	—	—
1844	72,500	200	300	375	600	1,350	1,850	3,000	—
1845	1,755,000	17.50	18.00	22.00	28.50	47.00	150	280	2,600
1845/1845	Inc. above	17.00	20.00	35.00	55.00	100.00	175	—	—
1845O	230,000	32.00	48.00	90.00	225	650	1,350	—	—
1846	31,300	150	250	365	575	1,600	9,000	5,500	—
1847	245,000	19.50	30.00	40.00	70.00	125	350	950	9,000
1848	451,500	19.50	25.00	28.50	52.50	95.00	175	750	7,000
1849	839,000	19.50	21.50	25.00	37.50	55.00	150	500	4,000
1849O	300,000	26.00	33.00	50.00	125	275	750	2,200	—
1850	1,931,500	19.50	21.50	24.50	34.50	50.00	150	280	5,900
1850O	510,000	25.00	32.00	40.00	75.00	135	300	1,250	—
1851	1,026,500	19.50	21.50	24.50	32.50	50.00	150	335	5,000
1851O	400,000	25.00	34.00	42.50	85.00	175	475	1,850	—
1852	1,535,500	16.50	18.00	20.00	26.50	45.00	150	280	2,550
1852O	430,000	28.50	34.00	53.50	145	250	400	1,800	—
1853	95,000	95.00	145	220	300	425	575	750	—

Seated Liberty Dime

Seated Liberty, stars around top 1/2 of border, arrows at date obverse
Value within wreath reverse

KM# 77 • 2.4900 g., 0.9000 **Silver**, 0.0720 oz. ASW • **Rev. Legend:** UNITED STATES OF AMERICA
Designer: Christian Gobrecht

Date	Mintage	G-4	VG-8	F-12	VF-20	XF-40	AU-50	MS-60	MS-65	Prf-65
1853	12,078,010	16.00	18.00	19.00	25.00	44.00	145	260	2,500	31,500
1853O	1,100,000	18.00	20.00	24.00	45.00	125	285	900	—	—
1854	4,470,000	16.00	18.00	19.00	22.00	44.00	145	260	2,500	31,500
1854O	1,770,000	17.00	20.00	22.00	26.00	60.00	160	600	—	—
1855	2,075,000	16.00	18.00	19.00	22.00	48.00	150	350	3,800	31,500

DIME

Seated Liberty Dime

Seated Liberty, stars around top 1/2 of border, date below obverse
Value within wreath reverse

KM# A63.2 • 2.4900 g., 0.9000 **Silver**, 0.0720 oz. ASW • **Rev. Legend:** UNITED STATES OF AMERICA
Designer: Christian Gobrecht

Date	Mintage	G-4	VG-8	F-12	VF-20	XF-40	AU-50	MS-60	MS-65	Prf-65
1856 small date	5,780,000	15.50	17.00	18.50	21.00	42.00	138	250	7,050	38,000
1856 large date	Inc. above	20.00	23.50	27.00	34.00	65.00	175	475	—	—
1856O	1,180,000	19.00	22.00	23.50	32.00	70.00	225	625	5,250	—
1856S	70,000	135	185	360	575	1,150	1,750	—	—	—
1857	5,580,000	15.50	17.00	18.50	21.00	42.00	138	250	2,600	3,400
1857O	1,540,000	16.50	18.00	19.50	26.00	55.00	175	375	2,600	—
1858	1,540,000	15.50	17.00	18.50	21.00	42.00	138	260	2,600	3,400
1858O	290,000	16.50	25.00	36.00	85.00	120	280	800	5,000	—
1858S	60,000	135	200	265	475	1,000	1,650	—	—	—
1859	430,000	16.00	20.00	23.50	38.00	55.00	138	350	—	3,400
1859O	480,000	16.00	20.00	25.00	40.00	80.00	240	550	—	—
1859S	60,000	100.00	175	350	600	1,350	2,750	—	—	—
1860S	140,000	37.50	55.00	70.00	145	325	625	—	—	—

Seated Liberty Dime

UNITED STATES OF AMERICA replaced stars obverse
Value within wreath reverse

KM# 92 • 2.4900 g., 0.9000 **Silver**, 0.0720 oz. ASW • **Obv. Legend** UNITED STATES OF AMERICA **Obv.**
Designer: Christian Gobrecht **Notes:** The 1873 "closed-3" and "open-3" varieties are distinguished by the
amount of space between the upper left and lower left serifs of the 3 in the date.

Date	Mintage	G-4	VG-8	F-12	VF-20	XF-40	AU-50	MS-60	MS-65	Prf-65
1860	607,000	17.50	19.00	29.00	32.00	44.00	115	275	1,350	1,400
1860O	40,000	400	600	900	1,950	3,650	6,500	8,500	—	—
1861	1,884,000	16.50	18.00	20.00	23.00	32.00	85.00	150	1,250	1,400
1861S	172,500	55.00	90.00	150	200	400	650	1,400	—	—
1862	847,550	17.50	19.00	21.00	24.00	45.00	75.00	165	1,250	1,400
1862S	180,750	45.00	60.00	95.00	175	300	675	1,000	—	—
1863	14,460	425	500	650	900	1,050	1,100	1,300	—	1,400
1863S	157,500	45.00	55.00	75.00	145	250	500	1,200	—	—
1864	11,470	425	500	650	800	1,000	1,150	1,200	—	1,400
1864S	230,000	35.00	45.00	75.00	120	225	375	1,200	—	—
1865	10,500	475	575	700	875	1,250	1,200	1,350	—	1,400
1865S	175,000	45.00	55.00	85.00	200	350	775	—	—	—
1866	8,725	500	600	775	950	1,300	1,200	1,800	—	1,750
1866S	135,000	50.00	65.00	100.00	150	275	400	1,900	—	—
1867	6,625	600	700	950	1,100	1,450	1,600	1,800	—	1,750
1867S	140,000	45.00	80.00	135	200	365	675	1,200	—	—
1868	464,000	25.00	30.00	36.00	50.00	90.00	175	300	—	1,400
1868S	260,000	32.00	38.00	50.00	115	175	275	600	—	—
1869	256,600	30.00	35.00	45.00	110	145	250	600	—	1,400
1869S	450,000	25.00	30.00	40.00	55.00	90.00	160	400	—	—
1870	471,000	17.50	22.00	30.00	40.00	50.00	85.00	150	—	1,400
1870S	50,000	300	375	500	650	850	1,050	2,000	—	—
1871	907,710	16.50	18.00	20.00	30.00	45.00	160	300	—	1,400
1871CC	20,100	2,000	3,500	4,500	9,500	12,500	25,000	—	—	—
1871S	320,000	35.00	55.00	85.00	135	195	325	900	—	—
1872	2,396,450	15.00	16.50	18.50	21.50	30.00	85.00	175	—	1,400
1872CC	35,480	650	1,250	1,850	3,000	7,500	—	—	—	—
1872S	190,000	40.00	65.00	85.00	165	250	400	1,100	—	—
1873 closed 3	1,568,600	16.50	18.00	20.00	24.00	32.50	75.00	200	—	1,400
1873 open 3	Inc. above	28.00	35.00	60.00	90.00	140	220	650	—	—
1873CC	12,400	—	—	—	—	—	—	—	—	—

Note: 1873-CC, Heritage Sale, April 1999, MS-64, $632,500.

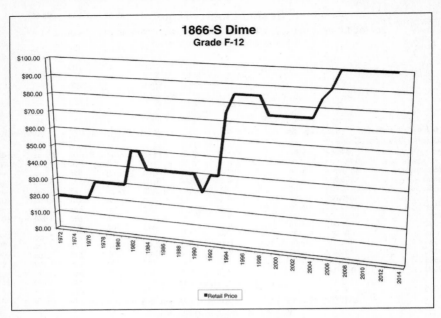

1866-S Dime
Grade F-12

Seated Liberty Dime
Seated Liberty, arrows at date obverse
Value within wreath reverse

KM# 105 • 2.5000 g., 0.9000 **Silver**, 0.0723 oz. ASW • **Obv. Legend** UNITED STATES OF AMERICA
Designer: Christian Gobrecht

Date	Mintage	G-4	VG-8	F-12	VF-20	XF-40	AU-50	MS-60	MS-65	Prf-65
1873	2,378,500	17.00	20.00	27.50	60.00	118	280	500	4,500	4,500
1873CC	18,791	1,350	2,850	4,250	9,500	16,500	—	—	—	—
1873S	455,000	22.00	30.00	40.00	80.00	200	425	1,500	—	—
1874	2,940,700	16.00	19.00	26.00	60.00	118	280	500	4,500	4,500
1874CC	10,817	5,000	7,000	10,500	18,500	34,000	—	—	—	—
1874S	240,000	50.00	60.00	85.00	150	265	450	1,500	—	—

Seated Liberty Dime
Seated Liberty, date below obverse
Value within wreath reverse

KM# A92 • 2.5000 g., 0.9000 **Silver**, 0.0723 oz. ASW • **Obv. Legend** UNITED STATES OF AMERICA
Designer: Christian Gobrecht **Notes:** On the 1876-CC doubled-obverse variety, doubling appears in the
words OF AMERICA in the legend.

Date	Mintage	G-4	VG-8	F-12	VF-20	XF-40	AU-50	MS-60	MS-65	Prf-65
1875	10,350,700	16.00	17.50	19.50	22.50	32.00	80.00	145	2,250	4,600
1875CC mint mark in wreath	4,645,000	29.00	32.00	36.00	52.00	68.00	130	190	2,700	—
1875CC mint mark under wreath	Inc. above	32.00	34.00	40.00	58.00	90.00	165	235	3,000	—

Date	Mintage	G-4	VG-8	F-12	VF-20	XF-40	AU-50	MS-60	MS-65	Prf-65
1875S mint mark in wreath	9,070,000	19.00	23.00	28.00	40.00	65.00	95.00	225	3,100	—
1875S mint mark under wreath	Inc. above	16.00	18.00	20.00	22.50	32.00	80.00	145	1,100	—
1876 Type 1 rev	11,461,150	15.00	17.00	19.00	22.50	30.00	75.00	145	1,100	1,200
1876 Type 2 rev	Inc. above	19.00	25.00	30.00	40.00	60.00	120	200	—	—
1876CC Type 1 rev	8,270,000	29.00	32.00	36.00	50.00	70.00	125	225	—	—
1876CC Type 2 rev	Inc. above	32.00	34.00	48.00	65.00	90.00	175	300	—	—
1876CC doubled die obverse	Inc. above	35.00	40.00	55.00	100.00	185	340	600	—	—
1876S Type 1 rev	10,420,000	15.00	16.50	18.50	22.50	30.00	75.00	145	1,750	—
1876S Type 2 rev	Inc. above	20.00	20.00	24.00	30.00	40.00	90.00	150	—	—
1877 Type 1 rev	7,310,510	15.00	16.50	18.50	22.50	30.00	75.00	145	1,100	1,200
1877 Type 2 rev	Inc. above	18.00	24.00	30.00	40.00	40.00	90.00	150	—	—
1877CC Type 1 rev	7,700,000	35.00	42.00	48.00	70.00	90.00	175	300	1,100	—
1877CC Type 2 rev	Inc. above	29.00	32.00	36.00	52.00	70.00	125	225	—	—
1877S Type 1 rev	2,340,000	—	—	—	—	—	—	—	—	—
1877S Type 2 rev	Inc. above	15.00	16.50	18.50	22.50	30.00	85.00	225	—	—
1878 Type 1 rev	1,678,800	28.00	35.00	50.00	65.00	100.00	175	—	—	—
1878 Type 2 rev	Inc. above	15.00	16.50	18.50	22.50	33.00	75.00	145	1,500	1,200
1878CC Type 1 rev	200,000	100.00	135	175	285	450	600	—	—	—
1878CC Type 2 rev	Inc. above	65.00	90.00	135	225	370	500	900	3,500	—
1879	15,100	275	310	375	500	625	700	800	1,750	1,500
1880	37,335	225	275	330	425	475	585	675	1,750	1,500
1881	24,975	240	300	350	450	500	610	700	2,500	1,600
1882	3,911,100	15.00	16.50	18.50	21.50	30.00	75.00	145	1,100	1,200
1883	7,675,712	15.00	16.50	18.50	21.50	30.00	75.00	145	1,100	1,200
1884	3,366,380	15.00	16.50	18.50	21.50	30.00	75.00	145	1,100	1,200
1884S	564,969	26.00	33.00	42.00	55.00	125	280	650	—	—
1885	2,533,427	15.00	16.50	18.50	21.50	30.00	75.00	145	1,100	1,200
1885S	43,690	475	575	850	1,400	2,400	3,350	5,000	—	—
1886	6,377,570	15.00	16.50	18.50	21.50	30.00	75.00	145	1,100	1,200
1886S	206,524	30.00	45.00	65.00	125	150	175	600	—	—
1887	11,283,939	15.00	16.50	18.50	21.50	30.00	75.00	145	1,100	1,200
1887S	4,454,450	15.00	16.50	18.50	21.50	30.00	75.00	145	1,100	—
1888	5,496,487	15.00	16.50	18.50	21.50	30.00	75.00	145	1,100	1,200
1888S	1,720,000	15.00	16.50	18.50	25.50	35.00	90.00	200	—	—
1889	7,380,711	15.00	16.50	18.50	21.50	30.00	75.00	145	1,100	1,200
1889S	972,678	15.00	18.50	25.00	45.00	70.00	150	475	4,500	—
1890	9,911,541	15.00	16.50	18.50	21.50	30.00	75.00	145	1,100	1,200
1890S	1,423,076	15.00	16.50	24.00	44.00	85.00	145	400	4,900	—
1891	15,310,600	15.00	16.50	18.50	21.50	30.00	75.00	145	1,100	1,200
1891O	4,540,000	16.00	17.50	20.50	25.50	35.00	90.00	175	1,750	—
1891O /horizontal O	Inc. above	65.00	95.00	125	175	225	400	—	—	—
1891S	3,196,116	15.00	17.00	19.00	21.50	30.00	75.00	175	1,650	—
1891S/S	Inc. above	25.00	30.00	40.00	85.00	135	250	—	—	—

Barber Dime

Laureate head right, date at angle below obverse
Value within wreath reverse

KM# 113 • 2.5000 g., 0.9000 **Silver**, 0.0723 oz. ASW, 17.9 mm. • **Obv. Legend** UNITED STATES OF AMERICA **Designer:** Charles E. Barber

Date	Mintage	G-4	VG-8	F-12	VF-20	XF-40	AU-50	MS-60	MS-65	Prf-65
1892	12,121,245	6.75	7.50	16.00	25.00	27.50	63.00	105	710	1,485
1892O	3,841,700	11.00	15.00	32.50	56.00	75.00	96.00	135	1,275	—
1892S	990,710	66.00	115	210	245	285	340	425	3,500	—
1893/2	3,340,792	135	155	175	225	300	325	450	4,850	—
1893	Inc. above	8.25	12.50	20.00	30.00	46.00	80.00	165	1,000	1,485
1893O	1,760,000	31.00	45.00	135	168	190	250	315	2,950	—
1893S	2,491,401	14.00	25.00	39.00	50.00	85.00	155	360	3,750	—
1894	1,330,972	25.00	45.00	122	165	190	235	310	1,150	1,485
1894O	720,000	70.00	105	215	280	425	650	1,550	15,500	—
1894S	24	—	—	—	—	—	—	—1,900,000	—

Note: 1894S, Eliasberg Sale, May 1996, Prf-64, $451,000.

Date	Mintage	G-4	VG-8	F-12	VF-20	XF-40	AU-50	MS-60	MS-65	Prf-65
1895	690,880	85.00	180	355	480	565	650	750	2,650	1,485
1895O	440,000	385	575	900	1,285	2,500	3,650	6,000	19,500	—
1895S	1,120,000	43.50	60.00	135	190	240	320	500	7,500	—
1896	2,000,762	11.50	23.00	56.00	82.00	100.00	120	145	1,450	1,485
1896O	610,000	80.00	155	305	375	465	700	975	9,500	—
1896S	575,056	85.00	160	310	335	385	525	770	4,650	—

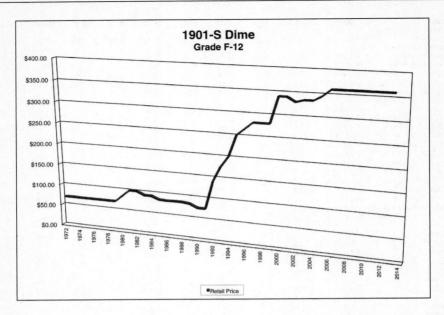

Date	Mintage	G-4	VG-8	F-12	VF-20	XF-40	AU-50	MS-60	MS-65	Prf-65
1897	10,869,264	3.50	3.75	8.00	15.00	31.50	73.00	125	710	1,485
1897O	666,000	69.50	115	290	385	480	600	975	4,450	—
1897S	1,342,844	21.00	45.00	98.00	125	185	265	435	3,950	—
1898	16,320,735	3.50	3.75	7.50	15.00	28.00	68.00	125	710	1,485
1898O	2,130,000	13.50	27.50	88.00	145	200	285	450	3,850	—
1898S	1,702,507	8.50	15.00	33.00	48.00	78.00	160	370	3,750	—
1899	19,580,846	3.50	3.75	7.50	12.00	26.00	68.00	110	710	1,485
1899O	2,650,000	10.00	19.50	72.00	110	150	230	415	4,450	—
1899S	1,867,493	9.00	16.00	34.00	37.00	46.00	105	300	4,350	—
1900	17,600,912	4.00	5.00	7.00	11.00	26.00	63.00	105	740	1,485
1900O	2,010,000	19.50	38.50	115	165	225	355	595	5,750	—
1900S	5,168,270	5.00	6.25	12.50	19.50	31.50	75.00	155	1,850	—
1901	18,860,478	4.00	5.00	6.50	10.00	27.50	63.00	105	755	1,485
1901O	5,620,000	4.00	5.50	16.00	27.50	67.50	175	450	4,350	—
1901S	593,022	80.00	150	360	475	520	675	985	5,350	—
1902	21,380,777	4.00	5.00	6.25	8.00	23.00	63.00	105	755	1,485
1902O	4,500,000	4.00	5.50	15.00	32.50	62.50	145	350	4,500	—
1902S	2,070,000	8.00	21.00	58.00	90.00	135	195	375	3,950	—
1903	19,500,755	4.00	5.00	6.25	8.00	25.00	63.00	105	1,100	1,485
1903O	8,180,000	4.00	5.50	13.50	23.50	50.00	110	250	4,850	—
1903S	613,300	84.00	130	350	490	750	840	1,100	3,150	—
1904	14,601,027	4.00	5.00	7.00	9.75	25.00	63.00	110	1,850	1,485
1904S	800,000	45.00	75.00	165	245	335	465	725	4,500	—
1905	14,552,350	4.25	5.25	6.75	9.75	25.00	63.00	105	735	1,485
1905O	3,400,000	4.25	14.50	36.50	57.50	92.00	155	285	1,650	—
1905O micro O	Inc. above	35.00	50.00	75.00	140	235	375	1,750	12,500	—
1905S	6,855,199	3.50	5.00	9.00	18.50	43.50	96.00	210	775	—
1906	19,958,406	3.25	4.50	4.50	7.25	22.00	58.00	100.00	735	1,485
1906D	4,060,000	3.75	4.85	7.00	15.00	35.00	78.00	175	1,650	—
1906O	2,610,000	5.50	13.00	50.00	78.00	100.00	135	195	1,150	—
1906S	3,136,640	4.25	6.25	12.50	22.50	44.00	110	240	1,350	—
1907	22,220,575	3.25	3.50	4.25	7.25	22.00	58.00	100.00	700	1,485
1907D	4,080,000	3.75	5.00	8.75	17.50	43.50	115	275	3,950	—
1907O	5,058,000	4.25	6.75	33.50	50.00	62.50	110	210	1,350	—
1907S	3,178,470	4.25	5.50	16.00	27.50	67.50	150	410	2,450	—
1908	10,600,545	3.25	3.50	4.25	7.25	22.00	58.00	100.00	700	1,485
1908D	7,490,000	3.25	3.50	5.75	9.75	29.00	63.00	125	990	—
1908O	1,789,000	5.25	11.00	44.50	64.00	92.00	150	290	1,350	—
1908S	3,220,000	4.50	6.25	11.50	22.00	46.00	175	310	2,350	—
1909	10,240,650	3.25	3.50	4.25	7.25	22.00	58.00	100.00	700	1,485
1909D	954,000	7.25	18.50	60.00	100.00	135	225	485	3,150	—
1909O	2,287,000	4.00	7.25	12.50	22.00	50.00	92.50	185	1,650	—
1909S	1,000,000	8.75	19.50	88.00	130	182	315	525	3,150	—
1910	11,520,551	3.25	3.50	4.00	9.75	22.00	58.00	100.00	700	1,485
1910D	3,490,000	3.50	4.00	8.50	19.00	47.50	100.00	210	1,650	—
1910S	1,240,000	5.25	9.00	50.00	74.00	110	195	425	2,450	—

Date	Mintage	G-4	VG-8	F-12	VF-20	XF-40	AU-50	MS-60	MS-65	Prf-65
1911	18,870,543	3.25	3.50	4.00	7.00	22.00	58.00	100.00	700	1,485
1911D	11,209,000	3.25	3.50	4.00	7.00	22.00	58.00	100.00	700	—
1911S	3,520,000	4.00	4.75	8.50	18.50	39.50	105	195	1,050	—
1912	19,350,700	3.25	3.50	4.00	7.00	22.00	58.00	100.00	700	1,485
1912D	11,760,000	3.25	3.50	4.00	7.00	22.00	58.00	100.00	700	—
1912S	3,420,000	3.50	4.50	5.60	12.50	34.00	92.50	155	775	—
1913	19,760,622	3.25	3.50	4.00	7.00	22.00	58.00	100.00	700	1,485
1913S	510,000	35.00	50.00	120	190	240	325	480	1,375	—
1914	17,360,655	3.25	3.50	4.00	7.00	22.00	58.00	100.00	700	1,485
1914D	11,908,000	3.25	3.50	4.00	7.00	22.00	58.00	100.00	700	—
1914S	2,100,000	3.50	4.50	8.00	17.50	39.50	78.00	150	1,250	—
1915	5,620,450	3.25	3.50	4.00	7.00	22.00	58.00	100.00	700	1,485
1915S	960,000	7.50	11.50	34.50	49.50	66.50	135	250	1,550	—
1916	18,490,000	3.25	3.50	4.00	8.00	22.00	58.00	100.00	700	—
1916S	5,820,000	3.50	4.50	5.00	8.50	25.50	63.00	105	795	—

Mercury Dime

Mint mark

1942/41

Full split bands

KM# 140 • 2.5000 g., 0.9000 **Silver**, 0.0723 oz. ASW, 17.8 mm. • **Designer:** Adolph A. Weinman **Notes:** All specimens listed as -65FSB are for fully struck MS-65 coins with fully split and rounded horizontal bands on the fasces.

Date	Mintage	G-4	VG-8	F-12	VF-20	XF-40	MS-60	MS-65	Prf-65	-65FSB
1916	22,180,080	3.80	4.75	6.00	7.00	12.00	29.00	110	—	165
1916D	264,000	850	1,500	2,750	3,950	5,750	13,200	26,500	—	48,500
1916S	10,450,000	4.00	5.00	9.25	15.00	25.00	44.00	210	—	800
1917	55,230,000	3.40	3.80	4.40	5.50	8.00	27.00	155	—	375
1917D	9,402,000	4.30	6.00	12.50	26.00	52.50	120	1,100	—	5,650
1917S	27,330,000	3.40	3.90	4.60	7.50	15.00	60.00	470	—	1,265
1918	26,680,000	3.40	4.60	5.75	12.00	34.00	67.00	420	—	1,325
1918D	22,674,800	3.40	4.50	6.50	13.00	32.00	100.00	600	—	27,500
1918S	19,300,000	3.40	3.90	4.40	11.00	24.00	92.00	660	—	7,450
1919	35,740,000	3.40	3.80	4.40	5.50	12.00	36.00	315	—	685
1919D	9,939,000	3.40	6.00	13.50	31.00	46.00	175	2,100	—	38,500
1919S	8,850,000	3.40	4.50	10.50	20.00	42.00	175	1,250	—	14,350
1920	59,030,000	3.40	3.80	4.40	4.50	8.50	28.00	235	—	540
1920D	19,171,000	3.40	4.50	4.75	9.00	24.00	110	750	—	4,750
1920S	13,820,000	3.40	3.90	7.00	9.00	21.00	110	1,300	—	8,250
1921	1,230,000	60.00	77.00	110	245	540	1,150	2,850	—	4,350
1921D	1,080,000	80.00	120	185	365	650	1,250	2,900	—	5,200
1923	50,130,000	3.40	3.80	4.40	4.50	7.00	28.00	115	—	340
1923S	6,440,000	3.40	4.50	8.25	19.00	75.00	155	1,150	—	7,450
1924	24,010,000	3.40	3.80	4.40	4.50	13.50	40.00	175	—	500
1924D	6,810,000	3.90	4.90	9.00	23.50	63.00	165	1,050	—	1,365
1924S	7,120,000	3.40	3.90	4.40	12.00	59.00	185	1,100	—	16,750
1925	25,610,000	3.40	3.80	4.40	5.50	11.00	28.00	210	—	990
1925D	5,117,000	4.90	5.00	12.75	46.50	135	335	1,750	—	3,500
1925S	5,850,000	3.40	3.90	7.75	18.50	85.00	180	1,400	—	4,650
1926	32,160,000	3.40	3.80	3.90	4.00	5.75	26.00	240	—	525
1926D	6,828,000	3.90	4.00	5.00	12.00	32.00	125	550	—	2,500
1926S	1,520,000	11.75	13.50	29.00	67.50	275	850	3,000	—	6,750
1927	28,080,000	3.40	3.80	4.40	4.50	6.00	26.00	138	—	350
1927D	4,812,000	3.90	5.00	7.75	25.50	88.00	165	1,285	—	8,500
1927S	4,770,000	3.40	3.90	5.50	11.00	30.00	270	1,400	—	7,600
1928	19,480,000	3.40	3.80	4.40	4.50	4.75	28.00	120	—	345
1928D	4,161,000	3.70	4.90	11.50	25.50	62.50	165	875	—	2,750
1928S Large S	7,400,000	4.40	5.40	7.50	12.00	40.00	225	750	—	6,500
1928S Small S	Inc. above	3.40	3.80	4.40	6.50	19.00	140	425	—	2,000

DIME

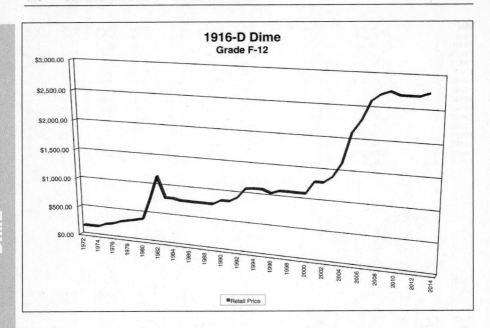

1916-D Dime
Grade F-12

Date	Mintage	G-4	VG-8	F-12	VF-20	XF-40	MS-60	MS-65	Prf-65	-65FSB
1929	25,970,000	3.40	3.80	4.40	4.50	4.50	21.00	60.00	—	175
1929D	5,034,000	3.40	3.90	4.40	8.00	15.00	28.00	75.00	—	225
1929S	4,730,000	3.40	3.80	4.40	5.00	7.50	32.50	90.00	—	560
1929S Doubled Die Obv	Inc. above	5.00	9.00	16.00	25.00	40.00	95.00	275	—	1,150
1930	6,770,000	3.40	3.80	2.40	2.60	7.00	26.00	120	—	575
1930S	1,843,000	3.40	3.90	4.80	6.50	19.00	80.00	200	—	685
1931	3,150,000	3.40	3.80	4.40	4.70	12.50	33.00	135	—	800
1931D	1,260,000	8.50	10.00	15.00	19.50	48.00	100.00	285	—	375
1931 Doubled Die Obv & Rev	Inc. above	—	—	—	50.00	70.00	135	485	—	650
1931S	1,800,000	4.00	5.00	5.50	11.00	23.50	100.00	275	—	2,500
1931S Doubled Die Obv	Inc. above	7.50	10.00	13.00	25.00	35.00	140	425	—	3,850
1934	24,080,000	2.10	2.20	2.30	2.40	6.50	28.00	42.00	—	130
1934D	6,772,000	2.80	2.90	3.90	7.50	14.00	48.00	78.00	—	320
1935	58,830,000	2.10	2.20	2.30	2.40	4.25	10.00	30.00	—	68.00
1935D	10,477,000	2.50	2.60	2.70	6.50	13.00	37.00	84.00	—	500
1935S	15,840,000	2.50	2.60	2.70	3.30	5.50	24.00	37.00	—	360
1936	87,504,130	2.10	2.20	2.30	2.40	2.80	9.00	26.50	1,950	84.00
1936 Doubled Die Obv	Inc. above	—	—	8.00	15.00	25.00	50.00	165	—	—
1936D	16,132,000	2.50	2.60	2.70	4.30	8.50	28.00	53.00	—	290
1936S	9,210,000	—	2.60	2.70	3.00	6.00	20.00	33.00	—	88.00
1937	56,865,756	2.10	2.20	2.30	2.40	3.75	8.00	24.00	800	52.00
1937 Doubled Die Obv	Inc. above	—	—	—	6.00	9.00	20.00	60.00	—	175
1937D	14,146,000	2.50	2.60	2.70	3.00	6.00	22.50	43.00	—	105
1937S	9,740,000	2.50	2.60	2.70	3.00	5.50	22.00	36.00	—	190
1937S Doubled Die Obv	Inc. above	—	—	—	5.00	8.00	28.00	80.00	—	275
1938	22,198,728	2.10	2.20	2.30	2.40	3.75	13.50	25.00	480	80.00
1938D	5,537,000	2.50	2.60	2.70	5.00	6.00	18.50	34.00	—	62.00
1938S	8,090,000	2.50	2.60	2.70	3.00	5.00	21.50	37.00	—	160
1939	67,749,321	2.10	2.20	2.30	2.40	2.80	9.00	25.00	425	170
1939 Doubled Die Obv	Inc. above	—	—	—	4.00	6.00	14.00	35.00	—	450
1939D	24,394,000	2.30	2.40	2.50	2.70	3.50	7.50	26.00	—	49.00
1939S	10,540,000	2.60	2.70	2.80	3.10	6.75	25.00	50.00	—	765
1940	65,361,827	2.10	2.20	2.30	2.40	2.80	6.00	30.00	325	48.00
1940D	21,198,000	2.30	2.40	2.50	2.70	4.20	8.00	32.00	—	48.00
1940S	21,560,000	2.30	2.40	2.50	2.70	4.20	8.50	32.00	—	95.00
1941	175,106,557	2.10	2.20	2.30	2.40	2.80	6.00	30.00	325	46.00
1941 Doubled Die Obv	Inc. above	—	—	—	10.00	16.00	55.00	140	—	295
1941D	45,634,000	2.30	2.40	2.50	2.70	3.20	8.00	23.00	—	46.00
1941D Doubled Die Obv	Inc. above	—	—	—	9.00	14.00	30.00	90.00	—	250
1941S Small S	43,090,000	2.30	2.40	2.50	2.70	3.20	7.00	30.00	—	46.00
1941S Large S	Inc. above	4.00	5.00	8.00	15.00	25.00	110	250	—	425
1941S Doubled Die Rev	Inc. above	4.00	4.50	5.00	5.50	6.00	18.00	50.00	—	85.00
1942	205,432,329	2.10	2.20	2.30	2.40	2.80	6.00	24.00	325	46.00

Date	Mintage	G-4	VG-8	F-12	VF-20	XF-40	MS-60	MS-65	Prf-65	-65FSB
1942/41	Inc. above	525	545	610	640	750	2,700	12,500	—	35,000
1942D	60,740,000	2.30	2.40	2.50	2.70	3.20	8.00	27.50	—	46.00
1942/41D	Inc. above	475	540	600	650	825	2,650	7,000	—	26,500
1942S	49,300,000	2.30	2.40	2.50	2.70	3.20	9.80	24.00	—	145
1943	191,710,000	2.10	2.20	2.30	2.40	2.80	6.00	31.00	—	50.00
1943D	71,949,000	2.30	2.40	2.50	2.70	3.20	7.80	30.00	—	47.00
1943S	60,400,000	2.30	2.40	2.50	2.70	3.20	9.50	26.50	—	66.00
1944	231,410,000	2.10	2.20	2.30	2.40	2.80	6.00	23.00	—	75.00
1944D	62,224,000	2.30	2.40	2.50	2.70	3.20	7.50	23.00	—	46.00
1944S	49,490,000	2.30	2.40	2.50	2.70	3.20	7.50	30.00	—	50.00
1945	159,130,000	2.10	2.20	2.30	2.40	2.80	6.00	23.00	—	97.50
1945D	40,245,000	2.30	2.40	2.50	2.70	3.20	6.50	24.00	—	46.50
1945S	41,920,000	2.30	2.40	2.50	2.70	3.20	7.00	24.00	—	105
1945S micro S	Inc. above	3.30	4.00	6.00	9.00	13.00	28.00	115	—	685

Roosevelt Dime

Mint mark 1946-64

KM# 195 • 2.5000 g., 0.9000 **Silver**, 0.0723 oz. ASW, 17.9 mm. • **Designer:** John R. Sinnock

Date	Mintage	G-4	VG-8	F-12	VF-20	XF-40	AU-50	MS-60	MS-65	Prf-65
1946	225,250,000	—	—	—	—	3.50	3.70	3.90	14.50	—
1946D	61,043,500	—	—	—	—	3.50	3.90	3.90	13.50	—
1946S	27,900,000	—	—	—	—	3.50	4.00	3.90	18.50	—
1947	121,520,000	—	—	—	—	3.50	3.60	3.70	15.00	—
1947D	46,835,000	—	—	—	—	3.50	3.60	4.50	16.00	—
1947S	34,840,000	—	—	—	—	3.50	3.60	3.70	15.00	—
1948	74,950,000	—	—	—	—	3.50	3.60	3.70	14.00	—
1948D	52,841,000	—	—	—	—	3.50	3.60	5.00	15.00	—
1948S	35,520,000	—	—	—	—	3.50	3.60	4.50	17.00	—
1949	30,940,000	—	—	3.30	3.30	3.50	8.50	16.00	65.00	—
1949D	26,034,000	—	—	3.30	3.30	3.50	5.50	9.00	25.00	—
1949S	13,510,000	—	—	3.30	3.50	8.00	15.00	35.00	65.00	—
1950	50,181,500	—	—	—	3.30	3.50	3.50	7.00	32.00	55.00
1950D	46,803,000	—	—	—	—	—	3.60	3.70	15.00	—
1950S	20,440,000	—	—	3.30	3.30	3.75	9.00	23.00	68.00	—
1951	102,937,602	—	—	—	—	—	3.80	3.90	11.00	60.00
1951D	56,529,000	—	—	—	—	—	3.70	3.90	11.00	—
1951S	31,630,000	—	—	—	3.30	3.50	4.00	10.00	34.00	—
1952	99,122,073	—	—	—	—	—	3.60	3.90	22.00	35.00
1952D	122,100,000	—	—	—	—	—	3.60	3.90	11.00	—
1952S	44,419,500	—	—	—	3.30	3.90	4.10	5.50	16.00	—
1953	53,618,920	—	—	—	—	—	3.60	3.90	12.00	42.00
1953D	136,433,000	—	—	—	—	—	3.60	4.20	11.00	—
1953S	39,180,000	—	—	—	—	—	4.00	5.50	12.50	—
1954	114,243,503	—	—	—	—	—	3.60	3.90	10.00	18.00
1954D	106,397,000	—	—	—	—	—	3.60	3.90	10.00	—
1954S	22,860,000	—	—	—	—	—	3.60	4.00	10.00	—
1955	12,828,381	—	—	—	3.30	3.50	3.60	3.90	8.50	17.00
1955D	13,959,000	—	—	—	3.30	3.50	3.60	3.90	8.50	—
1955S	18,510,000	—	—	—	3.30	3.50	3.60	3.90	8.00	—
1956	109,309,384	—	—	—	—	—	3.60	3.90	9.50	8.00
1956D	108,015,100	—	—	—	—	—	3.60	4.00	9.00	—
1957	161,407,952	—	—	—	—	—	3.60	3.90	8.50	5.00
1957D	113,354,330	—	—	—	—	—	3.60	3.90	7.50	—
1958	32,785,652	—	—	—	—	—	3.60	3.90	11.00	6.00
1958D	136,564,600	—	—	—	—	—	3.60	3.90	10.00	—
1959	86,929,291	—	—	—	—	—	3.60	3.90	8.00	4.50
1959D	164,919,790	—	—	—	—	—	3.60	3.90	8.50	—
1960	72,081,602	—	—	—	—	—	3.60	3.20	8.50	4.50
1960D	200,160,400	—	—	—	—	—	3.60	3.90	7.50	—
1961	96,758,244	—	—	—	—	—	3.60	3.90	8.00	4.00
1961D	209,146,550	—	—	—	—	—	3.60	3.90	6.50	—
1962	75,668,019	—	—	—	—	—	3.60	3.90	6.50	4.00
1962D	334,948,380	—	—	—	—	—	3.60	3.90	7.00	—
1963	126,725,645	—	—	—	—	—	3.60	3.90	7.50	3.75
1963D	421,476,530	—	—	—	—	—	3.60	3.90	7.00	—
1964	933,310,762	—	—	—	—	—	3.60	3.90	7.50	3.75
1964D	1,357,517,180	—	—	—	—	—	3.60	3.90	7.00	—

DIME

Roosevelt Dime

Mint mark 1968- present   1982 No mint mark

KM# 195a • 2.2680 g., Copper-Nickel Clad Copper, 17.91 mm. • Designer: John R. Sinnock **Notes:**
The 1979-S and 1981-S Type II proofs have clearer mint marks than the Type I proofs of those years. On the
1982 no-mint-mark variety, the mint mark was inadvertently left off.

Date	Mintage	MS-65	Prf-65	Date	Mintage	MS-65	Prf-65
1965	1,652,140,570	6.00	—	1986P	682,649,693	3.50	—
1965SMS	—	2.00	—	1986D	473,326,970	3.50	—
1966	1,382,734,540	6.50	—	1986S	3,010,497	—	4.00
1966SMS	—	2.25	—	1987P	762,709,481	4.50	—
1967	2,244,007,320	7.00	—	1987D	653,203,402	4.50	—
1967SMS	—	3.50	—	1987S	4,227,728	—	4.00
1968	424,470,000	6.50	—	1988P	1,030,550,000	5.50	—
1968D	480,748,280	6.50	—	1988D	962,385,488	5.50	—
1968S	3,041,506	—	4.00	1988S	3,262,948	—	3.00
1968 no S error	—	—	7,500	1989P	1,298,400,000	4.00	—
1969	145,790,000	7.00	—	1989D	896,535,597	5.00	—
1969D	563,323,870	6.00	—	1989S	3,220,194	—	4.00
1969S	2,934,631	—	4.00	1990P	1,034,340,000	4.50	—
1970	345,570,000	5.50	—	1990D	839,995,824	5.50	—
1970D	754,942,100	5.00	—	1990S	3,299,559	—	4.00
1970S	2,632,810	—	4.00	1991P	927,220,000	5.00	—
1970S No S	—	—	1,300	1991D	601,241,114	5.00	—
1971	162,690,000	10.00	—	1991S	2,867,787	—	3.00
1971D	377,914,240	8.00	—	1992P	593,500,000	4.50	—
1971S	3,220,733	—	4.00	1992D	616,273,932	4.50	—
1972	431,540,000	7.50	—	1992S	2,858,981	—	4.00
1972D	330,290,000	8.50	—	1993P	766,180,000	3.50	—
1972S	3,260,996	—	4.00	1993D	750,110,166	4.50	—
1973	315,670,000	6.00	—	1993S	2,633,439	—	7.00
1973D	455,032,426	5.50	—	1994P	1,189,000,000	4.00	—
1973S	2,760,339	—	4.00	1994D	1,303,268,110	5.50	—
1974	470,248,000	5.50	—	1994S	2,484,594	—	5.00
1974D	571,083,000	4.50	—	1995P	1,125,500,000	4.00	—
1974S	2,612,568	—	4.00	1995D	1,274,890,000	4.50	—
1975	585,673,900	4.50	—	1995S	2,010,384	—	20.00
1975D	313,705,300	4.50	—	1996P	1,421,163,000	3.00	—
1975S	2,845,450	—	4.00	1996D	1,400,300,000	5.00	—
1976	568,760,000	4.50	—	1996W	1,457,949	24.00	—
1976D	695,222,774	4.50	—	1996S	2,085,191	—	3.50
1976S	4,149,730	—	4.00	1997P	991,640,000	4.00	—
1977	796,930,000	4.50	—	1997D	979,810,000	3.00	—
1977D	376,607,228	8.00	—	1997S	1,975,000	—	14.00
1977S	3,251,152	—	4.00	1998P	1,163,000,000	2.75	—
1978	663,980,000	5.00	—	1998D	1,172,250,000	2.75	—
1978D	282,847,540	4.50	—	1998S	2,078,494	—	4.00
1978S	3,127,781	—	4.00	1999P	2,164,000,000	2.75	—
1979	315,440,000	5.50	—	1999D	1,397,750,000	2.75	—
1979D	390,921,184	5.00	—	1999S	2,557,897	—	4.00
1979S type I	3,677,175	—	5.00	2000P	1,842,500,000	2.75	—
1979S type II	Inc. above	—	2.00	2000D	1,818,700,000	2.75	—
1980P	735,170,000	6.00	—	2000S	3,097,440	—	1.00
1980D	719,354,321	5.00	—	2001P	1,369,590,000	2.75	—
1980S	3,554,806	—	4.00	2001D	1,412,800,000	2.75	—
1981P	676,650,000	4.00	—	2001S	2,249,496	—	3.75
1981D	712,284,143	4.00	—	2002P	1,187,500,000	2.75	—
1981S type I	—	—	4.00	2002D	1,379,500,000	3.00	—
1981S type II	—	—	6.50	2002S	2,268,913	—	2.50
1982P	519,475,000	8.50	—	2003P	1,085,500,000	3.00	—
1982 no mint mark	Inc. above	300	—	2003D	986,500,000	3.00	—
1982D	542,713,584	3.20	—	2003S	2,076,165	—	2.60
1982S	3,857,479	—	4.00	2004P	1,328,000,000	3.00	—
1983P	647,025,000	6.00	—	2004D	1,159,500,000	3.00	—
1983D	730,129,224	4.00	—	2004S	1,804,396	—	4.75
1983S	3,279,126	—	4.00	2005P	1,412,000,000	2.75	—
1984P	856,669,000	4.00	—	2005P Satin Finish	—	4.00	—
1984D	704,803,976	3.50	—	2005D	1,423,500,000	2.75	—
1984S	3,065,110	—	4.00	2005D Satin Finish	—	4.00	—
1985P	705,200,962	5.00	—	2005S	—	—	2.60
1985D	587,979,970	3.50	—	2006P	1,381,000,000	2.50	—
1985S	3,362,821	—	4.00	2006P Satin Finish	—	4.00	—

Date	Mintage	MS-65	Prf-65
2006D	1,447,000,000	2.50	—
2006D Satin Finish	—	4.00	—
2006S	—	—	2.50
2007P	—	2.00	—
2007P Satin Finish	—	3.00	—
2007D	—	2.00	—
2007D Satin Finish	—	3.00	—
2007S	—	—	2.50
2008P	—	1.25	—
2008 Satin Finish	—	2.50	—
2008D	—	1.25	—
2008 Satin Finish	—	2.50	—
2008S	—	—	2.50
2009P	—	1.25	—
2009 Satin Finish	—	1.00	—
2009D	—	1.25	—

Date	Mintage	MS-65	Prf-65
2009 Satin Finish	—	1.00	—
2009S	—	—	2.50
2010P	—	4.00	—
2010P Satin Finish	—	2.00	—
2010D	—	4.00	—
2010D Satin Finish	—	2.00	—
2010S	—	—	2.50
2011P	—	4.00	—
2011D	—	4.00	—
2011S	—	—	2.50
2012P	—	4.00	—
2012D	—	4.00	—
2012S	—	—	2.50
2013P	—	4.00	—
2013D	—	4.00	—
2013S	—	—	2.50

Roosevelt Dime

KM# 195b • 2.5000 g., 0.9000 **Silver**, 0.0723 oz. ASW, 17.9 mm. • **Designer:** John R. Sinnock

Date	Mintage	Prf-65
1992S	1,317,579	5.00
1993S	761,353	9.00
1994S	785,329	9.00
1995S	838,953	12.00
1996S	830,021	8.00
1997S	821,678	14.00
1998S	878,792	8.00
1999S	804,565	8.00
2000S	965,921	5.50
2001S	849,600	5.00
2002S	888,826	5.00

Date	Mintage	Prf-65
2003S	1,090,425	4.75
2004S	—	5.00
2005S	—	5.00
2006S	—	4.50
2007S	—	6.00
2008S	—	6.50
2009S	—	6.75
2010S	—	6.75
2011S	—	6.75
2012S	—	6.75
2013S	—	6.75

20 CENTS

**Seated Liberty within circle of stars, date below obverse
Eagle with arrows in talons, value below reverse**

KM# 109 • 5.0000 g., 0.9000 **Silver**, 0.1447 oz. ASW, 22 mm. • **Rev. Legend:** UNITED STATES OF AMERICA **Designer:** William Barber

Date	Mintage	G-4	VG-8	F-12	VF-20	XF-40	AU-50	MS-60	MS-65	Prf-65
1875	39,700	165	210	270	325	415	550	835	5,500	9,500
1875S Clear S	110	120	135	200	235	350	600	5,500	—
1875S	1,155,000	100.00	110	120	175	210	320	500	4,900	—
Note: 1875-S exists as a branch mint proof										
1875S over horizontal S	Inc. above	100.00	110	120	175	210	320	500	4,900	—
Note: Also known as filled S										
1875S as $	Inc. above	—	120	130	150	225	260	375	1,300	—
1875CC	133,290	335	385	475	600	775	1,150	1,650	10,000	—
1876	15,900	185	225	285	350	410	535	800	5,600	9,400
1876CC	10,000	—	—	—	—	—	60,000	—	—	175,000
Note: Only one circulated example known. Eliasberg Sale, April 1997, MS-65, $148,500. Heritage 1999 ANA, MS-63, $86,500.										
1877 proof only	510	—	—	2,700	2,900	3,300	3,500	—	—	10,000
1878 proof only	600	—	—	2,000	2,300	2,400	2,800	—	—	9,500

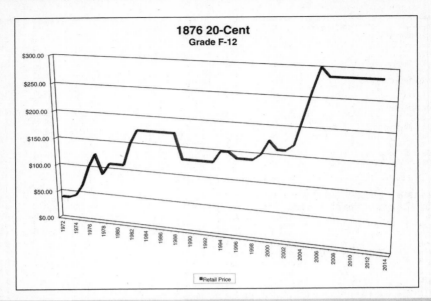

1876 20-Cent
Grade F-12

QUARTER

Draped Bust Quarter
Draped bust right obverse　Small eagle reverse

KM# 25 • 6.7400 g., 0.8920 **Silver**, 0.1933 oz. ASW, 27.5 mm. • **Designer:** Robert Scot

Date	Mintage	G-4	VG-8	F-12	VF-20	XF-40	AU-50	MS-60	MS-65
1796	6,146	12,000	17,500	25,500	36,500	52,500	59,000	83,000	325,000

Draped Bust Quarter
Draped bust right, flanked by stars, date at angle below obverse
Heraldic eagle reverse

KM# 36 • 6.7400 g., 0.8920 **Silver**, 0.1933 oz. ASW, 27.5 mm. • **Obv. Legend** LIBERTY **Rev. Legend:**
UNITED STATES OF AMERICA **Designer:** Robert Scot

Date	Mintage	G-4	VG-8	F-12	VF-20	XF-40	AU-50	MS-60	MS-65
1804	6,738	5,500	6,750	9,250	14,500	32,500	56,500	92,500	425,000
1805	121,394	555	675	1,075	1,750	3,900	6,000	11,500	95,000
1806/5	206,124	585	710	1,150	2,150	4,200	6,300	12,500	100,000
1806	Inc. above	525	635	975	1,650	3,950	5,850	11,000	93,500
1807	220,643	525	635	975	1,650	3,950	5,850	11,500	95,000

1804 Quarter
Grade XF-40

Liberty Cap Quarter
Draped bust left, flanked by stars, date below obverse
Eagle with arrows in talons, banner above, value below reverse

KM# 44 • 6.7400 g., 0.8920 **Silver**, 0.1933 oz. ASW, 27 mm. • **Rev. Legend:** UNITED STATES OF AMERICA **Designer:** John Reich **Notes:** Varieties of the 1819 strikes are distinguished by the size of the 9 in the date. Varieties of the 1820 strikes are distinguished by the size of the 0 in the date. One 1822 variety and one 1828 variety have "25" engraved over "50" in the denomination. The 1827 restrikes were produced privately using dies sold as scrap by the U.S. Mint.

Date	Mintage	G-4	VG-8	F-12	VF-20	XF-40	AU-50	MS-60	MS-65
1815	89,235	120	160	215	435	1,550	2,250	3,800	39,000
1818/15	361,174	120	180	275	750	1,650	2,350	4,200	29,000
1818	Inc. above	110	135	180	400	1,500	2,150	3,750	28,000
1819 small 9	144,000	95.00	135	180	480	1,700	2,275	3,750	35,000
1819 large 9	Inc. above	95.00	145	190	540	1,800	2,350	4,750	42,500
1820 small 0	127,444	95.00	135	180	400	1,500	2,150	3,750	35,000
1820 large 0	Inc. above	95.00	140	185	800	1,950	3,150	5,500	42,500
1821	216,851	115	160	205	425	1,500	2,100	3,550	28,000
1822	64,080	150	240	350	850	1,800	3,000	4,250	38,500
1822 25/50C.	Inc. above	2,750	6,500	4,850	11,000	18,500	25,000	36,500	125,000
1823/22	17,800	35,000	35,000	48,500	70,000	85,000	110,000	150,000	—
Note: 1823/22, Superior, Aug. 1990, Proof, $62,500.									
1824/2	—	950	1,350	2,250	4,000	5,850	9,000	22,500	—
1825/22	168,000	170	275	400	2,250	5,500	8,800	18,500	38,000
1825/23	Inc. above	160	235	375	700	1,700	2,350	3,850	35,000
1825/24	Inc. above	140	225	350	650	1,650	2,250	3,750	32,500
1827 original curl base 2	4,000	—	—	—	70,000	75,000	80,000	—	—
Note: Eliasberg, April 1997, VF-20, $39,600.									
1827 restrike, square base 2	Inc. above	—	—	—	—	—	—	—	—
Note: 1827 restrike, Eliasberg, April 1997, Prf-65, $77,000.									
1828	102,000	95.00	135	180	400	1,400	2,050	3,550	28,000
1828 25/50C.	Inc. above	500	850	1,550	1,900	3,000	4,250	9,500	—

Liberty Cap Quarter

Draped bust left, flanked by stars, date below obverse
Eagle with arrows in talons, value below reverse

KM# 55 • 0.8920 **Silver**, 24.3 mm. • **Rev. Legend:** UNITED STATES OF AMERICA **Designer:** William Kneass **Notes:** Varieties of the 1831 strikes are distinguished by the size of the lettering on the reverse.

Date	Mintage	G-4	VG-8	F-12	VF-20	XF-40	AU-50	MS-60	MS-65
1831 small letter rev.	398,000	68.00	120	145	165	410	800	1,250	25,000
1831 large letter rev.	Inc. above	90.00	135	165	200	455	845	1,295	25,000
1832	320,000	68.00	110	135	150	385	775	1,225	27,000
1833	156,000	80.00	120	145	165	420	810	1,260	22,500
1834	286,000	68.00	110	135	150	385	775	1,225	25,000
1834 0 over O	Inc. above	—	—	—	—	—	—	—	—
1835	1,952,000	68.00	110	135	150	385	825	1,275	22,500
1836	472,000	68.00	110	135	150	385	775	1,225	25,000
1837	252,400	68.00	110	135	150	385	775	1,225	22,500
1838	832,000	68.00	110	135	150	385	775	1,225	25,000

Seated Liberty Quarter

Seated Liberty, stars around top 1/2 of border, date below obverse
Eagle with arrows in talons, value below reverse

KM# 64.1 • 6.6800 g., 0.9000 **Silver**, 0.1933 oz. ASW, 24.3 mm. • **Rev. Legend:** UNITED STATES OF AMERICA **Designer:** Christian Gobrecht

Date	Mintage	G-4	VG-8	F-12	VF-20	XF-40	AU-50	MS-60	MS-65
1838	Inc. above	35.00	42.00	53.00	90.00	365	660	1,265	36,500
1839	491,146	37.00	46.00	58.00	96.00	380	685	1,340	38,000
1840O	425,200	40.00	54.00	75.00	135	425	700	1,650	48,500

Seated Liberty Quarter

Drapery added to Liberty's left elbow, stars around top 1/2 of border obverse
Eagle with arrows in talons, value below reverse

KM# 64.2 • 6.6800 g., 0.9000 **Silver**, 0.1933 oz. ASW, 24.3 mm. • **Rev. Legend:** UNITED STATES OF AMERICA **Designer:** Christian Gobrecht

Date	Mintage	G-4	VG-8	F-12	VF-20	XF-40	AU-50	MS-60	MS-65
1840	188,127	31.00	36.50	55.00	100.00	225	350	800	14,500
1840O	Inc. above	34.00	55.00	90.00	200	350	525	1,100	17,500
1841	120,000	52.00	75.00	95.00	190	275	400	950	11,000
1841O	452,000	30.00	33.50	50.00	85.00	190	325	750	10,000

Date	Mintage	G-4	VG-8	F-12	VF-20	XF-40	AU-50	MS-60	MS-65
1842 small date	88,000	—	—	—	—	—	—	—	—
Note: 1842 small date, Eliasberg, April 1997, Prf-63, $66,000.									
1842 large date	Inc. above	80.00	140	235	325	390	750	1,750	14,500
1842O small date	769,000	500	1,000	1,750	2,650	4,500	9,000	25,000	—
1842O large date	Inc. above	31.00	44.50	55.00	95.00	275	400	1,500	—
1843	645,600	28.00	31.50	34.00	44.00	75.00	185	400	6,750
1843O	968,000	31.00	44.50	55.00	145	400	825	2,200	—
1844	421,200	28.00	31.50	34.00	44.00	95.00	215	450	8,250
1844O	740,000	31.00	44.50	52.00	90.00	200	375	1,250	8,000
1845	922,000	28.00	31.50	34.00	44.00	110	200	485	6,250
1846	510,000	30.00	33.50	36.00	46.00	200	275	510	10,000
1847	734,000	28.00	31.50	34.00	44.00	85.00	200	450	6,650
1847O	368,000	36.00	55.00	100.00	200	475	1,750	3,650	—
1848	146,000	38.00	52.00	90.00	175	275	465	1,075	—
1849	340,000	30.00	33.50	38.00	75.00	145	290	700	13,500
1849O	—	550	800	1,300	2,200	4,000	5,750	10,000	—
1850	190,800	31.00	350	75.00	135	180	360	850	10,500
1850O	412,000	31.00	44.50	85.00	150	245	575	1,550	15,000
1851	160,000	36.00	65.00	125	200	285	400	875	8,000
1851O	88,000	200	350	550	950	1,650	3,000	5,850	—
1852	177,060	42.00	62.00	85.00	185	285	400	750	6,200
1852O	96,000	210	300	600	1,250	2,850	4,250	12,500	—
1853 recut date	44,200	350	450	1,050	1,250	1,750	2,500	3,850	11,000

Seated Liberty Quarter
Seated Liberty, arrows at date obverse   Rays around eagle reverse

KM# 78 • 6.2200 g., 0.9000 **Silver**, 0.1800 oz. ASW, 24.3 mm. • **Rev. Legend:** UNITED STATES OF AMERICA **Designer:** Christian Gobrecht

Date	Mintage	G-4	VG-8	F-12	VF-20	XF-40	AU-50	MS-60	MS-65	Prf-65
1853	15,210,020	27.50	31.00	34.00	44.00	150	320	900	17,000	175,000
1853/4	Inc. above	40.00	70.00	110	200	400	950	1,950	45,000	—
1853O	1,332,000	29.50	45.00	54.00	85.00	300	1,100	2,950	25,000	—

Seated Liberty Quarter
Seated Liberty, arrows at date obverse   Eagle with arrows in talons, value below reverse

KM# 81 • 6.2200 g., 0.9000 **Silver**, 0.1800 oz. ASW, 24.3 mm. • **Rev. Legend:** UNITED STATES OF AMERICA **Designer:** Christian Gobrecht

Date	Mintage	G-4	VG-8	F-12	VF-20	XF-40	AU-50	MS-60	MS-65	Prf-65
1854	12,380,000	27.50	31.00	33.00	42.00	70.00	245	460	8,900	37,500
1854O	1,484,000	29.50	33.00	35.00	60.00	125	265	900	10,000	—
1854O huge O	Inc. above	800	1,400	2,650	4,350	7,500	11,500	—	—	—
1855	2,857,000	27.50	31.00	33.00	42.00	75.00	245	460	8,900	37,500
1855O	176,000	40.00	60.00	115	250	475	1,250	3,000	—	—
1855S	396,400	45.00	60.00	120	225	550	1,350	2,400	29,500	—

QUARTER

Seated Liberty Quarter
Seated Liberty, date below obverse   Eagle with arrows in talons, value below reverse

KM# A64.2 • 6.2200 g., 0.9000 **Silver**, 0.1800 oz. ASW, 24.3 mm. • **Rev. Legend:** UNITED STATES OF AMERICA **Designer:** Christian Gobrecht

Date	Mintage	G-4	VG-8	F-12	VF-20	XF-40	AU-50	MS-60	MS-65	Prf-65
1856	7,264,000	28.00	31.50	34.00	44.00	75.00	185	280	4,150	18,500
1856O	968,000	30.00	33.50	40.00	60.00	110	300	925	9,000	—
1856S	286,000	60.00	120	200	350	1,600	2,250	5,000	—	—
1856S/S	Inc. above	150	275	500	1,250	2,450	3,500	—	—	—
1857	9,644,000	28.00	31.50	34.00	44.00	75.00	185	280	4,000	11,500
1857O	1,180,000	30.00	33.50	36.00	46.00	125	380	1,025	—	—
1857S	82,000	100.00	150	250	400	700	1,350	2,900	—	—
1858	7,368,000	28.00	31.50	34.00	44.00	75.00	185	280	4,000	8,500
1858O	520,000	32.00	35.50	40.00	60.00	135	425	1,450	24,000	—
1858S	121,000	75.00	120	250	800	2,850	3,750	13,500	—	—
1859	1,344,000	30.00	33.50	36.00	46.00	80.00	185	400	7,300	7,000
1859O	260,000	32.00	33.50	50.00	65.00	185	475	1,100	12,500	—
1859S	80,000	150	250	400	900	3,250	9,850	—	—	—
1860	805,400	32.00	35.50	38.00	48.00	85.00	195	444	4,500	5,650
1860O	388,000	32.00	44.00	52.00	70.00	120	360	950	13,000	—
1860S	56,000	450	1,000	2,200	3,700	14,500	24,500	—	—	—
1861	4,854,600	30.00	33.50	36.00	46.00	80.00	195	310	3,600	5,650
1861S	96,000	90.00	160	235	750	3,850	9,000	—	—	—
1862	932,550	32.00	36.50	42.00	52.00	90.00	190	350	4,350	5,650
1862S	67,000	65.00	130	250	475	880	1,650	3,500	—	—
1863	192,060	45.00	57.00	75.00	140	250	360	650	4,850	5,650
1864	94,070	80.00	100.00	130	225	360	440	775	5,000	5,650
1864S	20,000	450	650	1,150	2,150	3,450	4,850	12,500	—	—
1865	59,300	75.00	95.00	150	235	340	450	850	6,950	5,650
1865S	41,000	105	180	255	400	800	1,150	2,800	12,000	—
1866 unique	—	—	—	—	—	—	—	—	—	—

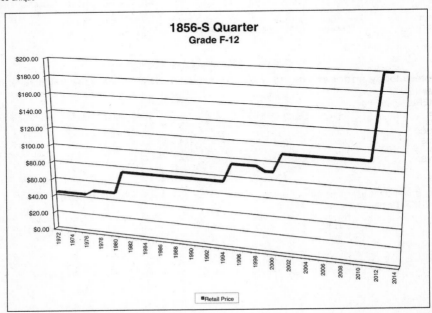

1856-S Quarter
Grade F-12

QUARTER

Seated Liberty Quarter

Seated Liberty, date below obverse   "In God We Trust" above eagle reverse

KM# 98 • 6.2200 g., 0.9000 **Silver**, 0.1800 oz. ASW, 24.3 mm. • **Rev. Legend:** UNITED STATES OF AMERICA **Designer:** Christian Gobrecht **Notes:** The 1873 closed-3 and open-3 varieties are distinguished by the amount of space between the upper left and lower left serifs in the 3.

Date	Mintage	G-4	VG-8	F-12	VF-20	XF-40	AU-50	MS-60	MS-65	Prf-65
1866	17,525	450	600	750	1,050	1,400	1,700	2,350	6,800	2,750
1866S	28,000	295	390	750	1,400	1,950	2,500	3,850	17,500	—
1867	20,625	260	325	500	850	1,325	1,575	1,950	—	2,550
1867S	48,000	250	450	850	1,350	2,850	7,000	14,000	—	—
1868	30,000	150	200	275	385	500	550	900	7,350	2,650
1868S	96,000	90.00	185	325	450	775	1,500	3,300	15,000	—
1869	16,600	300	450	560	700	935	1,050	1,600	7,500	2,650
1869S	76,000	100.00	185	325	475	840	1,400	2,650	15,500	—
1870	87,400	55.00	65.00	130	190	275	400	850	6,500	2,650
1870CC	8,340	8,500	14,500	18,500	24,500	40,000	55,000	75,000	—	—
1871	119,160	30.00	47.50	60.00	125	225	350	725	7,500	2,500
1871CC	10,890	3,250	7,500	10,000	15,500	26,500	40,000	66,500	—	—
1871S	30,900	400	525	850	1,150	1,400	2,600	4,450	11,500	—
1872	182,950	30.00	55.00	75.00	110	185	300	600	7,350	2,550
1872CC	22,850	1,250	1,850	3,250	6,000	13,000	20,000	44,500	—	—
1872S	83,000	850	1,250	2,250	3,350	5,000	6,750	8,750	52,500	—
1873 closed 3	212,600	250	425	550	800	1,650	2,200	7,500	—	2,650
1873 open 3	Inc. above	32.00	4,750	62.00	130	175	250	450	5,850	—
1873CC 6 known	4,000	—	75,000	—	—	100,000	124,000	140,000	—	—

Note: 1873CC, Heritage, April 1999, MS-62, $106,375.

Seated Liberty Quarter

Seated Liberty, arrows at date obverse   "In God We Trust" above eagle reverse

KM# 106 • 6.2500 g., 0.9000 **Silver**, 0.1808 oz. ASW, 24.3 mm. • **Rev. Legend:** UNITED STATES OF AMERICA **Designer:** Christian Gobrecht

Date	Mintage	G-4	VG-8	F-12	VF-20	XF-40	AU-50	MS-60	MS-65	Prf-65
1873	1,271,700	28.00	32.00	37.50	60.00	190	425	725	3,900	8,000
1873CC	12,462	2,950	5,750	10,500	16,500	26,500	47,500	93,500	—	—
1873S	156,000	35.00	45.00	85.00	175	325	525	1,450	20,000	—
1874	471,900	28.00	32.00	37.50	60.00	190	425	725	3,650	8,000
1874S	392,000	33.00	37.00	47.50	110	275	485	900	3,650	—

Seated Liberty Quarter

Seated Liberty, date below obverse   "In God We Trust" above eagle reverse

KM# A98 • 6.2500 g., 0.9000 **Silver**, 0.1808 oz. ASW, 24.3 mm. • **Rev. Legend:** UNITED STATES OF AMERICA **Designer:** Christian Gobrecht **Notes:** The 1876-CC fine-reeding variety has a more finely reeded edge.

QUARTER

Date	Mintage	G-4	VG-8	F-12	VF-20	XF-40	AU-50	MS-60	MS-65	Prf-65
1875	4,293,500	27.50	31.50	33.50	40.00	62.50	150	255	1,775	2,350
1875CC	140,000	95.00	155	270	450	825	1,250	3,650	30,000	—
1875S	680,000	40.00	50.00	67.00	110	175	275	575	3,350	—
1876	17,817,150	27.50	31.50	33.50	40.00	62.50	150	255	1,850	2,350
1876CC Ty1 rev. sm wide CC	4,944,000	60.00	80.00	95.00	125	165	310	550	5,500	—
1876CC Ty1 rev. sm close CC	Inc. above	55.00	73.00	87.50	110	150	275	500	4,250	—
1876CC Ty1 rev. tall CC	Inc. above	50.00	68.00	80.00	100.00	135	235	450	4,000	—
1876CC Ty2 rev. sm CC	Inc. above	50.00	68.00	80.00	100.00	135	235	450	4,150	—
1876CC Ty2 rev tall CC	Inc. above	58.00	75.00	90.00	115	155	300	525	4,400	—
1876S	8,596,000	27.50	31.50	33.50	40.00	62.50	150	255	2,350	—
1877	10,911,710	27.50	31.50	33.50	40.00	62.50	150	255	1,775	2,350
1877CC	4,192,000	50.00	68.00	80.00	100.00	135	235	450	2,600	—
1877S	8,996,000	27.50	31.50	33.50	40.00	62.50	150	255	1,825	—
1877S over horizontal S	Inc. above	34.00	44.00	85.00	175	250	335	650	4,350	—
1878	2,260,800	27.50	31.50	33.50	40.00	62.50	160	275	2,750	2,350
1878CC	996,000	55.00	75.00	90.00	140	150	265	550	3,650	—
1878S	140,000	150	225	345	475	785	1,075	1,950	—	—
1879	14,700	180	235	255	325	375	440	575	1,875	2,350
1880	14,955	155	215	275	325	375	435	575	2,100	2,350
1881	12,975	200	250	280	350	400	455	550	2,250	2,350
1882	16,300	210	260	290	350	400	420	600	2,150	2,350
1883	15,439	200	240	280	365	400	465	585	2,650	2,350
1884	8,875	225	285	475	550	550	600	725	2,150	2,350
1885	14,530	165	225	340	280	400	475	610	2,800	2,350
1886	5,886	325	450	550	750	675	750	925	3,250	2,350
1887	10,710	225	300	385	450	500	550	700	2,500	2,350
1888	10,833	200	275	325	425	475	520	660	2,000	2,350
1888S	1,216,000	27.50	31.50	33.50	40.00	62.50	160	340	4,000	—
1889	12,711	185	275	300	350	425	475	600	1,850	2,350
1890	80,590	60.00	75.00	100.00	135	200	300	440	1,825	2,350
1891	3,920,600	27.50	31.50	33.50	40.00	62.50	150	255	1,775	2,350
1891O	68,000	185	325	500	750	2,350	1,250	4,650	26,500	—
1891S	2,216,000	28.50	32.50	35.50	43.00	68.00	160	295	2,100	—

Barber Quarter

Laureate head right, flanked by stars, date below obverse
Heraldic eagle reverse

KM# 114 • 6.2500 g., 0.9000 **Silver**, 0.1808 oz. ASW, 24.3 mm. • **Obv. Legend** IN GOD WE TRUST **Rev. Legend:** UNITED STATES OF AMERICA **Designer:** Charles E. Barber

Date	Mintage	G-4	VG-8	F-12	VF-20	XF-40	AU-50	MS-60	MS-65	Prf-65
1892	8,237,245	11.00	14.50	30.00	65.00	100.00	167	285	—	2,450
1892 Type 2 Rev	Inc. above	10.50	12.00	26.00	46.00	72.00	122	220	1,350	2,450
1892O	2,640,000	22.00	30.00	55.00	90.00	155	245	400	—	—
1892O Type 2 Rev	Inc. above	15.00	22.50	44.50	64.00	100.00	160	290	1,600	—
1892S	964,079	50.00	75.00	135	200	300	480	650	—	—
1892S Type 2 Rev	Inc. above	35.00	59.00	95.00	145	205	320	475	4,500	—
1893	5,484,838	10.50	12.50	32.00	39.00	70.00	122	220	1,550	2,450
1893O	3,396,000	13.50	22.00	44.00	75.00	165	285	390	—	—
1893O MM far right	Inc. above	12.00	15.50	32.00	60.00	120	175	265	1,850	—
1893S	1,454,535	26.00	47.50	82.00	158	255	390	635	—	—
1893S MM far right	Inc. above	21.00	38.00	69.00	128	195	320	450	6,350	—
1894	3,432,972	11.00	12.00	32.50	48.00	93.50	140	235	1,300	2,450
1894O	2,852,000	12.50	24.00	50.00	95.00	165	285	415	—	—
1894O MM far right	Inc. above	12.50	18.50	44.00	82.00	142	220	325	2,000	—
1894S	2,648,821	12.00	17.00	50.00	95.00	180	265	410	—	—
1894S MM far right	Inc. above	11.00	13.50	37.50	72.00	130	195	295	2,650	—
1895	4,440,880	10.50	13.00	30.00	39.00	78.00	135	235	1,650	2,450
1895O	2,816,000	17.50	27.50	60.00	92.00	175	290	525	—	—
1895O MM far right	Inc. above	12.50	19.50	46.00	77.50	145	230	390	2,650	—
1895S	1,764,681	28.00	40.00	85.00	165	235	375	560	—	—
1895S MM far right	Inc. above	22.00	36.00	77.00	128	190	300	425	3,650	—
1896	3,874,762	10.50	12.00	25.00	41.50	82.00	135	225	1,150	2,450
1896O	1,484,000	62.00	95.00	200	365	625	775	815	6,950	—
1896S	188,039	845	1,625	2,550	4,000	5,350	6,250	9,750	50,000	—
1897	8,140,731	10.50	12.00	21.50	33.50	70.00	122	220	1,450	2,450

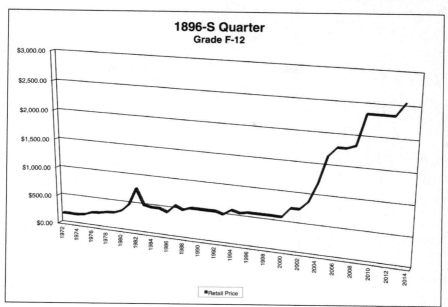

1896-S Quarter
Grade F-12

Date	Mintage	G-4	VG-8	F-12	VF-20	XF-40	AU-50	MS-60	MS-65	Prf-65
1897O	1,414,800	45.00	75.00	200	390	420	625	900	3,550	—
1897S	542,229	130	160	320	475	625	925	1,400	6,850	—
1898	11,100,735	10.50	12.00	22.50	35.00	75.00	122	220	1,150	2,450
1898O	1,868,000	16.00	28.50	75.00	165	300	430	665	8,950	—
1898S	1,020,592	12.50	19.00	50.00	74.00	100.00	220	385	7,950	—
1899	12,624,846	10.50	12.00	22.50	35.00	75.00	120	220	1,150	2,450
1899O	2,644,000	14.00	21.00	38.50	72.00	145	290	425	2,850	—
1899S	708,000	18.00	28.50	70.00	95.00	145	275	410	3,650	—
1900	10,016,912	10.50	12.00	23.50	36.00	71.50	130	220	1,550	2,450
1900O	3,416,000	16.00	29.00	69.50	120	175	345	575	3,750	—
1900S	1,858,585	10.50	15.00	38.00	50.00	80.00	135	375	4,950	—
1901	8,892,813	30.00	36.00	45.00	75.00	88.00	200	215	1,550	2,450
1901O	1,612,000	70.00	112	215	385	625	820	1,065	5,450	—
1901S	72,664	5,200	9,500	18,500	26,500	31,000	38,000	41,500	77,500	—
1902	12,197,744	8.70	9.40	19.50	32.50	65.00	121	220	1,100	2,450
1902O	4,748,000	10.50	16.00	52.50	89.00	150	245	485	4,000	—
1902S	1,524,612	14.50	22.00	55.00	92.00	170	260	525	3,600	—
1903	9,670,064	8.70	9.40	20.00	34.00	70.00	121	220	2,150	2,450
1903O	3,500,000	10.50	13.50	41.50	65.00	130	260	435	4,850	—
1903S	1,036,000	15.50	26.00	46.00	89.00	150	285	435	2,450	—
1904	9,588,813	8.70	9.80	20.00	35.00	69.00	120	230	1,200	2,450
1904O	2,456,000	32.00	45.00	90.00	165	235	460	850	2,650	—
1905	4,968,250	30.00	36.00	50.00	65.00	72.00	125	220	1,500	2,450
1905O	1,230,000	44.00	62.50	125	245	265	365	500	6,850	—
1905S	1,884,000	32.00	42.00	72.00	105	115	220	345	3,650	—
1906	3,656,435	8.70	9.40	18.50	32.50	95.00	121	215	1,100	2,450
1906D	3,280,000	8.70	9.70	25.00	42.50	69.00	155	230	1,675	—
1906O	2,056,000	10.50	13.50	40.00	60.00	112	200	290	1,150	—
1907	7,192,575	8.70	9.80	17.00	32.50	62.00	121	215	1,100	2,450
1907D	2,484,000	8.70	9.50	29.00	50.00	76.00	175	240	2,650	—
1907O	4,560,000	10.50	13.50	19.00	38.50	66.00	135	215	1,950	—
1907S	1,360,000	10.50	18.50	47.50	75.00	135	275	465	5,650	—
1908	4,232,545	8.70	9.40	18.50	33.50	66.00	121	215	1,100	2,450
1908D	5,788,000	8.70	9.40	17.50	35.00	66.00	117	250	1,100	—
1908O	6,244,000	8.70	12.50	17.50	38.50	72.00	120	215	1,100	—
1908S	784,000	18.50	40.00	90.00	165	295	500	775	4,750	—
1909	9,268,650	8.70	9.40	17.50	33.50	63.00	117	215	1,100	2,450
1909D	5,114,000	8.70	9.50	22.00	41.50	85.00	160	215	1,350	—
1909O	712,000	42.00	110	310	485	650	1,000	1,525	8,750	—
1909S	1,348,000	10.50	15.00	37.50	57.50	90.00	200	300	2,250	—
1910	2,244,551	8.70	10.00	30.00	46.00	78.00	140	215	1,100	2,450
1910D	1,500,000	8.90	11.00	47.50	72.00	130	260	375	1,875	—
1911	3,720,543	8.70	9.40	19.50	33.50	72.50	125	225	1,100	2,450
1911D	933,600	31.00	44.00	160	310	460	650	900	5,750	—

QUARTER

QUARTER

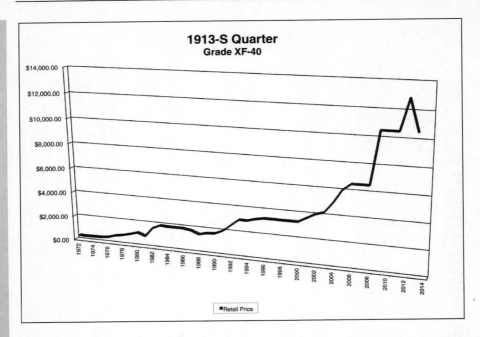

1913-S Quarter
Grade XF-40

Date	Mintage	G-4	VG-8	F-12	VF-20	XF-40	AU-50	MS-60	MS-65	Prf-65
1911S	988,000	10.50	13.00	53.00	92.00	210	300	385	1,425	—
1912	4,400,700	8.70	9.40	17.50	33.50	55.00	117	215	1,100	2,485
1912S	708,000	10.50	13.00	46.00	84.00	130	230	400	1,675	—
1913	484,613	16.00	26.00	75.00	190	390	535	900	4,450	2,485
1913D	1,450,800	12.50	14.50	38.50	58.50	90.00	185	275	1,200	—
1913S	40,000	1,800	2,450	5,350	7,950	10,500	13,250	15,500	31,500	—
1914	6,244,610	8.70	9.40	17.00	32.00	55.00	117	215	1,100	2,550
1914D	3,046,000	8.70	9.40	17.00	28.00	55.00	117	215	1,100	—
1914S	264,000	125	210	425	610	885	1,025	1,400	3,450	—
1915	3,480,450	8.70	9.40	17.00	28.00	61.00	117	215	1,100	2,485
1915D	3,694,000	8.70	9.40	17.00	28.00	61.00	117	215	1,100	—
1915S	704,000	28.00	42.00	63.50	92.00	110	220	285	1,200	—
1916	1,788,000	8.70	9.40	17.00	28.00	55.00	117	215	1,100	—
1916D	6,540,800	8.70	9.40	17.00	28.00	55.00	117	215	1,100	—
1916D/D	Inc. above	12.00	15.00	26.00	50.00	100.00	150	400	—	—

Standing Liberty Quarter
Right breast exposed; Type 1 obverse

Right breast exposed

KM# 141 • 6.2500 g., 0.9000 **Silver**, 0.1808 oz. ASW, 24.3 mm. • **Designer:** Hermon A. MacNeil

Date	Mintage	G-4	VG-8	F-12	VF-20	XF-40	AU-50	MS-60	MS-65	-65FH
1916	52,000	2,850	5,650	6,900	9,000	10,000	12,000	14,500	26,500	37,500
1917	8,792,000	—	50.00	66.50	89.00	118	170	205	685	1,500
1917D	1,509,200	28.00	67.50	98.00	130	200	255	310	900	2,550
1917S	1,952,000	30.00	75.00	110	155	220	280	340	1,150	4,100

Standing Liberty Quarter
Right breast covered; Type 2 obverse
Three stars below eagle reverse

Mint mark   Right breast covered

KM# 145 • 6.2500 g., 0.9000 **Silver**, 0.1808 oz. ASW, 24.3 mm. • **Designer:** Hermon A. MacNeil

Date	Mintage	G-4	VG-8	F-12	VF-20	XF-40	AU-50	MS-60	MS-65	-65FH
1917	13,880,000	25.00	35.00	52.00	72.00	96.50	145	200	610	900
1917D	6,224,400	40.00	45.00	88.00	120	160	210	265	1,550	3,350
1917S	5,522,000	40.00	45.00	63.00	75.00	108	155	215	1,100	3,650
1918	14,240,000	17.00	21.00	29.00	35.00	46.00	80.00	135	560	1,750
1918D	7,380,000	26.00	36.00	66.00	78.00	122	195	250	1,485	4,850
1918S	11,072,000	17.00	21.00	32.00	35.00	48.00	95.00	185	1,250	13,500
1918/17S	Inc. above	1,550	2,250	3,850	5,200	7,500	13,500	17,850	110,000	320,000
1919	11,324,000	33.00	44.00	55.00	74.00	80.00	118	175	600	1,650
1919D	1,944,000	85.00	110	195	345	565	695	825	2,950	28,500
1919S	1,836,000	80.00	105	185	285	510	585	750	4,200	30,000
1920	27,860,000	15.00	18.00	25.00	37.00	51.00	90.00	165	600	2,100
1920D	3,586,400	48.00	65.00	88.00	120	160	215	325	2,250	7,200
1920S	6,380,000	19.00	25.00	30.00	37.00	57.00	110	235	2,650	24,000
1921	1,916,000	165	210	450	635	825	1,125	1,625	3,850	5,500
1923	9,716,000	15.00	18.00	35.00	37.00	55.00	95.00	155	620	4,000
1923S	1,360,000	300	425	675	1,000	1,500	2,000	2,600	5,500	7,500
1924	10,920,000	15.00	18.00	25.00	34.00	45.00	90.00	170	585	1,650
1924D	3,112,000	56.00	68.00	108	135	185	220	300	610	5,750
1924S	2,860,000	27.00	32.00	43.00	57.00	105	220	315	1,850	6,500
1925	12,280,000	8.00	8.60	9.40	16.50	44.00	90.00	150	575	950
1926	11,316,000	8.00	8.20	8.70	12.80	28.00	72.50	135	535	2,250
1926D	1,716,000	6.50	10.00	20.00	40.00	75.00	118	170	485	22,500
1926S	2,700,000	8.30	8.50	11.00	30.00	110	225	325	2,175	28,000
1927	11,912,000	8.00	8.20	8.70	10.50	40.00	97.50	92.00	485	1,300
1927D	976,400	14.00	19.00	32.00	70.00	140	210	250	600	2,650
1927S	396,000	35.00	48.00	110	285	1,000	2,650	4,750	12,000	165,000
1928	6,336,000	8.00	8.20	8.70	11.50	28.00	72.50	92.00	485	2,150
1928D	1,627,600	8.50	8.70	9.60	20.00	42.50	90.00	135	485	5,650
1928S Large S	2,644,000	9.90	10.60	12.00	25.00	65.00	115	200	—	—
1928S Small S	Inc. above	8.30	8.50	9.30	16.50	38.00	75.00	125	525	900
1929	11,140,000	8.00	8.20	8.70	11.50	28.00	72.50	92.00	485	900
1929D	1,358,000	8.50	8.70	9.60	16.00	38.50	79.00	135	485	5,850
1929S	1,764,000	8.30	8.50	9.20	15.00	34.00	75.00	120	485	875
1930	5,632,000	8.00	8.20	8.70	10.50	28.00	72.50	92.00	485	875
1930S	1,556,000	8.30	8.50	8.70	10.50	34.00	70.00	115	485	925

Washington Quarter

Mint mark 1932-64

KM# 164 • 6.2500 g., 0.9000 **Silver**, 0.1808 oz. ASW, 24.3 mm. • **Designer:** John Flanagan

Date	Mintage	G-4	VG-8	F-12	VF-20	XF-40	AU-50	MS-60	MS-65	Prf-65
1932	5,404,000	6.80	6.39	7.00	7.10	9.50	14.50	25.00	300	—
1932D	436,800	115	125	140	180	290	440	1,150	12,500	—
1932S	408,000	125	140	150	165	225	260	465	4,000	—
1934 Medium Motto	31,912,052	6.38	7.40	7.80	8.10	9.50	10.50	26.00	100.00	—
1934 Heavy Motto	Inc. above	6.60	6.70	9.00	12.50	18.00	30.00	50.00	265	—
1934 Light motto	Inc. above	7.20	8.00	10.00	12.00	15.00	26.00	45.00	340	—
1934 Doubled Die Obverse	Inc. above	75.00	100.00	165	200	320	450	850	4,250	—
1934D Medium Motto	3,527,200	6.60	6.70	11.50	18.50	29.00	85.00	235	825	—
1934D Heavy Motto	Inc. above	6.80	7.50	12.50	20.00	34.00	100.00	265	1,350	—
1935	32,484,000	6.60	6.80	7.10	7.60	9.31	10.00	20.00	110	—
1935D	5,780,000	7.30	7.60	8.30	16.50	33.50	125	245	595	—
1935S	5,660,000	6.80	7.00	8.10	9.20	15.50	36.50	95.00	310	—

QUARTER

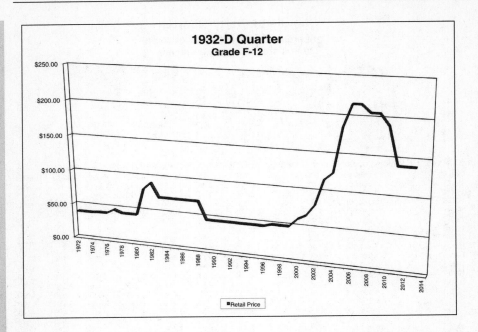

1932-D Quarter
Grade F-12

Date	Mintage	G-4	VG-8	F-12	VF-20	XF-40	AU-50	MS-60	MS-65	Prf-65
1936	41,303,837	6.60	6.80	7.10	7.60	9.10	9.50	26.00	100.00	1,550
1936D	5,374,000	7.30	7.60	10.50	26.00	52.00	255	585	975	—
1936S	3,828,000	7.00	7.30	8.10	8.60	14.50	48.50	108	345	—
1937	19,701,542	6.60	6.80	7.10	9.00	10.00	16.50	22.00	90.00	475
1937 Double Die Obverse	Inc. above	75.00	100.00	235	340	450	850	1,850	11,500	—
1937D	7,189,600	6.80	7.00	8.10	8.40	16.50	38.00	67.50	150	—
1937S	1,652,000	7.30	7.60	8.40	22.00	34.00	95.00	160	430	—
1938	9,480,045	6.80	7.00	8.10	8.50	18.00	49.00	90.00	215	350
1938S	2,832,000	7.30	7.50	7.70	9.75	22.50	55.00	108	215	—
1939	33,548,795	6.60	6.80	7.10	7.60	8.70	7.00	15.50	55.00	250
1939D	7,092,000	6.80	7.00	7.60	9.10	12.00	19.50	42.00	122	—
1939S	2,628,000	7.30	7.60	8.10	12.00	26.00	60.00	105	275	—
1940	35,715,246	6.60	6.80	7.10	7.60	8.60	7.50	17.50	53.50	160
1940D	2,797,600	6.80	7.00	7.10	12.50	26.00	65.00	130	300	—
1940S	8,244,000	6.80	7.00	7.10	7.20	9.00	16.50	28.50	52.00	—
1941	79,047,287	—	—	—	—	6.90	7.10	9.50	36.00	175
1941 Double Die Obv.	Inc. above	—	—	—	20.00	40.00	50.00	65.00	120	—
1941D	16,714,800	—	—	—	7.40	8.50	15.00	33.00	66.00	—
1941S	16,080,000	—	—	—	7.60	7.70	12.50	30.00	65.00	—
1941 Lg S	Inc. above	—	7.60	12.00	20.00	30.00	50.00	100.00	350	—
1942	102,117,123	—	—	—	—	6.70	6.90	8.50	29.00	135
1942D	17,487,200	—	—	—	7.40	8.50	11.00	18.00	38.00	—
1942D Double Die Obv.	Inc. above	—	115	250	440	650	1,350	2,150	5,000	—
1942D Double Die Rev.	Inc. above	—	22.00	40.00	60.00	75.00	150	350	1,850	—
1942S	19,384,000	—	—	—	7.50	11.00	22.50	70.00	135	—
1943	99,700,000	—	—	—	—	6.70	6.90	8.50	39.00	—
1943 Double Die Obv.	Inc. above	—	12.00	20.00	35.00	50.00	90.00	175	450	—
1943D	16,095,600	—	—	—	7.60	8.70	16.50	29.00	50.00	—
1943S	21,700,000	—	—	7.30	7.60	8.00	14.50	27.00	51.50	—
1943S Double Die Obv.	Inc. above	30.00	60.00	80.00	110	150	265	400	1,200	—
1943 Trumpet tail S	Inc. above	10.00	15.00	25.00	40.00	60.00	100.00	175	675	—
1944	104,956,000	—	—	—	—	6.70	6.90	7.60	29.00	—
1944D	14,600,800	—	—	—	7.30	7.40	11.00	19.00	38.50	—
1944S	12,560,000	—	—	—	7.30	7.40	9.50	14.50	31.00	—
1945	74,372,000	—	—	—	—	6.70	6.90	7.60	34.00	—
1945D	12,341,600	—	—	—	7.40	7.50	11.00	18.00	37.00	—
1945S	17,004,001	—	—	—	7.10	7.30	7.50	8.50	32.00	—
1946	53,436,000	—	—	—	—	6.70	6.90	7.60	38.00	—
1946D	9,072,800	—	—	—	7.30	7.90	8.10	9.75	40.00	—
1946S	4,204,000	—	—	—	7.30	7.90	8.10	8.70	34.00	—
1947	22,556,000	—	—	—	—	7.90	8.10	11.50	39.00	—
1947D	15,338,400	—	—	—	7.30	7.80	8.00	11.00	39.00	—
1947S	5,532,000	—	—	—	7.30	7.80	8.00	9.25	28.00	—

Date	Mintage	G-4	VG-8	F-12	VF-20	XF-40	AU-50	MS-60	MS-65	Prf-65
1948	35,196,000	—	—	—	7.30	7.80	8.00	7.70	30.00	—
1948D	16,766,800	—	—	—	7.30	7.90	8.20	13.00	45.00	—
1948S	15,960,000	—	—	—	7.30	7.70	7.90	8.60	40.00	—
1949	9,312,000	—	—	—	7.40	6.50	15.00	36.00	62.00	—
1949D	10,068,400	—	—	—	7.20	7.90	9.50	16.50	48.00	—
1950	24,971,512	—	—	—	—	7.40	9.00	11.00	30.00	65.00
1950D	21,075,600	—	—	—	—	6.90	7.10	7.70	32.00	—
1950D/S	Inc. above	30.00	37.00	45.00	75.00	140	225	350	5,000	—
1950S	10,284,004	—	—	—	—	7.50	7.50	13.50	34.00	—
1950S/D	Inc. above	32.00	44.00	65.00	125	180	285	400	1,250	—
1950S/S	Inc. above	6.00	7.00	8.00	10.00	14.00	18.00	35.00	135	—
1951	43,505,602	—	—	—	—	6.70	6.90	9.00	27.00	60.00
1951D	35,354,800	—	—	—	—	7.00	7.50	8.50	26.00	—
1951S	9,048,000	—	—	6.50	7.50	7.50	11.00	21.00	40.00	—
1952	38,862,073	—	—	—	—	6.70	7.70	10.90	28.00	46.00
1952D	49,795,200	—	—	—	—	6.70	6.90	8.60	32.00	—
1952S	13,707,800	—	—	—	7.40	7.50	11.00	15.00	32.00	—
1953	18,664,920	—	—	—	—	7.40	8.20	10.00	25.00	44.00
1953D	56,112,400	—	—	—	—	6.70	6.90	8.10	22.00	—
1953S	14,016,000	—	—	—	—	6.70	6.90	8.30	28.00	—
1954	54,645,503	—	—	—	—	6.70	6.90	7.60	24.00	18.00
1954D	42,305,500	—	—	—	—	6.70	6.90	7.60	24.00	—
1954S	11,834,722	—	—	—	—	6.70	6.90	8.10	22.00	—
1955	18,558,381	—	—	—	—	6.70	6.90	7.60	26.00	22.00
1955D	3,182,400	—	—	—	—	7.50	7.80	8.60	24.00	—
1956	44,813,384	—	—	—	—	6.70	6.90	7.60	22.00	15.00
1956 Double Bar 5	Inc. above	—	7.40	7.50	7.60	8.00	9.00	20.00	125	—
1956 Type B rev, proof rev die	Inc. above	—	—	8.00	12.00	18.00	25.00	35.00	275	—
1956D	32,334,500	—	—	—	—	6.70	6.90	7.60	15.00	—
1957	47,779,952	—	—	—	—	6.70	6.90	7.60	14.00	12.00
1957 Type B rev, proof rev die	Inc. above	—	—	—	7.40	10.00	20.00	40.00	125	—
1957D	77,924,160	—	—	—	—	6.70	6.90	7.60	16.00	—
1958	7,235,652	—	—	—	—	6.70	6.90	7.60	12.00	12.00
1958 Type B rev, proof rev die	Inc. above	—	—	—	7.40	10.00	16.00	24.00	90.00	—
1958D	78,124,900	—	—	—	—	6.70	6.90	7.60	15.00	—
1959	25,533,291	—	—	—	—	6.70	6.90	7.60	12.00	12.00
1959 Type B rev, proof rev die	Inc. above	—	—	—	7.60	8.00	12.00	18.00	65.00	—
1959D	62,054,232	—	—	—	—	6.70	6.90	7.60	18.00	—
1960	30,855,602	—	—	—	—	6.70	6.90	7.60	14.00	12.00
1960 Type B rev, proof rev die	Inc. above	—	—	—	6.90	10.00	16.00	24.00	90.00	—
1960D	63,000,324	—	—	—	—	6.70	6.90	7.60	14.00	—
1961	40,064,244	—	—	—	—	6.70	6.90	7.60	15.00	12.00
1961 Type B rev, proof rev die	Inc. above	—	—	—	7.60	10.00	14.00	20.00	200	—
1961D	83,656,928	—	—	—	—	6.70	6.90	7.60	20.00	—
1962	39,374,019	—	—	—	—	6.70	6.90	7.60	15.00	12.00
1962 Type B rev, proof rev die	Inc. above	—	—	—	8.00	12.00	15.00	30.00	175	—
1962D	127,554,756	—	—	—	—	6.70	6.90	7.60	22.00	—
1963	77,391,645	—	—	—	—	6.70	6.90	7.60	12.00	12.00
1963 Type B rev, proof rev die	Inc. above	—	—	—	7.60	7.70	8.00	15.00	50.00	—
1963D	135,288,184	—	—	—	—	6.70	6.90	7.60	15.00	—
1964	564,341,347	—	—	—	—	6.70	6.90	7.60	12.00	12.00
1964 Type B rev, proof rev die	Inc. above	—	—	—	7.60	9.00	10.00	18.00	75.00	—
1964 SMS	Inc. above	—	—	—	—	—	250	750	1,400	—
1964D	704,135,528	—	—	—	—	6.70	6.90	7.60	12.00	—
1964D Type C rev, clad rev die	Inc. above	—	—	—	40.00	55.00	75.00	125	450	—

KM# 164a • 5.6700 g., **Copper-Nickel Clad Copper**, 24.3 mm. • **Designer:** John Flanagan

Date	Mintage	MS-65	Prf-65
1965	1,819,717,540	12.00	—
1965 SMS	2,360,000	9.00	—
1966	821,101,500	7.50	—
1966 SMS	2,261,583	9.00	—
1967	1,524,031,848	12.00	—
1967 SMS	1,863,344	9.00	—
1968	220,731,500	15.00	—
1968D	101,534,000	8.00	—
1968S	3,041,506	—	2.00
1969	176,212,000	14.00	—
1969D	114,372,000	10.00	—
1969S	2,934,631	—	2.25
1970	136,420,000	12.00	—
1970D	417,341,364	6.00	—
1970S	2,632,810	—	2.00
1971	109,284,000	15.00	—
1971D	258,634,428	6.50	—

Date	Mintage	MS-65	Prf-65
1971S	3,220,733	—	2.00
1972	215,048,000	7.50	—
1972D	311,067,732	10.00	—
1972S	3,260,996	—	2.00
1973	346,924,000	10.00	—
1973D	232,977,400	11.00	—
1973S	2,760,339	—	1.75
1974	801,456,000	8.00	—
1974D	353,160,300	15.00	—
1974S	2,612,568	—	2.10
1975 none minted	—	—	—
1975D none minted	—	—	—
1975S none minted	—	—	—

QUARTER

Bicentennial design, drummer boy reverse

Mint mark
1968-present

KM# 204 • 5.6700 g., **Copper-Nickel Clad Copper**, 24.3 mm. • **Rev. Designer:** Jack L. Ahr

Date	Mintage	MS-60	MS-65	Prf-65
1976	809,784,016	.50	8.00	—
1976D	860,118,839	.50	10.00	—
1976S	4,149,730	—	—	3.25

KM# 204a • 5.7500 g., **Silver Clad**, 24.3 mm. • **Rev. Designer:** Jack L. Ahr

Date	Mintage	MS-60	MS-65	Prf-65
1976S	4,908,319	1.50	6.00	—
1976S	3,998,621	1.50	6.00	4.50

Regular design resumed reverse

KM# A164a • 5.6700 g., **Copper-Nickel Clad Copper**, 24.3 mm. • **Edge Desc:** Reeded **Notes:** KM#164 design and composition resumed. The 1979-S and 1981 Type II proofs have clearer mint marks than the Type I proofs for those years.

Date	Mintage	MS-65	Prf-65
1977	468,556,000	10.00	—
1977D	256,524,978	8.00	—
1977S	3,251,152	—	2.75
1978	521,452,000	9.00	—
1978D	287,373,152	11.00	—
1978S	3,127,781	—	2.75
1979	515,708,000	10.00	—
1979D	489,789,780	9.00	—
1979S T-I	3,677,175	—	2.50
1979S T-II	Inc. above	—	4.00
1980P	635,832,000	8.00	—
1980D	518,327,487	8.50	—
1980S	3,554,806	—	2.75
1981P	601,716,000	8.00	—
1981D	575,722,833	6.50	—
1981S T-I	4,063,083	—	2.75
1981S T-II	Inc. above	—	7.50
1982P	500,931,000	28.00	—
1982D	480,042,788	15.00	—
1982S	3,857,479	—	2.75
1983P	673,535,000	45.00	—
1983D	617,806,446	30.00	—
1983S	3,279,126	—	3.00
1984P	676,545,000	14.50	—

Date	Mintage	MS-65	Prf-65
1984D	546,483,064	12.50	—
1984S	3,065,110	—	2.75
1985P	775,818,962	12.50	—
1985D	519,962,888	10.00	—
1985S	3,362,821	5.00	2.75
1986P	551,199,333	12.00	—
1986D	504,298,660	15.00	—
1986S	3,010,497	—	3.00
1987P	582,499,481	10.50	—
1987D	655,594,696	10.00	—
1987S	4,227,728	—	2.75
1988P	562,052,000	16.00	—
1988D	596,810,688	14.00	—
1988S	3,262,948	—	2.75
1989P	512,868,000	18.00	—
1989D	896,535,597	7.50	—
1989S	3,220,194	—	2.75
1990P	613,792,000	17.00	—
1990D	927,638,181	7.00	—
1990S	3,299,559	—	4.50
1991P	570,968,000	15.00	—
1991D	630,966,693	12.00	—
1991S	2,867,787	—	2.75
1992P	384,764,000	20.00	—
1992D	389,777,107	27.50	—
1992S	2,858,981	—	2.75
1993P	639,276,000	11.00	—
1993D	645,476,128	14.00	—
1993S	2,633,439	—	2.75
1994P	825,600,000	18.00	—
1994D	880,034,110	10.00	—
1994S	2,484,594	—	2.75
1995P	1,004,336,000	12.00	—
1995D	1,103,216,000	10.00	—
1995S	2,117,496	—	8.50
1996P	925,040,000	12.00	—
1996D	906,868,000	14.00	—
1996S	1,750,244	—	4.50
1997P	595,740,000	12.50	—
1997D	599,680,000	16.00	—
1997S	2,055,000	—	8.50
1998P	896,268,000	13.50	—
1998D	821,000,000	13.50	—
1998S	2,086,507	—	8.50

KM# A164b • 6.2500 g., 0.9000 **Silver**, 0.1808 oz. ASW, 24.3 mm. •

Date	Mintage	Prf-65
1992S	1,317,579	6.80
1993S	761,353	6.80
1994S	785,329	8.00
1995S	838,953	8.00
1996S	775,021	8.00
1997S	741,678	8.00
1998S	878,792	6.80

50 State Quarters

Connecticut

KM# 297 • 5.6700 g., **Copper-Nickel Clad Copper**, 24.3 mm. •

Date	Mintage	MS-63	MS-65	Prf-65
1999P	688,744,000	.80	6.00	—
1999D	657,480,000	.80	5.00	—
1999S	3,713,359	—	—	3.50

KM# 297a • 6.2500 g., 0.9000 **Silver**, 0.1808 oz. ASW, 24.3 mm. •

Date	Mintage	MS-63	MS-65	Prf-65
1999S	804,565	—	—	20.00

Delaware

KM# 293 • 5.6700 g., **Copper-Nickel Clad Copper**, 24.3 mm. •

Date	Mintage	MS-63	MS-65	Prf-65
1999P	373,400,000	1.00	5.00	—
1999D	401,424,000	1.00	7.00	—
1999S	3,713,359	—	—	3.50

KM# 293a • 6.2500 g., 0.9000 **Silver**, 0.1808 oz. ASW, 24.3 mm. •

Date	Mintage	MS-63	MS-65	Prf-65
1999S	804,565	—	—	20.00

Georgia

KM# 296 • 5.6700 g., **Copper-Nickel Clad Copper**, 24.3 mm. •

Date	Mintage	MS-63	MS-65	Prf-65
1999P	451,188,000	1.00	4.50	—
1999D	488,744,000	1.00	4.50	—
1999S	3,713,359	—	—	3.50

KM# 296a • 6.2500 g., 0.9000 **Silver**, 0.1808 oz. ASW, 24.3 mm. •

Date	Mintage	MS-63	MS-65	Prf-65
1999S	804,565	—	—	20.00

New Jersey

KM# 295 • 5.6700 g., **Copper-Nickel Clad Copper**, 24.3 mm. •

Date	Mintage	MS-63	MS-65	Prf-65
1999P	363,200,000	1.00	5.00	—
1999D	299,028,000	1.00	4.00	—
1999S	3,713,359	—	—	3.50

KM# 295a • 6.2500 g., 0.9000 **Silver**, 0.1808 oz. ASW, 24.3 mm. •

Date	Mintage	MS-63	MS-65	Prf-65
1999S	804,565	—	—	20.00

Pennsylvania

KM# 294 • 5.6700 g., **Copper-Nickel Clad Copper**, 24.3 mm. •

Date	Mintage	MS-63	MS-65	Prf-65
1999P	349,000,000	1.00	5.00	—
1999D	358,332,000	1.00	4.00	—
1999S	3,713,359	—	—	3.50

KM# 294a • 6.2500 g., 0.9000 **Silver**, 0.1808 oz. ASW, 24.3 mm. •

Date	Mintage	MS-63	MS-65	Prf-65
1999S	804,565	—	—	20.00

Maryland

KM# 306 • 5.6700 g., **Copper-Nickel Clad Copper**, 24.3 mm. •

Date	Mintage	MS-63	MS-65	Prf-65
2000P	678,200,000	.80	6.00	—
2000D	556,526,000	.80	6.00	—
2000S	4,078,747	—	—	3.00

KM# 306a • 6.2500 g., 0.9000 **Silver**, 0.1808 oz. ASW, 24.3 mm. •

Date	Mintage	MS-63	MS-65	Prf-65
2000S	965,921	—	—	9.00

QUARTER

Massachusetts

KM# 305 • 5.6700 g., **Copper-Nickel Clad Copper**, 24.3 mm. •

Date	Mintage	MS-63	MS-65	Prf-65
2000P	629,800,000	.80	7.00	—
2000D	535,184,000	.80	8.00	—
2000S	4,078,747	—	—	3.00

KM# 305a • 6.2500 g., 0.9000 **Silver**, 0.1808 oz. ASW, 24.3 mm. •

Date	Mintage	MS-63	MS-65	Prf-65
2000S	965,921	—	—	9.00

New Hampshire

KM# 308 • 5.6700 g., **Copper-Nickel Clad Copper**, 24.3 mm. •

Date	Mintage	MS-63	MS-65	Prf-65
2000P	673,040,000	.80	8.00	—
2000D	495,976,000	.80	9.00	—
2000S	4,078,747	—	—	3.00

KM# 308a • 6.2500 g., 0.9000 **Silver**, 0.1808 oz. ASW, 24.3 mm. •

Date	Mintage	MS-63	MS-65	Prf-65
2000S	965,921	—	—	9.00

South Carolina

KM# 307 • 5.6700 g., **Copper-Nickel Clad Copper**, 24.3 mm. •

Date	Mintage	MS-63	MS-65	Prf-65
2000P	742,756,000	.80	6.00	—
2000D	566,208,000	.80	9.00	—
2000S	4,078,747	—	—	3.00

KM# 307a • 6.2500 g., 0.9000 **Silver**, 0.1808 oz. ASW, 24.3 mm. •

Date	Mintage	MS-63	MS-65	Prf-65
2000S	965,921	—	—	9.00

Virginia

KM# 309 • 5.6700 g., **Copper-Nickel Clad Copper**, 24.3 mm. •

Date	Mintage	MS-63	MS-65	Prf-65
2000P	943,000,000	.80	6.50	—
2000D	651,616,000	.80	6.50	—
2000S	4,078,747	—	—	3.00

KM# 309a • 6.2500 g., 0.9000 **Silver**, 0.1808 oz. ASW, 24.3 mm. •

Date	Mintage	MS-63	MS-65	Prf-65
2000S	965,921	—	—	9.50

Kentucky

KM# 322 • 5.6700 g., **Copper-Nickel Clad Copper**, 24.3 mm. •

Date	Mintage	MS-63	MS-65	Prf-65
2001P	353,000,000	1.00	6.50	—
2001D	370,564,000	1.00	7.00	—
2001S	3,094,140	—	—	4.00

KM# 322a • 6.2500 g., 0.9000 **Silver**, 0.1808 oz. ASW, 24.3 mm. •

Date	Mintage	MS-63	MS-65	Prf-65
2001S	889,697	—	—	9.50

New York

KM# 318 • 5.6700 g., **Copper-Nickel Clad Copper**, 24.3 mm. •

Date	Mintage	MS-63	MS-65	Prf-65
2001P	655,400,000	.80	5.50	—
2001D	619,640,000	.80	5.50	—
2001S	3,094,140	—	—	4.00

KM# 318a • 6.2500 g., 0.9000 **Silver**, 0.1808 oz. ASW, 24.3 mm. •

Date	Mintage	MS-63	MS-65	Prf-65
2001S	889,697	—	—	9.50

QUARTER

North Carolina

KM# 319 • 5.6700 g., **Copper-Nickel Clad Copper**, 24.3 mm. •

Date	Mintage	MS-63	MS-65	Prf-65
2001P	627,600,000	1.00	5.50	—
2001D	427,876,000	1.00	6.50	—
2001S	3,094,140	—	—	4.00

KM# 319a • 6.2500 g., 0.9000 **Silver**, 0.1808 oz. ASW, 24.3 mm. •

Date	Mintage	MS-63	MS-65	Prf-65
2001S	889,697	—	—	9.50

Indiana

KM# 334 • 5.6700 g., **Copper-Nickel Clad Copper**, 24.3 mm. •

Date	Mintage	MS-63	MS-65	Prf-65
2002P	362,600,000	.80	5.00	—
2002D	327,200,000	.80	5.00	—
2002S	3,084,245	—	—	2.30

KM# 334a • 6.2500 g., 0.9000 **Silver**, 0.1808 oz. ASW, 24.3 mm. •

Date	Mintage	MS-63	MS-65	Prf-65
2002S	892,229	—	—	8.50

Rhode Island

KM# 320 • 5.6700 g., **Copper-Nickel Clad Copper**, 24.3 mm. •

Date	Mintage	MS-63	MS-65	Prf-65
2001P	423,000,000	.80	5.50	—
2001D	447,100,000	.80	6.00	—
2001S	3,094,140	—	—	4.00

KM# 320a • 6.2500 g., 0.9000 **Silver**, 0.1808 oz. ASW, 24.3 mm. •

Date	Mintage	MS-63	MS-65	Prf-65
2001S	889,697	—	—	9.50

Louisiana

KM# 333 • 5.6700 g., **Copper-Nickel Clad Copper**, 24.3 mm. •

Date	Mintage	MS-63	MS-65	Prf-65
2002P	362,000,000	.80	5.50	—
2002D	402,204,000	.80	6.00	—
2002S	3,084,245	—	—	2.30

KM# 333a • 6.2500 g., 0.9000 **Silver**, 0.1808 oz. ASW, 24.3 mm. •

Date	Mintage	MS-63	MS-65	Prf-65
2002S	892,229	—	—	8.50

Vermont

KM# 321 • 5.6700 g., **Copper-Nickel Clad Copper**, 24.3 mm. •

Date	Mintage	MS-63	MS-65	Prf-65
2001P	423,400,000	.80	6.50	—
2001D	459,404,000	.80	6.50	—
2001S	3,094,140	—	—	4.00

KM# 321a • 6.2500 g., 0.9000 **Silver**, 0.1808 oz. ASW, 24.3 mm. •

Date	Mintage	MS-63	MS-65	Prf-65
2001S	889,697	—	—	9.50

Mississippi

KM# 335 • 5.6700 g., **Copper-Nickel Clad Copper**, 24.3 mm. •

Date	Mintage	MS-63	MS-65	Prf-65
2002P	290,000,000	.80	5.00	—
2002D	289,600,000	.80	5.00	—
2002S	3,084,245	—	—	2.30

KM# 335a • 6.2500 g., 0.9000 **Silver**, 0.1808 oz. ASW, 24.3 mm. •

Date	Mintage	MS-63	MS-65	Prf-65
2002S	892,229	—	—	8.50

QUARTER

Ohio

KM# 332 • 5.6700 g., **Copper-Nickel Clad Copper**, 24.3 mm. •

Date	Mintage	MS-63	MS-65	Prf-65
2002P	217,200,000	.80	5.50	—
2002D	414,832,000	.80	5.50	—
2002S	3,084,245	—	—	2.30

KM# 332a • 6.2500 g., 0.9000 **Silver**, 0.1808 oz. ASW, 24.3 mm. •

Date	Mintage	MS-63	MS-65	Prf-65
2002S	892,229	—	—	8.50

Tennessee

KM# 331 • 5.6700 g., **Copper-Nickel Clad Copper**, 24.3 mm. •

Date	Mintage	MS-63	MS-65	Prf-65
2002P	361,600,000	1.40	6.50	—
2002D	286,468,000	1.40	7.00	—
2002S	3,084,245	—	—	2.30

KM# 331a • 6.2500 g., 0.9000 **Silver**, 0.1808 oz. ASW, 24.3 mm. •

Date	Mintage	MS-63	MS-65	Prf-65
2002S	892,229	—	—	8.50

Alabama

KM# 344 • 5.6700 g., **Copper-Nickel Clad Copper**, 24.3 mm. •

Date	Mintage	MS-63	MS-65	Prf-65
2003P	225,000,000	.65	5.00	—
2003D	232,400,000	.65	5.00	—
2003S	3,408,516	—	—	2.30

KM# 344a • 6.2500 g., 0.9000 **Silver**, 0.1808 oz. ASW, 24.3 mm. •

Date	Mintage	MS-63	MS-65	Prf-65
2003S	1,257,555	—	—	8.50

Arkansas

KM# 347 • 5.6700 g., **Copper-Nickel Clad Copper**, 24.3 mm. •

Date	Mintage	MS-63	MS-65	Prf-65
2003P	228,000,000	.65	5.00	—
2003D	229,800,000	.65	5.00	—
2003S	3,408,516	—	—	2.30

KM# 347a • 6.2500 g., 0.9000 **Silver**, 0.1808 oz. ASW, 24.3 mm. •

Date	Mintage	MS-63	MS-65	Prf-65
2003S	1,257,555	—	—	8.50

Illinois

KM# 343 • 5.6700 g., **Copper-Nickel Clad Copper**, 24.3 mm. •

Date	Mintage	MS-63	MS-65	Prf-65
2003P	225,800,000	1.10	5.00	—
2003D	237,400,000	1.10	5.00	—
2003S	3,408,516	—	—	2.30

KM# 343a • 6.2500 g., 0.9000 **Silver**, 0.1808 oz. ASW, 24.3 mm. •

Date	Mintage	MS-63	MS-65	Prf-65
2003S	1,257,555	—	—	8.50

Maine

KM# 345 • 5.6700 g., **Copper-Nickel Clad Copper**, 24.3 mm. •

Date	Mintage	MS-63	MS-65	Prf-65
2003P	217,400,000	.65	5.00	—
2003D	213,400,000	.65	5.00	—
2003S	3,408,516	—	—	2.30

KM# 345a • 6.2500 g., 0.9000 **Silver**, 0.1808 oz. ASW, 24.3 mm. •

Date	Mintage	MS-63	MS-65	Prf-65
2003S	1,257,555	—	—	8.50

Missouri

KM# 346 • 5.6700 g., **Copper-Nickel Clad Copper**, 24.3 mm. •

Date	Mintage	MS-63	MS-65	Prf-65
2003P	225,000,000	.65	5.00	—
2003D	228,200,000	.65	5.00	—
2003S	3,408,516	—	—	2.30

KM# 346a • 6.2500 g., 0.9000 **Silver**, 0.1808 oz. ASW, 24.3 mm. •

Date	Mintage	MS-63	MS-65	Prf-65
2003S	1,257,555	—	—	8.50

Florida

KM# 356 • 5.6700 g., **Copper-Nickel Clad Copper**, 24.3 mm. •

Date	Mintage	MS-63	MS-65	Prf-65
2004P	240,200,000	.65	5.00	—
2004D	241,600,000	.65	5.00	—
2004S	2,740,684	—	—	2.30

KM# 356a • 6.2500 g., 0.9000 **Silver**, 0.1808 oz. ASW, 24.3 mm. •

Date	Mintage	MS-63	MS-65	Prf-65
2004S	1,775,370	—	—	8.50

Iowa

KM# 358 • 5.6700 g., **Copper-Nickel Clad Copper**, 24.3 mm. •

Date	Mintage	MS-63	MS-65	Prf-65
2004P	213,800,000	.65	5.00	—
2004D	251,800,000	.65	5.00	—
2004S	2,740,684	—	—	2.30

KM# 358a • 6.2500 g., 0.9000 **Silver**, 0.1808 oz. ASW, 24.3 mm. •

Date	Mintage	MS-63	MS-65	Prf-65
2004S	—	—	—	8.50

Michigan

KM# 355 • 5.6700 g., **Copper-Nickel Clad Copper**, 24.3 mm. •

Date	Mintage	MS-63	MS-65	Prf-65
2004P	233,800,000	.65	5.00	—
2004D	225,800,000	.65	5.00	—
2004S	2,740,684	—	—	2.30

KM# 355a • 6.2500 g., 0.9000 **Silver**, 0.1808 oz. ASW, 24.3 mm. •

Date	Mintage	MS-63	MS-65	Prf-65
2004S	1,775,370	—	—	8.50

Texas

KM# 357 • 5.6700 g., **Copper-Nickel Clad Copper**, 24.3 mm. •

Date	Mintage	MS-63	MS-65	Prf-65
2004P	278,800,000	.65	5.00	—
2004D	263,000,000	.65	5.00	—
2004S	2,740,684	—	—	2.30

KM# 357a • 6.2500 g., 0.9000 **Silver**, 0.1808 oz. ASW, 24.3 mm. •

Date	Mintage	MS-63	MS-65	Prf-65
2004S	1,775,370	—	—	8.50

Wisconsin

KM# 359 • 5.6700 g., **Copper-Nickel Clad Copper**, 24.3 mm. •

Date	Mintage	MS-63	MS-65	Prf-65
2004P	226,400,000	.65	5.00	—
2004D	226,800,000	.65	5.00	—
2004D Extra Leaf Low	Est. 9,000	135	190	—
2004D Extra Leaf High	Est. 3,000	175	285	—
2004S	—	—	—	2.30

KM# 359a • 6.2500 g., 0.9000 **Silver**, 0.1808 oz. ASW, 24.3 mm. •

Date	Mintage	MS-63	MS-65	Prf-65
2004S	1,775,370	—	—	8.50

QUARTER

California

KM# 370 • 5.6700 g., **Copper-Nickel Clad Copper**, 24.3 mm. •

Date	Mintage	MS-63	MS-65	Prf-65
2005P	257,200,000	.65	5.00	—
2005P Satin Finish	Inc. above	1.50	4.50	—
2005D	263,200,000	.65	5.00	—
2005D Satin Finish	Inc. above	1.50	4.50	—
2005S	3,262,960	—	—	2.30

KM# 370a • 6.2500 g., 0.9000 **Silver**, 0.1808 oz. ASW, 24.3 mm. •

Date	Mintage	MS-63	MS-65	Prf-65
2005S	1,679,600	—	—	8.50

Kansas

KM# 373 • 5.6700 g., **Copper-Nickel Clad Copper**, 24.3 mm. •

Date	Mintage	MS-63	MS-65	Prf-65
2005P	263,400,000	.65	5.00	—
2005P Satin Finish	Inc. above	1.50	4.50	—
2005D	300,000,000	.65	5.00	—
2005D Satin Finish	Inc. above	1.50	4.50	—
2005S	3,262,960	—	—	2.30

KM# 373a • 6.2500 g., 0.9000 **Silver**, 0.1808 oz. ASW, 24.3 mm. •

Date	Mintage	MS-63	MS-65	Prf-65
2005S	1,679,600	—	—	8.50

Minnesota

KM# 371 • 5.6700 g., **Copper-Nickel Clad Copper**, 24.3 mm. •

Date	Mintage	MS-63	MS-65	Prf-65
2005P	226,400,000	.65	5.00	—
2005P Satin Finish	Inc. above	1.50	4.50	—
2005D	226,800,000	.65	5.00	—
2005D Satin Finish	Inc. above	1.50	4.50	—
2005S	3,262,960	—	—	2.30

KM# 371a • 6.2500 g., 0.9000 **Silver**, 0.1808 oz. ASW, 24.3 mm. •

Date	Mintage	MS-63	MS-65	Prf-65
2005S	1,679,600	—	—	8.50

Oregon

KM# 372 • 5.6700 g., **Copper-Nickel Clad Copper**, 24.3 mm. •

Date	Mintage	MS-63	MS-65	Prf-65
2005P	316,200,000	.65	5.00	—
2005P Satin Finish	Inc. above	1.50	4.50	—
2005D	404,000,000	.65	5.00	—
2005D Satin Finish	Inc. above	1.50	4.50	—
2005S	3,262,960	—	—	2.30

KM# 372a • 6.2500 g., 0.9000 **Silver**, 0.1808 oz. ASW, 24.3 mm. •

Date	Mintage	MS-63	MS-65	Prf-65
2005S	1,679,600	—	—	8.50

West Virginia

KM# 374 • 5.6700 g., **Copper-Nickel Clad Copper**, 24.3 mm. •

Date	Mintage	MS-63	MS-65	Prf-65
2005P	365,400,000	.65	5.00	—
2005P Satin Finish	Inc. above	1.50	4.50	—
2005D	356,200,000	.65	5.00	—
2005D Satin Finish	Inc. above	1.50	4.50	—
2005S	3,262,960	—	—	2.30

KM# 374a • 6.2500 g., 0.9000 **Silver**, 0.1808 oz. ASW, 24.3 mm. •

Date	Mintage	MS-63	MS-65	Prf-65
2005S	1,679,600	—	—	8.50

Colorado

KM# 384 • 5.6700 g., **Copper-Nickel Clad Copper**, 24.3 mm. •

Date	Mintage	MS-63	MS-65	Prf-65
2006P	274,800,000	.65	5.00	—
2006P Satin Finish	Inc. above	1.50	4.50	—
2006D	294,200,000	.65	5.00	—
2006D Satin Finish	Inc. above	1.50	4.50	—
2006S	2,862,078	—	—	2.30

KM# 384a • 6.2500 g., 0.9000 **Silver**, 0.1808 oz. ASW, 24.3 mm. •

Date	Mintage	MS-63	MS-65	Prf-65
2006S	1,571,839	—	—	8.50

QUARTER

Nebraska

KM# 383 • 5.6700 g., **Copper-Nickel Clad Copper**, 24.3 mm. •

Date	Mintage	MS-63	MS-65	Prf-65
2006P	318,000,000	.65	5.00	—
2006P Satin Finish	Inc. above	1.50	4.50	—
2006D	273,000,000	.65	5.00	—
2006D Satin Finish	Inc. above	1.50	4.50	—
2006S	2,862,078	—	—	2.30

KM# 383a • 6.2500 g., 0.9000 **Silver**, 0.1808 oz. ASW, 24.3 mm. •

Date	Mintage	MS-63	MS-65	Prf-65
2006S	1,571,839	—	—	8.50

Nevada

KM# 382 • 5.6700 g., **Copper-Nickel Clad Copper**, 24.3 mm. •

Date	Mintage	MS-63	MS-65	Prf-65
2006P	277,000,000	.65	5.00	—
2006P Satin Finish	Inc. above	1.50	4.50	—
2006D	312,800,000	.65	5.00	—
2006D Satin Finish	Inc. above	1.50	4.50	—
2006S	2,862,078	—	—	2.30

KM# 382a • 6.2500 g., 0.9000 **Silver**, 0.1808 oz. ASW, 24.3 mm. •

Date	Mintage	MS-63	MS-65	Prf-65
2006S	1,571,839	—	—	8.50

North Dakota

KM# 385 • 5.6700 g., **Copper-Nickel Clad Copper**, 24.3 mm. •

Date	Mintage	MS-63	MS-65	Prf-65
2006P	305,800,000	.65	5.00	—
2006P Satin Finish	Inc. above	1.50	4.50	—
2006D	359,000,000	.65	5.00	—
2006D Satin Finish	Inc. above	1.50	4.50	—
2006S	2,862,078	—	—	2.30

KM# 385a • 6.2500 g., 0.9000 **Silver**, 0.1808 oz. ASW, 24.3 mm. •

Date	Mintage	MS-63	MS-65	Prf-65
2006S	1,571,839	—	—	8.50

South Dakota

KM# 386 • 5.6700 g., **Copper-Nickel Clad Copper**, 24.3 mm. •

Date	Mintage	MS-63	MS-65	Prf-65
2006P	245,000,000	.65	5.00	—
2006P Satin Finish	Inc. above	1.50	4.50	—
2006D	265,800,000	.65	5.00	—
2006D Satin Finish	Inc. above	1.50	4.50	—
2006S	2,862,078	—	—	2.30

KM# 386a • 6.2500 g., 0.9000 **Silver**, 0.1808 oz. ASW, 24.3 mm. •

Date	Mintage	MS-63	MS-65	Prf-65
2006S	1,571,839	—	—	8.50

Idaho

KM# 398 • 5.6700 g., **Copper-Nickel Clad Copper**, 24.3 mm. •

Date	Mintage	MS-63	MS-65	Prf-65
2007P	294,600,000	.65	5.00	—
2007P Satin finish	—	1.50	4.50	—
2007D	286,800,000	.65	5.00	—
2007D Satin finish	—	1.50	4.50	—
2007S	2,374,778	—	—	2.30

KM# 398a • 6.2500 g., 0.9000 **Silver**, 0.1808 oz. ASW, 24.3 mm. •

Date	Mintage	MS-63	MS-65	Prf-65
2007S	1,299,878	—	—	8.50

Montana

KM# 396 • 5.6700 g., **Copper-Nickel Clad Copper**, 24.3 mm. •

Date	Mintage	MS-63	MS-65	Prf-65
2007P	257,000,000	.65	5.00	—
2007 Satin Finish	—	1.50	4.50	—
2007 Satin Finish	—	1.50	4.50	—
2007D	256,240,000	.65	5.00	—
2007S	2,374,778	—	—	2.30

KM# 396a • 6.2500 g., 0.9000 **Silver**, 0.1808 oz. ASW, 24.3 mm. •

Date	Mintage	MS-63	MS-65	Prf-65
2007S	1,299,878	—	—	8.50

QUARTER

Utah

KM# 400 • 5.6700 g., **Copper-Nickel Clad Copper**, 24.3 mm. •

Date	Mintage	MS-63	MS-65	Prf-65
2007P	255,000,000	.65	5.00	—
2007P Satin finish	—	1.50	4.50	—
2007D	253,200,000	.65	5.00	—
2007D Satin finish	—	1.50	4.50	—
2007S	2,374,778	—	—	2.30

KM# 400a • 6.2500 g., 0.9000 **Silver**, 0.1808 oz. ASW •

Date	Mintage	MS-63	MS-65	Prf-65
2007S	1,299,878	—	—	8.50

Washington

KM# 397 • 5.6700 g., **Copper-Nickel Clad Copper**, 24.3 mm. •

Date	Mintage	MS-63	MS-65	Prf-65
2007P	265,200,000	.65	5.00	—
2007P Satin Finish	—	1.50	4.50	—
2007D	280,000,000	.65	5.00	—
2007D Satin Finish	—	1.50	4.50	—
2007S	2,374,778	—	—	2.30

KM# 397a • 6.2500 g., 0.9000 **Silver**, 0.1808 oz. ASW, 24.3 mm. •

Date	Mintage	MS-63	MS-65	Prf-65
2007S	1,299,878	—	—	8.50

Wyoming

KM# 399 • 5.6700 g., **Copper-Nickel Clad Copper**, 24.3 mm. •

Date	Mintage	MS-63	MS-65	Prf-65
2007P	243,600,000	.65	5.00	—
2007P Satin finish	—	1.50	4.50	—
2007D	320,800,000	.65	5.00	—
2007 Satin finish	—	1.50	4.50	—
2007S	2,374,778	—	—	2.30

KM# 399a • 6.2500 g., 0.9000 **Silver**, 0.1808 oz. ASW, 24.3 mm. •

Date	Mintage	MS-63	MS-65	Prf-65
2007S	1,299,878	—	—	8.50

Alaska

KM# 424 • 5.6700 g., **Copper-Nickel Clad Copper**, 24.3 mm. •

Date	Mintage	MS-63	MS-65	Prf-65
2008P	251,800,000	.65	5.00	—
2008P Satin finish	—	1.50	4.50	—
2008D	254,000,000	.65	5.00	—
2008D Satin finish	—	1.50	4.50	—
2008S	2,100,000	—	—	2.30

KM# 424a • 6.2500 g., 0.9000 **Silver**, 0.1808 oz. ASW, 24.3 mm. •

Date	Mintage	MS-63	MS-65	Prf-65
2008S	1,200,000	—	—	8.50

Arizona

KM# 423 • 5.6700 g., **Copper-Nickel Clad Copper**, 24.3 mm. •

Date	Mintage	MS-63	MS-65	Prf-65
2008P	244,600,000	.65	5.00	—
2008P Satin finish	—	1.50	4.50	—
2008D	265,000,000	.65	5.00	—
2008D Satin finish	—	1.50	4.50	—
2008S	2,100,000	—	—	2.30

KM# 423a • 6.2500 g., 0.9000 **Silver**, 0.1808 oz. ASW, 24.3 mm. •

Date	Mintage	MS-63	MS-65	Prf-65
2008S	1,200,000	—	—	8.50

Hawaii

KM# 425 • 5.6700 g., **Copper-Nickel Clad Copper**, 24.3 mm. •

Date	Mintage	MS-63	MS-65	Prf-65
2008P	254,000,000	.65	5.00	—
2008P Satin finish	—	1.50	4.50	—
2008D	263,600,000	.65	5.00	—
2008D Satin finish	—	1.50	4.50	—
2008S	2,100,000	—	—	2.30

KM# 425a • 6.2500 g., 0.9000 **Silver**, 0.1808 oz. ASW, 24.3 mm. •

Date	Mintage	MS-63	MS-65	Prf-65
2008S	1,200,000	—	—	8.50

QUARTER

New Mexico

KM# 422 • 5.6700 g., **Copper-Nickel Clad Copper**, 24.3 mm. •

Date	Mintage	MS-63	MS-65	Prf-65
2008P	244,200,000	.65	5.00	—
2008P Satin finish	—	1.50	4.50	—
2008D	244,400,000	.65	5.00	—
2008D Satin finish	—	1.50	4.50	—
2008S	2,100,000	—	—	2.30

KM# 422a • 6.2500 g., 0.9000 **Silver**, 0.1808 oz. ASW, 24.3 mm. •

Date	Mintage	MS-63	MS-65	Prf-65
2008S	1,200,000	—	—	8.50

Oklahoma

KM# 421 • 5.6700 g., **Copper-Nickel Clad Copper**, 24.3 mm. •

Date	Mintage	MS-63	MS-65	Prf-65
2008P	222,000,000	.65	5.00	—
2008P Satin finish	—	1.50	4.50	—
2008D	194,600,000	.65	5.00	—
2008D Satin finish	—	1.50	4.50	—
2008S	2,100,000	—	—	2.30

KM# 421a • 6.2500 g., 0.9000 **Silver**, 0.1808 oz. ASW, 24.3 mm. •

Date	Mintage	MS-63	MS-65	Prf-65
2008S	1,200,000	—	—	8.50

DC and Territories

American Samoa

KM# 448 • 5.6700 g., **Copper-Nickel Clad Copper**, 24.3 mm. • **Rev. Designer:** Charles Vickers

Date	Mintage	MS-63	MS-65	Prf-65
2009P	42,600,000	.75	5.00	—
2009D	39,600,000	.75	5.00	—
2009S	—	—	—	3.75

KM# 448a • 6.2500 g., 0.9000 **Silver**, 0.1808 oz. ASW, 24.3 mm. •

Date	Mintage	MS-63	MS-65	Prf-65
2009S	—	—	—	7.75

Guam

KM# 447 • 5.6700 g., **Copper-Nickel Clad Copper**, 24.3 mm. • **Rev. Designer:** James Licaretz

Date	Mintage	MS-63	MS-65	Prf-65
2009P	45,000,000	.75	5.00	—
2009D	42,600,000	.75	5.00	—
2009S	—	—	—	3.75

KM# 447a • 6.2500 g., 0.9000 **Silver**, 0.1808 oz. ASW, 24.3 mm. •

Date	Mintage	MS-63	MS-65	Prf-65
2009S	—	—	—	7.75

District of Columbia

KM# 445 • 5.6700 g., **Copper-Nickel Clad Copper**, 24.3 mm. • **Rev. Designer:** Don Everhart

Date	Mintage	MS-63	MS-65	Prf-65
2009P	83,600,000	.75	5.00	—
2009D	88,800,000	.75	5.00	—
2009S	—	—	—	3.75

KM# 445a • 6.2500 g., 0.9000 **Silver**, 0.1808 oz. ASW, 24.3 mm. •

Date	Mintage	MS-63	MS-65	Prf-65
2009S	—	—	—	7.75

Northern Mariana Islands

KM# 466 • 5.6700 g., **Copper-Nickel Clad Copper** • **Rev. Designer:** Pheve Hemphill

Date	Mintage	MS-63	MS-65	Prf-65
2009P	35,200,000	.75	5.00	—
2009D	37,600,000	.75	5.00	—
2009S	—	—	—	3.75

KM# 466a • 6.2500 g., 0.9000 **Silver**, 0.1808 oz. ASW •

Date	Mintage	MS-63	MS-65	Prf-65
2009S	—	—	—	7.75

QUARTER

QUARTER

Puerto Rico

KM# 446 • 5.6700 g., **Copper-Nickel Clad Copper**, 24.3 mm. • **Rev. Designer:** Joseph Menna

Date	Mintage	MS-63	MS-65	Prf-65
2009P	53,200,000	.75	5.00	—
2009D	86,000,000	.75	5.00	—
2009S	—	—	—	3.75

KM# 446a • 6.2500 g., 0.9000 **Silver**, 0.1808 oz. ASW, 24.3 mm. •

Date	Mintage	MS-63	MS-65	Prf-65
2009S	—	—	—	7.75

US Virgin Islands

KM# 449 • 5.6700 g., **Copper-Nickel Clad Copper**, 24.3 mm. • **Rev. Designer:** Joseph Menna

Date	Mintage	MS-63	MS-65	Prf-65
2009P	41,000,000	.75	5.00	—
2009D	41,000,000	.75	5.00	—
2009S	—	—	—	3.75

KM# 449a • 6.2500 g., 0.9000 **Silver**, 0.1808 oz. ASW, 24.3 mm. •

Date	Mintage	MS-63	MS-65	Prf-65
2009S	—	—	—	7.75

America the Beautiful

Grand Canyon National Park

KM# 472 • 5.6700 g., **Copper-Nickel Clad Copper**, 24.3 mm. •

Date	Mintage	MS-63	MS-65	Prf-65
2010P	—	.75	5.00	—
2010D	—	.75	5.00	—
2010S	—	—	—	3.75

KM# 472a • 6.2500 g., 0.9000 **Silver**, 0.1808 oz. ASW •

Date	Mintage	MS-63	MS-65	Prf-65
2010	—	—	—	7.75

Mount Hood National Park

KM# 473 • 5.6700 g., **Copper-Nickel Clad Copper** •

Date	Mintage	MS-63	MS-65	Prf-65
2010P	—	.75	5.00	—
2010D	—	.75	5.00	—
2010S	—	—	—	3.75

KM# 473a • 6.2500 g., 0.9000 **Silver**, 0.1808 oz. ASW •

Date	Mintage	MS-63	MS-65	Prf-65
2010	—	—	—	7.75

Hot Springs, Ark.

KM# 469 • 5.6700 g., **Copper-Nickel Clad Copper**, 24.3 mm. •

Date	Mintage	MS-63	MS-65	Prf-65
2010P	—	.75	5.00	—
2010D	—	.75	5.00	—
2010S	—	—	—	3.75

KM# 469a • 6.2500 g., 0.9000 **Silver**, 0.1808 oz. ASW •

Date	Mintage	MS-63	MS-65	Prf-65
2010S	—	—	—	7.75

Yellowstone National Park

KM# 470 • 5.6700 g., **Copper-Nickel Clad Copper**, 24.3 mm. •

Date	Mintage	MS-63	MS-65	Prf-65
2010P	—	.75	5.00	—
2010D	—	.75	5.00	—
2010S	—	—	—	3.75

KM# 470a • 6.2500 g., 0.9000 **Silver**, 0.1808 oz. ASW •

Date	Mintage	MS-63	MS-65	Prf-65
2010	—	—	—	7.75

Yosemite National Park

KM# 471 • 5.6700 g., **Copper-Nickel Clad Copper**, 24.3 mm. •

Date	Mintage	MS-63	MS-65	Prf-65
2010P	—	.75	5.00	—
2010D	—	.75	5.00	—
2010S	—	—	—	3.75

KM# 471a • 6.2500 g., 0.9000 **Silver**, 0.1808 oz. ASW •

Date	Mintage	MS-63	MS-65	Prf-65
2010	—	—	—	7.75

Chickasaw National Recreation Area

KM# 498 • 5.6700 g., **Copper-Nickel Clad Copper**, 24 mm. •

Date	Mintage	MS-63	MS-65	Prf-65
2011P	—	.75	5.00	—
2011D	—	.75	5.00	—
2011S	—	—	—	3.75

KM# 498a • 6.2500 g., 0.9000 **Silver**, 0.1808 oz. ASW •

Date	Mintage	MS-63	MS-65	Prf-65
2011S	—	—	—	7.75

Gettysburg National Military Park

KM# 494 • 5.6700 g., **Copper-Nickel Clad Copper**, 24 mm. •

Date	Mintage	MS-63	MS-65	Prf-65
2011P	—	.75	5.00	—
2011D	—	.75	5.00	—
2011S	—	—	—	3.75

KM# 494a • 6.2500 g., 0.9000 **Silver**, 0.1808 oz. ASW •

Date	Mintage	MS-63	MS-65	Prf-65
2011S	—	—	—	7.75

Glacier National Park

KM# 495 • 5.6700 g., **Copper-Nickel Clad Copper**, 24 mm. •

Date	Mintage	MS-63	MS-65	Prf-65
2011P	—	.75	5.00	—
2011D	—	.75	5.00	—
2011S	—	—	—	3.75

KM# 495a • 6.2500 g., 0.9000 **Silver**, 0.1808 oz. ASW •

Date	Mintage	MS-63	MS-65	Prf-65
2011S	—	—	—	7.75

Olympic National Park

KM# 496 • 5.6700 g., **Copper-Nickel Clad Copper**, 24 mm. •

Date	Mintage	MS-63	MS-65	Prf-65
2011P	—	.75	5.00	—
2011D	—	.75	5.00	—
2011S	—	—	—	3.75

KM# 496a • 6.2500 g., 0.9000 **Silver**, 0.1808 oz. ASW •

Date	Mintage	MS-63	MS-65	Prf-65
2011S	—	—	—	7.75

Vicksburg National Military Park

KM# 497 • 5.6700 g., **Copper-Nickel Clad Copper**, 24 mm. •

Date	Mintage	MS-63	MS-65	Prf-65
2011P	—	.75	5.00	—
2011D	—	.75	5.00	—
2011S	—	—	—	3.75

KM# 497a • 6.2500 g., 0.9000 **Silver**, 0.1808 oz. ASW •

Date	Mintage	MS-63	MS-65	Prf-65
2011S	—	—	—	7.75

Acadia National Park

KM# 521 • 5.6700 g., **Copper-Nickel Clad Copper**, 24.3 mm. •

Date	Mintage	MS-63	MS-65	Prf-65
2012P	—	.75	5.00	—
2012D	—	.75	5.00	—
2012S	—	—	—	3.75

QUARTER

KM# 521a • 6.2500 g., 0.9000 **Silver**, 0.1808 oz. ASW, 24.3 mm. •

Date	Mintage	MS-63	MS-65	Prf-65
2012S	—	—	—	7.75

Chaco Culture National Historic Park

KM# 520 • 5.7100 g., Copper-Nickel Clad Copper, 24.3 mm. •

Date	Mintage	MS-63	MS-65	Prf-65
2012P	—	.75	8.00	—
2012D	—	.75	8.00	—
2012S	—	—	—	4.00

KM# 520a • 6.2500 g., 0.9000 **Silver**, 0.1808 oz. ASW, 24.3 mm. •

Date	Mintage	MS-63	MS-65	Prf-65
2012	—	—	—	7.75

Denali National Park

KM# 523 • 5.6700 g., Copper-Nickel Clad Copper, 24.3 mm. •

Date	Mintage	MS-63	MS-65	Prf-65
2012P	—	.75	5.00	—
2012D	—	.75	5.00	—
2012S	—	—	—	3.75

KM# 523a • 6.2500 g., 0.9000 **Silver**, 0.1808 oz. ASW, 24.3 mm. •

Date	Mintage	MS-63	MS-65	Prf-65
2012	—	—	—	7.75

El Yunque National Forest

KM# 519 • 5.6700 g., Copper-Nickel Clad Copper, 24.3 mm. •

Date	Mintage	MS-63	MS-65	Prf-65
2012P	—	.75	5.00	—
2012D	—	.75	5.00	—
2012S	—	—	—	3.75

KM# 519a • 6.2500 g., 0.9000 **Silver**, 0.1808 oz. ASW, 24.3 mm. •

Date	Mintage	MS-63	MS-65	Prf-65
2012S	—	—	—	7.75

Hawai'i Volcanoes National Park

KM# 522 • 5.6700 g., Copper-Nickel Clad Copper, 24.3 mm. •

Date	Mintage	MS-63	MS-65	Prf-65
2012P	—	.75	5.00	—
2012D	—	.75	5.00	—
2012S	—	—	—	3.75

KM# 522a • 6.2500 g., 0.9000 **Silver**, 0.1808 oz. ASW, 24.3 mm. •

Date	Mintage	MS-63	MS-65	Prf-65
2012	—	—	—	7.75

HALF DOLLAR

Flowing Hair Half Dollar

KM# 16 • 13.4800 g., 0.8920 **Silver**, 0.3866 oz. ASW, 32.5 mm. • **Designer:** Robert Scot **Notes:** The 1795 "recut date" variety had the date cut into the dies twice, so both sets of numbers are visible on the coin. The 1795 "3 leaves" variety has three leaves under each of the eagle's wings on the reverse.

Date	Mintage	G-4	VG-8	F-12	VF-20	XF-40	MS-60
1794	23,464	2,850	5,750	8,850	19,500	37,500	225,000
1795	299,680	1,025	1,450	2,850	4,850	13,850	46,500
1795 recut date	Inc. above	1,040	1,470	2,895	5,200	14,250	46,500
1795 3 leaves	Inc. above	2,600	3,150	5,350	8,350	17,500	59,500

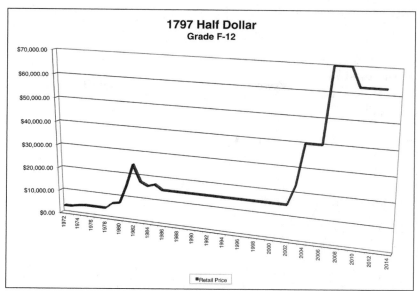

1797 Half Dollar
Grade F-12

Draped Bust Half Dollar
Draped bust right obverse   Small eagle reverse

KM# 26 • 13.4800 g., 0.8920 **Silver**, 0.3866 oz. ASW, 32.5 mm. • **Designer:** Robert Scot

Date	Mintage	G-4	VG-8	F-12	VF-20	XF-40	MS-60
1796 15 obverse stars	3,918	36,500	46,000	62,000	73,500	118,000	300,000
1796 16 obverse stars	Inc. above	39,500	50,000	67,000	79,500	128,000	320,000
1797	Inc. above	36,700	46,300	62,500	74,300	121,000	310,000

Draped Bust Half Dollar
Draped bust right, flanked by stars, date at angle below obverse   Heraldic eagle reverse

KM# 35 • 13.4800 g., 0.8920 **Silver**, 0.3866 oz. ASW, 32.5 mm. • **Obv. Legend** LIBERTY **Rev. Legend:** UNITED STATES OF AMERICA **Designer:** Robert Scot **Notes:** The two varieties of the 1803 strikes are distinguished by the size of the 3 in the date. The several varieties of the 1806 strikes are distinguished by the style of 6 in the date, size of the stars on the obverse, and whether the stem of the olive branch held by the reverse eagle extends through the claw.

Date	Mintage	G-4	VG-8	F-12	VF-20	XF-40	MS-60
1801	30,289	850	1,250	2,550	4,250	10,500	50,000
1802	29,890	900	1,350	2,750	4,500	11,000	52,000
1803 small 3	188,234	255	325	425	825	2,325	17,250
1803 large 3	Inc. above	195	235	295	715	1,925	14,750
1805	211,722	195	235	295	685	1,865	10,750
1805/4	Inc. above	270	385	570	1,515	3,325	30,000
1806 knobbed 6, large stars	839,576	195	235	295	665	1,825	—
1806 knobbed 6, small stars	Inc. above	195	235	295	680	2,025	13,500
1806 knobbed 6, stem not through claw	Inc. above	20,000	35,000	42,000	57,500	95,000	—
1806 pointed-top 6, stem not through claw	Inc. above	195	235	295	665	1,825	15,250
1806 pointed-top 6, stem through claw	Inc. above	195	235	295	665	1,825	9,750
1806/5	Inc. above	215	270	355	775	2,050	10,075
1806 /inverted 6	Inc. above	255	355	845	1,615	4,375	28,500
1807	301,076	195	235	295	665	1,825	9,750

Capped Bust

Draped bust left, flanked by stars, date at angle below obverse
"50 C." below eagle reverse

KM# 37 • 13.4800 g., 0.8920 **Silver**, 0.3866 oz. ASW, 32.5 mm. • **Rev. Legend:** UNITED STATES OF AMERICA **Designer:** John Reich **Notes:** There are three varieties of the 1807 strikes. Two are distinguished by the size of the stars on the obverse. The third was struck from a reverse die that had a 5 cut over a 2 in the "50C" denomination. Two varieties of the 1811 are distinguished by the size of the 8 in the date. A third has a period between the 8 and second 1 in the date. One variety of the 1817 has a period between the 1 and 7 in the date. Two varieties of the 1820 are distinguished by the size of the date. On the 1823 varieties, the "broken 3" appears to be almost separated in the middle of the 3 in the date; the "patched 3" has the error reparied; the "ugly 3" has portions of its detail missing. The 1827 "curled-2" and "square-2" varieties are distinguished by the numeral's base -- either curled or square. Among the 1828 varieties, "knobbed 2" and "no knob" refers to whether the upper left serif of the digit is rounded. The 1830 varieties are distinguished by the size of the 0 in the date. The four 1834 varieties are distinguished by the sizes of the stars, date and letters in the inscriptions. The 1836 "50/00" variety was struck from a reverse die that has "50" recut over "00" in the denomination.

Date	Mintage	G-4	VG-8	F-12	VF-20	XF-40	AU-50	MS-60	MS-65
1807 small stars	750,500	125	175	350	750	1,900	6,500	9,850	54,000
1807 large stars	Inc. above	115	165	300	660	1,750	5,650	8,900	—
1807 50/20 C.	Inc. above	85.00	125	195	450	1,500	3,150	6,500	30,000
1807 bearded goddess	—	450	775	1,500	3,350	6,850	22,500	—	—
1808	1,368,600	67.00	84.00	97.00	145	350	550	1,800	20,000
1808/7	Inc. above	90.00	110	135	240	440	1,850	5,400	32,500
1809 Normal edge	1,405,810	65.00	82.00	94.00	140	375	750	1,500	12,650
1809 XXXX edge	Inc. above	80.00	105	135	185	550	950	4,450	—
1809 IIIIII edge	Inc. above	85.00	110	140	210	450	850	4,000	—
1810	1,276,276	64.00	81.00	91.00	135	265	650	1,950	19,500
1811 small 8	1,203,644	70.00	80.00	88.00	125	350	800	2,350	28,500
1811 large 8	Inc. above	80.00	107	119	175	425	1,000	2,400	28,500
1811 dated 18.11	Inc. above	78.00	100.00	110	165	650	1,250	3,500	28,500
1812	1,628,059	64.00	81.00	88.00	114	254	440	1,350	13,450
1812/1 small 8	Inc. above	80.00	97.00	119	200	500	1,350	2,500	—
1812/1 large 8	Inc. above	1,650	2,450	4,500	6,750	12,000	21,000	—	—
1812 Single leaf below wing	Inc. above	750	950	1,250	2,400	4,000	6,800	12,500	—
1813	1,241,903	64.00	81.00	88.00	114	184	480	1,400	12,650
1813 50/UNI reverse	1,241,903	74.00	101	124	179	650	1,350	3,650	27,500
1814	1,039,075	64.00	81.00	88.00	124	285	650	1,650	11,450
1814/3	Inc. above	100.00	165	245	300	850	1,650	3,250	—
1814 E/A in States	Inc. above	85.00	110	150	225	385	950	3,950	—
1814 Single leaf below wing	Inc. above	75.00	97.00	124	194	575	1,350	2,250	—
1815/2	47,150	1,100	1,550	2,250	3,650	5,500	7,950	14,500	85,000
1817	1,215,567	67.00	84.00	91.00	119	195	450	1,300	11,650
1817/3	Inc. above	115	175	280	525	1,150	2,350	4,850	—
1817/4	—	60,000	80,000	150,000	200,000	240,000	—	—	—
1817 dated 181.7	Inc. above	100.00	87.00	94.00	104	575	1,350	3,950	27,500
1817 Single leaf below wing	Inc. above	75.00	98.00	124	209	550	2,100	2,750	—

HALF DOLLAR

Date	Mintage	G-4	VG-8	F-12	VF-20	XF-40	AU-50	MS-60	MS-65
1818	1,960,322	64.00	81.00	88.00	119	225	440	1,350	11,250
1818/7 Large 8	Inc. above	100.00	115	145	190	325	950	1,850	17,500
1818/7 Small 8	Inc. above	98.00	110	130	150	250	850	1,650	16,500
1819	2,208,000	64.00	81.00	88.00	119	175	430	1,350	13,650
1819/8 small 9	Inc. above	75.00	92.00	109	184	290	650	1,900	11,650
1819/8 large 9	Inc. above	85.00	105	150	275	385	850	2,000	25,650
1820 Curl Base 2, small date	751,122	70.00	85.00	96.00	124	285	950	2,250	11,650
1820 Square Base 2 with knob, large date	Inc. above	72.00	90.00	104	139	400	800	2,400	13,150
1820 Square Base 2 without know, large date	Inc. above	72.00	90.00	104	154	475	1,100	2,500	26,500
1820 E's without Serifs	Inc. above	260	450	900	2,150	3,500	5,500	—	—
1820/19 Square Base 2	Inc. above	110	130	165	240	775	1,650	3,250	25,000
1820/19 Curled Base 2	Inc. above	95.00	115	140	200	650	1,450	2,900	24,500
1821	1,305,797	58.00	76.00	89.00	101	185	575	1,350	11,250
1822	1,559,573	58.00	76.00	89.00	101	180	450	1,250	10,950
1822/1	Inc. above	83.00	100.00	129	275	385	800	1,900	
1823	1,694,200	58.00	76.00	89.00	101	175	425	1,150	11,150
1823 broken 3	Inc. above	68.00	88.00	104	139	500	1,500	3,200	—
1823 patched 3	Inc. above	73.00	94.00	119	159	550	950	2,000	15,150
1823 ugly 3	Inc. above	78.00	99.00	129	184	750	1,750	4,200	—
1824	3,504,954	58.00	76.00	89.00	101	175	360	1,075	10,150
1824/21	Inc. above	63.00	82.00	99.00	126	275	650	2,000	15,650
1824/4	Inc. above	61.00	80.00	91.00	114	225	500	1,350	—
1824 1824/various dates	Inc. above	60.00	79.00	91.00	104	300	875	2,000	15,150
1825	2,943,166	58.00	76.00	89.00	101	175	385	1,050	10,150
1826	4,004,180	58.00	76.00	89.00	101	175	385	1,050	10,150
1827 curled 2	5,493,400	61.00	81.00	99.00	134	185	485	1,400	12,650
1827 square 2	Inc. above	58.00	76.00	89.00	101	175	385	1,050	10,150
1827/6	Inc. above	85.00	95.00	120	155	265	650	1,450	11,650
1828 curled-base 2, no knob	3,075,200	58.00	76.00	89.00	101	175	385	1,150	11,150
1828 curled-base 2, knobbed 2	Inc. above	78.00	99.00	129	184	245	460	1,300	—
1828 small 8s, square-base 2, large letters	Inc. above	60.00	80.00	99.00	124	175	385	1,050	12,650
1828 small 8s, square-base 2, small letters	Inc. above	58.00	76.00	89.00	106	250	750	1,900	—
1828 large 8s, square-base 2	Inc. above	58.00	76.00	89.00	101	175	385	1,050	11,150
1829	3,712,156	55.00	72.00	79.00	89.00	159	350	1,000	10,150
1829 Large letters	Inc. above	59.00	79.00	89.00	104	180	420	1,250	12,650
1829/7	Inc. above	78.00	99.00	129	174	200	475	1,250	12,650
1830 Small O rev	4,764,800	55.00	72.00	79.00	89.00	159	350	1,000	10,150
1830 Large O	Inc. above	60.00	78.00	88.00	109	189	550	2,000	13,150
1830 Large letter rev	Inc. above	1,500	2,250	3,000	3,750	4,800	9,800	—	—
1831	5,873,660	55.00	72.00	79.00	89.00	159	350	1,000	10,150
1832 small letters	4,797,000	55.00	72.00	79.00	89.00	159	350	1,000	10,150
1832 large letters	Inc. above	58.00	75.00	85.00	99.00	175	410	1,350	12,650
1833	5,206,000	55.00	72.00	79.00	89.00	159	360	1,000	10,150
1834 small date, large stars, small letters	6,412,004	55.00	74.00	81.00	91.00	163	360	1,025	10,400
1834 small date, small stars, small letters	Inc. above	55.00	74.00	81.00	9.00	163	360	1,025	10,400
1834 large date, small letters	Inc. above	55.00	74.00	81.00	91.00	163	360	1,025	10,400
1834 large date, large letters	Inc. above	55.00	72.00	79.00	89.00	159	350	1,000	10,150
1835	5,352,006	55.00	72.00	79.00	89.00	159	350	1,000	10,150
1836	6,545,000	55.00	72.00	79.00	89.00	159	350	1,000	10,150
1836	Inc. above	80.00	95.00	120	265	450	1,000	2,500	—
1836 50/00	Inc. above	93.00	112	129	165	300	800	1,750	19,500

Bust Half Dollar

Draped bust left, flanked by stars, date at angle below obverse
"50 Cents" below eagle reverse

KM# 58 • 13.4800 g., 0.8920 **Silver**, 0.3866 oz. ASW, 30 mm. • **Rev. Legend:** UNITED STATES OF AMERICA **Designer:** Christian Gobrecht **Edge Desc:** Reeded.

Date	Mintage	G-4	VG-8	F-12	VF-20	XF-40	AU-50	MS-60	MS-65
1836	1,200	850	1,075	1,600	2,000	3,350	4,400	8,850	66,500
1837	3,629,820	58.00	73.00	83.00	115	200	400	1,160	23,500

Bust Half Dollar

Draped bust left, flanked by stars, date at angle below obverse
"50 Cents" below eagle reverse

KM# 58a • 13.3600 g., 0.9000 **Silver**, 0.3866 oz. ASW, 30 mm. • **Rev. Legend:** UNITED STATES OF AMERICA **Designer:** Christian Gobrecht **Edge Desc:** Reeded.

Date	Mintage	G-4	VG-8	F-12	VF-20	XF-40	AU-50	MS-60	MS-65
1837	3,629,820	58.00	73.00	80.00	115	200	345	1,100	24,500

HALF DOLLAR

Bust Half Dollar

Draped bust left, flanked by stars, date below obverse
HALF DOL. below eagle reverse

KM# 65 • 13.3600 g., 0.9000 **Silver**, 0.3866 oz. ASW, 30 mm. • **Rev. Legend:** UNITED STATES OF
AMERICA **Designer:** Christian Gobrecht

Date	Mintage	G-4	VG-8	F-12	VF-20	XF-40	AU-50	MS-60	MS-65
1838	3,546,000	58.00	70.00	82.00	120	205	420	1,200	17,500
1838O proof only	Est. 20	—	—	—	—	250,000	300,000	—	—
1839	1,392,976	60.00	76.00	92.00	130	245	410	1,350	39,500
1839O	116,000	240	325	425	650	1,350	2,350	4,500	46,500

Seated Liberty Half Dollar

Seated Liberty, date below obverse
"Half Dol." below eagle reverse

KM# 68 • 13.3600 g., 0.9000 **Silver**, 0.3866 oz. ASW, 30.6 mm. • **Rev. Legend:** UNITED STATES OF
AMERICA **Designer:** Christian Gobrecht

Date	Mintage	G-4	VG-8	F-12	VF-20	XF-40	AU-50	MS-60	MS-65
1839 no drapery from elbow	Inc. above	45.00	90.00	365	575	1,200	2,450	6,250	200,000
1839 drapery	Inc. above	50.00	57.00	75.50	110	185	2,550	1,000	25,000
1840 small letters	1,435,008	52.00	57.00	70.00	108	170	325	600	7,500
1840 reverse 1838	Inc. above	150	175	275	350	850	1,350	3,400	30,000
1840O	855,100	51.00	58.00	75.50	114	215	275	450	—
1841	310,000	52.00	65.00	110	165	235	325	1,200	6,850
1841O	401,000	50.00	65.00	75.00	106	265	2,515	600	7,000
1842 small date	2,012,764	48.00	55.00	80.00	135	200	325	1,300	13,500
1842 medium date	Inc. above	44.00	54.00	74.50	88.00	147	2,505	750	8,800
1842O small date	957,000	650	950	1,400	2,450	4,650	7,750	16,500	—
1842O medium date	Inc. above	42.00	58.00	75.50	85.00	175	500	1,250	10,500
1843	3,844,000	44.00	53.00	71.50	89.00	142	2,510	500	4,500
1843O	2,268,000	59.00	67.00	73.50	89.00	1,100	2,525	550	—
1844	1,766,000	49.00	55.00	71.50	65.00	160	210	440	4,500
1844O	2,005,000	46.00	55.00	71.50	70.00	165	225	550	—
1844/1844O	Inc. above	500	850	1,150	1,400	3,000	5,750	10,000	—
1845	589,000	49.00	57.00	79.50	125	220	325	850	12,000
1845O	2,094,000	46.00	55.00	71.50	70.00	165	240	550	9,400
1845O no drapery	Inc. above	45.00	70.00	100.00	165	350	375	750	—
1846 medium date	2,210,000	46.00	55.00	71.50	70.00	175	200	500	9,000
1846 tall date	Inc. above	47.00	61.00	90.50	135	350	250	650	12,000
1846 /horizontal 6	Inc. above	160	250	325	450	675	1,000	2,500	—
1846O medium date	2,304,000	49.00	57.00	79.50	70.00	220	225	550	12,000
1846O tall date	Inc. above	200	325	425	675	1,750	2,000	6,650	—
1847/1846	1,156,000	2,000	2,750	4,000	5,500	10,000	12,500	21,000	—
1847	Inc. above	44.00	59.00	74.50	91.00	137	2,500	480	9,000
1847O	2,584,000	46.00	55.00	71.50	89.00	152	2,560	640	7,000
1848	580,000	44.00	75.00	110	185	275	485	1,000	9,000
1848O	3,180,000	46.00	55.00	71.50	75.00	175	285	750	9,000

Date	Mintage	G-4	VG-8	F-12	VF-20	XF-40	AU-50	MS-60	MS-65
1849	1,252,000	49.00	59.00	75.50	91.00	140	365	1,250	15,000
1849O	2,310,000	46.00	55.00	71.50	70.00	175	250	650	9,000
1850	227,000	275	325	450	585	700	1,000	1,500	—
1850O	2,456,000	50.00	57.00	73.50	80.00	175	275	650	9,000
1851	200,750	335	475	550	850	1,350	1,200	2,250	—
1851O	402,000	49.00	55.00	67.50	120	225	300	700	9,000
1852	77,130	425	500	700	925	1,100	1,350	1,700	—
1852O	144,000	70.00	125	210	350	750	1,250	3,850	26,000
1853O mintage unrecorded	—	—	250,000	—	—	600,000	—	—	—

Note: 1853O, Eliasberg Sale, 1997, VG-8, $154,000.

Seated Liberty Half Dollar
Seated Liberty, arrows at date obverse
Rays around eagle reverse

KM# 79 • 12.4400 g., 0.9000 **Silver**, 0.3599 oz. ASW • **Rev. Legend:** UNITED STATES OF AMERICA
Designer: Christian Gobrecht

Date	Mintage	G-4	VG-8	F-12	VF-20	XF-40	AU-50	MS-60	MS-65	Prf-65
1853	3,532,708	36.50	48.00	72.00	97.50	265	610	1,500	24,500	175,000
1853O	1,328,000	41.50	56.50	77.00	124.5	285	695	2,250	29,500	—

Seated Liberty Half Dollar
Seated Liberty, arrows at date obverse
HALF DOL. below eagle reverse

KM# 82 • 12.4400 g., 0.9000 **Silver**, 0.3599 oz. ASW • **Rev. Legend:** UNITED STATES OF AMERICA
Designer: Christian Gobrecht

Date	Mintage	G-4	VG-8	F-12	VF-20	XF-40	AU-50	MS-60	MS-65	Prf-65
1854	2,982,000	36.50	48.00	60.00	73.50	135	270	675	8,000	37,500
1854O	5,240,000	36.50	48.00	60.00	73.50	135	270	600	8,000	—
1855	759,500	38.50	50.00	64.00	87.00	167	325	700	9,000	39,500
1855/4	Inc. above	65.00	75.00	135	195	400	600	2,000	17,500	37,000
1855O	3,688,000	39.50	55.00	60.00	73.50	135	270	650	8,000	—
1855S	129,950	350	575	800	1,600	3,650	6,850	19,500	—	—

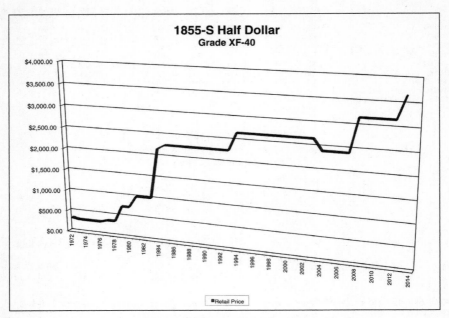

Seated Liberty Half Dollar

Seated Liberty, date below obverse
HALF DOL. below eagle reverse

KM# A68 • 12.4400 g., 0.9000 **Silver**, 0.3599 oz. ASW **• Rev. Legend:** UNITED STATES OF AMERICA
Designer: Christian Gobrecht

Date	Mintage	G-4	VG-8	F-12	VF-20	XF-40	AU-50	MS-60	MS-65	Prf-65
1856O	2,658,000	44.00	52.00	67.50	80.00	130	190	385	12,500	—
1856	938,000	44.00	52.00	67.50	80.00	130	215	425	6,500	12,500
1856S	211,000	85.00	110	165	275	750	1,250	3,500	19,000	—
1857	1,988,000	44.00	52.00	67.50	80.00	120	190	385	5,150	12,500
1857O	818,000	38.00	55.00	70.50	85.00	150	275	885	12,500	—
1857S	158,000	90.00	125	185	375	1,050	975	3,500	19,000	—
1858	4,226,000	44.00	52.00	67.50	80.00	120	215	385	6,500	12,500
1858O	7,294,000	44.00	52.00	67.50	80.00	120	215	385	12,500	—
1858S	476,000	50.00	65.00	85.00	140	365	400	950	12,500	—
1859	748,000	40.00	57.00	71.50	90.00	130	200	650	6,600	5,500
1859O	2,834,000	44.00	52.00	67.50	80.00	120	215	450	6,500	—
1859S	566,000	45.00	58.00	79.50	100.00	275	375	750	12,500	—
1860	303,700	48.00	56.00	71.50	100.00	150	350	1,000	6,500	5,500
1860O	1,290,000	44.00	52.00	67.50	80.00	125	230	450	5,150	—
1860S	472,000	49.00	57.00	72.50	88.00	215	245	850	12,500	—
1861	2,888,400	44.00	55.00	67.50	80.00	125	190	440	5,150	5,500
1861O	2,532,633	52.00	59.00	72.50	88.00	175	235	450	5,150	—
1861O CSA Obv, cracked die	Inc. above	150	350	500	750	1,200	1,750	—	—	—
1861S	939,500	49.00	60.00	74.50	93.00	165	195	975	9,500	—
1862	253,550	56.00	65.00	92.50	120	235	295	750	5,150	5,500
1862S	1,352,000	44.00	59.00	67.50	80.00	120	195	460	9,000	—
1863	503,660	59.00	73.00	92.50	110	190	250	750	5,150	5,500
1863S	916,000	52.00	69.00	82.50	90.00	220	195	460	9,000	—

Date	Mintage	G-4	VG-8	F-12	VF-20	XF-40	AU-50	MS-60	MS-65	Prf-65
1864	379,570	64.00	75.00	97.50	150	275	250	750	5,150	5,500
1864S	658,000	56.00	69.00	81.50	125	250	215	675	9,000	—
1865	511,900	48.00	71.00	90.50	100.00	265	275	750	5,150	5,500
1865S	675,000	56.00	63.00	82.50	100.00	250	235	500	9,000	—
1866 proof, unique	—	—	—	—	—	—	—	—	—	—
1866S	60,000	485	650	950	1,250	2,550	3,350	5,400	68,000	—

Seated Liberty Half Dollar

Seated Liberty, date below obverse
IN GOD WE TRUST above eagle reverse

KM# 99 • 12.4400 g., 0.9000 **Silver**, 0.3599 oz. ASW • **Rev. Legend:** UNITED STATES OF AMERICA
Designer: Christian Gobrecht

Date	Mintage	G-4	VG-8	F-12	VF-20	XF-40	AU-50	MS-60	MS-65	Prf-65
1866	745,625	51.50	64.50	82.00	95.00	175	225	350	4,800	3,750
1866S	994,000	48.50	62.50	80.00	85.00	200	275	650	5,000	—
1867	449,925	53.50	67.50	88.00	130	275	250	350	4,800	3,750
1867S	1,196,000	47.50	61.50	70.00	70.00	200	250	350	7,000	—
1868	418,200	58.50	70.00	105	185	275	300	525	7,100	3,750
1868S	1,160,000	43.50	51.50	70.00	70.00	175	250	350	7,000	—
1869	795,900	48.50	64.50	78.00	85.00	165	190	385	4,600	3,750
1869S	656,000	50.50	66.50	80.00	95.00	210	265	600	7,000	—
1870	634,900	47.50	54.40	70.00	80.00	165	250	475	7,000	3,750
1870CC	54,617	1,200	1,850	4,500	7,250	16,000	30,000	100,000	—	—
1870S	1,004,000	43.50	54.50	72.00	95.00	200	275	575	7,000	—
1871	1,204,560	40.50	51.50	71.00	75.00	160	165	350	7,000	3,750
1871CC	153,950	325	400	600	1,275	2,850	10,000	15,000	—	—
1871S	2,178,000	42.50	50.50	68.00	70.00	175	215	400	7,000	—
1872	881,550	44.50	59.50	68.00	75.00	185	195	430	2,850	3,750
1872CC	272,000	110	175	325	750	2,100	4,000	8,000	50,000	—
1872S	580,000	48.50	60.50	86.00	135	300	375	975	7,000	—
1873 closed 3	801,800	43.50	57.50	83.00	115	165	250	545	4,500	3,750
1873 open 3	Inc. above	3,450	4,450	5,600	6,600	7,750	13,500	30,000	—	—
1873CC	122,500	225	325	550	950	2,350	6,500	12,000	80,000	—
1873S no arrows	5,000	—	—	—	—	—	—	—	—	—

Note: 1873S no arrows, no specimens known to survive.

Seated Liberty Half Dollar

Seated Liberty, arrows at date obverse
IN GOD WE TRUST above eagle reverse

KM# 107 • 12.5000 g., 0.9000 **Silver**, 0.3617 oz. ASW • **Rev. Legend:** UNITED STATES OF AMERICA
Designer: Christian Gobrecht

Date	Mintage	G-4	VG-8	F-12	VF-20	XF-40	AU-50	MS-60	MS-65	Prf-65
1873	1,815,700	48.00	67.00	85.00	124	235	400	850	17,500	9,000
1873CC	214,560	150	400	650	1,100	2,350	2,400	5,700	42,000	—
1873S	233,000	55.00	110	150	245	475	675	2,200	40,000	—
1874	2,360,300	44.00	56.00	72.00	90.00	215	440	900	15,500	9,000
1874CC	59,000	500	1,000	2,200	3,250	5,400	5,600	10,500	—	—
1874S	394,000	43.00	65.00	85.00	185	365	685	1,850	20,000	—

Seated Liberty Half Dollar
Seated Liberty, date below obverse
IN GOD WE TRUST above eagle reverse

KM# A99 • 12.5000 g., 0.9000 **Silver**, 0.3617 oz. ASW • **Rev. Legend:** UNITED STATES OF AMERICA
Designer: Christian Gobrecht

Date	Mintage	G-4	VG-8	F-12	VF-20	XF-40	AU-50	MS-60	MS-65	Prf-65
1875	6,027,500	38.50	47.50	66.00	88.00	128	2,465	6,310	3,500	3,375
1875CC	1,008,000	50.00	80.00	110	225	325	325	650	8,350	—
1875S	3,200,000	38.50	47.50	66.00	95.00	130	2,450	6,250	2,700	—
1876	8,419,150	36.50	47.50	66.00	88.00	118	2,450	6,250	5,300	3,775
1876CC	1,956,000	50.00	60.00	75.00	115	265	275	560	4,200	—
1876S	4,528,000	36.50	47.50	66.00	88.00	118	2,450	6,250	2,700	—
1877	8,304,510	36.50	47.50	66.00	88.00	118	2,450	6,250	2,700	3,825
1877CC	1,420,000	50.00	68.00	100.00	125	265	275	630	3,250	—
1877S	5,356,000	36.50	47.50	66.00	88.00	118	2,450	6,250	2,700	—
1878	1,378,400	38.50	55.50	86.00	112	150	2,450	425	3,650	3,900
1878CC	62,000	750	1,150	2,000	2,350	3,150	4,850	7,000	43,500	—
1878S	12,000	28,500	42,000	47,500	58,000	60,000	85,000	70,000	175,000	—
1879	5,900	275	310	375	450	525	575	700	3,650	3,150
1880	9,755	260	300	350	410	500	535	700	3,750	3,150
1881	10,975	270	325	345	400	455	565	700	4,000	3,150
1882	5,500	340	410	460	600	650	600	750	3,850	3,150
1883	9,039	325	390	480	560	625	575	775	3,950	3,150
1884	5,275	385	425	500	610	700	635	800	3,850	3,150
1885	6,130	390	450	485	575	660	700	825	3,850	3,150
1886	5,886	400	550	630	725	850	875	1,000	3,900	3,150
1887	5,710	475	600	700	800	875	950	1,100	3,900	3,150
1888	12,833	280	310	365	410	525	550	800	3,900	3,150
1889	12,711	275	315	400	465	510	550	800	3,900	3,150
1890	12,590	275	310	365	415	500	550	800	3,850	3,150
1891	200,600	55.00	75.00	94.00	125	155	240	480	3,850	3,150

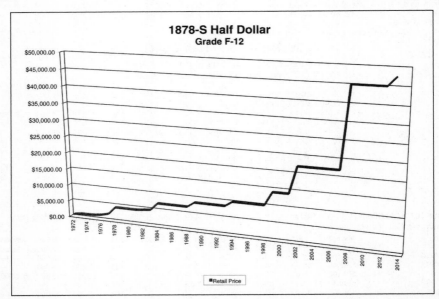

1878-S Half Dollar
Grade F-12

Barber Half Dollar

Laureate head right, flanked by stars, date below obverse
Heraldic eagle reverse

Mint mark

KM# 116 • 12.5000 g., 0.9000 **Silver**, 0.3617 oz. ASW, 30.6 mm. • **Obv. Legend** IN GOD WE TRUST
Rev. Legend: UNITED STATES OF AMERICA **Designer:** Charles E. Barber

Date	Mintage	G-4	VG-8	F-12	VF-20	XF-40	AU-50	MS-60	MS-65	Prf-65
1892	935,245	29.50	44.00	73.50	120	195	385	505	3,150	3,750
1892O	390,000	310	420	515	600	630	690	850	4,350	—
1892O micro O	Inc. above	2,000	3,750	4,500	7,000	10,000	17,500	24,000	64,000	—
1892S	1,029,028	250	330	425	550	600	700	985	4,850	—
1893	1,826,792	20.00	36.00	78.00	150	205	385	540	5,250	3,750
1893O	1,389,000	36.00	70.00	130	230	360	435	635	9,650	—
1893S	740,000	165	240	325	525	595	675	1,275	25,000	—
1894	1,148,972	32.50	54.00	115	210	280	395	540	3,850	3,750
1894O	2,138,000	22.00	36.00	95.00	180	310	400	555	6,250	—
1894S	4,048,690	22.00	28.00	67.00	125	230	400	575	9,850	—
1895	1,835,218	22.00	28.00	72.00	165	225	400	595	3,650	3,750
1895O	1,766,000	23.00	43.00	110	195	285	425	650	6,950	—
1895S	1,108,086	32.00	56.00	130	235	315	440	635	8,250	—
1896	950,762	22.50	30.00	88.00	160	265	395	625	5,450	3,750
1896O	924,000	45.00	60.00	215	290	510	885	1,750	19,500	—
1896S	1,140,948	120	145	210	350	515	800	1,575	10,500	—
1897	2,480,731	19.80	21.00	47.50	105	195	385	520	3,950	3,750
1897O	632,000	170	230	485	835	1,050	1,350	1,850	9,650	—
1897S	933,900	155	230	385	560	840	1,050	1,650	7,350	—
1898	2,956,735	19.80	21.00	38.50	94.00	185	375	520	3,500	3,750
1898O	874,000	37.50	95.00	240	400	525	640	1,250	9,450	—
1898S	2,358,550	28.50	53.00	87.50	175	340	440	985	10,250	—
1899	5,538,846	19.00	21.00	39.50	98.00	185	405	525	3,950	3,750
1899O	1,724,000	26.00	38.00	85.00	180	300	410	700	8,150	—
1899S	1,686,411	25.00	45.00	92.00	155	220	395	660	6,900	—
1900	4,762,912	20.30	22.00	38.50	95.00	190	375	515	3,950	3,750
1900O	2,744,000	19.00	23.00	62.00	175	290	400	900	15,500	—
1900S	2,560,322	19.00	22.00	46.50	98.00	215	375	640	9,500	—
1901	4,268,813	19.00	23.00	38.50	94.00	195	385	550	4,250	3,750
1901O	1,124,000	19.00	30.00	85.00	235	365	500	1,350	14,850	—
1901S	847,044	34.00	55.00	175	375	675	1,050	1,950	16,500	—
1902	4,922,777	18.80	19.00	38.50	90.00	190	375	505	4,450	3,750
1902O	2,526,000	20.30	22.00	55.00	115	230	395	775	10,500	—
1902S	1,460,670	20.80	25.00	66.00	165	265	420	750	7,750	—
1903	2,278,755	20.30	22.00	47.50	105	205	375	500	7,650	3,750
1903O	2,100,000	19.80	20.00	55.00	135	215	385	665	9,500	—
1903S	1,920,772	20.00	22.00	60.00	145	265	400	675	5,350	—
1904	2,992,670	19.80	21.00	35.00	95.00	190	385	510	4,650	3,750
1904O	1,117,600	22.00	33.00	90.00	235	385	610	1,375	12,500	—
1904S	553,038	42.00	95.00	300	700	1,250	2,450	9,850	46,000	—
1905	662,727	23.50	34.00	95.00	195	270	410	625	6,600	3,750
1905O	505,000	30.00	45.00	130	235	340	460	760	5,200	—
1905S	2,494,000	20.00	24.00	50.00	130	230	410	615	9,350	—
1906	2,638,675	18.80	19.00	32.00	85.00	185	385	500	3,300	3,750
1906D	4,028,000	18.80	19.00	35.00	89.00	185	375	495	3,800	—
1906O	2,446,000	18.80	19.00	44.00	205	195	400	600	6,350	—
1906S	1,740,154	20.30	21.00	57.50	118	220	420	590	5,750	—
1907	2,598,575	18.80	19.00	30.00	83.00	185	375	495	3,250	3,750
1907D	3,856,000	18.80	19.00	30.00	75.00	185	375	495	3,000	—
1907O	3,946,000	18.80	19.00	32.00	89.00	190	375	535	3,100	—
1907S	1,250,000	22.00	25.00	85.00	170	365	665	1,275	12,500	—
1908	1,354,545	18.80	19.00	30.00	85.00	185	375	495	3,300	3,750
1908D	3,280,000	18.80	19.00	30.00	80.00	185	375	495	3,000	—
1908O	5,360,000	18.80	19.00	30.00	89.00	185	385	540	3,000	—
1908S	1,644,828	20.30	25.00	72.00	165	285	440	875	6,350	—
1909	2,368,650	19.80	21.00	32.00	83.00	185	375	565	3,000	3,750
1909O	925,400	23.10	24.00	56.00	150	315	525	775	3,950	—
1909S	1,764,000	19.10	20.00	37.50	100.00	195	395	600	3,750	—

HALF DOLLAR

Date	Mintage	G-4	VG-8	F-12	VF-20	XF-40	AU-50	MS-60	MS-65	Prf-65
1910	418,551	20.00	30.00	95.00	180	330	485	610	3,900	3,750
1910S	1,948,000	22.30	24.00	36.00	100.00	200	395	640	6,650	—
1911	1,406,543	18.80	19.00	30.00	83.00	185	375	495	3,000	3,750
1911D	695,080	19.80	21.00	40.00	91.00	195	385	565	3,950	—
1911S	1,272,000	20.30	21.00	42.00	98.00	185	385	580	5,950	—
1912	1,550,700	18.80	19.00	30.00	83.00	185	375	495	3,500	3,750
1912D	2,300,800	18.80	19.00	30.00	81.00	185	375	495	3,000	—
1912S	1,370,000	21.10	22.00	43.50	100.00	210	375	535	4,600	—
1913	188,627	77.00	88.00	235	435	615	875	1,225	4,950	3,900
1913D	534,000	19.00	22.00	44.00	100.00	200	395	515	4,850	—
1913S	604,000	21.00	25.00	53.50	110	235	425	755	4,450	—
1914	124,610	145	180	335	575	775	1,025	1,475	8,500	4,100
1914S	992,000	20.80	23.00	41.00	98.00	190	395	575	4,650	—
1915	138,450	112	168	285	380	575	920	1,350	6,350	4,100
1915D	1,170,400	18.80	19.00	30.00	80.00	185	375	495	3,000	—
1915S	1,604,000	22.30	23.00	43.50	94.00	200	390	510	3,000	—

Walking Liberty Half Dollar
Liberty walking left wearing U.S. flag gown, sunrise at left obverse
Eagle advancing left reverse

Obverse mint mark
1916-1917

Reverse mint mark
1917-1947

KM# 142 • 12.5000 g., 0.9000 **Silver**, 0.3617 oz. ASW, 30.6 mm. • **Designer:** Adolph A. Weinman **Notes:**
The mint mark appears on the obverse below the word "Trust" on 1916 and some 1917 issues. Starting with
some 1917 issues and continuing through the remainder of the series, the mint mark was changed to the
reverse, at about the 8 o'clock position near the rim.

Date	Mintage	G-4	VG-8	F-12	VF-20	XF-40	AU-50	MS-60	MS-65	Prf-65
1916	608,000	47.00	55.00	95.00	170	240	275	345	1,950	—
1916D	1,014,400	48.50	55.00	80.00	135	220	255	360	2,500	—
1916S	508,000	108	135	280	440	600	720	1,050	6,250	—
1917	12,292,000	14.20	14.50	15.20	19.50	42.00	72.00	130	1,050	—
1917D obv. mint mark	765,400	23.50	33.00	80.00	155	235	335	625	7,900	—
1917S obv. mint mark	952,000	27.00	44.00	135	365	700	1,200	2,300	22,500	—
1917D rev. mint mark	1,940,000	14.20	14.50	45.00	135	275	555	940	18,500	—
1917S rev. mint mark	5,554,000	14.20	14.50	16.50	32.00	65.00	155	330	13,850	—
1918	6,634,000	14.20	14.50	15.50	64.00	150	265	565	3,800	—
1918D	3,853,040	14.20	14.50	35.00	90.00	225	500	1,300	24,500	—
1918S	10,282,000	14.20	14.50	16.00	34.00	60.00	190	485	17,750	—
1919	962,000	26.00	32.50	78.50	265	535	885	1,325	7,750	—
1919D	1,165,000	25.00	38.50	95.00	320	765	1,750	5,950	130,000	—
1919S	1,552,000	17.50	28.50	72.00	310	825	1,750	3,300	20,000	—
1920	6,372,000	14.20	14.50	15.50	42.00	75.00	155	330	5,250	—
1920D	1,551,000	14.20	14.50	65.00	240	460	920	1,485	17,500	—
1920S	4,624,000	14.20	14.50	19.00	78.00	235	510	850	14,500	—
1921	246,000	165	210	350	750	1,575	2,650	4,500	19,500	—
1921D	208,000	310	370	550	950	2,200	3,150	5,650	29,500	—
1921S	548,000	45.00	65.00	210	750	4,850	7,950	12,950	130,000	—
1923S	2,178,000	14.20	14.50	27.50	110	295	650	1,375	16,500	—
1927S	2,392,000	14.50	14.80	16.50	46.00	165	425	990	9,750	—
1928S Large S	1,940,000	14.50	17.50	28.00	110	325	600	1,650	—	—
1928S Small S	Inc. above	14.20	14.50	18.50	66.00	195	450	985	10,750	—
1929D	1,001,200	14.20	14.50	17.50	32.00	98.00	195	390	3,350	—
1929S	1,902,000	14.20	14.50	15.50	28.50	115	220	400	3,750	—
1933S	1,786,000	14.20	14.50	17.60	20.00	58.00	240	590	4,500	—
1934	6,964,000	14.00	14.50	15.20	15.80	17.60	25.00	85.00	565	—
1934D	2,361,400	14.20	14.90	18.90	17.50	36.00	88.00	150	1,625	—
1934S	3,652,000	14.00	14.70	15.80	18.00	30.00	100.00	385	4,800	—
1935	9,162,000	14.00	14.50	15.20	15.80	17.76	21.50	45.00	365	—
1935D	3,003,800	14.00	14.70	15.80	16.20	33.00	66.00	140	2,450	—
1935S	3,854,000	14.00	14.70	15.60	13.50	32.00	95.00	285	2,850	—
1936	12,617,901	14.00	14.50	15.20	15.80	17.76	21.00	37.50	265	6,600

HALF DOLLAR

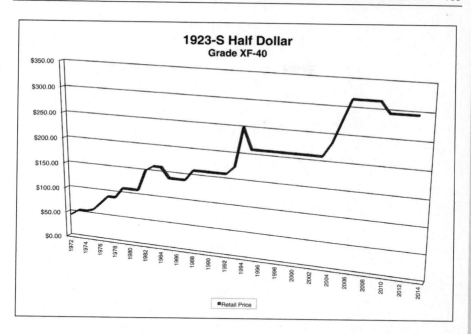

Date	Mintage	G-4	VG-8	F-12	VF-20	XF-40	AU-50	MS-60	MS-65	Prf-65
1936D	4,252,400	14.00	14.70	15.60	16.00	20.00	52.00	78.00	665	—
1936S	3,884,000	14.00	14.70	15.60	16.00	21.50	58.00	132	1,000	—
1937	9,527,728	14.00	14.50	15.20	15.80	17.76	22.00	38.00	285	1,700
1937D	1,676,000	14.00	14.70	17.20	17.60	33.50	105	220	965	—
1937S	2,090,000	14.00	14.70	15.80	17.20	25.50	62.00	168	785	—
1938	4,118,152	14.00	14.70	15.60	16.20	19.21	38.00	66.00	460	1,275
1938D	491,600	70.00	75.00	100.00	125	185	250	475	1,750	—
1939	6,820,808	14.00	14.30	15.00	15.80	17.76	22.00	41.00	210	1,150
1939D	4,267,800	14.00	14.50	15.20	16.80	18.51	26.00	45.00	225	—
1939S	2,552,000	14.00	14.70	15.60	16.00	25.00	76.00	145	375	—
1940	9,167,279	14.00	14.30	15.00	15.40	16.80	17.60	31.00	185	1,000
1940S	4,550,000	14.00	14.50	15.20	15.80	17.76	21.00	50.00	315	—
1941	24,207,412	14.00	14.30	15.00	15.36	16.10	17.60	30.00	155	850
1941D	11,248,400	14.00	14.50	15.20	15.80	16.20	18.00	37.50	180	—
1941S	8,098,000	14.00	14.50	15.20	15.80	19.60	27.50	70.00	925	—
1942	47,839,120	14.00	14.30	15.00	15.36	15.80	17.60	30.00	130	850
1942D	10,973,800	14.00	14.50	15.20	15.80	16.20	19.00	37.00	315	—
1942S	12,708,000	14.00	14.50	15.20	15.80	16.20	18.60	37.00	475	—
1943	53,190,000	14.00	14.30	15.00	15.36	16.10	17.60	30.00	140	—
1943D	11,346,000	14.00	14.50	15.20	15.80	16.20	25.00	42.00	240	—
1943D Double Die Obverse	—	14.20	15.00	17.00	19.00	22.00	30.00	55.00	450	—
1943S	13,450,000	14.00	14.50	15.20	15.80	16.20	18.50	42.00	290	—
1944	28,206,000	14.00	14.30	15.00	15.36	16.10	17.60	30.00	170	—
1944D	9,769,000	14.00	14.50	15.20	15.80	16.20	20.00	37.00	165	—
1944S	8,904,000	14.00	14.50	15.20	15.80	16.20	18.00	36.00	500	—
1945	31,502,000	14.00	14.30	15.00	15.36	16.10	17.60	30.00	130	—
1945D	9,966,800	14.00	14.50	15.20	15.80	16.20	19.00	36.00	130	—
1945S	10,156,000	14.00	14.50	15.20	15.80	16.20	17.50	36.00	135	—
1946 Double Die Reverse	Inc. above	16.00	24.00	35.00	50.00	85.00	175	325	2,750	—
1946	12,118,000	14.00	14.30	15.00	15.36	16.10	17.60	30.00	155	—
1946D	2,151,000	14.00	14.70	15.20	15.80	25.50	38.50	47.50	125	—
1946S	3,724,000	14.00	14.50	15.20	15.80	16.90	19.00	43.50	175	—
1947	4,094,000	14.00	14.30	15.00	15.80	16.20	22.00	50.00	220	—
1947D	3,900,600	14.00	14.70	15.20	15.80	16.20	31.50	52.50	145	—

Franklin Half Dollar
Franklin bust right obverse
Liberty Bell, small eagle at right reverse

Mint mark

KM# 199 • 12.5000 g., 0.9000 **Silver**, 0.3617 oz. ASW, 30.6 mm. • **Designer:** John R. Sinnock

Date	Mintage	G-4	VG-8	F-12	VF-20	XF-40	AU-50	MS-60	MS-65	-65FBL	-65CAM
1948	3,006,814	—	13.80	13.90	14.50	15.10	15.30	17.00	75.00	190	—
1948D	4,028,600	—	13.80	13.90	14.50	14.60	15.00	16.00	125	260	—
1949	5,614,000	—	—	—	—	15.60	14.00	38.50	120	250	—
1949D	4,120,600	—	—	—	14.30	16.60	25.00	43.50	900	1,750	—
1949S	3,744,000	—	—	—	14.50	16.50	30.00	62.50	160	700	—
1950	7,793,509	—	—	—	—	13.90	13.00	26.00	110	285	2,000
1950D	8,031,600	—	—	—	—	14.90	15.10	22.00	425	900	—
1951	16,859,602	—	—	—	—	13.60	16.60	17.60	75.00	340	1,450
1951D	9,475,200	—	—	—	—	17.90	17.50	26.00	170	540	—
1951S	13,696,000	—	—	—	13.90	14.60	15.00	23.50	125	750	—
1952	21,274,073	—	—	—	—	13.80	16.60	17.00	70.00	210	775
1952D	25,395,600	—	—	—	—	13.80	16.60	17.00	130	450	—
1952S	5,526,000	—	—	13.90	16.50	16.00	32.00	52.00	140	1,500	—
1953	2,796,920	—	—	13.90	14.00	14.40	16.00	25.00	140	1,000	475
1953D	20,900,400	—	—	—	—	13.60	13.80	14.00	150	400	—
1953S	4,148,000	—	—	—	13.90	14.60	18.50	25.00	65.00	16,000	—
1954	13,421,503	—	—	—	—	13.60	14.60	14.80	75.00	225	175
1954D	25,445,580	—	—	—	—	13.60	14.60	14.80	110	235	—
1954S	4,993,400	—	—	—	—	14.00	14.60	15.10	42.00	440	—
1955	2,876,381	—	15.50	16.00	17.50	18.00	18.50	20.00	70.00	140	120
1955 Bugs Bunny	Inc. above	—	20.00	22.00	23.00	25.00	26.00	28.00	120	750	—
1956 Type 1 rev.	4,701,384	—	13.50	13.60	13.70	14.00	14.80	15.40	55.00	125	300
1956 Type 2 rev.	Inc. above	—	—	—	—	—	—	—	—	—	40.00
1957 Type 1 rev.	6,361,952	—	—	—	—	13.60	14.80	15.70	63.00	95.00	55.00
1957 Type 2 rev.	Inc. above	—	—	—	—	—	—	—	—	—	—
1957D	19,966,850	—	—	—	—	13.60	14.80	15.50	60.00	100.00	—
1958 Type 1 rev.	4,917,652	—	—	—	—	13.60	14.80	15.50	55.00	110	60.00
1958 Type 2 rev.	Inc. above	—	—	—	—	14.30	20.00	26.00	—	—	—
1958D	23,962,412	—	—	—	—	13.60	14.80	15.50	55.00	80.00	—
1959 Type 1 rev.	7,349,291	—	—	—	—	13.60	14.80	15.50	110	250	75.00
1959 Type 2 rev.	Inc. above	—	—	—	—	14.10	16.00	30.00	115	—	—
1959D	13,053,750	—	—	—	—	13.60	14.80	15.50	125	215	—
1960 Type 1 rev.	7,715,602	—	—	—	—	13.60	14.80	15.50	110	340	45.00
1960 Type 2 rev.	Inc. above	—	—	—	—	—	—	—	—	—	—
1960D	18,215,812	—	—	—	—	13.60	14.80	15.50	400	1,350	—
1961 Type 1 rev.	11,318,244	—	—	—	—	13.60	14.80	15.50	125	1,300	40.00
1961 Type 2 rev.	Inc. above	—	—	—	—	25.00	—	—	—	—	—
1961 Double die rev.	Inc. above	—	—	—	—	—	—	—	—	—	3,500
1961D	20,276,442	—	—	—	—	13.60	14.80	15.50	155	875	—
1962 Type 1 rev.	12,932,019	—	—	—	—	13.60	14.80	15.50	145	1,850	35.00
1962 Type 2 rev.	Inc. above	—	—	—	—	—	—	—	—	—	—
1962D	35,473,281	—	—	—	—	13.60	14.80	15.50	175	800	—
1963 Type 1 rev.	25,239,645	—	—	—	—	13.60	14.80	15.50	55.00	1,200	35.00
1963 Type 2 rev.	Inc. above	—	—	—	—	—	—	—	—	—	—
1963D	67,069,292	—	—	—	—	13.60	14.80	15.50	75.00	165	—

HALF DOLLAR

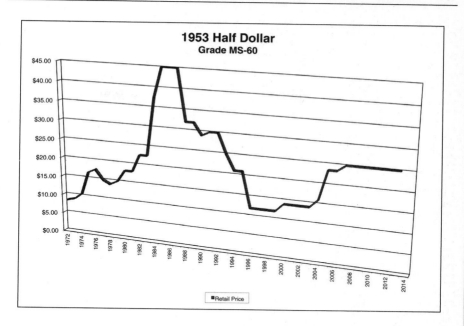

1953 Half Dollar
Grade MS-60

Retail Price

Kennedy Half Dollar

Mint mark 1964

Mint mark 1968 - present

KM# 202 • 12.5000 g., 0.9000 **Silver**, 0.3617 oz. ASW, 30.6 mm. • **Obv. Designer:** Gilroy Roberts **Rev. Designer:** Frank Gasparro **Edge Desc:** Reeded

Date	Mintage	XF-40	MS-60	MS-65	Prf-65
1964	277,254,766	10.10	10.30	22.00	15.00
1964 Accented Hair	Inc. above	—	—	—	40.00
1964D	156,205,446	10.20	10.50	24.00	—

KM# 202a • 11.5000 g., 0.4000 **Silver**, 0.1479 oz. ASW, 30.6 mm. • **Obv. Designer:** Gilroy Roberts **Rev. Designer:** Frank Gasparro **Edge Desc:** Reeded

Date	Mintage	MS-60	MS-65	Prf-65
1965	65,879,366	5.00	14.50	—
1965 SMS	2,360,000	—	15.00	—
1966	108,984,932	5.00	22.50	—
1966 SMS	2,261,583	—	17.00	—
1967	295,046,978	5.00	18.50	—
1967 SMS	1,863,344	—	18.00	—
1968D	246,951,930	5.00	16.50	—
1968S	3,041,506	—	—	7.49
1969D	129,881,800	5.00	20.00	—
1969S	2,934,631	—	—	7.49
1970D	2,150,000	8.50	40.00	—
1970S	2,632,810	—	—	12.00

HALF DOLLAR

KM# 202b • 11.3400 g., **Copper-Nickel Clad Copper**, 30.6 mm. • **Obv. Designer:** Gilroy Roberts **Rev. Designer:** Frank Gasparro

Date	Mintage	XF-40	MS-60	MS-65	Prf-65
1971	155,640,000	—	1.00	17.50	—
1971D	302,097,424	—	1.00	12.00	—
1971S	3,244,183	—	—	—	5.00
1972	153,180,000	—	1.00	15.50	—
1972D	141,890,000	—	1.00	14.50	—
1972S	3,267,667	—	—	—	5.00
1973	64,964,000	—	1.00	20.00	—
1973D	83,171,400	—	—	12.00	—
1973S	2,769,624	—	—	—	5.00
1974	201,596,000	—	1.00	25.00	—
1974D	79,066,300	—	1.00	17.00	—
1974D DDO	Inc. above	24.00	32.00	165	—
1974S	2,617,350	—	—	—	5.00
1975 none minted	—	—	—	—	—
1975D none minted	—	—	—	—	—
1975S none minted	—	—	—	—	—

Bicentennial design, Independence Hall reverse

KM# 205 • 11.2000 g., **Copper-Nickel**, 30.6 mm. • **Rev. Designer:** Seth Huntington

Date	Mintage	MS-60	MS-65	Prf-65
1976D	234,308,000	1.00	16.50	—
1976D	287,565,248	1.00	14.00	—
1976S	7,059,099	—	—	5.00

Bicentennial design, Independence Hall reverse

KM# 205a • 11.5000 g., 0.4000 **Silver**, 0.1479 oz. ASW, 30.6 mm. • **Rev. Designer:** Seth Huntington

Date	Mintage	MS-60	MS-65	Prf-65
1976S	4,908,319	—	12.00	7.60
1976S	3,998,621	—	—	7.60

Regular design resumed reverse

KM# A202b • 11.3400 g., **Copper-Nickel Clad Copper**, 30.61 mm. • **Edge Desc:** Reeded **Notes:** KM#202b design and composition resumed. The 1979-S and 1981-S Type II proofs have clearer mint marks than the Type I proofs of those years.

Date	Mintage	MS-65	Prf-65
1977	43,598,000	12.50	—
1977D	31,449,106	16.50	—

Date	Mintage	MS-65	Prf-65
1977S	3,251,152	—	4.50
1978	14,350,000	12.00	—
1978D	13,765,799	15.00	—
1978S	3,127,788	—	5.00
1979	68,312,000	13.50	—
1979D	15,815,422	13.50	—
1979S Type I	3,677,175	—	5.00
1979S Type II	Inc. above	—	18.00
1980P	44,134,000	12.50	—
1980D	33,456,449	17.50	—
1980S	3,547,030	—	5.00
1981P	29,544,000	15.50	—
1981D	27,839,533	20.00	—
1981S Type I	4,063,083	—	5.00
1981S Type II	Inc. above	—	18.50
1982P	10,819,000	18.50	—
1982P no initials FG	Inc. above	110	—
1982D	13,140,102	20.00	—
1982S	38,957,479	—	5.00
1983P	34,139,000	22.50	—
1983D	32,472,244	12.50	—
1983S	3,279,126	—	5.00
1984P	26,029,000	12.00	—
1984D	26,262,158	18.00	—
1984S	3,065,110	—	6.00
1985P	18,706,962	16.50	—
1985D	19,814,034	12.50	—
1985S	3,962,138	—	5.00
1986P	13,107,633	17.50	—
1986D	15,336,145	14.00	—
1986S	2,411,180	—	6.00
1987P	2,890,758	16.50	—
1987D	2,890,758	12.50	—
1987S	4,407,728	—	5.00
1988P	13,626,000	16.50	—
1988D	12,000,096	10.00	—
1988S	3,262,948	—	5.00
1989P	24,542,000	13.00	—
1989S	3,220,194	—	5.00
1989D	23,000,216	13.00	—
1990P	22,780,000	17.50	—
1990D	20,096,242	20.00	—
1990S	3,299,559	—	5.00
1991P	14,874,000	12.50	—
1991D	15,054,678	16.00	—
1991S	2,867,787	—	5.00
1992P	17,628,000	10.00	—
1992D	17,000,106	10.00	—
1992S	2,858,981	—	5.00
1993P	15,510,000	12.00	—
1993D	15,000,006	10.00	—
1993S	2,633,439	—	5.00
1994P	23,718,000	12.00	—
1994D	23,828,110	8.50	—
1994S	2,484,594	—	5.00
1995P	26,496,000	10.00	—
1995D	26,288,000	8.00	—
1995S	2,010,384	—	12.00
1996P	24,442,000	10.00	—
1996D	24,744,000	10.00	—
1996S	2,085,191	—	9.00
1997P	20,882,000	14.00	—
1997D	19,876,000	13.50	—
1997S	1,975,000	—	10.00
1998P	15,646,000	12.50	—
1998D	15,064,000	12.50	—
1998S	2,078,494	—	7.00
1999P	8,900,000	11.00	—
1999D	10,682,000	10.00	—
1999S	2,557,897	—	8.00
2000P	22,600,000	12.00	—
2000D	19,466,000	12.00	—
2000S	3,082,944	—	5.00
2001P	21,200,000	10.00	—
2001D	19,504,000	9.00	—
2001S	2,235,000	—	5.00
2002P	3,100,000	10.00	—
2002D	2,500,000	10.50	—
2002S	2,268,913	—	5.00

Date	Mintage	MS-65	Prf-65
2003P	2,500,000	6.00	—
2003D	2,500,000	6.00	—
2003S	2,076,165	—	5.00
2004P	2,900,000	4.50	—
2004D	2,900,000	4.50	—
2004S	1,789,488	—	6.00
2005P	3,800,000	6.00	—
2005P Satin finish	1,160,000	8.00	—
2005D	3,500,000	5.00	—
2005D Satin finish	1,160,000	10.00	—
2005S	2,275,000	—	5.00
2006P	2,400,000	4.50	—
2006P Satin finish	847,361	12.00	—
2006D	2,000,000	4.50	—
2006D Satin finish	847,361	14.00	—
2006S	1,934,965	—	6.00
2007P	—	4.50	—
2007P Satin finish	—	8.00	—
2007D	—	4.50	—
2007D Satin finish	—	8.00	—
2007S	—	—	6.00
2008P	—	4.50	—
2008P Satin finish	—	8.50	—
2008D	—	4.50	—
2008D Satin finish	—	8.50	—
2008S	—	—	9.00
2009P	—	4.50	—
2009P Satin finish	—	8.50	—
2009D	—	4.50	—
2009D Satin finish	—	8.50	—
2009S	—	—	6.00
2010P	—	4.50	—
2010P Satin finish	—	8.50	—
2010D	—	4.50	—
2010D Satin finish	—	8.50	—
2010S	—	—	13.00
2011P	—	4.50	—
2011D	—	4.50	—
2011S	—	—	9.00
2012P	—	4.50	—
2012D	—	4.50	—
2012S	—	—	9.00
2013P	—	4.50	—
2013D	—	4.50	—
2013S	—	—	9.00

KM# A202c • 12.5000 g., 0.9000 **Silver**, 0.3617 oz. ASW, 30.6 mm. • **Designer:** Gilroy Roberts

Date	Mintage	Prf-65
1992S	1,317,579	11.00
1993S	761,353	13.00
1994S	785,329	11.00
1995S	838,953	46.00
1996S	830,021	13.00
1997S	821,678	35.00
1998S	878,792	11.00
1998S Matte Proof	62,350	225
1999S	804,565	13.00
2000S	965,921	11.00
2001S	849,600	11.00
2002S	888,816	11.00
2003S	1,040,425	11.00
2004S	1,175,935	11.00
2005S	1,069,679	12.00
2006S	988,140	12.00
2007S	1,384,797	13.50
2008S	620,684	12.00
2009S	—	11.00
2010S	—	12.00
2011S	—	12.00
2012S	—	12.00
2013S	—	12.00

DOLLAR

Flowing Hair Dollar

KM# 17 • 26.9600 g., 0.8920 **Silver**, 0.7731 oz. ASW, 39-40 mm. • **Designer:** Robert Scot **Notes:** The two 1795 varieties have either two or three leaves under each of the eagle's wings on the reverse.

Date	Mintage	F-12	VF-20	XF-40	AU-50	MS-60	MS-63
1794	1,758	120,000	170,000	245,000	365,000	575,000	950,000
1795 2 leaves	203,033	4,450	7,800	16,150	25,500	80,500	196,500
1795 3 leaves	Inc. above	4,200	7,250	14,500	22,500	69,500	182,500
1795 Silver plug	Inc. above	9,850	13,950	28,500	48,500	115,000	235,000

DOLLAR

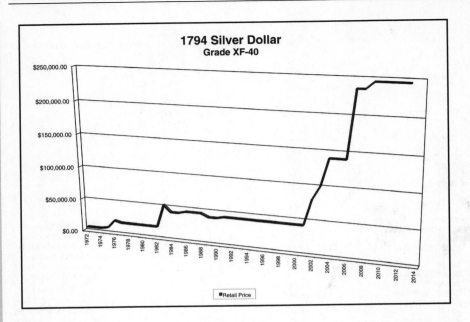

Draped Bust Dollar
Small eagle reverse

KM# 18 • 26.9600 g., 0.8920 **Silver**, 0.7731 oz. ASW, 39-40 mm. • **Designer:** Robert Scot

Date	Mintage	F-12	VF-20	XF-40	AU-50	MS-60	MS-63
1795 Off-center bust	Inc. above	3,850	5,850	12,500	17,000	52,000	126,000
1795 Centered bust	—	3,900	5,950	12,700	17,250	52,500	126,000
1796 small date, small letters	72,920	4,100	6,300	13,750	18,500	70,000	—
1796 small date, large letters	Inc. above	3,875	6,400	13,700	19,400	—	—
1796 large date, small letters	Inc. above	4,250	6,750	14,350	19,200	57,000	136,000
1797 9 stars left, 7 stars right, small letters	7,776	5,200	9,000	18,850	36,500	—	—
1797 9 stars left, 7 stars right, large letters	Inc. above	4,250	6,850	13,950	20,300	55,500	—
1797 10 stars left, 6 stars right	Inc. above	4,050	6,350	13,600	18,500	53,500	125,000
1798 13 stars	327,536	4,150	6,300	13,750	21,000	85,000	—
1798 15 stars	Inc. above	4,700	7,450	16,150	25,500	95,000	—

Draped Bust Dollar

Draped bust right, flanked by stars, date below obverse   Heraldic eagle reverse

KM# 32 • 26.9600 g., 0.8920 **Silver**, 0.7731 oz. ASW, 39-40 mm. • **Obv. Legend** LIBERTY **Rev. Legend:** UNITED STATES OF AMERICA **Designer:** Robert Scot **Notes:** The 1798 "knob 9" variety has a serif on the lower left of the 9 in the date. The 1798 varieties are distinguished by the number of arrows held by the eagle on the reverse and the number of berries on the olive branch. On the 1798 "high-8" variety, the 8 in the date is higher than the other numerals. The 1799 varieties are distinguished by the number and positioning of the stars on the obverse and by the size of the berries in the olive branch on the reverse. On the 1700 "irregular date" variety, the first 9 in the date is smaller than the other numerals. Some varieties of the 1800 strikes had letters in the legend cut twice into the dies; as between the numerals in the date are wider than other varieties and the 8 is lower than the other numerals. The 1800 "small berries" variety refers to the size of the berries in the olive branch on the reverse. The 1800 "12 arrows" and "10 arrows" varieties refer to the number of arrows held by the eagle. The 1800 "Americai" variety appears to have the faint outline of an "I" after "America" in the reverse legend. The "close" and "wide" varieties of the 1802 refer to the amount of space between the numerals in the date. The 1800 large-3 and small-3 varieties are distinguished by the size of the 3 in the date.

Date	Mintage	F-12	VF-20	XF-40	AU-50	MS-60	MS-63
1798 knob 9, 4 stripes	423,515	1,785	2,735	5,550	9,850	21,750	95,000
1798 knob 9, 10 arrows	Inc. above	1,785	2,735	5,550	9,850	21,750	87,000
1798 knob 9, 5 stripes	Inc. above	—	—	—	—	—	124,500
1798 pointed 9, 4 berries	Inc. above	1,785	2,735	5,550	9,850	21,750	43,500
1798 5 berries, 12 arrows	Inc. above	1,785	2,735	5,550	9,850	21,750	43,500
1798 high 8	Inc. above	1,785	2,735	5,550	9,850	21,750	43,500
1798 13 arrows	Inc. above	1,785	2,735	5,550	9,850	21,750	45,000
1799/98 13-star reverse	Inc. above	2,000	2,950	4,300	8,600	23,500	45,000
1799/98 15-star reverse	Inc. above	1,875	2,850	4,000	8,300	24,500	47,500
1799 irregular date, 13-star reverse	Inc. above	1,825	3,000	3,900	8,200	23,500	45,000
1799 irregular date, 15-star reverse	Inc. above	1,825	3,200	5,550	9,850	21,500	42,500
1799 perfect date, 7- and 6-star obverse, no berries	Inc. above	1,750	2,700	3,850	8,150	18,500	42,500
1799 perfect date, 7- and 6-star obverse, small berries	Inc. above	1,750	2,700	3,850	8,150	18,500	42,500
1799 perfect date, 7- and 6-star obverse, medium large berries	Inc. above	1,750	2,700	3,850	8,150	18,500	42,500
1799 perfect date, 7- and 6-star obverse, extra large berries	Inc. above	1,750	2,700	3,850	8,150	18,500	51,500
1799 8 stars left, 5 stars right on obverse	Inc. above	1,825	2,800	3,900	8,200	24,000	45,000
1800 "R" in "Liberty" double cut	220,920	1,825	2,775	5,550	9,850	21,500	45,000
1800 first "T" in "States" double cut	Inc. above	1,800	2,750	5,550	9,850	21,500	45,000
1800 both letters double cut	Inc. above	1,800	2,750	5,550	9,850	21,500	45,000
1800 "T" in "United" double cut	Inc. above	1,800	2,750	5,550	9,850	21,500	45,000
1800 very wide date, low 8	Inc. above	1,800	2,750	5,550	9,850	21,500	—
1800 small berries	Inc. above	1,850	2,800	3,900	8,200	22,000	48,500
1800 dot date	Inc. above	2,000	3,000	4,300	8,600	21,500	45,000
1800 12 arrows	Inc. above	1,825	3,200	5,550	9,850	31,000	—
1800 10 arrows	Inc. above	1,825	3,200	5,550	9,850	—	—
1800 "Americai"	Inc. above	2,000	3,300	4,300	8,600	21,500	49,000
1801	54,454	2,050	3,200	4,000	8,300	25,000	—
1801 proof restrike	—	—	—	—	—	—	—
1802/1 close	Inc. above	2,000	3,300	4,300	8,600	20,500	—
1802/1 wide	Inc. above	2,000	3,300	4,300	8,600	20,500	—
1802 close, perfect date	Inc. above	1,850	2,800	3,900	8,200	20,500	—
1802 wide, perfect date	Inc. above	1,825	2,775	3,950	8,250	21,500	—
1802 proof restrike, mintage unrecorded	—	—	—	—	—	—	—
1803 large 3	85,634	1,875	3,000	4,000	8,300	20,500	47,500
1803 small 3	Inc. above	2,000	3,300	4,300	8,600	21,500	48,500
1803 proof restrike, mintage unrecorded	—	—	—	—	—	—	—
1804 15 known	—	—	—	—	3,000,000	—	—

Note: 1804, Childs Sale, Aug. 1999, Prf-68, $4,140,000.

DOLLAR

Gobrecht Dollar

"C Gobrecht F." in base obverse   Eagle flying left amid stars reverse

KM# 59.1 • 26.7300 g., 0.9000 **Silver**, 0.7734 oz. ASW, 38.1 mm. • **Obv. Designer:** Christian Gobrecht
Rev. Legend: UNITED STATES OF AMERICA **Edge Desc:** Plain.

Date	Mintage	VF-20	XF-40	AU-50	Prf-60
1836	1,000	11,500	14,850	—	25,500

"C. Gobrecht F." in base obverse   Eagle flying in plain field reverse

KM# 59.2 • 26.7300 g., 0.9000 **Silver**, 0.7734 oz. ASW, 38.1 mm. • **Obv. Designer:** Christian Gobrecht.
Edge Desc: Plain.

Date	Mintage	VF-20	XF-40	AU-50	Prf-60
1836 Restrike	—	—	—	—	24,000

"C. Gobrecht F." in base obverse

KM# 59a.1 • 26.7300 g., 0.9000 **Silver**, 0.7734 oz. ASW, 38.1 mm. • **Obv. Legend** Eagle flying left amid stars. **Edge Desc:** Plain.

Date	Mintage	VF-20	XF-40	AU-50	Prf-60
1836	600	—	—	—	—

"C. Gobrecht F." in base obverse   Eagle flying left amid stars reverse

KM# 59a.2 • 26.7300 g., 0.9000 **Silver**, 0.7734 oz. ASW, 38.1 mm. • **Edge Desc:** Reeded.

Date	Mintage	VF-20	XF-40	AU-50	Prf-60
1836 Restrike	—	—	—	—	—

Designer's name omitted in base obverse   Eagle in plain field reverse

KM# 59a.3 • 26.7300 g., 0.9000 **Silver**, 0.7734 oz. ASW, 38.1 mm. • **Edge Desc:** Reeded.

Date	Mintage	VF-20	XF-40	AU-50	Prf-60
1839	300	—	—	—	38,000

Designer's name omitted in base obverse   Eagle in plain field reverse

KM# 59a.4 • 26.7300 g., 0.9000 **Silver**, 0.7734 oz. ASW, 38.1 mm. •

Date	Mintage	VF-20	XF-40	AU-50	Prf-60
1839 Restrike	—	—	—	—	36,500

Note: All other combinations are restrikes of the late 1850's.

Seated Liberty Dollar
Seated Liberty, date below obverse   No motto above eagle reverse

KM# 71 • 26.7300 g., 0.9000 **Silver**, 0.7734 oz. ASW, 38.1 mm. • **Rev. Legend:** UNITED STATES OF AMERICA **Designer:** Christian Gobrecht

Date	Mintage	G-4	VG-8	F-12	VF-20	XF-40	AU-50	MS-60	MS-63	MS-65	Prf-65
1840	61,005	290	320	340	420	680	1,075	4,000	21,500	—	—
1841	173,000	265	295	315	395	610	1,000	2,950	5,500	100,000	—
1842	184,618	265	295	315	395	630	925	2,650	4,700	—	—
1843	165,100	265	295	315	395	465	925	2,750	9,000	—	—
1844	20,000	280	313	360	455	785	1,250	6,450	15,000	100,000	—
1845	24,500	300	335	385	455	900	1,750	10,500	26,500	—	75,000
1846	110,600	275	313	345	490	650	1,100	2,750	5,200	98,000	125,000
1846O	59,000	285	330	370	480	775	1,325	8,750	20,000	—	—
1847	140,750	265	295	315	395	465	900	2,950	7,500	100,000	—
1848	15,000	325	385	515	795	1,250	1,700	4,100	12,500	100,000	—
1849	62,600	275	305	350	420	600	1,000	3,200	7,950	100,000	155,000
1850	7,500	465	545	380	845	1,750	2,650	7,850	15,000	—	80,000
1850O	40,000	335	400	515	750	1,550	3,950	12,850	34,500	—	—
1851	1,300	4,000	4,850	5,750	7,750	18,000	27,000	43,500	68,500	150,000	225,000
1851 Restrike	—	—	—	—	—	—	—	—	—	—	90,000
1852	1,100	3,500	4,150	5,200	7,000	15,000	26,000	38,500	60,000	150,000	200,000
1852 Restrike	—	—	—	—	—	—	—	—	—	—	70,000
1853	46,110	335	400	550	660	1,100	1,425	4,000	7,950	100,000	90,000
1853 Restrike	—	—	—	—	—	—	—	—	—	—	—
1854	33,140	1,100	1,450	2,000	2,850	4,500	5,750	8,500	13,500	100,000	80,000
1855	26,000	900	1,150	1,500	2,150	3,750	4,950	8,850	31,500	—	55,000
1856	63,500	400	450	650	775	1,650	2,850	4,350	11,500	—	39,500
1857	94,000	450	525	675	800	1,500	1,850	3,650	9,000	95,000	39,500
1858 proof only	Est. 800	3,200	3,600	4,000	4,800	7,250	8,850	—	—	—	42,500
Note: Later restrike.											
1859	256,500	285	335	400	515	655	1,000	2,850	5,850	95,000	17,500
1859O	360,000	265	295	315	395	465	800	2,250	4,150	56,000	—
1859S	20,000	330	390	515	750	1,550	3,500	15,000	36,500	—	—
1860	218,930	275	310	380	510	660	900	2,550	5,500	90,000	15,700
1860O	515,000	265	295	315	395	465	800	2,250	3,850	56,000	—
1861	78,500	600	750	900	985	1,750	1,975	2,950	5,650	90,000	15,700
1862	12,090	440	600	850	945	1,450	1,650	3,250	5,750	90,000	15,700
1863	27,660	375	525	575	660	985	1,400	3,250	6,000	90,000	18,000
1864	31,170	350	410	500	565	920	1,375	3,350	6,400	90,000	15,700
1865	47,000	300	350	420	585	1,050	1,750	3,250	6,250	90,000	15,700
1866 2 known without motto	—	—	—	—	—	—	—	—	—	—	—

DOLLAR

Seated Liberty Dollar

Seated Liberty, date below obverse   IN GOD WE TRUST above eagle reverse

KM# 100 • 26.7300 g., 0.9000 **Silver**, 0.7734 oz. ASW, 38.1 mm. • **Rev. Legend:** UNITED STATES OF
AMERICA **Designer:** Christian Gobrecht **Notes:** In 1866 the motto IN GOD WE TRUST was added to the
reverse above the eagle.

Date	Mintage	G-4	VG-8	F-12	VF-20	XF-40	AU-50	MS-60	MS-63	MS-65	Prf-65
1866	49,625	320	350	440	590	795	1,250	2,400	5,000	85,000	16,000
1867	47,525	315	345	405	565	670	895	2,435	5,050	85,000	16,000
1868	162,700	325	355	395	535	650	920	3,500	7,350	85,000	16,000
1869	424,300	290	320	370	490	640	985	2,400	5,000	85,000	16,000
1870	416,000	280	320	350	430	595	970	2,300	4,950	67,500	16,000
1870CC	12,462	475	600	825	1,375	3,650	8,250	27,500	44,500	—	
1870S 12-15 known	—	150,000	235,000	350,000	600,000	850,000	1,350,000	1,850,000	2,500,000	—	—

Note: 1870S, Eliasberg Sale, April 1997, EF-45 to AU-50, $264,000.

Date	Mintage	G-4	VG-8	F-12	VF-20	XF-40	AU-50	MS-60	MS-63	MS-65	Prf-65
1871	1,074,760	270	300	330	410	545	970	2,300	4,950	67,500	16,000
1871CC	1,376	2,000	2,850	4,750	7,450	14,500	25,000	68,500	175,000	—	
1872	1,106,450	270	300	330	410	495	820	2,300	4,850	67,500	16,000
1872CC	3,150	900	1,400	2,850	4,300	4,850	13,500	28,500	120,000	385,000	—
1872S	9,000	310	365	550	700	2,000	4,500	11,000	26,000	—	—
1873	293,600	275	310	340	420	510	840	2,350	4,900	67,500	16,000
1873CC	2,300	6,250	7,250	11,500	19,000	31,500	43,500	125,000	225,000	625,000	—
1873S none known	700	—	—	—	—	—	—	—	—	—	—

Trade Dollar

Seated Liberty, IN GOD WE TRUST in base above date obverse
TRADE DOLLAR below eagle reverse

KM# 108 • 27.2200 g., 0.9000 **Silver**, 0.7876 oz. ASW, 38.1 mm. • **Rev. Legend:** UNITED STATES OF
AMERICA. **Designer:** William Barber

Date	Mintage	G-4	VG-8	F-12	VF-20	XF-40	AU-50	MS-60	MS-65	Prf-65
1873	397,500	115	155	165	185	280	360	1,200	15,500	10,250
1873CC	124,500	245	295	335	460	875	1,875	10,000	120,000	—
1873S	703,000	115	155	160	210	280	355	1,475	18,500	—
1874	987,800	125	155	160	185	280	365	1,100	18,250	10,250
1874CC	1,373,200	255	295	335	385	625	775	3,450	33,000	—
1874S	2,549,000	115	155	160	170	280	340	1,125	17,500	—
1875	218,900	145	185	350	425	550	800	2,450	18,000	15,000
1875CC	1,573,700	235	275	315	350	525	800	2,650	38,500	—
1875S	4,487,000	105	155	155	160	260	330	1,050	12,500	—
1875S/CC	Inc. above	210	285	365	560	925	1,450	4,650	59,000	—
1876	456,150	115	155	160	170	280	340	1,100	12,500	10,250
1876CC	509,000	245	285	310	365	585	985	8,000	76,500	—

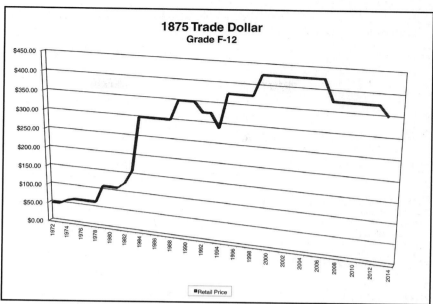

1875 Trade Dollar
Grade F-12

Date	Mintage	G-4	VG-8	F-12	VF-20	XF-40	AU-50	MS-60	MS-65	Prf-65
1876CC	Inc. above	—	—	375	650	1,250	2,000	8,500	—	—
1876S	5,227,000	105	145	150	160	255	330	1,050	17,500	—
1877	3,039,710	115	155	160	170	265	340	1,150	23,500	10,250
1877CC	534,000	255	295	335	425	700	825	2,650	59,000	—
1877S	9,519,000	105	145	150	160	255	330	1,050	12,500	—
1878 proof only	900	—	—	—	1,200	1,300	1,500	—	—	11,000
1878CC	97,000	425	625	935	1,475	2,750	4,000	13,500	112,500	—
1878S	4,162,000	105	145	150	160	225	330	1,050	12,500	—
1879 proof only	1,541	—	—	—	1,175	1,275	1,400	—	—	10,250
1880 proof only	1,987	—	—	—	1,150	1,250	1,350	—	—	10,250
1881 proof only	960	—	—	—	1,200	1,300	1,400	—	—	10,250
1882 proof only	1,097	—	—	—	1,175	1,275	1,375	—	—	10,250
1883 proof only	979	—	—	—	1,200	1,300	1,400	—	—	10,250
1884 proof only	10	—	—	—	—	—	100,000	—	—	650,000

Note: 1884, Eliasberg Sale, April 1997, Prf-66, $396,000.

1885 proof only	5	—	—	—	—	—	—	—	—	3,000,000

Note: 1885, Eliasberg Sale, April 1997, Prf-65, $907,500.

Morgan Dollar

Laureate head left, date below flanked by stars obverse   Eagle within 1/2 wreath reverse

8 Tail feathers   7 Tail feathers   7/8 Tail feathers

KM# 110 • 26.7300 g., 0.9000 **Silver**, 0.7734 oz. ASW, 38.1 mm. • **Obv. Legend** E.PLURIBUS.UNUM **Rev. Legend:** UNITED STATES OF AMERICA **Designer:** George T. Morgan **Notes:** "65DMPL" values are for coins grading MS-65 deep-mirror prooflike. The 1878 "8 tail feathers" and "7 tail feathers" varieties are distinguished by the number of feathers in the eagle's tail. On the "reverse of 1878" varieties, the top of the top feather in the arrows held by the eagle is straight across and the eagle's breast is concave. On the "reverse of 1879 varieties," the top feather in the arrows held by the eagle is slanted and the eagle's breast is convex. The 1890-CC "tail-bar" variety has a bar extending from the arrow feathers to the wreath on the reverse, the result of a die gouge. The Pittman Act of 1918 authorized the melting of 270 Million pieces of various dates. They were not individually recorded.

Date	Mintage	VG-8	F-12	VF-20	XF-40	AU-50	MS-60	MS-63	MS-64	MS-65	65DMPL	Prf-65
1878 8 tail feathers	750,000	38.70	47.40	53.00	53.00	72.00	165	250	490	1,600	23,500	8,350
1878 7 over 8 tail feathers	9,759,550	38.20	47.40	53.00	52.00	68.00	178	275	485	2,400	17,000	
1878 7 tail feathers, reverse of 1878	Inc. above	37.20	47.40	49.50	51.00	52.50	77.00	115	255	1,150	11,650	11,500
1878 7 tail feathers, reverse of 1879	Inc. above	37.20	47.40	49.00	50.00	51.00	90.00	195	505	2,650	24,500	185,000
1878CC	2,212,000	88.00	96.00	100.00	125	150	255	390	555	1,850	10,800	—
1878S	9,744,000	37.20	38.40	39.00	42.30	44.30	63.00	88.00	120	300	10,500	—
1879	14,807,100	35.20	36.40	37.00	38.30	41.80	59.00	83.50	145	875	17,250	7,550
1879CC	756,000	145	155	280	735	2,250	4,450	7,550	9,650	31,000	49,000	—
1879CC capped CC	Inc. above	145	182	250	640	1,850	4,100	6,300	9,350	43,000	63,500	—
1879O	2,887,000	37.60	39.00	40.50	41.50	47.30	84.00	225	530	4,150	28,500	—
1879S reverse of 1878	9,110,000	40.20	42.40	47.00	51.00	71.00	168	590	1,600	6,000	24,000	—
1879S reverse of 1879	9,110,000	35.20	36.40	37.00	38.30	41.80	57.00	68.50	89.50	162	1,300	—
1880	12,601,335	35.20	36.40	37.00	40.50	42.30	54.00	70.50	104.5	800	6,350	7,350
1880CC reverse of 1878	591,000	175	210	245	300	355	575	700	1,160	2,375	21,500	
1880CC 80/79 reverse of 1878	Inc. above	190	230	270	335	410	640	850	1,750	4,000	—	—
1880CC 8/7 reverse of 1878	Inc. above	170	200	235	290	360	600	720	1,300	2,800	—	—
1880CC reverse of 1879	Inc. above	170	200	240	285	345	500	630	660	1,150	9,850	—
1880CC 8/7 high 7 reverse of 1879	Inc. above	175	205	245	290	355	525	655	775	1,800		
1880CC 8/7 low 7 reverse of 1879	Inc. above	175	205	245	290	355	525	655	775	1,800	—	—
1880O	5,305,000	35.50	36.40	37.00	39.30	42.30	79.00	375	2,000	29,500	70,000	—
1880S	8,900,000	35.20	36.40	37.00	38.30	41.80	54.00	68.50	87.50	162	725	—
1880S 8/7 crossbar	—	39.20	41.40	44.00	45.00	75.00	90.00	265	335	450	—	—
1881	9,163,975	35.20	36.40	37.00	38.30	39.80	58.50	73.50	140	685	21,750	7,650
1881CC	296,000	375	385	410	425	460	540	585	605	890	3,050	—
1881O	5,708,000	35.20	36.40	37.00	39.60	42.30	52.00	72.50	190	1,375	35,000	—
1881S	12,760,000	35.20	36.40	37.00	39.60	41.80	54.00	68.50	89.50	167	850	—
1882	11,101,100	35.20	36.40	37.00	39.60	42.30	55.50	75.50	121	520	6,800	7,350
1882CC	1,133,000	92.00	96.00	110	130	155	220	265	280	495	1,950	—
1882O	6,090,000	35.50	36.40	37.00	39.30	41.80	58.00	71.50	119	1,175	4,950	—
1882O/S	Inc. above	46.00	47.00	55.00	67.50	99.50	245	775	2,000	61,500	65,000	—
1882S	9,250,000	35.20	36.40	37.00	38.30	41.80	53.00	73.00	88.00	174	4,000	—
1883	12,291,039	35.20	36.40	37.00	38.30	42.30	56.00	72.50	110	225	1,650	7,500
1883CC	1,204,000	92.00	96.00	110	125	148	210	248	260	475	1,450	—
1883O	8,725,000	35.20	36.40	37.00	38.30	39.80	48.50	68.50	87.50	174	1,400	—
1883S	6,250,000	35.20	37.40	40.50	43.30	145	665	2,650	5,350	51,500	94,500	—
1884	14,070,875	35.20	36.40	37.00	38.30	39.80	54.00	71.50	110	335	4,350	7,350
1884CC	1,136,000	138	145	150	155	160	210	248	260	430	1,450	—
1884O	9,730,000	35.20	36.40	37.00	38.30	39.80	52.00	70.50	87.50	194	1,000	—
1884S	3,200,000	35.20	36.90	39.00	43.00	310	7,500	35,500	110,000	235,000	220,000	—
1885	17,787,767	35.20	36.40	37.00	38.30	39.80	52.00	71.50	87.50	162	845	7,350
1885CC	228,000	550	565	580	595	610	660	695	755	1,135	2,400	—
1885O	9,185,000	35.20	36.40	37.00	38.30	39.80	51.00	68.50	87.50	174	1,000	—
1885S	1,497,000	39.00	39.50	40.00	64.00	110	265	355	710	2,225	42,500	—
1886	19,963,886	35.20	36.40	37.00	38.30	40.90	52.00	68.50	87.50	175	1,275	7,350
1886O	10,710,000	35.20	36.40	37.50	46.30	78.00	770	3,150	10,650	190,000	300,000	—
1886S	750,000	54.00	62.50	85.00	115	145	335	535	860	3,375	30,000	—
1887	20,290,710	35.20	36.40	37.00	38.30	39.80	52.00	68.50	87.50	162	1,200	7,350

Date	Mintage	VG-8	F-12	VF-20	XF-40	AU-50	MS-60	MS-63	MS-64	MS-65	65DMPL	Prf-65
1887/6	Inc. above	38.70	39.90	41.50	55.00	165	400	565	875	2,300	44,750	—
1887O	11,550,000	35.20	36.40	39.00	41.30	42.80	63.00	150	390	2,550	12,000	—
1887/6O	—	38.70	39.90	41.50	65.00	190	495	2,050	4,800	29,500	—	—
1887S	1,771,000	35.70	36.90	40.50	42.30	46.30	138	290	710	2,500	29,500	—
1888	19,183,833	35.20	36.40	37.00	38.30	39.80	54.00	68.50	91.50	240	3,000	7,500
1888O	12,150,000	35.20	36.40	37.00	40.30	42.30	54.00	72.50	99.00	655	2,850	—
1888O Hot Lips	Inc. above	55.00	125	250	600	3,000	—	—	—	—	—	—
1888S	657,000	115	190	210	225	235	335	495	915	3,400	16,500	—
1889	21,726,811	35.20	36.40	37.00	38.30	39.80	53.00	68.50	101.5	375	4,050	7,350
1889CC	350,000	660	940	1,300	3,150	6,900	25,500	43,500	66,000	320,000	—	—
1889O	11,875,000	35.50	36.40	39.00	40.30	41.80	180	390	960	7,850	14,500	—
1889S	700,000	51.00	60.00	65.00	82.00	125	265	390	675	2,150	38,500	—
1890	16,802,590	35.20	36.40	37.00	38.30	39.80	54.00	72.00	160	2,525	19,750	7,350
1890CC	2,309,041	85.00	96.00	105	140	235	455	825	1,425	5,250	15,500	—
1890CC tail bar	Inc. above	155	175	225	400	700	1,450	3,600	5,500			—
1890O	10,701,000	35.70	36.40	39.00	40.30	44.30	77.00	96.00	285	2,425	10,000	—
1890S	8,230,373	35.50	36.70	37.50	40.30	44.30	63.00	93.50	275	1,050	10,500	—
1891	8,694,206	35.70	37.40	38.00	40.30	44.30	64.00	165	775	9,000	27,500	7,350
1891CC	1,618,000	85.00	96.00	105	135	215	390	715	1,225	5,100	34,500	—
1891CC Spitting Eagle	Inc. above	105	115	135	185	260	425	900	1,600	6,000	—	—
1891O	7,954,529	35.70	36.80	37.50	40.30	42.30	175	350	770	8,550	37,500	—
1891S	5,296,000	35.70	36.90	38.00	40.30	43.30	63.00	135	310	1,650	21,500	—
1892	1,037,245	42.70	43.90	45.00	46.80	88.00	285	510	1,045	4,850	20,500	7,500
1892CC	1,352,000	190	210	290	485	725	1,375	2,225	2,825	8,900	39,500	—
1892O	2,744,000	38.70	40.40	43.00	44.00	67.50	285	420	1,225	7,750	52,500	—
1892S	1,200,000	38.90	43.90	136	315	1,650	44,500	66,500	112,500	205,000	225,000	—
1893	378,792	245	250	260	300	400	685	1,100	2,000	7,500	66,000	7,500
1893CC	677,000	255	310	660	1,500	2,500	4,400	7,150	11,400	70,000	90,000	—
1893O	300,000	195	215	380	620	850	2,775	6,650	16,500	210,000	215,000	—
1893S	100,000	3,000	4,150	5,750	9,500	21,000	130,000	205,000	365,000	715,000	735,000	—
1894	110,972	1,200	1,235	1,425	1,500	1,825	3,500	5,200	10,150	38,500	78,000	7,500
1894O	1,723,000	55.00	57.00	59.00	96.00	310	800	4,000	11,750	68,500	61,500	—
1894S	1,260,000	62.00	65.00	110	150	510	785	1,185	1,925	6,550	26,000	—
1895 proof only	12,880	21,500	29,500	36,500	38,000	40,000	—	—	—	—	—	75,000
1895O	450,000	315	350	480	595	1,225	15,500	57,500	85,000	165,000	—	—
1895S	400,000	465	525	900	1,325	1,865	3,850	6,450	8,550	28,000	42,500	—
1896	9,967,762	35.20	36.40	37.00	38.30	39.80	52.00	69.50	93.00	235	1,450	7,350
1896O	4,900,000	35.70	37.40	38.00	45.80	155	1,450	6,700	44,000	180,000	180,000	—
1896S	5,000,000	39.70	40.90	60.00	235	895	1,825	3,550	5,500	19,500	110,000	—
1897	2,822,731	35.20	36.40	37.00	40.30	42.30	51.00	66.00	99.00	355	3,950	7,350
1897O	4,004,000	35.70	37.40	39.00	54.30	110	770	4,400	15,900	70,000	72,500	—
1897S	5,825,000	35.70	37.40	38.00	40.30	45.30	77.00	122	165	610	3,250	—
1898	5,884,735	35.20	36.40	37.00	38.80	42.30	50.50	69.50	88.00	265	1,440	7,350
1898O	4,440,000	35.20	36.40	37.00	38.80	42.30	54.50	69.50	91.00	177	1,000	—
1898S	4,102,000	39.70	40.90	41.00	55.00	105	270	470	660	2,500	18,000	—
1899	330,846	170	182	195	205	245	265	290	390	935	2,850	7,350
1899O	12,290,000	35.20	36.40	37.00	38.30	39.80	54.50	68.50	94.50	178	1,550	—
1899S	2,562,000	39.70	40.90	41.50	58.50	145	410	495	825	2,275	26,000	—
1900	8,880,938	35.20	36.40	37.00	38.30	42.30	50.50	68.50	94.50	173	42,500	7,350
1900O	12,590,000	35.20	36.40	37.00	38.30	42.30	54.50	68.50	89.50	173	6,250	—
1900O/CC	Inc. above	39.50	47.50	62.50	100.00	190	305	770	935	1,800	19,000	—
1900S	3,540,000	39.20	41.90	42.50	45.80	85.00	320	400	660	1,800	38,500	—
1901	6,962,813	43.00	48.50	57.50	105	280	2,750	17,250	55,000	375,000	—	7,850
1901 doubled die reverse	Inc. above	275	450	900	2,000	3,850	—	—	—	—	—	—
1901O	13,320,000	32.80	38.40	39.00	40.30	45.30	54.50	71.00	84.00	198	10,000	—
1901S	2,284,000	32.80	38.90	39.00	51.00	200	510	775	1,000	3,150	24,500	—
1902	7,994,777	32.80	38.40	39.00	40.30	41.80	66.00	115	155	480	19,500	7,350
1902O	8,636,000	35.20	36.40	37.00	38.30	39.80	54.50	68.50	88.50	198	16,000	—
1902S	1,530,000	99.00	105	148	195	275	380	620	885	3,000	15,000	—
1903	4,652,755	47.00	48.00	49.00	50.00	52.00	66.00	82.50	116	320	36,850	7,350
1903O	4,450,000	325	350	375	390	398	412	455	475	635	5,950	—
1903S	1,241,000	95.00	130	210	365	1,725	4,350	6,500	7,400	11,750	40,000	—
1903S Micro S	Inc. above	135	225	450	1,150	3,000	—	—	—	—	—	—
1904	2,788,650	37.20	38.40	39.00	40.30	41.80	105	255	600	2,850	86,500	7,350
1904O	3,720,000	35.70	37.90	38.50	40.30	43.30	56.50	72.50	91.50	163	1,175	—
1904S	2,304,000	43.00	48.50	87.00	230	525	1,780	4,100	4,950	10,350	19,000	—
1921	44,690,000	33.80	34.60	35.60	36.70	38.20	45.00	52.00	80.00	185	11,500	—
1921D	20,345,000	34.10	35.00	35.90	37.10	41.00	54.50	74.00	122	420	10,000	—
1921S	21,695,000	34.10	35.00	35.90	37.10	41.00	54.50	74.00	155	1,525	31,000	—

DOLLAR

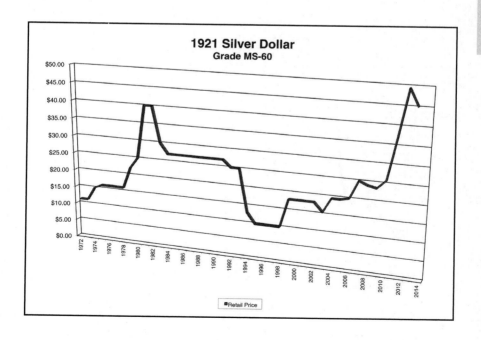

Peace Dollar
Liberty Head left obverse   Eagle facing right perched on rock reverse

Mint mark

KM# 150 • 26.7300 g., 0.9000 **Silver**, 0.7734 oz. ASW, 38.1 mm. • **Designer:** Anthony DeFrancisci

Date	Mintage	G-4	VG-8	F-12	VF-20	XF-40	AU-50	MS-60	MS-63	MS-64	MS-65
1921	1,006,473	95.00	120	126	133	143	165	270	420	750	2,000
1922	51,737,000	28.70	31.80	32.40	33.30	34.60	37.00	44.00	50.00	78.00	138
1922D	15,063,000	28.70	32.00	32.70	33.60	34.80	37.90	51.00	71.00	99.00	580
1922S	17,475,000	28.70	32.00	32.70	33.60	34.80	37.90	49.00	83.00	240	2,400
1923	30,800,000	28.70	31.80	32.40	33.30	34.60	37.00	44.00	50.00	78.00	138
1923D	6,811,000	28.70	32.00	32.70	33.60	34.80	41.00	70.00	143	320	1,155
1923S	19,020,000	28.70	32.00	32.70	33.60	34.80	37.90	50.00	83.00	330	6,200
1924	11,811,000	28.70	31.80	32.70	33.30	34.60	37.00	44.00	50.00	78.00	161
1924S	1,728,000	30.70	32.80	35.40	37.30	41.50	60.00	235	485	1,400	9,100
1925	10,198,000	28.70	31.80	32.40	33.30	34.60	37.00	46.00	50.00	78.00	150
1925S	1,610,000	28.70	31.80	33.30	37.30	34.60	46.00	90.00	220	1,075	25,000
1926	1,939,000	28.70	31.80	33.50	34.60	34.60	37.00	55.00	90.00	112	510
1926D	2,348,700	28.70	31.80	33.30	34.40	34.60	39.00	84.00	165	345	885
1926S	6,980,000	29.30	32.40	33.00	33.90	35.20	40.00	59.00	102	255	1,000
1927	848,000	31.00	35.00	37.40	39.30	40.60	50.00	79.00	180	495	2,900
1927D	1,268,900	31.00	35.00	37.40	39.30	40.60	80.00	200	370	990	4,600
1927S	866,000	31.00	35.00	37.40	39.30	40.60	80.00	200	460	1,150	9,900
1928	360,649	345	380	385	390	395	415	525	875	1,185	4,600
1928S	1,632,000	34.00	35.00	40.00	42.50	48.00	66.00	178	460	1,060	24,000
1934	954,057	35.00	44.00	45.00	46.00	47.50	50.00	115	215	360	750
1934D Large D	1,569,500	36.00	45.00	46.00	50.00	54.00	65.00	180	600	925	3,000
1934D Small D	Inc. above	35.00	44.00	45.00	46.00	47.50	50.00	155	385	510	1,675
1934S	1,011,000	38.00	45.00	53.00	80.00	172	475	1,925	3,300	4,600	8,100
1935	1,576,000	35.00	44.00	45.00	46.00	47.50	52.50	72.00	160	205	700
1935S 3 Rays	1,964,000	35.00	44.00	45.00	46.00	47.50	92.00	270	380	635	1,325
1935S 4 Rays	—	36.00	45.00	46.00	50.00	55.00	115	300	475	725	1,750

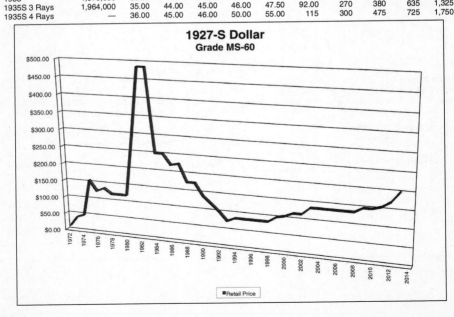

1927-S Dollar
Grade MS-60

Eisenhower Dollar

KM# 203 • 22.8000 g., **Copper-Nickel Clad Copper**, 38 mm. • **Designer:** Frank Gasparro

Date	Mintage	Proof	MS-63	Prf-65
1971	47,799,000	—	10.00	—
1971D	68,587,424	—	8.00	—
1972 Low Relief	75,890,000	—	18.00	—
1972 High Relief	Inc. above	—	175	—
1972 Modified High Relief	Inc. above	—	35.00	—
1972D	92,548,511	—	9.00	—
1973	2,000,056	—	12.00	—
1973D	2,000,000	—	12.00	—
1973S	—	2,769,624	—	12.00
1974	27,366,000	—	15.00	—
1974D	35,466,000	—	7.50	—
1974S	—	2,617,350	—	11.00

KM# 203a • 24.5900 g., 0.4000 **Silver**, 0.3162 oz. ASW, 38.1 mm. • **Designer:** Frank Gasparro

Date	Mintage	Proof	MS-63	Prf-65
1971S	6,868,530	—	15.80	11.00
1971S	—	4,265,234	—	—
1971S Peg Leg "R" Variety	Inc. above	—	—	17.00
1971S Partial Peg Leg "R" Variety	Inc. above	—	—	18.00
1972S	2,193,056	—	15.80	—
1972S	—	1,811,631	—	9.00
1973S	1,833,140	—	15.80	—
1973S	—	1,005,617	—	45.00
1974S	1,720,000	—	15.80	—
1974S	—	1,306,579	—	11.00

Bicentennial design, moon behind Liberty Bell reverse

Type I Squared "T"	Type II Slant-top "T"

KM# 206 • 22.6800 g., **Copper-Nickel Clad Copper**, 38.1 mm. • **Rev. Designer:** Dennis R. Williams **Notes:** In 1976 the lettering on the reverse was changed to thinner letters, resulting in the Type II variety for that year. The Type I variety was minted 1975 and dated 1976.

Date	Mintage	Proof	MS-63	Prf-65
1976 type I	117,337,000	—	12.00	—
1976 type II	Inc. above	—	8.00	—
1976D type I	103,228,274	—	7.50	—
1976D type II	Inc. above	—	6.00	—
1976S type I	—	2,909,369	—	10.00
1976S type II	—	4,149,730	—	9.00

Bicentennial design, moon behind Liberty Bell reverse

KM# 206a • 24.5900 g., 0.4000 **Silver**, 0.3162 oz. ASW • **Rev. Designer:** Dennis R. Williams

Date	Mintage	Proof	MS-63	Prf-65
1976S	4,908,319	—	15.80	14.00
1976S	—	3,998,621	—	—

Regular design resumed reverse

KM# A203 • **Copper-Nickel Clad Copper**, 38.1 mm. •

Date	Mintage	Proof	MS-63	Prf-65
1977	12,596,000	—	5.00	—
1977D	32,983,006	—	4.00	—
1977S	—	3,251,152	—	9.00
1978	25,702,000	—	4.00	—
1978D	33,012,890	—	4.75	—
1978S	—	3,127,788	—	9.00

DOLLAR

Susan B. Anthony Dollar

Susan B. Anthony bust right obverse
Eagle landing on moon, symbolic of
Apollo manned moon landing reverse

KM# 207 • 8.1000 g., **Copper-Nickel Clad Copper**, 26.5 mm. • **Designer:** Frank Gasparro **Edge Desc:** Reeded **Notes:** The 1979-S and 1981-S Type II coins have a clearer mint mark than the Type I varieties for those years.

Date	Mintage	MS-63	MS-65	Prf-65
1979P Near date	360,222,000	45.00	125	—
1979P	Inc. above	2.50	12.50	—
1979D	288,015,744	2.50	12.50	—
1979S Proof, Type I	(3,677,175)	—	—	6.00
1979S Proof, Type II	Inc. above	—	—	85.00
1979S	109,576,000	2.50	13.00	—
1980P	27,610,000	2.50	14.00	—
1980D	41,628,708	2.50	12.00	—
1980S	20,422,000	5.00	20.00	—
1980S Proof	3,547,030	—	—	5.00
1981P	3,000,000	5.00	18.00	—
1981D	3,250,000	5.00	13.50	—
1981S	3,492,000	5.00	30.00	—
1981S Proof, Type I	4,063,083	—	—	7.00
1981S Proof, Type II	Inc. above	—	—	225
1999P	29,592,000	3.00	10.00	—
1999P Proof	Est. 750,000	—	—	22.00
1999D	11,776,000	3.00	10.00	—

Sacagawea Dollar

Sacagawea bust right,
with baby on back obverse
Eagle in flight left reverse

KM# 310 • 8.0700 g., **Copper-Zinc-Manganese-Nickel Clad Copper**, 26.5 mm. •

Date	Mintage	MS-63	MS-65	Prf-65
2000P	767,140,000	2.00	7.50	—
2000P Goodacre Presentation	5,000	—	575	—
2000D	518,916,000	2.00	11.00	—
2000D from Millennium Set	5,500	10.00	50.00	—
2000S	4,048,000	—	—	5.00
2001P	62,468,000	2.25	6.00	—
2001D	70,909,500	2.25	8.00	—
2001S	3,084,000	—	—	16.00
2002P	3,865,610	3.00	9.00	—
2002D	3,732,000	2.75	10.00	—
2002S	3,157,739	—	—	10.00
2003P	3,090,000	4.50	10.00	—
2003D	3,090,000	4.75	12.00	—
2003S	3,116,590	—	—	8.00
2004P	2,660,000	3.50	6.00	—

Date	Mintage	MS-63	MS-65	Prf-65
2004D	2,660,000	4.00	8.00	—
2004S	2,992,069	—	—	7.50
2005P	2,520,000	3.00	9.00	—
2005P Satin Finish	1,160,000	5.00	9.00	—
2005D	2,520,000	3.00	10.00	—
2005D Satin Finish	1,160,000	5.00	9.00	—
2005S	3,273,000	—	—	6.00
2006P	4,900,000	3.25	6.00	—
2006P Satin Finish	847,361	4.50	9.00	—
2006D	2,800,000	3.50	10.00	—
2006D Satin Finish	847,361	4.00	6.00	—
2006S	3,054,436	—	—	9.00
2007P	3,640,000	2.25	5.50	—
2007P Satin Finish	895,628	4.00	6.00	—
2007D	3,920,000	2.25	7.50	—
2007D Satin Finish	895,628	4.00	6.00	—
2007S	2,577,166	—	—	6.50
2008P	1,820,000	2.00	7.00	—
2008P Satin Finish	745,464	4.00	6.00	—
2008D	1,820,000	3.50	10.00	—
2008D Satin Finish	745,464	4.00	6.00	—
2008S	2,169,561	—	—	16.00

Native American Dollar - Planting crops reverse

Sacagawea bust right with
baby on back obverse
Native American female planting corn,
beans and squash reverse

KM# 467 • 8.0700 g., **Copper-Zinc-Manganese-Nickel Clad Copper**, 26.5 mm. • **Edge Lettering:** E PLURIBUS UNUM, date, mint mark **Notes:** Date and mint mark on edge

Date	Mintage	MS-63	MS-65	Prf-65
2009P	37,380,000	2.00	5.00	—
2009D	33,880,000	4.00	7.00	—
2009S	—	2.00	5.00	—

Native American Dollar - Hiawatha belt reverse

Sacagawea bust right with
baby on back obverse
Hiawatha belt and
bundle of five arrows reverse

KM# 474 • 8.0700 g., **Copper-Zinc-Manganese-Nickel Clad Copper**, 26.5 mm. • **Edge Lettering:** E PLURIBUS UNUM, date, mint mark **Notes:** Date and mint mark on edge

Date	Mintage	MS-63	MS-65	Prf-65
2010P	—	2.00	5.00	—

DOLLAR

Date	Mintage	MS-63	MS-65	Prf-65
2010D	—	2.00	7.00	—
2010S	—	—	5.00	22.50

Native American Dollar - Peace Pipe reverse

Sacagawea bust right with baby on back obverse
Hands passing peace pipe reverse

KM# 503 • 8.0700 g., **Copper-Zinc-Manganese-Nickel Clad Copper**, 26.5 mm. • **Obv. Designer:** Glenna Goodacre **Rev. Designer:** Richard Masters and Joseph Menna **Edge Lettering:**E PLURIBUS UNUM, date, mint mark **Notes:** Date and mint mark on edge

Date	Mintage	MS-63	MS-65	Prf-65
2011P	—	2.00	5.50	—
2011D	—	2.00	5.00	—
2011S	—	—	—	8.00

Native American Dollar - Horse reverse

Sacagawea bust right with baby on back obverse
Horse and Native American profile facing left reverse

KM# 528 • 8.0700 g., **Copper-Zinc-Manganese-Nickel Clad Copper**, 26.5 mm. • **Edge Lettering:**E PLURIBUS UNUM, date, mint mark **Notes:** Date and mint mark on edge

Date	Mintage	MS-63	MS-65	Prf-65
2012P	—	2.00	7.00	—
2012D	—	2.00	7.00	—
2012S	—	—	—	8.00

Native American Dollar - Delaware Treaty of 1778

KM# 551 • 8.0700 g., **Copper-Zinc-Manganese-Nickel Clad Copper**, 26.5 mm. • **Edge Desc:**E PLURIBUS UNUM, date, mint mark **Notes:** Date and mint mark on edge.

Date	Mintage	MS-63	MS-65	Prf-65
2013P	—	2.00	3.00	—
2013D	—	2.00	3.00	—
2013S	—	—	—	5.00

Presidential Dollars

George Washington

KM# 401 • 8.0700 g., **Copper-Zinc-Manganese-Nickel Clad Copper**, 26.5 mm. • **Edge Lettering:**IN GOD WE TRUST date, mint mark E PLURIBUS UNUM **Notes:** Date and mint mark incuse on edge.

Date	Mintage	MS-63	MS-65	Prf-65
2007P	176,680,000	2.00	5.00	—
(2007) Plain edge error	Inc. above	75.00	—	—
2007D	163,680,000	2.00	5.00	—
2007S	3,883,103	—	—	5.00

James Madison

KM# 404 • 8.0700 g., **Copper-Zinc-Manganese-Nickel Clad Copper**, 26.5 mm. • **Edge Letter-**ing:IN GOD WE TRUST date, mint mark E PLURIBUS UNUM **Notes:** Date and mint mark incuse on edge.

Date	Mintage	MS-63	MS-65	Prf-65
2007P	84,560,000	2.00	5.00	—
2007D	87,780,000	2.00	5.00	—
2007S	3,876,829	—	—	5.00

John Adams

KM# 402 • 8.0700 g., **Copper-Zinc-Manganese-Nickel Clad Copper**, 26.5 mm. • **Edge Letter-**ing:IN GOD WE TRUST date, mint mark E PLURIBUS UNUM **Notes:** Date and mint mark incuse on edge.

Date	Mintage	MS-63	MS-65	Prf-65
2007P	112,420,000	2.00	5.00	—
2007P Double edge lettering	Inc. above	250	—	—
2007D	112,140,000	2.00	5.00	—
2007S	3,877,409	—	—	5.00

DOLLAR

DOLLAR

Thomas Jefferson

KM# 403 • 8.0700 g., **Copper-Zinc-Manganese-Nickel Clad Copper**, 26.5 mm. • **Edge Lettering:**IN GOD WE TRUST date, mint mark E PLURIBUS UNUM **Notes:** Date and mint mark incuse on edge.

Date	Mintage	MS-63	MS-65	Prf-65
2007P	100,800,000	2.00	5.00	—
2007D	102,810,000	2.00	5.00	—
2007S	3,877,573	—	—	5.00

John Quincy Adams

KM# 427 • 8.0700 g., **Copper-Zinc-Manganese-Nickel Clad Copper**, 26.5 mm. • **Edge Lettering:**IN GOD WE TRUST date, mint mark E PLURIBUS UNUM **Notes:** Date and mint mark incuse on edge.

Date	Mintage	MS-63	MS-65	Prf-65
2008P	57,540,000	2.00	5.00	—
2008D	57,720,000	2.00	5.00	—
2008S	3,000,000	—	—	5.00

Andrew Jackson

KM# 428 • 8.0700 g., **Copper-Zinc-Manganese-Nickel Clad Copper**, 26.5 mm. • **Edge Lettering:**IN GOD WE TRUST date, mint mark E PLURIBUS UNUM **Notes:** Date and mint mark incuse on edge.

Date	Mintage	MS-63	MS-65	Prf-65
2008P	61,180,000	2.00	5.00	—
2008D	61,070,000	2.00	5.00	—
2008S	3,000,000	—	—	5.00

Martin van Buren

KM# 429 • 8.0700 g., **Copper-Zinc-Manganese-Nickel Clad Copper**, 26.5 mm. • **Edge Lettering:**IN GOD WE TRUST date, mint mark E PLURIBUS UNUM **Notes:** Date and mint mark incuse on edge.

Date	Mintage	MS-63	MS-65	Prf-65
2008P	51,520,000	2.00	5.00	—
2008D	50,960,000	2.00	5.00	—
2008S	3,000,000	—	—	5.00

James Monroe

KM# 426 • 8.0700 g., **Copper-Zinc-Manganese-Nickel Clad Copper**, Date and mint mark incuse on edge., 26.5 mm. • **Edge Lettering:**IN GOD WE TRUST date, mint mark E PLURIBUS UNUM

Date	Mintage	MS-63	MS-65	Prf-65
2008P	64,260,000	2.00	5.00	—
2008D	60,230,000	2.00	5.00	—
2008S	3,000,000	—	—	5.00

James K. Polk

KM# 452 • 8.0700 g., **Copper-Zinc-Manganese-Nickel Clad Copper**, 26.5 mm. • **Edge Lettering:**E PLURIBUS UNUM, date, mint mark **Notes:** Date and mint mark on edge

Date	Mintage	MS-63	MS-65	Prf-65
2009P	46,620,000	2.00	5.00	—
2009D	41,720,000	2.00	5.00	—
2009S	—	—	—	5.00

John Tyler

KM# 451 • 8.0700 g., **Copper-Zinc-Manganese-Nickel Clad Copper**, 26.5 mm. • **Edge Lettering:**E PLURIBUS UNUM, date, mint mark **Notes:** Date and mint mark on edge.

Date	Mintage	MS-63	MS-65	Prf-65
2009P	43,540,000	2.00	5.00	—
2009D	43,540,000	2.00	5.00	—
2009S	—	—	—	5.00

William Henry Harrison

KM# 450 • 8.0700 g., **Copper-Zinc-Manganese-Nickel Clad Copper**, 26.5 mm. • **Edge Lettering:**E PLURIBUS UNUM, date, mint mark **Notes:** Date and mint mark on edge

Date	Mintage	MS-63	MS-65	Prf-65
2009P	43,260,000	2.00	5.00	—
2009D	55,160,000	2.00	5.00	—
2009S	—	—	—	5.00

Zachary Taylor

KM# 453 • 8.0700 g., **Copper-Zinc-Manganese-Nickel Clad Copper**, 26.5 mm. • **Edge Lettering:**E PLURIBUS UNUM, date, mint mark **Notes:** Date and mint mark on edge.

Date	Mintage	MS-63	MS-65	Prf-65
2009P	41,580,000	2.00	5.00	—
2009D	36,680,000	2.00	5.00	—
2009S	—	—	—	5.00

Abraham Lincoln

KM# 478 • 8.0700 g., **Copper-Zinc-Manganese-Nickel Clad Copper**, 26.5 mm. • **Edge Letter-**

ing:E PLURIBUS UNUM, date, mint mark **Notes:** Date and mint mark on edge.

Date	Mintage	MS-63	MS-65	Prf-65
2010P	—	2.00	5.00	—
2010D	—	2.00	5.00	—
2010S	—	—	—	5.00

Franklin Pierce

KM# 476 • 8.0700 g., **Copper-Zinc-Manganese-Nickel Clad Copper**, 26.5 mm. • **Edge Lettering:**E PLURIBUS UNUM, date, mint mark **Notes:** Date and mint mark on edge.

Date	Mintage	MS-63	MS-65	Prf-65
2010P	—	2.00	5.00	—
2010D	—	2.00	5.00	—
2010S	—	—	—	5.00

James Buchanan

KM# 477 • 8.0700 g., **Copper-Zinc-Manganese-Nickel Clad Copper**, 26.5 mm. • **Edge Lettering:**E PLURIBUS UNUM, date, mint mark **Notes:** Date and mint mark on edge.

Date	Mintage	MS-63	MS-65	Prf-65
2010P	—	2.00	5.00	—
2010D	—	2.00	5.00	—
2010S	—	—	—	5.00

Millard Filmore

KM# 475 • 8.0700 g., **Copper-Zinc-Manganese-Nickel Clad Copper**, 26.5 mm. • **Edge Lettering:**E PLURIBUS UNUM, date, mint mark **Notes:** Date and mint mark on edge.

Date	Mintage	MS-63	MS-65	Prf-65
2010P	—	2.00	5.00	—
2010D	—	2.00	5.00	—
2010S	—	—	—	5.00

DOLLAR

DOLLAR

Andrew Johnson

KM# 499 • 8.0700 g., **Copper-Zinc-Manganese-Nickel Clad Copper**, 26.5 mm. • **Edge Lettering:**E PLURIBUS UNUM, date, mint mark **Notes:** Date and mint mark on edge.

Date	Mintage	MS-63	MS-65	Prf-65
2011P	—	2.00	5.00	—
2011D	—	2.00	5.00	—
2011S	—	—	—	5.00

James Garfield

KM# 502 • 8.0700 g., **Copper-Zinc-Manganese-Nickel Clad Copper**, 26.5 mm. • **Edge Lettering:**E PLURIBUS UNUM, date, mint mark **Notes:** Date and mint mark on edge.

Date	Mintage	MS-63	MS-65	Prf-65
2011P	—	2.00	5.00	—
2011D	—	2.00	5.00	—
2011S	—	—	—	5.00

Rutherford B. Hayes

KM# 501 • 8.0700 g., **Copper-Zinc-Manganese-Nickel Clad Copper**, 26.5 mm. • **Edge Lettering:**E PLURIBUS UNUM, date, mint mark **Notes:** Date and mint mark on edge.

Date	Mintage	MS-63	MS-65	Prf-65
2011P	—	2.00	5.00	—
2011D	—	2.00	5.00	—
2011S	—	—	—	5.00

Ulysses S. Grant

KM# 500 • 8.0700 g., **Copper-Zinc-Manganese-Nickel Clad Copper**, 26.5 mm. • **Edge Lettering:**E PLURIBUS UNUM, date, mint mark **Notes:** Date and mint mark on edge.

Date	Mintage	MS-63	MS-65	Prf-65
2011P	—	2.00	5.00	—
2011D	—	2.00	5.00	—
2011S	—	—	—	5.00

Benjamin Harrison

KM# 526 • 8.0700 g., **Copper-Zinc-Manganese-Nickel Clad Copper**, 26.5 mm. • **Edge Lettering:**E PLURIBUS UNUM, date, mintmark **Notes:** Date at mint mark on edge

Date	Mintage	MS-63	MS-65	Prf-65
2012P	—	2.00	5.00	—
2012D	—	2.00	5.00	—
2012S	—	—	—	5.00

Chester A. Arthur

KM# 524 • 8.0700 g., **Copper-Zinc-Manganese-Nickel Clad Copper**, 26.5 mm. • **Edge Lettering:**E PLURIBUS UNUM, date, mintmark **Notes:** Date and mintmark on edge

Date	Mintage	MS-63	MS-65	Prf-65
2012P	—	2.00	5.00	—
2012D	—	2.00	5.00	—
2012S	—	—	—	5.00

Grover Cleveland, first term

KM# 525 • 8.0700 g., **Copper-Zinc-Manganese-Nickel Clad Copper**, 26.5 mm. • **Edge Lettering:**E PLURIBUS UNUM, date, mintmark **Notes:** Date and mint mark on edge

Date	Mintage	MS-63	MS-65	Prf-65
2012P	—	2.00	5.00	—
2012D	—	2.00	5.00	—
2012S	—	—	—	5.00

Grover Cleveland, second term

KM# 527 • 8.0700 g., **Copper-Zinc-Manganese-Nickel Clad Copper**, 26.5 mm. • **Edge Lettering:**E PLURIBUS UNUM, date, mintmark **Notes:** Date and mint mark on edge

Date	Mintage	MS-63	MS-65	Prf-65
2012P	—	2.00	5.00	—
2012D	—	2.00	5.00	—
2012S	—	—	—	5.00

GOLD
Liberty Head - Type 1
Liberty head left within circle of stars obverse   Value, date within 3/4 wreath reverse

KM# 73 • 1.6720 g., 0.9000 **Gold**, 0.0484 oz. AGW, 13 mm. • **Rev. Legend:** UNITED STATES OF AMERICA **Designer:** James B. Longacre **Notes:** On the "closed wreath" varieties of 1849, the wreath on the reverse extends closer to the numeral 1.

Date	Mintage	F-12	VF-20	XF-40	AU-50	MS-60
1849 open wreath	688,567	175	225	265	300	650
1849 small head, no L	—	—	—	—	—	—
1849 closed wreath	Inc. above	175	210	245	270	335
1849C closed wreath	11,634	800	950	1,450	2,400	8,850
1849C open wreath	Inc. above	135,000	240,000	320,000	475,000	600,000
1849D open wreath	21,588	1,050	1,300	1,875	2,600	6,000
1849O open wreath	215,000	195	235	310	390	800
1850	481,953	175	210	245	270	335
1850C	6,966	900	1,150	1,600	2,350	9,000
1850D	8,382	1,050	1,250	1,725	2,950	12,500
1850O	14,000	200	275	390	775	3,300
1851	3,317,671	175	210	245	270	335
1851C	41,267	840	1,150	1,500	1,700	3,150
1851D	9,882	1,000	1,250	1,675	2,500	5,650
1851O	290,000	160	195	240	265	775
1852	2,045,351	175	210	245	270	335
1852C	9,434	845	1,040	1,400	1,700	5,100
1852D	6,360	1,025	1,250	1,675	2,300	10,000
1852O	140,000	130	175	260	385	1,400
1853	4,076,051	175	210	245	270	335
1853C	11,515	900	1,100	1,400	2,000	5,600
1853D	6,583	1,040	1,250	1,700	2,650	9,700
1853O	290,000	135	160	235	270	665
1854	736,709	175	210	245	270	335
1854D	2,935	1,050	1,400	2,350	6,000	13,000
1854S	14,632	260	360	525	775	2,450

Indian Head - Type 2
Indian head with headdress left obverse   Value, date within wreath reverse

KM# 83 • 1.6720 g., 0.9000 **Gold**, 0.0484 oz. AGW, 15 mm. • **Obv. Legend** UNITED STATES OF AMERICA **Designer:** James B. Longacre

Date	Mintage	F-12	VF-20	XF-40	AU-50	MS-60
1854	902,736	250	280	410	535	1,680
1855	758,269	250	280	410	535	1,680
1855C	9,803	975	1,450	3,750	11,500	33,000
1855D	1,811	3,250	4,750	9,800	22,000	48,000
1855O	55,000	345	440	600	1,500	7,800
1856S	24,600	525	820	1,325	2,500	8,650

Indian Head - Type 3
Indian head with headdress left obverse   Value, date within wreath reverse

KM# 86 • 1.6720 g., 0.9000 **Gold**, 0.0484 oz. AGW, 15 mm. • **Obv. Legend** UNITED STATES OF AMERICA **Designer:** James B. Longacre **Notes:** The 1856 varieties are distinguished by whether the 5 in the date is slanted or upright. The 1873 varieties are distinguished by the amount of space between the upper left and lower left serifs in the 3.

DOLLAR

DOLLAR

Date	Mintage	F-12	VF-20	XF-40	AU-50	MS-60	Prf-65
1856 upright 5	1,762,936	225	260	310	335	510	—
1856 slanted 5	Inc. above	220	250	285	300	360	55,000
1856D	1,460	2,350	3,650	5,800	8,000	32,000	—
1857	774,789	210	245	285	300	360	32,000
1857C	13,280	900	1,150	1,750	3,750	13,250	—
1857D	3,533	1,000	1,300	2,300	4,400	11,000	—
1857S	10,000	260	520	650	1,300	6,200	—
1858	117,995	210	245	285	300	360	28,500
1858D	3,477	1,025	1,250	1,600	2,850	10,000	—
1858S	10,000	300	400	575	1,450	5,350	—
1859	168,244	210	245	285	300	360	17,000
1859C	5,235	885	1,050	1,700	4,250	9,850	—
1859D	4,952	1,050	1,500	2,100	3,250	10,500	—
1859S	15,000	210	265	525	1,250	5,500	—
1860	36,668	210	245	285	300	360	16,500
1860D	1,566	2,150	2,500	4,200	7,000	19,500	—
1860S	13,000	300	380	500	750	2,900	—
1861	527,499	210	245	285	300	360	14,850
1861D mintage unrecorded	—	4,950	7,000	11,000	21,000	41,500	—
1862	1,361,390	210	245	285	300	360	15,000
1863	6,250	370	500	925	2,100	3,900	18,000
1864	5,950	290	370	475	825	1,050	18,000
1865	3,725	290	370	590	750	1,600	18,000
1866	7,130	300	385	470	685	1,025	18,000
1867	5,250	325	420	525	675	1,160	17,500
1868	10,525	265	290	415	500	1,025	19,000
1869	5,925	315	460	530	725	1,150	17,000
1870	6,335	255	290	410	500	875	16,000
1870S	3,000	300	475	785	1,250	2,650	—
1871	3,930	260	290	390	480	750	18,000
1872	3,530	260	295	400	480	975	18,500
1873 closed 3	125,125	325	425	825	950	1,650	—
1873 open 3	Inc. above	210	245	285	300	360	—
1874	198,820	210	245	285	300	360	30,000
1875	420	1,650	2,350	4,650	5,200	10,000	32,500
1876	3,245	240	300	360	475	725	16,750
1877	3,920	210	210	340	460	725	18,000
1878	3,020	195	250	365	480	675	15,500
1879	3,030	210	225	285	330	525	14,000
1880	1,636	235	180	300	300	475	14,000
1881	7,707	235	270	300	300	460	11,500
1882	5,125	245	275	300	300	460	10,500
1883	11,007	235	265	300	300	460	11,000
1884	6,236	235	265	—	300	460	10,000
1885	12,261	235	265	300	300	460	10,000
1886	6,016	235	265	300	300	460	10,000
1887	8,543	235	265	300	300	460	10,000
1888	16,580	235	265	300	300	460	10,000
1889	30,729	235	265	300	300	390	10,000

$2.50 (QUARTER EAGLE)

GOLD
Liberty Cap
Liberty cap on head, right, flanked by stars obverse   Heraldic eagle reverse

KM# 27 • 4.3700 g., 0.9160 **Gold,** 0.1287 oz. AGW, 20 mm. • **Obv. Legend** LIBERTY **Rev. Legend:** UNITED STATES OF AMERICA **Designer:** Robert Scot **Notes:** The 1796 "no stars" variety does not have stars on the obverse. The 1804 varieties are distinguished by the number of stars on the obverse.

Date	Mintage	F-12	VF-20	XF-40	MS-60
1796 no stars	963	55,000	71,500	100,000	245,000
1796 stars	432	26,500	32,500	65,000	185,000
1797	427	20,000	25,000	45,000	125,000
1798 close date	1,094	6,250	8,650	16,500	60,000
1798 wide date	Inc. above	5,250	7,650	15,500	57,500
1802/1	3,035	4,250	6,650	14,500	34,500

Date	Mintage	F-12	VF-20	XF-40	MS-60
1804 13-star reverse	3,327	45,000	65,000	125,000	—
1804 14-star reverse	Inc. above	4,550	7,150	15,500	46,500
1805	1,781	4,250	6,650	14,500	37,000
1806/4	1,616	4,250	6,650	15,000	38,000
1806/5	Inc. above	6,250	8,650	21,500	95,000
1807	6,812	4,250	6,650	14,500	34,500

Turban Head

Turban on head left flanked by stars obverse   Banner above eagle reverse

KM# 40 • 4.3700 g., 0.9160 **Gold**, 0.1287 oz. AGW, 20 mm. • **Rev. Legend:** UNITED STATES OF AMERICA **Designer:** John Reich

Date	Mintage	F-12	VF-20	XF-40	MS-60
1808	2,710	26,500	36,500	54,500	175,000

Turban Head

Turban on head left within circle of stars obverse   Banner above eagle reverse

KM# 46 • 4.3700 g., 0.9160 **Gold**, 0.1287 oz. AGW, 18.5 mm. • **Rev. Legend:** UNITED STATES OF AMERICA **Designer:** John Reich

Date	Mintage	F-12	VF-20	XF-40	MS-60
1821	6,448	5,950	7,150	10,350	30,000
1824/21	2,600	5,950	7,150	10,250	29,500
1825	4,434	5,950	7,150	10,250	27,500
1826/25	760	6,450	7,900	11,000	100,000
1827	2,800	6,050	7,350	10,750	29,500

Turban Head

Turban on head left within circle of stars obverse   Banner above eagle reverse

KM# 49 • 4.3700 g., 0.9160 **Gold**, 0.1287 oz. AGW, 18.2 mm. • **Rev. Legend:** UNITED STATES OF AMERICA **Designer:** John Reich

Date	Mintage	F-12	VF-20	XF-40	MS-60
1829	3,403	5,400	6,250	7,950	18,500
1830	4,540	5,400	6,250	7,950	18,500
1831	4,520	5,400	6,250	7,950	19,000
1832	4,400	5,400	6,250	7,950	18,500
1833	4,160	5,400	6,250	7,950	19,000
1834	4,000	8,900	11,750	15,450	48,500

Classic Head

Classic head left within circle of stars obverse   No motto above eagle reverse

KM# 56 • 4.1800 g., 0.8990 **Gold**, 0.1208 oz. AGW, 18.2 mm. • **Rev. Legend:** UNITED STATES OF AMERICA **Designer:** William Kneass

Date	Mintage	VF-20	XF-40	AU-50	MS-60	MS-65
1834	112,234	475	675	965	3,300	27,000
1835	131,402	475	675	950	3,200	32,000
1836	547,986	475	675	940	3,100	29,000
1837	45,080	500	800	1,500	4,000	35,000
1838	47,030	500	625	1,100	3,200	30,000
1838C	7,880	1,700	3,000	8,000	27,000	55,000
1839	27,021	500	900	1,900	5,500	—
1839C	18,140	1,500	2,650	4,500	26,500	—
1839/8	Inc. above	—	—	—	—	—
1839D	13,674	1,750	3,450	8,000	24,000	—
1839O	17,781	700	1,100	2,500	7,250	—

Coronet Head

Coronet head left within circle of stars obverse   No motto above eagle reverse

1848 "Cal." reverse

KM# 72 • 4.1800 g., 0.9000 **Gold**, 0.1209 oz. AGW, 18 mm. • **Rev. Legend:** UNITED STATES OF AMERICA **Designer:** Christian Gobrecht

Date	Mintage	F-12	VF-20	XF-40	AU-50	MS-60	Prf-65
1840	18,859	275	375	900	2,950	6,000	—
1840C	12,822	1,250	1,400	1,600	6,000	13,000	—
1840D	3,532	2,500	3,200	8,700	15,500	35,000	—
1840O	33,580	325	400	825	2,100	11,000	—
1841	—	—	48,000	100,000	—	—	—
1841C	10,281	1,100	1,500	2,000	3,500	18,500	—
1841D	4,164	1,350	2,100	4,750	11,000	25,000	—
1842	2,823	1,100	900	2,600	6,500	20,000	140,000
1842C	6,729	1,250	1,700	3,500	8,000	27,000	—
1842D	4,643	1,300	2,100	4,000	11,750	—	—
1842O	19,800	325	390	1,200	2,500	14,000	—
1843	100,546	275	345	450	915	3,000	140,000
1843C small date, Crosslet 4	26,064	1,500	2,400	5,500	9,000	29,000	—
1843C large date, Plain 4	Inc. above	1,200	1,600	2,200	3,500	8,800	
1843D small date, Crosslet 4	36,209	1,350	1,800	2,350	3,250	10,500	—
1843O small date, Crosslet 4	288,002	285	315	375	400	1,700	—
1843O large date, Plain 4	76,000	295	370	465	1,600	8,000	—
1844	6,784	350	400	850	2,000	7,500	140,000
1844C	11,622	1,050	1,600	2,600	7,000	20,000	—
1844D	17,332	1,100	1,650	2,200	3,200	7,800	—
1845	91,051	325	395	360	600	1,275	140,000
1845D	19,460	1,100	1,900	2,600	3,900	15,000	—
1845O	4,000	575	1,050	2,300	9,000	20,000	—
1846	21,598	320	365	500	950	6,000	140,000
1846C	4,808	1,100	1,575	3,500	8,950	18,750	—
1846D	19,303	1,000	1,400	2,000	3,000	12,000	—
1846O	66,000	350	385	400	1,150	6,500	—
1847	29,814	275	350	360	825	3,800	—
1847C	23,226	900	1,800	2,300	3,500	7,250	—
1847D	15,784	950	1,650	2,250	3,250	10,500	—
1847O	124,000	275	365	400	1,000	4,000	—
1848	7,497	340	500	850	2,400	7,000	125,000
1848 "CAL."	1,389	35,000	40,000	45,000	50,000	55,000	—
1848C	16,788	950	1,600	2,100	3,800	13,750	—
1848D	13,771	1,100	2,000	2,500	4,500	12,000	—
1849	23,294	295	375	475	1,000	2,600	—
1849C	10,220	975	1,475	2,150	5,150	23,500	—
1849D	10,945	1,050	2,000	2,500	4,500	18,000	—
1850	252,923	265	310	360	385	1,100	—
1850C	9,148	800	1,500	2,000	3,600	13,500	—
1850D	12,148	950	1,700	2,350	3,450	1,600	—
1850O	84,000	300	345	485	1,300	4,500	—
1851	1,372,748	265	300	330	345	495	—
1851C	14,923	900	1,650	2,250	3,450	9,850	—
1851D	11,264	1,000	1,800	2,500	3,850	12,000	—
1851O	148,000	300	335	370	900	4,450	—
1852	1,159,681	265	300	330	345	495	—
1852C	9,772	975	1,500	2,050	4,250	16,500	—
1852D	4,078	1,100	1,650	2,950	7,000	17,500	—

Date	Mintage	F-12	VF-20	XF-40	AU-50	MS-60	Prf-65
1852O	140,000	300	335	365	1,000	5,000	—
1853	1,404,668	265	300	330	345	495	—
1853D	3,178	1,250	1,975	3,450	4,850	18,000	—
1854	596,258	265	300	330	345	495	—
1854C	7,295	1,100	1,450	2,450	4,750	13,500	—
1854D	1,760	2,100	3,350	6,950	11,500	27,500	—
1854O	153,000	300	335	365	420	1,600	—
1854S	246	95,000	175,000	300,000	—	—	—
1855	235,480	270	305	335	350	495	—
1855C	3,677	1,050	1,675	3,250	6,350	19,500	—
1855D	1,123	2,100	3,350	7,500	16,500	50,000	—
1856	384,240	270	305	335	350	515	75,000
1856C	7,913	985	1,600	2,500	4,000	14,500	—
1856D	874	3,850	6,500	12,850	30,000	72,500	—
1856O	21,100	300	345	750	1,350	7,500	—
1856S	71,120	300	335	425	950	4,350	—
1857	214,130	270	305	335	350	515	75,000
1857D	2,364	1,025	1,650	2,775	3,700	13,200	—
1857O	34,000	300	335	425	1,050	4,450	—
1857S	69,200	300	335	365	875	5,350	—
1858	47,377	275	310	340	395	1,250	59,000
1858C	9,056	965	1,500	2,100	3,350	9,250	—
1859	39,444	275	310	350	425	1,250	61,000
1859D	2,244	1,150	1,850	3,100	3,950	18,500	—
1859S	15,200	310	365	950	2,350	5,000	—
1860	22,675	275	310	340	450	1,150	58,000
1860C	7,469	985	1,475	2,175	3,100	20,000	—
1860S	35,600	310	365	625	1,150	3,850	—
1861	1,283,878	270	305	335	350	850	31,500
1861S	24,000	320	400	900	3,250	7,250	—
1862	98,543	310	340	600	1,950	5,150	32,500
1862/1	Inc. above	650	875	1,850	3,450	7,500	—
1862S	8,000	650	875	2,050	4,200	17,500	—
1863	30	—	—	—	—	—	95,000
1863S	10,800	465	475	1,475	3,150	13,500	—
1864	2,874	3,750	5,450	11,500	22,500	47,500	27,000
1865	1,545	2,950	4,750	7,750	18,000	37,500	30,000
1865S	23,376	320	335	595	1,450	4,400	—
1866	3,110	775	1,250	3,150	5,750	11,500	25,000
1866S	38,960	365	400	625	1,500	5,950	—
1867	3,250	350	395	850	1,150	4,750	27,000
1867S	28,000	300	335	575	1,600	4,100	—
1868	3,625	300	335	395	640	1,625	27,000
1868S	34,000	270	305	365	1,050	3,850	—
1869	4,345	300	335	435	685	2,750	24,500
1869S	29,500	300	365	445	800	4,000	—
1870	4,555	290	375	550	900	4,150	33,500
1870S	16,000	270	345	465	1,000	4,900	—
1871	5,350	295	360	385	850	3,100	36,500
1871S	22,000	270	345	415	550	2,350	—
1872	3,030	305	450	800	1,250	4,650	33,500
1872S	18,000	275	340	485	1,150	4,350	—
1873 closed 3	178,025	270	330	375	395	435	42,500
1873 open 3	Inc. above	270	325	355	375	405	—
1873S	27,000	280	345	395	900	2,800	—
1874	3,940	285	345	425	850	2,250	42,500
1875	420	1,950	3,500	5,500	11,000	24,000	70,000
1875S	11,600	270	330	375	850	3,950	—
1876	4,221	285	345	675	1,250	3,350	27,500
1876S	5,000	285	345	625	1,150	2,850	—
1877	1,652	310	395	875	1,250	3,250	35,000
1877S	35,400	265	325	355	415	750	—
1878	286,260	265	320	345	370	410	35,000
1878S	178,000	265	320	345	375	415	—
1879	88,990	270	325	355	385	435	26,000
1879S	43,500	270	340	365	765	2,500	—
1880	2,996	275	345	385	750	1,400	26,000
1881	691	950	2,150	3,150	5,250	9,850	26,500
1882	4,067	270	330	375	550	1,050	23,500
1883	2,002	280	395	750	1,350	3,350	23,500
1884	2,023	275	375	440	750	1,600	23,500
1885	887	400	750	1,850	2,650	4,850	22,500
1886	4,088	275	340	375	650	1,150	23,500
1887	6,282	275	340	365	500	850	17,500
1888	16,098	270	335	365	450	520	18,000
1889	17,648	270	335	365	450	535	20,500
1890	8,813	275	340	365	500	600	18,500
1891 DDR	Inc. above	275	335	365	475	585	—
1891	11,040	—	—	—	—	—	17,500

$2.50

Date	Mintage	F-12	VF-20	XF-40	AU-50	MS-60	Prf-65
1892	2,545	275	330	365	500	950	15,500
1893	30,106	270	330	355	375	400	15,500
1894	4,122	275	330	365	440	800	18,000
1895	6,199	265	325	355	400	525	16,750
1896	19,202	265	325	350	370	400	16,750
1897	29,904	270	325	350	370	400	16,750
1898	24,165	265	325	345	365	385	15,000
1899	27,350	265	325	345	365	385	15,000
1900	67,205	265	325	345	365	385	15,000
1901	91,322	265	325	345	365	385	15,000
1902	133,733	265	320	345	365	385	15,000
1903	201,257	265	320	345	365	385	15,000
1904	160,960	265	320	345	365	385	15,000
1905	217,944	265	320	345	365	385	15,000
1906	176,490	265	320	345	365	385	15,000
1907	336,448	265	320	345	365	385	15,000

Indian Head

KM# 128 • 4.1800 g., 0.9000 **Gold**, 0.1209 oz. AGW, 18 mm. • **Designer:** Bela Lyon Pratt

Date	Mintage	VF-20	XF-40	AU-50	MS-60	MS-63	MS-65	Prf-65
1908	565,057	325	330	345	410	990	3,150	25,000
1909	441,899	325	330	345	420	1,650	6,540	53,000
1910	492,682	325	330	345	410	1,550	7,500	35,000
1911	704,191	325	330	345	410	1,005	8,500	25,000
1911D D strong D	55,680	2,750	3,850	4,750	8,750	20,500	77,500	—
1911 1D weak D	Inc. above	1,150	1,950	2,850	4,950	—	—	—
1912	616,197	325	330	350	435	1,750	11,850	25,000
1913	722,165	325	330	345	410	930	7,500	25,000
1914	240,117	330	355	405	595	4,950	34,500	30,000
1914D	448,000	325	330	355	425	1,500	36,500	—
1915	606,100	325	330	340	410	965	6,500	32,500
1925D	578,000	325	330	340	400	715	2,550	—
1926	446,000	325	330	340	400	715	2,550	—
1927	388,000	325	330	340	400	715	2,550	—
1928	416,000	325	330	340	400	715	2,550	—
1929	532,000	325	340	355	430	805	7,000	—

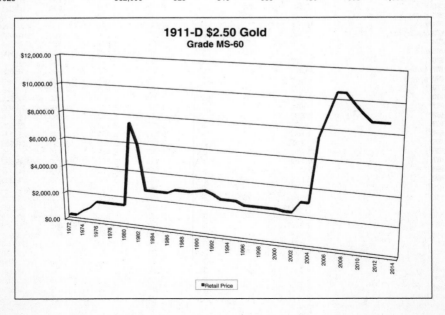

1911-D $2.50 Gold
Grade MS-60

■ Retail Price

$2.50

$3

GOLD
Indian head with headdress, left obverse   Value, date within wreath reverse

KM# 84 • 5.0150 g., 0.9000 **Gold**, 0.1451 oz. AGW, 20.5 mm. • **Obv. Legend** UNITED STATES OF AMERICA **Designer:** James B. Longacre **Notes:** The 1873 "closed-3" and "open-3" varieties are distinguished by the amount of space between the upper left and lower left serifs of the 3 in the date.

Date	Mintage	VF-20	XF-40	AU-50	MS-60	MS-65	Prf-65
1854	138,618	860	1,150	1,290	2,650	19,500	175,000
1854D	1,120	8,300	16,500	35,000	77,500	—	—
1854O	24,000	1,150	2,650	5,000	50,000	—	—
1855	50,555	840	1,175	1,750	3,200	44,000	150,000
1855S	6,600	1,055	2,750	6,950	25,000	—	—
1856	26,010	830	1,125	1,650	3,250	45,000	115,000
1856S	34,500	930	1,600	2,650	12,500	—	—
1857	20,891	830	1,125	1,415	3,500	44,000	105,000
1857S	14,000	980	2,775	5,350	21,000	—	—
1858	2,133	980	1,900	3,650	9,300	50,000	95,000
1859	15,638	930	1,725	1,975	3,250	32,500	60,000
1860	7,155	930	1,625	2,150	3,600	33,000	60,000
1860S	7,000	980	2,450	8,650	26,000	—	—
1861	6,072	955	2,550	3,650	6,900	37,500	60,000
1862	5,785	955	2,350	3,650	6,900	44,500	60,000
1863	5,039	930	2,350	3,650	6,900	34,500	60,000
1864	2,680	980	2,350	3,650	6,900	39,500	60,000
1865	1,165	1,275	2,700	6,500	11,700	55,000	60,000
1866	4,030	1,000	1,500	2,250	3,500	38,500	60,000
1867	2,650	1,025	1,550	2,650	3,600	39,500	60,000
1868	4,875	875	1,475	2,125	3,350	33,000	60,000
1869	2,525	1,150	1,550	2,350	4,300	50,000	60,000
1870	3,535	1,030	1,625	2,450	4,400	—	60,000
1870S unique	—	—	4,000,000	—	—	—	—
Note: H. W. Bass Collection. AU50, cleaned. Est. value, $1,250,000.							
1871	1,330	1,030	1,575	2,375	4,000	42,500	60,000
1872	2,030	930	1,525	2,250	3,850	4,500	60,000
1873 closed 3, mintage unknown	—	4,000	9,000	16,000	27,500	—	95,000
1873 open 3, proof only	25	—	—	—	—	—	90,000
1874	41,820	830	1,125	1,265	2,250	16,750	62,500
1875 proof only	20	20,000	28,000	47,500	—	—	225,000
1876	45	6,000	11,500	18,000	—	—	97,500
1877	1,488	1,350	3,150	7,500	23,000	—	65,000
1878	82,324	830	1,125	1,265	2,250	14,500	65,000
1879	3,030	880	1,325	2,000	3,200	22,500	50,000
1880	1,036	950	2,100	3,375	4,700	27,000	42,000
1881	554	1,400	3,350	6,750	12,000	38,500	36,500
1882	1,576	955	1,475	2,350	3,600	30,000	35,500
1883	989	1,000	1,625	2,950	3,800	34,500	35,500
1884	1,106	1,285	2,000	2,800	3,650	34,500	35,500
1885	910	1,300	2,050	3,450	5,200	38,500	34,500
1886	1,142	1,250	2,250	2,875	5,000	47,500	34,500
1887	6,160	930	1,550	2,175	3,250	22,500	34,500
1888	5,291	980	1,525	2,125	3,150	15,000	34,500
1889	2,429	955	1,475	2,000	3,200	22,500	34,500

$5 (HALF EAGLE)

GOLD
Liberty Cap
Liberty Cap on head, right, flanked by stars obverse   Small eagle reverse

KM# 19 • 8.7500 g., 0.9160 **Gold**, 0.2577 oz. AGW •

Date	Mintage	F-12	VF-20	XF-40	MS-60
1795	8,707	19,500	25,000	31,000	79,500
1796/95	6,196	20,500	25,350	32,750	84,500
1797 15 obverse stars	Inc. above	23,000	27,500	42,250	—
1797 16 obverse stars	Inc. above	21,000	25,850	41,000	210,000
1798	—	112,000	185,000	350,000	—

Liberty Cap
Liberty cap on head, right, flanked by stars obverse   Large Heraldic eagle reverse

KM# 28 • 8.7500 g., 0.9160 **Gold**, 0.2577 oz. AGW, 25 mm. • **Obv. Legend** LIBERTY **Rev. Legend:** UNITED STATES OF AMERICA **Designer:** Robert Scot

Date	Mintage	F-12	VF-20	XF-40	MS-60
1795	Inc. above	10,000	16,500	22,500	85,000
1797/95	3,609	10,850	17,500	24,000	155,000
1797 15 star obv.; Unique	—	—	—	—	—
Note: Smithsonian collection					
1797 16 star obv.; Unique	—	—	—	—	—
Note: Smithsonian collection					
1798 small 8	24,867	4,850	6,650	10,100	—
1798 large 8, 13-star reverse	Inc. above	4,050	5,050	8,350	33,500
1798 large 8, 14-star reverse	Inc. above	5,050	6,650	10,950	—
1799 small reverse stars	7,451	3,850	4,900	11,100	21,500
1799 large reverse stars	Inc. above	3,950	4,750	14,200	31,700
1800	37,628	3,850	4,650	7,100	15,850
1802/1	53,176	3,850	4,650	7,100	15,850
1803/2	33,506	3,850	4,650	7,100	15,850
1804 small 8	30,475	3,850	4,650	7,100	15,850
1804 small 8 over large 8	Inc. above	3,950	4,850	7,600	17,850
1805	33,183	3,850	4,650	7,100	15,850
1806 pointed 6	64,093	3,850	4,650	7,100	17,750
1806 round 6	Inc. above	3,850	4,650	7,100	15,850
1807	32,488	3,850	4,650	7,100	15,850

Turban Head

Capped draped bust, left, flanked by stars obverse   Heraldic eagle reverse

KM# 38 • 8.7500 g., 0.9160 **Gold**, 0.2577 oz. AGW, 25 mm. • **Rev. Legend:** UNITED STATES OF AMERICA **Designer:** John Reich

Date	Mintage	F-12	VF-20	XF-40	MS-60
1807	51,605	3,100	3,850	5,100	13,850
1808	55,578	3,600	4,500	5,950	18,850
1808/7	Inc. above	3,100	3,850	5,100	13,850
1809/8	33,875	3,100	3,850	5,100	13,850
1810 small date, small 5	100,287	17,500	32,500	48,500	125,000
1810 small date, large 5	Inc. above	3,100	3,850	5,100	16,250
1810 large date, small 5	Inc. above	17,500	37,500	60,000	135,000
1810 large date, large 5	Inc. above	3,100	3,850	5,100	13,850
1811 small 5	99,581	3,100	3,850	5,100	13,850
1811 tall 5	Inc. above	3,100	3,850	5,100	13,850
1812	58,087	3,100	3,850	5,100	13,850

Turban Head

Capped head, left, within circle of stars obverse   Heraldic eagle reverse

KM# 43 • 8.7500 g., 0.9160 **Gold**, 0.2577 oz. AGW, 25 mm. • **Rev. Legend:** UNITED STATES OF AMERICA **Designer:** John Reich

Date	Mintage	F-12	VF-20	XF-40	MS-60
1813	95,428	3,100	3,850	5,500	13,250
1814/13	15,454	5,000	6,250	8,250	19,000
1815	635	32,500	50,000	200,000	250,000
Note: 1815, private sale, Jan. 1994, MS-61, $150,000					
1818	48,588	5,000	6,450	13,500	20,000
1818 5D over 50 Inc. Above	—	5,500	6,450	10,500	23,500
1819	51,723	8,800	16,500	50,000	64,000
1819 5D over 50 Inc. Above	—	5,500	11,000	35,000	64,000
1820 curved-base 2, small letters	263,806	5,250	6,600	12,850	22,500
1820 curved-base 2, large letters	Inc. above	5,100	6,400	12,000	20,000
1820 square-base 2	Inc. above	5,000	6,250	11,500	19,000
1821	34,641	12,000	22,000	43,000	115,000
1822 3 known	—	—	—	1,250,000	—
1823	14,485	5,500	6,250	11,500	19,000
1824	17,340	5,500	10,500	32,000	38,000
1825/21	29,060	5,750	9,500	25,000	39,500
1825/24	Inc. above	—	—	550,000	750,000
Note: 1825/4, Bowers & Merena, March 1989, XF, $148,500.					
1826	18,069	5,500	7,800	16,500	30,000
1827	24,913	6,000	10,000	23,500	34,500
1828/7	28,029	15,000	28,500	66,000	125,000
Note: 1828/7, Bowers & Merena, June 1989, XF, $20,900.					
1828	Inc. above	6,000	13,000	30,000	60,000
1829 large planchet	57,442	15,000	28,500	65,000	125,000
Note: 1829 large planchet, Superior, July 1985, MS-65, $104,500.					
1829 small planchet	Inc. above	37,500	54,000	86,500	140,000
Note: 1829 small planchet, private sale, 1992 (XF-45), $89,000.					
1830 small "5D."	126,351	16,500	27,500	44,650	70,000
1830 large "5D."	Inc. above	16,500	27,500	44,650	70,000
1831	140,594	16,500	27,500	44,650	70,000
1832 curved-base 2, 12 stars	157,487	50,000	80,000	175,000	—
1832 square-base 2, 13 stars	Inc. above	16,500	27,500	44,650	70,000

Date	Mintage	F-12	VF-20	XF-40	MS-60
1833 small date	193,630	17,500	29,500	54,650	90,000
1833 large date	Inc. above	16,500	27,500	44,650	70,000
1834 plain 4	50,141	16,500	27,500	44,650	70,000
1834 crosslet 4	Inc. above	17,500	29,500	54,650	80,000

Classic Head

Classic head, left, within circle of stars obverse   No motto above eagle reverse

KM# 57 • 8.3600 g., 0.8990 **Gold**, 0.2416 oz. AGW, 22.5 mm. • **Rev. Legend:** UNITED STATES OF AMERICA **Designer:** William Kneass

Date	Mintage	VF-20	XF-40	AU-50	MS-60	MS-65
1834 plain 4	658,028	550	790	1,400	3,000	48,000
1834 crosslet 4	Inc. above	1,650	2,900	6,000	20,000	—
1835	371,534	550	790	1,450	3,150	—
1836	553,147	550	790	1,450	2,950	70,000
1837	207,121	550	790	1,650	3,500	75,000
1838	286,588	550	890	1,450	3,700	58,000
1838C	17,179	2,550	5,500	13,000	42,500	—
1838D	20,583	2,100	4,650	9,750	31,000	—

Coronet Head

Coronet head, left, within circle of stars obverse   No motto above eagle reverse

KM# 69 • 8.3590 g., 0.9000 **Gold**, 0.2419 oz. AGW, 21.6 mm. • **Rev. Legend:** UNITED STATES OF AMERICA **Designer:** Christian Gobrecht **Notes:** Varieties for 1843 are distinguished by the size of the numerals in the date. One 1848 variety has "Cal." incsribed on the reverse, indicating it was made from California gold. The 1873 "closed-3" and "open-3" varieties are distinguished by the amount of space between the upper left and lower left serifs in the 3 in the date.

Date	Mintage	F-12	VF-20	XF-40	MS-60	Prf-65
1839	118,143	532	562	591	4,000	—
1839/8 curved date	Inc. above	552	582	611	2,250	—
1839C	17,205	1,250	2,300	2,900	24,000	—
1839D	18,939	1,125	2,200	3,200	22,000	—
1840	137,382	522	552	570	3,700	—
1840C	18,992	1,200	2,200	3,000	26,000	—
1840D	22,896	1,200	2,200	3,000	16,000	—
1840O	38,700	532	582	611	11,000	—
1841	15,833	532	562	591	5,500	—
1841C	21,467	1,200	1,850	2,400	20,000	—
1841D	30,495	1,400	1,800	2,350	15,000	—
1841O 2 known	50	—	—	—	—	—
1842 small letters	27,578	200	345	1,100	—	—
1842 large letters	Inc. above	532	750	2,000	11,000	—
1842C small date	28,184	4,500	10,000	23,000	110,000	—
1842C large date	Inc. above	900	1,800	2,200	18,000	—
1842D small date	59,608	1,000	2,000	2,300	15,000	—
1842D large date	Inc. above	1,400	2,350	6,500	48,000	—
1842O	16,400	550	1,000	3,400	22,000	—
1843	611,205	522	552	581	1,850	—
1843C	44,201	1,250	1,850	2,500	14,000	—
1843D	98,452	1,250	1,950	2,600	13,000	—
1843O small letters	19,075	552	582	1,700	26,000	—
1843O large letters	82,000	532	586	1,175	12,000	—
1844	340,330	522	552	581	2,000	—
1844C	23,631	1,300	1,900	3,000	24,000	—

Date	Mintage	F-12	VF-20	XF-40	MS-60	Prf-65
1844D	88,982	1,500	1,950	2,400	12,000	—
1844O	364,600	556	586	590	4,700	—
1845	417,099	522	552	581	2,000	—
1845D	90,629	1,300	1,900	2,400	12,500	—
1845O	41,000	556	415	800	9,900	—
1846	395,942	522	552	581	2,400	—
1846C	12,995	1,350	1,900	3,000	24,000	—
1846D	80,294	1,250	1,800	2,400	13,000	—
1846O	58,000	556	375	1,000	11,500	—
1847	915,981	522	552	581	1,650	—
1847C	84,151	1,350	1,800	2,400	13,000	—
1847D	64,405	1,400	2,000	2,000	10,000	—
1847O	12,000	550	2,200	6,750	28,000	—
1848	260,775	522	552	581	1,500	—
1848C	64,472	1,400	1,900	2,250	19,250	—
1848D	47,465	1,450	2,000	2,350	14,500	—
1849	133,070	522	552	581	2,800	—
1849C	64,823	1,500	1,900	2,400	14,000	—
1849D	39,036	1,550	2,000	2,600	16,500	—
1850	64,491	522	552	581	4,250	—
1850C	63,591	1,350	1,850	2,300	14,000	—
1850D	43,984	1,450	1,950	2,500	33,000	—
1851	377,505	522	552	581	2,800	—
1851C	49,176	1,300	1,900	2,350	17,500	—
1851D	62,710	1,400	1,950	2,400	15,000	—
1851O	41,000	280	590	1,500	13,000	—
1852	573,901	522	552	581	1,400	—
1852C	72,574	1,350	1,900	2,450	7,750	—
1852D	91,584	1,450	2,000	2,450	13,000	—
1853	305,770	522	552	581	1,400	—
1853C	65,571	1,500	1,950	2,350	8,500	—
1853D	89,678	1,550	2,000	2,500	11,000	—
1854	160,675	522	552	581	2,000	—
1854C	39,283	1,400	1,900	2,300	14,000	—
1854D	56,413	1,400	1,875	2,200	11,500	—
1854O	46,000	552	582	611	8,250	—
1854S	268	—	—	—	—	—
Note: 1854S, Bowers & Merena, Oct. 1982, AU-55, $170,000.						
1855	117,098	522	552	581	1,800	—
1855C	39,788	1,400	1,900	2,300	16,000	—
1855D	22,432	1,500	1,950	2,400	19,000	—
1855O	11,100	315	675	2,100	20,000	—
1855S	61,000	552	390	1,000	15,500	—
1856	197,990	552	552	581	2,300	—
1856C	28,457	1,450	1,875	2,400	20,000	—
1856D	19,786	1,475	1,950	2,600	15,000	—
1856O	10,000	370	650	1,600	14,000	—
1856S	105,100	532	300	591	6,750	—
1857	98,188	522	552	581	1,600	123,500
1857C	31,360	1,400	1,900	2,500	9,500	—
1857D	17,046	1,500	2,000	2,650	14,500	—
1857O	13,000	340	640	1,400	15,000	—
1857S	87,000	532	562	591	11,000	—
1858	15,136	532	562	591	3,850	190,000
1858C	38,856	1,400	1,900	2,350	11,000	—
1858D	15,362	1,500	2,000	2,450	12,500	—
1858S	18,600	532	825	2,350	31,000	—
1859	16,814	532	562	591	7,000	—
1859C	31,847	1,400	1,900	2,450	16,000	—
1859D	10,366	1,600	2,150	2,600	16,000	—
1859S	13,220	615	1,800	4,150	30,000	—
1860	19,825	532	562	591	3,650	100,000
1860C	14,813	1,500	2,100	3,000	15,000	—
1860D	14,635	1,500	1,900	2,600	15,000	—
1860S	21,200	500	1,100	2,100	27,000	—
1861	688,150	522	552	591	1,450	100,000
1861C	6,879	1,500	2,400	3,900	25,000	—
1861D	1,597	3,000	4,700	7,000	50,000	—
1861S	18,000	500	1,100	4,500	36,500	—
1862	4,465	532	800	1,850	20,000	96,000
1862S	9,500	1,500	3,000	6,000	62,000	—
1863	2,472	532	1,200	3,750	27,500	90,000
1863S	17,000	600	1,450	4,100	35,500	—
1864	4,220	532	650	1,850	15,000	72,000
1864S	3,888	2,300	4,750	16,000	55,000	—
1865	1,295	500	1,450	4,100	20,000	82,500
1865S	27,612	475	1,400	2,400	20,000	—
1866S	9,000	750	1,750	4,000	40,000	—

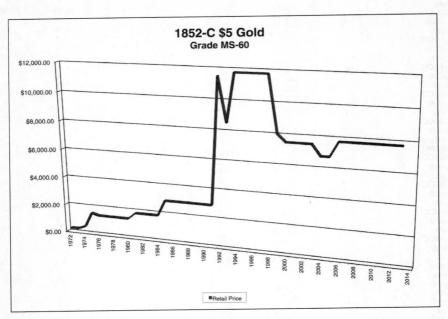

1852-C $5 Gold
Grade MS-60

Coronet Head

Coronet head, left, within circle of stars obverse   IN GOD WE TRUST above eagle reverse

KM# 101 • 8.3590 g., 0.9000 **Gold**, 0.2419 oz. AGW, 21.6 mm. • **Rev. Legend:** UNITED STATES OF AMERICA **Designer:** Christian Gobrecht

Date	Mintage	VF-20	XF-40	AU-50	MS-60	MS-63	MS-65	Prf-65
1866	6,730	750	1,650	3,500	16,500	—	—	70,000
1866S	34,920	900	2,600	8,800	25,000	—	—	—
1867	6,920	500	1,500	3,300	11,500	—	—	70,000
1867S	29,000	1,400	2,900	8,000	34,500	—	—	—
1868	5,725	650	1,000	3,500	11,500	—	—	70,000
1868S	52,000	486	1,550	4,000	20,000	—	—	—
1869	1,785	925	2,400	3,500	17,500	34,000	—	65,000
1869S	31,000	500	1,750	4,000	26,000	—	—	—
1870	4,035	800	2,000	2,850	18,000	—	—	75,000
1870CC	7,675	5,250	15,000	30,000	110,000	137,500	200,000	—
1870S	17,000	950	2,600	8,250	29,000	—	—	—
1871	3,230	900	1,700	3,300	12,500	—	—	70,000
1871CC	20,770	1,250	3,000	12,000	60,000	—	—	—
1871S	25,000	500	950	2,950	13,000	—	—	—
1872	1,690	850	1,925	3,000	15,000	18,000	—	60,000
1872CC	16,980	1,250	5,000	20,000	60,000	—	—	—
1872S	36,400	537	800	3,400	13,500	—	—	—
1873 closed 3	49,305	472	486	500	1,200	6,500	24,000	70,000
1873 open 3	63,200	467	477	487	850	3,650	—	—
1873CC	7,416	2,600	12,500	27,500	60,000	—	—	—
1873S	31,000	525	1,400	3,250	21,000	—	—	—
1874	3,508	660	1,675	2,500	13,000	26,000	—	66,000
1874CC	21,198	850	1,700	9,500	36,000	—	—	—
1874S	16,000	640	2,100	4,800	22,500	—	—	—
1875	220	34,000	45,000	60,000	190,000	—	—	185,000
1875CC	11,828	1,400	4,500	11,500	52,000	—	—	—
1875S	9,000	715	2,250	5,000	16,500	32,500	—	—
1876	1,477	1,100	2,500	4,125	11,000	14,500	55,000	60,000

Date	Mintage	VF-20	XF-40	AU-50	MS-60	MS-63	MS-65	Prf-65
1876CC	6,887	1,450	5,000	14,000	46,500	82,500	165,000	—
1876S	4,000	2,000	3,600	9,500	30,000	—	—	—
1877	1,152	900	2,750	4,000	13,750	29,000	—	75,000
1877CC	8,680	1,000	3,300	11,000	52,500	—	—	—
1877S	26,700	499	650	1,400	9,200	—	—	—
1878	131,740	469	480	524	550	2,000	—	50,000
1878CC	9,054	3,100	7,200	20,000	60,000	—	—	—
1878S	144,700	467	475	3,000	675	4,250	—	—
1879	301,950	467	475	485	520	2,000	12,000	55,000
1879CC	17,281	1,000	1,500	3,150	22,000	—	—	—
1879S	426,200	469	480	524	950	3,300	—	—
1880	3,166,436	462	470	480	500	840	7,500	54,000
1880CC	51,017	625	815	1,375	9,900	—	—	—
1880S	1,348,900	462	470	480	490	800	5,750	—
1881	5,708,802	462	470	480	500	775	4,800	54,000
1881/80	Inc. above	465	600	750	1,500	4,500	—	—
1881CC	13,886	650	1,500	7,000	22,500	60,000	—	—
1881S	969,000	462	470	480	500	775	7,150	—
1882	2,514,568	462	470	480	500	800	6,150	54,000
1882CC	82,817	625	625	900	7,500	40,000	—	—
1882S	969,000	462	470	480	510	800	4,500	—
1883	233,461	479	487	497	530	1,200	—	40,000
1883CC	12,958	625	1,100	3,200	18,000	—	—	—
1883S	83,200	479	478	490	1,000	2,950	—	—
1884	191,078	479	480	497	650	2,250	—	35,000
1884CC	16,402	625	975	3,000	17,000	—	—	—
1884S	177,000	479	487	497	490	2,000	—	—
1885	601,506	462	470	480	505	825	4,800	35,000
1885S	1,211,500	462	470	480	510	790	4,000	—
1886	388,432	462	470	480	510	1,125	5,600	44,000
1886S	3,268,000	462	470	480	510	815	4,500	—
1887	87	—	14,500	20,000	—	—	—	120,000
1887S	1,912,000	462	470	480	510	800	4,800	—
1888	18,296	477	485	497	550	1,500	—	29,000
1888S	293,900	467	475	547	1,200	4,000	—	—
1889	7,565	576	584	557	1,150	2,400	—	30,000
1890	4,328	499	507	550	2,200	6,500	—	27,000
1890CC	53,800	576	584	615	1,600	7,500	55,000	—
1891	61,413	469	480	524	640	2,000	5,400	29,000
1891CC	208,000	561	565	800	1,350	3,500	28,500	—
1892	753,572	462	470	480	530	1,350	7,000	30,000
1892CC	82,968	562	584	750	1,500	6,500	33,500	—
1892O	10,000	524	1,000	1,375	3,300	15,000	—	—
1892S	298,400	462	470	485	525	2,850	—	—
1893	1,528,197	462	470	480	510	1,150	3,900	34,000
1893CC	60,000	596	634	825	1,550	6,650	—	—
1893O	110,000	477	581	585	950	5,950	—	—
1893S	224,000	462	470	485	510	1,040	9,000	—
1894	957,955	462	470	480	500	905	2,600	35,000
1894O	16,600	479	487	570	1,300	5,500	—	—
1894S	55,900	489	487	575	2,900	10,000	—	—
1895	1,345,936	462	470	480	495	905	4,500	29,000
1895S	112,000	467	487	497	3,150	6,500	26,000	—
1896	59,063	462	470	485	510	1,650	4,500	30,000
1896S	155,400	469	480	524	1,150	6,000	24,500	—
1897	867,883	462	470	480	495	905	4,500	35,000
1897S	354,000	462	470	485	865	5,150	—	—
1898	633,495	462	470	480	500	905	6,000	30,000
1898S	1,397,400	462	470	480	495	1,310	—	—
1899	1,710,729	462	470	480	495	890	3,600	30,000
1899S	1,545,000	462	470	480	495	1,260	9,600	—
1900	1,405,730	462	470	480	495	890	3,600	30,000
1900S	329,000	462	470	480	500	1,260	14,000	—
1901	616,040	462	470	480	495	890	3,650	27,000
1901S	3,648,000	462	470	480	495	890	3,600	—
1902	172,562	462	470	480	495	890	4,400	27,000
1902S	939,000	462	470	480	495	890	3,600	—
1903	227,024	462	470	480	500	905	4,000	27,000
1903S	1,855,000	462	470	480	495	890	3,600	—
1904	392,136	462	470	480	495	890	3,600	27,000
1904S	97,000	469	480	524	885	4,000	9,600	—
1905	302,308	462	470	480	500	905	4,000	27,000
1905S	880,700	462	470	480	495	3,350	9,600	—
1906	348,820	462	470	480	495	890	3,600	26,000
1906D	320,000	462	470	480	495	905	3,200	—
1906S	598,000	462	470	480	500	1,190	4,400	—
1907	626,192	462	470	480	495	890	3,400	23,000
1907D	888,000	462	470	480	495	890	3,400	—
1908	421,874	462	470	485	510	905	3,400	—

Indian Head

KM# 129 • 8.3590 g., 0.9000 **Gold**, 0.2419 oz. AGW, 21.6 mm. • **Designer:** Bela Lyon Pratt

Date	Mintage	VF-20	XF-40	AU-50	MS-60	MS-63	MS-65	Prf-65
1908	578,012	463	475	489	585	1,850	12,500	25,500
1908D	148,000	463	475	489	585	2,000	36,500	—
1908S	82,000	538	600	1,150	2,350	7,000	21,500	—
1909	627,138	463	475	489	565	1,850	13,500	37,000
1909D	3,423,560	463	475	489	565	1,600	12,500	—
1909O	34,200	3,950	4,850	7,650	31,500	75,000	460,000	—
1909S	297,200	493	515	549	1,350	13,250	51,000	—
1910	604,250	463	475	489	565	1,650	13,750	28,500
1910D	193,600	463	475	489	585	4,175	38,500	—
1910S	770,200	503	530	559	975	8,500	49,500	—
1911	915,139	463	475	489	565	1,565	13,500	28,500
1911D	72,500	625	825	1,600	6,850	41,000	265,000	—
1911S	1,416,000	473	510	544	600	5,850	43,000	—
1912	790,144	463	475	489	565	1,565	13,500	28,500
1912S	392,000	508	540	634	1,675	14,500	142,500	—
1913	916,099	463	475	489	565	1,565	13,500	28,000
1913S	408,000	503	535	674	1,450	13,250	120,000	—
1914	247,125	463	475	489	585	2,250	15,500	28,500
1914D	247,000	463	475	489	585	2,550	23,500	—
1914S	263,000	508	530	584	1,375	14,350	105,000	—
1915	588,075	463	475	489	565	1,565	105,000	39,000
1915S	164,000	518	550	669	1,950	17,000	14,500	—
1916S	240,000	488	510	569	770	6,750	110,000	—
1929	662,000	11,500	14,750	18,000	27,500	45,000	88,500	—

$10 (EAGLE)

GOLD
Liberty Cap
Small eagle reverse

KM# 21 • 17.5000 g., 0.9160 **Gold**, 0.5154 oz. AGW, 33 mm. • **Designer:** Robert Scot

Date	Mintage	F-12	VF-20	XF-40	MS-60
1795 13 leaves	5,583	28,500	33,850	48,500	122,500
1795 9 leaves	Inc. above	30,000	45,000	73,500	250,000
1796	4,146	27,500	36,000	50,000	135,000
1797 small eagle	3,615	31,500	40,000	55,000	200,000

Liberty Cap

Liberty cap on head, right, flanked by stars obverse   Heraldic eagle reverse

KM# 30 • 17.5000 g., 0.9160 **Gold**, 0.5154 oz. AGW, 33 mm. • **Obv. Legend** LIBERTY **Rev. Legend:** UNITED STATES OF AMERICA **Designer:** Robert Scot

Date	Mintage	F-12	VF-20	XF-40	MS-60
1797 large eagle	10,940	9,800	12,850	21,400	58,500
1798/97 9 stars left, 4 right	900	13,500	19,000	34,500	127,500
1798/97 7 stars left, 6 right	842	28,500	38,500	87,500	235,000
1799 large star obv	37,449	9,350	10,750	18,200	37,500
1799 small star obv	Inc. above	9,350	10,750	18,200	37,500
1800	5,999	9,500	10,750	18,350	39,500
1801	44,344	9,250	10,900	17,400	37,500
1803 extra star	15,017	9,600	11,850	19,550	67,500
1803 large stars rev	Inc. above	9,250	11,400	17,800	37,500
1804 crosslet 4	3,757	16,500	22,750	31,500	92,500
1804 plain 4	—	—	—	—	400,000

Coronet Head

Old-style head, left, within circle of stars obverse   No motto above eagle reverse

KM# 66.1 • 16.7180 g., 0.9000 **Gold**, 0.4837 oz. AGW, 27 mm. • **Rev. Legend:** UNITED STATES OF AMERICA **Designer:** Christian Gobrecht

Date	Mintage	F-12	VF-20	XF-40	MS-60	Prf-65
1838	7,200	1,750	2,650	6,850	43,500	1,500,000
1839/8 Type of 1838	25,801	1,100	1,450	5,850	28,500	1,500,000
1839 large letters	Inc. above	800	1,150	2,150	32,000	—

Coronet Head

New-style head, left, within circle of stars obverse   No motto above eagle reverse

KM# 66.2 • 16.7180 g., 0.9000 **Gold**, 0.4837 oz. AGW, 27 mm. • **Rev. Legend:** UNITED STATES OF AMERICA **Designer:** Christian Gobrecht

Date	Mintage	F-12	VF-20	XF-40	MS-60	Prf-65
1839 small letters	12,447	975	1,550	6,850	75,000	—
1840	47,338	994	1,059	1,333	11,500	—
1841	63,131	974	1,049	1,233	9,000	—
1841O	2,500	1,750	3,450	6,950	—	—
1842 small date	81,507	974	1,049	1,158	15,000	—

$10

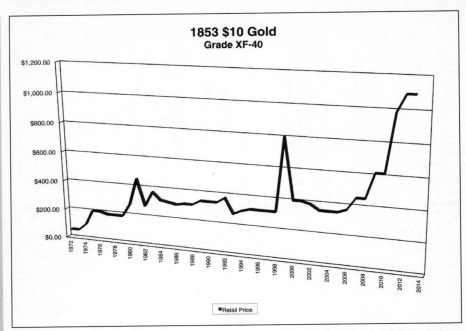

1853 $10 Gold
Grade XF-40

Date	Mintage	F-12	VF-20	XF-40	MS-60	Prf-65
1842 large date	Inc. above	974	1,049	1,148	9,500	—
1842O	27,400	974	1,059	1,463	22,500	—
1843	75,462	974	1,049	1,263	16,750	—
1843O	175,162	974	1,059	1,218	12,000	—
1844	6,361	800	1,350	3,200	16,750	—
1844O	118,700	974	1,059	1,403	15,000	—
1845	26,153	1,009	1,219	1,343	17,500	—
1845O	47,500	994	1,059	875	16,500	—
1845O repunched	Inc. above	1,069	1,419	3,850	—	—
1846	20,095	1,019	1,289	1,250	—	—
1846O	81,780	974	1,059	1,150	—	—
1846/5	Inc. above	1,069	1,419	1,135	—	—
1847	862,258	974	1,049	1,093	3,450	—
1847O	571,500	974	1,049	1,093	6,500	—
1848	145,484	974	1,049	1,158	5,000	—
1848O	38,850	1,049	1,239	1,850	17,750	—
1849	653,618	974	1,049	1,093	3,400	—
1849O	23,900	1,049	1,239	2,450	27,500	—
1850 large date	291,451	974	1,049	1,093	4,500	—
1850 small date	Inc. above	1,049	1,239	1,150	8,500	—
1850O	57,500	994	1,074	1,275	19,500	—
1851	176,328	974	1,049	1,093	5,150	—
1851O	263,000	974	1,059	1,148	6,650	—
1852	263,106	974	1,049	1,093	5,250	—
1852O	18,000	1,049	1,219	1,650	27,500	—
1853	201,253	994	1,059	1,093	3,600	—
1853/2	Inc. above	994	1,074	1,428	14,950	—
1853O	51,000	974	1,074	1,158	14,500	—
1854	54,250	974	1,049	1,118	6,250	—
1854O small date	52,500	994	1,074	1,398	11,000	—
1854O large date	Inc. above	1,049	1,214	925	9,450	—
1854S	123,826	974	1,049	1,118	10,500	—
1855	121,701	974	1,049	1,093	4,750	—
1855O	18,000	994	1,074	2,100	28,000	—
1856	60,490	974	1,049	1,093	4,250	—
1856O	14,500	1,049	1,374	2,150	18,500	—
1856S	68,000	974	1,049	1,168	9,000	—
1857	16,606	994	1,074	1,050	13,500	—
1857O	5,500	1,149	1,800	3,650	—	—
1857S	26,000	994	1,059	1,050	11,500	—
1858	2,521	3,000	5,200	8,250	35,000	—
1858O	20,000	974	1,049	1,418	10,000	—
1858S	11,800	900	1,600	3,950	—	—
1859	16,093	994	1,074	1,278	10,500	—

Date	Mintage	F-12	VF-20	XF-40	MS-60	Prf-65
1859O	2,300	2,000	4,250	10,500	—	—
1859S	7,000	1,450	2,600	5,250	—	—
1860	15,105	1,019	1,114	1,328	8,450	175,000
1860O	11,100	1,039	1,214	1,850	13,750	—
1860S	5,000	1,400	2,950	6,400	—	—
1861	113,233	974	1,049	1,093	6,250	170,000
1861S	15,500	690	1,600	3,750	—	—
1862	10,995	1,049	1,204	1,200	—	170,000
1862S	12,500	700	2,000	3,450	—	—
1863	1,248	2,400	4,000	10,000	52,500	165,000
1863S	10,000	700	1,600	3,750	29,500	—
1864	3,580	775	1,800	4,950	18,000	165,000
1864S	2,500	2,600	5,100	17,500	—	—
1865	4,005	900	1,950	4,850	34,500	165,000
1865S	16,700	1,700	4,850	12,500	—	—
1865S over inverted 186	Inc. above	1,300	3,450	8,750	50,000	—
1866S	8,500	1,000	2,650	5,950	—	—

Coronet Head

New-style head, left, within circle of stars obverse   IN GOD WE TRUST above eagle reverse

KM# 102 • 16.7180 g., 0.9000 **Gold**, 0.4837 oz. AGW, 27 mm. • **Rev. Legend:** UNITED STATES OF AMERICA **Designer:** Christian Gobrecht

Date	Mintage	VF-20	XF-40	AU-50	MS-60	MS-63	MS-65	Prf-65
1866	3,780	850	2,450	5,000	—	—	—	110,000
1866S	11,500	1,550	3,850	8,000	—	—	—	—
1867	3,140	1,500	2,600	5,000	33,000	—	—	—
1867S	9,000	2,350	6,650	9,850	—	—	—	—
1868	10,655	1,008	1,100	2,250	19,000	—	—	110,000
1868S	13,500	1,350	2,400	3,900	—	—	—	—
1869	1,855	1,550	3,000	5,650	36,000	—	—	—
1869S	6,430	1,500	2,700	6,250	25,000	—	—	—
1870	4,025	985	1,650	3,950	—	—	—	—
1870CC	5,908	13,000	30,000	52,500	—	—	—	—
1870S	8,000	1,150	2,850	7,400	33,500	—	—	—
1871	1,820	1,500	3,000	5,000	20,000	—	—	110,000
1871CC	8,085	2,600	6,400	22,500	65,000	—	—	—
1871S	16,500	1,300	2,200	6,000	30,000	—	—	—
1872	1,650	2,400	5,500	8,700	15,000	34,000	—	90,000
1872CC	4,600	2,850	9,850	24,500	—	—	—	—
1872S	17,300	850	1,175	1,900	—	—	—	—
1873 closed 3	825	4,500	9,750	17,500	55,000	—	—	—
1873CC	4,543	6,000	13,500	31,000	—	—	—	—
1873S	12,000	1,150	2,850	5,100	27,500	—	—	—
1874	53,160	934	966	980	2,100	7,250	42,500	120,000
1874CC	16,767	1,150	3,650	11,000	52,500	75,000	—	—
1874S	10,000	1,275	3,400	7,250	—	—	—	—
1875	120	40,000	67,500	80,000	—	—	—	—

Note: 1875, Akers, Aug. 1990, Proof, $115,000.

Date	Mintage	VF-20	XF-40	AU-50	MS-60	MS-63	MS-65	Prf-65
1875CC	7,715	4,250	9,850	25,000	71,500	—	—	—
1876	732	3,000	8,500	18,500	—	—	—	—
1876CC	4,696	3,600	7,750	21,500	—	—	—	—
1876S	5,000	1,300	2,950	7,500	—	—	—	—
1877	817	3,350	6,350	9,850	37,500	—	—	—
1877CC	3,332	2,400	6,750	15,000	—	—	—	—
1877S	17,000	936	1,250	2,450	33,500	—	—	—
1878	73,800	924	966	980	975	6,750	29,000	—
1878CC	3,244	3,850	10,000	19,000	—	—	—	—
1878S	26,100	936	975	2,150	16,500	29,500	—	—
1879	384,770	927	966	980	1,117	5,000	15,750	83,000
1879/78	Inc. above	934	978	1,265	1,250	2,850	—	—
1879CC	1,762	6,650	12,500	26,000	—	—	—	—
1879O	1,500	2,150	5,450	10,250	—	—	—	—
1879S	224,000	927	966	980	1,150	6,500	49,500	—
1880	1,644,876	909	928	942	972	3,650	—	—
1880CC	11,190	900	1,000	1,950	15,500	—	—	—
1880O	9,200	1,029	1,450	1,850	20,000	—	—	—

$10

Date	Mintage	VF-20	XF-40	AU-50	MS-60	MS-63	MS-65	Prf-65
1880S	506,250	909	928	942	992	4,850	25,000	—
1881	3,877,260	909	928	942	972	1,385	16,500	63,000
1881CC	24,015	1,055	1,200	1,800	6,850	36,500	—	—
1881O	8,350	1,009	1,150	1,500	6,950	—	—	—
1881S	970,000	909	928	942	982	1,385	—	—
1882	2,324,480	909	928	942	972	1,385	19,500	63,000
1882CC	6,764	985	1,750	3,250	—	—	—	—
1882O	10,820	937	1,115	1,250	6,350	18,500	—	—
1882S	132,000	937	966	980	1,054	3,650	—	—
1883	208,740	909	928	942	982	3,100	—	63,000
1883CC	12,000	1,109	1,250	2,600	22,500	—	—	—
1883O	800	3,000	7,950	10,500	—	—	—	—
1883S	38,000	937	966	980	1,275	10,500	23,500	—
1884	76,905	937	966	980	1,152	5,100	15,000	53,000
1884CC	9,925	1,129	1,450	2,350	12,850	55,000	—	—
1884S	124,250	909	928	942	1,067	6,500	—	—
1885	253,527	909	928	942	972	4,850	—	53,000
1885S	228,000	909	928	942	972	4,400	—	—
1886	236,160	909	928	942	972	5,100	—	53,000
1886S	826,000	909	928	942	982	1,500	—	—
1887	53,680	937	966	980	1,050	6,150	—	53,000
1887S	817,000	909	928	942	982	2,950	—	—
1888	132,996	937	966	980	1,212	6,600	—	—
1888O	21,335	937	966	980	1,152	5,750	—	—
1888S	648,700	909	928	942	972	2,700	—	—
1889	4,485	967	1,155	1,100	2,700	—	—	53,000
1889S	425,400	909	928	942	982	1,500	18,500	—
1890	58,043	947	966	1,000	1,015	5,500	16,000	46,000
1890CC	17,500	1,049	1,148	1,200	3,850	18,500	—	—
1891	91,868	967	1,006	1,020	1,050	4,500	—	48,000
1891CC	103,732	1,049	1,108	1,125	1,300	7,150	—	—
1892	797,552	909	928	942	972	1,385	9,100	48,000
1892CC	40,000	1,049	1,108	1,165	3,800	22,500	—	—
1892O	28,688	967	969	980	1,030	11,000	—	—
1892S	115,500	937	990	1,004	1,034	4,500	—	—
1893	1,840,895	909	928	942	972	1,385	16,500	46,000
1893CC	14,000	1,049	1,148	1,800	8,500	—	—	—
1893O	17,000	937	966	1,022	1,252	5,450	—	—
1893S	141,350	937	966	980	1,010	4,950	19,500	—
1894	2,470,778	909	928	942	972	1,510	—	46,000
1894O	107,500	937	966	975	1,000	6,350	—	—
1894S	25,000	937	990	1,100	3,950	—	—	—
1895	567,826	909	928	942	972	1,385	17,500	43,500
1895O	98,000	937	966	992	1,122	8,000	—	—
1895S	49,000	937	978	1,040	2,400	9,500	—	—
1896	76,348	909	928	942	982	2,550	30,000	43,500
1896S	123,750	937	961	1,002	2,500	12,000	28,500	—
1897	1,000,159	909	928	942	972	1,510	10,000	—
1897O	42,500	937	966	980	1,105	5,850	27,500	—
1897S	234,750	937	961	975	1,125	5,750	22,500	—
1898	812,197	909	928	942	972	1,510	9,000	43,500
1898S	473,600	937	861	975	1,042	5,100	18,500	—
1899	1,262,305	909	928	942	972	1,385	6,500	43,500
1899O	37,047	937	966	982	1,152	8,450	—	—
1899S	841,000	909	928	942	982	3,650	12,850	—
1900	293,960	909	928	942	982	1,385	9,500	43,500
1900S	81,000	937	966	980	1,205	6,750	—	—
1901	1,718,825	909	928	942	972	1,385	4,050	43,500
1901O	72,041	937	966	980	1,092	3,750	12,500	—
1901S	2,812,750	909	928	942	972	1,385	6,250	—
1902	82,513	909	928	942	982	2,800	11,750	43,500
1902S	469,500	909	928	942	972	1,385	6,250	—
1903	125,926	909	928	942	982	2,450	13,500	43,500
1903O	112,771	937	966	980	1,082	3,250	18,000	—
1903S	538,000	909	928	942	982	1,410	5,350	—
1904	162,038	909	928	942	982	2,000	9,500	46,000
1904O	108,950	937	966	980	1,082	3,700	16,500	—
1905	201,078	909	928	942	972	1,450	8,500	43,500
1905S	369,250	937	961	1,007	1,100	5,600	22,500	—
1906	165,497	909	928	942	982	2,450	10,000	43,500
1906D	981,000	909	928	942	972	1,385	7,000	—
1906O	86,895	937	966	980	1,122	4,900	14,500	—
1906S	457,000	937	961	980	1,132	5,000	15,500	—
1907	1,203,973	909	928	942	972	1,385	3,950	43,500
1907D	1,030,000	909	928	942	982	2,250	—	—
1907S	210,500	937	961	1,002	1,172	5,450	17,000	—

Indian Head
No motto next to eagle reverse

KM# 125 • 16.7180 g., 0.9000 **Gold**, 0.4837 oz. AGW, 27 mm. • **Designer:** Augustus Saint-Gaudens
Notes: 1907 varieties are distinguished by whether the edge is rolled or wired, and whether the legend E
PLURIBUS UNUM has periods between each word.

Date	Mintage	VF-20	XF-40	AU-50	MS-60	MS-63	MS-65	Prf-65
1907 wire edge, periods before and after legend	500	13,850	17,500	21,000	26,500	44,500	72,500	—
1907 same, without stars on edge, unique	—	—	—	—	—	—	—	—
1907 rolled edge, periods	42	26,000	38,500	49,000	66,500	113,000	265,000	—
1907 without periods	239,406	1,013	1,030	1,052	1,215	3,400	10,500	—
1908 without motto	33,500	998	1,015	1,037	1,200	4,650	15,500	—
1908D without motto	210,000	998	1,015	1,037	1,240	7,000	37,500	—

Indian Head
IN GOD WE TRUST left of eagle reverse

KM# 130 • 16.7180 g., 0.9000 **Gold**, 0.4837 oz. AGW, 27 mm. • **Designer:** Augustus Saint-Gaudens

Date	Mintage	VF-20	XF-40	AU-50	MS-60	MS-63	MS-65	Prf-65
1908	341,486	993	1,010	1,032	1,185	2,450	12,250	75,000
1908D	836,500	998	1,030	1,052	1,205	7,000	29,000	—
1908S	59,850	1,008	1,085	1,150	2,950	11,500	25,500	—
1909	184,863	993	1,010	1,032	1,165	3,950	18,500	80,000
1909D	121,540	998	1,015	1,037	1,230	6,100	36,500	—
1909S	292,350	998	1,015	1,037	1,375	6,350	19,000	—
1910	318,704	993	1,010	1,032	1,155	1,500	12,750	76,500
1910D	2,356,640	988	1,005	1,032	1,155	1,500	10,250	—
1910S	811,000	998	1,015	1,037	1,500	8,850	54,500	—
1911	505,595	988	1,005	1,027	1,170	1,550	10,000	75,000
1911D	30,100	1,200	1,400	1,700	9,000	31,000	140,000	—
1911S	51,000	1,028	1,150	1,200	2,050	10,000	21,500	—
1912	405,083	993	1,010	1,032	1,155	1,475	12,000	75,000
1912S	300,000	998	1,015	1,037	1,600	7,300	46,000	—
1913	442,071	993	1,010	1,032	1,155	1,500	11,000	75,000
1913S	66,000	1,043	1,200	1,300	4,650	31,500	125,000	—
1914	151,050	993	1,010	1,032	1,065	2,250	12,000	75,000
1914D	343,500	993	1,010	1,032	1,155	2,550	18,000	—
1914S	208,000	1,003	1,165	1,250	1,400	7,750	33,500	—
1915	351,075	993	1,010	1,032	1,155	2,000	12,000	75,000
1915S	59,000	1,043	1,075	1,200	3,150	15,500	58,500	—
1916S	138,500	1,028	1,045	1,100	1,425	6,350	26,500	—
1920S	126,500	12,500	16,850	19,750	37,000	88,500	275,000	—
1926	1,014,000	988	1,005	1,027	1,150	1,300	3,600	—
1930S	96,000	8,500	11,250	14,850	23,500	46,500	79,500	—
1932	4,463,000	988	1,005	1,027	1,150	1,300	3,600	—
1933	312,500	—	140,000	160,000	180,000	225,000	600,000	—

$10

$20

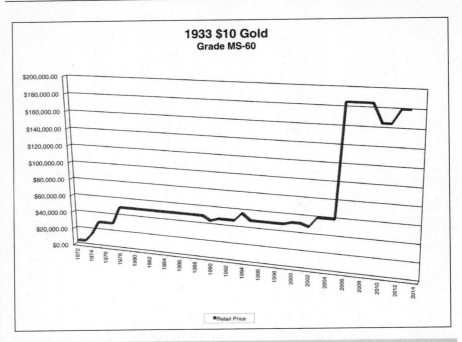

1933 $10 Gold
Grade MS-60

$20 (DOUBLE EAGLE)

GOLD
Liberty Head
Coronet head, left, within circle of stars obverse
TWENTY D. below eagle, no motto above eagle reverse

KM# 74.1 • 33.4360 g., 0.9000 **Gold**, 0.9675 oz. AGW, 34 mm. • **Rev. Legend:** UNITED STATES OF
AMERICA **Designer:** James B. Longacre

Date	Mintage	VF-20	XF-40	AU-50	MS-60	MS-63	MS-65	Prf-65
1849 unique, in Smithsonian collection	1	—	—	—	—	—	—	—
1850	1,170,261	2,170	2,270	3,000	8,500	43,500	175,000	—
1850O	141,000	2,250	3,500	9,800	45,000	—	—	—
1851	2,087,155	2,210	2,400	2,800	3,850	13,500	—	—
1851O	315,000	2,285	3,100	4,250	23,000	58,500	—	—
1852	2,053,026	2,210	2,400	2,700	3,950	17,500	—	—
1852O	190,000	2,240	2,950	4,150	22,500	—	—	—
1853	1,261,326	2,210	2,400	2,400	5,000	27,500	—	—
1853/2	Inc. above	2,290	2,390	6,850	33,500	—	—	—
1853O	71,000	2,300	3,650	4,850	32,500	65,000	—	—
1854	757,899	2,210	2,400	2,700	9,250	26,500	—	—
1854	Inc. above	2,450	2,350	6,000	—	—	—	—
1854O	3,250	95,000	225,000	365,000	—	—	—	—
1854S	141,468	2,290	2,390	3,000	6,000	15,500	52,500	—
1855	364,666	2,210	2,400	2,350	8,850	66,500	—	—

Date	Mintage	VF-20	XF-40	AU-50	MS-60	MS-63	MS-65	Prf-65
1855O	8,000	3,650	19,500	24,500	110,000	—	—	—
1855S	879,675	2,190	2,400	2,800	7,200	19,500	—	—
1856	329,878	2,210	2,400	2,600	8,400	24,500	—	—
1856O	2,250	97,500	165,000	300,000	525,000	750,000	—	—
1856S	1,189,750	2,190	2,400	2,600	5,900	15,000	30,000	—
1857	439,375	2,210	2,400	2,700	3,400	26,500	—	—
1857O	30,000	2,265	2,950	6,400	31,000	115,000	—	—
1857S	970,500	2,190	2,400	2,700	4,500	7,250	12,850	—
1858	211,714	2,265	2,390	2,600	5,500	34,500	—	—
1858O	35,250	2,490	3,850	7,500	42,000	—	—	—
1858S	846,710	2,190	2,420	2,890	8,500	—	—	—
1859	43,597	2,265	2,450	4,400	28,000	—	—	280,000
1859O	9,100	6,400	16,500	44,000	110,000	—	—	—
1859S	636,445	2,190	2,400	2,850	5,000	35,000	—	—
1860	577,670	2,190	2,400	2,700	3,950	18,000	63,500	—
1860O	6,600	3,650	14,500	24,000	100,000	—	—	—
1860S	544,950	2,210	2,690	2,890	7,350	18,500	48,000	—
1861	2,976,453	2,190	2,400	2,675	3,950	12,850	41,500	275,000
1861O	17,741	5,650	17,500	24,000	88,000	—	—	—
1861S	768,000	2,210	2,500	2,725	10,500	31,500	—	—

Liberty

**Coronet head, left, within circle of stars obverse
Paquet design, TWENTY D. below eagle reverse**

KM# 93 • 33.4360 g., 0.9000 **Gold**, 0.9675 oz. AGW • **Rev. Legend:** UNITED STATES OF AMERICA
Notes: In 1861 the reverse was redesigned by Anthony C. Paquet, but it was withdrawn soon after its
release. The letters in the inscriptions on the Paquet-reverse variety are taller than on the regular reverse.

Date	Mintage	VF-20	XF-40	AU-50	MS-60	MS-63	MS-65	Prf-65
1861 2 Known	—	—	—	—	—	—	—	—

Note: 1861 Paquet reverse, Bowers & Merena, Nov. 1988, MS-67, $660,000.

Date	Mintage	VF-20	XF-40	AU-50	MS-60	MS-63	MS-65	Prf-65
1861S	—	19,500	54,000	92,500	275,000	—	—	—

Note: Included in mintage of 1861S, KM#74.1

Liberty

Longacre design resumed reverse

KM# A74.1 • 33.4360 g., 0.9000 **Gold**, 0.9675 oz. AGW •

Date	Mintage	VF-20	XF-40	AU-50	MS-60	MS-63	MS-65	Prf-65
1862	92,133	2,190	3,500	6,000	17,500	36,500	—	250,000
1862S	854,173	2,175	2,275	2,100	12,400	36,000	—	—
1863	142,790	2,190	2,650	3,950	19,500	39,500	—	250,000
1863S	966,570	2,175	2,355	2,555	7,350	28,500	—	—
1864	204,285	2,190	2,290	2,450	14,500	40,000	—	250,000
1864S	793,660	2,175	2,335	2,535	8,600	32,000	—	—
1865	351,200	2,190	2,355	2,640	6,200	26,000	—	250,000
1865S	1,042,500	2,175	2,355	2,550	4,200	9,000	19,500	—
1866S	Inc. below	2,750	11,500	37,500	—	—	—	—

Liberty
Coronet head, left, within circle of stars obverse
TWENTY D. below eagle. IN GOD WE TRUST above eagle reverse

KM# 74.2 • 33.4360 g., 0.9000 **Gold**, 0.9675 oz. AGW, 34 mm. • **Rev. Legend:** UNITED STATES OF AMERICA **Designer:** James B. Longacre

Date	Mintage	VF-20	XF-40	AU-50	MS-60	MS-63	MS-65	Prf-65
1866	698,775	2,110	2,237	2,277	6,950	28,500	—	200,000
1866S	842,250	2,110	2,247	2,287	15,500	—	—	—
1867	251,065	2,110	2,257	2,277	3,250	30,000	—	200,000
1867S	920,750	2,110	2,247	2,100	15,000	—	—	—
1868	98,600	2,150	2,347	2,250	11,500	50,000	—	200,000
1868S	837,500	2,110	2,217	2,150	10,000	—	—	—
1869	175,155	2,120	2,207	2,100	6,800	22,750	—	210,000
1869S	686,750	2,110	2,237	2,100	7,000	45,000	—	—
1870	155,185	2,130	2,237	2,300	9,250	50,000	—	215,000
1870CC	3,789	200,000	275,000	400,000	—	—	—	—
1870S	982,000	2,110	2,192	2,232	5,450	34,000	—	—
1871	80,150	2,120	2,192	2,100	4,500	24,500	—	—
1871CC	17,387	9,500	19,500	45,000	97,500	300,000	650,000	—
1871S	928,000	2,110	2,207	2,272	4,750	22,000	—	—
1872	251,880	2,110	2,237	2,302	3,750	24,500	—	—
1872CC	26,900	2,550	5,450	8,950	38,500	—	—	—
1872S	780,000	2,110	2,237	2,277	3,250	23,500	—	—
1873 closed 3	Est. 208,925	2,110	2,297	2,337	3,350	—	—	200,000
1873 open 3	Est. 1,500,900	2,110	2,237	2,287	2,533	12,000	85,000	—
1873CC	22,410	2,900	4,750	11,750	37,500	115,000	—	—
1873S closed 3	1,040,600	2,110	2,207	2,280	2,448	20,000	—	—
1873S open 3	Inc. above	2,110	2,237	2,277	5,900	29,500	—	—
1874	366,800	2,110	2,237	2,277	2,523	19,500	—	—
1874CC	115,085	2,100	2,450	3,400	11,500	—	—	—
1874S	1,214,000	2,110	2,207	2,280	2,415	24,000	—	—
1875	295,740	2,110	2,237	2,277	2,445	13,500	—	—
1875CC	111,151	1,950	2,250	2,650	4,850	26,500	—	—
1875S	1,230,000	2,110	2,207	2,280	2,554	16,850	—	—
1876	583,905	2,110	2,227	2,280	2,350	13,500	78,500	—
1876CC	138,441	1,960	2,300	2,700	7,750	—	—	—
1876S	1,597,000	2,110	2,207	2,280	2,533	12,400	90,000	—

Liberty
Coronet head, left, within circle of stars obverse   TWENTY DOLLARS below eagle reverse

KM# 74.3 • 33.4360 g., 0.9000 **Gold**, 0.9675 oz. AGW • **Rev. Legend:** UNITED STATES OF AMERICA

Date	Mintage	VF-20	XF-40	AU-50	MS-60	MS-63	MS-65	Prf-65
1877	397,670	1,925	2,057	2,102	2,270	11,500	—	—
1877CC	42,565	2,100	2,450	3,650	19,500	—	—	—
1877S	1,735,000	1,915	1,957	2,032	2,240	15,500	—	—

Date	Mintage	VF-20	XF-40	AU-50	MS-60	MS-63	MS-65	Prf-65
1878	543,645	1,935	2,057	2,112	2,360	12,500	—	—
1878CC	13,180	2,450	3,950	7,250	30,000	—	—	—
1878S	1,739,000	1,915	1,932	1,957	2,240	20,500	—	—
1879	207,630	1,995	2,057	2,062	2,240	16,500	—	—
1879CC	10,708	3,000	4,850	8,850	34,000	77,500	—	—
1879O	2,325	12,500	21,500	27,500	88,500	127,500	—	—
1879S	1,223,800	1,915	1,932	1,957	2,150	30,000	—	—
1880	51,456	2,025	2,087	2,137	3,150	25,000	—	110,000
1880S	836,000	1,915	1,932	1,967	2,050	17,500	—	—
1881	2,260	12,500	21,000	34,500	79,000	—	—	110,000
1881S	727,000	1,915	1,932	1,967	2,340	20,000	—	—
1882	630	13,500	39,500	88,000	130,000	225,000	—	130,000
1882CC	39,140	2,065	2,450	2,600	8,850	65,000	—	—
1882S	1,125,000	1,915	1,932	1,947	2,310	18,500	—	—
1883 proof only	92	—	—	27,500	—	—	—	195,000
1883CC	59,962	2,065	2,450	2,600	7,850	30,000	—	—
1883S	1,189,000	1,915	1,932	1,957	2,240	8,500	—	—
1884 proof only	71	—	—	35,000	—	—	—	225,000
1884CC	81,139	2,065	2,450	2,750	5,000	25,000	—	—
1884S	916,000	1,915	1,932	1,957	2,180	6,150	46,500	—
1885	828	8,450	13,850	18,500	60,000	100,000	—	115,000
1885CC	9,450	2,500	3,850	6,450	19,500	48,500	—	—
1885S	683,500	1,915	1,932	1,967	2,180	5,700	29,500	—
1886	1,106	10,500	18,500	37,500	70,000	140,000	—	105,000
1887	121	—	—	26,500	—	—	—	142,500
1887S	283,000	1,915	1,932	1,957	2,240	15,000	36,500	—
1888	226,266	1,915	1,932	1,977	2,290	7,900	36,500	93,500
1888S	859,600	1,915	1,932	1,957	2,180	4,650	—	—
1889	44,111	2,075	2,187	2,302	2,630	13,500	36,500	105,000
1889CC	30,945	2,065	2,450	3,000	7,950	25,500	—	—
1889S	774,700	1,915	1,932	1,957	2,190	5,400	—	—
1890	75,995	1,915	1,957	2,032	2,240	10,000	—	100,000
1890CC	91,209	2,065	2,375	2,450	4,850	32,500	—	—
1890S	802,750	1,915	1,932	1,957	2,180	6,350	30,000	—
1891	1,442	8,500	15,000	22,500	75,000	125,000	—	108,000
1891CC	5,000	4,950	9,000	11,000	24,500	71,500	—	—
1891S	1,288,125	1,915	1,932	1,957	2,180	3,000	—	—
1892	4,523	2,000	3,650	6,250	13,500	35,000	—	90,000
1892CC	27,265	2,065	2,375	2,850	7,500	36,500	—	—
1892S	930,150	1,915	1,932	2,012	2,170	2,950	24,500	—
1893	344,339	1,915	1,952	2,022	2,210	2,100	—	95,000
1893CC	18,402	2,162	2,375	2,850	7,000	29,500	—	—
1893S	996,175	1,875	1,887	1,907	2,015	2,850	28,500	—
1894	1,368,990	1,875	1,887	1,907	2,015	2,340	26,500	85,000
1894S	1,048,550	1,875	1,887	1,907	2,015	2,450	27,500	—
1895	1,114,656	1,875	1,887	1,907	2,015	2,340	17,500	82,500
1895S	1,143,500	1,875	1,887	1,907	2,015	2,340	15,500	—
1896	792,663	1,875	1,887	1,907	2,015	2,340	19,500	200,000
1896S	1,403,925	1,875	1,887	1,907	2,015	2,340	23,500	—
1897	1,383,261	1,875	1,887	1,907	2,015	2,440	18,500	200,000
1897S	1,470,250	1,875	1,887	1,907	2,015	2,340	21,500	—
1898	170,470	1,880	1,917	2,007	2,315	4,500	—	200,000
1898S	2,575,175	1,875	1,887	1,907	2,015	2,340	7,950	—
1899	1,669,384	1,875	1,887	1,907	2,015	2,340	12,500	200,000
1899S	2,010,300	1,875	1,887	1,907	2,015	2,340	21,500	—
1900	1,874,584	1,875	1,887	1,907	2,015	2,375	5,900	200,000
1900S	2,459,500	1,875	1,887	1,907	2,015	2,340	23,000	—
1901	111,526	1,875	1,887	1,907	2,015	2,475	5,850	200,000
1901S	1,596,000	1,875	1,887	1,907	2,015	3,850	21,500	—
1902	31,254	1,875	2,082	2,167	2,425	11,750	37,500	200,000
1902S	1,753,625	1,875	1,887	1,907	2,015	2,900	23,500	—
1903	287,428	1,875	1,887	1,907	2,015	2,375	5,500	200,000
1903S	954,000	1,875	1,887	1,907	2,015	2,405	13,500	—
1904	6,256,797	1,875	1,887	1,907	2,015	2,340	3,900	200,000
1904S	5,134,175	1,875	1,887	1,907	2,015	2,340	5,400	—
1905	59,011	1,880	1,907	1,942	2,315	14,500	—	200,000
1905S	1,813,000	1,875	1,887	1,907	2,015	3,250	20,500	—
1906	69,690	1,880	1,892	1,962	2,195	6,850	26,500	200,000
1906D	620,250	1,875	1,887	1,907	2,015	3,450	22,500	—
1906S	2,065,750	1,875	1,887	1,907	2,015	2,350	19,500	—
1907	1,451,864	1,875	1,887	1,907	2,015	2,340	8,200	200,000
1907D	842,250	1,875	1,887	1,907	2,015	2,650	7,350	—
1907S	2,165,800	1,875	1,887	1,907	2,015	2,650	27,000	—

$20

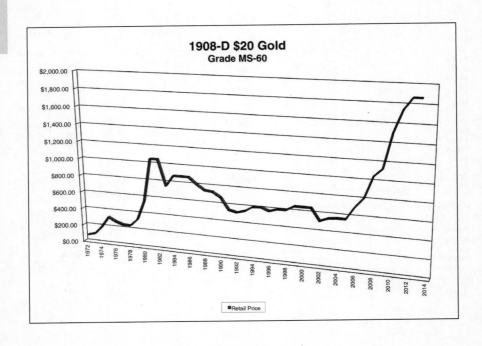

Saint-Gaudens

Roman numerals in date obverse   No motto below eagle reverse

KM# 126 • 33.4360 g., 0.9000 **Gold**, 0.9675 oz. AGW, 34 mm. • **Designer:** Augustus Saint-Gaudens
Edge Desc: Plain.

Date	Mintage	VF-20	XF-40	AU-50	MS-60	MS-63	MS-65	Prf-65
MCMVII (1907) high relief, unique, AU-55, $150,000	—	—	—	—	—	—	—	—
MCMVII (1907) high relief, wire rim	11,250	7,650	8,750	10,350	14,000	24,500	45,000	—
MCMVII (1907) high relief, flat rim	Inc. above	7,900	9,250	11,350	15,250	26,000	46,500	—

Saint-Gaudens

Arabic numerals in date obverse   No motto below eagle reverse

KM# 127 • 33.4360 g., 0.9000 **Gold**, 0.9675 oz. AGW, 34 mm. • **Designer:** Augustus Saint-Gaudens
Edge Desc: Lettered; large letters.

Date	Mintage	VF-20	XF-40	AU-50	MS-60	MS-63	MS-65	Prf-65
1907 large letters on edge, unique	—	—	—	—	—	—	—	—
1907 small letters on edge	361,667	1,796	1,829	1,839	1,865	2,185	4,600	—
1908	4,271,551	1,786	1,819	1,819	1,825	1,975	2,450	—
1908D	663,750	1,796	1,829	1,929	1,850	2,085	11,800	—

Saint-Gaudens

Roman numerals in date obverse   No motto below eagle reverse

KM# Pn1874 • 33.4360 g., 0.9000 **Gold**, 0.9675 oz. AGW, 34 mm. • **Designer:** Augustus Saint-Gaudens
Edge Desc: Plain. **Notes:** The "Roman numerals" varieties for 1907 use Roman numerals for the date instead of Arabic numerals. The lettered-edge varieties have "E Pluribus Unum" on the edge, with stars between the words.

Date	Mintage	VF-20	XF-40	AU-50	MS-60	MS-63	MS-65	Prf-65
1907 extremely high relief, unique	—	—	—	—	—	—	—	—
1907 extremely high relief, lettered edge	—	—	—	—	—	—	—	—

Note: 1907 extremely high relief, lettered edge, Prf-68, private sale, 1990, $1,500,000.

Saint-Gaudens
IN GOD WE TRUST below eagle reverse

KM# 131 • 33.4360 g., 0.9000 **Gold**, 0.9675 oz. AGW, 34 mm. • **Designer:** Augustus Saint-Gaudens

Date	Mintage	VF-20	XF-40	AU-50	MS-60	MS-63	MS-65	Prf-65
1908	156,359	1,791	1,824	1,829	1,875	2,300	28,000	76,500
1908 Roman finish; Prf64 Rare	—							
Note: Rare								
1908D	349,500	1,796	1,829	1,839	1,865	2,105	7,000	—
1908S	22,000	2,450	3,150	4,850	10,650	24,500	52,500	—
1909/8	161,282	1,796	1,829	1,879	1,850	6,250	52,000	—
1909	Inc. above	1,806	1,849	1,849	1,925	3,150	46,000	92,500
1909D	52,500	1,836	1,869	1,974	3,100	8,950	57,500	—
1909S	2,774,925	1,796	1,829	1,839	1,845	2,060	7,000	—
1910	482,167	1,791	1,824	1,829	1,875	2,075	9,000	84,500
1910D	429,000	1,791	1,824	1,829	1,850	2,045	3,450	—
1910S	2,128,250	1,796	1,829	1,844	1,855	2,110	11,350	—
1911	197,350	1,796	1,829	1,849	1,865	2,900	23,500	76,500
1911D	846,500	1,791	1,824	1,829	1,850	2,045	2,950	—
1911S	775,750	1,791	1,824	1,829	1,855	2,045	6,850	—
1912	149,824	1,796	1,829	1,844	1,890	2,050	31,000	76,500
1913	168,838	1,796	1,829	1,844	1,895	3,250	53,500	82,500
1913D	393,500	1,791	1,824	1,829	1,850	2,125	7,850	—
1913S	34,000	1,846	1,879	1,879	2,000	4,350	36,500	—
1914	95,320	1,806	1,839	1,879	1,275	3,900	25,000	81,500
1914D	453,000	1,791	1,824	1,829	1,850	2,055	3,450	—
1914S	1,498,000	1,791	1,824	1,829	1,850	2,045	3,150	—
1915	152,050	1,796	1,829	1,839	1,855	2,650	28,000	125,000
1915S	567,500	1,791	1,824	1,829	1,850	2,045	3,000	—
1916S	796,000	1,796	1,829	1,839	1,890	2,075	3,250	—
1920	228,250	1,786	1,819	1,849	1,850	2,450	118,000	—
1920S	558,000	14,500	18,500	28,500	53,000	105,000	355,000	—
1921	528,500	35,000	43,500	56,500	125,000	300,000	975,000	—
1922	1,375,500	1,786	1,819	1,819	1,825	1,995	6,850	—
1922S	2,658,000	1,906	1,150	1,300	2,450	5,650	63,500	—
1923	566,000	1,786	1,819	1,819	1,830	1,995	8,000	—
1923D	1,702,250	1,796	1,829	1,829	1,835	1,995	2,560	—
1924	4,323,500	1,786	1,819	1,819	1,825	1,975	2,450	—
1924D	3,049,500	2,009	2,042	2,100	3,950	11,200	115,000	—
1924S	2,927,500	1,665	1,750	2,200	3,800	12,250	180,000	—
1925	2,831,750	1,786	1,819	1,819	1,830	1,975	2,450	—
1925D	2,938,500	1,951	2,100	2,375	4,450	11,500	148,000	—
1925S	3,776,500	1,900	2,850	4,850	9,850	23,500	210,000	—
1926	816,750	1,786	1,819	1,819	1,830	1,975	2,450	—
1926D	481,000	10,000	15,500	19,350	27,500	35,000	235,000	—
1926S	2,041,500	1,989	1,550	1,725	3,050	5,650	37,500	—
1927	2,946,750	1,786	1,819	1,819	1,830	1,975	2,450	—
1927D	180,000	155,000	200,000	245,000	325,000	1,500,000	1,950,000	—
1927S	3,107,000	6,850	8,850	13,250	26,750	54,000	160,000	—
1928	8,816,000	1,786	1,819	1,819	1,830	1,975	2,450	—
1929	1,779,750	10,000	13,500	15,500	19,300	38,500	112,000	—
1930S	74,000	35,000	41,000	49,500	72,500	105,000	235,000	—
1931	2,938,250	10,500	13,500	20,500	31,500	63,500	120,000	—
1931D	106,500	8,850	11,500	21,500	42,500	83,500	140,000	—
1932	1,101,750	12,500	14,500	17,850	26,500	73,500	110,000	—
1933	445,500	—	—	—	—	—	9,000,000	—

Note: Sotheby/Stack's Sale, July 2002. Thirteen known, only one currently available.

MINT SETS

Mint, or uncirculated, sets contain one uncirculated coin of each denomination from each mint produced for circulation that year. Values listed here are only for those sets sold by the U.S. Mint. Sets were not offered in years not listed. In years when the Mint did not offer the sets, some private companies compiled and marketed uncirculated sets. Mint sets from 1947 through 1958 contained two examples of each coin mounted in cardboard holders, which caused the coins to tarnish. Beginning in 1959, the sets have been packaged in sealed Pliofilm packets and include only one specimen of each coin struck for that year (both P & D mints). Listings for 1965, 1966 and 1967 are for "special mint sets," which were of higher quality than regular mint sets and were prooflike. They were packaged in plastic cases. The 1970 large-date and small-date varieties are distinguished by the size of the date on the coin. The 1976 three-piece set contains the quarter, half dollar and dollar with the Bicentennial design. The 1971 and 1972 sets do not include a dollar coin; the 1979 set does not include an S-mint-marked dollar. Mint sets issued prior to 1959 were double sets (containing two of each coin) packaged in cardboard with a paper overlay. Origional sets will always be toned and can bring large premiums if nicely preserved with good color.

Date	Sets Sold	Issue Price	Value	Date	Sets Sold	Issue Price	Value
1947 Est. 5,000	—	4.87	1,325	1980	2,815,066	9.00	5.75
1948 Est. 6,000	—	4.92	750	1981 Type I	2,908,145	11.00	8.00
1949 Est. 5,200	—	5.45	935	1981 Susan B. Anthony			
1950 None issued	—	—	—	PDS Souvenir Set	—	—	22.00
1951	8,654	6.75	900	1982 Souvenir set	—	—	59.00
1952	11,499	6.14	825	1982 & 1983 None			
1953	15,538	6.14	565	issued	—	—	—
1954	25,599	6.19	265	1983 Souvenir set	—	—	65.00
1955 flat pack	49,656	3.57	168	1984	1,832,857	7.00	3.65
1956	45,475	3.34	165	1985	1,710,571	7.00	3.60
1957	32,324	24.50	275	1986	1,153,536	7.50	8.00
1958	50,314	4.43	150	1987	2,890,758	7.00	3.85
1959	187,000	2.40	58.50	1988	1,646,204	7.00	5.25
1960 large date	260,485	2.40	50.00	1989	1,987,915	7.00	3.10
1961	223,704	2.40	53.50	1990	1,809,184	7.00	3.30
1962	385,285	2.40	49.75	1991	1,352,101	7.00	4.40
1963	606,612	2.40	47.50	1992	1,500,143	7.00	3.10
1964	1,008,108	2.40	47.50	1993	1,297,094	8.00	6.00
1965 Special Mint Set	2,360,000	4.00	9.60	1994	1,234,813	8.00	3.85
1966 Special Mint Set	2,261,583	4.00	9.10	1995	1,038,787	8.00	5.00
1967 Special Mint Set	1,863,344	4.00	9.35	1996	1,457,949	8.00	17.00
1968	2,105,128	2.50	7.25	1997	950,473	8.00	7.20
1969	1,817,392	2.50	7.75	1998	1,187,325	8.00	4.25
1970 large date	2,038,134	2.50	18.25	1999 9 piece	1,421,625	14.95	8.00
1970 small date	Inc. above	2.50	62.50	2000	1,490,160	14.95	7.70
1971	2,193,396	3.50	3.30	2001	1,066,900	14.95	9.50
1972	2,750,000	3.50	2.75	2002	1,139,388	14.95	10.25
1973	1,767,691	8.00	8.60	2003	1,002,555	14.95	8.25
1974	1,975,981	6.75	6.90	2004	844,484	16.95	13.00
1975	1,921,488	6.00	7.15	2005	—	16.95	8.50
1976 3 coins	4,908,319	9.00	20.00	2006	—	16.95	12.25
1976	1,892,513	6.00	6.30	2007	—	—	17.60
1977	2,006,869	7.00	7.15	2008	—	—	59.50
1978	2,162,609	7.00	5.25	2009 18 piece clad set	—	—	24.50
1979 Type I	2,526,000	8.00	5.00	2010 28 piece clad set	—	—	29.70
1979 Susan B Anthony				2010 14 piece clad	—	—	24.50
PDS Souvenir Set	—	—	6.50	2011 14 piece clad set	532,059	—	33.00
1980 Susan B. Anthony				2012 14 piece clad set	365,298	—	35.00
PDS Souvenir Set	—	—	6.50				

PROOF SETS

Proof coins are produced through a special process involving specially selected, highly polished planchets and dies. They usually receive two strikings from the coin press at increased pressure. The result is a coin with mirrorlike surfaces and, in recent years, a cameo effect on its raised design surfaces. Proof sets have been sold off and on by the U.S. Mint since 1858. Listings here are for sets from what is commonly called the modern era, since 1936. Values for earlier proofs are included in regular date listings. Sets were not offered in years not listed. Since 1968, proof coins have been produced at the San Francisco Mint; before that they were produced at the Philadelphia Mint. In 1942 the five-cent coin was struck in two compositions. Some proof sets that year contain only one type (five-coin set); others contain both types. Two types of packaging were used in 1955 -- a box and a flat, plastic holder. The 1960 large-date and small-date sets are distinguished by the size of the date on the cent. Some 1968 sets are missing the mint mark on the dime, the result of an error in the preparation of an obverse die. The 1970 large-date and small-date sets are distinguished by the size of the date on the cent. Some 1970 sets are missing the mint mark on the dime, the result of an error in the preparation of an obverse die. Some 1971 sets are missing the mint mark on the five-cent piece, the result of an error in the preparation of an obverse die. The 1976 three-piece set contains the quarter, half dollar and dollar with the Bicentennial designs. The 1979 and 1981 Type II sets have clearer mint marks than the Type I sets for those years. Some 1983 sets are missing the mint mark on the dime, the result of an error in the preparation of an obverse die. Prestige sets contain the five regular-issue coins plus a commemorative silver dollar from that year. Sets issued prior to 1956 came in transparent envelopes stapled together in

a small square box. In mid 1955 sets were changed to a flat clear cellophane envelope. In 1968 sets were changed to a clear hard plastic case as they still are currently issued.

Date	Sets Sold	Issue Price	Value	Date	Sets Sold	Issue Price	Value
1795 (2006) XPn1-XPn3	—	—	—	1979S Type I	3,677,175	9.00	8.00
1836 (2006) XPn4, 10-11	—	—	—	1979S Type II	Inc. above	9.00	70.00
1863 (2006) XPn12-14	—	—	—	1980S	3,547,030	10.00	5.25
1871 (2006) XPn15-17	—	—	—	1981S Type I	4,063,083	11.00	5.50
1879 (2006) XPn18-20	—	—	—	1981S Type II	Inc. above	11.00	285
1879 (2006) XPn21-23	—	—	—	1982S	3,857,479	11.00	3.60
1936	3,837	1.89	7,500	1983S	3,138,765	11.00	3.60
1937	5,542	1.89	4,350	1983S Prestige Set	140,361	59.00	42.50
1938	8,045	1.89	1,900	1983S no mint mark dime	Inc. above	11.00	600
1939	8,795	—	1,800	1984S	2,748,430	11.00	5.85
1940	11,246	—	1,385	1984S Prestige Set	316,680	59.00	38.50
1941	15,287	—	1,450	1985S	3,362,821	11.00	4.10
1942 6 coins	21,120	1.89	1,475	1986S	2,411,180	11.00	5.75
1942 5 coins	Inc. above	1.89	1,250	1986S Prestige Set	599,317	48.50	38.50
1950	51,386	2.10	540	1987S	3,972,233	11.00	4.40
1951	57,500	2.10	565	1987S Prestige Set	435,495	45.00	38.50
1952	81,980	2.10	225	1988S	3,031,287	11.00	6.60
1953	128,800	2.10	210	1988S Prestige Set	231,661	45.00	38.50
1954	233,300	2.10	107	1989S	3,009,107	11.00	4.40
1955 box	378,200	2.10	90.00	1989S Prestige Set	211,087	45.00	45.50
1955 flat pack	Inc. above	2.10	115	1990S	2,793,433	11.00	5.00
1956	669,384	2.10	53.00	1990S no S 1¢	3,555	11.00	5,100
1957	1,247,952	2.10	30.00	1990S Prestige Set	506,126	45.00	38.50
1958	875,652	2.10	35.00	1990S Prestige Set, no S			
1959	1,149,291	2.10	31.00	1¢	Inc. above	45.00	5,100
1960 large date	1,691,602	2.10	28.50	1991S	2,610,833	11.00	5.25
1960 small date	Inc. above	2.10	33.50	1991S Prestige Set	256,954	59.00	41.50
1961	3,028,244	2.10	27.00	1992S	2,675,618	12.00	5.75
1962	3,218,019	2.10	27.00	1992S Prestige Set	183,285	59.00	43.50
1963	3,075,645	2.10	27.00	1992S Silver	1,009,585	21.00	24.00
1964	3,950,762	2.10	27.00	1992S Silver premier	308,055	37.00	24.50
1965 Special Mint Set	—	—	—	1993S	2,337,819	12.50	4.60
1966 Special Mint Set	—	—	—	1993S Prestige Set	224,045	57.00	55.00
1967 Special mint set	—	—	—	1993S Silver	570,213	21.00	32.50
1968S	3,041,509	5.00	7.75	1993S Silver premier	191,140	37.00	34.00
1968S no mint mark dime	Inc. above	5.00	16,500	1994S	2,308,701	13.00	4.95
1969S	2,934,631	5.00	7.25	1994S Prestige Set	175,893	57.00	51.00
1970S large date	2,632,810	5.00	9.35	1994S Silver	636,009	21.00	26.00
1970S small date	Inc. above	5.00	71.50	1994S Silver premier	149,320	37.50	27.50
1970S no mint mark dime	Inc. above	5.00	820	1995S	2,010,384	12.50	10.50
1971S	3,224,138	5.00	4.50	1995S Prestige Set	107,112	57.00	77.00
1971S no mint mark nickel				1995S Silver	549,878	21.00	43.50
Est. 1,655	1,655	5.00	1,350	1995S Silver premier	130,107	37.50	59.00
1972S	3,267,667	5.00	5.50	1996S	2,085,191	16.00	7.50
1973S	2,769,624	7.00	9.00	1996S Prestige Set	55,000	57.00	270
1974S	2,617,350	7.00	10.75	1996S Silver	623,655	21.00	26.50
1975S	2,909,369	7.00	8.40	1996S Silver premier	151,366	37.50	33.50
1975S no mint mark dime	Inc. above	7.00	275,000	1997S	1,975,000	12.50	11.25
1976S 3 coins	3,998,621	13.00	31.50	1997S Prestige Set	80,000	57.00	68.50
1976S	4,149,730	7.00	7.15	1997S Silver	605,473	21.00	32.50
1977S	3,251,152	9.00	8.25	1997S Silver premier	136,205	37.50	39.50
1978S	3,127,788	9.00	7.15	1998S	2,078,494	12.50	9.65

PROOF SETS

Date	Sets Sold	Issue Price	Value	Date	Sets Sold	Issue Price	Value
1998S Silver	638,134	21.00	28.50	2007S Silver 5 quarter set	—	22.95	33.70
1998S Silver premier	240,658	37.50	31.00	2007S 14 piece clad	—	—	14.50
1999S 9 piece	2,557,899	19.95	10.00	2007S Silver 14 piece	—	—	55.50
1999S 5 quarter set	1,169,958	13.95	6.15	2007S Presidental $ set	—	—	6.50
1999S Silver	804,565	31.95	120	2007S American Legacy	—	—	120
2000S 10 piece	3,097,442	19.95	6.35	2008 14 piece clad set	—	—	78.00
2000S 5 quarter set	995,803	13.95	3.60	2008S 14 piece silver set	734,045	—	61.00
2000S Silver	965,421	31.95	50.10	2008S Presidental $ set	—	—	11.00
2001S 10 piece	2,249,498	19.95	12.75	2008S American Legacy	—	—	120
2001S 5 quarter set	774,800	13.95	7.50	2008S 5 quarter clad set	—	22.95	47.50
2001S Silver	849,600	31.95	50.10	2008S 5 quarter silver set	—	—	33.70
2002S 10 piece	2,319,766	19.95	7.75	2009S 18 piece clad set	1,477,967	—	22.50
2002S 5 quarter set	764,419	13.95	4.50	2009S 18 piece silver set	694,406	—	70.00
2002S Silver	892,229	31.95	50.10	2009S Presidential $ set	627,925	—	8.25
2003 X#207, 208, 209.2	—	44.00	28.75	2009S Lincoln Chronicle	—	—	135
2003S 10 piece	2,175,684	16.75	8.00	2009S Lincoln 4 piece	—	—	15.50
2003S 5 quarter set	1,225,507	13.95	3.60	2009S 6 quarter clad set	—	—	10.50
2003S Silver	1,142,858	31.95	49.50	2009S 6 quarter silver set	—	—	39.90
2004S 11 piece	1,804,396	22.95	9.10	2010S 14 piece clad set	1,103,950	—	62.50
2004S 5 quarter set	987,960	23.95	30.10	2010S 14 piece silver set	583,912	—	63.80
2004S Silver 11 piece	1,187,673	37.95	49.50	2010S Presidential $ set	535,462	—	14.50
2004S Silver 5 quarter set	594,137	—	32.90	2010S 6 quarter set	276,335	—	32.00
2005S American Legacy	—	—	79.50	2010S 5 quarter silver set	274,003	—	32.90
2005S 11 piece	—	22.95	6.00	2011S 5 quarter silver set	147,005	—	29.20
2005S 5 quarter set	—	15.95	35.00	2011S 14 piece silver set	572,247	—	70.00
2005S Silver 11 piece	—	37.95	50.50	2011S 5 quarter clad set	151,434	—	14.50
2005S Silver 5 quarter set	—	23.95	32.90	2011S Presidential $ set	299,161	—	20.00
2005S American Legacy	—	—	84.50	2011S 14 piece clad set	1,095,318	—	39.75
2006S 10 piece clad	—	22.95	10.75	2012S 5 quarter silver set	—	—	45.00
2006S 5 quarter set	—	15.95	4.50	2012S 14 piece silver set	—	—	88.00
2006S Silver 10 piece	—	37.95	50.50	2012S 6 quarter set	—	—	20.00
2006S Silver 5 quarter set	—	23.95	32.90	2012S 14 piece clad set	—	—	48.50
2006S American Legacy	—	—	81.00	2012S Presidential $ set	—	—	36.50
2007S 5 quarter set	—	13.95	4.50				

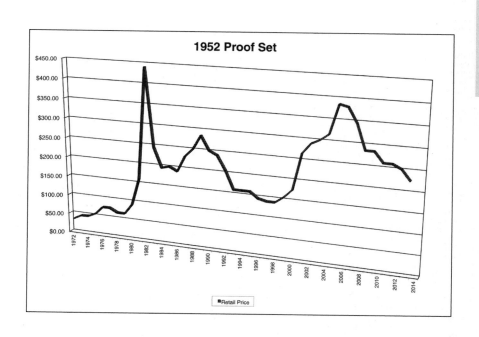

1952 Proof Set

■ Retail Price

UNCIRCULATED ROLLS

Listings are for rolls containing uncirculated coins. Large date and small date varieties for 1960 and 1970 apply to the one cent coins.

Date	Cents	Nickels	Dimes	Quarters	Halves	Date	Cents	Nickels	Dimes	Quarters	Halves
1934	585	3,500	2,350	1,650	2,350	1959	2.50	5.00	140	280	280
1934D	2,650	4,350	2,950	9,000	—	1959D	2.10	5.25	140	280	280
1934S	—	—	—	—	—	1960 large date	1.60	4.40	140	280	280
1935	885	1,700	1,450	1,725	1,250	1960 small date	220	—	—	—	—
1935D	750	3,150	2,950	8,850	4,000	1960D large date	1.60	5.00	140	280	280
1935S	2,500	1,725	1,950	4,650	6,500	1960D small date	2.85	—	—	—	—
1936	285	1,450	885	1,300	1,750	1961	1.60	4.25	140	280	280
1936D	400	1,450	1,700	—	2,750	1961D	1.90	4.50	140	280	280
1936S	885	1,800	1,675	6,250	3,500	1962	1.65	5.25	140	280	280
1937	250	1,100	710	1,250	1,150	1962D	1.65	5.50	140	280	280
1937D	250	1,200	1,550	3,450	5,000	1963	1.50	4.25	140	280	280
1937S	335	1,285	1,650	4,850	3,450	1963D	1.65	4.75	140	280	280
1938	665	535	1,100	3,100	1,850	1964	1.50	3.50	140	280	280
1938D	710	485	1,000	—	—	1964D	1.60	3.50	140	280	280
1938S	440	355	1,350	3,250	—	1965	2.25	8.75	8.00	25.00	120
1938D Buffalo	—	1,065	—	—	—	1966	3.75	6.00	10.00	53.00	120
1939	180	160	630	1,040	1,250	1967	4.50	9.75	8.50	25.00	120
1939D	535	3,850	610	1,875	1,975	1968	1.75	—	8.50	25.00	—
1939S	265	2,750	1,900	3,200	2,350	1968D	1.70	6.00	9.50	33.00	120
1940	225	145	535	1,850	975	1968S	1.90	6.25	—	—	—
1940D	265	120	780	5,350	—	1969	7.75	—	44.00	100.00	—
1940S	300	265	675	1,275	1,200	1969D	2.00	6.25	21.50	82.00	120
1941	170	215	430	475	750	1969S	3.75	6.75	—	—	—
1941D	335	330	710	2,750	1,200	1970	2.10	—	8.00	26.00	—
1941S	360	295	535	2,450	3,000	1970D	2.10	4.00	7.75	16.00	235
1942	140	315	465	450	690	1970S	3.00	4.50	—	—	—
1942P	—	600	—	—	—	1970S small date	2,650	—	—	—	—
1942D	140	2,550	740	1,060	1,350	1971	17.00	26.50	16.00	50.00	26.00
1942S	585	525	1,050	5,350	1,475	1971D	3.00	7.50	9.50	19.50	15.50
1943	60.00	275	470	365	725	1971S	4.00	—	—	—	—
1943D	170	210	610	2,000	1,775	1972	2.00	6.50	11.00	23.00	32.00
1943S	310	325	650	2,100	1,365	1972D	6.00	5.75	10.00	21.50	23.00
1944	30.00	720	460	280	715	1972S	4.75	—	—	—	—
1944D	38.00	680	635	725	1,250	1973	1.75	6.25	10.50	22.00	25.50
1944S	120	565	660	950	1,300	1973D	1.75	6.25	9.00	23.00	18.00
1945	125	375	410	325	730	1973S	3.00	—	—	—	—
1945D	110	315	500	1,000	1,000	1974	1.75	4.50	7.50	18.50	15.00
1945S	80.00	270	525	575	950	1974D	1.75	5.75	7.75	17.50	21.00
1946	39.00	80.00	140	365	1,025	1974S	3.50	—	—	—	—
1946D	36.50	75.00	140	380	900	1975	3.75	12.50	8.75	—	—
1946S	185	50.00	140	275	900	1975D	1.75	5.25	15.50	—	—
1947	220	58.00	215	735	1,000	1976	1.75	13.50	21.00	17.50	18.00
1947D	46.50	72.00	275	385	1,000	1976D	2.50	11.00	18.00	17.50	15.50
1947S	39.00	72.00	210	415	—	1977	1.75	6.25	9.75	16.50	21.50
1948	72.50	55.00	188	270	450	1977D	2.85	5.75	8.50	17.50	24.00
1948D	175	155	325	645	425	1978	3.00	4.50	7.25	16.00	32.00
1948S	165	80.00	255	475	—	1978D	10.00	5.00	8.00	16.50	46.50
1949	180	330	1,200	2,350	1,300	1979	1.75	4.75	8.75	17.00	22.50
1949D	125	215	550	1,285	1,475	1979D	3.00	5.75	8.00	22.50	22.50
1949S	140	138	2,350	—	2,250	1980	1.75	4.25	8.00	16.50	20.50
1950	115	120	525	395	750	1980D	2.50	4.50	7.50	16.50	20.50
1950D	42.00	385	200	440	875	1981	1.75	4.25	7.50	16.50	16.50
1950S	78.00	—	1,550	850	—	1981D	1.85	4.25	8.00	16.50	19.00
1951	165	230	140	435	390	1982 Small date	25.00	325	270	250	98.00
1951D	26.50	285	140	325	800	1982D Large date	4.00	54.00	66.00	165	80.00
1951S	60.00	265	690	1,350	750	1982 Large date	2.50	—	—	—	—
1952	165	145	140	535	385	1982 Copper plated Zinc	8.00	—	—	—	—
1952D	26.50	260	140	300	230	1982 Small date, copper plated zinc	3.00	—	—	—	—
1952S	300	42.00	290	1,000	1,585	1982D Large date, copper plated zinc	35.00	—	—	—	—
1953	42.00	24.50	140	635	490	1982D Small date, copper plated zinc	2.50	—	—	—	—
1953D	22.50	17.00	140	280	280	1983	7.50	90.00	235	945	80.00
1953S	35.00	39.00	140	280	850	1983D	17.50	39.00	39.00	410	120
1954	39.00	57.50	140	280	280	1984	5.50	22.00	8.50	17.00	26.00
1954D	22.50	24.00	140	280	280	1984D	14.50	6.50	21.00	29.00	37.00
1954S	22.50	39.50	140	280	400	1985	4.25	10.00	9.75	31.00	76.00
1955	24.50	19.00	140	280	300	1985D	9.75	8.00	9.25	22.00	44.00
1955D	19.00	7.00	170	280	—	1986	20.00	8.75	25.00	85.00	75.00
1955S	27.50	—	140	—	—	1986D	31.50	24.50	22.50	210	90.00
1956	10.50	7.50	140	280	280						
1956D	12.50	9.25	140	280	—						
1957	10.00	12.50	140	280	280						
1957D	9.50	4.75	140	280	280						
1958	10.50	6.50	140	280	280						
1958D	9.75	5.50	140	280	280						

Date	Cents	Nickels	Dimes	Quarters	Halves
1987	6.50	6.00	7.75	15.50	52.00
1987D	13.50	4.50	8.75	15.50	52.00
1988	6.25	5.50	9.75	39.00	75.00
1988D	12.50	9.00	9.25	22.50	45.00
1989	3.25	5.50	12.00	19.50	42.00
1989D	3.50	8.75	12.50	17.00	25.00
1990	4.00	11.50	14.50	20.00	39.00
1990D	5.85	13.75	10.00	25.00	52.00
1991	2.60	12.00	10.00	29.00	37.50
1991D	11.50	12.00	11.00	31.00	33.00
1992	3.00	46.00	8.00	42.00	21.00
1992D	5.00	9.00	8.00	27.50	50.00
1993	3.25	13.50	9.50	39.00	64.00
1993D	7.50	17.50	13.00	36.00	17.00
1994	2.00	7.75	12.00	42.00	15.00
1994D	2.00	8.00	12.00	47.50	20.00
1995	1.85	10.50	16.50	45.00	17.00
1995D	2.00	20.00	19.50	53.00	40.00
1996	2.25	8.75	11.00	19.00	17.00
1996D	2.85	8.25	11.50	27.50	19.00
1997	2.75	14.50	29.00	22.50	20.00
1997D	3.35	60.00	11.00	39.00	16.50
1998	2.00	13.75	9.75	17.00	20.00
1998D	1.85	14.00	12.00	18.00	16.50
1999P	2.35	5.50	8.50	—	20.00
1999D	2.25	6.25	8.50	—	19.00
2000P	2.50	6.25	7.75	—	15.00
2000D	1.75	4.75	7.00	—	17.00
2001P	3.75	4.75	7.75	—	16.50
2001D	2.00	6.50	7.25	—	16.00
2002P	2.00	4.00	7.25	—	20.00
2002D	3.25	4.10	7.25	—	20.00
2003P	3.35	7.50	7.00	—	22.50
2003D	2.00	3.50	7.00	—	19.50
2004P Peace Medal Nickel	1.75	6.75	7.00	—	30.00
2004D Peace Medal Nickel	2.50	7.00	7.00	—	30.00
2004P Keelboat Nickel	—	4.00	—	—	—
2004D Keelboat Nickel	—	3.50	—	—	—
2005P Bison Nickel	1.75	3.25	7.00	—	21.00
2005D Bison Nickel	2.75	3.25	7.00	—	21.00
2005P Ocean in view Nickel	—	3.25	—	—	—
2005D Ocean in view Nickel	—	3.25	—	—	—
2006P	2.75	3.25	8.50	—	29.00
2006D	1.75	3.25	8.50	—	29.00
2007P	1.75	3.50	8.00	—	21.00
2007D	1.75	3.50	7.75	—	21.00
2008P	1.75	3.75	8.00	—	24.50
2008D	1.75	3.75	7.50	—	25.50
2009P Log Cabin	2.00	23.00	13.50	—	18.50
2009D Log Cabin	2.15	13.50	13.50	—	18.50
2009P Log Splitter	1.75	—	—	—	—
2009D Log Splitter	1.75	—	—	—	—
2009P Professional	1.75	—	—	—	—
2009D Professional	1.75	—	—	—	—
2009P President	2.00	—	—	—	—
2009D President	2.00	—	—	—	—

50 STATE QUARTERS UNCIRCULATED ROLLS

Listings are for rolls containing uncirculated coins.

State	Philadelphia	Denver
1999 Delaware	15.00	15.50
1999 Pennsylvania	16.00	16.50
1999 New Jersey	16.00	15.50
1999 Georgia	28.00	30.00
1999 Connecticut	26.00	27.00
2000 Massachusetts	14.00	15.00
2000 Maryland	14.00	15.50
2000 South Carolina	15.50	15.50
2000 New Hampshire	13.50	14.50
2000 Virginia	14.50	14.50
2001 New York	14.00	14.00
2001 North Carolina	14.50	15.00
2001 Rhode Island	14.00	15.50
2001 Vermont	14.50	14.50
2001 Kentucky	16.50	18.50
2002 Mississippi	16.50	16.50
2002 Tennessee	30.00	39.50
2002 Ohio	21.50	21.50
2002 Louisiana	14.00	14.00
2002 Indiana	14.50	15.50
2003 Illinois	39.00	45.00
2003 Alabama	17.00	18.50
2003 Maine	14.50	15.50
2003 Missouri	14.50	14.75
2003 Arkansas	14.50	15.50
2004 Michigan	13.75	14.50
2004 Florida	13.75	14.50
2004 Texas	14.00	15.00
2004 Iowa	14.00	14.50
2004 Wisconsin	15.50	16.50
2005 California	21.00	22.50
2005 Minnesota	17.50	17.50
2005 Oregon	13.75	13.75
2005 Kansas	13.75	14.50
2005 West Virginia	13.50	13.75
2006 Nevada	13.75	13.75
2006 Nebraska	13.75	14.00
2006 Colorado	13.75	14.00
2006 North Dakota	13.75	14.50
2006 South Dakota	13.75	13.75
2007 Montana	14.00	17.00
2007 Washington	18.00	18.75
2007 Idaho	15.50	15.50
2007 Wyoming	14.75	15.00
2007 Utah	15.00	14.50
2008 Oklahoma	13.75	13.75
2008 New Mexico	14.00	15.50
2008 Arizona	15.50	13.75
2008 Alaska	13.50	13.75
2008 Hawaii	13.50	13.50

UNCIRCULATED ROLLS

COMMEMORATIVE COINAGE 1892-1954

All commemorative half dollars of 1892-1954 have the following specifications: diameter — 30.6 millimeters; weight — 12.5000 grams; composition — 0.9000 silver, 0.3617 ounces actual silver weight. Values for PDS sets contain one example each from the Philadelphia, Denver and San Francisco mints. Type coin prices are the most inexpensive single coin available from the date and mint mark combinations listed.

QUARTER

KM# 115 COLUMBIAN EXPOSITION
Weight: 6.2500 g. **Composition:** 0.9000 Silver, 0.1808 oz. ASW **Diameter:** 24.3mm. **Obv:** Queen Isabella bust left **Rev:** Female kneeling with distaff adn spindle

Date	Mintage	AU-50	MS-60	MS-63	MS-64	MS-65
1893	24,214	450	525	650	950	2,750

HALF DOLLAR

KM# 117 COLUMBIAN EXPOSITION   Obv: Christopher Columbus bust right **Obv. Designer:** Charles E. Barber **Rev:** Santa Maria sailing left, two globes below **Rev. Designer:** George T. Morgan

Date	Mintage	AU-50	MS-60	MS-63	MS-64	MS-65
1892	950,000	18.50	28.00	80.00	135	525
1893	1,550,405	17.00	28.00	75.00	145	465

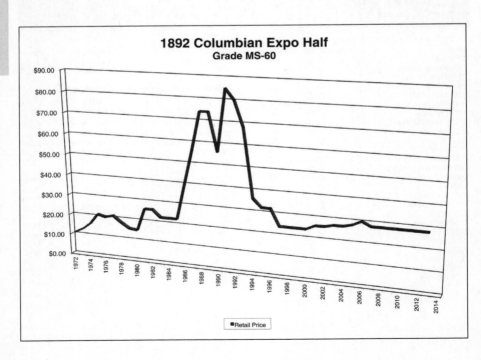

1892 Columbian Expo Half
Grade MS-60

KM# 135 PANAMA-PACIFIC EXPOSITION
Obv: Columbia standing, sunset in background
Rev: Eagle standing on shield **Designer:** Charles E. Barber

Date	Mintage	AU-50	MS-60	MS-63	MS-64	MS-65
1915S	27,134	465	535	825	1,250	2,650

KM# 143 ILLINOIS CENTENNIAL-LINCOLN
Obv: Abraham Lincon bust right **Obv. Designer:** George T. Morgan **Rev:** Eagle standing left **Rev. Designer:** John R. Sinnock

Date	Mintage	AU-50	MS-60	MS-63	MS-64	MS-65
1918	100,058	135	150	165	200	565

KM# 146 MAINE CENTENNIAL
Obv: Arms of the State of Maine **Rev:** Legend within wreath **Designer:** Anthony de Francisci

Date	Mintage	AU-50	MS-60	MS-63	MS-64	MS-65
1920	50,028	130	165	185	250	500

KM# 147.1 PILGRIM TERCENTENARY
Obv: William bradford half-length left **Rev:** Mayflower sailing left **Designer:** Cyrus E. Dallin

Date	Mintage	AU-50	MS-60	MS-63	MS-64	MS-65
1920	152,112	80.00	100.00	110	120	375

KM# 147.2 PILGRIM TERCENTENARY
Obv: William Bradford half-length left, 1921 added at left **Rev:** Mayflower sailing left **Designer:** Cyrus E. Dallin

Date	Mintage	AU-50	MS-60	MS-63	MS-64	MS-65
1921	20,053	170	200	220	235	515

2x2

KM# 148.1 ALABAMA CENTENNIAL
Obv: William W. Bibb and T.E. Kilby conjoint busts left. "2x2" at right above stars **Rev:** Ealge left on shield **Designer:** Laura G. Fraser **Notes:** "Fake 2x2" counterstamps exist.

Date	Mintage	AU-50	MS-60	MS-63	MS-64	MS-65
1921	6,006	315	330	525	675	1,600

KM# 148.2 ALABAMA CENTENNIAL
Obv: William W. Bibb and T.E. Kilby conjoint busts left **Obv. Designer:** Laura G. Fraser **Rev:** Eagle standing left on shield

Date	Mintage	AU-50	MS-60	MS-63	MS-64	MS-65
1921	59,038	190	215	525	685	1,800

COMMEMORATIVES

COMMEMORATIVES

KM# 149.1 MISSOURI CENTENNIAL
Obv: Frontiersman in coonskin cap left **Rev:** Frontiersman and Native American standing left **Designer:** Robert Aitken

Date	Mintage	AU-50	MS-60	MS-63	MS-64	MS-65
1921	15,428	400	600	885	1,275	3,650

2x4

KM# 149.2 MISSOURI CENTENNIAL
Obv: Frontiersman in coonskin cap left, 2(star)4 in field at left **Rev:** Frontiersman and Native American standing left **Designer:** Robert Aitken **Notes:** "Fake "2*4" counterstamps exist.

Date	Mintage	AU-50	MS-60	MS-63	MS-64	MS-65
1921	5,000	620	720	1,050	1,500	3,450

KM# 151.1 GRANT MEMORIAL
Obv: Grant bust right **Rev:** Birthplace in Point Pleasant, Ohio **Designer:** Laura G. Fraser

Date	Mintage	AU-50	MS-60	MS-63	MS-64	MS-65
1922	67,405	120	125	155	250	700

KM# 151.2 GRANT MEMORIAL **Obv:** Grant bust left, star above the word GRANT **Rev:** Birthplace in Point Pleasant, Ohio **Designer:** Laura G. Fraser **Notes:** "Fake star" counterstamps exist.

Date	Mintage	AU-50	MS-60	MS-63	MS-64	MS-65
1922	4,256	925	1,275	1,750	3,450	7,850

KM# 153 MONROE DOCTRINE CENTENNIAL
Obv: James Monroe and John Quincy Adams conjoint busts left **Rev:** Western Hemisphere portraied by two female figures **Designer:** Chester Beach

Date	Mintage	AU-50	MS-60	MS-63	MS-64	MS-65
1923S	274,077	56.00	72.50	125	250	1,950

KM# 154 HUGUENOT-WALLOON TERCENTENARY **Obv:** Huguenot leader Gaspard de Coligny and William I of Orange conjoint busts right **Rev:** Nieuw Nederland sailing left **Designer:** George T. Morgan

Date	Mintage	AU-50	MS-60	MS-63	MS-64	MS-65
1924	142,080	135	145	150	215	385

KM# 155 CALIFORNIA DIAMOND JUBILEE
Obv: Fourty-Niner kneeling panning for gold **Rev:**
Grizzly bear walking left **Designer:** Jo Mora

Date	Mintage	AU-50	MS-60	MS-63	MS-64	MS-65
1925S	86,594	195	225	270	485	900

KM# 156 LEXINGTON-CONCORD
SESQUICENTENNIAL Obv: Concord's Minute
Man statue **Rev:** Old Belfry at Lexington **Designer:**
Chester Beach

Date	Mintage	AU-50	MS-60	MS-63	MS-64	MS-65
1925	162,013	95.00	105	110	145	615

KM# 157 STONE MOUNTAIN MEMORIAL Obv:
Generals Robert E. Lee and Thomas "Stonewall"
Jackson mounted left. **Rev:** Eagle on rock at right
Designer: Gutzon Borglum

Date	Mintage	AU-50	MS-60	MS-63	MS-64	MS-65
1925	1,314,709	62.00	67.50	80.00	190	315

KM# 158 FORT VANCOUVER CENTENNIAL
Obv: John McLoughlin bust left **Rev:** Frontiersmen
standing with musket, Ft. Vancouver in background
Designer: Laura G. Fraser

Date	Mintage	AU-50	MS-60	MS-63	MS-64	MS-65
1925	14,994	320	360	420	475	1,250

KM# 159 OREGON TRAIL MEMORIAL
Obv: Native American standing in full headdress
and holding bow, US Map in background **Rev:**
Conestoga wagon pulled by oxen left towards
sunset **Designer:** James E. and Laura G. Fraser

Date	Mintage	AU-50	MS-60	MS-63	MS-64	MS-65
1926	47,955	135	165	175	195	315
1926S	83,055	135	165	180	195	320
1928	6,028	220	245	275	285	375
1933D	5,008	365	380	385	390	465
1934D	7,006	195	205	215	220	365
1936	10,006	165	190	205	220	340
1936S	5,006	175	190	210	235	350
1937D	12,008	175	200	210	225	325
1938	6,006	155	170	205	210	335
1938D	6,005	155	170	205	220	335
1938S	6,006	155	170	205	215	335
1939	3,004	510	585	600	620	675
1939D	3,004	510	585	610	620	675
1939S	3,005	510	585	590	600	665

KM# 160 U.S. SESQUICENTENNIAL
Obv: George Washington and Calvin Coolidge
conjoint busts right **Rev:** Liberty Bell **Designer:**
John R. Sinnock

Date	Mintage	AU-50	MS-60	MS-63	MS-64	MS-65
1926	141,120	85.00	110	118	465	4,800

KM# 162 VERMONT SESQUICENTENNIAL
Obv: Ira Allen bust right **Obv. Designer:** Charles
Keck **Rev:** Catamount advancing left

Date	Mintage	AU-50	MS-60	MS-63	MS-64	MS-65
1927	28,142	250	275	290	335	880

COMMEMORATIVES

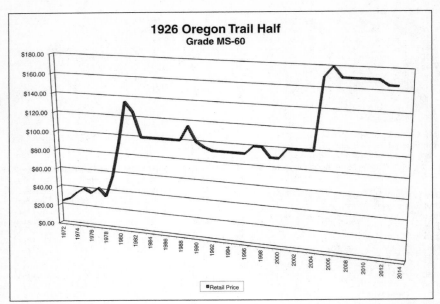

Date	Mintage	AU-50	MS-60	MS-63	MS-64	MS-65
1936S	9,662	105	110	120	130	255
1937	5,505	105	115	120	135	275
1937D	5,505	105	115	120	130	265
1937S	5,506	105	115	120	135	290
1938	3,156	155	180	190	200	590
1938D	3,155	160	180	190	200	580
1938S	3,156	160	180	190	200	640
1939	2,104	320	375	380	400	940
1939D	2,104	320	375	380	400	910
1939S	2,105	320	375	380	400	925

KM# 163 HAWAIIAN SESQUICENTENNIAL
Obv: Captain James Cook bust left **Rev:** Native Hawaiian standing over view of Diamond Head **Designer:** Juliette May Fraser and Chester Beach **Notes:** Counterfeits exist.

Date	Mintage	AU-50	MS-60	MS-63	MS-64	MS-65
1928	10,008	1,785	2,650	3,350	3,775	6,200

KM# 165.1 DANIEL BOONE BICENTENNIAL
Obv: Daniel Boone bust left **Rev:** Daniel Boone and Native American standing **Designer:** Augustus Lukeman

Date	Mintage	AU-50	MS-60	MS-63	MS-64	MS-65
1934	10,007	120	125	135	140	250
1935	10,010	120	125	135	140	250
1935D	5,005	130	135	145	155	295
1935S	5,005	130	135	145	155	285

KM# 168 ARKANSAS CENTENNIAL
Obv: Liberty and Indian Chief's conjoint heads left **Rev:** Eagle with outstreatched wings and Flag of Arkansas in background **Designer:** Edward E. Burr

Date	Mintage	AU-50	MS-60	MS-63	MS-64	MS-65
1935	13,012	90.00	100.00	110	120	215
1935D	5,505	105	110	120	130	250
1935S	5,506	105	110	120	130	250
1936	9,660	90.00	100.00	110	120	225
1936D	9,660	105	110	120	130	255

KM# 165.2 DANIEL BOONE BICENTENNIAL
Obv: Daniel Boone bust left **Rev:** Daniel Boone and Native American standing, "1934" added above the word "PIONEER." **Designer:** Augustus Lukeman

Date	Mintage	AU-50	MS-60	MS-63	MS-64	MS-65
1935	10,008	125	135	140	145	260
1935D	2,003	360	390	425	450	835
1935S	2,004	360	390	425	450	815
1936	12,012	120	125	135	140	250
1936D	5,005	130	135	145	155	295
1936S	5,006	130	135	145	155	285

Date	Mintage	AU-50	MS-60	MS-63	MS-64	MS-65
1937	9,810	135	135	138	145	260
1937D	2,506	320	375	385	400	515
1937S	2,506	320	375	385	400	540
1938	2,100	340	380	390	400	535
1938D	2,100	340	380	390	410	525
1938S	2,100	340	380	390	400	565

KM# 167 TEXAS CENTENNIAL
Obv: Eagle standing left, large star in background
Rev: Winged Victory kneeling beside Alamo
Mission, small busts of Sam Houston and Stephen
Austin at sides **Designer:** Pompeo Coppini

Date	Mintage	AU-50	MS-60	MS-63	MS-64	MS-65
1934	61,463	135	140	150	165	300
1935	9,994	140	145	155	160	300
1935D	10,007	140	145	155	160	300
1935S	10,008	140	145	155	160	300
1936	8,911	140	145	155	160	310
1936D	9,039	140	145	155	160	310
1936S	9,055	140	145	155	160	325
1937	6,571	140	145	155	160	310
1937D	6,605	140	145	155	160	300
1937S	6,637	140	145	155	160	300
1938	3,780	235	250	260	305	425
1938D	3,775	240	255	265	305	415
1938S	3,814	235	250	260	305	415

KM# 166 MARYLAND TERCENTENARY
Obv: Lord Baltimore, Cecil Calvert bust right
Rev: Maryland state arms **Designer:** Hans Schuler

Date	Mintage	AU-50	MS-60	MS-63	MS-64	MS-65
1934	25,015	150	175	185	200	375

KM# 171 SAN DIEGO-PACIFIC INTERNATIONAL
EXPOSITION Obv: Seated female with bear at her
side **Rev:** State of California exposition building
Designer: Robert Aitken

Date	Mintage	AU-50	MS-60	MS-63	MS-64	MS-65
1935S	70,132	95.00	98.00	105	110	240
1936D	30,092	100.00	120	125	135	275

KM# 169 CONNECTICUT TERCENTENARY
Obv: Eagle standing left **Rev:** Charter oak tree
Designer: Henry Kreiss

Date	Mintage	AU-50	MS-60	MS-63	MS-64	MS-65
1935	25,018	240	265	275	325	500

KM# 170 HUDSON, N.Y., SESQUICENTENNIAL
Obv: Hudson's ship, the Half Moon sailing right
Rev: Seal of the City of Hudson **Designer:** Chester
Beach

Date	Mintage	AU-50	MS-60	MS-63	MS-64	MS-65
1935	10,008	750	875	1,050	1,550	2,100

KM# 172 OLD SPANISH TRAIL Obv: Long-horn
cow's head facing **Rev:** The 1535 route of Cabeza
de Vaca's expedition and a yucca tree **Designer:**
L.W. Hoffecker **Notes:** Counterfeits exist.

Date	Mintage	AU-50	MS-60	MS-63	MS-64	MS-65
1935	10,008	1,250	1,375	1,650	1,750	2,000

KM# 173 ALBANY, N.Y., CHARTER
ANNIVERSARY Obv: Beaver knawing on maple
branch **Rev:** Standing figures of Thomas Dongan,
Peter Schyuyler and Robert Livingston **Designer:**
Gertrude K. Lathrop

Date	Mintage	AU-50	MS-60	MS-63	MS-64	MS-65
1936	17,671	300	310	330	350	440

COMMEMORATIVES

KM# 174 SAN FRANCISCO-OAKLAND BAY BRIDGE Obv: Grizzly bear facing **Rev:** Oakland Bay Bridge **Designer:** Jacques Schnier

Date	Mintage	AU-50	MS-60	MS-63	MS-64	MS-65
1936	71,424	155	160	165	185	365

**KM# 175 BRIDGEPORT, CONN., CENTENNIAL
Obv:** P.T. Barnum bust left **Rev:** Eagle standing right **Designer:** Henry Kreiss

Date	Mintage	AU-50	MS-60	MS-63	MS-64	MS-65
1936	25,015	130	140	150	175	320

KM# 176 CINCINNATI MUSIC CENTER Obv: Stephen Foster bust right **Rev:** Kneeling female with lyre **Designer:** Constance Ortmayer

Date	Mintage	AU-50	MS-60	MS-63	MS-64	MS-65
1936	5,005	295	310	335	410	725
1936D	5,005	295	310	335	410	750
1936S	5,006	295	310	335	410	750

KM# 177 CLEVELAND-GREAT LAKES EXPOSITION Obv: Moses Cleaveland bust left **Rev:** Dividers and map of the Great Lakes **Designer:** Brenda Putnam

Date	Mintage	AU-50	MS-60	MS-63	MS-64	MS-65
1936	50,030	110	115	120	160	215

**KM# 178 COLUMBIA, S.C., SESQUICENTENNIAL
Obv:** Figure of Justice between capitols of 1786 and 1936 **Rev:** Palmetto tree **Designer:** A. Wolfe Davidson

Date	Mintage	AU-50	MS-60	MS-63	MS-64	MS-65
1936	9,007	250	265	270	275	310
1936D	8,009	260	270	280	285	340
1936S	8,007	260	270	280	285	340

**KM# 179 DELAWARE TERCENTENARY
Obv:** Old Swedes Church in Wilmington **Rev:** Kalmar Nyckel sailing left **Designer:** Carl L. Schmitz

Date	Mintage	AU-50	MS-60	MS-63	MS-64	MS-65
1936	20,993	255	265	275	290	465

**KM# 180 ELGIN, ILL., CENTENNIAL
Obv:** Pioneer head left **Rev:** Statue group **Designer:** Trygve Rovelstad

Date	Mintage	AU-50	MS-60	MS-63	MS-64	MS-65
1936	20,015	195	205	215	225	355

KM# 181 BATTLE OF GETTYSBURG 75TH ANNIVERSARY Obv: Union and Confederate veteran conjoint busts right **Rev:** Double blased fasces seperating two shields **Designer:** Frank Vittor

Date	Mintage	AU-50	MS-60	MS-63	MS-64	MS-65
1936	26,928	435	460	485	565	925

KM# 182 LONG ISLAND TERCENTENARY
Obv: Dutch settler and Native American conjoint head right **Rev:** Dutch sailing vessel **Designer:** Howard K. Weinman

Date	Mintage	AU-50	MS-60	MS-63	MS-64	MS-65
1936	81,826	85.00	92.00	98.00	105	325

KM# 183 LYNCHBURG, VA., SESQUICENTENNIAL
Obv: Sen. Carter Glass bust left **Rev:** Liberty standing, old Lynchburg courthouse at right **Designer:** Charles Keck

Date	Mintage	AU-50	MS-60	MS-63	MS-64	MS-65
1936	20,013	220	230	265	275	365

KM# 184 NORFOLK, VA., BICENTENNIAL
Obv: Seal of the City of Norfolk **Rev:** Royal Mace of Norfolk **Designer:** William M. and Marjorie E. Simpson

Date	Mintage	AU-50	MS-60	MS-63	MS-64	MS-65
1936	16,936	425	435	445	460	575

KM# 185 RHODE ISLAND TERCENTENARY
Obv: Roger Williams in canoe hailing Native American **Rev:** Shield with anchor **Designer:** Arthur G. Carey and John H. Benson

Date	Mintage	AU-50	MS-60	MS-63	MS-64	MS-65
1936	20,013	98.00	105	110	120	290
1936D	15,010	100.00	110	120	125	305
1936S	15,011	100.00	110	120	130	320

KM# 186 ROANOKE ISLAND, N.C.
Obv: Sir Walter Raleigh bust left **Rev:** Ellinor Dare holding baby Virginia, two small ships flanking **Designer:** William M. Simpson

Date	Mintage	AU-50	MS-60	MS-63	MS-64	MS-65
1937	29,030	220	225	235	245	315

KM# 187 ARKANSAS CENTENNIAL
Obv: Eagle with wings outstreatched, Arkansas flag in backgorund **Obv. Designer:** Henry Kreiss **Rev:** Sen. Joseph T. Robinson bust right **Rev. Designer:** Edward E. Burr

Date	Mintage	AU-50	MS-60	MS-63	MS-64	MS-65
1936	25,265	140	175	210	220	385

KM# 188 WISCONSIN TERRITORIAL CENTENNIAL
Obv: Badger from the Territorial seal **Rev:** Pick axe and mound of lead ore **Designer:** David Parsons

Date	Mintage	AU-50	MS-60	MS-63	MS-64	MS-65
1936	25,015	215	240	255	265	365

KM# 189 YORK COUNTY, MAINE, TERCENTENARY
Obv: Stockade **Rev:** York County seal **Designer:** Walter H. Rich

Date	Mintage	AU-50	MS-60	MS-63	MS-64	MS-65
1936	25,015	210	215	225	235	340

COMMEMORATIVES

KM# 190 BATTLE OF ANTIETAM 75TH
ANNIVERSARY **Obv:** Generals Robert E. Lee
and George McClellan conjoint busts left **Rev:**
Burnside Bridge **Designer:** William M. Simpson

Date	Mintage	AU-50	MS-60	MS-63	MS-64	MS-65
1937	18,028	695	735	750	775	950

KM# 191 NEW ROCHELLE, N.Y.
Obv: John Pell and a calf **Rev:** Fleur-de-lis from the
seal of the city **Designer:** Gertrude K. Lathrop

Date	Mintage	AU-50	MS-60	MS-63	MS-64	MS-65
1938	15,266	375	385	425	440	600

KM# 198 BOOKER T. WASHINGTON
Obv: Booker T. Washington bust right **Rev:** Cabin
and NYU's Hall of Fame **Designer:** Isaac S.
Hathaway **Notes:** Actual mintages are higher, but
unsold issues were melted to produce Washington
Carver issues.

Date	Mintage	AU-50	MS-60	MS-63	MS-64	MS-65
1946	1,000,546	14.00	18.00	21.00	23.00	64.00
1946D	200,113	16.50	20.00	32.00	37.00	72.00
1946S	500,729	15.00	18.50	23.00	27.00	66.00
1947	100,017	30.00	36.00	56.00	65.00	80.00
1947D	100,017	32.00	38.00	62.00	70.00	100.00
1947S	100,017	32.00	38.00	59.00	65.00	76.00
1948	8,005	46.00	64.00	77.00	80.00	84.00
1948D	8,005	46.00	62.00	77.00	80.00	84.00
1948S	8,005	46.00	65.00	78.00	82.00	88.00
1949	6,004	67.00	82.00	85.00	96.00	115
1949D	6,004	67.00	82.00	85.00	96.00	115
1949S	6,004	67.00	82.00	85.00	102	105
1950	6,004	46.00	68.00	78.00	82.00	90.00
1950D	6,004	46.00	68.00	75.00	82.00	88.00
1950S	512,091	18.00	20.00	24.00	26.00	65.00
1951	51,082	17.00	22.00	24.00	26.00	65.00
1951D	7,004	47.00	68.00	80.00	85.00	90.00
1951S	7,004	47.00	68.00	80.00	84.00	88.00

KM# 197 IOWA STATEHOOD CENTENNIAL
Obv: First Capitol building at Iowa City **Rev:** Iowa
state seal **Designer:** Adam Pietz

Date	Mintage	AU-50	MS-60	MS-63	MS-64	MS-65
1946	100,057	100.00	105	108	112	160

KM# 200 BOOKER T. WASHINGTON AND
GEORGE WASHINGTON CARVER **Obv:** Booker
T. Washington and George Washington Carver
conjoint busts right **Rev:** Map of the United States
Designer: Isaac S. Hathaway

Date	Mintage	AU-50	MS-60	MS-63	MS-64	MS-65
1951	110,018	18.00	20.00	25.00	44.00	290
1951D	10,004	42.00	50.00	80.00	82.00	140
1951S	10,004	42.00	50.00	80.00	86.00	90.00
1952	2,006,292	17.00	18.00	24.00	42.00	83.00
1952D	8,006	40.00	50.00	80.00	85.00	190
1952S	8,006	40.00	50.00	80.00	84.00	185
1953	8,003	40.00	50.00	80.00	85.00	260
1953D	8,003	40.00	50.00	80.00	85.00	175
1953S	108,020	17.00	18.00	24.00	42.00	120
1954	12,006	39.00	48.00	70.00	75.00	200
1954D	12,006	39.00	48.00	70.00	80.00	83.00
1954S	122,024	17.00	18.00	24.00	42.00	83.00

DOLLAR

KM# 118 LA FAYETTE **Weight:** 26.7300 g.
Composition: 0.9000 Silver, 0.7734 oz. ASW

Diameter: 38.1mm. **Obv:** George Washington and Marquis de La Fayette conjoint busts right **Rev:** La Fayette on horseback left **Designer:** Charles E. Barber

Date	Mintage	AU-50	MS-60	MS-63	MS-64	MS-65
1900	36,026	550	950	1,875	3,250	11,500

KM# 119 LOUISIANA PURCHASE EXPOSITION - JEFFERSON
Weight: 1.6720 g. **Composition:** 0.9000 Gold, 0.0484 oz. AGW **Diameter:** 15mm. **Obv:** Jefferson bust left **Rev:** Legend and laurel branch **Designer:** Charles E. Barber

Date	Mintage	AU-50	MS-60	MS-63	MS-64	MS-65
1903	17,500	600	660	925	1,450	2,150

KM# 120 LOUISIANA PURCHASE EXPOSITION - MCKINLEY
Weight: 1.6720 g. **Composition:** 0.9000 Gold, 0.0484 oz. AGW **Diameter:** 15mm. **Obv:** William McKinley bust left **Obv. Designer:** Charles E. Barber **Rev:** Legend and laurel branch

Date	Mintage	AU-50	MS-60	MS-63	MS-64	MS-65
1903	17,500	590	650	800	1,400	2,100

KM# 121 LEWIS AND CLARK EXPOSITION
Weight: 1.6720 g. **Composition:** 0.9000 Gold, 0.0484 oz. AGW **Diameter:** 15mm. **Obv:** Lewis bust left **Obv. Designer:** Charles E. Barber **Rev:** Clark bust left

Date	Mintage	AU-50	MS-60	MS-63	MS-64	MS-65
1904	10,025	950	1,100	1,850	3,650	7,900
1905	10,041	975	1,450	2,250	3,950	15,000

KM# 136 PANAMA-PACIFIC EXPOSITION
Weight: 1.6720 g. **Composition:** 0.9000 Gold, 0.0484 oz. AGW **Diameter:** 15mm. **Obv:** Canal laborer bust left **Obv. Designer:** Charles Keck **Rev:** Value within two dolphins

Date	Mintage	AU-50	MS-60	MS-63	MS-64	MS-65
1915S	15,000	565	625	775	1,100	1,700

KM# 144 MCKINLEY MEMORIAL
Weight: 1.6720 g. **Composition:** 0.9000 Gold, 0.0484 oz. AGW **Diameter:** 15mm. **Obv:** William McKinley head left **Obv. Designer:** Charles E.

Barber **Rev:** Memorial building at Niles, Ohio **Rev. Designer:** George T. Morgan

Date	Mintage	AU-50	MS-60	MS-63	MS-64	MS-65
1916	9,977	520	600	685	1,000	1,750
1917	10,000	575	700	900	1,475	2,250

KM# 152.1 GRANT MEMORIAL
Weight: 1.6720 g. **Composition:** 0.9000 Gold, 0.0484 oz. AGW **Diameter:** 15mm. **Obv:** U.S. Grant bust right **Obv. Designer:** Laura G. Fraser **Rev:** Birthplace **Notes:** Without an incuse "star" above the word GRANT on the obverse.

Date	Mintage	AU-50	MS-60	MS-63	MS-64	MS-65
1922	5,000	1,875	1,900	2,350	3,650	4,900

Star

KM# 152.2 GRANT MEMORIAL
Weight: 1.6720 g. **Composition:** 0.9000 Gold, 0.0484 oz. AGW **Diameter:** 15mm. **Obv:** U.S. Grant bust right **Obv. Designer:** Laura G. Fraser **Rev:** Birthplace **Notes:** Variety with an incuse "star" above the word GRANT on the obverse.

Date	Mintage	AU-50	MS-60	MS-63	MS-64	MS-65
1922	5,016	1,650	1,775	2,100	2,150	3,100

$2.50 (QUARTER EAGLE)

KM# 137 PANAMA-PACIFIC EXPOSITION
Weight: 4.1800 g. **Composition:** 0.9000 Gold, 0.1209 oz. AGW **Diameter:** 18mm. **Obv:** Columbia holding cadueus while seated on a hippocamp **Obv. Designer:** Charles E. Barber **Rev:** Eagle standing left **Rev. Designer:** George T. Morgan

Date	Mintage	AU-50	MS-60	MS-63	MS-64	MS-65
1915S	6,749	1,550	1,950	4,100	5,650	6,750

KM# 161 U.S. SESQUICENTENNIAL
Weight: 4.1800 g. **Composition:** 0.9000 Gold, 0.1209 oz. AGW **Diameter:** 18mm. **Obv:** Liberty standing holding torch and scroll **Obv. Designer:** John R. Sinnock **Rev:** Independence Hall

Date	Mintage	AU-50	MS-60	MS-63	MS-64	MS-65
1926	46,019	425	500	800	1,375	3,450

COMMEMORATIVES

COMMEMORATIVES

$50

KM# 138 PANAMA-PACIFIC EXPOSITION
ROUND   Weight: 83.5900 g. **Composition:**
0.9000 Gold, 2.4186 oz. AGW **Diameter:** 44mm.
Obv: Minerva bust helmeted left **Obv. Designer:**
Robert Aitken **Rev:** Owl pearched on California pin
branch

Date	Mintage	AU-50	MS-60	MS-63	MS-64	MS-65
1915S	483	46,500	57,500	90,000	105,000	160,000

KM# 139 PANAMA-PACIFIC EXPOSITION
OCTAGONAL   Weight: 83.5900 g. **Composition:**
0.9000 Gold, 2.4186 oz. AGW **Diameter:** 44mm.
Obv: Minerva bust helmeted left **Obv. Designer:**
Robert Aitken **Rev:** Owl pearched on California
pine branch

Date	Mintage	AU-50	MS-60	MS-63	MS-64	MS-65
1915S	645	50,000	52,500	84,500	98,000	146,000

COMMEMORATIVE COINAGE 1982-PRESENT

All commemorative silver dollar coins of 1982-present have the following specifications: diameter — 38.1 millimeters; weight — 26.7300 grams; composition — 0.9000 silver, 0.7736 ounces actual silver weight. All commemorative $5 coins of 1982-present have the following specificiations: diameter — 21.6 millimeters; weight — 8.3590 grams; composition: 0.9000 gold, 0.242 ounces actual gold weight.

Note: In 1982, after a hiatus of nearly 20 years, coinage of commemorative half dollars resumed. Those designated with a 'W' were struck at the West Point Mint. Some issues were struck in copper-nickel. Those struck in silver have the same size, weight and composition as the prior commemorative half-dollar series.

HALF DOLLAR

KM# 208 GEORGE WASHINGTON, 250TH BIRTH ANNIVERSARY
Weight: 12.5000 g. **Composition:** 0.9000 Silver, 0.3617 oz. ASW **Diameter:** 30.6mm. **Obv:** George Washington on horseback facing **Obv. Designer:** Elizabeth Jones **Rev:** Mount Vernon **Rev. Designer:** Matthew Peloso

Date	UNC Mintage	Proof Mintage	MS-65	Prf-65
1982D	2,210,458	—	13.70	—
1982S	—	4,894,044	—	13.70

KM# 212 STATUE OF LIBERTY CENTENNIAL
Weight: 11.3400 g. **Composition:** Copper-Nickel Clad Copper **Obv:** State of Liberty and sunrise **Obv. Designer:** Edgar Z. Steever **Rev:** Emigrant family looking toward mainland **Rev. Designer:** Sherl Joseph Winter

Date	UNC Mintage	Proof Mintage	MS-65	Prf-65
1986D	928,008	—	3.25	—
1986S	—	6,925,627	—	3.50

KM# 224 CONGRESS BICENTENNIAL
Weight: 11.3400 g. **Composition:** Copper-Nickel Clad Copper **Obv:** Statue of Freedom head **Designer:** Patricia L. Verani **Rev:** Capitol building **Rev. Designer:** William Woodward and Edgar Z. Steever

Date	UNC Mintage	Proof Mintage	MS-65	Prf-65
1989D	163,753	—	7.50	—
1989S	—	762,198	—	7.50

KM# 228 MOUNT RUSHMORE 50TH ANNIVERSARY
Weight: 11.3400 g. **Composition:** Copper-Nickel Clad Copper **Obv. Designer:** Marcel Jovine **Rev:** Mount Rushmore portraits **Rev. Designer:** T. James Ferrell

Date	UNC Mintage	Proof Mintage	MS-65	Prf-65
1991D	172,754	—	17.50	—
1991S	—	753,257	—	16.00

KM# 233 1992 OLYMPICS
Weight: 11.3400 g. **Composition:** Copper-Nickel Clad Copper **Obv:** Torch and laurel **Obv.**

COMMEMORATIVES

COMMEMORATIVES

Designer: William Cousins **Rev:** Female gymnast and large flag **Rev. Designer:** Steven M. Bieda

Date	UNC Mintage	Proof Mintage	MS-65	Prf-65
1992P	161,607	—	8.50	—
1992S	—	519,645	—	8.50

KM# 237 COLUMBUS VOYAGE - 500TH ANNIVERSARY **Weight:** 11.3400 g.
Composition: Copper-Nickel Clad Copper **Obv:** Columbus standing on shore **Obv. Designer:** T. James Ferrell **Rev:** Nina, Pinta and Santa Maria sailing right **Rev. Designer:** Thomas D. Rogers, Sr.

Date	UNC Mintage	Proof Mintage	MS-65	Prf-65
1992D	135,702	—	11.50	—
1992S	—	390,154	—	8.75

KM# 240 JAMES MADISON - BILL OF RIGHTS
Weight: 12.5000 g. **Composition:** 0.9000 Silver, 0.3617 oz. ASW **Obv:** James Madison writing, Montpelier in background **Obv. Designer:** T. James Ferrell **Rev:** Statue of Liberty torch **Rev. Designer:** Dean McMullen

Date	UNC Mintage	Proof Mintage	MS-65	Prf-65
1993W	193,346	—	19.00	—
1993S	—	586,315	—	19.00

KM# 243 WORLD WAR II 50TH ANNIVERSARY
Weight: 11.3400 g. **Composition:** Copper-Nickel Clad Copper **Obv:** Three portraits, plane above, large V in backgound **Obv. Designer:** George Klauba and T. James Ferrell **Rev:** Pacific island battle scene **Rev. Designer:** William J. Leftwich and T. James Ferrell

Date	UNC Mintage	Proof Mintage	MS-65	Prf-65
(1993)P	197,072	—	17.00	—
(1993)P	—	317,396	—	16.50

KM# 246 1994 WORLD CUP SOCCER
Weight: 11.3400 g. **Composition:** Copper-Nickel Clad Copper **Obv:** Soccer player with ball **Obv. Designer:** Richard T. LaRoche **Rev:** World Cup 94 logo **Rev. Designer:** Dean McMullen

Date	UNC Mintage	Proof Mintage	MS-65	Prf-65
1994D	168,208	—	8.25	—
1994P	—	609,354	—	8.00

KM# 254 CIVIL WAR BATTLEFIELD PRESERVATION **Weight:** 11.3400 g.
Composition: Copper-Nickel Clad Copper **Obv:** Drummer and fenceline **Obv. Designer:** Don Troiani **Rev:** Canon overlooking battlefield **Rev. Designer:** T. James Ferrell

Date	UNC Mintage	Proof Mintage	MS-65	Prf-65
1995S	119,510	—	36.50	—
1995S	—	330,099	—	33.50

KM# 257 1996 ATLANTA OLYMPICS - BASKETBALL **Weight:** 11.3400 g.
Composition: Copper-Nickel Clad Copper **Obv:** Three players, one jumping for a shot **Obv. Designer:** Clint Hansen and Al Maletsky **Rev:** Hemisphere and Atlanta Olympics logo **Rev. Designer:** T. James Ferrell

Date	UNC Mintage	Proof Mintage	MS-65	Prf-65
1995S	—	169,655	—	18.00
1995S	171,001	—	17.00	—

COMMEMORATIVES

KM# 262 1996 ATLANTA OLYMPICS - BASEBALL Weight: 11.3400 g. Composition: Copper-Nickel Clad Copper Obv: Baseball batter at plate, catcher and umpire Obv. Designer: Edgar Z. Steever Rev: Hemisphere and Atlanta Olympics logo Rev. Designer: T. James Ferrell

Date	UNC Mintage	Proof Mintage	MS-65	Prf-65
1995S	164,605	—	19.50	—
1995S	—	118,087	—	17.50

KM# 323 U. S. CAPITOL VISITOR CENTER Weight: 11.3400 g. Composition: Copper-Nickel Clad Copper Obv: Capitol sillouete, 1800 structure in detail Obv. Designer: Dean McMullen Rev: Legend within circle of stars Rev. Designer: Alex Shagin and Marcel Jovine

Date	UNC Mintage	Proof Mintage	MS-65	Prf-65
2001P	99,157	—	14.50	—
2001P	—	77,962	—	15.50

KM# 271 1996 ATLANTA OLYMPICS - SOCCER Weight: 11.3400 g. Composition: Copper-Nickel Clad Copper Obv: Two female soccer players Rev: Atlanta Olympics logo

Date	UNC Mintage	Proof Mintage	MS-65	Prf-65
1996S	52,836	—	130	—
1996S	—	122,412	—	88.00

KM# 348 FIRST FLIGHT CENTENNIAL Weight: 11.3400 g. Composition: Copper-Nickel Clad Copper Obv: Wright Monument at Kitty Hawk Obv. Designer: John Mercanti Rev: Wright Flyer in flight Rev. Designer: Donna Weaver

Date	UNC Mintage	Proof Mintage	MS-65	Prf-65
2003P	57,726	—	15.00	—
2003P	—	111,569	—	17.00

KM# 267 1996 ATLANTA OLYMPICS - SWIMMING Weight: 11.3400 g. Composition: Copper-Nickel Clad Copper Obv: Swimmer right in butterfly stroke Obv. Designer: William J. Krawczewicz and Edgar Z. Steever Rev: Atlanta Olympics logo Rev. Designer: Malcolm Farley and Thomas D. Rogers, Sr.

Date	UNC Mintage	Proof Mintage	MS-65	Prf-65
1996S	49,533	—	140	—
1996S	—	114,315	—	31.00

KM# 438 AMERICAN BALD EAGLE Weight: 11.3400 g. Composition: Copper-Nickel Clad Copper Diameter: 30.6mm. Obv: Two eaglets in nest with egg Obv. Designer: Susan Gamble and Joseph Menna Rev: Eagle Challenger facing right, American Flag in background Rev. Designer: Donna Weaver and Charles Vickers

Date	UNC Mintage	Proof Mintage	MS-65	Prf-65
2008S	120,180	—	12.50	—
2008S	—	222,577	—	14.00

COMMEMORATIVES

KM# 506 U.S. ARMY Weight: 11.3400 g.
Composition: Copper-Nickel Clad Copper
Diameter: 30.6mm. **Obv:** Army contributions
during peacetime, surveying, building a flood wall
and space exploration **Obv. Designer:** Donna
Weaver and Charles L. Vickers **Rev:** Continental
soldier with musket **Rev. Designer:** Thomas
Cleveland and Joseph Menna

Date	UNC Mintage	Proof Mintage	MS-65	Prf-65
2011D	39,461	—	69.00	—
2011		68,349	—	35.00

DOLLAR

**KM# 209 1984 LOS ANGELES OLYMPICS -
DISCUS Obv:** Trippled discus thrower and five
star logo **Obv. Designer:** Elizabeth Jones **Rev:**
Eagle bust left

Date	UNC Mintage	Proof Mintage	MS-65	Prf-65
1983P	294,543	—	34.80	—
1983D	174,014	—	34.70	—
1983S	174,014	—	34.80	—
1983S		1,577,025	—	36.80

**KM# 210 1984 LOS ANGELES OLYMPICS -
STADIUM STATUES Obv:** Statues at exterior of
Los Angeles Memorial Coliseum **Obv. Designer:**
Robert Graham **Rev:** Eagle standing on rock

Date	UNC Mintage	Proof Mintage	MS-65	Prf-65
1984P	217,954	—	34.80	—
1984D	116,675	—	35.30	—
1984S	116,675	—	35.30	—
1984S		1,801,210	—	36.80

**KM# 214 STATUE OF LIBERTY CENTENNIAL
Obv:** Statue of Liberty and Ellis Island great hall
Obv. Designer: John Mercanti **Rev:** Statue of
Liberty torch **Rev. Designer:** John Mercanti and
Matthew Peloso

Date	UNC Mintage	Proof Mintage	MS-65	Prf-65
1986P	723,635	—	34.80	—
1986S		6,414,638	—	36.80

**KM# 220 CONSTITUTION BICENTENNIAL
Obv:** Feather pen and document **Obv. Designer:**
Patricia L. Verani **Rev:** Group of people

Date	UNC Mintage	Proof Mintage	MS-65	Prf-65
1987P	451,629	—	34.80	—
1987S		2,747,116	—	36.80

KM# 222 1988 OLYMPICS
Obv: Olympic torch and Statue of Liberty torch within laurel wreath **Obv. Designer:** Patricia L. Verani **Rev:** Olympic rights within olive wreath **Rev. Designer:** Sherl Joseph Winter

Date	UNC Mintage	Proof Mintage	MS-65	Prf-65
1988D	191,368	—	34.80	—
1988S	—	1,359,366	—	36.80

KM# 227 EISENHOWER CENTENNIAL
Obv: Two Eisenhower profiles, as general, left, as President, right **Obv. Designer:** John Mercanti **Rev:** Eisenhower home at Gettysburg **Rev. Designer:** Marcel Jovine and John Mercanti

Date	UNC Mintage	Proof Mintage	MS-65	Prf-65
1990W	241,669	—	34.80	—
1990P	1,144,461	—	—	36.80

KM# 225 CONGRESS BICENTENNIAL
Obv: Statue of Freedom in clouds and sunburst **Rev:** Mace from the House of Represenatives **Designer:** William Woodward and Chester Y. Martin

Date	UNC Mintage	Proof Mintage	MS-65	Prf-65
1989D	135,203	—	34.80	—
1989S	—	762,198	—	36.80

KM# 229 MOUNT RUSHMORE 50TH ANNIVERSARY
Obv: Mount Rushmore portraits, wreath below **Obv. Designer:** Marika Somogyi and Chester Martin **Rev:** Great seal in rays, United States map in background **Rev. Designer:** Frank Gasparro

Date	UNC Mintage	Proof Mintage	MS-65	Prf-65
1991P	133,139	—	39.80	—
1991S	—	738,419	—	42.80

COMMEMORATIVES

COMMEMORATIVES

KM# 231 KOREAN WAR - 38TH ANNIVERSARY
Obv: Solder advancing right up a hill; planes above, ships below **Obv. Designer:** John Mercanti **Rev:** Map of Korean pensiluar, eagle's head **Rev. Designer:** T. James Ferrell

Date	UNC Mintage	Proof Mintage	MS-65	Prf-65
1991D	213,049	—	37.80	—
1991P	—	618,488	—	36.80

KM# 234 1992 OLYMPICS - BASEBALL
Obv: Baseball pitcher, Nolan Ryan as depicted on card **Obv. Designer:** John R. Deecken and Chester Y. Martin **Rev:** Shield flanked by stylized wreath, olympic rings above **Rev. Designer:** Marcel Jovine

Date	UNC Mintage	Proof Mintage	MS-65	Prf-65
1992D	187,552	—	37.80	—
1992S	—	504,505	—	38.80

KM# 232 USO 50TH ANNIVERSARY
Obv: USO banner **Obv. Designer:** Robert Lamb **Rev:** Eagle pearched right atop globe **Rev. Designer:** John Mercanti

Date	UNC Mintage	Proof Mintage	MS-65	Prf-65
1991D	124,958	—	37.80	—
1991S	—	321,275	—	38.80

KM# 236 WHITE HOUSE BICENTENNIAL
Obv: White House's north portico **Obv. Designer:** Edgar Z. Steever **Rev:** John Hoban bust left, main entrance doorway **Rev. Designer:** Chester Y. Martin

Date	UNC Mintage	Proof Mintage	MS-65	Prf-65
1992D	123,803	—	37.80	—
1992W	—	375,851	—	38.80

**KM# 238 COLUMBUS DISCOVERY - 500TH
ANNIVERSARY   Obv:** Columbus standing with
banner, three ships in background **Obv. Designer:**
John Mercanti **Rev:** Half view of Santa Maria on
left, Space Shuttle Discovery on right **Rev.
Designer:** Thomas D. Rogers, Sr.

Date	UNC Mintage	Proof Mintage	MS-65	Prf-65
1992D	106,949	—	40.80	—
1992P	—	385,241	—	37.80

**KM# 244 WORLD WAR II 50TH ANNIVERSARY
Obv:** Soldier on Normandy beach **Rev:** Insignia of the
Supreme Headquarters of the AEF above
Eisenhower quote **Designer:** Thomas D. Rogers, Sr.

Date	UNC Mintage	Proof Mintage	MS-65	Prf-65
1993D	94,708	—	36.80	—
1993W	—	342,041	—	40.80

**KM# 241 JAMES MADISON - BILL OF RIGHTS
Obv:** James Madison bust right, at left **Obv.
Designer:** William Krawczewicz and Thomas D.
Rogers, Sr. **Rev:** Montpelier home **Rev. Designer:**
Dean McMullen and Thomas D. Rogers, Sr.

Date	UNC Mintage	Proof Mintage	MS-65	Prf-65
1993D	98,383	—	37.80	—
1993S	—	534,001	—	38.80

**KM# 247 1994 WORLD CUP SOCCER
Obv:** Two players with ball **Obv. Designer:** Dean
McMullen and T. James Ferrell **Rev:** World Cup 94
logo **Rev. Designer:** Dean McMullen

Date	UNC Mintage	Proof Mintage	MS-65	Prf-65
1994D	81,698	—	38.80	—
1994S	—	576,978	—	36.80

COMMEMORATIVES

COMMEMORATIVES

KM# 249 THOMAS JEFFERSON 250TH BIRTH ANNIVERSARY Obv: Jefferson's head left Rev: Monticello home Designer: T. James Ferrell

Date	UNC Mintage	Proof Mintage	MS-65	Prf-65
1993P	266,927	—	36.80	—
1993S	—	332,891	—	40.80

KM# 251 NATIONAL PRISONER OF WAR MUSEUM Obv: Eagle in flight left within circle of barbed wire Obv. Designer: Thomas Nielson and Alfred Maletsky Rev: National Prisioner of War Museum Rev. Designer: Edgar Z. Steever

Date	UNC Mintage	Proof Mintage	MS-65	Prf-65
1994W	54,790	—	84.00	—
1994P	—	220,100	—	39.80

KM# 250 VIETNAM VETERANS MEMORIAL Obv: Outstretched hand touching names on the Wall, Washington Monument in background Obv. Designer: John Mercanti Rev: Service Medals Rev. Designer: Thomas D. Rogers, Sr.

Date	UNC Mintage	Proof Mintage	MS-65	Prf-65
1994W	57,317	—	79.00	—
1994P	—	226,262	—	63.00

KM# 252 WOMEN IN MILITARY SERVICE MEMORIAL Obv: Five uniformed women left Obv. Designer: T. James Ferrell Rev: Memorial at Arlington National Cemetery Rev. Designer: Thomas D. Rogers, Sr.

Date	UNC Mintage	Proof Mintage	MS-65	Prf-65
1994W	53,054	—	38.80	—
1994P	—	213,201	—	38.80

KM# 253 U.S. CAPITOL BICENTENNIAL

Obv: Capitol dome, Statue fo Freedom surrounded by stars **Obv. Designer:** William C. Cousins **Rev:** Eagle on shield, flags flanking **Rev. Designer:** John Mercanti

Date	UNC Mintage	Proof Mintage	MS-65	Prf-65
1994D	68,352	—	38.80	—
1994S	—	279,416	—	40.80

KM# 259 1996 ATLANTA PARALYMPICS - BLIND RUNNER

Obv: Blind runner **Obv. Designer:** Jim C. Sharpe and Thomas D. Rogers, Sr. **Rev:** Two clasped hands, Atlanta Olympic logo above **Rev. Designer:** William J. Krawczewicz and T. James Ferrell

Date	UNC Mintage	Proof Mintage	MS-65	Prf-65
1995D	28,649	—	67.00	—
1995P	—	138,337	—	45.00

KM# 255 CIVIL WAR

Obv: Soldier giving water to wounded soldier **Obv. Designer:** Don Troiani and Edgar Z. Steever **Rev:** Chamberlain quote and battlefield monument **Rev. Designer:** John Mercanti

Date	UNC Mintage	Proof Mintage	MS-65	Prf-65
1995P	45,866	—	65.00	—
1995S	—	437,114	—	54.00

KM# 260 1996 ATLANTA OLYMPICS - GYMNASTICS

Obv: Two gymnasts, female on floor exercise and male on rings **Obv. Designer:** James C. Sharpe and Thomas D. Rogers, Sr. **Rev:** Two clasped hands, Atlanta Olympic logo above **Rev. Designer:** William J. Krawczewicz and T. James Ferrell

Date	UNC Mintage	Proof Mintage	MS-65	Prf-65
1995D	42,497	—	55.00	—
1995P	—	182,676	—	36.80

COMMEMORATIVES

KM# 263 1996 ATLANTA OLYMPICS - CYCLING
Obv: Three cyclists approaching **Obv. Designer:**
John Mercanti **Rev:** Two clasped hands, Atlanta
Olympic logo above **Rev. Designer:** William J.
Krawczewicz and T. James Ferrell

Date	UNC Mintage	Proof Mintage	MS-65	Prf-65
1995D	19,662	—	135	—
1995P	—	118,795	—	45.00

KM# 266 SPECIAL OLYMPICS WORLD GAMES
Obv: Eunice Schriver head left; founder of the
Special Olympics **Obv. Designer:** Jamie Wyeth
and T. James Ferrell **Rev:** Special Olympics Logo
on an award medal, rose, quote from Schriver
Rev. Designer: Thomas D. Rogers, Sr.

Date	UNC Mintage	Proof Mintage	MS-65	Prf-65
1995W	89,301	—	40.80	—
1995P	—	351,764	—	41.80

KM# 264 1996 ATLANTA OLYMPICS - TRACK
AND FIELD **Obv:** Two runners on a track, one
crossing finish line **Obv. Designer:** John Mercanti
Rev: Two clasped hands, Atlanta Olympic logo
above **Rev. Designer:** William J. Krawczewicz and
T. James Ferrell

Date	UNC Mintage	Proof Mintage	MS-65	Prf-65
1995D	24,796	—	88.00	—
1995P	—	136,935	—	38.80

KM# 268 1996 ATLANTA PARALYMPICS -
WHEELCHAIR RACER **Obv:** Wheelchair racer
approaching with uplifted arms **Obv. Designer:**
James C. Sharpe and Alfred F. Maletsky **Rev:**
Atlanta Olympics logo **Rev. Designer:** Thomas D.
Rogers, Sr.

Date	UNC Mintage	Proof Mintage	MS-65	Prf-65
1996D	14,497	—	305	—
1996P	—	84,280	—	71.00

KM# 269 1996 ATLANTA OLYMPICS - TENNIS
Obv: Female tennis player **Obv. Designer:** James C. Sharpe and T. James Ferrell **Rev:** Atlanta Olympics logo **Rev. Designer:** Thomas D. Rogers, Sr.

Date	UNC Mintage	Proof Mintage	MS-65	Prf-65
1996D	15,983	—	245	—
1996P	—	92,016	—	83.00

KM# 272 1996 ATLANTA OLYMPICS - ROWING
Obv: Four man crew rowing left **Obv. Designer:** Bart Forbes and T. James Ferrell **Rev:** Atlanta Olympic logo **Rev. Designer:** Thomas D. Rogers, Sr.

Date	UNC Mintage	Proof Mintage	MS-65	Prf-65
1996D	16,258	—	290	—
1996P	—	151,890	—	62.00

KM# A272 1996 ATLANTA OLYMPICS - HIGH JUMP
Obv: High jumper **Obv. Designer:** T. James Ferrell **Rev. Designer:** Thomas D. Rogers, Sr.

Date	UNC Mintage	Proof Mintage	MS-65	Prf-65
1996D	15,697	—	310	—
1996P	—	124,502	—	43.00

KM# 275 NATIONAL COMMUNITY SERVICE
Obv: Female standing with lamp and shield **Obv. Designer:** Thomas D. Rogers, Sr. **Rev:** Legend within wreath **Rev. Designer:** William C. Cousins

Date	UNC Mintage	Proof Mintage	MS-65	Prf-65
1996S	23,500	—	170	—
1996S	—	101,543	—	51.00

KM# 276 SMITHSONIAN INSTITUTION 150TH ANNIVERSARY Obv: Original Smithsonian building, the "Castle" designed by James Renwick Obv. Designer: Thomas D. Rogers, Sr. Rev: Female seated with torch and scroll on globe Rev. Designer: John Mercanti

Date	UNC Mintage	Proof Mintage	MS-65	Prf-65
1996D	31,230	—	122	—
1996P	—	129,152	—	49.00

KM# 279 JACKIE ROBINSON Obv: Jackie Robinson sliding into base Obv. Designer: Alfred Maletsky Rev: Anniversary logo Rev. Designer: T. James Ferrell

Date	UNC Mintage	Proof Mintage	MS-65	Prf-65
1997S	30,007	—	72.00	—
1997S	—	110,495	—	90.00

KM# 278 U.S. BOTANIC GARDENS 175TH ANNIVERSARY Obv: National Botanic Gardens Conservatory building Obv. Designer: Edgar Z. Steever Rev: Rose Rev. Designer: William C. Cousins

Date	UNC Mintage	Proof Mintage	MS-65	Prf-65
1997P	57,272	—	42.00	—
1997P	—	264,528	—	42.00

KM# 281 NATIONAL LAW ENFORCEMENT OFFICERS MEMORIAL Obv: Male and female officer admiring name on monument Rev: Rose on a plain shield Designer: Alfred F. Maletsky

Date	UNC Mintage	Proof Mintage	MS-65	Prf-65
1997P	—	110,428	—	78.00
1997P	28,575	—	135	—

COMMEMORATIVES

KM# 287 ROBERT F. KENNEDY Obv: Kennedy bust facing **Obv. Designer:** Thomas D. Rogers, Sr. **Rev:** Eagle on sheild, Senate Seal **Rev. Designer:** James M. Peed and Thomas D. Rogers, Sr.

Date	UNC Mintage	Proof Mintage	MS-65	Prf-65
1998S	106,422	—	47.50	—
1998S	—	99,020	—	47.50

KM# 298 DOLLEY MADISON Obv: Madison bust right, at left **Obv. Designer:** Tiffany & Co. and T. James Ferrell **Rev. Designer:** Tiffany & Co. and Thomas D. Rogers, Sr. **Rev:** Montpelier home

Date	UNC Mintage	Proof Mintage	MS-65	Prf-65
1999P	22,948	—	38.30	—
1999P	—	158,247	—	38.30

KM# 288 BLACK REVOLUTIONARY WAR PATRIOTS Obv: Crispus Attucks bust right **Obv. Designer:** John Mercanti **Rev:** Family standing **Rev. Designer:** Edward Dwight and Thomas D. Rogers, Sr.

Date	UNC Mintage	Proof Mintage	MS-65	Prf-65
1998S	37,210	—	145	—
1998S	—	75,070	—	89.00

KM# 299 YELLOWSTONE Obv: Old Faithful gyser erupting **Obv. Designer:** Edgar Z. Steever **Rev:** Bison and vista as on National Parks shield **Rev. Designer:** William C. Cousins

Date	UNC Mintage	Proof Mintage	MS-65	Prf-65
1999P	23,614	—	44.00	—
1999P	—	128,646	—	40.30

COMMEMORATIVES

COMMEMORATIVES

KM# 311 LIBRARY OF CONGRESS
BICENTENNIAL   Obv: Open and closed book, torch in background **Obv. Designer:** Thomas D. Rogers, Sr. **Rev:** Skylight dome above the main reading room **Rev. Designer:** John Mercanti

Date	UNC Mintage	Proof Mintage	MS-65	Prf-65
2000P	52,771	—	40.80	—
2000P	—	196,900	—	38.30

KM# 324 CAPITOL VISITOR CENTER
Obv: Original and current Capital facades **Obv. Designer:** Marika Somogyi **Rev:** Eagle with sheild and ribbon **Rev. Designer:** John Mercanti

Date	UNC Mintage	Proof Mintage	MS-65	Prf-65
2001P	66,636	—	40.80	—
2001P	—	143,793	—	40.80

KM# 313 LEIF ERICSON   Obv:** Ericson bust helmeted right **Obv. Designer:** John Mercanti **Rev:** Viking ship sailing left **Rev. Designer:** T. James Ferrell

Date	UNC Mintage	Proof Mintage	MS-65	Prf-65
2000P	28,150	—	69.00	—
2000 Iceland	—	15,947	—	26.80
2000P	—	58,612	—	62.50

KM# 325 NATIVE AMERICAN - BISON
Obv: Native American bust right **Rev:** Bison standing left **Designer:** James E. Fraser

Date	UNC Mintage	Proof Mintage	MS-65	Prf-65
2001D	197,131	—	165	—
2001P	—	272,869	—	169

KM# 336 2002 WINTER OLYMPICS - SALT LAKE CITY Obv: Salt Lake City Olympic logo Obv. Designer: John Mercanti Rev: Stylized skyline with mountains in background Rev. Designer: Donna Weaver

Date	UNC Mintage	Proof Mintage	MS-65	Prf-65
2002P	35,388	—	40.80	—
2002P	—	142,873	—	38.30

KM# 349 FIRST FLIGHT CENTENNIAL Obv: Orville and Wilbur Wright busts left Obv. Designer: T. James Ferrell Rev: Wright Flyer over dunes Rev. Designer: Norman E. Nemeth

Date	UNC Mintage	Proof Mintage	MS-65	Prf-65
2003P	53,761	—	40.80	—
2003P	—	193,086	—	46.80

KM# 338 U.S. MILITARY ACADEMY AT WEST POINT -BICENTENNIAL Obv: Cadet Review flagbearers, Academy buildings in background Obv. Designer: T. James Ferrell Rev: Academy emblems - Corinthian helmet and sword Rev. Designer: John Mercanti

Date	UNC Mintage	Proof Mintage	MS-65	Prf-65
2002W	103,201	—	38.30	—
2002W	—	288,293	—	39.80

KM# 362 THOMAS A. EDISON - ELECTRIC LIGHT 125TH ANNIVERSARY Obv: Edison half-length figure facing holding light bulb Obv. Designer: Donna Weaver Rev: Light bulb and rays Rev. Designer: John Mercanti

Date	UNC Mintage	Proof Mintage	MS-65	Prf-65
2004P	68,031	—	40.80	—
2004P	—	213,409	—	41.80

KM# 363 LEWIS AND CLARK CORPS OF DISCOVERY BICENTENNIAL Obv: Lewis and Clark standing Rev: Jefferson era clasped hands peace medal Designer: Donna Weaver

Date	UNC Mintage	Proof Mintage	MS-65	Prf-65
2004P	90,323	—	40.80	—
2004P	—	288,492	—	46.80

KM# 376 U.S. MARINE CORPS, 230TH ANNIVERSARY Obv: Flag Raising at Mt. Suribachi on Iwo Jima Obv. Designer: Norman E. Nemeth Rev: Marine Corps emblem Rev. Designer: Charles Vickers

Date	UNC Mintage	Proof Mintage	MS-65	Prf-65
2005P	130,000	—	48.00	—
2005P	—	370,000	—	52.50

KM# 375 JOHN MARSHALL, 250TH BIRTH ANNIVERSARY Obv: Marshall bust left Obv. Designer: John Mercanti Rev: Marshall era Supreme Court Chamber Rev. Designer: Donna Weaver

Date	UNC Mintage	Proof Mintage	MS-65	Prf-65
2005P	48,953	—	37.30	—
2005P	—	141,993	—	35.80

KM# 387 BENJAMIN FRANKLIN, 300TH BIRTH ANNIVERSARY Obv: Youthful Franklin flying kite Obv. Designer: Norman E. Nemeth Rev: Revolutionary era "JOIN, or DIE" snake cartoon illustration Rev. Designer: Charles Vickers

Date	UNC Mintage	Proof Mintage	MS-65	Prf-65
2006P	58,000	—	40.80	—
2006P	—	142,000	—	45.00

KM# 388 BENJAMIN FRANKLIN, 300TH BIRTH
ANNIVERSARY Obv: Bust 3/4 right, signature in oval below **Obv. Designer:** Don Everhart II
Rev: Continental Dollar of 1776 in center
Rev. Designer: Donna Weaver

Date	UNC Mintage	Proof Mintage	MS-65	Prf-65
2006P	58,000		40.80	—
2006P	—	142,000	—	51.00

KM# 405 JAMESTOWN - 400TH ANNIVERSARY
Obv: Two settlers and Native American **Obv. Designer:** Donna Weaver and Don Everhart II
Rev: Three ships **Rev. Designer:** Susan Gamble and Charles Vickers

Date	UNC Mintage	Proof Mintage	MS-65	Prf-65
2007P	79,801	—	40.80	—
2007P	—	258,802	—	38.30

KM# 394 SAN FRANCISCO MINT MUSEUM
Obv: 3/4 view of building **Obv. Designer:** Sherl J. Winter **Rev:** Reverse of 1880s Morgan silver dollar **Rev. Designer:** George T. Morgan

Date	UNC Mintage	Proof Mintage	MS-65	Prf-65
2006S	65,609	—	40.80	—
2006S	—	255,700	—	40.80

KM# 418 CENTRAL HIGH SCHOOL
DESEGREGATION Obv: Children's feet walking left with adult feet in military boots **Obv. Designer:** Richard Masters and Charles Vickers **Rev:** Little Rock's Central High School **Rev. Designer:** Don Everhart II

Date	UNC Mintage	Proof Mintage	MS-65	Prf-65
2007P	66,093	—	40.80	—
2007P	—	124,618	—	43.00

COMMEMORATIVES

KM# 439 AMERICAN BALD EAGLE
Obv: Eagle with flight, mountain in background at right **Obv. Designer:** Joel Iskowitz and Don Everhart II **Rev:** Great Seal of the United States **Rev. Designer:** James Licaretz

Date	UNC Mintage	Proof Mintage	MS-65	Prf-65
2008P	110,073	—	44.00	—
2008P	—	243,558	—	38.30

KM# 454 LINCOLN BICENTENNIAL
Obv: 3/4 portrait facing right **Obv. Designer:** Justin Kunz and Don Everhart II **Rev:** Part of Gettysburg Address within wreath **Rev. Designer:** Phebe Hemphill

Date	UNC Mintage	Proof Mintage	MS-65	Prf-65
2009P	125,000	—	55.00	—
2009P	—	375,000	—	55.00

KM# 479 AMERICAN VETERANS DISABLED FOR LIFE
Obv: Soldier's feet, crutches **Obv. Designer:** Don Everhart II **Rev:** Legend within wreath **Rev. Designer:** Thomas Cleveland and Joseph Menna

Date	UNC Mintage	Proof Mintage	MS-65	Prf-65
2010W	77,859	—	40.80	—
2010W	—	189,881	—	42.30

KM# 455 LOUIS BRAILLE BIRTH BICENTENNIAL
Obv: Louis Braille bust facing **Obv. Designer:** Joel Iskowitz and Phebe Hemphill **Rev:** School child reading book in Braille, BRL in Braille code above **Rev. Designer:** Susan Gamble and Joseph Menna

Date	UNC Mintage	Proof Mintage	MS-65	Prf-65
2009P	82,639	—	38.50	—
2009P	—	135,235	—	38.30

KM# 480 BOY SCOUTS OF AMERICA, 100TH ANNIVERSARY
Obv: Cub Scout, Boy Scout and Venturer saluting **Obv. Designer:** Donna Weaver **Rev:** Boy Scouts of America logo **Rev. Designer:** Jim Licaretz

Date	UNC Mintage	Proof Mintage	MS-65	Prf-65
2010P	—	—	38.50	—
2010P	—	—	—	42.00

KM# 504 MEDAL OF HONOR
Obv: Medal of Honor designs for Army, Navy and Air Force awards **Obv. Designer:** James Licaretz **Rev:** Army infantry doldier carrying another to safety **Rev. Designer:** Richard Masters and Phebe Hemphill

Date	UNC Mintage	Proof Mintage	MS-65	Prf-65
2011S	44,769	—	46.50	—
2011S	—	112,850	—	43.50

KM# 507 U.S. ARMY Obv: Male and femlae soldier heads looking outward **Obv. Designer:** Richard Masters and Michael Gaudioso **Rev:** Seven core values of the Army, Eagle from the great seal **Rev. Designer:** Susan Gamble and Don Everhart, II

Date	UNC Mintage	Proof Mintage	MS-65	Prf-65
2011S	—	—	45.00	—
2011S	—	—	—	43.50

KM# 529 NATIONAL INFANTRY MUSEUM AND SOLDIER CENTER

Date	UNC Mintage	Proof Mintage	MS-65	Prf-65
2012	—	—	—	—
2012	—	—	—	—

KM# 530 STAR-SPANGLED BANNER

Date	UNC Mintage	Proof Mintage	MS-65	Prf-65
2012	—	—	—	—
2012	—	—	—	—

$5 (HALF EAGLE)

KM# 215 STATUE OF LIBERTY CENTENNIAL
Obv: Statue of Liberty head right **Rev:** Eagle in flight left **Designer:** Elizabeth Jones

Date	UNC Mintage	Proof Mintage	MS-65	Prf-65
1986W	95,248	—	442	—
1986W	—	404,013	—	442

KM# 221 CONSTITUTION BICENTENNIAL
Obv: Eagle left with quill pen in talon **Rev:** Upright quill pen **Designer:** Marcel Jovine

Date	UNC Mintage	Proof Mintage	MS-65	Prf-65
1987W	214,225	—	442	—
1987W	—	651,659	—	442

KM# 223 1988 OLYMPICS Obv: Nike head wearing olive wreath **Obv. Designer:** Elizabeth Jones **Rev:** Stylized olympic couldron **Rev. Designer:** Marcel Jovine

Date	UNC Mintage	Proof Mintage	MS-65	Prf-65
1988W	62,913	—	442	—
1988W	—	281,456	—	442

KM# 226 CONGRESS BICENTENNIAL Obv: Capitol dome **Rev:** Eagle atop of the canopy from the Old Senate Chamber **Designer:** John Mercanti

Date	UNC Mintage	Proof Mintage	MS-65	Prf-65
1989W	46,899	—	442	—
1989W	—	164,690	—	442

KM# 230 MOUNT RUSHMORE 50TH ANNIVERSARY Obv: Eagle in flight towards Mount Rushmore **Obv. Designer:** John Mercanti **Rev:** Legend at center **Rev. Designer:** Robert Lamb and William C. Cousins

Date	UNC Mintage	Proof Mintage	MS-65	Prf-65
1991W	31,959	—	442	—
1991W	—	111,991	—	442

KM# 235 1992 OLYMPICS Obv: Sprinter, U.S. Flag in background **Obv. Designer:** James C. Sharpe and T. James Ferrell **Rev:** Heraldic eagle, olympic rings above **Rev. Designer:** James M. Peed

Date	UNC Mintage	Proof Mintage	MS-65	Prf-65
1992W	27,732	—	442	—
1992W	—	77,313	—	442

KM# 239 COLUMBUS QUINCENTENARY Obv: Columbus' profile left, at right, map of Western Hemisphere at left **Obv. Designer:** T. James Ferrell **Rev:** Arms of Spain, and parchment map **Rev. Designer:** Thomas D. Rogers, Sr.

Date	UNC Mintage	Proof Mintage	MS-65	Prf-65
1992W	79,730	—	—	442
1992W	24,329	—	442	—

COMMEMORATIVES

COMMEMORATIVES

KM# 242 JAMES MADISON - BILL OF RIGHTS
Obv: Madison at left holding document **Obv.**
Designer: Scott R. Blazek **Rev:** Eagle above
legend, torch and laurel at sides **Rev. Designer:**
Joseph D. Peña

Date	UNC Mintage	Proof Mintage	MS-65	Prf-65
1993W	—	78,651	—	442
1993W	22,266	—	442	—

KM# 245 WORLD WAR II 50TH ANNIVERSARY
Obv: Soldier with expression of victory **Obv.**
Designer: Charles J. Madsen and T. James Ferrell
Rev: Morse code dot-dot-dot-dash for V, large in
background; V for Victory **Rev. Designer:** Edward
S. Fisher and T. James Ferrell

Date	UNC Mintage	Proof Mintage	MS-65	Prf-65
1993W	—	65,461	—	442
1993W	23,089	—	442	—

KM# 248 1994 WORLD CUP SOCCER
Obv: World Cup trophy **Obv. Designer:** William J.
Krawczewicz **Rev:** World Cup 94 logo **Rev.**
Designer: Dean McMullen

Date	UNC Mintage	Proof Mintage	MS-65	Prf-65
1994W	22,464	—	442	—
1994W	—	89,619	—	442

KM# 256 CIVIL WAR **Obv:** Bugler on horseback
right **Rev:** Eagle on shield **Designer:** Don Troiani
and Alfred F. Maletsky

Date	UNC Mintage	Proof Mintage	MS-65	Prf-65
1995W	12,735	—	950	—
1995W	—	55,246	—	442

KM# 261 1996 OLYMPICS - TORCH RUNNER
Obv: Torch runner, Atlanta skyline and logo in
background **Rev:** Eagle advancing right **Designer:**
Frank Gasparro

Date	UNC Mintage	Proof Mintage	MS-65	Prf-65
1995W	—	57,442	—	442
1995W	14,675	—	885	—

KM# 265 1996 OLYMPICS - STADIUM
Obv: Atlanta Stadium and logo **Obv. Designer:**
Marvel Jovine and William C. Cousins **Rev:** Eagle
advancing right **Rev. Designer:** Frank Gasparro

Date	UNC Mintage	Proof Mintage	MS-65	Prf-65
1995W	—	43,124	—	442
1995W	10,579	—	2,500	—

KM# 270 1996 OLYMPICS - CAULDRON
Obv: Torch bearer lighting cauldron **Obv.**
Designer: Frank Gasparro and T. James Ferrell
Rev: Atlanta Olympics logo flanked by laurel **Rev.**
Designer: William J. Krawczewicz and Thomas D.
Rogers, Sr.

Date	UNC Mintage	Proof Mintage	MS-65	Prf-65
1996W	—	38,555	—	442
1996W	9,210	—	2,600	—

KM# 274 1996 OLYMPICS - FLAG BEARER
Obv: Flag bearer advancing **Obv. Designer:**
Patricia Verani and John Mercanti **Rev:** Atlanta
Olympic logo flanked by laurel **Rev. Designer:**
William J. Krawczewicz and Thomas D. Rogers, Sr.

Date	UNC Mintage	Proof Mintage	MS-65	Prf-65
1996W	—	32,886	—	442
1996W	9,174	—	2,600	—

KM# 277 SMITHSONIAN INSTITUTION 150TH ANNIVERSARY Obv: Smithson bust left Obv. Designer: Alfred Maletsky Rev: Sunburst museum logo Rev. Designer: T. James Ferrell

Date	UNC Mintage	Proof Mintage	MS-65	Prf-65
1996W	9,068	—	850	—
1996W	—	29,474	—	442

KM# 280 JACKIE ROBINSON
Obv: Robinson head right Obv. Designer: William C. Cousins Rev: Legend on baseball Rev. Designer: James M. Peed

Date	UNC Mintage	Proof Mintage	MS-65	Prf-65
1997W	5,202	—	2,900	—
1997W	—	24,072	—	590

KM# 282 FRANKLIN DELANO ROOSEVELT
Obv: Roosevelt bust right Obv. Designer: T. James Ferrell Rev: Eagle shield Rev. Designer: James M. Peed and Thomas D. Rogers, Sr.

Date	UNC Mintage	Proof Mintage	MS-65	Prf-65
1997W	11,894	—	1,275	—
1997W	—	29,474	—	442

KM# 300 GEORGE WASHINGTON DEATH BICENTENNIAL Obv: Washington's head right Rev: Eagle with wings outstretched Designer: Laura G. Fraser

Date	UNC Mintage	Proof Mintage	MS-65	Prf-65
1999W	22,511	—	452	—
1999W	—	41,693	—	447

KM# 326 CAPITOL VISITOR CENTER
Obv: Column at right Rev: First Capital building Designer: Elizabeth Jones

Date	UNC Mintage	Proof Mintage	MS-65	Prf-65
2001W	6,761	—	1,750	—
2001W	—	27,652	—	442

KM# 337 2002 WINTER OLYMPICS
Obv: Salt Lake City Olympics logo Rev: Stylized cauldron Designer: Donna Weaver

Date	UNC Mintage	Proof Mintage	MS-65	Prf-65
2002W	10,585	—	452	—
2002W	—	32,877	—	442

KM# 395 SAN FRANCISCO MINT MUSEUM
Obv: Front entrance façade Obv. Designer: Charles Vickers and Joseph Menna Rev: Eagle as on 1860's $5. Gold Rev. Designer: Christian Gobrecht

Date	UNC Mintage	Proof Mintage	MS-65	Prf-65
2006S	16,230	—	442	—
2006S	—	41,517	—	442

KM# 406 JAMESTOWN - 400TH ANNIVERSARY
Obv: Settler and Native American Obv. Designer: John Mercanti Rev: Jamestown Memorial Church ruins Rev. Designer: Susan Gamble and Norman Nemeth

Date	UNC Mintage	Proof Mintage	MS-65	Prf-65
2007W	18,843	—	442	—
2007W	—	47,050	—	442

COMMEMORATIVES

KM# 440 AMERICAN BALD EAGLE
Obv: Two eagles on branch **Obv. Designer:** Susan Gamble adn Phebe Hemphill **Rev:** Eagle with shield **Rev. Designer:** Don Everhart II

Date	UNC Mintage	Proof Mintage	MS-65	Prf-65
2008W	13,467	—	457	—
2008W	—	59,269	—	442

KM# 505 MEDAL OF HONOR
Obv: 1861 Medal of Honor design for the Navy **Obv. Designer:** Joseph Menna **Rev:** Minerva standing with shield and Union flag, field artillery canon flanking **Rev. Designer:** Joel Iskowitz and Michael Gaudioso

Date	UNC Mintage	Proof Mintage	MS-65	Prf-65
2011S	8,251	—	585	—
2011S	—	18,012	—	500

KM# 508 U.S. ARMY
Obv: Five Soldiers of different eras **Obv. Designer:** Joel Iskowitz and Phebe Hemphill **Rev:** Elements from the Army's emblem **Rev. Designer:** Joseph Menna

Date	UNC Mintage	Proof Mintage	MS-65	Prf-65
2011P	8,062	—	585	—
2011P	—	17,173	—	495

KM# 531 STAR-SPANGLED BANNER

Date	UNC Mintage	Proof Mintage	MS-65	Prf-65
2012	—	—	—	—
2012	—	—	—	—

$10 (EAGLE)

KM# 211 1984 OLYMPICS
Weight: 16.7180 g. **Composition:** 0.9000 Gold, 0.4837 oz. AGW **Diameter:** 27mm. **Obv:** Male and female runner with torch **Obv. Designer:** James M. Peed and John Mercanti **Rev:** Heraldic eagle **Rev. Designer:** John Mercanti

Date	UNC Mintage	Proof Mintage	MS-65	Prf-65
1984W	75,886	—	883	—
1984P	—	33,309	—	893
1984D	—	34,533	—	893
1984S	—	48,551	—	893
1984W	—	381,085	—	893

KM# 312 LIBRARY OF CONGRESS
Weight: 16.2590 g. **Composition:** Bi-Metallic **Obv:** Torch and partial facade **Obv. Designer:** John Mercanti **Rev:** Stylized eagle within laurel wreath **Rev. Designer:** Thomas D. Rogers, Sr.

Date	UNC Mintage	Proof Mintage	MS-65	Prf-65
2000W	6,683	—	4,500	—
2000W	—	27,167	—	1,300

KM# 350 FIRST FLIGHT CENTENNIAL
Weight: 16.7180 g. **Composition:** 0.9000 Gold, 0.4837 oz. AGW **Obv:** Orvile and Wilbur Wright busts facing **Obv. Designer:** Donna Weaver **Rev:** Wright flyer and eagle **Rev. Designer:** Norman Nemeth

Date	UNC Mintage	Proof Mintage	MS-65	Prf-65
2003P	10,129	—	1,050	—
2003P	—	21,846	—	893

$20 (DOUBLE EAGLE)

KM# 464   **Weight:** 31.1050 g. **Composition:** 0.9990 Gold, 0.9990 oz. AGW **Diameter:** 27mm. **Obv:** Ultra high relief Liberty holding torch, walking forward **Rev:** Eagle in flight left, sunrise in background **Designer:** Augustus Saint-Gaudens

Date	UNC Mintage	Proof Mintage	MS-65	Prf-65
2009	115,178	—	2,750	—

MODERN COMMEMORATIVE COIN SETS

Olympic, 1983-1984

Date	Price
1983 & 1984 3 coin set: 1983 and one 1984 uncirculated dollar and 1984W uncirculated gold $10; KM209, 210, 211.	952
1983S & 1984S 3 coin set: proof 1983 and 1984 dollar and 1984W gold $10; KM209, 210, 211.	956
1983 & 1984 6 coin set in a cherrywood box: 1983S and 1984S uncirculated and proof dollars, 1984W uncirculated and proof gold $10; KM209, 210, 211.	1,909
1983S & 1984S 2 coin set: proof dollars.	74.00
1983 collectors 3 coin set: 1983 PDS uncirculated dollars; KM209.	104
1984 collectors 3 coin set: 1984 PDS uncirculated dollars; KM210.	105

Statue of Liberty

Date	Price
1986 2 coin set: uncirculated silver dollar and clad half dollar; KM212, 214.	38.00
1986 2 coin set: proof silver dollar and clad half dollar; KM212, 214.	40.00
1986 3 coin set: uncirculated silver dollar, clad half dollar and gold $5; KM212, 214, 215.	480
1986 3 coin set: proof silver dollar, clad half dollar and gold $5; KM212, 214, 215.	483
1986 6 coin set: 1 each of the proof and uncirculated issues; KM212, 214, 215.	963

Constitution

Date	Price
1987 2 coin set: uncirculated silver dollar and gold $5; KM220, 221.	477
1987 2 coin set: proof silver dollar and gold $5; KM220, 221.	479
1987 4 coin set: silver dollar and $5 gold proof and uncirculated issues; KM220, 221.	958

Olympic, 1988

Date	Price
1988 2 coin set: uncirculated silver dollar and gold $5; KM222, 223.	477
1988 2 coin set: proof silver dollar and gold $5; KM222, 223.	479
1988 4 coin set: silver dollar and $5 gold proof and uncirculated issues; KM222, 223.	958

Congress

Date	Price
1989 2 coin set: uncirculated silver dollar and clad half dollar; KM224, 225.	42.00
1989 2 coin set: proof silver dollar and clad half dollar; KM224, 225.	44.00
1989 3 coin set: uncirculated silver dollar, clad half and gold $5; KM224, 225, 226.	485
1989 3 coin set: proof silver dollar, clad half and gold $5; KM224, 225, 226.	487
1989 6 coin set: 1 each of the proof and uncirculated issues; KM224, 225, 226.	973

Mt. Rushmore

Date	Price
1991 2 coin set: uncirculated half dollar and silver dollar; KM228, 229.	57.00
1991 2 coin set: proof half dollar and silver dollar; KM228, 229.	60.00
1991 3 coin set: uncirculated half dollar, silver dollar and gold $5; KM228, 229, 230.	500
1991 3 coin set: proof half dollar, silver dollar and gold $5; KM228, 229, 230.	502
1991 6 coin set: 1 each of proof and uncirculated issues; KM228, 229, 230.	1,004

Olympic, 1992

Date	Price
1992 2 coin set: uncirculated half dollar and silver dollar; KM233, 234.	46.00
1992 2 coin set: proof half dollar and silver dollar; KM233, 234.	47.00
1992 3 coin set: uncirculated half dollar, silver dollar and gold $5; KM233, 234, 235.	489
1992 3 coin set: proof half dollar, silver dollar and gold $5; KM233, 234, 235.	490
1992 6 coin set: 1 each of proof and uncirculated issues; KM233, 234, 235.	978

Columbus Quincentenary

Date	Price
1992 2 coin set: uncirculated half dollar and silver dollar; KM237, 238.	52.00
1992 2 coin set: proof half dollar and silver dollar; KM237, 238.	47.00
1992 3 coin set: uncirculated half dollar, silver dollar and gold $5; KM237, 238, 239.	495
1992 3 coin set: proof half dollar, silver dollar and gold $5; KM237, 238, 239.	489
1992 6 coin set: 1 each of proof and uncirculated issues; KM237, 238, 239.	985

Jefferson

Date	Price
1993 Jefferson: dollar, 1994 matte proof nickel and $2 note; KM249, 192.	109

Madison / Bill of Rights

Date	Price
1993 2 coin set: uncirculated half dollar and silver dollar; KM240, 241.	57.00
1993 2 coin set: proof half dollar and silver dollar; KM240, 241.	58.00
1993 3 coin set: uncirculated half dollar, silver dollar and gold $5; KM240, 241, 242.	499
1993 3 coin set: proof half dollar, silver dollar and gold $5; KM240, 241, 242.	500
1993 6 coin set: 1 each of proof and uncirculated issues; KM240, 241, 242.	999
Coin and stamp set; KM#240 and 20c stamp	21.00

COMMEMORATIVE SETS

COMMEMORATIVE SETS

World War II

Date	Price
1993 2 coin set: uncirculated half dollar and silver dollar; KM243, 244.	54.00
1993 2 coin set: proof half dollar and silver dollar; KM243, 244.	57.00
1993 3 coin set: uncirculated half dollar, silver dollar and gold $5; KM243, 244, 245.	496
1993 3 coin set: proof half dollar, silver dollar and gold $5; KM243, 244, 245.	500
1993 6 coin set: 1 each of proof and uncirculated issues; KM243, 244, 245.	1,000

U.S. Veterans

Date	Price
1994 3 coin set: uncirculated POW, Vietnam, Women dollars; KM250, 251, 252.	202
1994 3 coin set: proof POW, Vietnam, Women dollars; KM250, 251, 252.	142

World Cup

Date	Price
1994 2 coin set: uncirculated half dollar and silver dollar; KM246, 247.	48.00
1994 2 coin set: proof half dollar and silver dollar; KM246, 247.	45.00
1994 3 coin set: uncirculated half dollar, silver dollar and gold $5; KM246, 247, 248.	490
1994 3 coin set: proof half dollar, silver dollar and gold $5; KM246, 247, 248.	487
1994 6 coin set: 1 each of proof and uncirculated issues; KM246, 247, 248.	983

Olympic, 1995-96

Date	Price
1995 4 coin set: uncirculated basketball half, $1 gymnast & blind runner, $5 torch runner; KM257, 259, 260, 261.	1,024
1995 4 coin set: proof basketball half, $1 gymnast & blind runner, $5 torch runner; KM257, 259, 260, 261.	533
1995P 2 coin set: proof $1 gymnast & blind runner; KM259, 260.	82.00
1995P 2 coin set: proof $1 track & field, cycling; KM263, 264.	84.00
1995-96 4 coin set: proof halves, basketball, baseball, swimming, soccer; KM257, 262, 267, 271.	75.00
1995 & 96 8 coins in cherry wood case: proof silver dollars: blind runner, gymnast, cycling, track & field, wheelchair, tennis, rowing, high jump; KM259, 260, 263, 264, 268, 269, 272, 272A.	425
1995 & 96 16 coins in cherry wood case: bu and proof silver dollars: blind runner, gymnast, cycling, track & field, wheelchair, tennis, rowing, high jump; KM259, 260, 263, 264, 268, 269, 272, 272A.	10,400
1995 & 96 16 coins in cherry wood case: proof half dollars: basketball, baseball, swimming, soccer, KM257, 262, 267, 271. Proof silver dollars: blind runner, gymnast, cycling, track & field, wheelchair, tennis, rowing, high jump, KM259, 260, 263, 264, 268, 269, 272, 272A. Proof $5 gold: torch runner, stadium, cauldron, flag bearer, KM 261, 265, 270, 274.	2,370
1995 & 96 32 coins in cherry wood case: bu & proof half dollars: basketball, baseball, swimming, soccer, KM257, 262, 267, 271. BU & proof silver dollars: blind runner, gymnast, cycling, track & field, wheelchair, tennis, rowing, high jump, KM259, 260, 263, 264, 268, 269, 272, 272A. BU & proof $5 gold: torch runner, stadium, cauldron, flag bearer, KM261, 265, 270, 274.	12,800
Young collector 4 coin set; Half dollars: KM#257, 262, 267, 271	205
1996P 2 coin set: proof $1 wheelchair & tennis; KM268, 269.	154
1996P 2 coin set: proof $1 rowing & high jump; KM272, 272A.	105

Civil War

Date	Price
1995 2 coin set: uncirculated half and dollar; KM254, 255.	102
1995 2 coin set: proof half and dollar; KM254, 255.	88.00
1995 3 coin set: uncirculated half, dollar and gold $5; KM254, 255, 256.	1,055
1995 3 coin set: proof half, dollar and gold $5; KM254, 255, 256.	530
1995 6 coin set: 1 each of proof and uncirculated issues; KM254, 255, 256.	1,585
Civil War Young Collectors set KM#245	37.50

Smithsonian

Date	Price
1996 2 coin set: proof dollar and $5 gold; KM276, 277.	495
1996 4 coin set: proof and B.U. ; KM276, 277.	1,465

Franklin Delano Roosevelt

Date	Price
1997W 2 coin set: uncirculated and proof; KM282.	3,500

Jackie Robinson

Date	Price
1997 2 coin set: proof dollar & $5 gold; KM279, 280.	680
1997 4 coin set: proof & BU; KM279, 280.	3,660
1997 legacy set.	650

Botanic Garden

Date	Price
1997 2 coin set: dollar, Jefferson nickel and $1 note; KM278, 192.	220

Black Patriots

Date	Price
1998S 2 coin set: uncirculated and proof; KM288.	220

Kennedy

Date	Price
1998 2 coin set: proof; KM287.	88.00
1998 2 coin collectors set: Robert Kennedy dollar and John Kennedy half dollar; KM287, 202b. Matte finished.	225

Dolley Madison

Date	Price
1999 2 coin set: proof and uncirculated silver dollars; KM298.	76.00

Yellowstone National Park

Date	Price
1999 2 coin set: proof and uncirculated silver dollars; KM299.	84.00

George Washington

Date	Price
1999 2 coin set: proof and uncirculated gold $5; KM300.	900

Millennium Coin & Currency

Date	Price
2000 2 coin set: uncirculated Sacagewea $1, silver Eagle & $1 note.	67.50

Leif Ericson

Date	Price
2000 2 coin set: proof and uncirculated silver dollars; KM313.	85.00

American Buffalo

Date	Price
2001 2 coin set: 90% silver unc. & proof $1.; KM325.	330
2001 coin & currency set 90% unc. dollar & replicas of 1899 $5 silver cert.; KM325.	180

Capitol Visitor Center

Date	Price
2001 3 coin set: proof half, silver dollar, gold $5; KM323, 324, 326.	495

Winter Olympics - Salt Lake City

Date	Price
2002 2 coin set: proof 90% silver dollar KM336 & $5.00 Gold KM337.	465
2002 4 coin set: 90% silver unc. & proof $1, KM336 & unc. & proof gold $5, KM337.	925

Thomas Alva Edison

Date	Price
2004 Uncirculated silver dollar and light bulb.	55.00

Lewis and Clark Bicentennial

Date	Price
2004 Coin and pouch set.	65.00
2004 coin and currency set: Uncirculated silver dollar, two 2005 nickels, replica 1901 $10 Bison note, silver plated peace medal, three stamps & two booklets.	58.00
2004 Westward Journey Nickel series coin and medal set: Proof Sacagawea dollar, two 2005 proof nickels and silver plated peace medal.	40.00

Chief Justice John Marshall

Date	Price
2005 Coin and Chronicles set: Uncirculated silver dollar, booklet and BEP intaglio portrait.	57.00

U.S. Marine Corps

Date	Price
2005 Uncirculated silver dollar and stamp set.	63.00

Benjamin Franklin Tercentennary

Date	Price
2006 Coin and Chronicles set: Uncirculated "Scientist" silver dollar, four stamps, Poor Richards Almanac and intaglio print.	49.00

Central High School Desegregation

Date	Price
2007 Little Rock Dollar and medal set, KM#418	47.80

American Bald Eagle

Date	Price
2008 Proof half dollar, dollar and $5 gold, KM438, KM439, KM440	490
2008 Bald Eagle young collector's set; Half Dollar, KM#438	23.00

Louis Braille

Date	Price
Braille Education set, KM#455	43.50

AMERICAN EAGLE SILVER BULLION

SILVER DOLLAR

KM# 273 • 31.1050 g., 0.9993 **Silver**, 0.9993 oz., 40.6mm. • **Obv. Desc:** Liberty walking left **Rev. Desc:** Eagle with shield **Obv. Designer:** Adolph A. Weinman **Rev. Designer:** John Mercanti

Date	Mintage	MS65	PRF65
1986	5,393,005	43.70	—
1986S	1,446,778	—	72.00
1987	11,442,335	40.00	—
1987S	904,732	—	72.00
1988	5,004,646	38.00	—
1988S	557,370	—	72.00
1989	5,203,327	37.20	—
1989S	617,694	—	72.00
1990	5,840,110	40.50	—
1990S	695,510	—	72.00
1991	7,191,066	37.00	—
1991S	511,924	—	72.00
1992	5,540,068	39.00	—
1992S	498,543	—	72.00
1993	6,763,762	38.00	—
1993P	405,913	—	88.00
1994	4,227,319	40.00	—
1994P	372,168	—	96.00
1995	4,672,051	40.50	—
1995P	407,822	—	90.00
1995W 10th Anniversary	30,102	—	3,600
1996	3,603,386	62.00	—
1996P	498,293	—	72.00
1997	4,295,004	41.00	—
1997P	440,315	—	72.00
1998	4,847,547	40.00	—
1998P	450,728	—	72.00
1999	7,408,640	39.00	—
1999P	549,330	—	72.00
2000P	600,743	—	65.00
2000	9,239,132	38.00	—

Date	Mintage	MS65	PRF65
2001	9,001,711	35.20	—
2001W	746,398	—	65.00
2002	10,539,026	35.20	—
2002W	647,342	—	69.00
2003	8,495,008	35.20	—
2003W	747,831	—	69.00
2004	8,882,754	35.20	—
2004W	801,602	—	75.00
2005	8,891,025	35.20	—
2005W	816,663	—	65.00
2006	10,676,522	36.50	—
2006W	1,093,600	—	65.00
2006P Reverse Proof	—	—	265
2006W Burnished Unc.	468,000	85.00	—
2006 20th Aniv. 3 pc. set	—	—	385
2007	9,028,036	35.50	—
2007W	821,759	—	65.00
2007W Burnished Unc.	690,891	39.20	—
2008	20,583,000	35.20	—
2008W Reverse of '07, U in United with rounded bottom.	—	475	—
2008	713,353	—	65.00
2008W Burnished Unc.	—	65.00	—
2009	30,459,000	35.20	—
2010	34,764,500	35.20	—
2010	—	—	65.00
2011	—	38.20	—
2011P Reverse Proof	100,000	—	275
2011S Unc.	100,000	285	—
2011W Burnished Unc.	100,000	50.00	—
2011W Proof	100,000	—	63.00
2012	—	35.20	—
2012 Reverse Proof	—	—	125
2012P Proof	—	—	90.00
2012W Burnished Unc.	—	55.00	—

AMERICA THE BEAUTIFUL SILVER BULLION

SILVER QUARTER

KM# 489 • 155.5500 g., 0.9990 **Silver**, 4.9958 oz. • **Subject:** Hot Springs, Ark. **Rev. Desc:** Park Headquarters and fountain **Rev. Designer:** Don Everhart II and Joseph Menna

Date	Mintage	MS65	PRF65
2010	33,000	290	—
2010P Vapor Blast finish	27,000	250	—

KM# 490 • 155.5500 g., 0.9990 **Silver**, 4.9958 oz. • **Subject:** Yellowstone National Park **Rev. Desc:**

Old Faithful geyser and bison **Rev. Designer:** Don Everhart II

Date	Mintage	MS65	PRF65
2010	33,000	275	—
2010P Vapor Blast finish	27,000	240	—

KM# 491 • 155.5500 g., 0.9990 **Silver**, 4.9958 oz. • **Subject:** Yosemite National Park **Rev. Desc:** El Capitan, largest monolith of granite in the world **Rev. Designer:** Joseph Menna and Phebe Hemphill

BULLION COINS

Date	Mintage	MS65	PRF65
2010	33,000	275	—
2010P Vapor blast finish	27,000	225	—

KM# 492 • 155.5500 g., 0.9990 **Silver**, 4.9958 oz.
• **Subject:** Grand Canyon National Park **Rev.**
Desc: Grabarues above the Nankoweap Delta in
Marble Canyon near the Colorado River **Rev.**
Designer: Phebe Hemphill

Date	Mintage	MS65	PRF65
2010	33,000	250	—
2010P Vapor blast finish	26,019	225	—

KM# 493 • 155.5500 g., 0.9990 **Silver**, 4.9958 oz.
• **Subject:** Mount Hood National Park **Rev. Desc:**
Mt. Hood with Lost Lake in the foreground **Rev.**
Designer: Phebe Hemphill

Date	Mintage	MS65	PRF65
2010	33,000	275	—
2010P Vapor blast finish	25,318	200	—

KM# 513 • 155.5500 g., 0.9990 **Silver**, 4.9958 oz.
• **Subject:** Gettysburg National Military Park **Rev.**
Desc: 72nd Pennsylvania Infantry Monumnet on
the battle line of the Union Army at Cemetery Ridge
Rev. Designer: Joel Iskowitz and Phebe Hemphill

Date	Mintage	MS65	PRF65
2011	126,700	200	—
2011P Vapor blast finish	24,625	190	—

KM# 514 • 155.5500 g., 0.9990 **Silver**, 4.9958 oz.
• **Subject:** Glacier National Park **Rev. Desc:**
Northeast slope of Mount Reynolds **Rev. Designer:**
Barbara Fox and Charles L. Vickers

Date	Mintage	MS65	PRF65
2011	126,700	200	—
2011P Vapor blast finish	20,503	190	—

KM# 515 • 155.5500 g., 0.9990 **Silver**, 4.9958 oz.
• **Subject:** Olympic National Park **Rev. Desc:**
Roosevelt elk on a gravel river bar along the Hoh
River, Mount Olympus in the background **Rev.**
Designer: Susan Gambel and Michael Gaudioso

Date	Mintage	MS65	PRF65
2011	85,900	200	—
2011P Vapor blast finish	17,988	190	—

KM# 516 • 155.5500 g., 0.9990 **Silver**, 4.9958 oz.
• **Subject:** Vicksburg National Military Park **Rev.**
Desc: U.S.S. Cairo on the Yazoo River **Rev.**
Designer: Thomas Cleveland and Joseph menna

Date	Mintage	MS65	PRF65
2011	39,500	200	—
2011P Vapor blast finish	18,181	190	—

KM# 517 • 155.5500 g., 0.9990 **Silver**, 4.9958 oz.
• **Subject:** Chickasaw National Recreation Area
Rev. Desc: Limestone Lincoln Bridge **Rev.**
Designer: Donna Weaver and James Licaretz

Date	Mintage	MS65	PRF65
2011	29,700	200	—
2011P Vapor blast finish	16,386	190	—

KM# 536 • 155.5500 g., 0.9990 **Silver**, 4.9958 oz.
• **Subject:** El Yungue National Forest

Date	Mintage	MS65	PRF65
2012	21,900	200	—
2012P Vapor blast finish	15,271	190	—

KM# 537 • 155.5200 g., 0.9990 **Silver**, 4.9949 oz.
• **Subject:** Chaco Culture National Historic Park

Date	Mintage	MS65	PRF65
2012	20,000	200	—
2012P Vapor blast finish	12,679	190	—

KM# 538 • 155.5200 g., 0.9990 **Silver**, 4.9949 oz.
• **Subject:** Acadia National Park

Date	Mintage	MS65	PRF65
2012	25,400	200	—
2012P Vapor blast finish	13,196	190	—

KM# 539 • 155.5200 g., 0.9990 **Silver**, 4.9949 oz.
• **Subject:** Hawaii Volcanoes National Park

Date	Mintage	MS65	PRF65
2012	20,000	200	—
2012P Vapor blast finish	13,789	190	—

KM# 540 • 155.5520 g., 0.9990 **Silver**, 4.9959 oz.
• **Subject:** Denali National Park

Date	Mintage	MS65	PRF65
2012	20,000	200	—
2012P Vapor blast finish	10,180	190	—

BULLION COINS

AMERICAN EAGLE GOLD BULLION

GOLD $5

KM# 216 • 3.3930 g., 0.9167 **Gold**, 0.1000 oz.,
16.5mm. • **Obv. Designer:** Augustus Saint-
Gaudens **Rev. Designer:** Miley Busiek

Date	Mintage	MS65	PRF65
MCMLXXXVI (1986)	912,609	197	—
MCMLXXXVII (1987)	580,266	197	—
MCMLXXXVIII (1988)	159,500	197	—
MCMLXXXVIII (1988)P	143,881	—	213
MCMLXXXIX (1989)	264,790	255	—
MCMLXXXIX (1989)P	84,647	—	213
MCMXC (1990)	210,210	197	—
MCMXC (1990)P	99,349	—	213
MCMXCI (1991)	165,200	245	—
MCMXCI (1991)P	70,334	—	213
1992	209,300	197	—
1992P	64,874	—	213

Date	Mintage	MS65	PRF65
1993	210,709	197	—
1993P	45,960	—	213
1994	206,380	197	—
1994W	62,849	—	213
1995	223,025	197	—
1995W	62,667	—	213
1996	401,964	197	—
1996W	57,047	—	213
1997	528,515	220	—
1997W	34,977	—	213
1998	1,344,520	220	—
1998W	39,395	—	213
1999	2,750,338	197	—
1999W	48,428	—	213
1999W Unfinished Proof die	—	800	—

Note: The 1999 W issues are standard matte finished gold
that were struck with unfinished proof dies.

Date	Mintage	MS65	PRF65
2000	569,153	197	—
2000W	49,971	—	213
2001	269,147	197	—
2001W	37,530	—	213
2002	230,027	245	—
2002W	40,864	—	213
2003	245,029	197	—
2003W	40,027	—	213
2004	250,016	197	—

BULLION COINS

Date	Mintage	MS65	PRF65
2004W	35,131	—	225
2005	300,043	197	—
2005W	49,265	—	225
2006	285,006	197	—
2006W	47,277	—	213
2006W Burnished Unc.	20,643	215	—
2007	190,010	197	—
2007W	58,553	—	213
2007W Burnished Unc.	22,501	175	—
2008	305,000	197	—
2008W	—	—	213
2008W Burnished Unc.	12,657	325	—
2009	27,000	197	—
2010	—	197	—
2010W	—	—	213
2011W	5,000	—	213
2011	—	197	—
2012	—	—	—

Date	Mintage	MS65	PRF65
2006W Burnished Unc.	15,188	785	—
2007	34,004	467	—
2007W	46,189	—	509
2007W Burnished Unc.	12,786	990	—
2008	—	467	—
2008W	28,000	—	509
2008W Burnished Unc.	8,883	1,750	—
2009	27,500	467	—
2010	—	467	—
2010W	—	—	509
2011W	4,000	—	509
2011	—	467	—
2012	—	467	—

GOLD $10

KM# 217 • 8.4830 g., 0.9167 Gold, 0.2500 oz. , 22mm. • Obv. Designer: Augustus Saint-Gaudens Rev. Designer: Miley Busiek

Date	Mintage	MS65	PRF65
MCMLXXXVI (1986)	726,031	550	—
MCMLXXXVII (1987)	269,255	550	—
MCMLXXXVIII (1988)	49,000	550	—
MCMLXXXVIII (1988)P	98,028	—	509
MCMLXXXIX (1989)	81,789	565	—
MCMLXXXIX (1989)P	54,170	—	509
MCMXC (1990)	41,000	550	—
MCMXC (1990)P	62,674	—	509
MCMXCI (1991)	36,100	550	—
MCMXCI (1991)P	50,839	—	509
1992	59,546	467	—
1992P	46,269	—	509
1993	71,864	467	—
1993P	33,775	—	509
1994	72,650	467	—
1994W	47,172	—	509
1995	83,752	467	—
1995W	47,526	—	509
1996	60,318	467	—
1996W	38,219	—	509
1997	108,805	467	—
1997W	29,805	—	509
1998	309,829	467	—
1998W	29,503	—	509
1999	564,232	467	—
1999W	34,417	—	509
1999W Unfinished Proof die	—	1,350	—

Note: The 1999 W issues are standard matte finished gold that were struck with unfinished proof dies.

Date	Mintage	MS65	PRF65
2000	128,964	467	—
2000W	36,036	—	509
2001	71,280	467	—
2001W	25,613	—	509
2002	62,027	467	—
2002W	29,242	—	509
2003	74,029	467	—
2003W	30,292	—	509
2004	72,014	467	—
2004W	28,839	—	509
2005	72,015	467	—
2005W	37,207	—	509
2006	60,004	467	—
2006W	36,127	—	509

GOLD $25

KM# 218 • 16.9660 g., 0.9167 Gold, 0.5000 oz. , 27mm. • Obv. Designer: Augustus Saint-Gaudens Rev. Designer: Miley Busiek

Date	Mintage	MS65	PRF65
MCMLXXXVI (1986)	599,566	995	—
MCMLXXXVII (1987)	131,255	9.40	—
MCMLXXXVII (1987)P	143,398	—	1,028
MCMLXXXVIII (1988)	45,000	1,650	—
MCMLXXXVIII (1988)P	76,528	—	1,028
MCMLXXXIX (1989)	44,829	1,700	—
MCMLXXXIX (1989)P	44,798	—	1,028
MCMXC (1990)	31,000	2,000	—
MCMXC (1990)P	51,636	—	1,028
MCMXCI (1991)	24,100	2,900	—
MCMXCI (1991)P	53,125	—	960
1992	54,404	1,100	—
1992P	40,976	—	1,028
1993	73,324	995	—
1993P	31,130	—	1,028
1994	62,400	995	—
1994W	44,584	—	1,028
1995	53,474	1,150	—
1995W	45,388	—	1,028
1996	39,287	1,500	—
1996W	35,058	—	1,028
1997	79,605	995	—
1997W	26,344	—	1,028
1998	169,029	934	—
1998W	25,374	—	1,028
1999	263,013	934	—
1999W	30,427	—	1,028
2000	79,287	995	—
2000W	32,028	—	1,028
2001	48,047	1,100	—
2001W	23,240	—	1,028
2002	70,027	995	—
2002W	26,646	—	1,028
2003	79,029	934	—
2003W	28,270	—	1,028
2004	98,040	934	—
2004W	27,330	—	1,028
2005	80,023	934	—
2005W	34,311	—	1,028
2006	66,004	937	—
2006W	34,322	—	1,028
2006W Burnished Unc.	15,164	1,650	—
2007	47,002	1,100	—
2007W	44,025	—	1,028
2007W Burnished Unc.	11,458	1,900	—
2008	61,000	937	—

Date	Mintage	MS65	PRF65
2008W	27,800	—	1,028
2008W Burnished Unc.	15,683	1,650	—
2009	55,000	937	—
2010	—	934	—
2010W	—	—	1,028
2011W	2,000	—	1,028
2011	—	934	—
2012	—	934	—

GOLD $50

KM# 219 • 33.9310 g., 0.9167 **Gold**, 100000 oz. , 32.7mm. • **Obv. Designer:** Augustus Saint-Gaudens **Rev. Designer:** Miley Busiek

Date	Mintage	MS65	PRF65
MCMLXXXVI (1986)	1,362,650	1,784	—
MCMLXXXVI (1986)W	446,290	—	1,985
MCMLXXXVII (1987)	1,045,500	1,784	—
MCMLXXXVII (1987)W	147,498	—	1,985
MCMLXXXVIII (1988)	465,000	1,784	—
MCMLXXXVIII (1988)W	87,133	—	1,985
MCMLXXXIX (1989)	415,790	1,784	—
MCMLXXXIX (1989)W	54,570	—	1,985
MCMXC (1990)	373,219	1,784	—
MCMXC (1990)W	62,401	—	1,985
MCMXCI (1991)	243,100	1,784	—
MCMXCI (1991)W	50,411	—	1,985

Date	Mintage	MS65	PRF65
1992	275,000	1,784	—
1992W	44,826	—	1,950
1993	480,192	1,784	—
1993W	34,369	—	1,950
1994	221,663	1,784	—
1994W	46,674	—	1,950
1995	200,636	1,784	—
1995W	46,368	—	1,950
1995W 10th Anniversary	—	—	—
1996	189,148	1,784	—
1996W	36,153	—	1,950
1997	664,508	1,784	—
1997W	28,034	—	1,950
1998	1,468,530	1,784	—
1998W	25,886	—	1,950
1999	1,505,026	1,784	—
1999W	31,427	—	1,950
1999W Die error	—	3,300	—

Note: The 1999 W issues are standard matte finished gold that were struck with unfinished proof dies.

Date	Mintage	MS65	PRF65
2000	433,319	1,784	—
2000W	33,007	—	1,950
2001	143,605	1,784	—
2001W	24,555	—	1,950
2002	222,029	1,784	—
2002W	27,499	—	1,950
2003	416,032	1,784	—
2003W	28,344	—	1,950
2004	417,149	1,784	—
2004W	28,215	—	1,950
2005	356,555	1,784	—
2005W	35,246	—	1,950
2006	237,510	1,784	—
2006W	47,000	—	1,950
2006W Reverse Proof	10,000	—	2,550
2006W Burnished Unc.	45,912	1,885	—
2007	140,016	1,800	—
2007W	51,810	—	1,950
2007W Burnished Unc.	18,609	1,980	—
2008W	710,000	1,784	—
2008W Proof	29,000	—	1,950
2008W Burnished Unc.	11,908	—	2,100
2008W Reverse of '07	—	—	—
2009	122,000	1,784	—
2010	—	1,784	—
2010W	—	—	1,950
2011	—	1,784	—
2011W	—	—	1,950
2011 Burnished Unc.	—	2,350	—
2012	—	1,784	—

AMERICAN EAGLE PLATINUM BULLION

PLATINUM $10

KM# 283 • 3.1100 g., 0.9995 **Platinum**, 0.0999 oz. , 17mm. • **Rev. Desc:** Eagle flying right over sunrise **Obv. Designer:** John Mercanti **Rev. Designer:** Thomas D. Rogers Sr

Date	Mintage	MS65	PRF65
1997	70,250	202	—
1997W	36,996	—	252
1998	39,525	202	—
1999	55,955	202	—
2000	34,027	202	—
2001	52,017	202	—
2002	23,005	202	—
2003	22,007	202	—

Date	Mintage	MS65	PRF65
2004	15,010	202	—
2005	14,013	202	—
2006	11,001	202	—
2006W Burnished Unc.	—	425	—
2007	13,003	285	—
2007W Burnished Unc.	—	265	—
2008	17,000	202	—
2008 Burnished Unc.	—	290	—

KM# 289 • 3.1100 g., 0.9995 **Platinum**, 0.0999 oz. • **Rev. Desc:** Eagle in flight over New England costal lighthouse **Obv. Designer:** John Mercanti

Date	Mintage	MS65	PRF65
1998W	19,847	—	247

BULLION COINS

KM# 301 • 3.1100 g., 0.9995 **Platinum**, 0.0999 oz. • **Rev. Desc:** Eagle in flight over Southeastern Wetlands **Obv. Designer:** John Mercanti

Date	Mintage	MS65	PRF65
1999W	19,133	—	247

KM# 314 • 3.1100 g., 0.9995 **Platinum**, 0.0999 oz. • **Rev. Desc:** Eagle in flight over Heartland **Obv. Designer:** John Mercanti

Date	Mintage	MS65	PRF65
2000W	15,651	—	247

KM# 327 • 3.1100 g., 0.9995 **Platinum**, 0.0999 oz. , 17mm. • **Rev. Desc:** Eagle in flight over Southwestern cactus desert **Obv. Designer:** John Mercanti

Date	Mintage	MS65	PRF65
2001W	12,174	—	247

KM# 339 • 3.1100 g., 0.9995 **Platinum**, 0.0999 oz. , 17mm. • **Rev. Desc:** Eagle fishing in America's Northwest **Obv. Designer:** John Mercanti

Date	Mintage	MS65	PRF65
2002W	12,365	—	247

KM# 351 • 3.1100 g., 0.9995 **Platinum**, 0.0999 oz. , 17mm. • **Rev. Desc:** Eagle pearched on a Rocky Mountain Pine branch against a flag backdrop **Obv. Designer:** John Mercanti **Rev. Designer:** Al Maletsky

Date	Mintage	MS65	PRF65
2003W	9,534	—	250

KM# 364 • 3.1100 g., 0.9995 **Platinum**, 0.0999 oz. , 17mm. • **Rev. Desc:** Chester French, 1907. The sculpture is outside the N.Y. Customs House, now part of the Smithsonian's Museum of the American Indian **Obv. Designer:** John Mercanti

Date	Mintage	MS65	PRF65
2004W	7,161	—	455

KM# 377 • 3.1100 g., 0.9995 **Platinum**, 0.0999 oz. , 17mm. • **Rev. Desc:** Eagle with cornucopiae **Obv. Designer:** John Mercanti **Rev. Designer:** Donna Weaver

Date	Mintage	MS65	PRF65
2005W	8,104	—	265

KM# 389 • 3.1100 g., 0.9995 **Platinum**, 0.0999 oz. , 17mm. • **Subject:** Legislative **Rev. Desc:** Liberty seated writing between two columns **Obv. Designer:** John Mercanti

Date	Mintage	MS65	PRF65
2006W	10,205	—	247

KM# 414 • 3.1100 g., 0.9995 **Platinum**, 0.0999 oz. , 17mm. • **Subject:** Executive Branch **Rev. Desc:** Eagle with shield **Obv. Designer:** John Mercanti

Date	Mintage	MS65	PRF65
2007W	8,176	—	285

KM# 434 • 3.1100 g., 0.9995 **Platinum**, 0.0999 oz. , 17mm. • **Rev. Desc:** Justice standing before eagle **Obv. Designer:** John Mercanti

Date	Mintage	MS65	PRF65
2008W	8,176	—	495

KM# 460 • 3.1100 g., 0.9995 **Platinum**, 0.0999 oz. , 17mm. • **Subject:** Judicial **Obv. Designer:** John Mercanti

Date	Mintage	MS65	PRF65
2009W	5,600	—	—

BULLION COINS

PLATINUM $25

KM# 284 • 7.7857 g., 0.9995 **Platinum**, 0.2502 oz. , 22mm. • **Rev. Desc:** Eagle in flight over sunrise **Obv. Designer:** John Mercanti **Rev. Designer:** Thomas D. Rogers Sr

Date	Mintage	MS65	PRF65
1997	27,100	502	—
1997W	18,628	—	493
1998	38,887	502	—
1999	39,734	502	—
2000	20,054	502	—
2001	21,815	502	—
2002	27,405	502	—
2003	25,207	502	—
2004	18,010	502	—
2005	12,013	502	—
2006	12,001	502	—
2006W Burnished Unc.	—	590	—
2007	8,402	502	—
2007W Burnished Unc.	—	590	—
2008	22,800	484	—
2008 Burnished Unc.	—	665	—

KM# 290 • 7.7857 g., 0.9995 **Platinum**, 0.2502 oz. • **Rev. Desc:** Eagle in flight over New England costal lighthouse **Obv. Designer:** John Mercanti

Date	Mintage	MS65	PRF65
1998W	14,873	—	493

KM# 302 • 7.7857 g., 0.9995 **Platinum**, 0.2502 oz. • **Rev. Desc:** Eagle in flight over Southeastern Wetlands **Obv. Designer:** John Mercanti

Date	Mintage	MS65	PRF65
1999W	13,507	—	493

KM# 315 • 7.7857 g., 0.9995 **Platinum**, 0.2502 oz. • **Rev. Desc:** Eagle in flight over Heartland **Obv. Designer:** John Mercanti

Date	Mintage	MS65	PRF65
2000W	11,995	—	493

KM# 328 • 7.7857 g., 0.9995 **Platinum**, 0.2502 oz. , 22mm. • **Rev. Desc:** Eagle in flight over Southwestern cactus desert **Obv. Designer:** John Mercanti

Date	Mintage	MS65	PRF65
2001W	8,847	—	493

KM# 340 • 7.7857 g., 0.9995 **Platinum**, 0.2502 oz. , 22mm. • **Rev. Desc:** Eagle fishing in America's Northwest **Obv. Designer:** John Mercanti

Date	Mintage	MS65	PRF65
2002W	9,282	—	493

KM# 352 • 7.7857 g., 0.9995 **Platinum**, 0.2502 oz. , 22mm. • **Rev. Desc:** Eagle pearched on a Rocky Mountain Pine branch against a flag backdrop. **Obv. Designer:** John Mercanti **Rev. Designer:** Al Maletsky

Date	Mintage	MS65	PRF65
2003W	7,044	—	493

KM# 365 • 7.7857 g., 0.9995 **Platinum,** 0.2502 oz. , 22mm. • **Rev. Desc:** Chester French, 1907. The sculpture is outside the N.Y. Customs House, now part of the Smithsonian's Museum of the American Indian **Obv. Designer:** John Mercanti

Date	Mintage	MS65	PRF65
2004W	5,193	—	1,000

KM# 378 • 7.7857 g., 0.9995 **Platinum,** 0.2502 oz. , 22mm. • **Rev. Desc:** Eagle with cornucopiae **Obv. Designer:** John Mercanti **Rev. Designer:** Donna Weaver

Date	Mintage	MS65	PRF65
2005W	6,592	—	610

KM# 390 • 7.7857 g., 0.9995 **Platinum,** 0.2502 oz. , 22mm. • **Subject:** Legislative **Rev. Desc:** Liberty seated writing between two columns **Obv. Designer:** John Mercanti

Date	Mintage	MS65	PRF65
2006W	7,813	—	502

KM# 415 • 7.7857 g., 0.9995 **Platinum,** 0.2502 oz. , 22mm. • **Subject:** Executive **Rev. Desc:** Eagle with shield **Obv. Designer:** John Mercanti

Date	Mintage	MS65	PRF65
2007W	6,017	—	502

KM# 435 • 7.7857 g., 0.9995 **Platinum,** 0.2502 oz. , 22mm. • **Rev. Desc:** Justice standing before eagle **Obv. Designer:** John Mercanti

Date	Mintage	MS65	PRF65
2008W	6,017	—	985

KM# 461 • 7.7857 g., 0.9995 **Platinum,** 0.2502 oz. , 22mm. • **Subject:** Judicial **Obv. Designer:** John Mercanti

Date	Mintage	MS65	PRF65
2009W	3,800	—	—

PLATINUM $50

KM# 285 • 15.5520 g., 0.9995 **Platinum,** 0.4997 oz. , 27mm. • **Rev. Desc:** Eagle flying right over

sunrise **Obv. Designer:** John Mercanti **Rev. Designer:** Thomas D. Rogers Sr

Date	Mintage	MS65	PRF65
1997	20,500	969	—
1997W	15,432	—	995
1998	32,419	969	—
1999	32,309	969	—
2000	18,892	969	—
2001	12,815	969	—
2002	24,005	969	—
2003	17,409	969	—
2004	13,236	969	—
2005	9,013	969	—
2006	9,602	969	—
2006W Burnished Unc.	—	1,073	—
2007	7,001	1,003	—
2007W Burnished Unc.	—	1,038	—
2008	14,000	969	—
2008W Burnished Unc.	—	1,200	—
2009	—	—	—

KM# 291 • 15.5520 g., 0.9995 **Platinum,** 0.4997 oz. • **Rev. Desc:** Eagle in flight over New England costal lighthouse **Obv. Designer:** John Mercanti

Date	Mintage	MS65	PRF65
1998W	13,836	—	986

KM# 303 • 15.5520 g., 0.9995 **Platinum,** 0.4997 oz. • **Rev. Desc:** Eagle in flight over Southeastern Wetlands **Obv. Designer:** John Mercanti

Date	Mintage	MS65	PRF65
1999W	11,103	—	986

KM# 316 • 15.5520 g., 0.9995 **Platinum,** 0.4997 oz. • **Rev. Desc:** Eagle in flight over Heartland **Obv. Designer:** John Mercanti

Date	Mintage	MS65	PRF65
2000W	11,049	—	986

KM# 329 • 15.5520 g., 0.9995 **Platinum**, 0.4997 oz. , 27mm. • **Rev. Desc:** Eagle in flight over Southwestern cactus desert **Obv. Designer:** John Mercanti

Date	Mintage	MS65	PRF65
2001W	8,254	—	986

KM# 341 • 15.5520 g., 0.9995 **Platinum**, 0.4997 oz. , 27mm. • **Rev. Desc:** Eagle fishing in America's Northwest **Obv. Designer:** John Mercanti

Date	Mintage	MS65	PRF65
2002W	8,772	—	986

KM# 353 • 15.5520 g., 0.9995 **Platinum**, 0.4997 oz. , 27mm. • **Rev. Desc:** Eagle pearched on a Rocky Mountain Pine branch against a flag backdrop. **Obv. Designer:** John Mercanti **Rev. Designer:** Al Maletsky

Date	Mintage	MS65	PRF65
2003W	7,131	—	986

KM# 366 • 15.5520 g., 0.9995 **Platinum**, 0.4997 oz. , 27mm. • **Rev. Desc:** Chester French, 1907. The sculpture is outside the N.Y. Customs House, now part of the Smithsonian's Museum of the American Indian **Obv. Designer:** John Mercanti

Date	Mintage	MS65	PRF65
2004W	5,063	—	1,550

KM# 379 • 15.5520 g., 0.9995 **Platinum**, 0.4997 oz. , 27mm. • **Rev. Desc:** Eagle with cornucopiae **Obv. Designer:** John Mercanti **Rev. Designer:** Donna Weaver

Date	Mintage	MS65	PRF65
2005W	5,942	—	1,175

KM# 391 • 15.5520 g., 0.9995 **Platinum**, 0.4997 oz. , 27mm. • **Subject:** Legislative **Rev. Desc:** Liberty seated writing between two columns **Obv. Designer:** John Mercanti

Date	Mintage	MS65	PRF65
2006W	7,649	—	986

KM# 416 • 15.5520 g., 0.9995 **Platinum**, 0.4997 oz. , 27mm. • **Subject:** Executive **Rev. Desc:** Eagle with shield **Obv. Designer:** John Mercanti

Date	Mintage	MS65	PRF65
2007W	22,873	—	986
2007W Reverse Proof	16,937	—	986

KM# 436 • 15.5520 g., 0.9995 **Platinum**, 0.4997 oz. , 27mm. • **Rev. Desc:** Justice standing before eagle **Obv. Designer:** John Mercanti

Date	Mintage	MS65	PRF65
2008W	22,873	—	1,400

KM# 462 • 15.5520 g., 0.9995 **Platinum**, 0.4997 oz. , 27mm. • **Subject:** Judicial **Obv. Designer:** John Mercanti

Date	Mintage	MS65	PRF65
2009	3,600	—	—

PLATINUM $100

KM# 286 • 31.1050 g., 0.9995 **Platinum**, 0.9995 oz. , 33mm. • **Rev. Desc:** Eagle in flight over sun rise **Obv. Designer:** John Mercanti **Rev. Designer:** Thomas D. Rogers Sr

Date	Mintage	MS65	PRF65
1997	56,000	1,938	—
1997W	15,885	—	1,989
1998	133,002	1,938	—
1999	56,707	1,938	—
2000	10,003	1,938	—
2001	14,070	1,938	—
2002	11,502	1,938	—
2003	8,007	1,938	—
2004	7,009	1,938	—
2005	6,310	1,938	—
2006	6,000	1,938	—
2006W Burnished Unc.	—	2,200	—
2007	7,202	1,990	—
2007W Burnished Unc.	—	2,100	—
2008	21,800	1,938	—
2008W Burnished Unc.	—	2,250	—
2009	—	—	—
2011	10,299	1,950	—

BULLION COINS

BULLION COINS

KM# 292 • 31.1050 g., 0.9995 **Platinum**, 0.9995 oz. • **Rev. Desc:** Eagle in flight over New England costal lighthouse **Obv. Designer:** John Mercanti

Date	Mintage	MS65	PRF65
1998W	14,912	—	1,989

KM# 304 • 31.1050 g., 0.9995 **Platinum**, 0.9995 oz. • **Rev. Desc:** Eagle in flight over Southeastern Wetlands **Obv. Designer:** John Mercanti

Date	Mintage	MS65	PRF65
1999W	12,363	—	1,971

KM# 317 • 31.1050 g., 0.9995 **Platinum**, 0.9995 oz. • **Rev. Desc:** Eagle in flight over Heartland **Obv. Designer:** John Mercanti

Date	Mintage	MS65	PRF65
2000W	12,453	—	1,971

KM# 330 • 31.1050 g., 0.9995 **Platinum**, 0.9995 oz. , 33mm. • **Rev. Desc:** Eagle in flight over Southwestern cactus desert **Obv. Designer:** John Mercanti

Date	Mintage	MS65	PRF65
2001W	8,969	—	1,971

KM# 342 • 31.1050 g., 0.9995 **Platinum**, 0.9995 oz. , 33mm. • **Rev. Desc:** Eagle fishing in America's Northwest **Obv. Designer:** John Mercanti

Date	Mintage	MS65	PRF65
2002W	9,834	—	1,971

KM# 354 • 31.1050 g., 0.9995 **Platinum**, 0.9995 oz. , 33mm. • **Rev. Desc:** Eagle pearched on a Rocky Mountain Pine branch against a flag backdrop **Obv. Designer:** John Mercanti **Rev. Designer:** Al Maletsky

Date	Mintage	MS65	PRF65
2003W	8,246	—	1,989

KM# 367 • 31.1050 g., 0.9995 **Platinum**, 0.9995 oz. , 33mm. • **Rev. Desc:** Inspired by the sculpture "America" by Daniel Chester French, 1907. The sculpture is outside the N.Y. Customs House, now part of the Smithsonian's Museum of the American Indian **Obv. Designer:** John Mercanti **Rev. Designer:** Donna Weaver

Date	Mintage	MS65	PRF65
2004W	6,007	—	2,373

KM# 380 • 31.1050 g., 0.9995 **Platinum**, 0.9995
oz. , 33mm. • **Rev. Desc:** Eagle with cornucopiae
Obv. Designer: John Mercanti **Rev. Designer:**
Donna Weaver

Date	Mintage	MS65	PRF65
2005W	6,602	—	2,400

KM# 392 • 31.1050 g., 0.9995 **Platinum**, 0.9995
oz. , 33mm. • **Subject:** Legislaive **Rev. Desc:**
Liberty seated writing between two columns **Obv.
Designer:** John Mercanti

Date	Mintage	MS65	PRF65
2006W	9,152	—	1,971

KM# 417 • 31.1050 g., 0.9995 **Platinum**, 0.9995
oz. , 33mm. • **Subject:** Executive Branch **Rev.
Desc:** Eagle with shield **Obv. Designer:** John
Mercanti

Date	Mintage	MS65	PRF65
2007W	8,363	—	1,971

KM# 437 • 31.1050 g., 0.9995 **Platinum**, 0.9995
oz. , 33mm. • **Rev. Desc:** Justice standing before
eagle **Obv. Designer:** John Mercanti

Date	Mintage	MS65	PRF65
2008W	8,363	—	3,000

KM# 463 • 31.1020 g., 0.9995 **Platinum**, 0.9994
oz. , 33mm. • **Subject:** A more perfect Union **Rev.
Desc:** Four portraits **Obv. Designer:** John Mercanti

Date	Mintage	MS65	PRF65
2009W Proof	4,900	—	2,250

KM# 488 • 31.1050 g., 0.9990 **Platinum**, 0.9990
oz. , 33mm. • **Rev. Desc:** Statue of Justice
holding scales **Obv. Designer:** John Mercanti

Date	Mintage	MS65	PRF65
2010W	—	—	2,200

KM# 518 • 31.1050 g., 0.9995 **Platinum**, 0.9995
oz. , 33mm. • **Subject:** To Insure Domestic
Tranquility

Date	Mintage	MS65	PRF65
2011W	—	—	1,658

KM# 541 • 31.1050 g., 0.9995 **Platinum**, 0.9995
oz. • **Subject:** To provide for the Common Justice

Date	Mintage	MS65	PRF65
2012	—	—	1,692

BISON BULLION COINAGE

GOLD $5

KM# 411 • 3.1100 g., 0.9999 **Gold**, 0.1000 oz. •
Obv. Desc: Indian Head right **Rev. Desc:** Bison

Date	Mintage	MS65	PRF65
2008W	19,300	—	660
2008W	19,000	575	—

GOLD $10

KM# 412 • 7.7857 g., 0.9999 **Gold**, 0.2503 oz. •
Obv. Desc: Indian Head right **Rev. Desc:** Bison

Date	Mintage	MS65	PRF65
2008W	13,900	—	1,550
2008W	10,500	1,375	—

GOLD $25

KM# 413 • 15.5520 g., 0.9990 **Gold**, 0.4995 oz. •
Obv. Desc: Indian Head right **Rev. Desc:** Bison

Date	Mintage	MS65	PRF65
2008W	12,500	—	1,850
2008W	17,000	1,350	—

GOLD $50

KM# 393 • 31.1050 g., 0.9999 **Gold**, 0.9999 oz. ,
32mm. • **Obv. Desc:** Indian head right **Rev.
Desc:** Bison standing left on mound **Designer:**
James E. Fraser

Date	Mintage	MS65	PRF65
2006W	246,267	—	1,912
2006W	337,012	1,784	—
2007W	136,503	1,784	—
2007W	58,998	—	1,912
2008W	189,500	1,784	—
2008W	19,500	3,200	—
2008W Moy Family Chop	—	—	3,950
2009W	—	1,784	—
2009W	—	—	1,882
2010W	49,374	—	1,912
2010	—	—	—
2011W	—	—	1,912
2011	—	—	—
2012W	—	—	—
2012	—	—	—

FIRST SPOUSE GOLD COINAGE

GOLD $10

KM# 407 • 15.5520 g., 0.9999 **Gold**, 0.4999 oz. ,
23.5mm. • **Subject:** Martha Washington **Obv. Desc:**
Bust 3/4 facing **Rev. Desc:** Martha Washington
seated sewing **Obv. Designer:** Joseph Menna
Rev. Designer: Susan Gamble and Don Everhart

Date	Mintage	MS65	PRF65
2007W	20,000	917	—
2007W	20,000	—	917

KM# 408 • 15.5520 g., 0.9999 **Gold**, 0.4999 oz. ,
26.5mm. • **Subject:** Abigail Adams **Obv. Desc:**

Bust 3/4 facing **Rev. Desc:** Abigail Adams seated
at desk writing to John during the Revolutionary
War **Obv. Designer:** Joseph Menna **Rev.
Designer:** Thomas Cleveland and Phebe Hemphill

Date	Mintage	MS65	PRF65
2007W	20,000	917	—
2007W	20,000	—	917

KM# 409 • 15.5520 g., 0.9999 **Gold**, 0.4999 oz. ,
26.5mm. • **Subject:** Jefferson - Bust coinage
design **Obv. Desc:** Bust design from coinage
Rev. Desc: Jefferson's tombstone **Obv. Designer:**
Robert Scot and Phebe Hemphill **Rev. Designer:**
Charles Vickers

Date	Mintage	MS65	PRF65
2007W	20,000	917	—
2007W	20,000	—	917

BULLION COINS

KM# 410 • 15.5520 g., 0.9999 **Gold**, 0.4999 oz. , 26.5mm. • **Subject:** Dolley Madison **Obv. Desc:** Bust 3/4 facing **Rev. Desc:** Dolley standing before painting of Washington, which she saved from the White House **Obv. Designer:** Don Everhart **Rev. Designer:** Joel Iskowitz and Don Everhart

Date	Mintage	MS65	PRF65
2007W	12,500	917	—
2007W	18,300	—	917

KM# 430 • 15.5520 g., 0.9990 **Gold**, 0.4995 oz. , 26.5mm. • **Subject:** Elizabeth Monroe **Obv. Desc:** Bust 3/4 facing right **Rev. Desc:** Elizabeth standing before mirror **Obv. Designer:** Joel Iskowitz and Don Everhart **Rev. Designer:** Donna Weaver and Charles Vickers

Date	Mintage	MS65	PRF65
2008W	4,500	975	—
2008W	7,900	—	950

KM# 431 • 15.5520 g., 0.9990 **Gold**, 0.4995 oz. , 26.5mm. • **Subject:** Lousia Adams **Obv. Desc:** Bust 3/4 facing right **Rev. Desc:** Lousia and son Charles before entrance **Obv. Designer:** Susan Gamble and Phebe Hemphill **Rev. Designer:** Joseph Menna

Date	Mintage	MS65	PRF65
2008W	4,200	1,175	—
2008W	7,400	—	1,125

KM# 432 • 15.5520 g., 0.9990 **Gold**, 0.4995 oz. , 26.5mm. • **Subject:** Jackson's Liberty **Obv. Desc:** Capped and draped bust left **Rev. Desc:** Andrew Jackson on horseback right **Obv. Designer:** John Reich **Rev. Designer:** Justin Kunz and Don Everhart

Date	Mintage	MS65	PRF65
2008W	4,800	1,575	—
2008W	7,800	—	1,325

KM# 433 • 15.5520 g., 0.9990 **Gold**, 0.4995 oz. , 26.5mm. • **Subject:** van Buren's Liberty **Obv. Desc:** Seated Liberty with shiled **Rev. Desc:** Youthful van Buren seated under tree, family tavern in distance **Obv. Designer:** Christian Gobrecht **Rev. Designer:** Thomas Cleveland and James Licaretz

Date	Mintage	MS65	PRF65
2008W	15,000	1,500	—
2008W	Inc. above	—	1,525

KM# 456 • 15.5520 g., 0.9990 **Gold**, 0.4995 oz. • **Subject:** Anna Harrison **Obv. Desc:** Bust 3/4 left **Rev. Desc:** Anna reading to her three children **Obv. Designer:** Donna Weaver and Joseph Menna **Rev. Designer:** Thomas Cleveland and Charles Vickers

Date	Mintage	MS65	PRF65
2009W	15,000	1,225	—
2009W	Inc. above	—	1,150

KM# 457 • 15.5520 g., 0.9990 **Gold**, 0.4995 oz. • **Subject:** Lettia Tyler **Obv. Desc:** Bust facing **Rev. Desc:** Letitia and two children playing outside of Cedar Grove Plantation **Obv. Designer:** Phebe Hemphill **Rev. Designer:** Susan Gamble and Norm Nemeth

Date	Mintage	MS65	PRF65
2009W	15,000	1,525	—
2009W	Inc. above	—	1,325

KM# 458 • 15.5520 g., 0.9990 **Gold**, 0.4995 oz. • **Subject:** Julia Tyler **Obv. Desc:** Bust facing **Rev. Desc:** Julia and John Tyler dancing **Designer:** Joel Iskowitz and Don Everhart

Date	Mintage	MS65	PRF65
2009W	15,000	1,650	—
2009W	Inc. above	—	1,800

BULLION COINS

BULLION COINS

KM# 459 • 15.5520 g., 0.9990 **Gold**, 0.4995 oz. •
Subject: Sarah Polk **Obv. Desc:** Bust 3/4 right
Rev. Desc: Sarah seated at desk as personal
secretary to James Polk **Designer:** Phebe Hemphill

Date	Mintage	MS65	PRF65
2009W	3,501	1,300	—
2009W	5,157	—	1,100

KM# 465 • 15.5520 g., 0.9990 **Gold**, 0.4995 oz. •
Subject: Margaret Taylor **Obv. Desc:** Bust 3/4 left
Rev. Desc: Margaret Taylor nurses wounded
soldier during the Seminole War **Obv. Designer:**
Phebe Hemphill and Charles Vickers **Rev.
Designer:** Mary Beth Zeitz and James Licaretz

Date	Mintage	MS65	PRF65
2009W	3,430	1,050	—
2009W	4,787	—	1,225

KM# 481 • 15.5200 g., 0.9990 **Gold**, 0.4985 oz. •
Subject: Abigail Filmore **Rev. Desc:** Abigail
Filmore placing books on library shelf **Obv.
Designer:** Phebe Hemphill **Rev. Designer:** Susan
Gamble and Joseph Menna

Date	Mintage	MS65	PRF65
2010W	15,000	1,300	—
2010W	Inc. above	—	1,025

KM# 482 • 15.5200 g., 0.9990 **Gold**, 0.4985 oz. •
Subject: Jane Pierce **Rev. Desc:** Jane Pierce
seated on porch **Obv. Designer:** Donna Weaver
and Don Everhart **Rev. Designer:** Donna Weaver
and Charles Vickers

Date	Mintage	MS65	PRF65
2010W	3,333	1,000	—
2010W	4,843	—	1,225

KM# 483 • 15.5200 g., 0.9990 **Gold**, 0.4985 oz. ,
26.5mm. • **Subject:** Buchanan's Liberty **Rev.
Desc:** Buchanan as clerk **Obv. Designer:** Christian
Gobrecht **Rev. Designer:** Joseph Menna

Date	Mintage	MS65	PRF65
2010W	5,348	1,000	—
2010W	7,304	—	1,075

KM# 484 • 15.5200 g., 0.9990 **Gold**, 0.4985 oz. •
Subject: Mary Todd Lincoln **Rev. Desc:** Mary
Lincoln visiting soldiers at hospital **Obv. Designer:**
Phebe Hemphill **Rev. Designer:** Joel Iskowitz and
Pheve Hemphill

Date	Mintage	MS65	PRF65
2010W	3,760	1,000	—
2010W	6,904	—	975

KM# 509 • 15.5500 g., 0.9990 **Gold**, 0.4994 oz. •
Subject: Eliza Johnson **Obv. Desc:** Bust of Eliza
Johnson

Date	Mintage	MS65	PRF65
2011W	15,000	1,075	—
2011W	Inc. above	—	1,075

KM# 510 • 15.5520 g., 0.9990 **Gold**, 0.4995 oz. ,
26.5mm. • **Subject:** Julia Grant **Obv. Desc:** Bust
of Julia Grant

Date	Mintage	MS65	PRF65
2011W	15,000	1,075	—
2011W	Inc. above	—	1,075

KM# 511 • 15.5520 g., 0.9990 **Gold**, 0.4995 oz. •
Subject: Lucy Hayes **Obv. Desc:** Bust of Lucy
Hayes

Date	Mintage	MS65	PRF65
2011W	15,000	1,325	—
2011W	3,826	—	1,075

KM# 512 • 15.5520 g., 0.9990 **Gold**, 0.4995 oz. •
Subject: Lucretia Garfield **Obv. Desc:** Bust of
Lucretia Garfield

Date	Mintage	MS65	PRF65
2011W	15,000	1,325	—
2011W	3,521	—	1,075

KM# 532 • 15.5520 g., 0.9990 **Gold**, 0.4995 oz. •
Obv. Desc: Alice Paul, suffragist

Date	Mintage	MS65	PRF65
2012W	2,021	1,050	—
2012W	2,802	—	1,075

KM# 533 • 15.5520 g., 0.9990 **Gold**, 0.4995 oz. •
Subject: Francis Cleveland (First Term) **Obv.
Desc:** Francis Cleveland

Date	Mintage	MS65	PRF65
2012W	1,565	1,050	—
2012W	2,152	—	1,075

KM# 534 • 15.5520 g., 0.9990 **Gold**, 0.4995 oz. •
Subject: Caroline Harrison **Obv. Desc:** Caroline
Harrison

Date	Mintage	MS65	PRF65
2012W	942	1,050	—
2012W	1,380	—	1,075

KM# 535 • 15.5520 g., 0.9990 **Gold**, 0.4995 oz. •
Subject: Francis Cleveland (Second Term) **Obv.
Desc:** Francis Cleveland

Date	Mintage	MS65	PRF65
2012	—	1,050	—
2012	—	—	1,075

BULLION COINS

CANADA

CONFEDERATION

CIRCULATION COINAGE

CENT

KM# 1 4.5400 g. Bronze   **Obv:** Laureate head left **Obv. Legend:** VICTORIA DEI GRATIA REGINA. CANADA **Rev:** Denomination and date within beaded circle, chain of leaves surrounds **Rev. Legend:** ONE CENT **Edge:** plain

Date	Mintage	VG-8	F-12	VF-20	XF-40	MS-60	MS-63	Proof
1858	421,000	75.00	100.00	125	200	500	2,000	—
1859/8 Wide 9	Inc. above	30.00	45.00	60.00	125	350	1,800	—
1859 Narrow 9	9,579,000	2.25	3.00	5.00	7.00	45.00	250	—
1859 Double punched narrow 9 type I	Inc. above	200	250	350	550	1,300	5,000	—
1859 Double punched narrow 9 type II	Inc. above	55.00	75.00	125	175	550	3,000	—

KM# 7 5.6700 g. Bronze 25.5 mm.   **Obv:** Crowned head left within beaded circle **Obv. Legend:** VICTORIA DEI GRATIA REGINA. CANADA **Obv. Designer:** Leonard C. Wyon **Rev:** Denomination and date within beaded circle, chain of leaves surrounds **Edge:** Plain

Date	Mintage	VG-8	F-12	VF-20	XF-40	MS-60	MS-63	Proof
1876H	4,000,000	3.00	4.00	6.00	9.00	45.00	250	—
1881H	2,000,000	4.00	5.00	11.00	18.00	75.00	300	—
1882H	4,000,000	3.00	3.50	4.00	7.50	40.00	250	—
1884	2,500,000	3.00	4.00	6.50	11.00	60.00	300	—
1886	1,500,000	4.00	7.00	13.00	20.00	95.00	450	—
1887	1,500,000	3.50	5.00	8.00	14.00	70.00	225	—
1888	4,000,000	3.00	4.00	5.00	7.50	40.00	175	—
1890H	1,000,000	8.00	12.00	19.00	30.00	125	450	—
1891 Large date	1,452,000	8.00	11.00	17.00	35.00	150	450	—
1891 S.D.L.L.	Inc. above	65.00	125	200	300	1,000	4,000	—
1891 S.D.S.L.	Inc. above	60.00	95.00	125	200	450	1,750	—
1892	1,200,000	5.50	8.00	12.00	15.00	60.00	225	—
1893	2,000,000	3.00	4.00	5.00	9.50	45.00	200	—
1894	1,000,000	11.00	15.00	20.00	40.00	125	300	—
1895	1,200,000	5.00	9.50	13.00	16.00	60.00	225	—
1896	2,000,000	3.00	5.00	6.50	7.50	40.00	150	—
1897	1,500,000	3.00	5.00	6.50	9.00	45.00	200	—
1898H	1,000,000	9.00	13.00	17.00	35.00	100.00	300	—
1899	2,400,000	3.00	3.50	5.00	7.00	45.00	150	—
1900	1,000,000	9.00	13.50	20.00	30.00	125	500	—
1900H	2,600,000	3.00	3.50	5.00	7.50	30.00	95.00	—
1901	4,100,000	3.00	4.00	6.00	11.00	45.00	100.00	—

KM# 8 5.6700 g. Bronze 25.5 mm. **Obv:** Kings bust right within beaded circle **Obv. Designer:** G. W. DeSaulles **Rev:** Denomination above date within circle, chain of leaves surrounds **Edge:** Plain

Date	Mintage	VG-8	F-12	VF-20	XF-40	MS-60	MS-63	Proof
1902	3,000,000	2.25	3.00	4.00	8.00	27.00	75.00	—
1903	4,000,000	2.25	3.00	4.00	8.00	30.00	90.00	—
1904	2,500,000	2.50	4.00	6.00	10.00	45.00	100.00	—
1905	2,000,000	4.00	6.00	9.00	13.00	55.00	150	—
1906	4,100,000	2.25	3.00	4.00	8.00	40.00	175	—
1907	2,400,000	2.50	3.00	5.00	10.00	40.00	175	—
1907H	800,000	14.50	21.00	30.00	55.00	175	600	—
1908	2,401,506	3.00	4.00	6.00	10.00	40.00	125	500
1909	3,973,339	2.00	3.00	4.00	7.00	30.00	100.00	—
1910	5,146,487	1.50	2.00	3.00	6.00	30.00	85.00	—

KM# 15 5.6700 g. Bronze 25.5 mm. **Obv:** King's bust left **Obv. Designer:** E. B. MacKennal **Rev:** Denomination above date within beaded circle, chain of leaves surrounds **Edge:** Plain

Date	Mintage	VG-8	F-12	VF-20	XF-40	MS-60	MS-63	Proof
1911	4,663,486	0.80	1.50	2.25	3.50	25.00	70.00	800

KM# 21 5.6700 g. Bronze 25.5 mm. **Obv:** King's bust left **Obv. Designer:** E. B. MacKennal **Rev:** Denomination above date within beaded circle, chain of leaves surrounds **Edge:** Plain

Date	Mintage	VG-8	F-12	VF-20	XF-40	MS-60	MS-63	Proof
1912	5,107,642	0.90	1.75	2.50	4.00	30.00	75.00	—
1913	5,735,405	0.90	1.75	2.50	5.00	27.50	95.00	—
1914	3,405,958	1.25	1.75	3.00	5.00	40.00	100.00	—
1915	4,932,134	0.90	1.50	2.50	5.00	35.00	95.00	—
1916	11,022,367	0.60	0.80	1.50	3.00	19.00	60.00	—
1917	11,899,254	0.60	0.80	1.00	2.50	16.00	55.00	—
1918	12,970,798	0.60	0.80	1.00	2.50	14.00	55.00	—
1919	11,279,634	0.60	0.80	1.00	2.50	14.00	55.00	—
1920	6,762,247	0.70	0.90	1.25	2.50	22.00	85.00	—

Dot below date

KM# 28 3.2400 g. Bronze 19.10 mm. **Obv:** King's bust left **Obv. Designer:** E. B. MacKennal **Rev:** Denomination above date, leaves flank **Rev. Designer:** Fred Lewis **Edge:** Plain

Date	Mintage	VG-8	F-12	VF-20	XF-40	MS-60	MS-63	Proof
1920	15,483,923	0.20	0.45	0.95	1.75	15.00	50.00	—
1921	7,601,627	0.45	0.75	1.75	5.00	35.00	250	—
1922	1,243,635	13.00	16.00	25.00	45.00	200	1,200	—
1923	1,019,002	29.00	35.00	40.00	60.00	300	2,000	—
1924	1,593,195	6.00	7.00	12.00	20.00	125	850	—
1925	1,000,622	22.00	25.00	30.00	50.00	200	1,200	—
1926	2,143,372	3.50	4.50	7.00	16.00	95.00	650	—
1927	3,553,928	1.25	1.75	3.50	8.00	40.00	225	—
1928	9,144,860	0.15	0.30	0.65	1.50	20.00	90.00	—
1929	12,159,840	0.15	0.30	0.65	1.50	20.00	80.00	—
1930	2,538,613	2.00	2.50	4.50	9.00	50.00	225	—
1931	3,842,776	0.65	1.00	2.50	6.00	40.00	200	—
1932	21,316,190	0.15	0.20	0.50	1.50	16.00	60.00	—
1933	12,079,310	0.15	0.30	0.50	1.50	16.00	55.00	—
1934	7,042,358	0.20	0.30	0.75	1.50	16.00	60.00	—
1935	7,526,400	0.20	0.30	0.75	1.50	16.00	50.00	—
1936	8,768,769	0.15	0.30	0.75	1.50	14.00	45.00	—
1936 dot below date; Rare	678,823	—	—	—	—	—	250,000	—

Note: Only one possible business strike is known to exist. No other examples (or possible business strikes) have ever surfaced.

1936 dot below date, specimen, 3 known		—	—	—	—	—	—	—

Note: At the David Akers auction of the John Jay Pittman collection (Part 1, 10-97), a gem specimen realized $121,000. At the David Akers auction of the John Jay Pittman collection (Part 3, 10-99), a near choice specimen realized $115,000.

Maple leaf

KM# 32 3.2400 g. Bronze 19.10 mm. **Obv:** Head left **Obv. Designer:** T. H. Paget **Rev:** Maple leaf divides date and denomination **Rev. Designer:** George E. Kruger-Gray **Edge:** Plain

Date	Mintage	VG-8	F-12	VF-20	XF-40	MS-60	MS-63	Proof
1937	10,040,231	0.45	0.60	0.85	1.00	2.50	12.00	—
1938	18,365,608	0.25	0.35	0.45	0.85	2.50	13.00	—
1939	21,600,319	0.20	0.30	0.50	0.80	2.00	8.00	—
1940	85,740,532	0.10	0.15	0.25	0.50	2.50	8.00	—
1941	56,336,011	0.10	0.15	0.25	0.50	8.00	50.00	—
1942	76,113,708	0.10	0.15	0.25	0.50	7.00	50.00	—
1943	89,111,969	0.10	0.15	0.25	0.45	3.50	22.00	—
1944	44,131,216	0.10	0.15	0.30	0.60	11.00	70.00	—
1945	77,268,591	0.10	0.15	0.20	0.35	2.50	22.00	—
1946	56,662,071	0.10	0.15	0.20	0.35	2.50	12.00	—
1947	31,093,901	0.10	0.15	0.20	0.35	2.50	9.00	—
1947 maple leaf	47,855,448	0.10	0.15	0.20	0.35	2.50	9.00	—

KM# 41 3.2400 g. Bronze 19.10 mm. **Obv:** Modified legend **Obv. Designer:** T. H. Paget **Rev. Designer:** George E. Kruger-Gray **Edge:** Plain

Date	Mintage	VG-8	F-12	VF-20	XF-40	MS-60	MS-63	Proof
1948	25,767,779	—	0.15	0.25	0.70	4.00	27.00	—
1949	33,128,933	—	0.10	0.15	0.35	2.50	9.00	—
1950	60,444,992	—	0.10	0.15	0.25	1.75	9.00	—
1951	80,430,379	—	0.10	0.15	0.20	1.75	14.00	—
1952	67,631,736	—	0.10	0.15	0.20	1.25	9.00	—

No strap　　　　With strap

KM# 49 3.2400 g. Bronze 19.10 mm. **Obv:** Laureate bust right **Obv. Designer:** Mary Gillick **Rev:** Maple leaf divides date and denomination **Rev. Designer:** George E. Kruger-Gray

Date	Mintage	VG-8	F-12	VF-20	XF-40	MS-60	MS-63	Proof
1953	67,806,016	0.10	0.10	0.10	0.25	0.80	2.50	—
Note: Without strap								
1953	Inc. above	0.50	1.00	1.50	2.50	12.00	60.00	—
Note: With strap								
1954	22,181,760	0.10	0.10	0.10	0.40	1.75	6.00	—
Note: With strap								
1954 Prooflike only	Inc. above	—	—	—	—	550	800	—
Note: Without strap								
1955	56,403,193	—	0.10	0.10	0.15	0.45	3.00	—
Note: With strap								

Date	Mintage	VG-8	F-12	VF-20	XF-40	MS-60	MS-63	Proof
1955	Inc. above	100.00	150	175	250	600	2,000	—
Note: Without strap								
1956	78,658,535	—	—	—	0.15	0.30	2.00	—
1957	100,601,792	—	—	—	0.10	0.10	1.00	—
1958	59,385,679	—	—	—	0.10	0.10	1.00	—
1959	83,615,343	—	—	—	0.10	0.10	0.60	—
1960	75,772,775	—	—	—	0.10	0.10	0.60	—
1961	139,598,404	—	—	—	—	0.10	0.60	—
1962	227,244,069	—	—	—	—	0.10	0.40	—
1963	279,076,334	—	—	—	—	0.10	0.40	—
1964	484,655,322	—	—	—	—	0.10	0.40	—

KM# 59.1 3.2400 g. Bronze 19.10 mm. **Obv:** Queens bust right **Obv. Designer:** Arnold Machin **Rev:** Maple leaf divides date and denomination **Rev. Designer:** George E. Kruger-Gray **Edge:** Plain

Date	Mintage	VG-8	F-12	VF-20	XF-40	MS-60	MS-63	Proof
1965	304,441,082	—	0.15	0.20	0.40	1.00	5.00	—
Note: Small beads, pointed 5								
1965	Inc. above	—	—	—	—	0.10	0.40	—
Note: Small beads, blunt 5								
1965	Inc. above	1.75	3.00	4.50	7.50	18.00	45.00	—
Note: Large beads, pointed 5								
1965	Inc. above	—	—	—	0.10	0.10	0.40	—
Note: Large beads, blunt 5								
1966	184,151,087	—	—	—	—	0.10	0.40	—
1968	329,695,772	—	—	—	—	0.10	0.40	—
1969	335,240,929	—	—	—	—	0.10	0.40	—
1970	311,145,010	—	—	—	—	0.10	0.40	—
1971	298,228,936	—	—	—	—	0.10	0.40	—
1972	451,304,591	—	—	—	—	0.10	0.40	—
1973	457,059,852	—	—	—	—	0.10	0.40	—
1974	692,058,489	—	—	—	—	0.10	0.40	—
1975	642,318,000	—	—	—	—	0.10	0.40	—
1976	701,122,890	—	—	—	—	0.10	0.40	—
1977	453,762,670	—	—	—	—	0.10	0.40	—

KM# 65 3.2400 g. Bronze 19.10 mm. **Subject:** Confederation Centennial **Obv:** Queen's bust right **Obv. Designer:** Arnold Machin **Rev:** Dove with wings spread, denomination above, two dates below **Rev. Designer:** Alex Coville

Date	Mintage	VG-8	F-12	VF-20	XF-40	MS-60	MS-63	Proof
1867-1967	345,140,645	—	—	—	—	0.10	0.40	1.00

KM# 59.2 3.2400 g. Bronze 19.10 mm. **Obv:** Queen's bust right **Obv. Designer:** Arnold Machin **Rev:** Maple leaves **Rev. Designer:** George E. Kruger-Gray **Edge:** Plain **Note:** Thin planchet.

Date	Mintage	VG-8	F-12	VF-20	XF-40	MS-60	MS-63	Proof
1978	911,170,647	—	—	—	—	0.10	0.30	—
1979	754,394,064	—	—	—	—	0.10	0.30	—

KM# 127 2.8000 g. Bronze 19.10 mm. **Obv:** Queen's bust right **Obv. Designer:** Arnold Machin **Rev. Designer:** George E. Kruger-Gray **Edge:** Plain **Note:** Reduced weight.

Date	Mintage	VG-8	F-12	VF-20	XF-40	MS-60	MS-63	Proof
1980	912,052,318	—	—	—	—	0.10	0.30	—

CENT

Date	Mintage	VG-8	F-12	VF-20	XF-40	MS-60	MS-63	Proof
1981	1,209,468,500	—	—	—	—	0.10	0.30	—
1981 Proof	199,000	—	—	—	—	—	—	1.50

KM# 132 2.5000 g. Bronze 19.10 mm.   **Obv:** Queen's bust right **Obv. Designer:** Arnold Machin **Rev:** Maple leaf divides date and denomination **Rev. Designer:** George E. Kruger-Gray **Edge:** Plain **Note:** Reduced weight.

Date	Mintage	VG-8	F-12	VF-20	XF-40	MS-60	MS-63	Proof
1982	911,001,000	—	—	—	—	0.10	0.30	—
1982 Proof	180,908	—	—	—	—	—	—	1.50
1983	975,510,000	—	—	—	—	0.10	0.30	—
1983 Proof	168,000	—	—	—	—	—	—	1.50
1984	838,225,000	—	—	—	—	0.10	0.30	—
1984 Proof	161,602	—	—	—	—	—	—	1.50
1985	771,772,500	0.95	1.75	2.50	3.50	10.00	19.00	—
Note: Pointed 5								
1985	Inc. above	—	—	—	—	0.10	0.30	—
Note: Blunt 5								
1985 Proof	157,037	—	—	—	—	—	—	1.50
Note: Blunt 5								
1986	740,335,000	—	—	—	—	0.10	0.30	—
1986 Proof	175,745	—	—	—	—	—	—	1.50
1987	774,549,000	—	—	—	—	0.10	0.30	—
1987 Proof	179,004	—	—	—	—	—	—	1.50
1988	482,676,752	—	—	—	—	0.10	0.30	—
1988 Proof	175,259	—	—	—	—	—	—	1.50
1989	1,077,347,200	—	—	—	—	0.10	0.30	—
1989 Proof	170,928	—	—	—	—	—	—	1.50

KM# 181 2.5000 g. Bronze 19.10 mm.   **Obv:** Crowned Queen's head right **Obv. Designer:** Dora dePedery-Hunt **Rev:** Maple leaf divides date and denomination **Rev. Designer:** George E. Kruger-Gray **Edge:** Plain

Date	Mintage	MS-63	Proof
1990	218,035,000	0.30	—
1990 Proof	140,649	—	2.50
1991	831,001,000	0.30	—
1991 Proof	131,888	—	3.50
1993	752,034,000	0.30	—
1993 Proof	145,065	—	2.00
1994	639,516,000	0.30	—
1994 Proof	146,424	—	2.50
1995	624,983,000	0.30	—
1995 Proof	—	—	2.50
1996	445,746,000	0.30	—
1996 Proof	—	—	2.50

KM# 204 Bronze 19.10 mm.   **Subject:** Confederation 125 **Obv:** Crowned Queen's head right **Obv. Designer:** Dora dePedery-Hunt **Rev:**

Maple leaf divides date and denomination **Rev. Designer:** George E. Kruger-Gray

Date	Mintage	MS-63	Proof
1992	673,512,000	0.30	—
1992 Proof	147,061	—	2.50

KM# 289 2.2500 g. Copper Plated Steel 19.05 mm.   **Obv:** Crowned head right **Obv. Designer:** Dora dePédery-Hunt **Rev:** Maple twig design **Rev. Designer:** George E. Kruger-Gray **Edge:** Round and plain

Date	Mintage	MS-63	Proof
1997	549,868,000	0.30	—
1997 Proof	—	—	2.75
1998	999,578,000	0.30	—
1998 Proof	—	—	3.00
1998W	—	1.75	—
1999P	—	6.00	—
1999	1,089,625,000	0.30	—
1999 Proof	—	—	4.00
1999W	—	—	—
2000	771,908,206	0.30	—
2000 Proof	—	—	4.00
2000W	—	1.75	—
2001	919,358,000	0.30	—
2001P Proof	—	—	5.00
2003	92,219,775	0.30	—
2003P Proof	—	—	5.00
2003P	235,936,799	1.50	—

KM# 289a Bronze 19.10 mm.

Date	Mintage	MS-63	Proof
1998	—	0.75	—
Note: In Specimen sets only			

KM# 309 5.6700 g. 0.9250 Copper Plated Silver 0.1686 oz.   **Subject:** 90th Anniversary Royal Canadian Mint - 1908-1998 **Obv. Designer:** Dora dePédery-Hunt **Rev. Designer:** G. W. DeSaulles

Date	Mintage	MS-63	Proof
1908-1998	25,000	16.00	—
Note: Antique finish			
1908-1998 Proof	—	—	—

KM# 332 5.6700 g. 0.9250 Silver 0.1686 oz. ASW **Subject:** 90th Anniversary Royal Canadian Mint - 1908-1998 **Obv:** Crowned Queen's head right, with "Canada" added to head **Obv. Designer:** Dora dePedery-Hunt **Rev:** Denomination above dates withn beaded circle, chain of leaves surrounds **Rev. Designer:** G. W. DeSaulles

Date	Mintage	MS-63	P/L	Proof
1908-1998 Proof	25,000	—	—	16.00

Note: Mirror finish

KM# 445 2.2500 g. Copper Plated Steel 19.1 mm. **Subject:** Elizabeth II Golden Jubilee **Obv:** Crowned head right, Jubilee commemorative dates 1952-2002 **Obv. Designer:** Dora dePédery-Hunt **Rev:** Denomination above maple leaves **Rev. Designer:** George E. Kruger-Gray **Edge:** Plain

Date	Mintage	MS-63	Proof
1952-2002	716,366,000	0.75	—
1952-2002	114,212,000	1.00	—
1952-2002P Proof	32,642	—	5.00

KM# 445a 0.9250 Silver **Subject:** Elizabeth II Golden Jubilee **Obv:** Crowned head right, Jubilee commemorative dates 1952-2002 **Obv. Designer:** Dora dePédery-Hunt **Rev:** Denomination above maple leaves **Rev. Designer:** George E. Kruger-Gray

Date	Mintage	MS-63	Proof
1952-2002	21,537	—	3.00

KM# 490 2.2500 g. Copper Plated Zinc 19.05 mm. **Obv:** New effigy of Queen Elizabeth II right **Obv. Designer:** Susanna Blunt **Rev:** Two maple leaves **Edge:** Plain

Date	Mintage	MS-63	Proof
2003	56,877,144	0.25	—
2004	653,317,000	0.25	—
2004 Proof	—	—	2.50
2005	759,658,000	0.25	—
2005 Proof	—	—	2.50
2006	886,275,000	0.25	—
2006 Proof	—	—	2.50

KM# 490a 2.2500 g. Copper Plated Steel 19.05 mm. **Obv:** Bust right **Obv. Designer:** Susanna Blunt **Rev:** Two maple leaves **Rev. Designer:** G. E. Kruger-Gray

Date	Mintage	MS-63	Proof
2003P	591,257,000	0.25	—
2003 WP	Inc. above	0.25	—
2004P	134,906,000	0.25	—
2005P	30,525,000	0.25	—
2006P	137,733,000	0.25	—
2006(ml)	Inc. above	0.25	—
2007(ml)	938,270,000	0.25	—
2007(ml) Proof	—	—	2.50
2008(ml)	787,625,000	0.25	—
2008(ml) Proof	—	—	2.50
2009(ml)	455,680,000	0.25	—
2009(ml) Proof	—	—	2.50
2010(ml)	—	0.25	—
2010(ml) Proof	—	—	2.50

Date	Mintage	MS-63	Proof
2011(ml)	—	0.25	—
2011(ml) Proof	—	—	2.50
2012(ml)	—	0.25	—
2012(ml) Proof	—	—	2.50

KM# 468 2.5000 g. Copper **Subject:** 50th Anniversary of the Coronation of Elizabeth II **Obv:** 1953 Effigy of the Queen, Jubilee commemorative dates 1953-2003 **Obv. Designer:** Mary Gillick

Date	Mintage	MS-63	Proof
1953-2003 Proof	—	—	2.50

KM# 490b 2.2500 g. Copper Plated Zinc **Obv:** Head right **Rev:** Maple leaf, selectively gold plated **Note:** Bound into Annual Report.

Date	Mintage	MS-63	Proof
2003 Proof	7,746	—	35.00

KM# 1023 Copper 19.1 mm. **Obv:** George V bust left **Rev:** Value within wreath, dual dates below

Date	Mintage	MS-63	Proof
1935-2010 Proof	—	—	10.00

KM# 1153 5.6700 g. Copper 19.1 mm. **Obv:** George V bust **Rev:** Value within wreath

Date	Mintage	MS-63	Proof
1911-2011 Proof	6,000	—	10.00

3 CENTS

KM# 410 3.1100 g. 0.9250 Silver Gilt 0.0925 oz. ASW 21.3 mm. **Subject:** 1st Canadian Postage Stamp **Obv:** Crowned head right **Obv. Designer:** Dora dePédery-Hunt **Rev:** Partial stamp design **Rev. Designer:** Sandford Fleming **Edge:** Plain

Date	Mintage	MS-63	Proof
2001 Proof	59,573	—	12.50

5 CENTS

Oval O's

Round O's

KM# 2 1.1620 g. 0.9250 Silver 0.0346 oz. ASW **Obv:** Head left **Obv. Legend:** VICTORIA DEI GRATIA REGINA. CANADA **Rev:** Denomination and date within wreath, crown above

Date	Mintage	VG-8	F-12	VF-20	XF-40	MS-60	MS-63	Proof
1858 Small date	1,500,000	19.00	30.00	45.00	80.00	250	550	—
1858 Large date over small date	Inc. above	150	225	350	550	1,500	3,500	—
1870	2,800,000	15.00	24.00	40.00	75.00	250	850	—
Note: Flat rim								
1870	Inc. above	15.00	24.00	40.00	75.00	250	600	—
Note: Wire rim								
1871	1,400,000	15.00	24.00	40.00	75.00	300	800	—
1872H	2,000,000	13.00	20.00	35.00	80.00	350	1,250	—
1874H Plain 4	800,000	22.00	45.00	90.00	150	450	1,000	—
1874H Crosslet 4	Inc. above	18.00	40.00	75.00	150	500	1,100	—
1875H Large date	1,000,000	300	500	800	1,400	5,000	15,000	—
1875H Small date	Inc. above	150	225	500	700	2,100	6,000	—
1880H	3,000,000	6.00	12.00	27.00	65.00	300	800	—
1881H	1,500,000	9.00	15.00	30.00	70.00	300	800	—
1882H	1,000,000	12.00	18.00	28.00	80.00	300	800	—
1883H	600,000	23.00	40.00	85.00	200	900	3,000	—
1884	200,000	125	200	350	750	3,500	9,000	—
1885 Small 5	1,000,000	16.00	24.00	50.00	125	750	2,900	—
1885 Large 5	Inc. above	15.00	27.00	55.00	150	850	3,000	—
1885 Large 5 over small 5	Inc. above	65.00	125	200	500	4,000	—	—
1886 Small 6	1,700,000	9.00	15.00	30.00	60.00	400	1,300	—
1886 Large 6	Inc. above	11.00	18.00	40.00	70.00	425	1,500	—
1887	500,000	30.00	60.00	75.00	175	500	1,000	—
1888	1,000,000	6.00	9.00	18.00	50.00	175	450	—
1889	1,200,000	24.00	40.00	90.00	175	600	1,600	—
1890H	1,000,000	6.00	12.00	22.00	50.00	200	450	—
1891	1,800,000	6.00	9.00	15.00	30.00	150	400	—
1892	860,000	6.00	10.00	20.00	50.00	250	700	—
1893	1,700,000	6.00	9.00	14.00	30.00	175	500	—
1894	500,000	19.00	30.00	75.00	125	450	1,400	—
1896	1,500,000	6.00	9.00	14.00	35.00	175	450	—
1897	1,319,283	4.50	6.50	20.00	45.00	150	450	—
1898	580,717	12.00	20.00	40.00	90.00	350	950	—
1899	3,000,000	4.50	6.50	12.00	25.00	125	350	—
1900 Oval 0's	1,800,000	4.50	6.50	12.00	25.00	125	400	—
1900 Round 0's	Inc. above	21.00	40.00	60.00	150	450	1,000	—
1901	2,000,000	6.00	8.00	16.00	35.00	175	500	—

KM# 9 1.1620 g. 0.9250 Silver 0.0346 oz. ASW 20.1 mm. **Obv. Designer:** G. W. DeSaulles **Rev. Designer:** Leonard C. Wyon

Date	Mintage	VG-8	F-12	VF-20	XF-40	MS-60	MS-63	Proof
1902	2,120,000	2.00	3.00	5.00	9.00	45.00	70.00	—
1902	2,200,000	2.00	4.00	7.00	14.00	45.00	80.00	—
Note: Large broad H								
1902	Inc. above	10.00	17.00	30.00	50.00	125	225	—
Note: Small narrow H								

KM# 13 1.1620 g. 0.9250 Silver 0.0346 oz. ASW 15.5 mm. **Obv:** King's bust right **Rev:** Denomination and date within wreath, crown at top

Date	Mintage	VG-8	F-12	VF-20	XF-40	MS-60	MS-63	Proof
1903 22 leaves	1,000,000	5.00	9.00	22.50	45.00	200	450	—
1903H 21 leaves	2,640,000	2.50	4.00	9.00	20.00	125	400	—
1904	2,400,000	3.00	5.00	9.00	30.00	225	650	—
1905	2,600,000	2.50	4.00	10.00	20.00	125	300	—
1906	3,100,000	2.50	3.00	7.00	17.00	125	250	—
1907	5,200,000	2.50	3.00	5.00	13.00	70.00	175	—
1908	1,220,524	7.00	13.00	30.00	50.00	125	225	—
1909 Round leaves	1,983,725	4.00	8.00	13.00	40.00	250	700	—
1909 Pointed leaves	Inc. above	16.00	24.00	55.00	125	700	1,700	—

Date	Mintage	VG-8	F-12	VF-20	XF-40	MS-60	MS-63	Proof
1910 Pointed leaves	3,850,325	2.50	3.00	6.00	12.00	65.00	125	—
1910 Round leaves	Inc. above	18.00	24.00	45.00	125	550	1,700	—

KM# 16 1.1620 g. 0.9250 Silver 0.0346 oz. ASW **Obv:** King's bust left **Obv. Designer:** E. B. MacKennal **Rev:** Denomination and date within wreath, crown above **Rev. Designer:** Leonard C. Wyon

Date	Mintage	VG-8	F-12	VF-20	XF-40	MS-60	MS-63	Proof
1911	3,692,350	2.50	4.00	7.00	12.00	80.00	125	—

KM# 22 1.1300 g. 0.9250 Silver 0.0336 oz. ASW 15.5 mm. **Obv:** King's bust left **Obv. Designer:** E. B. MacKennal **Rev:** Denomination and date within wreath, crown above **Rev. Designer:** Leonard C. Wyon

Date	Mintage	VG-8	F-12	VF-20	XF-40	MS-60	MS-63	Proof
1912	5,863,170	2.50	3.00	6.00	10.00	70.00	200	—
1913	5,488,048	2.50	3.00	5.00	8.00	35.00	70.00	—
1914	4,202,179	2.50	3.00	6.00	10.00	65.00	200	—
1915	1,172,258	14.00	20.00	35.00	65.00	350	800	—
1916	2,481,675	4.00	7.00	12.00	28.00	125	300	—
1917	5,521,373	2.50	3.00	4.00	9.00	40.00	100.00	—
1918	6,052,298	2.50	3.00	4.00	8.00	40.00	85.00	—
1919	7,835,400	2.50	3.00	4.00	8.00	40.00	85.00	—

KM# 22a 1.1664 g. 0.8000 Silver 0.0300 oz. ASW 15.48 mm. **Obv. Designer:** E. B. MacKennal **Rev. Designer:** Leonard C. Wyon

Date	Mintage	VG-8	F-12	VF-20	XF-40	MS-60	MS-63	Proof
1920	10,649,851	2.00	2.50	3.00	6.50	28.00	65.00	—
1921	2,582,495	4,000	5,000	6,500	9,000	16,000	28,000	—

Note: Approximately 460 known; balance remelted. Stack's A.G. Carter Jr. Sale (12-89) choice BU, finest known, realized $57,200

Near 6   Far 6

KM# 29 4.6000 g. Nickel 21.2 mm. **Obv:** King's bust left **Obv. Designer:** E. B. MacKennal **Rev:** Maple leaves divide denomination and date **Rev. Designer:** W. H. J. Blakemore

Date	Mintage	VG-8	F-12	VF-20	XF-40	MS-60	MS-63	Proof
1922	4,794,119	0.30	0.95	1.75	7.00	60.00	125	—
1923	2,502,279	0.40	1.25	5.50	16.00	150	400	—
1924	3,105,839	0.30	1.00	4.00	10.00	100.00	300	—
1925	201,921	65.00	80.00	150	300	1,600	5,000	—
1926 Near 6	938,162	3.00	7.00	16.00	75.00	450	1,600	—
1926 Far 6	Inc. above	150	175	300	600	2,000	6,000	—
1927	5,285,627	0.30	0.65	3.00	14.50	75.00	200	—
1928	4,577,712	0.30	0.65	3.00	14.50	65.00	125	—
1929	5,611,911	0.30	0.65	3.00	14.50	80.00	200	—
1930	3,704,673	0.30	1.25	3.00	15.00	125	250	—
1931	5,100,830	0.30	1.25	3.50	18.00	175	650	—
1932	3,198,566	0.30	1.00	3.50	16.00	150	500	—
1933	2,597,867	0.40	1.50	6.00	18.00	200	800	—
1934	3,827,304	0.30	1.00	3.00	16.00	150	500	—
1935	3,900,000	0.30	1.00	3.00	11.00	125	350	—
1936	4,400,450	0.30	0.65	1.75	9.00	60.00	150	—

KM# 33 4.5000 g. Nickel 21.2 mm.   **Obv:** Head left **Obv. Designer:** T. H. Paget **Rev:** Beaver on rock divides denomination and date **Rev. Designer:** George E. Kruger-Gray

Date	Mintage	VG-8	F-12	VF-20	XF-40	MS-60	MS-63	Proof
1937 Dot	4,593,263	0.20	0.30	1.25	2.50	12.00	24.00	—
1938	3,898,974	0.30	0.90	2.00	7.00	80.00	175	—
1939	5,661,123	0.20	0.35	1.25	3.00	55.00	90.00	—
1940	13,920,197	0.20	0.30	0.75	2.25	20.00	55.00	—
1941	8,681,785	0.20	0.30	0.75	2.25	28.00	70.00	—
1942 Round	6,847,544	0.20	0.30	0.75	1.75	20.00	50.00	—

KM# 39 Tombac Brass 21.2 mm.   **Obv:** Head left **Obv. Designer:** T. H. Paget **Rev:** Beaver on rock divides denomination and date **Rev. Designer:** George E. Kruger-Gray **Shape:** 12-sided

Date	Mintage	VG-8	F-12	VF-20	XF-40	MS-60	MS-63	Proof
1942	3,396,234	0.40	0.65	1.25	1.75	4.00	16.00	—

KM# 40 Tombac Brass 21.2 mm.   **Subject:** Victory **Obv:** Head left **Obv. Designer:** T. H. Paget **Rev:** Torch on "V" divides date **Rev. Designer:** Thomas Shingles

Date	Mintage	VG-8	F-12	VF-20	XF-40	MS-60	MS-63	Proof
1943	24,760,256	0.20	0.30	0.40	0.80	3.50	12.00	—
1944	8,000	—	—	—	—	—	—	—

Note: 1 known

KM# 40a 4.4000 g. Chrome Plated Steel 21.2 mm.   **Obv:** Head left **Rev:** Torch on "V" divides date

Date	Mintage	VG-8	F-12	VF-20	XF-40	MS-60	MS-63	Proof
1944	11,532,784	0.10	0.20	0.45	0.90	2.50	6.50	—
1945	18,893,216	0.10	0.20	0.40	0.80	2.50	6.50	—

Dot   Maple leaf

KM# 39a 4.5000 g. Nickel 21.2 mm.   **Obv:** Head left **Obv. Designer:** T. H. Paget **Rev:** Beaver on rock divides denomination and date **Rev. Designer:** George E. Kruger-Gray

Date	Mintage	VG-8	F-12	VF-20	XF-40	MS-60	MS-63	Proof
1946	6,952,684	0.10	0.25	0.50	2.00	16.00	40.00	—
1947	7,603,724	0.20	0.25	0.50	1.25	12.00	28.00	—

5 CENTS

Date	Mintage	VG-8	F-12	VF-20	XF-40	MS-60	MS-63	Proof
1947 Dot	Inc. above	18.00	22.00	35.00	75.00	200	400	—
1947 Maple leaf	9,595,124	0.20	0.25	0.45	1.25	12.00	25.00	—

KM# 42 4.5400 g. Nickel 21.2 mm. **Obv:** Head left, modified legend **Obv. Designer:** T. H. Paget **Rev:** Beaver on rock divides date and denomination **Rev. Designer:** George E. Kruger-Gray

Date	Mintage	VG-8	F-12	VF-20	XF-40	MS-60	MS-63	Proof
1948	1,810,789	0.40	0.50	1.00	3.00	20.00	40.00	—
1949	13,037,090	0.15	0.25	0.45	0.75	7.00	16.00	—
1950	11,970,521	0.15	0.25	0.45	0.75	7.00	16.00	—

KM# 42a Chromium And Nickel Plated Steel 21.2 mm. **Obv:** Head left **Obv. Designer:** T. H. Paget **Rev:** Beaver on rock divides date and denomination **Rev. Designer:** George E. Kruger-Gray

Date	Mintage	VG-8	F-12	VF-20	XF-40	MS-60	MS-63	Proof
1951	4,313,410	0.10	0.20	0.45	0.80	3.50	11.00	—
Note: Low relief; Second "A" in GRATIA points between denticles								
1951	Inc. above	400	550	750	1,200	2,400	3,500	—
Note: High relief; Second "A" in GRATIA points to a denticle								
1952	10,891,148	0.10	0.20	0.45	0.80	3.50	8.00	—

KM# 48 4.5500 g. Nickel 21.2 mm. **Subject:** Nickel Bicentennial **Obv:** Head left **Obv. Designer:** T. H. Paget **Rev:** Buildings with center tower divide dates and denomination **Rev. Designer:** Stephen Trenka **Shape:** 12-sided

Date	Mintage	VG-8	F-12	VF-20	XF-40	MS-60	MS-63	Proof
1951	9,028,507	0.15	0.25	0.30	0.45	1.75	8.00	—

KM# 50 Chromium And Nickel Plated Steel 21.2 mm. **Obv:** Laureate queen's bust, right **Obv. Designer:** Mary Gillick **Rev:** Beaver on rock divides date and denomination **Rev. Designer:** George E. Kruger-Gray **Shape:** 12-sided

Date	Mintage	VG-8	F-12	VF-20	XF-40	MS-60	MS-63	Proof
1953	16,635,552	0.10	0.20	0.40	0.90	3.00	7.00	—
Note: Without strap								
1953	Inc. above	175	250	350	550	1,600	3,500	—
Note: With strap, far leaf								
1953	Inc. above	300	450	700	900	1,300	3,500	—
Note: Without strap, near leaf								
1953	Inc. above	0.10	0.20	0.40	0.90	5.00	8.00	—
Note: With strap								
1954	6,998,662	0.10	0.25	0.50	1.00	6.00	12.00	—

KM# 50a 4.5900 g. Nickel 21.2 mm. **Obv:** Laureate queen's bust right **Obv. Designer:** Mary Gillick **Rev:** Beaver on rock divides date and denomination **Rev. Designer:** George E. Kruger-Gray

Date	Mintage	VG-8	F-12	VF-20	XF-40	MS-60	MS-63	Proof
1955	5,355,028	0.15	0.20	0.40	0.75	3.50	6.50	—
1956	9,399,854	—	0.15	0.30	0.45	2.50	5.00	—
1957	7,387,703	—	—	0.25	0.30	1.25	3.50	—
1958	7,607,521	—	—	0.25	0.30	1.25	3.50	—
1959	11,552,523	—	—	—	0.20	0.45	1.75	—
1960	37,157,433	—	—	—	0.20	0.45	1.75	—
1961	47,889,051	—	—	—	—	0.40	1.25	—
1962	46,307,305	—	—	—	—	0.40	1.25	—

KM# 57 Nickel 21.2 mm.   **Obv:** Laureate queen's bust right **Obv. Designer:** Mary Gillick **Rev:** Beaver on rock divides date and denomination **Rev. Designer:** George E. Kruger-Gray **Shape:** Round

Date	Mintage	VG-8	F-12	VF-20	XF-40	MS-60	MS-63	Proof
1963	43,970,320	—	—	—	—	0.30	0.80	—
1964	78,075,068	—	—	—	—	0.30	0.80	—
1964	—	18.00	20.00	21.00	24.00	40.00	125	—

Note: Extra water line

KM# 60.1 4.5400 g. Nickel 21.2 mm.   **Obv:** Queen's bust right **Obv. Designer:** Arnold Machin **Rev:** Beaver on rock divides date and denomination **Rev. Designer:** George E. Kruger-Gray

Date	Mintage	MS-63	Proof
1965	84,876,018	0.80	—
1966	27,976,648	0.80	—
1968	101,930,379	0.80	—
1969	27,830,229	0.80	—
1970	5,726,010	1.75	—
1971	27,312,609	0.80	—
1972	62,417,387	0.80	—
1973	53,507,435	0.80	—
1974	94,704,645	0.80	—
1975	138,882,000	0.80	—
1976	55,140,213	0.80	—
1977	89,120,791	0.80	—
1978	137,079,273	0.80	—

KM# 66 Nickel 21.2 mm.   **Subject:** Confederation Centennial **Obv:** Queen's bust right **Obv. Designer:** Arnold Machin **Rev:** Snowshoe rabbit bounding left divides dates and denomination **Rev. Designer:** Alex Coville

Date	Mintage	MS-63	Proof
1867-1967	36,876,574	0.80	1.00

KM# 60.2 Nickel 21.2 mm.   **Obv:** Queen's bust right **Obv. Designer:** Arnold Machin **Rev:** Beaver on rock divides date and denomination **Rev. Designer:** George E. Kruger-Gray

Date	Mintage	MS-63	Proof
1979	186,295,825	0.30	—
1980	134,878,000	0.30	—
1981	99,107,900	0.30	—
1981 Proof	199,000	—	1.50

KM# 60.2a 4.6000 g. Copper-Nickel 21.2 mm. **Obv:** Queen's bust right **Obv. Designer:** Arnold Machin **Rev:** Beaver on rock divides date and denomination **Rev. Designer:** George E. Kruger-Gray

Date	Mintage	MS-63	Proof
1982	64,924,400	0.30	—
1982 Proof	180,908	—	1.50
1983	72,596,000	0.30	—
1983 Proof	168,000	—	1.50
1984	84,088,000	0.30	—
1984 Proof	161,602	—	1.50
1985	126,618,000	0.30	—

Date	Mintage	MS-63	Proof
1985 Proof	157,037	—	1.50
1986	156,104,000	0.30	—
1986 Proof	175,745	—	1.50
1987	106,299,000	0.30	—
1987 Proof	179,004	—	1.50
1988	75,025,000	0.30	—
1988 Proof	175,259	—	1.50
1989	141,570,538	0.30	—
1989 Proof	170,928	—	1.50

KM# 182 4.6000 g. Copper-Nickel 19.55 mm. **Obv:** Crowned head right **Obv. Designer:** Dora dePedery-Hunt **Rev:** Beaver on rock divides dates and denomination **Rev. Designer:** George E. Kruger-Gray **Edge:** Plain

Date	Mintage	MS-63	Proof
1990	42,537,000	0.30	—
1990 Proof	140,649	—	2.50
1991	10,931,000	0.55	—
1991 Proof	131,888	—	7.00
1993	86,877,000	0.30	—
1993 Proof	143,065	—	2.50
1994	99,352,000	0.30	—
1994 Proof	146,424	—	3.00
1995	78,528,000	0.30	—
1995 Proof	50,000	—	2.50
1996 Far 6	36,686,000	2.25	—
1996 Near 6	Inc. above	2.25	—
1996 Proof	—	—	6.00
1997	27,354,000	0.30	—
1997 Proof	—	—	5.00
1998	156,873,000	0.30	—
1998W	—	1.50	—
1998 Proof	—	—	5.00
1999	124,861,000	0.30	—
1999W	—	—	—
1999 Proof	—	—	5.00
2000	108,514,000	0.30	—
2000W	—	1.50	—
2000 Proof	—	—	5.00
2001	30,035,000	12.50	—
2001P Proof	—	—	10.00
2003	—	0.30	—

KM# 205 4.6000 g. Copper-Nickel 21.2 mm.
Subject: Confederation 125 **Obv:** Crowned head
right **Obv. Designer:** Dora dePedery-Hunt **Rev:**
Beaver on rock divides date and denomination **Rev.
Designer:** George E. Kruger-Gray

Date	Mintage	MS-63	Proof
1992 Proof	147,061	—	4.00
1992	53,732,000	0.30	—

KM# 182b 3.9000 g. Nickel Plated Steel
21.2 mm. **Obv:** Crowned head right **Obv.
Designer:** Dora dePedery-Hunt **Rev:** Beaver on
rock divides date and denomination **Rev. Designer:**
George E. Kruger-Gray **Edge:** Plain

Date	Mintage	MS-63	Proof
1999 P	Est. 20,000	15.00	—
2000 P	Est. 2,300,000	3.50	—
2001 P	136,650,000	0.35	—
2003 P	32,986,921	0.35	—

KM#182a 5.3500 g. 0.9250 Silver 0.1591 oz. ASW
21.2 mm. **Obv:** Crowned head right **Obv.
Designer:** Dora dePedery-Hunt **Rev:** Beaver on
rock divides date and denomination **Rev. Designer:**
George E. Kruger-Gray

Date	Mintage	MS-63	Proof
1996 Proof	—	—	8.00
1997 Proof	—	—	8.00
1998 Proof	—	—	8.00
1998O Proof	—	—	8.00
1999 Proof	—	—	8.00
2000 Proof	—	—	8.00
2001 Proof	—	—	8.00
2003 Proof	—	—	8.00

KM# 310 1.1670 g. 0.9250 Silver 0.0347 oz.
ASW **Subject:** 90th Anniversary Royal Canadian
Mint **Obv:** Crowned head right **Obv. Designer:** Dora
dePedery-Hunt **Rev:** Denomination and date within
wreath, crown above **Rev. Designer:** W. H. J.
Blackmore

Date	Mintage	MS-63	Proof
1908-1998	25,000	12.00	—
1908-1998 Proof	25,000	—	12.00

KM# 400 0.9250 Silver 21.2 mm. **Subject:** First
French-Canadian Regiment **Obv:** Crowned head
right **Obv. Designer:** Dora dePedery-Hunt **Rev:**
Regimental drums, sash and baton, denomination
above, date at right **Rev. Designer:** R. C. M. Staff
Edge: Plain

Date	Mintage	MS-63	Proof
2000 Proof	—	—	9.00

KM# 413 5.3500 g. 0.9250 Silver 0.1591 oz. ASW
21.2 mm. **Subject:** Royal Military College **Obv:**
Crowned head right **Rev:** Marching cadets and arch
Rev. Designer: Gerald T. Locklin **Edge:** Plain

Date	Mintage	MS-63	Proof
2001 Proof	25,834	—	8.00

KM# 446 3.9500 g. Nickel Plated Steel
21.2 mm. **Subject:** Elizabeth II Golden Jubilee
Obv: Crowned head right, Jubilee commemorative
dates 1952-2002 **Obv. Designer:** Dora dePedery-
Hunt **Rev. Designer:** George E. Kruger-Gray **Note:**
Magnetic.

Date	Mintage	MS-63	Proof
1952-2002P	135,960,000	0.45	—
1952-2002P Proof	32,642	—	10.00

KM#446a 5.3500 g. 0.9250 Silver 0.1591 oz. ASW
21.2 mm. **Subject:** Elizabeth II Golden Jubilee
Obv: Queen, Jubilee commemorative dates 1952-
2002

Date	Mintage	MS-63	Proof
1952-2002 Proof	21,573	—	11.50

KM# 453 5.3500 g. 0.9250 Silver 0.1591 oz. ASW
21.2 mm. **Subject:** Vimy Ridge - WWI **Obv:**
Crowned head right **Rev:** Vimy Ridge Memorial,
allegorical figure and dates 1917-2002 **Rev.
Designer:** S. A. Allward

Date	Mintage	MS-63	Proof
2002 Proof	22,646	—	11.50

KM# 491 3.9500 g. Nickel Plated Steel
21.2 mm. **Obv:** Bare head right **Obv. Designer:**
Susanna Blunt **Rev:** Beaver divides date and
denomination **Rev. Designer:** George E. Kruger-
Gray **Note:** Magnetic.

Date	Mintage	MS-63	Proof
2003P	61,392,180	0.45	—
2004P	132,097,000	0.45	—
2004P Proof	—	—	2.50
2005P	89,664,000	0.45	—

5 CENTS

Date	Mintage	MS-63	Proof
2005P Proof	—	—	2.50
2006P	139,308,000	0.50	—
2006P Proof	—	—	2.50
2006(ml)	184,874,000	0.45	—
2006(ml) Proof	—	—	2.50
2007(ml)	221,472,000	0.45	—
2007(ml) Proof	—	—	2.50
2008(ml)	278,530,000	0.45	—
2008(ml) Proof	—	—	2.50
2009(ml)	266,488,000	0.45	—
2009(ml) Proof	—	—	2.50
2010(ml)	—	0.45	—
2010(ml) Proof	—	—	2.50
2011(ml)	—	0.45	—
2011(ml) Proof	—	—	2.50
2012(ml)	—	0.45	—
2012(ml) Proof	—	—	2.50
2013(ml)	—	0.45	—
2013(ml) Proof	—	—	2.50

KM# 469 5.3500 g. 0.9250 Silver 0.1591 oz. ASW 21.2 mm. **Subject:** 50th Anniversary of the Coronation of Elizabeth II **Obv:** Crowned head right, Jubilee commemorative dates 1953-2003 **Obv. Designer:** Mary Gillick

Date	Mintage	MS-63	Proof
1953-2003 Proof	21,573	—	11.50

KM# 491a 5.3500 g. 0.9250 Silver 0.1591 oz. ASW 21.1 mm. **Obv:** Crowned head right **Obv. Designer:** Susanna Blunt **Rev:** Beaver divides date and denomination **Edge:** Plain

Date	Mintage	MS-63	Proof
2004 Proof	—	—	6.50

KM# 506 5.3500 g. 0.9250 Silver 0.1591 oz. ASW 21.3 mm. **Obv:** Bare head right **Rev:** "Victory " design of the KM-40 reverse **Edge:** Plain **Shape:** 12-sided

Date	Mintage	MS-63	Proof
1944-2004 Proof	20,019	—	15.00

KM# 627 3.9500 g. Nickel Plated Steel 21.2 mm. **Subject:** 60th Anniversary, Victory in Europe 1945-2005 **Obv:** Head right **Rev:** Large V **Edge:** Plain

Date	Mintage	MS-63	Proof
2005P	59,269,192	4.50	—

KM# 758 5.3000 g. 0.9250 Silver 0.1576 oz. ASW **Obv:** George VI head left **Rev:** Torch and large V

Date	Mintage	MS-63	Proof
2005 Proof	42,792	—	35.00

KM# 758a 5.3000 g. 0.9250 Silver selectively gold plated 0.1576 oz. ASW **Obv:** George VI head left **Rev:** Torch and large V **Note:** Bound into Annual Report.

Date	Mintage	MS-63	Proof
2005 Proof	6,065	—	40.00

KM# 491b 4.6000 g. Copper-Nickel **Obv:** Bust right **Rev:** Beaver

Date	Mintage	MS-63	Proof
2006	43,008,000	5.00	—

KM# 1024 Nickel 21.2 mm. **Obv:** George V bust left **Rev:** Denomination and 1935-2010 anniversary dates, two maple leaves below

Date	Mintage	MS-63	Proof
1935-2010 Proof	—	—	15.00

KM# 1154 1.5590 g. 0.9250 Silver 0.0464 oz. ASW 15.5 mm. **Obv:** George V bust **Rev:** Value within wreath

Date	Mintage	MS-63	P/L	Proof
1911-2011 Proof	6,000	—	—	15.00

10 CENTS

KM# 3 2.3240 g. 0.9250 Silver 0.0691 oz. ASW 18.03 mm. **Obv:** Head left **Obv. Legend:** VICTORIA DEI GRATIA REGINA. CANADA **Rev:** Denomination and date within wreath, crown above **Edge:** Reeded

Date	Mintage	VG-8	F-12	VF-20	XF-40	MS-60	MS-63	Proof
1858/5	900	1,400	2,100	4,000	12,000	—	—	
1858	1,250,000	20.00	35.00	65.00	125	350	850	—
1870 Narrow 0	1,600,000	18.00	40.00	75.00	125	400	1,300	—
1870 Wide 0	Inc. above	35.00	65.00	125	225	600	2,100	—
1871	800,000	29.00	50.00	125	200	600	2,500	—
1871H	1,870,000	35.00	60.00	125	225	600	2,100	—
1872H	1,000,000	150	225	400	600	1,750	4,000	—
1874H	600,000	14.00	24.00	50.00	125	350	1,100	—
1875H	1,000,000	400	800	1,200	2,000	7,000	16,000	—
1880H	1,500,000	18.00	30.00	65.00	125	350	1,200	—

Date	Mintage	VG-8	F-12	VF-20	XF-40	MS-60	MS-63	Proof
1881H	950,000	21.00	35.00	70.00	150	400	1,300	—
1882H	1,000,000	21.00	35.00	70.00	150	450	1,500	—
1883H	300,000	65.00	125	250	500	1,300	3,000	—
1884	150,000	300	500	950	1,700	6,000	20,000	—
1885	400,000	65.00	125	250	500	1,700	7,000	—
1886 Small 6	800,000	30.00	65.00	125	300	1,500	4,000	—
1886 Large 6	Inc. above	40.00	80.00	150	350	1,500	4,000	—
1887	350,000	65.00	125	225	450	1,700	4,000	—
1888	500,000	16.00	27.00	55.00	125	350	1,100	—
1889	600,000	750	1,200	2,000	4,000	13,000	35,000	—
1890H	450,000	21.00	45.00	90.00	200	500	1,100	—
1891 21 leaves	800,000	21.00	45.00	90.00	200	500	1,300	—
1891 22 leaves	Inc. above	21.00	45.00	90.00	200	500	1,200	—
1892/1	520,000	250	400	700	1,400	4,000	—	—
1892	Inc. above	20.00	35.00	75.00	150	450	1,200	—
1893 Flat-top 3	500,000	45.00	80.00	150	300	1,000	2,300	—
1893 Round-top 3	Inc. above	850	1,400	2,700	5,000	13,000	35,000	—
1894	500,000	45.00	80.00	150	250	750	1,800	—
1896	650,000	14.00	24.00	45.00	90.00	300	750	—
1898	720,000	14.00	24.00	45.00	90.00	300	750	—
1899 Small 9's	1,200,000	12.00	22.00	40.00	75.00	225	600	—
1899 Large 9's	Inc. above	24.00	45.00	85.00	150	500	1,200	—
1900	1,100,000	8.50	18.00	40.00	85.00	225	650	—
1901	1,200,000	12.00	24.00	50.00	100.00	250	850	—

KM# 10 2.3240 g. 0.9250 Silver 0.0691 oz. ASW 18.03 mm.   **Obv:** Crowned bust right **Obv. Designer:** G. W. DeSaulles **Rev:** Denomination and date within wreath, crown above **Rev. Designer:** Leonard C. Wyon **Edge:** Reeded

Date	Mintage	VG-8	F-12	VF-20	XF-40	MS-60	MS-63	Proof
1902	720,000	9.00	18.00	35.00	100.00	450	1,200	—
1902H	1,100,000	4.00	9.00	20.00	45.00	150	350	—
1903	500,000	15.00	35.00	90.00	300	1,200	2,300	—
1903H	1,320,000	8.00	18.00	35.00	90.00	350	800	—
1904	1,000,000	12.00	27.50	50.00	150	400	1,000	—
1905	1,000,000	7.00	27.50	60.00	150	600	1,400	—
1906	1,700,000	7.00	13.00	35.00	80.00	350	900	—
1907	2,620,000	5.00	12.00	25.00	45.00	300	600	—
1908	776,666	9.00	27.50	60.00	150	300	600	—
1909	1,697,200	7.00	20.00	45.00	125	500	1,200	—
Note: "Victorian" leaves, similar to 1902-08 coins								
1909	Inc. above	11.00	30.00	60.00	150	750	1,800	—
Note: Broad leaves, similar to 1910-12 coins								
1910	4,468,331	4.00	9.00	20.00	40.00	150	400	—

KM# 17 2.3240 g. 0.9250 Silver 0.0691 oz. ASW 23.5 mm.   **Obv:** Crowned bust left **Obv. Designer:** E. B. MacKennal **Rev:** Denomination and date within wreath, crown above **Rev. Designer:** Leonard C. Wyon **Edge:** Reeded

Date	Mintage	VG-8	F-12	VF-20	XF-40	MS-60	MS-63	Proof
1911	2,737,584	5.00	12.00	20.00	45.00	150	300	—

Small leaves

Large leaves

KM# 23 2.3240 g. 0.9250 Silver 0.0691 oz. ASW 17.8 mm.   **Obv:** Crowned bust left **Obv. Designer:** E. B. MacKennal **Rev:** Denomination and date within wreath, crown above **Rev. Designer:** Leonard C. Wyon **Edge:** Reeded

Date	Mintage	VG-8	F-12	VF-20	XF-40	MS-60	MS-63	Proof
1912	3,235,557	BV	5.00	11.00	35.00	250	650	—
1913	3,613,937	BV	3.50	9.00	30.00	200	500	—
Note: Small leaves								
1913	Inc. above	125	225	450	1,350	8,500	27,500	—
Note: Large leaves								
1914	2,549,811	BV	4.00	9.00	30.00	175	500	—
1915	688,057	7.00	16.00	40.00	125	500	950	—
1916	4,218,114	BV	3.50	6.00	25.00	100.00	225	—
1917	5,011,988	BV	3.50	4.00	12.00	75.00	125	—
1918	5,133,602	BV	3.50	4.00	10.00	65.00	100.00	—
1919	7,877,722	BV	3.50	4.00	10.00	65.00	100.00	—

KM# 23a 2.3320 g. 0.8000 Silver 0.0600 oz. ASW 17.9 mm.   **Obv:** Crowned bust left **Obv. Designer:** E. B. MacKennal **Rev:** Denomination and date within wreath, crown above **Edge:** Reeded

Date	Mintage	VG-8	F-12	VF-20	XF-40	MS-60	MS-63	Proof
1920	6,305,345	BV	2.75	3.50	12.00	75.00	125	—
1921	2,469,562	BV	2.75	6.00	20.00	90.00	225	—
1928	2,458,602	BV	2.75	4.00	12.00	80.00	150	—
1929	3,253,888	BV	3.50	3.50	12.00	75.00	125	—
1930	1,831,043	BV	3.50	4.50	14.00	80.00	175	—
1931	2,067,421	BV	3.50	4.00	12.00	70.00	125	—
1932	1,154,317	BV	3.00	9.00	23.00	125	250	—
1933	672,368	2.50	5.00	12.00	35.00	200	400	—
1934	409,067	4.00	7.00	22.00	60.00	350	650	—
1935	384,056	4.00	7.00	19.00	60.00	350	600	—
1936	2,460,871	BV	3.50	3.00	9.00	60.00	100.00	—
1936	—	—	—	—	—	—	150,000	—

Note: Dot on reverse. Specimen, 4 known; David Akers sale of John Jay Pittman collection, Part 1, 10-97, a gem specimen realized $120,000

Maple leaf

KM# 34 2.3328 g. 0.8000 Silver 0.0600 oz. ASW 18.03 mm.   **Obv:** Head left **Obv. Designer:** T. H. Paget **Rev:** Bluenose sailing left, date at right, denomination below **Rev. Designer:** Emanuel Hahn **Edge:** Reeded

Date	Mintage	VG-8	F-12	VF-20	XF-40	MS-60	MS-63	Proof
1937	2,500,095	—	BV	3.50	4.00	16.00	24.00	—
1938	4,197,323	—	BV	4.50	7.00	60.00	100.00	—
1939	5,501,748	—	BV	3.50	6.00	50.00	90.00	—
1940	16,526,470	—	—	BV	4.00	20.00	40.00	—
1941	8,716,386	—	BV	3.00	7.00	50.00	100.00	—
1942	10,214,011	—	—	BV	5.00	40.00	60.00	—
1943	21,143,229	—	—	BV	4.00	20.00	35.00	—
1944	9,383,582	—	—	BV	5.00	28.00	45.00	—
1945	10,979,570	—	—	BV	4.00	20.00	35.00	—
1946	6,300,066	—	—	BV	5.00	30.00	45.00	—
1947	4,431,926	—	BV	3.00	7.00	40.00	60.00	—
1947	9,638,793	—	—	BV	4.00	15.00	20.00	—

Note: Maple leaf

KM# 43 2.3328 g. 0.8000 Silver 0.0600 oz. ASW 18.03 mm.   **Obv:** Head left, modified legend **Obv. Designer:** T. H. Paget **Rev:** Bluenose sailing left, date at right, denomination below **Rev. Designer:** Emanuel Hahn

Date	Mintage	VG-8	F-12	VF-20	XF-40	MS-60	MS-63	Proof
1948	422,741	BV	3.50	7.50	13.00	60.00	80.00	—
1949	11,336,172	—	—	BV	2.50	12.00	18.00	—
1950	17,823,075	—	—	BV	2.50	10.00	15.00	—
1951	15,079,265	—	—	BV	2.50	7.00	12.00	—
1951	—	—	6.00	8.00	12.00	40.00	65.00	—
Note: Doubled die								
1952	10,474,455	—	—	BV	2.50	6.00	10.00	—

KM# 51 2.3100 g. 0.8000 Silver 0.0594 oz. ASW 18 mm.   **Obv:** Laureate bust right **Obv. Designer:** Mary Gllick **Rev:** Bluenose sailing left, date at right, denomination below **Rev. Designer:** Emanuel Hahn

Date	Mintage	VG-8	F-12	VF-20	XF-40	MS-60	MS-63	Proof
1953	17,706,395	—	—	—	BV	6.00	12.00	—
Note: Without straps								
1953	Inc. above	—	—	—	BV	4.00	8.00	—
Note: With straps								
1954	4,493,150	—	—	—	BV	12.00	20.00	—
1955	12,237,294	—	—	—	BV	4.50	8.00	—
1956	Inc. above	—	3.50	4.00	7.00	15.00	24.00	—
Note: Dot below date								
1956	16,732,844	—	—	—	BV	3.00	6.00	—
1957	16,110,229	—	—	—	BV	3.50	4.00	—
1958	10,621,236	—	—	—	BV	3.50	4.00	—
1959	19,691,433	—	—	—	BV	3.00	4.00	—
1960	45,446,835	—	—	—	BV	3.00	4.00	—
1961	26,850,859	—	—	—	BV	3.00	4.00	—
1962	41,864,335	—	—	—	—	BV	2.50	—
1963	41,916,208	—	—	—	—	BV	2.50	—
1964	49,518,549	—	—	—	—	BV	2.50	—

KM# 61 2.3328 g. 0.8000 Silver 0.0600 oz. ASW 18.03 mm.   **Obv:** Young bust right **Obv. Designer:** Arnold Machin **Rev:** Bluenose sailing left, date at right, denomination below

Date	Mintage	VG-8	F-12	VF-20	XF-40	MS-60	MS-63	Proof
1965	56,965,392	—	—	—	—	BV	2.50	—
1966	34,567,898	—	—	—	—	BV	2.50	—

KM# 67 2.3328 g. 0.8000 Silver 0.0600 oz. ASW 18.03 mm.   **Subject:** Confederation Centennial **Obv:** Bust right **Rev:** Atlantic mackerel left, denomination above, dates below **Rev. Designer:** Alex Colville

Date	Mintage	VG-8	F-12	VF-20	XF-40	MS-60	MS-63	Proof
1867-1967	62,998,215	—	—	—	—	BV	2.50	—
ND1867-1967	—	—	—	—	—	—	—	2.50

KM# 67a 2.3328 g. 0.5000 Silver 0.0375 oz. ASW 18.03 mm.   **Subject:** Confederation Centennial **Obv:** Young bust right **Rev:** Atlantic mackerel left, denomination above, dates below

Date	Mintage	VG-8	F-12	VF-20	XF-40	MS-60	MS-63	Proof
1867-1967	Inc. above	—	—	—	—	BV	2.00	—

Ottawa

KM# 72 2.3328 g. 0.5000 Silver 0.0375 oz. ASW 18.03 mm.   **Obv:** Bust right **Obv. Designer:** Arnold Machin **Rev:** Bluenose sailing left, date at right, denomination below **Rev. Designer:** Emanuel Hahn **Note:** Ottawa Mint reeding has pointed deep areas in the edge reeding.

Date	Mintage	VG-8	F-12	VF-20	XF-40	MS-60	MS-63	Proof
1968	70,460,000	—	—	—	—	BV	1.50	—

Ottawa

KM# 72a Nickel 18.03 mm.   **Obv:** Young bust right **Obv. Designer:** Arnold Machin **Rev:** Bluenose sailing left, date at right, denomination below **Rev. Designer:** Emanuel Hahn **Note:** Ottawa Mint reeding has pointed deep areas in the edge reeding.

Date	Mintage	VG-8	F-12	VF-20	XF-40	MS-60	MS-63	Proof
1968	87,412,930	—	—	—	0.10	0.15	0.40	—

Philadelphia

KM# 73 2.3300 g. Nickel 18.03 mm.   **Obv:** Young bust right **Obv. Designer:** Arnold Machin **Rev:** Bluenose sailing left, date at right, denomination below **Rev. Designer:** Emanuel Hahn **Note:** Philadelphia Mint reeding has flat deep areas in the edge reeding.

Date	Mintage	VG-8	F-12	VF-20	XF-40	MS-60	MS-63	Proof
1968	85,170,000	—	—	—	0.10	0.15	0.40	—
1969	—	—	10,000	12,000	16,000	25,000	—	—

Note: Large date, large ship, 10-20 known

KM# 77.1 2.0700 g. Nickel 18.03 mm.   **Obv:** Young bust right **Obv. Designer:** Arnold Machin **Rev:** Redesigned smaller Bluenose sailing left, date at right, denomination below **Rev. Designer:** Emanuel Hahn **Edge:** Reeded

Date	Mintage	MS-63	Proof
1969	55,833,929	0.50	—
1970	5,249,296	1.00	—
1971	41,016,968	0.50	—
1972	60,169,387	0.50	—
1973	167,715,435	0.50	—
1974	201,566,565	0.50	—
1975	207,680,000	0.50	—
1976	95,018,533	0.50	—
1977	128,452,206	0.50	—
1978	170,366,431	0.50	—

KM# 77.2 2.0700 g. Nickel 18.03 mm.   **Obv:** Smaller young bust right **Obv. Designer:** Arnold Machin **Rev:** Redesigned smaller Bluenose sailing left, denomination below, date at right **Rev. Designer:** Emanuel Hahn **Edge:** Reeded

Date	Mintage	MS-63	Proof
1979	237,321,321	0.35	—
1980	170,111,533	0.35	—
1981	123,912,900	0.35	—
1981 Proof	199,000	—	1.50
1982	93,475,000	0.35	—
1982 Proof	180,908	—	1.50
1983	111,065,000	0.35	—
1983 Proof	168,000	—	1.50
1984	121,690,000	0.35	—
1984 Proof	161,602	—	1.50
1985	143,025,000	0.35	—
1985 Proof	157,037	—	1.50
1986	168,620,000	0.35	—
1986 Proof	175,745	—	1.50
1987	147,309,000	0.35	—
1987 Proof	179,004	—	1.50
1988	162,998,558	0.35	—
1988 Proof	175,259	—	1.50
1989	199,104,414	0.35	—
1989 Proof	170,528	—	1.50

KM# 183 2.1400 g. Nickel 18.03 mm.   **Obv:** Crowned head right **Obv. Designer:** Dora dePedery-Hunt **Rev:** Bluenose sailing left, date at right, denomination below **Rev. Designer:** Emanuel Hahn **Edge:** Reeded

Date	Mintage	MS-63	Proof
1990	65,023,000	0.35	—
1990 Proof	140,649	—	2.50
1991	50,397,000	0.45	—
1991 Proof	131,888	—	4.00
1993	135,569,000	0.35	—
1993 Proof	143,065	—	2.00
1994	145,800,000	0.35	—
1994 Proof	146,424	—	2.50
1995	123,875,000	0.35	—
1995 Proof	50,000	—	2.50
1996	51,814,000	0.35	—
1996 Proof	—	—	2.50
1997	43,126,000	0.35	—
1997 Proof	—	—	2.50
1998	203,514,000	0.35	—
1998W	—	1.50	—
1998 Proof	—	—	2.50
1999	258,462,000	0.35	—
1999 Proof	—	—	2.50
2000	159,125,000	0.35	—
2000 Proof	—	—	2.50
2000W	—	1.50	—

KM# 206 Nickel 18.03 mm.   **Subject:** Confederation 125 **Obv:** Crowned head right **Rev:** Bluenose sailing left, date at right, denomination below

Date	Mintage	MS-63	Proof
1867-1992	174,476,000	0.35	—
1867-1992 Proof	147,061	—	3.00

KM# 183a 2.4000 g. 0.9250 Silver 0.0714 oz. ASW 18.03 mm.   **Obv:** Crowned head right **Rev:** Bluenose sailing left, date at right, denomination below

Date	Mintage	MS-63	Proof
1996 Proof	—	—	5.50
1997 Proof	—	—	5.50
1998 Proof	—	—	4.00
1998O Proof	—	—	4.00
1999 Proof	—	—	5.00

Date	Mintage	MS-63	Proof
2000 Proof	—	—	5.00
2001 Proof	—	—	5.00
2002 Proof	—	—	7.50
2003 Proof	—	—	7.50

KM# 299 2.4000 g. 0.9250 Silver 0.0714 oz. ASW 18.03 mm. **Subject:** John Cabot **Obv:** Crowned head right **Rev:** Ship with full sails divides dates, denomination below **Rev. Designer:** Donald H. Curley

Date	Mintage	MS-63	Proof
1997 Proof	49,848	—	17.50

KM# 311 2.3200 g. 0.9250 Silver 0.0690 oz. ASW 18.03 mm. **Subject:** 90th Anniversary Royal Canadian Mint **Obv:** Crowned head right **Rev:** Denomination and date within wreath, crown above

Date	Mintage	MS-63	Proof
1908-1998 Matte	25,000	—	10.00
1908-1998 Proof	25,000	—	10.00

KM# 183b 1.7700 g. Nickel Plated Steel 18.03 mm. **Obv:** Crowned head right **Obv. Designer:** Dora dePedery-Hunt **Rev:** Bluenose sailing left, date at right, denomination below **Rev. Designer:** Emanuel Hahn **Edge:** Reeded

Date	Mintage	MS-63	Proof
1999 P	Est. 20,000	15.00	—
2000 P	Est. 200	1,000	—
2001 P	266,000,000	0.45	—
2003 P	162,398,000	0.20	—

KM# 409 2.4000 g. 0.9250 Silver 0.0714 oz. ASW 18.03 mm. **Subject:** First Canadian Credit Union **Obv:** Crowned head right **Rev:** Alphonse Desjardins' house (founder of the first credit union in Canada), dates at right, denomination below **Edge:** Reeded

Date	Mintage	MS-63	Proof
2000 Proof	66,336	—	8.00

KM# 412a 2.4000 g. 0.9250 Silver 0.0714 oz. ASW 18 mm. **Subject:** Year of the Volunteer **Obv:** Crowned head right **Rev:** Three portraits left above banner, radiant sun below **Edge:** Reeded

Date	Mintage	MS-63	Proof
2001P Proof	40,634	—	9.00

KM# 412 1.7700 g. Nickel Plated Steel 18 mm. **Subject:** Year of the Volunteer **Obv:** Crowned head right **Rev:** Three portraits left and radiant sun **Edge:** Reeded

Date	Mintage	MS-63	Proof
2001P	224,714,000	4.50	—

KM# 447 1.7700 g. Nickel Plated Steel 18 mm. **Subject:** Elizabeth II Golden Jubilee **Obv:** Crowned head right, Jubilee commemorative dates 1952-2002

Date	Mintage	MS-63	Proof
1952-2002P	252,563,000	1.00	—
1952-2002 Proof	32,642	—	2.50

KM# 447a 2.3200 g. 0.9250 Silver 0.0690 oz. ASW 18 mm. **Subject:** Elizabeth II Golden Jubilee **Obv:** Crowned head right, Jubilee commemorative dates 1952-2002

Date	Mintage	MS-63	Proof
2002 Proof	21,537	—	12.50

KM# 492 1.7700 g. Nickel Plated Steel 18 mm. **Obv:** Head right **Obv. Designer:** Susanna Blunt **Rev:** Bluenose sailing left

Date	Mintage	MS-63	Proof
2003P	—	1.25	—
2004P	211,924,000	0.60	—
2004P Proof	—	—	2.50
2005P	212,175,000	0.60	—
2005P Proof	—	—	2.50
2006P	312,122,000	0.60	—
2006P Proof	—	—	2.50
2007(ml) Straight 7	304,110,000	0.60	—
2007(ml) Curved 7	Inc. above	0.60	—
2007(ml) Proof	—	—	2.50
2008(ml)	467,495,000	0.60	—
2008(ml) Proof	—	—	2.50
2009(ml)	370,700,000	0.60	—
2009(ml) Proof	—	—	2.50
2010(ml)	—	0.60	—
2010(ml) Proof	—	—	2.50
2011(ml)	—	0.60	—
2011(ml) Proof	—	—	2.50
2012(ml)	—	0.60	—
2012(ml) Proof	—	—	2.50
2013(ml)	—	0.60	—
2013(ml) Proof	—	—	2.50

KM# 470 2.3200 g. 0.9250 Silver 0.0690 oz. ASW **Subject:** 50th Anniversary of the Coronation of Elizabeth II **Obv:** Head right **Rev:** Bluenose sailing left

Date	Mintage	MS-63	Proof
1953-2003 Proof	21,537	—	12.00

KM# 492a 2.4000 g. 0.9250 Silver 0.0714 oz. ASW 18 mm. **Obv:** Bare head right **Obv. Designer:** Susanna Blunt **Rev:** Sailboat **Edge:** Reeded

Date	Mintage	MS-63	Proof
2004 Proof	—	—	6.00

10 CENTS

KM# 524 2.4000 g. 0.9250 Silver 0.0714 oz. ASW 18 mm. **Subject:** Golf, Championship of Canada, Centennial. **Obv:** Head right

Date	Mintage	MS-63	Proof
2004	39,486	12.50	—

KM# 1155 2.4000 g. 0.9250 Silver 0.0714 oz. ASW 18.03 mm. **Obv:** George V bust **Rev:** Value within wreath

Date	Mintage	MS-63	Proof
1911-2011 Proof	6,000	—	20.00

KM# 1025 Silver 18.03 mm. **Obv:** George V bust left **Rev:** Value within wreath, dual dates below

Date	Mintage	MS-63	Proof
1935-2010 Proof	—	—	20.00

20 CENTS

KM# 4 4.6480 g. 0.9250 Silver 0.1382 oz. ASW **Obv:** Head left **Obv. Legend:** VICTORIA DEI GRATIA REGINA. CANADA **Rev:** Denomination and date within wreath, crown above

Date	Mintage	VG-8	F-12	VF-20	XF-40	MS-60	MS-63	Proof
1858	750,000	60.00	100.00	125	225	900	2,500	—

25 CENTS

KM# 5 5.8100 g. 0.9250 Silver 0.1728 oz. ASW 23.88 mm. **Obv:** Crowned head left **Obv. Legend:** VICTORIA DEI GRATIA REGINA. CANADA **Obv. Designer:** Leonard C. Wyon **Rev:** Denomination and date within wreath, crown above

Date	Mintage	VG-8	F-12	VF-20	XF-40	MS-60	MS-63	Proof
1870	900,000	22.00	45.00	85.00	200	750	2,000	—
1871	400,000	27.00	50.00	125	250	1,000	2,400	—
1871H	748,000	35.00	60.00	150	300	1,100	2,100	—
1872H	Inc. above	—	—	—	—	2,500	6,000	—
Note: Inverted "A" for "V" in Victoria								
1872H	2,240,000	13.00	25.00	45.00	125	550	1,800	—
1874H	1,600,000	13.00	25.00	45.00	125	450	1,400	—
1875H	1,000,000	400	700	1,700	3,000	20,000	35,000	—
1880H Narrow 0	400,000	60.00	125	300	600	1,700	3,500	—
1880H Wide 0	Inc. above	150	350	600	1,400	4,500	8,000	—
1880H Narrow/wide 0	Inc. above	100.00	225	400	950	2,800	—	—
1881H	820,000	30.00	55.00	125	300	1,300	4,000	—
1882H	600,000	30.00	65.00	125	300	1,200	3,000	—
1883H	960,000	20.00	40.00	85.00	200	600	1,700	—
1885	192,000	150	300	5,500	1,100	4,000	10,000	—
1886/3	540,000	90.00	200	400	750	2,400	4,500	—
1886	Inc. above	45.00	90.00	200	450	1,700	4,500	—
1887	100,000	150	300	550	1,200	7,500	12,500	—
1888	400,000	26.00	40.00	90.00	200	750	2,200	—
1889	66,324	175	350	650	1,400	4,500	13,000	—
1890H	200,000	30.00	60.00	150	300	1,000	2,300	—
1891	120,000	125	225	400	750	1,800	3,500	—
1892	510,000	20.00	40.00	85.00	200	750	2,300	—

Date	Mintage	VG-8	F-12	VF-20	XF-40	MS-60	MS-63	Proof
1893	100,000	150	300	550	1,000	2,000	3,000	—
1894	220,000	30.00	65.00	150	300	850	2,000	—
1899	415,580	12.00	25.00	60.00	150	600	1,500	—
1900	1,320,000	11.00	20.00	50.00	125	550	1,200	—
1901	640,000	15.00	24.00	65.00	200	650	1,400	—

KM# 11 5.8100 g. 0.9250 Silver 0.1728 oz. ASW 23.4 mm.   **Obv:** Crowned bust right **Obv. Designer:** G. W. DeSaulles **Rev:** Denomination and date within wreath, crown above

Date	Mintage	VG-8	F-12	VF-20	XF-40	MS-60	MS-63	Proof
1902	464,000	16.00	35.00	85.00	250	1,000	2,600	—
1902H	800,000	11.00	22.50	65.00	150	350	700	—
1903	846,150	20.00	40.00	100.00	300	1,100	2,600	—
1904	400,000	28.00	75.00	200	500	2,250	7,000	—
1905	800,000	20.00	45.00	150	400	2,000	6,000	—
1906 Large crown	1,237,843	14.00	30.00	75.00	250	800	2,400	—
1906 Small crown, Rare	Inc. above	3,500	5,500	100,000	19,000	30,000	40,000	—
1907	2,088,000	11.00	22.50	70.00	175	600	1,700	—
1908	495,016	24.00	50.00	100.00	250	550	1,000	—
1909	1,335,929	16.00	40.00	100.00	250	850	2,400	—

KM# 11a 5.8319 g. 0.9250 Silver 0.1734 oz. ASW   **Obv:** Crowned bust right **Rev:** Denomination and date within wreath, crown above

Date	Mintage	VG-8	F-12	VF-20	XF-40	MS-60	MS-63	Proof
1910	3,577,569	10.00	22.50	55.00	100.00	350	850	—

KM# 18 5.8319 g. 0.9250 Silver 0.1734 oz. ASW   **Obv:** Crowned bust left **Obv. Legend:** GEORGIVS V REX ET IND IMP **Obv. Designer:** E. B. MacKennal **Rev:** Denomination and date within wreath, crown above

Date	Mintage	VG-8	F-12	VF-20	XF-40	MS-60	MS-63	Proof
1911	1,721,341	18.00	20.00	55.00	125	350	650	—

KM# 24 5.8319 g. 0.9250 Silver 0.1734 oz. ASW 23.5 mm.   **Obv:** Crowned bust left **Obv. Legend:** GEORGIVS V DEI GRA REX ET IND IMP **Obv. Designer:** E. B. MacKennal **Rev:** Denomination and date within wreath, crown above

Date	Mintage	VG-8	F-12	VF-20	XF-40	MS-60	MS-63	Proof
1912	2,544,199	9.00	15.00	30.00	70.00	400	1,500	—
1913	2,213,595	8.00	14.00	30.00	65.00	350	1,250	—
1914	1,215,397	9.00	17.00	40.00	80.00	650	2,100	—
1915	242,382	28.00	70.00	225	600	3,500	8,500	—
1916	1,462,566	7.50	12.00	25.00	50.00	250	800	—
1917	3,365,644	7.50	9.00	18.00	40.00	150	300	—
1918	4,175,649	BV	9.00	14.00	35.00	125	225	—
1919	5,852,262	BV	9.00	14.00	35.00	125	225	—

Dot below wreath

KM# 24a 5.8319 g. 0.8000 Silver 0.1500 oz. ASW   **Obv:** Crowned bust left **Obv. Designer:** E. B. MacKennal
Rev: Denomination and date within wreath, crown below

Date	Mintage	VG-8	F-12	VF-20	XF-40	MS-60	MS-63	Proof
1920	1,975,278	BV	9.00	18.00	40.00	200	550	—
1921	597,337	17.00	35.00	125	300	1,450	3,500	—
1927	468,096	40.00	70.00	125	300	1,000	2,100	—
1928	2,114,178	BV	9.00	18.00	50.00	175	450	—
1929	2,690,562	BV	9.00	18.00	45.00	150	400	—
1930	968,748	BV	9.00	27.00	50.00	250	650	—
1931	537,815	BV	10.00	30.00	65.00	300	650	—
1932	537,994	BV	10.00	30.00	65.00	300	650	—
1933	421,282	BV	10.00	35.00	85.00	250	450	—
1934	384,350	BV	12.00	45.00	90.00	350	650	—
1935	537,772	BV	10.00	35.00	65.00	200	400	—
1936	972,094	BV	8.00	14.00	28.00	100.00	225	—
1936 Dot below wreath	153,322	40.00	95.00	225	450	1,050	2,400	—

Note: David Akers John Jay Pittman sale Part Three, 10-99, nearly Choice Unc. realized $6,900; considered a possible specimen example

Maple leaf after date

KM# 35 5.8320 g. 0.8000 Silver 0.1500 oz. ASW 23.5 mm.   **Obv:** Head left **Obv. Designer:** T. H. Paget
Rev: Caribou left, denomination above, date at right **Rev. Designer:** Emanuel Hahn

Date	Mintage	VG-8	F-12	VF-20	XF-40	MS-60	MS-63	Proof
1937	2,690,176	—	BV	7.00	7.50	20.00	40.00	—
1938	3,149,245	—	BV	8.00	15.00	80.00	150	—
1939	3,532,495	—	BV	8.00	11.00	65.00	125	—
1940	9,583,650	—	—	BV	5.00	20.00	40.00	—
1941	6,654,672	—	—	BV	6.00	23.00	45.00	—
1942	6,935,871	—	—	BV	6.00	24.00	45.00	—
1943	13,559,575	—	—	BV	6.00	23.00	45.00	—
1944	7,216,237	—	—	BV	6.00	30.00	65.00	—
1945	5,296,495	—	—	BV	6.00	23.00	55.00	—
1946	2,210,810	—	BV	6.00	12.00	55.00	100.00	—
1947	1,524,554	—	BV	6.00	12.00	65.00	100.00	—
1947 Dot after 7	Inc. above	65.00	90.00	125	225	450	900	—
1947 Maple leaf after 7	4,393,938	—	—	BV	6.00	20.00	30.00	—

KM# 44 5.8319 g. 0.8000 Silver 0.1500 oz. ASW 23.5 mm.   **Obv:** Head left, modified legend **Obv. Designer:**
T. H. Paget **Rev:** Caribou left, denomination above, date at right **Rev. Designer:** Emanuel Hahn

Date	Mintage	VG-8	F-12	VF-20	XF-40	MS-60	MS-63	Proof
1948	2,564,424	—	—	BV	12.00	70.00	125	—
1949	7,988,830	—	—	BV	12.00	15.00	30.00	—
1950	9,673,335	—	—	BV	12.00	12.00	23.00	—
1951	8,290,719	—	—	BV	12.00	11.00	18.00	—
1952	8,859,642	—	—	BV	12.00	10.00	17.00	—

25 CENTS

KM# 52 5.8319 g. 0.8000 Silver 0.1500 oz. ASW 23.8 mm. **Obv:** Laureate bust right **Obv. Designer:** Mary Gillick **Rev:** Caribou left, denomination above, date at right **Rev. Designer:** Emanuel Hahn

Date	Mintage	VG-8	F-12	VF-20	XF-40	MS-60	MS-63	Proof
1953 Without strap	10,546,769	—	—	—	BV	8.00	15.00	—
1953 With strap	Inc. above	—	—	BV	6.00	11.00	27.50	—
1954	2,318,891	—	—	BV	11.00	30.00	60.00	—
1955	9,552,505	—	—	BV	6.00	9.00	17.00	—
1956	11,269,353	—	—	—	BV	8.00	12.00	—
1957	12,770,190	—	—	—	BV	8.00	10.00	—
1958	9,336,910	—	—	—	BV	8.00	10.00	—
1959	13,503,461	—	—	—	—	BV	8.00	—
1960	22,835,327	—	—	—	—	BV	8.00	—
1961	18,164,368	—	—	—	—	BV	8.00	—
1962	29,559,266	—	—	—	—	BV	8.00	—
1963	21,180,652	—	—	—	—	BV	8.00	—
1964	36,479,343	—	—	—	—	BV	8.00	—

KM# 62 5.8319 g. 0.8000 Silver 0.1500 oz. ASW 23.8 mm. **Obv:** Young bust right **Obv. Designer:** Arnold Machin **Rev:** Caribou left, denomination above, date at right **Rev. Designer:** Emanuel Hahn

Date	Mintage	VG-8	F-12	VF-20	XF-40	MS-60	MS-63	Proof
1965	44,708,869	—	—	—	—	BV	8.00	—
1966	25,626,315	—	—	—	—	BV	8.00	—

KM# 68 5.8319 g. 0.8000 Silver 0.1500 oz. ASW 23.8 mm. **Subject:** Confederation Centennial **Obv:** Young bust right **Rev:** Lynx striding left divides dates and denomination **Rev. Designer:** Alex Colville

Date	Mintage	VG-8	F-12	VF-20	XF-40	MS-60	MS-63	Proof
1867-1967	48,855,500	—	—	—	—	BV	6.00	—

KM# 68a 5.8319 g. 0.5000 Silver 0.0937 oz. ASW 23.8 mm. **Subject:** Confederation Centennial **Obv:** Young bust right **Rev:** Lynx striding left divides dates and denomination

Date	Mintage	VG-8	F-12	VF-20	XF-40	MS-60	MS-63	Proof
1867-1967	Inc. above	—	—	—	BV	3.25	4.50	—

25 CENTS

KM# 62a 5.8319 g. 0.5000 Silver 0.0937 oz. ASW 23.8 mm. **Obv:** Young bust right **Obv. Designer:** Machin **Rev:** Caribou left, denomination above, date at right

Date	Mintage	MS-63	Proof
1968	71,464,000	4.50	—

KM# 62b 5.0600 g. Nickel 23.8 mm.   **Obv:** Young bust right **Obv. Designer:** Machin **Rev:** Caribou left, denomination above, date at right

Date	Mintage	MS-63	Proof
1968	88,686,931	0.80	—
1969	133,037,929	0.80	—
1970	10,302,010	2.00	—
1971	48,170,428	0.80	—
1972	43,743,387	0.80	—
1974	192,360,598	0.80	—
1975	141,148,000	0.80	—
1976	86,898,261	0.80	—
1977	99,634,555	0.80	—
1978	176,475,408	0.80	—

KM# 81.1 Nickel 23.8 mm.   **Subject:** Royal Candian Mounted Police Centennial **Obv:** Young bust right **Rev:** Mountie divides dates, denomination above **Rev. Designer:** Paul Cedarberg **Note:** 120 beads.

Date	Mintage	MS-63	Proof
1873-1973	134,958,587	1.25	—

KM# 81.2 Nickel 23.8 mm.   **Subject:** RCMP Centennial **Obv:** Young bust right **Rev:** Mountie divides dates, denomination above **Note:** Large bust, 132 beads.

Date	Mintage	MS-63	Proof
1873-1973	Inc. above	750	—

KM# 74 5.0700 g. Nickel 23.88 mm.   **Obv:** Small young bust right **Obv. Designer:** Machin **Rev. Designer:** Emanuel Hahn

Date	Mintage	MS-63	Proof
1979	131,042,905	0.75	—
1980	76,178,000	0.75	—
1981	131,580,272	0.75	—
1981 Proof	199,000	—	2.00
1982	171,926,000	0.75	—
1982 Proof	180,908	—	2.00
1983	13,162,000	1.50	—
1983 Proof	168,000	—	3.00
1984	121,668,000	0.75	—
1984 Proof	161,602	—	2.00
1985	158,734,000	0.75	—
1985 Proof	157,037	—	2.00
1986	132,220,000	0.75	—
1986 Proof	175,745	—	2.00
1987	53,408,000	1.25	—
1987 Proof	179,004	—	2.00

Date	Mintage	MS-63	Proof
1988	80,368,473	0.95	—
1988 Proof	175,259	—	2.00
1989	119,796,307	0.75	—
1989 Proof	170,928	—	2.00

KM# 184 5.0700 g. Nickel 23.88 mm.   **Obv:** Crowned head right **Obv. Designer:** Dora dePedery-Hunt **Rev:** Caribou left, denomination above, date at right **Rev. Designer:** Emanuel Hahn

Date	Mintage	MS-63	Proof
1990	31,258,000	0.90	—
1990 Proof	140,649	—	2.50
1991	459,000	12.00	—
1991 Proof	131,888	—	20.00
1993	73,758,000	0.70	—
1993 Proof	143,065	—	2.00
1994	77,670,000	0.70	—
1994 Proof	146,424	—	3.00
1995	89,210,000	0.70	—
1995 Proof	50,000	—	3.00
1996	28,106,000	0.70	—
1996 Proof	—	—	6.00
1997	—	0.70	—
1997 Proof	—	—	6.00
1998W	—	5.00	—
1999	258,888,000	0.75	—
1999 Proof	—	—	6.00
2000	434,087,000	0.75	—
2000 Proof	—	—	6.00
2000W	—	5.00	—
2001	8,415,000	5.00	—
2001 Proof	—	—	7.50

KM# 203 5.0000 g. Nickel 23.9 mm.   **Series:** 125th Anniversary of Confederation **Subject:** New Brunswick **Obv:** Crowned head right **Rev:** Covered bridge in Newton, denomination below **Rev. Designer:** Ronald Lambert

Date	Mintage	MS-63	Proof
1992	12,174,000	0.70	—

KM# 203a 5.8319 g. 0.9250 Silver 0.1734 oz. ASW 23.8 mm.   **Series:** 125th Anniversary of Confederation **Subject:** New Brunswick **Obv:** Crowned head right **Rev:** Covered bridge in Newton, denomination below

Date	Mintage	MS-63	Proof
1992 Proof	149,579	—	8.50

KM# 207 Nickel 23.8 mm. **Subject:** Confederation 125 **Obv:** Crowned head right **Obv. Designer:** Dora dePedery-Hunt **Rev:** Caribou left, denomination above, date at right **Rev. Designer:** Emanuel Hahn

Date	Mintage	MS-63	Proof
1867-1992	442,986	12.50	—
1867-1992 Proof	147,061	—	20.00

KM# 212 Nickel 23.8 mm. **Series:** 125th Anniversary of Confederation **Subject:** Northwest Territories **Obv:** Crowned head right **Rev. Designer:** Beth McEachen

Date	Mintage	MS-63	Proof
1992	12,582,000	0.70	—

KM#212a 5.8319 g. 0.9250 Silver 0.1734 oz. ASW 23.8 mm. **Series:** 125th Anniversary of Confederation **Subject:** Northwest Territories **Obv:** Crowned head right

Date	Mintage	MS-63	Proof
1992 Proof	149,579	—	8.50

KM# 213 Nickel 23.8 mm. **Series:** 125th Anniversary of Confederation **Subject:** Newfoundland **Rev:** Fisherman rowing a dory, denomination below **Rev. Designer:** Christopher Newhook

Date	Mintage	MS-63	Proof
1992	11,405,000	0.70	—

KM#213a 5.8319 g. 0.9250 Silver 0.1734 oz. ASW 23.8 mm. **Series:** 125th Anniversary of Confederation **Subject:** Newfoundland **Rev:** Fisherman rowing a dory, denomination below

Date	Mintage	MS-63	Proof
1992 Proof	149,579	—	8.50

KM# 214 Nickel 23.8 mm. **Series:** 125th Anniversary of Confederation **Subject:** Manitoba **Obv:** Crowned head right **Rev. Designer:** Muriel Hope

Date	Mintage	MS-63	Proof
1992	11,349,000	0.70	—

KM#214a 5.8319 g. 0.9250 Silver 0.1734 oz. ASW 23.8 mm. **Series:** 125th Anniversary of Confederation **Subject:** Manitoba **Obv:** Crowned head right

Date	Mintage	MS-63	Proof
1992 Proof	149,579	—	8.50

KM# 220 Nickel 23.8 mm. **Series:** 125th Anniversary of Confederation **Subject:** Yukon **Obv:** Crowned head right **Rev. Designer:** Libby Dulac

Date	Mintage	MS-63	Proof
1992	10,388,000	0.70	—

KM#220a 5.8319 g. 0.9250 Silver 0.1734 oz. ASW 23.8 mm. **Series:** 125th Anniversary of Confederation **Subject:** Yukon **Obv:** Crowned head right

Date	Mintage	MS-63	Proof
1992 Proof	149,579	—	8.50

KM# 221 Nickel 23.8 mm. **Series:** 125th Anniversary of Confederation **Subject:** Alberta **Obv:** Crowned head right **Rev:** Rock formations in the badlands near Drumhelter, denomination below **Rev. Designer:** Mel Heath

Date	Mintage	MS-63	Proof
1992	12,133,000	0.70	—

KM#221a 5.8319 g. 0.9250 Silver 0.1734 oz. ASW 23.8 mm. **Series:** 125th Anniversary of Confederation **Subject:** Alberta **Obv:** Crowned head right **Rev:** Rock formations in the badlands near Drumhelter, denomination below **Rev. Designer:** Mel Heath

Date	Mintage	MS-63	Proof
1992 Proof	—	—	8.50

KM# 222 Nickel 23.8 mm. **Series:** 125th Anniversary of Confederation **Subject:** Prince Edward Island **Obv:** Crowned head right **Rev. Designer:** Nigel Roe

Date	Mintage	MS-63	Proof
1992	13,001,000	0.70	—

KM# 222a 5.8319 g. 0.9250 Silver 0.1734 oz. ASW 23.8 mm. **Series:** 125th Anniversary of Confederation **Subject:** Prince Edward Island **Obv:** Crowned head right **Rev. Designer:** Nigel Roe

Date	Mintage	MS-63	Proof
1992 Proof	149,579	—	8.50

KM# 223 Nickel 23.8 mm. **Series:** 125th Anniversary of Confederation **Subject:** Ontario **Obv:** Crowned head right **Rev:** Jack pine, denomination below **Rev. Designer:** Greg Salmela

Date	Mintage	MS-63	Proof
1992	14,263,000	0.70	—

KM# 223a 5.8319 g. 0.9250 Silver 0.1734 oz. ASW 23.8 mm. **Series:** 125th Anniversary of Confederation **Subject:** Ontario **Obv:** Crowned head right **Rev:** Jack pine, denomination below **Rev. Designer:** Greg Salmela

Date	Mintage	MS-63	Proof
1992 Proof	149,579	—	8.50

KM# 231 5.0300 g. Nickel 23.8 mm. **Series:** 125th Anniversary of Confederation **Subject:** Nova Scotia **Obv:** Crowned head right **Rev:** Lighthouse, denomination below **Rev. Designer:** Bruce Wood

Date	Mintage	MS-63	Proof
1992	13,600,000	0.70	—

KM# 231a 5.8319 g. 0.9250 Silver 0.1734 oz. ASW 23.8 mm. **Series:** 125th Anniversary of Confederation **Subject:** Nova Scotia **Obv:** Crowned head right **Rev:** Lighthouse, denomination below **Rev. Designer:** Bruce Wood

Date	Mintage	MS-63	Proof
1992 Proof	149,579	—	8.50

KM# 232 Nickel 23.8 mm. **Series:** 125th Anniversary of Confederation **Subject:** British Columbia **Obv:** Crowned head right, dates below **Rev:** Large rock, whales, denomination below **Rev. Designer:** Carla Herrera Egan

Date	Mintage	MS-63	Proof
1992	14,001,000	0.70	—

KM# 232a 5.8319 g. 0.9250 Silver 0.1734 oz. ASW 23.8 mm. **Series:** 125th Anniversary of Confederation **Subject:** British Columbia **Obv:** Crowned head right, dates below **Rev:** Large rock, whales, denomination below **Rev. Designer:** Carla Herrera Egan

Date	Mintage	MS-63	Proof
1992 Proof	149,579	—	8.50

KM# 233 Nickel 23.8 mm. **Series:** 125th Anniversary of Confederation **Subject:** Saskatchewan **Obv:** Crowned head right **Rev:** Buildings behind wall, grain stalks on right, denomination below **Rev. Designer:** Brian Cobb

Date	Mintage	MS-63	Proof
1992	14,165,000	0.70	—

KM# 233a 5.8319 g. 0.9250 Silver 0.1734 oz. ASW 23.8 mm. **Series:** 125th Anniversary of Confederation **Subject:** Saskatchewan **Obv:** Crowned head right **Rev:** Buildings behind wall, grain stalks on right, denomination below **Rev. Designer:** Brian Cobb

Date	Mintage	MS-63	Proof
1992 Proof	149,579	—	8.50

KM# 234 Nickel 23.8 mm. **Series:** 125th Anniversary of Confederation **Subject:** Quebec **Obv:** Crowned head right **Rev:** Boats on water, large rocks in background, denomination below **Rev. Designer:** Romualdas Bukauskas

Date	Mintage	MS-63	Proof
1992	13,607,000	0.70	—

KM# 234a 5.8319 g. 0.9250 Silver 0.1734 oz. ASW 23.8 mm. **Series:** 125th Anniversary of Confederation **Subject:** Quebec **Obv:** Crowned head right **Rev:** Boats on water, large rocks in background, denomination below **Rev. Designer:** Romualdas Bukauskas

Date	Mintage	MS-63	Proof
1992 Proof	149,579	—	8.50

KM# 184a 5.9000 g. 0.9250 Silver 0.1755 oz. ASW 23.88 mm. **Obv:** Crowned head right **Rev:** Caribou left, denomination above, date at right

Date	Mintage	MS-63	Proof
1996 Proof	—	—	9.50
1997 Proof	—	—	9.50
1998 Proof	—	—	8.50
1998O Proof	—	—	8.50
1999 Proof	—	—	8.50
2001 Proof	—	—	9.50
2003 Proof	—	—	9.50

25 CENTS

KM# 312 0.9250 Silver 23.88 mm.   **Subject:** 90th Anniversary Royal Canadian Mint **Obv:** Crowned head right **Rev:** Denomination and date within wreath, crown above

Date	Mintage	MS-63	Proof
1998 Matte	25,000	—	15.00
1998 Proof	—	—	15.00

KM# 184b 4.4000 g. Nickel Plated Steel 23.88 mm.   **Obv:** Crowned head right **Rev:** Caribou left, denomination above, date at right

Date	Mintage	MS-63	Proof
1999 P	Est. 20,000	20.00	—
2000 P	—	5,500	—
Note: 3-5 known			
2001 P	55,773,000	0.95	—
2001 P Proof	—	—	5.00
2002 P	156,105,000	2.50	—
2002 P Proof	—	—	5.00
2003 P	87,647,000	2.50	—
2003 P Proof	—	—	5.00

KM# 342 5.0700 g. Nickel 23.8 mm.   **Series:** Millennium **Subject:** January - A Country Unfolds **Obv:** Crowned head right **Rev:** Totem pole, portraits **Rev. Designer:** P. Ka-Kin Poon

Date	Mintage	MS-63	Proof
1999	12,181,200	0.65	—

KM#342a 5.8319 g. 0.9250 Silver 0.1734 oz. ASW 23.8 mm.   **Series:** Millennium **Subject:** January **Obv:** Crowned head right **Rev:** Totem pole, portraits **Rev. Designer:** P. Ka-kin Poon

Date	Mintage	MS-63	Proof
1999 Proof	113,645	—	9.50

KM# 343 5.0900 g. Nickel 23.8 mm.   **Series:** Millennium **Subject:** February - Etched in Stone **Obv:** Crowned head right **Rev:** Native petroglyphs **Rev. Designer:** L. Springer

Date	Mintage	MS-63	Proof
1999	14,469,250	0.65	—

KM#343a 5.8319 g. 0.9250 Silver 0.1734 oz. ASW 23.8 mm.   **Series:** Millennium **Subject:** February **Obv:** Crowned head right **Rev:** Native petroglyphs **Rev. Designer:** L. Springer

Date	Mintage	MS-63	Proof
1999 Proof	113,645	—	9.50

KM# 344 5.0700 g. Nickel 23.8 mm.   **Series:** Millennium **Subject:** March - The Log Drive **Obv:** Crowned head right **Rev:** Lumberjack **Rev. Designer:** M. Lavoie

Date	Mintage	MS-63	Proof
1999	15,033,500	0.65	—

KM#344a 5.8319 g. 0.9250 Silver 0.1734 oz. ASW 23.8 mm.   **Series:** Millennium **Subject:** March **Obv:** Crowned head right **Rev:** Lumberjack **Rev. Designer:** M. Lavoie

Date	Mintage	MS-63	Proof
1999 Proof	113,645	—	9.50

KM# 345 5.0700 g. Nickel 23.8 mm.   **Series:** Millennium **Subject:** April - Our Northern Heritage **Obv:** Crowned head right **Rev:** Owl, polar bear **Rev. Designer:** Ken Ojnak Ashevac

Date	Mintage	MS-63	Proof
1999	15,446,000	0.65	—

KM#345a 5.8319 g. 0.9250 Silver 0.1734 oz. ASW 23.8 mm.   **Series:** Millennium **Subject:** April **Obv:** Crowned head right **Rev:** Owl, polar bear **Rev. Designer:** Ken Ojnak Ashevac

Date	Mintage	MS-63	Proof
1999 Proof	113,645	—	9.50

KM# 346 5.0700 g. Nickel 23.8 mm.   **Series:** Millennium **Subject:** May - The Voyageures **Obv:** Crowned head right **Rev:** Voyageurs in canoe **Rev. Designer:** S. Mineok

Date	Mintage	MS-63	Proof
1999	15,566,100	0.65	—

KM#346a 5.8319 g. 0.9250 Silver 0.1734 oz. ASW 23.8 mm.   **Series:** Millennium **Subject:** May **Obv:** Crowned head right **Rev:** Voyageurs in canoe **Rev. Designer:** S. Mineok

Date	Mintage	MS-63	Proof
1999 Proof	113,645	—	9.50

25 CENTS

KM# 347 5.0300 g. Nickel 23.8 mm. **Series:** Millennium **Subject:** June - From Coast to Coast **Obv:** Crowned head right **Rev:** 19th-century locomotive **Rev. Designer:** G. Ho **Edge:** Reeded

Date	Mintage	MS-63	Proof
1999	20,432,750	0.65	—

KM#347a 5.8319 g. 0.9250 Silver 0.1734 oz. ASW 23.8 mm. **Series:** Millennium **Subject:** June **Obv:** Crowned head right **Rev:** 19th-century locomotive **Rev. Designer:** G. Ho **Edge:** Reeded

Date	Mintage	MS-63	Proof
1999 Proof	113,645	—	9.50

KM# 350 5.0700 g. Nickel 23.8 mm. **Series:** Millennium **Subject:** September - Canada Through a Child's Eye **Obv:** Crowned head right **Rev:** Childlike artwork **Rev. Designer:** Claudia Bertrand

Date	Mintage	MS-63	Proof
1999	31,539,350	0.65	—

KM#350a 5.8319 g. 0.9250 Silver 0.1734 oz. ASW 23.8 mm. **Series:** Millennium **Subject:** September **Obv:** Crowned head right **Rev:** Childlike artwork **Rev. Designer:** Claudia Bertrand

Date	Mintage	MS-63	Proof
1999 Proof	113,645	—	9.50

KM# 348 5.0700 g. Nickel 23.8 mm. **Series:** Millennium **Subject:** July - A Nation of People **Obv:** Crowned head right **Rev:** 6 stylized portraits **Rev. Designer:** M. H. Sarkany

Date	Mintage	MS-63	Proof
1999	17,321,000	0.65	—

KM#348a 5.8319 g. 0.9250 Silver 0.1734 oz. ASW 23.8 mm. **Series:** Millennium **Subject:** July **Obv:** Crowned head right **Rev:** 6 stylized portraits **Rev. Designer:** M.H. Sarkany

Date	Mintage	MS-63	Proof
1999 Proof	113,645	—	9.50

KM# 351 5.0700 g. Nickel 23.8 mm. **Series:** Millennium **Subject:** October - Tribute to the First Nations **Obv:** Crowned head right **Rev:** Aboriginal artwork **Rev. Designer:** J. E. Read

Date	Mintage	MS-63	Proof
1999	32,136,650	0.65	—

KM#351a 5.8319 g. 0.9250 Silver 0.1734 oz. ASW 23.8 mm. **Series:** Millennium **Subject:** October **Obv:** Crowned head right **Rev:** Aboriginal artwork **Rev. Designer:** J.E. Read

Date	Mintage	MS-63	Proof
1999 Proof	113,645	—	9.50

KM# 349 5.0700 g. Nickel 23.8 mm. **Series:** Millennium **Subject:** August - The Pioneer Spirit **Obv:** Crowned head right **Rev:** Hay harvesting **Rev. Designer:** A. Botelho

Date	Mintage	MS-63	Proof
1999	18,153,700	0.65	—

KM#349a 5.8319 g. 0.9250 Silver 0.1734 oz. ASW 23.8 mm. **Series:** Millennium **Subject:** August **Obv:** Crowned head right **Rev:** Hay harvesting **Rev. Designer:** A. Botelho

Date	Mintage	MS-63	Proof
1999 Proof	113,645	—	9.50

KM# 352 5.0700 g. Nickel 23.8 mm. **Series:** Millennium **Subject:** November - The Airplane Opens the North **Obv:** Crowned head right **Rev:** Bush plane with landing skis **Rev. Designer:** B. R. Brown

Date	Mintage	MS-63	Proof
1999	27,162,800	0.65	—

KM#352a 5.8319 g. 0.9250 Silver 0.1734 oz. ASW 23.8 mm. **Series:** Millennium **Subject:** November **Obv:** Crowned head right **Rev:** Bush plane with landing skis **Rev. Designer:** B.R. Brown

Date	Mintage	MS-63	Proof
1999 Proof	113,645	—	9.50

KM# 353 5.0700 g. Nickel 23.8 mm. **Series:** Millennium **Subject:** December - This is Canada **Obv:** Crowned head right **Rev:** Eclectic geometric design **Rev. Designer:** J. L. P. Provencher

Date	Mintage	MS-63	Proof
1999	43,339,200	0.70	—

KM#353a 5.1000 g. 0.9250 Silver 0.1517 oz. ASW 23.8 mm. **Series:** Millennium **Subject:** December **Obv:** Crowned head right **Rev:** Eclectic geometric design **Rev. Designer:** J.L.P. Provencher

Date	Mintage	MS-63	Proof
1999 Proof	113,645	—	9.50

KM# 373 Nickel 23.8 mm. **Subject:** Health **Obv:** Crowned head right, denomination below **Rev:** Ribbon and caduceus, date above **Rev. Designer:** Anny Wassef

Date	Mintage	MS-63	Proof
2000	35,470,900	0.65	—

KM# 373a 0.9250 Silver 23.8 mm. **Subject:** Health **Obv:** Crowned head right, denomination below **Rev:** Ribbon and caduceus, date above **Rev. Designer:** Anny Wassef

Date	Mintage	MS-63	Proof
2000 Proof	76,956	—	9.50

KM# 374 5.1000 g. Nickel 23.85 mm. **Subject:** Freedom **Obv:** Crowned head right, denomination below **Rev:** 2 children on maple leaf and rising sun, date above **Rev. Designer:** Kathy Vinish

Date	Mintage	MS-63	Proof
2000	35,188,900	0.65	—

KM# 374a 0.9250 Silver 23.8 mm. **Subject:** Freedom **Obv:** Crowned head right, denomination below **Rev:** 2 children on maple leaf and rising sun, date above **Rev. Designer:** Kathy Vinish

Date	Mintage	MS-63	Proof
2000 Proof	76,956	—	9.00

KM# 375 Nickel 23.8 mm. **Subject:** Family **Obv:** Crowned head right, denomination below **Rev:** Wreath of native carvings, date above **Rev. Designer:** Wade Stephen Baker

Date	Mintage	MS-63	Proof
2000	35,107,700	0.65	—

KM# 375a 0.9250 Silver 23.8 mm. **Subject:** Family **Obv:** Crowned head right, denomination below **Rev:** Wreath of native carvings, date above **Rev. Designer:** Wade Stephen Baker

Date	Mintage	MS-63	Proof
2000 Proof	76,956	—	9.00

KM# 376 5.0800 g. Nickel 23.8 mm. **Subject:** Community **Obv:** Crowned head right, denomination below **Rev:** Map on globe, symbols surround, date above **Rev. Designer:** Michelle Thibodeau

Date	Mintage	MS-63	Proof
2000	35,155,400	0.65	—

KM# 376a 0.9250 Silver 23.8 mm. **Subject:** Community **Obv:** Crowned head right, denomination below **Rev:** Map on globe, symbols surround, date above **Rev. Designer:** Michelle Thibodeau

Date	Mintage	MS-63	Proof
2000 Proof	76,956	—	9.00

KM# 377 Nickel 23.8 mm. **Subject:** Harmony **Obv:** Crowned **Rev:** Maple leaf, date above **Rev. Designer:** Haver Demirer

Date	Mintage	MS-63	Proof
2000	35,184,200	0.65	—

KM# 377a 0.9250 Silver 23.8 mm. **Subject:** Harmony **Obv:** Crowned head right, denomination below **Rev:** Maple leaf **Rev. Designer:** Haver Demirer

Date	Mintage	MS-63	Proof
2000 Proof	76,956	—	9.00

25 CENTS

KM# 378 Nickel 23.8 mm. **Subject:** Wisdom **Obv:** Crowned head right, denomination below **Rev:** Man with young child, date above **Rev. Designer:** Cezar Serbanescu

Date	Mintage	MS-63	Proof
2000	35,123,950	0.65	—

KM# 378a 0.9250 Silver 23.8 mm. **Subject:** Wisdom **Obv:** Crowned head right, denomination below **Rev:** Man with young child **Rev. Designer:** Cezar Serbanescu

Date	Mintage	MS-63	Proof
2000 Proof	76,956	—	9.00

KM# 379 Nickel 23.8 mm. **Subject:** Creativity **Obv:** Crowned head right, denomination below **Rev:** Canoe full of children, date above **Rev. Designer:** Kong Tat Hui

Date	Mintage	MS-63	Proof
2000	35,316,770	0.65	—

KM# 379a 0.9250 Silver 23.8 mm. **Subject:** Creativity **Obv:** Crowned head right, denomination below **Rev:** Canoe full of children **Rev. Designer:** Kong Tat Hui

Date	Mintage	MS-63	Proof
2000 Proof	76,956	—	9.00

KM# 380 Nickel 23.8 mm. **Subject:** Ingenuity **Obv:** Crowned head right, denomination below **Rev:** Crescent-shaped city views, date above **Rev. Designer:** John Jaciw

Date	Mintage	MS-63	Proof
2000	36,078,360	0.65	—

KM# 380a 0.9250 Silver 23.8 mm. **Subject:** Ingenuity **Obv:** Crowned head right, denomination below **Rev:** Crescent-shaped city views **Rev. Designer:** John Jaciw

Date	Mintage	MS-63	Proof
2000 Proof	76,956	—	9.00

KM# 381 Nickel 23.8 mm. **Subject:** Achievement **Obv:** Crowned head right, denomination below **Rev:** Rocket above jagged design, date above **Rev. Designer:** Daryl Dorosz

Date	Mintage	MS-63	Proof
2000	35,312,750	0.65	—

KM# 381a 0.9250 Silver 23.8 mm. **Subject:** Achievement **Obv:** Crowned head right, denomination below **Rev:** Rocket above jagged design **Rev. Designer:** Daryl Dorosz

Date	Mintage	MS-63	Proof
2000 Proof	76,956	—	9.00

KM# 382 Nickel 23.8 mm. **Subject:** Natural legacy **Obv:** Crowned head right, denomination below **Rev:** Environmental elements, date above **Rev. Designer:** Randy Trantau

Date	Mintage	MS-63	Proof
2000	36,236,900	0.65	—

KM# 382a 0.9250 Silver 23.8 mm. **Subject:** Natural legacy **Obv:** Crowned head right, denomination below **Rev:** Environmental elements **Rev. Designer:** Randy Trantau

Date	Mintage	MS-63	Proof
2000 Proof	76,956	—	9.00

KM# 383 Nickel 23.8 mm. **Subject:** Celebration **Obv:** Crowned head right, denomination below **Rev:** Fireworks, children behind flag, date above **Rev. Designer:** Laura Paxton

Date	Mintage	MS-63	Proof
2000	35,144,100	0.65	—

KM# 383a 0.9250 Silver 23.8 mm. **Subject:** Celebration **Obv:** Crowned head right, denomination below **Rev:** Fireworks, children behind flag **Rev. Designer:** Laura Paxton

Date	Mintage	MS-63	Proof
2000 Proof	76,956	—	9.00

KM# 384.1 Nickel 23.8 mm. **Subject:** Pride **Obv:** Crowned head right, denomination below **Rev:** Large ribbon 2 in red with 3 small red maple leaves on large maple leaf, date above **Rev. Designer:** Donald F. Warkentin **Edge:** Reeded **Note:** Colorized version.

Date	Mintage	MS-63	Proof
2000	49,399	6.50	—

KM# 384.2 Nickel 23.8 mm. **Subject:** Pride **Obv:** Crowned head right, denomination below **Rev:** Large ribbon 2 with three small maple leaves on large maple leaf, date above **Rev. Designer:** Donald F. Warkentin

Date	Mintage	MS-63	Proof
2000	50,666,800	0.65	—

KM# 384.2a 0.9250 Silver 23.8 mm. **Subject:** Pride **Obv:** Crowned head right, denomination below **Rev:** Ribbon 2 with 3 small maple leaves on large maple leaf **Rev. Designer:** Donald F. Warkentin

Date	Mintage	MS-63	Proof
2000 Proof	76,956	—	9.00

KM# 419 4.4000 g. Nickel Plated Steel 23.9 mm. **Subject:** Canada Day **Obv:** Crowned head right **Rev:** Maple leaf at center, children holding hands below **Rev. Designer:** Silke Ware **Edge:** Reeded

Date	Mintage	MS-63	Proof
2001	96,352	7.00	—

KM# 448 4.4000 g. Nickel Plated Steel 23.9 mm. **Subject:** Elizabeth II Golden Jubilee **Obv:** Crowned head right **Rev:** Caribou left

Date	Mintage	MS-63	Proof
1952-2002P	152,485,000	2.00	—
1952-2002P Proof	32,642	—	6.00

KM# 448a 5.9000 g. 0.9250 Silver 0.1755 oz. ASW 23.9 mm. **Subject:** Elizabeth II Golden Jubilee **Obv:** Crowned head right, Jubilee commemorative dates 1952-2002

Date	Mintage	MS-63	Proof
1952-2002 Proof	100,000	—	12.50

KM# 451 4.4000 g. Nickel Plated Steel 23.9 mm. **Rev:** Small human figures supporting large maple leaf

Date	Mintage	MS-63	Proof
2002P	30,627,000	5.00	—

KM# 451a 4.4000 g. Nickel Plated Steel 23.9 mm. **Subject:** Canada Day **Obv:** Crowned

head right **Rev:** Human figures supporting large red maple leaf **Edge:** Reeded

Date	Mintage	MS-63	Proof
2002P	49,901	6.00	—

KM# 493 4.4000 g. Nickel Plated Steel 23.9 mm. **Obv:** Bare head right **Obv. Designer:** Susanna Blunt **Rev:** Caribou left, denomination above, date at right

Date	Mintage	MS-63	Proof
2003P	66,861,633	2.00	—
2003P W	—	—	—
2004P	177,466,000	2.50	—
2004P Proof	—	—	5.00
2005P	206,346,000	2.50	—
2005P Proof	—	—	5.00
2006P	423,189,000	2.50	—
2006P Proof	—	—	5.00
2007(ml)	386,763,000	2.50	—
2007(ml) Proof	—	—	5.00
2008(ml)	387,222,000	2.50	—
2008(ml) Proof	—	—	5.00
2009(ml)	266,766,000	2.50	—
2009(ml) Proof	—	—	5.00
2010(ml)	—	2.50	—
2010(ml) Proof	—	—	5.00
2011(ml)	—	2.50	—
2011(ml) Proof	—	—	5.00
2012(ml)	—	2.50	—
2012(ml) Proof	—	—	5.00
2013(ml)	—	2.50	—
2013(ml) Proof	—	—	5.00

KM# 471 5.9000 g. 0.9250 Silver 0.1755 oz. ASW 23.9 mm. **Subject:** 50th Anniversary of the Coronation of Elizabeth II **Obv:** 1953 Effigy of the Queen, Coronation Jubilee dates 1953-2003 **Obv. Designer:** Mary Gillick

Date	Mintage	MS-63	Proof
1953-2003 Proof	21,537	—	12.50

KM# 474 4.4000 g. 0.9250 Silver 0.1308 oz. ASW 23.9 mm. **Subject:** Canada Day **Obv:** Queen's head right **Rev:** Polar bear and red colored maple leaves

Date	Mintage	MS-63	Proof
2003 Proof	63,511	—	12.00

KM# 493a 5.9000 g. 0.9250 Silver 0.1755 oz. ASW 23.9 mm. **Obv:** Bare head right **Obv. Designer:** Suanne Blunt **Rev:** Caribou **Edge:** Reeded

Date	Mintage	MS-63	Proof
2004 Proof	—	—	6.50

25 CENTS

25 CENTS

KM# 510 4.4000 g. Nickel Plated Steel
23.9 mm.   **Obv:** Bare head right **Rev:** Red poppy
in center of maple leaf **Edge:** Reeded

Date	Mintage	MS-63	Proof
2004	28,500,000	5.00	—

KM# 510a 5.9000 g. 0.9250 Silver 0.1755 oz. ASW
23.9 mm.   **Obv:** Bare head right **Rev:** Poppy at
center of maple leaf, selectively gold plated **Edge:**
Reeded **Note:** Housed in Annual Report.

Date	Mintage	MS-63	Proof
2004 Proof	12,677	—	20.00

KM# 525 4.4000 g. Nickel Plated Steel
23.9 mm.   **Obv:** Bare head right **Rev:** Maple leaf,
colorized

Date	Mintage	MS-63	Proof
2004	16,028	8.00	—

KM# 628 4.4000 g. Nickel Plated Steel
23.9 mm.   **Subject:** First Settlement, Ile Ste Croix
1604-2004 **Obv:** Bare head right **Rev:** Sailing ship
Bonne-Renommee

Date	Mintage	MS-63	Proof
2004P	15,400,000	5.00	—

KM# 698 4.4000 g. Nickel Plated Steel
23.88 mm.   **Rev:** Santa, colorized

Date	Mintage	MS-63	Proof
2004	62,777	5.00	—

KM# 699 4.4000 g. Nickel Plated Steel
23.9 mm.   **Series:** Canada Day **Rev:** Moose head,
humorous

Date	Mintage	MS-63	Proof
2004	44,752	5.00	—

KM# 529 4.4000 g. Nickel Plated Steel
23.9 mm.   **Subject:** WWII, 60th Anniversary **Obv:**
Head right **Rev:** Three soldiers and flag

Date	Mintage	MS-63	Proof
1945-2005	3,500	20.00	—

KM# 530 4.4000 g. Nickel Plated Steel
23.9 mm.   **Subject:** Alberta **Obv:** Head right **Rev:**
Oil rig and sunset

Date	Mintage	MS-63	Proof
2005P	20,640,000	7.00	—

KM# 531 4.4000 g. Nickel Plated Steel
23.9 mm.   **Subject:** Canada Day **Obv:** Head right
Rev: Beaver, colorized

Date	Mintage	MS-63	Proof
2005P	58,370	8.50	—

KM# 532 4.4000 g. Nickel Plated Steel
23.9 mm.   **Subject:** Saskatchewan **Obv:** Head
right **Rev:** Bird on fencepost

Date	Mintage	MS-63	Proof
2005P	19,290,000	7.00	—

KM# 533 4.4000 g. Nickel Plated Steel
23.9 mm.   **Obv:** Head right **Rev:** Stuffed bear in
Christmas stocking, colorized

Date	Mintage	MS-63	Proof
2005P	72,831	10.00	—

KM# 535 4.4000 g. Nickel Plated Steel
23.9 mm.   **Subject:** Year of the Veteran **Obv:**
Head right **Rev:** Conjoined busts of young and
veteran left **Edge:** Reeded

Date	Mintage	MS-63	Proof
2005P	29,390,000	7.00	—

KM# 576 4.4000 g. Nickel Plated Steel
23.9 mm.   **Subject:** Quebec Winter Carnival **Obv:**
Head right **Rev:** Snowman, colorized

Date	Mintage	MS-63	Proof
2006	8,200	10.00	—

KM# 534 4.4000 g. Nickel Plated Steel
23.9 mm.   **Subject:** Toronto Maple Leafs **Obv:**
Head right **Rev:** Colorized team logo

Date	Mintage	MS-63	Proof
2006P	11,765	12.50	—

KM# 575 4.4000 g. Nickel Plated Steel
23.9 mm.   **Subject:** Montreal Canadiens **Obv:**
Head right **Rev:** Colorized logo

Date	Mintage	MS-63	Proof
2006P	11,765	12.50	—

KM# 629 4.4000 g. Nickel Plated Steel
23.9 mm. **Obv:** Head right **Rev:** Medal of Bravery
Edge: Reeded

Date	Mintage	MS-63	Proof
2006(ml)	20,040,000	2.50	—

KM# 632 12.6100 g. Nickel Plated Steel 35 mm.
Subject: Queen Elizabeth II 80th Birthday **Rev:**
Crown, colorized

Date	Mintage	MS-63	Proof
1926-2006 Specimen	24,977	25.00	—

KM# 633 4.4300 g. Nickel Plated Steel
23.9 mm. **Subject:** Canada Day **Obv:** Crowned
head right **Rev:** Boy marching with flag, colorized

Date	Mintage	MS-63	Proof
2006P	30,328	6.00	—

KM# 634 4.4300 g. Nickel Plated Steel
23.88 mm. **Subject:** Breast Cancer **Rev:** Four
ribbons, all colorized **Note:** Sold housed in a
bookmark.

Date	Mintage	MS-63	Proof
2006P	40,911	10.00	—

KM# 636 4.4000 g. Nickel Plated Steel
23.88 mm. **Obv:** Head right **Obv. Designer:**
Susana Blunt **Rev:** Medal of Bravery design (maple
leaf within wreath)

Date	Mintage	MS-63	Proof
2006	20,045,111	7.00	—

KM# 637 4.4300 g. Nickel Plated Steel
23.88 mm. **Subject:** Wedding **Rev:** Colorized
bouquet of flowers

Date	Mintage	MS-63	Proof
2007(ml)	10,318	5.00	—

KM# 642 4.4300 g. Nickel Plated Steel
23.88 mm. **Subject:** Ottawa Senators **Obv:** Head
right **Rev:** Logo

Date	Mintage	MS-63	Proof
2006P	11,765	12.50	—

KM# 644 4.4300 g. Nickel Plated Steel
23.88 mm. **Subject:** Calgary Flames **Obv:** Head
right **Rev:** Logo

Date	Mintage	MS-63	Proof
2007(ml)	1,082	12.50	—

KM# 645 4.4300 g. Nickel Plated Steel
23.88 mm. **Subject:** Edmonton Oilers **Obv:** Head
right **Rev:** Logo

Date	Mintage	MS-63	Proof
2007(ml)	2,214	12.50	—

KM# 647 4.4300 g. Nickel Plated Steel **Subject:**
Santa and Rudolph **Rev:** Colorized Santa in sled
lead by Rudolph

Date	Mintage	MS-63	Proof
2006P	99,258	5.00	—

KM# 682 4.4300 g. Nickel Plated Steel **Subject:**
Curling **Obv:** Head right

Date	Mintage	MS-63	Proof
2007	22,400,000	7.50	—
2008 Mule	—	—	—

KM# 683 4.4300 g. Nickel Plated Steel **Subject:**
Ice Hockey **Obv:** Head right

Date	Mintage	MS-63	Proof
2007	22,400,000	7.50	—
2008 Mule	—	—	—

25 CENTS

KM# 684 4.4300 g. Nickel Plated Steel
23.8 mm.   **Subject:** Paraolympic Winter Games
Obv: Head right **Rev:** Wheelchair curling

Date	Mintage	MS-63	Proof
2007	22,400,000	7.50	—
2008 Mule	—	—	—

KM# 685 4.4300 g. Nickel Plated Steel   **Subject:**
Biathlon **Obv:** Head right

Date	Mintage	MS-63	Proof
2007	22,400,000	7.50	—
2008 Mule	—	—	—

KM# 638 4.4300 g. Nickel Plated Steel
23.88 mm.   **Subject:** Birthday **Rev:** Colorized
balloons

Date	Mintage	MS-63	Proof
2007(ml)	24,531	5.00	—

KM# 639 4.4300 g. Nickel Plated Steel
23.88 mm.   **Subject:** Baby birth **Rev:** Colorized
baby rattle **Edge:** Reeded

Date	Mintage	MS-63	Proof
2007(ml)	30,090	5.00	—

KM# 640 4.4300 g. Nickel Plated Steel
23.88 mm.   **Subject:** Oh Canada **Obv:** Head right
Rev: Maple leaf, colorized

Date	Mintage	MS-63	Proof
2006(ml)	23,582	8.50	—

KM# 641 4.4300 g. Nickel Plated Steel
23.88 mm.   **Subject:** Congratulations **Obv:** Head
right **Rev:** Fireworks, colorized

Date	Mintage	MS-63	Proof
2006(ml)	9,671	8.00	—

KM# 643 4.4300 g. Nickel Plated Steel
23.88 mm.   **Subject:** Vancouver Canucks **Obv:**
Head right **Rev:** Logo

Date	Mintage	MS-63	Proof
2007(ml)	1,526	12.50	—

KM# 686 4.4300 g. Nickel Plated Steel
23.8 mm.   **Subject:** Alpine Skiing **Obv:** Head right

Date	Mintage	MS-63	Proof
2007	22,400,000	7.50	—
2008 Mule	—	—	—

KM# 701 4.4300 g. Nickel Plated Steel
23.88 mm.   **Subject:** Birthday **Rev:** Party hat,
multicolor

Date	Mintage	MS-63	Proof
2007	11,376	8.00	—

KM# 702 4.4300 g. Nickel Plated Steel
23.88 mm.   **Subject:** Congratulations **Rev:**
Trophy, multicolor

Date	Mintage	MS-63	Proof
2007	—	8.00	—

KM# 703 4.4300 g. Nickel Plated Steel
23.88 mm.   **Subject:** Wedding **Rev:** Cake,
multicolor

Date	Mintage	MS-63	Proof
2007	—	8.00	—

KM# 704 4.4300 g. Nickel Plated Steel
23.88 mm.   **Subject:** Canada Day **Rev:** Mountie,
colorized

Date	Mintage	MS-63	Proof
2007(ml)	27,743	8.00	—

KM# 705 4.4300 g. Nickel Plated Steel
23.88 mm.   **Subject:** Christmas **Rev:** Multicolor
tree

Date	Mintage	MS-63	Proof
2007	66,267	8.00	—

KM# 706 12.6100 g. Nickel Plated Steel 35.0 mm.
Subject: Red-breasted Nuthatch **Obv:** Head right
Obv. Legend: ELIZABETH II - D • G • REGINA **Obv.
Designer:** Susanna Blunt **Rev:** Nuthatch perched on
pine branch multicolor **Rev. Legend:** CANADA **Rev.
Designer:** Arnold Nogy **Edge:** Plain

Date	Mintage	MS-63	Proof
2007(ml) Specimen	11,909	295	—

KM# 760 4.4300 g. Nickel Plated Steel 23.88 mm. **Subject:** Baby **Rev:** Multicolor blue teddy bear

Date	Mintage	MS-63	Proof
2008	29,639	8.00	—

KM# 761 4.4300 g. Nickel Plated Steel 23.88 mm. **Subject:** Birthday **Rev:** Multicolor party hat

Date	Mintage	MS-63	Proof
2008	11,376	8.00	—

KM# 707 12.6100 g. Nickel Plated Steel 35 mm. **Obv:** Elizabeth II **Rev:** Multicolor ruby-throated hummingbird and flower **Edge:** Plain

Date	Mintage	MS-63	Proof
2007 Specimen	17,174	135	—

KM# 762 4.4300 g. Nickel Plated Steel 23.88 mm. **Subject:** Congratulations **Rev:** Multicolor trophy

Date	Mintage	MS-63	Proof
2008	6,821	8.00	—

KM# 708 12.6100 g. Nickel Plated Steel 35 mm. **Subject:** Queen's 60th Wedding Anniversary **Rev:** Royal carriage in color

Date	Mintage	MS-63	Proof
1947-2007 Specimen	15,235	25.00	—

KM# 713 4.4000 g. Nickel Plated Steel **Rev:** Toronto Maple Leaf logo, colorized

Date	Mintage	MS-63	Proof
2007(ml)	5,365	5.00	—

KM# 714 4.4000 g. Nickel Plated Steel **Rev:** Ottawa Senators logo, colorized

Date	Mintage	MS-63	Proof
2007(ml)	2,474	5.00	—

KM# 723 4.4000 g. Nickel Plated Steel **Rev:** Montreal Canadiens logo, colorized

Date	Mintage	MS-63	Proof
2007(ml)	4,091	5.00	—

KM# 763 4.4300 g. Nickel Plated Steel 23.88 mm. **Subject:** Wedding **Rev:** Multicolor wedding cake

Date	Mintage	MS-63	Proof
2008	7,407	8.00	—

KM# 764 4.4300 g. Nickel Plated Steel 23.88 mm. **Subject:** Santa Claus **Rev:** Multicolor Santa

Date	Mintage	MS-63	Proof
2008	42,344	8.00	—

KM# 1039 4.4300 g. Nickel Plated Steel 23.9 mm. **Subject:** Canada Day **Rev:** Colorized moose head

Date	Mintage	MS-63	Proof
2008	11,538	12.50	—

KM# 765 4.4300 g. Nickel Plated Steel 23.9 mm. **Subject:** Vancouver Olympics **Rev:** Freestyle skiing

Date	Mintage	MS-63	Proof
2008	—	2.00	—

KM# 766 4.4300 g. Nickel Plated Steel 23.8 mm.
Subject: Vancouver Olympics **Rev:** Figure skating

Date	Mintage	MS-63	Proof
2008	—	2.00	—

KM#768 4.4300 g. Nickel Plated Steel 23.88 mm.
Subject: Vancouver Olympics **Rev:** Snowboarding

Date	Mintage	MS-63	Proof
2008	—	2.00	—

KM# 769 4.4300 g. Nickel Plated Steel
23.88 mm.   **Subject:** Vancouver Olympics **Rev:**
Olympic mascot - Miga

Date	Mintage	MS-63	Proof
2008	—	3.00	—

KM# 770 4.4300 g. Nickel Plated Steel
23.88 mm.   **Subject:** Vancouver Olympics **Rev:**
Olympic mascot - Quatchi

Date	Mintage	MS-63	Proof
2008	—	3.00	—

KM# 771 4.4300 g. Nickel Plated Steel
23.88 mm.   **Subject:** Vancouver Olympics **Rev:**
Olympic mascot - Sumi

Date	Mintage	MS-63	Proof
2008	—	3.00	—

KM#772 4.4300 g. Nickel Plated Steel 23.88 mm.
Subject: Oh Canada **Rev:** Multicolor red flag

Date	Mintage	MS-63	Proof
2008	—	8.00	—

KM# 773 12.6100 g. Nickel Plated Steel 35 mm.
Obv: Bust right **Obv. Designer:** Susanna Blunt **Rev:**

Downy woodpecker in tree, multicolor **Rev. Designer:**
Arnold Nogy **Edge:** Plain **Note:** Prev. KM#717.

Date	Mintage	MS-63	Proof
2008(ml) Specimen	14,282	275	—

KM# 774 12.6100 g. Nickel Plated Steel 35 mm.
Obv: Bust right **Obv. Designer:** Susanna Blunt
Rev: Northern cardinal perched on branch -
multicolor **Rev. Designer:** Arnold Nogy **Edge:** Plain
Note: Prev. KM#718.

Date	Mintage	MS-63	Proof
2008(ml) Specimen	11,604	275	—

KM# 775 4.4300 g. Nickel Plated Steel
23.8 mm.   **Subject:** End of WWI, 90th Anniversary
Rev: Multicolor poppy

Date	Mintage	MS-63	Proof
1918-2008	10,167	8.00	—

KM# 776 12.6100 g. Nickel Plated Steel 35 mm.
Subject: Anne of Green Gables **Rev:** Image of
young girl, multicolor **Rev. Designer:** Ben Stahl

Date	Mintage	MS-63	Proof
1908-2008 Specimen	32,795	20.00	—

KM# 841 4.4300 g. Nickel Plated Steel
23.8 mm. **Subject:** Vancouver Olympics **Rev:**
Bobsleigh

Date	Mintage	MS-63	Proof
2008	—	3.00	—

KM# 1041 4.4300 g. Nickel Plated Steel
Subject: WWI **Rev:** Three military men standing
over tomb

Date	Mintage	MS-63	Proof
2008(ml)	10,167	12.50	—

KM# 840 4.4300 g. Nickel Plated Steel
23.8 mm. **Subject:** Valcouver 2010 Olympics
Rev: Cross-country skiing

Date	Mintage	MS-63	Proof
2009	—	3.00	—

KM# 842 4.4300 g. Nickel Plated Steel
23.9 mm. **Subject:** Edmonton Olympics **Rev:**
Speed skating

Date	Mintage	MS-63	Proof
2009	—	3.00	—

KM# 885 4.4000 g. Nickel Plated Steel
23.88 mm. **Subject:** Canada Day **Rev:** Animals
in boat with flag **Rev. Legend:** Canada 25 cents

Date	Mintage	MS-63	Proof
2009	11,091	5.00	—

KM# 886 12.6100 g. Nickel Plated Steel 35 mm.
Subject: Notre-Dame-Du-Saguenay **Obv:** Bust
right **Obv. Legend:** Elizabeth II DG Regina **Obv.
Designer:** Susanna Blunt **Rev:** Color photo of fjord
and statue **Rev. Legend:** Canada 25 cents

Date	Mintage	MS-63	Proof
2009 Specimen	16,653	25.00	—

KM# 915 4.4300 g. Nickel Plated Steel
23.9 mm. **Subject:** Surprise Birthday **Obv:** Bust
right **Obv. Designer:** Susanna Blunt **Rev:** Colorized

Date	Mintage	MS-63	Proof
2009	9,663	12.50	—

KM# 916 4.4300 g. Nickel Plated Steel
23.9 mm. **Subject:** Share the Excitement **Obv:**
Bust right **Obv. Designer:** Susanna Blunt **Rev:**
Colorized

Date	Mintage	MS-63	Proof
2009	4,126	12.50	—

KM# 917 4.4300 g. Nickel Plated Steel
23.9 mm. **Subject:** Share the Love **Obv:** Bust
right **Obv. Designer:** Susanna Blunt **Rev:** Two
doves, coolored

Date	Mintage	MS-63	Proof
2009	7,571	12.50	—

KM# 918 4.4300 g. Nickel Plated Steel
23.9 mm. **Subject:** Thank You **Obv:** Bust right
Obv. Designer: Susanna Blunt **Rev:** Colorized

Date	Mintage	MS-63	Proof
2009	4,415	12.50	—

KM# 933 4.4000 g. Nickel Plated Steel
23.9 mm. **Rev:** Santa Claus, multicolor

Date	Mintage	MS-63	Proof
2009	933	16.50	—

KM# 934 4.4000 g. Nickel Plated Steel 23.9 mm.
Rev: Multicolor teddy bear, crescent moon

Date	Mintage	MS-63	Proof
2009	25,182	16.50	—

KM# 935 4.4000 g. Nickel Plated Steel
23.9 mm. **Subject:** Oh Canada **Rev:** Maple
leaves, yellow color

Date	Mintage	MS-63	Proof
2009	14,451	16.50	—

KM# 952 4.4000 g. Nickel Plated Steel
23.9 mm. **Rev:** Sledge hockey

Date	Mintage	MS-63	Proof
2009	—	3.00	—

KM# 1063 Nickel Plated Steel **Subject:** Men's
Hockey **Rev:** Hockey player and maple leaf outline

Date	Mintage	MS-63	Proof
2009	—	2.50	—

KM# 1063a Nickel Plated Steel **Subject:** Men's
Hockey **Rev:** Hockey player and maple leaf outline
in red

Date	Mintage	MS-63	Proof
2009	—	7.50	—

KM# 1064 Nickel Plated Steel 23.9 mm.
Subject: Women's Hockey **Rev:** Hockey player and
maple leaf outline

Date	Mintage	MS-63	Proof
2009	—	2.50	—

KM# 1064a Nickel Plated Steel **Subject:**
Women's Hockey **Rev:** Hockey player and male leaf
outline in red

Date	Mintage	MS-63	Proof
2009	—	7.50	—

KM# 1065 Nickel Plated Steel 23.9 mm.
Subject: Klassen - Female hockey player **Rev:**
Skater and maple leaf outline

Date	Mintage	MS-63	Proof
2009	—	2.50	—

KM# 1065a Nickel Plated Steel   **Subject:**
Klassen - female skater **Rev:** Skater and maple leaf
outline in red

Date	Mintage	MS-63	Proof
2009	—	7.50	—

KM# 880 4.4000 g. Nickel Plated Steel
23.88 mm.   **Subject:** Miga Mascot Vancouver
Olympics **Rev:** Mica Mascot - color **Rev. Legend:**
Vancouver 2010 25 cents

Date	Mintage	MS-63	Proof
2010	14,654	3.00	—

KM# 881 4.4000 g. Nickel Plated Steel
23.88 mm.   **Subject:** Quatchi Mascot - Vancouver
Olympics **Obv:** Bust right **Rev:** Quatchi Mascot color
Rev. Legend: Vancouver 2010 25 cents

Date	Mintage	MS-63	Proof
2010	15,310	3.00	—

KM# 882 4.4000 g. Nickel Plated Steel
23.88 mm.   **Subject:** Sumi Mascot **Rev:** Sumi
Mascot color **Rev. Legend:** Vancouver 2010 25
cents

Date	Mintage	MS-63	Proof
2010	15,333	3.00	—

KM# 953 4.4000 g. Nickel Plated Steel
23.9 mm.   **Rev:** Ice hockey

Date	Mintage	MS-63	Proof
2010	—	3.00	—

KM# 953a 4.4000 g. Nickel Plated Steel
23.9 mm.   **Rev:** Ice Hockey - red enamel

Date	Mintage	MS-63	Proof
2010	—	8.00	—

KM# 954 4.4000 g. Nickel Plated Steel
23.9 mm.   **Rev:** Curling

Date	Mintage	MS-63	Proof
2010	—	3.00	—

KM# 954a 4.4000 g. Nickel Plated Steel
23.9 mm.   **Rev:** Curling red enamel

Date	Mintage	MS-63	Proof
2010	—	8.00	—

KM# 955 4.4000 g. Nickel Plated Steel
23.9 mm.   **Rev:** Wheelchair curling

Date	Mintage	MS-63	Proof
2010	—	3.00	—

KM# 955a 4.4000 g. Nickel Plated Steel
23.9 mm.   **Rev:** Wheelchair curling - red enamel

Date	Mintage	MS-63	Proof
2010	—	8.00	—

KM# 956 4.4000 g. Nickel Plated Steel
23.9 mm.   **Rev:** Biathlon

Date	Mintage	MS-63	Proof
2010	—	3.00	—

KM# 956a 4.4000 g. Nickel Plated Steel
23.9 mm.   **Rev:** Biathlon - red enamel

Date	Mintage	MS-63	Proof
2010	—	8.00	—

KM# 957 4.4000 g. Nickel Plated Steel
23.9 mm.   **Rev:** Alpine skiing

Date	Mintage	MS-63	Proof
2010	—	3.00	—

KM# 957a 4.4000 g. Nickel Plated Steel
23.9 mm.   **Rev:** Alpine skiing - red enamel

Date	Mintage	MS-63	Proof
2010	—	8.00	—

KM# 958 4.4000 g. Nickel Plated Steel
23.9 mm.   **Rev:** Snowboarding

Date	Mintage	MS-63	Proof
2010	—	3.00	—

KM# 958a 4.4000 g. Nickel Plated Steel
23.9 mm.   **Rev:** Snowboarding - red enamel

Date	Mintage	MS-63	Proof
2010	—	8.00	—

KM# 959 23.9000 g. Nickel Plated Steel
23.9 mm.   **Rev:** Free-style skiing

Date	Mintage	MS-63	Proof
2010	—	3.00	—

KM# 959a 4.4000 g. Nickel Plated Steel
23.9 mm.   **Rev:** Free-style skiing - red enamel

Date	Mintage	MS-63	Proof
2010	—	8.00	—

KM# 960 4.4000 g. Nickel Plated Steel
23.9 mm.   **Rev:** Alpine skiing

Date	Mintage	MS-63	Proof
2010	—	3.00	—

KM# 960a 4.4000 g. Nickel Plated Steel
23.9 mm.   **Rev:** Alpine skiing - red enamel

Date	Mintage	MS-63	Proof
2010	—	8.00	—

KM# 988 4.4000 g. Nickel Plated Steel
23.88 mm.   **Rev:** Blue baby carriage

Date	Mintage	MS-63	Proof
2010	—	10.00	—

KM# 989 4.4000 g. Nickel Plated Steel
23.9 mm.   **Rev:** Purple gift box

Date	Mintage	MS-63	Proof
2010	—	10.00	—

KM# 991 4.4000 g. Nickel Plated Steel
23.9 mm.   **Rev:** Three maple leaves

Date	Mintage	MS-63	Proof
2010	—	12.50	—

KM# 992 4.4000 g. Nickel Plated Steel
23.9 mm.   **Rev:** Three zinnias

Date	Mintage	MS-63	Proof
2010	—	12.50	—

KM# 993 4.4300 g. Nickel Plated Steel
23.9 mm.   **Rev:** Pink hearts and roses

Date	Mintage	MS-63	Proof
2010	—	10.00	—

KM# 994 12.6100 g. Nickel Plated Steel 35 mm.
Rev: Goldfinch, multicolor **Rev. Designer:** Arnold
Nogy

Date	Mintage	MS-63	Proof
2010 Specimen	Est. 14,000	90.00	

KM# 1001 12.6100 g. Nickel Plated Steel
35 mm.   **Subject:** Blue Jay **Rev:** Multicolor blue
jay on yellow maple leaves

Date	Mintage	MS-63	Proof
2010 Specimen	Est. 14,000	90.00	25.00

KM# 1006 0.5000 g. 0.9990 Gold 0.0161 oz. AGW
11 mm.   **Rev:** Caribou head left

Date	Mintage	MS-63	Proof
2010 Proof	15,000	—	80.00

KM# 1021 Nickel Plated Steel 23.9 mm.   **Rev:**
Santa Claus in color

Date	Mintage	MS-63	Proof
2010	—	15.00	—

KM# 1026 Silver 23.8 mm.   **Obv:** George V bust
left **Rev:** Value within wreath, dual dates below

Date	Mintage	MS-63	Proof
1935-2010 Proof	—	—	25.00

KM# 1028 4.4000 g. Nickel Plated Steel
23.9 mm.   **Rev:** Soldier standing, two red poppies,
large maple leaf behind

Date	Mintage	MS-63	Proof
2010	—	15.00	—

25 CENTS

KM# 1110 12.6100 g. Nickel Plated Steel
35 mm. **Subject:** Royal Wedding **Rev:** Colored
portraits left of William and Katherine

Date	Mintage	MS-63	Proof
2011 Specimen	—	25.00	—

KM#1156 5.9000 g. 0.9250 Silver 0.1755 oz. ASW
23.8 mm. **Obv:** George V bust **Rev:** Value within
wreath

Date	Mintage	MS-63	P/L	Proof
1911-2011 Proof	6,000	—	—	25.00

KM# 1079 12.6100 g. Nickel Plated Steel
35 mm. **Rev:** Barn Swallow in color **Rev.**
Designer: Arnold Nagy

Date	Mintage	MS-63	Proof
2011 Specimen	Est. 14,000	55.00	—

KM# 1080 4.4300 g. Nickel Plated Steel
23.88 mm. **Subject:** Oh Canada! **Rev:** Maple leaf
and circular legend

Date	Mintage	MS-63	Proof
2011	—	2.50	—

KM# 1081 4.4300 g. Nickel Plated Steel
23.88 mm. **Subject:** Wedding **Rev:** Two rings

Date	Mintage	MS-63	Proof
2011	—	2.50	—

KM# 1082 4.4300 g. Nickel Plated Steel
23.88 mm. **Subject:** Birthday **Rev:** Year in four
baloons

Date	Mintage	MS-63	Proof
2011	—	2.50	—

KM# 1083 4.4300 g. Nickel Plated Steel
23.88 mm. **Subject:** New Baby! **Rev:** Baby's feet

Date	Mintage	MS-63	Proof
2011	—	2.50	—

KM# 1084 4.4300 g. Nickel Plated Steel
23.88 mm. **Rev:** Tooth Fairy

Date	Mintage	MS-63	Proof
2011	—	2.50	—

KM# 1113 12.6100 g. Nickel Plated Steel 35 mm.
Rev: Fantasy Furry Woods creature in color

Date	Mintage	MS-63	Proof
2011	—	20.00	—

25 CENTS

KM# 1114 12.6100 g. Nickel Plated Steel
35 mm.   **Rev:** Fantasy sea serpent in color

Date	Mintage	MS-63	Proof
2011	—	20.00	—

KM# 1115 12.6100 g. Nickel Plated Steel
35 mm.   **Rev:** Tulip and ladybug in color

Date	Mintage	MS-63	Proof
2011	—	35.00	—

KM# 1116 12.6100 g. Nickel Plated Steel
35 mm.   **Rev:** Black capped chickadee in color

Date	Mintage	MS-63	Proof
2011 Specimen	—	55.00	—

KM# 1148 4.4300 g. Nickel Plated Steel
23.9 mm.   **Obv:** Bust right **Rev:** Snowflake

Date	Mintage	MS-63	Proof
2011	—	7.50	—

KM# 1168 4.4000 g. Nickel Plated Steel
23.9 mm.   **Obv:** Bust right **Rev:** Stylized bison

Date	Mintage	MS-63	Proof
2011	—	2.50	—

KM# 1168a 4.4000 g. Nickel Plated Steel with
color 23.9 mm.   **Obv:** Bust right **Rev:** Stylized
bison, green circle in background

Date	Mintage	MS-63	Proof
2011	—	9.50	—

KM# 1169 4.4000 g. Nickel Plated Steel
23.9 mm.   **Obv:** Bust right **Rev:** Stylized falcon

Date	Mintage	MS-63	Proof
2011	—	2.50	—

KM# 1169a 4.4000 g. Nickel Plated Steel with
color 23.9 mm.   **Obv:** Bust right **Rev:** Stylized
falcon with yellow circle in background

Date	Mintage	MS-63	Proof
2011	—	9.50	—

KM# 1170 4.4000 g. Nickel Plated Steel
23.9 mm.   **Obv:** Bust right **Rev:** Stylized orca
whale

Date	Mintage	MS-63	Proof
2011	—	2.50	—

KM# 1170a 4.4000 g. Nickel Plated Steel with color 23.9 mm. **Obv:** Bust right **Rev:** Stylized orca whale with blue circle in background

Date	Mintage	MS-63	Proof
2011	—	9.50	—

KM# 1171 0.5000 g. 0.9990 Gold 0.0161 oz. AGW 11 mm. **Obv:** Bust right **Rev:** Cougar head left

Date	Mintage	MS-63	Proof
2011 Proof	—	—	80.00

KM# 1172 12.6100 g. Copper Plated Silver gold plated 35 mm. **Obv:** Bust right **Rev:** Wayne Greskey in hockey helmet left

Date	Mintage	MS-63	Proof
2011 Specimen	—	35.00	—

KM# 1192 4.4300 g. Nickel Plated Steel 23.9 mm. **Subject:** Canadian Broadcasting Company, 75th Anniversary **Obv:** Bust right **Rev:** Old-time radio microphone

Date	Mintage	MS-63	Proof
2011	—	2.50	—

KM# 1193 12.6100 g. Nickel Plated Steel 35 mm. **Subject:** Mythical Creature - Mishepishu **Obv:** Bust right **Rev:** Horned lizard in color

Date	Mintage	MS-63	Proof
2011	—	15.00	—

KM# 1227 4.4300 g. Nickel Plated Steel 23.9 mm. **Obv:** Bust right **Rev:** Tooth Fairy in flight

Date	Mintage	MS-63	Proof
2012	—	2.50	—

KM# 1228 4.4300 g. Nickel Plated Steel 23.9 mm. **Subject:** Baby **Rev:** Baby's mobile

Date	Mintage	MS-63	Proof
2012	—	2.50	—

KM# 1229 4.4300 g. Nickel Plated Steel 23.9 mm. **Subject:** Wedding **Rev:** Two wedding rings with small feet

Date	Mintage	MS-63	Proof
2012	—	2.50	—

KM# 1230 4.4300 g. Nickel Plated Steel 23.9 mm. **Subject:** Birthday **Rev:** Cone with character face

Date	Mintage	MS-63	Proof
2012	—	2.50	—

KM# 1231 4.4300 g. Nickel Plated Steel 23.9 mm. **Subject:** Oh, Canada ! **Rev:** Maple leaves with character faces

Date	Mintage	MS-63	Proof
2012	—	2.50	—

KM# 1232 4.4300 g. Nickel Plated Steel 23.88 mm. **Subject:** Winnipeg Jets **Rev:** Jet superimposed on Maple leaf

Date	Mintage	MS-63	Proof
2012	—	2.50	—

KM# 1233 12.6100 g. Nickel Plated Steel
35 mm.   **Subject:** Titanic, 100th Anniversary **Obv:**
Bust right **Rev:** Two views of Titanic, one at
dockside, one nighttime at sea

Date	Mintage	MS-63	Proof
2012	—	20.00	—

KM# 1247 12.6100 g. Nickel Plated Steel
35 mm.   **Subject:** Coast Guard, 100th anniversary
Rev: Rescue craft in rough seas

Date	Mintage	MS-63	Proof
2012	—	30.00	—

KM# 1252 12.6100 g. Nickel Plated Steel
35 mm.   **Subject:** Pachyrhinosaurus Lakusta
Note: Skelton glows in the dark.

Date	Mintage	MS-63	Proof
2012	—	25.00	—

KM# 1253 12.6100 g. Nickel Plated Steel
35 mm.   **Subject:** Rose Breasted Grosbeak

Date	Mintage	MS-63	Proof
2012	—	35.00	—

KM# 1265 12.6100 g. Nickel Plated Steel
35 mm.   **Subject:** Aster and Bee

Date	Mintage	MS-63	Proof
2012	—	35.00	—

KM# 1313 0.5000 g. Silver 35 mm.   **Subject:**
Grey Cup, 100th Anniversary **Obv:** Bust right **Obv.
Designer:** Susana Blunt **Rev:** B.C. Lions logo in
color

Date	Mintage	MS-63	Proof
2012 Proof	—	—	25.00

KM# 1314 0.5000 g. Copper-Nickel 35 mm.
Subject: Grey Cup, 100th Anniversary **Obv:** Bust
right **Obv. Designer:** Susana Blunt **Rev:** Calgary
Stampeeders logo in color

Date	Mintage	MS-63	Proof
2012 Proof	—	—	25.00

KM# 1315 0.5000 g. Copper-Nickel 35 mm.
Subject: Grey Cup, 100th Anniversary **Obv:** Bust
right **Obv. Designer:** Susana Blunt **Rev:** Edmonton
Eskimos logo in color

Date	Mintage	MS-63	Proof
2012 Proof	—	—	25.00

KM# 1316 0.5000 g. Copper-Nickel 35 mm.
Subject: Grey Cup, 100th Anniversary **Obv:** Bust
right **Obv. Designer:** Susana Blunt **Rev:** Hamilton
Tiger-Cats logo in color

KM# 1317 0.5000 g. Copper-Nickel 35 mm.
Subject: Grey Cup, 100th Anniversary **Obv:** Bust
right **Obv. Designer:** Susana Blunt **Rev:** Montreal
Alouettes logo in color

Date	Mintage	MS-63	Proof
2012 Proof	—	—	25.00

KM# 1318 0.5000 g. Copper-Nickel 35 mm.
Subject: Grey Cup, 100th Anniversary **Obv:** Bust
right **Obv. Designer:** Susana Blunt **Rev:**
Saskatchewan Roughriders logo in color

Date	Mintage	MS-63	Proof
2012 Proof	—	—	25.00

KM# 1319 0.5000 g. Copper-Nickel 35 mm.
Subject: Grey Cup, 100th Anniversary **Obv:** Bust
right **Obv. Designer:** Susana Blunt **Rev:** Toronto
Argonauts logo in color

Date	Mintage	MS-63	Proof
2012 Proof	—	—	25.00

KM# 1320 0.5000 g. Copper-Nickel 35 mm.
Subject: Grey Cup, 100th Anniversary **Obv:** Bust
right **Obv. Designer:** Susana Blunt **Rev:** Winnipeg
Blue Bombers logo in color

Date	Mintage	MS-63	Proof
2012 Proof	—	—	25.00

25 CENTS

50 CENTS

KM# 6 11.6200 g. 0.9250 Silver 0.3456 oz. ASW 29.72 mm. **Obv:** VICTORIA DEI GRATIA REGINA. CANADA **Obv. Designer:** Leonard C. Wyon **Rev:** Denomination and date within wreath, crown above **Edge:** Reeded

Date	Mintage	VG-8	F-12	VF-20	XF-40	MS-60	MS-63	Proof
1870	450,000	900	1,400	2,400	5,000	25,000	40,000	—
1870 LCW	Inc. above	45.00	75.00	175	400	3,500	10,000	—
1871	200,000	75.00	150	350	650	7,000	15,000	—
1871H	45,000	150	225	450	1,100	8,500	22,000	—
1872H	80,000	55.00	95.00	200	450	4,000	10,500	—
1872H Inverted A for V in Victoria	Inc. above	500	700	1,900	5,000	25,000	—	—
1881H	150,000	60.00	125	225	550	5,500	16,000	—
1888	60,000	225	400	750	1,400	9,500	22,000	—
1890H	20,000	1,200	1,900	3,500	6,000	30,000	65,000	—
1892	151,000	70.00	125	350	650	9,000	21,000	—
1894	29,036	500	900	1,500	2,500	14,000	35,000	—
1898	100,000	75.00	150	350	750	9,000	26,000	—
1899	50,000	200	350	700	1,600	14,000	35,000	—
1900	118,000	60.00	100.00	200	500	5,000	10,500	—
1901	80,000	80.00	150	300	750	7,000	17,500	—

Victorian leaves

KM# 12 11.6200 g. 0.9250 Silver 0.3456 oz. ASW 29.72 mm. **Obv:** Crowned bust right **Obv. Designer:** G. W. DeSaulles **Rev:** Denomination and date within wreath, crown above **Edge:** Reeded

Date	Mintage	VG-8	F-12	VF-20	XF-40	MS-60	MS-63	Proof
1902	120,000	28.00	55.00	150	350	1,950	4,500	—
1903H	140,000	35.00	70.00	225	550	2,100	5,500	—
1904	60,000	175	300	750	1,500	5,000	14,500	—
1905	40,000	225	450	950	2,100	9,000	22,500	—
1906	350,000	24.00	45.00	150	400	1,950	4,500	—
1907	300,000	24.00	50.00	125	350	1,900	5,000	—
1908	128,119	40.00	95.00	250	600	1,500	2,800	—
1909	302,118	28.00	90.00	250	750	3,000	12,000	—
1910 Victoria leaves	649,521	35.00	70.00	175	550	2,400	7,500	—

Edwardian leaves

KM# 12a 11.6200 g. 0.9250 Silver 0.3456 oz. ASW 29.72 mm. **Obv:** Crowned bust right **Obv. Designer:** G. W. DeSaulles **Rev:** Denomination and date within wreath **Edge:** Reeded

Date	Mintage	VG-8	F-12	VF-20	XF-40	MS-60	MS-63	Proof
1910 Edwardian leaves	Inc. above	23.00	40.00	100.00	400	1,550	4,500	—

KM# 19 11.6200 g. 0.9250 Silver 0.3456 oz. ASW 29.72 mm.   **Obv:** Crowned bust left **Obv. Designer:** E. B. MacKennal **Rev:** Denomination and date within wreath, crown above **Edge:** Reeded

Date	Mintage	VG-8	F-12	VF-20	XF-40	MS-60	MS-63	Proof
1911	209,972	25.00	100.00	350	800	1,950	4,000	—

KM# 25 11.6200 g. 0.9250 Silver 0.3456 oz. ASW 29.72 mm.   **Obv:** Crowned bust left, modified legend **Obv. Designer:** E. B. MacKennal **Rev:** Denomination and date within wreath, crown above **Edge:** Reeded

Date	Mintage	VG-8	F-12	VF-20	XF-40	MS-60	MS-63	Proof
1912	285,867	16.00	40.00	150	350	1,650	4,000	—
1913	265,889	16.00	40.00	175	400	1,900	6,500	—
1914	160,128	40.00	100.00	300	850	4,000	11,500	—
1916	459,070	15.00	24.00	75.00	200	950	2,900	—
1917	752,213	15.00	22.00	55.00	150	700	1,650	—
1918	754,989	15.00	20.00	40.00	125	600	1,400	—
1919	1,113,429	15.00	20.00	40.00	125	550	1,400	—

KM# 25a 11.6638 g. 0.8000 Silver 0.3000 oz. ASW 29.72 mm.   **Obv:** Crowned bust left **Obv. Designer:** E. B. MacKennal **Rev:** Denomination and date within wreath, crown below **Edge:** Reeded

Date	Mintage	VG-8	F-12	VF-20	XF-40	MS-60	MS-63	Proof
1920	584,691	14.50	22.00	55.00	200	850	2,100	—
1921	—	35,000	40,000	50,000	55,000	70,000	125,000	—

Note: 75 to 100 known; David Akers John Jay Pittman sale, Part Three, 10-99, Gem Unc. realized $63,250

Date	Mintage	VG-8	F-12	VF-20	XF-40	MS-60	MS-63	Proof
1929	228,328	14.00	22.00	50.00	150	700	1,650	—
1931	57,581	20.00	40.00	100.00	300	1,200	2,400	—
1932	19,213	150	250	500	1,100	5,000	9,500	—
1934	39,539	28.00	40.00	125	300	950	1,950	—
1936	38,550	24.00	45.00	100.00	300	750	1,400	—

KM# 36 11.6638 g. 0.8000 Silver 0.3000 oz. ASW 29.72 mm. **Obv:** Head left **Obv. Designer:** T. H. Paget **Rev:** Crowned arms with supporters, denomination above, date below **Rev. Designer:** George E. Kruger-Gray **Edge:** Reeded

Date	Mintage	VG-8	F-12	VF-20	XF-40	MS-60	MS-63	Proof
1937	192,016	BV	13.00	14.00	18.00	40.00	95.00	—
1938	192,018	BV	15.00	20.00	40.00	175	450	—
1939	287,976	BV	13.00	15.00	28.00	100.00	300	—
1940	1,996,566	—	—	BV	28.00	35.00	75.00	—
1941	1,714,874	—	—	BV	28.00	35.00	75.00	—
1942	1,974,164	—	—	BV	28.00	35.00	75.00	—
1943	3,109,583	—	—	BV	28.00	35.00	75.00	—
1944	2,460,205	—	—	BV	28.00	35.00	75.00	—
1945	1,959,528	—	—	BV	28.00	35.00	75.00	—
1946	950,235	—	BV	13.00	18.00	80.00	175	—
1946 hoof in 6	Inc. above	28.00	40.00	60.00	225	1,650	4,500	—
1947 straight 7	424,885	—	BV	13.00	20.00	95.00	250	—
1947 curved 7	Inc. above	—	BV	13.00	30.00	125	350	—
1947 maple leaf, straight 7	38,433	28.00	40.00	55.00	100.00	250	400	—
1947 maple leaf, curved 7	Inc. above	1,500	1,950	3,000	3,500	7,000	15,000	—

KM# 45 11.6638 g. 0.8000 Silver 0.3000 oz. ASW 29.72 mm. **Obv:** Head left, modified legend **Obv. Designer:** T. H. Paget **Rev:** Crowned arms with supporters, denomination above, date below **Rev. Designer:** George E. Kruger-Gray **Edge:** Reeded

Date	Mintage	VG-8	F-12	VF-20	XF-40	MS-60	MS-63	Proof
1948	37,784	90.00	125	150	175	300	450	—
1949	858,991	—	—	BV	13.00	55.00	125	—
1949 hoof over 9	Inc. above	20.00	22.50	45.00	90.00	500	1,150	—
1950 no lines in 0	2,384,179	14.00	16.00	18.00	45.00	200	350	—
1950 lines in 0	Inc. above	—	—	BV	12.00	16.00	45.00	—
1951	2,421,730	—	—	—	BV	14.00	30.00	—
1952	2,596,465	—	—	—	BV	14.00	24.00	—

KM# 53 11.6638 g. 0.8000 Silver 0.3000 oz. ASW 29.72 mm. **Obv:** Laureate bust right **Obv. Designer:** Mary Gillick **Rev:** Crowned arms with supporters, denomination above, date below **Edge:** Reeded

Date	Mintage	VG-8	F-12	VF-20	XF-40	MS-60	MS-63	Proof
1953	1,630,429	—	—	—	BV	13.00	22.50	—
Note: small date								
1953	Inc. above	—	—	BV	12.00	28.00	55.00	—
Note: large date, straps								
1953	Inc. above	—	BV	12.00	20.00	95.00	225	—

Date	Mintage	VG-8	F-12	VF-20	XF-40	MS-60	MS-63	Proof
Note: large date without straps								
1954	506,305	—	—	BV	14.00	28.00	50.00	—
1955	753,511	—	—	BV	12.00	19.00	30.00	—
1956	1,379,499	—	—	—	BV	12.00	20.00	—
1957	2,171,689	—	—	—	BV	12.00	15.00	—
1958	2,957,266	—	—	—	BV	12.00	13.00	—

KM# 56 11.6638 g. 0.8000 Silver 0.3000 oz. ASW 29.7 mm.   **Obv:** Luareate bust right **Obv. Designer:** Mary Gillick **Rev:** Crown divides date above arms with supporters, denomination at right **Rev. Designer:** Thomas Shingles **Edge:** Reeded

Date	Mintage	VG-8	F-12	VF-20	XF-40	MS-60	MS-63	Proof
1959	3,095,535	—	—	—	—	BV	12.00	—
Note: horizontal shading								
1960	3,488,897	—	—	—	—	BV	12.00	—
1961	3,584,417	—	—	—	—	BV	12.00	—
1962	5,208,030	—	—	—	—	BV	12.00	—
1963	8,348,871	—	—	—	—	BV	12.00	—
1964	9,377,676	—	—	—	—	BV	12.00	—

KM# 63 11.6638 g. 0.8000 Silver 0.3000 oz. ASW 29.72 mm.   **Obv:** Young bust right **Obv. Designer:** Arnold Machin **Rev:** Crown divides date above arms with supporters, denomination at right **Rev. Designer:** Thomas Shingles **Edge:** Reeded

Date	Mintage	VG-8	F-12	VF-20	XF-40	MS-60	MS-63	Proof
1965	12,629,974	—	—	—	—	BV	12.00	—
1966	7,920,496	—	—	—	—	BV	12.00	—

KM# 69 11.6638 g. 0.8000 Silver 0.3000 oz. ASW 29.72 mm.   **Subject:** Confederation Centennial **Obv:** Young bust right **Rev:** Seated wolf howling divides denomination at top, dates at bottom **Rev. Designer:** Alex Colville **Edge:** Reeded

Date	Mintage	VG-8	F-12	VF-20	XF-40	MS-60	MS-63	Proof
1867-1967	4,211,392	—	—	—	—	BV	12.00	14.00

KM# 75.1 8.1000 g. Nickel 27.13 mm.   **Obv:** Young bust right **Obv. Designer:** Arnold Machin **Rev:** Crown divides date above arms with supporters, denomination at right **Rev. Designer:** Thomas Shingles **Edge:** Reeded

Date	Mintage	VG-8	F-12	VF-20	XF-40	MS-60	MS-63	Proof
1968	3,966,932	—	—	—	0.50	0.80	1.25	—
1969	7,113,929	—	—	—	0.50	0.80	1.25	—
1970	2,429,526	—	—	—	0.50	0.80	1.25	—

50 CENTS

Date	Mintage	VG-8	F-12	VF-20	XF-40	MS-60	MS-63	Proof
1971	2,166,444	—	—	—	0.50	0.80	1.25	—
1972	2,515,632	—	—	—	0.50	0.80	1.25	—
1973	2,546,096	—	—	—	0.50	0.80	1.25	—
1974	3,436,650	—	—	—	0.50	0.80	1.25	—
1975	3,710,000	—	—	—	0.50	0.80	1.25	—
1976	2,940,719	—	—	—	0.50	0.80	1.25	—

KM# 75.2 8.1000 g. Nickel 27.13 mm.   **Obv:** Small young bust right **Obv. Designer:** Arnold Machin **Rev:** Crown divides date above arms with supporters, denomination at right **Rev. Designer:** Thomas Shingles **Edge:** Reeded

Date	Mintage	VG-8	F-12	VF-20	XF-40	MS-60	MS-63	Proof
1977	709,839	—	—	0.50	0.75	1.25	2.00	—

KM# 75.3 8.1000 g. Nickel 27.13 mm.   **Obv:** Young bust right **Obv. Designer:** Arnold Machin **Rev:** Crown divides date above arms with supporters, denomination at right, redesigned arms **Rev. Designer:** Thomas Shingles **Edge:** Reeded

Date	Mintage	VG-8	F-12	VF-20	XF-40	MS-60	MS-63	Proof
1978	3,341,892	—	—	—	0.50	0.65	1.00	—
Note: square jewels								
1978	Inc. above	—	—	1.00	2.50	4.50	6.00	—
Note: round jewels								
1979	3,425,000	—	—	—	0.50	0.65	1.00	—
1980	1,574,000	—	—	—	0.50	0.65	1.00	—
1981	2,690,272	—	—	—	0.50	0.65	1.00	—
1981 Proof	199,000	—	—	—	—	—	—	3.00
1982	2,236,674	—	—	—	30.00	65.00	95.00	—
Note: small beads								
1982 Proof	180,908	—	—	—	—	—	—	3.00
Note: small beads								
1982	Inc. above	—	—	—	0.50	0.65	1.00	—
Note: large beads								
1983	1,177,000	—	—	—	0.50	0.65	1.00	—
1983 Proof	168,000	—	—	—	—	—	—	3.00
1984	1,502,989	—	—	—	0.50	0.65	1.00	—
1984 Proof	161,602	—	—	—	—	—	—	3.00
1985	2,188,374	—	—	—	0.50	0.65	1.00	—
1985 Proof	157,037	—	—	—	—	—	—	3.00
1986	781,400	—	—	—	0.50	0.80	1.00	—
1986 Proof	175,745	—	—	—	—	—	—	3.00
1987	373,000	—	—	—	0.50	0.80	1.00	—
1987 Proof	179,004	—	—	—	—	—	—	3.50
1988	220,000	—	—	—	0.50	0.80	1.00	—
1988 Proof	175,259	—	—	—	—	—	—	3.00
1989	266,419	—	—	—	0.50	0.80	1.00	—
1989 Proof	170,928	—	—	—	—	—	—	3.00

KM# 185 8.1000 g. Nickel 27.13 mm.   **Obv:** Crowned head right **Obv. Designer:** Dora dePedery-Hunt **Rev:** Crown divides date above arms with supporters, denomination at right **Rev. Designer:** Thomas Shingles **Edge:** Reeded

Date	Mintage	VG-8	F-12	VF-20	XF-40	MS-60	MS-63	Proof
1990	207,000	—	—	—	0.50	0.80	1.00	—
1990 Proof	140,649	—	—	—	—	—	—	5.00
1991	490,000	—	—	—	0.50	0.85	1.00	—
1991 Proof	131,888	—	—	—	—	—	—	7.00
1993	393,000	—	—	—	0.50	0.85	1.00	—
1993 Proof	143,065	—	—	—	—	—	—	3.00
1994	987,000	—	—	—	0.50	0.75	1.00	—
1994 Proof	146,424	—	—	—	—	—	—	4.00
1995	626,000	—	—	—	0.50	0.75	1.00	—
1995 Proof	50,000	—	—	—	—	—	—	4.00
1996	458,000	—	—	—	0.50	0.65	1.00	—
1996 Proof	—	—	—	—	—	—	—	4.00

KM# 208 8.1000 g. Nickel 27.1 mm.   **Subject:** Confederation 125 **Obv:** Crowned head right **Obv. Designer:** Dora dePedery-Hunt **Rev:** Crown divides date above arms with supporters, denomination at right **Rev. Designer:** Thomas Shingles **Edge:** Reeded

Date	Mintage	MS-63	Proof
1992	445,000	1.00	—
1992 Proof	147,061	—	5.00

KM# 261 11.6638 g. 0.9250 Silver 0.3469 oz. ASW   **Obv:** Crowned head right **Rev:** Atlantic Puffin, denomination and date at right **Rev. Designer:** Sheldon Beveridge

Date	Mintage	MS-63	Proof
1995 Proof	—	—	24.00

KM# 262 11.6638 g. 0.9250 Silver 0.3469 oz. ASW   **Obv:** Crowned head right **Rev:** Whooping crane left, denomination and date at right **Rev. Designer:** Stan Witten

Date	Mintage	MS-63	Proof
1995 Proof	—	—	24.00

KM# 263 11.6638 g. 0.9250 Silver 0.3469 oz. ASW   **Obv:** Crowned head right **Rev:** Gray Jays, denomination and date at right **Rev. Designer:** Sheldon Beveridge

Date	Mintage	MS-63	Proof
1995 Proof	—	—	24.00

50 CENTS

KM# 264 11.6638 g. 0.9250 Silver 0.3469 oz. ASW **Obv:** Crowned head right **Rev:** White-tailed ptarmigans, date and denomination at right **Rev. Designer:** Cosme Saffioti

Date	Mintage	MS-63	Proof
1995 Proof	—	—	22.00

KM# 283 11.6638 g. 0.9250 Silver 0.3469 oz. ASW 27 mm. **Obv:** Crowned head right **Rev:** Moose calf left, denomination and date at right **Rev. Designer:** Ago Aarand

Date	Mintage	MS-63	Proof
1996 Proof	—	—	20.00

KM# 284 11.6638 g. 0.9250 Silver 0.3469 oz. ASW 27 mm. **Obv:** Crowned head right **Rev:** Wood ducklings, date and denomination at right **Rev. Designer:** Sheldon Beveridge

Date	Mintage	MS-63	Proof
1996 Proof	—	—	20.00

KM# 285 11.6638 g. 0.9250 Silver 0.3469 oz. ASW 27 mm. **Obv:** Crowned head right **Rev:** Cougar kittens, date and denomination at right **Rev. Designer:** Stan Witten

Date	Mintage	MS-63	Proof
1996 Proof	—	—	20.00

KM# 286 11.6638 g. 0.9250 Silver 0.3469 oz. ASW 27 mm. **Obv:** Crowned head right **Rev:** Bear cubs standing, date and denomination at right **Rev. Designer:** Sheldon Beveridge

Date	Mintage	MS-63	Proof
1996 Proof	—	—	20.00

KM# 185a 11.6380 g. 0.9250 Silver 0.3461 oz. ASW **Obv:** Crowned head right **Obv. Designer:** Dora dePedery-Hunt **Rev:** Crown divides date above arms with supporters, denomination at right **Rev. Designer:** Thomas Shingles

Date	Mintage	MS-63	Proof
1996 Proof	—	—	13.00

KM# 290 8.1000 g. Nickel 27.1 mm. **Obv:** Crowned head right **Obv. Designer:** Dora dePedery-Hunt **Rev:** Redesigned arms **Rev. Designer:** Cathy Bursey-Sabourin **Edge:** Reeded

Date	Mintage	MS-63	Proof
1997	387,000	1.00	—
1997 Proof	—	—	5.00
1998	308,000	1.00	—
1998 Proof	—	—	—
1998W	—	2.00	—
1999	496,000	1.00	—
1999 Proof	—	—	5.00
2000	559,000	1.00	—
2000 Proof	—	—	5.00
2000W	—	1.50	—
2001P	—	1.50	—
2001P Proof	—	—	5.00
2003P	—	1.50	—
2003P Proof	—	—	5.00

KM# 292 11.6638 g. 0.9250 Silver 0.3469 oz. ASW 27 mm. **Obv:** Crowned head right **Rev:** Duck Toling Retriever, date and denomination at right **Rev. Designer:** Stan Witten

Date	Mintage	MS-63	Proof
1997 Proof	—	—	17.00

50 CENTS

KM# 293 11.6638 g. 0.9250 Silver 0.3469 oz.
ASW   **Obv:** Crowned head right **Rev:** Labrador
leaping left, date and denomination at right **Rev.
Designer:** Sheldon Beveridge

Date	Mintage	MS-63	Proof
1997 Proof	—	—	17.00

KM# 294 11.6638 g. 0.9250 Silver 0.3469 oz.
ASW   **Obv:** Crowned head right **Rev:**
Newfoundland right, date and denomination at right
Rev. Designer: William Woodruff

Date	Mintage	MS-63	Proof
1997 Proof	—	—	17.00

KM#295 11.6638 g. 0.9250 Silver 0.3469 oz. ASW
27.1 mm.   **Obv:** Crowned head right **Rev:** Eskimo
dog leaping forward, date and denomination at right
Rev. Designer: Cosme Saffioti

Date	Mintage	MS-63	Proof
1997 Proof	—	—	17.00

KM# 290a 11.6640 g. 0.9250 Silver 0.3469 oz.
ASW 27.13 mm.   **Obv:** Crowned head right **Obv.
Designer:** Dora dePedery-Hunt **Rev:** Redesigned
arms **Rev. Designer:** Cathy Bursey-Sabourin
Edge: Reeded

Date	Mintage	MS-63	Proof
1997 Proof	—	—	13.00
1998 Proof	—	—	13.00
1999 Proof	—	—	13.00
2000 Proof	—	—	13.00
2001 Proof	—	—	13.00
2003 Proof	—	—	13.00

KM# 313 11.6638 g. 0.9250 Silver 0.3469 oz.
ASW   **Subject:** 90th Anniversary Royal Canadian
Mint **Obv:** Crowned head right **Rev:** Denomination
and date within wreath, crown above **Rev.
Designer:** W. H. J. Blakemore

Date	Mintage	MS-63	Proof
1908-1998 Matte	25,000	—	15.00
1908-1998 Proof	25,000	—	15.00

KM# 318 11.6638 g. 0.9250 Silver 0.3469 oz.
ASW   **Obv:** Crowned head right **Rev:** Killer
Whales, date and denomination at right **Rev.
Designer:** William Woodruff

Date	Mintage	MS-63	Proof
1998 Proof	—	—	17.00

KM#319 11.6638 g. 0.9250 Silver 0.3469 oz. ASW
27 mm.   **Obv:** Crowned head right **Rev:**
Humpback whale, date and denomination at right
Rev. Designer: Sheldon Beveridge

Date	Mintage	MS-63	Proof
1998 Proof	—	—	17.00

KM# 320 11.6638 g. 0.9250 Silver 0.3469 oz.
ASW   **Obv:** Crowned head right **Rev:** Beluga
whales, date and denomination at right **Rev.
Designer:** Cosme Saffioti

Date	Mintage	MS-63	Proof
1998 Proof	—	—	17.00

KM# 321 11.6638 g. 0.9250 Silver 0.3469 oz. ASW 27 mm. **Obv:** Crowned head right **Rev:** Blue whale, date and denomination at right **Rev. Designer:** Stan Witten

Date	Mintage	MS-63	Proof
1998 Proof	—	—	17.00

KM# 327 11.6638 g. 0.9250 Silver 0.3469 oz. ASW **Subject:** 110 Years Canadian Soccer **Obv:** Crowned head right **Rev:** Soccer players, dates above, denomination at right **Rev. Designer:** Stan Witten

Date	Mintage	MS-63	Proof
1998 Proof	—	—	13.00

KM# 314 11.6638 g. 0.9250 Silver 0.3469 oz. ASW **Subject:** 110 Years Canadian Speed and Figure Skating **Obv:** Crowned head right **Rev:** Speed skaters, dates below, denomination above **Rev. Designer:** Sheldon Beveridge

Date	Mintage	MS-63	Proof
1998 Proof	—	—	13.00

KM# 315 11.6638 g. 0.9250 Silver 0.3469 oz. ASW **Subject:** 100 Years Canadian Ski Racing **Obv:** Crowned head right **Rev:** Skiers, dates below, denomination upper left **Rev. Designer:** Ago Aarand

Date	Mintage	MS-63	Proof
1998 Proof	—	—	13.00

KM# 328 11.6638 g. 0.9250 Silver 0.3469 oz. ASW **Subject:** 20 Years Canadian Auto Racing **Obv:** Crowned head right **Rev:** Race car divides date and denomination **Rev. Designer:** Cosme Saffioti

Date	Mintage	MS-63	Proof
1998 Proof	—	—	13.00

KM# 290b 6.9000 g. Nickel Plated Steel 27.13 mm. **Obv:** Crowned head right **Obv. Designer:** Dora dePedery-Hunt **Rev:** Redesigned arms **Rev. Designer:** Cathy Bursey-Sabourin **Edge:** Reeded

Date	Mintage	MS-63	Proof
1999 P	Est. 20,000	15.00	—
2000 P	Est. 50	3,500	—
2001 P	389,000	1.50	—
2003 P	—	5.00	—

Note: Available only in RCM presentation coin clocks

KM# 335 11.6638 g. 0.9250 Silver 0.3469 oz. ASW **Series:** Canadian Cats **Obv:** Crowned head right **Rev:** Cymric cat, date below, denomination at bottom **Rev. Designer:** Susan Taylor

Date	Mintage	MS-63	Proof
1999 Proof	—	—	35.00

KM# 336 11.6638 g. 0.9250 Silver 0.3469 oz. ASW **Series:** Canadian Cats **Obv:** Crowned head right **Rev:** Tonkinese cat, date below, denomination at bottom **Rev. Designer:** Susan Taylor

Date	Mintage	MS-63	Proof
1999 Proof	—	—	35.00

50 CENTS

KM# 337 11.6638 g. 0.9250 Silver 0.3469 oz.
ASW   **Series:** Canadian Cats **Obv:** Crowned head
right **Rev:** Cougar, date and denomination below
Rev. Designer: Susan Taylor

Date	Mintage	MS-63	Proof
1999 Proof	—	—	35.00

KM# 338 11.6638 g. 0.9250 Silver 0.3469 oz.
ASW   **Series:** Canadian Cats **Obv:** Crowned head
right **Rev:** Lynx, date and denomination below **Rev.
Designer:** Susan Taylor

Date	Mintage	MS-63	Proof
1999 Proof	—	—	35.00

KM# 333 11.6638 g. 0.9250 Silver 0.3469 oz.
ASW   **Subject:** 1904 Canadian Open **Obv:**
Crowned head right **Rev:** Golfers, date at right,
denomination below **Rev. Designer:** William
Woodruff

Date	Mintage	MS-63	Proof
1999 Proof	—	—	15.00

KM# 334 11.6638 g. 0.9250 Silver 0.3469 oz.
ASW   **Subject:** First U.S.-Canadian Yacht Race
Obv: Crowned head right **Rev:** Yachts, dates at left,
denomination below **Rev. Designer:** Stan Witten

Date	Mintage	MS-63	Proof
1999 Proof	—	—	13.00

KM# 371 9.3600 g. 0.9250 Silver 0.2783 oz. ASW
27.1 mm.   **Subject:** Basketball **Obv:** Crowned
head right **Rev:** Basketball players **Rev. Designer:**
Sheldon Beveridge **Edge:** Reeded

Date	Mintage	MS-63	Proof
1999 Proof	—	—	11.00

KM# 372 9.3600 g. 0.9250 Silver 0.2783 oz. ASW
27.1 mm.   **Obv:** Crowned head right **Rev:** Football
players **Rev. Designer:** Cosme Saffioti **Edge:**
Reeded

Date	Mintage	MS-63	Proof
1999 Proof	—	—	12.00

KM# 389 9.3500 g. 0.9250 Silver 0.2781 oz.
ASW   **Obv:** Crowned head right **Rev:** Great
horned owl, facing, date and denomination at right
Rev. Designer: Susan Taylor

Date	Mintage	MS-63	Proof
2000 Proof	—	—	20.00

KM# 390 9.3500 g. 0.9250 Silver 0.2781 oz.
ASW   **Obv:** Crowned head right **Rev:** Red-tailed
hawk, dates and denomination at right

Date	Mintage	MS-63	Proof
2000 Proof	—	—	20.00

KM# 391 9.3500 g. 0.9250 Silver 0.2781 oz.
ASW   **Obv:** Crowned head right **Rev:** Osprey,
dates and denomination at right **Rev. Designer:**
Susan Taylor

Date	Mintage	MS-63	Proof
2000 Proof	—	—	20.00

KM# 392 9.3500 g. 0.9250 Silver 0.2781 oz.
ASW **Obv:** Crowned head right **Rev:** Bald eagle,
dates and denomination at right **Rev. Designer:**
William Woodruff

Date	Mintage	MS-63	Proof
2000 Proof	—	—	20.00

KM# 393 9.3500 g. 0.9250 Silver 0.2781 oz.
ASW **Subject:** Steeplechase **Obv:** Crowned
head right **Rev:** Steeplechase, dates and
denomination below **Rev. Designer:** Susan Taylor

Date	Mintage	MS-63	Proof
1840-2000 Proof	—	—	12.00

KM# 394 9.3500 g. 0.9250 Silver 0.2781 oz.
ASW **Subject:** Bowling **Obv:** Crowned head right
Rev. Designer: William Woodruff

Date	Mintage	MS-63	Proof
2000 Proof	—	—	12.00

KM# 385 9.3500 g. 0.9250 Silver 0.2781 oz. ASW
Subject: Ice Hockey **Obv:** Crowned head right **Rev:**
4 hockey players **Rev. Designer:** Stanley Witten

Date	Mintage	MS-63	Proof
2000 Proof	—	—	12.00

KM# 386 9.3500 g. 0.9250 Silver 0.2781 oz.
ASW **Subject:** Curling **Obv:** Crowned head right
Rev: Motion study of curlers, dates and
denomination below **Rev. Designer:** Cosme Saffioti

Date	Mintage	MS-63	Proof
1910-2000 Proof	—	—	12.00

KM# 420 9.3000 g. 0.9250 Silver 0.2766 oz. ASW
27.13 mm. **Series:** Festivals - Quebec **Obv:**
Crowned head right **Rev:** Snowman and Chateau
Frontenac **Rev. Designer:** Sylvie Daigneault **Edge:**
Reeded

Date	Mintage	MS-63	Proof
2001 Proof	58,123	—	8.50

KM# 421 9.3000 g. 0.9250 Silver 0.2766 oz. ASW
27.13 mm. **Series:** Festivals - Nunavut **Obv:**
Crowned head right **Rev:** Dancer, dog sled and
snowmobiles **Rev. Designer:** John Mardon **Edge:**
Reeded

Date	Mintage	MS-63	Proof
2001 Proof	58,123	—	8.50

KM# 422 9.3000 g. 0.9250 Silver 0.2766 oz. ASW
27.13 mm. **Series:** Festivals - Newfoundland
Obv: Crowned head right **Rev:** Sailor and musical
people **Rev. Designer:** David Craig **Edge:** Reeded

Date	Mintage	MS-63	Proof
2001 Proof	58,123	—	8.50

KM# 423 9.3000 g. 0.9250 Silver 0.2766 oz. ASW
27.13 mm. **Series:** Festivals - Prince Edward
Island **Obv:** Crowned head right **Rev:** Family,
juggler and building **Rev. Designer:** Brenda
Whiteway **Edge:** Reeded

Date	Mintage	MS-63	Proof
2001 Proof	58,123	—	8.50

KM# 424 9.3000 g. 0.9250 Silver 0.2766 oz. ASW
27.13 mm. **Series:** Folklore - The Sled **Obv:**

50 CENTS

Crowned head right **Rev:** Family scene **Rev.
Designer:** Valentina Hotz-Entin **Edge:** Reeded

Date	Mintage	MS-63	Proof
2001 Proof	28,979	—	9.00

KM# 425 9.3000 g. 0.9250 Silver 0.2766 oz. ASW
27.13 mm. **Series:** Folklore - The Maiden's Cave
Obv: Crowned head right **Rev:** Woman shouting
Rev. Designer: Peter Kiss **Edge:** Reeded

Date	Mintage	MS-63	Proof
2001 Proof	28,979	—	9.00

KM# 426 9.3000 g. 0.9250 Silver 0.2766 oz. ASW
27.13 mm. **Series:** Folklore - The Small Jumpers
Obv: Crowned head right **Rev:** Jumping children on
seashore **Rev. Designer:** Miynki Tanobe **Edge:**
Reeded

Date	Mintage	MS-63	Proof
2001 Proof	28,979	—	9.00

KM# 509 6.9000 g. Nickel Plated Steel
27.13 mm. **Obv:** Crowned head right **Rev:**
National arms **Edge:** Reeded

Date	Mintage	MS-63	Proof
2001 P	—	1.50	—

KM# 444 6.9000 g. Nickel Plated Steel
27.13 mm. **Subject:** Queen's Golden Jubilee
Obv: Coronation crowned head right and
monogram **Rev:** Canadian arms **Rev. Designer:**
Bursey Sabourin **Edge:** Reeded

Date	Mintage	MS-63	Proof
1952-2002P	14,440,000	2.50	—

KM# 444a 9.3000 g. 0.9250 Silver 0.2766 oz. ASW
27.13 mm. **Subject:** Elizabeth II Golden Jubilee
Obv: Crowned head right, Jubilee commemorative
dates 1952-2002

Date	Mintage	MS-63	Proof
1952-2002 Proof	100,000	—	17.50

KM# 444b 9.3000 g. 0.9250 Silver Gilt 0.2766 oz.
ASW 27.13 mm. **Subject:** Queen's Golden
Jubilee **Obv:** Crowned head right and monogram
Rev: Canadian arms **Edge:** Reeded **Note:** Special
24 karat gold-plated issue of KM#444.

Date	Mintage	MS-63	Proof
1952-2002 Proof	32,642	—	35.00

KM# 454 9.3000 g. 0.9250 Silver 0.2766 oz. ASW
27.13 mm. **Subject:** Nova Scotia Annapolis
Valley Apple Blossom Festival **Obv:** Crowned head
right **Rev. Designer:** Bonnie Ross

Date	Mintage	MS-63	Proof
2002 Proof	59,998	—	9.50

KM# 455 9.3000 g. 0.9250 Silver 0.2766 oz. ASW
27.13 mm. **Subject:** Stratford Festival **Obv:**
Crowned head right **Rev:** Couple with building in
background **Rev. Designer:** Laurie McGaw

Date	Mintage	MS-63	Proof
2002 Proof	59,998	—	9.50

KM# 456 9.3000 g. 0.9250 Silver 0.2766 oz. ASW
27.13 mm. **Subject:** Folklorama **Obv:** Crowned
head right **Rev. Designer:** William Woodruff

Date	Mintage	MS-63	Proof
2002 Proof	59,998	—	9.50

KM# 457 9.3000 g. 0.9250 Silver 0.2766 oz. ASW
27.13 mm. **Subject:** Calgary Stampede **Obv:**
Crowned head right **Rev. Designer:** Stan Witten

Date	Mintage	MS-63	Proof
2002 Proof	59,998	—	9.50

KM# 458 9.3000 g. 0.9250 Silver 0.2766 oz. ASW
27.13 mm. **Subject:** Squamish Days Logger
Sports **Obv:** Crowned head right **Rev. Designer:**
Jose Osio

Date	Mintage	MS-63	Proof
2002 Proof	59,998	—	9.50

KM# 459 9.3000 g. 0.9250 Silver 0.2766 oz. ASW
27.13 mm. **Series:** Folklore and Legends **Obv:**
Crowned head right **Rev:** The Shoemaker in
Heaven **Rev. Designer:** Francine Gravel

Date	Mintage	MS-63	Proof
2002 Proof	19,267	—	11.00

KM# 460 9.3000 g. 0.9250 Silver 0.2766 oz. ASW
27.13 mm. **Series:** Folklore and Legends
Subject: The Ghost Ship **Obv:** Crowned head right
Rev. Designer: Colette Boivin

Date	Mintage	MS-63	Proof
2002 Proof	19,267	—	11.00

KM# 461 9.3000 g. 0.9250 Silver 0.2766 oz. ASW
27.13 mm. **Series:** Folklore and Legends
Subject: The Pig That Wouldn't Get Over the Stile
Obv: Crowned head right **Rev. Designer:** Laura
Jolicoeur

Date	Mintage	MS-63	Proof
2002 Proof	19,267	—	11.00

KM# 494 6.9000 g. Nickel Plated Steel
27.13 mm. **Obv:** Crowned head right **Obv.**
Designer: Susanna Blunt **Rev:** National arms **Rev.**
Designer: Cathy Bursey-Sabourin **Edge:** Reeded

Date	Mintage	MS-63	Proof
2003P W	—	5.00	—
2003P W Proof	—	—	7.50
2004P	—	5.00	—
2004P Proof	—	—	7.50
2005P	200,000	1.50	—
2005P Proof	—	—	5.00
2006P	98,000	1.50	—
2006P Proof	—	—	5.00
2007(ml)	250,000	1.50	—
2007(ml) Proof	—	—	5.00
2008(ml)	211,000	1.50	—
2008(ml) Proof	—	—	5.00
2009(ml)	150,000	1.50	—
2009(ml) Proof	—	—	5.00
2010(ml)	—	1.50	—
2010(ml) Proof	—	—	5.00
2011(ml)	—	1.50	—
2011(ml) Proof	—	—	5.00
2012(ml)	—	1.50	—
2012(ml) Proof	—	—	5.00
2013(ml)	—	1.50	—
2013(ml) Proof	—	—	5.00

KM# 472 11.6200 g. 0.9250 Silver 0.3456 oz. ASW
27.13 mm. **Subject:** 50th Anniversary of the
Coronation of Elizabeth II **Obv:** Crowned head right,
Jubilee commemorative dates 1952-2002 **Obv.**
Designer: Mary Gillick

Date	Mintage	MS-63	Proof
2003 Proof	30,000	—	15.00

KM# 475 9.3000 g. 0.9250 Silver 0.2766 oz. ASW
27.13 mm. **Obv:** Crowned head right **Obv.**
Designer: Dora dePédery-Hunt **Rev:** Golden
daffodil **Rev. Designer:** Christie Paquet, Stan
Witten

Date	Mintage	MS-63	Proof
2003 Proof	36,293	—	25.00

KM# 476 9.3000 g. 0.9250 Silver 0.2766 oz. ASW
27.13 mm. **Subject:** Yukon International
Storytelling Festival **Obv:** Crowned head right **Obv.**
Designer: Dora dePédery-Hunt **Rev. Designer:**
Ken Anderson, Jose Oslo

Date	Mintage	MS-63	Proof
2003 Proof	—	—	11.00

KM# 477 9.3000 g. 0.9250 Silver 0.2766 oz. ASW
27.13 mm. **Subject:** Festival Acadien de
Caraquet **Obv:** Crowned head right **Obv. Designer:**
Dora dePédery-Hunt **Rev:** Sailboat and couple **Rev.**
Designer: Susan Taylor, Hudson Design Group

Date	Mintage	MS-63	Proof
2003 Proof	—	—	11.00

KM# 478 9.3000 g. 0.9250 Silver 0.2766 oz. ASW
27.13 mm. **Subject:** Back to Batoche **Obv:**
Crowned head right **Obv. Designer:** Dora dePédery-
Hunt **Rev. Designer:** David Hannan, Stan Witten

Date	Mintage	MS-63	Proof
2003 Proof	—	—	11.00

KM# 479 9.3000 g. 0.9250 Silver 0.2766 oz. ASW
27.13 mm. **Subject:** Great Northern Arts Festival
Obv: Crowned head right **Obv. Designer:** Dora
dePédery-Hunt **Rev. Designer:** Dawn Oman,
Susan Taylor

Date	Mintage	MS-63	Proof
2003 Proof	—	—	11.00

KM# 494a 9.3000 g. 0.9250 Silver 0.2766 oz. ASW
27.13 mm. **Obv:** Crowned head right **Obv.**
Designer: Susanna Blunt **Rev:** Canadian coat of
arms **Edge:** Reeded

Date	Mintage	MS-63	Proof
2004 Proof	—	—	7.50

KM# 526 1.2700 g. 0.9999 Gold 0.0408 oz. AGW
14 mm. **Subject:** Moose **Obv:** Head right **Rev:**
Moose head facing right

Date	Mintage	MS-63	Proof
2004 Proof	—	—	85.00

KM# 606 9.3000 g. 0.9250 Silver 0.2766 oz. ASW
27.13 mm. **Obv:** Head right **Obv. Designer:**
Susanna Blunt **Rev:** Clouded Sulphur Butterfly,
hologram **Rev. Designer:** Susan Taylor

Date	Mintage	MS-63	Proof
2004 Proof	15,281	—	45.00

KM# 712 9.3000 g. 0.9250 Silver 0.2766 oz. ASW
27.13 mm. **Rev:** Hologram of Tiger Swallowtail
butterfly

Date	Mintage	MS-63	Proof
2004 Proof	20,462	—	45.00

50 CENTS

KM# 536 9.3000 g. 0.9250 Silver with partial gold plating 0.2766 oz. ASW 27.13 mm. **Subject:** Golden rose **Obv:** Head right **Obv. Designer:** Susanna Blunt **Rev. Designer:** Christie Paquet

Date	Mintage	MS-63	Proof
2005 Proof	17,418	—	40.00

KM# 537 9.3000 g. 0.9250 Silver 0.2766 oz. ASW 27.13 mm.   **Obv:** Head right **Obv. Designer:** Susanna Blunt **Rev:** Great Spangled Fritillary butterfly, hologram **Rev. Designer:** Jianping Yan

Date	Mintage	MS-63	Proof
2005 Proof	20,000	—	50.00

KM# 538 9.3000 g. 0.9250 Silver 0.2766 oz. ASW 27.13 mm. **Subject:** Toronto Maple Leafs **Obv:** Head right **Obv. Designer:** Susanna Blunt **Rev:** Darryl Sittler

Date	Mintage	MS-63	Proof
2005 Specimen	25,000	—	16.00

KM# 539 9.3000 g. 0.9250 Silver 0.2766 oz. ASW 27.13 mm. **Subject:** Toronto Maple Leafs **Obv:** Head right **Obv. Designer:** Susanna Blunt **Rev:** Dave Keon

Date	Mintage	MS-63	Proof
2005 Specimen	25,000	—	16.00

KM# 540 9.3000 g. 0.9250 Silver 0.2766 oz. ASW 27.13 mm. **Subject:** Toronto Maple Leafs **Obv:** Head right **Obv. Designer:** Susanna Blunt **Rev:** Jonny Bover, goalie

Date	Mintage	MS-63	Proof
2005 Specimen	25,000	—	16.00

KM# 541 9.3000 g. 0.9250 Silver 0.2766 oz. ASW 27.13 mm. **Subject:** Toronto Maple Leafs **Obv:** Head right **Obv. Designer:** Susanna Blunt **Rev:** Tim Horton

Date	Mintage	MS-63	Proof
2005 Specimen	25,000	—	16.00

KM# 543 9.3000 g. 0.9250 Silver 0.2766 oz. ASW **Subject:** WWII - Battle of Britain **Obv:** Head right **Rev:** Fighter plane in sky

Date	Mintage	MS-63	Proof
2005 Specimen	20,000	—	22.50

KM# 544 9.3000 g. 0.9250 Silver 0.2766 oz. ASW 27.13 mm.   **Subject:** WWII - Battle of Scheldt **Obv:** Head right **Obv. Designer:** Susanna Blunt **Rev:** Four soldiers walking down road **Rev. Designer:** Peter Mossman

Date	Mintage	MS-63	Proof
2005 Specimen	20,000	—	19.00

KM# 545 9.3000 g. 0.9250 Silver 0.2766 oz. ASW 27.13 mm.   **Subject:** WWII - Battle of the Atlantic **Obv:** Head right **Obv. Designer:** Susanna Blunt **Rev:** Merchant ship sinking **Rev. Designer:** Peter Mossman

Date	Mintage	MS-63	Proof
2005 Specimen	20,000	—	19.00

KM# 546 9.3000 g. 0.9250 Silver 0.2766 oz. ASW 27.13 mm.   **Subject:** WWII - Conquest of Sicily **Obv:** Head right **Obv. Designer:** Susanna Blunt **Rev:** Tank among town ruins **Rev. Designer:** Peter Mossman

Date	Mintage	MS-63	Proof
2005 Specimen	20,000	—	19.00

KM# 547 9.3000 g. 0.9250 Silver 0.2766 oz. ASW 27.13 mm.   **Subject:** WWII - Liberation of the Netherlands **Obv:** Head right **Obv. Designer:** Susanna Blunt **Rev:** Soldiers in parade, one holding flag **Rev. Designer:** Peter Mossman

Date	Mintage	MS-63	Proof
2005 Specimen	20,000	—	19.00

KM# 548 9.3000 g. 0.9250 Silver 0.2766 oz. ASW 27.13 mm.   **Subject:** WWII - Raid of Dieppe **Obv:** Head right **Obv. Designer:** Susanna Blunt **Rev:** Three soldiers exiting landing craft **Rev. Designer:** Peter Mossman

Date	Mintage	MS-63	Proof
2005 Specimen	20,000	—	19.00

KM# 577 9.3000 g. 0.9250 Silver 0.2766 oz. ASW 27.13 mm. **Subject:** Montreal Canadiens **Obv:** Head right **Obv. Designer:** Susanna Blunt **Rev:** Guy LaFleur

Date	Mintage	MS-63	Proof
2005 Specimen	25,000	—	17.50

KM# 578 9.3000 g. 0.9250 Silver 0.2766 oz. ASW 27.13 mm.   **Subject:** Montreal Canadiens **Obv:** Head right **Obv. Designer:** Susanna Blunt **Rev:** Jaque Plante

Date	Mintage	MS-63	Proof
2005 Specimen	25,000	—	17.50

KM# 579 9.3000 g. 0.9250 Silver 0.2766 oz. ASW 27.13 mm.   **Subject:** Montreal Canadiens **Obv:** Head right **Obv. Designer:** Susanna Blunt **Rev:** Jean Beliveau

Date	Mintage	MS-63	Proof
2005 Specimen	25,000	—	17.50

KM# 580 9.3000 g. 0.9250 Silver 0.2766 oz. ASW 27.13 mm.   **Subject:** Montreal Canadiens **Obv:** Head right **Obv. Designer:** Susanna Blunt **Rev:** Maurice Richard

Date	Mintage	MS-63	Proof
2005 Specimen	25,000	—	17.50

50 CENTS

KM# 599 9.3000 g. 0.9250 Silver 0.2766 oz. ASW
27.13 mm. **Obv:** Head right **Obv. Designer:**
Susanna Blunt **Rev:** Monarch butterfly, colorized
Rev. Designer: Susan Taylor

Date	Mintage	MS-63	Proof
2005 Proof	20,000	—	50.00

KM# 648 9.3000 g. 0.9250 Silver partially gilt
0.2766 oz. ASW **Subject:** Golden Daisy **Obv:**
Head right

Date	Mintage	MS-63	Proof
2006 Proof	18,190	—	30.00

KM# 649 9.3000 g. 0.9250 Silver 0.2766 oz. ASW
27.13 mm. **Subject:** Short-tailed swallowtail
Obv: Head right **Rev:** Colorized butterfly

Date	Mintage	MS-63	Proof
2006 Proof	24,568	—	45.00

KM# 650 9.3000 g. 0.9250 Silver 0.2766 oz. ASW
27.13 mm. **Obv:** Head right **Rev:** Butterfly, silvery
blue hologram

Date	Mintage	MS-63	Proof
2006 Proof	16,000	—	45.00

KM# 651 9.3000 g. 0.9250 Silver 0.2766 oz.
ASW **Subject:** Cowboy **Obv:** Head right

Date	Mintage	MS-63	Proof
2006	—	17.50	—

KM# 494b 6.9000 g. Nickel Plated Steel partially
gilt 27.13 mm. **Rev:** State Arms, gilt **Note:**
Housed in Mint Annual Report

Date	Mintage	MS-63	Proof
2006	—	15.00	—

KM# 716 9.3000 g. 0.9250 Silver 0.2766 oz.
ASW **Rev:** Multicolor holiday ornaments

Date	Mintage	MS-63	Proof
2006	16,989	17.50	—

KM# 715 9.3000 g. 0.9250 Silver with partial gold
plating 0.2766 oz. ASW 27.12 mm. **Rev:** Forget-
me-not flower

Date	Mintage	MS-63	Proof
2007 Proof	22,882	—	29.00

KM# 778 20.0000 g. 0.9250 Silver colorized green
0.5948 oz. ASW 34.06 mm. **Subject:** Milk
delivery **Obv:** Bust right **Rev:** Cow head and milk
can **Shape:** Triangle

Date	Mintage	MS-63	Proof
2008 Proof	24,448	—	35.00

KM# 779 9.3000 g. 0.9250 Silver 0.2766 oz. ASW
35 mm. **Rev:** Multicolor snowman

Date	Mintage	MS-63	Proof
2008	21,679	17.50	—

KM#780 9.3000 g. 0.9250 Silver 0.2766 oz. ASW
Subject: Ottawa Mint Centennial 1908-2008

Date	Mintage	MS-63	Proof
2008 Proof	3,248	—	20.00

KM# 845 9.3000 g. 0.9250 Silver 0.2766 oz. ASW
27.13 mm. **Rev:** Calgary Flames lenticular

design, old and new logos

Date	Mintage	MS-63	Proof
2009	—	12.00	—

KM# 846 9.3000 g. 0.9250 Silver 0.2766 oz. ASW
27.13 mm. **Rev:** Edmonton Oiler's lenticular
design, old and new logos

Date	Mintage	MS-63	Proof
2009	—	12.00	—

KM# 847 9.3000 g. 0.9250 Silver 0.2766 oz. ASW
27.13 mm. **Rev:** Montreal Canadiens lenticular
design, old and new logos

Date	Mintage	MS-63	Proof
2009	—	12.00	—

KM# 848 9.3000 g. 0.9250 Silver 0.2766 oz. ASW
27.13 mm. **Rev:** Ottawa Senators lenticular
design, old and new logos

Date	Mintage	MS-63	Proof
2009	—	12.00	—

KM# 849 9.3000 g. 0.9250 Silver 0.2766 oz. ASW
27.13 mm. **Rev:** Toronto Maple Leafs lenticular
design, old and new logos

Date	Mintage	MS-63	Proof
2009	—	12.00	—

KM# 850 9.3000 g. 0.9250 Silver 0.2766 oz. ASW
27.13 mm. **Rev:** Vancouver Canucks lenticular
design, old and new logos

Date	Mintage	MS-63	Proof
2009	—	12.00	—

KM# 857 6.9000 g. Nickel Plated Steel 35 mm.
Rev: Calgary Flames lenticular old and new logos

Date	Mintage	MS-63	Proof
2009	—	25.00	—

KM# 858 6.9000 g. Nickel Plated Steel 35 mm.
Rev: Edmonton Oilers lenticular old and new logos

Date	Mintage	MS-63	Proof
2009	—	25.00	—

KM# 859 35.0000 g. Nickel Plated Steel 35 mm.
Rev: Montreal Canadians lenticular old and new logo

Date	Mintage	MS-63	Proof
2009	—	25.00	—

KM# 860 6.9000 g. Nickel Plated Steel 35 mm.
Rev: Ottawa Senators lenticular old and new logos

Date	Mintage	MS-63	Proof
2009	—	25.00	—

KM# 861 6.9000 g. Nickel Plated Steel 35 mm.
Rev: Toronto Maple Leafs lenticular old and new logos

Date	Mintage	MS-63	Proof
2009	—	25.00	—

KM# 862 6.9000 g. Nickel Plated Steel 35 mm.
Rev: Vancouver Canucks lenticular old and new logos

Date	Mintage	MS-63	Proof
2009	—	25.00	—

KM# 887 19.1000 g. Copper-Nickel 34.06 mm.
Subject: Six-string national guitar **Obv:** Bust right
Obv. Legend: Elizabeth II DG Regina **Obv.
Designer:** Susanna Blunt **Rev:** Hologram with 6
"strings" **Rev. Legend:** 50 CENTS Canada **Shape:**
Triangle

Date	Mintage	MS-63	Proof
2009 Proof	13,602	—	50.00

KM# 936 9.3000 g. Nickel   **Rev:** Vancouver
Canucks goalie jersey

Date	Mintage	MS-63	Proof
2009	3,563	15.00	—

KM# 937 6.9000 g. Nickel Plated Steel 35 mm.
Rev: Calgary Flames player - colorized

Date	Mintage	MS-63	Proof
2009	3,518	15.00	—

KM# 938 6.9000 g. Nickel Plated Steel 35 mm.
Rev: Edmonton Oilers player

Date	Mintage	MS-63	Proof
2009	3,562	15.00	—

KM# 939 6.9000 g. Nickel Plated Steel 35 mm.
Rev: Toronto Maple Leafs player

Date	Mintage	MS-63	Proof
2009	5,918	15.00	—

KM# 940 6.9000 g. Nickel Plated Steel 35 mm.
Rev: Montreal Canadiens player

Date	Mintage	MS-63	Proof
2009	9,865	15.00	—

KM# 941 6.9000 g. Nickel Plated Steel 35 mm.
Rev: Ottawa Senators player

Date	Mintage	MS-63	Proof
2009	3,293	15.00	—

KM# 1035 12.6100 g. Brass Plated Steel
35 mm. **Subject:** Christmas toy train **Rev:**
movement from far to close

Date	Mintage	MS-63	Proof
2009	19,103	17.50	—

KM# 961 6.9000 g. Nickel Plated Steel 35 mm.
Rev: Bob sleigh

Date	Mintage	MS-63	Proof
2010	—	12.00	—

KM# 961a 6.9000 g. Nickel Plated Steel 35 mm.
Rev: Bob sleigh - red enamel

Date	Mintage	MS-63	Proof
2010	—	12.00	—

KM# 962 6.9000 g. Nickel Plated Steel 35 mm.
Rev: Speed skating

Date	Mintage	MS-63	Proof
2010	—	12.00	—

KM# 962a 6.9000 g. Nickel Plated Steel 35 mm.
Rev: Speed skating - red enamel

Date	Mintage	MS-63	Proof
2010	—	12.00	—

KM# 963 6.9000 g. Nickel Plated Steel 35 mm.
Rev: Miga and Quatchi in bob sleigh

Date	Mintage	MS-63	Proof
2010	2,119	12.00	—

KM# 964 6.9000 g. Nickel Plated Steel 35 mm.
Rev: Miga in hockey

Date	Mintage	MS-63	Proof
2010	5,275	12.00	—

KM# 965 6.9000 g. Nickel Plated Steel 35 mm.
Rev: Quatchi in ice hockey

Date	Mintage	MS-63	Proof
2010	5,614	12.00	—

KM# 966 6.9000 g. Nickel Plated Steel 35 mm.
Rev: Sumi Para Sledge

Date	Mintage	MS-63	Proof
2010	3,707	12.00	—

KM# 967 6.9000 g. Nickel Plated Steel 35 mm.
Rev: Miga and Quatchi Figure-skating **Edge:**
Reeded

Date	Mintage	MS-63	Proof
2010	2,981	12.00	—

KM# 968 6.9000 g. Nickel Plated Steel 35 mm.
Rev: Free-style mascot

Date	Mintage	MS-63	Proof
2010	2,114	12.00	—

KM# 969 6.9000 g. Nickel Plated Steel 35 mm.
Rev: Skeleton mascot

Date	Mintage	MS-63	Proof
2010	1,672	12.00	—

KM# 970 6.9000 g. Nickel Plated Steel 35 mm.
Rev: Parallel giant slalom mascot

Date	Mintage	MS-63	Proof
2010	1,730	12.00	—

KM# 971 6.9000 g. Nickel Plated Steel 35 mm.
Rev: Alpine skiing mascot

Date	Mintage	MS-63	Proof
2010	2,309	12.00	—

KM# 972 6.9000 g. Nickel Plated Steel 35 mm.
Rev: Para Olympic alpine skiing mascot

Date	Mintage	MS-63	Proof
2010	1,902	12.00	—

KM# 973 6.9000 g. Nickel Plated Steel 35 mm.
Rev: Snowboard mascot

Date	Mintage	MS-63	Proof
2010	2,090	12.00	—

KM# 974 6.9000 g. Nickel Plated Steel 35 mm.
Rev: Speed-skating mascott

Date	Mintage	MS-63	Proof
2010	1,825	12.00	—

KM# 986 12.6100 g. Brass Plated Steel 35 mm.
Rev: Dasplerosaurus Torosus - 3-D lenticular movement

Date	Mintage	MS-63	Proof
2010	—	20.00	—

KM# 1015 12.6100 g. Brass Plated Steel 35 mm. **Rev:** Sinosauropteryx

Date	Mintage	MS-63	Proof
2010	—	20.00	—

KM# 1016 12.6100 g. Brass Plated Steel 35 mm. **Rev:** Albertosaurus

Date	Mintage	MS-63	Proof
2010	—	20.00	—

KM# 1043 Nickel Plated Steel 34 mm. **Rev:** Santa Claus transforms into Rudolf the red-nosed reindeer

Date	Mintage	MS-63	Proof
2010	—	17.50	—

KM# 1157 11.6200 g. 0.9250 Silver 0.3456 oz.
ASW 29.72 mm. **Obv:** George V bust **Rev:** Value within wreath

Date	Mintage	MS-63	P/L	Proof
1911-2011 Proof	6,000	—	—	45.00

KM# 1180 6.9000 g. Nickel Plated Steel 27.13 mm. **Obv:** Bust right **Rev:** Winnipeg Jets Logo, jet over maple leaf **Edge:** Reeded

Date	Mintage	MS-63	Proof
2011	—	15.00	—

KM# 1191 12.6100 g. Copper Plated Steel 35 mm. **Obv:** Bust right **Rev:** Santa Claus checking list, and in sled over house

Date	Mintage	MS-63	Proof
2011	—	27.50	—

KM# 1202 1.2700 g. 0.9999 Gold 0.0408 oz. AGW 13.92 mm. **Rev:** Wood Bison **Rev. Designer:** Corrine Hunt **Edge:** Reeded

Date	Mintage	MS-63	Proof
2011 Proof	Est. 2,500	—	100

KM# 1204 1.2700 g. 0.9999 Gold 0.0408 oz. AGW 13.92 mm. **Subject:** Boreal Forest **Rev:** Bird and tree **Rev. Designer:** Corrine Hunt **Edge:** Reeded

Date	Mintage	MS-63	Proof
2011 Proof	Est. 2,500	—	100

KM# 1206 1.2700 g. 0.9999 Gold 0.0408 oz. AGW
13.92 mm. **Rev:** Peregrine Falcon perched on
branch **Rev. Designer:** Corrine Hunt

Date	Mintage	MS-63	Proof
2011 Proof	Est. 2,500	—	100

KM# 1208 1.2700 g. 0.9999 Gold 0.0408 oz. AGW
13.92 mm. **Rev:** Orca Whale **Rev. Designer:**
Corrine Hunt **Edge:** Reeded

Date	Mintage	MS-63	Proof
2011 Proof	Est. 2,500	—	100

KM# 1234 12.6100 g. Nickel Plated Steel
35 mm. **Subject:** Titanic, 100th Anniversary **Obv:**
Bust right **Rev:** Titanic sailing forward towards
iceberg, colored sea

Date	Mintage	MS-63	Proof
2012 Proof	—	—	65.00

KM# 1264 1.2700 g. 0.9990 Gold 0.0408 oz. AGW
13.92 mm. **Subject:** Gold Rush

KM# 1293 9.3000 g. 0.9250 Silver 0.2766 oz. ASW
27.13 mm. **Subject:** Elizabeth II Diamond Jubilee
Rev: Diamond Jubilee logo in color

Date	Mintage	MS-63	Proof
2012	—	—	—

DOLLAR

KM# 30 23.3276 g. 0.8000 Silver 0.6000 oz. ASW 36 mm. **Subject:** Silver Jubilee **Obv:** Bust left **Obv.**
Designer: Percy Metcalfe **Rev:** Voyager, date and denomination below **Rev. Designer:** Emanuel Hahn

Date	Mintage	F-12	VF-20	XF-40	AU-50	MS-60	MS-63	Proof
1935	428,707	23.00	27.00	35.00	40.00	45.00	70.00	4,500

KM# 31 23.3276 g. 0.8000 Silver 0.6000 oz. ASW 36 mm. **Obv:** Crowned bust left **Obv. Designer:** E. B.
MacKennal **Rev:** Voyageur, date and denomination below **Rev. Designer:** Emanuel Hahn

Date	Mintage	F-12	VF-20	XF-40	AU-50	MS-60	MS-63	Proof
1936	339,600	25.00	28.00	32.00	40.00	50.00	100.00	4,500

Pointed 7   Blunt 7   Maple leaf

KM# 37   23.3276 g. 0.8000 Silver 0.6000 oz. ASW 36 mm.   **Obv:** Head left **Obv. Designer:** T. H. Paget **Rev:** Voyageur, date and denomination below **Rev. Designer:** Emanuel Hahn

Date	Mintage	F-12	VF-20	XF-40	AU-50	MS-60	MS-63	Proof
1937	207,406	25.00	28.00	32.00	40.00	50.00	95.00	—
1937 Mirror Proof	1,295	—	—	—	—	—	—	1,050
1937 Matte Proof	Inc. above	—	—	—	—	—	—	450
1938	90,304	35.00	45.00	70.00	85.00	100.00	250	8,000
1945	38,391	125	175	225	300	350	750	2,900
1946	93,055	26.00	40.00	55.00	70.00	100.00	400	2,400
1947 Pointed 7		80.00	125	175	200	400	2,000	4,500
1947 Blunt 7	65,595	60.00	90.00	125	150	175	400	5,000
1947 Maple leaf	21,135	150	200	225	300	400	800	2,900

KM# 38   23.3276 g. 0.8000 Silver 0.6000 oz. ASW 36 mm.   **Subject:** Royal Visit **Obv:** Head left **Obv. Designer:** T. H. Paget **Rev:** Tower at center of building, date and denomination below **Rev. Designer:** Emanuel Hahn

Date	Mintage	F-12	VF-20	XF-40	AU-50	MS-60	MS-63	Proof
1939	1,363,816	—	—	BV	23.00	24.00	35.00	—
1939		—	—	—	—	—	—	800
Note: Matte specimen								
1939 Proof		—	—	—	—	—	—	1,350
Note: Mirror specimen								

KM# 46   23.3276 g. 0.8000 Silver 0.6000 oz. ASW 36 mm.   **Obv:** Head left, modified left legend **Obv. Designer:** T. H. Paget **Rev:** Voyageur, date and denomination below **Rev. Designer:** Emanuel Hahn

Date	Mintage	F-12	VF-20	XF-40	AU-50	MS-60	MS-63	Proof
1948	18,780	750	950	1,300	1,400	1,700	3,000	5,000
1950	261,002	—	23.00	24.00	25.00	30.00	75.00	1,800
Note: With 3 water lines								
1950 Matte Proof	—	—	—	—	—	—	—	—
Note: With 4 water lines, 1 known								
1950	Inc. above	23.00	28.00	35.00	40.00	55.00	125	2,600
Note: Amprior with 2-1/2 water lines								
1951	416,395	—	—	BV	22.00	25.00	40.00	1,000
Note: With 3 water lines								
1951	Inc. above	40.00	60.00	90.00	125	225	450	3,000
Note: Amprior with 1-1/2 water lines								
1952	406,148	—	—	BV	22.00	24.00	35.00	1,500
Note: With 3 water lines								
1952	Inc. above	BV	23.00	30.00	35.00	55.00	100.00	1,900
Note: Short water links								
1952	Inc. above	—	BV	22.00	24.00	26.00	60.00	—
Note: Without water lines								

KM# 47 23.3276 g. 0.8000 Silver 0.6000 oz. ASW 36 mm. **Subject:** Newfoundland **Obv:** Head left **Obv. Designer:** T. H. Paget **Rev:** "The Matthew", John Cabot's ship, date and denomination below **Rev. Designer:** Thomas Shingles

Date	Mintage	F-12	VF-20	XF-40	AU-50	MS-60	MS-63	Proof
1949	672,218	BV	23.00	25.00	27.50	30.00	35.00	400
1949 Proof	—	—	—	—	—	—	—	2,600

KM# 54 23.3276 g. 0.8000 Silver 0.6000 oz. ASW 36 mm. **Obv:** Laureate bust right **Obv. Designer:** Mary Gillick **Rev:** Voyageur, date and denomination below **Rev. Designer:** Emanuel Hahn **Note:** All genuine circulation strike 1955 Amprior dollars have a die break running along the top of TI in the word GRATIA on the obverse.

Date	Mintage	F-12	VF-20	XF-40	AU-50	MS-60	MS-63	Proof
1953	1,074,578	—	—	—	BV	23.00	30.00	1,600
Note: Without strap, wire rim								
1953	Inc. above	—	—	—	BV	23.00	30.00	—
Note: With strap, flat rim								
1954	246,606	—	BV	23.00	25.00	30.00	50.00	—
1955	268,105	—	BV	23.00	24.00	30.00	50.00	—
Note: With 3 water lines								
1955	Inc. above	85.00	95.00	100.00	125	150	300	—
Note: Amprior with 1-1/2 water lines* and die break								
1956	209,092	BV	22.00	24.00	26.00	35.00	85.00	—
1957	496,389	—	—	—	BV	23.00	26.00	—
Note: With 3 water lines								
1957	Inc. above	—	BV	24.00	26.00	28.00	50.00	—
Note: With 1 water line								
1959	1,443,502	—	—	—	—	BV	24.00	—
1960	1,420,486	—	—	—	—	BV	24.00	—
1961	1,262,231	—	—	—	—	BV	24.00	—
1962	1,884,789	—	—	—	—	BV	24.00	—
1963	4,179,981	—	—	—	—	BV	24.00	—

KM# 55 23.3276 g. 0.8000 Silver 0.6000 oz. ASW 36 mm.   **Subject:** British Columbia **Obv:** Laureate bust right **Obv. Designer:** Mary Gillick **Rev:** Totem Pole, dates at left, denomination below **Rev. Designer:** Stephan Trenka

Date	Mintage	F-12	VF-20	XF-40	AU-50	MS-60	MS-63	Proof
1858-1958	3,039,630	—	—	—	BV	23.00	26.00	—

KM# 58 23.3276 g. 0.8000 Silver 0.6000 oz. ASW 36 mm.   **Subject:** Charlottetown **Obv:** Laureate bust right **Rev:** Design at center, dates at outer edges, denomination below **Rev. Designer:** Dinko Voldanovic

Date	Mintage	F-12	VF-20	XF-40	AU-50	MS-60	MS-63	Proof
1864-1964	7,296,832	—	—	—	—	BV	24.00	—
1864-1964 Specimen proof	Inc. above	—	—	—	—	—	—	300

Large beads	Medium beads	Small beads

KM# 64.1 23.3276 g. 0.8000 Silver 0.6000 oz. ASW 36 mm.   **Obv:** Young bust right **Obv. Designer:** Arnold Machin **Rev:** Voyageur, date and denomination below **Rev. Designer:** Emanual Hahn

Date	Mintage	F-12	VF-20	XF-40	AU-50	MS-60	MS-63	Proof
1965	10,768,569	—	—	—	—	BV	24.00	400
Note: Small beads, pointed 5								
1965	Inc. above	—	—	—	—	BV	24.00	400
Note: Small beads, blunt 5								
1965	Inc. above	—	—	—	—	BV	24.00	—
Note: Large beads, blunt 5								
1965	Inc. above	—	—	—	BV	23.00	28.00	—
Note: Large beads, pointed 5								

Date	Mintage	F-12	VF-20	XF-40	AU-50	MS-60	MS-63	Proof
1965	Inc. above	—	—	BV	23.00	26.00	45.00	—
Note: Medium beads, pointed 5								
1966	9,912,178	—	—	—	—	BV	24.00	—
Note: Large beads								
1966	485	—	—	2,400	2,600	2,900	4,000	—
Note: Small beads								

KM# 70 23.3280 g. 0.8000 Silver 0.6000 oz. ASW 36 mm. **Subject:** Confederation Centennial **Obv:** Young bust right **Obv. Designer:** Arnold Machin **Rev:** Goose left, dates below, denomination above **Rev. Designer:** Alex Colville

Date	Mintage	MS-63	Proof
1867-1967	6,767,496	24.00	25.00

KM# 76.1 15.6400 g. Nickel 32 mm. **Obv:** Young bust right **Obv. Designer:** Arnold Machin **Rev:** Voyageur, date and denomination below **Rev. Designer:** Emanuel Hahn

Date	Mintage	MS-63	P/L	Proof
1968 Small island	—	10.00	7.50	—
1968	1,408,143	2.50	1.75	—
1968 No Island	—	12.00	4.50	—
1968	—	—	30.00	—
Note: Doubled die; exhibits extra water lines				
1968	5,579,714	2.00	—	—
1969	4,809,313	2.50	—	—
1969	594,258	—	1.75	125
1972	2,676,041	3.50	—	—
1972	405,865	—	2.25	—

KM# 78 15.6000 g. Nickel 32 mm. **Subject:** Manitoba **Obv:** Young bust right **Rev:** Pasque flower

divides dates and denomination **Rev. Designer:** Raymond Taylor

Date	Mintage	MS-63	P/L	Proof
1870-1970	4,140,058	3.50	—	—
1870-1970	645,869	—	2.25	80.00

KM# 79 15.7000 g. Nickel 32.1 mm. **Subject:** British Columbia **Obv:** Young bust right **Rev:** Shield divides dates, denomination below, flowers above **Rev. Designer:** Thomas Shingles

Date	Mintage	MS-63	P/L	Proof
1871-1971	4,260,781	3.50	—	—
1871-1971	468,729	—	2.25	125

KM# 80 23.3276 g. 0.5000 Silver 0.3750 oz. ASW 36 mm. **Subject:** British Columbia **Obv:** Young bust right **Rev:** Crowned arms with supporters divide dates, maple at top divides denomination, crowned lion atop crown on shield **Rev. Designer:** Patrick Brindley

Date	Mintage	MS-63	P/L	Proof
1871-1971 Specimen	585,674	—	14.00	—

KM# 64.2a 23.3276 g. 0.5000 Silver 0.3750 oz. ASW 36 mm. **Obv:** Smaller young bust right **Obv. Designer:** Arnold Machin **Rev:** Voyageur **Rev. Designer:** Emanuel Hahn

Date	Mintage	MS-63	P/L	Proof
1972 Specimen	341,598	—	13.00	—
1972 Proof	Inc. above	—	—	15.00

DOLLAR

KM# 82 Nickel 32 mm.   **Subject:** Prince Edward Island **Obv:** Young bust right **Rev:** Building, inscription below divides dates, denomination above **Rev. Designer:** Terry Manning

Date	Mintage	MS-63	P/L	Proof
1873-1973	3,196,452	2.00	—	—
1873-1973 (c)	466,881	—	2.50	—

KM# 83 23.3276 g. 0.5000 Silver 0.3750 oz. ASW 36 mm.   **Obv:** Young bust right **Rev:** Mountie left, dates below, denomination at right **Rev. Designer:** Paul Cedarberg

Date	Mintage	MS-63	P/L	Proof
1873-1973 Specimen	1,031,271	—	14.00	—
1873-1973 Specimen	—	—	25.00	—

Note: Dollar housed in special blue case with RCMP crest.

KM# 88 Nickel 32 mm.   **Subject:** Winnipeg Centennial **Obv:** Young bust right **Rev:** Zeros frame pictures, dates below, denomination at bottom **Rev. Designer:** Paul Pederson and Patrick Brindley

Date	Mintage	MS-63	P/L	Proof
1874-1974	2,799,363	2.00	—	—
1874-1974 (c)	363,786	—	2.50	—

KM# 88a 23.3276 g. 0.5000 Silver 0.3750 oz. ASW 36 mm.   **Subject:** Winnipeg Centennial **Obv:** Young bust right **Rev:** Zeros frame pictures, dates below, denomination at bottom **Rev. Designer:** Paul Pederson and Patrick Brindley

Date	Mintage	MS-63	P/L	Proof
1974-1974 Specimen	728,947	—	14.00	—

KM# 76.2 15.6200 g. Nickel 32 mm.   **Obv:** Smaller young bust right **Obv. Designer:** Arnold Machin **Rev:** Voyageur **Rev. Designer:** Emanuel Hahn

Date	Mintage	MS-63	P/L	Proof
1975	3,256,000	1.50	—	—
1975	322,325	—	2.50	—
1976	2,498,204	1.50	—	—
1976	274,106	—	2.50	—

KM# 97 23.3276 g. 0.5000 Silver 0.3750 oz. ASW 36 mm.   **Subject:** Calgary **Obv:** Youmg bust right **Rev:** Figure on bucking horse, dates divided below, denomination above **Rev. Designer:** Donald D. Paterson

Date	Mintage	MS-63	P/L	Proof
1875-1975 Specimen	930,956	—	14.00	—

KM# 76.3 Nickel 32 mm.   **Obv:** Young bust right **Obv. Designer:** Arnold Machin **Rev:** Voyageur **Rev. Designer:** Emanuel Hahn **Note:** Only known in prooflike sets with 1976 obverse slightly modified.

Date	Mintage	MS-63	P/L	Proof
1975	Inc. above	—	3.00	—

Note: mule with 1976 obv.

KM# 106 23.3276 g. 0.5000 Silver 0.3750 oz. ASW 36 mm. **Subject:** Parliament Library **Obv:** Young bust right **Rev:** Library building, dates below, denomination above **Rev. Designer:** Walter Ott and Patrick Brindley

Date	Mintage	MS-63	P/L	Proof
1876-1976 Specimen	578,708	—	14.00	—
1876-1976 Proof	Inc. above	—	—	25.00

Note: Blue case VIP

KM# 117 Nickel 32 mm. **Obv:** Young bust right **Obv. Designer:** Arnold Machin **Rev:** Voyageur modified **Rev. Designer:** Emanuel Hahn

Date	Mintage	MS-63	P/L	Proof
1977	1,393,745	3.50	—	—
1977	—	—	4.00	—

KM# 118 23.3276 g. 0.5000 Silver 0.3750 oz. ASW 36 mm. **Subject:** Silver Jubilee **Obv:** Young bust right, dates below **Rev:** Throne, denomination below **Rev. Designer:** Raymond Lee

Date	Mintage	MS-63	P/L	Proof
1952-1977 Specimen	744,848	—	14.00	—
1952-1977 Specimen	Inc. above	—	45.00	—

Note: red case VIP

KM# 120.1 15.5000 g. Nickel 32.1 mm. **Obv:** Young bust right **Obv. Designer:** Arnold Machin **Rev:** Voyageur, date and denomination below **Rev. Designer:** Emanuel Hahn **Note:** Modified design.

Date	Mintage	MS-63	Proof
1978	2,948,488	1.50	—
1979	2,954,842	1.50	—
1980	3,291,221	1.50	—
1981	2,778,900	1.50	—
1981 Proof	—	—	5.25
1982	1,098,500	1.50	—
1982 Proof	180,908	—	5.25
1983	2,267,525	1.50	—
1983 Proof	166,779	—	5.25
1984	1,223,486	1.50	—
1984 Proof	161,602	—	6.00
1985	3,104,092	1.50	—
1985 Proof	153,950	—	7.00
1986	3,089,225	2.00	—
1986 Proof	176,224	—	7.50
1987	287,330	3.50	—
1987 Proof	175,686	—	7.50

KM# 121 23.3276 g. 0.5000 Silver 0.3750 oz. ASW 36 mm. **Subject:** XI Commonwealth Games **Obv:** Young bust right **Rev:** Commonwealth games, logo at center **Rev. Designer:** Raymond Taylor

Date	Mintage	MS-63	P/L	Proof
1978 Specimen	709,602	—	14.00	—

KM# 124 23.3276 g. 0.5000 Silver 0.3750 oz. ASW 36 mm. **Subject:** Griffon **Obv:** Young bust right **Rev:** Ship, dates below, denomination above **Rev. Designer:** Walter Schluep

Date	Mintage	MS-63	P/L	Proof
1979 Specimen	826,695	—	14.00	—

DOLLAR

KM#128 23.3276 g. 0.5000 Silver 0.3750 oz. ASW 36 mm. **Subject:** Arctic Territories **Obv:** Young bust right **Rev:** Bear right, date below, denomination above **Rev. Designer:** Donald D. Paterson

Date	Mintage	MS-63	P/L	Proof
1980 Specimen	539,617	—	22.00	—

KM#130 23.3276 g. 0.5000 Silver 0.3750 oz. ASW 36 mm. **Subject:** Transcontinental Railroad **Obv:** Young bust right **Rev:** Train engine and map, date below, denomination above **Rev. Designer:** Christopher Gorey

Date	Mintage	MS-63	Proof
1981	699,494	14.00	—
1981 Proof	—	—	15.00

KM#133 23.3276 g. 0.5000 Silver 0.3750 oz. ASW 36 mm. **Subject:** Regina **Obv:** Young bust right **Rev:** Cattle skull divides dates and denomination below **Rev. Designer:** Huntley Brown

Date	Mintage	MS-63	Proof
1882-1982	144,930	14.00	—
1882-1982 Proof	758,958	—	14.00

KM#134 15.4200 g. Nickel 32 mm. **Subject:** Constitution **Obv:** Young bust right **Rev:** Meeting of Government **Rev. Designer:** Ago Aarand

Date	Mintage	MS-63	P/L	Proof
1867-1982	9,709,422	3.00	6.00	—

KM#138 23.3276 g. 0.5000 Silver 0.3750 oz. ASW 36 mm. **Subject:** Edmonton University Games **Obv:** Young bust right **Rev:** Athlete within game logo, date and denomination below **Rev. Designer:** Carola Tietz

Date	Mintage	MS-63	Proof
1983	159,450	14.00	—
1983 Proof	506,847	—	14.00

KM#140 23.3276 g. 0.5000 Silver 0.3750 oz. ASW 36 mm. **Subject:** Toronto Sesquicentennial **Obv:** Young bust right **Rev. Designer:** D. J. Craig

Date	Mintage	MS-63	Proof
1984	133,610	14.00	—
1984 Proof	732,542	—	14.00

KM#141 15.5000 g. Nickel 32 mm. **Subject:** Jacques Cartier **Obv:** Young bust right **Rev:** Cross with shield above figures **Rev. Designer:** Hector Greville

Date	Mintage	MS-63	Proof
1534-1984	7,009,323	3.50	—
1534-1984 Proof	87,760	—	6.00

KM# 143 23.3276 g. 0.5000 Silver 0.3750 oz. ASW
36 mm. **Subject:** National Parks **Obv:** Young
bust right **Rev:** Moose right, dates above,
denomination below **Rev. Designer:** Karel Rohlicek

Date	Mintage	MS-63	Proof
1885-1985	163,314	14.00	—
1885-1985 Proof	733,354	—	14.00

KM# 120.2 Nickel 32.13 mm. **Obv:** Young bust
right **Rev:** Voyageur **Note:** Mule with New Zealand
50 cent, KM-37 obverse.

Date	Mintage	MS-63	Proof
1985	—	3,000	—

KM# 149 23.3276 g. 0.5000 Silver 0.3750 oz. ASW
36 mm. **Subject:** Vancouver **Obv:** Young bust
right **Rev:** Train left, dates divided below,
denomination above **Rev. Designer:** Elliot John
Morrison

Date	Mintage	MS-63	Proof
1886-1986	125,949	14.00	—
1886-1986 Proof	680,004	—	14.00

KM# 157 7.0000 g. Aureate-Bronze Plated Nickel
26.5 mm. **Obv:** Young bust right **Obv. Designer:**
Arnold Machin **Rev:** Loon right, date and
denomination below **Rev. Designer:** Robert R.
Carmichael **Shape:** 11-sided

Date	Mintage	MS-63	Proof
1987	205,405,000	2.25	—
1987 Proof	178,120	—	8.00
1988	138,893,539	2.25	—
1988 Proof	175,259	—	6.75
1989	184,773,902	3.00	—
1989 Proof	170,928	—	6.75

KM# 154 23.3276 g. 0.5000 Silver 0.3750 oz. ASW
36 mm. **Subject:** John Davis **Obv:** Young bust
right **Rev:** Ship "John Davis" with masts, rock in
background, dates below, denomination at bottom
Rev. Designer: Christopher Gorey

Date	Mintage	MS-63	Proof
1587-1987	118,722	14.00	—
1587-1987 Proof	602,374	—	14.00

KM# 161 23.3276 g. 0.5000 Silver 0.3750 oz. ASW
36 mm. **Subject:** Ironworks **Obv:** Young bust
right **Rev:** Ironworkers, date and denomination
below **Rev. Designer:** Robert R. Carmichael

Date	Mintage	MS-63	Proof
1988	106,872	14.00	—
1988 Proof	255,013	—	17.50

KM# 168 23.3276 g. 0.5000 Silver 0.3750 oz. ASW
36 mm. **Subject:** MacKenzie River **Obv:** Young
bust right **Rev:** People in canoe, date above,
denomination below **Rev. Designer:** John Mardon

Date	Mintage	MS-63	Proof
1989	99,774	14.00	—
1989 Proof	244,062	—	17.50

KM# 186 7.0000 g. Aureate-Bronze Plated Nickel 26.5 mm. **Obv:** Crowned head right **Obv. Designer:** Dora dePedery-Hunt **Rev:** Loon right, date and denomination **Rev. Designer:** Robert R. Carmichael **Shape:** 11-sided

Date	Mintage	MS-63	Proof
1990	68,402,000	1.75	—
1990 Proof	140,649	—	7.00
1991	23,156,000	1.75	—
1991 Proof	131,888	—	13.00
1993	33,662,000	2.00	—
1993 Proof	143,065	—	6.00
1994	16,232,530	2.00	—
1994 Proof	104,485	—	7.00
1995	27,492,630	2.25	—
1995 Proof	101,560	—	7.00
1996	17,101,000	2.00	—
1996 Proof	112,835	—	7.50
1997	—	5.00	—
1997 Proof	113,647	—	8.00
1998	—	2.50	—
1998W Prooflike	—	—	—
1998 Proof	93,632	—	10.00
1999	—	2.00	—
1999 Proof	95,113	—	8.00
2000	—	2.00	—
2000W Prooflike	—	—	—
2000 Proof	90,921	—	8.00
2001	—	2.50	—
2001 Proof	74,194	—	8.00
2002	—	4.50	—
2002 Proof	65,315	—	7.50
2003	—	5.50	—

Note: Mintage of 5,101,000 includes both KM186 and KM495 examples.

2003 Proof	—	—	12.00

KM#170 23.3276 g. 0.5000 Silver 0.3750 oz. ASW 36 mm. **Subject:** Henry Kelsey **Obv:** Crowned head right **Rev:** Kelsey with natives, dates below, denomination above **Rev. Designer:** D. J. Craig

Date	Mintage	MS-63	Proof
1690-1990	99,455	14.00	—
1690-1990 Proof	254,959	—	20.00

KM#179 23.3276 g. 0.5000 Silver 0.3750 oz. ASW 36 mm. **Subject:** S.S. Frontenac **Obv:** Crowned head right **Rev:** Ship, "Frontenac," date and denomination below, **Rev. Designer:** D. J. Craig

Date	Mintage	MS-63	Proof
1991	73,843	14.00	—
1991 Proof	195,424	—	25.00

KM#210 25.1750 g. 0.9250 Silver 0.7487 oz. ASW 36 mm. **Subject:** Stagecoach service **Obv:** Crowned head right **Rev:** Stagecoach, date and denomination below **Rev. Designer:** Karsten Smith

Date	Mintage	MS-63	Proof
1992	78,160	25.00	—
1992 Proof	187,612	—	25.00

KM# 209 Aureate 26.5 mm. **Subject:** Loon right, dates and denomination **Obv:** Crowned head right **Rev. Designer:** Robert R. Carmichael

Date	Mintage	MS-63	Proof
1867-1992	4,242,085	2.00	—
1867-1992 Proof	147,061	—	8.00

KM# 218 Aureate 26 mm. **Subject:** Parliament **Obv:** Crowned head right, dates below **Rev:** Backs of three seated figures in front of building, denomination below **Rev. Designer:** Rita Swanson

Date	Mintage	MS-63	Proof
1867-1992	23,915,000	2.25	—
1867-1992 Proof	24,227	—	9.00

KM#235 25.1750 g. 0.9250 Silver 0.7487 oz. ASW 36 mm. **Subject:** Stanley Cup hockey **Obv:** Crowned head right **Rev:** Hockey players between cups, dates below, denomination above **Rev. Designer:** Stewart Sherwood

Date	Mintage	MS-63	Proof
1993	88,150	25.00	—
1993 Proof	294,314	—	25.00

KM# 248 7.0000 g. Aureate-Bronze Plated Nickel 26 mm. **Subject:** War Memorial **Obv:** Crowned head right, date below **Rev:** Memorial, denomination at right **Rev. Designer:** R. C. M. Staff

Date	Mintage	MS-63	Proof
1994	20,004,830	2.25	—
1994 Proof	54,524	—	7.50

KM#251 25.1750 g. 0.9250 Silver 0.7487 oz. ASW 36 mm. **Subject:** Last RCMP sled-dog patrol

Obv: Crowned head right **Rev:** Dogsled, denomination divides dates below **Rev. Designer:** Ian Sparks

Date	Mintage	MS-63	Proof
1969-1994	61,561	25.00	—
1969-1994 Proof	170,374	—	25.00

KM# 258 7.0000 g. Aureate 26 mm. **Subject:** Peacekeeping Monument in Ottawa **Obv:** Crowned head right, date below **Rev:** Monument, denomination above right **Rev. Designer:** J. K. Harmon, R. G. Henriquez and C. H. Oberlander **Note:** Mintage included with KM#186.

Date	Mintage	MS-63	Proof
1995	18,502,750	2.25	—
1995 Proof	43,293	—	7.50

KM#259 25.1750 g. 0.9250 Silver 0.7487 oz. ASW 36 mm. **Subject:** Hudson Bay Company **Obv:** Crowned head right **Rev:** Explorers and ship, date and denomination below **Rev. Designer:** Vincent McIndoe

Date	Mintage	MS-63	Proof
1995	61,819	25.00	—
1995 Proof	166,259	—	30.00

KM#274 25.1750 g. 0.9250 Silver 0.7487 oz. ASW 36 mm. **Subject:** McIntosh Apple **Obv:** Crowned head right **Rev:** Apple, dates and denomination below **Rev. Designer:** Roger Hill

Date	Mintage	MS-63	Proof
1796-1996	58,834	25.00	—
1796-1996 Proof	133,779	—	25.00

DOLLAR

KM#282 25.1750 g. 0.9250 Silver 0.7487 oz. ASW
36 mm.   **Subject:** 25th Anniversary Hockey
Victory **Obv:** Crowned head right **Rev:** The winning
goal by Paul Aenderson. Based on a painting by
Andre l'Archeveque, dates at right, denomination at
bottom **Rev. Designer:** Walter Burden

Date	Mintage	MS-63	Proof
1972-1997	155,252	25.00	—
1972-1997 Proof	184,965	—	30.00

KM#291 7.0000 g. Aureate-Bronze Plated Nickel
26 mm.   **Subject:** Loon Dollar 10th Anniversary
Obv: Crowned head right **Rev:** Loon in flight left,
dates above, denomination below **Rev. Designer:**
Jean-Luc Grondin

Date	Mintage	MS-63	P/L	Proof
1987-1997	—	—	22.00	—

KM#296 25.1750 g. 0.9250 Silver 0.7487 oz. ASW
36 mm.   **Subject:** Loon Dollar 10th Anniversary
Obv: Crowned head right **Rev:** Loon in flight left,
dates above, denomination below **Rev. Designer:**
Jean-Luc Grondin

Date	Mintage	MS-63	Proof
1987-1997 Proof	24,995	—	95.00

KM#306 25.1750 g. 0.9250 Silver 0.7487 oz. ASW
36 mm.   **Subject:** 120th Anniversary Royal
Canadian Mounted Police **Obv:** Crowned head right
Rev: Mountie on horseback, dates at left,
denomination above **Rev. Designer:** Adeline
Halvorson **Note:** Individually cased prooflikes,
proofs or specimens are from broken-up prooflike
or specimen sets.

Date	Mintage	MS-63	P/L	Proof
1873-1998	79,777	—	25.00	—
1873-1998 Proof	120,172	—	—	35.00

KM#355 25.1750 g. 0.9250 Silver 0.7487 oz. ASW
36 mm.   **Subject:** International Year of Old
Persons **Obv:** Crowned head right **Rev:** Figures
amid trees, date and denomination below **Rev.
Designer:** S. Armstrong-Hodgson

Date	Mintage	MS-63	Proof
1999 Proof	24,976	—	40.00

KM#356 25.1750 g. 0.9250 Silver 0.7487 oz. ASW
36 mm.   **Subject:** Discovery of Queen Charlotte
Isle **Obv:** Crowned head right **Rev:** Ship and three
boats, dates at right, denomination below **Rev.
Designer:** D. J. Craig

Date	Mintage	MS-63	P/L	Proof
1999	67,655	—	25.00	—
1999 Proof	126,435	—	—	35.00

DOLLAR

KM# 401 25.1750 g. 0.9250 Silver 0.7487 oz. ASW 36 mm. **Subject:** Voyage of Discovery **Obv:** Crowned head right **Rev:** Human and space shuttle, date above, denomination below **Rev. Designer:** D. F. Warkentine

Date	Mintage	MS-63	P/L	Proof
2000	60,100	—	25.00	—
2000 Proof	114,130	—	—	30.00

KM# 414 25.1750 g. 0.9250 Silver 0.7487 oz. ASW 36 mm. **Subject:** National Ballet **Obv:** Crowned head right **Rev:** Ballet dancers **Rev. Designer:** Scott McKowen **Edge:** Reeded

Date	Mintage	MS-63	Proof
2001	65,000	27.50	—
2001 Proof	225,000	—	35.00

KM# 434 25.1750 g. 0.9250 Silver 0.7487 oz. ASW 36 mm. **Obv:** Crowned head right **Rev:** Recycled 1911 pattern dollar design: denomination, country name and dates in crowned wreath **Edge:** Reeded

Date	Mintage	MS-63	Proof
1911-2001 Proof	24,996	—	55.00

KM# 186a Gilt Aureate-Bronze Plated Nickel 26.5 mm. **Subject:** Olympic Win

Date	Mintage	MS-63	Proof
2002 Proof	—	—	40.00

KM# 443 25.1750 g. 0.9250 Silver 0.7487 oz. ASW 36 mm. **Subject:** Queen's Golden Jubilee **Obv:** Crowned head right, with anniversary date at left **Obv. Designer:** Dora dePédery-Hunt **Rev:** Queen in her coach and a view of the coach, denomination below **Edge:** Reeded

Date	Mintage	MS-63	Proof
1952-2002	65,140	28.50	—
1952-2002 Proof	29,688	—	40.00

KM# 443a 25.1800 g. 0.9250 Silver Gilt 0.7488 oz. ASW 36 mm. **Subject:** Queen's Golden Jubilee **Obv:** Crowned head right with anniversary date **Rev:** Queen in her coach and a view of the coach **Edge:** Reeded **Note:** Special 24 karat gold plated issue of KM#443.

Date	Mintage	MS-63	Proof
2002 Proof	32,642	—	45.00

KM# 462 7.0000 g. Aureate-Bronze Plated Nickel **Obv:** Commemorative dates 1952-2002 **Obv. Designer:** Dora dePédery-Hunt **Rev:** Family of Loons

Date	Mintage	MS-63	Proof
2002 Specimen	67,672	—	35.00

KM# 467 7.0000 g. Aureate-Bronze Plated Nickel **Subject:** Elizabeth II Golden Jubilee **Obv:** Crowned head right, Jubilee commemorative dates 1952-2002 **Obv. Designer:** Dora dePédery-Hunt

Date	Mintage	MS-63	Proof
2002	2,302,000	2.50	—
2002 Proof	—	—	8.00

KM# 467a Gold **Subject:** 50th Anniversary, Accession to the Throne **Obv:** Crowned head right **Note:** Sold on the internet.

Date	Mintage	MS-63	Proof
2002	1	—	55,500

KM# 503 25.1750 g. 0.9250 Silver 0.7487 oz. ASW 36 mm. **Subject:** Queen Mother **Obv:** Crowned head right **Obv. Designer:** Dora de Pedery-Hunt **Rev:** Queen Mother facing

Date	Mintage	MS-63	Proof
2002 Proof	9,994	—	250

KM# 450 25.1750 g. 0.9999 Silver 0.8093 oz. ASW 36 mm. **Subject:** Cobalt Mining Centennial **Obv:**

Queens portrait right **Obv. Designer:** Dora dePédery-Hunt **Rev:** Mine tower and fox **Edge:** Reeded

Date	Mintage	MS-63	Proof
2003	51,130	30.00	—
2003 Proof	88,536	—	45.00

KM# 495 7.0000 g. Aureate-Bronze Plated Nickel 26.5 mm. **Obv:** Bare head right **Obv. Designer:** Susanna Blunt **Rev:** Loon right **Rev. Designer:** Robert R. Carmichael **Shape:** 11-sided

Date	Mintage	MS-63	Proof
2003	5,102,000	5.50	—

Note: Mintage of 5,101,000 includes both KM 186 and 495 examples.

Date	Mintage	MS-63	Proof
2003W Prooflike	—	—	—
2003 Proof	62,507	—	7.50
2004	10,894,000	1.75	—
2004 Proof	—	—	12.00
2005	44,375,000	3.00	—
2005 Proof	—	—	7.50
2006	49,111,000	3.00	—
2006 Proof	—	—	7.50
2006(ml)	49,111,000	3.00	—
2006(ml) Proof	—	—	7.50
2007(ml)	38,045,000	3.00	—
2007(ml) Proof	—	—	7.50
2008(ml)	29,561,000	3.00	—
2008(ml) Proof	—	—	7.50
2009(ml)	39,601,000	3.00	—
2009(ml) Proof	—	—	7.50
2010(ml)	—	3.00	—
2010(ml) Proof	—	—	7.50
2011(ml)	—	3.00	—
2011(ml) Proof	—	—	7.50
2012(ml)	—	3.00	—
2012(ml) Proof	—	—	7.50

KM# 473 25.1750 g. 0.9999 Silver 0.8093 oz. ASW **Subject:** 50th Anniversary of the Coronation of Elizabeth II **Obv:** 1953 effigy of the Queen, Jubilee dates 1953-2003 **Obv. Designer:** Mary Gillick **Rev:** Voyageur, date and denomination below

Date	Mintage	MS-63	Proof
1953-2003 Proof	21,537	—	45.00

KM# 480 25.1750 g. 0.9999 Silver 0.8093 oz. ASW **Subject:** Coronation of Queen Elizabeth II **Obv:** Head right **Rev:** Voyaguers **Rev. Designer:** Emanuel Hahn

Date	Mintage	MS-63	Proof
1953-2003 Proof	29,586	—	50.00

KM# 480a Gold **Subject:** 50th Anniversary of Coronation **Obv. Designer:** Mary Gilick **Rev:** Voyageur **Note:** Sold on the internet.

Date	Mintage	MS-63	Proof
1953-2003	1	—	62,750

KM# 507 7.0000 g. Aureate-Bronze Plated Nickel 26.5 mm. **Obv:** Bare head right, date below **Obv. Designer:** Susanna Blunt **Rev:** Loon **Edge:** Plain **Shape:** 11-sided

Date	Mintage	MS-63	Proof
2004 Proof	25,105	—	75.00

KM# 511 25.1750 g. 0.9999 Silver 0.8093 oz. ASW 36 mm. **Obv:** Elizabeth II **Rev:** Poppy on maple leaf **Edge:** Reeded

Date	Mintage	MS-63	Proof
2004 Proof	24,527	—	50.00

KM# 512 25.1750 g. 0.9999 Silver 0.8093 oz. ASW 36 mm. **Subject:** First French Settlement in America **Obv:** Crowned head right **Rev:** Sailing ship **Edge:** Reeded

Date	Mintage	MS-63	Proof
2004	42,582	30.00	—
2004 Fleur-dis-lis privy mark	8,315	60.00	—
2004 Proof	106,974	—	50.00

KM# 513 7.0000 g. Aureate-Bronze Plated Nickel 26.5 mm. **Subject:** Olympics **Obv:** Bare head right **Rev:** Maple leaf, Olympic flame and rings above loon **Edge:** Plain **Shape:** 11-sided

Date	Mintage	MS-63	Proof
2004	6,526,000	8.00	—

KM# 513a 9.3100 g. 0.9250 Silver 0.2769 oz. ASW 26.5 mm. **Subject:** Olympics **Obv:** Bare head right **Rev:** Multicolor maple leaf, Olympic flame and rings above loon **Edge:** Plain **Shape:** 11-sided

Date	Mintage	MS-63	Proof
2004 Proof	19,994	—	50.00

KM# 549 25.1750 g. 0.9250 Silver 0.7487 oz. ASW 36.07 mm. **Subject:** 40th Anniversary of National

Flag **Obv:** Head right **Obv. Designer:** Susanna
Blunt **Rev. Designer:** William Woodruff

Date	Mintage	MS-63	Proof
2005	50,948	27.50	—
2005 Proof	95,431	—	40.00

KM# 549a 25.1750 g. 0.9250 Silver partially gilt
0.7487 oz. ASW 36.07 mm. **Subject:** 40th
Anniversary of National Flag **Obv:** Head right

Date	Mintage	MS-63	Proof
2005	62,562	75.00	—

KM# 549b 25.1800 g. 0.9250 Silver 0.7488 oz.
ASW 36.07 mm. **Subject:** 40th Anniversary
National Flag **Rev:** National flag, colorized

Date	Mintage	MS-63	Proof
2005 Proof	4,898	—	350

KM# 552 7.0000 g. Aureate-Bronze Plated Nickel
26.5 mm. **Obv:** Head right **Rev:** Terry Fox walking
left

Date	Mintage	MS-63	Proof
2005	1,290,900	3.50	—

KM# 553 7.0000 g. Aureate-Bronze Plated Nickel
Subject: Tuffed Puffin **Obv:** Head right **Obv.
Designer:** Susanna Blunt

Date	Mintage	MS-63	Proof
2005	39,818	—	30.00

KM# 581 9.3100 g. 0.9250 Silver 0.2769 oz.
ASW **Subject:** Lullabies Loonie **Obv:** Head right
Obv. Designer: Susanna Blunt **Rev:** Loon and
moon, teddy bear in stars

Date	Mintage	MS-63	Proof
2006	18,103	4.50	—

KM# 582 7.0000 g. Aureate-Bronze Plated Nickel
26.5 mm. **Subject:** Snowy owl **Obv:** Head right
Obv. Designer: Susanna Blunt **Rev:** Snowy owl
with year above

Date	Mintage	MS-63	Proof
2006 Specimen	39,935	—	30.00

KM# 583 25.1750 g. 0.9250 Silver 0.7487 oz. ASW
36 mm. **Obv:** Head right **Rev:** Victoria Cross

Date	Mintage	MS-63	Proof
2006	27,254	25.00	—
2006 Proof	53,822	—	45.00

KM# 583a 25.1750 g. 0.9250 Silver partially gilt
0.7487 oz. ASW 36 mm. **Obv:** Head right **Rev:**
Victoria Cross gilt

Date	Mintage	MS-63	Proof
2006 Proof	53,822	—	75.00

KM# 630 7.0000 g. Aureate Bronze 26.5 mm.
Obv: Bust right **Rev:** Loon splashing in water

Date	Mintage	MS-63	Proof
2006	—	3.00	—

DOLLAR

DOLLAR

KM# 630a 9.3100 g. 0.9250 Silver with enamel 0.2769 oz. ASW 26.5 mm.   **Subject:** Olympic Games **Obv:** Crowned head right **Rev:** Loon in flight, colored olympic logo above

Date	Mintage	MS-63	Proof
2006	19,956	30.00	—

KM# 654 7.0000 g. 0.9250 Silver 0.2082 oz. ASW   **Obv:** Head right **Rev:** Snowflake, colorized **Note:** Sold in a CD package.

Date	Mintage	MS-63	Proof
2006(ml)	34,014	35.00	—

KM# 655 7.0000 g. 0.9250 Silver 0.2082 oz. ASW   **Subject:** Baby Rattle **Obv:** Head right **Rev:** Baby rattle

Date	Mintage	MS-63	Proof
2006	3,207	20.00	—

KM# 655a 7.0000 g. 0.9250 Silver 0.2082 oz. ASW   **Obv:** Bust right **Rev:** Baby Rattle, partially gilt

Date	Mintage	MS-63	Proof
2006	1,911	15.00	—

KM# 656 28.1750 g. 0.9250 Silver 0.8379 oz. ASW   **Subject:** Medal of Bravery **Obv:** Head right

Date	Mintage	MS-63	Proof
2006 Proof	8,343	—	50.00

KM# 656a 28.1750 g. 0.9250 Silver with multicolor enamel 0.8379 oz. ASW   **Subject:** Medal of Bravery **Obv:** Head right **Rev:** Maple leaf within wreath. Colorized.

Date	Mintage	MS-63	Proof
2006 Proof	4,999	—	150

KM# 1287 7.0000 g. Aureate Bronze 26.5 mm. **Rev:** Goose in flight

Date	Mintage	MS-63	Proof
2006 Proof	—	—	20.00

KM# 688 7.0000 g. Aureate-Bronze Plated Nickel 26.5 mm.   **Obv:** Head right **Rev:** Trumpeter Swan

Date	Mintage	MS-63	Proof
2007(ml)	40,000	20.00	—

KM# 653 25.1750 g. 0.9250 Silver 0.7487 oz. ASW 36.07 mm.   **Subject:** Thayendanegea **Obv:** Head right **Rev:** Bust 3/4 facing right

Date	Mintage	MS-63	Proof
2007	16,378	30.00	—
2007 Proof	—	—	40.00

KM# 653a 25.1750 g. 0.9250 Silver partially gilt 0.7487 oz. ASW 36.07 mm. **Subject:** Thayendanega **Rev:** Bust 3/4 right, partially gold plated

Date	Mintage	MS-63	Proof
2007 Proof	60,000	—	125

KM# 720 25.1800 g. 0.9250 Silver 0.7488 oz. ASW 36.07 mm. **Obv:** Bust right **Rev:** Thayendanega multicolor

Date	Mintage	MS-63	Proof
2007 Proof	4,760	—	120

KM# 700 7.0000 g. 0.9250 Silver 0.2082 oz. ASW 23.88 mm. **Rev:** Alphabet Letter Blocks

Date	Mintage	MS-63	Proof
2007	3,207	—	25.00

KM# 719 25.1800 g. 0.9250 Silver 0.7488 oz. ASW 36.07 mm. **Subject:** Celebration of the Arts **Rev:** Book, TV set, musical instruments, film montage **Rev. Designer:** Friedrich Peter **Edge:** Reeded

Date	Mintage	MS-63	Proof
2007	6,466	—	55.00

KM# A727 7.0000 g. Aureate-Bronze Plated Nickel 26.5 mm. **Subject:** Vancouver Olympic Games **Rev:** Loon splashing in water, Olympics logo at right

Date	Mintage	MS-63	Proof
2007(ml)	19,973	3.00	—

KM# 724 7.0000 g. Nickel 26.5 mm. **Rev:** Ottawa Senators, multicolor logo in circle

Date	Mintage	MS-63	Proof
2008	1,633	25.00	—

KM# 725 7.0000 g. Aureate-Bronze Plated Nickel 26.5 mm. **Obv:** Bust right **Rev:** Toronto Maple Leafs, multicolor logo in circle

Date	Mintage	MS-63	Proof
2008	—	25.00	—

KM# 726 7.0000 g. Aureate-Bronze Plated Nickel 26.5 mm. **Obv:** Bust left **Rev:** Vancouver Canucks, logo in center

Date	Mintage	MS-63	Proof
2008	1,302	25.00	—

KM# 767 25.1800 g. 0.9250 Silver 0.7488 oz. ASW 36.07 mm. **Rev:** Poppy at center of large maple leaf

Date	Mintage	MS-63	Proof
2008 Proof	—	—	50.00

KM# 781 25.1800 g. 0.9250 Silver partially gilt 0.7488 oz. ASW 36.07 mm. **Subject:** Ottawa Mint Centennial 1908-2008 **Rev:** Maple leaf transforming into a common loon, gilt rim and 100 **Rev. Designer:** Jason Bowman

Date	Mintage	MS-63	Proof
2008 Proof	15,000	—	65.00

KM# 784 7.0000 g. Aureate-Bronze Plated Nickel 26.5 mm. **Rev:** Common elder

Date	Mintage	MS-63	Proof
2008 Specimen	21,227	—	50.00

DOLLAR

KM#785 25.1800 g. 0.9250 Silver 0.7488 oz. ASW 36.07 mm.   **Subject:** Founding of Quebec 400th Anniversary **Rev:** Samuel de Champlain, ship and town view **Rev. Designer:** Susanne Duranceau

Date	Mintage	MS-63	Proof
2008	35,000	25.00	—
2008 Proof	65,000	—	40.00

KM# 785a 25.1800 g. 0.9250 Silver partially gilt. 0.7488 oz. ASW 36.07 mm.   **Subject:** Founding of Quebec 400th Anniversary **Rev:** Samuel de Champlain selectively gold plated, ship, town view **Rev. Designer:** Susanne Duranceau

Date	Mintage	MS-63	Proof
2008 Proof	38,630	—	75.00

KM# 787 7.0000 g. Aureate-Bronze Plated Nickel 26.5 mm.   **Subject:** Lucky Loonie **Rev:** Loon splashing and Olympic logo at right **Rev. Designer:** Steve Hepurn

Date	Mintage	MS-63	Proof
2008	—	20.00	—

KM#787a 9.3100 g. 0.9250 Silver 0.2769 oz. ASW 26.5 mm.   **Rev:** Loon splashing with Olympic logo

and maple leaf in color above **Rev. Designer:** Steve Hepurn

Date	Mintage	MS-63	Proof
2008 Proof	52,987	—	25.00

KM# 791 6.5000 g. Nickel 26.5 mm.   **Rev:** Edmonton Oilers

Date	Mintage	MS-63	Proof
2008	—	25.00	—

KM# 792 6.5000 g. Nickel 26.5 mm.   **Rev:** Montreal Canadiens

Date	Mintage	MS-63	Proof
2008	—	25.00	—

KM# 793 6.5000 g. Nickel 26.5 mm.   **Rev:** Ottawa Senators

Date	Mintage	MS-63	Proof
2008	—	25.00	—

KM# 794 6.5000 g. Nickel 26.5 mm.   **Rev:** Toronto Maple Leafs

Date	Mintage	MS-63	Proof
2008	—	25.00	—

KM# 795 6.5000 g. Nickel 26.5 mm. **Rev:**
Vancouver Canucks

Date	Mintage	MS-63	Proof
2008	—	25.00	—

KM# 851 33.6500 g. Nickel 26.5 mm. **Rev:**
Calgary Flames Road Jersey

Date	Mintage	MS-63	Proof
2009	382	25.00	—

KM# 852 33.6500 g. Nickel 26.5 mm. **Rev:**
Edmonton Oilers Road Jersey

Date	Mintage	MS-63	Proof
2009	472	25.00	—

KM# 853 33.6500 g. Nickel 26.5 mm. **Rev:**
Montreal Canadians Road Jersey

Date	Mintage	MS-63	Proof
2009	4,857	25.00	—

KM# 854 33.6500 g. Nickel 26.5 mm. **Rev:**
Ottawa Senators Road Jersey

Date	Mintage	MS-63	Proof
2009	387	25.00	—

KM# 855 33.6500 g. Nickel 26.5 mm. **Rev:**
Toronto Maple Leafs Road Jersey

Date	Mintage	MS-63	Proof
2009	1,328	25.00	—

KM# 856 33.6500 g. Nickel 26.5 mm. **Rev:**
Vancouver Canucks Road Jersey

Date	Mintage	MS-63	Proof
2009	794	25.00	—

KM# 864 7.0000 g. Aureate-Bronze Plated Nickel 26.5 mm. **Subject:** Montreal Canadiens, 100th Anniversary **Obv:** Bust right **Rev:** Montreal Canadiens logo and large 100 **Shape:** 11-sided

Date	Mintage	MS-63	Proof
2009	—	25.00	—

KM#865 25.1700 g. 0.9250 Silver 0.7485 oz. ASW 36.07 mm. **Subject:** Montreal Canadiens 100th Anniversary **Obv:** Bust right **Obv. Designer:** Susanna Blunt **Rev:** Montreal Canadiens logo partially gilt

Date	Mintage	MS-63	Proof
2009 Proof in black case	15,000	—	75.00
2009 Proof in acrillic stand	5,000	—	150

DOLLAR

KM# 889 25.1800 g. 0.9250 Silver 0.7488 oz. ASW 36.07 mm. **Subject:** 100th Anniversary of flight in Canada **Obv:** Bust right **Obv. Legend:** Elizabeth II DG Regina **Obv. Designer:** Susanna Blunt **Rev:** Silhouette with arms spread, 3 planes, plane cutout **Rev. Legend:** Canada Dollar 1909-2009 **Rev. Designer:** Jason Bouwman

Date	Mintage	MS-63	Proof
2009	13,074	40.00	—
2009 Proof	52,549	—	50.00

KM# 889a 25.1800 g. 0.9250 Silver partially gilt 0.7488 oz. ASW 36.07 mm. **Obv:** Bust right **Rev:** Boy silouette with arms spread, 3 planes, plane shadow partially gilt

Date	Mintage	MS-63	Proof
2009(ml) Proof	27,549	—	65.00

KM# 914 7.0000 g. Aureate-Bronze Plated Nickel 26.5 mm. **Obv:** Bust right **Obv. Designer:** Susanna Blunt **Rev:** Blue heron in flight

Date	Mintage	MS-63	Proof
2009 Specimen	21,677	50.00	—

KM# 883 7.0000 g. Aureate-Bronze Plated Nickel 26.5 mm. **Subject:** Lucky Loonie **Obv:** Bust right **Obv. Legend:** Elizabeth II DG Regina **Rev:** Canadian Olympic logo **Rev. Legend:** Canada Dollar

Date	Mintage	MS-63	Proof
2010	12,000	20.00	—

KM# 883a 9.3100 g. 0.9250 Silver 0.2769 oz. ASW 26.5 mm. **Subject:** Lucky Loonie **Obv:** Bust right **Obv. Legend:** Elizabeth II DG Regina **Rev:** Canadian Olympic logo in color **Rev. Legend:** Vancouver 2010 Canada Dollar **Shape:** 11-sided

Date	Mintage	MS-63	Proof
2010 Proof	40,000	—	55.00

KM# 1046 Aureate-Bronze Plated Nickel 26.5 mm. **Subject:** Roughriders **Rev:** S logo **Shape:** 11-sided

Date	Mintage	MS-63	Proof
2010(ml)		7.50	—

KM# 975 0.9250 Silver 36 mm. **Rev:** Sun mask **Rev. Designer:** Xwa lack Tun

Date	Mintage	MS-63	Proof
2010 Proof	1,278	—	200

KM# 995 25.1700 g. 0.9250 Silver 0.7485 oz. ASW 36.07 mm. **Rev:** HMCS Sackville **Rev. Designer:** Yves Berube

Date	Mintage	MS-63	Proof
2010 Proof	Est. 50,000	—	55.00

KM# 995a 25.1700 g. 0.9250 Silver partially gilt 0.7485 oz. ASW 36.07 mm. **Subject:** Navy Centennial **Rev:** HMCS Sackville, sea waves in gilt

Date	Mintage	MS-63	Proof
2010	—	—	110

KM# 996 7.0000 g. Aureate-Bronze Plated Nickel 26.5 mm. **Rev:** Northern Harrier Hawk

Date	Mintage	MS-63	Proof
2010	35,000	30.00	—
2010(ml)	—	—	50.00

KM# 1017 7.0000 g. Aureate-Bronze Plated Nickel 26.5 mm. **Rev:** Male and female sailors saluting, HMCS Halifax and anchor above

Date	Mintage	MS-63	Proof
2010	—	5.00	—

KM# 1027 25.1800 g. 0.9250 Silver 0.7488 oz. ASW 36.07 mm. **Obv:** George V bust left **Rev:** Voyaguers, dual dates below

Date	Mintage	MS-63	Proof
2010 Proof	7,500	—	70.00

KM# 1050 25.1800 g. 0.9250 Silver 0.7488 oz. ASW 36.07 mm. **Rev:** Red poppy in large field of poppies **Edge:** Reeded

Date	Mintage	MS-63	Proof
2010 Proof	5,000	—	150

KM# 1086 7.0000 g. Aureate-Bronze Plated Nickel 26.5 mm. **Rev:** Great Grey Owl **Rev. Designer:** Arnold Nagy

Date	Mintage	MS-63	Proof
2011	35,000	13.50	—

KM# 1017a 7.0000 g. Aureate Bronze gilt 26.5 mm. **Rev:** Male and female sailors saluting, HMCS Halifax in background and anchor above

Date	Mintage	MS-63	Proof
2010 Proof	—	—	50.00

KM# 1087 25.1800 g. 0.9250 Silver 0.7488 oz. ASW 36.07 mm. **Subject:** Parks Canada, 100th Anniversary **Rev:** Female head looking downward

DOLLAR

into hands holding nature scene **Rev. Designer:**
Luc Normandin

Date	Mintage	MS-63	Proof
2011	25,000	50.00	—
2011 Proof	—	—	60.00

KM# 1087a 25.1800 g. 0.9250 Silver partially gilt
0.7488 oz. ASW 36.07 mm.   **Subject:** Parks
Canada, 100th Anniversary **Rev:** Female head
looking downward to hands holding nature scene,
partially gilt **Rev. Designer:** Luc Normandin

Date	Mintage	MS-63	Proof
2011 Proof	45,000	—	75.00

KM# 1112 25.1700 g. 0.9250 Silver 0.7485 oz.
ASW 36.07 mm.   **Obv:** Crowned bust left of
George V **Obv. Designer:** E. B. MacKennal **Rev:**
Value and date within maple wreath **Rev. Designer:**
W.H.J. Blakemore

Date	Mintage	MS-63	Proof
2011 Proof	Est. 15,000	—	115

KM# 1166 7.0000 g. Aureate-Bronze Plated
Nickel 26.5 mm.   **Subject:** Canada Parks **Obv:**
Bust right **Rev:** Stylized animals

Date	Mintage	MS-63	Proof
2011	—	5.00	—

KM# 1255 6.2700 g. Brass Plated Steel
26.5 mm.   **Rev:** Loon with security feature above
Shape: 11-sided

Date	Mintage	MS-63	Proof
2012	—	5.00	—
2012 Proof	—	—	7.50
2013	—	5.00	—
2013 Proof	—	—	7.50

KM# 1216 9.3100 g. 0.9250 Silver 0.2769 oz. ASW
26.5 mm.   **Obv:** Bust right, SP/PA below **Rev:**
Loon, 1987-2012 below

Date	Mintage	MS-63	Proof
2012 Specimen	—	—	55.00

KM# 1222 7.0000 g. Aureate-Bronze Plated
Nickel 26.5 mm.   **Obv:** Bust right **Rev:** Loon and
two young, 1987-2012 dates

Date	Mintage	MS-63	Proof
2012 Specimen	—	—	40.00

KM# 1225 25.1800 g. 0.9250 Silver 0.7488 oz.
ASW 36.07 mm.   **Subject:** War of 1812, 200th
Anniversary **Obv:** Bust right **Rev:** Two soldiers and
guide on patrol

Date	Mintage	MS-63	Proof
2012	—	50.00	—
2012 Proof	—	—	60.00

KM# 1225a 25.1800 g. 0.9250 Silver partially gilt
0.7488 oz. ASW 36.07 mm.   **Subject:** War of
1812, 200th Anniversary **Obv:** Bust right, gilt rim
Rev: Two solders and guide, partially gilt

Date	Mintage	MS-63	Proof
2012 Proof	—	—	65.00

KM# 1244 25.1800 g. 0.9250 Silver 0.7488 oz. ASW 36.07 mm. **Subject:** Calgary Stampede

Date	Mintage	MS-63	Proof
2012	—	—	55.00

KM# 1254 7.8900 g. 0.9990 Silver 0.2534 oz. ASW 26.5 mm. **Subject:** Loonie, 25th Anniversary **Rev:** Two loons and large 25

Date	Mintage	MS-63	Proof
1987-2012 Proof	15,000	—	35.00

KM# 1256 6.2700 g. Brass Plated Steel 26.5 mm. **Subject:** Lucky Loonie **Rev:** Loon and Olympic logo **Shape:** 11-sided

Date	Mintage	MS-63	Proof
2012	—	10.00	—

KM# 1256a 12.1600 g. 0.9250 Silver 0.3616 oz. ASW 26.5 mm. **Subject:** Lucky loonie **Rev:** Loon and olympic logo in color

Date	Mintage	MS-63	Proof
2012 Proof	—	—	35.00

KM# 1274 25.1800 g. 0.9250 Silver 0.7488 oz. ASW 36.07 mm. **Subject:** Artistic Loonie **Rev:** Four Loons in color

Date	Mintage	MS-63	Proof
2012 Proof	—	—	125

KM# 1294 6.2700 g. Brass Plated Steel 26.5 mm. **Subject:** Grey Cup, 100th Anniversary **Obv:** Bust right **Shape:** 11-sided

Date	Mintage	MS-63	Proof
2012	—	5.00	—

KM# 1295 25.1800 g. 0.9250 Silver 0.7488 oz. ASW 36.07 mm. **Subject:** Grey Cup, 100th Anniversary

Date	Mintage	MS-63	Proof
2012 Proof	—	—	85.00

DOLLAR (Louis)

KM# 652 1.5000 g. 0.9990 Gold 0.0482 oz. AGW 14.1 mm. **Subject:** Gold Louis **Obv:** Bust right **Obv. Designer:** Susanna Blunt **Rev:** Crowned double L monogram within wreath

Date	Mintage	MS-63	Proof
2006 Proof	5,648	—	110

KM# 756 1.5550 g. 0.9990 Gold 0.0499 oz. AGW 14.1 mm. **Obv:** Bust right **Obv. Designer:** Susanna Blunt **Rev:** Crown above two oval shields

Date	Mintage	MS-63	Proof
2007 Proof	4,023	—	110

KM# 834 1.5550 g. 0.9990 Gold 0.0499 oz. AGW 14.1 mm. **Obv:** Bust right **Obv. Designer:** Susanna Blunt **Rev:** Crowned double L monogram, three lis around

Date	Mintage	MS-63	Proof
2008 Proof	3,793	—	110

2 DOLLARS

KM# 270 7.3000 g. Bi-Metallic Aluminum-Bronze center in Nickel ring 28 mm. **Obv:** Crowned head right within circle, date below **Obv. Designer:** Dora dePedery-Hunt **Rev:** Polar bear right within circle, denomination below **Rev. Designer:** Brent Townsend **Edge:** Segmented reeding

Date	Mintage	MS-63	P/L	Proof
1996	375,483,000	3.25	5.00	—
1996 Proof	—	—	—	10.00
1997	16,942,000	3.25	—	—
1998	4,926,000	3.25	—	—
1998W	Inc. above	3.25	—	—
1999	25,130,000	3.25	—	—
2000	29,847,000	3.25	—	—
2000W	Inc. above	3.25	—	—
2001	27,008,000	5.00	—	—
2001 Proof	74,944	—	—	12.50
2002	11,910,000	5.00	—	—
2002 Proof	65,315	—	—	12.50
2003	7,123,697	5.00	—	—
2003 Proof	62,007	—	—	12.50

KM# 270b 25.0000 g. 0.9250 Bi-Metallic Gold plated silver center on Silver planchet 0.7435 oz. 28 mm. **Obv:** Crowned head right within circle, date below **Rev:** Polar bear right within circle, denomination below **Edge:** 4.5mm thick

Date	Mintage	MS-63	Proof
1996 Proof	10,000	—	55.00
1998 Proof	—	—	—

KM# 270c 8.8300 g. 0.9250 Silver gold plated center 0.2626 oz. ASW 28 mm.   **Obv:** Crowned head right within circle, date below **Rev:** Polar bear right within circle, denomination below **Note:** 1.9mm thick.

Date	Mintage	MS-63	Proof
1996 Proof	10,000	—	12.00
1997 Proof	—	—	10.00
1998O Proof	—	—	12.00
1999 Proof	—	—	12.00
2000 Proof	—	—	12.00
2001 Proof	—	—	12.00

KM# 270a 10.8414 g. Bi-Metallic .999 Gold 5.7456g center in .999 Silver 5.0958g ring 28 mm.   **Obv:** Crowned head right within circle, date below **Rev:** Polar bear right within circle, denomination below

Date	Mintage	MS-63	Proof
1996 Proof	5,000	—	375

KM# 357 7.3000 g. Bi-Metallic Aluminum-Bronze center in Nickel ring 28 mm.   **Subject:** Nunavut **Obv:** Crowned head right **Rev:** Inuit person with drum, denomination below **Rev. Designer:** G. Arnaktavyok **Edge:** Segmented reeding

Date	Mintage	MS-63	Proof
1999	—	4.00	—

KM# 357a 8.5200 g. 0.9250 Silver gold plated center. 0.2534 oz. ASW 28 mm.   **Subject:** Nunavut **Obv:** Crowned head right **Rev:** Drum dancer **Edge:** Interrupted reeding

Date	Mintage	MS-63	Proof
1999 Proof	39,873	—	15.00

KM# 357b Gold Yellow gold center in White Gold ring   **Subject:** Nunavut **Obv:** Crowned head right **Rev:** Drum dancer

Date	Mintage	MS-63	Proof
1999 Proof	4,298	—	400

KM# 399 7.3000 g. Bi-Metallic Aluminum-Bronze center in Nickel ring 28 mm.   **Subject:** Knowledge **Obv:** Crowned head right within circle, denomination below **Rev:** Polar bear and 2 cubs right within circle, date above **Rev. Designer:** Tony Bianco **Edge:** Segmented reeding

Date	Mintage	MS-63	Proof
2000 Specimen	1,500	5.00	—

KM# 399a 8.5200 g. 0.9250 Silver gold plated center. 0.2534 oz. ASW   **Subject:** Knowledge **Obv:** Crowned head right within circle, denomination below **Rev:** Polar bear and 2 cubs within circle, date above

Date	Mintage	MS-63	Proof
2000 Proof	39,768	—	15.00

KM# 399b 6.3100 g. 0.9160 Gold Yellow gold center in White Gold ring 0.1858 oz. AGW **Subject:** Knowledge **Obv:** Crowned head right within circle, denomination below **Rev:** Polar bear and two cubs right within circle, date above

Date	Mintage	MS-63	Proof
2000 Proof	5,881	—	350

KM# 449 7.3000 g. Bi-Metallic Aluminum-Bronze center in Nickel ring 28 mm.   **Subject:** Elizabeth II Golden Jubilee **Obv:** Crowned head right, jubilee commemorative dates below **Edge:** Segmented reeding

Date	Mintage	MS-63	Proof
1952-2002	27,020,000	4.00	—

KM# 449a 8.8300 g. 0.9250 Silver gold plated center 0.2626 oz. ASW 28 mm.   **Subject:** Elizabeth II Golden Jubilee **Obv:** Crowned head right, jubilee commemorative dates below

Date	Mintage	MS-63	Proof
1952-2002 Proof	100,000	—	14.00

KM# 496 7.3000 g. Bi-Metallic Aluminum-Bronze center in Nickel ring 28 mm.   **Obv:** Head right **Obv. Designer:** Susanna Blunt **Rev:** Polar bear advancing right **Rev. Designer:** Brent Townsend **Edge:** Segmented reeding

Date	Mintage	MS-63	Proof
2003	11,244,000	5.00	—
2003W	71,142	25.00	—
2004	12,908,000	5.00	—
2004 Proof	—	—	12.50
2005	38,317,000	5.00	—
2005 Proof	—	—	12.50
2006(ml)	35,319,000	5.00	—
2006(ml) Proof	—	—	12.50
2007(ml)	38,957,000	5.00	—
2007(ml) Proof	—	—	12.50
2008(ml)	18,400,000	5.00	—
2008(ml) Proof	—	—	12.50
2009(ml)	38,430,000	5.00	—
2009(ml) Proof	—	—	12.50
2010(ml)	—	5.00	—
2010(ml) Proof	—	—	12.50
2011(ml)	—	5.00	—
2011(ml) Proof	—	—	12.50
2012(ml)	—	5.00	—
2012(ml) Proof	—	—	12.50

KM# 270d 8.8300 g. 0.9250 Silver gold plated center 0.2626 oz. ASW   **Subject:** 100th Anniversary of the Cobalt Silver Strike **Obv:** Crowned head right, within circle, date below **Rev:** Polar bear right, within circle, denomination below

Date	Mintage	MS-63	Proof
2003 Proof	100,000	—	25.00

KM# 496a 10.8414 g. 0.9250 Bi-Metallic Gold plated Silver center in Silver ring 0.3224 oz. 28 mm. **Obv:** Head right **Obv. Designer:** Susanna Blunt **Rev:** Polar Bear **Edge:** Segmented reeding

Date	Mintage	MS-63	Proof
2004 Proof	—	—	25.00

KM# 835 8.8000 g. 0.9250 Silver 0.2617 oz. ASW 27.95 mm. **Rev:** Proud Polar Bear advancing right

Date	Mintage	MS-63	Proof
2004 Proof	12,607	—	40.00

KM# 837 7.3000 g. Bi-Metallic Aluminum-Bronze center in Nickel ring **Obv:** Bust left, date at top **Rev:** Polar Bear advancing right

Date	Mintage	MS-63	Proof
2006(ml)	—	7.50	—
2007(ml)	38,957,000	7.50	—

KM# 631 7.3000 g. Bi-Metallic Aluminum-Bronze center in Nickel ring 28 mm. **Subject:** 10th Anniversary of $2 coin **Obv:** Crowned head right **Edge:** Segmented reeding

Date	Mintage	MS-63	Proof
2006(ml)	5,005,000	25.00	—
2006(ml) Proof	—	—	40.00

KM# 631a Bi-Metallic 22 Kt Gold ring around 4.1 Kt. Gold core **Subject:** 10th Anniversary of $2 coin **Obv:** Crowned head right **Rev:** Polar bear

Date	Mintage	MS-63	Proof
2006 Proof	2,068	—	400

KM# 836 7.3000 g. Bi-Metallic Aluminum-Bronze center in Nickel ring 28 mm. **Subject:** $2 coin, 10th Anniversary **Rev:** "Churchill" Polar Bear, northern lights **Edge:** Segmented reeding

Date	Mintage	MS-63	Proof
2006(ml)	31,636	7.50	—

KM# 796 8.8300 g. 0.9250 Silver 0.2626 oz. ASW 28.07 mm. **Rev:** Bear, gold plated center

Date	Mintage	MS-63	Proof
2008	—	25.00	—

KM# 1040 7.3000 g. Bi-Metallic Aluminum-Bronze center in Nickel ring 28 mm. **Subject:** Quebec

400th Anniversary **Rev:** Lis and small sailing ship **Edge:** Segmented reeding

Date	Mintage	MS-63	Proof
2008	—	7.50	—

KM# 1020 7.3000 g. Bi-Metallic Aluminum-Bronze center in Nickel ring 28 mm. **Rev:** Two lynx cubs **Rev. Designer:** Christie Paquet **Edge:** Segmented reeding

Date	Mintage	MS-63	Proof
2010 Specimen	15,000	—	40.00

KM# 1088 7.3000 g. Bi-Metallic Aluminum-Bronze center in Nickel ring 28 mm. **Rev:** Elk Calf **Rev. Designer:** Christine Paquet **Edge:** Segmented reeding

Date	Mintage	MS-63	Proof
2011	—	7.50	—

KM# 1167 7.3000 g. Bi-Metallic Aluminum-Bronze center in Nickel ring 28 mm. **Subject:** Canada Parks **Obv:** Bust right **Rev:** Stylized trees

Date	Mintage	MS-63	Proof
2011	—	7.50	—

KM# 1257 6.9200 g. Bi-Metallic Brass Plated Aluminum-Bronze center in Nickel Plated Steel ring 28 mm. **Rev:** Polar bear with security device above **Edge:** Lettered and segmented reeding

Date	Mintage	MS-63	Proof
2012	—	7.50	—
2012 Proof	—	—	10.00
2013	—	7.50	—
2013 Proof	—	—	10.00

KM# 1258 6.9200 g. Bi-Metallic Brass Plated Aluminum-Bronze center in Nickel Plated Steel ring 28 mm. **Subject:** H.M.S. Shannon **Edge:** Lettered and segmented reeding

Date	Mintage	MS-63	Proof
2012	—	10.00	—

KM# 1263 7.3000 g. Bi-Metallic Aluminum-Bronze center in Nickel ring 28 mm. **Rev:** Wolf cubs

Date	Mintage	MS-63	Proof
2012	—	10.00	—

3 DOLLARS

KM# 657 11.7200 g. 0.9250 Silver gilt 0.3485 oz. ASW 27x27 mm. **Rev:** Beaver within wreath **Shape:** Square

Date	Mintage	MS-63	Proof
2006 Proof	19,963	—	225

KM# 1051 11.6000 g. 0.9250 Silver gilt 0.3450 oz. ASW 27x27 mm. **Subject:** Wildlife conservation **Rev:** Stylized polar bear and northern lights **Shape:** square

Date	Mintage	MS-63	Proof
2010 Specimen	15,000	55.00	—

KM# 978 7.9600 g. Silver Partially Gilt 27 mm. **Rev:** Return of the Tyee (giant salmon)

Date	Mintage	MS-63	Proof
2010 Proof	15,000	—	50.00

KM# 1011 11.6000 g. 0.9250 Silver gilt 0.3450 oz. ASW 27x27 mm. **Rev:** Barn Owl **Rev. Designer:** Jason Bouwman **Shape:** Square

Date	Mintage	MS-63	Proof
2010 Proof	15,000	—	65.00

KM# 1089 11.6000 g. 0.9250 Silver gilt 0.3450 oz. ASW 27x27 mm. **Rev:** Orca Whale **Rev. Designer:** Jason Bouwman **Shape:** Square

Date	Mintage	MS-63	Proof
2011 Proof	15,000	—	65.00

KM# 1090 7.9600 g. 0.9990 Silver with red and yellow partial gilding 0.2557 oz. ASW 27 mm. **Obv:** Bust right **Rev:** Eskimo mother kneeling, child on back, partially gilt **Rev. Designer:** Andrew Oappik

Date	Mintage	MS-63	Proof
2011 Proof	10,000	—	65.00

KM# 1117 7.9600 g. 0.9999 Silver 0.2559 oz. ASW 27 mm. **Subject:** January birthstone, Garnet **Obv:** Bust left **Rev:** Birthstone at cener of artistic sunburst **Edge:** Reeded

Date	Mintage	MS-63	Proof
2011 Proof	—	—	45.00

KM# 1118 7.9600 g. 0.9999 Silver 0.2559 oz. ASW 27 mm. **Subject:** February birthstone, Amythest **Obv:** Bust right **Rev:** Birthstone at cener of artistic sunburst **Edge:** Reeded

Date	Mintage	MS-63	Proof
2011 Proof	—	—	45.00

KM# 1119 7.9600 g. 0.9999 Silver 0.2559 oz. ASW 27 mm. **Subject:** March birthstone, Aquamarine **Obv:** Bust right **Rev:** Birthstone at cener of artistic sunburst **Edge:** Reeded

Date	Mintage	MS-63	Proof
2011 Proof	—	—	45.00

KM# 1120 7.9600 g. 0.9999 Silver 0.2559 oz. ASW 27 mm. **Subject:** April birthstone, diamond **Obv:** Bust right **Rev:** Birthstone at cener of artistic sunburst **Edge:** Reeded

Date	Mintage	MS-63	Proof
2011 Proof	—	—	45.00

KM# 1121 7.9600 g. 0.9999 Silver 0.2559 oz. ASW 27 mm. **Subject:** May birthstone **Obv:** Bust right **Rev:** Birthstone at cener of artistic sunburst **Edge:** Reeded

Date	Mintage	MS-63	Proof
2011 Proof	—	—	45.00

KM# 1122 7.9600 g. 0.9999 Silver 0.2559 oz. ASW 27 mm. **Subject:** June birthstone, Alexandrite **Obv:** Bust right **Rev:** Birthstone at cener of artistic sunburst

Date	Mintage	MS-63	Proof
2011 Proof	—	—	45.00

KM# 1123 7.9600 g. 0.9999 Silver 0.2559 oz. ASW 27 mm. **Subject:** July birthstone, Ruby **Obv:** Bust right **Rev:** Birthstone at cener of artistic sunburst

Date	Mintage	MS-63	Proof
2011 Proof	—	—	45.00

KM# 1124 7.9600 g. 0.9999 Silver 0.2559 oz. ASW 27 mm. **Subject:** August birthstone, Priedot **Obv:** Bust right **Rev:** Birthstone at cener of artistic sunburst

Date	Mintage	MS-63	Proof
2011 Proof	—	—	45.00

KM# 1126 7.9600 g. 0.9999 Silver 0.2559 oz. ASW 27 mm. **Subject:** October birthstone **Obv:** Bust right **Rev:** Birthstone at cener of artistic sunburst

Date	Mintage	MS-63	Proof
2011 Proof	—	—	45.00

KM# 1127 7.9600 g. 0.9999 Silver 0.2559 oz. ASW 27 mm. **Subject:** November birthstone **Obv:** Bust right **Rev:** Birthstone at cener of artistic sunburst

Date	Mintage	MS-63	Proof
2011 Proof	—	—	45.00

KM# 1128 7.9600 g. 0.9999 Silver 0.2559 oz. ASW 27 mm. **Subject:** December birhtstone **Obv:** Bust right **Rev:** Birthstone at cener of artistic sunburst

Date	Mintage	MS-63	Proof
2011 Proof	—	—	45.00

KM# 1151 11.8000 g. 0.9250 Silver gold plated 0.3509 oz. ASW 27x27 mm. **Obv:** Bust right **Rev:** Black footed ferret

Date	Mintage	MS-63	Proof
2011 Proof	Est. 15,000	—	65.00

3 DOLLARS

KM#1300 7.9600 g. 0.9999 Silver 0.2559 oz. ASW
27 mm.   **Subject:** January birthstone, Garnet
Obv: Bust right **Obv. Designer:** Susana Blunt **Rev:**
Birthstone at center of wreath **Rev. Designer:**
Maurice Gervias

Date	Mintage	MS-63	Proof
2013 Proof	—	—	50.00

KM#1301 7.9600 g. 0.9990 Silver 0.2557 oz. ASW
27 mm.   **Subject:** February birthstone, Amythest
Obv: Bust right **Obv. Designer:** Susana Blunt **Rev:**
Birthstone at center of wreath **Rev. Designer:**
Maurice Gervais

Date	Mintage	MS-63	Proof
2013 Proof	—	—	65.00

KM#1302 7.9600 g. 0.9990 Silver 0.2557 oz. ASW
27 mm.   **Subject:** March birthstone, Aquamarine
Obv: Bust right **Obv. Designer:** Susana Blunt **Rev:**
Birthstone at center of wreath **Rev. Designer:**
Maurice Gervais

Date	Mintage	MS-63	Proof
2013 Proof	—	—	50.00

KM#1303 7.9600 g. 0.9990 Silver 0.2557 oz. ASW
27 mm.   **Subject:** April birthstone, Diamond **Obv:**
Bust right **Obv. Designer:** Susana Blunt **Rev:**
Birthstone at center of wreath **Rev. Designer:**
Maurice Gervais

Date	Mintage	MS-63	Proof
2013 Proof	—	—	50.00

KM#1304 7.9600 g. 0.9990 Silver 0.2557 oz. ASW
27 mm.   **Subject:** May birthstone **Obv:** Bust right
Obv. Designer: Susana Blunt **Rev:** Birthstone at
center of wreath **Rev. Designer:** Maurice Gervais

Date	Mintage	MS-63	Proof
2013 Proof	—	—	50.00

KM#1305 7.9600 g. 0.9990 Silver 0.2557 oz. ASW
27 mm.   **Subject:** June birthstone, Alexandrite
Obv: Bust right **Obv. Designer:** Susana Blunt **Rev:**
Birthstone at center of wreath **Rev. Designer:**
Maurice Gervais

Date	Mintage	MS-63	Proof
2013 Proof	—	—	50.00

KM#1306 7.9600 g. 0.9990 Silver 0.2557 oz. ASW
27 mm.   **Subject:** July birthstone - Ruby **Obv:**
Bust right **Obv. Designer:** Susana Blunt **Rev:**
Birthstone at center of wreath **Rev. Designer:**
Maurice Gervais

Date	Mintage	MS-63	Proof
2013 Proof	—	—	50.00

KM#1307 7.9600 g. 0.9990 Silver 0.2557 oz. ASW
27 mm.   **Subject:** August birthstone - Priedot
Obv: Bust right **Obv. Designer:** Susana Blunt **Rev:**
Birthstone at center of wreath **Rev. Designer:**
Maurice Gervais

Date	Mintage	MS-63	Proof
2013 Proof	—	—	50.00

KM#1308 7.9600 g. 0.9990 Silver 0.2557 oz. ASW
27 mm.   **Subject:** September birthstone **Obv:**
Bust right **Obv. Designer:** Susana Blunt **Rev:**
Birthstone at center of wreath **Rev. Designer:**
Maruice Gervais

Date	Mintage	MS-63	Proof
2013 Proof	—	—	50.00

KM#1309 7.9600 g. 0.9990 Silver 0.2557 oz. ASW
27 mm.   **Subject:** October birthstone **Obv:** Bust
right **Obv. Designer:** Susana Blunt **Rev:** Birthstone
at center of wreath **Rev. Designer:** Maurice Gervais

Date	Mintage	MS-63	Proof
2013 Proof	—	—	50.00

KM#1310 7.9600 g. 0.9990 Silver 0.2557 oz. ASW
27 mm.   **Subject:** November birthstone **Obv:** Bust
right **Obv. Designer:** Susana Blunt **Rev:** Birthstone
at center of wreath **Rev. Designer:** Maurice Gervais

Date	Mintage	MS-63	Proof
2013 Proof	—	—	50.00

KM#1311 7.9600 g. 0.9990 Silver 0.2557 oz. ASW
27 mm.   **Subject:** December birthstone **Obv:** Bust
right **Obv. Designer:** Susana Blunt **Rev:** Birthstone
at center of wreath **Rev. Designer:** Maurice Gervais

Date	Mintage	MS-63	Proof
2013 Proof	—	—	50.00

4 DOLLARS

KM#728 15.8700 g. 0.9250 Silver 0.4719 oz. ASW
34 mm.   **Subject:** Dinosaur fossil **Obv:** Bust right
Rev: Parasaurolophus, selective enameling

Date	Mintage	MS-63	Proof
2007 Proof	14,946	—	125

KM#797 15.8700 g. 0.9990 Silver 0.5097 oz. ASW
34 mm.   **Subject:** Dinosaur fossil **Obv:** Bust right
Rev: Triceratops, enameled **Rev. Designer:** Kerri
Burnett

Date	Mintage	MS-63	Proof
2008 Proof	13,046	—	75.00

KM#890 15.8700 g. 0.9990 Silver 0.5097 oz. ASW
34 mm.   **Subject:** Tyrannosaurus Rex **Obv:** Bust
right **Obv. Legend:** Elizabeth II DG Regina **Obv.
Designer:** Susanna Blunt **Rev:** T-Rex skeleton in
selective aging **Rev. Legend:** Canada 4 Dollars
Rev. Designer: Kerri Burnette

Date	Mintage	MS-63	Proof
2009 Proof	13,572	—	60.00

KM# 942 15.8700 g. Silver 34 mm. **Rev:** Kids hanging stocking on fireplace, Christmas tree on right

Date	Mintage	MS-63	Proof
2009 Proof	6,011	—	45.00

KM# 1014 15.8700 g. 0.9990 Silver selectively plated 0.5097 oz. ASW 34 mm. **Rev:** Euoplocephalus **Rev. Designer:** Kerri Burnett

Date	Mintage	MS-63	Proof
2010 Proof	Est. 13,000	—	60.00

KM# 1022 Silver selective plating **Rev:** Dromaeosaurus

Date	Mintage	MS-63	Proof
2010 Proof	8,982	—	85.00

KM# 1129 15.8700 g. 0.9999 Silver 0.5102 oz. ASW 34 mm. **Obv:** Bust right **Rev:** Baby's footprint **Edge:** Reeded

Date	Mintage	MS-63	Proof
2011 Proof	Est. 10,000	—	60.00

SOVEREIGN

KM# 14 7.9881 g. 0.9170 Gold 0.2355 oz. AGW **Rev:** St. George slaying dragon, mint mark below horse's rear hooves

Date	Mintage	F-12	VF-20	XF-40	AU-50	MS-60	MS-63
1908C	636	1,800	2,500	3,500	4,000	4,500	5,500
1909C	16,273	—	—	BV	450	650	2,900
1910C	28,012	—	—	BV	450	650	2,900

KM# 20 7.9881 g. 0.9170 Gold 0.2355 oz. AGW **Rev:** St. George slaying dragon, mint mark below horse's rear hooves

Date	Mintage	F-12	VF-20	XF-40	AU-50	MS-60	MS-63
1911C	256,946	—	—	—	BV	450	650
1911C Specimen	—	—	—	—	—	—	—
1913C	3,715	650	800	1,050	1,300	1,800	3,500
1914C	14,871	—	BV	450	500	650	1,150
1916C About 20 known	—	16,000	17,000	18,000	20,000	24,000	40,000
Note: Stacks' A.G. Carter Jr. Sale 12-89 Gem BU realized $82,500							
1917C	58,845	—	—	—	BV	450	700

Date	Mintage	F-12	VF-20	XF-40	AU-50	MS-60	MS-63
1918C	106,514	—	—	—	BV	450	1,000
1919C	135,889	—	—	—	BV	450	800

5 DOLLARS

KM# 26 8.3592 g. 0.9000 Gold 0.2419 oz. AGW **Obv:** Crowned bust left **Obv. Designer:** E. B. MacKennal
Rev: Arms within wreath, date and denomination below **Rev. Designer:** W. H. J. Blakemore

Date	Mintage	F-12	VF-20	XF-40	AU-50	MS-60	MS-63
1912	165,680	—	—	—	BV	450	650
1913	98,832	—	—	—	BV	450	800
1914	31,122	—	BV	450	600	900	3,000

Date	Mintage	MS-63	Proof
1973	—	24.00	—
1973 Proof	165,203	—	24.00

KM# 89 24.3000 g. 0.9250 Silver 0.7226 oz. ASW
38 mm.   **Subject:** 1976 Montreal Olympics **Obv:**
Young bust right, small maple leaf below, date at
right **Rev:** Olympic rings, denomination below **Rev.
Designer:** Anthony Mann **Note:** Series II.

Date	Mintage	MS-63	Proof
1974	—	24.00	—
1974 Proof	97,431	—	24.00

KM# 84 24.3000 g. 0.9250 Silver 0.7226 oz. ASW
38 mm.   **Subject:** 1976 Montreal Olympics **Obv:**
Young bust right, small maple below, date at right
Rev: Sailboat "Kingston", date at left, denomination
below **Rev. Designer:** Georges Huel **Note:** Series I.

Date	Mintage	MS-63	Proof
1973	—	24.00	—
1973 Proof	165,203	—	24.00

KM# 90 24.3000 g. 0.9250 Silver 0.7226 oz. ASW
38 mm.   **Subject:** 1976 Montreal Olympics **Obv:**
Young bust right, small maple leaf below, date at
right **Rev:** Athlete with torch, denomination below
Rev. Designer: Anthony Mann **Note:** Series II.

Date	Mintage	MS-63	Proof
1974	—	24.00	—
1974 Proof	97,431	—	24.00

KM# 85 24.3000 g. 0.9250 Silver 0.7226 oz. ASW
38 mm.   **Subject:** 1976 Montreal Olympics **Obv:**
Young bust right, small maple leaf below, date at
right **Rev:** North American map, denominaton below
Rev. Designer: Georges Huel **Note:** Series I.

SOVEREIGN

KM# 91 24.3000 g. 0.9250 Silver 0.7226 oz. ASW 38 mm. **Subject:** 1976 Montreal Olympics **Obv:** Young bust right, small maple leaf below, date at right **Rev:** Rower, denomination below **Rev. Designer:** Ken Danby **Note:** Series III.

Date	Mintage	MS-63	Proof
1974	—	24.00	—
1974 Proof	104,684	—	24.00

KM# 92 24.3000 g. 0.9250 Silver 0.7226 oz. ASW 38 mm. **Subject:** 1976 Montreal Olympics **Obv:** Young bust right, small maple leaf below, date at right **Rev:** Canoeing, denomination below **Rev. Designer:** Ken Danby **Note:** Series III.

Date	Mintage	MS-63	Proof
1974	—	24.00	—
1974 Proof	104,684	—	24.00

KM# 98 24.3000 g. 0.9250 Silver 0.7226 oz. ASW 38 mm. **Subject:** 1976 Montreal Olympics **Obv:** Young bust right, small maple leaf below, date at right **Rev:** Marathon, denomination below **Rev. Designer:** Leo Yerxa **Note:** Series IV.

Date	Mintage	MS-63	Proof
1975	—	24.00	—
1975 Proof	89,155	—	24.00

KM# 99 24.3000 g. 0.9250 Silver 0.7226 oz. ASW 38 mm. **Subject:** Montreal 1976 - 21st Summer Olympic Games **Obv:** Young bust right, small maple leaf below, date at right **Rev:** Women's javelin event,

denomination below **Rev. Designer:** Leo Yerxa **Note:** Series IV.

Date	Mintage	MS-63	Proof
1975	—	24.00	—
1975 Proof	89,155	—	24.00

KM# 100 24.3000 g. 0.9250 Silver 0.7226 oz. ASW 38 mm. **Subject:** 1976 Montreal Olympics **Obv:** Young bust right, small maple leaf below, date at right **Rev:** Swimmer, denomination below **Rev. Designer:** Lynda Cooper **Note:** Series V.

Date	Mintage	MS-63	Proof
1975	—	24.00	—
1975 Proof	89,155	—	24.00

KM# 101 24.3000 g. 0.9250 Silver 0.7226 oz. ASW 38 mm. **Subject:** Montreal 1976 - 21st Summer Olympic Games **Obv:** Young bust right, small maple leaf below, date at right **Rev:** Platform Diver, denomination below **Rev. Designer:** Lynda Cooper **Note:** Series V.

Date	Mintage	MS-63	Proof
1975	—	24.00	—
1975 Proof	89,155	—	24.00

KM# 107 24.3000 g. 0.9250 Silver 0.7226 oz. ASW 38 mm. **Subject:** 1976 Montreal Olympics **Obv:** Young bust right, small maple leaf below, date at right **Rev:** Fencing, denomination below **Rev. Designer:** Shigeo Fukada **Note:** Series VI.

Date	Mintage	MS-63	Proof
1976	—	24.00	—
1976 Proof	82,302	—	24.00

KM# 108 24.3000 g. 0.9250 Silver 0.7226 oz. ASW 38 mm. **Subject:** 1976 Montreal Olympics **Obv:** Young bust right, small maple leaf below, date at right **Obv. Legend:** Boxing **Rev:** Boxers, denomination below **Rev. Designer:** Shigeo Fukada **Note:** Series VI.

Date	Mintage	MS-63	Proof
1976	—	24.00	—
1976 Proof	82,302	—	24.00

KM# 109 24.3000 g. 0.9250 Silver 0.7226 oz. ASW
38 mm.   **Subject:** 1976 Montreal Olympics **Obv:**
Young bust right, small maple leaf below, date at right
Rev: Olympic village, denomination below **Rev.**
Designer: Elliot John Morrison **Note:** Series VII.

Date	Mintage	MS-63	Proof
1976	—	24.00	—
1976 Proof	76,908	—	24.00

KM#110 24.3000 g. 0.9250 Silver 0.7226 oz. ASW
38 mm.   **Subject:** 1976 Montreal Olympics **Obv:**
Young bust right, maple leaf below, date at right
Rev: Olympic flame, denomination below **Rev.**
Designer: Elliot John Morrison **Note:** Series VII.

Date	Mintage	MS-63	Proof
1976	—	24.00	—
1976 Proof	79,102	—	24.00

KM# 316 31.3900 g. 0.9999 Silver 1.0091 oz.
ASW   **Subject:** Dr. Norman Bethune **Obv:** Young
bust right **Rev:** Bethune and party, date at upper
right **Rev. Designer:** Harvey Chan

Date	Mintage	MS-63	Proof
1998 Proof	61,000	—	40.00

KM# 398 Copper-Nickel-Zinc   **Obv:** Young bust
right **Rev:** Viking ship under sail **Rev. Designer:**
Donald Curley **Note:** Sold in sets with Norway 20
kroner, KM#465.

Date	Mintage	MS-63	Proof
1999 Proof	28,450	—	18.50

KM#435 16.8600 g. 0.9250 Silver 0.5014 oz. ASW
28.4 mm.   **Subject:** Guglielmo Marconi **Obv:**
Crowned head right **Rev:** Gold-plated cameo
portrait of Marconi **Rev. Designer:** Cosme Saffioti
Edge: Reeded **Note:** Only issued in two coin set
with British 2 pounds KM#1014a.

Date	Mintage	MS-63	Proof
2001 Proof	15,011	—	30.00

KM# 519 8.3600 g. 0.9000 Gold 0.2419 oz. AGW
21.6 mm.   **Obv:** Crowned head right **Rev:** National
arms **Edge:** Reeded

Date	Mintage	MS-63	Proof
1912-2002 Proof	2,002	—	450

KM# 603 31.1050 g. 0.9999 Silver 0.9999 oz.
ASW   **Obv:** Head right **Rev:** Loon splashing in the
water, hologram

Date	Mintage	MS-63	Proof
2002 Satin Proof	30,000	—	45.00

KM#518 31.1200 g. 0.9999 Silver 1.0004 oz. ASW
38 mm.   **Subject:** F.I.F.A. World Cup Soccer ,
Germany 2006 **Obv:** Crowned head right,
denomination **Rev:** Goalie on knees **Edge:** Reeded

Date	Mintage	MS-63	Proof
2003 Proof	21,542	—	40.00

KM#514 31.1200 g. 0.9999 Silver 1.0004 oz. ASW
38 mm.   **Obv:** Crowned head right **Rev:** Moose
Edge: Reeded

Date	Mintage	MS-63	Proof
2004 Proof	12,822	—	175

KM# 527 31.1200 g. 0.9999 Silver 1.0004 oz.
ASW **Subject:** Golf, Championship of Canada,
Centennial **Obv:** Head right

Date	Mintage	MS-63	Proof
2004 Proof	18,750	—	30.00

KM# 554 31.1200 g. 0.9999 Silver 1.0004 oz.
ASW **Subject:** Alberta **Obv. Designer:** Head
right **Rev. Designer:** Michelle Grant

Date	Mintage	MS-63	Proof
2005 Proof	20,000	—	35.00

KM# 555 31.1200 g. 0.9999 Silver 1.0004 oz.
ASW **Subject:** Saskatchewan **Obv:** Head right
Obv. Designer: Susanna Blunt **Rev. Designer:**
Paulett Sapergia

Date	Mintage	MS-63	Proof
2005 Proof	20,000	—	35.00

KM# 556.1 31.1200 g. 0.9990 Silver 0.9995 oz.
ASW 38.02 mm. **Subject:** 60th Anniversay
Victory WWII - Veterans **Obv:** Bust right **Rev:** Large
V and heads of sailor, soldier and aviator on large
maple leaf **Edge:** Reeded

Date	Mintage	MS-63	Proof
2005	25,000	32.00	—

KM# 556.2 31.1200 g. 0.9999 Silver 1.0004 oz.
ASW 38.02 mm. **Subject:** 60th Anniversary
Victory WW II - Veterans **Obv:** Bust right **Rev:** Large
V and heads of sailor, soldier and aviator on maple
leaf with small maple leaf added at left and right
Edge: Reeded

Date	Mintage	MS-63	Proof
2005	10,000	125	—

KM# 557 31.1200 g. 0.9999 Silver 1.0004 oz. ASW
36 mm. **Subject:** Walrus and calf **Obv:** Head right
Obv. Designer: Susanna Blunt **Rev:** Two walrusus
and calf **Rev. Designer:** Pierre Leduc

Date	Mintage	MS-63	Proof
2005 Proof	5,519	—	45.00

KM# 558 31.1200 g. 0.9999 Silver 1.0004 oz. ASW
36 mm. **Subject:** White tailed deer **Obv:** Head
right **Obv. Designer:** Susanna Blunt **Rev:** Two deer
standing **Rev. Designer:** Xerxes Irani

Date	Mintage	MS-63	Proof
2005 Proof	6,439	—	45.00

KM# 585 31.1200 g. 0.9999 Silver 1.0004 oz. ASW
36 mm. **Obv:** Head right **Obv. Designer:**
Susanna Blunt **Rev:** Peregrine Falcon feeding
young ones **Rev. Designer:** Dwayne Harty

Date	Mintage	MS-63	Proof
2006 Proof	7,226	—	50.00

KM# 586 31.1200 g. 0.9999 Silver 1.0004 oz. ASW
36 mm. **Subject:** Sable Island horses **Obv:** Head
right **Obv. Designer:** Susanna Blunt **Rev:** Horse
and foal standing **Rev. Designer:** Christie Paquet

Date	Mintage	MS-63	Proof
2006 Proof	10,108	—	50.00

5 DOLLARS

5 DOLLARS

KM# 658 31.1200 g. 0.9999 Silver 1.0004 oz. ASW 36.07 mm.   **Subject:** Breast Cancer Awareness **Rev:** Colorized pink ribbon

Date	Mintage	MS-63	Proof
2006 Proof	11,048	—	50.00

KM# 659 31.1200 g. 0.9999 Silver 1.0004 oz. ASW   **Subject:** C.A.F. Snowbirds Acrobatic Jet Flying Team **Rev:** Image of fighter jets and piolt

Date	Mintage	MS-63	Proof
2006 Proof	10,034	—	50.00

KM# 1036 31.1200 g. 0.9990 Silver 0.9995 oz. ASW   **Subject:** 80th Anniversary **Rev:** Two deer standing, one eating branch

Date	Mintage	MS-63	Proof
2009 Proof	27,872	—	70.00

KM# 1130 8.5000 g. Bi-Metallic Niobium center in .925 Silver ring 28 mm.   **Subject:** Summer - Buck Moon **Obv:** Bust right **Rev:** Buck against summer moon

Date	Mintage	MS-63	Proof
2011 Proof	7,500	—	125

KM# 1131 8.5000 g. Bi-Metallic Niobium center in .925 Silver ring 28 mm.   **Subject:** Fall Moon **Obv:** Bust right **Rev:** Native American hunter seated tracking prey before Harvest Moon

Date	Mintage	MS-63	Proof
2011 Proof	7,500	—	125

KM# 1132 8.5000 g. Bi-Metallic Niobium center in .925 Silver ring 28 mm.   **Subject:** Winter Moon **Obv:** Bust right **Rev:** Wolf howling before Winter Moon

Date	Mintage	MS-63	Proof
2011 Proof	7,500	—	125

KM# 1133 8.5000 g. Bi-Metallic Niobium center in .925 Silver ring 28 mm.   **Subject:** Spring Moon **Obv:** Bust right **Rev:** Phlox blossoming agains a Spring Moon

Date	Mintage	MS-63	Proof
2011 Proof	7,500	—	125

KM# 1149 3.1300 g. 0.9999 Gold 0.1006 oz. AGW 16 mm.   **Subject:** Norman Bethune **Obv:** Bust right **Rev:** Half-length figure at right, looking left

Date	Mintage	MS-63	Proof
2011 Proof	Est. 5,000	—	300

KM# 1236 8.3600 g. 0.9000 Gold 0.2419 oz. AGW 21.6 mm.   **Obv:** Bust right **Rev:** Crowned monogram in wreath

Date	Mintage	MS-63	Proof
1952-2012 Proof	—	—	500

KM# 1194 3.1300 g. 0.9990 Gold 0.1005 oz. AGW 16 mm.   **Obv:** Bust right **Rev:** Royal Cypher, wreath below

Date	Mintage	MS-63	Proof
2012 Proof	—	—	200

KM# 1220 3.1300 g. 0.9999 Gold 0.1006 oz. AGW
16 mm. **Subject:** Year of the Dragon **Obv:** Bust
right **Rev:** Dragon forpart right

Date	Mintage	MS-63	Proof
2012 Specimen	Est. 38,888	—	225

KM# 1248 31.1200 g. 0.9990 Silver 0.9995 oz.
ASW 36 mm. **Subject:** Rich Hansen **Rev:**
Wheelchair bound athlethe

Date	Mintage	MS-63	Proof
2012	—	—	75.00

KM# 1261 8.5000 g. Bi-Metallic Niobium center in
.925 Silver ring. 28 mm. **Rev:** Flowers and moon,
field in color

Date	Mintage	MS-63	Proof
2012	—	—	125

KM# 1281 3.1300 g. 0.9990 Gold 0.1005 oz. AGW
16 mm. **Subject:** Year of the Dragon

Date	Mintage	MS-63	Proof
2012 Proof	—	—	200

KM# 1298 3.1300 g. 0.9990 Gold 0.1005 oz.
AGW **Subject:** Year of the Snake

Date	Mintage	MS-63	Proof
2013 Proof	—	—	225

KM# 515 28.8000 g. 0.9250 Silver 0.8565 oz. ASW
39 mm. **Obv:** Head right **Obv. Designer:**
Susanna Blunt **Rev:** Grizzly bear walking left **Edge:**
Reeded

Date	Mintage	MS-63	Proof
2004 Proof	12,942	—	85.00

KM# 597 32.1500 g. 0.9999 Silver partially gilt
1.0335 oz. ASW **Subject:** Canadian Pacific
Railway, 120th Anniversary **Obv:** Head right **Obv.
Designer:** Susanna Blunt **Rev:** Railway bridge,
center is gilt

Date	Mintage	MS-63	Proof
2005 Proof	9,892	—	65.00

KM# 598 32.1500 g. 0.9999 Silver partially gilt
1.0335 oz. ASW **Subject:** Canadian Pacific
Railway, 120th Anniversary **Obv:** Head right **Rev:**
Railway memorial to the Chinese workers, center gilt

Date	Mintage	MS-63	Proof
2005 Proof	9,892	—	65.00

KM# 730 25.1800 g. 0.9999 Silver 0.8094 oz. ASW
36.07 mm. **Obv:** Queens's head at top in circle,
three Chinese characters **Rev:** Dragon and other
creatures

Date	Mintage	MS-63	Proof
2007 Proof	19,996	—	50.00

KM# 731 25.1800 g. 0.9990 Silver 0.8087 oz. ASW
36.1 mm.   **Rev:** Maple leaf, long life hologram

Date	Mintage	MS-63	Proof
2007	15,000	—	55.00

KM# 943 25.1800 g. 0.9250 Silver 0.7488 oz. ASW
36.1 mm.   **Rev:** Hologram maple of wisdom at top
left, crystal in center, dragons around

Date	Mintage	MS-63	Proof
2009 Proof	7,273	—	90.00

KM# 1012 25.3000 g. 0.9250 Silver 0.7524 oz.
ASW 36.07 mm.   **Rev:** Horses around central
maple leaf hologram **Rev. Designer:** Simon Ng

Date	Mintage	MS-63	Proof
2010 Proof	8,888	—	100

10 DOLLARS

KM# 27 16.7185 g. 0.9000 Gold 0.4837 oz. AGW
26.92 mm.   **Obv:** Crowned bust left **Obv.**

Designer: E. B. MacKennal **Rev:** Arms within
wreath, date and denomination below **Rev.**
Designer: W. H. J. Blakemore

Date	Mintage	AU-50	MS-60	MS-63
1912	74,759	BV	900	2,700
1913	149,232	BV	900	3,000
1914	140,068	BV	1,150	3,000

KM# 86.1 48.6000 g. 0.9250 Silver 1.4453 oz.
ASW 45 mm.   **Subject:** 1976 Montreal Olympics
Obv: Young bust right, maple leaf below, date at
right **Rev:** World map, denomination below **Rev.**
Designer: Georges Huel **Note:** Series I.

Date	Mintage	MS-63	Proof
1973	103,426	47.50	—
1973 Proof	165,203	—	47.50

KM# 87 48.6000 g. 0.9250 Silver 1.4453 oz. ASW
45 mm.   **Subject:** 1976 Montreal Olympics **Obv:**
Young bust right, small maple leaf below, date at
right **Rev:** Montreal skyline, denomination below
Rev. Designer: Georges Huel **Note:** Series I.

Date	Mintage	MS-63	Proof
1973	—	47.50	—
1973 Proof	165,203	—	47.50

KM# 86.2 48.6000 g. 0.9250 Silver 1.4453 oz. ASW 45 mm. **Subject:** 1976 Montreal Olympics **Obv:** Young bust right, small maple leaf below, date at right **Rev:** World map **Rev. Designer:** Georges Huel **Note:** Series I.

Date	Mintage	MS-63	Proof
1974	320	325	—

Note: Error: mule

KM# 93 48.6000 g. 0.9250 Silver 1.4453 oz. ASW 45 mm. **Subject:** 1976 Montreal Olympics **Obv:** Young bust right, small maple leaf below, date at right **Rev:** Head of Zeus, denomination below **Rev. Designer:** Anthony Mann **Note:** Series II.

Date	Mintage	MS-63	Proof
1974	—	47.50	—
1974 Proof	104,684	—	47.50

KM# 94 48.6000 g. 0.9250 Silver 1.4453 oz. ASW 45 mm. **Subject:** 1976 Montreal Olympics **Obv:** Young bust right, small maple leaf below, date at right **Rev:** Temple of Zeus, denomination below **Rev. Designer:** Anthony Mann **Note:** Series II.

Date	Mintage	MS-63	Proof
1974	—	47.50	—
1974 Proof	104,684	—	47.50

KM# 95 48.6000 g. 0.9250 Silver 1.4453 oz. ASW 45 mm. **Subject:** 1976 Montreal Olympics **Obv:** Young bust right, small maple leaf below, date at right **Rev:** Cycling, denomination below **Rev. Designer:** Ken Danby **Note:** Series III.

Date	Mintage	MS-63	Proof
1974	—	47.50	—
1974 Proof	97,431	—	47.50

KM# 96 48.6000 g. 0.9250 Silver 1.4453 oz. ASW 45 mm. **Subject:** 1976 Montreal Olympics **Obv:** Young bust right, small maple leaf below, date at right **Rev:** Lacrosse, denomination below **Rev. Designer:** Ken Danby **Note:** Series III.

Date	Mintage	MS-63	Proof
1974	—	47.50	—
1974 Proof	97,431	—	47.50

KM# 102 48.6000 g. 0.9250 Silver 1.4453 oz. ASW 45 mm. **Subject:** 1976 Montreal Olympics **Obv:** Young bust right, small maple leaf below, date at right **Rev:** Men's hurdles, denomination below **Rev. Designer:** Leo Yerxa **Note:** Series IV.

Date	Mintage	MS-63	Proof
1975	—	47.50	—
1975 Proof	82,302	—	47.50

KM# 103 48.6000 g. 0.9250 Silver 1.4453 oz. ASW 45 mm. **Subject:** Montreal 1976 - 21st Summer Olympic Games **Obv:** Young bust right, small maple leaf below, date at right **Rev:** Women's shot put,

denomination below **Rev. Designer:** Leo Yerxa
Note: Series IV.

Date	Mintage	MS-63	Proof
1975	—	47.50	—
1975 Proof	82,302	—	47.50

KM# 104 48.6000 g. 0.9250 Silver 1.4453 oz. ASW
45 mm.   **Subject:** 1976 Montreal Olympics **Obv:**
Young bust right, small maple leaf below, date at
right **Rev:** Sailing, denomination below **Rev.
Designer:** Lynda Cooper **Note:** Series V.

Date	Mintage	MS-63	Proof
1975	—	47.50	—
1975 Proof	89,155	—	47.50

KM# 105 48.6000 g. 0.9250 Silver 1.4453 oz. ASW
45 mm.   **Subject:** 1976 Montreal Olympics **Obv:**
Young bust right, small maple leaf below, date at
right **Rev:** Canoeing, denomination below **Rev.
Designer:** Lynda Cooper **Note:** Series V.

Date	Mintage	MS-63	Proof
1975	—	47.50	—
1975 Proof	89,155	—	47.50

KM# 111 48.6000 g. 0.9250 Silver 1.4453 oz. ASW
45 mm.   **Subject:** 1976 Montreal Olympics **Obv:**
Young bust right, small maple leaf below, date at
right **Rev:** Football, denomination below **Rev.
Designer:** Shigeo Fukada **Note:** Series VI.

Date	Mintage	MS-63	Proof
1976	—	47.50	—
1976 Proof	76,908	—	47.50

KM# 112 48.6000 g. 0.9250 Silver 1.4453 oz. ASW
45 mm.   **Subject:** 1976 Montreal Olympics **Obv:**
Young bust right, small maple leaf below, date at
right **Rev:** Field hockey **Rev. Designer:** Shigeo
Fukada **Note:** Series VI.

Date	Mintage	MS-63	Proof
1976	—	47.50	—
1976 Proof	76,908	—	47.50

KM# 113 48.6000 g. 0.9250 Silver 1.4453 oz. ASW
45 mm.   **Subject:** 1976 Montreal Olympics **Obv:**
Young bust right, small maple leaf below, date at
right **Rev:** Olympic Stadium, denomination below
Rev. Designer: Elliot John Morrison **Note:** Series
VII.

Date	Mintage	MS-63	Proof
1976	—	47.50	—
1976 Proof	79,102	—	47.50

KM# 114 48.6000 g. 0.9250 Silver 1.4453 oz. ASW
45 mm.   **Subject:** 1976 Montreal Olympics **Obv:**
Young bust right, small maple leaf below, date at right
Rev: Olympic Velodrome, denomination below **Rev.
Designer:** Elliot John Morrison **Note:** Series VII.

Date	Mintage	MS-63	Proof
1976	—	47.50	—
1976 Proof	79,102	—	47.50

KM# 520 16.7200 g. 0.9000 Gold 0.4838 oz. AGW
26.92 mm. **Obv:** Crowned head right **Rev:**
National arms **Edge:** Reeded

Date	Mintage	MS-63	Proof
1912-2002 Proof	2,002	—	850

KM# 559 25.1750 g. 0.9999 Silver 0.8093 oz. ASW
36 mm. **Subject:** Pope John Paul II **Obv:** Head right

Date	Mintage	MS-63	Proof
2005 Proof	24,716	—	45.00

KM# 757 25.1750 g. 0.9999 Silver 0.8093 oz.
ASW **Subject:** Year of the Veteran **Rev:** Profile
left of young and old veteran

Date	Mintage	MS-63	Proof
2005 Proof	6,549	—	225

KM# 661 25.1750 g. 0.9999 Silver 0.8093 oz.
ASW **Subject:** National Historic Sites **Obv:** Head
right **Rev:** Fortress of Louisbourg

Date	Mintage	MS-63	Proof
2006 Proof	5,544	—	40.00

KM# 1010 15.8700 g. 0.9990 Silver 0.5097 oz.
ASW **Subject:** 75th Anniversary Canadian Bank
Notes **Rev:** Female seated

Date	Mintage	MS-63	Proof
2010 Proof	7,500	—	50.00

KM# 1096 27.7800 g. 0.9250 Silver 0.8261 oz.
ASW 40 mm. **Obv:** Bust right **Rev:** Blue whale
diving in sea

Date	Mintage	MS-63	Proof
2010 Proof	10,000	—	85.00

KM# 1199 15.8700 g. 0.9999 Silver 0.5102 oz.
ASW 34 mm. **Subject:** Winter Scene - Skating
Rev: Three kids skating on pond, colored holly at left

Date	Mintage	MS-63	Proof
2011 Proof	Est. 8,000	—	40.00

KM# 1198 15.8700 g. 0.9990 Silver 0.5097 oz.
ASW 34 mm. **Subject:** Highway of Heroes **Obv:**
Bust right **Obv. Designer:** Susanna Blunt **Rev:**
Citizens on Highway 401 overpass with signs and
flags, large maple leaf in background, Memorial

Cross medal at top left. **Rev. Designer:** Stan Witten and Major Carl Gauthier **Edge:** Reeded

Date	Mintage	MS-63	Proof
2011	25,000	—	70.00

KM# 1200 15.8700 g. 0.9999 Silver 0.5102 oz. ASW 34 mm. **Subject:** Winter scene - Two houses **Rev:** Two houses in snowy lane, colored holly flanking

Date	Mintage	MS-63	Proof
2011 Proof	Est. 8,000	—	40.00

KM# 1201 15.8700 g. 0.9999 Silver 0.5102 oz. ASW 34 mm. **Obv:** Bust right **Rev:** Wood Bison **Rev. Designer:** Corrine Hunt

Date	Mintage	MS-63	Proof
2011 Proof	Est. 10,000	—	50.00

KM# 1203 15.8700 g. 0.9999 Silver 0.5102 oz. ASW 34 mm. **Subject:** Boreal Forest **Rev:** Bird and tree **Rev. Designer:** Corrine Hunt

Date	Mintage	MS-63	Proof
2011 Proof	Est. 10,000	—	50.00

KM# 1205 15.8700 g. 0.9999 Silver 0.5102 oz. ASW 34 mm. **Obv:** Bust right **Rev:** Peregrine Falcon perched on branch **Rev. Designer:** Corrine Hunt

Date	Mintage	MS-63	Proof
2011 Proof	Est. 10,000	—	50.00

KM# 1207 15.8700 g. 0.9999 Silver 0.5102 oz. ASW 34 mm. **Obv:** Bust right **Rev:** Orca Whale **Rev. Designer:** Corrine Hunt

Date	Mintage	MS-63	Proof
2011 Proof	Est. 10,000	—	50.00

KM# 1221 15.8700 g. 0.9990 Silver 0.5097 oz. ASW 34 mm. **Subject:** Year of the Dragon **Obv:**

Bust right **Rev:** Dragon forepart right

Date	Mintage	MS-63	Proof
2012 Specimen	58,888	—	40.00

KM# 1235 25.1750 g. 0.9990 Silver 0.8086 oz. ASW 36 mm. **Obv:** Bust right **Rev:** Titanic sailing at right, map of Eastern Canada at left

Date	Mintage	MS-63	Proof
2012 Proof	—	—	100

KM# 1249 15.8700 g. 0.9990 Silver 0.5097 oz. ASW 34 mm. **Subject:** H.M.S. Shannon

Date	Mintage	MS-63	Proof
2012	—	—	65.00

KM# 1259 15.8700 g. 0.9990 Silver 0.5097 oz. ASW 34 mm. **Subject:** Praying Mantis

Date	Mintage	MS-63	Proof
2012 Proof	—	—	45.00

KM# 1282 7.7700 g. 0.9990 Gold 0.2496 oz. AGW 20 mm. **Subject:** Year of the Dragon

Date	Mintage	MS-63	Proof
2012 Proof	—	—	450

10 DOLLARS

KM# 1299 31.1050 g. Silver **Subject:** Year of the Snake

Date	Mintage	MS-63	Proof
2013 Proof	—	—	50.00

15 DOLLARS

KM# 215 33.6300 g. 0.9250 Silver 1.0000 oz. ASW 39 mm. **Subject:** 1992 Olympics **Obv:** Crowned head right, date at left, denomination below **Rev:** Coaching track **Rev. Designer:** Stewart Sherwood

Date	Mintage	MS-63	Proof
1992 Proof	275,000	—	35.00

KM# 216 33.6300 g. 0.9250 Silver 1.0000 oz. ASW **Subject:** 1992 Olympics **Obv:** Crowned head right, date at left, denomination below **Rev:** High jump, rings, speed skating **Rev. Designer:** David Craig

Date	Mintage	MS-63	Proof
1992 Proof	275,000	—	35.00

KM# 304 33.6300 g. 0.9250 Silver with gold insert 1.0000 oz. ASW 40 mm. **Subject:** Year of the

Tiger **Obv:** Crowned head right **Rev:** Tiger within octagon at center, animal figures surround **Rev. Designer:** Harvey Chan

Date	Mintage	MS-63	Proof
1998 Proof	68,888	—	375

KM# 331 33.6300 g. 0.9250 Silver with gold insert 1.0000 oz. ASW **Subject:** Year of the Rabbitt **Obv:** Crowned head right **Rev:** Rabbit within octagon at center, animal figures surround **Rev. Designer:** Harvey Chan

Date	Mintage	MS-63	Proof
1999 Proof	77,791	—	100

KM# 387 33.6300 g. 0.9250 Silver with gold insert 1.0000 oz. ASW **Subject:** Year of the Dragon **Obv:** Crowned head right **Rev. Designer:** Harvey Chan

Date	Mintage	MS-63	Proof
2000 Proof	88,634	—	150

KM# 415 33.6300 g. 0.9250 Silver with gold insert 1.0000 oz. ASW 40 mm. **Subject:** Year of the Snake **Obv:** Crowned head right **Rev:** Snake within circle of lunar calendar signs **Rev. Designer:** Harvey Chain **Edge:** Reeded

Date	Mintage	MS-63	Proof
2001 Proof	60,754	—	85.00

KM# 463 33.6300 g. 0.9250 Silver with gold insert 1.0000 oz. ASW **Subject:** Year of the Horse **Obv:** Crowned head right **Obv. Designer:** Dora dePédery-Hunt **Rev:** Horse in center with Chinese Lunar calendar around **Rev. Designer:** Harvey Chain

Date	Mintage	MS-63	Proof
2002 Proof	59,395	—	85.00

KM# 481 33.6300 g. 0.9250 Silver with gold insert 1.0000 oz. ASW 40 mm. **Subject:** Year of the Sheep **Obv:** Crowned head right **Rev:** Sheep in center with Chinese Lunar calendar around **Rev. Designer:** Harvey Chain

Date	Mintage	MS-63	Proof
2003 Proof	53,714	—	85.00

KM# 415 33.6300 g. 0.9250 Silver with gold insert 1.0000 oz. ASW 40 mm. **Subject:** Year of the Snake **Obv:** Crowned head right **Rev:** Snake within circle of lunar calendar signs **Rev. Designer:** Harvey Chain **Edge:** Reeded

Date	Mintage	MS-63	Proof
2001 Proof	60,754	—	85.00

KM# 463 33.6300 g. 0.9250 Silver with gold insert 1.0000 oz. ASW **Subject:** Year of the Horse **Obv:** Crowned head right **Obv. Designer:** Dora dePédery-Hunt **Rev:** Horse in center with Chinese Lunar calendar around **Rev. Designer:** Harvey Chain

Date	Mintage	MS-63	Proof
2002 Proof	59,395	—	85.00

KM# 481 33.6300 g. 0.9250 Silver with gold insert 1.0000 oz. ASW 40 mm. **Subject:** Year of the Sheep **Obv:** Crowned head right **Rev:** Sheep in center with Chinese Lunar calendar around **Rev. Designer:** Harvey Chain

Date	Mintage	MS-63	Proof
2003 Proof	53,714	—	85.00

KM# 610 33.6300 g. 0.9250 Silver Gold octagon applique in center 1.0000 oz. ASW **Subject:** Year of the Monkey **Obv:** Crowned head right **Rev:** Monkey in center with Chinese Lunar calendar around

Date	Mintage	MS-63	Proof
2004 Proof	46,175	—	150

KM# 560 33.6300 g. 0.9250 Silver with gold insert 1.0000 oz. ASW **Subject:** Year of the Rooster **Obv:** Crowned head right **Rev:** Rooster in center with Chinese Lunar calendar around

Date	Mintage	MS-63	Proof
2005 Proof	44,690	—	125

KM# 587 33.6300 g. 0.9250 Silver with gold insert 1.0000 oz. ASW **Subject:** Year of the Dog **Obv:** Crowned head left **Rev:** Dog in center with Chinese Lunar calendar around

Date	Mintage	MS-63	Proof
2006 Proof	41,617	—	100

KM# 732 33.6300 g. 0.9250 Silver with gold insert 1.0000 oz. ASW 40 mm. **Subject:** Year of the Pig **Rev:** Pig at center of lunar characters

Date	Mintage	MS-63	Proof
2007 Proof	48,888	—	100

KM# 801 33.6300 g. 0.9250 Silver with gold insert 1.0000 oz. ASW 40 mm. **Subject:** Year of the Rat **Rev:** Rat, gold octagonal insert at center

Date	Mintage	MS-63	Proof
2008 Proof	48,888	—	90.00

KM# 803 30.0000 g. 0.9250 Silver 0.8921 oz. ASW 36.15 mm. **Rev:** Queen Victoria's coinage portrait

Date	Mintage	MS-63	Proof
2008	3,442	100.00	—

KM# 804 30.0000 g. 0.9250 Silver 0.8921 oz. ASW 36.15 mm. **Rev:** Edward VII coinage portrait **Rev. Designer:** G. W. DeSaulles

Date	Mintage	MS-63	Proof
2008	6,261	100.00	—

KM# 805 20.0000 g. 0.9250 Silver 0.5948 oz. ASW 36.15 mm. **Rev:** George V coinage portrait

Date	Mintage	MS-63	Proof
2008	—	100.00	—

KM# 806 31.5600 g. 0.9250 Silver 0.9385 oz. ASW 49.8 x 28.6 mm. **Rev:** Queen of Spades, multicolor playing card

Date	Mintage	MS-63	Proof
2008 Proof	8,714	—	90.00

KM# 807 31.5600 g. 0.9250 Silver 0.9385 oz. ASW
28.6x49.8 mm. **Rev:** Jack of Hearts, multicolor
playing card

Date	Mintage	MS-63	Proof
2008 Proof	11,362	—	85.00

KM# 920 31.5600 g. 0.9250 Silver 0.9385 oz. ASW
49.8 x 28.6 mm. **Obv:** Bust right **Obv. Designer:**
Susanna Blunt **Rev:** King of hearts, multicolor
Shape: Rectangle

Date	Mintage	MS-63	Proof
2009 Proof	5,798	—	120

KM# 919 31.5600 g. 0.9250 Silver 0.9385 oz. ASW
49.8 x 28.6 mm. **Obv:** Bust right **Obv. Designer:**
Susanna Blunt **Rev:** Ten of spades, multicolor
Shape: rectangle

Date	Mintage	MS-63	Proof
2009 Proof	5,921	—	150

KM# 866 33.6300 g. 0.9250 Silver with gold insert
1.0000 oz. ASW 40 mm. **Subject:** Year of the Ox
Rev: Ox, octagon gold insert

Date	Mintage	MS-63	Proof
2009 Proof	48,888	—	90.00

KM# 922 30.0000 g. 0.9250 Silver 0.8921 oz. ASW
36.15 mm. **Obv:** Bust right **Obv. Designer:**
Susanna Blunt **Rev:** Paget portrait of George VI

Date	Mintage	MS-63	Proof
2009(ml) Prooflike	—	100.00	—

KM#923 30.0000 g. 0.9250 Silver 0.8921 oz. ASW
36.15 mm.   **Obv:** Bust right **Obv. Designer:**
Susanna Blunt **Rev:** Gillick portrait of Queen
Elizabeth II

Date	Mintage	MS-63	Proof
2009(ml) Prooflike	2,643	100.00	—

KM# 1038   Silver 38 mm.   **Subject:** Year of the
tiger **Rev:** Tiger in forest **Shape:** scalloped

Date	Mintage	MS-63	Proof
2009 Proof	10,268	—	85.00

KM#980 34.0000 g. 0.9250 Silver 1.0111 oz. ASW
40 mm.   **Rev:** Tiger in gold insert

Date	Mintage	MS-63	Proof
2010 Proof	48,888	—	100

KM# 1032 0.9990 Silver   **Subject:** Year of the
tiger **Rev:** Tiger walking tiger

Date	Mintage	MS-63	Proof
2010 Proof	9,999	—	85.00

KM# 1055 31.1050 g. 0.9990 Silver 0.9990 oz.
ASW 38 mm.   **Rev:** Rabbit sitting, head turned left
Shape: scalloped

Date	Mintage	MS-63	Proof
2011 Proof	19,888	—	85.00

KM# 1091 25.1100 g. 0.9250 Silver 0.7467 oz.
ASW 36.15 mm.   **Rev:** Prince Charles bust **Rev.
Designer:** Laurie McGaw

Date	Mintage	MS-63	Proof
2011 Prooflike	10,000	100.00	—

KM# 1092 25.1100 g. 0.9250 Silver 0.7467 oz.
ASW 36.15 mm.   **Rev:** Prince William **Rev.
Designer:** Laurie McGaw

Date	Mintage	MS-63	Proof
2011 Prooflike	10,000	100.00	—

KM# 1093 25.1800 g. 0.9250 Silver 0.7488 oz.
ASW 36.15 mm. **Rev:** Prince Harry bust 1/4 right
Rev. Designer: Laurie McGaw

Date	Mintage	MS-63	Proof
2011 Prooflike	10,000	100.00	—

KM# 1094 31.3900 g. 0.9990 Silver 1.0082 oz.
ASW 38 mm. **Rev:** Rabbit bounding left **Rev.
Designer:** Aries Cheung

Date	Mintage	MS-63	Proof
2011 Proof	9,999	—	100

KM# 1152 31.3900 g. 0.9999 Silver 1.0091 oz.
ASW 38 mm. **Obv:** Bust right **Rev:** Magpie, bird
of happyness in flight at top, lotus flowers at bottom,
maple leaf hologram at center

Date	Mintage	MS-63	Proof
2011 Proof	Est. 8,888	—	100

KM# 1183 31.1050 g. 0.9990 Silver 0.9990 oz.
ASW 36.5 mm. **Subject:** Year of the Dragon **Obv:**
Bust right **Rev:** Dragon right

Date	Mintage	MS-63	Proof
2012 Proof	—	—	75.00

KM# 1186 31.1050 g. 0.9990 Silver 0.9990 oz.
ASW 36.5 mm. **Subject:** Year of the Dragon **Obv:**
Bust right **Rev:** Dragon left **Shape:** Scalloped

Date	Mintage	MS-63	Proof
2012 Proof	—	—	75.00

KM# 1260 31.3900 g. 0.9990 Silver 1.0082 oz.
ASW 36.5 mm. **Subject:** Good Fortune **Rev:**
Deer and doe froclicking around central hologram

Date	Mintage	MS-63	Proof
2012 Proof	—	—	75.00

20 DOLLARS

KM# 71 18.2733 g. 0.9000 Gold 0.5287 oz. AGW
27.05 mm. **Subject:** Centennial **Obv:** Crowned
head right **Rev:** Crowned and supported arms
Edge: Reeded

Date	Mintage	MS-63	Proof
1967 Proof	337,688	—	1,000

KM# 145 33.6300 g. 0.9250 Silver 1.0000 oz. ASW
40 mm. **Subject:** 1988 Calgary Olympics **Obv:**
Young bust right, maple leaf below, date at right
Rev: Downhill skier, denomination below **Rev.**
Designer: Ian Stewart **Edge:** Lettered

Date	Mintage	MS-63	Proof
1985 Proof	406,360	—	35.00
1985 Proof	Inc. above	—	200

Note: Plain edge

KM# 146 33.6300 g. 0.9250 Silver 1.0000 oz. ASW
40 mm. **Subject:** 1988 Calgary Olympics **Obv:**
Young bust right, small maple leaf below, date at
right **Rev:** Speed skater, denomination below **Rev.**
Designer: Friedrich Peter **Edge:** Lettered

Date	Mintage	MS-63	Proof
1985 Proof	354,222	—	35.00
1985 Proof	Inc. above	—	200

Note: Plain edge

KM# 150 33.6300 g. 0.9250 Silver 1.0000 oz. ASW
40 mm. **Subject:** Calgary 1988 - 15th Winter

Olympic Games **Obv:** Young bust right, small maple
leaf below, date at right **Rev:** Cross-country skier,
denomination below **Rev. Designer:** Ian Stewart
Edge: Lettered

Date	Mintage	MS-63	Proof
1986 Proof	303,199	—	35.00

KM# 147 33.6300 g. 0.9250 Silver 1.0000 oz. ASW
40 mm. **Subject:** 1988 Calgary Olympics **Obv:**
Young bust right, small maple leaf below, date at
right **Rev:** Biathlon, denomination below **Rev.**
Designer: John Mardon **Edge:** Lettered

Date	Mintage	MS-63	Proof
1986 Proof	308,086	—	35.00
1986 Proof	Inc. above	—	200

Note: Plain edge

KM# 148 33.6300 g. 0.9250 Silver 1.0000 oz. ASW
40 mm. **Subject:** 1988 Calgary Olympics **Obv:**
Young bust right, small maple leaf below, date at
right **Rev:** Hockey, denomination below **Rev.**
Designer: Ian Stewart **Edge:** Lettered

Date	Mintage	MS-63	Proof
1986 Proof	396,602	—	35.00
1986 Proof	Inc. above	—	200

Note: Plain edge

KM# 151 33.6300 g. 0.9250 Silver 1.0000 oz. ASW
40 mm. **Subject:** 1988 Calgary Olympics **Obv:**
Young bust right, small maple leaf below, date at
right **Rev:** Free-style skier, denomination below
Rev. Designer: Walter Ott **Edge:** Lettered

Date	Mintage	MS-63	Proof
1986 Proof	294,322	—	35.00
1986 Proof	Inc. above	—	200

Note: Plain edge

KM# 155 34.1070 g. 0.9250 Silver 1.0143 oz. ASW
40 mm. **Subject:** Calgary 1988 - 15th Winter
Olympic Games **Obv:** Young bust right, small maple
leaf below, date at right **Rev:** Figure skating pairs
event, denomination below **Rev. Designer:**
Raymond Taylor **Edge:** Lettered

Date	Mintage	MS-63	Proof
1987 Proof	334,875	—	35.00

KM# 156 34.1070 g. 0.9250 Silver 1.0143 oz. ASW 40 mm. **Subject:** 1988 Calgary Olympics **Obv:** Young bust right, small maple leaf below, date at right **Rev:** Curling, denomination below **Rev. Designer:** Ian Stewart **Edge:** Lettered

Date	Mintage	MS-63	Proof
1987 Proof	286,457	—	35.00

KM# 159 34.1070 g. 0.9250 Silver 1.0143 oz. ASW 40 mm. **Subject:** 1988 Calgary Olympics **Obv:** Young bust right, small maple leaf below, date at right **Rev:** Ski jumper, denomination below **Rev. Designer:** Raymond Taylor **Edge:** Lettered

Date	Mintage	MS-63	Proof
1987 Proof	290,954	—	35.00

KM# 160 34.1070 g. 0.9250 Silver 1.0143 oz. ASW 40 mm. **Subject:** 1988 Calgary Olympics **Obv:** Young bust right, maple leaf below, date at right **Rev:** Bobsled, denomination below **Rev. Designer:** John Mardon **Edge:** Lettered

Date	Mintage	MS-63	Proof
1987 Proof	274,326	—	35.00

KM# 172 31.1030 g. 0.9250 Silver gold cameo insert 0.9249 oz. ASW 38 mm. **Subject:** Aviation **Obv:** Crowned head right, date below **Rev:**

Lancaster, Fauquier in cameo, denomination below **Rev. Designer:** Robert R. Carmichael

Date	Mintage	MS-63	Proof
1990 Proof	43,596	—	125

KM# 173 31.1030 g. 0.9250 Silver with Gold cameo insert. 0.9249 oz. ASW 38 mm. **Subject:** Aviation **Obv:** Crowned head right, date below **Rev:** Anson and Harvard, Air Marshal Robert Leckie in cameo, denomination below **Rev. Designer:** Geoff Bennett

Date	Mintage	MS-63	Proof
1990 Proof	41,844	—	45.00

KM# 196 31.1030 g. 0.9250 Silver gold cameo insert 0.9249 oz. ASW 38 mm. **Subject:** Aviation **Obv:** Crowned head right, date below **Rev:** Silver Dart, John A. D. McCurdy and F. W. "Casey" Baldwin in cameo, denomination below **Rev. Designer:** George Velinger

Date	Mintage	MS-63	Proof
1991 Proof	28,791	—	45.00

KM# 197 31.1030 g. 0.9250 Silver gold cameo insert 0.9249 oz. ASW 38 mm. **Subject:** Aviation **Obv:** Crowned head right, date below **Rev:** de Haviland Beaver, Philip C. Garratt in cameo, denomination below **Rev. Designer:** Peter Massman

Date	Mintage	MS-63	Proof
1991 Proof	29,399	—	45.00

KM# 224 31.1030 g. 0.9250 Silver gold cameo insert 0.9249 oz. ASW 38 mm.   **Subject:** Aviation **Obv:** Crowned head right, date below **Rev:** Curtiss JN-4 Canick ("Jenny"), Sir Frank W. Baillie in cameo, denomination below **Rev. Designer:** George Velinger

Date	Mintage	MS-63	Proof
1992 Proof	33,105	—	45.00

KM# 237 31.1030 g. 0.9250 Silver with Gold cameo insert. 0.9249 oz. ASW 38 mm.   **Subject:** Aviation **Obv:** Crowned head right, date below **Rev:** Lockheed 14, Zebulon Lewis Leigh in cameo, denomination below **Rev. Designer:** Robert R. Carmichael

Date	Mintage	MS-63	Proof
1993 Proof	32,550	—	45.00

KM# 225 31.1030 g. 0.9250 Silver with Gold cameo insert. 0.9249 oz. ASW 38 mm.   **Subject:** Aviation **Obv:** Crowned head right, date below **Rev:** de Haviland Gypsy Moth, Murton A. Seymour in cameo, denomination below **Rev. Designer:** John Mardon

Date	Mintage	MS-63	Proof
1992 Proof	32,537	—	45.00

KM# 246 31.1030 g. 0.9250 Silver with Gold cameo insert. 0.9249 oz. ASW 38 mm.   **Subject:** Aviation **Obv:** Crowned head right, date below **Rev:** Curtiss HS-2L seaplane, Stewart Graham in cameo, denomination below **Rev. Designer:** John Mardon

Date	Mintage	MS-63	Proof
1994 Proof	31,242	—	45.00

KM# 236 31.1030 g. 0.9250 Silver with Gold cameo insert. 0.9249 oz. ASW 38 mm.   **Subject:** Aviation **Obv:** Crowned head right, date below **Rev:** Fairchild 71C float plane, James A. Richardson, Sr. in cameo, denomination below **Rev. Designer:** Robert R. Carmichael

Date	Mintage	MS-63	Proof
1993 Proof	32,199	—	45.00

KM# 247 31.1030 g. 0.9250 Silver with Gold cameo insert. 0.9249 oz. ASW 38 mm.   **Subject:** Aviation **Obv:** Crowned head right, date below **Rev:** Vickers Vedette, Wilfred T. Reid in cameo, denomination below **Rev. Designer:** Robert R. Carmichael

Date	Mintage	MS-63	Proof
1994 Proof	30,880	—	45.00

KM# 271 31.1030 g. 0.9250 Silver gold cameo insert 0.9249 oz. ASW 38 mm. **Subject:** Aviation **Obv:** Crowned head right, date below **Rev:** C-FEA1 Fleet Cannuck, denomination below **Rev. Designer:** Robert Bradford

Date	Mintage	MS-63	Proof
1995 Proof	17,438	—	45.00

KM# 277 31.1030 g. 0.9250 Silver gold cameo insert 0.9249 oz. ASW 38 mm. **Subject:** Aviation **Obv:** Crowned head right, date below **Obv. Legend:** CF-105 Arrow, denomination below **Rev. Designer:** Jim Bruce

Date	Mintage	MS-63	Proof
1996 Proof	27,163	—	100

KM# 272 31.1030 g. 0.9250 Silver gold cameo insert 0.9249 oz. ASW 38 mm. **Subject:** Aviation **Obv:** Crowned head right, date below **Rev:** DHC-1 Chipmunk, denomination below **Rev. Designer:** Robert Bradford

Date	Mintage	MS-63	Proof
1995 Proof	17,722	—	45.00

KM# 297 31.1030 g. 0.9250 Silver gold cameo insert 0.9249 oz. ASW 38 mm. **Subject:** Aviation **Obv:** Crowned head right, date below **Rev:** Canadair F-86 Sabre, denomination below **Rev. Designer:** Ross Buckland

Date	Mintage	MS-63	Proof
1997 Proof	14,389	—	45.00

KM# 276 31.1030 g. 0.9250 Silver gold cameo insert 0.9249 oz. ASW 38 mm. **Subject:** Aviation **Obv:** Crowned head right, date below **Rev:** CF-100 Cannuck, denomination below **Rev. Designer:** Jim Bruce

Date	Mintage	MS-63	Proof
1996 Proof	18,508	—	45.00

KM# 298 31.1030 g. 0.9250 Silver with Gold cameo insert. 0.9249 oz. ASW 38 mm. **Subject:** Aviation **Obv:** Crowned head right, date below **Rev:** Canadair CT-114 Tutor, denomination below **Rev. Designer:** Ross Buckland

Date	Mintage	MS-63	Proof
1997 Proof	15,669	—	45.00

KM# 329 31.1030 g. 0.9250 Silver gold cameo insert 0.9249 oz. ASW 38 mm. **Subject:** Aviation **Obv:** Crowned head, right, date below **Rev:** CP-107 Argus, denomination below

Date	Mintage	MS-63	Proof
1998 Proof	Est. 50,000	—	50.00

KM# 330 31.1030 g. 0.9250 Silver gold cameo insert 0.9249 oz. ASW 38 mm. **Subject:** Aviation **Obv:** Crowned head right, date below **Rev:** CP-215 Waterbomber, denomination below **Rev. Designer:** Peter Mossman

Date	Mintage	MS-63	Proof
1998 Proof	Est. 50,000	—	75.00

KM# 339 31.1030 g. 0.9250 Silver gold cameo insert 0.9249 oz. ASW 38 mm. **Subject:** Aviation **Obv:** Crowned head right, date below **Rev:** DHC-6 Twin Otter, denomination below **Rev. Designer:** Neil Aird

Date	Mintage	MS-63	Proof
1999 Proof	Est. 50,000	—	95.00

KM# 340 31.1030 g. 0.9250 Silver gold cameo insert 0.9249 oz. ASW 38 mm. **Subject:** Aviation **Obv:** Crowned head right, date below **Rev:** DHC-8 Dash 8, denomination below

Date	Mintage	MS-63	Proof
1999 Proof	50,000	—	100

KM# 395 0.9250 Silver 38 mm. **Subject:** First Canadian locomotive **Obv:** Crowned head right, date below **Rev:** Locomotive below multicolored cameo, denomination below

Date	Mintage	MS-63	Proof
2000 Proof	—	—	50.00

KM# 396 0.9250 Silver 38 mm. **Subject:** First Canadian self-propelled car **Obv:** Crowned head right, date below **Rev:** Car below multicolored cameo, denomination below

Date	Mintage	MS-63	Proof
2000 Proof	—	—	50.00

KM# 397 0.9250 Silver 38 mm. **Subject:** Bluenose sailboat **Obv:** Crowned head right, date below **Rev:** Bluenose sailing left below multicolored cameo, denomination below

Date	Mintage	MS-63	Proof
2000 Proof	—	—	150

KM# 428 31.1030 g. 0.9250 Silver 0.9249 oz. ASW 38 mm. **Series:** Transportation - Russell Touring Car **Obv:** Crowned head right **Rev:** Russell touring car with hologram cameo **Rev. Designer:** John Mardon **Edge:** Segmented reeding

Date	Mintage	MS-63	Proof
2001 Proof	15,000	—	45.00

KM# 464 31.1030 g. 0.9250 Silver 0.9249 oz. ASW **Obv:** Crowned head right **Obv. Designer:** Dora dePédery-Hunt **Rev:** Gray-Dort Model 25-SM with cameo hologram **Rev. Designer:** John Mardon

Date	Mintage	MS-63	Proof
2002 Proof	15,000	—	45.00

KM# 465 31.1030 g. 0.9250 Silver 0.9249 oz. ASW **Obv:** Crowned head right **Obv. Designer:** Dora dePédery-Hunt **Rev:** Sailing ship William D. Lawrence **Rev. Designer:** Bonnie Ross

Date	Mintage	MS-63	Proof
2002 Proof	15,000	—	45.00

KM# 411 31.1035 g. 0.9250 Silver 0.9250 oz. ASW 38 mm. **Subject:** Transportation - Steam Locomotive **Obv:** Crowned head right **Obv. Designer:** Dora dePédery-Hunt **Rev:** First Canadian Steel Steam Locomotive and cameo hologram **Rev. Designer:** Don Curely **Edge:** Segmented reeding

Date	Mintage	MS-63	Proof
2001 Proof	15,000	—	45.00

KM# 482 31.3900 g. 0.9999 Silver 1.0091 oz. ASW 38 mm. **Obv:** Crowned head right **Obv. Designer:** Dora dePédery-Hunt **Rev:** Niagara Falls hologram **Rev. Designer:** Gary Corcoran

Date	Mintage	MS-63	Proof
2003 Proof	29,967	—	75.00

KM# 483 31.1030 g. 0.9250 Silver with selective gold plating 0.9249 oz. ASW **Subject:** The HMCS Bras d'or (FHE-400) **Obv:** Crowned head right **Obv. Designer:** Dora dePédery-Hunt **Rev:** Ship in water **Rev. Designer:** Donald Curley, Stan Witten

Date	Mintage	MS-63	Proof
2003 Proof	15,000	—	45.00

KM# 427 31.1030 g. 0.9250 Silver 0.9249 oz. ASW 38 mm. **Series:** Transportation - The Marco Polo **Obv:** Crowned head right **Rev:** Sailship with hologram cameo **Rev. Designer:** J. Franklin Wright **Edge:** Segmented reeding

Date	Mintage	MS-63	Proof
2001 Proof	15,000	—	45.00

KM#523   31.3900 g. 0.9990 Silver 1.0082 oz. ASW
38 mm.   Obv: Crowned head right Obv.
Designer: Dora dePédery-Hunt Rev: Canadian
Rockies, multicolor

Date	Mintage	MS-63	Proof
2003 Proof	29,967	—	50.00

KM#484   31.1030 g. 0.9250 Silver with selective gold
plating 0.9249 oz. ASW   Subject: Canadian
National FA-1 diesel-electric locomotive Obv:
Crowned head right Obv. Designer: Dora dePédery-
Hunt Rev. Designer: John Mardon, William Woodruff

Date	Mintage	MS-63	Proof
2003 Proof	15,000	—	45.00

KM# 485   31.1030 g. 0.9250 Silver with selective
gold plating 0.9249 oz. ASW   Obv: Crowned head
right Obv. Designer: Dora dePédery-Hunt Rev:
The Bricklin SV-1 Rev. Designer: Brian Hughes,
José Oslo

Date	Mintage	MS-63	Proof
2003 Proof	15,000	—	45.00

KM#611   31.3900 g. 0.9999 Silver 1.0091 oz. ASW
38 mm.   Obv: Head right Obv. Designer:
Susanna Blunt Rev: Iceberg, hologram

Date	Mintage	MS-63	Proof
2004 Proof	24,879	—	45.00

KM# 838   31.3900 g. 0.9999 Silver partially gilt
1.0091 oz. ASW 38 mm.   Rev: Hopewell Rocks, gilt

Date	Mintage	MS-63	Proof
2004 Proof	16,918	—	45.00

KM#561   31.3900 g. 0.9999 Silver 1.0091 oz. ASW
38 mm.   Obv: Head right Obv. Designer:
Susanna Blunt Rev: Three-masted sailing ship,
hologram of the sea Rev. Designer: Bonnie Ross

Date	Mintage	MS-63	Proof
2005 Proof	18,276	—	55.00

KM# 562   31.3900 g. 0.9999 Silver 1.0091 oz. ASW
38 mm.   Subject: Northwest Territories Diamonds
Obv: Head right Obv. Designer: Susanna Blunt Rev:
Multicolor diamond hologram on landscape Rev.
Designer: José Oslo Edge: Reeded

Date	Mintage	MS-63	Proof
2005 Proof	35,000	—	50.00

KM# 563   31.3900 g. 0.9999 Silver 1.0091 oz.
ASW   Subject: Mingan Archepelago Obv: Head
right Obv. Designer: Susanna Blunt Rev: Cliffs with
whale tail out of water Rev. Designer: Pierre Leduc

Date	Mintage	MS-63	Proof
2005 Proof	—	—	45.00

KM# 564   31.3900 g. 0.9999 Silver 1.0091 oz.
ASW   Subject: Rainforests of the Pacific
Northwest Obv: Head right Rev: Open winged bird

Date	Mintage	MS-63	Proof
2005 Proof	—	—	45.00

KM#565 31.3900 g. 0.9999 Silver 1.0091 oz. ASW 38 mm. **Subject:** Toronto Island National Park **Obv:** Head right **Rev:** Toronto Island Lighthouse, Toronto skyline in background

Date	Mintage	MS-63	Proof
2005 Proof	—	—	55.00

KM# 588 31.3900 g. 0.9999 Silver 1.0091 oz. ASW **Subject:** Georgian Bay National Park **Obv:** Head right **Rev:** Canoe and small trees on island

Date	Mintage	MS-63	Proof
2006 Proof	—	—	60.00

KM#589 31.1000 g. 0.9999 Silver 0.9997 oz. ASW 38 mm. **Obv:** Head right **Rev:** Notre Dame Basilica, Montreal, as a hologram

Date	Mintage	MS-63	Proof
2006 Proof	15,000	—	50.00

KM#663 31.3900 g. 0.9999 Silver 1.0091 oz. ASW 38 mm. **Subject:** Nahanni National Park **Obv:** Head right **Rev:** Bear walking along sream, cliff in background

Date	Mintage	MS-63	Proof
2006 Proof	—	—	60.00

KM#664 31.3900 g. 0.9999 Silver 1.0091 oz. ASW 38 mm. **Subject:** Jasper National Park **Obv:**

Head right **Rev:** Cowboy on horseback in majestic scene

Date	Mintage	MS-63	Proof
2006 Proof	—	—	60.00

KM#665 31.1000 g. 0.9999 Silver 0.9997 oz. ASW 38 mm. **Obv:** Head right **Rev:** Holographic rendering of CN Tower

Date	Mintage	MS-63	Proof
2006 Proof	15,000	—	60.00

KM# 666 31.1000 g. 0.9999 Silver 0.9997 oz. ASW **Obv:** Head right **Rev:** Holographic view of Pengrowth Saddledome in Calgary

Date	Mintage	MS-63	Proof
2006 Proof	15,000	—	55.00

KM# 667 31.3900 g. 0.9999 Silver 1.0091 oz. ASW **Subject:** Tall Ship **Obv:** Head right **Rev:** Ketch and holographic image of thunderstorm in sky

Date	Mintage	MS-63	Proof
2006 Proof	10,299	—	60.00

20 DOLLARS

KM# 734 31.1000 g. 0.9990 Silver 0.9988 oz. ASW
38 mm.   **Rev:** Holiday sleigh ride

Date	Mintage	MS-63	Proof
2007 Proof	6,804	—	70.00

KM# 735 31.1000 g. 0.9990 Silver 0.9988 oz. ASW
38 mm.   **Rev:** Snowflake, aquamarine crystal

Date	Mintage	MS-63	Proof
2007 Proof	4,989	—	175

KM# 737 31.1000 g. 0.9990 Silver 0.9988 oz. ASW
38 mm.   **Subject:** International Polar Year

Date	Mintage	MS-63	Proof
2007 Proof	9,164	—	65.00

KM# 737a 27.7800 g. 0.9250 Silver 0.8261 oz.
ASW 40 mm.   **Subject:** International Polar Year
Rev: Blue plasma coating

Date	Mintage	MS-63	Proof
2007 Proof	3,005	—	250

KM# 738 31.3900 g. 0.9999 Silver 1.0091 oz. ASW
38 mm.   **Subject:** Tall ships **Rev:** Brigantine in
harbor, hologram

Date	Mintage	MS-63	Proof
2007 Proof	16,000	—	60.00

KM# 839 31.3900 g. 0.9999 Silver 1.0091 oz.
ASW   **Rev:** Northern lights in hologram

Date	Mintage	MS-63	Proof
2007	—	35.00	—

KM# 808 31.5000 g. 0.9250 Silver 0.9368 oz. ASW
38 mm.   **Subject:** Agriculture trade **Rev:** Team of
horses plowing

Date	Mintage	MS-63	Proof
2008 Proof	5,802	—	70.00

KM# 809 31.1050 g. 0.9990 Silver 0.9990 oz. ASW
38 mm. **Rev:** Royal Hudson Steam locomotive

Date	Mintage	MS-63	Proof
2008 Proof	8,345	—	70.00

KM# 810 31.3900 g. 0.9990 Silver 1.0082 oz. ASW
38 mm. **Rev:** Green leaf and crystal raindrop **Rev. Designer:** Stanley Witten

Date	Mintage	MS-63	Proof
2008 Proof	15,000	—	175

KM# 811 31.1050 g. 0.9990 Silver 0.9990 oz. ASW **Rev:** Snowflake, amethyst crystal

Date	Mintage	MS-63	Proof
2008 Proof	7,172	—	95.00

KM# 813 31.1050 g. 0.9990 Silver 0.9990 oz. ASW
38 mm. **Rev:** Carolers around tree

Date	Mintage	MS-63	Proof
2008 Proof	10,000	—	70.00

KM# 872 31.1050 g. 0.9990 Silver 0.9990 oz. ASW
38 mm. **Rev:** Snowflake, sapphire crystal

Date	Mintage	MS-63	Proof
2008 Proof	7,765	—	95.00

KM# 893 31.3900 g. 0.9990 Silver 1.0082 oz. ASW
38 mm. **Subject:** Coal mining trade **Obv:** Bust right **Obv. Legend:** Elizabeth II DG Regina **Obv. Designer:** Susanna Blunt **Rev:** Miner pushing cart with coal **Rev. Legend:** Canada 20 Dollars **Rev. Designer:** John Marder

Date	Mintage	MS-63	Proof
2009 Proof	10,000	—	75.00

KM# 891 31.3900 g. 0.9990 Silver 1.0082 oz. ASW
38 mm. **Subject:** Great Canadian Locomotives - Jubilee **Obv:** Bust right **Obv. Legend:** Elizabeth II DG Regina **Obv. Designer:** Susanna Blunt **Rev:** Jubilee locomotive side view **Rev. Legend:** Canada 20 Dollars **Edge Lettering:** Jubilee

Date	Mintage	MS-63	Proof
2009 Proof	6,036	—	70.00

KM# 870 27.7800 g. 0.9250 Silver 0.8261 oz. ASW
40 mm. **Rev:** Calgary Flames goalie mask multicolor on goal net

Date	Mintage	MS-63	Proof
2009 Proof	10,000	—	70.00

KM#871 27.7800 g. 0.9250 Silver 0.8261 oz. ASW
40 mm.   **Rev:** Edmonton Oilers goalie mask,
multicolor on goal net

Date	Mintage	MS-63	Proof
2009 Proof	10,000	—	70.00

KM# 872A 27.7800 g. 0.9250 Silver 0.8261 oz.
ASW 40 mm.   **Rev:** Montreal Canadians goalie
mask multicolor

Date	Mintage	MS-63	Proof
2009 Proof	10,000	—	70.00

KM#873 27.7800 g. 0.9250 Silver 0.8261 oz. ASW
40 mm.   **Rev:** Ottawa Senators goalie mask on
goal net

Date	Mintage	MS-63	Proof
2009 Proof	10,000	—	70.00

KM#874 27.7800 g. 0.9250 Silver 0.8261 oz. ASW

40 mm.   **Rev:** Toronto Maple Leafs goalie mask,
multicolor on goal net

Date	Mintage	MS-63	Proof
2009 Proof	10,000	—	70.00

KM#875 27.7800 g. 0.9250 Silver 0.8261 oz. ASW
40 mm.   **Rev:** Vancouver Canucks goalie mask,
multicolor on goal net

Date	Mintage	MS-63	Proof
2009 Proof	10,000	—	70.00

KM#876 31.5000 g. 0.9250 Silver 0.9368 oz. ASW
40 mm.   **Rev:** Summer moon mask

Date	Mintage	MS-63	Proof
2009 Proof	2,834	—	225

KM#944 31.1050 g. 0.9990 Silver 0.9990 oz. ASW
38 mm.   **Rev:** Snowflake - light blue crystal

Date	Mintage	MS-63	Proof
2009 Proof	7,477	—	100

KM#945 31.1050 g. 0.9990 Silver 0.9990 oz. ASW
38 mm.   **Rev:** Snowflake - light red crystal

Date	Mintage	MS-63	Proof
2009 Proof	7,004	—	100

KM# 892 31.3900 g. 0.9990 Silver 1.0082 oz. ASW 38 mm. **Subject:** Crystal raindrop **Obv:** Bust right **Rev:** Maple leaf and rain drop - fall colors **Rev. Designer:** Celia Godkin

Date	Mintage	MS-63	Proof
2009 Proof	9,998	—	85.00

KM# 1013 31.3900 g. 0.9990 Silver 1.0082 oz. ASW 38 mm. **Rev:** Maple leaf and crystal **Rev. Designer:** Celia Godkin

Date	Mintage	MS-63	Proof
2010 Proof	10,000	—	100

KM# 987 31.3900 g. 0.9999 Silver 1.0091 oz. ASW 38 mm. **Rev:** Lotus Water Lilly in multicolor and crystal **Rev. Designer:** Cladio D'Angelo

Date	Mintage	MS-63	Proof
2010 Proof	10,000	—	120

KM# 1018 31.3900 g. 0.9990 Silver 1.0082 oz. ASW 38 mm. **Rev:** Steam Locomotive Selkirk

Date	Mintage	MS-63	Proof
2010 Proof	10,000	—	80.00

KM# 1009 31.3900 g. 0.9990 Silver 1.0082 oz. ASW **Subject:** 75th Anniversary of Canadian Bank Notes **Rev:** Female and farmer seated

Date	Mintage	MS-63	Proof
2010 Proof	7,500	—	70.00

KM# 1048 31.1050 g. 0.9999 Silver 0.9999 oz. ASW 38 mm. **Rev:** Snowflake, blue crystals

Date	Mintage	MS-63	Proof
2010 Proof	7,500	—	95.00

KM# 1049 31.1050 g. 0.9999 Silver 0.9999 oz. ASW 38 mm. **Rev:** Snowflake, tanzanite crystals

Date	Mintage	MS-63	Proof
2010 Proof	7,500	—	95.00

20 DOLLARS

KM# 1066 31.9900 g. 0.9990 Silver 1.0274 oz.
ASW 38 mm.   **Rev:** Pinecone with ruby crystals
Rev. Designer: Susan Taylor

Date	Mintage	MS-63	Proof
2010 Proof	5,000	—	120

KM# 1067 31.9900 g. 0.9990 Silver 1.0274 oz.
ASW 38 mm.   **Rev:** Pinecone with moonlight blue
crystals **Rev. Designer:** Susan Taylor

Date	Mintage	MS-63	Proof
2010 Proof	5,000	—	120

KM# 1075 27.7800 g. 0.9250 Silver 0.8261 oz.
ASW 40 mm.   **Subject:** Winter Scene **Rev:** Horse
pulling cut Christmas Tree **Rev. Designer:** Rene
Clark

Date	Mintage	MS-63	Proof
2011 Proof	8,000	—	70.00

KM# 1111 31.3900 g. 0.9990 Silver 1.0082 oz.
ASW 40 mm.   **Subject:** Royal Wedding **Rev:**
Portraits of Katherine and William facing each other,
crystal insert

Date	Mintage	MS-63	Proof
2011 Proof	—	—	80.00

KM# 1134 31.3900 g. 0.9999 Silver 1.0091 oz.
ASW 38 mm.   **Subject:** Canadian Pacific's D-10
Steam Locomotive **Obv:** Bust right **Rev:** Steam
locomotive right **Edge:** Lettered

Date	Mintage	MS-63	Proof
2011 Proof	10,000	—	80.00

KM# 1135 31.3900 g. 0.9999 Silver 1.0091 oz.
ASW 38 mm.   **Obv:** Bust right **Rev:** Tulip in color
and Vienitian glass lady bug

Date	Mintage	MS-63	Proof
2011 Proof	5,000	—	1,000

KM# 1145 31.3900 g. 0.9999 Silver 1.0091 oz.
ASW 38 mm.   **Obv:** Bust right **Rev:** Wild rose in
color, swarovski crystrals

Date	Mintage	MS-63	Proof
2011 Proof	Est. 10,000	—	135

KM# 1182 31.9900 g. 0.9999 Silver 1.0284 oz.
ASW 38 mm.   **Obv:** Bust right **Rev:** Christmas tree
with six crystals

Date	Mintage	MS-63	Proof
2011 Proof	—	—	75.00

KM# 1147 31.3900 g. 0.9999 Silver 1.0091 oz.
ASW 38 mm.   **Obv:** Bust right **Rev:** Maple leaves,
seeds in color, swarovski crystal drop

Date	Mintage	MS-63	Proof
2011 Proof	—	—	110

KM# 1187 31.3900 g. 0.9990 Silver 1.0082 oz.
ASW 38 mm.   **Obv:** Bust right **Rev:** Snowflake
with emerald crystals

Date	Mintage	MS-63	Proof
2011 Proof	15,000	—	85.00

KM# 1188 31.8900 g. 0.9990 Silver 1.0242 oz.
ASW 38 mm.   **Obv:** Bust right **Rev:** Snowflake
with topaz crystals

Date	Mintage	MS-63	Proof
2011 Proof	15,000	—	85.00

KM# 1181 31.3900 g. 0.9990 Silver 1.0082 oz.
ASW 38 mm.   **Obv:** Bust right **Rev:** Winnipeg Jets
Logo, jet over maple leaf

Date	Mintage	MS-63	Proof
2011 Proof	15,000	—	95.00

KM# 1189 31.8900 g. 0.9990 Silver 1.0242 oz.
ASW 38 mm.   **Obv:** Bust right **Rev:** Three
snowflakes with three Hyacinth red crystals

Date	Mintage	MS-63	Proof
2011 Proof	15,000	—	85.00

KM# 1190 31.8900 g. 0.9990 Silver 1.0242 oz.
ASW 38 mm.   **Obv:** Bust right **Rev:** Three
snowflakes with three Montana blue crystals

Date	Mintage	MS-63	Proof
2011 Proof	15,000	—	85.00

20 DOLLARS

KM# 1137 31.3900 g. 0.9990 Silver 1.0082 oz.
ASW 38 mm.   **Subject:** Elizabeth II, 60th
Anniversary of reign **Obv:** Bust right **Rev:** Crowned
bust right with swarovski crystal insert **Edge:**
Reeded

Date	Mintage	MS-63	Proof
2012 Proof	15,000	—	80.00

KM# 1177 27.7800 g. 0.9250 Silver 0.8261 oz.
ASW 38 mm.   **Obv:** Bust right **Rev:** Youthful busts
right of Elizabeth II and Prince Philip

Date	Mintage	MS-63	Proof
2012 Proof	—	—	85.00

KM# 1178 27.7800 g. 0.9250 Silver 0.8261 oz.
ASW 38 mm.   **Obv:** Bust right **Rev:** Royal cypher,
wreath below

Date	Mintage	MS-63	Proof
2012 Proof	—	—	85.00

KM# 1238 30.7500 g. 0.9999 Silver 0.9885 oz.
ASW 36 mm.   **Subject:** Elizabeth II, Diamond
Jubilee **Obv:** Bust right **Rev:** Elizabeth II profile left,
high releif **Rev. Designer:** Laurie McGaw

Date	Mintage	MS-63	Proof
2012 Proof	7,500	—	75.00

KM# 1239 7.9600 g. 0.9990 Silver 0.2557 oz. ASW
27 mm.   **Subject:** Elizabeth II, Diamond Jubilee
Obv: Young portrait right **Obv. Designer:** Mary
Gilick **Rev:** Elizabeth II with hat at left **Rev.
Designer:** Laurie McGaw

Date	Mintage	MS-63	Proof
1952-2012 Proof	25,000	—	30.00

KM# 1246 27.7800 g. 0.9250 Silver 0.8261 oz.
ASW 38 mm.   **Subject:** Coast Guard, 50th
Anniversary

Date	Mintage	MS-63	Proof
2012	—	—	100

KM# 1250 27.7800 g. 0.9250 Silver 0.8261 oz.
ASW 38 mm.   **Subject:** F.H. Varley

Date	Mintage	MS-63	Proof
2012	—	—	75.00

KM# 1251 27.7800 g. 0.9250 Silver 0.8261 oz.
ASW 38 mm.   **Subject:** Arthur Lismer

Date	Mintage	MS-63	Proof
2012 Proof	—	—	75.00

KM# 1266 31.1000 g. 0.9990 Silver 0.9988 oz. ASW 38 mm. **Subject:** Aster and bee

Date	Mintage	MS-63	Proof
2012 Proof	—	—	100

KM# 1269 31.3900 g. 0.9990 Silver 1.0082 oz. ASW 38 mm. **Subject:** Sugar Maple Leaf **Rev:** Leaves in color, crystal

Date	Mintage	MS-63	Proof
2012 Proof	—	—	130

KM# 1270 31.3900 g. 0.9990 Silver 1.0082 oz. ASW 38 mm. **Rev:** Rhododendron

Date	Mintage	MS-63	Proof
2012 Proof	—	—	125

KM# 1280 31.1050 g. 0.9990 Silver 0.9990 oz. ASW 38 mm. **Subject:** Bateman Moose

Date	Mintage	MS-63	Proof
2012 Proof	—	—	135

KM# 1283 15.5500 g. 0.9990 Gold 0.4994 oz. AGW 25 mm. **Subject:** Year of the Dragon

Date	Mintage	MS-63	Proof
2012 Proof	—	—	900

25 DOLLARS

KM#742 27.7800 g. 0.9250 Silver 0.8261 oz. ASW 40 mm. **Subject:** Vancouver Olympics **Rev:** Alpine skiing, hologram

Date	Mintage	MS-63	Proof
2007 Proof	45,000	—	50.00

KM#743 27.7800 g. 0.9250 Silver 0.8261 oz. ASW 40 mm. **Subject:** Vancouver Olympics **Rev:** Athletics pride hologram

Date	Mintage	MS-63	Proof
2007 Proof	45,000	—	65.00

25 DOLLARS

KM#744 27.7500 g. 0.9250 Silver 0.8252 oz. ASW
40 mm.   **Subject:** Vancouver Olympics **Rev:**
Biathleon hologram

Date	Mintage	MS-63	Proof
2007 Proof	54,000	—	50.00

KM#745 27.7800 g. 0.9250 Silver 0.8261 oz. ASW
40 mm.   **Subject:** Vancouver Olympics **Rev:**
Curling hologram

Date	Mintage	MS-63	Proof
2007 Proof	—	—	50.00

KM#746 27.7800 g. 0.9250 Silver 0.8261 oz. ASW
40 mm.   **Subject:** Vancouver Olympics **Rev:**
Hockey, hologram

Date	Mintage	MS-63	Proof
2007 Proof	45,000	—	50.00

KM#814 27.7800 g. 0.9250 Silver 0.8261 oz. ASW
40 mm.   **Subject:** Vancouver Olympics **Rev:**
Bobsleigh, hologram

Date	Mintage	MS-63	Proof
2008 Proof	45,000	—	50.00

KM#815 27.7800 g. 0.9250 Silver 0.8261 oz. ASW
40 mm.   **Subject:** Vancouver Olympics **Rev:**
Figure skating, hologram

Date	Mintage	MS-63	Proof
2008 Proof	45,000	—	50.00

KM#816 27.7800 g. 0.9250 Silver 0.8261 oz. ASW
40 mm.   **Subject:** Vancouver Olympics **Rev:**
Freestyle skating, hologram

Date	Mintage	MS-63	Proof
2008 Proof	45,000	—	50.00

KM# 817 27.7800 g. 0.9250 Silver 0.8261 oz. ASW 40 mm. **Subject:** Vancouver Olympics **Rev:** Snowboarding, hologram

Date	Mintage	MS-63	Proof
2008 Proof	45,000	—	50.00

KM# 818 27.7800 g. 0.9250 Silver 0.8261 oz. ASW 40 mm. **Subject:** Vancouver Olympics **Rev:** Home of the 2010 Olympics

Date	Mintage	MS-63	Proof
2008 Proof	45,000	—	50.00

KM# 903 27.7800 g. 0.9250 Silver 0.8261 oz. ASW 40 mm. **Subject:** 2010 Vancouver Olympics **Obv:** Bust right **Obv. Designer:** Susanna Blunt **Rev:** Cross Country Skiing and hologram at left

Date	Mintage	MS-63	Proof
2009 Proof	45,000	—	50.00

KM# 904 27.7800 g. 0.9250 Silver 0.8261 oz. ASW 40 mm. **Subject:** 2010 Vancouver Olympics **Obv:** Bust right **Obv. Designer:** Susanna Blunt **Rev:** Olympians holding torch, hologram at left

Date	Mintage	MS-63	Proof
2009 Proof	45,000	—	50.00

KM# 905 27.7800 g. 0.9250 Silver 0.8261 oz. ASW 40 mm. **Subject:** 2010 Vancouver Olympics **Obv:** Bust right **Obv. Designer:** Susanna Blunt **Rev:** Sled, hologram at left

Date	Mintage	MS-63	Proof
2009 Proof	45,000	—	50.00

KM# 906 27.7800 g. 0.9250 Silver 0.8261 oz. ASW 40 mm. **Subject:** 2010 Vancouver Olympics **Obv:** Bust right **Obv. Designer:** Susanna Blunt **Rev:** Ski Jumper, hologram at left

Date	Mintage	MS-63	Proof
2009 Proof	45,000	—	50.00

25 DOLLARS

KM# 907 27.7800 g. 0.9250 Silver 0.8261 oz. ASW
40 mm.   **Subject:** 2010 Vancouver Olympics
Obv: Bust right **Obv. Designer:** Susanna Blunt
Rev: Speed Skaters, hologram at left

Date	Mintage	MS-63	Proof
2009 Proof	45,000	—	50.00

KM# 1146 62.4100 g. 0.9999 Silver selectively gilt
2.0062 oz. ASW 60 mm.   **Obv:** Bust right **Rev:**
Toronto map and skyline, partilly gilt **Edge:** Reeded

Date	Mintage	MS-63	Proof
2011 Proof	Est. 7,500	—	180

KM# 1173 31.3900 g. 0.9999 Silver 1.0091 oz.
ASW 38 mm.   **Obv:** Bust right **Rev:** Wayne
Greskey skating right, father's portrait in circle at
right, 99 in hologram at lower right

Date	Mintage	MS-63	Proof
2011 Proof	—	—	85.00

30 DOLLARS

KM# 590 31.5000 g. 0.9250 Silver 0.9368 oz.
ASW   **Subject:** Pacific Northwest Wood Carvings
Obv: Head right **Rev:** Welcome figure totem pole

Date	Mintage	MS-63	Proof
2006 Proof	9,904	—	75.00

KM# 668 31.5000 g. 0.9250 Silver 0.9368 oz.
ASW   **Subject:** Canadarm and Col. C. Hadfield
Obv: Head right **Rev:** Hologram of Canadarm

Date	Mintage	MS-63	Proof
2006 Proof	9,357	—	90.00

KM# 669 31.5000 g. 0.9250 Silver 0.9368 oz.
ASW   **Subject:** National War Memorial **Obv:**
Head right **Rev:** Statue of three soldiers

Date	Mintage	MS-63	Proof
2006 Proof	8,876	—	85.00

KM# 670 31.5000 g. 0.9250 Silver 0.9368 oz.
ASW   **Subject:** Beaumont Hamel Newfoundland
Obv: Head right **Rev:** Caribou statue on rock
outcrop

Date	Mintage	MS-63	Proof
2006 Proof	15,325	—	95.00

KM# 671 31.5000 g. 0.9250 Silver 0.9368 oz.
ASW   **Obv:** Head right **Rev:** Dog Sled Team in color

Date	Mintage	MS-63	Proof
2006 Proof	7,384	—	85.00

KM# 739 31.5000 g. 0.9250 Silver 0.9368 oz. ASW
40 mm.   **Rev:** Niagra Falls panoramic hologram

Date	Mintage	MS-63	Proof
2007 Proof	7,384	—	85.00

KM#741 31.5000 g. 0.9250 Silver 0.9368 oz. ASW
40 mm. **Rev:** War Memorial, Vimy Ridge

Date	Mintage	MS-63	Proof
2007 Proof	5,335	—	85.00

KM#819 31.5000 g. 0.9250 Silver 0.9368 oz. ASW
40 mm. **Subject:** IMAX **Rev:** Youth reaching out
to shark on large screen

Date	Mintage	MS-63	Proof
2008 Proof	3,861	—	75.00

KM#895 33.7500 g. 0.9250 Silver 1.0037 oz. ASW
40 mm. **Subject:** International year of astronomy
Obv: Bust right **Obv. Legend:** Elizabeth II 30
Dollars DG Regina **Obv. Designer:** Susanna Blunt
Rev: Observatory with planets and colored sky **Rev.
Legend:** Canada **Rev. Designer:** Colin Mayne

Date	Mintage	MS-63	Proof
2009 Proof	7,174	—	90.00

50 DOLLARS

KM# 566 12.0000 g. 0.5833 Gold 0.2250 oz. AGW
27 mm. **Subject:** End of World War II, 60th
Anniversary **Obv:** Head right **Rev:** Large V and
three portraits

Date	Mintage	MS-63	Proof
2005 Specimen	4,000	—	375

KM# 672 31.1600 g. 0.9995 Palladium
1.0013 oz. **Subject:** Constellation in Spring sky
position **Rev:** Large Bear at top

Date	Mintage	MS-63	Proof
2006 Proof	297	—	1,250

KM# 673 31.1600 g. 0.9995 Palladium
1.0013 oz. **Subject:** Constellation in Summer sky
position **Rev:** Large Bear at left

Date	Mintage	MS-63	Proof
2006 Proof	296	—	1,250

KM# 674 31.1600 g. 0.9995 Palladium
1.0013 oz. **Subject:** Constellation in Autumn sky
position **Rev:** Large Bear towards bottom

Date	Mintage	MS-63	Proof
2006 Proof	296	—	1,250

50 DOLLARS

KM# 675 31.1600 g. 0.9995 Palladium
1.0013 oz.   **Subject:** Constellation in Winter sky
position **Rev:** Large Bear towards right

Date	Mintage	MS-63	Proof
2006 Proof	293	—	1,250

KM# 783 156.7700 g. 0.9990 Silver 5.0350 oz.
ASW 65 mm.   **Subject:** Ottawa Mint Centennial
1908-2008 **Rev:** Mint building facade **Note:** Photo
reduced.

Date	Mintage	MS-63	Proof
2008 Proof	2,078	—	400

KM# 709 155.5000 g. 0.9999 Silver 4.9987 oz.
ASW   **Subject:** Queen's 60th Wedding
Anniversary **Rev:** Coat of Arms and Mascots of
Elizabeth and Philip

Date	Mintage	MS-63	Proof
2007 Proof	1,957	—	350

KM# 896 156.7700 g. 0.9990 Silver 5.0350 oz.
ASW 65.25 mm.   **Subject:** 150 Anniversary of the
start of construction of the parliament buildings **Obv:**
Bust right **Obv. Legend:** Elizabeth II Canada DG
Regina **Obv. Designer:** Susanna Blunt **Rev:**
Incomplete west block, original architecture **Rev.
Legend:** 50 Dollars 1859-2009

Date	Mintage	MS-63	Proof
2009 Proof	910	—	450

KM# 1284 31.1050 g. 0.9990 Gold 0.9990 oz. AGW 30 mm. **Subject:** Year of the Dragon

Date	Mintage	MS-63	Proof
2012 Proof	—	—	1,750

KM# 1296 Gold **Obv:** Bust right **Obv. Designer:** Susana Blunt **Rev:** High relief bust **Note:** Ultra high relief

Date	Mintage	MS-63	Proof
2012	500	—	—

75 DOLLARS

KM# 567 31.4400 g. 0.4166 Gold 0.4211 oz. AGW 36.07 mm. **Subject:** Pope John Paul II **Obv:** Head right **Rev:** Pope giving blessing

Date	Mintage	MS-63	Proof
2005 Proof	1,870	—	825

KM# 747 12.0000 g. 0.5830 Gold 0.2249 oz. AGW 27 mm. **Subject:** Vancouver Olympics - Athletics Pride **Rev:** Athletics celebrating, holding flag aloft

Date	Mintage	MS-63	Proof
2007 Proof	4,524	—	440

KM# 748 12.0000 g. 0.5830 Gold 0.2249 oz. AGW 27 mm. **Obv:** Bust right **Obv. Designer:** Susanna Blunt **Rev:** Canada geese in flight left, multicolor

Date	Mintage	MS-63	Proof
2007 Proof	4,418	—	440

KM# 1008 157.6000 g. 0.9990 Silver 5.0617 oz. ASW 65.25 mm. **Subject:** 75th Anniverary of Canadian Bank Notes **Rev:** Female seated speaking into microphone **Note:** Photo reduced.

Date	Mintage	MS-63	Proof
2010 Proof	2,000	—	400

KM# 1243 156.7700 g. 0.9250 Silver 4.6621 oz. ASW 65.25 mm. **Subject:** Calgary Stampede

Date	Mintage	MS-63	Proof
2012	—	—	400

KM# 749 12.0000 g. 0.5830 Gold 0.2249 oz. AGW 27 mm. **Rev:** Mountie, multicolor

Date	Mintage	MS-63	Proof
2007 Proof	6,687	—	440

KM# 820 12.0000 g. 0.5830 Gold partially silver plated 0.2249 oz. AGW 27 mm. **Rev:** 2010 Olympic Inukshuk Stone man, partially silver plated

Date	Mintage	MS-63	P/L	Proof
2008 Proof	—	—	—	420

KM# 821 12.0000 g. 0.5830 Gold 0.2249 oz. AGW 27 mm. **Rev:** Four Host Nations mask emblems, colored **Rev. Designer:** Jody Broomfield

Date	Mintage	MS-63	Proof
2008 Proof	8,000	—	440

KM# 947 12.0000 g. 0.5830 Gold 0.2249 oz. AGW 27 mm. **Subject:** Vancouver Olympics **Rev:** Tent building at Olympic site, color

Date	Mintage	MS-63	Proof
2008 Proof	8,000	—	440

KM# 908 12.0000 g. 0.5830 Gold 0.2249 oz. AGW 27 mm. **Subject:** 2010 Vancouver Olympics **Obv:** Bust right **Obv. Designer:** Susana Blunt **Rev:** Multicolor moose

Date	Mintage	MS-63	Proof
2009 Proof	4,075	—	440

KM# 909 12.0000 g. 0.5830 Gold 0.2249 oz. AGW 27 mm. **Subject:** 2010 Vancouver Olympics **Obv:** Bust right **Obv. Designer:** Susanna Blunt **Rev:** Multicolor athletics and torch

Date	Mintage	MS-63	Proof
2009 Proof	4,479	—	440

KM# 910 12.0000 g. 0.5830 Gold 0.2249 oz. AGW 27 mm. **Subject:** 2010 Vancouver Olympics **Obv:** Bust right **Obv. Designer:** Susanna Blunt **Rev:** Wolf, multicolor

Date	Mintage	MS-63	Proof
2009 Proof	4,161	—	440

KM# 1002 12.0000 g. 0.5830 Gold 0.2249 oz. AGW 27 mm. **Rev:** Spring color maple leaves

Date	Mintage	MS-63	Proof
2010 Proof	1,000	—	500

KM# 1003 12.0000 g. 0.5830 Gold 0.2249 oz. AGW 27 mm. **Rev:** Summer color maple leaves

Date	Mintage	MS-63	Proof
2010 Proof	1,000	—	500

KM# 1004 12.0000 g. 0.5830 Gold 0.2249 oz.
AGW 27 mm. **Rev:** Fall color maple leaves

Date	Mintage	MS-63	Proof
2010 Proof	1,000	—	500

KM# 1005 12.0000 g. 0.5830 Gold 0.2249 oz.
AGW 27 mm. **Rev:** Winter color maple leaves

Date	Mintage	MS-63	Proof
2010 Proof	1,000	—	500

100 DOLLARS

KM# 115 13.3375 g. 0.5830 Gold 0.2500 oz. AGW
27 mm. **Subject:** 1976 Montreal Olympics **Obv:**
Young bust right, maple leaf below, date at right,
beaded borders **Rev:** Past and present Olympic
figures, denomination at right **Rev. Designer:** Dora
dePedery-Hunt

Date	Mintage	MS-63	Proof
1976	650,000	475	—

KM# 116 16.9655 g. 0.9170 Gold 0.5002 oz. AGW
25 mm. **Subject:** 1976 Montreal Olympics **Obv:**
Young bust right, maple leaf below, date at right,
plain borders **Rev:** Past and present Olympic
figures, denomination at right **Rev. Designer:** Dora
dePedery-Hunt

Date	Mintage	MS-63	Proof
1976 Proof	337,342	—	950

KM# 119 16.9655 g. 0.9170 Gold 0.5002 oz.
AGW **Subject:** Queen's silver jubilee **Obv:** Young
bust right **Rev:** Bouquet of provincial flowers,
denomination below **Rev. Designer:** Raymond Lee

Date	Mintage	MS-63	Proof
1952-1977 Proof	180,396	—	950

KM# 122 16.9655 g. 0.9170 Gold 0.5002 oz.
AGW **Subject:** Canadian unification **Obv:** Young
bust right, denomination at left, date upper right **Rev:**
Geese (representing the provinces) in flight
formation **Rev. Designer:** Roger Savage

Date	Mintage	MS-63	Proof
1978 Proof	200,000	—	950

KM# 126 16.9655 g. 0.9170 Gold 0.5002 oz.
AGW **Subject:** International Year of the Child
Obv: Young bust right **Rev:** Children with hands
joined divide denomination and date **Rev.
Designer:** Carola Tietz

Date	Mintage	MS-63	Proof
1979 Proof	250,000	—	950

KM# 129 16.9655 g. 0.9170 Gold 0.5002 oz.
AGW **Subject:** Arctic Territories **Obv:** Young bust
right, denomination at left, date above right **Rev:**
Kayaker **Rev. Designer:** Arnaldo Marchetti

Date	Mintage	MS-63	Proof
1980 Proof	300,000	—	950

KM# 131 16.9655 g. 0.9170 Gold 0.5002 oz.
AGW   **Subject:** National anthem **Obv:** Young bust
right, denomination at left, date above right **Rev:**
Music score on map **Rev. Designer:** Roger Savage

Date	Mintage	MS-63	Proof
1981 Proof	102,000	—	950

KM# 137 16.9655 g. 0.9170 Gold 0.5002 oz.
AGW   **Subject:** New Constitution **Obv:** Young
bust right, denomination at left **Rev:** Open book,
maple leaf on right page, date below **Rev. Designer:**
Friedrich Peter

Date	Mintage	MS-63	Proof
1982 Proof	121,708	—	950

KM# 139 16.9655 g. 0.9170 Gold 0.5002 oz.
AGW   **Subject:** 400th Anniversary of St. John's,
Newfoundland **Obv:** Young bust right **Rev:** Anchor
divides building and ship, denomination below,
dates above **Rev. Designer:** John Jaciw

Date	Mintage	MS-63	Proof
1583-1983 Proof	83,128	—	950

KM# 142 16.9655 g. 0.9170 Gold 0.5002 oz.
AGW   **Subject:** Jacques Cartier **Obv:** Young bust
right **Rev:** Cartier head on right facing left, ship on
left, date lower right, denomination above **Rev.
Designer:** Carola Tietz

Date	Mintage	MS-63	Proof
1534-1984 Proof	67,662	—	950

KM# 144 16.9655 g. 0.9170 Gold 0.5002 oz.
AGW   **Subject:** National Parks **Obv:** Young bust
right **Rev:** Bighorn sheep, denomination divides
dates below **Rev. Designer:** Hector Greville

Date	Mintage	MS-63	Proof
1885-1985 Proof	61,332	—	950

KM# 152 16.9655 g. 0.9170 Gold 0.5002 oz.
AGW   **Subject:** Peace **Obv:** Young bust right **Rev:**
Maple leaves and letters intertwined, date at right,
denomination below **Rev. Designer:** Dora
dePedery-Hunt

Date	Mintage	MS-63	Proof
1986 Proof	76,409	—	950

KM# 158 13.3375 g. 0.5830 Gold 0.2500 oz.
AGW   **Subject:** 1988 Calgary Olympics **Obv:**
Young bust right, maple leaf below, date at right
Rev: Torch and logo, denomination below **Rev.
Designer:** Friedrich Peter **Edge Lettering:** In
English and French

Date	Mintage	MS-63	Proof
1987 Proof, letter edge	142,750	—	475
1987 Proof, plain edge	Inc. above	—	475

KM# 162 13.3375 g. 0.5830 Gold 0.2500 oz.
AGW   **Subject:** Bowhead Whales, balaera
mysticetus **Rev:** Whales left, date below, within
circle, denomination below **Rev. Designer:** Robert
R. Carmichael

Date	Mintage	MS-63	Proof
1988 Proof	52,594	—	475

KM# 169 13.3375 g. 0.5830 Gold 0.2500 oz.
AGW **Subject:** Sainte-Marie **Obv:** Young bust
right **Rev:** Huron Indian, Missionary and Mission
building, denomination below, dates above **Rev.
Designer:** D. J. Craig

Date	Mintage	MS-63	Proof
1639-1989 Proof	59,657	—	475

KM# 171 13.3375 g. 0.5830 Gold 0.2500 oz.
AGW **Subject:** International Literacy Year **Obv:**
Crowned head right, date below **Rev:** Woman with
children, denomination below **Rev. Designer:** John
Mardon

Date	Mintage	MS-63	Proof
1990 Proof	49,940	—	475

KM# 180 13.3375 g. 0.5830 Gold 0.2500 oz.
AGW **Subject:** S.S. Empress of India **Obv:**
Crowned head right, date below **Rev:** Ship, "SS
Empress", denomination below **Rev. Designer:**
Karsten Smith

Date	Mintage	MS-63	Proof
1991 Proof	33,966	—	475

KM# 211 13.3375 g. 0.5830 Gold 0.2500 oz.
AGW **Subject:** Montreal **Obv:** Crowned head
right, date below **Rev:** Half figure in foreground with
paper, buildings in back, denomination below **Rev.
Designer:** Stewart Sherwood

Date	Mintage	MS-63	Proof
1992 Proof	28,162	—	475

KM# 245 13.3375 g. 0.5830 Gold 0.2500 oz.
AGW **Subject:** Antique Automobiles **Obv:**
Crowned head right, date below **Rev:** German Bene
Victoria; Simmonds Steam Carriage; French
Panhard-Levassor's Daimler; American Duryea;
Canadian Featherston Haugh in center,
denomination below **Rev. Designer:** John Mardon

Date	Mintage	MS-63	Proof
1993 Proof	25,971	—	475

KM# 249 13.3375 g. 0.5830 Gold 0.2500 oz.
AGW **Subject:** World War II Home Front **Obv:**
Crowned head right, date below **Rev:** Kneeling
figure working on plane, denomination below **Rev.
Designer:** Paraskeva Clark

Date	Mintage	MS-63	Proof
1994 Proof	16,201	—	475

KM# 260 13.3375 g. 0.5830 Gold 0.2500 oz.
AGW **Subject:** Louisbourg **Obv:** Crowned head
right, date below **Rev:** Ship and buildings, dates and
denomination above **Rev. Designer:** Lewis Parker

Date	Mintage	MS-63	Proof
1995 Proof	16,916	—	475

KM# 273 13.3375 g. 0.5830 Gold 0.2500 oz.
AGW **Subject:** Klondike Gold Rush Centennial
Obv: Crowned head right, date below **Rev:** Scene

of Kate Carmack panning for gold, dates above, denomination lower left **Rev. Designer:** John Mantha

Date	Mintage	MS-63	Proof
1896-1996 Proof	17,973	—	450

KM# 287 13.3375 g. 0.5830 Gold 0.2500 oz. AGW **Subject:** Alexander Graham Bell **Obv:** Crowned head right, date below **Rev:** A. G. Bell head right, globe and telephone, denomination upper right **Rev. Designer:** Donald H. Carley

Date	Mintage	MS-63	Proof
1997 Proof	14,775	—	475

KM# 307 13.3375 g. 0.5830 Gold 0.2500 oz. AGW **Subject:** Discovery of Insulin **Obv:** Crowned head right, date below **Rev:** Nobel prize award figurine, dates at left, denomination at right **Rev. Designer:** Robert R. Carmichael

Date	Mintage	MS-63	Proof
1998 Proof	11,220	—	475

KM# 341 13.3375 g. 0.5830 Gold 0.2500 oz. AGW **Subject:** 50th Anniversary Newfoundland Unity With Canada **Obv:** Crowned head right, date below **Rev:** Two designs at front, mountains in back, denomination below **Rev. Designer:** Jackie Gale-Vaillancourt

Date	Mintage	MS-63	Proof
1999 Proof	10,242	—	475

KM# 402 13.3375 g. 0.5830 Gold 0.2500 oz. AGW 27 mm. **Subject:** McClure's Arctic expedition **Obv:** Crowned head right, date below **Rev:** Six men pulling supply sled to an icebound ship, denomination below **Rev. Designer:** John Mardon **Edge:** Reeded

Date	Mintage	MS-63	Proof
2000 Proof	9,767	—	475

KM# 416 13.3375 g. 0.5830 Gold alloyed with 5.5579 g of .999 Silver, .1787 oz ASW 0.2500 oz. AGW 27 mm. **Subject:** Library of Parliament **Obv:** Crowned head right **Obv. Designer:** Dora dePedery-Hunt **Rev:** Statue in domed building **Rev. Designer:** Robert R. Carmichael **Edge:** Reeded

Date	Mintage	MS-63	Proof
2001 Proof	8,080	—	475

KM# 452 13.3375 g. 0.5830 Gold 0.2500 oz. AGW 27 mm. **Subject:** Discovery of Oil in Alberta **Obv:** Crowned head right **Rev:** Oil well with black oil spill on ground **Rev. Designer:** John Marden **Edge:** Reeded

Date	Mintage	MS-63	Proof
2002 Proof	9,994	—	475

KM# 486 13.3375 g. 0.5830 Gold 0.2500 oz. AGW **Subject:** 100th Anniversary of the Discovery of Marquis Wheat **Obv:** Head right

Date	Mintage	MS-63	Proof
2003 Proof	9,993	—	475

KM# 528 12.0000 g. 0.5830 Gold 0.2249 oz. AGW **Subject:** St. Lawrence Seaway, 50th Anniversary **Obv:** Head right

Date	Mintage	MS-63	Proof
2004 Proof	7,454	—	425

KM# 593 12.0000 g. 0.5833 Gold 0.2250 oz. AGW **Subject:** 130th Anniversary, Supreme Court **Obv:** Head right

Date	Mintage	MS-63	Proof
2005 Proof	5,092	—	425

KM# 591 12.0000 g. 0.5833 Gold 0.2250 oz.
AGW **Subject:** 75th Anniversary, Hockey Classic
between Royal Military College and U.S. Military
Academy **Obv:** Head right

Date	Mintage	MS-63	Proof
2006 Proof	5,439	—	425

KM# 689 12.0000 g. 0.5833 Gold 0.2250 oz. AGW
27 mm. **Subject:** 140th Anniversary Dominion
Obv: Head right

Date	Mintage	MS-63	Proof
2007 Proof	4,453	—	425

KM# 823 12.0000 g. 0.5830 Gold 0.2249 oz. AGW
27 mm. **Rev:** Fraser River

Date	Mintage	MS-63	Proof
2008 Proof	3,089	—	425

KM# 898 12.0000 g. 0.5830 Gold 0.2249 oz. AGW
27 mm. **Subject:** 10th Anniversary of Nunavut
Obv: Bust right **Obv. Legend:** Elizabeth II DG
Regina **Obv. Designer:** Susanna Blunt **Rev:** Inuit
dancer with 3 faces behind **Rev. Legend:** Canada
100 Dollars 1999-2009

Date	Mintage	MS-63	Proof
2009 Proof	2,309	—	425

KM# 997 12.0000 g. 0.5830 Gold 0.2249 oz. AGW
27 mm. **Rev:** Henry Hudson, Map of Hudson's
Bay **Rev. Designer:** John Mantha

Date	Mintage	MS-63	Proof
2010 Proof	Est. 5,000	—	425

KM# 1073 12.0000 g. 0.5830 Gold 0.2249 oz.
AGW 27 mm. **Subject:** Canadian Railroads,
175th Anniversary **Rev:** Early steam locomotive

Date	Mintage	MS-63	Proof
2011	3,000	—	425

150 DOLLARS

KM# 388 13.6100 g. 0.7500 Gold 0.3282 oz.
AGW **Subject:** Year of the Dragon **Obv:** Crowned
head right **Rev. Designer:** Harvey Chan

Date	Mintage	MS-63	Proof
2000 Proof	8,851	—	625

KM# 417 13.6100 g. 0.7500 Gold 0.3282 oz. AGW
28 mm. **Subject:** Year of the Snake **Obv:**
Crowned head right **Obv. Designer:** Dora
dePedery-Hunt **Rev:** Multicolor snake hologram
Edge: Reeded

Date	Mintage	MS-63	Proof
2001 Proof	6,571	—	625

KM# 604 13.6100 g. 0.7500 Gold 0.3282 oz.
AGW **Obv:** Head right **Rev:** Stylized horse left

Date	Mintage	MS-63	Proof
2002 Proof	6,843	—	625

KM# 487 13.6100 g. 0.7500 Gold 0.3282 oz. AGW
28 mm. **Subject:** Year of the Ram **Obv:** Crowned
head right **Rev:** Stylized ram left, hologram **Rev.
Designer:** Harvey Chan

Date	Mintage	MS-63	Proof
2003 Proof	3,927	—	625

KM# 614 13.6100 g. 0.7500 Gold 0.3282 oz.
AGW **Obv:** Head right **Rev:** Year of the Monkey,
hologram

Date	Mintage	MS-63	Proof
2004 Proof	3,392	—	625

KM# 568 13.6100 g. 0.7500 Gold 0.3282 oz.
AGW **Subject:** Year of the Rooster **Obv:** Head
right **Rev:** Rooster left, hologram

Date	Mintage	MS-63	Proof
2005 Proof	3,731	—	625

KM# 592 13.6100 g. 0.7500 Gold 0.3282 oz. AGW
28 mm. **Subject:** Year of the Dog, hologram **Obv:**
Head right **Rev:** Stylized dog left

Date	Mintage	MS-63	Proof
2006 Proof	2,604	—	625

KM# 733 11.8400 g. 0.7500 Gold 0.2855 oz. AGW
28 mm. **Subject:** Year of the Pig **Obv:** Head right
Rev: Pig in center with Chinese lunar calendar
around, hologram

Date	Mintage	MS-63	Proof
2007 Proof	826	—	733

KM# 802 11.8400 g. 0.7500 Gold 0.2855 oz. AGW
28 mm. **Subject:** Year of the Rat **Rev:** Rat,
hologram

Date	Mintage	MS-63	Proof
2008 Proof	582	—	550

KM# 899 10.4000 g. 0.9990 Gold 0.3340 oz. AGW
22.5 mm. **Subject:** Blessings of wealth **Obv:** Bust
right **Obv. Legend:** Elizabeth II, DG Regina, Fine
Gold 99999 or PUR **Obv. Designer:** Susanna Blunt
Rev: Three goldfish surround peony, clouds **Rev.
Legend:** Canada 150 Dollars (Chinese symbols of
good fortune) **Rev. Designer:** Harvey Chan **Edge:**
Scalloped

Date	Mintage	MS-63	Proof
2009 Proof	1,273	—	650

KM# 867 11.8400 g. 0.7500 Gold 0.2855 oz. AGW
28 mm. **Subject:** Year of the Ox **Rev:** Ox, hologram

Date	Mintage	MS-63	Proof
2009 Proof	486	—	550

KM# 979 11.8400 g. 0.7500 Gold 0.2855 oz. AGW
28 mm. **Subject:** Year of the Tiger **Rev:** Tiger in
hologram

Date	Mintage	MS-63	Proof
2010 Proof	1,507	—	550

KM# 1030 10.4000 g. 0.9999 Gold 0.3343 oz.
AGW **Subject:** Blessing of Wealth **Shape:**
Scalloped

Date	Mintage	MS-63	Proof
2010 Proof	1,388	—	650

KM# 1031 Gold **Subject:** Year of the Tiger **Rev:**
Tiger walking

Date	Mintage	MS-63	Proof
2010 Proof	2,500	—	600

KM# 1053 13.6100 g. 0.7500 Gold 0.3282 oz.
AGW 28 mm. **Subject:** Year of the rabbit **Rev:**
Rabbit hologram

Date	Mintage	MS-63	Proof
2011 Proof	Est. 4,888	—	600

KM# 1184 13.6100 g. 0.7500 Gold 0.3282 oz.
AGW 28 mm. **Subject:** Year of the Dragon **Obv:**
Bust right **Rev:** Dragon left

Date	Mintage	MS-63	Proof
2012 Proof	—	—	650

KM# 1262 10.4000 g. 0.9990 Gold 0.3340 oz.
AGW 22.5 mm. **Subject:** Good Fortune Panda

Date	Mintage	MS-63	Proof
2012 Proof	—	—	650

175 DOLLARS

KM# 217 16.9700 g. 0.9170 Gold 0.5003 oz.
AGW **Subject:** 1992 Olympics **Obv:** Crowned
head right, date at left, denomination below **Rev:**
Passing the torch **Rev. Designer:** Stewart
Sherwood **Edge:** Lettered

Date	Mintage	MS-63	Proof
1992 Proof	22,092	—	950

200 DOLLARS

KM# 178 17.1350 g. 0.9166 Gold 0.5049 oz. AGW
29 mm. **Subject:** Canadian flag silver jubilee
Obv: Crowned head right, date below **Rev:** People
with flag, denomination above **Rev. Designer:**
Stewart Sherwood

Date	Mintage	MS-63	Proof
1990 Proof	20,980	—	975

KM# 202 17.1350 g. 0.9166 Gold 0.5049 oz. AGW
29 mm. **Subject:** Hockey **Obv:** Crowned head
right **Rev:** Hockey players, denomination above
Rev. Designer: Stewart Sherwood

Date	Mintage	MS-63	Proof
1991 Proof	10,215	—	975

KM# 230 17.1350 g. 0.9166 Gold 0.5049 oz. AGW
29 mm. **Subject:** Niagara Falls **Obv:** Crowned
head right **Rev:** Niagara Falls, denomination above
Rev. Designer: John Mardon

Date	Mintage	MS-63	Proof
1992 Proof	9,465	—	975

KM# 244 17.1350 g. 0.9166 Gold 0.5049 oz. AGW
29 mm. **Subject:** Mounted police **Obv:** Crowned
head right, date below **Rev:** Mountie with children,
denomination above **Rev. Designer:** Stewart
Sherwood

Date	Mintage	MS-63	Proof
1993 Proof	10,807	—	975

KM# 250 17.1350 g. 0.9166 Gold 0.5049 oz. AGW
29 mm. **Subject:** Interpretation of 1908 novel by
Lucy Maud Montgomery, 1874-1942, Anne of Green
Gables **Obv:** Crowned head right **Rev:** Figure sitting
in window, denomination above **Rev. Designer:**
Phoebe Gilman

Date	Mintage	MS-63	Proof
1994 Proof	10,655	—	975

200 DOLLARS

KM# 265 17.1350 g. 0.9166 Gold 0.5049 oz. AGW
29 mm. **Subject:** Maple-syrup production **Obv:**
Crowned head right, date below **Rev:** Maple syrup
making, denomination at right **Rev. Designer:** J. D.
Mantha

Date	Mintage	MS-63	Proof
1995 Proof	6,579	—	975

KM# 275 17.1350 g. 0.9166 Gold 0.5049 oz. AGW
29 mm. **Subject:** Transcontinental Canadian
Railway **Obv:** Crowned head right, date below **Rev:**
Train going through mountains, denomination below
Rev. Designer: Suzanne Duranceau

Date	Mintage	MS-63	Proof
1996 Proof	8,047	—	975

KM# 288 17.1350 g. 0.9166 Gold 0.5049 oz. AGW
29 mm. **Subject:** Haida mask **Obv:** Crowned
head right, date below **Rev:** Haida mask **Rev.
Designer:** Robert Davidson

Date	Mintage	MS-63	Proof
1997 Proof	11,610	—	975

KM# 317 17.1350 g. 0.9166 Gold 0.5049 oz. AGW
29 mm. **Subject:** Legendary white buffalo **Obv:**
Crowned head right, date below **Rev:** Buffalo **Rev.
Designer:** Alex Janvler

Date	Mintage	MS-63	Proof
1998 Proof	7,149	—	975

KM# 358 17.1350 g. 0.9166 Gold 0.5049 oz. AGW
29 mm. **Subject:** Mikmaq butterfly **Obv:** Crowned
head right **Rev:** Butterfly within design **Rev.
Designer:** Alan Syliboy

Date	Mintage	MS-63	Proof
1999 Proof	6,510	—	975

KM# 403 17.1350 g. 0.9166 Gold 0.5049 oz. AGW
29 mm. **Subject:** Motherhood **Obv:** Crowned
head right, date above, denomination at right **Rev:**
Inuit mother with infant **Rev. Designer:** Germaine
Arnaktauyak **Edge:** Reeded

Date	Mintage	MS-63	Proof
2000 Proof	6,284	—	975

KM# 418 17.1350 g. 0.9166 Gold 0.5049 oz. AGW
29 mm. **Subject:** Cornelius D. Krieghoff's "The
Habitant farm" **Obv:** Queens head right **Edge:**
Reeded

Date	Mintage	MS-63	Proof
2001 Proof	5,406	—	975

KM# 466 17.1350 g. 0.9166 Gold 0.5049 oz. AGW
29 mm. **Subject:** Thomas Thompson "The Jack
Pine" (1916-17) **Obv:** Crowned head right

Date	Mintage	MS-63	Proof
2002 Proof	5,264	—	975

KM# 488 17.1350 g. 0.9166 Gold 0.5049 oz.
AGW   **Subject:** Fitzgerald's "Houses" (1929)
Obv: Crowned head right **Rev:** House with trees

Date	Mintage	MS-63	Proof
2003 Proof	4,118	—	975

KM# 516 16.0000 g. 0.9166 Gold 0.4715 oz. AGW
29 mm.   **Subject:** "Fragments" **Obv:** Crowned
head right **Rev:** Fragmented face **Edge:** Reeded

Date	Mintage	MS-63	Proof
2004 Proof	3,917	—	900

KM# 569 16.0000 g. 0.9166 Gold 0.4715 oz.
AGW   **Subject:** Fur traders **Obv:** Head right **Rev:**
Men in canoe riding wave

Date	Mintage	MS-63	Proof
2005 Proof	3,669	—	900

KM# 594 16.0000 g. 0.9166 Gold 0.4715 oz.
AGW   **Subject:** Timber trade **Obv:** Head right
Rev: Lumberjacks felling tree

Date	Mintage	MS-63	Proof
2006 Proof	3,218	—	900

KM# 691 16.0000 g. 0.9166 Gold 0.4715 oz. AGW
29 mm.   **Subject:** Fishing Trade **Obv:** Head right
Rev: Two fishermen hauling net

Date	Mintage	MS-63	Proof
2007 Proof	2,137	—	900

KM# 824 16.0000 g. 0.9170 Gold 0.4717 oz. AGW
29 mm.   **Subject:** Commerce **Rev:** Horse drawn
plow

Date	Mintage	MS-63	Proof
2008 Proof	1,951	—	900

KM# 894 16.0000 g. 0.9160 Gold 0.4712 oz. AGW
29 mm.   **Subject:** Coal mining trade **Obv:** Bust
right **Obv. Legend:** Elizabeth II DG Regina **Obv.**
Designer: Susanna Blunt **Rev:** Miner pushing cart
with black coal **Rev. Legend:** Canada 200 Dollars
Rev. Designer: John Marder

Date	Mintage	MS-63	Proof
2009 Proof	2,241	—	900

KM# 1000 16.0000 g. 0.9160 Gold 0.4712 oz.
AGW 29 mm.   **Subject:** Petroleum and Oil Trade
Rev: Oil railcar and well head

Date	Mintage	MS-63	Proof
2010 Proof	Est. 4,000	—	900

KM# 1060 16.0000 g. 0.9167 Gold 0.4715 oz.
AGW 29 mm.   **Rev:** Olympic athletics with medal,
flag and flowers

Date	Mintage	MS-63	Proof
2010 Proof	—	—	900

KM# 1074 16.0000 g. 0.9167 Gold 0.4715 oz.
AGW 29 mm.   **Rev:** SS Beaver - Seam Sail ship
Rev. Designer: John Mardon

Date	Mintage	MS-63	Proof
2011 Proof	2,800	—	900

KM# 1143 16.0000 g. 0.9167 Gold 0.4715 oz.
AGW 27 mm.   **Subject:** Wedding, Prince William
and Katherine Middleton **Obv:** Bust right **Rev:** Half-
length figures facing, swarovski crystal **Edge:**
Reeded

Date	Mintage	MS-63	Proof
2011 Proof	2,000	—	900

KM# 1174 16.0000 g. 0.9160 Gold 0.4712 oz.
AGW 29 mm.   **Obv:** Bust right **Rev:** Wayne
Greskey skating right, father's portrait in circle at
right, 99 in color at lower right **Rev. Designer:** Glen
Green

Date	Mintage	MS-63	Proof
2011 Proof	999	—	900

KM# 1219 16.0000 g. 0.9167 Gold 0.4715 oz.
AGW 29 mm.   **Obv:** Bust right **Rev:** Prospector
panning for gold in stream

Date	Mintage	MS-63	Proof
2012 Proof	—	—	900

KM# 1223 16.0000 g. 0.9167 Gold 0.4715 oz.
AGW 29 mm.   **Obv:** Bust right **Rev:** Vikings and
ship

Date	Mintage	MS-63	Proof
2012 Proof	—	—	900

KM# 1279 31.1050 g. 0.9990 Gold 0.9990 oz.
AGW 30 mm.   **Subject:** Bateman Moose

Date	Mintage	MS-63	Proof
2012 Proof	—	—	1,850

250 DOLLARS

KM# 677 45.0000 g. 0.5833 Gold 0.8439 oz. AGW
40 mm.   **Rev:** Dog Sled Team

Date	Mintage	MS-63	Proof
2006 Proof	953	—	1,625

KM# 751 1000.0000 g. 0.9999 Silver 32.146 oz.
ASW 101.6 mm.   **Subject:** Vancouver Olympics,
2010 **Rev:** Early Canada motif **Note:** Illustration
reduced.

Date	Mintage	MS-63	Proof
2007 Proof	2,500	—	1,250

KM# 833 1000.0000 g. 0.9990 Silver 32.117 oz.
ASW 101.6 mm. **Subject:** Vancouver Olympics
2010 **Rev:** Towards confederation **Note:** Illustration
reduced.

Date	Mintage	MS-63	Proof
2008 Proof	2,500	—	1,350

KM# 981 1000.0000 g. 0.9990 Silver 32.117 oz.
ASW 101.6 mm. **Rev:** Eagle head

Date	Mintage	MS-63	Proof
2010 Antique Patina	500	1,350	—
2010 Proof	500	—	1,400

KM# 913 1000.0000 g. 0.9999 Silver 32.146 oz.
ASW 101.5 mm. **Obv. Designer:**
Susanna Blunt **Rev:** Mask with fish - Surviving the
flood **Note:** Illustration reduced.

Date	Mintage	MS-63	Proof
2009 Proof	815	—	1,350

KM# 981a 1000.0000 g. 0.9990 Silver 32.117 oz.
ASW 101.6 mm. **Rev:** Eagle head, blue enamel

Date	Mintage	MS-63	Proof
2010 Proof	500	—	1,400

KM# 949 1000.0000 g. 0.9990 Silver 32.117 oz.
ASW 101.6 mm. **Rev:** Modern Canada

Date	Mintage	MS-63	Proof
2009 Proof	905	—	1,350

KM# 1044 1000.0000 g. 0.9990 Silver 32.117 oz. ASW 101.6 mm.   **Subject:** Baniff, 125th Anniversary of resort founding **Rev:** Features of Baniff

Date	Mintage	MS-63	Proof
2010 Proof	750	—	1,650

KM# 1285 1000.0000 g. 0.9990 Silver 32.117 oz. ASW 101 mm.   **Subject:** Olympic views

Date	Mintage	MS-63	Proof
2010 Proof	—	—	1,350

KM# 1150 1000.0000 g. 0.9999 Silver 32.146 oz. ASW 100 mm.   **Rev:** Lacrosse

Date	Mintage	MS-63	Proof
2011 Proof	—	—	1,350

KM# 1185 1000.0000 g. 0.9990 Silver 32.117 oz. ASW 101.6 mm.   **Subject:** Year of the Dragon **Obv:** Bust left **Rev:** Dragon left

Date	Mintage	MS-63	Proof
2012 Proof	—	—	1,550

KM# 1277 1000.0000 g. 0.9990 Silver 32.117 oz. ASW 101 mm.   **Subject:** Bateman Moose

Date	Mintage	MS-63	Proof
2012 Proof	—	—	1,650

300 DOLLARS

KM# 501 60.0000 g. 0.5833 Gold 1.1252 oz. AGW 50 mm.   **Obv:** Triple cameo portraits of Queen Elizabeth II by Gillick, Machin and de Pedery-Hunt, each in 14K gold, rose in center **Rev:** Dates "1952-2002" and denomination in legend, rose in center **Note:** Housed in anodized gold-colored aluminum box with cherrywood stained siding

Date	Mintage	MS-63	Proof
1952-2002 Proof	999	—	2,150

KM# 570.5 45.0000 g. 0.5830 Gold 0.8434 oz.
AGW 40 mm. **Subject:** Standard Time - Atlantic
8 AM **Obv:** Head right **Rev:** Roman numeral clock
with world inside

Date	Mintage	MS-63	Proof
2005 Proof	200	—	1,650

KM# 570.6 45.0000 g. 0.5830 Gold 0.8434 oz.
AGW 40 mm. **Subject:** Standard Time -
Newfoundland 8:30 **Obv:** Head right **Rev:** Roman
numeral clock with world inside

Date	Mintage	MS-63	Proof
2005 Proof	200	—	1,650

KM# 596 60.0000 g. 0.5833 Gold 1.1252 oz. AGW
50 mm. **Subject:** Shinplaster **Obv:** Head right
Rev: Britannia bust, spear over shoulder

Date	Mintage	MS-63	Proof
2005 Proof	994	—	2,150

KM# 517 60.0000 g. 0.5833 Gold 1.1252 oz. AGW
50 mm. **Obv:** Four coinage portraits of Elizabeth
II **Rev:** Canadian arms above value **Edge:** Plain

Date	Mintage	MS-63	Proof
2004 Proof	998	—	2,150

KM# 600 60.0000 g. 0.5833 Gold 1.1252 oz. AGW
40 mm. **Subject:** Welcome Figure Totem Pole
Obv: Head right **Rev:** Men with totem pole

Date	Mintage	MS-63	Proof
2005 Proof	948	—	2,150

KM# 570.1 45.0000 g. 0.5833 Gold 0.8439 oz.
AGW 40 mm. **Subject:** Standard Time - 4 AM
Pacific **Obv:** Head right **Rev:** Roman numeral clock
with world inside

Date	Mintage	MS-63	Proof
2005 Proof	200	—	1,650

KM# 570.2 45.0000 g. 0.5830 Gold 0.8434 oz.
AGW 40 mm. **Subject:** Standard Time - Mountian
5 AM **Obv:** Head right **Rev:** Roman numeral clock
with world inside.

Date	Mintage	MS-63	Proof
2005 Proof	200	—	1,650

KM# 570.3 45.0000 g. 0.5830 Gold 0.8434 oz.
AGW 40 mm. **Subject:** Standard Time - Central
6 PM **Obv:** Head right **Rev:** Roman numeral clock
with world inside

Date	Mintage	MS-63	Proof
2005 Proof	200	—	1,650

KM# 570.4 45.0000 g. 0.5830 Gold 0.8434 oz.
AGW 40 mm. **Subject:** Standard Time - Eastern
7 AM **Obv:** Head right **Rev:** Roman numeral clock
with world inside

Date	Mintage	MS-63	Proof
2005 Proof	200	—	1,650

KM# 678 45.0000 g. 0.5833 Gold 0.8439 oz. AGW
40 mm. **Rev:** Hologram of Canadarm, Col. C.
Hadfield in spacewalk

Date	Mintage	MS-63	Proof
2006 Proof	581	—	1,650

KM# 679 60.0000 g. 0.5833 Gold 1.1252 oz. AGW
50 mm. **Subject:** Queen Elizabeth's 80th
Birthday **Rev:** State Crown, colorized

Date	Mintage	MS-63	Proof
2006 Proof	996	—	2,150

KM# 680 60.0000 g. 0.5833 Gold 1.1252 oz. AGW
50 mm. **Subject:** Crystal Snowflake

Date	Mintage	MS-63	Proof
2006 Proof	998	—	2,150

KM# 595 60.0000 g. 0.5833 Gold 1.1252 oz. AGW
50 mm. **Subject:** Shinplaster **Obv:** Head right
Rev: Seated Britannia with shield

Date	Mintage	MS-63	Proof
2006 Proof	940	—	2,150

KM# 692 60.0000 g. 0.5833 Gold 1.1252 oz. AGW
50 mm. **Subject:** Shinplaster **Rev:** 1923 25 cent
bank note

Date	Mintage	MS-63	Proof
2007 Proof	778	—	2,150

KM# 740 45.0000 g. 0.5830 Gold 0.8434 oz. AGW
40 mm. **Rev:** Canadian Rockies panoramic
hologram

Date	Mintage	MS-63	Proof
2007 Proof	511	—	1,750

KM# 826 60.0000 g. 0.5830 Gold 1.1246 oz. AGW
50 mm. **Rev:** Newfoundland and Labrador Coat of Arms

Date	Mintage	MS-63	Proof
2008 Proof	472	—	2,150

KM# 827 45.0000 g. 0.5830 Gold 0.8434 oz. AGW
40 mm. **Subject:** Canadian achievements IMAX
Rev: Kid in audience reaching out to shark on big
screen

Date	Mintage	MS-63	Proof
2008 Proof	—	—	1,650

KM# 828 60.0000 g. 0.5830 Gold 1.1246 oz. AGW
50 mm. **Rev:** Four seasons moon mask in color,
blue design in border

Date	Mintage	MS-63	Proof
2008 Proof	544	—	3,800

KM# 752 60.0000 g. 0.5830 Gold 1.1246 oz. AGW
50 mm. **Subject:** Vancouver Olympics **Rev:**
Olympic ideals, classic figures and torch

Date	Mintage	MS-63	Proof
2007 Proof	953	—	2,150

KM# 825 45.0000 g. 0.5830 Gold 0.8434 oz. AGW
50 mm. **Rev:** Alberta Coat of Arms

Date	Mintage	MS-63	Proof
2008 Proof	344	—	1,750

KM# 830 60.0000 g. 0.5830 Gold 1.1246 oz. AGW
50 mm. **Subject:** Vancouver Olympics **Rev:**
Olympic competition, athletics and torch

Date	Mintage	MS-63	Proof
2008 Proof	334	—	2,250

KM# 900 60.0000 g. 0.5830 Gold 1.1246 oz. AGW 50 mm. **Subject:** Yukon Coat of Arms **Obv:** Bust right **Obv. Legend:** Elizabeth II DG Regina **Obv. Designer:** Susanna Blunt **Rev:** Yukon Coat of Arms **Rev. Legend:** Canada 300 Dollars

Date	Mintage	MS-63	Proof
2009 Proof	325	—	2,150

KM# 877 60.0000 g. 0.5830 Gold 1.1246 oz. AGW 50 mm. **Rev:** Summer moon mask, enameled

Date	Mintage	MS-63	Proof
2009 Proof	—	—	2,250

KM# 911 60.0000 g. 0.5830 Gold 1.1246 oz. AGW 50 mm. **Subject:** 2010 Vancouver Olympics **Obv:** Bust right **Obv. Designer:** Susanna Blunt

Rev: Athletics with torch - Olympic firendship

Date	Mintage	MS-63	Proof
2009 Proof	880	—	2,150

KM# 999 54.0000 g. 0.5830 Gold 1.0121 oz. AGW 50 mm. **Rev:** British Columbia Arms

Date	Mintage	MS-63	Proof
2010 Proof	500	—	1,900

KM# 1047 60.0000 g. 0.5830 Gold 1.1246 oz. AGW 50 mm. **Rev:** Snowflake, white crystals

Date	Mintage	MS-63	Proof
2010 Proof	750	—	2,150

KM# 1078 60.0000 g. 0.5830 Gold 1.1246 oz. AGW 50 mm. **Rev:** New Brunswick Coat of arms

Date	Mintage	MS-63	Proof
2010 Proof	500	—	2,150

KM# 1095 60.0000 g. 0.9167 Gold 1.7683 oz.
AGW 50 mm.   **Rev:** Manitoba Coat of arms

Date	Mintage	MS-63	Proof
2011 Proof	500	—	3,300

KM# 1215 60.0000 g. 0.9170 Gold 1.7689 oz. AGW
50 mm.   **Obv:** Bust right **Rev:** Arms of Nova Scotia

Date	Mintage	MS-63	Proof
2011 Proof	—	—	3,300

KM# 1240 45.0000 g. 0.5830 Gold 0.8434 oz.
AGW 40 mm.   **Subject:** Elizabeth II, Diamond
Jubilee **Obv:** Bust right **Rev:** Youthful bust with
crown right, insert crystal at right

Date	Mintage	MS-63	Proof
1952-2012 Proof	—	—	1,600

KM# 1224 60.0000 g. 0.9167 Gold 1.7683 oz.
AGW 50 mm.   **Obv:** Bust right **Rev:** Shield of
Quebec

Date	Mintage	MS-63	Proof
2012 Proof	—	—	3,300

KM# 1242 16.0000 g. 0.9160 Gold 0.4712 oz.
AGW 29 mm.   **Subject:** Calgary Stampede

Date	Mintage	MS-63	Proof
2012	—	—	900

KM# 1195 Gold 50 mm.   **Obv:** Bust right **Rev:**
Youthful Elizabeth II right, hands uplifted, crystal

Date	Mintage	MS-63	Proof
2012 Proof	—	—	1,650

KM# 1278 31.1090 g. 0.9990 Platinum 0.9991 oz.
APW 30 mm.   **Subject:** Bateman Moose

Date	Mintage	MS-63	Proof
2012 Proof	—	—	1,750

350 DOLLARS

KM# 502 38.0500 g. 0.9999 Gold 1.2232 oz. AGW 34 mm. **Subject:** The Wild Rose **Obv:** Crowned head right **Obv. Designer:** Dora de Pedery-Hunt **Rev:** Wild rose plant **Rev. Designer:** Dr. Andreas Kare Hellum

Date	Mintage	MS-63	Proof
2002 Proof	2,001	—	2,350

KM# 308 38.0500 g. 0.9999 Gold 1.2232 oz. AGW **Subject:** Flowers of Canada's Coat of Arms **Obv:** Crowned head right, date behind, denomination at bottom **Rev:** Flowers **Rev. Designer:** Pierre Leduc

Date	Mintage	MS-63	Proof
1998 Proof	664	—	2,350

KM#370 38.0500 g. 0.9999 Gold 1.2232 oz. AGW **Rev:** Lady's slipper **Rev. Designer:** Henry Purdy

Date	Mintage	MS-63	Proof
1999 Proof	1,990	—	2,350

KM# 504 38.0500 g. 0.9999 Gold 1.2232 oz. AGW 34 mm. **Subject:** The White Trillium **Obv:** Crowned head right **Obv. Designer:** Dora de Pedery-Hunt **Rev:** White Trillium

Date	Mintage	MS-63	Proof
2003 Proof	1,865	—	2,350

KM# 601 38.0500 g. 0.9999 Gold 1.2232 oz. AGW **Subject:** Western Red Lilly **Obv:** Head right **Rev:** Western Red Lilies

Date	Mintage	MS-63	Proof
2005 Proof	1,634	—	2,350

KM# 404 38.0500 g. 0.9999 Gold 1.2232 oz. AGW 34 mm. **Obv:** Crowned head right **Rev:** Three Pacific Dogwood flowers **Rev. Designer:** Caren Heine **Edge:** Reeded

Date	Mintage	MS-63	Proof
2000 Proof	1,506	—	2,350

KM# 626 38.0500 g. 0.9999 Gold 1.2232 oz. AGW 34 mm. **Subject:** Iris Vericolor **Obv:** Crowned head right **Rev:** Iris

Date	Mintage	MS-63	Proof
2006 Proof	1,995	—	2,350

KM# 433 38.0500 g. 0.9999 Gold 1.2232 oz. AGW 34 mm. **Subject:** The Mayflower Flower **Obv:** Crowned head right **Rev:** Two flowers **Rev. Designer:** Bonnie Ross **Edge:** Reeded

Date	Mintage	MS-63	Proof
2001 Proof	1,988	—	2,350

KM# 754 35.0000 g. 0.9999 Gold 1.1251 oz. AGW 34 mm. **Rev:** Purple violet

Date	Mintage	MS-63	Proof
2007 Proof	1,392	—	2,200

KM# 832 35.0000 g. 0.9999 Gold 1.1251 oz. AGW 34 mm. **Rev:** Purple saxifrage

Date	Mintage	MS-63	Proof
2008 Proof	1,313	—	2,200

350 DOLLARS

KM# 901 35.0000 g. 1.0000 Gold 1.1252 oz. AGW
34 mm. **Subject:** Pitcher plant **Obv:** Bust right
Obv. Legend: Elizabeth II Canada DG Regina Fine
Gold 350 Dollars or PUR 99999 **Obv. Designer:**
Susana Blunt **Rev:** Cluster of pitcher flowers **Rev.
Legend:** Julie Wilson

Date	Mintage	MS-63	Proof
2009 Proof	1,003	—	2,200

KM# 1019 35.0000 g. 0.9990 Gold 1.1241 oz.
AGW 34 mm. **Rev:** Praire Crocus **Rev. Designer:**
Celia Godkin

Date	Mintage	MS-63	Proof
2010 Proof	Est. 1,400	—	2,200

KM# 1136 35.0000 g. 0.9999 Gold 1.1251 oz.
AGW 34 mm. **Obv:** Bust right **Rev:** Mountain
Avens in bloom **Edge:** Reeded

Date	Mintage	MS-63	Proof
2011 Proof	1,300	—	2,200

500 DOLLARS

KM# 710 156.5000 g. 0.9999 Gold 5.0309 oz.
AGW 60 mm. **Subject:** Queen's 60th Wedding
Rev: Coat of Arms and Mascots of Elizabeth and
Philip

Date	Mintage	MS-63	Proof
2007	198	9,150	—

KM# 782 155.7600 g. 0.9990 Gold 5.0026 oz.
AGW 60 mm. **Subject:** Ottawa Mint Centennial
1908-2008 **Rev:** Mint building facade **Note:**
Illustration reduced.

Date	Mintage	MS-63	Proof
2008	248	9,150	—

KM# 897 156.0500 g. 0.9990 Gold 5.0119 oz.
AGW 60 mm. **Subject:** 150th Anniversary of the
start of construction of the Parliament Buildings
Obv: Bust right **Rev:** Incomplete west block, original
architecture **Rev. Legend:** 500 Dollars 1859-2009

Date	Mintage	MS-63	Proof
2009 Proof	77	—	9,150

KM# 1007 156.5000 g. 0.9990 Gold 5.0263 oz.
AGW 60 mm. **Subject:** 75th Anniversary of
Canadian Bank Notes **Rev:** Abundance seated
under tree

Date	Mintage	MS-63	Proof
2010 Proof	200	—	9,150

350 DOLLARS

KM# 1288 1000.0000 g. 0.9990 Gold 32.117 oz.
AGW 101 mm. **Subject:** Old town view

Date	Mintage	MS-63	Proof
2008 Proof	—	—	57,000

KM# 1179 156.5000 g. 0.9999 Gold 5.0309 oz.
AGW 60 mm. **Obv:** Crowned bust of George V
Rev: Arms of Canada, dual dates and denomination
below **Edge:** Serially numbered

Date	Mintage	MS-63	Proof
1912-2012 Proof	200	—	9,150

2500 DOLLARS

KM# 902 1000.0000 g. 0.9990 Silver 32.117 oz.
ASW 101.6 mm. **Series:** History and Culture
Collection **Subject:** Modern Canada **Obv:** Bust right
Obv. Legend: Vancouver 2010, 2500 Dollars,
Elizabeth II **Obv. Designer:** Susanna Blunt **Rev:**
Canadian landscape with modern elements

Date	Mintage	MS-63	Proof
2009 Proof	2,500	—	1,250

KM# 902a 1000.0000 g. 0.9990 Gold 32.117 oz.
AGW 101.6 mm. **Series:** History and Culture
Collection **Subject:** Modern Canada **Obv:** Bust right
Obv. Legend: Vancouver 2010, 2500 Dollars,
Elizabeth II **Obv. Designer:** Susana Blunt **Rev:**
Canadian landscape with modern elements

Date	Mintage	MS-63	Proof
2009 Proof	50	—	57,000

KM# 681 1000.0000 g. 0.9999 Gold 32.146 oz.
AGW 101.6 mm. **Subject:** Kilo **Rev:** Common
Characters, Early Canada

Date	Mintage	MS-63	Proof
2007	20	57,000	—

KM# 912 1000.0000 g. 0.9999 Gold 32.146 oz. AGW 101 mm.   **Obv:** Bust right **Obv. Designer:** Susanna Blunt **Rev:** Mask with fish - Surviving the flood

Date	Mintage	MS-63	Proof
2009 Proof	40	—	58,000

KM# 984 1000.0000 g. 0.9990 Gold 32.117 oz. AGW 101 mm.

Date	Mintage	MS-63	Proof
2010 Proof	20	—	60,000

KM# 1045 1000.0000 g. 0.9999 Gold 32.146 oz. AGW 101 mm.   **Subject:** Baniff, 125th

Anniversary **Rev:** Highlights of Baniff

Date	Mintage	MS-63	Proof
2010	—	—	60,000

KM# 1286 1000.0000 g. 0.9990 Gold 32.117 oz. AGW 101 mm.   **Subject:** Olympic views

Date	Mintage	MS-63	Proof
2010 Proof	—	—	60,000

KM# 1197 1000.0000 g. 0.9999 Gold 32.146 oz. AGW 101 mm.   **Obv:** Bust right **Rev:** Early lacrosse game

Date	Mintage	MS-63	Proof
2011 Proof	35	—	60,000

KM# 1276 1000.0000 g. 0.9990 Gold 32.117 oz. AGW 101 mm.   **Subject:** Bateman Moose

Date	Mintage	MS-63	Proof
2012 Proof	—	—	58,000

SILVER BULLION COINAGE

DOLLAR

KM# 617 1.5550 g. 0.9999 Silver 0.0500 oz. ASW 16 mm. **Obv:** Crowned head right **Rev:** Holographic Maple leaf **Edge:** Reeded

Date	Mintage	MS-63	Proof
2003 Proof	—	—	4.50

KM# 621 1.5550 g. 0.9999 Silver 0.0500 oz. ASW 17 mm. **Obv:** Crowned head right **Rev:** Maple leaf **Edge:** Reeded

Date	Mintage	MS-63	Proof
2004 Mint logo privy mark Proof	13,859	—	4.50

KM#718 15.5500 g. 0.9990 Silver 0.4994 oz. ASW 32 mm. **Obv:** Bust right **Rev:** Grey Wolf standing with moon in background **Rev. Designer:** William Woodruff **Edge:** Reeded

Date	Mintage	MS-63	Proof
2005	106,800	40.00	—
2006	—	40.00	—
2007	—	40.00	—

2 DOLLARS

KM# 618 3.1100 g. 0.9999 Silver 0.1000 oz. ASW 20.1 mm. **Obv:** Crowned head right **Rev:** Holographic Maple leaf **Edge:** Reeded

Date	Mintage	MS-63	Proof
2003 Proof	—	—	7.50

KM# 622 3.1100 g. 0.9999 Silver 0.1000 oz. ASW 21 mm. **Obv:** Crowned head right **Rev:** Maple leaf **Edge:** Reeded

Date	Mintage	MS-63	Proof
2004 Mint logo privy mark Proof	13,859	—	7.50

KM# 571 3.1100 g. 0.9999 Silver 0.1000 oz. ASW 21 mm. **Obv:** Head right **Rev:** Lynx

Date	Mintage	MS-63	Proof
2005 Proof	—	—	7.50

3 DOLLARS

KM# 619 7.7760 g. 0.9999 Silver 0.2500 oz. ASW 26.9 mm. **Obv:** Crowned head right **Rev:** Holographic Maple leaf **Edge:** Reeded

Date	Mintage	MS-63	Proof
2003 Proof	—	—	15.00

KM# 623 7.7760 g. 0.9999 Silver 0.2500 oz. ASW 27 mm. **Obv:** Crowned head right **Rev:** Maple leaf **Edge:** Reeded

Date	Mintage	MS-63	Proof
2004 Mint logo privy mark Proof	13,859	—	12.50

KM# 572 7.7760 g. 0.9999 Silver 0.2500 oz. ASW 27 mm. **Obv:** Head right **Rev:** Lynx

Date	Mintage	MS-63	Proof
2005 Proof	—	—	12.50

4 DOLLARS

KM#620 15.5500 g. 0.9999 Silver 0.4999 oz. ASW
33.9 mm.   **Obv:** Crowned head right **Rev:**
Holographic Maple leaf **Edge:** Reeded

Date	Mintage	MS-63	Proof
2003 Proof	—	—	25.00

KM#624 15.5500 g. 0.9999 Silver 0.4999 oz. ASW
34 mm.   **Obv:** Crowned head right **Rev:** Maple leaf
Edge: Reeded

Date	Mintage	MS-63	Proof
2004 Mint logo privy mark Reverse Proof	13,859	—	22.50

KM#573 15.5500 g. 0.9999 Silver 0.4999 oz. ASW
34 mm.   **Obv:** Head right **Rev:** Lynx

Date	Mintage	MS-63	Proof
2005 Proof	—	—	22.50

5 DOLLARS

KM# 163 31.1000 g. 0.9999 Silver 0.9997 oz.
ASW   **Obv:** Young bust right, denomination and
date below **Obv. Designer:** Arnold Machin **Rev:**
Maple leaf flanked by 9999

Date	Mintage	MS-63	Proof
1988	1,155,931	35.00	—
1989 Proof	29,999	—	40.00
1989	3,332,200	35.00	—

KM# 187 31.1000 g. 0.9999 Silver 0.9997 oz.
ASW   **Obv:** Crowned head right, date and
denomination below **Obv. Designer:** Dora de
Pedery-Hunt **Rev:** Maple leaf flanked by 9999

Date	Mintage	MS-63	Proof
1990	1,708,800	35.00	—
1991	644,300	35.00	—
1992	343,800	35.00	—
1993	889,946	35.00	—
1994	1,133,900	35.00	—
1995	326,244	35.00	—
1996	250,445	42.50	—
1997	100,970	35.00	—
1998 Tiger privy mark	25,000	35.00	—
1998	591,359	35.00	—
1998 Titanic privy mark	26,000	85.00	—

Date	Mintage	MS-63	Proof
1998 R.C.M.P. privy mark	25,000	35.00	—
1998 90th Anniversary R.C.M. privy mark	13,025	35.00	—
1999	1,229,442	35.00	—
1999 Rabbit privy mark	25,000	35.00	—
1999 "Y2K" privy mark	9,999	37.50	—
2000 Expo Hanover privy mark	—	45.00	—
2000 Dragon privy mark	25,000	35.00	—
2000	403,652	35.00	—
2001	398,563	35.00	—
2001 Reverse proof, Snake privy mark	25,000	—	45.00
2002	576,196	35.00	—
2002 Reverse proof, Horse privy mark	25,000	—	45.00
2003	—	35.00	—
2003 Reverse proof, sheep privy mark	25,000	—	45.00

KM# 363 31.1000 g. 0.9999 Silver 0.9997 oz. ASW **Obv:** Crowned head right, date and denomination below **Rev:** Maple leaf flanked by 9999

Date	Mintage	MS-63	Proof
1999/2000 Fireworks privy mark	298,775	35.00	—

KM# 437 31.1035 g. 0.9999 Silver 0.9999 oz. ASW 38 mm. **Obv:** Crowned head right, date and denomination below **Rev:** Radiant maple leaf hologram **Edge:** Reeded

Date	Mintage	MS-63	Proof
2001 Good fortune privy mark	29,906	75.00	—

KM# 436 31.1035 g. 0.9999 Silver 0.9999 oz. ASW 38 mm. **Obv:** Crowned head right, date and denomination below **Rev:** Three maple leaves in autumn colors, 9999 flanks **Rev. Designer:** Debbie Adams **Edge:** Reeded

Date	Mintage	MS-63	Proof
2001 Proof	49,709	—	40.00

KM# 505 31.1035 g. 0.9999 Silver 0.9999 oz. ASW 38 mm. **Obv:** Crowned head right, date and denomination below **Rev:** Two maple leaves in spring color (green) **Edge:** Reeded

Date	Mintage	MS-63	Proof
2002	29,509	37.50	—

KM# 521 31.1035 g. 0.9999 Silver 0.9999 oz. ASW **Obv:** Head right **Rev:** Maple leaf, summer colors **Rev. Designer:** Stan Witten

Date	Mintage	MS-63	Proof
2003	29,416	37.50	—

KM# 508 31.1035 g. 0.9999 Silver 0.9999 oz. ASW 38 mm. **Obv:** Crowned head right, date and denomination below **Obv. Designer:** Dora de Pedery-Hunt **Rev:** Holographic Maple leaf flanked by 9999 **Edge:** Reeded

Date	Mintage	MS-63	Proof
2003 Proof	—	—	37.50

KM# 607 31.1200 g. 0.9999 Silver 1.0004 oz.
ASW **Obv:** Head right **Rev:** Maple leaf, winter colors

Date	Mintage	MS-63	Proof
2004	—	37.50	—

KM#625 31.1035 g. 0.9999 Silver 0.9999 oz. ASW
38 mm.   **Obv:** Bust right **Obv. Designer:** Susanna
Blunt **Rev:** Maple leaf **Edge:** Reeded

Date	Mintage	MS-63	Proof
2004 Mint logo privy mark Specimen	13,859	—	37.50
2004 Monkey privy mark Specimen	25,000	—	37.50
2004 D-Day privy mark Specimen	11,698	—	37.50
2004 Desjardins privy mark	15,000	37.50	—
2004 Capricorn privy Mark Reverse proof	5,000	—	37.50
2004 Aquarius privy mark Reverse proof	5,000	—	37.50
2004 Pisces privy mark Reverse proof	5,000	—	37.50
2004 Aries privy mark Reverse proof	5,000	—	37.50
2004 Taurus privy mark Reverse proof	5,000	—	37.50
2004 Gemini privy mark Reverse proof	5,000	—	37.50
2004 Cancer privy mark Reverse proof	5,000	—	37.50
2004 Leo privy mark Reverse proof	5,000	—	37.50
2004 Virgo privy mark Reverse proof	5,000	—	37.50
2004 Libra privy mark Reverse proof	5,000	—	37.50
2004 Scorpio privy mark Reverse proof	5,000	—	37.50
2004 Sagittarius privy mark Reverse proof	5,000	—	50.00
2005	—	35.00	—
2005 Tulip privy mark Reverse proof	3,500	—	50.00
2005 Tank privy mark Reverse proof	7,000	—	60.00
2005 USS Missouri privy mark Reverse proof	7,000	—	60.00
2005 Rooster privy mark Reverse proof	15,000	—	50.00
2006	—	35.00	—

Date	Mintage	MS-63	Proof
2006 Dog privy mark Reverse proof	—	—	50.00
2007	—	35.00	—
2007 F12 privy mark Reverse proof	—	—	130
2007 Pig privy mark Reverse proof	—	—	50.00
2008	—	35.00	—
2008 F12 privy mark Reverse proof	—	—	130
2008 Rat privy mark Reverse proof	—	—	50.00
2009	—	35.00	—
2009 Brandenberg Gate privy mark Reverse proof	—	—	50.00
2009 Tower Bridge privy mark Reverse proof	—	—	50.00
2009 Ox Privy mark Reverse proof	—	—	50.00
2010	—	35.00	—
2010 Fabulous 15 privy mark Reverse proof	—	—	50.00
2011	—	35.00	—
2012	—	35.00	—
2012 Dragon privy mark Reverse proof	—	—	50.00
2012 Titanic privy mark Reverse proof	—	—	50.00
2012 Pisa privy mark	—	35.00	—
2012 Fabulous 15 privy mark Reverse proof	—	—	75.00
2013	—	35.00	—

KM# 522 31.1050 g. 0.9999 Silver 0.9999 oz.
ASW   **Obv:** Head right **Rev:** Maple leaf, winter
color **Rev. Designer:** Stan Witten

Date	Mintage	MS-63	Proof
2004	26,763	35.00	—

KM#574 31.1035 g. 0.9999 Silver 0.9999 oz. ASW
38 mm.   **Obv:** Head right **Rev:** Lynx

Date	Mintage	MS-63	Proof
2005 Proof	—	—	37.50

KM# 924 31.1050 g. 0.9999 Silver 0.9999 oz.
ASW   **Rev:** Maple Leaf, laser engraved **Rev.
Designer:** Joan Nguyen

Date	Mintage	MS-63	Proof
2005 Proof	25,000	—	60.00

SILVER BULLION

KM#550 31.1035 g. 0.9999 Silver 0.9999 oz. ASW 38 mm. **Obv:** Head right **Rev:** Big Leaf Maple and seed pod, color **Rev. Designer:** Stan Witten

Date	Mintage	MS-63	Proof
2005	21,233	35.00	—

KM# 660 31.1035 g. 0.9990 Silver 0.9990 oz. ASW **Obv:** Bust right **Obv. Designer:** Susanna Blunt **Rev:** Silver maple, colorized **Rev. Designer:** Stan Witten

Date	Mintage	MS-63	Proof
2006	14,157	37.50	—

KM# 625a 31.1050 g. 0.9999 Silver 0.9999 oz. ASW 38 mm. **Rev:** Maple leaf, gilt

Date	Mintage	MS-63	Proof
2007	—	75.00	—
2008	—	75.00	—
2009	—	75.00	—
2009 Tower Bridge Privy Mark	—	75.00	—
2010	—	75.00	—

KM#729 31.1050 g. 0.9990 Silver 0.9990 oz. ASW 38 mm. **Obv:** Bust right **Rev:** Maple leaf orange multicolor

Date	Mintage	MS-63	Proof
2007 Proof	—	—	45.00

KM# 925 31.1050 g. 0.9990 Silver 0.9990 oz. ASW **Obv:** Bust right **Obv. Designer:** Susanna Blunt **Rev:** Sugar maple, colorized **Rev. Designer:** Stan Witten

Date	Mintage	MS-63	Proof
2007	11,495	37.50	—

KM#928 31.3900 g. 0.9990 Silver 1.0082 oz. ASW 38 mm. **Rev:** Orange sugar maple leaf **Rev. Designer:** Stan Witten

Date	Mintage	MS-63	Proof
2007 Specimen	20,000	—	75.00

KM#798 31.1050 g. 0.9990 Silver 0.9990 oz. ASW 38 mm. **Subject:** Maple Leaf 20th Anniversary **Rev:** Maple Leaf, selective gold plating

Date	Mintage	MS-63	Proof
2008 Proof	10,000	—	75.00

KM#799 31.1050 g. 0.9990 Silver 0.9990 oz. ASW 38 mm. **Subject:** Breast Cancer Awareness **Rev:** Multicolor, green maple leaf and pink ribbon

Date	Mintage	MS-63	Proof
2008	11,048	85.00	—

SILVER BULLION

KM# 800 31.1050 g. 0.9990 Silver 0.9990 oz. ASW
38 mm.   **Subject:** Vancouver Olympics **Obv:** Bust
right **Obv. Designer:** Susanna Blunt **Rev:** Maple
leaf, Olympic logo at left, turtle

Date	Mintage	MS-63	Proof
2008	—	37.50	—
2009	—	37.50	—
2010	—	37.50	—

KM# 800a 31.1050 g. 0.9999 Silver partially gilt
0.9999 oz. ASW 38 mm.   **Rev:** Maple leaf gilt,
olympic logo at left

Date	Mintage	MS-63	Proof
2008	—	50.00	—

KM# 1056 31.1050 g. 0.9999 Silver 0.9999 oz.
ASW 38 mm.   **Rev:** Maple leaf in brown color, card
diamond

Date	Mintage	MS-63	Proof
2008	—	50.00	—

KM# 1057 31.1050 g. 0.9999 Silver 0.9999 oz.
ASW 38 mm.   **Rev:** Maple Leaf in green color, card
heart

Date	Mintage	MS-63	Proof
2008	—	50.00	—

KM# 1058 31.1050 g. 0.9999 Silver 0.9999 oz.
ASW 38 mm.   **Rev:** Maple leaf in green color, card
club

Date	Mintage	MS-63	Proof
2008	—	50.00	—

KM# 1059 31.1050 g. 0.9999 Silver 0.9999 oz.
ASW 38 mm.   **Rev:** Maple Leaf in red color, card
spade

Date	Mintage	MS-63	Proof
2008	—	50.00	—

KM#863 31.1050 g. 0.9999 Silver 0.9999 oz. ASW
38 mm. **Subject:** Vancouver Olympics **Rev:**
Thunderbird Totem **Rev. Designer:** Rick Harry

Date	Mintage	MS-63	Proof
2009	—	50.00	—

KM# 863a 31.1050 g. 0.9999 Silver partially gilt
0.9999 oz. ASW 38 mm. **Rev:** Thunderbird, gilt

Date	Mintage	MS-63	Proof
2009	—	60.00	—

KM# 1061 31.1050 g. 0.9999 Silver 0.9999 oz.
ASW 38 mm. **Rev:** Maple leaf in red color, support
our troops yellow ribbon

Date	Mintage	MS-63	Proof
2009	—	70.00	—

KM# 998 31.1200 g. 0.9990 Silver 0.9995 oz. ASW
38 mm. **Rev:** Olympic Hockey

Date	Mintage	MS-63	Proof
2010 Proof	—	—	42.50

KM# 998a 31.1050 g. 0.9999 Silver partially gilt
0.9999 oz. ASW 38 mm. **Rev:** Hockey player, gilt
maple leaves flanking

Date	Mintage	MS-63	Proof
2010	—	50.00	—

KM# 1077 31.3900 g. 0.9990 Silver 1.0082 oz.
ASW 34 mm. **Rev:** Maple leaf on 45 degree angle
left **Note:** Piedfort.

Date	Mintage	MS-63	Proof
2010 Reverse Proof	9,000	—	80.00

KM# 1289 31.1050 g. 0.9999 Silver 0.9999 oz.
ASW 38 mm. **Rev:** Maple leaf in green with crystal

Date	Mintage	MS-63	Proof
2010	—	65.00	—

KM# 1290 31.1050 g. 0.9990 Silver 0.9990 oz.
ASW 38 mm. **Rev:** Maple leaf in red with crystal

Date	Mintage	MS-63	Proof
2010	—	65.00	—

KM# 1291 31.1050 g. 0.9999 Silver 0.9999 oz.
ASW 38 mm. **Rev:** Maple leaf in dark green with
crystal

Date	Mintage	MS-63	Proof
2010	—	65.00	—

SILVER BULLION

KM# 1241 31.1350 g. 0.9999 Silver 1.0009 oz.
ASW 38 mm. **Obv. Designer:**
Susana Blunt **Rev:** Moose left **Rev. Designer:**
William Woodruff **Edge:** Reeded

Date	Mintage	MS-63	Proof
2012	1,000,000	42.00	—

KM# 1297 31.1050 g. 0.9990 Silver 0.9990 oz.
ASW 38 mm. **Obv:** Bust right **Rev:** Antelope

Date	Mintage	MS-63	Proof
2013	—	—	—

10 DOLLARS

KM# 1052 31.1050 g. 0.9999 Silver 0.9999 oz.
ASW 38 mm. **Rev:** Wolf standing with moonlight
in background

Date	Mintage	MS-63	Proof
2011	1,000,000	42.00	—

KM# 1158 31.1050 g. 0.9999 Silver 0.9999 oz.
ASW 38 mm. **Obv:** Bust right **Rev:** Branch with
three maple leaves

Date	Mintage	MS-63	Proof
2011 Proof	—	—	50.00

KM# 1109 31.1050 g. 0.9990 Silver 0.9990 oz.
ASW 38 mm. **Rev:** Grizzly Bear walking right

Date	Mintage	MS-63	Proof
2011	1,000,000	40.00	—

KM# 1164 31.1050 g. 0.9990 Silver 0.9990 oz.
ASW 38 mm. **Obv. Designer:** Susanna Blunt
Rev: Cougar **Rev. Designer:** William Woodruff

Date	Mintage	MS-63	Proof
2012	1,000,000	40.00	—

KM# 1268 31.1050 g. 0.9990 Silver 0.9990 oz.
ASW 38 mm. **Subject:** Maple Leaf Forever

Date	Mintage	MS-63	Proof
2012 Proof	—	—	50.00

SILVER BULLION

20 DOLLARS

KM# 1062 7.9600 g. 0.9999 Silver 0.2559 oz. ASW 27 mm. **Rev:** Five Maple leaves at left **Note:** Thick planchet

Date	Mintage	MS-63	Proof
2011	200,000	25.00	—

KM# 1176 7.9600 g. 0.9999 Silver 0.2559 oz. ASW 27 mm. **Obv:** Bust right **Rev:** Canoe and reflection **Rev. Designer:** Jason Bouwman **Edge:** Reeded **Note:** Thick planchet.

Date	Mintage	MS-63	Proof
2011	200,000	30.00	—

KM# 1226 7.9600 g. 0.9999 Silver 0.2559 oz. ASW 27 mm. **Obv:** Bust right **Rev:** Waterline view of polar bear swimming **Edge:** Reeded

Date	Mintage	MS-63	Proof
2012	250,000	25.00	—

KM# 1237 15.5500 g. 0.9999 Silver 0.4999 oz. ASW 27 mm. **Obv:** Bust right **Rev:** Maple leafs floating on water

Date	Mintage	MS-63	Proof
2012	—	20.00	—

50 DOLLARS

KM# 326 311.0350 g. 0.9999 Silver 9.9986 oz. ASW **Subject:** 10th Anniversary Silver Maple Leaf **Obv:** Crowned head right **Rev:** Maple leaf flanked by 9999 **Edge:** 10th ANNIVERSARY 10e ANNIVERSAIRE

Date	Mintage	MS-63	Proof
1998 Proof	25,000	—	350

250 DOLLARS

KM# 676 1000.0000 g. 0.9999 Silver 32.146 oz. ASW **Subject:** Kilo

Date	Mintage	MS-63	Proof
2006	—	1,350	—

KM# 1160 1000.0000 g. 0.9999 Silver 32.146 oz. ASW 101 mm. **Obv. Designer:** Susana Blunt **Rev:** Three maple leaves on branch **Rev. Designer:** Debbie Adams

Date	Mintage	MS-63	Proof
2011 Proof	999	—	2,000

SILVER BULLION

KM# 1272 1000.0000 g. 0.9990 Silver 32.117 oz. ASW 101 mm. **Subject:** Maple Leaf Forever

Date	Mintage	MS-63	Proof
2012 Proof	—	—	1,450

500 DOLLARS

KM# 1245 5000.0000 g. 0.9999 Silver 160.73 oz. ASW 101 mm. **Subject:** Haida sculpture

Date	Mintage	MS-63	Proof
2012 Proof	100	—	7,500

GOLD BULLION COINAGE

50 CENTS

KM# 542 1.2700 g. 0.9990 Gold 0.0408 oz. AGW 13.92 mm. **Rev:** Voyagers with northern lights above **Rev. Designer:** Emanuel Hahn

Date	Mintage	MS-63	Proof
2005 Proof	Est. 25,000	—	100

KM# 717 1.2400 g. 0.9990 Gold 0.0398 oz. AGW 13.9 mm. **Rev:** Wolf

Date	Mintage	MS-63	Proof
2006 Proof	—	—	100

KM# 926 1.2400 g. 0.9990 Gold 0.0398 oz. AGW 13.9 mm. **Rev:** Cowboy and bronco rider

Date	Mintage	MS-63	Proof
2006 Proof	—	—	100

KM# 927 1.2400 g. 0.9990 Gold 0.0398 oz. AGW 13.9 mm. **Subject:** Gold Louis

Date	Mintage	MS-63	Proof
2007 Proof	—	—	100

KM# 777 1.2400 g. 0.9990 Gold 0.0398 oz. AGW 13.9 mm. **Subject:** DeHavilland beaver

Date	Mintage	MS-63	Proof
2008 Proof	20,000	—	100

KM# 888 1.2700 g. 0.9990 Gold 0.0408 oz. AGW 13.92 mm. **Subject:** Red maple **Obv:** Bust right **Obv. Legend:** Elizabeth II 50 cents **Obv. Designer:** Susanna Blunt **Rev:** Two maple leaves **Rev. Legend:** Canada, Fine gold 1/25 oz or PUR 9999

Date	Mintage	MS-63	Proof
2009 Proof	150,000	—	90.00

KM# 985 1.2400 g. 0.9990 Gold 0.0398 oz. AGW 13.92 mm. **Subject:** RCMP **Obv:** Bust right **Rev:** Mountie on horseback **Rev. Designer:** Janet Griffin-Scott

Date	Mintage	MS-63	Proof
2010 Proof	Est. 14,000	—	100

SILVER BULLION

KM# 1085 1.2700 g. 0.9990 Gold 0.0408 oz. AGW 13.92 mm. **Rev:** Geese in flight left **Rev. Designer:** Emily Damstra

Date	Mintage	MS-63	Proof
2011 Proof	10,000	—	90.00

KM# 1214 1.2700 g. 1.0000 Gold 0.0408 oz. AGW 13.92 mm. **Obv:** Bust right **Rev:** Three maple leaves, 2007-2012 above

Date	Mintage	MS-63	Proof
2012 Proof	—	—	90.00

KM# 1218 1.2700 g. 0.9999 Gold 0.0408 oz. AGW 13.92 mm. **Obv:** Bust right **Rev:** Schooner sailing left

Date	Mintage	MS-63	Proof
2012 Proof	—	—	90.00

DOLLAR

KM# 238 1.5551 g. 0.9999 Gold 0.0500 oz. AGW **Obv:** Crowned head right, denomination and date below **Rev:** Maple leaf flanked by 9999

Date	Mintage	MS-63	Proof
1993	37,080	BV+25%	—
1994	78,860	BV+25%	—
1995	85,920	BV+25%	—
1996	56,520	BV+25%	—
1997	59,720	BV+25%	—
1998	44,260	BV+25%	—
1999 oval "20 YEARS ANS" privy mark	—	BV+30%	—
2000 oval "2000" privy mark	—	BV+30%	—
2001	—	BV+30%	—

KM# 365 1.5551 g. 0.9999 Gold 0.0500 oz. AGW **Obv:** Crowned head right **Rev:** Maple leaf hologram

Date	Mintage	MS-63	Proof
1999	500	115	—

KM# 438 1.5810 g. 0.9990 Gold 0.0508 oz. AGW 14.1 mm. **Subject:** Holographic Maple Leaves **Obv:** Crowned head right **Rev:** Three maple leaves multicolor hologram **Edge:** Reeded

Date	Mintage	MS-63	Proof
2001	600	85.00	—

KM# 1138 1.5600 g. 0.9999 Gold 0.0501 oz. AGW 14 mm. **Obv:** Bust right **Rev:** Maple leaf

Date	Mintage	MS-63	Proof
1911-2011	—	100.00	—

KM# 1213 1.5810 g. 1.0000 Gold 0.0508 oz. AGW 14.1 mm. **Obv:** Bust right **Rev:** Three maple leaves, 2007-2012 above

Date	Mintage	MS-63	Proof
2012 Proof	—	—	110

2 DOLLARS

KM# 256 2.0735 g. 0.9999 Gold 0.0667 oz. AGW **Obv:** Crowned head right, denomination and date below **Rev:** Maple leaf flanked by 9999

Date	Mintage	MS-63	Proof
1994	5,493	140	—

5 DOLLARS

KM# 135 3.1200 g. 0.9999 Gold 0.1003 oz. AGW **Obv:** Young bust right, date and denomination below **Obv. Designer:** Arnold Machin **Rev:** Maple leaf flanked by 9999

Date	Mintage	MS-63	Proof
1982	246,000	BV+14%	—
1983	304,000	BV+14%	—
1984	262,000	BV+14%	—
1985	398,000	BV+14%	—
1986	529,516	BV+14%	—
1987	459,000	BV+14%	—
1988	506,500	BV+14%	—
1989	539,000	BV+14%	—
1989 Proof	16,992	—	200

KM# 188 3.1200 g. 0.9999 Gold 0.1003 oz. AGW **Obv:** Elizabeth II effigy **Obv. Designer:** Dora dePedery-Hunt **Rev:** Maple leaf

Date	Mintage	MS-63	Proof
1990	476,000	BV+14%	—
1991	322,000	BV+14%	—
1992	384,000	BV+14%	—
1993	248,630	BV+14%	—
1994	313,150	BV+14%	—
1995	294,890	BV+14%	—
1996	179,220	BV+14%	—
1997	188,540	BV+14%	—
1998	301,940	BV+14%	—
1999 oval "20 Years ANS" privy mark	—	BV+19%	—
2000 oval "2000" privy mark	—	BV+19%	—
2001	—	BV+14%	—

KM# 366 3.1200 g. 0.9999 Gold 0.1003 oz. AGW **Rev:** Maple leaf hologram

Date	Mintage	MS-63	Proof
1999	500	210	—

KM# 439 3.1310 g. 0.9999 Gold 0.1006 oz. AGW 16 mm. **Subject:** Holographic Maple Leaves **Obv:** Crowned head right **Rev:** Three maple leaves multicolor hologram **Edge:** Reeded

Date	Mintage	MS-63	Proof
2001	600	200	—

KM# 929 3.1300 g. 0.9990 Gold 0.1005 oz. AGW 16 mm. **Obv. Designer:** Susan Blunt **Rev:** Maple leaf **Rev. Designer:** Walter Ott

Date	Mintage	MS-63	Proof
2007	—	—	200
2008	—	—	200
2009	—	—	200
2010	—	—	200
2011	—	—	200

KM# 1139 3.1300 g. 0.9990 Gold 0.1005 oz. AGW
16 mm.   **Obv:** Bust right **Rev:** Maple leaf

Date	Mintage	MS-63	Proof
1911-2011	—	225	—

KM# 1212 3.1300 g. 1.0000 Gold 0.1006 oz. AGW
16 mm.   **Obv:** Bust right **Rev:** Three maple leaves,
2007-2012 above

Date	Mintage	MS-63	Proof
2012 Proof	—	—	200

KM# 1267 3.1300 g. 0.9990 Gold 0.1005 oz. AGW
16 mm.   **Subject:** Maple Leaf Forever

Date	Mintage	MS-63	Proof
2012 Proof	—	—	200

10 DOLLARS

KM# 136 7.7850 g. 0.9999 Gold 0.2503 oz.
AGW   **Obv:** Young bust right, date and
denomination below **Obv. Designer:** Arnold Machin
Rev: Maple leaf flanked by 9999

Date	Mintage	MS-63	Proof
1982	184,000	BV+10%	—
1983	308,800	BV+10%	—
1984	242,400	BV+10%	—
1985	620,000	BV+10%	—
1986	915,200	BV+10%	—
1987	376,000	BV+10%	—
1988	436,000	BV+10%	—
1989 Proof	6,998	—	500
1989	328,800	BV+10%	—

KM# 189 7.7850 g. 0.9999 Gold 0.2503 oz.
AGW   **Obv:** Crowned head right, date and
denomination below **Obv. Designer:** Dora
dePedery-Hunt **Rev:** Maple leaf flanked by 9999

Date	Mintage	MS-63	Proof
1990	253,600	BV+10%	—
1991	166,400	BV+10%	—
1992	179,600	BV+10%	—
1993	158,452	BV+10%	—
1994	148,792	BV+10%	—
1995	127,596	BV+10%	—
1996	89,148	BV+10%	—
1997	98,104	BV+10%	—
1998	85,472	BV+10%	—
1999 oval "20 Years ANS" privy mark	—	BV+15%	—
2000 oval "2000" privy mark	—	BV+15%	—
2001	—	BV+15%	—

KM# 367 7.7850 g. 0.9999 Gold 0.2503 oz.
AGW   **Rev:** Maple leaf hologram

Date	Mintage	MS-63	Proof
1999	—	485	—

KM# 440 7.7970 g. 0.9999 Gold 0.2506 oz. AGW
20 mm.   **Subject:** Holographic Maples Leaves
Obv: Crowned head right **Rev:** Three maple leaves
multicolor hologram **Edge:** Reeded

Date	Mintage	MS-63	Proof
2001	15,000	475	—

KM# 1140 7.7970 g. 0.9999 Gold 0.2506 oz. AGW
20 mm.   **Obv:** Bust right **Rev:** Maple leaf

Date	Mintage	MS-63	Proof
1911-2011	—	485	—

KM# 1312 6.2200 g. 0.9990 Gold 0.1998 oz. AGW
Obv: Bust right **Rev:** Maple leaf **Note:** Piedfort

Date	Mintage	MS-63	Proof
2011	—	400	—

KM# 1211 7.7970 g. 1.0000 Gold 0.2507 oz. AGW
20 mm.   **Obv:** Bust right **Rev:** Three maple leaves,
2007-2012 above

Date	Mintage	MS-63	Proof
2012 Proof	—	—	475

KM# 1275 7.7700 g. 0.9999 Gold 0.2498 oz. AGW
20 mm.   **Subject:** War of 1812

Date	Mintage	MS-63	Proof
2012 Proof	—	—	500

20 DOLLARS

KM# 153 15.5515 g. 0.9999 Gold 0.4999 oz. AGW
32 mm.   **Obv:** Young bust right, date and
denomination below **Obv. Designer:** Arnold Machin
Rev: Maple leaf flanked by 9999

Date	Mintage	MS-63	Proof
1986	529,200	BV+7%	—
1987	332,800	BV+7%	—
1988	538,400	BV+7%	—
1989 Proof	6,998	—	935
1989	259,200	BV+7%	—

KM# 190 15.5515 g. 0.9999 Gold 0.4999 oz.
AGW   **Obv:** Crowned head right, date and
denomination below **Obv. Designer:** Dora

dePedery-Hunt **Rev:** Maple leaf flanked by 9999

Date	Mintage	MS-63	Proof
1990	174,400	BV+7%	—
1991	96,200	BV+7%	—
1992	108,000	BV+7%	—
1993	99,492	BV+7%	—
1994	104,766	BV+7%	—
1995	103,162	BV+7%	—
1996	66,246	BV+7%	—
1997	63,354	BV+7%	—
1998	65,366	BV+7%	—
1999 oval "20 Years ANS" privy mark	—	BV+12%	—
2000 oval "2000" privy mark	—	BV+12%	—
2001	—	BV+12%	—

KM# 368 15.5515 g. 0.9999 Gold 0.4999 oz. AGW **Rev:** Maple leaf hologram

Date	Mintage	MS-63	Proof
1999	500	935	—

KM# 441 15.5840 g. 0.9999 Gold 0.5010 oz. AGW 25 mm. **Subject:** Holographic Maples Leaves **Obv:** Crowned head right **Rev:** Three maple leaves multicolor hologram **Edge:** Reeded

Date	Mintage	MS-63	Proof
2001	600	925	—

50 DOLLARS

KM# 125.1 31.1030 g. 0.9990 Gold 0.9989 oz. AGW **Obv:** Young bust right, denomination and date below **Rev:** Maple leaf flanked by .999

Date	Mintage	MS-63	Proof
1979	1,000,000	BV+4%	—
1980	1,251,500	BV+4%	—
1981	863,000	BV+4%	—
1982	883,000	BV+4%	—

KM# 125.2 31.1030 g. 0.9999 Gold 0.9998 oz. AGW **Obv:** Young bust right, date and denomination below **Rev:** Maple leaf flanked by .9999

Date	Mintage	MS-63	Proof
1983	843,000	BV+4%	—
1984	1,067,500	BV+4%	—
1985	1,908,000	BV+4%	—
1986	779,115	BV+4%	—
1987	978,000	BV+4%	—
1988	826,500	BV+4%	—
1989	856,000	BV+4%	—
1989 Proof	17,781	—	1,900

KM# 191 31.1030 g. 0.9999 Gold 0.9998 oz.

AGW **Obv:** Crowned head right, date and denomination below **Obv. Designer:** Dora dePedery-Hunt **Rev:** Maple leaf flanked by .9999

Date	Mintage	MS-63	Proof
1990	815,000	BV+4%	—
1991	290,000	BV+4%	—
1992	368,900	BV+4%	—
1993	321,413	BV+4%	—
1994	180,357	BV+4%	—
1995	208,729	BV+4%	—
1996	143,682	BV+4%	—
1997	478,211	BV+4%	—
1998	593,704	BV+4%	—
1999 oval "20 Years ANS" privy mark	—	BV+7%	—
2000 oval "2000" privy mark	—	BV+7%	—
2000 oval fireworks privy mark	—	BV+7%	—
2001	—	BV+7%	—

KM# 305 31.1030 g. 0.9999 Gold 0.9998 oz. AGW **Obv:** Crowned head denomination below, within circle, dates below **Rev:** Mountie at gallop right, within circle **Rev. Designer:** Ago Aarand **Shape:** 10-sided

Date	Mintage	MS-63	Proof
1997	12,913	1,850	—

KM# 369 31.1030 g. 0.9999 Gold 0.9998 oz. AGW **Obv:** Crowned head right, date and denomination below **Rev:** Maple leaf hologram flanked by 9999, with fireworks privy mark

Date	Mintage	MS-63	Proof
2000	500	1,850	—

KM# 442 31.1500 g. 0.9999 Gold 1.0014 oz. AGW 30 mm. **Subject:** Holographic Maples Leaves **Obv:** Crowned head right **Rev:** Three maple leaves multicolor hologram **Edge:** Reeded

Date	Mintage	MS-63	Proof
2001	600	1,850	—

KM# 1042 31.1050 g. 0.9990 Gold 0.9990 oz.

AGW 30 mm.   **Rev:** Vancouver logo and maple
leaf **Edge:** Reeded

Date	Mintage	MS-63	Proof
2008P	—	1,850	—

KM# 1042a 31.1050 g. 0.9999 Gold partially
enameled 0.9999 oz. AGW 30 mm.   **Rev:** Maple
leaf in red enamel, olympic logo at left

Date	Mintage	MS-63	Proof
2008	—	1,850	—

KM# 1037 31.1050 g. 0.9999 Gold 0.9999 oz.
AGW 30 mm.   **Rev:** Thunderbird **Edge:** Reeded

Date	Mintage	MS-63	Proof
2009	—	1,850	—

KM# 1037a 31.1050 g. 0.9999 Gold 0.9999 oz.
AGW 30 mm.   **Rev:** Thunderbird, stars in red
enamel highlights

Date	Mintage	MS-63	Proof
2009	—	1,850	—

KM# 1029 31.1050 g. 0.9999 Gold 0.9999 oz.
AGW 30 mm.   **Rev:** Hockey player flanked by
maple leaves

Date	Mintage	MS-63	Proof
2010	—	1,850	—

KM# 1029a 31.1050 g. 0.9999 Gold 0.9999 oz.
AGW 30 mm.   **Rev:** Hockey player, red enameled
maple leaves flanking

Date	Mintage	MS-63	Proof
2010	—	1,850	—

KM# 1141 31.1050 g. 0.9999 Gold 0.9999 oz.
AGW 30 mm.   **Obv:** Bust right **Rev:** Maple leaf

Date	Mintage	MS-63	Proof
1911-2011	—	1,850	—

KM# 1210 31.1050 g. 1.0000 Gold 100000 oz.
AGW 30 mm.   **Obv:** Bust right **Rev:** Three maple
leaves, 2007-2012 above

Date	Mintage	MS-63	Proof
2012 Proof	—	—	1,850

200 DOLLARS

KM# 750 31.1050 g. 1.0000 Gold 100000 oz. AGW
30 mm.   **Rev:** Three maple leaves

Date	Mintage	MS-63	Proof
2007 Proof, T/E privy mark	500	—	1,850

GOLD BULLION

KM#786 31.1050 g. 1.0000 Gold 100000 oz. AGW
30 mm. **Obv:** Bust right on lathe-work
background **Rev:** Two maple leaves on lathe-work
background

Date	Mintage	MS-63	Proof
2008 Proof	—	—	1,850

KM# 1162 31.1050 g. 1.0000 Gold 100000 oz.
AGW **Rev:** Maple leaf with lathe backgound

Date	Mintage	MS-63	Proof
2009 Proof	—	—	1,850

KM# 1163 31.1050 g. 0.9990 Gold 0.9990 oz.
AGW **Subject:** Celebrating win **Rev:** Three
athletics with hands raised

Date	Mintage	MS-63	Proof
2010 Proof	—	—	1,850

KM# 1165 31.1050 g. 1.0000 Gold 100000 oz.
AGW 30 mm. **Obv. Designer:** Susanna Blunt
Rev: Mountie on horseback, lathe backgound **Rev.
Designer:** Ago Aarand

Date	Mintage	MS-63	P/L	Proof
2011	—	1,850	—	—

2500 DOLLARS

KM# 1161 1000.0000 g. 0.9999 Gold 32.146 oz.
AGW 101 mm. **Rev:** Three maple leaves on
branch

Date	Mintage	MS-63	Proof
2011	—	—	56,000

KM# 1271 1000.0000 g. 0.9990 Gold 32.117 oz.
AGW 101 mm. **Subject:** Maple Leaf Forever

Date	Mintage	MS-63	Proof
2012 Proof	—	—	56,000

100000 DOLLARS

KM# 1209 10000.0000 g. 1.0000 Gold 321.49 oz.
AGW **Obv:** Bust right **Rev:** Bill Reid's sculpture:
Spirit of Haida Gwaii **Note:** The sculpture is at the
Canadian Embassy in Washington, D.C.

Date	Mintage	MS-63	Proof
2011 Proof	—	—	565,000

1000000 DOLLARS

KM# 755 100000.0000 g. 0.9999 Gold 3214.6 oz.
AGW **Obv:** Bust right **Rev:** Three maple leaves
Note: Cast

Date	Mintage	MS-63	Proof
2007	10	5,630,000	—

GOLD BULLION

PLATINUM BULLION COINAGE

DOLLAR

KM# 239 1.5552 g. 0.9995 Platinum 0.0500 oz. APW   **Obv:** Crowned head right, date and denomination below **Rev:** Maple leaf flanked by 9995

Date	Mintage	MS-63	Proof
1993	2,120	BV+30%	—
1994	4,260	BV+30%	—
1995	460	150	—
1996	1,640	BV+30%	—
1997	1,340	BV+30%	—
1998	2,000	BV+30%	—
1999	2,000	BV+30%	—

2 DOLLARS

KM# 257 2.0735 g. 0.9995 Platinum 0.0666 oz. APW   **Obv:** Crowned head right, date and denomination below **Rev:** Maple leaf flanked by 9995

Date	Mintage	MS-63	Proof
1994	1,470	240	—

5 DOLLARS

KM# 164 3.1203 g. 0.9995 Platinum 0.1003 oz. APW   **Obv:** Young bust right, date and denomination below **Obv. Designer:** Arnold Machin **Rev:** Maple leaf flanked by 9995

Date	Mintage	MS-63	Proof
1988	74,000	BV+18%	—
1989 Proof	11,999	—	250
1989	18,000	BV+18%	—

KM# 192 3.1203 g. 0.9995 Platinum 0.1003 oz. APW   **Obv. Designer:** dePedery-Hunt **Rev:** Maple leaf

Date	Mintage	MS-63	Proof
1990	9,000	BV+18%	—
1991	13,000	BV+18%	—
1992	16,000	BV+18%	—
1993	14,020	BV+18%	—
1994	19,190	BV+18%	—
1995	8,940	BV+18%	—
1996	8,820	BV+18%	—
1997	7,050	BV+18%	—
1998	5,710	BV+18%	—
1999	2,000	BV+18%	—

10 DOLLARS

KM# 165 7.7857 g. 0.9995 Platinum 0.2502 oz. APW   **Obv:** Young bust right, date and denomination below **Obv. Designer:** Machin **Rev:** Maple leaf flanked by 9995

Date	Mintage	MS-63	Proof
1988	93,600	BV+13%	—
1989	3,200	BV+13%	—
1989 Proof	1,999	—	550

KM# 193 7.7857 g. 0.9995 Platinum 0.2502 oz. APW   **Obv. Designer:** dePedery-Hunt **Rev:** Maple leaf

Date	Mintage	MS-63	Proof
1990	1,600	BV+13%	—
1991	7,200	BV+13%	—
1992	11,600	BV+13%	—
1993	8,048	BV+13%	—
1994	9,456	BV+13%	—
1995	6,524	BV+13%	—
1996	6,160	BV+13%	—
1997	4,552	BV+13%	—
1998	3,816	BV+13%	—
1999	2,000	BV+13%	—

20 DOLLARS

KM# 166 15.5519 g. 0.9995 Platinum 0.4997 oz. APW   **Obv:** Young bust right, denomination and date below **Obv. Designer:** Machin **Rev:** Maple leaf flanked by 9995

Date	Mintage	MS-63	Proof
1988	23,600	BV+9%	—
1989 Proof	1,999	—	1,000
1989	4,800	BV+9%	—

KM# 194 15.5519 g. 0.9995 Platinum 0.4997 oz. APW   **Obv. Designer:** dePedery-Hunt **Rev:** Maple leaf

Date	Mintage	MS-63	Proof
1990	2,600	BV+9%	—
1991	5,600	BV+9%	—
1992	12,800	BV+9%	—
1993	6,022	BV+9%	—
1994	6,710	BV+9%	—
1995	6,308	BV+9%	—
1996	5,490	BV+9%	—
1997	3,990	BV+9%	—
1998	5,486	BV+9%	—
1999	500	BV+15%	—

PLATINUM BULLION

30 DOLLARS

KM# 174 3.1100 g. 0.9990 Platinum 0.0999 oz.
APW **Obv:** Crowned head right **Rev:** Polar bear swimming, denomination below **Rev. Designer:** Robert Bateman

Date	Mintage	MS-63	Proof
1990 Proof	2,629	—	210

KM# 198 3.1100 g. 0.9990 Platinum 0.0999 oz.
APW **Obv:** Crowned head right **Rev:** Snowy owl, denomination below **Rev. Designer:** Glen Loates

Date	Mintage	MS-63	Proof
1991 Proof	3,500	—	210

KM# 226 3.1100 g. 0.9990 Platinum 0.0999 oz.
APW **Obv:** Crowned head right **Rev:** Cougar head and shoulders, denomination below **Rev. Designer:** George McLean

Date	Mintage	MS-63	Proof
1992 Proof	3,500	—	210

KM# 240 3.1100 g. 0.9990 Platinum 0.0999 oz.
APW **Obv:** Crowned head right **Rev:** Arctic fox, denomination below **Rev. Designer:** Claude D'Angelo

Date	Mintage	MS-63	Proof
1993 Proof	3,500	—	210

KM# 252 3.1100 g. 0.9990 Platinum 0.0999 oz.
APW **Obv:** Crowned head right **Rev:** Sea otter, denomination below **Rev. Designer:** Ron S. Parker

Date	Mintage	MS-63	Proof
1994 Proof	1,500	—	210

KM# 266 3.1100 g. 0.9990 Platinum 0.0999 oz.
APW **Obv:** Crowned head right, date below **Rev:** Canadian lynx, denomination below **Rev. Designer:** Michael Dumas

Date	Mintage	MS-63	Proof
1995 Proof	620	—	210

KM# 278 3.1100 g. 0.9990 Platinum 0.0999 oz.
APW **Obv:** Crowned head right, date below **Rev:** Falcon portrait, denomination below **Rev. Designer:** Dwayne Harty

Date	Mintage	MS-63	Proof
1996 Proof	489	—	210

KM# 300 3.1100 g. 0.9995 Platinum 0.0999 oz.
APW **Obv:** Crowned head right, date below **Rev:** Bison head, denomination below **Rev. Designer:** Chris Bacon

Date	Mintage	MS-63	Proof
1997 Proof	5,000	—	210

KM# 322 3.1100 g. 0.9990 Platinum 0.0999 oz.
APW **Obv:** Crowned head right, date below **Rev:** Grey wolf **Rev. Designer:** Kerr Burnett

Date	Mintage	MS-63	Proof
1998 Proof	2,000	—	210

KM# 359 3.1100 g. 0.9995 Platinum 0.0999 oz.
APW **Obv:** Crowned head right, date below **Rev:** Musk ox **Rev. Designer:** Mark Hobson

Date	Mintage	MS-63	Proof
1999 Proof	1,500	—	210

KM# 405 3.1100 g. 0.9995 Platinum 0.0999 oz.
APW 16 mm. **Obv:** Crowned head right, date below **Rev:** Pronghorn antelope head, denomination below **Rev. Designer:** Mark Hobson **Edge:** Reeded

Date	Mintage	MS-63	Proof
2000 Proof	600	—	210

KM# 429 3.1100 g. 0.9995 Platinum 0.0999 oz.
APW 16 mm. **Obv:** Crowned head right **Rev:**

Harlequin duck's head **Rev. Designer:** Cosme
Saffioti and Susan Taylor **Edge:** Reeded

Date	Mintage	MS-63	Proof
2001 Proof	448	—	200

KM# 1097 3.1100 g. 0.9995 Platinum 0.0999 oz.
APW 16 mm. **Rev:** Great Blue Heron

Date	Mintage	MS-63	Proof
2002 Proof	344	—	200

KM# 1101 3.1100 g. 0.9995 Platinum 0.0999 oz.
APW 16 mm. **Rev:** Atlantic Walrus

Date	Mintage	MS-63	Proof
2003	365	—	250

KM# 1105 3.1100 g. 0.9995 Platinum 0.0999 oz.
APW 16 mm. **Rev:** Grizzly Bear

Date	Mintage	MS-63	Proof
2004 Proof	380	—	250

50 DOLLARS

KM# 167 31.1030 g. 0.9995 Platinum 0.9994 oz.
APW **Obv:** Young bust right, denomination and
date below **Obv. Designer:** Machin **Rev:** Maple leaf
flanked by 9995

Date	Mintage	MS-63	Proof
1988	37,500	BV+4%	—
1989 Proof	5,965	—	1,900
1989	10,000	BV+4%	

KM# 195 31.1030 g. 0.9995 Platinum 0.9994 oz.
APW **Obv. Designer:** dePedery-Hunt **Rev:**
Maple leaf

Date	Mintage	MS-63	Proof
1990	15,100	BV+4%	—
1991	31,900	BV+4%	—
1992	40,500	BV+4%	—
1993	17,666	BV+4%	—
1994	36,245	BV+4%	—
1995	25,829	BV+4%	—
1996	62,273	BV+4%	—
1997	25,480	BV+4%	—
1998	10,403	BV+4%	—
1999	1,300	BV+10%	—

75 DOLLARS

KM# 175 7.7760 g. 0.9990 Platinum 0.2497 oz.
APW **Obv:** Crowned head right **Rev:** Polar bear
resting, denomination below **Rev. Designer:** Robert
Bateman

Date	Mintage	MS-63	Proof
1990 Proof	2,629	—	520

KM# 199 7.7760 g. 0.9990 Platinum 0.2497 oz.
APW **Obv:** Crowned head right **Rev:** Snowy owls
perched on branch, denomination below **Rev.
Designer:** Glen Loates

Date	Mintage	MS-63	Proof
1991 Proof	3,500	—	520

KM# 227 7.7760 g. 0.9990 Platinum 0.2497 oz.
APW **Obv:** Crowned head right **Rev:** Cougar
prowling, denomination below **Rev. Designer:**
George McLean

Date	Mintage	MS-63	Proof
1992 Proof	3,500	—	520

KM# 241 7.7760 g. 0.9990 Platinum 0.2497 oz.
APW **Obv:** Crowned head right **Rev:** Two Arctic
foxes, denomination below **Rev. Designer:** Claude
D'Angelo

Date	Mintage	MS-63	Proof
1993 Proof	3,500	—	520

KM# 253 7.7760 g. 0.9990 Platinum 0.2497 oz.
APW **Obv:** Crowned head right, date below **Rev:**
Sea otter eating urchin, denomination below **Rev.
Designer:** Ron S. Parker

Date	Mintage	MS-63	Proof
1994 Proof	1,500	—	520

KM# 267 7.7760 g. 0.9990 Platinum 0.2497 oz.
APW **Obv:** Crowned head right, date below **Rev:**
Two lynx kittens, denomination below **Rev.
Designer:** Michael Dumas

Date	Mintage	MS-63	Proof
1995 Proof	1,500	—	520

PLATINUM BULLION

KM# 279 7.7760 g. 0.9990 Platinum 0.2497 oz.
APW **Obv:** Crowned head right, date below **Rev:**
Peregrine falcon, denomination below **Rev.**
Designer: Dwayne Harty

Date	Mintage	MS-63	Proof
1996 Proof	1,500	—	520

KM# 301 7.7760 g. 0.9990 Platinum 0.2497 oz.
APW **Obv:** Crowned head right, date below **Rev:**
Two bison calves, denomination below **Rev.**
Designer: Chris Bacon

Date	Mintage	MS-63	Proof
1997 Proof	1,500	—	520

KM# 323 7.7760 g. 0.9990 Platinum 0.2497 oz.
APW **Obv:** Crowned head right, date below **Rev:**
Gray wolf **Rev. Designer:** Kerr Burnett

Date	Mintage	MS-63	Proof
1998 Proof	1,000	—	520

KM# 360 7.7760 g. 0.9990 Platinum 0.2497 oz.
APW **Obv:** Crowned head right, date below **Rev:**
Musk ox **Rev. Designer:** Mark Hobson

Date	Mintage	MS-63	Proof
1999 Proof	500	—	520

KM# 406 7.7760 g. 0.9990 Platinum 0.2497 oz.
APW 20 mm. **Obv:** Crowned head right **Rev:**
Standing pronghorn antelope, denomination below
Rev. Designer: Mark Hobson **Edge:** Reeded

Date	Mintage	MS-63	Proof
2000 Proof	600	—	520

KM# 430 7.7760 g. 0.9995 Platinum 0.2499 oz.
APW 20 mm. **Obv:** Crowned head right **Rev:**
Harlequin duck in flight **Rev. Designer:** Cosme
Saffioti and Susan Taylor **Edge:** Reeded

Date	Mintage	MS-63	Proof
2001 Proof	448	—	500

KM# 1098 7.7700 g. 0.9995 Platinum 0.2497 oz.
APW 20 mm. **Rev:** Great Blue Heron

Date	Mintage	MS-63	Proof
2002 Proof	344	—	525

KM# 1102 7.7700 g. 0.9995 Platinum 0.2497 oz.
APW 20 mm. **Rev:** Atlantic Walrus

Date	Mintage	MS-63	Proof
2003 Proof	365	—	550

KM# 1106 7.7700 g. 0.9995 Platinum 0.2497 oz.
APW 20 mm. **Rev:** Grizzly Bear

Date	Mintage	MS-63	Proof
2004 Proof	380	—	550

150 DOLLARS

KM# 176 15.5520 g. 0.9990 Platinum 0.4995 oz.
APW **Obv:** Crowned head right **Rev:** Polar bear
walking, denomination below **Rev. Designer:**
Robert Bateman

Date	Mintage	MS-63	Proof
1990 Proof	2,629	—	1,000

KM# 200 15.5520 g. 0.9990 Platinum 0.4995 oz.
APW **Obv:** Crowned head right **Rev:** Snowy owl
flying, denomination below **Rev. Designer:** Glen
Loates

Date	Mintage	MS-63	Proof
1991 Proof	3,500	—	1,000

KM# 228 15.5520 g. 0.9990 Platinum 0.4995 oz.
APW **Obv:** Crowned head right **Rev:** Cougar
mother and cub, denomination below **Rev.**
Designer: George McLean

Date	Mintage	MS-63	Proof
1992 Proof	3,500	—	1,000

KM# 242 15.5520 g. 0.9990 Platinum 0.4995 oz.
APW **Obv:** Crowned head right **Rev:** Arctic fox
by lake, denomination below **Rev. Designer:**
Claude D'Angelo

Date	Mintage	MS-63	Proof
1993 Proof	3,500	—	1,000

PLATINUM BULLION

PLATINUM BULLION

KM# 254 15.5520 g. 0.9990 Platinum 0.4995 oz.
APW   **Obv:** Crowned head right, date below **Rev:**
Sea otter mother carrying pup, denomination below
Rev. Designer: Ron S. Parker

Date	Mintage	MS-63	Proof
1994 Proof	—	—	1,000

KM# 268 15.5520 g. 0.9990 Platinum 0.4995 oz.
APW   **Obv:** Crowned head right, date below **Rev:**
Prowling lynx, denomination below **Rev. Designer:**
Michael Dumas

Date	Mintage	MS-63	Proof
1995 Proof	226	—	1,000

KM# 280 15.5520 g. 0.9990 Platinum 0.4995 oz.
APW   **Obv:** Crowned head right, date below **Rev:**
Peregrine falcon on branch, denomination below
Rev. Designer: Dwayne Harty

Date	Mintage	MS-63	Proof
1996 Proof	100	—	1,000

KM# 302 15.5520 g. 0.9990 Platinum 0.4995 oz.
APW   **Obv:** Crowned head right, date below **Rev:**
Bison bull, denomination below **Rev. Designer:**
Chris Bacon

Date	Mintage	MS-63	Proof
1997 Proof	4,000	—	1,000

KM# 324 15.5520 g. 0.9990 Platinum 0.4995 oz.
APW   **Obv:** Crowned head right, date below **Rev:**
Two gray wolf cubs, denomination below **Rev.**
Designer: Kerr Burnett

Date	Mintage	MS-63	Proof
1998 Proof	2,000	—	1,000

KM# 361 15.5520 g. 0.9990 Platinum 0.4995 oz.
APW   **Obv:** Crowned head right **Rev:** Musk ox,
denomination below **Rev. Designer:** Mark Hobson

Date	Mintage	MS-63	Proof
1999 Proof	500	—	1,000

KM# 407 15.5500 g. 0.9990 Platinum 0.4994 oz.
APW 25 mm.   **Obv:** Crowned head right **Rev:** Two
pronghorn antelope, denomination below **Rev.**
Designer: Mark Hobson **Edge:** Reeded

Date	Mintage	MS-63	Proof
2000 Proof	600	—	1,000

KM# 431 15.5500 g. 0.9995 Platinum 0.4997 oz.
APW 25 mm.   **Obv:** Crowned head right **Rev:** Two
harlequin ducks **Rev. Designer:** Cosme Saffioti and
Susan Taylor **Edge:** Reeded

Date	Mintage	MS-63	Proof
2001 Proof	448	—	1,000

KM# 1099 15.5500 g. 0.9995 Platinum 0.4997 oz.
APW 25 mm.   **Rev:** Great Blue Heron

Date	Mintage	MS-63	Proof
2002 Proof	344	—	1,000

KM# 1103 15.5500 g. 0.9995 Platinum 0.4997 oz.
APW 25 mm.   **Rev:** Atlantic Walrus

Date	Mintage	MS-63	Proof
2003 Proof	365	—	1,000

KM# 1107 15.5500 g. 0.9995 Platinum 0.4997 oz.
APW 25 mm.   **Rev:** Grizzly Bear

Date	Mintage	MS-63	Proof
2004 Proof	380	—	1,000

300 DOLLARS

KM# 177 31.1035 g. 0.9990 Platinum 0.9990 oz.
APW   **Obv:** Crowned head right **Rev:** Polar bear
mother and cub, denomination below **Rev.**
Designer: Robert Bateman

Date	Mintage	MS-63	Proof
1990 Proof	2,629	—	1,950

KM# 201 31.1035 g. 0.9990 Platinum 0.9990 oz.
APW   **Obv:** Crowned head right **Rev:** Snowy owl
with chicks, denomination below **Rev. Designer:**
Glen Loates

Date	Mintage	MS-63	Proof
1991 Proof	3,500	—	1,950

KM# 229 31.1035 g. 0.9990 Platinum 0.9990 oz.
APW   **Obv:** Crowned head right **Rev:** Cougar
resting in tree, denomination below **Rev. Designer:**
George McLean

Date	Mintage	MS-63	Proof
1992 Proof	3,500	—	1,950

KM# 243 31.1035 g. 0.9990 Platinum 0.9990 oz.
APW   **Obv:** Crowned head right **Rev:** Mother fox
and three kits, denomination below **Rev. Designer:**
Claude D'Angelo

Date	Mintage	MS-63	Proof
1993 Proof	3,500	—	1,950

KM# 255 31.1035 g. 0.9990 Platinum 0.9990 oz.
APW   **Obv:** Crowned head right, date below **Rev:**
Two otters swimming, denomination below **Rev.**
Designer: Ron S. Parker

Date	Mintage	MS-63	Proof
1994 Proof	—	—	1,950

KM# 269 31.1035 g. 0.9990 Platinum 0.9990 oz.
APW   **Obv:** Crowned head right, date below **Rev:**
Female lynx and three kittens, denomination below
Rev. Designer: Michael Dumas

Date	Mintage	MS-63	Proof
1995 Proof	1,500	—	1,950

KM# 281 31.1035 g. 0.9990 Platinum 0.9990 oz.
APW   **Obv:** Crowned head right, date below **Rev:**
Peregrine falcon feeding nestlings, denomination
below **Rev. Designer:** Dwayne Harty

Date	Mintage	MS-63	Proof
1996 Proof	1,500	—	1,950

PLATINUM BULLION

KM# 303 31.1035 g. 0.9990 Platinum 0.9990 oz. APW **Obv:** Crowned head right, date below **Rev:** Bison family, denomination below **Rev. Designer:** Chris Bacon

Date	Mintage	MS-63	Proof
1997 Proof	1,500	—	1,950

KM# 325 31.1035 g. 0.9990 Platinum 0.9990 oz. APW **Obv:** Crowned head right, date below **Rev:** Gray wolf and two cubs, denomination below **Rev. Designer:** Kerr Burnett

Date	Mintage	MS-63	Proof
1998 Proof	—	—	1,950

KM# 362 31.1035 g. 0.9990 Platinum 0.9990 oz. APW **Obv:** Crowned head right, date below **Rev:** Musk ox **Rev. Designer:** Mark Hobson

Date	Mintage	MS-63	Proof
1999 Proof	500	—	1,950

KM# 408 31.1035 g. 0.9990 Platinum 0.9990 oz. APW 30 mm. **Obv:** Crowned head right, date below **Rev:** Four pronghorn antelope, denomination below **Rev. Designer:** Mark Hobson **Edge:** Reeded

Date	Mintage	MS-63	Proof
2000 Proof	600	—	1,950

KM# 432 31.1035 g. 0.9995 Platinum 0.9995 oz. APW 30 mm. **Obv:** Crowned head right **Rev:** Two standing harlequin ducks **Rev. Designer:** Cosme Saffioti and Susan Taylor **Edge:** Reeded

Date	Mintage	MS-63	Proof
2001 Proof	448	—	1,900

KM# 1100 31.1050 g. 0.9995 Platinum 0.9995 oz. APW 30 mm. **Rev:** Great Blue Heron

Date	Mintage	MS-63	Proof
2002 Proof	344	—	1,950

KM# 1104 31.1050 g. 0.9995 Platinum 0.9995 oz. APW 30 mm. **Rev:** Atlantic Walrus

Date	Mintage	MS-63	Proof
2003 Proof	365	—	1,950

KM# 1108 31.1050 g. 0.9995 Platinum 0.9995 oz. APW 30 mm. **Rev:** Grizzly Bear

Date	Mintage	MS-63	Proof
2004 Proof	380	—	1,950

KM# 753 31.1050 g. 0.9999 Platinum 0.9999 oz. APW **Rev:** Wooly mammoth

Date	Mintage	MS-63	Proof
2007 Proof	400	—	3,200

KM# 831 31.1050 g. 0.9990 Platinum 0.9990 oz. APW **Rev:** Saber Tooth Scimitar cat

Date	Mintage	MS-63	Proof
2008 Proof	200	—	3,500

KM# 951 31.1600 g. 0.9990 Platinum 1.0008 oz. APW 30 mm. **Rev:** Steppe Bison

Date	Mintage	MS-63	Proof
2009 Proof	200	—	3,500

KM# 1159 31.1050 g. 0.9990 Platinum 0.9990 oz. APW 30 mm. **Rev:** Ground Sloth

Date	Mintage	MS-63	P/L	Proof
2010 Proof	200	—	—	1,900

PLATINUM BULLION

KM# 1175 31.1050 g. 0.9995 Platinum 0.9995 oz. APW 30 mm. **Obv:** Bust right **Rev:** Cougar head left

Date	Mintage	MS-63	Proof
2011 Proof	200	—	1,950

KM# 1273 31.1050 g. 0.9990 Platinum 0.9990 oz. APW 30 mm. **Subject:** Maple Leaf Forever

Date	Mintage	MS-63	Proof
2012 Proof	—	—	1,950

SETS

Custom Proof-Like Sets (CPL)

KM#	Date	Mintage	Identification	Issue Price	Mkt. Value
CPL1	1971 (7)	33,517	KM59.1 (2 pcs.), 60.1, 62b, 75.1, 77.1 ,79	6.50	5.00
CPL2	1971 (6)	38,198	KM59.1 (2 pcs.), 60.1, 62b, 75.1, 77.1	6.50	5.00
CPL3	1973 (6)	35,676	KM59.1 (2 pcs.), 60.1, 75.1, 77.1, 81.1 obv. 120 beads, 82	6.50	6.50
CPL4	1973 (6)	Inc. above	KM59.1 (2 pcs.), 60.1, 75.1, 77.1, 81.1 obv. 132 beads, 82	6.50	200
CPL5	1974 (5)	44,296	KM59.1 (2 pcs.), 60.1, 62b-75.1, 88	8.00	5.00
CPL6	1975 (6)	36,851	KM59.1 (2 pcs.), 60.1, 62b-75.1, 76.2, 77.1	8.00	5.00
CPL7	1976 (6)	28,162	KM59.1 (2 pcs.), 60.1, 62b-75.1, 76.2, 77.1	8.00	5.50
CPL8	1977 (6)	44,198	KM59.1 (2 pcs.), 60.1, 62b-75.2, 77.1, 117	8.15	7.50
CPL9	1978 (6)	41,000	KM59.1 (2 pcs.), 60.1, 62b-75.3, 77.1, 120.1	—	5.00
CPL10	1979 (6)	31,174	KM59.2 (2 pcs.), 60.2, 74, 75.3, 77.2, 120.1	10.75	5.00
CPL11	1980 (7)	41,447	KM60.2, 74, 75.3, 77.2, 120.1, 127 (2 pcs.)	10.75	6.00

Mint Sets

KM#	Date	Mintage	Identification	Issue Price	Mkt. Value
MS1	1973 (4)	Inc. above	KM84, 85, 86.1, 87; Olympic Commemoratives, Series I	45.00	135
MS2	1974 (4)	Inc. above	KM89, 90, 93, 94; Olympic Commemoratives, Series II	48.00	135
MS3	1974 (4)	Inc. above	KM91-92, 95-96; Olympic Commemorative, Series III	48.00	135
MS4	1975 (4)	Inc. above	KM98, 99, 102, 103; Olympic Commemoratives, Series IV	48.00	135
MS5	1975 (4)	Inc. above	KM100, 101, 104, 105; Olympic Commemoratives, Series V	60.00	135
MS6	1976 (4)	Inc. above	KM107, 108, 111, 112; Olympic Commemoratives, Series VI	60.00	135
MS7	1976 (4)	Inc. above	KM109, 110, 113, 114; Olympic Commemoratives, Series VII	60.00	135
MS8	2001 (5)	600	KM438-442	1,996	2,950
MS10	2002 (7)	—	KM#444-449, 467, Oh! Canada! 135th Birthday Gift set.	17.00	16.00
MS11	2002 (7)	—	KM#444-449, 467, Tiny Treasures Uncirculated Gift Set	17.00	16.00
MS12	2003 (7)	135,000	KM#289, 182b, 183b, 184b, 290, 186, 270	12.00	16.00
MS13	2003 (7)	75,000	KM490-496	13.25	20.00
MS14	2003 (7)	—	KM289, 182-184, 290, 186, 270, Oh! Canada!	17.75	16.00
MS15	2003 (7)	—	KM289, 182-184, 290, 186, 270, Tiny Treasures Uncirculated Gift Set	17.75	16.00

Olympic Commemoratives (OCP)

KM#	Date	Mintage	Identification	Issue Price	Mkt. Value
OCP1	1973 (4)	Inc. above	KM84-87, Series I	78.50	135
OCP2	1974 (4)	Inc. above	KM89-90, 93-94, Series II	88.50	135
OCP3	1974 (4)	Inc. above	KM91-92, 95-96, Series III	88.50	135
OCP4	1975 (4)	Inc. above	KM98-99, 102-103, Series IV	88.50	135
OCP5	1975 (4)	Inc. above	KM100-101, 104-105, Series V	88.50	135
OCP6	1976 (4)	Inc. above	KM107-108, 111-112, Series VI	88.50	135
OCP7	1976 (4)	Inc. above	KM109-110, 113-114, Series VII	88.50	135

Proof Sets

KM#	Date	Mintage	Identification	Issue Price	Mkt. Value
PS1	1981 (7)	199,000	KM60.2, 74, 75.3, 77.2, 120.1, 127, 130	36.00	30.00
PS2	1982 (7)	180,908	KM60.2a, 74, 75.3, 77.2, 120.1, 132, 133	36.00	37.50
PS3	1983 (7)	166,779	KM60.2a, 74, 75.3, 77.2, 120.1, 132, 138	36.00	27.50
PS4	1984 (7)	161,602	KM60.2a, 74, 75.3, 77.2, 120.1, 132, 140	30.00	27.50
PS5	1985 (7)	157,037	KM60.2a, 74, 75.3, 77.2, 120.1, 132, 143	30.00	30.00
PS6	1986 (7)	175,745	KM60.2a, 74, 75.3, 77.2, 120.1, 132, 149	30.00	29.00
PS7	1987 (7)	179,004	KM60.2a, 74, 75.3, 77.2, 120.1, 132, 154	34.00	30.00
PS8	1988 (7)	175,259	KM60.2a, 74, 75.3, 77.2, 132, 157, 161	37.50	34.00
PS9	1989 (7)	170,928	KM60.2a, 74, 75.3, 77.2, 132, 157, 168	40.00	34.00
PS10	1989 (4)	6,823	KM125.2, 135-136, 153	1,190	2,900
PS11	1989 (4)	1,995	KM164-167	1,700	3,750

KM#	Date	Mintage	Identification	Issue Price	Mkt. Value
PS12	1989 (3)	2,550	KM125.2, 163, 167	1,530	3,500
PS13	1989 (3)	9,979	KM135, 163, 164	165	475
PS14	1990 (7)	158,068	KM170, 181, 182, 183, 184, 185, 186	41.00	42.50
PS15	1990 (4)	2,629	KM174-177	1,720	3,700
PS16	1991 (7)	14,629	KM179, 181, 182, 183, 184, 185, 186	—	80.00
PS17	1991 (4)	873	KM198-201	1,760	3,700
PS18	1992 (11)	84,397	KM203a, 212a-214a, 218, 220a-223a, 231a-234a	—	92.50
PS19	1992 (7)	147,061	KM204-210	42.75	65.00
PS20	1992 (4)	3,500	KM226-229	1,680	3,700
PS21	1993 (7)	143,065	KM181, 182, 183, 184, 185, 186, 235	42.75	40.00
PS22	1993 (4)	3,500	KM240-243	1,329	3,700
PS23	1994 (7)	47,303	KM181-186, 248	47.50	30.00
PS24	1994 (7)	99,121	KM181-186, 251	43.00	45.00
PS25	1994 (4)	1,500	KM252-255	915	3,700
PS26	1995 (7)	Inc. above	KM181-186, 259	37.45	52.00
PS27	1995 (7)	50,000	KM181-185, 258, 259	49.45	52.00
PS28	1995 (4)	Inc. above	KM261-264	42.00	95.00
PS29	1995 (4)	682	KM266-269	1,555	3,700
PS30	1995 (2)	Inc. above	KM261-262	22.00	48.00
PS31	1995 (2)	Inc. above	KM263-264	22.00	46.00
PS32	1996 (4)	423	KM278-281	1,555	3,700
PS33	1996 (7)	Inc. above	KM181, 182a, 183a, 184a, 185a, 186, 274	49.00	60.00
PS34	1996 (4)	Inc. above	KM283-286	44.45	80.00
PS35	1997 (7)	Inc. above	KM182a, 183a, 184a, 270c, 282, 289, 290	60.00	75.00
PS36	1997 (4)	Inc. above	KM292-295	44.45	68.00
PS37	1997 (4)	Inc. above	KM300-303	1,530	3,700
PS38	1998 (8)	Inc. above	KM182a, 183a, 184a, 186, 270b, 289, 290a, 306	59.45	80.00
PS39	1998 (5)	25,000	KM309-313	73.50	55.00
PS40	1998 (2)	61,000	KM316 w/China Y-727	72.50	40.00
PS41	1998 (4)	Inc. above	KM318-321	44.45	68.00
PS42	1998 (4)	1,000	KM322-325	1,552	3,700
PS43	1998 (5)	25,000	KM310-313, 332	73.50	68.00
PS44	1999 (7)	Inc. above	KM182a-184a, 186, 270c, 289, 290a,	59.45	55.00
PS45	1999 (4)	Inc. above	KM335-338	39.95	140
PS46	1999 (12)	Inc. above	KM342a-353a	99.45	115
PS47	1999 (4)	Inc. above	KM359-362	1,425	3,700
PS48	2000 (12)	—	KM373a-383a, 384.2a	101	110
PS49	2000 (4)	—	KM389-392	44.00	80.00
PS50	2000 (4)	600	KM405-408	1,416	3,700
PS51	2001 (4)	—	KM429, 430, 431, 432	—	3,600
PS54	2002 (2)	—	KM#519, 520	750	1,125
PS57	2004 (8)	—	KM#490, 491a-494a, 495, 496a, 512	—	115
PS58	2004 (5)	25,000	KM#621-625	—	100.00

Proof-Like Dollars

KM#	Date	Mintage	Identification	Issue Price	Mkt. Value
D1.1	1951 (1)	—	KM46, Canoe	—	150
D1.2	1951 (1)	—	KM46, Arnprior	—	1,300
D2.1	1952 (1)	—	KM46, water lines	—	1,150
D2.2	1952 (1)	—	KM46, without water lines	—	150
D3	1953 (1)	1,200	KM54, Canoe w/shoulder fold	—	400
D4	1954 (1)	5,300	KM54, Canoe	1.25	175
D5	1955 (1)	7,950	KM54, Canoe	1.25	125
D5a	1955 (1)	Inc. above	KM54, Arnprior	1.25	250
D6	1956 (1)	10,212	KM54, Canoe	1.25	95.00
D7	1957 (1)	16,241	KM54, Canoe	1.25	50.00
D8	1958 (1)	33,237	KM55, British Columbia	1.25	35.00
D9	1959 (1)	45,160	KM54, Canoe	1.25	24.00
D10	1960 (1)	82,728	KM54, Canoe	1.25	22.00
D11	1961 (1)	120,928	KM54, Canoe	1.25	22.00
D12	1962 (1)	248,901	KM54, Canoe	1.25	22.00
D13	1963 (1)	963,525	KM54, Canoe	1.25	22.00
D14	1964 (1)	2,862,441	KM58, Charlottetown	1.25	22.00
D15	1965 (1)	2,904,352	KM64.1, Canoe	—	22.00
D16	1966 (1)	672,514	KM64.1, Canoe	—	22.00
D17	1967 (1)	1,036,176	KM70, Confederation	—	22.00

Proof-Like Sets (PL)

KM#	Date	Mintage	Identification	Issue Price	Mkt. Value
PL1	1953 (6)	1,200	KM49 w/o shoulder fold, 50-54	2.20	2,000
PL3	1954 (6)	3,000	KM49-54	2.50	650
PL4	1954 (6)	Inc. above	KM49 w/o shoulder fold, 50-54	2.50	1,450
PL5	1955 (6)	6,300	KM49, 50a, 51-54	2.50	400
PL6	1955 (6)	Inc. above	KM49, 50a, 51-54, Arnprior	2.50	500
PL7	1956 (6)	6,500	KM49, 50a, 51-54	2.50	200
PL8	1957 (6)	11,862	KM49, 50a, 51-54	2.50	150
PL9	1958 (6)	18,259	KM49, 50a, 51-53, 55	2.50	125
PL10	1959 (6)	31,577	KM49, 50a, 51, 52, 54, 56	2.50	60.00
PL11	1960 (6)	64,097	KM49, 50a, 51, 52, 54, 56	3.00	45.00

SETS

KM#	Date	Mintage	Identification	Issue Price	Mkt. Value
PL12	1961 (6)	98,373	KM49, 50a, 51, 52, 54, 56	3.00	45.00
PL13	1962 (6)	200,950	KM49, 50a, 51, 52, 54, 56	3.00	40.00
PL14	1963 (6)	673,006	KM49, 51, 52, 54, 56, 57	3.00	40.00
PL15	1964 (5)	1,653,162	KM49, 51, 52, 56-58	3.00	40.00
PL16	1965 (4)	2,904,352	KM59.1-60.1, 61-63, 64.1	4.00	40.00
PL17	1966 (5)	672,514	KM59.1-60.1, 61-63, 64.1	4.00	40.00
PL18	1967 (6)	961,887	KM65-70 (pliofilm flat pack)	4.00	40.00
PL18A	1967 (6)	70,583	KM65-70 and Silver Medal (red box)	12.00	65.00
PL18B	1967 (7)	337,688	KM65-71 (black box)	40.00	1,100
PL19	1968 (6)	521,641	KM59.1-60.1, 62b, 72a, 75.1-76.1	4.00	2.25
PL20	1969 (4)	326,203	KM59.1-60.1, 62b, 75.1-77.1	4.00	3.00
PL21	1970 (4)	349,120	KM59.1-60.1, 62b, 75.1, 77.1, 78	4.00	3.50
PL22	1971 (4)	253,311	KM59.1-60.1, 62b, 75.1, 77.1, 79	4.00	3.00
PL23	1972 (3)	224,275	KM59.1-60.1, 62b-77.1	4.00	3.00
PL24	1973 (4)	243,695	KM59.1-60.1, 62b-75.1 obv. 120 beads, 77.1, 81.1, 82	4.00	4.00
PL25	1973 (3)	Inc. above	KM59.1-60.1, 62b-75.1 obv. 132 beads, 77.1, 81.2, 82	4.00	250
PL26	1974 (6)	213,589	KM59.1-60.1, 62b-75.1, 77.1, 88	5.00	3.00
PL27.1	1975 (4)	197,372	KM59.1, 60.1, 62b-75.1, 76.2, 77.1	5.00	3.50
PL27.2	1975 (6)	Inc. above	KM59.1, 60.1, 62b-75.1, 76.3, 77.1	5.00	5.00
PL28	1976 (4)	171,737	KM59.1, 60.1, 62b-75.1, 76.2, 77.1	5.15	3.00
PL29	1977 (4)	225,307	KM59.1, 60.1, 62b, 75.2, 77.1, 117.1	5.15	3.00
PL30	1978 (6)	260,000	KM59.1-60.1, 62b, 75.3, 77.1, 120.1	5.25	4.25
PL31	1979 (6)	187,624	KM59.2-60.2, 74, 75.3, 77.2, 120.1	6.25	4.25
PL32	1980 (6)	410,842	KM60.2, 74, 75.3, 77.2, 120.1, 127	6.50	4.50
PL33	1981 (5)	186,250	KM60.2, 74, 75.3, 77.2, 120.1, 123	5.00	4.00
PL34	1982 (5)	203,287	KM60.2, 74, 75.3, 77.2, 120.1, 123	6.00	4.00
PL36	1983 (6)	190,838	KM60.2a, 74, 75.3, 77.2, 120.1, 132	5.00	5.00
PL36.1	1983 (6)	Inc. above	KM60.2a, 74, 75.3, 77.2, 120.1, 132; set in folder packaged by British Royal Mint Coin Club	—	10.00
PL37	1984 (6)	181,249	KM60.2a, 74, 75.3, 77.2, 120.1, 132	5.25	5.00
PL38	1985 (6)	173,924	KM60.2a, 74, 75.3, 77.2, 120.1, 132	5.25	24.00
PL39	1986 (6)	167,338	KM60.2a, 74, 75.3, 77.2, 120.1, 132	5.25	6.50
PL40	1987 (6)	212,136	KM60.2a, 74, 75.3, 77.2, 120.1, 132	5.25	7.00
PL41	1988 (6)	182,048	KM60.2a, 74, 75.3, 77.2, 132, 157	6.05	5.50
PL42	1989 (6)	173,622	KM60.2a, 74, 75.3, 77.2, 132, 157	6.60	8.00
PL43	1990 (6)	170,791	KM181-186	7.40	8.00
PL44	1991 (6)	147,814	KM181-186	7.40	25.00
PL45	1992 (6)	217,597	KM204-209	8.25	17.50
PL46	1993 (6)	171,680	KM181-186	8.25	5.00
PL47	1994 (6)	141,676	KM181-185, 258	8.50	5.50
PL48	1994 (6)	18,794	KM181-185, 258 (Oh Canada holder)	—	8.50
PL49	1995 (6)	143,892	KM181-186	6.95	5.50
PL50	1995 (6)	50,927	KM181-186 (Oh Canada holder)	14.65	8.50
PL51	1995 (6)	36,443	KM181-186 (Baby Gift holder)	—	9.00
PL52	1996 (4)	116,736	KM181-186	—	27.00
PL53	1996 (6)	29,747	KM181-186 (Baby Gift holder)	—	14.00
PL54	1996 (10)	Inc. above	KM181a-185a, 186	8.95	65.00
PL55	1996 (6)	Inc. above	KM181a-185a, 186 (Oh Canada holder)	14.65	12.00
PL56	1996 (6)	Inc. above	KM181a-185a, 186 (Baby Gift holder)	—	12.00
PL57	1997 (7)	Inc. above	KM182a-184a, 209, 270, 289-290	10.45	8.00
PL58	1997 (7)	Inc. above	KM182a-184a, 270, 289-291 (Oh Canada holder)	16.45	30.00
PL59	1997 (5)	Inc. above	KM182a-184a, 209, 270, 289-290 (Baby Gift holder)	18.50	25.00
PL60	1998 (7)	Inc. above	KM182-184, 186, 270, 289-290	10.45	25.00
PL61	1998 (7)	Inc. above	KM182-184, 186, 270, 289-290 (Oh Canada holder)	16.45	25.00
PL62	1998 (7)	Inc. above	KM182-184, 186, 270, 289-290 (Tiny Treasures holder)	16.45	25.00
PL63	1999 (12)	Inc. above	KM342-353	16.95	10.00
PL64	2000 (12)	—	KM373-384	16.95	10.00

Specimen Sets (SS)

KM#	Date	Mintage	Identification	Issue Price	Mkt. Value
SS1	1858 (4)	Inc. above	KM1-4, Reeded edge	—	12,000
SS2	1858 (4)	Inc. above	KM1-4, Plain edge	—	10,000
SS3	1858 (4)	Inc. above	KM1-4; Double Set	—	20,000
SS4	1858 (1)	Inc. above	KM1 (overdate), 2-4; Double Set	—	20,000
SS5	1870 (1)	100	KM2, 3, 5, 6 (reeded edges)	—	40,000
SS6	1870 (1)	Inc. above	KM2, 3, 5, 6; Double Set (plain edges)	—	80,000
SS7	1872 (4)	Inc. above	KM2, 3, 5, 6	—	12,500
SS8	1875 (2)	Inc. above	KM2 (Large date), 3, 5	—	100,000
SS9	1880 (2)	Inc. above	KM2, 3, 5 (Narrow 0)	—	55,000
SS10	1881 (5)	Inc. above	KM7, 2, 3, 5, 6	—	35,000
SS11	1892 (2)	Inc. above	KM3, 5	—	10,000
SS12	1902 (5)	100	KM8-12	—	60,000
SS13	1902 (3)	Inc. above	KM9 (Large H), 10, 11	—	40,000
SS14	1903 (3)	Inc. above	KM10, 12, 13	—	7,000
SS15	1908 (5)	1,000	KM8, 10-13	—	3,500
SS16	1911 (5)	1,000	KM15-19	—	5,500
SS17	1911/12 (7)	5	KM15-20, 26-27	—	75,000
SS18	1921 (5)	Inc. above	KM22a-25a, 28	—	225,000
SS19	1922 (2)	Inc. above	KM28, 29	—	2,500

KM#	Date	Mintage	Identification	Issue Price	Mkt. Value
SS20	1923 (2)	Inc. above	KM28, 29	—	5,000
SS21	1924 (2)	Inc. above	KM28, 29	—	4,000
SS22	1925 (2)	Inc. above	KM28, 29	—	7,000
SS23	1926 (2)	Inc. above	KM28, 29 (Near 6)	—	5,000
SS24	1927 (3)	Inc. above	KM24a, 28, 29	—	8,000
SS25	1928 (4)	Inc. above	KM23a, 24a, 28, 29	—	12,000
SS26	1929 (5)	Inc. above	KM23a,-25a, 28, 29	—	35,000
SS27	1930 (4)	Inc. above	KM23a, 24a. 28, 29	—	25,000
SS28	1931 (5)	Inc. above	KM23a-25a, 28, 29	—	60,000
SS29	1932 (5)	Inc. above	KM23a-25a, 28, 29	—	20,000
SS30	1934 (2)	Inc. above	KM23-25, 28, 29	—	50,000
SS31	1936 (5)	Inc. above	KM23a-25a, 28, 29	—	12,000
SS32	1936 (5)	Inc. above	KM23a(dot), 24a(dot), 25a, 28(dot), 29, 30	—	550,000
SS33	1937 (6)	1,025	KM32-37, Matte Finish	—	1,600
SS34	1937 (4)	Inc. above	KM32-35, Mirror Fields	—	1,200
SS35	1937 (6)	75	KM32-37, Mirror Fields	—	3,000
SS36	1938 (6)	Inc. above	KM32-37	—	40,000
SS-A36	1939 (5)	Inc. above	KM32-35, 38, Matte Finish	—	—
SS-B36	1939 (5)	Inc. above	KM32-35, 38, Mirror Fields	—	—
SS-C36	1942 (2)	Inc. above	KM32, 33	—	1,000
SS-D36	1943 (2)	Inc. above	KM32, 40	—	1,000
SS37	1944 (5)	3	KM32, 34-37, 40a	—	20,000
SS-A37	1944 (2)	Inc. above	KM32, 40a	—	1,000
SS38	1945 (5)	6	KM32, 34-37, 40a	—	12,500
SS-A38	1945 (2)	Inc. above	KM32, 40a	—	1,000
SS39	1946 (5)	15	KM32, 34-37, 39a	—	9,000
SS40	1947 (6)	Inc. above	KM32, 34-36(7 curved), 37(7 pointed),	—	8,750
SS41	1947 (6)	Inc. above	KM32, 34-36(7 curved), 37(blunt 7), 39a	—	6,200
SS42	1947 (6)	Inc. above	KM32, 34-36(7 curved right), 37, 39a	—	4,250
SS43	1948 (6)	30	KM41-46	—	10,000
SS44	1949 (4)	20	KM41-45, 47	—	8,000
SS44A	1949 (2)	Inc. above	KM47 (Proof)	—	2,600
SS45	1950 (4)	12	KM41-46	—	4,000
SS46	1950 (4)	Inc. above	KM41-45, 46 (Arnprior)	—	7,000
SS47	1951 (5)	12	KM41, 48, 42a, 43-46 (w/water lines)	—	4,000
SS48	1952 (5)	2,317	KM41, 42a, 43-46 (water lines)	—	3,500
SS48A	1952 (5)	Inc. above	KM41, 42a, 43-46 (w/o water lines)	—	2,900
SS49	1953 (6)	28	KM49 w/o straps, 50-54	—	3,500
SS50	1953 (6)	Inc. above	KM49 w/ straps, 50-54	—	875
SS51	1964 (5)	Inc. above	KM49, 51, 52, 56-58	—	2,400
SS52	1965 (4)	Inc. above	KM59.1-60.1, 61-63, 64.1	—	2,400
SS56	1971 (6)	66,860	KM59.1-60.1, 62b-75.1, 77.1, 79 (2 pcs.); Double Dollar Prestige Sets	12.00	14.50
SS57	1972 (5)	36,349	KM59.1,-60.1, 62b-75.1, 76.1 (2 pcs.)	12.00	18.00
SS58	1973 (6)	119,819	KM59.1-60.1, 75.1, 77.1, 81.1, 82, 83	12.00	16.00
SS59	1973 (6)	Inc. above	KM59.1-60.1, 75.1, 77.1, 81.2, 82, 83		1,600
SS60	1974 (5)	85,230	KM59.1-60.1, 62b-75.1, 77.1, 88, 88a	15.00	12.50
SS61	1975 (5)	97,263	KM59.1-60.1, 62b-75.1, 76.2, 77.1, 97	15.00	12.50
SS62	1976 (5)	87,744	KM59.1-60, 62b-75.1, 76.2, 77.1, 106	16.00	14.00
SS63	1977 (5)	142,577	KM59.1-60.1, 62b, 75.2, 77.1, 117.1, 118	16.50	14.50
SS64	1978 (6)	147,000	KM59.1-60.1, 62b, 75.3, 77.1, 120.1, 121	16.50	10.00
SS65	1979 (6)	155,698	KM59.2-60.2, 74, 75.3, 77.2, 120, 124	18.50	15.50
SS66	1980 (6)	162,875	KM60.2, 74-75.3, 77.2, 120, 127, 128	30.50	25.00
SS67	1981 (6)	71,300	KM60.2, 74, 75.3, 77.2, 120.1, 127; Regular Specimen Sets	10.00	5.50
SS68	1982 (10)	62,298	KM60.2a, 74, 75.3, 77.2, 120.1, 132	11.50	100.00
SS69	1983 (6)	60,329	KM60.2a, 74, 75.3, 77.2, 120.1, 132	12.75	9.00
SS70	1984 (2)	60,400	KM60.2a, 74, 75.3, 77.2, 120.1, 132	10.00	5.50
SS71	1985 (6)	61,553	KM60.2a, 74, 75.3, 77.2, 120.1, 132	10.00	23.50
SS72	1986 (6)	67,152	KM60.2a, 74, 75.3, 77.2, 120.1, 132	10.00	9.00
SS72A	1987 (6)	75,194	KM60.2a, 74, 75.3, 77.2, 120.1, 132	11.00	7.50
SS73	1988 (6)	70,205	KM60.2a, 74, 75.3, 77.2, 132, 157	12.30	7.50
SS74	1989 (6)	75,306	KM60.2a, 74, 75.3, 77.2, 132, 157	14.50	9.50
SS75	1990 (6)	76,611	KM181-186	15.50	8.50
SS76	1991 (6)	68,552	KM181-186	15.50	17.50
SS77	1992 (6)	78,328	KM204-209	16.25	17.50
SS78	1993 (6)	77,351	KM181-186; Regular Specimen Sets Resumed	16.25	13.00
SS79	1994 (6)	77,349	KM181-186	16.50	9.50
SS80	1995 (6)	Inc. above	KM181-186	13.95	9.50
SS82	1996 (4)	Inc. above	KM181a-185a, 186	18.95	35.00
SS83	1997 (7)	Inc. above	KM182a-184a, 270, 289-291	19.95	47.50
SS84	1998 (7)	Inc. above	KM182-184, 186, 270, 289, 290	19.95	18.00
SS85	1999 (7)	Inc. above	KM182-184, 186, 270, 289a, 290	19.95	20.00
SS91	2003 (3)	75,000	KM#(uncertain), 270, 289, 290	30.00	50.00

V.I.P. Specimen Sets (VS)

KM#	Date	Mintage	Identification	Issue Price	Mkt. Value
VS1	1969 (0)	4		—	2,000
VS2	1970 (0)	100	KM59.1-60.1, 74.1-75.1, 77.1, 78	—	525
VS3	1971 (0)	69	KM59.1-60.1, 74.1-75.1, 77.1, 79(2 pcs.)	—	525

KM#	Date	Mintage	Identification	Issue Price	Mkt. Value
VS4	1972 (0)	25	KM59.1-60.1, 74.1-75.1, 76.1, (2 pcs.), 77.1	—	650
VS5	1973 (0)	26	KM59.1-60.1, 75.1, 77.1, 81.1, 82, 83	—	650
VS6	1974 (0)	72	KM59.1-60.1, 74.1-75.1, 77.1, 88, 88a	—	525
VS7	1975 (0)	94	KM59.1-60.1, 74.1-75.1, 76.2, 77.1, 97	—	525
VS8	1976 (0)	Inc. above	KM59.1-60.1, 74.1-75.1, 76.2, 77.1, 106	—	525

NEW BRUNSWICK
PROVINCE

STERLING COINAGE

HALFPENNY TOKEN

KM# 1 Copper   **Obv:** Crowned head left **Obv. Legend:** VICTORIA DEI GRATIA REGINA **Rev:** Three masted ship **Rev. Legend:** NEW BRUNSWICK

Date	Mintage	VG-8	F-12	VF-20	XF-40	MS-60	MS-63	Proof
1843	480,000	4.00	7.50	15.00	45.00	300	400	—
1843 Proof	—	—	—	—	—	—	—	750

KM# 3 Copper   **Obv:** Head left **Obv. Legend:** VICTORIA DEI GRATIA REGINA **Rev:** Three masted ship **Rev. Legend:** NEW BRUNSWICK

Date	Mintage	VG-8	F-12	VF-20	XF-40	MS-60	MS-63	Proof
1854	864,000	4.00	7.50	15.00	45.00	300	400	—

KM# 3a Bronze   **Obv:** Head left **Obv. Legend:** VICTORIA DEI GRATIA REGINA **Rev:** Three masted ship **Rev. Legend:** NEW BRUNSWICK

Date	Mintage	VG-8	F-12	VF-20	XF-40	MS-60	MS-63	Proof
1854 Proof	—	—	—	—	—	—	—	400

1 PENNY TOKEN

NEW BRUNSWICK

KM# 2 Copper   **Obv:** Crowned head left **Obv. Legend:** VICTORIA DEI GRATIA REGINA **Rev:** Three masted ship **Rev. Legend:** NEW BRUNSWICK

Date	Mintage	VG-8	F-12	VF-20	XF-40	MS-60	MS-63	Proof
1843	480,000	5.00	9.50	23.00	65.00	250	350	—
1843 Proof								800

KM# 4 Copper   **Obv:** Head left **Obv. Legend:** VICTORIA DEI GRATIA REGINA **Rev:** Three masted ship **Rev. Legend:** NEW BRUNSWICK

Date	Mintage	VG-8	F-12	VF-20	XF-40	MS-60	MS-63	Proof
1854	432,000	3.75	7.50	22.00	65.00	300	400	—

DECIMAL COINAGE

HALF CENT

KM# 5 Bronze   **Obv:** Laureate bust left **Obv. Legend:** VICTORIA D:G: BRITT: REG: F:D: **Rev:** Crown and date within beaded circle, wreath surrounds

Date	Mintage	VG-8	F-12	VF-20	XF-40	MS-60	MS-63	Proof
1861	222,800	125	175	225	350	650	1,500	—
1861 Proof	—	—	—	—	—	—	—	2,200

CENT

KM# 6 Bronze   **Obv:** Laureate bust left **Obv. Legend:** VICTORIA D:G: BRITT: REG: F:D: **Rev:** Crown and date within beaded circle, wreath surrounds **Rev. Legend:** NEW BRUNSWICK

Date	Mintage	VG-8	F-12	VF-20	XF-40	MS-60	MS-63	Proof
1861	1,000,000	3.50	6.00	9.00	14.00	100.00	450	—
1861 Proof	—	—	—	—	—	—	—	450
1864 short 6	1,000,000	3.50	6.00	9.00	20.00	125	550	—
1864 long 6	Inc. above	4.00	6.50	13.00	24.00	175	650	—

NEW BRUNSWICK

NEW BRUNSWICK • 20 CENTS 465

5 CENTS

KM# 7 1.1620 g. 0.9250 Silver 0.0346 oz. ASW **Obv:** Laureate head left **Obv. Legend:** VICTORIA D: G: REG: / NEW BRUNSWICK **Rev:** Denomination and date within wreath, crown above

Date	Mintage	VG-8	F-12	VF-20	XF-40	MS-60	MS-63	Proof
1862	100,000	65.00	100.00	225	500	1,700	3,200	—
1862 Proof	—	—	—	—	—	—	—	3,500
1864 small 6	100,000	65.00	100.00	225	1,000	2,200	4,900	—
1864 large 6	Inc. above	75.00	125	300	600	2,500	5,000	—

10 CENTS

KM# 8 2.3240 g. 0.9250 Silver 0.0691 oz. ASW **Obv:** Laureate head left **Obv. Legend:** VICTORIA D: G: REG: / NEW BRUNSWICK **Rev:** Denomination and date within wreath, crown above

Date	Mintage	VG-8	F-12	VF-20	XF-40	MS-60	MS-63	Proof
1862	150,000	65.00	100.00	225	450	1,600	3,000	—
1862 recut 2	Inc. above	95.00	175	350	750	2,900	6,700	—
1862 Proof	—	—	—	—	—	—	—	2,850
1864	100,000	65.00	100.00	225	450	2,700	6,300	—

20 CENTS

KM# 9 4.6480 g. 0.9250 Silver 0.1382 oz. ASW **Obv:** Laureate head left **Obv. Legend:** VICTORIA D: G: REG: / NEW BRUNSWICK **Rev:** Denomination and date within wreath, crown above

Date	Mintage	VG-8	F-12	VF-20	XF-40	MS-60	MS-63	Proof
1862	150,000	29.00	50.00	100.00	225	1,050	4,400	—
1862 Proof	—	—	—	—	—	—	—	2,850
1864	150,000	29.00	50.00	100.00	225	1,600	4,600	—

NEWFOUNDLAND

PROVINCE

CIRCULATION COINAGE

LARGE CENT

KM# 1 Bronze **Obv:** Laureate bust left **Obv. Legend:** VICTORIA D:G: BRITT: REG:F:D: **Rev:** Crown and date within circle, florals surround **Rev. Legend:** NEWFOUNDLAND

Date	Mintage	VG-8	F-12	VF-20	XF-40	MS-60	MS-63	Proof
1865	240,000	3.50	5.50	12.00	30.00	175	900	—
1872H	200,000	2.50	4.00	7.00	17.00	70.00	250	—
1872H Proof	—	—	—	—	—	—	—	800
1873	200,025	4.00	6.50	20.00	40.00	300	1,600	—
1873 Proof	—	—	—	—	—	—	—	3,000
1876H	200,000	3.50	7.00	15.00	60.00	300	1,600	—
1876H Proof, reported not confirmed	—	—	—	—	—	—	—	—
1880 round 0, even date	400,000	3.00	3.50	7.00	20.00	125	500	—
1880 round and low 0	Inc. above	4.50	12.00	20.00	50.00	400	2,600	—
1880 oval 0	Inc. above	200	300	500	950	2,000	6,000	—
1880 oval 0 Proof	—	—	—	—	—	—	—	2,500
1885	40,000	27.50	50.00	75.00	125	500	2,400	—
1885 Proof	—	—	—	—	—	—	—	2,500
1888	50,000	30.00	55.00	80.00	175	750	4,800	—
1890	200,000	3.00	6.00	15.00	45.00	300	1,200	—
1894	200,000	3.00	5.00	10.00	25.00	140	1,200	—
1894 Proof	—	—	—	—	—	—	—	1,500
1896	200,000	3.00	3.50	7.00	27.00	120	500	—
1896 Proof	—	—	—	—	—	—	—	1,500

KM# 9 Bronze **Obv:** Crowned bust right **Obv. Designer:** G.W. DeSaulles **Rev:** Crown and date within center circle, wreath surrounds, denomination above **Rev. Designer:** Horace Morehen

Date	Mintage	VG-8	F-12	VF-20	XF-40	MS-60	MS-63	Proof
1904H	100,000	10.00	18.00	30.00	75.00	400	1,300	—
1904H Proof	—	—	—	—	—	—	—	6,000
1907	200,000	3.00	5.00	11.00	35.00	250	1,000	—
1909	200,000	3.00	5.00	9.00	27.50	125	250	—
1909 Proof	—	—	—	—	—	—	—	600

KM# 16 Bronze **Obv:** Crowned bust left **Obv. Designer:** E.B. MacKennal **Rev:** Crown and date within center circle, wreath surrounds, denomination above **Rev. Designer:** Horace Morehen

Date	Mintage	VG-8	F-12	VF-20	XF-40	MS-60	MS-63	Proof
1913	400,000	1.50	2.50	3.50	9.00	60.00	125	—
1917C	702,350	1.50	2.50	3.50	8.00	100.00	400	—
1917C Proof	—	—	—	—	—	—	—	950
1919C	300,000	1.50	2.50	4.00	14.00	225	750	—
1919C Proof	—	—	—	—	—	—	—	2,500
1920C	302,184	1.50	2.50	6.00	24.00	350	1,900	—
1929	300,000	1.50	2.50	3.50	7.00	85.00	175	—
1929C Proof	—	—	—	—	—	—	—	3,000
1936	300,000	1.50	2.00	2.50	5.00	40.00	100.00	—

SMALL CENT

KM# 18 3.2000 g. Bronze 19 mm. **Obv:** Crowned head left **Obv. Designer:** Percy Metcalfe **Rev:** Pitcher plant divides date, denomination below **Rev. Designer:** Walter J. Newman

Date	Mintage	VG-8	F-12	VF-20	XF-40	MS-60	MS-63	Proof
1938	500,000	0.45	0.95	1.25	3.50	24.00	70.00	—
1938 Proof	—	—	—	—	—	—	—	6,000
1940	300,000	1.25	2.25	4.50	14.00	95.00	600	—
1940 Re-engraved date	Inc. above	45.00	60.00	85.00	150	650	2,400	—
1940 Proof	—	—	—	—	—	—	—	2,500
1941C	827,662	0.45	0.70	0.95	2.50	29.00	200	—
1941C Re-engraved date	Inc. above	16.00	24.00	40.00	95.00	400	2,000	—
1942	1,996,889	0.45	0.70	0.95	2.50	40.00	250	—
1943C	1,239,732	0.45	0.70	0.95	2.50	22.50	100.00	—
1944C	1,328,776	1.50	2.50	9.00	35.00	300	2,000	—
1947C	313,772	1.25	1.75	4.00	19.00	100.00	350	—
1947C Proof	—	—	—	—	—	—	—	3,000

5 CENTS

KM# 2 1.1782 g. 0.9250 Silver 0.0350 oz. ASW **Obv:** Laureate head left **Obv. Legend:** VICTORIA D: G: REG: / NEWFOUNDLAND **Rev:** Denomination and date within ornamental circle **Edge:** Reeded

Date	Mintage	VG-8	F-12	VF-20	XF-40	MS-60	MS-63	Proof
1865	80,000	35.00	50.00	150	300	1,200	3,000	—
1865 Proof	—	—	—	—	—	—	—	4,000
1870	40,000	65.00	125	225	500	1,900	3,000	—
1870 Proof	—	—	—	—	—	—	—	4,000
1872H	40,000	40.00	70.00	125	175	600	2,400	—
1873	44,260	125	200	450	1,100	4,600	—	—
1873H	Inc. above	950	1,400	2,000	3,700	12,500	22,000	—
1873 Proof	—	—	—	—	—	—	—	10,000
1876H	20,000	125	200	350	650	1,200	2,750	—
1880	40,000	45.00	65.00	150	300	1,600	2,400	—
1880 Proof	—	—	—	—	—	—	—	5,000
1881	40,000	45.00	65.00	150	300	1,900	2,500	—
1881 Proof	—	—	—	—	—	—	—	5,000
1882H	60,000	23.00	45.00	90.00	200	800	2,000	—
1882H Proof	—	—	—	—	—	—	—	2,000
1885	16,000	130	210	335	750	2,400	4,500	—
1885 Proof	—	—	—	—	—	—	—	7,500
1888	40,000	40.00	75.00	225	375	1,900	4,900	—
1888 Proof	—	—	—	—	—	—	—	7,500
1890	160,000	11.00	21.00	45.00	125	800	2,000	—
1890 Proof	—	—	—	—	—	—	—	5,000
1894	160,000	10.00	19.00	30.00	100.00	800	2,500	—
1894 Proof	—	—	—	—	—	—	—	5,000
1896	400,000	4.00	8.00	20.00	50.00	700	2,700	—
1896 Proof	—	—	—	—	—	—	—	5,000

KM#7 1.1782 g. 0.9250 Silver 0.0350 oz. ASW **Obv:** Crowned bust right **Rev:** Denomination and date within circle

Date	Mintage	VG-8	F-12	VF-20	XF-40	MS-60	MS-63	Proof
1903	100,000	5.00	11.00	29.00	70.00	450	1,700	—
1903 Proof	—	—	—	—	—	—	—	3,000
1904H	100,000	4.00	7.00	19.00	45.00	225	450	—
1904H Proof	—	—	—	—	—	—	—	1,800
1908	400,000	4.00	7.00	18.00	45.00	250	1,100	—

KM# 13 1.1782 g. 0.9250 Silver 0.0350 oz. ASW **Obv:** Crowned bust left **Obv. Designer:** E.B. MacKennal **Rev:** Denomination and date within circle **Rev. Designer:** G.W. DeSaulles

NEWFOUNDLAND

Date	Mintage	VG-8	F-12	VF-20	XF-40	MS-60	MS-63	Proof
1912	300,000	2.00	3.00	6.00	24.00	125	250	—
1912 Proof	—	—	—	—	—	—	—	2,400
1917C	300,319	2.00	5.00	8.00	27.00	350	1,200	—
1917C Proof	—	—	—	—	—	—	—	2,400
1919C	100,844	6.00	11.00	27.00	100.00	1,200	3,500	—
1919C Proof	—	—	—	—	—	—	—	2,400
1929	300,000	2.00	3.00	4.00	14.00	175	400	—

KM# 19 1.1782 g. 0.9250 Silver 0.0350 oz. ASW **Obv:** Crowned head left **Obv. Designer:** Percy Metcalfe **Rev:** Denomination and date within circle **Rev. Designer:** G.W. DeSaulles

Date	Mintage	VG-8	F-12	VF-20	XF-40	MS-60	MS-63	Proof
1938	100,000	1.50	2.50	3.00	11.00	100.00	300	—
1938 Proof	—	—	—	—	—	—	—	1,600
1940C	200,000	1.50	2.50	3.00	11.00	100.00	350	—
1940C Proof	—	—	—	—	—	—	—	3,200
1941C	621,641	BV	1.75	2.50	4.00	22.00	35.00	—
1942C	298,348	BV	1.75	2.50	5.00	28.00	60.00	—
1943C	351,666	BV	1.50	2.50	5.00	22.00	45.00	—

KM# 19a 1.1664 g. 0.8000 Silver 0.0300 oz. ASW 15.67 mm. **Obv:** Crowned head left **Obv. Designer:** Percy Metcalfe **Rev:** Denomination and date within circle **Rev. Designer:** G.W. DeSaulles **Edge:** Reeded

Date	Mintage	VG-8	F-12	VF-20	XF-40	MS-60	MS-63	Proof
1944C	286,504	1.50	1.75	2.50	9.00	70.00	150	—
1945C	203,828	1.50	1.75	2.50	4.00	22.50	35.00	—
1946C	2,041	550	600	700	900	2,100	3,000	3,000
1946C Prooflike	—	—	—	—	—	—	4,000	—
1947C	38,400	3.00	5.00	8.00	30.00	100.00	250	—
1947C Prooflike	—	—	—	—	—	—	2,100	—

10 CENTS

KM# 3 2.3564 g. 0.9250 Silver 0.0701 oz. ASW **Obv:** Laureate head left **Obv. Legend:** VICTORIA D: G: REG: / NEWFOUNDLAND **Rev:** Denomination and date within ornamental circle

Date	Mintage	VG-8	F-12	VF-20	XF-40	MS-60	MS-63	Proof
1865	80,000	27.00	45.00	75.00	250	1,100	2,250	—
1865 Proof, plain edge	—	—	—	—	—	—	—	5,500
1870	30,000	150	250	450	725	2,350	5,000	—
1870 Proof	—	—	—	—	—	—	—	10,000
1872H	40,000	22.00	35.00	80.00	200	800	1,700	—
1873 flat 3	23,614	55.00	70.00	250	650	4,000	5,000	—
1873 round 3	Inc. above	55.00	70.00	250	650	4,000	5,000	—
1873 Proof	—	—	—	—	—	—	—	12,000
1876H	10,000	55.00	70.00	225	350	1,400	2,500	—
1880/70	10,000	55.00	100.00	250	400	1,800	2,950	—
1880 Proof	—	—	—	—	—	—	—	7,500
1882H	20,000	30.00	55.00	150	475	2,200	6,700	—
1882H Proof	—	—	—	—	—	—	—	3,000
1885	8,000	70.00	130	300	800	2,200	4,250	—
1885 Proof	—	—	—	—	—	—	—	8,000
1888	30,000	35.00	70.00	200	700	4,000	5,000	—
1888 Proof	—	—	—	—	—	—	—	8,000

Date	Mintage	VG-8	F-12	VF-20	XF-40	MS-60	MS-63	Proof
1890	100,000	9.00	19.00	35.00	150	1,100	3,200	—
1890 Proof	—	—	—	—	—	—	—	5,000
1894	100,000	8.50	12.00	25.00	125	1,200	3,000	—
1894 Proof	—	—	—	—	—	—	—	5,000
1896	230,000	5.00	10.00	25.00	90.00	1,200	3,200	—
1896 Proof	—	—	—	—	—	—	—	5,000

KM# 8 2.3564 g. 0.9250 Silver 0.0701 oz. ASW **Obv:** Crowned bust right **Rev:** Denomination and date within circle

Date	Mintage	VG-8	F-12	VF-20	XF-40	MS-60	MS-63	Proof
1903	100,000	11.00	30.00	90.00	250	2,400	5,500	—
1903 Proof	—	—	—	—	—	—	—	3,750
1904H	100,000	6.00	14.00	35.00	100.00	350	600	—
1904H Proof	—	—	—	—	—	—	—	2,250

KM# 14 2.3564 g. 0.9250 Silver 0.0701 oz. ASW **Obv:** Crowned bust left **Obv. Designer:** E.B. MacKennal **Rev. Designer:** G.W. DeSaulles

Date	Mintage	VG-8	F-12	VF-20	XF-40	MS-60	MS-63	Proof
1912	150,000	4.00	5.50	14.00	45.00	225	350	—
1917C	250,805	3.50	5.00	14.00	45.00	450	1,450	—
1919C	54,342	4.00	11.00	22.00	70.00	250	350	—

KM# 20 2.3564 g. 0.9250 Silver 0.0701 oz. ASW **Obv:** Crowned head left **Obv. Designer:** Percy Metcalfe **Rev:** Denomination and date within circle **Rev. Designer:** G.W. DeSaulles

Date	Mintage	VG-8	F-12	VF-20	XF-40	MS-60	MS-63	Proof
1938	100,000	3.50	4.00	4.50	18.00	200	800	—
1938 Proof	—	—	—	—	—	—	—	3,200
1940	100,000	3.00	3.50	4.50	14.00	100.00	400	—
1940 Proof	—	—	—	—	—	—	—	4,000
1941C	483,630	BV	3.00	3.50	7.00	50.00	125	—
1942C	293,736	BV	3.00	3.50	7.00	70.00	200	—
1943C	104,706	BV	3.00	3.50	9.00	250	800	—
1944C	151,471	BV	3.50	11.00	27.00	350	1,300	—

KM# 20a 2.3328 g. 0.8000 Silver 0.0600 oz. ASW **Obv:** Crowned head left **Obv. Designer:** Percy Metcalfe **Rev. Designer:** G.W. DeSaulles

Date	Mintage	VG-8	F-12	VF-20	XF-40	MS-60	MS-63	Proof
1945C	175,833	BV	2.50	3.00	7.00	100.00	400	—
1946C	38,400	3.50	4.50	9.00	30.00	125	300	—
1946C Proof	—	—	—	—	—	—	—	1,200
1946C	38,400	3.50	4.50	9.00	30.00	125	300	—
1947C	61,988	3.00	3.50	7.00	20.00	100.00	350	—

20 CENTS

KM# 4 4.7127 g. 0.9250 Silver 0.1401 oz. ASW 23.19 mm. **Obv:** Laureate head left **Rev:** Denomination and date within ornamental circle

Date	Mintage	VG-8	F-12	VF-20	XF-40	MS-60	MS-63	Proof
1865	100,000	16.00	30.00	60.00	225	950	2,600	—
1865 Proof, plain edge	—	—	—	—	—	—	—	6,500
1865 Proof, reeded edge	—	—	—	—	—	—	—	10,000
1870	50,000	21.00	45.00	100.00	250	1,250	2,600	—
1870 Proof, plain edge	—	—	—	—	—	—	—	6,500
1870 Proof, reeded edge	—	—	—	—	—	—	—	6,500
1872H	90,000	12.00	25.00	60.00	140	750	1,800	—
1873	45,797	21.00	65.00	175	550	5,400	8,000	—
1873 Proof	—	—	—	—	—	—	—	12,000
1876H	50,000	25.00	50.00	80.00	300	1,350	2,700	—
1880/70	30,000	27.00	55.00	100.00	350	2,000	3,000	—
1880 Proof	—	—	—	—	—	—	—	8,000
1881	60,000	12.00	25.00	80.00	300	1,200	2,900	—
1881 Proof	—	—	—	—	—	—	—	8,000
1882H	100,000	9.00	19.00	50.00	140	1,000	3,400	—
1882H Proof	—	—	—	—	—	—	—	3,500
1885	40,000	14.00	30.00	80.00	300	2,900	4,500	—
1885 Proof	—	—	—	—	—	—	—	10,000
1888	75,000	12.00	25.00	70.00	225	1,400	4,200	—
1888 Proof	—	—	—	—	—	—	—	10,000
1890	100,000	9.00	15.00	45.00	225	1,400	3,500	—
1890 Proof	—	—	—	—	—	—	—	6,500
1894	100,000	12.00	24.00	50.00	175	1,200	—	—
1894 Proof	—	—	—	—	—	—	—	6,500
1896 small 96	125,000	6.00	12.00	35.00	150	1,400	3,600	—
1896 large 96	Inc. above	7.00	15.00	50.00	200	1,700	4,500	—
1896 large 96, Proof	—	—	—	—	—	—	—	6,500
1899 hook 99	125,000	27.00	50.00	125	350	1,800	4,900	—
1899 large 99	Inc. above	5.00	12.00	30.00	125	1,400	3,600	—
1900	125,000	5.00	8.00	25.00	80.00	1,100	3,400	—
1900 Proof	—	—	—	—	—	—	—	6,500

KM# 10 4.7127 g. 0.9250 Silver 0.1401 oz. ASW **Obv:** Crowned bust right **Obv. Designer:** G.W. DeSaulles **Rev:** Denomination and date within circle **Rev. Designer:** W.H.J. Blakemore

Date	Mintage	VG-8	F-12	VF-20	XF-40	MS-60	MS-63	Proof
1904H	75,000	13.00	35.00	65.00	300	2,700	7,000	—
1904H Proof	—	—	—	—	—	—	—	2,400

KM# 15 4.7127 g. 0.9250 Silver 0.1401 oz. ASW **Obv:** Crowned bust left **Obv. Designer:** E.B. MacKennal **Rev:** Denomination and date within circle **Rev. Designer:** W.H.J. Blakemore

Date	Mintage	VG-8	F-12	VF-20	XF-40	MS-60	MS-63	Proof
1912	350,000	5.50	8.00	18.00	65.00	300	750	—
1912 Proof	—	—	—	—	—	—	—	2,500

25 CENTS

KM# 17 5.8319 g. 0.9250 Silver 0.1734 oz. ASW   **Obv:** Crowned bust left **Obv. Designer:** E.B. MacKennal **Rev:** Denomination and date within circle **Rev. Designer:** W.H.J. Blakemore

Date	Mintage	VG-8	F-12	VF-20	XF-40	MS-60	MS-63	Proof
1917C	464,779	7.00	8.00	10.00	18.00	200	400	—
1917C Proof	—	—	—	—	—	—	—	3,000
1919C	163,939	7.00	8.00	15.00	35.00	450	2,000	—
1919C Proof	—	—	—	—	—	—	—	3,000

50 CENTS

KM# 6 11.7818 g. 0.9250 Silver 0.3504 oz. ASW 29.85 mm.   **Obv:** Laureate head left **Obv. Legend:** VICTORIA DEI GRATIA REGINA NEWFOUNDLAND **Rev:** Denomination and date within ornamental circle

Date	Mintage	VG-8	F-12	VF-20	XF-40	MS-60	MS-63	Proof
1870	50,000	26.00	50.00	150	600	3,500	8,500	—
1870 Proof, plain edge	—	—	—	—	—	—	—	25,000
1870 Proof, reeded edge	—	—	—	—	—	—	—	25,000
1872H	48,000	18.00	35.00	90.00	400	1,600	3,600	—
1873	37,675	40.00	75.00	200	650	9,600	11,000	—
1873 Proof	—	—	—	—	—	—	—	40,000
1874	80,000	25.00	45.00	125	550	8,900	10,000	—
1874 Proof	—	—	—	—	—	—	—	40,000
1876H	28,000	35.00	85.00	150	450	2,250	5,250	—
1880	24,000	45.00	95.00	250	900	6,500	16,000	—
1880 Proof	—	—	—	—	—	—	—	40,000
1881	50,000	20.00	35.00	135	400	3,300	9,300	—
1881 Proof	—	—	—	—	—	—	—	40,000
1882H	100,000	12.00	30.00	95.00	350	1,600	5,400	—
1882H Proof	—	—	—	—	—	—	—	8,000
1885	40,000	30.00	60.00	175	650	2,800	7,100	—
1885 Proof	—	—	—	—	—	—	—	40,000
1888	20,000	50.00	90.00	250	925	11,000	13,000	—
1888 Proof	—	—	—	—	—	—	—	40,000
1894	40,000	12.00	28.00	75.00	300	3,700	9,700	—
1896	60,000	8.50	16.00	65.00	300	3,000	8,100	—
1896 Proof	—	—	—	—	—	—	—	25,000
1898	76,607	8.50	13.00	60.00	200	3,100	8,100	—
1899 wide 9's	150,000	8.50	13.00	60.00	200	2,800	7,200	—
1899 narrow 9's	Inc. above	8.50	13.00	45.00	150	2,600	7,700	—
1900	150,000	8.50	13.00	45.00	175	2,600	7,200	—

NEWFOUNDLAND

KM# 11 11.7800 g. 0.9250 Silver 0.3503 oz. ASW 30 mm.   **Obv:** Crowned bust right **Obv. Designer:** G.W.
DeSaulles **Rev. Designer:** W.H.J. Blakemore

Date	Mintage	VG-8	F-12	VF-20	XF-40	MS-60	MS-63	Proof
1904H	140,000	14.00	16.00	20.00	60.00	350	1,000	—
1904H Proof	—	—	—	—	—	—	—	2,900
1907	100,000	14.00	16.00	25.00	75.00	400	1,200	—
1908	160,000	14.00	16.00	20.00	60.00	300	800	—
1909	200,000	14.00	16.00	22.00	60.00	350	1,000	—

KM# 12 11.7800 g. 0.9250 Silver 0.3503 oz. ASW 30 mm.   **Obv:** Crowned bust left **Obv. Designer:** E.B.
MacKennal **Rev:** Denomination and date within circle **Rev. Designer:** W.H.J. Blakemore

Date	Mintage	VG-8	F-12	VF-20	XF-40	MS-60	MS-63	Proof
1911	200,000	13.50	15.00	15.00	45.00	300	750	—
1917C	375,560	13.00	14.00	15.00	40.00	175	500	—
1917C Proof	—	—	—	—	—	—	—	3,250
1918C	294,824	13.00	14.00	15.00	40.00	175	500	—
1919C	306,267	13.00	14.00	15.00	40.00	300	1,200	—
1919C Proof	—	—	—	—	—	—	—	3,250

2 DOLLARS

KM# 5 3.3284 g. 0.9170 Gold 0.0981 oz. AGW   **Obv:** Laureate head left **Obv. Legend:** VICTORIA D: G:
REG: / NEWFOUNDLAND **Rev:** Denomination and date within circle

Date	Mintage	F-12	VF-20	XF-40	AU-50	MS-60	MS-63
1865	10,000	150	225	300	375	1,100	8,500
1865 plain edge, Specimen-63, $15,000.	Est. 10	—	—	—	—	—	—
1870	10,000	150	225	300	450	1,500	7,500
1870 reeded edge, Specimen-63 $20,000.	Est. 5	—	—	—	—	—	—
1872	6,050	220	400	500	900	2,200	8,800
1872 Specimen-63 $12,500.	Est. 10	—	—	—	—	—	—
1880	2,500	800	1,000	1,200	2,300	4,650	14,250
1880/70	—	—	—	—	—	—	—
Note: Specimen. Bowers and Merena Norweb sale 11-96, specimen 64 realized $70,400.							
1881	10,000	150	200	250	325	1,600	2,500
1881 Specimen; Rare	—	—	—	—	—	—	—
1882H	25,000	150	200	250	300	700	2,200
1882H Specimen $4,250.	—	—	—	—	—	—	—
1885	10,000	150	200	250	300	850	2,750
1885 Specimen	—	—	—	—	—	—	—
Note: Bowers and Merena Norweb sale 11-96, specimen 66 realized $44,000							
1888	25,000	150	175	200	250	600	2,000
1888 Specimen; Rare	—	—	—	—	—	—	—

NOVA SCOTIA
PROVINCE

DECIMAL COINAGE

HALF CENT

KM# 7 Bronze **Obv:** Laureate bust left **Obv. Legend:** VICTORIA D:G: BRITT: REG:F:D: **Rev:** Crown and date within beaded circle, wreath of roses surrounds **Rev. Legend:** NOVA SCOTIA

Date	Mintage	VG-8	F-12	VF-20	XF-40	MS-60	MS-63	Proof
1861	400,000	5.00	7.00	8.00	13.00	60.00	300	—
1864	400,000	5.00	7.00	8.00	13.00	55.00	250	—
1864 Proof	—	—	—	—	—	—	—	300

CENT

KM# 8.2 Bronze **Obv:** Laureate bust left **Obv. Legend:** VICTORIA D:G: BRITT: REG:F:D: **Rev:** Crown and date within beaded circle, wreath of roses surrounds **Rev. Legend:** NOVA SCOTIA **Note:** Prev. KM#8. Small rosebud right of SCOTIA. The Royal Mint report records mintage of 1 million for 1862, which is considered incorrect.

Date	Mintage	VG-8	F-12	VF-20	XF-40	MS-60	MS-63	Proof
1861	800,000	3.00	4.50	5.00	11.00	125	400	—
1862	Est. 1,000,000	45.00	75.00	150	300	1,300	—	—
1864	800,000	3.00	4.50	5.00	16.00	150	450	—

STERLING COINAGE

HALFPENNY TOKEN

KM# 1 Copper **Obv:** Laureate head left **Obv. Legend:** PROVINCE OF NOVA SCOTIA **Rev:** Thistle

Date	Mintage	VG-8	F-12	VF-20	XF-40	MS-60	MS-63	Proof
1823	400,000	3.00	6.00	13.00	60.00	275	—	—
1823 without hyphen	Inc. above	5.00	10.00	35.00	125	325	—	—
1824	118,636	6.00	12.00	27.00	65.00	450	—	—
1832	800,000	3.00	5.00	13.50	40.00	225	—	—

NOVA SCOTIA

KM# 1a Copper   **Obv:** Laureate head left, draped collar **Obv. Legend:** PROVINCE OF NOVA SCOTIA
Rev: Thistle

Date	Mintage	VG-8	F-12	VF-20	XF-40	MS-60	MS-63	Proof
1382 1382 (error)	—	500	700	1,650	—	—	—	—
1832/1382	—	10.00	15.00	50.00	150	—	—	—
1832 (imitation)	—	3.00	9.00	27.00	75.00	125	200	—

KM# 3 Copper   **Obv:** Head left **Obv. Legend:** PROVINCE OF NOVA SCOTIA **Rev:** Thistle

Date	Mintage	VG-8	F-12	VF-20	XF-40	MS-60	MS-63	Proof
1840 small 0	300,000	3.50	10.00	25.00	65.00	185	—	—
1840 large 0	Inc. above	4.00	10.00	40.00	125	250	—	—
1840 medium 0	Inc. above	3.50	9.00	25.00	65.00	185	—	—
1843	300,000	3.00	6.00	24.00	65.00	185	—	—

KM# 5 Copper

Date	Mintage	VG-8	F-12	VF-20	XF-40	MS-60	MS-63	Proof
1856 without LCW	720,000	3.00	4.00	7.50	23.00	175	—	—
1856 without LCW, Proof	—	—	—	—	—	—	—	600
1856 without LCW, inverted A for V in PROVINCE, Proof	—	—	—	—	—	—	—	600

KM# 5a Bronze

Date	Mintage	VG-8	F-12	VF-20	XF-40	MS-60	MS-63	Proof
1856 with LCW, Proof	—	—	—	—	—	—	—	600

1 PENNY TOKEN

KM# 2 Copper   **Obv:** Laureate head left **Obv. Legend:** PROVINCE OF NOVA SCOTIA **Rev:** Thistle

Date	Mintage	VG-8	F-12	VF-20	XF-40	MS-60	MS-63	Proof
1824	217,776	4.00	10.00	26.00	85.00	400	—	—
1832	200,000	4.00	8.00	15.00	55.00	350	—	—

KM# 2a Copper   **Obv:** Laureate head left **Obv. Legend:** PROVINCE OF NOVA SCOTIA **Rev:** Thistle

Date	Mintage	VG-8	F-12	VF-20	XF-40	MS-60	MS-63	Proof
1832 (imitation)	—	3.75	7.50	22.50	85.00	—	—	—

KM# 4 Copper 32 mm.   **Obv:** Head left **Obv. Legend:** PROVINCE OF NOVA SCOTIA **Rev:** Thistle

Date	Mintage	VG-8	F-12	VF-20	XF-40	MS-60	MS-63	Proof
1840	150,000	3.50	9.00	23.00	65.00	450	—	—
1843/0	150,000	45.00	75.00	250	—	—	—	—
1843	Inc. above	4.00	12.00	24.00	65.00	450	—	—

KM# 6 Copper   **Obv:** Crowned head left **Obv. Legend:** VICTORIA D: G: BRITANNIA R: REG: F: D: **Rev:** Plant **Rev. Legend:** PROVINCE OF NOVA SCOTIA

Date	Mintage	VG-8	F-12	VF-20	XF-40	MS-60	MS-63	Proof
1856 without LCW	360,000	4.00	7.50	13.00	35.00	300	—	—
1856 with LCW	Inc. above	2.50	5.00	12.00	35.00	350	—	—

KM# 6a Bronze   **Obv:** Crowned head left **Obv. Legend:** VICTORIA D: G: BRITANNIA R: REG: F: D: **Rev:** Plant **Rev. Legend:** PROVINCE OF NOVA SCOTIA

Date	Mintage	VG-8	F-12	VF-20	XF-40	MS-60	MS-63	Proof
1856 Proof	—	—	—	—	—	—	—	400

PRINCE EDWARD ISLAND

PROVINCE

CUT & COUNTERMARKED COINAGE

ca. 1813

SHILLING

KM# 1 Silver   **Countermark:** Sunburst **Note:** Countermark on center plug of Spanish or Spanish Colonial 8 Reales.

Date	Mintage	VG-8	F-12	VF-20	XF-40	MS-60	MS-63	Proof
ND	1,000	2,500	4,500	7,500	—	—	—	—

5 SHILLING

KM# 3 Silver   **Countermark:** Sunburst **Note:** Countermark on holed Lima 8 Reales, KM#106.2.

Date	Mintage	VG-8	F-12	VF-20	XF-40	MS-60	MS-63	Proof
ND1809-11	1,000	2,500	4,500	7,500	—	—	—	—

KM# 2.1 Silver   **Countermark:** Sunburst **Note:** Countermark on holed Mexico City 8 Reales, KM#109.

Date	Mintage	VG-8	F-12	VF-20	XF-40	MS-60	MS-63	Proof
1791-1808	—	1,500	2,250	3,750	—	—	—	—

KM# 2.2 Silver   **Countermark:** Sunburst **Note:** Countermark on holed Mexico City 8 Reales, KM#110.

Date	Mintage	VG-8	F-12	VF-20	XF-40	MS-60	MS-63	Proof
ND1808-11	—	1,500	2,250	3,750	—	—	—	—

DECIMAL COINAGE

CENT

KM# 4 Bronze   **Obv:** Crowned head left within beaded circle **Obv. Legend:** VICTORIA QUEEN **Rev:** Trees within beaded circle **Rev. Legend:** PRINCE EDWARD ISLAND

Date	Mintage	VG-8	F-12	VF-20	XF-40	MS-60	MS-63	Proof
1871	2,000,000	2.50	4.00	6.50	20.00	100.00	185	—
1871 Proof	—	—	—	—	—	—	—	2,000

MEXICO

The United States of Mexico, located immediately south of the United States has an area of 759,529 sq. mi. (1,967,183 sq. km.) and an estimated population of 100 million. Capital: Mexico City. The economy is based on agriculture, manufacturing and mining. Oil, cotton, silver, coffee, and shrimp are exported.

Mexico was the site of highly advanced Indian civilizations 1,500 years before conquistador Hernando Cortes conquered the wealthy Aztec empire of Montezuma, 1519-21, and founded a Spanish colony, which lasted for nearly 300 years. During tvohe Spanish period, Mexico, then called New Spain, stretched from Guatemala to the present states of Wyoming and California, its present northern boundary having been established by the secession of Texas during 1836 and the war of 1846-48 with the United States.

Independence from Spain was declared by Father Miguel Hidalgo on Sept. 16, 1810, (Mexican Independence Day) and was achieved by General Agustin de Iturbide in1821. Iturbide became emperor in 1822 but was deposed when a republic was established a year later. For more than fifty years following the birth of the republic, the political scene of Mexico was characterized by turmoil, which saw two emperors (including the unfortunate Maximilian), several dictators and an average of one new government every nine months passing swiftly from obscurity to oblivion. The land, social, economic and labor reforms promulgated by the Reform Constitution of Feb. 5, 1917 established the basis for sustained economic development and participative democracy that have made Mexico one of the most politically stable countries of modern Latin America.

SPANISH COLONY

COB COINAGE

KM# 24 1/2 REAL
1.6900 g., 0.9310 Silver 0.0506 oz. ASW **Ruler:** Philip V **Obv:** Legend around crowned PHILIPVS monogram **Rev:** Legend around cross, lions and castles **Mint:** Mexico City **Note:** Mint mark M, Mo. For this series completeness of date is a stronger determining factor of price than grade. The values listed below reflect a range for examples with an average amount of date visible.

Date	Mintage	VG	F	VF	XF
ND(1701-28) Date off flan	—	25.00	40.00	65.00	—
1701 L	—	125	200	300	—
1702 L	—	125	200	300	—
1703 L	—	125	200	300	—
1704 L	—	125	200	300	—
1705 L	—	125	200	300	—
1706 J	—	125	200	300	—
1707 J	—	125	200	300	—
1708 J	—	125	200	285	—
1709 J	—	125	200	285	—
1710 J	—	125	200	285	—
1711 J	—	125	200	285	—
1712 J	—	125	200	285	—
1713 J	—	125	200	285	—
1714 J	—	125	200	285	—
1715 J	—	125	200	285	—
1716 J	—	125	200	285	—
1717 J	—	125	200	285	—
1718/7	—	—	—	—	—
1718 J	—	125	200	285	—
1719 J	—	125	200	285	—
1720 J	—	125	200	285	—
1721 J	—	125	200	285	—
1722 J	—	125	200	285	—
1723 J	—	125	200	285	—
1724 J	—	125	200	285	—
1724 D	—	125	200	285	—
1725 D	—	125	200	285	—
1726 D	—	125	200	285	—
1727 D	—	125	200	285	—
1728 D	—	125	200	285	—

KM# 25 1/2 REAL
1.6900 g., 0.9310 Silver 0.0506 oz. ASW **Ruler:** Luis I **Obv:** Legend around crowned LVDOVICVS monogram **Rev:** Legend around cross, lions and castles **Note:** Mint mark M, Mo.

Date	Mintage	VG	F	VF	XF
ND(1724-25) Date off flan	—	125	200	250	—
1724 D Rare	—	—	—	—	—
1725 D Rare	—	—	—	—	—

KM# 24a 1/2 REAL
1.6900 g., 0.9160 Silver 0.0498 oz. ASW **Ruler:** Philip V **Obv:** Legend around crowned PHILIPVS monogram **Rev:** Legend around cross, lions and castles **Mint:** Mexico City **Note:** Mint mark M, Mo.

Date	Mintage	VG	F	VF	XF
ND(1729-33) Date off flan	—	25.00	40.00	65.00	—
1729 R	—	90.00	120	150	—
1730 R	—	90.00	120	150	—
1730 F Rare	—	—	—	—	—
1731 F	—	90.00	120	150	—
1732/1 F	—	90.00	120	150	—
1732 F	—	90.00	120	150	—
1733/2 F	—	90.00	120	150	—
1733 F	—	90.00	120	150	—

KM# 30 REAL
3.3800 g., 0.9310 Silver 0.1012 oz. ASW **Ruler:** Philip V **Obv:** Legend and date around crowned arms **Obv. Legend:** PHILIPVS V DEI G **Rev:** Lions and castles in angles of cross **Mint:** Mexico City **Note:** Mint mark M, Mo. For this series completeness of date is a stronger determining factor of price than grade. The values listed below reflect a range for examples with an average amount of date visible.

Date	Mintage	VG	F	VF	XF
ND(1701-28) Date off flan	—	35.00	55.00	75.00	—
1701 L	—	165	275	400	—
1702 L	—	165	275	400	—
1703 L	—	165	275	400	—
1704 L	—	165	275	400	—
1705 L	—	165	275	400	—
1706 J	—	165	275	400	—
1707 J	—	165	275	400	—
1708 J	—	165	275	400	—
1709 J	—	165	275	400	—
1710 J	—	165	275	400	—
1711 J	—	165	275	400	—
1712 J	—	165	275	400	—

SPANISH COLONIAL • COB

Date	Mintage	VG	F	VF	XF
1713 J	—	165	275	400	—
1714 J	—	165	275	400	—
1715 J	—	150	275	400	—
1716 J	—	150	275	400	—
1717 J	—	150	275	400	—
1718 J	—	150	275	400	—
1719 J	—	150	275	400	—
1720/19 J Rare	—	—	—	—	—
1720 J	—	150	275	400	—
1721 J	—	150	275	400	—
1722 J	—	150	275	400	—
1723 J	—	150	275	400	—
1726 D	—	150	275	400	—
1727 D	—	150	275	400	—
1728 D	—	150	275	400	—

KM# A31   REAL

3.3834 g., 0.9310 Silver 0.1013 oz. ASW **Ruler:** Luis I **Mint:** Mexico City **Note:** A significant portion of the legend must be visibile for proper attribution. Mint mark M, Mo.

Date	Mintage	Good	VG	F	VF	XF
1724 D Rare	—	—	—	—	—	—
1725 D Rare	—	—	—	—	—	—

KM# 30a   REAL

3.3800 g., 0.9160 Silver 0.0995 oz. ASW **Ruler:** Philip V **Obv:** Legend and date around crowned arms **Obv. Legend:** PHILIPVS V DEI G **Rev:** Lions and castles in angles of cross **Mint:** Mexico City **Note:** Mint mark M, Mo.

Date	Mintage	VG	F	VF	XF
ND(1729-32) Date off flan	—	30.00	50.00	70.00	—
1729 R	—	90.00	125	175	—
1730 R	—	90.00	125	175	—
1730 F	—	90.00	125	175	—
1730 G	—	90.00	125	175	—
1731 F	—	90.00	125	175	—
1732 F	—	90.00	125	175	—

KM# 35   2 REALES

6.7700 g., 0.9310 Silver 0.2026 oz. ASW **Ruler:** Philip V **Obv:** Legend and date around crowned arms **Obv. Legend:** PHILIPVS V DEI G **Rev:** Lions and castles in angles of cross **Mint:** Mexico City **Note:** Mint mark M, Mo. For this series completeness of date is a stronger determining factor of price than grade. The values listed below reflect a range for examples with an average amount of date visible.

Date	Mintage	VG	F	VF	XF
ND(1701-28) Date off flan	—	45.00	65.00	90.00	—
1701 L	—	175	300	450	—
1702 L	—	175	300	450	—
1703 L	—	175	300	450	—
1704 L	—	175	300	450	—
1705 L	—	175	300	450	—
1706 J	—	175	300	450	—
1707 J	—	175	300	450	—
1708 J	—	175	300	450	—
1710 J	—	175	300	450	—
1711 J	—	175	300	450	—
1712 J	—	175	300	450	—
1713 J	—	175	300	450	—
1714 J	—	185	325	475	—
1715 J	—	185	325	475	—
1716 J	—	185	325	475	—
1717 J	—	185	325	475	—
1718 J	—	185	325	475	—
1719 J	—	185	325	475	—
1720 J	—	185	325	475	—
1721 J	—	185	325	475	—
1722 J	—	185	325	475	—
1723 J	—	185	325	475	—
1724 J	—	185	325	475	—
1725 D Rare	—	—	—	—	—
1726 D	—	185	325	475	—
1727 D	—	185	325	475	—
1728 D	—	185	325	475	—

KM# 35a   2 REALES

6.7700 g., 0.9160 Silver 0.1994 oz. ASW **Ruler:** Philip V **Obv:** Legend and date around crowned arms **Obv. Legend:** PHILIPVS V DEI G **Rev:** Lions and castles in angles of cross **Mint:** Mexico City **Note:** Mint mark M, Mo.

Date	Mintage	VG	F	VF	XF
ND(1729-32) Date off flan	—	40.00	60.00	90.00	—
1729 R	—	125	175	225	—
1730 R	—	125	175	225	—
1730 G Rare	—	—	—	—	—
1730 G/R Rare	—	—	—	—	—
1731 F	—	125	175	225	—
1731/0 F Reported, not confirmed	—	—	—	—	—
1732 F	—	125	175	225	—
1733 F Rare	—	—	—	—	—

KM# 40   4 REALES

13.5400 g., 0.9310 Silver 0.4053 oz. ASW **Ruler:** Philip V **Obv:** Legend and date around crowned arms **Obv. Legend:** PHILIPVS V DEI G **Rev:** Lions and castles in angles of cross **Mint:** Mexico City **Note:** Mint mark M, Mo. For this series completeness of date is a stronger determining factor of price than grade. The values listed below reflect a range for examples with an average amount of date visible.

Date	Mintage	VG	F	VF	XF
ND (1701-28) Date off flan	—	50.00	75.00	100	—
1701 L	—	225	475	800	—
1702 L	—	225	475	800	—
1703 L	—	225	475	800	—
1704 L	—	225	475	800	—
1705 L	—	225	475	800	—
1706 J	—	225	475	800	—
1707 J	—	225	475	800	—
1708 J	—	225	475	800	—
1709 J	—	225	475	800	—
1710 J	—	225	475	800	—
1711 J	—	200	425	700	—
1712 J	—	200	425	700	—
1713 J	—	200	425	700	—
1714 J	—	200	425	700	—
1715 J Rare	—	—	—	—	—
1716 J	—	250	600	1,000	—
1717 J	—	250	600	1,000	—
1718 J	—	250	600	1,000	—
1719 J	—	250	600	1,000	—
1720 J	—	250	600	1,000	—
1721 J	—	250	600	1,000	—
1722 J	—	250	600	1,000	—
1723 J	—	250	600	1,000	—
1726 D	—	250	600	1,000	—
1727 D	—	250	600	1,000	—
1728 D	—	250	600	1,000	—

SPANISH COLONIAL • COB

KM# 42   4 REALES

13.5400 g., 0.9310 Silver 0.4053 oz. ASW **Ruler:**
Luis I **Obv:** Legend around crowned arms **Obv.**
Legend: LVDOVICVS I DEI G **Rev:** Lions and castles
in angles of cross, legend around **Mint:** Mexico City
Note: A significant portion of the legend must be visible
for proper attribution. Mint mark M, Mo.

Date	Mintage	Good	VG	F	VF	XF
1724 D Rare	—	—	—	—	—	—
1725 D Rare	—	—	—	—	—	—

KM# 40a   4 REALES

13.5400 g., 0.9160 Silver 0.3987 oz. ASW **Ruler:**
Philip V **Obv:** Legend and date around crowned arms
Obv. Legend: PHILIPVS V DEI G **Rev:** Lions and
castles in angles of cross **Mint:** Mexico City **Note:**
Mint mark M, Mo.

Date	Mintage	VG	F	VF	XF
ND(1729-33) Date off flan	—	50.00	75.00	100	—
1729 R	—	150	250	350	—
1730 R	—	150	250	350	—
1730 F/G	—	150	250	375	—
1730 G	—	150	250	350	—
1731/0 F	—	150	250	375	—
1731 F	—	150	250	350	—
1732/1 F	—	150	250	350	—
1732 F	—	150	250	350	—
1733 F Rare	—	—	—	—	—
1733/2 F Rare	—	—	—	—	—

KM# 41   4 REALES

13.5400 g., 0.9160 Silver 0.3987 oz. ASW **Ruler:**
Philip V **Obv:** Legend and date around crowned arms
Obv. Legend: PHILIPVS V DEI G **Rev:** Lions and
castles in angles of cross, legend around **Mint:**
Mexico City **Note:** Klippe. Similar to KM#40a. Mint
mark M, Mo.

Date	Mintage	Good	VG	F	VF	XF
1733 MF	—	—	450	600	750	—
1734 MF Rare	—	—	—	—	—	—
1734/3 MF	—	—	450	600	750	—

KM# 47   8 REALES

27.0700 g., 0.9310 Silver 0.8102 oz. ASW **Ruler:**
Philip V **Obv:** Legend and date around crowned arms
Obv. Legend: PHILIPVS V DEI G **Rev:** Lions and
castles in angles of cross, legend around **Mint:**
Mexico City **Note:** Mint mark M, Mo. For this series
completeness of date is a stronger determining factor
of price than grade. The values listed below reflect a
range for examples with an average amount of date
visible.

Date	Mintage	VG	F	VF	XF
ND(1701-28) Date off flan	—	70.00	90.00	120	—
1701 L Rare	—	—	—	—	—
1702 L Rare	—	—	—	—	—
1703 L Rare	—	—	—	—	—
1704 L Rare	—	—	—	—	—
1705 L Rare	—	—	—	—	—
1706 J Rare	—	—	—	—	—
1707 J Rare	—	—	—	—	—
1708 J Rare	—	—	—	—	—
1709 J Rare	—	—	—	—	—
1710 J Rare	—	—	—	—	—
1711 J	—	200	1,100	2,000	—
1712 J	—	200	1,100	2,000	—
1713 J	—	200	1,100	2,000	—
1714 J	—	200	1,100	2,000	—
1715 J	—	200	1,200	2,250	—
1716 J	—	575	2,300	4,500	—
1717 J	—	575	2,300	4,500	—
1718/7 J	—	575	2,300	4,500	—
1718 J	—	525	2,000	4,000	—
1719 J	—	525	2,000	4,000	—
1720 J	—	525	2,000	4,000	—
1721 J	—	525	2,000	4,000	—
1722 J	—	525	2,000	4,000	—
1723 J	—	525	2,000	4,000	—
1724 D	—	525	2,000	4,000	—
1725 D	—	525	2,000	4,000	—
1726 D	—	525	2,000	4,000	—
1727 D	—	525	2,000	4,000	—
1728 D	—	600	2,400	5,000	—

SPANISH COLONIAL - COB

KM# 46   8 REALES
27.0700 g., 0.9310 Silver 0.8102 oz. ASW **Ruler:**
Charles II **Obv:** Legend and date around crowned
arms **Obv. Legend:** CAROLVS II DEI G **Rev:** Legend
around cross, lions and castles **Note:** Struck at
Mexico City Mint, mint mark M, Mo.

Date	Mintage	Good	VG	F	VF	XF
1701 L Rare	—	—	—	—	—	—

KM# 49   8 REALES
27.0700 g., 0.9310 Silver 0.8102 oz. ASW **Ruler:**
Luis I **Obv:** Legend and date around crowned arms
Obv. Legend: LVDOVICVS I DEI G **Rev:** Lions and
castles in angles of cross, legend around **Rev.**
Legend: INDIARVM * REX HISPANIARV ... **Mint:**
Mexico City **Note:** A significant portion of the legend
must be visible for proper attribution. Mint mark M,
Mo.

Date	Mintage	VG	F	VF	XF
ND(1724-25) Date off flan; Rare	—	—	—	—	—
1724 D Rare	—	—	—	—	—
1725 D Rare	—	—	—	—	—

KM# 47a   8 REALES
27.0700 g., 0.9160 Silver 0.7972 oz. ASW **Ruler:**
Philip V **Obv:** Legend and date around crowned arms
Obv. Legend: PHILIPVS V DEI G **Rev:** Lions and
castles in angles of cross, legend around **Mint:**
Mexico City **Note:** Mint mark M, Mo.

Date	Mintage	VG	F	VF	XF
ND(1729-33) Date off flan	—	70.00	100	125	—
1729 R	—	150	225	350	—
1730 G/R	—	150	225	350	—
1730 G	—	150	225	350	—
1730 R	—	150	225	350	—
1730 F Reported, not confirmed	—	—	—	—	—
1731/0 F	—	150	225	350	—
1731/0 F/G Rare	—	—	—	—	—
1731 F	—	135	210	325	—
1732/1 F	—	135	210	325	—
1732 F	—	135	210	350	—
1733/2 F	—	200	300	400	—
1733 F	—	200	300	400	—

KM# 48   8 REALES
0.9160 g., Silver **Ruler:** Philip V **Obv:** Legend
around crowned arms **Rev:** Lions and castles in
angles of cross, legend around **Mint:** Mexico City
Note: Klippe. Similar to KM#47a. Mint mark M, Mo.

Date	Mintage	VG	F	VF	XF
ND(1733-34) Date off flan	—	200	350	500	—
1733 F	—	550	750	1,150	—
1733 MF	—	450	600	750	—
1734/3 MF	—	500	750	1,000	—
1734 MF	—	500	750	1,000	—

KM# 50   ESCUDO
3.3800 g., 0.9170 Gold 0.0996 oz. AGW **Ruler:**
Charles II **Obv:** Legend and date around crowned
arms **Obv. Legend:** CAROLVS II DEI G **Rev:** Lions
and castles in angles of cross, legend around **Mint:**
Mexico City

Date	Mintage	VG	F	VF	XF	Unc
1701/0MXo L Rare	—	—	—	—	—	—

KM# 51.1   ESCUDO
3.3800 g., 0.9170 Gold 0.0996 oz. AGW **Ruler:**
Philip V **Obv:** Legend and date around crowned arms

SPANISH COLONIAL · COB

Obv. Legend: PHILIPVS V DEI G **Rev:** Lions and castles in angles of cross, legend around **Mint:** Mexico City

Date	Mintage	VG	F	VF	XF
ND(1702-13) Date off flan	—	—	1,000	1,350	1,500
1702MXo L Rare	—	—	—	—	—
1703/2MXo L Rare	—	—	—	—	—
1704MXo L Rare	—	—	—	—	—
1707MXo J Rare	—	—	—	—	—
1708MXo J Rare	—	—	—	—	—
1709MXo J Rare	—	—	—	—	—
1710MXo J Rare	—	—	—	—	—
1711MXo J	—	—	1,500	2,500	3,500
1712MXo J	—	—	1,500	2,500	3,500
1713MXo J	—	—	1,500	2,500	3,500

KM# 51.2   ESCUDO

3.3800 g., 0.9170 Gold 0.0996 oz. AGW   **Ruler:** Philip V **Obv:** Legend and date around crowned arms **Obv. Legend:** PHILIPVS V DEI G **Rev:** Lions and castles in angles of cross, legend around **Mint:** Mexico City

Date	Mintage	F	VF	XF
1712Mo J	—	2,000	3,000	4,000
1714Mo J	—	1,400	2,000	3,000
1714Mo J J's 1's (J7J4J) Rare	—	—	—	—
1715Mo J	—	2,000	3,000	4,000
1727Mo J Rare	—	—	—	—
1728Mo J Rare	—	—	—	—
1731 F Rare	—	—	—	—

Note: Die-struck counterfeits of 1731 F exist

KM# 52   2 ESCUDOS

6.7700 g., 0.9170 Gold 0.1996 oz. AGW   **Ruler:** Philip V **Obv:** Legend and date around crowned arms **Obv. Legend:** CAROLVS II DEI G **Rev:** Legend around cross **Mint:** Mexico City

Date	Mintage	VG	F	VF	XF	Unc
1701MXo L Rare	—	—	—	—	—	—

KM# 53.1   2 ESCUDOS

6.7700 g., 0.9170 Gold 0.1996 oz. AGW   **Ruler:** Philip V **Obv:** Legend and date around crowned arms **Obv. Legend:** PHILIPVS V DEI G **Rev:** Legend around cross **Mint:** Mexico City

Date	Mintage	VG	F	VF	XF
ND(1704-13) Date off flan	—	—	1,250	1,500	2,000
1704MXo L Rare	—	—	—	—	—
1708MXo J Rare	—	—	—	—	—
1710MXo J Rare	—	—	—	—	—
1711MXo J	—	—	2,500	3,500	4,500
1712MXo J	—	—	2,500	3,500	4,500
1713MXo J	—	—	2,500	3,500	4,500

KM# 53.2   2 ESCUDOS

6.7700 g., 0.9170 Gold 0.1996 oz. AGW   **Ruler:** Philip V **Obv:** Legend and date around crowned arms **Obv. Legend:** PHILIPVS V DEI G **Rev:** Legend around cross **Mint:** Mexico City **Note:** Struck counterfeits exist for 1731.

Date	Mintage	VG	F	VF	XF
ND(1714-31) Date off flan	—	—	1,500	1,750	2,500
1714Mo J	—	—	—	2,500	3,500
1715Mo J	—	—	—	3,000	4,000
1717Mo J Rare	—	—	—	—	—
1722Mo J Rare	—	—	—	—	—
1729Mo R Rare	—	—	—	—	—
1731Mo F Rare	—	—	—	—	—

KM# A54   2 ESCUDOS

6.7700 g., 0.9170 Gold 0.1996 oz. AGW   **Ruler:** Luis I **Obv:** Legend and date around crowned arms **Obv. Legend:** LVDOVICVS I DEI G. **Rev:** Legend around cross **Mint:** Mexico City **Note:** A significant portion of the legend must be visible for proper attribution.

Date	Mintage	VG	F	VF	XF	Unc
NDMo D Rare	—	—	—	—	—	—

KM# 54   4 ESCUDOS

13.5400 g., 0.9170 Gold 0.3992 oz. AGW   **Ruler:** Charles II **Obv:** Legend and date around crowned arms **Obv. Legend:** CAROLVS II DEI G **Rev:** Legend around cross **Mint:** Mexico City

Date	Mintage	VG	F	VF	XF	Unc
1701MXo L Rare	—	—	—	—	—	—

KM# 55.1   4 ESCUDOS

13.5400 g., 0.9170 Gold 0.3992 oz. AGW   **Ruler:** Philip V **Obv:** Legend and date around crowned arms

SPANISH COLONIAL · COB

Obv. Legend: PHILIPVS V DEI G **Rev:** Legend around cross **Mint:** Mexico City

Date	Mintage	VG	F	VF	XF
ND(1705-13) Date off flan	—	—	2,500	3,000	4,000
1705MXo J Rare	—	—	—	—	—
1706MXo L Rare	—	—	—	—	—
1711MXo J	—	—	3,500	4,750	6,000
1712MXo J	—	—	3,500	4,750	6,000
1713MXo J	—	—	3,500	4,750	6,000

KM# 55.2 4 ESCUDOS
13.5400 g., 0.9170 Gold 0.3992 oz. AGW **Ruler:** Philip V **Obv:** Legend and date around crowned arms **Obv. Legend:** PHILIPVS V DEI G **Rev:** Legend around cross **Mint:** Mexico City

Date	Mintage	VG	F	VF	XF
ND(1714-20) Date off flan	—	—	2,500	3,500	4,500
1714Mo J	—	—	—	5,500	7,000
1715Mo J	—	—	—	5,500	7,000
1720Mo J Rare	—	—	—	—	—

KM# 57.1 8 ESCUDOS
27.0700 g., 0.9170 Gold 0.7981 oz. AGW **Ruler:** Philip V **Obv:** Legend and date around crowned arms **Obv. Legend:** PHILIPVS V DEI G **Rev:** Legend around cross **Mint:** Mexico City

Date	Mintage	VG	F	VF	XF
ND(1701-13) Date off flan	—	—	2,500	3,500	4,500
1701MXo L Rare	—	—	—	—	—
1703MXo L Rare	—	—	—	—	—
1706MXo J Rare	—	—	—	—	—
1708MXo J Rare	—	—	—	—	—
1709MXo J Rare	—	—	—	—	—
1710MXo J Rare	—	—	—	—	—
1711MXo J	—	—	3,500	4,500	6,000
1712MXo J	—	—	3,500	4,500	6,000
1713MXo J	—	—	3,500	4,500	6,000

KM# 57.2 8 ESCUDOS
27.0700 g., 0.9170 Gold 0.7981 oz. AGW **Ruler:**

Philip V **Obv:** Legend and date around crowned arms **Obv. Legend:** PHILIPVS V DEI G **Rev:** Legend around cross **Mint:** Mexico City

Date	Mintage	F	VF	XF
ND(1714-32)Mo Date off flan	—	2,750	3,750	5,000
1714Mo J	—	4,000	5,500	7,500
1714Mo Date over GRAT on obverse	—	6,000	7,500	9,000
1715Mo J	—	5,000	6,500	8,000
1717/6Mo J Rare	—	—	—	—
1720/19Mo J Rare	—	—	—	—
1723Mo J Rare	—	—	—	—
1727/6Mo D Rare	—	—	—	—
1728/7Mo D Rare	—	—	—	—
1729Mo R Rare	—	—	—	—
1730Mo R Rare	—	—	—	—
1730Mo F Rare	—	—	—	—
1731Mo F Rare	—	—	—	—
1732Mo F Rare	—	—	—	—

KM# 57.3 8 ESCUDOS
27.0700 g., 0.9170 Gold 0.7981 oz. AGW **Ruler:** Philip V **Obv:** Date around crowned arms **Obv. Legend:** PHILIPVS V DEI G **Rev:** Legend and date around cross **Mint:** Mexico City

Date	Mintage	VG	F	VF	XF
1714Mo J Date on reverse	—	—	6,000	7,500	9,000

KM# 58 8 ESCUDOS
27.0700 g., 0.9170 Gold 0.7981 oz. AGW **Ruler:** Luis I **Obv:** Legend and date around crowned arms **Obv. Legend:** LVDOVICVS I DEI G **Rev:** Legend around cross **Mint:** Mexico City **Note:** A significant portion of the legend must be visible for proper attribution.

Date	Mintage	VG	F	VF	XF
ND(1724-25)Mo D Rare	—	—	—	—	—

ROYAL COINAGE

Struck on specially prepared round planchets using well centered dies in excellent condition to prove the quality of the minting to the Viceroy or even to the King.

KM# R24 1/2 REAL
1.6917 g., 0.9310 Silver 0.0506 oz. ASW **Ruler:** Philip V **Mint:** Mexico City **Note:** Normally found holed. Mint mark Mo.

Date	Mintage	Good	VG	F	VF	XF
1715Mo J	—	—	250	400	575	750
1719Mo J	—	—	250	400	575	750
1721Mo J	—	—	250	400	575	750
1722Mo J	—	—	250	400	575	750
1726Mo D	—	—	250	400	575	750
1727Mo D	—	—	250	400	575	750

KM# R25 1/2 REAL
1.6917 g., 0.9310 Silver 0.0506 oz. ASW **Ruler:** Luis I **Obv:** Legend around crowned LVDOVICVS monogram **Rev:** Lions and castles in angles of cross, legend around **Mint:** Mexico City **Note:** Mint mark Mo.

Date	Mintage	Good	VG	F	VF	XF
1724Mo D Rare	—	—	—	—	—	—

KM# R24a 1/2 REAL
1.6917 g., 0.9170 Silver 0.0499 oz. ASW **Ruler:**
Philip V **Mint:** Mexico City **Note:** Normally found
holed. Mint mark Mo.

Date	Mintage	Good	VG	F	VF	XF
1730Mo D	—	—	250	400	575	750

KM# R30 REAL
3.3834 g., 0.9310 Silver 0.1013 oz. ASW **Ruler:**
Philip V **Obv. Legend:** PHILIPVS V DEI G **Mint:**
Mexico City **Note:** Mint mark Mo.

Date	Mintage	Good	VG	F	VF	XF
1715Mo J Rare	—	—	—	—	—	—
1716Mo J Rare	—	—	—	—	—	—
1718Mo J Rare	—	—	—	—	—	—

KM# R35 2 REALES
6.7668 g., 0.9310 Silver 0.2025 oz. ASW **Ruler:**
Philip V **Obv. Legend:** PHILIPVS V DEI G **Mint:**
Mexico City **Note:** Mint mark Mo.

Date	Mintage	Good	VG	F	VF	XF
1715Mo J Rare	—	—	—	—	—	—

KM# R35a 2 REALES
6.7668 g., 0.9170 Silver 0.1995 oz. ASW **Ruler:**
Philip V **Mint:** Mexico City **Note:** Mint mark Mo.

Date	Mintage	Good	VG	F	VF	XF
1730Mo R Rare	—	—	—	—	—	—

KM# R40 4 REALES
13.5337 g., 0.9310 Silver 0.4051 oz. ASW **Ruler:**
Philip V **Obv. Legend:** PHILIPVS V DEI G **Mint:**
Mexico City **Note:** Mint mark Mo.

Date	Mintage	Good	VG	F	VF	XF
1716Mo J Rare	—	—	—	—	—	—
1719Mo J Rare	—	—	—	—	—	—
1721Mo J Rare	—	—	—	—	—	—
1722Mo J Rare	—	—	—	—	—	—
1723Mo J Rare	—	—	—	—	—	—

KM# R47 8 REALES
27.0674 g., 0.9310 Silver 0.8102 oz. ASW **Ruler:**
Philip V **Obv. Legend:** PHILIPVS V DEI G **Mint:**
Mexico City **Note:** Struck at Mexico City Mint, mint
mark Mo.

Date	Mintage	Good	VG	F	VF	XF
1702Mo L Rare	—	—	—	—	—	—
1703Mo L Rare	—	—	—	—	—	—
1705Mo J Rare	—	—	—	—	—	—
1706Mo J Rare	—	—	—	—	—	—
1709Mo J Rare	—	—	—	—	—	—
1711Mo J Rare	—	—	—	—	—	—
1714Mo J Rare	—	—	—	—	—	—
1715Mo J Rare	—	—	—	—	—	—
1716Mo J Rare	—	—	—	—	—	—
1717Mo J Rare	—	—	—	—	—	—
1719Mo J Rare	—	—	—	—	—	—
1721Mo J Rare	—	—	—	—	—	—
1722Mo J Rare	—	—	—	—	—	—
1723Mo J Rare	—	—	—	—	—	—
1724Mo D Rare	—	—	—	—	—	—
1725Mo D Rare	—	—	—	—	—	—
1726/5Mo D Rare	—	—	—	—	—	—
1726Mo D Rare	—	—	—	—	—	—
1727Mo D Rare	—	—	—	—	—	—

KM# R49 8 REALES
27.0674 g., 0.9310 Silver 0.8102 oz. ASW **Ruler:**
Luis I **Note:** Mint mark Mo.

Date	Mintage	Good	VG	F	VF	XF
1724 D Rare	—	—	—	—	—	—
1725 D Rare	—	—	—	—	—	—

KM# R47a 8 REALES
27.0674 g., 0.9170 Silver 0.7980 oz. ASW **Ruler:**
Philip V **Mint:** Mexico City **Note:** Mint mark Mo.

Date	Mintage	Good	VG	F	VF	XF
1729Mo R Rare	—	—	—	—	—	—
1730Mo R/D Rare	—	—	—	—	—	—
1730Mo G Rare	—	—	—	—	—	—

KM# R51.2 ESCUDO
3.3834 g., 0.9170 Gold 0.0997 oz. AGW **Ruler:**
Philip V **Mint:** Mexico City

Date	Mintage	Good	VG	F	VF	XF
1714Mo J Rare	—	—	—	—	—	—
1715Mo J Rare	—	—	—	—	—	—

KM# R53.1 2 ESCUDOS
6.7668 g., 0.9170 Gold 0.1995 oz. AGW **Ruler:**
Philip V **Mint:** Mexico City

Date	Mintage	Good	VG	F	VF	XF
1711MXo J Rare	—	—	—	—	—	—
1712MXo J Rare	—	—	—	—	—	—

KM# R55.1 4 ESCUDOS
13.5337 g., 0.9170 Gold 0.3990 oz. AGW **Ruler:**
Philip V **Mint:** Mexico City **Note:** Mint mark M, Mo.

Date	Mintage	Good	VG	F	VF	XF
1711 Rare	—	—	—	—	—	—

KM# R55.2 4 ESCUDOS
13.5337 g., 0.9170 Gold 0.3990 oz. AGW **Ruler:**
Philip V **Mint:** Mexico City **Note:** Mint mark M, Mo.

Date	Mintage	Good	VG	F	VF	XF
1714 Rare	—	—	—	—	—	—

SPANISH COLONIAL • ROYAL

KM# R57.1 8 ESCUDOS
27.0674 g., 0.9170 Gold 0.7980 oz. AGW **Ruler:**
Philip V **Mint:** Mexico City

Date	Mintage	Good	VG	F	VF	XF
1702MXo L Rare	—	—	—	—	—	—
1711MXo J Rare	—	—	—	—	—	—
1712MXo J Rare	—	—	—	—	—	—
1713MXo J Rare	—	—	—	—	—	—

KM# R57.3 8 ESCUDOS
27.0674 g., 0.9170 Gold 0.7980 oz. AGW **Ruler:**
Philip V **Mint:** Mexico City

Date	Mintage	Good	VG	F	VF	XF
1714Mo J Rare	—	—	—	—	—	—
1715Mo J Rare	—	—	—	—	—	—
1717Mo J Rare	—	—	—	—	—	—
1718Mo J Rare	—	—	—	—	—	—
1723Mo J Rare	—	—	—	—	—	—

MILLED COINAGE

KM# 59 1/8 PILON (1/16 Real)
Copper **Ruler:** Ferdinand VII **Obv:** Crowned
monogram **Rev:** Castles and lions in wreath **Mint:**
Mexico City **Note:** Mint mark Mo.

Date	Mintage	VG	F	VF	XF	Unc
1814	—	12.00	25.00	55.00	145	—
1815	—	12.00	25.00	55.00	145	—

KM# 63 1/4 TLACO (1/8 Real)
Copper **Ruler:** Ferdinand VII **Obv:** Crowned
monogram flanked by value and mint mark **Obv.**
Legend: FERDIN. VII... **Rev:** Arms without shield
within wreath **Mint:** Mexico City **Note:** Mint mark Mo.

Date	Mintage	VG	F	VF	XF	Unc
1814	—	14.00	30.00	60.00	180	—
1815	—	14.00	30.00	60.00	180	—
1816	—	14.00	30.00	60.00	180	—

KM# 62 1/4 REAL
0.8458 g., 0.8960 Silver 0.0244 oz. ASW **Ruler:**
Charles IV **Obv:** Crowned rampant lion, left **Rev:**
Castle **Mint:** Mexico City **Note:** Mint mark Mo.

Date	Mintage	VG	F	VF	XF	Unc
1796	—	35.00	65.00	125	200	—
1797	—	35.00	65.00	125	200	—
1798	—	35.00	65.00	125	200	—
1799/8	—	35.00	65.00	125	200	—
1799	—	35.00	65.00	125	200	—
1800	—	35.00	65.00	125	200	—
1801/0	—	10.00	20.00	40.00	70.00	—
1801	—	10.00	20.00	40.00	70.00	—
1802	—	10.00	20.00	40.00	70.00	—
1803	—	10.00	20.00	40.00	70.00	—
1804	—	10.00	20.00	40.00	75.00	—
1805/4	—	12.50	25.00	55.00	85.00	—
1805	—	10.00	22.00	50.00	75.00	—
1806	—	10.00	22.00	50.00	80.00	—

Date	Mintage	VG	F	VF	XF	Unc
1807/797	—	15.00	30.00	55.00	85.00	—
1807	—	12.50	25.00	50.00	80.00	—
1808	—	12.50	25.00	50.00	80.00	—
1809/8	—	12.50	25.00	50.00	80.00	—
1809	—	12.50	25.00	50.00	80.00	—
1810	—	12.50	25.00	50.00	75.00	—
1811	—	12.50	25.00	50.00	75.00	—
1812	—	12.50	25.00	50.00	75.00	—
1813	—	10.00	20.00	40.00	70.00	—
1815	—	12.50	22.00	50.00	75.00	—
1816	—	10.00	20.00	40.00	70.00	—

KM# 64 2/4 SENAL (1/4 Real)
Copper **Ruler:** Ferdinand VII **Obv:** Legend around
crowned monogram flanked by mint mark and value
Obv. Legend: FERDIN. VII... **Rev:** Arms without shield
within wreath **Mint:** Mexico City **Note:** Mint mark Mo.

Date	Mintage	VG	F	VF	XF	Unc
1814	—	14.00	30.00	60.00	180	—
1815/4	—	18.00	36.00	70.00	200	—
1815	—	14.00	30.00	60.00	180	—
1816	—	14.00	30.00	60.00	180	—
1821	—	25.00	48.00	90.00	240	—

KM# 65 1/2 REAL
1.6917 g., 0.9170 Silver 0.0499 oz. ASW **Ruler:**
Philip V **Obv:** Crowned shield flanked by M F,
rosettes and small cross **Obv. Legend:** PHILIP • V
• D • G • HISPAN • ET IND • REX **Rev:** Crowned
globes flanked by crowned pillars with banner, date
below **Mint:** Mexico City **Note:** Mint mark M, Mo, MX.

Date	Mintage	VG	F	VF	XF	Unc
1732 Rare	—	—	—	—	—	—
1732 F	—	500	800	1,200	2,000	—
1733 MF (MX)	—	400	600	1,000	1,500	—
1733 F	—	200	325	550	800	—
1733/2 MF	—	300	400	600	800	—
1733 MF	—	300	400	600	800	—
1734/3 MF	—	20.00	50.00	100	150	—
1734 MF	—	20.00	50.00	100	150	—
1735/4 MF	—	20.00	50.00	100	150	—
1735 MF	—	20.00	50.00	100	150	—
1736/5 MF	—	20.00	50.00	100	150	—
1736 MF	—	20.00	50.00	100	150	—
1737/6 MF	—	20.00	50.00	100	150	—
1737 MF	—	20.00	50.00	100	150	—
1738/7 MF	—	20.00	50.00	100	150	—
1738 MF	—	20.00	50.00	100	150	—
1739 MF	—	20.00	50.00	100	150	—
1740/30 MF	—	20.00	50.00	100	150	—
1740 MF	—	20.00	50.00	100	150	—
1741 MF	—	20.00	50.00	100	150	—

KM# 66 1/2 REAL
1.6900 g., 0.9170 Silver 0.0498 oz. ASW **Ruler:**
Philip V **Obv:** Crowned shield flanked by stars **Obv.**
Legend: PHS • V • D • G • HISP • ET IND • R **Rev:**
Crowned globes flanked by crowned pillars with
banner, date below **Mint:** Mexico City **Note:** Mint
mark M, Mo.

Date	Mintage	VG	F	VF	XF	Unc
1742 M	—	15.00	40.00	75.00	125	—
1743 M	—	15.00	40.00	75.00	125	—

SPANISH COLONIAL · ROYAL

Date	Mintage	VG	F	VF	XF	Unc
1744/3 M	—	15.00	40.00	75.00	125	—
1744 M	—	15.00	40.00	75.00	125	—
1745 M Rare	—	—	—	—	—	—

Note: Legend variation: PHS. V. D. G. HISP. EST IND. R

Date	Mintage	VG	F	VF	XF	Unc
1745 M	—	15.00	40.00	75.00	125	—
1746/5 M	—	15.00	40.00	75.00	125	—
1746 M	—	15.00	40.00	75.00	125	—
1747 M	—	15.00	40.00	75.00	125	—

KM# 67.1 1/2 REAL
1.6900 g., 0.9170 Silver 0.0498 oz. ASW **Ruler:**
Ferdinand VI **Obv:** Royal crown **Obv. Legend:** FRD
• VI • D • G • HIPS • ET IND • R **Mint:** Mexico City
Note: Mint mark M, Mo.

Date	Mintage	VG	F	VF	XF	Unc
1747/6 M	—	15.00	40.00	75.00	125	—
1747 M	—	15.00	40.00	75.00	125	—
1748/7 M	—	15.00	40.00	75.00	125	—
1748 M	—	15.00	40.00	75.00	125	—
1749 M	—	15.00	40.00	75.00	125	—
1750 M	—	15.00	40.00	75.00	125	—
1751 M	—	15.00	40.00	75.00	125	—
1752 M	—	15.00	40.00	75.00	125	—
1753 M	—	15.00	40.00	75.00	125	—
1754 M	—	15.00	40.00	75.00	125	—
1755/6 M	—	15.00	40.00	75.00	125	—
1755 M	—	15.00	40.00	75.00	125	—
1756/5 M	—	15.00	40.00	75.00	125	—
1756 M	—	15.00	40.00	75.00	125	—
1757/6 M	—	15.00	40.00	75.00	125	—
1757 M	—	15.00	40.00	75.00	125	—

KM# 67.2 1/2 REAL
1.6917 g., 0.9170 Silver 0.0499 oz. ASW **Ruler:**
Ferdinand VI **Obv:** Different crown **Mint:** Mexico City
Note: Mint mark M, Mo.

Date	Mintage	VG	F	VF	XF	Unc
1757 M	—	15.00	40.00	75.00	125	—
1758/7 M	—	15.00	40.00	75.00	125	—
1758 M	—	15.00	40.00	75.00	125	—
1759 M	—	15.00	40.00	75.00	125	—
1760/59 M	—	15.00	40.00	75.00	125	—
1760 M	—	15.00	40.00	75.00	125	—

KM# 68 1/2 REAL
1.6900 g., 0.9170 Silver 0.0498 oz. ASW **Ruler:**
Charles III **Obv:** Crowned shield flanked by stars
Obv. Legend: CAR • III • D • G • HISP • ET IND • R
Rev: Crowned globes flanked by crowned pillars with
banner, date below **Mint:** Mexico City **Note:** Mint
mark M, Mo.

Date	Mintage	VG	F	VF	XF	Unc
1760/59 M	—	15.00	40.00	75.00	125	—
1760 M	—	15.00	40.00	75.00	125	—
1761 M	—	15.00	40.00	75.00	125	—
1762 M	—	15.00	40.00	75.00	125	—
1763/2 M	—	15.00	40.00	75.00	125	—
1763 M	—	15.00	40.00	75.00	125	—
1764 M	—	15.00	40.00	75.00	125	—
1765/4 M	—	15.00	40.00	75.00	125	—
1765 M	—	15.00	40.00	75.00	125	—
1766 M	—	15.00	40.00	75.00	125	—
1767 M	—	15.00	40.00	75.00	125	—
1768/6 M	—	15.00	40.00	75.00	125	—
1768 M	—	15.00	40.00	75.00	125	—
1769 M	—	15.00	40.00	75.00	125	—
1770 M	—	15.00	40.00	75.00	125	—
1770 F	—	15.00	40.00	75.00	125	—
1771 F	—	15.00	40.00	75.00	125	—

KM# 69.2 1/2 REAL
1.6917 g., 0.9030 Silver 0.0491 oz. ASW **Ruler:**
Charles III **Obv:** Armored bust of Charles III, right
Obv. Legend: CAROLUS • III • DEI • GRATIA **Rev:**
Crown above shield flanked by pillars with banner,
normal initials and mint mark **Mint:** Mexico City **Note:**
Mint mark Mo.

Date	Mintage	VG	F	VF	XF
1772Mo FF	—	15.00	40.00	70.00	110
1773Mo FM	—	12.00	35.00	60.00	100
1773Mo FM CAROLS (error)	—	75.00	150	250	400
1774Mo FM	—	10.00	25.00	50.00	90.00
1775Mo FM	—	10.00	25.00	50.00	90.00
1776Mo FM	—	20.00	40.00	70.00	110
1777/6Mo FM	—	10.00	25.00	50.00	90.00
1777Mo FM	—	10.00	25.00	50.00	90.00
1778Mo FF	—	10.00	25.00	50.00	90.00
1779Mo FF	—	10.00	25.00	50.00	90.00
1780/79Mo FF	—	10.00	25.00	50.00	90.00
1780Mo FF	—	10.00	25.00	50.00	90.00
1781Mo FF	—	10.00	25.00	50.00	90.00
1782/1Mo FF	—	10.00	25.00	50.00	90.00
1782Mo FF	—	10.00	25.00	50.00	90.00
1783Mo FF	—	10.00	25.00	50.00	90.00
1783Mo FM	—	10.00	25.00	50.00	90.00
1784Mo FF	—	10.00	25.00	50.00	90.00
1784Mo FM	—	10.00	25.00	50.00	90.00

KM# 69.1 1/2 REAL
1.6900 g., 0.9030 Silver 0.0491 oz. ASW **Ruler:**
Charles III **Obv. Legend:** CAROLUS • III • DEI •
GRATIA **Rev:** Inverted FM and mint mark **Mint:**
Mexico City **Note:** Mint mark Mo.

Date	Mintage	VG	F	VF	XF	Unc
1772Mo FM	—	12.00	35.00	60.00	100	—
1773Mo FM	—	10.00	25.00	50.00	90.00	—

KM# 69.2a 1/2 REAL
1.6917 g., 0.8960 Silver 0.0487 oz. ASW **Ruler:**
Charles III **Rev:** Normal initials and mint mark **Note:**
Mint mark M, Mo.

Date	Mintage	VG	F	VF	XF	Unc
1785/4 FM	—	10.00	25.00	50.00	90.00	—
1785 FM	—	10.00	25.00	50.00	90.00	—
1786 FM	—	10.00	25.00	50.00	90.00	—
1787 FM	—	10.00	25.00	50.00	90.00	—
1788 FM	—	10.00	25.00	50.00	90.00	—
1789 FM	—	12.00	35.00	60.00	100	—

KM# 70 1/2 REAL
1.6917 g., 0.8960 Silver 0.0487 oz. ASW **Ruler:**
Charles IV **Obv:** Armored bust of Charles IV, right
Obv. Legend: CAROLUS • IV •... **Rev:** Crown above
shield flanked by pillars with banner **Mint:** Mexico
City **Note:** Mint mark M, Mo.

Date	Mintage	VG	F	VF	XF	Unc
1789 FM	—	12.00	35.00	60.00	100	—
1790 FM	—	12.00	35.00	60.00	100	—

KM# 71   1/2 REAL
1.6917 g., 0.8960 Silver 0.0487 oz. ASW **Ruler:**
Charles IV **Obv:** Armored bust of Charles IIII, right
Obv. Legend: CAROLUS • IIII •... **Rev:** Crown above
shield flanked by pillars with banner **Mint:** Mexico
City **Note:** Mint mark M, Mo.

Date	Mintage	VG	F	VF	XF	Unc
1790 FM	—	12.00	35.00	60.00	100	—

KM# 72   1/2 REAL
1.6900 g., 0.9030 Silver 0.0491 oz. ASW **Ruler:**
Charles IV **Obv:** Armored bust of Charles IIII, right
Obv. Legend: CAROLUS • IIII • ... **Rev:** Crowned
shield flanked by pillars with banner **Rev. Legend:**
IND • R • .... **Mint:** Mexico City **Note:** Mint mark Mo.

Date	Mintage	VG	F	VF	XF	Unc
1792 FM	—	10.00	20.00	55.00	85.00	—
1793 FM	—	10.00	20.00	55.00	85.00	—
1794/3 FM	—	10.00	20.00	55.00	85.00	—
1794 FM	—	10.00	20.00	55.00	85.00	—
1795 FM	—	10.00	20.00	55.00	85.00	—
1796 FM	—	10.00	20.00	55.00	85.00	—
1797 FM	—	10.00	20.00	55.00	85.00	—
1798/7 FM	—	10.00	20.00	55.00	85.00	—
1798 FM	—	10.00	20.00	55.00	85.00	—
1799 FM	—	10.00	20.00	55.00	85.00	—
1800/799 FM	—	10.00	20.00	55.00	85.00	—
1800 FM	—	10.00	20.00	55.00	85.00	—
1801 FM	—	8.00	17.00	33.00	85.00	—
1801 FT	—	4.00	11.00	25.00	50.00	—
1802 FT	—	4.00	11.00	25.00	50.00	—
1803 FT	—	6.00	13.00	27.50	55.00	—
1804 TH	—	4.00	11.00	25.00	50.00	—
1805 TH	—	4.00	11.00	25.00	50.00	—
1806 TH	—	4.00	11.00	25.00	50.00	—
1807/6 TH	—	6.00	13.00	27.50	55.00	—
1807 TH	—	4.00	11.00	25.00	50.00	—
1808/7 TH	—	6.00	13.00	27.50	55.00	—
1808 TH	—	4.00	11.00	25.00	50.00	—

KM# 73   1/2 REAL
1.6900 g., 0.9030 Silver 0.0491 oz. ASW **Ruler:**
Ferdinand VII **Obv:** Armored laureate bust right **Obv.**
Legend: FERDIN.VII... **Rev:** Crowned shield flanked
by pillars **Rev. Legend:** IND.R.... **Mint:** Mexico City
Note: Mint mark Mo.

Date	Mintage	VG	F	VF	XF	Unc
1808 TH	—	4.00	9.00	22.50	40.00	—
1809 TH	—	4.00	9.00	22.50	40.00	—
1810 TH	—	6.00	11.00	25.00	50.00	—
1810 HJ	—	4.00	9.00	22.50	40.00	—
1811 HJ	—	4.00	9.00	22.50	40.00	—
1812/1 HJ	—	8.00	17.00	38.50	85.00	—
1812 HJ	—	4.00	9.00	22.50	40.00	—
1812 JJ	—	13.00	27.50	49.50	105	—
1813/2 JJ	—	13.00	27.50	49.50	105	—
1813 TH	—	4.00	9.00	22.50	40.00	—
1813 JJ	—	7.00	13.00	27.50	80.00	—
1813 HJ	—	8.00	17.00	38.50	95.00	—
1814/3 JJ	—	8.00	17.00	38.50	95.00	—
1814 JJ	—	6.00	11.00	25.00	50.00	—

KM# 74   1/2 REAL
1.6900 g., 0.9030 Silver 0.0491 oz. ASW **Ruler:**
Ferdinand VII **Obv:** Draped laureate bust right **Obv.**
Legend: FERDIN.VII.... **Rev:** Crowned shield
flanked by pillars **Rev. Legend:** IND.R.... **Mint:**
Mexico City **Note:** Mint mark Mo.

Date	Mintage	VG	F	VF	XF	Unc
1815 JJ	—	4.00	9.00	22.50	45.00	—
1816 JJ	—	4.00	9.00	22.50	45.00	—
1817/6 JJ	—	13.00	27.50	55.00	125	—
1817 JJ	—	4.00	9.00	30.75	50.00	—
1818/7 JJ	—	4.00	9.00	27.50	55.00	—
1818 JJ	—	4.00	9.00	27.50	55.00	—
1819/8 JJ	—	7.00	13.00	38.50	95.00	—
1819 JJ	—	4.00	9.00	22.50	45.00	—
1820 JJ	—	4.00	9.00	27.50	55.00	—
1821 JJ	—	4.00	9.00	22.50	45.00	—

KM# 75.1   REAL
3.3834 g., 0.9170 Silver 0.0997 oz. ASW **Ruler:**
Philip V **Obv:** Crowned shield flanked by MF I ** **Obv.**
Legend: PHILIP • V • D • G • HISPAN • ET IND •
REX **Rev:** Crowned globes flanked by crowned
pillars with banner, date below **Mint:** Mexico City
Note: Mint mark M, Mo, (MX).

Date	Mintage	VG	F	VF	XF	Unc
1732 Rare	—	—	—	—	—	—
1732 F	—	—	—	—	—	—
1733 F (MX)	—	150	350	425	750	—
1733 MF (MX)	—	150	350	425	750	—
1733 F Rare	—	—	—	—	—	—
1733 MF	—	100	200	300	500	—
1734/3 MF	—	35.00	60.00	125	175	—
1734 MF	—	35.00	60.00	125	175	—
1735 MF	—	35.00	60.00	125	175	—
1736 MF	—	35.00	60.00	125	175	—
1737 MF	—	35.00	60.00	125	175	—
1738 MF	—	35.00	60.00	125	175	—
1739 MF	—	35.00	60.00	125	175	—
1740 MF	—	35.00	60.00	125	175	—
1741 MF	—	35.00	60.00	125	175	—

KM# 75.2   REAL
3.3834 g., 0.9170 Silver 0.0997 oz. ASW **Ruler:**
Philip V **Obv. Legend:** PHS • V • D • G • HISP • ET
• IND • R **Note:** Mint mark M, Mo.

Date	Mintage	VG	F	VF	XF	Unc
1742 M	—	35.00	60.00	110	165	—
1743 M	—	35.00	60.00	110	165	—
1744/3 M	—	35.00	60.00	110	165	—
1744 M	—	35.00	60.00	110	165	—
1745 M	—	35.00	60.00	110	165	—
1746/5 M	—	35.00	60.00	110	165	—
1746 M	—	35.00	60.00	110	165	—
1747 M	—	35.00	60.00	110	165	—

SPANISH COLONIAL - MILLED

KM# 76.1 REAL
3.3800 g., 0.9170 Silver 0.0996 oz. ASW **Ruler:**
Ferdinand VI **Obv:** Crowned shield flanked by R I
Obv. Legend: FRD • VI • D • G • HISP • ET IND • R
Rev: Crowned globes flanked by crowned pillars with
banner, date below **Mint:** Mexico City **Note:** Mint
mark M, Mo.

Date	Mintage	VG	F	VF	XF	Unc
1747 M	—	30.00	50.00	100	150	—
1748/7 M	—	30.00	50.00	100	150	—
1748 M	—	30.00	50.00	100	150	—
1749 M	—	30.00	50.00	100	150	—
1750/40 M	—	30.00	50.00	100	150	—
1750 M	—	30.00	50.00	100	150	—
1751 M	—	30.00	50.00	100	150	—
1752 M	—	30.00	50.00	100	150	—
1753 M	—	30.00	50.00	100	150	—
1754 M	—	30.00	50.00	100	150	—
1755/4 M	—	30.00	50.00	100	150	—
1755 M	—	30.00	50.00	100	150	—
1756 M	—	30.00	50.00	100	150	—
1757 M	—	30.00	50.00	100	150	—
1758/5 M	—	30.00	50.00	100	150	—
1758 M	—	30.00	50.00	100	150	—

KM# 76.2 REAL
3.3834 g., 0.9170 Silver 0.0997 oz. ASW **Ruler:**
Ferdinand VI **Obv:** Royal and Imperial crowns **Note:**
Mint mark M, Mo.

Date	Mintage	VG	F	VF	XF	Unc
1757 M	—	30.00	50.00	100	150	—
1758/7 M	—	30.00	50.00	100	150	—
1758 M	—	30.00	50.00	100	150	—
1759 M	—	30.00	50.00	100	150	—
1760 M	—	30.00	50.00	100	150	—

KM# 77 REAL
3.3800 g., 0.9170 Silver 0.0996 oz. ASW **Ruler:**
Charles III **Obv:** Crowned shield flanked by R I **Obv.
Legend:** CAR • III • D • G • HISP • ET IND • R **Rev:**
Crowned globes flanked by crowned pillars with banner,
date below **Mint:** Mexico City **Note:** Mint mark M, Mo.

Date	Mintage	VG	F	VF	XF	Unc
1760 M	—	30.00	50.00	100	150	—
1761/0 M	—	30.00	50.00	100	150	—
1761 M	—	30.00	50.00	100	150	—
1762 M	—	30.00	50.00	100	150	—
1763/2 M	—	30.00	50.00	100	150	—
1763 M	—	30.00	50.00	100	150	—
1764 M	—	30.00	50.00	100	150	—
1765 M	—	30.00	50.00	100	150	—
1766 M	—	30.00	50.00	100	150	—
1767 M	—	30.00	50.00	100	150	—
1768 M	—	30.00	50.00	100	150	—
1769 M	—	30.00	50.00	100	150	—
1769/70 M	—	30.00	50.00	100	150	—
1770 M	—	30.00	50.00	100	150	—
1770 F	—	30.00	50.00	100	200	—
1771 F	—	30.00	50.00	100	200	—

KM# 78.1 REAL
3.3834 g., 0.9030 Silver 0.0982 oz. ASW **Ruler:**
Charles III **Obv. Legend:** CAROLUS • III • DEI •
GRATIA **Rev:** Inverted FM and mint mark **Note:** Mint
mark M, Mo.

Date	Mintage	VG	F	VF	XF	Unc
1772 FM	—	25.00	40.00	80.00	125	—
1773 FM	—	25.00	40.00	80.00	125	—

KM# 78.2 REAL
3.3800 g., 0.9030 Silver 0.0981 oz. ASW **Ruler:**
Charles III **Obv:** Armored bust of Charles III, right
Obv. Legend: CAROLUS • III • DEI • GRATIA **Rev.
Legend:** Crowned shield flanked by pillars with
banner, normal initials and mint mark **Mint:** Mexico
City **Note:** Mint mark M, Mo.

Date	Mintage	VG	F	VF	XF	Unc
1774 FM	—	20.00	35.00	65.00	100	—
1775/4 FM	—	20.00	35.00	65.00	100	—
1775 FM	—	20.00	35.00	65.00	100	—
1776 FM	—	20.00	35.00	65.00	100	—
1777 FM	—	20.00	35.00	65.00	100	—
1778 FF/M	—	20.00	35.00	65.00	100	—
1778 FF	—	20.00	35.00	65.00	100	—
1779 FF	—	20.00	35.00	65.00	100	—
1780 FF	—	20.00	35.00	65.00	100	—
1780 F F/M	—	20.00	35.00	65.00	100	—
1781 FF	—	20.00	35.00	65.00	100	—
1782 FF	—	20.00	35.00	65.00	100	—
1783 FF	—	20.00	35.00	65.00	100	—
1784 FF	—	20.00	35.00	65.00	100	—

KM# 78.2a REAL
3.3834 g., 0.8960 Silver 0.0975 oz. ASW **Ruler:**
Charles III **Rev:** Normal initials and mint mark **Note:**
Mint mark M, Mo.

Date	Mintage	VG	F	VF	XF	Unc
1785 FF	—	20.00	35.00	65.00	100	—
1785 FM	—	20.00	35.00	65.00	100	—
1786 FM	—	20.00	35.00	65.00	100	—
1787 FF	—	20.00	35.00	65.00	125	—
1787 FM	—	20.00	35.00	65.00	100	—
1788 FF	—	50.00	100	200	—	—
1788 FM	—	20.00	35.00	65.00	100	—
1789 FM	—	20.00	35.00	65.00	100	—

KM# 79 REAL
3.3800 g., 0.9030 Silver 0.0981 oz. ASW **Ruler:**
Charles IV **Obv:** Armored bust of Charles III, right
Obv. Legend: CAROLUS • IV • ... **Rev:** Crown above
shield flanked by pillars with banner **Mint:** Mexico
City **Note:** Mint mark M, Mo.

Date	Mintage	VG	F	VF	XF	Unc
1789 FM	—	20.00	35.00	65.00	150	—
1790 FM	—	20.00	35.00	65.00	150	—

KM# 80 REAL
3.3800 g., 0.9030 Silver 0.0981 oz. ASW **Ruler:**
Charles IV **Obv:** Armored bust of Charles IIII, right
Obv. Legend: CAROLUS • IIII • ... **Rev:** Crowned

shield flanked by pillars with banner **Mint:** Mexico City **Note:** Mint mark M, Mo.

Date	Mintage	VG	F	VF	XF	Unc
1790 FM	—	20.00	35.00	70.00	165	—

KM# 81   REAL
3.3834 g., 0.8960 Silver 0.0975 oz. ASW **Ruler:** Charles IV **Obv:** Armored bust of Charles IIII, right **Obv. Legend:** CAROLUS • IIII • ... **Rev:** Crowned shield flanked by pillars with banner **Rev. Legend:** IND • REX ... **Mint:** Mexico City **Note:** Mint mark Mo.

Date	Mintage	VG	F	VF	XF	Unc
1792 FM	—	15.00	30.00	60.00	90.00	—
1793 FM	—	15.00	30.00	60.00	150	—
1794 FM	—	25.00	50.00	100	250	—
1795 FM	—	15.00	30.00	60.00	150	—
1796 FM	—	15.00	30.00	60.00	90.00	—
1797/6 FM	—	15.00	30.00	60.00	90.00	—
1797 FM	—	15.00	30.00	60.00	90.00	—
1798/7 FM	—	15.00	30.00	60.00	90.00	—
1798 FM	—	15.00	30.00	60.00	90.00	—
1799 FM	—	15.00	30.00	60.00	90.00	—
1800 FM	—	15.00	30.00	60.00	90.00	—
1801 FT/M	—	6.00	11.00	27.50	65.00	—
1801 FT	—	6.00	11.00	27.50	65.00	—
1801 FM	—	9.00	17.00	30.75	65.00	—
1802 FM	—	6.00	11.00	27.50	65.00	—
1802 FT	—	6.00	11.00	27.50	65.00	—
1802 FT/M	—	6.00	11.00	27.50	65.00	—
1802/1 FT	—	6.00	11.00	27.50	65.00	—
1803 FT	—	6.00	11.00	27.50	65.00	—
1804 TH	—	6.00	11.00	27.50	65.00	—
1805 TH	—	6.00	11.00	27.50	65.00	—
1806 TH	—	6.00	11.00	27.50	65.00	—
1807/6 TH	—	6.00	11.00	27.50	65.00	—
1807 TH	—	6.00	11.00	27.50	65.00	—
1808/7 TH	—	6.00	11.00	27.50	65.00	—
1808 FM	—	6.00	11.00	27.50	65.00	—

KM# 82   REAL
3.3800 g., 0.9030 Silver 0.0981 oz. ASW **Ruler:** Ferdinand VII **Obv:** Armored laureate bust right **Obv. Legend:** FERDIN.VII... **Rev:** Crowned shield flanked by pillars **Rev. Legend:** IND.REX.... **Mint:** Mexico City **Note:** Mint mark Mo.

Date	Mintage	VG	F	VF	XF	Unc
1809 TH	—	10.00	18.00	32.00	95.00	—
1810/09 TH	—	10.00	18.00	32.00	95.00	—
1810 TH	—	10.00	18.00	32.00	95.00	—
1811 TH	—	27.50	38.50	65.00	250	—
1811 HJ	—	10.00	18.00	32.00	95.00	—
1812 HJ	—	6.00	12.00	32.00	85.00	—
1812 JJ	—	12.00	22.50	45.00	135	—
1813 HJ	—	12.00	22.50	45.00	135	—
1813 JJ	—	55.00	110	165	250	—
1814 HJ	—	17.00	33.00	165	155	—
1814 JJ	—	55.00	110	195	300	—

KM# 83   REAL
3.3800 g., 0.9030 Silver 0.0981 oz. ASW **Ruler:** Ferdinand VII **Obv:** Draped laureate bust right **Obv. Legend:** FERDIN.VII... **Rev:** Crowned shield flanked by pillars **Rev. Legend:** IND.REX... **Mint:** Mexico City **Note:** Mint mark Mo.

Date	Mintage	VG	F	VF	XF	Unc
1814 JJ	—	27.50	55.00	110	350	—
1815 HJ	—	17.00	33.00	65.00	150	—
1815 JJ	—	12.00	22.50	45.00	125	—
1816 JJ	—	6.00	12.00	27.50	75.00	—
1817 JJ	—	6.00	12.00	27.50	75.00	—
1818 JJ	—	33.00	65.00	140	500	—
1819 JJ	—	6.00	12.00	27.50	75.00	—
1820 JJ	—	6.00	12.00	27.50	75.00	—
1821/0 JJ	—	10.00	18.00	33.00	115	—
1821 JJ	—	6.00	12.00	27.50	55.00	—

KM# 84   2 REALES
6.7668 g., 0.9170 Silver 0.1995 oz. ASW **Ruler:** Philip V **Obv:** Crowned shield flanked by M F 2 **Obv. Legend:** PHILIP • V • D • G • HISPAN • ET IND • REX **Rev:** Crowned globes flanked by crowned pillars with banner, date below **Rev. Legend:** VTRAQUE VNUM **Mint:** Mexico City **Note:** Mint mark M, Mo, (MX).

Date	Mintage	VG	F	VF	XF	Unc
1732 Rare	—					—
1732 F	—	800	1,300	1,750	2,750	—
1733 F	—	600	800	1,350	2,250	—
1733 MF (MX)	—	350	600	1,000	1,650	—
1733 MF	—	600	900	1,500	2,500	—
1734/3 MF	—	45.00	75.00	135	200	—
1734 MF	—	45.00	75.00	135	200	—
1735/3 MF	—	45.00	75.00	135	200	—
1735/4 MF	—	45.00	75.00	135	200	—
1735 MF	—	45.00	75.00	135	200	—
1736/3 MF	—	45.00	75.00	135	200	—
1736/4 MF	—	45.00	75.00	135	200	—
1736/5 MF	—	45.00	75.00	135	200	—
1736 MF	—	45.00	75.00	135	200	—
1737/3 MF	—	45.00	75.00	135	200	—
1737 MF	—	45.00	75.00	135	200	—
1738/7 MF	—	45.00	75.00	135	200	—
1738 MF	—	45.00	75.00	135	200	—
1739 MF	—	45.00	75.00	135	200	—
1740/30 MF	—	45.00	75.00	135	200	—
1740 MF	—	45.00	75.00	135	200	—
1741 MF	—	45.00	75.00	135	200	—

SPANISH COLONIAL - MILLED

KM# 85 2 REALES
6.7700 g., 0.9170 Silver 0.1996 oz. ASW **Ruler:**
Philip V **Obv:** Crowned shield flanked by R 2 **Obv.**
Legend: PHS • V • D • G • HISP • ET IND • R * **Rev:**
Crowned globes flanked by crowned pillars with
banner, date below **Rev. Legend:** VTRA QUE
VNUM **Mint:** Mexico City **Note:** Mint mark M, Mo.

Date	Mintage	F	VF	XF	Unc	BU
1742 M	—	70.00	125	185	—	—
1743/2 M	—	70.00	125	185	—	—
1743 M	—	70.00	125	185	—	—
1744/3 M	—	70.00	125	185	—	—
1744 M	—	70.00	125	185	—	—
1745/4 M	—	70.00	125	185	—	—
1745 M	—	70.00	125	185	—	—
1745 M HIP Rare	—	—	—	—	—	—
1746/5 M	—	70.00	125	185	—	—
1746 M	—	70.00	125	185	—	—
1747 M	—	70.00	125	185	—	—
1750 M Rare	—	—	—	—	—	—

Note: Posthumous mule.

KM# 86.1 2 REALES
6.7668 g., 0.9170 Silver 0.1995 oz. ASW **Ruler:**
Ferdinand VI **Obv:** Crowned shield flanked by R 2
Obv. Legend: FRD • VI • D • G • HISP • ET IND • R
Rev: Crowned globes flanked by crowned pillars with
banner, date below **Rev. Legend:** VTRA QUE VNUM
Mint: Mexico City **Note:** Mint mark M, Mo.

Date	Mintage	VG	F	VF	XF	Unc
1747 M	—	35.00	60.00	110	175	—
1748/7 M	—	35.00	60.00	110	175	—
1748 M	—	35.00	60.00	110	175	—
1749 M	—	35.00	60.00	110	175	—
1750 M	—	35.00	60.00	110	175	—
1751/41 M	—	35.00	60.00	110	175	—
1751 M	—	35.00	60.00	110	175	—
1752 M	—	35.00	60.00	110	175	—
1753/2 M	—	35.00	60.00	110	175	—
1753 M	—	35.00	60.00	110	175	—
1754 M	—	35.00	60.00	110	175	—
1755/4 M	—	35.00	60.00	110	175	—
1755 M	—	35.00	60.00	110	175	—
1756/55 M	—	35.00	60.00	110	175	—
1756 M	—	35.00	60.00	110	175	—
1757/6 M	—	35.00	60.00	110	175	—
1757 M	—	35.00	60.00	110	175	—

KM# 86.2 2 REALES
6.7668 g., 0.9170 Silver 0.1995 oz. ASW **Ruler:**
Ferdinand VI **Obv:** Royal and Imperial crowns **Note:**
Mint mark M, Mo.

Date	Mintage	VG	F	VF	XF	Unc
1757 M	—	35.00	60.00	110	175	—
1758 M	—	35.00	60.00	110	175	—
1759/8 M	—	35.00	60.00	110	175	—
1759 M	—	35.00	60.00	110	175	—
1760 M	—	35.00	60.00	110	175	—

KM# 87 2 REALES
6.7700 g., 0.9170 Silver 0.1996 oz. ASW **Ruler:**
Charles III **Obv:** Crowned shield flanked by R 2 **Obv.**
Legend: CAR • III • D • G • HISP • ET IND • R **Rev:**
Crowned globes flanked by crowned pillars with
banner, date below **Rev. Legend:** VTRA QUE VNUM
Mint: Mexico City **Note:** Mint mark M, Mo.

Date	Mintage	VG	F	VF	XF	Unc
1760 M	—	35.00	60.00	110	175	—
1761 M	—	35.00	60.00	110	175	—
1762/1 M	—	35.00	60.00	110	175	—
1762 M	—	35.00	60.00	110	175	—
1763/2 M	—	35.00	60.00	110	175	—
1763 M	—	35.00	60.00	110	175	—
1764 M	—	35.00	60.00	110	175	—
1765 M	—	35.00	60.00	110	175	—
1766 M	—	35.00	60.00	110	175	—
1767 M	—	35.00	60.00	110	175	—
1768/6 M	—	35.00	60.00	110	175	—
1768 M	—	35.00	60.00	110	175	—
1769 M	—	35.00	60.00	110	175	—
1770 M	—	350	550	—	—	—
1770 F Rare	—	—	—	—	—	—
1771 F	—	35.00	60.00	110	175	—

KM# 88.1 2 REALES
6.7668 g., 0.9030 Silver 0.1964 oz. ASW **Ruler:**
Charles III **Obv:** Armored bust of Charles III, right
Obv. Legend: CAROLUS • III • DEI • GRATIA **Rev:**
Inverted FM and mint mark **Note:** Mint mark M, Mo.

Date	Mintage	VG	F	VF	XF	Unc
1772 FM	—	30.00	50.00	100	150	—
1773 FM	—	30.00	50.00	100	150	—

SPANISH COLONIAL · MILLED

KM# 88.2   2 REALES
6.7700 g., 0.9030 Silver 0.1965 oz. ASW **Ruler:**
Charles III **Obv:** Armored bust of Charles III, right **Obv.**
Legend: CAROLUS • III • DEI • GRATIA • **Rev:**
Crowned shield flanked by pillars with banner, normal
initials and mint mark **Rev. Legend:** • HISPAN • ET IND
• REX • ... **Mint:** Mexico City **Note:** Mint mark M, Mo.

Date	Mintage	VG	F	VF	XF
1773 FM	—	25.00	40.00	80.00	125
1774 FM	—	25.00	40.00	80.00	125
1775 FM	—	25.00	40.00	80.00	125
1776 FM	—	25.00	40.00	80.00	125
1777 FM	—	25.00	40.00	80.00	125
1778/7 FF	—	25.00	40.00	80.00	125
1778 F F/M	—	25.00	40.00	80.00	125
1778 FF	—	25.00	40.00	80.00	125
1779/8 FF	—	25.00	40.00	80.00	125
1779 FF	—	25.00	40.00	80.00	125
1780 FF	—	25.00	40.00	80.00	125
1781 FF	—	25.00	40.00	80.00	125
1782/1 FF	—	25.00	40.00	80.00	125
1782 FF	—	25.00	40.00	80.00	125
1783 FF	—	25.00	40.00	80.00	125
1784 FF	—	25.00	40.00	80.00	125
1784 FF DEI GRTIA (error)	—	100	150	250	600
1784 FM	—	70.00	120	225	575

KM# 88.2a   2 REALES
6.7668 g., 0.8960 Silver 0.1949 oz. ASW **Ruler:**
Charles III **Obv:** Armored bust of Charles III, right
Rev: Crowned shield flanked by pillars with banner
Mint: Mexico City **Note:** Mint mark Mo.

Date	Mintage	VG	F	VF	XF	Unc
1785Mo FM	—	25.00	40.00	80.00	125	—
1786Mo FF	—	200	350	550	950	—
1786Mo FM	—	25.00	40.00	80.00	125	—
1787Mo FM	—	25.00	40.00	80.00	125	—
1788/98Mo FM	—	25.00	40.00	80.00	125	—
1788Mo FM	—	25.00	40.00	80.00	125	—
1789Mo FM	—	25.00	40.00	50.00	150	—

KM# 89   2 REALES
6.7700 g., 0.9030 Silver 0.1965 oz. ASW **Ruler:**
Charles IV **Obv:** Armored bust of Charles IV, right
Obv. Legend: CAROLUS • IV • DEI • GRATIA • **Rev:**
Crowned shield flanked by pillars with banner **Rev.**
Legend: • HISPAN • ET IND • REX • ... **Mint:** Mexico
City **Note:** Mint mark M, Mo.

Date	Mintage	VG	F	VF	XF	Unc
1789 FM	—	25.00	40.00	75.00	200	—
1790 FM	—	25.00	40.00	75.00	200	—

KM# 90   2 REALES
6.7700 g., 0.9030 Silver 0.1965 oz. ASW **Ruler:**
Charles IV **Obv:** Armored bust of Charles IIII, right
Obv. Legend: CAROLUS • IIII • DEI • GRATIA • **Rev.**
Legend: • HISPAN • ET IND REX • ... **Mint:** Mexico
City **Note:** Mint mark M, Mo.

Date	Mintage	VG	F	VF	XF	Unc
1790 FM	—	25.00	40.00	80.00	200	—

KM# 91   2 REALES
6.7668 g., 0.8960 Silver 0.1949 oz. ASW **Ruler:**
Charles IV **Obv:** Armored bust of Charles IIII, right
Obv. Legend: CAROLUS • IIII • DEI • GRATIA • **Rev:**
Crowned shield flanked by pillars with banner **Rev.**
Legend: • HISPAN • ET IND REX • ... **Mint:** Mexico
City **Note:** Mint mark Mo.

Date	Mintage	VG	F	VF	XF	Unc
1792 FM	—	20.00	35.00	60.00	200	—
1793 FM	—	20.00	35.00	60.00	200	—
1794/3 FM	—	50.00	100	200	450	—
1794 FM	—	40.00	75.00	150	400	—
1795 FM	—	20.00	35.00	70.00	100	—
1796 FM	—	20.00	35.00	70.00	100	—
1797 FM	—	20.00	35.00	70.00	100	—
1798 FM	—	20.00	35.00	70.00	100	—
1799/8 FM	—	20.00	35.00	70.00	100	—
1799 FM	—	20.00	35.00	70.00	100	—
1800 FM	—	20.00	35.00	70.00	100	—
1801 FT/M	—	8.00	18.00	36.00	100	—
1801 FT	—	8.00	18.00	36.00	100	—
1801 FM	—	25.00	48.00	90.00	300	—
1802 FT	—	8.00	18.00	36.00	100	—
1803 FT	—	8.00	18.00	36.00	100	—
1804/3 TH	—	8.00	18.00	36.00	100	—
1804 TH	—	8.00	18.00	36.00	100	—
1805 TH	—	8.00	18.00	36.00	100	—
1806/5 TH	—	8.00	18.00	38.50	110	—
1806 TH	—	8.00	18.00	36.00	100	—
1807/5 TH	—	8.00	18.00	38.50	110	—
1807/6 TH	—	18.00	36.00	70.00	240	—
1807 TH	—	8.00	18.00	36.00	100	—
1808/7 TH	—	8.00	18.00	38.50	110	—
1808 TH	—	8.00	18.00	36.00	100	—

SPANISH COLONIAL - MILLED

KM# 92   2 REALES
6.7700 g., 0.9030 Silver 0.1965 oz. ASW   **Ruler:**
Ferdinand VII **Obv:** Armored laureate bust right **Obv.**
Legend: FERDIN.VII... **Rev:** Crowned shield flanked
by pillars **Rev. Legend:** IND.REX... **Mint:** Mexico
City **Note:** Mint mark Mo.

Date	Mintage	VG	F	VF	XF	Unc
1809 TH	—	15.00	30.00	75.00	200	—
181/00 TH	—	15.00	30.00	75.00	200	—
181/00 HJ	—	15.00	30.00	75.00	200	—
181/00 HJ/TH	—	15.00	30.00	75.00	200	—
1810 TH	—	15.00	30.00	75.00	200	—
1810 HJ	—	15.00	30.00	75.00	200	—
1811 TH	—	150	250	350	750	—
1811/0 HJ/TH	—	40.00	80.00	150	300	—
1811 HJ	—	15.00	30.00	75.00	200	—
1811 HJ/TH	—	40.00	80.00	150	300	—

KM# 93   2 REALES
6.7700 g., 0.9030 Silver 0.1965 oz. ASW   **Ruler:**
Ferdinand VII **Obv:** Draped laureate bust right **Obv.**
Legend: FERDIN.VII... **Rev:** Crowned shield flanked
by pillars **Rev. Legend:** IND.REX... **Mint:** Mexico
City **Note:** Mint mark Mo.

Date	Mintage	VG	F	VF	XF	Unc
1812 TH	—	60.00	125	250	550	—
1812 HJ	—	40.00	100	200	500	—
1812 JJ	—	10.00	20.00	60.00	200	—
1813 TH	—	15.00	30.00	100	400	—
1813 JJ	—	20.00	60.00	125	350	—
1813 HJ	—	40.00	100	200	500	—
1814/2 JJ	—	15.00	30.00	100	400	—
1814/3 JJ	—	15.00	30.00	100	400	—
1814 JJ	—	15.00	30.00	100	400	—
1815 JJ	—	7.00	15.00	30.00	85.00	—
1816 JJ	—	7.00	15.00	30.00	85.00	—
1817 JJ	—	7.00	15.00	30.00	85.00	—
1818 JJ	—	7.00	15.00	30.00	85.00	—
1819/8 JJ	—	7.00	15.00	30.00	85.00	—
1819 JJ	—	7.00	15.00	30.00	85.00	—
1820 JJ	—	175	—	—	—	—
1821/0 JJ	—	8.00	16.00	32.00	90.00	—
1821 JJ	—	7.00	15.00	30.00	85.00	—

KM# 94   4 REALES
13.5337 g., 0.9170 Silver 0.3990 oz. ASW   **Ruler:**
Philip V **Obv:** Crowned shield flanked by F 4 **Obv.**
Legend: PHILLIP • V • D • G • HISPAN • ET IND •
REX **Rev:** Crowned globes flanked by crowned
pillars with banner, date below **Rev. Legend:**
VTRAQUE VNUM **Mint:** Mexico City **Note:** Mint mark
M, Mo, MX.

Date	Mintage	VG	F	VF	XF
1732 Rare; Specimen	—	—	—	—	—
1732 F	—	2,000	3,000	5,000	10,000
1733/2 F	—	1,500	2,000	4,000	6,500
1733 MF	—	1,100	1,650	2,250	4,250
1733 MF (MX)	—	1,500	2,200	3,250	5,500
1733 MX/XM	—	1,500	2,200	3,250	5,500
1734/3 MF	—	150	300	600	1,200
1734 MF	—	150	300	600	1,200
1735/4 MF	—	125	200	300	600
1735 MF	—	125	200	300	600
1736 MF	—	125	200	300	600
1737 MF	—	125	200	300	600
1738/7 MF	—	125	200	300	600
1738 MF	—	125	200	300	600
1739 MF	—	125	200	300	600
1740/30 MF	—	125	200	325	625
1740 MF	—	125	200	300	600
1741 MF	—	125	200	300	600
1742/1 MF	—	125	200	300	600
1742/32 MF	—	125	200	300	600
1742 MF	—	110	185	300	600
1743 MF	—	110	185	300	600
1744/3 MF	—	125	200	325	625
1744 MF	—	110	185	300	600
1745 MF	—	110	185	300	600
1746 MF	—	110	185	300	600
1747 MF	—	150	275	400	650

KM# 95   4 REALES
13.5400 g., 0.9170 Silver 0.3992 oz. ASW   **Ruler:**
Ferdinand VI **Obv:** Crowned shield flanked by M F 4
Obv. Legend: FERDND • VI • D • G • HISPAN • ET
IND • REX **Rev:** Crowned globes flanked by crowned
pillars with banner, date below **Rev. Legend:** ...QUE
VNUM **Mint:** Mexico City **Note:** Struck at Mexico City
Mint, mint mark M, Mo.

Date	Mintage	VG	F	VF	XF	Unc
1747 MF	—	125	175	300	550	—
1748/7 MF	—	125	175	300	550	—
1748 MF	—	125	175	250	500	—

SPANISH COLONIAL - MILLED

Date	Mintage	VG	F	VF	XF	Unc
1749 MF	—	150	225	350	650	—
1750/40 MF	—	125	175	250	500	—
1751/41 MF	—	125	175	250	500	—
1751 MF	—	125	175	250	500	—
1752 MF	—	125	175	250	500	—
1753 MF	—	125	175	300	550	—
1754 MF	—	250	375	500	850	—
1755 MM	—	125	175	250	500	—
1756 MM	—	125	175	300	550	—
1757 MM	—	125	175	300	550	—
1758 MM	—	125	175	250	500	—
1759 MM	—	125	175	250	500	—
1760/59 MM	—	125	175	350	600	—
1760 MM	—	125	175	350	600	—

KM# 96   4 REALES
13.5400 g., 0.9170 Silver 0.3992 oz. ASW   **Ruler:**
Charles III **Obv:** Crowned shield flanked by F M 4 **Obv.**
Legend: CAROLVS • III • D • G • HISPAN • ET IND
• REX **Rev:** Crowned globes flanked by crowned
pillars with banner, date below **Rev. Legend:** ...AQUE
VNUM **Mint:** Mexico City **Note:** Mint mark M, Mo.

Date	Mintage	VG	F	VF	XF
1760 MM	—	125	175	250	900
1761 MM	—	125	175	250	900
1761 MM Cross between H and I	—	125	175	250	900
1762 MM	—	125	175	250	500
1763/1 MM	—	125	175	300	600
1763 MM	—	125	175	300	600
1764 MM	—	400	600	1,000	2,000
1764 MF	—	350	500	1,000	2,000
1765 MF	—	350	500	1,000	2,000
1766 MF	—	250	350	550	1,250
1767 MF	—	125	175	300	600
1768 MF	—	125	175	250	500
1769 MF	—	125	175	250	500
1770 MF	—	125	175	250	500
1771 MF	—	125	200	325	700

KM# 97.1   4 REALES
13.5337 g., 0.9030 Silver 0.3929 oz. ASW   **Ruler:**
Charles III **Obv:** Armored bust of Charles III, right **Obv.**
Legend: CAROLUS • III • DEI • GRATIA • **Rev:**
Crowned shield flanked by pillars with banner, inverted
FM and mint mark **Rev. Legend:** • HISPAN • ET IND
REX • ... **Mint:** Mexico City **Note:** Mint mark M, Mo.

Date	Mintage	VG	F	VF	XF	Unc
1772 FM	—	100	125	250	500	—
1773 FM	—	100	175	300	650	—

KM# 97.2   4 REALES
13.5400 g., 0.9030 Silver 0.3931 oz. ASW   **Ruler:**
Charles III **Obv:** Armored bust of Charles III, right **Obv.**
Legend: CAROLUS • III • DEI • GRATIA • **Rev:**
Crowned shield flanked by pillars with banner, normal
initials and mint mark **Rev. Legend:** • HISPAN • ET
IND REX • ... **Mint:** Mexico City **Note:** Mint mark M, Mo.

Date	Mintage	VG	F	VF	XF	Unc
1774 FM	—	70.00	100	200	500	—
1775 FM	—	70.00	100	200	500	—
1776 FM	—	70.00	100	200	500	—
1777 FM	—	70.00	100	200	500	—
1778 FF	—	70.00	100	200	500	—
1779 FF	—	70.00	100	200	500	—
1780 FF	—	70.00	100	200	500	—
1781 FF	—	70.00	100	200	500	—
1782 FF	—	70.00	100	200	500	—
1783 FF	—	70.00	100	200	500	—
1784 FF	—	70.00	100	200	500	—
1784 FM	—	100	200	350	600	—

KM# 97.2a   4 REALES
13.5337 g., 0.8960 Silver 0.3898 oz. ASW   **Ruler:**
Charles III **Obv:** Armored bust of Charles III, right
Obv. Legend: CAROLUS • III • DEI • GRATIA • **Rev:**
Crowned shield flanked by pillars with banner, normal
initials and mint mark **Rev. Legend:** • HISPAN • ET
IND REX • ... **Note:** Mint mark M, Mo.

Date	Mintage	VG	F	VF	XF	Unc
1785 FM	—	100	200	350	600	—
1786 FM	—	70.00	100	200	500	—
1787 FM	—	70.00	100	200	500	—
1788 FM	—	70.00	100	200	500	—
1789 FM	—	70.00	100	200	500	—

KM# 98   4 REALES
13.5400 g., 0.9030 Silver 0.3931 oz. ASW   **Ruler:**
Charles IV **Obv:** Armored bust of Charles III, right
Obv. Legend: CAROLUS • IV • DEI • GRATIA • **Rev.**
Crowned shield flanked by pillars with banner **Rev.**
Legend: • HISPAN • ET IND REX • ... **Mint:** Mexico
City **Note:** Mintint mark M, Mo, using old bust punch.

Date	Mintage	VG	F	VF	XF	Unc
1789 FM	—	75.00	125	250	550	—
1790 FM	—	70.00	100	200	500	—

SPANISH COLONIAL - MILLED

KM# 99 4 REALES
13.5400 g., 0.9030 Silver 0.3931 oz. ASW **Ruler:**
Charles IV **Obv:** Armored bust of Charles III, right
Obv. Legend: CAROLUS • IIII • DEI • GRATIA • **Rev:**
Crowned shield flanked by pillars with banner **Rev.**
Legend: • HISPAN • ET IND • REX • ... **Mint:** Mexico
City **Note:** Mint mark M, Mo, using old bust punch.

Date	Mintage	VG	F	VF	XF	Unc
1790 FM	—	75.00	125	250	550	—

KM# 101 4 REALES
13.5400 g., 0.9030 Silver 0.3931 oz. ASW **Ruler:**
Ferdinand VII **Obv:** Armored laureate bust right **Obv.**
Legend: FERDIN.VII... **Rev:** Crowned shield flanked
by pillars **Rev. Legend:** IND.REX... **Mint:** Mexico
City **Note:** Mint mark Mo.

Date	Mintage	VG	F	VF	XF	Unc
1809 HJ	—	75.00	135	250	775	—
1810 HJ	—	75.00	135	250	775	—
1811 HJ	—	75.00	135	250	775	—
1812 HJ	—	400	650	900	1,850	—

KM# 100 4 REALES
13.5337 g., 0.8960 Silver 0.3898 oz. ASW **Ruler:**
Charles IV **Obv:** Armored bust of Charles IIII, right
Obv. Legend: CAROLUS • IIII • DEI • GRATIA • **Rev:**
Crowned shield flanked by pillars with banner **Rev.**
Legend: • HISPAN • ET IND • REX • ... **Mint:** Mexico
City **Note:** Mint mark Mo.

Date	Mintage	VG	F	VF	XF	Unc
1792 FM	—	65.00	95.00	165	450	—
1793 FM	—	85.00	140	220	550	—
1794/3 FM	—	65.00	95.00	165	450	—
1794 FM	—	65.00	95.00	165	450	—
1795 FM	—	65.00	95.00	165	450	—
1796 FM	—	165	275	450	875	—
1797 FM	—	75.00	130	220	550	—
1798/7 FM	—	65.00	95.00	165	450	—
1798 FM	—	65.00	95.00	165	450	—
1799 FM	—	65.00	95.00	165	450	—
1800 FM	—	65.00	95.00	165	450	—
1801 FM	—	38.50	70.00	165	475	—
1801 FT	—	65.00	130	220	575	—
1802 FT	—	220	325	550	1,100	—
1803 FT	—	85.00	150	250	625	—
1803 FM	—	220	325	550	1,100	—
1804 TH	—	44.00	85.00	195	525	—
1805 TH	—	38.50	70.00	165	475	—
1806 TH	—	38.50	70.00	165	475	—
1807 TH	—	38.50	70.00	165	475	—
1808/7 TH	—	44.00	85.00	195	525	—
1808 TH	—	44.00	85.00	195	525	—

KM# 102 4 REALES
13.5400 g., 0.9030 Silver 0.3931 oz. ASW **Ruler:**
Ferdinand VII **Obv:** Draped laureate bust right **Obv.**
Legend: FERDIN.VII... **Rev:** Crowned shield flanked
by pillars **Rev. Legend:** IND.REX... **Mint:** Mexico
City **Note:** Mint mark Mo.

Date	Mintage	VG	F	VF	XF	Unc
1816 JJ	—	150	200	325	800	—
1817 JJ	—	250	400	500	1,000	—
1818/7 JJ	—	250	400	500	1,000	—
1819 JJ	—	175	250	325	800	—
1820 JJ	—	175	250	325	800	—
1821 JJ	—	75.00	135	250	700	—

KM# 103 8 REALES
27.0674 g., 0.9170 Silver 0.7980 oz. ASW **Ruler:**

SPANISH COLONIAL - MILLED

Philip V **Obv:** Crowned shield flanked by M F 8 **Obv.
Legend:** PHILIP • V • D • G • HISPAN • ET IND • REX
Rev: Crowned globes flanked by crowned pillars with
banner, date below **Rev. Legend:** ...VNUM **Mint:**
Mexico City **Note:** Mint mark M, Mo, MX.

Date	Mintage	VG	F	VF	XF
1732 F	—	2,750	4,750	8,500	18,000
1733/2 F (MX)	—	3,000	5,250	9,500	—
1733 F	—	2,000	3,000	5,500	11,000
1733 MF Large crown; Rare	—	—	—	—	—
1733 F (MX) Rare	—	—	—	—	—

Note: Bonhams Patterson sale 7-96 VF 1733 F (MX) realized $11,710

Date	Mintage	VG	F	VF	XF
1733 MF (MX) Rare	—	—	—	—	—
1733 MF Small crown	—	700	1,500	2,250	4,200
1734/3 MF	—	125	175	275	700
1734 MF	—	125	175	250	550
1735 MF	—	125	175	250	550
1736/5 MF	—	125	175	275	700
1736 MF	—	125	175	250	550
1736 MF Small planchet	—	125	175	250	550
1737 MF	—	100	150	250	475
1738/6 MF	—	100	150	250	475
1738/7 MF	—	100	150	250	475
1738 MF	—	100	150	250	475
1739 MF	—	100	150	250	475
1739/6 MF 9 over inverted 6	—	100	150	250	475
1740/30 MF	—	100	150	275	600
1740/39 MF	—	100	150	275	600
1740 MF	—	100	150	250	475
1741/31 MF	—	100	150	250	475
1741 MF	—	100	150	250	475
1742/32 MF	—	100	150	250	600
1742/1 MF	—	100	150	250	475
1742 MF	—	100	150	250	475
1743/2 MF	—	100	150	250	475
1743 MF	—	100	150	250	475
1744/34 MF	—	100	150	250	475
1744/3 MF	—	100	150	250	475
1744 MF	—	100	150	250	475
1745/4 MF	—	100	150	250	500
1745 MF	—	100	150	250	475
1746/5 MF	—	100	150	275	700
1746 MF	—	100	150	250	475
1747 MF	—	100	150	250	475

IND • REX **Rev:** Crowned globes flanked by crowned
pillars with banner, date below **Rev. Legend:**
...VNUM M **Mint:** Mexico City **Note:** Mint mark M, Mo.

Date	Mintage	VG	F	VF	XF	Unc
1747 MF	—	100	140	200	350	—
1748/7 MF	—	100	140	200	550	—
1748 MF	—	100	140	200	350	—
1749 MF	—	100	140	200	350	—
1749/8 MF	—	100	140	200	350	—
1750 MF	—	100	140	200	350	—
1751/0 MF	—	100	140	200	350	—
1751 MF	—	100	140	200	350	—
1752/1 MF	—	100	140	200	350	—
1752 MF	—	100	140	200	350	—
1753/2 MF	—	100	140	200	350	—
1753 MF	—	100	140	200	350	—
1754/3 MF	—	100	140	200	400	—
1754 MF	—	100	140	200	350	—
1754 MM/MF	—	300	700	1,500	4,200	—
1754 MM	—	300	700	1,500	4,200	—

KM# 104.2 8 REALES
27.0674 g., 0.9170 Silver 0.7980 oz. ASW **Ruler:**
Ferdinand VI **Obv:** Crowned shield flanked by M M
8 **Obv. Legend:** FERDND • VI • D • G • HISPAN •
ET IND • REX **Rev:** Imperial crown on left pillar **Rev.
Legend:** ...VNUM M **Mint:** Mexico City **Note:** Mint
mark M, Mo.

Date	Mintage	VG	F	VF	XF	Unc
1754 MM	—	100	140	200	450	—
1754 MM/MF	—	100	140	250	600	—
1754 MF	—	150	285	550	1,150	—
1755/4 MM	—	100	140	200	400	—
1755 MM	—	100	140	200	350	—
1756/5 MM	—	100	140	200	350	—
1756 MM	—	100	140	200	350	—
1757/6 MM	—	100	140	200	350	—
1757 MM	—	100	140	200	400	—
1758 MM	—	100	140	200	350	—
1759 MM	—	100	140	200	350	—
1760/59 MM	—	100	140	200	350	—
1760 MM	—	100	140	200	350	—

KM# 104.1 8 REALES
27.0674 g., 0.9170 Silver 0.7980 oz. ASW **Ruler:**
Ferdinand VI **Obv:** Crowned shield flaned by M F 8
Obv. Legend: FERDND • VI • D • G • HISPAN • ET

KM# 105 8 REALES
27.0674 g., 0.9170 Silver 0.7980 oz. ASW **Ruler:**
Charles III **Obv:** Crowned shield flanked by M M 8

Obv. Legend: CAROLUS • III • D • G • HISPAN • ET IND • REX **Rev:** Crowned globes flanked by crowned pillars with banner, date below **Rev. Legend:** ...E VNUM M **Mint:** Mexico City **Note:** Mint mark M, Mo.

Date	Mintage	VG	F	VF	XF	Unc
1760/59 MM	—	450	700	—	—	—
Note: CAROLUS. III/Ferdin. Vi						
1760 MM	—	100	140	200	400	—
Note: CAROLUS. III/FERDIN. VI. recut die						
1760 MM	—	100	140	200	350	—
1761/50 MM	—	100	140	200	400	—
Note: Tip of cross between I and S in legend						
1761/51 MM	—	100	140	200	400	—
Note: Tip of cross between I and S in legend						
1761/0 MM	—	100	140	200	400	—
Note: Tip of cross between H and I in legend						
1761 MM	—	100	140	200	325	—
Note: Cross under I in legend						
1761 MM	—	100	140	200	325	—
Note: Tip of cross between H and I in legend						
1761 MM	—	100	140	200	400	—
Note: Tip of cross between I and S in legend						
1762/1 MM	—	100	140	200	550	—
Note: Tip of cross between H and I in legend						
1762/1 MM	—	100	140	200	550	—
1762 MM	—	100	140	200	325	—
Note: Tip of cross between H and I in legend						
1762 MM	—	100	140	200	300	—
Note: Tip of cross between I and S in legend						
1762 MF	—	500	750	1,250	2,750	—
1763/2 MM	—	300	450	750	1,600	—
1763 MM	—	450	650	1,150	2,700	—
1763/1 MF	—	100	140	200	300	—
1763/2 MF	—	100	140	200	300	—
1763 MF	—	100	140	200	300	—
1764 MF	—	100	140	200	325	—
Note: CAR/CRA						
1764 MF	—	100	140	200	300	—
1765 MF	—	100	140	200	300	—
1766/5 MF	—	100	150	200	700	—
1766 MF	—	100	140	200	300	—
1767/6 MF	—	100	140	200	300	—
1767 MF	—	100	140	200	300	—
1768/7 MF	—	100	165	250	725	—
1768 MF	—	100	140	200	300	—
1769 MF	—	100	140	200	300	—
1770/60 MF	—	100	185	300	775	—
1770 MF	—	100	140	200	300	—
1770/60 FM	—	100	185	300	775	—
1770/69 FM	—	100	185	300	775	—
1770 FM/F	—	100	40.00	200	300	—
1770 FM	—	100	140	200	300	—
1771/0 FM	—	100	140	200	300	—
1771 FM	—	100	140	200	300	—

KM# 106.1   8 REALES
27.0674 g., 0.9030 Silver 0.7858 oz. ASW   **Ruler:** Charles III **Obv:** Armored bust of Charles III, right **Obv. Legend:** CAROLUS • III • DEI • GRATIA • **Rev:** Crowned shield flanked by pillars with banner, Assayer initials and mint mark inverted from remainder of legend **Rev. Legend:** • HISPAN • ET IND • REX • ... **Mint:** Mexico City **Note:** Mint mark M, Mo. Mintmark and assayer initials bottom facing rim.

Date	Mintage	VG	F	VF	XF	Unc
1772 FM	—	100	150	225	425	—
1772 MF	—	150	350	750	1,500	—
1773 FM	—	75.00	100	160	290	—

KM# 106.2   8 REALES
27.0674 g., 0.9030 Silver 0.7858 oz. ASW   **Ruler:** Charles III **Obv:** Armored bust of Charles III, right **Obv. Legend:** CAROLUS • III • DEI • GRATIA • **Rev:** Crowned shield flanked by pillars with banner, normal initials and mint mark **Rev. Legend:** • HISPAN • ET IND • REX • ... **Note:** Mint mark M, Mo.

Date	Mintage	VG	F	VF	XF	Unc
1773 FM	—	75.00	100	150	270	—
1774 FM	—	75.00	100	150	270	—
1775 FM	—	75.00	100	150	270	—
1776 FM	—	100	150	225	425	—
1776 FF	—	75.00	100	150	270	—
1777/6 FM	—	75.00	100	150	270	—
1777 FM	—	75.00	100	150	270	—
1777 FF	—	75.00	100	150	270	—
1778 FM	—	—	—	—	—	—
Note: Superior Casterline sale 5-89 VF realized $17,600						
1778/7 FF	—	75.00	100	150	270	—
1778 FF	—	75.00	100	150	270	—
1779 FF	—	75.00	100	150	270	—
1780 FF	—	75.00	100	150	270	—
1781 FF	—	75.00	100	150	270	—
1782 FF	—	75.00	100	150	270	—
1783 FF	—	75.00	100	150	270	—
1783 FM	—	4,000	6,000	9,000	—	—
1784 FF	—	150	300	600	1,500	—
1784 FM	—	75.00	100	150	270	—

KM# 106.2a   8 REALES
27.0674 g., 0.8960 Silver 0.7797 oz. ASW   **Ruler:** Charles III **Obv:** Armored bust of Charles III, right

SPANISH COLONIAL - MILLED

Obv. Legend: CAROLUS • III • DEI • GRATIA • **Rev:** Crowned shield flanked by pillars with banner, normal initials and mint mark **Rev. Legend:** • HISPAN • ET IND • REX • ... **Note:** Mint mark M, Mo.

Date	Mintage	VG	F	VF	XF	Unc
1785 FM	—	75.00	100	140	200	—
1786/5 FM	—	75.00	100	200	400	—
1786 FM	—	75.00	100	140	200	—
1787/6 FM	—	100	250	450	1,200	—
1787 FM	—	75.00	100	140	200	—
1788 FM	—	75.00	100	140	200	—
1789 FM	—	75.00	100	150	225	—

KM# 107   8 REALES
27.0674 g., 0.9030 Silver 0.7858 oz. ASW **Ruler:** Charles IV **Obv:** Armored bust of Charles III, right **Obv. Legend:** CAROLUS • IV • DEI • GRATIA • **Rev:** Crowned shield flanked by pillars with banner **Rev. Legend:** • HISPAN • ET IND • REX • ... **Mint:** Mexico City **Note:** Mint mark M, Mo, using old bust punch.

Date	Mintage	VG	F	VF	XF	Unc
1789 FM	—	75.00	100	160	300	—
1790 FM	—	75.00	100	150	270	—

KM# 108   8 REALES
27.0674 g., 0.9030 Silver 0.7858 oz. ASW **Ruler:** Charles IV **Obv:** Armored bust of Charles III, right **Obv. Legend:** CAROLUS • IIII • DEI • GRATIA • **Rev:** Crowned shield flanked by pillars with banner **Rev. Legend:** • HISPAN • ET IND • REX • ... **Mint:** Mexico City **Note:** Mint mark M, Mo, using old portait punch.

Date	Mintage	VG	F	VF	XF	Unc
1790 FM	—	75.00	100	150	270	—

KM# 109   8 REALES
27.0674 g., 0.8960 Silver 0.7797 oz. ASW **Ruler:** Charles IV **Obv:** Armored bust of Charles IIII, right **Obv. Inscription:** CAROLUS • IIII • DEI • GRATIA • **Rev:** Crowned shield flanked by pillars with banner **Rev. Legend:** • HISPAN • ET IND • REX • ... **Mint:** Mexico City **Note:** Mint mark Mo.

Date	Mintage	VG	F	VF	XF	Unc
1791 FM	—	60.00	90.00	135	210	—
1792 FM	—	60.00	90.00	135	210	—
1793 FM	—	60.00	90.00	135	210	—
1794 FM	—	60.00	90.00	135	210	—
1795/4 FM	—	60.00	90.00	135	210	—
1795 FM	—	60.00	90.00	135	210	—
1796 FM	—	60.00	90.00	135	210	—
1797 FM	—	60.00	90.00	135	210	—
1798 FM	—	60.00	90.00	135	210	—
1799 FM	—	60.00	90.00	135	210	—
1800/700 FM	—	60.00	90.00	135	210	—
1800 FM	—	60.00	90.00	135	210	—
1801/0 FT/FM	—	60.00	90.00	135	210	—
1801/791 FM	—	46.25	80.00	130	400	—
1801/0 FM	—	46.25	80.00	130	400	—
1801 FM	—	27.50	55.00	135	400	—
1801 FT/M	—	46.25	80.00	150	425	—
1801 FT	—	27.50	46.25	65.00	170	—
1802/1 FT	—	46.25	80.00	150	425	—
1802 FT	—	27.50	46.25	65.00	170	—
1802 FT/M	—	27.50	46.25	65.00	170	—
1803 FT	—	27.50	46.25	65.00	180	—
1803 FT/M	—	27.50	46.25	65.00	170	—
1803 TH	—	100	200	325	725	—
1804 TH	—	27.50	46.25	65.00	170	—
Note: CARLUS (error)						
1804/3 TH	—	46.25	80.00	150	425	—
1805/4 TH	—	55.00	110	175	450	—
1805 TH	—	27.50	46.25	65.00	170	—
Note: Narrow date						
1805 TH	—	27.50	46.25	65.00	170	—
Note: Wide date						
1806 TH	—	27.50	46.25	65.00	170	—
1807/6 TH	—	200	325	475	1,100	—
1807 TH	—	27.50	46.25	65.00	170	—
1808/7 TH	—	27.50	46.25	65.00	170	—
1808 TH	—	27.50	46.25	65.00	170	—

SPANISH COLONIAL · MILLED

KM# 110   8 REALES

27.0674 g., 0.8960 Silver 0.7797 oz. ASW **Ruler:**
Ferdinand VII **Obv:** Armored laureate bust right **Obv.**
Legend: FERDIN • VII... **Rev:** Crowned shield
flanked by pillars **Rev. Legend:** IND • REX... **Mint:**
Mexico City **Note:** Mint mark Mo.

Date	Mintage	VG	F	VF	XF	Unc
1808 TH	—	33.00	55.00	100	240	—
1809/8 TH	—	33.00	55.00	100	240	—
1809 TH	—	27.50	47.50	70.00	200	—
1809 HJ	—	33.00	55.00	100	240	—
1809 HJ/TH	—	27.50	47.50	70.00	200	—
1810/09 HJ	—	33.00	55.00	100	240	—
1810 TH	—	100	200	400	950	—
1810 HJ/TH	—	33.00	55.00	100	240	—
1810 HJ	—	33.00	55.00	100	240	—
1811/0 HJ	—	27.50	47.50	70.00	200	—
1811 HJ	—	27.50	47.50	70.00	200	—
1811 HJ/TH	—	27.50	45.00	65.00	170	—

KM# 111   8 REALES

27.0700 g., 0.9030 Silver 0.7859 oz. ASW **Ruler:**
Ferdinand VII **Obv:** Draped laureate bust right **Obv.**
Legend: FERDIN • VII... **Rev:** Crowned shield

flanked by pillars **Rev. Legend:** IND • REX... **Mint:**
Mexico City **Note:** Mint mark Mo.

Date	Mintage	VG	F	VF	XF	Unc
1811 HJ	—	27.50	55.00	80.00	210	—
1812 HJ	—	65.00	100	170	425	—
1812 JJ/HJ	—	27.50	45.00	65.00	170	—
1812 JJ	—	27.50	45.00	65.00	170	—
1813 HJ	—	65.00	100	170	425	—
1813 JJ	—	27.50	45.00	65.00	170	—
1814/3 HJ	—	1,550	3,300	6,600	—	—
1814/3 JJ	—	27.50	45.00	65.00	170	—
1814 JJ	—	27.50	45.00	65.00	170	—
1815/4 JJ	—	27.50	45.00	65.00	170	—
1815 JJ	—	27.50	45.00	65.00	170	—
1816/5 JJ	—	27.50	45.00	65.00	150	—
1816 JJ	—	27.50	45.00	65.00	150	—
1817 JJ	—	27.50	45.00	65.00	150	—
1818 JJ	—	27.50	45.00	65.00	150	—
1819 JJ	—	27.50	45.00	65.00	150	—
1820 JJ	—	27.50	45.00	65.00	150	—
1821 JJ	—	27.50	45.00	65.00	150	—

KM# 112   1/2 ESCUDO

1.6917 g., 0.8750 Gold 0.0476 oz. AGW **Ruler:**
Ferdinand VII **Obv:** Laureate head right **Obv. Legend:**
FERD • VII • D • G • HISP • ET IND **Rev:** Crowned oval
shield **Mint:** Mexico City **Note:** Mint mark Mo.

Date	Mintage	VG	F	VF	XF	Unc
1814 JJ	—	100	150	225	375	550
1815/4 JJ	—	150	200	250	400	875
1815 JJ	—	150	200	250	400	—
1816 JJ	—	100	150	225	375	550
1817 JJ	—	150	200	250	400	—
1818 JJ	—	150	200	250	400	—
1819 JJ	—	150	200	250	400	—
1820 JJ	—	200	300	400	550	—

KM# 113   ESCUDO

3.3834 g., 0.9170 Gold 0.0997 oz. AGW **Ruler:**
Philip V **Obv:** Armored bust right **Obv. Legend:**
PHILIP • V • D • G • HISPAN • ET IND • REX **Rev:**
Crowned shield flanked by M F I **Mint:** Mexico City

Date	Mintage	VG	F	VF	XF	Unc
1732 F	—	1,000	2,000	3,000	4,000	—
1733/2 F	—	1,000	2,000	3,000	4,000	—
1734/3 MF	—	200	300	400	850	—
1735/4 MF	—	200	300	400	850	—
1735 MF	—	200	300	400	850	—
1736/5 MF	—	200	300	400	850	—
1736 MF	—	200	300	400	850	—
1737 MF	—	200	300	600	1,200	—
1738/7 MF	—	200	300	600	1,200	—
1738 MF	—	200	300	600	1,200	—
1739 MF	—	200	300	600	1,200	—
1740/30 MF	—	200	300	600	1,200	—
1741 MF	—	200	300	600	1,200	—
1742 MF	—	200	300	600	1,200	—
1743/2 MF	—	200	300	450	800	—
1743 MF	—	200	300	400	700	—
1744/3 MF	—	200	300	400	700	—
1744 MF	—	200	300	400	700	—
1745 MF	—	200	300	400	700	—
1746/5 MF	—	200	300	400	700	—
1747 MF Rare	—	—	—	—	—	—

SPANISH COLONIAL - MILLED

KM# 114 ESCUDO
3.3834 g., 0.9170 Gold 0.0997 oz. AGW **Ruler:**
Ferdinand VI **Obv:** Armored bust right **Obv. Legend:**
FERD • VI • D • G • HISPAN • ET IND • REX **Rev:**
Crowned shield flanked by M F I **Mint:** Mexico City
Note: Mint mark M, Mo.

Date	Mintage	VG	F	VF	XF	Unc
1747 MF	—	1,650	3,000	5,000	7,500	—

KM# 115.1 ESCUDO
3.3834 g., 0.9170 Gold 0.0997 oz. AGW **Ruler:**
Ferdinand VI **Obv:** Short armored bust right **Obv.**
Legend: FERD • VI • D • G • HISPAN • ET IND •
REX **Rev:** Crowned shield **Mint:** Mexico City **Note:**
Mint mark M, Mo.

Date	Mintage	VG	F	VF	XF	Unc
1748 MF	—	250	350	550	950	—
1749 MF	—	300	450	700	1,150	—
1750 MF	—	200	300	400	800	—
1751 MF	—	200	300	400	800	—

KM# 115.2 ESCUDO
3.3834 g., 0.9170 Gold 0.0997 oz. AGW **Ruler:**
Ferdinand VI **Obv:** Short armored bust right **Obv.**
Legend: FERD • VI • D • G • HISPAN • ET IND •
REX **Rev:** Without 1 S flanking crowned shield **Mint:**
Mexico City

Date	Mintage	VG	F	VF	XF	Unc
1752 MF	—	200	300	375	750	—
1753/2 MF	—	200	300	400	800	—
1753 MF	—	200	300	400	800	—
1754 MF	—	200	300	400	800	—
1755 MM	—	200	300	400	800	—
1756 MM	—	200	300	400	800	—

KM# A116 ESCUDO
3.3834 g., 0.9170 Gold 0.0997 oz. AGW **Ruler:**
Ferdinand VI **Obv:** Armored bust right **Obv. Legend:**
FERDIND • VI • D • G • HISPAN • ETIND • REX •
Rev: Crowned shield **Rev. Legend:** M • NOMINA
MAGNA SEQUOR • M **Mint:** Mexico City

Date	Mintage	VG	F	VF	XF	Unc
1757 MM	—	200	300	400	800	—
1759 MM	—	200	300	400	800	—

KM# 116 ESCUDO
3.3834 g., 0.9170 Gold 0.0997 oz. AGW **Ruler:**
Charles III **Obv:** Armored bust right **Obv. Legend:**
CAROLVS • III • D • G • HISPAN • ET IND • REX
Rev: Crowned shield **Rev. Legend:** M • NOMINA
MAGNA SEQUOR • M• **Mint:** Mexico City **Note:** Mint
mark M, Mo.

Date	Mintage	VG	F	VF	XF	Unc
1760 MM	—	400	800	1,500	2,500	—
1761/0 MM	—	400	800	1,500	2,500	—
1761 MM	—	400	800	1,500	2,500	—

KM# 117 ESCUDO
3.3834 g., 0.9170 Gold 0.0997 oz. AGW **Ruler:**
Charles III **Obv:** Large armored bust right **Obv.**
Legend: CAR • III • D • G • HISP • ET IND • R **Rev:**
Crowned shield **Rev. Legend:** IN • UTROQ • FELIX
• **Mint:** Mexico City **Note:** Mint mark M, Mo.

Date	Mintage	VG	F	VF	XF	Unc
1762 MM	—	250	375	600	1,000	—
1763 MM	—	275	425	700	1,100	—
1764 MM	—	250	375	600	1,000	—
1765 MF	—	250	375	600	1,000	—
1766 MF	—	250	375	600	1,000	—
1767 MF	—	250	375	600	1,000	—
1768 MF	—	250	375	600	1,000	—
1769 MF	—	250	375	600	1,000	—
1770 MF	—	250	375	600	1,000	—
1771 MF	—	250	375	600	1,000	—

KM# 118.1 ESCUDO
3.3834 g., 0.9010 Gold 0.0980 oz. AGW **Ruler:**
Charles III **Obv:** Large armored bust right **Obv.**
Legend: CAROL • III • D • G • HISPAN • ET IND •
R **Rev:** Crowned shield flanked by 1 S within order
chain **Rev. Legend:** FELIX • A • D • ... **Mint:** Mexico
City **Note:** Mint mark M, Mo.

Date	Mintage	VG	F	VF	XF	Unc
1772 MF	—	175	250	350	475	—
1772 FM	—	175	250	275	475	—
1773 FM	—	175	250	275	475	—

KM# 118.2 ESCUDO
3.3834 g., 0.9010 Gold 0.0980 oz. AGW **Ruler:**

Charles III **Obv:** Large armored bust right **Obv.**
Legend: CAROL • III • D • G • HISPAN • ET IND •
R **Rev:** crowned shield in order chain, initials and
mint mark inverted **Rev. Legend:** FELIX • A • D • ...
Mint: Mexico City **Note:** Mint mark M, Mo.

Date	Mintage	VG	F	VF	XF	Unc
1773 FM	—	175	250	350	475	—
1774 FM	—	175	250	350	475	—
1775 FM	—	175	250	350	475	—
1776 FM	—	225	300	400	575	—
1777 FM	—	175	250	350	475	—
1778 FF	—	175	250	350	475	—
1779 FF	—	175	250	350	475	—
1780 FF	—	175	250	350	475	—
1781 FF	—	175	250	350	475	—
1782 FF	—	175	250	350	475	—
1783/2 FF	—	175	250	350	475	—
1783 FF	—	175	250	350	475	—
1784/3 FF	—	175	250	350	475	—
1784/3 FM/F	—	175	250	350	475	—

KM# 118.2a ESCUDO
3.3800 g., 0.8750 Gold 0.0951 oz. AGW **Ruler:**
Charles III **Obv:** Large armored bust right **Obv.**
Legend: CAROL • III • D • G • HISPAN • ET IND •
R • **Rev:** Crowned shield in order chain, initials and
mint mark inverted **Rev. Legend:** FELIX • A • D • ...
Mint: Mexico City **Note:** Mint mark M, Mo.

Date	Mintage	VG	F	VF	XF	Unc
1785 FM	—	175	250	350	475	—
1786 FM	—	175	250	350	475	—
1787 FM	—	175	250	350	475	—
1788 FM	—	175	250	350	475	—

KM# 118.1a ESCUDO
3.3834 g., 0.8750 Gold 0.0952 oz. AGW **Ruler:**
Charles III **Obv:** Large armored bust right **Obv.**
Legend: CAROL • III • D • G • HISPAN • ET IND •
R **Rev:** Crowned shield in order chain, initial letters
and mint mark upright **Rev. Legend:** FELIX • A • D
• ... **Mint:** Mexico City **Note:** Mint mark M, Mo.

Date	Mintage	VG	F	VF	XF	Unc
1788 FM	—	175	250	350	475	—

KM# 119 ESCUDO
3.3834 g., 0.8750 Gold 0.0952 oz. AGW **Ruler:**
Charles IV **Obv:** Armored bust of Charles III, right
Obv. Legend: CAROL • IV • D • G • ... **Rev:** Crowned
shield in order chain, initial letters and mint mark
upright **Rev. Legend:** FELIX • A • D • ... **Mint:** Mexico
City **Note:** Mint mark M, Mo, using old portrait punch.

Date	Mintage	VG	F	VF	XF	Unc
1789 FM	—	300	550	1,000	2,000	—
1790 FM	—	300	550	1,000	2,000	—

KM# 120 ESCUDO
3.3834 g., 0.8750 Gold 0.0952 oz. AGW **Ruler:**
Charles IV **Obv:** Armored bust right **Obv. Legend:**
CAROL • IIII • D • G • ... **Rev:** Crowned shield in order
chain, initial letters and mint mark upright **Rev.
Legend:** FELIX • A • D • ... **Mint:** Mexico City **Note:**
Mint mark Mo.

Date	Mintage	VG	F	VF	XF	Unc
1792 MF	—	150	225	300	375	—
1793 FM	—	150	225	300	375	—
1794 FM	—	150	225	300	375	—
1795 FM	—	150	225	300	375	—
1796 FM	—	150	225	300	375	—
1797 FM	—	150	225	300	375	—
1798 FM	—	150	225	300	375	—
1799 FM	—	150	225	300	375	—
1800 FM	—	150	225	300	375	—
1801 FM	—	155	185	265	375	—
1801 FT	—	155	185	265	375	700
1802 FT	—	155	185	265	375	—
1803 FT	—	155	185	265	375	—
1804/3 TH	—	155	185	265	375	800
1804 TH	—	155	185	265	375	800
1805 TH	—	155	185	265	375	—
1806/5 TH	—	155	185	265	375	—
1806 TH	—	155	185	265	375	—
1807 TH	—	155	185	265	375	—
1808 TH	—	155	185	265	375	—

KM# 121 ESCUDO
3.3834 g., 0.8750 Gold 0.0952 oz. AGW **Ruler:**
Ferdinand VII **Obv:** Armored bust right **Obv.**
Legend: FERDIN.VII... **Rev:** Crowned shield divides
designed wreath **Rev. Legend:** FELIX. A. D, initial
letters and mint mark upright **Mint:** Mexico City **Note:**
Mint mark Mo.

Date	Mintage	VG	F	VF	XF	Unc
1809 HJ/TH	—	150	180	235	400	750
1809 HJ	—	150	180	235	400	750
1811/0 HJ	—	150	180	235	400	—
1812 HJ	—	165	250	300	500	—

KM# 122 ESCUDO
3.3834 g., 0.8750 Gold 0.0952 oz. AGW **Ruler:**
Ferdinand VII **Obv:** Laureate head right **Obv.**
Legend: FERDIN • VII • D • G... **Rev:** Crowned shield
divides designed wreath, initial letters and mint mark
upright **Rev. Legend:** FELIX • A • D... **Mint:** Mexico
City **Note:** Mint mark Mo.

SPANISH COLONIAL - MILLED

Date	Mintage	VG	F	VF	XF	Unc
1814 HJ	—	165	250	300	500	900
1815 HJ	—	165	250	300	500	900
1815 JJ	—	165	250	300	500	900
1816 JJ	—	180	275	325	550	950
1817 JJ	—	165	250	300	500	900
1818 JJ	—	165	250	300	500	900
1819 JJ	—	165	250	300	500	900
1820 JJ	—	165	250	300	500	900

KM# 124   2 ESCUDOS
6.7660 g., 0.9170 Gold 0.1995 oz. AGW **Ruler:** Philip V **Obv:** Armored bust right **Obv. Legend:** PHILIP • V • D • G • HISPAN • ET IND • REX **Rev:** Crowned shield flanked by M F 2 **Rev. Legend:** INITIUM SAPIENTIAE TIMOR DOMINI **Mint:** Mexico City

Date	Mintage	VG	F	VF	XF	Unc
1732 F	—	1,000	1,500	2,000	3,000	—
1733 F	—	750	1,000	1,500	2,500	—
1734/3 MF	—	400	500	900	1,400	—
1735 MF	—	400	500	900	1,400	—
1736/5 MF	—	400	500	900	1,400	—
1736 MF	—	400	500	900	1,400	—
1737 MF	—	400	500	900	1,400	—
1738/7 MF	—	400	500	900	1,400	—
1739 MF	—	400	500	900	1,400	—
1740/30 MF	—	400	500	900	1,400	—
1741 MF	—	400	500	900	1,400	—
1742 MF	—	400	500	900	1,400	—
1743 MF	—	400	500	900	1,400	—
1744/2 MF	—	400	500	900	1,400	—
1744 MF	—	400	500	900	1,400	—
1745 MF	—	400	500	900	1,400	—
1746/5 MF	—	400	500	900	1,400	—
1747 MF	—	400	500	900	1,400	—

KM# 125   2 ESCUDOS
6.7660 g., 0.9170 Gold 0.1995 oz. AGW **Ruler:** Ferdinand VI **Obv:** Large armored bust right **Obv. Legend:** FERD • VI • D • G • ... **Rev:** Crowned shield flanked by M F 2 **Rev. Legend:** INITIUM... **Mint:** Mexico City

Date	Mintage	VG	F	VF	XF	Unc
1747 MF	—	3,000	5,500	9,000	15,000	—

KM# 126.1   2 ESCUDOS
6.7660 g., 0.9170 Gold 0.1995 oz. AGW **Ruler:**

Ferdinand VI **Obv:** Head right **Obv. Legend:** FERD • VI • D • G • ... **Rev:** Crowned shield **Rev. Legend:** NOMINA MAGNA SEQUOR **Mint:** Mexico City **Note:** Mint mark M, Mo.

Date	Mintage	VG	F	VF	XF	Unc
1748 MF	—	450	750	1,500	3,000	—
1749/8 MF	—	450	750	1,500	3,000	—
1750 MF	—	400	700	1,400	2,850	—
1751 MF	—	400	700	1,400	2,850	—

KM# 126.2   2 ESCUDOS
6.7660 g., 0.9170 Gold 0.1995 oz. AGW **Ruler:** Ferdinand VI **Obv:** Head right **Obv. Legend:** FERD • VI • D • G • ... **Rev:** Without 2 S by crowned shield **Rev. Legend:** NOMINA MAGNA SEQUOR **Mint:** Mexico City **Note:** Mint mark M, Mo.

Date	Mintage	VG	F	VF	XF	Unc
1752 MF	—	400	700	1,400	2,850	—
1753 MF	—	400	700	1,400	2,850	—
1754 MF	—	600	850	1,750	3,500	—
1755 MM	—	400	700	1,400	2,850	—
1756 MM	—	600	850	1,750	3,500	—

KM# 127   2 ESCUDOS
6.7660 g., 0.9170 Gold 0.1995 oz. AGW **Ruler:** Ferdinand VI **Obv:** Armored bust right **Obv. Legend:** FERDIND • VI • D • G • ... **Rev:** Without 2 S by crowned shield **Rev. Legend:** NOMINA MAGNA SEQUOR **Mint:** Mexico City **Note:** Mint mark M, Mo.

Date	Mintage	VG	F	VF	XF	Unc
1757 MM	—	450	750	1,500	3,000	—
1759 MM	—	450	750	1,500	3,000	—

KM# 128   2 ESCUDOS
6.7660 g., 0.9170 Gold 0.1995 oz. AGW **Ruler:** Charles III **Obv:** Armored bust right **Obv. Legend:** CAROLVS • III • D • G • ... **Rev:** Without 2 S by crowned shield **Rev. Legend:** NOMINA MAGNA SEQUOR **Mint:** Mexico City **Note:** Mint mark M, Mo.

Date	Mintage	VG	F	VF	XF	Unc
1760 MM	—	550	1,000	2,000	4,000	—
1761 MM	—	550	1,000	2,000	4,000	—

SPANISH COLONIAL - MILLED

KM# 129 2 ESCUDOS

6.7668 g., 0.9170 Gold 0.1995 oz. AGW **Ruler:** Charles III **Obv:** Large armored bust right **Obv. Legend:** CAROLUS • III • D • G • ... **Rev:** Without 2 S by crowned shield **Rev. Legend:** IN • UTROQ • FELIX • AUSPICE • DEO **Mint:** Mexico City **Note:** Mint mark M, Mo.

Date	Mintage	VG	F	VF	XF	Unc
1762 MF	—	500	900	1,850	3,750	—
1763 MF	—	500	900	1,850	3,750	—
1764/3 MF	—	500	900	1,850	3,750	—
1765 MF	—	500	900	1,850	3,750	—
1766 MF	—	500	900	1,850	3,750	—
1767 MF	—	500	900	1,850	3,750	—
1768 MF	—	500	900	1,850	3,750	—
1769 MF	—	500	900	1,850	3,750	—
1770 MF	—	500	900	1,850	3,750	—
1771 MF	—	500	900	1,850	3,750	—

KM# 130.1 2 ESCUDOS

6.7668 g., 0.9010 Gold 0.1960 oz. AGW **Ruler:** Charles III **Obv:** Older, armored bust right **Obv. Legend:** CAROLUS • III • D • G • ... **Rev:** Crowned shield in order chain, initials and mint mark upright **Rev. Legend:** IN • UTROQ • FELIX • AUSPICE • DEO **Mint:** Mexico City **Note:** Mint mark M, Mo.

Date	Mintage	VG	F	VF	XF	Unc
1772 FM	—	300	400	550	1,000	—
1773 FM	—	300	400	550	1,000	—

KM# 130.2 2 ESCUDOS

6.7668 g., 0.9010 Gold 0.1960 oz. AGW **Ruler:** Charles III **Obv:** Older, armored bust right **Obv. Legend:** CAROLUS • III • D • G • ... **Rev:** Crowned shield in order chain, initials and mint mark inverted **Rev. Legend:** IN • UTROQ • FELIX • AUSPICE • DEO **Mint:** Mexico City **Note:** Mint mark M, Mo.

Date	Mintage	VG	F	VF	XF	Unc
1773 FM	—	300	400	550	1,000	—
1774 FM	—	300	400	550	1,000	—
1775 FM	—	300	400	550	1,000	—
1776 FM	—	350	500	675	1,000	—
1777 FM	—	300	400	500	900	—
1778 FF	—	300	400	500	900	—
1779 FF	—	300	400	500	900	—
1780 FF	—	300	400	500	900	—
1781 FM/M	—	300	400	500	900	—
1781 FF	—	300	400	500	900	—
1782 FF	—	300	400	500	900	—
1783 FF	—	300	400	500	900	—
1784 FF	—	300	400	500	900	—
1784 FM/F	—	300	400	500	900	—

KM# 130.2a 2 ESCUDOS

6.7668 g., 0.8750 Gold 0.1904 oz. AGW **Ruler:** Charles III **Obv:** Older, armored bust right **Obv. Legend:** CAROLUS • III • D • G • ... **Rev:** Crowned shield in order chain, initials and mint mark inverted **Rev. Legend:** IN • UTROQ • FELIX • AUSPICE • DEO **Mint:** Mexico City **Note:** Mint mark M, Mo.

Date	Mintage	VG	F	VF	XF	Unc
1785 FM	—	300	400	500	900	—
1786 FM	—	300	400	500	900	—
1787 FM	—	300	400	500	900	—
1788 FM	—	300	400	500	900	—

KM# 130.1a 2 ESCUDOS

6.7668 g., 0.8750 Gold 0.1904 oz. AGW **Ruler:** Charles III **Obv:** Older, armored bust right **Obv. Legend:** CAROLUS • III • D • G • ... **Rev:** Crowned shield in order chain, initials and mint mark upright **Rev. Legend:** IN • UTROQ • FELIX • AUSPICE • DEO **Mint:** Mexico City **Note:** Mint mark M, Mo.

Date	Mintage	VG	F	VF	XF	Unc
1788 FM	—	300	400	500	900	—

KM# 131 2 ESCUDOS

6.7668 g., 0.8750 Gold 0.1904 oz. AGW **Ruler:** Charles IV **Obv:** Armored bust of Charles III, right **Obv. Legend:** CAROL • IV • D • G • ... **Rev:** Crowned shield in order chain, initials and mint mark upright **Rev. Legend:** IN • UTROQ • FELIX • AUSPICE • DEO **Mint:** Mexico City **Note:** Mint mark M, Mo, using old portrait punch.

Date	Mintage	VG	F	VF	XF	Unc
1789 FM	—	650	1,200	2,000	3,500	—
1790 FM	—	650	1,200	2,000	3,500	—

KM# 132 2 ESCUDOS

6.7668 g., 0.8750 Gold 0.1904 oz. AGW **Ruler:** Charles IV **Obv:** Armored bust of Charles IIII, right **Obv. Legend:** CAROL • IIII • D • G • ... **Rev:** Crowned shield flanked by 2 S in order chain **Rev. Legend:** IN • UTROQ • FELIX • AUSPICE • DEO; initials and mint mark upright **Mint:** Mexico City **Note:** Mint mark Mo.

Date	Mintage	VG	F	VF	XF	Unc
1791 FM Mo over inverted Mo	—	300	400	600	950	—
1792 FM	—	250	350	450	575	—
1793 FM	—	250	350	450	575	—
1794 FM	—	250	350	450	575	—
1795 FM	—	250	350	450	575	—
1796 FM	—	250	350	450	575	—
1797 FM	—	250	350	450	575	—
1798 FM	—	250	350	450	575	—
1799 FM	—	250	350	450	575	—
1800 FM	—	250	350	450	575	—
1801 FT	—	300	350	425	600	—
1802 FT	—	300	350	425	600	1,000
1803 FT	—	300	350	425	600	—
1804 TH	—	300	350	425	600	—
1805 TH	—	300	350	425	600	—
1806/5 TH	—	300	350	425	600	—
1807 TH	—	300	350	425	600	—
1808 TH	—	300	350	425	600	1,500

KM# 134 2 ESCUDOS

6.7668 g., 0.8750 Gold 0.1904 oz. AGW **Ruler:** Ferdinand VII **Obv:** Laureate head right **Obv.**

SPANISH COLONIAL • MILLED

Legend: FERDIN • VII • D • G... **Rev:** Crowned shield
divides designed wreath, initials and mint mark upright
Rev. Legend: IN • UTROQ • FELIX • AUSPICE • DEO
Mint: Mexico City **Note:** Mint mark Mo.

Date	Mintage	VG	F	VF	XF	Unc
1814Mo HJ	—	300	450	750	1,250	—
1815 JJ	—	300	450	750	1,250	—
1816 JJ	—	300	450	750	1,250	—
1817 JJ	—	300	450	750	1,250	—
1818 JJ	—	300	450	750	1,250	3,750
1819 JJ	—	300	450	750	1,250	—
1820 JJ	—	300	450	750	1,250	—
1821 JJ	—	300	450	750	1,250	—

KM# 135   4 ESCUDOS
13.5337 g., 0.9170 Gold 0.3990 oz. AGW   **Ruler:**
Philip V **Obv:** Armored bust right **Obv. Legend:**
PHILIP • V • D • G • HISPAN • ET IND • REX **Rev:**
Crowned shield flanked by F 4 **Rev. Legend:** INITIUM
SAPIENTIAE TIMOR DOMINI **Mint:** Mexico City

Date	Mintage	VG	F	VF	XF	Unc
1732 Rare	—	—	—	—	—	—
1732 F Rare	—	—	—	—	—	—
1733 F Rare	—	—	—	—	—	—
1734/3 F	—	1,200	1,800	3,350	5,400	—
1734 MF	—	1,000	1,600	3,000	5,100	—
1735 MF	—	1,000	1,600	3,000	5,400	—
1736 MF	—	1,000	1,600	3,000	5,400	—
1737 MF	—	900	1,500	2,900	4,800	—
1738/7 MF	—	900	1,500	2,900	4,800	—
1738 MF	—	900	1,500	2,900	4,800	—
1739 MF	—	900	1,500	2,900	4,800	—
1740/30 MF	—	900	1,500	2,900	4,800	—
1740 MF	—	900	1,500	2,900	4,800	—
1741 MF	—	900	1,500	2,900	4,800	—
1742/32 MF	—	900	1,500	2,900	4,800	—
1743 MF	—	900	1,500	2,900	4,800	—
1744 MD	—	900	1,500	2,900	4,800	—
1745 MF	—	900	1,500	2,900	4,800	—
1746 MF	—	900	1,500	2,900	4,800	—
1747 MF	—	900	1,500	2,900	4,800	—
1746/5 MF	—	900	1,500	2,900	4,800	—

KM# 136   4 ESCUDOS
13.5337 g., 0.9170 Gold 0.3990 oz. AGW   **Ruler:**
Ferdinand VI **Obv:** Large, armored bust right **Obv.
Legend:** FERDND • VI • D • G • ... **Rev:** Crowned
shield flanked by F 4 **Rev. Legend:** INITIUM
SAPIENTIAE TIMOR DOMINI **Mint:** Mexico City
Note: Mint mark M, Mo.

Date	Mintage	VG	F	VF	XF	Unc
1747 MF	—	7,500	13,500	20,000	30,000	—

KM# 137   4 ESCUDOS
13.5337 g., 0.9170 Gold 0.3990 oz. AGW   **Ruler:**
Ferdinand VI **Obv:** Armored bust right **Obv. Legend:**
FERDND • VI • D • G • ... **Rev:** Crowned shield flanked
by 4 S **Rev. Legend:** NOMINA MAGNA SEQUOR
Mint: Mexico City **Note:** Mint mark M, Mo.

Date	Mintage	VG	F	VF	XF	Unc
1748 MF	—	1,500	3,000	5,000	8,000	—
1749 MF	—	1,500	3,000	5,000	8,000	—
1750/48 MF	—	1,500	3,000	5,000	8,000	—
1750 MF	—	1,500	3,000	5,000	8,000	—
1751 MF	—	1,500	3,000	5,000	8,000	—

KM# 138   4 ESCUDOS
13.5337 g., 0.9170 Gold 0.3990 oz. AGW   **Ruler:**
Ferdinand VI **Obv:** Small, armored bust right **Obv.
Legend:** FERDND • VI • D • G • ... **Rev:** Crowned
shield, without value **Rev. Legend:** NOMINA
MAGNA... **Mint:** Mexico City **Note:** Mint mark M, Mo.

Date	Mintage	VG	F	VF	XF	Unc
1752 MF	—	1,000	2,000	3,500	6,000	—
1753 MF	—	1,000	2,000	3,500	6,000	—
1754 MF	—	1,000	2,000	3,500	6,000	—
1755 MM	—	1,000	2,000	3,500	6,000	—
1756 MM	—	1,000	2,000	3,500	6,000	—

KM# 139   4 ESCUDOS
13.5337 g., 0.9170 Gold 0.3990 oz. AGW   **Ruler:**
Ferdinand VI **Obv:** Armored bust right **Obv. Legend:**
FERDND • VI • D • G • ... **Rev:** Crowned shield, without
value **Rev. Legend:** NOMINA MAGNA... **Mint:**
Mexico City **Note:** Mint mark M, Mo.

Date	Mintage	VG	F	VF	XF	Unc
1757 MM	—	1,250	2,500	4,000	6,500	—
1759 MM	—	1,250	2,500	4,000	6,500	—

SPANISH COLONIAL · MILLED

KM# 140 4 ESCUDOS
13.5337 g., 0.9170 Gold 0.3990 oz. AGW **Ruler:**
Charles III **Obv:** Armored bust right **Obv. Legend:**
CAROLVS • III • D • G •... **Rev:** Crowned shield,
without value **Rev. Legend:** NOMINA MAGNA
SEQUOR **Mint:** Mexico City **Note:** Mint mark M, Mo.

Date	Mintage	VG	F	VF	XF	Unc
1760 MM	—	3,500	6,500	10,000	20,000	—
1761 MM	—	3,500	6,500	10,000	20,000	—

KM# 141 4 ESCUDOS
13.5337 g., 0.9170 Gold 0.3990 oz. AGW **Ruler:**
Charles III **Obv:** Large, armored bust right **Obv.
Legend:** CAROLUS • III • D • G •... **Rev:** Crowned
shield in order chain, without value **Rev. Legend:** IN
• UTROQ • FELIX • AUSPICE • DEO **Mint:** Mexico
City **Note:** Mint mark M, Mo.

Date	Mintage	VG	F	VF	XF	Unc
1762 MF	—	2,500	4,500	7,500	15,000	—
1763 MF	—	2,500	4,500	7,500	15,000	—
1764 MF	—	2,500	4,500	7,500	15,000	—
1765 MF	—	2,500	4,500	7,500	15,000	—
1766/5 MF	—	2,500	4,500	7,500	15,000	—
1767 MF	—	2,500	4,500	7,500	15,000	—
1768 MF	—	2,500	4,500	7,500	15,000	—
1769 MF	—	2,500	4,500	7,500	15,000	—
1770 MF	—	2,500	4,500	7,500	15,000	—
1771 MF	—	2,500	4,500	7,500	15,000	—

KM# 142.1 4 ESCUDOS
13.5337 g., 0.9010 Gold 0.3920 oz. AGW **Ruler:**
Charles III **Obv:** Large, armored bust right **Obv.
Legend:** CAROL • III • D • G •... **Rev:** Crowned shield
in order chain, initials and mint mark upright **Rev.
Legend:** IN • UTROQ • FELIX • AUSPICE • DEO
Mint: Mexico City **Note:** Mint mark M, Mo.

Date	Mintage	VG	F	VF	XF	Unc
1772 FM	—	600	975	1,500	3,000	—
1773 FM	—	600	975	1,500	3,000	—

KM# 142.2 4 ESCUDOS
13.5337 g., 0.9010 Gold 0.3920 oz. AGW **Ruler:**
Charles III **Obv:** Large, armored bust right **Obv.
Legend:** CAROL • III • D • G •... **Rev:** Crowned shield
flanked by 4 S in order chain, initials and mint mark
inverted **Rev. Legend:** IN•UTROQ•FELIX•AUSPICE
• DEO **Mint:** Mexico City **Note:** Mint mark M, Mo.

Date	Mintage	VG	F	VF	XF	Unc
1773 FM	—	525	725	1,100	2,200	—
1774 FM	—	525	725	1,100	2,200	—
1775 FM	—	525	725	1,100	2,200	—
1776 FM	—	525	725	1,100	2,200	—
1777 FM	—	525	725	1,100	2,200	—
1778 FF	—	525	725	1,100	2,200	—
1779 FF	—	525	725	1,100	2,200	—
1780 FF	—	525	725	1,100	2,200	—
1781 FF	—	525	725	1,100	2,200	—
1782 FF	—	525	725	1,100	2,200	—
1783 FF	—	525	725	1,100	2,200	—
1784 FF	—	525	725	1,100	2,200	—
1784/3 FM/F	—	525	725	1,100	2,200	—

KM# 142.2a 4 ESCUDOS
13.5337 g., 0.8750 Gold 0.3807 oz. AGW **Ruler:**
Charles III **Obv:** Large, armored bust right **Obv.
Legend:** CAROL • III • D • G •... **Rev:** Crowned shield
in order chain, initials and mint mark inverted **Rev.
Legend:** IN • UTROQ • FELIX • AUSPICE • DEO
Mint: Mexico City **Note:** Mint mark M, Mo.

Date	Mintage	VG	F	VF	XF	Unc
1785 FM	—	525	725	1,100	2,200	—
1786 FM/F	—	525	725	1,100	2,200	—
1786 FM	—	525	725	1,100	2,200	—
1787 FM	—	525	725	1,100	2,200	—
1788 FM	—	525	725	1,100	2,200	—

KM# 142.1a 4 ESCUDOS
13.5337 g., 0.8750 Gold 0.3807 oz. AGW **Ruler:**
Charles III **Obv:** Large, armored bust right **Obv.
Legend:** CAROL • III • D • G •... **Rev:** Crowned shield
in order chain, initials and mint mark upright **Rev.
Legend:** IN • UTROQ • FELIX • AUSPICE • DEO
Mint: Mexico City **Note:** Mint mark M, Mo.

Date	Mintage	VG	F	VF	XF	Unc
1788 FM	—	600	975	1,500	3,000	—

KM# 143.1 4 ESCUDOS
13.5337 g., 0.8750 Gold 0.3807 oz. AGW **Ruler:**
Charles IV **Obv:** Armored bust of Charles III, right
Obv. Legend: CAROL • IV • D • G •... **Rev:** Crowned
shield in order chain, initials and mint mark upright
Rev. Legend: IN • UTROQ • FELIX • AUSPICE •
DEO **Mint:** Mexico City **Note:** Mint mark M, Mo, using
old portrait punch.

Date	Mintage	VG	F	VF	XF	Unc
1789 FM	—	550	750	1,100	2,150	—
1790 FM	—	550	750	1,100	2,150	—

KM# 143.2   4 ESCUDOS
13.5337 g., 0.8750 Gold 0.3807 oz. AGW **Ruler:**
Charles IV **Obv:** Armored bust of Charles III, right
Obv. Legend: CAROL • IIII • D • G • ... **Rev:** Crowned
shield in order chain, initials and mint mark upright
Rev. Legend: IN • UTROQ • FELIX • AUSPICE •
DEO **Mint:** Mexico City **Note:** Mint mark M, Mo, using
old portrait punch.

Date	Mintage	VG	F	VF	XF	Unc
1790 FM	—	600	1,000	1,800	3,000	—

KM# 144   4 ESCUDOS
13.5337 g., 0.8750 Gold 0.3807 oz. AGW **Ruler:**
Charles IV **Obv:** Armored bust of Charles IIII, right
Obv. Legend: CAROL • IIII • D • G • ... **Rev:** Crowned
shield flanked by 4 S in order chain **Rev. Legend:** IN
• UTROQ • FELIX • AUSPICE • DEO; initials and mint
mark upright **Mint:** Mexico City **Note:** Mint mark Mo.

Date	Mintage	VG	F	VF	XF	Unc
1792 FM	—	500	600	750	1,500	—
1793 FM	—	500	600	750	1,500	—
1794/3 FM	—	500	600	750	1,500	—
1795 FM	—	500	600	750	1,500	—
1796 FM	—	500	600	750	1,500	—
1797 FM	—	500	600	750	1,500	—
1798/7 FM	—	500	600	750	1,500	—
1798 FM	—	500	600	750	1,500	—
1799 FM	—	500	600	750	1,500	—
1800 FM	—	500	600	750	1,500	—
1801 FM	—	600	650	800	1,500	—
1801 FT	—	600	650	800	1,500	—
1802 FT	—	600	700	800	1,650	—
1803 FT	—	600	650	800	1,500	—
1803/2	—	600	750	900	1,500	—
1804/3 TH	—	600	650	800	1,500	—
1804 TH	—	600	650	800	1,500	—
1805 TH	—	600	650	800	1,500	—
1806/5 TH	—	600	650	800	1,500	—
1807 TH	—	600	700	900	1,650	—
1808/0 TH	—	600	650	800	1,500	—
1808 TH	—	600	650	800	1,500	—

KM# 145   4 ESCUDOS
13.5337 g., 0.8750 Gold 0.3807 oz. AGW **Ruler:**
Ferdinand VII **Obv:** Armored bust right **Obv. Legend:**
FERDIN • VII D • G... **Rev:** Crowned shield divides
designed wreath, initials and mint mark upright **Rev.**

Legend: IN • UTROQ • FELIX • AUSPICE • DEO **Mint:**
Mexico City **Note:** Mint mark Mo.

Date	Mintage	VG	F	VF	XF	Unc
1810 HJ	—	650	750	1,150	2,500	—
1811 HJ	—	650	750	1,150	2,500	—
1812 HJ	—	650	750	1,150	2,500	—

KM# 146   4 ESCUDOS
13.5337 g., 0.8750 Gold 0.3807 oz. AGW   **Ruler:**
Ferdinand VII **Obv:** Laureate head right **Obv.
Legend:** FERDIN. VII D. G... **Rev:** Crowned shield
divides designed wreath **Rev. Legend:** IN. UTROQ.
FELIX. AUSPICE. DEO; initials and mint mark
upright **Mint:** Mexico City **Note:** Mint mark Mo.

Date	Mintage	VG	F	VF	XF	Unc
1814 HJ	—	675	800	1,250	2,700	—
1815 HJ	—	675	800	1,250	2,700	—
1815 JJ	—	675	800	1,250	2,700	—
1816 JJ	—	675	800	1,250	2,700	—
1817 JJ	—	675	800	1,250	2,700	—
1818 JJ	—	675	800	1,250	2,700	—
1819 JJ	—	675	800	1,250	2,700	—
1820 JJ	—	675	800	1,250	2,700	—

KM# 148   8 ESCUDOS
27.0674 g., 0.9170 Gold 0.7980 oz. AGW **Ruler:**
Philip V **Obv:** Large, armored bust right **Obv.
Legend:** PHILIP • V • D • G • HISPAN • ET IND •
REX **Rev:** Crowned shield flanked by M F 8 in order
chain **Rev. Legend:** INITIUM SAPIENTIAE TIMOR
DOMINI **Mint:** Mexico City **Note:** Mint mark M, Mo.

Date	Mintage	VG	F	VF	XF	Unc
1732 Rare	—	—	—	—	—	—
1732 F Rare	—	—	—	—	—	—
1733 F Rare	—	—	—	—	—	—
Note: Heritage World Coin Auctions #3004, 1-09, MS64 realized $54,625						
1734 MF	—	1,500	2,000	3,300	5,800	—
1734 MF/F	—	1,500	2,000	3,300	5,800	—
1735 MF	—	1,500	1,800	3,000	5,400	—
1736 MF	—	1,500	1,800	3,000	5,400	—
1737 MF	—	1,500	1,800	3,000	5,400	—
1738/7 MF	—	1,500	1,800	3,000	5,400	—
1738 MF	—	1,500	1,800	3,000	5,400	—
1739 MF	—	1,500	1,800	3,000	5,400	—
1740 MF	—	1,500	1,800	3,000	5,400	—
1740/30 MF	—	1,500	1,800	3,000	5,400	—
1741 MF	—	1,500	1,800	3,000	5,400	—
1742 MF	—	1,500	1,800	3,000	5,400	—
1743 MF	—	1,500	1,800	3,000	5,400	—

SPANISH COLONIAL · MILLED

Date	Mintage	VG	F	VF	XF	Unc
1744 MF	—	1,500	1,800	3,000	5,400	—
1744/3 MF	—	1,500	1,800	3,000	5,400	—
1745 MF	—	1,500	1,800	3,000	5,400	—
1745/4 MF	—	1,500	1,800	3,000	5,400	—
1746 MF	—	1,500	1,800	3,000	5,400	—
1746/5 MF	—	1,500	1,800	3,000	5,400	—
1747 MF	—	1,500	2,100	3,400	6,000	—

KM# 151　8 ESCUDOS
27.0674 g., 0.9170 Gold 0.7980 oz. AGW　**Ruler:** Ferdinand VI **Obv:** Armored bust right **Obv. Legend:** FERDND • VI • D • G • ... **Rev:** Crowned shield in order chain **Rev. Legend:** NOMINA MAGNA SEQUOR **Mint:** Mexico City **Note:** Mint mark M, Mo.

Date	Mintage	VG	F	VF	XF	Unc
1752 MF	—	1,500	2,400	4,200	7,200	—
1753 MF	—	1,500	2,400	4,200	7,200	—
1754 MF	—	1,500	2,400	4,200	7,200	—
1755 MM	—	1,500	2,400	4,200	7,200	—
1756 MM	—	1,500	2,400	4,200	7,200	—

KM# 149　8 ESCUDOS
27.0674 g., 0.9170 Gold 0.7980 oz. AGW　**Ruler:** Ferdinand VI **Obv:** Large, armored bust right **Obv. Legend:** FERDND • VI • D • G • ... **Rev:** Crowned shield flanked by M F 8 in order chain **Rev. Legend:** INITIUM SAPIENTIAE TIMOR DOMINI **Mint:** Mexico City **Note:** Mint mark M, Mo.

Date	Mintage	VG	F	VF	XF	Unc
1747 MF	—	9,000	15,000	22,000	35,000	—

KM# 152　8 ESCUDOS
27.0674 g., 0.9170 Gold 0.7980 oz. AGW　**Ruler:** Ferdinand VI **Obv:** Armored bust right **Obv. Legend:** FERDND • VI • D • G • ... **Rev:** Crowned shield in order chain **Rev. Legend:** NOMINA MAGNA SEQUOR **Mint:** Mexico City **Note:** Mint mark M, Mo.

Date	Mintage	VG	F	VF	XF	Unc
1757 MM	—	1,500	2,400	4,200	7,200	—
1758 MM	—	1,500	2,400	4,200	7,200	—
1759 MM	—	1,500	2,400	4,200	7,200	—

KM# 150　8 ESCUDOS
27.0674 g., 0.9170 Gold 0.7980 oz. AGW　**Ruler:** Ferdinand VI **Obv:** Small, armored bust right **Obv. Legend:** FERDND • VI • D • G • ... **Rev:** Crowned shield flanked by 8 S in order chain **Rev. Legend:** NOMINA MAGNA SEQUOR **Mint:** Mexico City **Note:** Mint mark M, Mo.

Date	Mintage	VG	F	VF	XF	Unc
1748 MF	—	1,500	2,400	4,200	7,200	—
1749/8 MF	—	1,500	2,400	4,200	7,200	—
1749 MF	—	1,500	2,400	4,200	7,200	—
1750 MF	—	1,500	2,400	4,200	7,200	—
1751/0 MF	—	1,800	2,400	4,200	7,200	—
1751 MF	—	1,500	2,400	4,200	7,200	—

KM# 153　8 ESCUDOS
27.0674 g., 0.9170 Gold 0.7980 oz. AGW　**Ruler:**

SPANISH COLONIAL - MILLED

Charles III **Obv:** Armored bust right **Obv. Legend:**
CAROLVS • III • D • G • ... **Rev:** Crowned shield in
order chain **Rev. Legend:** NOMINA MAGNA
SEQUOR **Mint:** Mexico City **Note:** Mint mark M, Mo.

Date	Mintage	VG	F	VF	XF	Unc
1760 MM	—	2,100	3,600	6,000	11,000	—
1761/0 MM	—	2,400	4,200	6,600	12,000	—
1761 MM	—	2,400	4,200	6,600	12,000	—

Date	Mintage	VG	F	VF	XF	Unc
1770 MF	—	1,900	3,150	5,000	9,400	—
1771 MF	—	2,200	3,750	6,300	11,500	—

KM# 154   8 ESCUDOS
27.0674 g., 0.9170 Gold 0.7980 oz. AGW **Ruler:**
Charles III **Obv:** Armored bust right **Obv. Legend:**
CAROLVS • III • D • G • ... **Rev:** Crowned shield in
order chain **Rev. Legend:** NOMINA MAGNA
SEQUOR **Mint:** Mexico City **Note:** Mint mark M, Mo.

Date	Mintage	VG	F	VF	XF	Unc
1761 MM	—	2,100	3,600	6,300	11,500	—

KM# 156.1   8 ESCUDOS
27.0674 g., 0.9010 Gold 0.7841 oz. AGW **Ruler:**
Charles III **Obv:** Large, armored bust right **Obv.
Legend:** CAROL • III • D • G • ... **Rev:** Crowned shield
flanked by 8 S in order chain, initials and mint mark
upright **Rev. Legend:** ... AUSPICE • DEO • **Mint:**
Mexico City **Note:** Mint mark M, Mo.

Date	Mintage	VG	F	VF	XF	Unc
1772 FM	—	1,100	1,500	2,000	2,750	—
1773 FM	—	1,100	1,500	2,000	2,750	—

KM# 155   8 ESCUDOS
27.0674 g., 0.9170 Gold 0.7980 oz. AGW **Ruler:**
Charles III **Obv:** Large, armored bust right **Obv.
Legend:** CAROLUS • III • D • G • ... **Rev:** Crowned
shield in order chain **Rev. Legend:** IN • UTROQ •
FELIX • AUSPICE • DEO • **Mint:** Mexico City **Note:**
Mint mark M, Mo.

Date	Mintage	VG	F	VF	XF	Unc
1762 MM	—	2,000	3,450	5,600	10,500	—
1763 MM	—	2,000	3,450	5,600	10,500	—
1764 MF	—	2,200	3,750	6,300	11,500	—
1764/2 MF	—	2,200	3,750	6,300	11,500	—
1764 MF	—	2,200	3,750	6,300	11,500	—
1765/4 MF	—	2,200	3,750	6,300	11,500	—
1765/4 MM	—	2,200	3,750	6,300	11,500	—
1765 MF	—	2,200	3,750	6,300	11,500	—
1765 MM	—	1,900	3,150	5,000	9,400	—
1766 MF	—	1,900	3,150	5,000	9,400	—
1767/6 MF	—	1,900	3,150	5,000	9,400	—
1767 MF	—	1,900	3,150	5,000	9,400	—
1768/7 MF	—	1,900	3,150	5,000	9,400	—
1768 MF	—	1,900	3,150	5,000	9,400	—
1769 MF	—	1,900	3,150	5,000	9,400	—

KM# 156.2   8 ESCUDOS
27.0674 g., 0.9010 Gold 0.7841 oz. AGW **Ruler:**
Charles III **Obv:** Large, armored bust right **Obv.
Legend:** CAROL • III • D • G • ... **Rev:** Crowned shield
flanked by 8 S in order chain, initials and mint mark
inverted **Rev. Legend:** ... AUSPICE • DEO • **Mint:**
Mexico City **Note:** Mint mark M, Mo.

Date	Mintage	VG	F	VF	XF	Unc
1773 FM	—	1,100	1,350	1,800	2,400	—
1774 FM	—	1,100	1,350	1,800	2,400	—
1775 FM	—	1,100	1,350	1,800	2,400	—
1776 FM	—	1,500	1,850	2,250	3,000	—
1777/6 FM	—	1,100	1,350	1,500	2,400	—
1777 FM	—	1,100	1,350	1,500	2,400	—
1778 FF	—	1,100	1,350	1,500	2,400	—
1779 FF	—	1,100	1,350	1,500	2,400	—
1780 FF	—	1,100	1,350	1,500	2,400	—
1781 FF	—	1,100	1,350	1,500	2,400	—
1782 FF	—	1,100	1,350	1,500	2,400	—
1783 FF	—	1,100	1,350	1,500	2,400	—
1784 FF	—	1,100	1,350	1,500	2,400	—
1784 FM/F	—	1,100	1,350	1,500	2,400	—
1784 FM	—	1,100	1,350	1,500	2,400	—
1785 FM	—	1,100	1,350	1,500	2,400	—

SPANISH COLONIAL - MILLED

KM# 156.2a 8 ESCUDOS
27.0674 g., 0.8750 Gold 0.7614 oz. AGW **Ruler:** Charles III **Obv:** Large, armored bust right **Obv. Legend:** CAROL • III • D • G • ... **Rev:** Crowned shield flanked by 8 S in order chain, initials and mint mark inverted **Rev. Legend:** ... AUSPICE • DEO • **Mint:** Mexico City **Note:** Mint mark M, Mo.

Date	Mintage	VG	F	VF	XF	Unc
1786 FM	—	1,100	1,350	1,800	2,400	—
1787 FM	—	1,100	1,350	1,800	2,400	—
1788 FM	—	1,100	1,350	1,800	2,400	—

KM# 157 8 ESCUDOS
27.0674 g., 0.8750 Gold 0.7614 oz. AGW **Ruler:** Charles IV **Obv:** Armored bust of Charles III, right **Obv. Legend:** CAROL • IV • D • G • ... **Rev:** Crowned shield flanked by 8 S in order chain **Rev. Legend:** IN • UTROQ • ... **Mint:** Mexico City **Note:** Mint mark M, Mo, using old portrait punch.

Date	Mintage	VG	F	VF	XF	Unc
1789 FM	—	1,100	1,500	2,000	2,750	—
1790 FM	—	1,100	1,500	2,000	2,750	—

KM# 156.1a 8 ESCUDOS
27.0674 g., 0.8750 Gold 0.7614 oz. AGW **Ruler:** Charles III **Obv:** Large, armored bust right **Obv. Legend:** CAROL • III • D • G • ... **Rev:** Crowned shield flanked by 8 S in order chain, initials and mint mark upright **Rev. Legend:** ... AUSPICE • DEO • **Mint:** Mexico City **Note:** Mint mark M, Mo.

Date	Mintage	VG	F	VF	XF	Unc
1788 FM	—	1,100	1,300	1,500	2,400	—

KM# 158 8 ESCUDOS
27.0674 g., 0.8750 Gold 0.7614 oz. AGW **Ruler:** Charles IV **Obv:** Armored bust of Charles III, right **Obv. Legend:** CAROL • IIII • D • G • ... **Rev:** Crowned shield flanked by 8 S in order chain **Rev. Legend:** IN • UTROQ • ... **Mint:** Mexico City **Note:** Mint mark M, Mo, using old portrait punch.

Date	Mintage	VG	F	VF	XF	Unc
1790 FM	—	1,100	1,500	2,000	2,750	—

KM# 159   8 ESCUDOS
27.0674 g., 0.8750 Gold 0.7614 oz. AGW   **Ruler:**
Charles IV **Obv:** Armored bust right **Obv. Legend:**
CAROL • IIII • D • G • ... **Rev:** Crowned shield flanked
by 8 S in order chain **Rev. Legend:** IN • UTROQ • ...
Mint: Mexico City **Note:** Mint mark Mo.

Date	Mintage	VG	F	VF	XF	Unc
1791 FM	—	1,000	1,250	1,500	2,000	—
1792 FM	—	1,000	1,250	1,500	2,000	—
1793 FM	—	1,000	1,250	1,500	2,000	—
1794 FM	—	1,000	1,250	1,500	2,000	—
1795 FM	—	1,000	1,250	1,500	2,000	—
1796/5 FM	—	1,000	1,250	1,500	2,000	—
1796 FM	—	1,000	1,250	1,500	2,000	—
1797 FM	—	1,000	1,250	1,500	2,000	—
1797 FM EPLIX	—	1,000	1,250	1,500	2,000	—
1798 FM	—	1,000	1,250	1,500	2,000	—
1799 FM	—	1,000	1,250	1,500	2,000	—
1800 FM	—	1,000	1,250	1,500	2,000	—
1801/0 FT	—	1,225	1,275	1,375	1,950	—
1801 FM	—	1,225	1,275	1,350	1,700	—
1801 FT	—	1,225	1,275	1,350	1,700	—
1802 FT	—	1,225	1,275	1,350	1,700	—
1803 FT	—	1,225	1,275	1,350	1,700	—
1804/3 TH	—	1,225	1,275	1,375	1,950	—
1804 TH	—	1,225	1,275	1,350	1,700	5,300
1805 TH	—	1,225	1,275	1,350	1,700	—
1806 TH	—	1,225	1,275	1,350	1,700	5,300
1807 TH Mo over inverted Mo	—	1,225	1,275	1,375	1,950	—
1807/6 TH	—	1,225	1,275	1,375	1,950	—
1808/7 TH	—	1,225	1,275	1,350	2,100	—
1807 TH	—	1,225	1,275	1,450	1,700	—
1808 TH	—	1,225	1,275	1,450	2,100	—

KM# 160   8 ESCUDOS
27.0674 g., 0.8750 Gold 0.7614 oz. AGW   **Ruler:**
Ferdinand VII **Obv:** Armored bust right **Obv.
Legend:** FERDIN • VII • D • G... **Rev:** Crowned shield
divides designed wreath **Rev. Legend:** IN UTROQ
• FELIX **Mint:** Mexico City **Note:** Mint mark Mo.

Date	Mintage	VG	F	VF	XF	Unc
1808 TH	—	1,225	1,250	1,400	2,250	—
1809 HJ	—	1,225	1,250	1,400	2,250	—
1810 HJ	—	1,225	1,250	1,400	2,250	—
1811 HJ H/T	—	1,225	1,250	1,400	2,250	—

Date	Mintage	VG	F	VF	XF	Unc
1811/0 HJ	—	1,225	1,250	1,400	2,250	—
1811 HJ	—	1,225	1,250	1,400	2,250	—
1811 JJ	—	1,225	1,250	1,400	2,250	—
1812 JJ	—	1,225	1,250	1,400	2,250	—

KM# 161   8 ESCUDOS
27.0674 g., 0.8750 Gold 0.7614 oz. AGW   **Ruler:**
Ferdinand VII **Obv:** Laureate head right **Obv.
Legend:** FERDIN • VII • D • G... **Rev:** Crowned shield
divides designed wreath **Rev. Legend:** IN UTROQ
• FELIX **Mint:** Mexico City **Note:** Mint mark Mo.

Date	Mintage	VG	F	VF	XF	Unc
1814 JJ	—	1,225	1,275	1,400	2,000	—
1815/4 JJ	—	1,225	1,275	1,400	2,150	—
1815/4 HJ	—	1,225	1,275	1,400	2,150	—
1815 JJ	—	1,225	1,275	1,400	2,000	—
1815 HJ	—	1,225	1,275	1,400	2,000	—
1816 JJ	—	1,225	1,275	1,400	2,150	—
1817 JJ	—	1,225	1,275	1,400	2,100	—
1818/7 JJ	—	1,225	1,275	1,400	2,100	—
1818 JJ	—	1,225	1,275	1,400	2,100	—
1819 JJ	—	1,225	1,275	1,400	2,100	—
1820 JJ	—	1,225	1,275	1,400	2,100	—
1821 JJ	—	1,225	1,275	1,400	2,250	—

PROCLAMATION MEDALLIC COINAGE

The Q used in the following listings refer to Standard Catalog of Mexican Coins, Paper Money, Stocks, Bonds, and Medals by Krause Publications, Inc., ©1981.

KM# Q22   1/2 REAL
1.6000 g., Silver   **Issuer:** Mexico City **Obv:** Crowned
shield flanked by crowned pillars with banner **Obv.
Legend:** A CARLOS IV REY DE ESPANA Y DE LAS
YNDIAS **Rev:** Legend, date within wreath **Rev.
Legend:** PROCLAMADO EN MEXICO ANO DE 1789

Date	Mintage	F	VF	XF	Unc	BU
1789	—	40.00	70.00	120	—	—

SPANISH COLONIAL - MILLED

KM# Q22a 1/2 REAL
Bronze **Issuer:** Mexico City **Obv:** Crowned shield flanked by crowned pillars with banner **Obv. Legend:** A CARLOS IV REY DE ESPANA Y DE LAS YNDIAS **Rev:** Legend, date within wreath **Rev. Legend:** PROCLAMADO EN MEXICO ANO DE 1789

Date	Mintage	F	VF	XF	Unc	BU
1789	—	45.00	90.00	150	—	—

KM# Q23 1/2 REAL
Silver **Issuer:** Mexico City **Obv:** Crowned arms in double-lined circle **Obv. Legend:** A CARLOS IV REY DE ESPANA Y DE LAS YNDIAS **Rev. Legend:** PROCLAMADO EN MEXICO ANO DE 1789

Date	Mintage	F	VF	XF	Unc	BU
1789	—	40.00	70.00	120	—	—

KM# Q23a 1/2 REAL
Bronze **Issuer:** Mexico City **Obv:** Crowned arms in double-lined circle **Obv. Legend:** A CARLOS IV REY DE ESPANA Y DE LAS YNDIAS **Rev. Legend:** PROCLAMADO EN MEXICO ANO DE 1789

Date	Mintage	F	VF	XF	Unc	BU
1789	—	45.00	90.00	150	—	—

KM# Q24 REAL
Silver **Issuer:** Mexico City **Obv:** Crowned shield flanked by crowned pillars with banner **Obv. Legend:** A CARLOS IV REY DE ESPANA Y DE LAS YNDIAS **Rev:** Legend, date, value within wreath **Rev. Legend:** PROCLAMADO EN MEXICO ANO DE 1789

Date	Mintage	F	VF	XF	Unc	BU
1789	—	40.00	70.00	120	—	—

KM# Q24a REAL
Bronze **Issuer:** Mexico City **Obv:** Crowned shield flanked by crowned pillars with banner **Obv. Legend:** A CARLOS IV REY DE ESPANA Y DE LAS YNDIAS **Rev:** Legend, date, value within wreath **Rev. Legend:** PROCLAMADO EN MEXICO ANO DE 1789

Date	Mintage	F	VF	XF	Unc	BU
1789	—	45.00	90.00	150	—	—

KM# Q-A24 REAL
Silver **Issuer:** Mexico City **Obv:** Crowned arms in double-lined circle **Obv. Legend:** A CARLOS IV REY DE ESPANA Y DE LAS YNDIAS **Rev. Legend:** PROCLAMADO EN MEXICO ANO DE 1789

Date	Mintage	F	VF	XF	Unc	BU
1789	—	40.00	70.00	120	—	—

KM# Q-A24a REAL
Copper **Issuer:** Mexico City **Obv:** Crowned arms in double-lined circle **Obv. Legend:** A CARLOS IV REY DE ESPANA Y DE LAS YNDIAS **Rev. Legend:** PROCLAMADO EN MEXICO ANO DE 1789

Date	Mintage	F	VF	XF	Unc	BU
1789	—	45.00	90.00	150	—	—

KM# Q8 REAL
Silver **Issuer:** Chiapa **Obv:** Crowned shield flanked by pillars **Obv. Legend:** FERNANDO. VII. REY DE ESPAÑA. Y DE SUS IND. **Rev:** Legend within wreath **Rev. Legend:** PROCLA/MADO ENCUID•R•DE/ CHIAPA•/•A1808•

Date	Mintage	F	VF	XF	Unc	BU
1808	—	25.00	40.00	70.00	125	—

KM# Q25 2 REALES
6.7000 g., Silver **Issuer:** Mexico City **Obv:** Crowned shield flanked by crowned pillars with banner **Obv. Legend:** A CARLOS IV REY DE ESPANA Y DE LAS YNDIAS **Rev:** Legend, date, value within wreath **Rev. Legend:** PROCLAMADO EN MEXICO ANO DE 1789

Date	Mintage	F	VF	XF	Unc	BU
1789	—	70.00	125	225	—	—

KM# Q25a 2 REALES
6.7000 g., Bronze **Issuer:** Mexico City **Obv:** Crowned shield flanked by crowned pillars with banner **Obv. Legend:** A CARLOS IV REY DE ESPANA Y DE LAS YNDIAS **Rev:** Legend, date, value within wreath **Rev. Legend:** PROCLAMADO EN MEXICO ANO DE 1789

Date	Mintage	F	VF	XF	Unc	BU
1789	—	60.00	115	180	—	—

KM# Q64 2 REALES
Silver **Issuer:** Queretaro **Obv:** Crowned shield flanked by pillars **Obv. Legend:** FERNANDO VII REY DE ESPANA **Rev:** Legend, date within wreath

Date	Mintage	F	VF	XF	Unc	BU
1808	—	25.00	45.00	90.00	150	—

KM# Q10 2 REALES
Silver **Issuer:** Chiapa **Obv:** Crowned shield flanked by pillars **Obv. Legend:** FERNANDO VII REY DE ESPANA Y DE SUS INDIAS **Rev:** Legend, date within wreath

Date	Mintage	F	VF	XF	Unc	BU
1808	—	45.00	70.00	100	175	—

SPANISH COLONIAL · PROCLAMATION

KM# Q27 4 REALES
13.6000 g., Silver **Issuer:** Mexico City **Obv:**
Crowned shield flanked by crowned pillars with
banner **Obv. Legend:** A CARLOS IV REY DE
ESPANA Y DE LAS YNDIAS **Rev:** Legend date,
value within wreath **Rev. Legend:** PROCLAMADO
EN MEXICO ANO DE 1789

Date	Mintage	F	VF	XF	Unc	BU
1789	—	200	375	675	1,150	—

KM# Q27a 4 REALES
13.6000 g., Bronze **Issuer:** Mexico City **Obv:**
Crowned shield flanked by crowned pillars with
banner **Obv. Legend:** A CARLOS IV REY DE
ESPANA Y DE LAS YNDIAS **Rev:** Legend, date,
value within wreath **Rev. Legend:** PROCLAMADO
EN MEXICO ANO DE 1789

Date	Mintage	F	VF	XF	Unc	BU
1789	—	140	250	450	—	—

KM# Q-A66 4 REALES
Silver **Issuer:** Queretaro **Obv:** Crowned shield
flanked by pillars **Obv. Legend:** FERNANDO VII
REY DE ESPANA **Rev:** Legend, date within wreath

Date	Mintage	F	VF	XF	Unc	BU
1808	—	100	160	295	475	—

KM# Q28 8 REALES
27.0000 g., Silver **Issuer:** Mexico City **Obv:**
Crowned shield flanked by crowned pillars with
banner **Obv. Legend:** A CARLOS IV REY DE
ESPANA Y DE LAS YNDIAS **Rev:** Legend, date,
value within wreath **Rev. Legend:** PROCLAMADO
EN MEXICO ANO DE 1789

Date	Mintage	F	VF	XF	Unc	BU
1789	—	400	700	1,200	2,000	—

KM# Q28a 8 REALES
27.0000 g., Bronze **Issuer:** Mexico City **Obv:**
Crowned shield flanked by crowned pillars with
banner **Obv. Legend:** A CARLOS IV REY DE
ESPANA Y DE LAS YNDIAS **Rev:** Legend, date,
value within wreath **Rev. Legend:** PROCLAMADO
EN MEXICO ANO DE 1789

Date	Mintage	F	VF	XF	Unc	BU
1789	—	140	250	450	—	—

KM# Q68 8 REALES
Silver **Issuer:** Queretaro **Obv:** Crowned shield
flanked by pillars **Obv. Legend:** FERNANDO VII
REY DE ESPANA **Rev:** Legend, date within wreath

Date	Mintage	F	VF	XF	Unc	BU
1808	—	220	425	575	950	—

WAR OF INDEPENDENCE

CHIHUAHUA

The Chihuahua Mint was established by a decree of
October 8, 1810 as a temporary mint. Their first coins were
cast 8 Reales using Mexico City coins as patterns and obliter-
ating/changing the mint mark and moneyer initials. Two c/m
were placed on the obverse - on the left, a T designating
receipt by the Royal Treasurer, crowned pillars of Hercules on
the right with pomegranate beneath, the comptrollers symbol.
In 1814, standard dies were made available, thus
machine struck 8 Reales were produced until 1822. Only the
one denomination was made at Chihuahua.
Mint mark: CA.

ROYALIST COINAGE

KM# 123 8 REALES
Cast Silver **Ruler:** Ferdinand VII **Countermark:** T
at left, pillars at right, pomegranate below **Obv:**
Armored bust right **Obv. Legend:** FERDIN• VII • DEI
• GRATIA **Rev:** Crowned shield flanked by pillars
Mint: Chihuahua

Date	Mintage	Good	VG	F	VF	XF
1810CA RP Rare	—	—	—	—	—	—
1811CA RP	—	45.00	70.00	120	200	—
1812CA RP	—	40.00	65.00	90.00	175	—
1813CA RP	—	35.00	50.00	70.00	120	—

KM# 111.1 8 REALES
27.0700 g., 0.9030 Silver 0.7859 oz. ASW **Ruler:**
Ferdinand VII **Obv:** Draped bust right **Obv. Legend:**
FERDIN • VII • DEI • GRATIA **Rev:** Crowned shield
flanked by pillars

Date	Mintage	VG	F	VF	XF	Unc
1815 RP	—	220	300	525	750	—
1816 RP	—	90.00	140	225	425	—
1817 RP	—	110	165	280	425	—
1818 RP	—	110	165	280	425	—
1819/8 RP	—	140	195	375	525	—
1819 RP	—	140	195	375	525	—
1820 RP	—	220	300	525	750	—
1821 RP	—	220	300	525	750	—
1822 RP	—	450	650	1,200	1,650	—

Note: KM#111.1 is normally found struck over earlier cast 8
Reales, KM#123 and Monclova (MVA) 1812 cast countermark 8 Reales, KM#202 and Zacatecas 8 Reales, KM#190

DURANGO

The Durango mint was authorized as a temporary mint
on the same day as the Chihuahua Mint, October 8, 1810.
The mint opened in 1811 and made coins of 6 denominations between 1811 and 1822.

Mint mark: D.

ROYALIST COINAGE

KM# 60 1/8 REAL
Copper **Ruler:** Ferdinand VII **Obv:** Crowned
monogram **Rev:** EN DURANGO, value, date **Mint:**
Durango

Date	Mintage	VG	F	VF	XF	Unc
1812D	—	40.00	75.00	125	250	—
1813D	—	65.00	135	185	375	—
1814D Rare	—	—	—	—	—	—

KM# 61 1/8 REAL
Copper **Ruler:** Ferdinand VII **Obv:** Crowned
monogram **Rev:** Value within spray, date below **Rev.
Legend:** ENDURANGO. **Mint:** Durango

Date	Mintage	VG	F	VF	XF	Unc
1814D	—	18.00	32.50	55.00	95.00	—
1815D	—	18.00	35.00	60.00	100	—
1816D	—	18.00	35.00	60.00	100	—
1817D	—	15.00	30.00	50.00	95.00	—
1818D	—	15.00	30.00	50.00	95.00	—
1818D	—	45.00	80.00	125	225	—

Note: OCTAVO DD REAL, error

KM# 74.1 1/2 REAL
1.6900 g., 0.9030 Silver 0.0491 oz. ASW **Ruler:**
Ferdinand VII **Obv:** Draped laureate bust right **Rev:**
Crowned shield flanked by pillars **Mint:** Durango

Date	Mintage	VG	F	VF	XF	Unc
1813D RM	—	275	500	825	2,050	—
1814D MZ	—	275	500	825	2,050	—
1816D MZ	—	275	500	825	2,050	—

KM# 83.1 REAL
3.3800 g., 0.9030 Silver 0.0981 oz. ASW **Ruler:**
Ferdinand VII **Obv:** Draped laureate bust right **Obv.
Legend:** FERDIN • VII... **Rev:** Crowned shield flanked
by pillars **Rev. Legend:** IND • REX... **Mint:** Durango

Date	Mintage	VG	F	VF	XF	Unc
1813D RM	—	275	500	725	1,800	—
1814D MZ	—	275	500	725	1,800	—
1815D MZ	—	275	500	725	1,800	—

KM# 92.2 2 REALES
6.7700 g., 0.9030 Silver 0.1965 oz. ASW **Ruler:**
Ferdinand VII **Obv:** Armored bust right **Rev:**
Crowned shield flanked by pillars **Rev. Legend:**
MON PROV DE DURANGO... **Mint:** Durango

Date	Mintage	VG	F	VF	XF	Unc
1811D RM	—	700	800	1,550	3,200	—

KM# 92.3 2 REALES
6.7700 g., 0.9030 Silver 0.1965 oz. ASW **Ruler:**
Ferdinand VII **Obv:** Armored bust right **Rev:**
Crowned shield flanked by pillars **Rev. Legend:**
HISPAN ET IND REX...

Date	Mintage	VG	F	VF	XF	Unc
1812 RM	—	425	650	1,250	2,750	—

KM# 93.1 2 REALES
6.7700 g., 0.9030 Silver 0.1965 oz. ASW **Ruler:**
Ferdinand VII **Obv:** Draped laureate bust right **Obv.
Legend:** FERDIN • VII... **Rev:** Crowned shield
flanked by pillars **Rev. Legend:** IND • REX... **Mint:**
Durango

Date	Mintage	VG	F	VF	XF	Unc
1812D RM	—	375	600	1,150	2,550	—
1813D RM	—	475	925	1,550	4,250	—
1813D MZ	—	475	925	1,550	4,250	—
1814D MZ	—	475	925	1,550	4,250	—
1815D MZ	—	475	925	1,550	4,250	—
1816D MZ	—	475	925	1,550	4,250	—
1817D MZ	—	475	925	1,550	4,250	—

WAR OF INDEPENDENCE

KM# 102.1   4 REALES
13.5400 g., 0.9030 Silver 0.3931 oz. ASW **Ruler:**
Ferdinand VII **Obv:** Draped laureate bust right **Obv.**
Legend: FERDIN • VII... **Rev:** Crowned shield
flanked by pillars **Rev. Legend:** IND • REX... **Mint:**
Durango

Date	Mintage	VG	F	VF	XF	Unc
1814D MZ	—	850	1,550	2,550	6,900	—
1816D MZ	—	700	1,400	2,150	6,200	—
1817D MZ	—	700	1,400	2,150	6,200	—

KM# 110.1   8 REALES
27.0700 g., 0.9030 Silver 0.7859 oz. ASW **Ruler:**
Ferdinand VII **Obv:** Armored bust right **Obv.**
Legend: FERD • VII... **Rev:** Crowned shield flanked
by pillars **Rev. Legend:** DURANGO • 8R R • M...
Mint: Durango

Date	Mintage	VG	F	VF	XF	Unc
1811D RM	—	2,800	5,500	9,000	—	—
1812D RM	—	450	825	1,250	4,400	—
1814D MZ	—	450	825	1,250	4,400	—

KM# 111.2   8 REALES
27.0700 g., 0.9030 Silver 0.7859 oz. ASW **Ruler:**
Ferdinand VII **Obv:** Draped laureate bust right **Obv.**
Legend: FERDIN • VII... **Rev:** Crowned shield flanked
by pillars **Rev. Legend:** IND • REX... **Mint:** Durango

Date	Mintage	VG	F	VF	XF	Unc
1812D RM	—	175	245	375	1,150	—
1813D RM	—	210	280	450	1,250	—
1813D MZ	—	175	245	375	1,100	—
1814/2D MZ	—	210	280	425	1,100	—
1814D MZ	—	210	280	425	1,100	—
1815D MZ	—	105	175	325	875	—
1816D MZ	—	70.00	105	175	500	—
1817D MZ	—	42.00	70.00	125	375	—
1818D MZ	—	70.00	105	175	525	—
1818D RM	—	70.00	105	175	500	—
1818D CG/RM	—	140	175	210	525	—
1818D CG	—	70.00	105	175	500	—
1819D CG/RM	—	70.00	140	210	450	—
1819D CG	—	42.00	85.00	140	375	—
1820D CG	—	42.00	85.00	140	375	—
1821D CG	—	42.00	55.00	110	325	—
1822D CG	—	42.00	70.00	125	375	—

Note: Occasionally these are found struck over cast Chihuahua 8 reales and are very rare in general, specimens dated prior to 1816 are rather crudely struck

GUADALAJARA

The Guadalajara Mint made its first coins in 1812 and the mint operated until April 30, 1815. It was to reopen in 1818 and continue operations until 1822. It was the only Royalist mint to strike gold coins, both 4 and 8 Escudos. In addition to these it struck the standard 5 denominations in silver.

Mint mark: GA.

ROYALIST COINAGE

KM# 74.2   1/2 REAL
1.6900 g., 0.9030 Silver 0.0491 oz. ASW **Ruler:**
Ferdinand VII **Obv:** Draped laureate bust right **Obv.**
Legend: FERDIN • VII... **Rev:** Crowned shield
flanked by pillars **Rev. Legend:** IND... **Mint:**
Guadalajara

Date	Mintage	VG	F	VF	XF	Unc
1812GA MR Rare	—	—	—	—	—	—
1814GA MR	—	60.00	145	290	425	—
1815GA MR	—	290	500	725	1,450	—

WAR OF INDEPENDENCE

KM# 83.2 REAL
3.3800 g., 0.9030 Silver 0.0981 oz. ASW **Ruler:**
Ferdinand VII **Obv:** Draped laureate bust right **Obv.**
Legend: FERDIN • VII... **Rev:** Crowned shield
flanked by pillars **Rev. Legend:** IND • REX... **Mint:**
Guadalajara

Date	Mintage	VG	F	VF	XF	Unc
1813GA MR	—	425	725	1,150	—	—
1814GA MR	—	215	290	500	925	—
1815GA MR	—	425	725	1,150	—	—

KM# 102.3 4 REALES
13.5400 g., 0.9030 Silver 0.3931 oz. ASW **Ruler:**
Ferdinand VII **Obv:** Draped laureate bust right **Obv.**
Legend: FERDIN • VII... **Rev:** Crowned shield
flanked by pillars **Rev. Legend:** IND • REX... **Mint:**
Guadalajara

Date	Mintage	VG	F	VF	XF	Unc
1814GA MR	—	85.00	165	325	650	—

KM# 93.2 2 REALES
6.7700 g., 0.9030 Silver 0.1965 oz. ASW **Ruler:**
Ferdinand VII **Obv:** Draped laureate bust right **Obv.**
Legend: FERDIN • VII... **Rev:** Crowned shield
flanked by pillars **Rev. Legend:** IND • REX.... **Mint:**
Guadalajara

Date	Mintage	VG	F	VF	XF	Unc
1812GA MR	—	350	600	950	3,000	—
1814/2GA MR	—	90.00	150	300	775	—
1814GA MR	—	90.00	150	300	775	—
1815/4GA MR	—	500	875	1,300	4,300	—
1815GA MR	—	475	850	1,200	4,200	—
1821GA FS	—	240	300	425	1,150	—

KM# 102.4 4 REALES
13.5400 g., 0.9030 Silver 0.3931 oz. ASW **Ruler:**
Ferdinand VII **Obv:** Draped laureate bust right **Obv.**
Legend: FERDIN • VII... **Rev:** Crowned shield
flanked by pillars **Rev. Legend:** IND • REX... **Mint:**
Guadalajara

Date	Mintage	VG	F	VF	XF	Unc
1814GA MR	—	100	195	425	750	—

KM# 102.2 4 REALES
13.5400 g., 0.9030 Silver 0.3931 oz. ASW **Ruler:**
Ferdinand VII **Obv:** Draped laureate bust right **Obv.**
Legend: FERDIN • VII... **Rev:** Crowned shield
flanked by pillars **Rev. Legend:** IND • REX... **Mint:**
Guadalajara

Date	Mintage	VG	F	VF	XF	Unc
1814GA MR	—	65.00	105	245	425	—
1815GA MR	—	130	245	500	825	—

KM# 111.3 8 REALES
27.0700 g., 0.9030 Silver 0.7859 oz. ASW **Ruler:**
Ferdinand VII **Obv:** Draped laureate bust right **Obv.**
Legend: FERDIN • VII... **Rev:** Crowned shield
flanked by pillars **Rev. Legend:** IND • REX... **Mint:**
Guadalajara

Date	Mintage	VG	F	VF	XF	Unc
1812GA MR	—	2,700	4,500	6,500	9,500	—
1813/2GA MR	—	110	180	270	725	—
1813GA MR	—	110	180	270	725	—
1814GA MR	—	36.00	65.00	110	325	—

Note: Several bust varieties exist for the 1814 issue

1815GA MR	—	230	300	550	1,150	—
1818GA FS	—	55.00	90.00	140	350	—
1821/18GA FS	—	55.00	90.00	140	350	—
1821GA FS	—	45.00	65.00	110	300	—
1821/2GA FS	—	55.00	90.00	140	350	—
1822GA FS	—	45.00	80.00	115	300	—

Note: Die varieties exist. Early dates are also encountered struck over other types

| 1822/1GA FS | — | 55.00 | 90.00 | 140 | 350 | — |

KM# 147   4 ESCUDOS
13.5400 g., 0.8750 Gold 0.3809 oz. AGW **Ruler:** Ferdinand VII **Obv:** Uniformed bust right **Rev:** Crowned shield divides designed wreath **Mint:** Guadalajara

Date	Mintage	VG	F	VF	XF	Unc
1812GA MR Rare	—	—	—	—	—	—

KM# 162   8 ESCUDOS
27.0700 g., 0.8750 Gold 0.7615 oz. AGW **Ruler:** Ferdinand VII **Obv:** Large uniformed bust right **Obv. Legend:** FERDIN • VII • D • G... **Rev:** Crowned shield divides designed wreath **Rev. Legend:** UTROQ • FELIX... **Mint:** Guadalajara

Date	Mintage	VG	F	VF	XF	Unc
1812GA MR Rare	—	—	—	—	—	—
1813GA MR	—	6,000	9,000	15,000	25,000	—

Note: Heritage Long Beach sale 5-08, Choice AU realized $37,500. American Numismatic Rarities Eliasberg sale 4-05, VF-30 realized $23,000.

KM# 163   8 ESCUDOS
27.0700 g., 0.8750 Gold 0.7615 oz. AGW **Ruler:**

Ferdinand VII **Obv:** Small uniformed bust right **Obv. Legend:** FERDIN • VII... **Rev:** Crowned shield divides designed wreath **Rev. Legend:** UTROQ • FELIX... **Mint:** Guadalajara

Date	Mintage	VG	F	VF	XF	Unc
1813GA MR	—	10,000	16,000	30,000	45,000	—

Note: Spink America Gerber sale 6-96 VF or better realized $46,200

KM# 161.1   8 ESCUDOS
27.0700 g., 0.8750 Gold 0.7615 oz. AGW **Ruler:** Ferdinand VII **Obv:** Laureate head right **Obv. Legend:** FERDIN • VII • D • G... **Rev:** Crowned shield divides designed wreath **Rev. Legend:** UTROQ • FELIX... **Mint:** Guadalajara

Date	Mintage	VG	F	VF	XF	Unc
1821GA FS	—	2,000	4,000	10,000	17,000	—

Note: American Numismatic Rarities Eliasberg sale 4-05, AU-55 realized $20,700.

KM# 164   8 ESCUDOS
27.0700 g., 0.8750 Gold 0.7615 oz. AGW **Ruler:** Ferdinand VII **Obv:** Draped laureate bust right **Rev:** Crowned shield flanked by pillars **Mint:** Guadalajara

Date	Mintage	VG	F	VF	XF	Unc
1821GA FS	—	5,500	8,000	14,500	23,000	—

GUANAJUATO

The Guanajuato Mint was authorized December 24, 1812 and started production shortly thereafter; closing for unknown reasons on May 15, 1813. The mint was reopened in April, 1821 by the insurgents, who struck coins of the old royal Spanish design to pay their army, even after independence, well into 1822.

Only the 2 and 8 Reales coins were made.

Mint mark: Go.

ROYALIST COINAGE

KM# 93.3   2 REALES
6.7700 g., 0.9030 Silver 0.1965 oz. ASW **Ruler:** Ferdinand VII **Obv:** Draped laureate bust right **Obv. Legend:** FERDIN • VII... **Rev:** Crowned shield flanked bu pillars **Rev. Legend:** IND • REX... **Mint:** Guanajuato

Date	Mintage	VG	F	VF	XF	Unc
1821Go JM	—	50.00	95.00	145	265	—
1822Go JM	—	43.25	70.00	110	210	—

KM# 111.4 8 REALES
27.0700 g., 0.9030 Silver 0.7859 oz. ASW **Ruler:**
Ferdinand VII **Obv:** Draped laureate bust right **Obv.**
Legend: FERDIN • VII... **Rev:** Crowned shield
flanked by pillars **Rev. Legend:** IND • REX... **Mint:**
Guanajuato

Date	Mintage	VG	F	VF	XF	Unc
1812Go JJ	—	3,700	6,500	—	—	—
1813Go JJ	—	180	250	400	875	—
1821Go JM	—	36.00	70.00	110	290	—
1822Go JM	—	30.00	50.00	85.00	265	—

NUEVA GALICIA

(Later became Jalisco State)

In early colonial times, Nueva Galicia was an extensive
province which substantially combined later provinces of
Zacatecas and Jalisco. These are states of Mexico today
although the name was revived during the War of Independence. The only issue was 2 Reales of rather enigmatic origin. No decrees or other authorization to strike this coin has
yet been located or reported.

INSURGENT COINAGE

KM# 218 2 REALES
0.9030 Silver **Obv:** N. G. in center, date **Obv.**
Legend: PROVYCIONAL... **Rev:** 2R in center **Rev.**
Legend: ... A. JUNIANA...

Date	Mintage	Good	VG	F	VF	XF
1813	—	1,250	3,150	5,600	—	—

Note: Excellent struck counterfeits exist

NUEVA VISCAYA

(Later became Durango State)

This 8 Reales, intended for the province of Nueva Vis-
caya, was minted in the newly-opened Durango Mint during
February and March of 1811, before the regular coinage of
Durango was started.

ROYALIST COINAGE

KM# 181 8 REALES
27.0700 g., 0.9030 Silver 0.7859 oz. ASW **Ruler:**
Ferdinand VII **Obv:** Crowned shield within sprays
Obv. Legend: MON • PROV • DE NUEV • VIZCAYA
Rev: Crowned shield flanked by pillars

Date	Mintage	Good	VG	F	VF	XF
1811 RM	—	1,250	2,800	3,550	6,900	—

Note: Several varieties exist.

OAXACA

The city of Oaxaca was in the midst of a coin shortage
when it became apparent the city would be taken by the
Insurgents. Royalist forces under Lt. Gen. Saravia had coins
made. They were cast in a blacksmith shop. 1/2, 1, and 8
Reales were made only briefly in 1812 before the Royalists
surrendered the city.

ROYALIST COINAGE

KM# 166 1/2 REAL
0.9030 Silver **Ruler:** Ferdinand VII **Obv:** Cross
separating castle, lion, Fo, 7o **Rev:** Legend around
shield **Rev. Legend:** PROV • D • OAXACA

Date	Mintage	Good	VG	F	VF	XF
1812	—	1,250	1,900	3,150	4,400	—

WAR OF INDEPENDENCE

KM# 167   REAL
0.9030 Silver   **Ruler:** Ferdinand VII **Obv:** Cross
separating castle, lion, Fo, 7o **Rev:** Legend around
shield **Rev. Legend:** PROV • D • OAXACA

Date	Mintage	Good	VG	F	VF	XF
1812	—	450	825	1,500	3,150	—

KM# 168   8 REALES
0.9030 Silver   **Obv:** Cross separating castle, lion,
Fo, 7o **Obv. Legend:** OAXACA 1812... **Rev:** Shield,
authorization mark above **Note:** These issues
usually display a second mark 'O' between the
crowned pillars on the obverse. Varieties of large and
small lion in shield also exist.

Date	Mintage	Good	VG	F	VF	XF
1812 "A"	—	1,500	2,100	3,500	5,700	—
1812 "B"	—	1,500	2,100	3,500	5,700	—
1812 "C"	—	1,500	2,100	3,500	5,700	—
1812 "D"	—	1,500	2,100	3,500	5,700	—
1812 "K"	—	1,500	2,100	3,500	5,700	—
1812 "L"	—	1,500	2,100	3,500	5,700	—
1812 "Mo"	—	1,500	2,100	3,500	5,700	—
1812 "N"	—	1,500	2,100	3,500	5,700	—
1812 "O"	—	1,500	2,100	3,500	5,700	—
1812 "R"	—	1,500	2,100	3,500	5,700	—
1812 "V"	—	1,500	2,100	3,500	5,700	—
1812 "Z"	—	1,500	2,100	3,500	5,700	—

INSURGENT COINAGE

Oaxaca was the hub of Insurgent activity in the south
where coinage started in July 1811 and continued until
October 1814. The Oaxaca issues represent episodic strikings, usually under dire circumstances by various individuals. Coins were commonly made of copper due to urgency
and were intended to be redeemed at face value in gold or
silver once silver was available to the Insurgents. Some
were later made in silver, but most appear to be of more
recent origin, to satisfy collectors.

KM# 219   1/2 REAL
Struck Copper **Issuer:** SUD, Under General Morelos
Obv: Bow, arrow, SUD **Rev:** Morelos monogram Mo,
date

Date	Mintage	Good	VG	F	VF	XF
1811	—	6.75	11.50	20.00	35.00	—
1812	—	6.75	11.50	20.00	35.00	—
1813	—	5.50	9.00	17.50	30.00	—
1814	—	9.00	16.50	25.00	40.00	—

Note: Uniface strikes exist of #219

KM# 220.1   1/2 REAL
Struck Silver **Issuer:** SUD, Under General Morelos
Obv: Bow, arrow, SUD **Rev:** Morelos monogram Mo,
date

Date	Mintage	Good	VG	F	VF	XF
1811	—	—	—	—	—	—
1812	—	—	—	—	—	—
1813	—	—	—	—	—	—

KM# 220.2   1/2 REAL
Struck Silver **Issuer:** SUD, Under General Morelos
Obv: Bow, arrow, SUD **Rev:** Morelos monogram Mo,
date

Date	Mintage	Good	VG	F	VF	XF
1811	—	—	—	—	—	—
1812	—	—	—	—	—	—
1813	—	33.00	65.00	130	200	—

Note: Use caution as silver specimens appear questionable
and may be considered spurious

KM# 221   1/2 REAL
Struck Silver **Issuer:** SUD, Under General Morelos
Obv: Bow, arrow **Obv. Legend:** PROVICIONAL DE
OAXACA **Rev:** Lion **Rev. Legend:** AMERICA
MORELOS

Date	Mintage	Good	VG	F	VF	XF
1812	—	46.25	80.00	130	200	—
1813	—	46.25	80.00	130	200	—

KM# 221a   1/2 REAL
Struck Copper **Issuer:** SUD, Under General Morelos
Obv: Bow, arrow **Obv. Legend:** PROVICIONAL DE
OAXACA **Rev:** Lion **Rev. Legend:** AMERICA
MORELOS

Date	Mintage	Good	VG	F	VF	XF
1812	—	36.25	55.00	90.00	130	—
1813	—	27.50	46.25	80.00	115	—

KM# A222   1/2 REAL
Struck Copper **Issuer:** SUD, Under General Morelos
Obv: Similar to KM#220 **Rev:** Similar to KM#221 but
with 1/2 at left of lion **Rev. Legend:** AMERICA
MORELOS

Date	Mintage	Good	VG	F	VF	XF
1813	—	36.25	55.00	90.00	130	—

KM# 243   1/2 REAL
Struck Copper   **Issuer:** Tierra Caliente (Hot Country), Under General Morelos **Obv:** Bow, T.C., SUD **Rev:** Morelos monogram, value, date

Date	Mintage	Good	VG	F	VF	XF
1813	—	49.50	90.00	170	265	—

KM# 222   REAL
Struck Copper   **Issuer:** SUD, Under General Morelos **Obv:** Bow, arrow, SUD **Rev:** Morelos monogram, 1 R., date

Date	Mintage	Good	VG	F	VF	XF
1811	—	6.00	12.00	25.00	50.00	—
1812	—	5.00	10.00	18.00	39.50	—
1813	—	5.00	10.00	18.00	39.50	—

KM# 222a   REAL
Struck Silver   **Issuer:** SUD, Under General Morelos **Obv:** Bow, arrow, SUD **Rev:** Morelos monogram, 1 R., date

Date	Mintage	Good	VG	F	VF	XF
1812	—	—	—	—	—	—
1813	—	—	—	—	—	—

KM# 223   REAL
Cast Silver   **Issuer:** SUD, Under General Morelos **Obv:** Bow, arrow, SUD with floral ornaments **Rev:** Morelos monogram, 1 R., date

Date	Mintage	Good	VG	F	VF	XF
1812	—	—	—	—	—	—
1813	—	36.25	80.00	150	210	—

Note: Use caution as many silver specimens appear questionable and may be considered spurious

KM# 224   REAL
Struck Copper   **Issuer:** SUD, Under General Morelos **Obv:** Bow, arrow/SUD **Rev:** Lion **Rev. Legend:** AMERICA MORELOS

Date	Mintage	Good	VG	F	VF	XF
1813	—	36.25	55.00	100	145	—

KM# 225   REAL
Silver   **Issuer:** SUD, Under General Morelos **Obv:** Bow, arrow/SUD **Rev:** Lion **Rev. Legend:** AMERICA MORELOS

Date	Mintage	Good	VG	F	VF	XF
1813 Rare	—	—	—	—	—	—

KM# 244   REAL
Struck Copper   **Issuer:** Tierra Caliente (Hot Country), Under General Morelos **Obv:** Bow, T.C., SUD **Rev:** Morelos monogram, value, date

Date	Mintage	Good	VG	F	VF	XF
1813	—	18.00	33.00	65.00	110	—

KM# 226.1   2 REALES
Struck Copper   **Issuer:** SUD, Under General Morelos **Obv:** Bow, arrow/SUD **Rev:** Morelos monogram, .2.R., date

Date	Mintage	Good	VG	F	VF	XF
1811	—	17.00	33.00	70.00	130	—
1811 inverted 2	—	20.00	39.50	80.00	155	—
1812	—	3.00	5.00	8.00	16.00	—
1813	—	4.00	7.00	11.00	20.00	—
1814	—	18.00	37.00	85.00	155	—

KM# 226.1a   2 REALES
Struck Silver   **Issuer:** SUD, Under General Morelos **Obv:** Bow, arrow/SUD **Rev:** Morelos monogram, .2.R., date

Date	Mintage	Good	VG	F	VF	XF
1812	—	215	350	600	900	—

KM# 229   2 REALES
Cast Silver   **Issuer:** SUD, Under General Morelos **Obv:** Bow, arrow, SUD **Rev:** Morelos monogram, value, date in center with ornamentation around

Date	Mintage	Good	VG	F	VF	XF
1812	—	80.00	130	200	300	—
1812 Filled in D in SUD	—	80.00	130	200	300	—

Note: Use caution as many silver specimens appear questionable and may be considered spurious

KM# 245   2 REALES
Struck Copper   **Issuer:** Tierra Caliente (Hot Country), Under General Morelos **Obv:** Bow, T.C., SUD **Rev:** Morelos monogram, value, date

Date	Mintage	Good	VG	F	VF	XF
1813	—	12.00	30.00	46.25	65.00	—

KM# 227   2 REALES
Struck Silver   **Issuer:** SUD, Under General Morelos **Obv:** Bow, arrow **Obv. Legend:** SUD-OXA **Rev:** Morelos monogram, value, date

Date	Mintage	Good	VG	F	VF	XF
1813	—	80.00	130	265	400	—
1814	—	80.00	130	265	400	—

KM# 228   2 REALES
Struck Silver   **Issuer:** SUD, Under General Morelos **Obv:** Bow, arrow **Obv. Legend:** SUD. OAXACA **Rev:** Morelos monogram, value, date

Date	Mintage	Good	VG	F	VF	XF
1814	—	80.00	130	265	425	—

WAR OF INDEPENDENCE

KM# 226.2   2 REALES
Struck Silver **Issuer:** SUD, Under General Morelos
Obv: Three large stars added **Rev:** Morelos
monogram, .2.R., date

Date	Mintage	Good	VG	F	VF	XF
1814	—	13.00	27.50	55.00	80.00	—

KM# 246   2 REALES
Struck Copper **Issuer:** Tierra Caliente (Hot
Country), Under General Morelos **Obv:** Bow, T.C.,
SUD **Rev:** Morelos monogram, value, date

Date	Mintage	Good	VG	F	VF	XF
1814	—	33.00	70.00	145	250	—

KM# 234   8 REALES
Copper **Issuer:** SUD, Under General Morelos **Obv:**
Bow, arrow, SUD in floral ornamentation **Rev:**
Morelos monogram, .8.R., date surrounded by ornate
flowery fields

Date	Mintage	Good	VG	F	VF	XF
1811	—	115	190	225	350	—
1812	—	10.00	15.00	25.00	50.00	—
1813	—	10.00	15.00	25.00	50.00	—
1814	—	19.00	27.50	47.00	95.00	—

KM# 235   8 REALES
Cast Silver **Issuer:** SUD, Under General Morelos
Obv: Bow, arrow, SUD in floral ornamentation **Rev:**
Morelos monogram, value, date surrounded by
ornate flowery fields

Date	Mintage	Good	VG	F	VF	XF
1811	—	—	—	—	—	—
1812	—	115	190	300	525	—
1813	—	90.00	150	265	450	—
1814	—	—	—	—	—	—

Note: Most silver specimens available in today's market are
considered spurious

KM# 234a   8 REALES
Struck Silver **Issuer:** SUD, under General Morelos
Obv: Bow, arrow, SUD in floral ornamentation **Rev:**
Morelos monogram, .8.R., date surrounded by ornate
flowery fields

Date	Mintage	Good	VG	F	VF	XF
1811	—	—	—	3,150	5,000	—
1812	—	—	—	1,500	2,500	—

KM# 233.5a   8 REALES
Silver **Issuer:** SUD, Under General Morelos **Obv:**

8 dots below bow, SUD, plain fields **Rev:** Morelos
monogram, 8.R., date

Date	Mintage	Good	VG	F	VF	XF
1812	—	—	—	1,500	2,500	—

KM# 236 8 REALES
0.9030 Struck Silver **Issuer:** SUD, Under General
Morelos **Obv:** M monogram **Obv. Legend:** PROV • D
• OAXACA **Rev:** Lion shield with or without bow above

Date	Mintage	Good	VG	F	VF	XF
1812 Rare	—	—	—	—	—	—

KM# 233.1 8 REALES
Copper **Issuer:** SUD, Under General Morelos **Obv:**
Bow, arrow, SUD **Rev:** Morelos monogram, 8.R.,
date, plain fields

Date	Mintage	Good	VG	F	VF	XF
1812	—	27.50	55.00	115	170	—

KM# 233.1a 8 REALES
Struck Silver **Issuer:** SUD, Under General Morelos
Obv: Bow, arrow, SUD **Rev:** Morelos monogram,
8.R., date, plain fields

Date	Mintage	Good	VG	F	VF	XF
1812	—	150	225	375	700	—

KM# 233.2 8 REALES
Copper **Issuer:** SUD, Under General Morelos **Obv:**
Bow, arrow, SUD **Rev:** Morelos monogram, 8 R,
date, plain fields

Date	Mintage	Good	VG	F	VF	XF
1812	—	15.00	20.00	31.25	37.50	—
1813	—	15.00	20.00	31.25	37.50	—
1814	—	25.00	31.25	37.50	50.00	—

Note: Similar to KM#233.4 but lines below bow slant left

KM# 242 8 REALES
Copper **Issuer:** Huautla, Under General Morelos
Obv: Legend around bow, arrow/SUD **Obv. Legend:**
MONEDA PROVI • CIONAL PS • ES • **Rev. Legend:**
FABRICADO EN HUAUTLA

Date	Mintage	Good	VG	F	VF	XF
1812	—	1,250	1,900	2,500	—	—

KM# 248 8 REALES
Struck Copper **Issuer:** Tierra Caliente (Hot
Country), Under General Morelos **Obv:** Bow, T.C.,
SUD **Rev:** Morelos monogram, value, date

Date	Mintage	Good	VG	F	VF	XF
1813	—	18.00	37.50	75.00	145	—

KM# 249 8 REALES
Cast Silver **Issuer:** Tierra Caliente (Hot Country),
Under General Morelos **Obv:** Bow, T.C., SUD **Rev:**
Morelos monogram, value, date

Date	Mintage	Good	VG	F	VF	XF
1813	—	—	—	—	—	—

Note: Use caution as many silver specimens appear questionable and may be considered spurious

WAR OF INDEPENDENCE

KM# 233.2a   8 REALES
Silver **Issuer:** SUD, Under General Morelos **Obv:** bow, arrow, SUD **Rev:** Morelos monogram, 8R, date, plain fields

Date	Mintage	Good	VG	F	VF	XF
1813	—	—	—	1,500	2,500	—

KM# 233.3   8 REALES
Struck Copper **Issuer:** SUD, Under General Morelos **Obv:** Bow, arrow, SUD, with left slant lines below bow **Rev:** Morelos monogram, 8.R., date, plain fields

Date	Mintage	Good	VG	F	VF	XF
1813	—	19.00	34.50	55.00	95.00	—

KM# 233.4   8 REALES
Struck Copper **Issuer:** SUD, Under General Morelos **Obv:** Bow, arrow, SUD, with right slant lines below bow **Rev:** Morelos monogram, 8.R., date, plain fields

Date	Mintage	Good	VG	F	VF	XF
1813	—	19.00	34.50	55.00	95.00	—

KM# 237   8 REALES
0.9250 Silver **Issuer:** SUD, Under General Morelos **Obv:** M monogram, without legend **Rev:** Lion shield with or without bow above

Date	Mintage	Good	VG	F	VF	XF
1813 Rare	—	—	—	—	—	—

KM# 238   8 REALES
0.9030 Struck Silver **Issuer:** SUD, Under General Morelos **Obv:** Bow/M/SUD **Rev:** PROV. DE. ... arms

Date	Mintage	Good	VG	F	VF	XF
1813 Rare	—	—	—	—	—	—

KM# 239   8 REALES
Cast Silver **Issuer:** SUD, Under General Morelos **Obv:** Bow, arrow **Obv. Legend:** SUD-OXA **Rev:** Morelos monogram

Date	Mintage	Good	VG	F	VF	XF
1814 Rare	—	—	—	—	—	—

KM# 240   8 REALES
Copper **Issuer:** SUD, Under General Morelos **Obv:** Bow, arrow **Obv. Legend:** SUD-OXA **Rev:** Morelos monogram, 8.R., date

Date	Mintage	Good	VG	F	VF	XF
1814	—	55.00	105	225	375	—

KM# 241   8 REALES
Copper **Issuer:** SUD, Under General Morelos **Obv:** Bow, arrow **Obv. Legend:** SUD-OAXACA **Rev:** Morelos monogram, 8.R., date

Date	Mintage	Good	VG	F	VF	XF
1814	—	125	250	450	700	—

PUEBLA

INSURGENT COINAGE

KM# 250   1/2 REAL
Copper **Issuer:** Zacatlan, struck by General Osorno **Obv:** Osorno monogram, ZACATLAN, date **Rev:** Crossed arrows, wreath, value

Date	Mintage	Good	VG	F	VF	XF
1813 Rare	—	—	—	—	—	—

KM# 251   REAL
Copper **Issuer:** Zacatlan, struck by General Osorno **Obv:** Osorno monogram, ZACATLAN, date **Rev:** Crossed arrows, wreath, value

Date	Mintage	Good	VG	F	VF	XF
1813	—	140	210	300	625	—

KM# 252   2 REALES
Copper **Issuer:** Zacatlan, struck by General Osorno **Obv:** Osorno monogram, ZACATLAN, date **Rev:** Crossed arrows, wreath, value

Date	Mintage	Good	VG	F	VF	XF
1813	—	170	240	375	700	—

REAL DEL CATORCE

(City in San Luis Potosi)

Real del Catorce is an important mining center in the Province of San Luis Potosi. In 1811 an 8 Reales coin was issued under very primitive conditions while the city was still in Royalist hands. Few survive.

ROYALIST COINAGE

KM# 169   8 REALES
0.9030 Silver   **Ruler:** Ferdinand VII **Obv. Legend:**
EL R • D • CATORC • POR FERNA • VII **Rev. Legend:**
MONEDA • PROVISIONAL • VALE • 8R

Date	Mintage	VG	F	VF	XF	Unc
1811	—	8,400	18,000	42,000	78,000	—

Note: Spink America Gerber Sale 6-96 VF or XF realized
$63,800

SAN FERNANDO DE BEXAR

TOKEN COINAGE

KM# Tn1   1/2 REAL (Jola)
Copper   **Ruler:** Ferdinand VII **Note:** Prev. KM#170.

Date	Mintage	Good	VG	F	VF	XF
1818	8,000	—	—	—	28,000	32,000

KM# Tn2   1/2 REAL (Jola)
Copper   **Ruler:** Ferdinand VII **Note:** Prev. KM#171.

Date	Mintage	Good	VG	F	VF	XF
1818	Inc. above	—	—	—	25,000	30,000

SAN LUIS POTOSI

Sierra de Pinos

ROYALIST COINAGE

KM# A172   1/4 REAL
Copper   **Ruler:** Ferdinand VII **Issuer:** Sierra de
Pinos, Villa

Date	Mintage	Good	VG	F	VF	XF
1814	—	125	190	325	500	—

KM# A172a   1/4 REAL
Silver   **Ruler:** Ferdinand VII

Date	Mintage	Good	VG	F	VF	XF
1814 Rare	—	—	—	—	—	—

SOMBRERETE

(Under Royalist Vargas)

The Sombrerete Mint opened on October 8, 1810 in an
area that boasted some of the richest mines in Mexico. The
mint operated only until July 16, 1811, only to reopen in
1812 and finally close for good at the end of the year. Mines
Administrator Fernando Vargas, was also in charge of the
coining, all coins bear his name.

ROYALIST COINAGE

KM# 172   1/2 REAL
0.9030 Silver   **Ruler:** Ferdinand VII **Obv:** Legend
around crowned globes **Obv. Legend:** FERDIN • VII
• SOMBRERETE... **Rev:** Legend above lys in oval,
sprays, date below **Rev. Legend:** VARGAS

Date	Mintage	Good	VG	F	VF	XF
1811	—	55.00	85.00	180	325	—
1812	—	60.00	110	210	350	—

KM# 173   REAL
0.9030 Silver   **Ruler:** Ferdinand VII **Obv:** Legend
around crowned globes **Obv. Legend:** FERDIN • VII
• SOMBRERETE... **Rev:** Legend above lys in oval
with denomination flanking, sprays, date below **Rev.
Legend:** VARGAS

Date	Mintage	Good	VG	F	VF	XF
1811	—	55.00	85.00	180	325	—

Note: For 1811, denomination reads as '1R' or 'R1'

1812	—	60.00	110	210	350	—

WAR OF INDEPENDENCE

KM# 174   2 REALES
0.9030 Silver **Ruler:** Ferdinand VII **Countermark:**
VARGAS **Obv:** Royal arms **Obv. Legend:** R • CAXA
• DE • SOMBRERETE **Rev:** 1811, S between
crowned pillars

Date	Mintage	Good	VG	F	VF	XF
1811 SE	—	120	300	550	900	—

KM# 175   4 REALES
0.9030 Silver **Ruler:** Ferdinand VII **Obv:** Crowned
Royal arms **Obv. Legend:** R • CAXA • DE •
SOMBRERETE **Rev:** Large legend **Rev. Legend:**
VARGAS / 1812 **Note:** Prev. KM#172.

Date	Mintage	Good	VG	F	VF	XF
1812	—	60.00	120	240	600	—

KM# 176   8 REALES
0.9030 Silver **Ruler:** Ferdinand VII **Countermark:**
VARGAS, date, S **Obv:** Royal arms **Obv. Legend:**
R • CAXA • DE SOMBRERETE **Rev:** Several
countermarks between crowned pillars

Date	Mintage	Good	VG	F	VF	XF
1810	—	1,200	2,100	3,300	5,400	10,500
1811	—	270	400	550	725	—

KM# 177   8 REALES
0.9030 Silver **Ruler:** Ferdinand VII **Obv:** Crowned
Royal arms **Obv. Legend:** R • CAXA • DE
SOMBRETE **Rev. Legend:** VARGAS / date /3, S
between crowned pillars

Date	Mintage	Good	VG	F	VF	XF
1811	—	170	240	475	950	—
1812	—	150	220	450	925	—

VALLADOLID MICHOACAN

ROYALIST COINAGE

KM# 178   8 REALES
0.9030 Silver **Ruler:** Ferdinand VII **Obv:** Royal arms
in wreath, value at sides **Rev. Legend:**
PROVISIONAL / DE VALLADOLID / 1813

Date	Mintage	Good	VG	F	VF	XF
1813 Rare	—	—	—	—	—	—

KM# 179   8 REALES
0.9030 Silver   **Ruler:** Ferdinand VII **Obv:** Draped
laureate bust right **Obv. Legend:** FERDIN • VII •...
Rev: Crowned shield flanked by pillars, P. D. V. in
legend **Rev. Legend:** REX • P • D • V...

Date	Mintage	Good	VG	F	VF	XF
1813 Rare	—	—	—	—	—	—

Note: Spink America Gerber sale 6-96 good realized
$23,100

VERACRUZ

In Zongolica, in the province of Veracruz, 2 priests and
a lawyer decided to raise an army to fight for independence.
Due to isolation from other Insurgent forces, they decided to
make their own coins. Records show that they intended to
mint coins of 1/2, 1, 2, 4, and 8 Reales, but specimens are
extant of only the three higher denominations.

INSURGENT COINAGE

KM# 253   2 REALES
0.9030 Silver **Issuer:** Zongolica **Obv:** Bow and
arrow **Obv. Legend:** VIVA FERNANDO VII Y

AMERICA **Rev:** Value, crossed palm branch, sword, date **Rev. Legend:** ZONGOLICA

Date	Mintage	Good	VG	F	VF	XF
1812	—	120	240	425	775	—

KM# 255   8 REALES
0.9030 Silver **Issuer:** Zongolica **Obv:** Bow and arrow **Obv. Legend:** VIVA FERNANDO VII Y AMERICA **Rev:** Value, crossed palm branch, sword, date **Rev. Legend:** ZONGOLICA **Note:** Similar to 2 Reales, KM#253.

Date	Mintage	Good	VG	F	VF	XF
1812 Rare	—	—	—	—	—	—

Note: Spink America Gerber sale 6-96 VF to XF realized $57,200

INSURGENT COUNTERMARKED COINAGE

CONGRESS OF CHILPANZINGO

Type A: Hand holding bow and arrow between quiver with arrows, sword and bow.

Type B: Crowned eagle on bridge.

KM# 256.1   1/2 REAL
Silver **Issuer:** Congress of Chilpanzingo **Countermark:** Type A hand holding bow and arrow between quiver with arrows, sword and bow **Note:** Countermark on cast Mexico City KM#72.

CM Date	Host Date	Good	VG	F	VF	XF
ND	1812	50.00	85.00	110	170	—

KM# 256.2   1/2 REAL
Silver **Issuer:** Congress of Chilpanzingo **Countermark:** Type A hand holding bow and arrow between quiver with arrows, sword and bow **Note:** Countermark on Zacatecas KM#181.

CM Date	Host Date	Good	VG	F	VF	XF
ND	1811	60.00	90.00	120	180	—

KM# A257   REAL
Cast Silver **Issuer:** Congress of Chilpanzingo **Countermark:** Type A hand holding bow and arrow between quiver with arrows, sword and bow **Note:** Countermark on cast Mexico City KM#81.

CM Date	Host Date	Good	VG	F	VF	XF
ND	1803	22.50	36.00	60.00	100	—

KM# 257.1   2 REALES
Silver **Issuer:** Congress of Chilpanzingo **Countermark:** Type B crowned eagle on bridge **Note:** Countermark on 1/4 cut of 8 Reales.

CM Date	Host Date	Good	VG	F	VF	XF
	ND Unique	—	—	—	—	—

KM# 257.2   2 REALES
Silver **Issuer:** Congress of Chilpanzingo **Countermark:** Type B crowned eagle on bridge **Note:** Countermark on Zacatecas KM#186.

CM Date	Host Date	Good	VG	F	VF	XF
ND	1811 Unique	—	—	—	—	—

KM# 258.1   8 REALES
Silver **Issuer:** Congress of Chilpanzingo
Countermark: Type A hand holding bow and arrow between quiver with arrows, sword and bow **Note:** Countermark on cast Mexico City KM#109.

CM Date	Host Date	Good	VG	F	VF	XF
ND	1805	55.00	80.00	100	180	—

Note: A countermark appears on coins dated 1805 TH

KM# 258.2   8 REALES
Silver **Issuer:** Congress of Chilpanzingo
Countermark: Type A hand holding bow and arrow between quiver with arrows, sword and bow **Note:** Countermark on cast Mexico City KM#110.

CM Date	Host Date	Good	VG	F	VF	XF
ND	1810 HJ	60.00	90.00	120	210	—

KM# 258.3   8 REALES
Silver **Issuer:** Congress of Chilpanzingo
Countermark: Type A hand holding bow and arrow between quiver with arrows, sword and bow **Note:** Countermark on cast Mexico City KM#111.

CM Date	Host Date	Good	VG	F	VF	XF
ND	1811 HJ	55.00	80.00	100	180	—
ND	1812 HJ	120	150	210	325	—

KM# 259.1   8 REALES
Silver **Issuer:** Congress of Chilpanzingo
Countermark: Type B crowned eagle on bridge
Note: Countermark on Chihuahua KM#111.1.

CM Date	Host Date	Good	VG	F	VF	XF
ND	1816 RP	240	300	350	475	—

KM# 259.2   8 REALES
Silver **Issuer:** Congress of Chilpanzingo
Countermark: Type B crowned eagle on bridge
Note: Countermark on cast Mexico City KM#111.

CM Date	Host Date	Good	VG	F	VF	XF
ND	1811 HJ	155	180	210	300	—

KM# 259.3   8 REALES
Silver **Issuer:** Congress of Chilpanzingo
Countermark: Type B crowned eagle on bridge
Note: Countermark on Valladolid KM#178.

CM Date	Host Date	Good	VG	F	VF	XF
ND	1813	1,250	2,500	3,750	6,300	—

KM# 259.4   8 REALES
Silver **Issuer:** Congress of Chilpanzingo
Countermark: Type B crowned eagle on bridge
Note: Countermark on Zacatecas KM#190.

CM Date	Host Date	Good	VG	F	VF	XF
ND	1810	500	625	750	975	—

DON JOSE MARIA DE LINARES

KM# 263.1   8 REALES
Silver **Issuer:** Don Jose Maria De Linares
Countermark: LINA/RES* **Note:** Countermark on Mexico City KM#110.

CM Date	Host Date	Good	VG	F	VF	XF
ND	1808 TH	325	375	475	700	—

KM# 263.2   8 REALES
Silver **Issuer:** Don Jose Maria De Linares
Countermark: LINA/RES * **Note:** Countermark on Zacatecas KM#190.

CM Date	Host Date	Good	VG	F	VF	XF
ND	1811	375	475	575	825	—

KM# 263.3   8 REALES
Silver **Issuer:** Don Jose Maria De Linares
Countermark: LINA/RES* **Note:** Countermark on Zacatecas KM#191.

CM Date	Host Date	Good	VG	F	VF	XF
ND	1812	325	375	475	700	—

WAR OF INDEPENDENCE

GENERAL VICENTE GUERRERO

The countermark of an eagle facing left within a pearled oval has been attributed by some authors as that of General Vicente Guerrero, a leader of the insurgents in the south, 1816-1821.

KM# 276   1/2 REAL
Silver **Issuer:** General Vicente Guerrero
Countermark: Eagle **Note:** Countermark on Mexico City KM#72.

CM Date	Host Date	Good	VG	F	VF	XF
ND	ND	48.00	70.00	95.00	210	—

KM# 277   REAL
Silver **Issuer:** General Vicente Guerrero
Countermark: Eagle **Note:** Countermark on Mexico City KM#78.

CM Date	Host Date	Good	VG	F	VF	XF
ND	1772 FM	43.75	65.00	95.00	205	—

KM# 278.1   2 REALES
Silver **Issuer:** General Vicente Guerrero
Countermark: Eagle **Note:** Countermark on Mexico City KM#88.

CM Date	Host Date	Good	VG	F	VF	XF
ND	1784 FM	40.00	60.00	100	225	—
ND	1798	40.00	60.00	100	225	—

KM# 278.2   2 REALES
Silver **Issuer:** General Vicente Guerrero
Countermark: Eagle **Note:** Countermark on Mexico City KM#91.

CM Date	Host Date	Good	VG	F	VF	XF
ND	1807 PJ	36.00	60.00	95.00	240	—

KM# 279   8 REALES
Silver **Issuer:** General Vicente Guerrero
Countermark: Eagle **Note:** Countermark on Zacatecas KM#191.

CM Date	Host Date	Good	VG	F	VF	XF
ND	1811	120	180	240	425	—

ENSAIE

KM# 260.3   8 REALES
Silver **Issuer:** Ensaie **Countermark:** Eagle over ENSAIE, crude sling below **Note:** Countermark on Zacatecas KM#190.

CM Date	Host Date	Good	VG	F	VF	XF
ND	1810	—	—	—	—	—
ND	1811	120	180	240	400	—

KM# 260.4   8 REALES
Silver **Issuer:** Ensaie **Countermark:** Eagle over ENSAIE, crude sling below **Note:** Countermark on Zacatecas KM#191.

CM Date	Host Date	Good	VG	F	VF	XF
ND	1810	600	850	1,100	1,500	—
ND	1811	300	350	450	650	—
ND	1812	240	300	350	550	—

KM# 260.1   8 REALES
Silver **Issuer:** Ensaie **Countermark:** Eagle over ENSAIE, crude sling below **Note:** Countermark on Mexico City KM#110.

CM Date	Host Date	Good	VG	F	VF	XF
ND	1811 HJ	180	240	325	450	—

WAR OF INDEPENDENCE

KM# 260.2   8 REALES
Silver **Issuer:** Ensaie **Countermark:** Eagle over
ENSAIE, crude sling below **Note:** Countermark on
Zacatecas KM#189.

CM Date	Host Date	Good	VG	F	VF	XF
ND	1811	240	475	725	1,000	—

JOSE MARIA LICEAGA

J.M.L. with banner on cross,
crossed olive branches.

(J.M.L./V., D.s, S.M., S.Y.S.L., Ve,
A.P., s.r.a., Sea, P.G., S., S.M., El)

KM# A260   1/2 REAL
Silver **Issuer:** Jose Maria Liceaga **Countermark:**
JML/SM with banner on cross, crossed olive
branches **Note:** Countermark on cast Mexico City 1/
2 Real.

CM Date	Host Date	Good	VG	F	VF	XF
ND	ND	125	190	250	375	—

KM# 261.6   2 REALES
Silver **Issuer:** Jose Maria Liceaga **Countermark:**
J.M.L./V. with banner on cross, crossed olive
branches **Note:** Countermark on Zacatecas
KM#187.

CM Date	Host Date	Good	VG	F	VF	XF
ND	1811	250	280	325	400	—

KM# 261.7   2 REALES
Silver **Issuer:** Jose Maria Liceaga **Countermark:**
J.M.L./DS with banner on cross, crossed olive
branches **Note:** Countermark on Zacatecas
KM#187.

CM Date	Host Date	Good	VG	F	VF	XF
ND	1811	250	295	350	450	—

KM# 261.8   2 REALES
Silver **Issuer:** Jose Maria Liceaga **Countermark:**
J.M.L./S.M. with banner on cross, crossed olive
branches **Note:** Countermark on Zacatecas
KM#187.

CM Date	Host Date	Good	VG	F	VF	XF
ND	1811	240	280	325	425	—

KM# 261.9   2 REALES
Silver **Issuer:** Jose Maria Liceaga **Countermark:**
J.M.L./S.Y. with banner on cross, crossed olive
branches **Note:** Countermark on Zacatecas
KM#187.

CM Date	Host Date	Good	VG	F	VF	XF
ND	1811	240	280	325	425	—

KM# 261.1   2 REALES
Silver **Issuer:** Jose Maria Liceaga **Countermark:**
J.M.L./Ve with banner on cross, crossed olive
branches **Note:** Countermark on 1/4 cut of 8 Reales.

CM Date	Host Date	Good	VG	F	VF	XF
ND	ND	210	270	400	—	—

KM# 261.2   2 REALES
Silver **Issuer:** Jose Maria Liceaga **Countermark:**
J.M.L./V with banner on cross, crossed olive branchs
Note: Countermark on Zacatecas KM#186.

CM Date	Host Date	Good	VG	F	VF	XF
ND	1811	250	280	325	400	—

KM# 261.3   2 REALES
Silver **Issuer:** Jose Maria Liceaga **Countermark:**
J.M.L./DS with banner on cross, crossed olive
branches **Note:** Countermark on Zacatecas
KM#186.

CM Date	Host Date	Good	VG	F	VF	XF
ND	1811	250	295	350	450	—

KM# 261.4   2 REALES
Silver **Issuer:** Jose Maria Liceaga **Countermark:**
J.M.L./S.M. with banner on cross, crossed olive
branches **Note:** Countermark on Zacatecas KM#186.

CM Date	Host Date	Good	VG	F	VF	XF
ND	1811	250	295	350	450	—

KM# 261.5   2 REALES
Silver **Issuer:** Jose Maria Liceaga **Countermark:**
J.M.L./S.Y. with banner on cross, crossed olive
branches **Note:** Countermark on Zacatecas KM#186.

CM Date	Host Date	Good	VG	F	VF	XF
ND	1811	250	295	350	450	—

KM# 262.1   8 REALES
Silver **Issuer:** Jose Maria Liceaga **Countermark:**

WAR OF INDEPENDENCE

J.M.L./D.S. with banner on cross, crossed olive branches **Note:** Countermark on Zacatecas KM#190.

CM Date	Host Date	Good	VG	F	VF	XF
ND	1811	325	400	525	775	—

KM# 262.4   8 REALES
Silver **Issuer:** Jose Maria Liceaga **Countermark:** J.M.L./S.F. with banner on cross, crossed olive branches **Note:** Countermark on Zacatecas KM#190.

CM Date	Host Date	Good	VG	F	VF	XF
ND	1811	250	350	475	725	—

KM# 262.6   8 REALES
Silver **Issuer:** Jose Maria Liceaga **Countermark:** J.M.L./V.E. with banner on cross, cross olive branches **Note:** Countermark on Zacatecas KM#190.

CM Date	Host Date	Good	VG	F	VF	XF
ND	1811	250	350	475	700	—

KM# 262.2   8 REALES
Silver **Issuer:** Jose Maria Liceaga **Countermark:** J.M.L./E with banner on cross, crossed olive branches **Note:** Countermark on Zacatecas KM#190.

CM Date	Host Date	Good	VG	F	VF	XF
ND	1811	280	375	500	750	—

KM# 262.3   8 REALES
Silver **Issuer:** Jose Maria Liceaga **Countermark:** J.M.L./P.G. with banner on cross, crossed olive branches **Note:** Countermark on Durango KM#111.2.

CM Date	Host Date	Good	VG	F	VF	XF
ND	1813 RM	250	350	475	725	—

KM# 262.12   8 REALES
Silver **Issuer:** Jose Maria Liceaga, Banner on cross, crossed olive branches **Countermark:** J.M.L. / P.G. **Note:** Countermark on Guanajuato 8 Reales, KM#111.4.

CM Date	Host Date	Good	VG	F	VF	XF
ND	ND1813	190	325	575	—	—

KM# 262.7   8 REALES
Silver **Issuer:** Jose Maria Liceaga, J.M.L with banner on cross, crossed olive branches. (J.M.L./V., D.s, S.M., S.Y.S.L., Ve, A.P., s.r.a., Sea, P.G., S., S.M., E.) **Countermark:** J.M.L./D.S. **Note:** Countermark on Zacatecas KM#190.

CM Date	Host Date	Good	VG	F	VF	XF
ND	1811	—	—	—	—	—

KM# 262.5   8 REALES
Silver **Issuer:** Jose Maria Liceaga **Countermark:** J.M.L./S.M. with banner on cross, crossed olive branches **Note:** Countermark on Zacatecas KM#190.

CM Date	Host Date	Good	VG	F	VF	XF
ND	1811	250	350	475	700	—

KM# 262.10   8 REALES
Silver **Issuer:** Jose Maria Liceaga, J.M.L. with banner on cross, crossed olive branches. (J.M.L./V. D.s., S.M., S.Y.S.L.,Ve, A.P., s.r.a., Sea, P.G., S., S.M., E.) **Countermark:** J.M.L./S.M. **Note:** Countermark on Zacatecas KM#190.

CM Date	Host Date	Good	VG	F	VF	XF
ND	1811	—	—	—	—	—

KM# 262.9   8 REALES
Silver **Issuer:** Jose Maria Liceaga, J.M.L. with banner on cross, crossed olive branches. (J.M.L./V. D.s., S.M., S.Y.S.L.,Ve, A.P., s.r.a., Sea, P.G., S., S.M., E.) **Countermark:** J.M.L./S.F. **Note:** Countermark on Zacatecas KM#190.

CM Date	Host Date	Good	VG	F	VF	XF
ND	1811	—	—	—	—	—

WAR OF INDEPENDENCE

KM# 262.11   8 REALES
Silver   **Issuer:** Jose Maria Liceaga, J.M.L. with
banner on cross, crossed olive branches. (J.M.L./V.
D.s., S.M., S.Y.S.L.,Ve, A.P., s.r.a., Sea, P.G., S.,
S.M., E.) **Countermark:** J.M.L./V.E. **Note:**
Countermark on Zacatecas KM#190.

CM Date	Host Date	Good	VG	F	VF	XF
ND	1811	—	—	—	—	—

KM# 262.8   8 REALES
Silver   **Issuer:** Jose Maria Liceaga

, J.M.L. with banner on cross, crossed olive branches.
(J.M.L./V. D.s., S.M., S.Y.S.L.,Ve, A.P., s.r.a., Sea,
P.G., S., S.M., E.) **Countermark:** J.M.L./E **Note:**
Countermark on Zacatecas KM#190.

CM Date	Host Date	Good	VG	F	VF	XF
ND	1811	—	—	—	—	—

L.V.S. - LABOR
VINCIT SEMPER

Some authorities believe L.V.S. is for La Villa de
Sombrerete.

KM# 264.1   8 REALES
Cast Silver   **Issuer:** Labor Vincit Semper, Some
authorities believe L.V.S. is for "La Villa de
Sombrerete" **Countermark:** L.V.S. **Note:**
Countermark on Chihuahua KM#123.

CM Date	Host Date	Good	VG	F	VF	XF
ND	1811 RP	350	450	575	750	—
ND	1812 RP	250	325	375	500	—

KM# 264.2   8 REALES
Silver   **Issuer:** Labor Vincit Semper, Some
authorities believe L.V.S. is for "La Villa de
Sombrerete" **Countermark:** L.V.S. **Note:**
Countermark on Chihuahua KM#111.1 overstruck on
KM#123.

CM Date	Host Date	Good	VG	F	VF	XF
ND	1816 RP	325	375	400	525	—
ND	1817 RP	325	375	400	525	—
ND	1818 RP	325	375	400	525	—

CM Date	Host Date	Good	VG	F	VF	XF
ND	1819 RP	500	575	625	875	—
ND	1820 RP	575	625	700	450	—

KM# 264.3   8 REALES
Silver   **Issuer:** Labor Vincit Semper, Some
authorities believe L.V.S. is for "La Villa de
Sombrerete" **Countermark:** L.V.S. **Note:**
Countermark on Guadalajara KM#111.3.

CM Date	Host Date	Good	VG	F	VF	XF
ND	1817	230	275	325	450	—

KM# 264.4   8 REALES
Silver   **Issuer:** Labor Vincit Semper, Some
authorities believe L.V.S. is for "La Villa de
Sombrerete" **Countermark:** L.V.S. **Note:**
Countermark on Nueva Vizcaya KM#165.

CM Date	Host Date	Good	VG	F	VF	XF
ND	1811 RM	1,250	3,450	5,800	9,100	—

KM# 264.5   8 REALES
Silver   **Issuer:** Labor Vincit Semper, Some
authorities believe L.V.S. is for "La Villa de
Sombrerete" **Countermark:** L.V.S. **Note:**
Countermark on Sombrerete KM#177.

CM Date	Host Date	Good	VG	F	VF	XF
ND	1811	375	450	575	825	—
ND	1812	375	450	575	825	—

KM# 264.6   8 REALES
Silver   **Issuer:** Labor Vincit Semper, Some
authorities believe L.V.S. is for "La Villa de
Sombrerete" **Countermark:** L.V.S. **Note:**
Countermark on Zacatecas KM#190.

CM Date	Host Date	Good	VG	F	VF	XF
ND	1811	450	500	575	825	—

KM# 264.7   8 REALES
Silver   **Issuer:** Labor Vincit Semper, Some
authorities believe L.V.S. is for "La Villa de
Sombrerete" **Countermark:** L.V.S. **Note:**
Countermark on Zacatecas KM#192.

CM Date	Host Date	Good	VG	F	VF	XF
ND	1813	450	500	575	825	—

MORELOS

Morelos monogram

Type A: Stars above and
below monogram in circle.

Type B: Dots above and below monogram in oval.

Type C: Monogram in rectangle.

Note: Many specimens of Type C available in todays market are considered spurious.

KM# A265 2 REALES
Copper Issuer: Morelos Countermark: Type A stars above and below monogram in circle Note: Countermark on Oaxaca Sud, KM#226.1.

CM Date	Host Date	Good	VG	F	VF	XF
ND	1812	—	—	—	—	—

KM# A267 8 REALES
Silver Note: Countermark Type C on Zacatecas KM#190.

CM Date	Host Date	Good	VG	F	VF	XF
ND	1811	375	450	575	950	—

KM# 265.1 8 REALES
Silver Issuer: Morelos Countermark: Type A star

above and below monogram in circle Note: Countermark on Mexico City KM#109.

CM Date	Host Date	Good	VG	F	VF	XF
ND	1797 FM	55.00	65.00	75.00	120	—
ND	1798 FM	55.00	65.00	75.00	120	—
ND	1800 FM	55.00	65.00	75.00	120	—
ND	1807 TH	55.00	65.00	75.00	120	—

KM# 265.2 8 REALES
Silver Issuer: Morelos Countermark: Type A stars above and below monogram in circle Note: Countermark on Mexico City KM#110.

CM Date	Host Date	Good	VG	F	VF	XF
ND	1809 TH	70.00	95.00	150	250	—
ND	1811 HJ	70.00	95.00	150	250	—

KM# 265.3 8 REALES
Silver Issuer: Morelos Countermark: Type A stars above and below monogram in circle Note: Countermark on Mexico City KM#111.

CM Date	Host Date	Good	VG	F	VF	XF
ND	1812 JJ	65.00	75.00	95.00	155	—

KM# 265.5 8 REALES
Cast Silver Issuer: Morelos Countermark: Type A stars above and below monogram in circle Note: Countermark on Supreme National Congress KM#206.

CM Date	Host Date	Good	VG	F	VF	XF
ND	1811	250	325	475	750	—

KM# 266.1 8 REALES
Silver Issuer: Morelos Countermark: Type B dots above and below monogram in oval Note: Countermark on Guatamala 8 Reales, C#67.

CM Date	Host Date	Good	VG	F	VF	XF
ND	1810 M Rare	—	—	—	—	—

WAR OF INDEPENDENCE

KM# 266.2   8 REALES

Silver **Issuer:** Morelos **Countermark:** Type B dots above and below monogram in oval **Note:** Countermark on Mexico City KM#110.

CM Date	Host Date	Good	VG	F	VF	XF
ND	1809 TH	55.00	70.00	80.00	125	—

KM# 267.1   8 REALES

Silver **Issuer:** Morelos **Countermark:** Type C monogram in rectangle **Note:** Countermark on Zacatecas KM#189. Many specimens of Type C available in today's market are considered spurious.

CM Date	Host Date	Good	VG	F	VF	XF
ND	1811	375	450	575	950	—

KM# 265.4   8 REALES

Copper **Issuer:** Morelos **Countermark:** Type A stars above and below monogram in circle **Note:** Countermark on Oaxaca Sud KM#233.2.

CM Date	Host Date	Good	VG	F	VF	XF
ND	1812	25.00	35.75	48.75	80.00	—
ND	1813	25.00	35.75	48.75	80.00	—
ND	1814	25.00	35.75	48.75	80.00	—

KM# 265.6   8 REALES

Silver **Issuer:** Morelos **Countermark:** Type A stars above and below monogram in circle **Note:** Countermark on Zacatecas KM#190.

CM Date	Host Date	Good	VG	F	VF	XF
ND	1811	450	750	1,100	—	—

KM# 265.7   8 REALES

Silver **Issuer:** Morelos **Countermark:** Type A stars above and below monogram in circle **Note:** Countermark on Zacatecas KM#191.

CM Date	Host Date	Good	VG	F	VF	XF
ND	1811	240	300	450	725	—

KM# 267.2   8 REALES

Silver **Issuer:** Morelos **Countermark:** Type C: monogram in rectangle **Note:** Countermark Type C on Zacatecas KM#190. Many specimens of Type C available in today's market are considered spurious.

CM Date	Host Date	Good	VG	F	VF	XF
ND	1811	375	450	575	950	—

NORTE

Issued by the Supreme National Congress and the Army of the North.

Countermark: Eagle on cactus; star to left; NORTE below.

KM# 268   1/2 REAL

Silver **Issuer:** Supreme National Congress and the Army of the North **Countermark:** Eagle on cactus; star to left; NORTE below **Note:** Countermark on Zacatecas KM#180.

CM Date	Host Date	Good	VG	F	VF	XF
ND	1811	275	325	425	550	—

KM# 269   2 REALES

Silver **Issuer:** Supreme National Congress and the Army of the North **Countermark:** Eagle on cactus; star to left; NORTE below **Note:** Countermark on Zacatecas KM#187.

CM Date	Host Date	Good	VG	F	VF	XF
ND	1811	250	300	350	500	—

KM# A269   2 REALES

Silver **Issuer:** Supreme National Congress and the Army of the North **Countermark:** Eagle on cactus; star to left; NORTE below **Note:** Countermark on Zacatecas KM#188.

CM Date	Host Date	Good	VG	F	VF	XF
ND	1812	—	—	—	—	—

KM# B269   4 REALES

Silver **Issuer:** Supreme National Congress and the Army of the North **Countermark:** Eagle on cactus; star to left; NORTE below **Note:** Countermark on Sombrerete KM#175.

CM Date	Host Date	Good	VG	F	VF	XF
ND	1812	110	165	220	325	—

WAR OF INDEPENDENCE

KM# 270.4 8 REALES
Silver **Issuer:** Supreme National Congress and the Army of the North **Countermark:** Eagle on cactus; star to left; NORTE below **Note:** Countermark on Zacatecas KM#191.

CM Date	Host Date	Good	VG	F	VF	XF
ND	1811	220	325	450	600	—
ND	1811	220	325	450	600	—
ND	1812	220	325	450	600	—

KM# 270.1 8 REALES
Silver **Issuer:** Supreme National Congress and the Army of the North **Countermark:** Eagle on cactus; star to left; NORTE below **Note:** Countermark on Chihuahua KM#111.1.

CM Date	Host Date	Good	VG	F	VF	XF
ND	1813 RP	275	375	500	600	—

KM# 270.3 8 REALES
Silver **Issuer:** Supreme National Congress and the Army of the North **Countermark:** Eagle on cactus; star to left; NORTE below **Note:** Countermark on Zacatecas KM#190.

CM Date	Host Date	Good	VG	F	VF	XF
ND	1811	350	450	575	775	—

OSORNO

Countermark: Osorno monogram.
(Jose Francisco Osorno)

KM# 271.1 1/2 REAL
Silver **Issuer:** Jose Francisco Osorno **Countermark:** Osorno monogram **Note:** Countermark on Mexico City KM#72.

CM Date	Host Date	Good	VG	F	VF	XF
ND	1798 FM	80.00	120	180	270	—
ND	1802 FT	80.00	120	180	270	—
ND	1806	80.00	120	180	270	—

KM# 271.2 1/2 REAL
Silver **Issuer:** Jose Francisco Osorno **Countermark:** Osorno monogram **Note:** Countermark on Mexico City KM#73.

CM Date	Host Date	Good	VG	F	VF	XF
ND	1809 TH	80.00	120	180	270	—

KM# 270.2 8 REALES
Silver **Issuer:** Supreme National Congress and the Army of the North **Countermark:** Eagle on cactus; star to left; NORTE below **Note:** Countermark on Guanajuato KM#111.4.

CM Date	Host Date	Good	VG	F	VF	XF
ND	1813 JM	450	625	800	975	—

KM# 272.1 REAL
Silver **Issuer:** Jose Francisco Osorno **Countermark:** Osorno monogram **Note:** Countermark on Mexico City KM#81.

CM Date	Host Date	Good	VG	F	VF	XF
ND	1803 FT	80.00	120	180	300	—

WAR OF INDEPENDENCE

KM# 272.2   REAL
Silver **Issuer:** Jose Francisco Osorno
Countermark: Osorno monogram **Note:**
Countermark on Potosi KM#70.

CM Date	Host Date	Good	VG	F	VF	XF
ND	ND	90.00	140	210	325	—

KM# 272.3   REAL
Silver **Issuer:** Jose Francisco Osorno
Countermark: Osorno monogram **Note:**
Countermark on Guatemala KM#54.

CM Date	Host Date	Good	VG	F	VF	XF
ND	1804	90.00	140	210	325	—

KM# A272.1   2 REALES
Silver **Issuer:** Jose Francisco Osorno
Countermark: Osorno monogram **Note:**
Countermark on Mexico City KM#88.2.

CM Date	Host Date	Good	VG	F	VF	XF
ND	1788 FM	90.00	150	210	325	—

KM# A272.2   2 REALES
Silver **Issuer:** Jose Francisco Osorno
Countermark: Osorno monogram **Note:**
Countermark on Mexico City KM#91.

CM Date	Host Date	Good	VG	F	VF	XF
ND	1808 TH	90.00	150	210	325	—

KM# A272.3   2 REALES
Silver **Issuer:** Jose Francisco Osorno
Countermark: Osorno monogram **Note:**
Countermark on Mexico City KM#92.

CM Date	Host Date	Good	VG	F	VF	XF
ND	1809 TH	90.00	150	210	325	—

KM# A272.4   2 REALES
Silver **Issuer:** Jose Francisco Osorno
Countermark: Osorno monogram **Note:**
Countermark on Zacatlian KM#252.

CM Date	Host Date	Good	VG	F	VF	XF
ND	1813	180	240	425	600	—

KM# 273.1   4 REALES
Silver **Issuer:** Jose Francisco Osorno
Countermark: Osorno monogram **Note:**
Countermark on Mexico City KM#97.2.

CM Date	Host Date	Good	VG	F	VF	XF
ND	1782 FF	100	180	240	350	—

KM# 273.2   4 REALES
Silver **Issuer:** Jose Francisco Osorno
Countermark: Osorno monogram **Note:**
Countermark on Mexico City KM#100.

CM Date	Host Date	Good	VG	F	VF	XF
ND	1799 FM	100	180	240	350	—

KM# 274.1   8 REALES
Silver **Issuer:** Jose Francisco Osorno
Countermark: Osorno monogram **Note:**
Countermark on Lima 8 Reales, C#101.

CM Date	Host Date	Good	VG	F	VF	XF
ND	1811 JP	240	270	300	425	—

WAR OF INDEPENDENCE

KM# 274.2 8 REALES
Silver **Issuer:** Jose Francisco Osorno
Countermark: Osorno monogram **Note:**
Countermark on Mexico City KM#110.

CM Date	Host Date	Good	VG	F	VF	XF
ND	1809 TH	150	180	270	450	—
ND	1810 HJ	150	180	270	450	—
ND	1811 HJ	150	180	270	450	—

VILLA / GRAN

(Julian Villagran)

KM# 298 2 REALES
Cast Silver , Julian Villagran **Countermark:** VILLA/
GRAN **Note:** Countermark on cast Mexico City
KM#91.

CM Date	Host Date	Good	VG	F	VF	XF
ND	1799 FM	180	240	300	425	—
ND	1802 FT	180	240	300	425	—

KM# 275 8 REALES
Cast Silver **Issuer:** Julian Villagran **Countermark:**

VILLA/GRAN Note: Countermark on cast Mexico
City KM#109.

CM Date	Host Date	Good	VG	F	VF	XF
ND	1796 FM	240	300	425	600	—
ND	1806 TH	240	300	425	600	—

ZMY

KM# 286 8 REALES
Silver **Issuer:** Unknown, presumed insurgent
Countermark: ZMY **Note:** Countermark on
Zacatecas KM#191.

CM Date	Host Date	Good	VG	F	VF	XF
ND	1812	120	180	240	425	—

COUNTERMARKED COINAGE

KM# 270.6 8 REALES
Silver **Issuer:** Issued by the Supreme National
Congress and the Army of the North **Countermark:**
Eagle on cactus; star to left; NORTE below. **Note:**
Countermark on Sombrerete KM# 177.

CM Date	Host Date	Good	VG	F	VF	XF
ND	1812	1,250	1,600	2,000	—	—

KM# 263.4 8 REALES
Silver **Issuer:** Don Jose Maria De Linares
Countermark: LINA/RES * **Note:** Countermark on
Zacatecas KM#190.

CM Date	Host Date	Good	VG	F	VF	XF
ND	1811	—	—	—	—	—

KM# 263.5 8 REALES
Silver **Issuer:** Don Jose Maria De Linares
Countermark: LINA/RES* **Note:** Countermark on
Zacatecas KM#192.

CM Date	Host Date	Good	VG	F	VF	XF
ND	1812	—	—	—	—	—

KM# 270.5 8 REALES
Silver **Issuer:** Norte, Issued by the Supreme
National Congress and the Army of the North
Countermark: Eagle on cactus; star to left; NORTE
below **Note:** Countermark on Zacatecas KM#190.

CM Date	Host Date	Good	VG	F	VF	XF
ND	1811	—	—	—	—	—

WAR OF INDEPENDENCE

KM# 265.8   8 REALES
Silver **Issuer:** Morelos, Type A: Stars above and below monogram in circle. Type B: Dots above and below monogram in oval. Type C: Monogram in rectangle. Many specimens of Type C available in today's market are considered spurious. **Countermark:** Type A **Note:** Countermark on Zacatecas KM#190.

CM Date	Host Date	Good	VG	F	VF	XF
ND	1811	—	—	—	—	—

KM# 264.8   8 REALES
Cast Silver **Issuer:** Labor Vincit Semper, L.V.S.; Some authorities believe L.V.S. is for "La Villa de Sombrerete" **Countermark:** L.V.S. **Note:** Countermark on Zacatecas KM#190.

CM Date	Host Date	Good	VG	F	VF	XF
ND	1811	—	—	—	—	—

MULTIPLE COUNTERMARKS

Many combinations of Royalist and Insurgent countermarks are usually found on the cast copies produced by Chihuahua and Mexico City and on the other crude provisional issues of this period. Struck Mexico City coins were used to make molds for casting necessity issues and countermarked afterwards to show issuing authority. Some were marked again by either both or separate opposing friendly forces to authorize circulation in their areas of occupation. Some countermarks are only obtainable with companion markings.

KM# 289   2 REALES
Silver **Issuer:** C.M.S. and S.C.M. **Countermark:** C.M.S. (Comandancia Militar Suriana) and eagle with S.C.M. (Soberano Congreso Mexicano) **Note:** Countermark on Mexico City KM#91.

CM Date	Host Date	Good	VG	F	VF	XF
ND	ND	—	—	—	—	—

KM# 295   2 REALES
Silver **Issuer:** Militar del Sur and Soberano Congreso Mexicano **Countermark:** M.d.S. and eagle with S.C.M **Note:** Countermark on Mexico City KM#91.

CM Date	Host Date	Good	VG	F	VF	XF
ND	ND	—	180	300	550	—

KM# 296   2 REALES
Silver **Issuer:** Jose Francisco Osorno and Julian Villagran **Countermark:** Osorno monogram and VILLA/GRAN **Note:** Countermark on cast Mexico City KM#110.

CM Date	Host Date	Good	VG	F	VF	XF
ND	1809 TH	—	—	—	—	—

KM# A286   2 REALES
Silver **Issuer:** Jose Maria Liceaga and VTIL **Countermark:** J.M.L./D.S. AND VTIL **Note:** Countermark on Zacatecas KM#186.

CM Date	Host Date	Good	VG	F	VF	XF
ND	1811	90.00	150	210	325	—

KM# B286   2 REALES
Silver **Issuer:** Jose Maria Liceaga and VTIL **Countermark:** J.M.L./V.E. and VTIL **Note:** Countermark on Zacatecas KM#186.

CM Date	Host Date	Good	VG	F	VF	XF
ND	1810	90.00	150	210	325	—
ND	1811	90.00	150	210	325	—

KM# 285.2   8 REALES
Silver **Issuer:** Chilpanzingo and Morelos **Countermark:** Chilpanzingo Type A and Morelos monogram Type A **Note:** Countermark on cast Mexico City KM#110.

CM Date	Host Date	Good	VG	F	VF	XF
ND	1810 HJ	42.00	55.00	70.00	180	—
ND	1811 HJ	42.00	55.00	70.00	180	—

KM# C286   8 REALES
Silver **Issuer:** Chilpanzingo and Morelos and LVS

Countermark: Chilpanzingo Type A, Morelos Type A and LVS monogram on cast Mexico City KM#110

CM Date	Host Date	Good	VG	F	VF	XF
ND	1809 HJ	60.00	90.00	150	400	—

KM# A298   8 REALES
Silver **Issuer:** S.J.N.G. and VTIL **Countermark:** S.J.N.G and VTIL on Zacatecas KM#191

CM Date	Host Date	Good	VG	F	VF	XF
ND	ND	42.00	60.00	90.00	240	—

KM# A297   8 REALES
Silver **Issuer:** Chilpanzingo and ENSAIE **Countermark:** Chilpanzingo Type B and ENSAIE **Note:** Countermark on Zacatecas KM#189.

CM Date	Host Date	Good	VG	F	VF	XF
ND	ND	210	300	425	—	—

KM# 297   8 REALES
Silver **Issuer:** Chilpanzingo and LVA **Countermark:** Chilpanzingo Type A and LVA **Note:** Countermark on Mexico City KM#109.

CM Date	Host Date	Good	VG	F	VF	XF
ND	1805 TH	55.00	90.00	175	350	—

KM# 288.2   8 REALES
Silver **Issuer:** Chilpanzingo and Suprema Junta Nacional Gubernativa **Countermark:** Chilpanzingo Type B **Note:** Countermark on Zacatecas KM#190. Prev. KM#288.

CM Date	Host Date	Good	VG	F	VF	XF
ND	1811	—	—	—	—	—

KM# 290.2   8 REALES
Silver **Issuer:** ENSAIE and VTIL **Countermark:** ENSAIE and VTIL **Note:** Countermark on Zacatecas KM#190. Prev. KM#290.

CM Date	Host Date	Good	VG	F	VF	XF
ND	1811	125	220	350	475	—

KM# 281   8 REALES
Silver **Issuer:** Chilpanzingo and LVS **Countermark:** Chilpanzingo Type A and script LVS **Note:** Countermark on cast Mexico City KM#110.

CM Date	Host Date	Good	VG	F	VF	XF
ND	1809 HJ	55.00	80.00	160	350	—

KM# 291   8 REALES
Silver **Issuer:** Jose Maria Liceaga and VTIL **Countermark:** J.M.L./D.S. and VTIL **Note:** Countermark on Mexico City KM#110.

CM Date	Host Date	Good	VG	F	VF	XF
ND	1810 HJ	105	190	325	575	—

KM# 282   8 REALES
Silver **Issuer:** La Comandancia Militar and Morelos **Countermark:** L.C.M and Morelos monogram Type A **Note:** Countermark on cast Mexico City KM#109.

CM Date	Host Date	Good	VG	F	VF	XF
ND	1792 FM	—	—	—	—	—

WAR OF INDEPENDENCE

KM# 283 8 REALES
Silver **Issuer:** Morelos and Morelos **Countermark:** Morelos Type A and C **Note:** Countermark on cast Mexico City KM#109.

CM Date	Host Date	Good	VG	F	VF	XF
ND	1806 TH	—	—	—	—	—

KM# 284 8 REALES
Silver **Issuer:** Chilpanzingo and Morelos **Countermark:** Chilpanzingo Type A and Morelos monogram Type A **Note:** Countermark on cast Mexico City KM#109.

CM Date	Host Date	Good	VG	F	VF	XF
ND	1806 TH	43.75	65.00	125	280	—
ND	1807 TH	43.75	65.00	125	280	—

KM# 285.1 8 REALES
Silver **Issuer:** Chilpanzingo and Morelos **Countermark:** Chilpanzingo Type A and Morelos monogram Type A **Note:** Countermark on struck Mexico City KM#110.

CM Date	Host Date	Good	VG	F	VF	XF
ND	1809 TH	55.00	80.00	170	375	—

KM# 285.3 8 REALES
Silver **Issuer:** Chilpanzingo and Morelos **Countermark:** Chilpanzingo Type A and Morelos monogram Type A **Note:** Countermark on cast Mexico City KM#111.

CM Date	Host Date	Good	VG	F	VF	XF
ND	1811 HJ	95.00	150	220	450	—

KM# A290 8 REALES
Silver **Issuer:** ENSAIE and Jose Maria Liceaga **Countermark:** ENSAIE and J.M.L. **Note:** Countermark on Zacatecas KM#190.

CM Date	Host Date	Good	VG	F	VF	XF
ND	1811	125	220	350	600	—

KM# 294 8 REALES
Silver **Issuer:** L.V.A. and Morelos **Countermark:** Script LVA and Morelos monogram Type A **Note:** Countermark on cast Mexico City KM#110.

CM Date	Host Date	Good	VG	F	VF	XF
ND	ND HJ	55.00	95.00	170	375	—

KM# 288.1 8 REALES
Silver **Issuer:** Chilpanzingo and Suprema Junta Nacional Gubernativa **Countermark:** Chilpanzingo Type B and S.J.N.G **Note:** Countermark on Zacatecas KM#189.

CM Date	Host Date	Good	VG	F	VF	XF
ND	1811	—	—	—	—	—

KM# 290.1 8 REALES
Silver **Issuer:** ENSAIE and VTIL **Countermark:** ENSAIE and VTIL **Note:** Countermark on Zacatecas KM#189.

CM Date	Host Date	Good	VG	F	VF	XF
ND	1811	125	220	350	600	—

KM# 280.1 8 REALES
Silver **Issuer:** Chilpanzingo and Crown and flag **Countermark:** Chilpanzingo Type B and Crown and flag **Note:** Countermark on Zacatecas KM#189.

CM Date	Host Date	Good	VG	F	VF	XF
ND	1811	—	—	—	—	—

KM# 280.2 8 REALES
Silver **Issuer:** Chilpanzingo and crown and flag **Countermark:** Chilpanzingo Type B and crown and flag **Note:** Countermark on Zacatecas KM#190.

CM Date	Host Date	Good	VG	F	VF	XF
ND	1811	—	—	—	—	—

WAR OF INDEPENDENCE

KM# 287 8 REALES
Silver **Issuer:** Chilpanzingo - Provisional De Valladolid **Countermark:** Chilpanzingo Type B and P.D.V **Note:** Countermark on Valladolid KM#178.

CM Date	Host Date	Good	VG	F	VF	XF
ND	1813	—	—	—	—	—

ZACATECAS

The city of Zacatecas, in a rich mining region has provided silver for the world since mid-1500. On November 14, 1810 a mint began production for the Royalist cause. Zacatecas was the most prolific during the War of Independence. Four of the 5 standard silver denominations were made here, 4 Reales were not. The first, a local type showing mountains of silver on the coins were made only in 1810 and 1811. Some 1811 coins were made by the Insurgents who took the city on April 15, 1811, later retaken by the Royalists on May 21, 1811. Zacatecas struck the standard Ferdinand VII bust type until 1822.

Mint marks: Z, ZS, Zs.

ROYALIST COINAGE

KM# 180 1/2 REAL
0.9030 Silver **Ruler:** Ferdinand VII **Obv:** Crowned shield flanked by pillars **Obv. Legend:** FERDIN • VII... **Rev:** Mountain within beaded circle **Mint:** Zacatecas **Note:** Mint marks: Z, ZS, Zs.

Date	Mintage	Good	VG	F	VF	XF
1810	—	90.00	150	240	475	—
1811	—	36.00	60.00	110	240	—

Note: Date aligned with legend

KM# 181 1/2 REAL
0.9030 Silver **Ruler:** Ferdinand VII **Obv:** Crowned shield flanked by pillars **Rev:** Mountain within beaded circle **Rev. Legend:** MONEDA PROVISIONAL DE ZACATECAS **Mint:** Zacatecas **Note:** Mint marks: Z, ZS, Zs.

Date	Mintage	Good	VG	F	VF	XF
1811	—	36.00	60.00	110	240	—

KM# 182 1/2 REAL
0.9030 Silver **Ruler:** Ferdinand VII **Obv:** Provincial bust right **Obv. Legend:** FERDIN • VII **Rev:** Crowned shield flanked by pillars **Rev. Legend:** MONEDA PROVISIONAL DE ZACATECAS **Mint:** Zacatecas **Note:** Mint marks: Z, ZS, Zs.

Date	Mintage	Good	VG	F	VF	XF
1811	—	36.00	48.00	80.00	170	—
1812	—	30.00	42.00	70.00	150	—

KM# 73.1 1/2 REAL
1.6900 g., 0.9030 Silver 0.0491 oz. ASW **Ruler:** Ferdinand VII **Obv:** Armored laureate bust right **Obv. Legend:** FERDIN • VII... **Rev:** Crowned shield flanked by pillars **Rev. Legend:** IND... **Mint:** Zacatecas **Note:** Mint marks: Z, ZS, Zs.

Date	Mintage	Good	VG	F	VF	XF
1813 AG	—	25.00	48.00	70.00	130	—
1813 FP	—	30.00	55.00	100	220	—
1814 AG	—	18.00	36.00	70.00	130	—
1815 AG	—	15.00	30.00	48.00	85.00	—
1816 AG	—	12.00	18.00	30.00	65.00	—
1817 AG	—	12.00	18.00	30.00	65.00	—
1818 AG	—	12.00	18.00	30.00	65.00	—
1819 AG	—	12.00	18.00	30.00	65.00	—

KM# 74.3 1/2 REAL
1.6900 g., 0.9030 Silver 0.0491 oz. ASW **Ruler:** Ferdinand VII **Obv:** Draped laureate bust right **Obv. Legend:** FERDIN • VII... **Rev:** Crowned shield flanked by pillars **Rev. Legend:** IND... **Mint:** Zacatecas **Note:** Mint marks: Z, ZS, Zs.

Date	Mintage	VG	F	VF	XF	Unc
1819 AG	—	10.00	14.00	30.00	60.00	—
1820 AG	—	10.00	14.00	30.00	60.00	—
1820 RG	—	6.00	12.00	25.00	55.00	—
1821 AG	—	180	300	550	1,000	—
1821 RG	—	6.00	12.00	25.00	55.00	—

KM# 183 REAL
0.9030 Silver **Ruler:** Ferdinand VII **Obv:** Crowned shield flanked by pillars **Rev:** Mountain within beaded circle **Mint:** Zacatecas **Note:** Mint marks: Z, ZS, Zs.

Date	Mintage	Good	VG	F	VF	XF
1810	—	120	180	350	600	—
1811	—	25.00	48.00	90.00	180	—

Note: Date aligned with legend

KM# 184 REAL
0.9030 Silver **Ruler:** Ferdinand VII **Obv:** Crowned shield flanked by pillars **Rev:** Mountain within beaded circle **Rev. Legend:** MONEDA PROVISIONAL DE ZACATECAS **Mint:** Zacatecas **Note:** Mint marks: Z, ZS, Zs.

Date	Mintage	Good	VG	F	VF	XF
1811	—	18.00	36.00	70.00	160	—

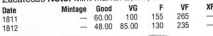

KM# 185 REAL
0.9030 Silver **Ruler:** Ferdinand VII **Obv:** Provincial bust right **Obv. Legend:** FERDIN • VII... **Rev:** Crowned shield flanked by pillars **Rev. Legend:** MONEDA PROVISIONAL DE ZACATECAS **Mint:** Zacatecas **Note:** Mint marks: Z, ZS, Zs.

Date	Mintage	Good	VG	F	VF	XF
1811	—	60.00	100	155	265	—
1812	—	48.00	85.00	130	235	—

KM# 82.1 REAL
3.3800 g., 0.9030 Silver 0.0981 oz. ASW **Ruler:** Ferdinand VII **Obv:** Armored laureate bust right **Obv. Legend:** FERDIN • VII... **Rev:** Crowned shield flanked by pillars **Rev. Legend:** IND • REX... **Mint:** Zacatecas **Note:** Mint marks: Z, ZS, Zs.

Date	Mintage	Good	VG	F	VF	XF
1813 FP	—	60.00	120	180	300	—
1814 AG	—	25.00	42.00	60.00	100	—
1814 FP	—	25.00	42.00	60.00	100	—
1815 AG	—	25.00	42.00	60.00	100	—
1816 AG	—	14.00	25.00	36.00	80.00	—
1817 AG	—	10.00	15.00	25.00	55.00	—
1818 AG	—	10.00	15.00	25.00	55.00	—
1819 AG	—	7.00	13.00	22.50	42.00	—

KM# 83.3 REAL
3.3800 g., 0.9030 Silver 0.0981 oz. ASW **Ruler:** Ferdinand VII **Obv:** Draped laureate bust right **Obv. Legend:** FERDIN • VII... **Rev:** Crowned shield flanked by pillars **Rev. Legend:** REX • Z... **Mint:** Zacatecas **Note:** Mint marks: Z, ZS, Zs.

Date	Mintage	VG	F	VF	XF	Unc
1820 AG	—	7.00	14.00	25.00	70.00	—
1820 RG	—	7.00	14.00	25.00	70.00	—
1821 AG	—	22.50	36.00	55.00	110	—
1821 AZ	—	14.00	25.00	48.00	100	—
1821 RG	—	8.00	15.00	30.00	80.00	—
1822 AZ	—	8.00	15.00	30.00	80.00	—
1822 RG	—	22.50	36.00	55.00	110	—

KM# 186 2 REALES
0.9030 Silver **Ruler:** Ferdinand VII **Obv:** Crowned shield flanked by pillars **Obv. Legend:** FERDIN • VII... **Rev:** Mountain within beaded circle **Rev. Legend:** MONEDA • PROVISION... **Mint:** Zacatecas **Note:** Mint marks: Z, ZS, Zs.

Date	Mintage	Good	VG	F	VF	XF
1810 Rare	—	—	—	—	—	—
1811	—	36.00	60.00	100	175	—

Note: Date aligned with legend

KM# 187 2 REALES
0.9030 Silver **Ruler:** Ferdinand VII **Obv:** Crowned shield flanked by pillars **Rev:** Mountain above L. V. O within beaded circle **Rev. Legend:** MONEDA PROVISIONAL DE ZACATECAS **Mint:** Zacatecas **Note:** Mint marks: Z, ZS, Zs.

Date	Mintage	Good	VG	F	VF	XF
1811	—	22.50	43.25	85.00	145	—

KM# 188 2 REALES
0.9030 Silver **Ruler:** Ferdinand VII **Obv:** Armored bust right **Obv. Legend:** FERDIN • VII... **Rev:** Crowned shield flanked by pillars **Rev. Legend:** MONEDA PROVISIONAL DE ZACATECAS **Mint:** Zacatecas **Note:** Mint marks: Z, ZS, Zs.

Date	Mintage	Good	VG	F	VF	XF
1811	—	46.25	85.00	180	300	—
1812	—	39.50	80.00	170	265	—

KM# 92.1 2 REALES
6.7700 g., 0.9030 Silver 0.1965 oz. ASW **Ruler:** Ferdinand VII **Obv:** Large armored bust right **Obv. Legend:** FERDIN • VII **Rev:** Crowned shield flanked by pillars **Rev. Inscription:** MONEDA • PROVISION... **Mint:** Zacatecas **Note:** Mint marks: Z, ZS, Zs.

Date	Mintage	Good	VG	F	VF	XF
1813 FP	—	42.00	60.00	90.00	150	—
1814 FP	—	42.00	60.00	90.00	150	—
1814 AG	—	42.00	60.00	90.00	150	—
1815 AG	—	9.00	18.00	36.00	65.00	—

WAR OF INDEPENDENCE

Date	Mintage	Good	VG	F	VF	XF
1816 AG	—	9.00	18.00	36.00	65.00	—
1817 AG	—	9.00	18.00	36.00	65.00	—
1818 AG	—	9.00	18.00	36.00	65.00	—

Date	Mintage	Good	VG	F	VF	XF
1810	—	350	600	900	1,500	—
1811	—	120	180	270	425	—

Note: Date aligned with legend. Also exists with incomplete date

KM# 93.4 2 REALES
6.7700 g., 0.9030 Silver 0.1965 oz. ASW **Ruler:**
Ferdinand VII **Obv:** Draped laureate bust right **Obv.
Legend:** FERDIN • VII **Rev:** Crowned shield flanked
by pillars **Rev. Legend:** IND • REX... **Mint:** Zacatecas
Note: Mint marks: Z, ZS, Zs.

Date	Mintage	VG	F	VF	XF	Unc
1818 AG	—	9.00	18.00	36.00	65.00	—
1819 AG	—	12.00	25.00	48.00	100	—
1819 AG	—	12.00	25.00	48.00	100	—

Note: Reversed 'S' in HISPAN

Date	Mintage	VG	F	VF	XF	Unc
1820 AG	—	12.00	25.00	48.00	100	—
1820 RG	—	12.00	25.00	48.00	100	—
1821 AG	—	12.00	25.00	48.00	100	—
1821 AZ/RG	—	12.00	25.00	48.00	100	—
1821 AZ	—	12.00	25.00	48.00	100	—
1821 RG	—	12.00	25.00	48.00	100	—
1822 AG	—	12.00	25.00	48.00	100	—
1822 RG	—	12.00	25.00	48.00	100	—

KM# A92 2 REALES
6.7700 g., 0.9030 Silver 0.1965 oz. ASW **Ruler:**
Ferdinand VII **Obv:** Small armored bust right **Obv.
Legend:** FERDIN • VII **Rev:** Crowned shield flanked
by pillars **Rev. Legend:** IND • REX... **Mint:** Zacatecas
Note: Mint marks: Z, ZS, Zs.

Date	Mintage	Good	VG	F	VF	XF
1819 AG	—	55.00	120	240	475	—

KM# 190 8 REALES
0.9030 Silver **Ruler:** Ferdinand VII **Obv:** Crowned
shield flanked by pillars **Obv. Legend:** FERDIN • VII
• DEI... **Rev:** Mountain above L. V. O within beaded
circle **Rev. Legend:** MONEDA PROVISIONAL DE
ZACATECAS **Mint:** Zacatecas

Date	Mintage	Good	VG	F	VF	XF
1811	—	80.00	120	160	425	775

Note: Date aligned with legend

Date	Mintage	Good	VG	F	VF	XF
1811 Error	—	—	—	—	3,600	6,000

FERDIN • VI

KM# 189 8 REALES
0.9030 Silver **Ruler:** Ferdinand VII **Obv:** Crowned
shield flanked by pillars **Rev:** Mountain above L.V.O.
within beaded circle **Rev. Legend:**
MONEDA.PROVISION... **Mint:** Zacatecas **Note:**
Mint Zacatecas.

KM# 191 8 REALES
0.9030 Silver **Ruler:** Ferdinand VII **Obv:** Armored
bust right **Obv. Legend:** FERDIN • VII • 8 • R • DEI...
Rev: Crowned shield flanked by pillars **Rev. Legend:**
MONEDA PROVISIONAL DE ZACATECAS **Mint:**
Zacatecas

Date	Mintage	Good	VG	F	VF	XF
1811	—	55.00	90.00	175	325	—
1812	—	60.00	100	190	350	—

KM# 192   8 REALES
0.9030 Silver   **Ruler:** Ferdinand VII **Obv:** Draped laureate bust right **Obv. Legend:** FERDIN • VII • DEI... **Rev:** Crowned shield flanked by pillars **Rev. Legend:** MONEDA PROVISIONAL DE ZACATECAS **Mint:** Zacatecas

Date	Mintage	Good	VG	F	VF	XF
1812	—	90.00	180	325	550	—

KM# 111.6   8 REALES
27.0700 g., 0.9030 Silver 0.7859 oz. ASW   **Ruler:** Ferdinand VII **Obv:** Draped laureate bust right **Obv. Legend:** FERDIN • VII • DEI • GRATIA **Rev:** Crowned shield flanked by pillars **Rev. Legend:** HISAV • ET IND • REX **Mint:** Zacatecas

Date	Mintage	VG	F	VF	XF	Unc
1821Zs	—	190	375	650	900	—

ROYALIST COUNTERMARKED COINAGE

LCM - LA COMANDANCIA MILITAR

Crown and Flag

This countermark exists in 15 various sizes.

KM# 193.1   2 REALES
0.9030 Silver   **Issuer:** La Comandancia Militar **Countermark:** LCM **Note:** Countermark on Mexico KM#92.

CM Date	Host Date	Good	VG	F	VF	XF
ND	1809 TH	100	200	300	550	—

KM# 111.5   8 REALES
27.0700 g., 0.9030 Silver 0.7859 oz. ASW   **Ruler:** Ferdinand VII **Obv:** Draped laureate bust right **Obv. Legend:** FERDIN • VII • DEI • GRATIA **Rev:** Crowned shield flanked by pillars **Rev. Legend:** HISPAN • ET IND • REX **Mint:** Zacatecas **Note:** Mint mark: Zs. Several bust types exist for the 1821 issues.

Date	Mintage	VG	F	VF	XF	Unc
1813 FP	—	90.00	150	210	325	—
1814 FP	—	180	300	425	550	—
1814 AG	—	120	180	240	350	—
1814 AG	—	150	210	270	400	—
Note: D over horizontal D in IND						
1814 AG/FP	—	120	180	240	350	—
1815 AG	—	60.00	120	180	300	—
1816 AG	—	42.00	60.00	80.00	150	—
1817 AG	—	42.00	60.00	80.00	150	—
1818 AG	—	36.00	48.00	60.00	120	—
1819 AG	—	36.00	48.00	60.00	120	—
1819 AG 'GRATIA' error	—	120	240	350	475	—
1820 AG 18/11 error	—	120	240	350	475	—
1820 AG	—	36.00	48.00	60.00	120	600
1820 RG	—	36.00	48.00	60.00	120	—
1821/81 RG	—	90.00	180	270	350	—
1821 RG	—	18.00	30.00	42.00	80.00	—
1821 AZ/RG	—	60.00	120	180	240	—
1821 AZ	—	60.00	120	180	240	—
1822 RG	—	48.00	70.00	120	210	775

KM# 193.2   2 REALES
0.9030 Silver   **Issuer:** La Comandancia Militar, (The LCM countermark exists in 15 various sizes) **Countermark:** LCM **Note:** Countermark on Mexico KM#186.

CM Date	Host Date	Good	VG	F	VF	XF
ND	1811	100	200	300	550	—

WAR OF INDEPENDENCE

KM# 194.1 8 REALES
Cast Silver **Issuer:** La Comandancia Militar, (The LCM countermark exists in 15 various sizes) **Countermark:** LCM **Note:** Countermark on Chihuahua KM#123.

CM Date	Host Date	Good	VG	F	VF	XF
ND	1811 RP	120	240	350	600	—
ND	1812 RP	120	240	350	600	—

KM# 194.2 8 REALES
0.9030 Silver **Issuer:** La Comandancia Militar, The LCM countermark exists in 15 different sizes **Countermark:** LCM **Note:** Countermark on Chihuahua KM#111.1 struck over KM#123.

CM Date	Host Date	Good	VG	F	VF	XF
ND	1815 RP	240	325	475	725	—
ND	1817 RP	150	210	270	425	—
ND	1820 RP	150	210	270	425	—
ND	1821 RP	150	210	270	425	—

KM# 194.3 8 REALES
0.9030 Silver **Issuer:** La Comandancia Militar, The LCM countermark exists in 15 different sizes **Countermark:** LCM **Note:** Countermark on Durango KM#111.2.

CM Date	Host Date	Good	VG	F	VF	XF
ND	1812 RM	85.00	150	240	350	—
ND	1821 CG	85.00	150	240	350	—

KM# 194.4 8 REALES
0.9030 Silver **Issuer:** La Comandancia Militar, The LCM countermark exists in 15 different sizes **Countermark:** LCM **Note:** Countermark on Guadalajara KM#111.3.

CM Date	Host Date	Good	VG	F	VF	XF
ND	1813 MR	180	270	350	600	—

KM# 194.5 8 REALES
0.9030 Silver **Issuer:** La Comandancia Militar, The LCM countermark exists in 15 different sizes **Countermark:** LCM **Note:** Countermark on Guanajuato KM#111.4.

CM Date	Host Date	Good	VG	F	VF	XF
ND	1813 JJ	270	425	575	850	—

KM# 194.6 8 REALES
0.9030 Silver **Issuer:** La Comandancia Militar, The LCM countermark exists in 15 different sizes **Countermark:** LCM **Note:** Countermark on Nueva Viscaya KM#165.

CM Date	Host Date	Good	VG	F	VF	XF
ND	1811 RM Rare	—	—	—	—	—

KM# 194.7 8 REALES
0.9030 Silver **Issuer:** La Comandancia Militar, The LCM countermark exists in 15 different sizes **Countermark:** LCM **Note:** Countermark on Mexico KM#111.

CM Date	Host Date	Good	VG	F	VF	XF
ND	1811 HJ	150	270	425	775	—
ND	1812 JJ	130	160	240	425	—
ND	1817 JJ	60.00	80.00	100	210	—
ND	1818 JJ	60.00	80.00	100	210	—
ND	1820 JJ	—	—	—	—	—

WAR OF INDEPENDENCE

KM# 194.8   8 REALES
0.9030 Silver **Issuer:** La Comandancia Militar, The LCM countermark exists in 15 different sizes **Countermark:** LCM **Note:** Countermark on Sombrerete KM#176.

CM Date	Host Date	Good	VG	F	VF	XF
ND	1811 Rare	—	—	—	—	—
ND	1812 Rare	—	—	—	—	—

KM# 194.9   8 REALES
0.9030 Silver **Issuer:** La Comandancia Militar, The LCM countermark exists in 15 different sizes **Countermark:** LCM **Note:** Countermark on Zacatecas KM#190.

CM Date	Host Date	Good	VG	F	VF	XF
ND	1811	270	425	600	—	—

KM# 194.10   8 REALES
0.9030 Silver **Issuer:** La Comandancia Militar, The LCM countermark exists in 15 different sizes **Countermark:** LCM **Note:** Countermark on Zacatecas KM#111.5.

CM Date	Host Date	Good	VG	F	VF	XF
ND	1813 FP	—	—	—	—	—
ND	1814 AG	—	—	—	—	—
ND	1822 RG	—	—	—	—	—

LCV -
LAS CAJAS DE VERACRUZ

The Royal Treasury of the City of Veracruz

KM# 195   7 REALES
Silver **Issuer:** Las Cajas de Veracruz, The Royal Treasury of the City of Veracruz **Countermark:** LCV **Note:** Countermark and 7 on underweight 8 Reales.

CM Date	Host Date	Good	VG	F	VF	XF
ND	ND Rare	—	—	—	—	—

Note: Most examples are counterfeit

KM# 196   7-1/4 REALES
Silver **Issuer:** Las Cajas de Veracruz, The Royal Treasury of the City of Veracruz **Countermark:** LCV **Note:** Countermark and 7-1/4 on underweight 8 Reales.

CM Date	Host Date	Good	VG	F	VF	XF
ND	ND Rare	—	—	—	—	—

Note: Most examples are counterfeit

KM# 197   7-1/2 REALES
Silver **Issuer:** Las Cajas de Veracruz, The Royal Treasury of the City of Veracruz **Countermark:** LCV **Note:** Countermark and 7-1/2 on underweight 8 Reales.

CM Date	Host Date	Good	VG	F	VF	XF
ND	ND Rare	—	—	—	—	—

Note: Most examples are counterfeit

KM# 198   7-3/4 REALES
Silver **Issuer:** Las Cajas de Veracruz, The Royal Treasury of the City of Veracruz **Countermark:** LCV **Note:** Countermark and 7-3/4 on underweight 8 Reales.

CM Date	Host Date	Good	VG	F	VF	XF
ND	ND	350	450	550	850	—

Note: Many examples are counterfeit

KM# A198   8 REALES
Cast Silver **Issuer:** Las Cajas de Veracruz, The Royal Treasury of the City of Veracruz **Countermark:** LCV **Note:** Countermark on Chihuahua KM#123.

CM Date	Host Date	Good	VG	F	VF	XF
ND	1811 RP	180	300	475	725	—

WAR OF INDEPENDENCE

KM# 199   8 REALES
Silver **Issuer:** Las Cajas de Veracruz, The Royal Treasury of the City of Veracruz **Countermark:** LCV **Note:** Countermark on Zacatecas KM#191.

CM Date	Host Date	Good	VG	F	VF	XF
ND	1811	210	270	325	450	—
ND	1812	210	270	325	450	—

MS (MONOGRAM) - MANUEL SALCEDO

KM# 200   8 REALES
Silver **Issuer:** Manuel Salcedo **Countermark:** MS monogram **Note:** Countermark on Mexico KM#110.

CM Date	Host Date	Good	VG	F	VF	XF
ND	1809 TH	180	300	475	725	—
ND	1810 HJ	180	300	475	725	—
ND	1811 HJ	180	300	475	725	—

MVA - MONCLOVA

KM# 202.3   8 REALES
Silver **Issuer:** Monclova, MVA **Countermark:** MVA/ 1812 **Note:** Countermark on cast Mexico KM#110.

CM Date	Host Date	Good	VG	F	VF	XF
1812	1809 HJ	120	180	300	450	—
1812	1809 TH	120	180	300	450	—
1812	1810 HJ	120	180	300	450	—

KM# 201   8 REALES
Silver **Issuer:** Monclova, MVA **Countermark:** MVA/ 1811 **Note:** Countermark on Chihuahua KM#111.1; struck over cast Mexico KM#110.

CM Date	Host Date	Good	VG	F	VF	XF
ND	1809	300	550	850	1,200	—
ND	1816 RP	300	550	850	1,200	—
ND	1821 RP	300	550	850	1,200	—

KM# 202.5   8 REALES
Silver **Issuer:** Monclova, MVA **Countermark:** MVA/ 1812 **Note:** Countermark on Zacatecas KM#189.

CM Date	Host Date	Good	VG	F	VF	XF
1812	1813	350	425	550	850	—

KM# 202.1   8 REALES
Silver **Issuer:** Monclova, MVA **Countermark:** MVA/ 1812 **Note:** Countermark on Chihuahua KM#111.1; struck over cast Mexico KM#109.

CM Date	Host Date	Good	VG	F	VF	XF
1812	1810	150	210	300	450	—

KM# 202.2   8 REALES
Silver **Issuer:** Monclova, MVA **Countermark:** MVA/1812 **Note:** Countermark on cast Mexico KM#109.

CM Date	Host Date	Good	VG	F	VF	XF
1812	1798 FM	120	180	300	450	—
1812	1802 FT	120	180	300	450	—

INSURGENT COINAGE

AMERICAN CONGRESS

KM# 216   REAL
0.9030 Silver   **Issuer:** American Congress **Obv:** Eagle on cactus **Obv. Legend:** CONGRESO AMERICANO **Rev:** F. 7 on spread mantle **Rev. Legend:** DEPOSIT D.L. AUCTORI J **Mint:** Mexico City

Date	Mintage	Good	VG	F	VF	XF
ND(1813)	—	42.00	90.00	150	270	—

KM# 217   REAL
0.9030 Silver   **Issuer:** American Congress **Obv:** Eagle on cactus **Obv. Legend:** CONGR. AMER. **Rev:** F. 7 on spread mantle **Rev. Legend:** DEPOS. D. L. AUT. D. **Mint:** Mexico City

Date	Mintage	Good	VG	F	VF	XF
ND(1813)	—	42.00	90.00	150	270	—

NATIONAL CONGRESS

KM# 209   1/2 REAL
Struck Copper   **Issuer:** National Congress **Obv:** Eagle on bridge **Obv. Legend:** VICE FERD. VII DEI GRATIA ET **Rev:** Value, bow quiver, etc **Rev. Legend:** S. P. CONG. NAT. IND.

Date	Mintage	Good	VG	F	VF	XF
1811	—	55.00	100	180	300	—
1812	—	33.00	70.00	120	210	—
1813	—	33.00	70.00	120	210	—
1814	—	55.00	100	180	300	—

KM# 210   1/2 REAL
0.9030 Silver **Issuer:** National Congress **Obv:** Eagle on bridge **Obv. Legend:** VICE FERD. VII DEI GRATIA ET **Rev:** Value, bow quiver, etc **Rev. Legend:** S. P. CONG. NAT. IND.

Date	Mintage	Good	VG	F	VF	XF
1812	—	33.00	70.00	120	210	—
1813	—	55.00	110	210	325	—

Note: 1812 exists with the date reading inwards and outwards

KM# 211   REAL
0.9030 Silver **Issuer:** National Congress **Obv:** Eagle on bridge **Obv. Legend:** VICE FERD. VII DEI GRATIA ET **Rev:** Value, bow quiver, etc **Rev. Legend:** S. P. CONG. NAT. IND.

Date	Mintage	Good	VG	F	VF	XF
1812	—	27.50	55.00	95.00	180	—
1813	—	27.50	55.00	95.00	180	—

Note: 1812 exists with the date reading either inward or outward

KM# 212   2 REALES
Struck Copper   **Issuer:** National Congress **Obv:** Eagle on bridge **Obv. Legend:** VICE FERD. VII DEI GRATIA ET **Rev:** Value, bow quiver, etc **Rev. Legend:** S. P. CONG. NAT. IND.

Date	Mintage	Good	VG	F	VF	XF
1812	—	120	180	270	425	—
1813	—	27.50	60.00	90.00	180	—
1814	—	39.00	90.00	130	220	—

KM# A213   2 REALES
Struck Silver **Issuer:** National Congress **Obv:** Eagle on bridge **Obv. Legend:** VICE FERD. VII DEI GRATIA ET **Rev:** Value, bow, quiver, etc **Rev. Legend:** S. P. CONG. NAT. IND.

Date	Mintage	Good	VG	F	VF	XF
1813	—	1,050	1,950	3,300	5,500	—

WAR OF INDEPENDENCE

KM# 213 2 REALES

0.9030 Silver **Issuer:** National Congress **Obv:** Eagle on bridge in shield, denomination at sides **Obv. Legend:** VICE FERD. VII DEI GRATIA ET **Rev:** Canon, quiver, arm, etc

Date	Mintage	Good	VG	F	VF	XF
1813	—	95.00	200	350	500	—

Note: These dies were believed to be intended for the striking of 2 Escudos

KM# 214 4 REALES

0.9030 Silver **Issuer:** National Congress **Obv:** Eagle on bridge **Obv. Legend:** VICE FERD. VII DEI GRATIA ET **Rev:** Value, bow, quiver, etc **Rev. Legend:** S. P. CONG. NAT. IND. **Mint:** Mexico City

Date	Mintage	Good	VG	F	VF	XF
1813	—	650	1,300	2,700	5,200	—

KM# 215.1 8 REALES

0.9030 Silver **Issuer:** National Congress **Obv:** Small crowned eagle **Obv. Legend:** VICE FERD. VII DEI GRATIA ET **Rev:** Value, bow, quiver, etc **Rev. Legend:** S. P. CONG. NAT. IND. **Mint:** Mexico City

Date	Mintage	Good	VG	F	VF	XF
1812Mo	—	650	1,250	2,600	4,950	—

KM# 215.2 8 REALES

0.9030 Silver **Issuer:** National Congress **Obv:** Large crowned eagle **Obv. Legend:** VICE FERD. VII DEI GRATIA ET **Rev:** Value, bow, quiver, etc **Rev. Legend:** S. P. CONG. NAT. IND. **Mint:** Mexico City

Date	Mintage	Good	VG	F	VF	XF
1813Mo	—	650	1,250	2,600	4,950	—

SUPREME NATIONAL CONGRESS OF AMERICA

PDV - Provisional de Valladolid

VTIL - Util = useful

(Refer to Multiple countermarks)

KM# 203 1/2 REAL

Struck Copper **Issuer:** Supreme National Congress of America **Obv:** Eagle on bridge **Obv. Legend:** FERDIN. VII DEI GRATIA **Rev:** Value, bow, quiver, etc **Rev. Legend:** S. P. CONG. NAT. IND. GUV.T.

Date	Mintage	Good	VG	F	VF	XF
1811	—	34.50	55.00	80.00	150	—
1812	—	34.50	55.00	80.00	150	—
1813	—	34.50	55.00	80.00	150	—
1814	—	34.50	55.00	80.00	150	—

KM# 204 REAL

Struck Copper **Issuer:** Supreme National Congress of America **Obv:** Eagle on bridge **Obv. Legend:** FERDIN. VII DEI GRATIA **Rev:** Value, bow, quiver, etc **Rev. Legend:** S. P. CONG. NAT. IND. GUV.T.

Date	Mintage	Good	VG	F	VF	XF
1811	—	55.00	95.00	155	250	—

KM# 205 2 REALES

Struck Copper **Issuer:** Supreme National Congress

of America **Obv:** Eagle on bridge **Obv. Legend:**
FERDIN. VII DEI GRATIA **Rev:** Value, bow, quiver, etc

Date	Mintage	Good	VG	F	VF	XF
1812	—	280	400	600	950	—

KM# 206   8 REALES
Cast Silver **Issuer:** Supreme National Congress of
America **Obv:** Eagle on bridge **Obv. Legend:** FERDIN.
VII DEI GRATIA **Rev:** Value, bow, quiver, etc

Date	Mintage	Good	VG	F	VF	XF
1811	—	190	325	450	700	—
1812	—	190	325	475	700	—

KM# 207   8 REALES
Struck Silver **Issuer:** Supreme National Congress of
America **Obv:** Eagle on bridge **Obv. Legend:** FERDIN.
VII DEI GRATIA **Rev:** Value, bow, quiver, etc

Date	Mintage	Good	VG	F	VF	XF
1811	—	—	—	—	—	—

Note: Ira & Larry Goldberg Millennia Sale 5-08, QU-55 realized $55,000.

Date	Mintage	Good	VG	F	VF	XF
1812	—	625	1,250	1,900	3,150	—

KM# 208   8 REALES
Struck Copper **Issuer:** Supreme National Congress
of America **Obv:** Eagle on bridge **Obv. Legend:**
FERDIN. VII... **Rev:** Bow, sword and quiver **Rev.
Legend:** PROVICIONAL POR LA SUPREMA
JUNTA DE AMERICA

Date	Mintage	Good	VG	F	VF	XF
1811	—	125	190	280	600	—
1812	—	125	190	280	600	—

EMPIRE OF ITURBIDE

RULER
Augustin I Iturbide, 1822-1823
MINT MARK
Mo - Mexico City
ASSAYERS' INITIALS
JA - Jose Garcia Ansaldo, 1812-1833
JM - Joaquin Davila Madrid, 1809-1833

MILLED COINAGE

KM# 299   1/8 REAL
Copper **Ruler:** Augustin I Iturbide **Obv:** Crowned
shield within sprays **Rev:** Inscription, date **Rev.
Inscription:** DE LA PROVINCIA DE NUEVA
VISCAYA **Mint:** Durango

Date	Mintage	Good	VG	F	VF	XF
1821D	—	22.50	50.00	85.00	150	—
1822D	—	7.50	13.50	28.50	60.00	—
1823D	—	9.00	13.50	26.50	55.00	—

KM# 300   1/4 REAL
Copper **Ruler:** Augustin I Iturbide **Obv:** Crowned
shield within sprays **Rev:** Inscription, date **Rev.
Inscription:** DE LA PROVINCIA DE NUEVA
VISCAYA **Mint:** Durango

Date	Mintage	Good	VG	F	VF	XF
1822D	—	160	275	400	550	—

KM# 301   1/2 REAL
0.9030 Silver **Ruler:** Augustin I Iturbide **Obv:** Head
right **Obv. Legend:** AUGUSTINUS DEI... **Rev:**
Crowned eagle **Rev. Legend:** I.M.E.X.I... **Mint:**
Mexico City

Date	Mintage	F	VF	XF	Unc	BU
1822Mo JM	—	22.50	55.00	110	375	700
1823Mo JM	—	17.00	42.00	85.00	325	—

KM# 302   REAL
0.9030 Silver **Ruler:** Augustin I Iturbide **Obv:** Head

right **Obv. Legend:** AUGUSTINUS DEI... **Rev:**
Crowned eagle **Rev. Legend:** MEX.I.IMPERATOR...
Mint: Mexico City

Date	Mintage	VG	F	VF	XF	Unc
1822Mo JM	—	100	175	350	550	1,150

KM# 303 2 REALES
6.7667 g., 0.9030 Silver 0.1964 oz. ASW **Ruler:**
Augustin I Iturbide **Obv:** Head right **Obv. Legend:**
AUGUSTINUS DEI... **Rev:** Crowned eagle **Rev.**
Legend: MEX • I • IMPERATOR... **Mint:** Mexico City

Date	Mintage	F	VF	XF	Unc	BU
1822Mo JM	—	60.00	120	350	1,000	—
1823Mo JM	—	40.00	80.00	250	850	1,600

KM# 304 8 REALES
27.0674 g., 0.9030 Silver 0.7858 oz. ASW **Ruler:**
Augustin I Iturbide **Obv:** Head right **Obv. Legend:**
AUGUST.... **Rev:** Crowned eagle **Rev. Legend:**
...MEX • I • IMPERATOR... **Mint:** Mexico City

Date	Mintage	F	VF	XF	Unc
1822Mo JM	—	75.00	150	375	1,300
1822Mo JM Proof, 3 known					

Note: Ponterio & Associates Sale #86, 04-97, choice AU
Proof realized $12,650

KM# 305 8 REALES
0.9030 Silver **Ruler:** Augustin I Iturbide **Obv:** Bust
similar to 8 Escudos, KM#131 **Rev:** Crowned eagle
Mint: Mexico City

Date	Mintage	F	VF	XF	Unc	BU
1822Mo JM Rare	—	—	—	—	—	—

KM# 306.1 8 REALES
0.9030 Silver **Ruler:** Augustin I Iturbide **Obv:** Head
right **Obv. Legend:** AUGUST... **Rev:** Crowned
eagle, 8 R.J.M. at upper left of eagle **Rev. Legend:**
MEX • I • IMPERATOR... **Mint:** Mexico City **Note:**
Type I.

Date	Mintage	F	VF	XF	Unc	BU
1822Mo JM	—	100	200	475	1,800	—

KM# 306.2 8 REALES
0.9030 Silver **Ruler:** Augustin I Iturbide **Obv:** Head
right **Rev:** Cross on crown **Mint:** Mexico City **Note:**
Type I.

Date	Mintage	F	VF	XF	Unc	BU
1822Mo JM	—	650	1,100	—	—	—

KM# 307 8 REALES
0.9030 Silver **Ruler:** Augustin I Iturbide **Obv:** Head
right **Rev:** Crowned eagle **Mint:** Mexico City **Note:**
Type II.

Date	Mintage	F	VF	XF	Unc	BU
1822Mo JM	—	150	350	850	3,750	—

KM# 308 8 REALES
0.9030 Silver **Ruler:** Augustin I Iturbide **Obv:** Head
right, continuous legend with long smooth truncation
Obv. Legend: AUGUSTINUS DEI... **Rev:** Crowned
eagle **Mint:** Mexico City **Note:** Type III.

Date	Mintage	F	VF	XF	Unc	BU
1822Mo JM	—	175	500	1,150	3,750	—

Note: Variety with long, straight truncation is valued at $5,000 in uncirculated condition

KM# 309   8 REALES
0.9030 Silver **Ruler:** Augustin I Iturbide **Obv:** Head right **Obv. Legend:** AUGUSTINUS DEI... **Rev:** Crowned eagle **Rev. Legend:** MEX • I • IMPERATOR... **Mint:** Mexico City **Note:** Type IV.

Date	Mintage	F	VF	XF	Unc	BU
1822Mo JM	—	50.00	120	300	1,300	—

KM# 310   8 REALES
0.9030 Silver **Ruler:** Augustin I Iturbide **Obv:** Head right, continuous legend with short irregular truncation **Obv. Legend:** AUGUSTINUS DEI... **Rev:** Crowned eagle, 8 R.J.M. below eagle **Rev. Legend:** MEX • I • IMPERATOR... **Mint:** Mexico City **Note:** Type V.

Date	Mintage	F	VF	XF	Unc	BU
1822Mo JM	—	50.00	120	300	1,500	—
1823Mo JM	—	50.00	120	300	1,500	—

KM# 311   8 REALES
0.9030 Silver **Ruler:** Augustin I Iturbide **Obv:** Head right, long truncation **Rev:** Crowned eagle **Mint:** Mexico City **Note:** Type VI.

Date	Mintage	F	VF	XF	Unc	BU
1822Mo JM Rare	—	—	—	—	—	—

KM# 312   4 SCUDOS
13.5334 g., 0.8750 Gold 0.3807 oz. AGW **Ruler:** Augustin I Iturbide **Obv:** Head right **Obv. Legend:** AUGUSTINUS DEI... **Rev:** Crowned eagle within ornate shield **Rev. Legend:** CONSTITUT.4.S.I.M... **Mint:** Mexico City

Date	Mintage	F	VF	XF	Unc	BU
1823Mo JM	—	1,350	2,750	6,250	12,000	—

KM# 313.1   8 SCUDOS
27.0674 g., 0.8750 Gold 0.7614 oz. AGW **Ruler:** Augustin I Iturbide **Obv:** Head right **Obv. Legend:** AUGUSTINUS . DEI... **Rev:** Crowned eagle **Rev. Legend:** CONSTITUT.8.S.I.M... **Mint:** Mexico City

Date	Mintage	F	VF	XF	Unc	BU
1822Mo JM	—	1,500	3,500	6,500	12,000	15,000

Note: American Numismatic Rarities Eliasberg sale 4-05, MS-62 realized $20,700. Superior Casterline sale 5-89 choice AU realized $11,000

KM# 313.2   8 SCUDOS
0.8750 Gold **Ruler:** Augustin I Iturbide **Obv:** Head right, error in legend **Obv. Legend:** AUGUSTINUS • DEI... **Rev:** Crowned eagle **Rev. Legend:** CONSTITUT • 8 • S • I • M... **Mint:** Mexico City

Date	Mintage	F	VF	XF	Unc	BU
1822Mo JM	—	1,350	3,650	6,750	12,500	16,000

KM# 314 8 SCUDOS
0.8750 Gold **Ruler:** Augustin I Iturbide **Obv:** Head right **Obv. Legend:** AUGUSTINUS DEI... **Rev:** Crowned eagle within ornate shield **Rev. Legend:** CONSTITUT • 8 • S • I • M... **Mint:** Mexico City

Date	Mintage	F	VF	XF	Unc	BU
1823Mo JM	—	1,300	2,700	6,000	11,000	—

REPUBLIC
First

MINT MARKS
A, AS - Alamos
CE - Real de Catorce
CA,CH - Chihuahua
C, Cn, Gn(error) - Culiacan
D, Do - Durango
EoMo - Estado de Mexico
Ga - Guadalajara
GC - Guadalupe y Calvo
G, Go - Guanajuato
H, Ho - Hermosillo
M, Mo - Mexico City
O, OA - Oaxaca
SLP, PI, P, I/P - San Luis Potosi
Z, Zs - Zacatecas
ASSAYERS' INITIALS

ALAMOS MINT
PG	1862-68	Pascual Gaxiola
DL, L	1866-79	Domingo Larraguibel
AM	1872-74	Antonio Moreno
ML, L	1878-95	Manuel Larraguibel

REAL DE CATORCE MINT
ML	1863	Mariano Cristobal Ramirez

CHIHUAHUA MINT
MR	1831-34	Mariano Cristobal Ramirez
AM	1833-39	Jose Antonio Mucharraz
MJ	1832	Jose Mariano Jimenez
RG	1839-56	Rodrigo Garcia
JC	1856-65	Joaquin Campa
BA	1858	Bruno Arriada
FP	1866	Francisco Potts
JC	1866-1868	Jose Maria Gomez del Campo
MM, M	1868-95	Manuel Merino
AV	1873-80	Antonio Valero
EA	1877	Eduardo Avila
JM	1877	Jacobo Mucharraz
GR	1877	Guadalupe Rocha
MG	1880-82	Manuel Gameros

CULIACAN MINT
CE	1846-70	Clemente Espinosa de los Monteros
C	1870	???
PV	1860-61	Pablo Viruega
MP, P	1871-76	Manuel Onofre Parodi
GP	1876	Celso Gaxiola & Manuel Onofre Parodi
CG, G	1876-78	Celso Gaxiola
JD, D	1878-82	Juan Dominguez
AM, M	1882-1899	Antonio Moreno
F	1870	Fernando Ferrari
JQ, Q	1899-1903	Jesus S. Quiroz

DURANGO MINT
RL	1825-1832	???
RM	1830-48	Ramon Mascarenas
OMC	1840	Octavio Martinez de Castro
CM	1848-76	Clemente Moron
JMR	1849-52	Jose Maria Ramirez
CP, P	1853-64, 1867-73	Carlos Leon de la Pena
LT	1864-65	???
JMP, P	1877	Carlos Miguel de la Palma
PE, E	1878	Pedro Espejo
TB, B	1878-80	Trinidad Barrera
JP	1880-94	J. Miguel Palma
MC, C	1882-90	Manuel M. Canseco or Melchor Calderon
JB	1885	Jocobo Blanco
ND, D	1892-95	Norberto Dominguez

ESTADO DE MEXICO MINT
L	1828-30	Luis Valazquez de la Cadena
F	1828-30	Francisco Parodi

GUADALAJARA MINT
FS	1818-35	Francisco Suarez
JM	1830-32	???
JG	1836-39, 1842-67	Juan de Dios Guzman
MC	1839-46	Manuel Cueras
JM	1867-69	Jesus P. Manzano
IC, C	1869-77	Ignacio Canizo y Soto
MC	1874-75	Manuel Contreras
JA, A	1877-81	Julio Arancivia
FS, S	1880-82	Fernando Sayago
TB, B	1883-84	Trinidad Barrera
AH, H	1884-85	Antonio Hernandez y Prado
JS, S	1885-95	Jose S. Schiafino

GUADALUPE Y CALVO MINT
MP	1844-52	Manuel Onofre Parodi

GUANAJUATO MINT
JJ	1825-26	Jose Mariano Jimenez
MJ, MR, JM, PG, PJ, PF		???
PM	1841-48, 1853-61	Patrick Murphy
YF	1862-68	Yldefonso Flores
YE	1862-63	Ynocencio Espinoza
FR	1870-78	Faustino Ramirez
SB, RR		???
RS	1891-1900	Rosendo Sandoval

HERMOSILLO MINT
PP	1835-36	Pedro Peimbert
FM	1871-76	Florencio Monteverde
MP	1866	Manuel Onofre Parodi
PR	1866-75	Pablo Rubio
R	1874-75	Pablo Rubio
GR	1877	Guadalupe Rocha
AF, F	1876-77	Alejandro Fourcade

FIRST REPUBLIC

JA, A	1877-83	Jesus Acosta
FM, M	1883-86	Fernando Mendez
FG, G	1886-95	Fausto Gaxiola

MEXICO CITY MINT

Because of the great number of assayers for this mint (Mexico City is a much larger mint than any of the others)there is much confusion as to which initial stands for which assayer at any one time. Therefore we feel that it would be of no value to list the assayers.

OAXACA MINT

AE	1859-91	Agustin Endner
E	1889-90	Agustin Endner
FR	1861-64	Francisco de la Rosa
EN	1890	Eduardo Navarro Luna
N	1890	Eduardo Navarro Luna

POTOSI MINT

JS	1827-42	Juan Sanabria
AM	1838, 1843-49	Jose Antonio Mucharraz
PS	1842-43, 1848-49, 1857-61, 1867-70	Pompaso Sanabria
S	1869-70	Pomposo Sanabria
MC	1849-59	Mariano Catano
RO	1859-65	Romualdo Obregon
MH, H	1870-85	Manuel Herrera Razo
O	1870-73	Juan R. Ochoa
CA, G	1867-70	Carlos Aguirre Gomez
BE, E	1879-81	Blas Escontria
LC, C	1885-86	Luis Cuevas
MR, R	1886-93	Mariano Reyes

ZACATECAS MINT

A	1825-29	Adalco
Z	1825-26	Mariano Zaldivar
V	1824-31	Jose Mariano Vela
O	1829-67	Manuel Ochoa
M	1831-67	Manuel Miner
VL	1860-66	Vicente Larranaga
JS	1867-68, 1876-86	J.S. de Santa Ana
YH	1868-74	Ygnacio Hierro
JA	1874-76	Juan H. Acuna
FZ	18861905	Francisco de P. Zarate

DIE VARIETIES

Similar basic designs were utilized by all the Mexican mints, but many variations are noticeable, particularly in the eagle, cactus and sprays.

1849 Mexico City, 8 Escudos
Illustration enlarged.
The later eagle featured undersized wings.

1844 Durango, 8 Escudos
Illustration enlarged.
The early renditions of the hand held Liberty cap over open book were massive in the gold escudo series.

1835 Durango, 8 Escudos
Illustration enlarged.
A large winged eagle was portrayed on the earlier coinage of the new republic.

1864 Durango, 8 Escudos
Illustration enlarged.
A finer, more petite style was adopted later on in the gold escudo series.

FIRST REPUBLIC

PROFILE EAGLE COINAGE

The first coins of the Republic were of the distinctive Profile Eagle style, sometimes called the "Hooked Neck Eagle". They were struck first in Mexico City in 1823 in denominations of eight reales and eight escudos. In 1824, they were produced at the Durango and Guanajuato mints in addition to Mexico City. Denominations included the one half, one, two and eight reales. No gold escudos of this design were struck in 1824. In 1825, only the eight reales were struck briefly at the Guanajuato mint.

NOTE: For a more extensive examination of Profile Eagle Coinage, please refer to Hookneck - El Aguila de Perfil by Clyde Hubbard and David O Harrow.

KM# 369   1/2 REAL
1.6900 g., 0.9030 Silver 0.0491 oz. ASW **Obv:** Full breast Profile eagle **Rev:** Cap and rays **Mint:** Mexico City **Note:** Die varieties exist.

Date	Mintage	F	VF	XF	Unc	BU
1824Mo JM	—	45.00	75.00	175	750	—

KM# 371.1   REAL
3.3800 g., 0.9030 Silver 0.0981 oz. ASW **Obv:** Thin Profile eagle **Rev:** Superscript S reversed **Mint:** Durango

Date	Mintage	F	VF	XF	Unc	BU
1824Do RL	—	5,500	9,500	13,000	—	—

KM# 371.2   REAL
3.3800 g., 0.9030 Silver 0.0981 oz. ASW **Obv:** Thin Profile eagle **Rev:** Superscript S normal **Mint:** Durango

Date	Mintage	F	VF	XF	Unc	BU
1824Do RL 3 known	—	—	—	—	—	—

Mint mark: Do

KM# 373.1   2 REALES
6.7600 g., 0.9030 Silver 0.1962 oz. ASW **Obv:**

Profile eagle, snake in beak **Obv. Legend:** REPUBLICA • MEXICANA **Rev:** Radiant cap **Mint:** Durango **Note:** Die varieties exist.

Date	Mintage	F	VF	XF	Unc	BU
1824Do RL	—	60.00	135	850	2,200	—

KM# 373.2   2 REALES
6.7600 g., 0.9030 Silver 0.1962 oz. ASW **Obv:** Profile eagle, snake in beak **Obv. Legend:** Thin profile **Rev:** Radiant cap **Rev. Legend:** Type 1, dot before 2R in legend **Mint:** Durango

Date	Mintage	F	VF	XF	Unc	BU
1824D RL	—	120	250	1,000	3,000	—

KM# 373.3   2 REALES
6.7600 g., 0.9030 Silver 0.1962 oz. ASW **Obv:** Profile eagle, snake in beak **Obv. Legend:** Thin profile **Rev:** Radiant cap **Rev. Legend:** Type II, no dot before 2R in legend **Mint:** Durango

Date	Mintage	F	VF	XF	Unc	BU
1824D RL	—	120	250	1,000	3,000	—

KM# 373.4   2 REALES
Obv: Profile eagle, snake in beak **Obv. Legend:** REPUBLICA • MEXICANA **Rev:** Radiant cap **Mint:** Mexico City **Note:** Varieties exist.

Date	Mintage	F	VF	XF	Unc	BU
1824Mo JM	—	40.00	90.00	450	2,000	—

Note: No coins are known with visible feather details on the eagle's breast

KM# A376.2   8 REALES
27.0700 g., 0.9030 Silver 0.7859 oz. ASW **Obv:** Full breast profile eagle, snake in beak **Obv. Legend:**

FIRST REPUBLIC

REPUBLICA MEXICANA **Rev:** Radiant cap **Edge:**
Standard or Republic **Mint:** Mexico City

Date	Mintage	F	VF	XF	Unc	BU
1823Mo JM	—	150	300	800	4,500	—
1824Mo JM	—	125	250	700	4,000	—

KM# A376.1   8 REALES
27.0700 g., 0.9030 Silver 0.7859 oz. ASW **Obv:** Full
breast profile eagle, snake in beak **Obv. Legend:**
REPUBLICA MEXICANA. **Rev:** Radiant cap **Mint:**
Guanajuato

Date	Mintage	F	VF	XF	Unc	BU
1824Go JM	—	250	400	1,100	3,500	—
1825/4Go JJ	—	600	1,200	2,750	7,000	—
1825Go JJ	—	500	750	1,400	5,500	—

KM# A376.3   8 REALES
27.0700 g., 0.9030 Silver 0.7859 oz. ASW **Obv:** Full
breast profile eagle, snake in beak **Rev:** Radiant cap
Edge: Colonial or circle and rectangle **Mint:** Mexico
City

Date	Mintage	F	VF	XF	Unc	BU
1823Mo JM Rare	—	—	—	—	—	—

The Round-Topped Three

KM# A376.4   8 REALES
27.0700 g., 0.9030 Silver 0.7859 oz. ASW **Obv:** Full
breast profile eagle, snake in beak **Rev:** Radiant cap,
round topped three **Edge:** Standard or Republic
Mint: Mexico City

Date	Mintage	F	VF	XF	Unc	BU
1823Mo JM	—	2,000	4,000	6,000	8,000	—

Note: Many die varieties exist; Illustrations of one of the die
differences is the size of the snake loop at the eagle's beak;
This difference is not apparent except on the 1824 Mo 8
Reales

KM# A376.5   8 REALES
27.0700 g., 0.9030 Silver 0.7859 oz. ASW **Obv:** Full

breast profile eagle, snake in beak, REPULICA
(error) **Rev:** Radiant cap **Mint:** Mexico City

Date	Mintage	F	VF	XF	Unc	BU
1824Mo JM	—	6,000	9,000	11,000	—	—

Note: Legible Libertads on the cap are not as prevalent on
the Mexico City 8 Reales as on the Durango 8 Reales; They
are much more numerous than on the Guanajuato 8 Reales

Typical Submissive
Snake Obverse

Typical Folded
Snake Obverse

NOTE: Legible Libertads on the Cap are common on
Durango eight reales.

Med. Libertad	Small Libertad	Large Libertad
Cap Reverse	Cap Reverse	Cap Reverse

NOTE: The three styles of obverses and the three styles
of reverses were combined   to make six distinct
varieties of coins.

KM# 376.1 8 REALES
27.0700 g., 0.9030 Silver 0.7859 oz. ASW **Obv:**
Thin profile eagle, defiant snake **Rev:** Radiant cap,
medium Libertad **Mint:** Durango

Date	Mintage	F	VF	XF	Unc	BU
1824Do RL	—	500	1,200	5,400	10,500	—

Note: Five die varieties are known, all are rare. Ira & Larry
Goldberg Millennia Sale 5-08, MS-64 realized $25,000.

KM# 376.2 8 REALES
27.0700 g., 0.9030 Silver 0.7859 oz. ASW **Obv:**
Thin profile eagle, defiant snake **Obv. Legend:**
REPUBLICA MEXICANA **Rev:** Radiant cap, small
Libertad **Mint:** Durango

Date	Mintage	F	VF	XF	Unc	BU
1824Do RL	—	300	500	1,900	5,300	—

Note: Eleven die varieties are known, some are rare

KM# 376.3 8 REALES
27.0700 g., 0.9030 Silver 0.7859 oz. ASW **Obv:**
Thin profile eagle, submissive snake **Obv. Legend:**
REPUBLICA • MEXICANA **Rev:** Radiant cap, small
Libertad **Mint:** Durango

Date	Mintage	F	VF	XF	Unc	BU
1824Do RL	—	200	400	1,500	4,150	—

Note: Seven die varieties are known, some are rare

KM# 376.4 8 REALES
27.0700 g., 0.9030 Silver 0.7859 oz. ASW **Obv:**
Thin profile eagle, submissive snake **Rev:** Radiant
cap, large Libertad **Mint:** Durango

Date	Mintage	F	VF	XF	Unc	BU
1824Do RL	—	200	400	1,500	4,150	—

Note: Twelve die varieties known, some are rare

KM# 376.5 8 REALES
27.0700 g., 0.9030 Silver 0.7859 oz. ASW **Obv:**
Thin profile eagle, folded snake **Rev:** Radiant cap,
small Libertad **Mint:** Durango

Date	Mintage	F	VF	XF	Unc	BU
1824Do RL	—	200	400	1,450	3,750	—

Note: Only one die variety is known

KM# 376.6 8 REALES
27.0700 g., 0.9030 Silver 0.7859 oz. ASW **Obv:**
Thin profile eagle, folded snake **Rev:** Radiant cap,
large Libertad **Mint:** Durango

Date	Mintage	F	VF	XF	Unc	BU
1824Do RL	—	200	450	1,800	4,500	—

Note: Eleven die varieties known, some are rare

Type I Obverse/Reverse

NOTE: The cap on the reverse of the curved tail Type I
points to the "A" of LIBERTAD.

KM# 382.1   8 ESCUDOS

27.0700 g., 0.8750 Gold 0.7615 oz. AGW **Obv:** Profile eagle, snake's tail curved **Obv. Legend:** REPUBLICA MEXICANA **Rev:** Open book, hand holding stick with cap, cap points to "A" of LIBERTAD **Rev. Legend:** LIBERTAD EN... **Mint:** Mexico City

Date	Mintage	F	VF	XF	Unc	BU
1823Mo JM	—	7,000	10,000	20,000	35,000	—

Note: American Numismatic Rarities Eliasberg sale 4-05, MS-61 realized $55,200.

Type II Obverse/Reverse

NOTE: The cap on the reverse of the looped tail Type II points to the "T" of LIBERTAD.

KM# 382.2   8 ESCUDOS

27.0700 g., 0.8750 Gold 0.7615 oz. AGW **Obv:** Profile eagle, snake's tail looped **Obv. Legend:** REPUBLICA MEXICANA **Rev:** Open book, hand holding stick with cap, cap points to "T" of LIBERTAD **Rev. Legend:** LIBERTAD EN... **Mint:** Mexico City

Date	Mintage	F	VF	XF	Unc	BU
1823Mo JM	—	6,000	9,000	18,000	35,000	—

Note: The quality of the strikes of Type I coins is almost always superior to that of the Type II; Details of the eagle feathers, cactus and lettering on the open book are better on most Type I coins but the Type II coins are scarcer; Type I coins outnumber Type II coins by about two to one

STATE COINAGE

KM# 316   1/16 REAL (Medio Octavo)

4.7500 g., Copper, 21 mm. **Obv:** Bow, quiver and flag **Obv. Legend:** DEPARTAMENTO DE JALISCO **Rev:** Seated figure, left, cap on pole **Edge:** Oblique reeding **Mint:** Guadalajara

Date	Mintage	Good	VG	F	VF	XF
1860	—	5.00	12.00	27.50	85.00	—

KM# 317   1/16 REAL (Medio Octavo)

4.7500 g., Copper, 21 mm. **Obv. Legend:** ESTADO LIBRE DE JALISCO **Edge:** Oblique reeding **Mint:** Guadalajara

Date	Mintage	Good	VG	F	VF	XF
1861	—	4.00	9.00	20.00	48.75	—

KM# 320   1/8 REAL (Octavo Real)

Copper **Obv:** Facing eagle, snake in beak, value at lower left **Rev:** Radiant Libertad above date within wreath **Rev. Legend:** LIBERTAD **Edge:** Oblique reeding **Mint:** Durango **Note:** Size varies 17-18mm. Weight varies 2.5-4 g. These pieces were frequently struck over 1/8 Real, dated 1821-23 of Nueva Vizcaya. All known examples struck over these coins are believed to be contemporary counterfeits.

Date	Mintage	Good	VG	F	VF	XF
1824D	—	8.00	19.00	55.00	130	—
1828D	—	225	375	600	1,500	—

KM# 338   1/8 REAL (Octavo Real)

4.0000 g., Brass, 21 mm. **Obv:** Monument **Obv. Legend:** ESTo LIBe FEDo DE ZACATECAS **Rev:** Floating angel holding radiant cap **Edge:** Oblique reeding **Mint:** Zacatecas

Date	Mintage	Good	VG	F	VF	XF
1825	—	5.00	8.00	18.00	37.50	—
1827	—	5.00	8.00	18.00	37.50	—
1827	—	18.00	30.00	60.00	150	—
Note: Inverted A for V in OCTAVO						
1827	—	22.50	37.50	75.00	180	—
Note: OCTAVA (error)						
1827 Inverted 1	—	18.00	30.00	60.00	150	—
1829 Rare	—	—	—	—	—	—
1830	—	4.00	8.00	12.00	30.00	—
1831	—	7.00	10.00	20.00	41.25	—
1832	—	4.00	8.00	12.00	30.00	—
1833	—	4.00	8.00	12.00	30.00	—
1835	—	5.00	9.00	15.00	37.50	—
1846	—	5.00	9.00	15.00	37.50	—
1851	—	55.00	105	175	325	—
1852	—	5.00	9.00	15.00	37.50	—
1858	—	4.00	8.00	12.00	30.00	—
1859	—	4.00	8.00	12.00	30.00	—
1862	—	4.00	8.00	12.00	30.00	—
1863 Reversed 6 in date	—	4.00	8.00	12.00	30.00	—

KM# 321   1/8 REAL (Octavo Real)

3.3000 g., Copper **Obv:** Child holding bow, right, small tree **Rev:** Radiant cap **Rev. Legend:** OCTo.

DE. R. DE DO **Edge:** Oblique reeding **Mint:** Durango **Note:** Size varies 18-19mm.

Date	Mintage	Good	VG	F	VF	XF
1828D	—	11.00	27.50	60.00	175	—

KM# 335   1/8 REAL (Octavo Real)
Copper **Obv. Legend:** ESTADO DE OCCIDENTE **Edge:** Oblique reeding **Mint:** Alamos **Note:** Size varies: 17-18mm, weight varies: 2-3 g. The C before date on reverse may be a mint mark standing for Concepcion de Alamos.

Date	Mintage	Good	VG	F	VF	XF
1828 Reverse S	—	55.00	100	180	—	—
1829	—	45.00	90.00	165	—	—

KM# 329   1/8 REAL (Octavo Real)
4.8000 g., Copper, 21 mm.   **Obv:** Bow, quiver and flag **Obv. Legend:** ESTADO LIBRE DE JALISCO **Rev:** Seated figure, left, cap on pole **Edge:** Oblique reeding **Mint:** Guadalajara

Date	Mintage	Good	VG	F	VF	XF
1828	—	5.00	8.00	12.00	33.75	—
1831	—	95.00	150	280	425	—
1832/28	—	7.00	10.00	17.00	41.25	—
1832	—	7.00	9.00	15.00	37.50	—
1833	—	5.00	8.00	14.00	35.25	—
1834	—	55.00	120	225	350	—

KM# 326   1/8 REAL (Octavo Real)
3.5000 g., Copper, 21 mm.   **Obv:** Seated figure **Obv. Legend:** ESTADO LIBRE DE GUANAJUATO **Rev:** Cap within center wreath of stylized rays, date below **Edge:** Ornamented with incuse dots **Mint:** Guanajuato

Date	Mintage	Good	VG	F	VF	XF
1829	—	5.00	8.00	15.00	39.75	—
1829	—	6.00	10.00	19.00	42.75	—
Note: Error with GUANJUATO						
1830	—	12.00	20.00	42.75	100	—

KM# 336   1/8 REAL (Octavo Real)
Copper, 21 mm.   **Obv:** Value above divides wreath, open book within **Obv. Legend:** ESTADO LIBRE DE SAN LUIS POTOSI **Rev:** Seated figure **Edge:** Oblique reeding **Mint:** San Luis Potosi **Note:** Weight varies (1829-31) 4.5-5.5 g; (1859) 4-4.5 g.

Date	Mintage	Good	VG	F	VF	XF
1829	—	9.00	17.00	39.75	95.00	—
1830	—	13.00	22.50	45.00	105	—
1831	—	9.00	14.00	27.50	70.00	—

Date	Mintage	Good	VG	F	VF	XF
1859	—	8.00	12.00	25.00	70.00	—
1865/1	—	—	—	—	—	—
Note: Reported, not confirmed						

KM# 318   1/8 REAL (Octavo Real)
3.5400 g., Copper, 20 mm.   **Obv. Legend:** ESTADO SOBERANO DE CHIHUAHUA **Edge:** Plain **Mint:** Chihuahua

Date	Mintage	Good	VG	F	VF	XF
1833	—	525	1,150	—	—	—
1834	—	525	1,150	—	—	—
1835/3	—	525	1,150	—	—	—

KM# 322   1/8 REAL (Octavo Real)
3.5000 g., Copper, 20 mm.   **Obv:** Profile eagle, snake in beak **Obv. Legend:** ESTADO DE DURANGO **Rev:** Value and date within circle and wreath **Mint:** Durango

Date	Mintage	Good	VG	F	VF	XF
1833	—	525	—	—	—	—

KM# 339   1/8 REAL (Octavo Real)
4.0000 g., Copper, 21 mm.   **Obv:** Monument **Obv. Legend:** DEPARTAMENTO DE ZACATECAS **Rev:** Floating angel holding radiant cap **Edge:** Oblique reeding **Mint:** Zacatecas

Date	Mintage	Good	VG	F	VF	XF
1836	—	8.00	13.00	27.50	60.00	—
1845	—	11.00	19.00	33.75	75.00	—
1846	—	13.00	15.00	30.00	70.00	—

KM# 323   1/8 REAL (Octavo Real)
3.5000 g., Copper   **Obv:** Facing eagle, snake in beak **Obv. Legend:** REPUBLICA MEXICANA **Rev:** Value and date within circle and wreath **Mint:** Durango **Note:** Size varies: 19-23mm.

Date	Mintage	Good	VG	F	VF	XF
1842/33	—	19.00	33.75	65.00	175	—
1842	—	13.00	22.50	48.75	150	—

KM# 324   1/8 REAL (Octavo Real)
Copper, 19 mm.   **Obv:** Facing eagle, snake in beak

FIRST REPUBLIC - STATE

Obv. Legend: REPUBLICA MEXICANA **Rev:** Value within circle **Rev. Legend:** DEPARTAMENTO DE DURANGO **Edge:** Ornamented with arc and dot pattern **Mint:** Durango **Note:** Weight varies: 3.5-3.8 g.

Date	Mintage	Good	VG	F	VF	XF
1845	—	33.75	85.00	175	375	—
1846 Rare	—	—	—	—	—	—
1847	—	5.00	11.00	27.50	55.00	—

KM# 325   1/8 REAL (Octavo Real)
Copper, 19 mm. **Obv:** Facing eagle, snake in beak **Obv. Legend:** REPUBLICA MEXICANA **Rev:** Value within circle **Rev. Legend:** ESTADO DE DURANGO **Edge:** Ornamented with arc and dot pattern **Mint:** Durango **Note:** Weight varies: 3.5-3.8 g.

Date	Mintage	Good	VG	F	VF	XF
1851	—	5.00	12.00	19.00	50.00	—
1852/1	—	5.00	10.00	17.00	50.00	—
1852	—	5.00	8.00	12.00	45.00	—
1854	—	11.00	20.00	42.75	95.00	—

KM# 319   1/8 REAL (Octavo Real)
3.5400 g., Copper, 20 mm. **Obv:** Standing figure facing holding bow and arrow **Obv. Legend:** ESTADO DE CHIHUAHUA **Rev:** Date and value within wreath **Edge:** Plain **Mint:** Chihuahua

Date	Mintage	Good	VG	F	VF	XF
1855	—	8.00	13.00	37.50	115	—

KM# 327   1/8 REAL (Octavo Real)
7.2000 g., Brass, 29 mm. **Obv:** Facing eagle, snake in beak **Obv. Legend:** ESTADO LIBRE DE GUANAJUATO **Rev:** Oval arms within sprays below radiant cap **Edge:** Plain **Mint:** Guanajuato

Date	Mintage	Good	VG	F	VF	XF
1856	—	11.00	18.00	30.00	115	—

KM# 330   1/8 REAL (Octavo Real)
9.5000 g., Copper, 28 mm. **Obv. Legend:** ESTADO

LIBRE DE JALISCO **Rev:** Seated figure, left, cap on pole **Edge:** Oblique reeding **Mint:** Guadalajara

Date	Mintage	Good	VG	F	VF	XF
1856	—	5.00	9.00	14.00	27.50	—
1857	—	5.00	9.00	14.00	27.50	—
1858	—	5.00	9.00	14.00	27.50	—
1861	—	115	205	300	450	—
1862/1	—	6.00	11.00	15.00	33.75	—
1862	—	6.00	11.00	15.00	33.75	—

KM# 328   1/8 REAL (Octavo Real)
Brass, 25 mm. **Obv:** Facing eagle, snake in beak **Obv. Legend:** ESTADO LIBRE DE GUANAJUATO **Rev:** Oval arms within sprays below radiant cap **Edge:** Plain **Mint:** Guanajuato **Note:** Weight varies: 7.1-7.2 g.

Date	Mintage	Good	VG	F	VF	XF
1856	—	6.00	11.00	19.00	55.00	—
1857	—	5.00	9.00	15.00	45.00	—

KM# 328a   1/8 REAL (Octavo Real)
Copper, 25 mm. **Obv:** Facing eagle, snake in beak **Obv. Legend:** ESTADO LIBRE DE GUANAJUATO **Rev:** Oval arms within sprays below radiant cap **Edge:** Plain **Mint:** Guanajuato **Note:** Weight varies: 7.1-7.2 g.

Date	Mintage	Good	VG	F	VF	XF
1857	—	11.00	25.00	48.75	85.00	—

KM# 331   1/8 REAL (Octavo Real)
9.5000 g., Copper, 28 mm. **Obv:** Bow, quiver and flag **Obv. Legend:** DEPARTAMENTO DE JALISCO **Edge:** Oblique reeding **Mint:** Guadalajara

Date	Mintage	Good	VG	F	VF	XF
1858	—	6.00	11.00	20.00	42.75	—
1859	—	5.00	9.00	12.00	30.00	—
1860/59	—	5.00	9.00	14.00	33.75	—
1860	—	5.00	9.00	14.00	33.75	—
1862	—	6.00	12.00	27.50	55.00	—

KM# 337   1/8 REAL (Octavo Real)
6.7000 g., Copper, 28 mm. **Obv. Legend:** ESTO LIBE Y SOBO DE SONORA **Edge:** Reeded **Mint:** Hermosillo

Date	Mintage	Good	VG	F	VF	XF
1859 Rare	—	—	—	—	—	—

KM# 366 1/4 REAL (Un Quarto/Una Quartilla)
8.0000 g., Brass **Obv:** Monument **Obv. Legend:**
ESTO LIBE FEDO DE ZACATECAS **Rev:** Floating
angel with radiant cap on tip of arrow **Edge:** Oblique
reeding **Mint:** Zacatecas **Note:** Size varies: 28-
29mm.

Date	Mintage	Good	VG	F	VF	XF
1824 Rare	—	—	—	—	—	—
1825	—	4.00	8.00	15.00	30.00	—
1826	—	115	195	325	500	—
1827/17	—	4.00	8.00	14.00	30.00	—
1829	—	4.00	8.00	14.00	30.00	—
1830	—	4.00	8.00	13.00	30.00	—
1831	—	60.00	130	210	325	—
1832	—	4.00	8.00	14.00	30.00	—
1833	—	4.00	8.00	14.00	30.00	—
1834 Rare	—	—	—	—	—	—
1835	—	4.00	8.00	14.00	30.00	—
1846	—	4.00	8.00	13.00	30.00	—
1847	—	4.00	8.00	13.00	30.00	—
1852	—	4.00	8.00	13.00	30.00	—
1853	—	4.00	8.00	13.00	30.00	—
1855	—	7.00	15.00	37.50	100	—
1858	—	4.00	8.00	13.00	30.00	—
1859	—	4.00	8.00	13.00	30.00	—
1860	—	115	190	300	475	—
1862/57	—	4.00	8.00	13.00	30.00	—
1862/59/7	—	12.00	27.50	55.00	115	—
1862	—	4.00	8.00	12.00	30.00	—
1863/2	—	4.00	8.00	12.00	30.00	—
1863	—	4.00	8.00	12.00	30.00	—
1864	—	6.00	17.00	37.50	90.00	—

KM# 359 1/4 REAL (Un Quarto/Una Quartilla)
Copper **Obv:** Value above divides wreath, open book
within **Obv. Legend:** ESTADO LIBRE DE SAN LUIS
POTOSI **Rev:** Seated figure with cap on tip of arrow
Rev. Legend: MEXICO LIBRE **Edge:** Oblique reeding
Mint: San Luis Potosi **Note:** Size varies: 25-31mm,
weight varies: (1828-32) 9-10 g.; (1859-60) 8-9 g.

Date	Mintage	Good	VG	F	VF
1828	—	3.00	6.00	14.00	27.50
1829	—	5.00	8.00	14.00	30.00
1830	—	3.00	6.00	12.00	25.00
1832	—	6.00	9.00	15.00	33.75
1859 Large LIBRE	—	4.00	6.00	12.00	27.50
1859 Small LIBRE	—	4.00	6.00	12.00	27.50
1860	—	4.00	6.00	12.00	27.50

KM# 351 1/4 REAL (Un Quarto/Una Quartilla)
7.0000 g., Copper, 27 mm. **Obv:** Seated figure with
head right **Obv. Legend:** ESTADO LIBRE DE
GUANAJUATO **Rev:** Cap within radiant wreath
Edge: Ornamented with incuse dots **Mint:**
Guanajuato

Date	Mintage	Good	VG	F	VF	XF
1828	—	6.00	12.00	27.50	60.00	—
1828	—	6.00	14.00	30.00	65.00	—
Note: Error with GUANJUATO						
1829	—	8.00	18.00	33.75	70.00	—

KM# 353 1/4 REAL (Un Quarto/Una Quartilla)
9.3500 g., Copper, 28 mm. **Obv:** Oblique reeding
Obv. Legend: ESTADO LIBRE DE JALISCO **Rev:**
Seated figure, left, cap on pole **Mint:** Guadalajara

Date	Mintage	Good	VG	F	VF	XF
1828	—	6.00	11.00	22.50	55.00	—
1829/8	—	5.00	9.00	20.00	49.50	—
1829	—	5.00	9.00	20.00	49.50	—
1830/20	—	5.00	8.00	15.00	42.75	—
1830/29	—	5.00	8.00	15.00	42.75	—
1830	—	5.00	8.00	15.00	42.75	—
1831 Rare	—	—	—	—	—	—
1832/20	—	5.00	8.00	15.00	42.75	—
1832/28	—	5.00	8.00	15.00	42.75	—
1832	—	4.00	8.00	14.00	41.25	—
1833/2	—	5.00	8.00	14.00	41.25	—
1834	—	4.00	8.00	14.00	41.25	—
1835/3	—	5.00	8.00	14.00	41.25	—
1835	—	4.00	8.00	14.00	41.25	—
1836 Rare	—	—	—	—	—	—

KM# 364 1/4 REAL (Un Quarto/Una Quartilla)
Copper **Obv:** Arrow divides quivers **Obv. Legend:**
EST. D. SONORA UNA CUART **Rev:** Stylized
radiant cap **Edge:** Oblique reeding **Mint:** Hermosillo
Note: Size varies: 21-22mm. Weight varies: 2.3-5.5
g.

Date	Mintage	Good	VG	F	VF	XF
1831 L.S. Rare	—	—	—	—	—	—
1832 L.S.	—	4.00	8.00	22.50	75.00	—
1833/2 L.S.	—	3.00	6.00	19.00	55.00	—
1833 L.S.	—	3.00	6.00	19.00	55.00	—

Date	Mintage	Good	VG	F	VF	XF
1834 L.S.	—	3.00	6.00	19.00	55.00	—
1835/3 L.S.	—	4.00	8.00	22.50	60.00	—
1835 L.S.	—	3.00	6.00	19.00	55.00	—
1836 L.S.	—	3.00	6.00	19.00	55.00	—

KM# 340   1/4 REAL (Un Quarto/Una Quartilla)
Copper, 27 mm. **Obv:** Child facing, holding bow and arrow **Obv. Legend:** ESTADO SOBERANO DE CHIHUAHUA **Rev:** Value and date within palm wreath **Edge:** Herringbone pattern **Mint:** Chihuahua

Date	Mintage	Good	VG	F	VF	XF
1833	—	11.00	25.00	55.00	130	—
1834	—	10.00	20.00	42.00	85.00	—
1835	—	8.00	15.00	33.00	75.00	—
1835 Plain edge	—	8.00	12.00	18.00	75.00	—

KM# 354   1/4 REAL (Un Quarto/Una Quartilla)
9.3500 g., Copper, 28 mm. **Obv. Legend:** DEPARTAMENTO DE JALISCO **Edge:** Oblique reeding **Mint:** Guadalajara

Date	Mintage	Good	VG	F	VF	XF
1836	—	180	300	525	—	—

KM# 367   1/4 REAL (Un Quarto/Una Quartilla)
8.0000 g., Brass **Obv:** Monument **Obv. Legend:** DEPARTAMENTO DE ZACATECAS **Rev:** Floating angel with radiant cap on tip of arrow **Edge:** Oblique reeding **Mint:** Zacatecas **Note:** Size varies: 28-29mm.

Date	Mintage	Good	VG	F	VF	XF
1836	—	6.00	13.00	20.00	37.50	—
1845 Rare	—	—	—	—	—	—
1846	—	5.00	10.00	14.00	30.00	—

KM# 345   1/4 REAL (Un Quarto/Una Quartilla)
7.0000 g., Copper, 27 mm. **Obv:** Facing eagle, snake in beak **Obv. Legend:** REPUBLICA MEXICANA **Rev:** Value and date within circle, DURANGO above in wreath **Mint:** Durango

Date	Mintage	Good	VG	F	VF	XF
1845 Rare	—	—	—	—	—	—

KM# 341   1/4 REAL (Un Quarto/Una Quartilla)
7.0800 g., Copper, 27 mm. **Obv:** Stylized figure facing, holding bow and arrow **Obv. Legend:** ESTADO LIBRE DE CHIHUAHUA **Rev:** Value and date within designed wreath **Edge:** Plain **Mint:** Chihuahua

Date	Mintage	Good	VG	F	VF	XF
1846	—	5.00	9.00	18.00	55.00	—
Note: With fraction bar						
1846	—	8.00	13.00	22.50	70.00	—
Note: Without fraction bar						

KM# 363   1/4 REAL (Un Quarto/Una Quartilla)
27.0000 g., Copper, 27 mm. **Obv:** Head left within wreath **Obv. Legend:** ESTADO LIBRE Y SOBERANO DE SINALOA **Rev:** Value and date within wreath **Edge:** Reeded **Mint:** Culiacan

Date	Mintage	Good	VG	F	VF	XF
1847	—	5.00	8.00	18.00	35.25	—
1848	—	5.00	8.00	17.00	33.00	—
1859	—	5.00	7.00	11.00	25.00	—
1861	—	2.75	5.00	6.00	15.00	—
1862	—	2.75	5.00	6.00	17.00	—
1863	—	4.00	6.00	8.00	17.00	—
1864/3	—	4.00	6.00	8.00	17.00	—
1864	—	2.75	5.00	7.00	15.00	—
1865	—	5.00	8.00	13.00	27.50	—
1866/5	7,401,000	4.00	5.00	8.00	17.00	—
1866	Inc. above	2.75	5.00	6.00	15.00	—

KM# 363a   1/4 REAL (Un Quarto/Una Quartilla)
7.0000 g., Brass, 27 mm. **Obv:** Head left within wreath **Obv. Legend:** ESTADO LIBRE Y SOBERANO DE SINALOA **Rev:** Value and date within wreath **Edge:** Reeded **Mint:** Culiacan

Date	Mintage	Good	VG	F	VF	XF
1847	—	8.00	15.00	27.50	60.00	—

KM# 342   1/4 REAL (Un Quarto/Una Quartilla)
7.0800 g., Copper, 27 mm. **Obv:** Stylized figure facing, holding bow and arrow **Obv. Legend:** ESTADO DE CHIHUAHUA **Rev:** Value and date within designed wreath **Edge:** Plain **Mint:** Chihuahua

Date	Mintage	Good	VG	F	VF	XF
1855	—	4.00	9.00	20.00	60.00	—
1856	—	4.00	9.00	20.00	60.00	—

KM# 343   1/4 REAL (Un Quarto/Una Quartilla)
7.0800 g., Copper, 27 mm.   **Obv:** Stylized figure facing, holding bow and arrow **Obv. Legend:** DEPARTAMENTO DE CHIHUAHUA **Rev:** Value and date within designed wreath **Edge:** Plain **Mint:** Chihuahua

Date	Mintage	Good	VG	F	VF
1855	—	5.00	9.00	20.00	55.00
1855 DE (reversed D)	—	7.00	13.00	27.50	60.00

KM# 352   1/4 REAL (Un Quarto/Una Quartilla)
14.0000 g., Copper, 32 mm.   **Obv:** Facing eagle, snake in beak **Obv. Legend:** EST. LIB. DE GUANAXUATO **Rev:** Oval arms within sprays below radiant cap **Rev. Legend:** OMNIA VINCIT LABOR **Edge:** Plain **Mint:** Guanajuato

Date	Mintage	Good	VG	F	VF	XF
1856	—	11.00	27.50	55.00	105	—
1857	—	10.00	20.00	41.25	75.00	—

KM# 352a   1/4 REAL (Un Quarto/Una Quartilla)
14.0000 g., Brass, 32 mm.   **Obv:** Facing eagle, snake in beak **Obv. Legend:** EST. LIB. DE GUANAXUATO **Rev:** Oval arms within sprays below radiant cap **Rev. Legend:** OMNIA VINCIT LABOR **Edge:** Plain **Mint:** Guanajuato

Date	Mintage	Good	VG	F	VF	XF
1856	—	5.00	10.00	20.00	45.00	—
1857	—	5.00	10.00	20.00	45.00	—

KM# 346   1/4 REAL (Un Quarto/Una Quartilla)
7.5000 g., Copper, 27 mm.   **Obv:** Facing eagle, snake in beak **Obv. Legend:** REPUBLICA MEXICANA **Rev:** Date, value **Rev. Legend:** DURANGO **Edge:** Ornamented with arc and dot pattern **Mint:** Durango

Date	Mintage	Good	VG	F	VF	XF
1858 Rare	—	—	—	—	—	—

KM# 347   1/4 REAL (Un Quarto/Una Quartilla)
7.5000 g., Copper, 27 mm.   **Obv:** Facing eagle, snake in beak **Obv. Legend:** ESTADO DE DURANGO **Rev:** Radiant cap above value and date within stylized sprays **Rev. Legend:** CONSTITUCION **Edge:** Ornamented with arc and dot pattern **Mint:** Durango **Note:** Brass examples have been reported, but not confirmed.

Date	Mintage	Good	VG	F	VF	XF
1858	—	6.00	13.00	33.00	75.00	—

KM# 355   1/4 REAL (Un Quarto/Una Quartilla)
19.0000 g., Copper, 32 mm.   **Obv:** Bow, quiver and flag **Obv. Legend:** ESTADO LIBRE DE JALISCO **Rev:** Seated figure, left, cap on pole **Edge:** Oblique reeding **Mint:** Guadalajara

Date	Mintage	Good	VG	F	VF	XF
1858	—	5.00	9.00	17.00	37.50	—
1861	—	6.00	12.00	25.00	49.50	—
1862	—	5.00	9.00	17.00	37.50	—

KM# 356   1/4 REAL (Un Quarto/Una Quartilla)
19.0000 g., Copper, 32 mm.   **Obv:** Bow, quiver and flag **Obv. Legend:** DEPARTAMENTO DE JALISCO **Rev:** Seated figure, left, cap on pole **Edge:** Oblique reeding **Mint:** Guadalajara

Date	Mintage	Good	VG	F	VF	XF
1858	—	5.00	9.00	14.00	30.00	—
1859/8	—	5.00	9.00	14.00	30.00	—
1859	—	5.00	9.00	14.00	30.00	—
1860	—	5.00	9.00	14.00	30.00	—

FIRST REPUBLIC - STATE

KM# 365   1/4 REAL (Un Quarto/Una Quartilla)
14.3000 g., Copper, 32 mm. **Obv:** Facing eagle, snake in beak **Obv. Legend:** ESTO. LIBE. Y SOBO. DE SONORA **Rev:** Seated figure, left, cap on pole **Edge:** Reeded **Mint:** Hermosillo

Date	Mintage	Good	VG	F	VF	XF
1859	—	5.00	12.00	18.00	45.00	—
1861/59	—	6.00	15.00	25.00	55.00	—
1861	—	5.00	12.00	18.00	45.00	—
1862	—	5.00	12.00	18.00	45.00	—
1863/2	—	12.00	27.50	55.00	130	—

KM# 344   1/4 REAL (Un Quarto/Una Quartilla)
Copper, 28 mm. **Obv:** Seated figure, right **Obv. Legend:** E. CHIHA LIBERTAD **Rev:** Value and date within wreath **Edge:** Plain **Mint:** Chihuahua **Note:** Weight varies 11-11.5 g.

Date	Mintage	Good	VG	F	VF	XF
1860	—	3.00	6.00	17.00	37.50	—
1861	—	3.00	6.00	17.00	37.50	—
1865/1	—	4.00	8.00	20.00	45.00	—
1865	—	9.00	20.00	42.75	100	—
1866/5	—	8.00	14.00	37.50	90.00	—
1866	—	3.00	6.00	17.00	37.50	—
Note: Coin rotation
1866	—	3.00	6.00	17.00	37.50	—
Note: Medal rotation

KM# 348   1/4 REAL (Un Quarto/Una Quartilla)
Copper, 27 mm. **Obv:** Facing eagle, snake in beak **Obv. Legend:** DEPARTAMENTO DE DURANGO **Rev:** Value and date within circular legend and wreath **Rev. Legend:** LIBERTAD EN EL ORDEN **Edge:** Ornamented with arc and dot pattern **Mint:** Durango **Note:** Weight varies: 7-7.5 g.

Date	Mintage	Good	VG	F	VF	XF
1860	—	4.00	11.00	25.00	65.00	—
1866	—	5.00	12.00	27.50	70.00	—

KM# 360   1/4 REAL (Un Quarto/Una Quartilla)
Copper **Obv:** Value above divides wreath, open book within **Obv. Legend:** ESTADO LIBRE DE SAN LUIS POTOSI **Rev:** Seated figure with cap on tip of arrow **Rev. Legend:** REPUBLICA MEXICANA **Edge:** Oblique reeding **Mint:** San Luis Potosi **Note:** Size varies: 25-31mm.

Date	Mintage	Good	VG	F	VF	XF
1862	1,367	4.00	6.00	12.00	25.00	—
1862 LIBR	Inc. above	6.00	9.00	14.00	27.50	—

KM# 349   1/4 REAL (Un Quarto/Una Quartilla)
7.0000 g., Copper **Obv:** Facing eagle, snake in beak **Obv. Legend:** ESTADO DE DURANGO **Rev:** Value and date above sprays **Rev. Legend:** INDEPENDENCIA Y LIBERTAD **Edge:** Ornamented with arc and dot pattern **Mint:** Durango **Note:** Size varies: 26-27mm.

Date	Mintage	Good	VG	F	VF	XF
1866	—	6.00	14.00	37.50	85.00	—

KM# 361   1/4 REAL (Un Quarto/Una Quartilla)
Copper **Obv. Legend:** ESTADO LIBRE Y SOBERANO DE S.L. POTOSI **Rev:** Radiant cap and value within wrath, date below **Rev. Legend:** LIBERTAD Y REFORMA **Edge:** Reeded or plain **Mint:** San Luis Potosi **Note:** Size varies: 27-28mm. Weight varies: 9-10 g.

Date	Mintage	Good	VG	F	VF	XF
1867	3,177,000	4.00	6.00	11.00	25.00	—
1867 AFG	Inc. above	4.00	6.00	11.00	25.00	—
Note: "AFG" are the coin designer/engraver initials

KM# 362   1/4 REAL (Un Quarto/Una Quartilla)
Copper **Obv. Legend:** ESTADO LIBRE Y SOBERANO DE S.L. POTOSI **Rev. Legend:** LIBERTAD Y REFORMA **Edge:** Plain **Mint:** San Luis Potosi

Date	Mintage	Good	VG	F	VF	XF
1867	Inc. above	4.00	6.00	11.00	25.00	—
1867 AFG	Inc. above	4.00	6.00	11.00	25.00	—
Note: "AFG" are the coin designer/engraver initials

KM# 350 1/4 REAL (Un Quarto/Una Quartilla)
7.5000 g., Copper, 27 mm. **Obv:** Facing eagle,
snake in beak **Obv. Legend:** ESTADO DE
DURANGO **Rev:** Date and circular legend, value
within **Rev. Legend:** SUFRAGIO LIBRE **Edge:**
Ornamented with arc and dot pattern **Mint:** Durango
Note: Brass examples have been reported, but not
confirmed.

Date	Mintage	Good	VG	F	VF	XF
1872	—	3.00	6.00	14.00	30.00	—

FEDERAL COINAGE

KM# 315 1/16 REAL (Medio Octavo)
1.7500 g., Copper, 17 mm. **Obv. Legend:**
REPUBLICA MEXICANA **Edge:** Ornamented with
small incuse rectangles **Mint:** Mexico City

Date	Mintage	VG	F	VF	XF	Unc
1831	—	10.00	20.00	50.00	100	—
1832/1	—	12.00	22.00	55.00	125	—
1832	—	10.00	20.00	50.00	100	—
1833	—	10.00	20.00	50.00	100	—

KM# 315a 1/16 REAL (Medio Octavo)
1.7500 g., Brass, 17 mm. **Obv. Legend:**
REPUBLICA MEXICANA **Edge:** Ornamented with
small incuse rectangles **Mint:** Mexico City

Date	Mintage	VG	F	VF	XF	Unc
1832	—	13.50	22.50	65.00	175	650
1833	—	10.00	17.50	50.00	150	—
1835	—	400	800	1,250	2,500	—

KM# 333 1/8 REAL (Octavo Real)
3.5000 g., Copper, 21 mm. **Obv:** Facing eagle,
snake in beak **Obv. Legend:** REPUBLICA
MEXICANA **Rev:** Value and date within wreath
Edge: Ornamented with small incuse rectangles
Mint: Mexico City

Date	Mintage	Good	VG	F	VF	XF
1829	—	7.50	12.00	25.00	55.00	—
1830	—	1.00	2.00	6.00	20.00	—
1831	—	1.50	3.50	7.00	25.00	—
1832	—	1.50	3.50	7.00	25.00	—
1833/2	—	1.50	3.50	7.00	25.00	—
1833	—	1.50	2.75	6.00	20.00	—
1834	—	1.50	2.75	6.00	20.00	—
1835	—	1.50	2.75	6.00	20.00	—
1835/4	—	1.75	3.50	7.00	25.00	—

KM# 332 1/8 REAL (Octavo Real)
7.0000 g., Copper, 27 mm. **Obv. Legend:**
REPUBLICA MEXICANA **Edge:** Ornamented with
small incuse rectangles **Mint:** Mexico City

Date	Mintage	VG	F	VF	XF	Unc
1829	—	450	900	1,500	2,500	—

KM# 334 1/8 REAL (Octavo Real)
14.0000 g., Copper **Obv:** Seated figure, right **Obv.
Legend:** LIBERTAD **Rev:** Value and date within
wreath **Edge:** Lettered (1841-42); Plain (1850-61)
Edge Lettering: REPUBLICA MEXICANA **Mint:**
Mexico City **Note:** Size varies: 29-30mm.

Date	Mintage	Good	VG	F	VF	XF
1841	—	6.00	15.00	30.00	75.00	—
1842	—	2.50	5.00	10.00	30.00	—
1850	—	12.50	20.00	30.00	80.00	175
1861	—	5.00	12.00	25.00	70.00	—

KM# 357 1/4 REAL (Un Quarto/Una Quartilla)
14.0000 g., Copper, 33 mm. **Obv:** Facing eagle,
snake in beak **Obv. Legend:** REPUBLICA
MEXICANA **Rev:** Value and date within wreath
Edge: Ornamented with small incuse rectangles
Mint: Mexico City

Date	Mintage	VG	F	VF	XF	Unc
1829	—	12.00	36.00	90.00	275	—

KM# 358 1/4 REAL (Un Quarto/Una Quartilla)
7.0000 g., Copper, 27 mm. **Obv:** Facing eagle,
snake in beak **Obv. Legend:** REPUBLICA
MEXICANA **Rev:** Value and date within wreath
Edge: Ornamented with small incuse rectangles
Mint: Mexico City **Note:** Reduced size.

Date	Mintage	VG	F	VF	XF	Unc
1829	—	12.00	25.00	50.00	180	—
1830	—	1.50	2.75	5.00	12.00	—
1831	—	1.50	2.75	5.00	12.00	—
1832	—	5.50	10.00	20.00	42.00	—
1833	—	1.50	2.75	5.00	12.00	—
1834/3	—	1.75	3.00	6.00	14.00	—
1834	—	1.50	2.75	5.00	12.00	—
1835	—	1.50	2.75	5.00	12.00	—
1836/5	—	1.75	3.00	6.00	14.00	—
1836	—	1.50	2.75	5.00	12.00	—
1837	—	6.50	13.50	22.50	55.00	—

KM# 358a.1   1/4 REAL (Un Quarto/Una Quartilla)
7.0000 g., Brass, 27 mm. **Countermark:** JM **Obv. Legend:** REPUBLICA MEXICANA **Edge:** Ornamented with small incuse rectangles **Mint:** Mexico City **Note:** Reduced size.

Date	Mintage	VG	F	VF	XF	Unc
1831		8.00	13.50	27.50	60.00	—

KM# 358a.2   1/4 REAL (Un Quarto/Una Quartilla)
7.0000 g., Brass, 27 mm. **Obv. Legend:** REPUBLICA MEXICANA **Edge:** Ornamented with small incuse rectangles **Mint:** Mexico City **Note:** Without countermark.

Date	Mintage	VG	F	VF	XF	Unc
1831	—	—	—	—	—	—

KM# 368.2   1/4 REAL (Un Quarto/Una Quartilla)
0.8450 g., 0.9030 Silver 0.0245 oz. ASW **Mint:** Durango **Note:** Struck at Durango Mint, mint mark Do.

Date	Mintage	VG	F	VF	XF	Unc
1842Do LR	—	12.00	20.00	40.00	140	—
1843Do	—	20.00	40.00	90.00	220	—

KM# 368   1/4 REAL (Un Quarto/Una Quartilla)
0.8450 g., 0.9030 Silver 0.0245 oz. ASW **Obv:** Head left **Rev:** Value **Mint:** Chihuahua **Note:** Mint mark CA.

Date	Mintage	VG	F	VF	XF	Unc
1843CA RG	—	75.00	125	300	550	—

KM# 368.3   1/4 REAL (Un Quarto/Una Quartilla)
0.8450 g., 0.9030 Silver 0.0245 oz. ASW **Mint:** Guadalajara **Note:** Mint mark Ga.

Date	Mintage	VG	F	VF	XF
1842Ga JG	—	3.00	7.00	10.00	25.00
1843/2Ga JG	—	—	—	—	—
1843Ga JG	—	7.00	11.00	15.00	36.00
1843Ga MC	—	5.00	8.00	11.00	30.00
1844Ga MC	—	5.00	8.00	11.00	30.00
1844Ga LR	—	3.00	6.00	12.00	25.00
1845Ga LR	—	10.00	25.00	48.00	90.00
1846Ga LR	—	12.00	30.00	48.00	70.00
1847Ga LR	—	10.00	25.00	48.00	70.00
1848Ga LR Rare	—	—	—	—	—
1850Ga LR Rare	—	—	—	—	—
1851Ga LR	—	7.00	12.00	25.00	60.00
1852Ga LR	—	60.00	120	160	240
1854/3Ga LR	—	60.00	120	160	240
1854Ga LR	—	12.00	25.00	60.00	120
1855Ga LR	—	12.00	25.00	60.00	120
1857Ga LR	—	12.00	25.00	60.00	120
1862Ga LR	—	12.00	25.00	60.00	120

KM# 368.5   1/4 REAL (Un Quarto/Una Quartilla)
0.8450 g., 0.9030 Silver 0.0245 oz. ASW **Mint:** Guanajuato **Note:** Mint mark Go.

Date	Mintage	VG	F	VF	XF
1842Go PM	—	5.00	15.00	35.00	90.00
1842Go LR	—	2.00	4.00	8.00	18.00
1843/2Go LR	—	4.00	6.00	10.00	25.00
1843Go LR	—	2.00	4.00	8.00	18.00
1844/3Go LR	—	—	—	—	—
1844Go LR	—	10.00	25.00	60.00	150
1845Go LR	—	8.00	17.00	40.00	95.00
1846/5Go LR	—	—	—	—	—
1846Go LR	—	6.00	15.00	30.00	70.00
1847Go LR	—	2.00	4.00	8.00	18.00
1848/7Go LR	—	2.00	4.00	8.00	18.00
1848Go LR	—	2.00	4.00	8.00	18.00
1849/7Go LR	—	8.00	15.00	30.00	70.00
1849Go LR	—	2.00	4.00	8.00	18.00
1850Go LR	—	2.00	4.00	8.00	15.00
1851Go LR	—	2.00	4.00	8.00	18.00
1852Go LR	—	2.00	4.00	8.00	18.00
1853Go LR	—	2.00	4.00	8.00	18.00
1855Go LR	—	4.00	8.00	15.00	36.00

KM# 368.6   1/4 REAL (Un Quarto/Una Quartilla)
0.8450 g., 0.9030 Silver 0.0245 oz. ASW **Mint:** Mexico City **Note:** Mint mark Mo.

Date	Mintage	VG	F	VF	XF
1856/4Go LR	—	20.00	40.00	60.00	120
1856Go LR	—	5.00	10.00	20.00	42.00
1862/1Go LR	—	3.00	5.00	10.00	25.00
1862Go LR	—	2.00	4.00	8.00	18.00
1863Go	—	2.00	4.00	8.00	18.00

KM# 368.6   1/4 REAL (Un Quarto/Una Quartilla)
0.8450 g., 0.9030 Silver 0.0245 oz. ASW **Mint:** Mexico City **Note:** Mint mark Mo.

Date	Mintage	VG	F	VF	XF
1842Mo LR	—	2.00	4.00	8.00	18.00
1843Mo LR	—	2.00	4.00	8.00	18.00
1844/3Mo LR	—	20.00	30.00	75.00	150
1844Mo LR	—	4.00	6.00	10.00	25.00
1845Mo LR	—	6.00	15.00	35.00	85.00
1846Mo LR	—	10.00	20.00	35.00	80.00
1850Mo LR Rare	—	—	—	—	—
1858Mo LR	—	4.00	8.00	15.00	36.00
1859Mo LR	—	4.00	6.00	10.00	25.00
1860Mo LR	—	4.00	6.00	10.00	25.00
1861Mo LR	—	4.00	6.00	10.00	25.00
1862Mo LR	—	4.00	6.00	10.00	25.00
1863/53Mo LR	—	4.00	6.00	10.00	25.00
1863Mo LR	—	4.00	6.00	10.00	25.00

KM# 368.7   1/4 REAL (Un Quarto/Una Quartilla)
0.8450 g., 0.9030 Silver 0.0245 oz. ASW **Mint:** San Luis Potosi **Note:** Mint mark SLP, PI, P, I/P.

Date	Mintage	VG	F	VF	XF
1842S.L.Pi	—	2.00	5.00	10.00	25.00
1843/2S.L.Pi	—	4.00	6.00	10.00	25.00
1843S.L.Pi	—	2.00	4.00	8.00	25.00
1844S.L.Pi	—	2.00	4.00	8.00	25.00
1845/3S.L.Pi	—	4.00	6.00	10.00	30.00
1845/4S.L.Pi	—	4.00	6.00	10.00	30.00
1845S.L.Pi	—	2.00	4.00	8.00	25.00
1847/5S.L.Pi	—	4.00	9.00	20.00	48.00
1847S.L.Pi	—	3.00	6.00	12.00	30.00
1851/47S.L.Pi	—	10.00	20.00	35.00	70.00
1854S.L.Pi	—	125	200	275	475
1856S.L.Pi	—	10.00	20.00	35.00	70.00
1857S.L.Pi	—	30.00	60.00	100	210
1862/57S.L.Pi	—	10.00	20.00	40.00	100

KM# 368.1   1/4 REAL (Un Quarto/Una Quartilla)
0.8450 g., 0.9030 Silver 0.0245 oz. ASW **Mint:** Culiacan **Note:** Mint mark C.

Date	Mintage	VG	F	VF	XF	Unc
1855C LR	—	50.00	100	225	525	—

KM# 368.4   1/4 REAL (Un Quarto/Una Quartilla)
0.8450 g., 0.9030 Silver 0.0245 oz. ASW **Mint:** Guadalupe y Calvo **Note:** Mint mark GC.

Date	Mintage	VG	F	VF	XF	Unc
1844GC LR	—	50.00	75.00	200	500	—

KM# 368.8   1/4 REAL (Un Quarto/Una Quartilla)
0.8450 g., 0.9030 Silver 0.0245 oz. ASW **Mint:** Zacatecas **Note:** Mint mark Zs.

Date	Mintage	VG	F	VF	XF	Unc
1842/1Zs LR	—	4.00	8.00	15.00	36.00	—
1842Zs LR	—	4.00	8.00	15.00	36.00	—

KM# 370.5   1/2 REAL
1.6900 g., 0.9030 Silver 0.0491 oz. ASW **Obv:** Facing eagle, snake in beak **Mint:** Guadalajara

Date	Mintage	F	VF	XF	Unc
1825Ga FS	—	25.00	40.00	85.00	220
1826Ga FS	—	10.00	15.00	38.50	90.00
1828/7Ga FS	—	12.50	20.00	40.00	90.00
1829Ga FS	—	7.50	15.00	33.00	75.00
1830/29Ga FS	—	40.00	60.00	110	220
1831Ga LP	—	350	—	—	—
1832Ga FS	—	10.00	20.00	38.50	90.00
1834/3Ga FS	—	65.00	100	195	275
1834Ga FS	—	10.00	20.00	38.50	90.00
1835/4/3Ga FS/LP	—	15.00	25.00	44.00	100
1837/6Ga JG	—	100	250	550	1,100
1838/7Ga JG	—	15.00	25.00	44.00	100
1839/8Ga JG/FS	—	35.00	75.00	165	275

FIRST REPUBLIC - FEDERAL

Date	Mintage	F	VF	XF	Unc
1839Ga MC	—	10.00	20.00	38.50	90.00
1840/39Ga MC/JG	—	—	—	—	—
1840Ga MC	—	15.00	25.00	44.00	100
1841Ga MC	—	20.00	35.00	55.00	110
1842/1Ga JG	—	15.00	25.00	44.00	100
1842Ga JG	—	10.00	20.00	38.50	90.00
1843/2Ga JG	—	15.00	30.00	55.00	110
1843Ga JG	—	10.00	20.00	38.50	90.00
1843Ga MC/JG	—	10.00	20.00	38.50	90.00
1843Ga MC	—	10.00	20.00	38.50	90.00
1844Ga MC	—	10.00	20.00	38.50	90.00
1845Ga MC	—	10.00	20.00	38.50	90.00
1845Ga JG	—	10.00	20.00	38.50	90.00
1846Ga MC	—	10.00	20.00	38.50	90.00
1846Ga JG	—	10.00	20.00	38.50	90.00
1847Ga JG	—	10.00	20.00	38.50	90.00
1848/7Ga JG	—	10.00	20.00	38.50	90.00
1849Ga JG	—	10.00	20.00	38.50	90.00
1850/49Ga JG	—	—	—	—	—
1850Ga JG	—	10.00	20.00	38.50	90.00
1851/0Ga JG	—	10.00	20.00	38.50	90.00
1852Ga JG	—	10.00	20.00	38.50	90.00
1853Ga JG	—	10.00	20.00	38.50	90.00
1854Ga JG	—	10.00	20.00	38.50	90.00
1855/4Ga JG	—	10.00	20.00	38.50	90.00
1855Ga JG	—	10.00	20.00	38.50	90.00
1856Ga JG	—	10.00	20.00	38.50	90.00
1857Ga JG	—	10.00	20.00	38.50	90.00
1858/7Ga JG	—	10.00	20.00	38.50	90.00
1858Ga JG	—	10.00	20.00	38.50	90.00
1859/7Ga JG	—	10.00	20.00	38.50	90.00
1860/59Ga JG	—	10.00	20.00	38.50	90.00
1861Ga JG	—	5.00	12.50	27.50	65.00
1862/1Ga JG	—	15.00	25.00	44.00	100

KM# 370.6 1/2 REAL
1.6900 g., 0.9030 Silver 0.0491 oz. ASW **Obv:** Facing eagle, snake in beak **Mint:** Guadalupe y Calvo

Date	Mintage	F	VF	XF	Unc
1844GC MP	—	50.00	100	165	425
1845GC MP	—	25.00	50.00	110	240
1846GC MP	—	25.00	50.00	110	240
1847GC MP	—	25.00	50.00	110	350
1848GC MP	—	20.00	40.00	85.00	180
1849GC MP	—	25.00	50.00	110	240
1850GC MP	—	30.00	60.00	140	300
1851GC MP	—	25.00	50.00	110	240

KM# 370.8 1/2 REAL
1.6900 g., 0.9030 Silver 0.0491 oz. ASW **Obv:** Facing eagle, snake in beak **Mint:** Hermosillo

Date	Mintage	F	VF	XF	Unc
1839Ho PP Unique	—	—	—	—	—
1862Ho FM	—	500	650	1,100	—
1867Ho PR/FM Inverted 6, and 7/1	—	100	175	275	600

KM# 370.9 1/2 REAL
1.6900 g., 0.9030 Silver 0.0491 oz. ASW **Obv:** Facing eagle, snake in beak **Mint:** Mexico City

Date	Mintage	F	VF	XF	Unc
1825Mo JM Short top 5	—	10.00	20.00	44.00	90.00
1825Mo JM Long top 5	—	10.00	20.00	44.00	90.00
1826/5Mo JM	—	10.00	20.00	44.00	90.00
1826Mo JM	—	5.00	10.00	22.50	65.00
1827/6Mo JM	—	5.00	10.00	22.50	65.00
1827Mo JM	—	5.00	10.00	22.50	65.00
1828/7Mo JM	—	7.50	15.00	27.50	95.00
1828Mo JM	—	10.00	20.00	44.00	100
1829Mo JM	—	7.50	15.00	27.50	85.00
1830Mo JM	—	5.00	10.00	22.50	65.00
1831Mo JM	—	5.00	10.00	22.50	65.00
1832Mo JM	—	7.50	12.50	30.25	65.00
1833Mo MJ	—	7.50	12.50	30.25	65.00
1834Mo ML	—	5.00	10.00	22.50	65.00
1835Mo ML	—	5.00	10.00	22.50	65.00
1836/5Mo ML/MF	—	7.50	15.00	27.50	70.00
1836Mo ML	—	7.50	15.00	27.50	70.00

Date	Mintage	F	VF	XF	Unc
1838Mo ML	—	5.00	10.00	22.50	65.00
1839/8Mo ML	—	5.00	10.00	27.50	70.00
1839Mo ML	—	5.00	10.00	22.50	55.00
1840Mo ML	—	5.00	10.00	22.50	55.00
1841Mo ML	—	5.00	10.00	22.50	55.00
1842Mo ML	—	15.00	35.00	90.00	220
1842Mo MM	—	5.00	10.00	22.50	55.00
1843Mo MM	—	10.00	20.00	44.00	90.00
1844Mo MF	—	5.00	10.00	22.50	55.00
1845/4Mo MF	—	5.00	10.00	27.50	65.00
1845Mo MF	—	5.00	10.00	22.50	55.00
1846Mo MF	—	5.00	10.00	22.50	55.00
1847Mo RC	—	10.00	20.00	44.00	90.00
1847Mo RC R/M	—	10.00	20.00	44.00	90.00
1848/7Mo GC/RC	—	5.00	10.00	22.50	55.00
1849Mo GC	—	5.00	10.00	22.50	55.00
1850Mo GC	—	5.00	10.00	22.50	55.00
1851Mo GC	—	5.00	10.00	22.50	55.00
1852Mo GC	—	5.00	10.00	22.50	55.00
1853Mo GC	—	5.00	10.00	22.50	55.00
1854Mo GC	—	5.00	10.00	22.50	55.00
1855Mo GC	—	5.00	10.00	22.50	55.00
1855Mo GF/GC	—	7.50	12.50	27.50	70.00
1856/5Mo GF	—	7.50	12.50	27.50	70.00
1857Mo GF	—	5.00	10.00	22.50	55.00
1858Mo FH	—	3.00	5.00	14.00	44.00
1858Mo FH F/G	—	5.00	10.00	22.50	55.00
1858/9Mo FH	—	5.00	10.00	22.50	55.00
1859Mo FH/GC	—	5.00	10.00	22.50	55.00
1859Mo FH	—	3.00	6.00	17.00	55.00
1860Mo FH/GC	—	5.00	10.00	22.50	55.00
1860Mo FH	—	3.00	6.00	17.00	55.00
1860Mo TH	—	25.00	50.00	110	220
1860/59Mo FH	—	7.50	12.50	27.50	70.00
1861Mo CH	—	3.00	6.00	17.00	49.50
1862/52Mo CH	—	5.00	10.00	22.50	55.00
1862Mo CH	—	3.00	6.00	17.00	49.50
1863/55Mo TH/GC	—	5.00	10.00	22.50	55.00
1863Mo CH/GC	—	5.00	10.00	22.50	55.00
1863Mo CH	—	3.00	6.00	17.00	49.50

KM# 370.10 1/2 REAL
1.6900 g., 0.9030 Silver 0.0491 oz. ASW **Obv:** Facing eagle, snake in beak **Mint:** San Luis Potosi

Date	Mintage	F	VF	XF	Unc
1831Pi JS	—	7.50	12.50	27.50	70.00
1841/36Pi JS	—	20.00	40.00	85.00	140
1842/1Pi PS	—	20.00	40.00	85.00	140
1842/1Pi PS P/J	—	60.00	80.00	165	325
1842Pi PS/PJ	—	50.00	75.00	140	275
1842 PS	—	60.00	80.00	165	325
1842Pi JS	—	20.00	40.00	85.00	140
1843/2Pi PS	—	17.50	25.00	44.00	90.00
1843Pi PS	—	15.00	25.00	38.50	75.00
1843Pi AM	—	10.00	15.00	27.50	65.00
1844Pi AM	—	10.00	15.00	33.00	70.00
1845Pi AM	—	250	375	550	1,650
1846/5Pi AM	—	40.00	75.00	140	220
1847/6Pi AM	—	15.00	25.00	44.00	90.00
1848Pi AM	—	15.00	25.00	44.00	90.00
1849Pi MC/AM	—	15.00	25.00	44.00	90.00
1849Pi MC	—	12.50	20.00	38.50	75.00
1850/49Pi MC	—	—	—	—	—
1850Pi MC	—	10.00	15.00	27.50	65.00
1850P MC	—	—	—	—	—
1851Pi MC	—	10.00	15.00	27.50	65.00
1852Pi MC	—	10.00	20.00	33.00	70.00
1853Pi MC	—	7.50	12.50	22.50	65.00
1854Pi MC	—	7.50	12.50	22.50	65.00
1855Pi MC	—	15.00	20.00	38.50	75.00
1856Pi MC	—	15.00	25.00	55.00	110
1856Pi (no I)	—	—	—	—	—
1857Pi MC	—	7.50	12.50	22.50	65.00
1857Pi PS	—	10.00	15.00	33.00	70.00
1858Pi MC	—	12.50	20.00	38.50	75.00
1858Pi PS	—	12.50	20.00	38.50	75.00
1859Pi MC Rare	—	—	—	—	—
1860/59Pi PS	—	125	200	650	—
1861Pi RO	—	10.00	15.00	33.00	65.00

Date	Mintage	F	VF	XF	Unc
1862/1Pi RO	—	15.00	25.00	55.00	140
1862Pi RO	—	15.00	25.00	55.00	140
1863/2Pi RO	—	15.00	25.00	49.50	110

KM# 370.2 1/2 REAL
1.6900 g., 0.9030 Silver 0.0491 oz. ASW **Obv:**
Facing eagle, snake in beak **Obv. Legend:**
REPUBLICA MEXICANA **Rev:** Radiant cap **Mint:**
Culiacan **Note:** Mint mark C.

Date	Mintage	F	VF	XF	Unc
1846 CE	—	30.00	50.00	85.00	165
1848/7 CE	—	15.00	25.00	49.50	100
1849/8 CE	—	15.00	25.00	49.50	100
1849 CE	—	—	—	—	—
1852 CE	—	12.50	20.00	44.00	90.00
1853/1 CE	—	12.50	20.00	44.00	90.00
1854 CE	—	20.00	35.00	55.00	110
1856 CE	—	12.50	20.00	44.00	90.00
1857/6 CE	—	20.00	35.00	55.00	110
1857 CE	—	15.00	25.00	49.50	100
1858 CE Error 1 for 1/2	—	12.50	20.00	44.00	90.00
1860/59 PV	—	20.00	35.00	55.00	110
1860 PV	—	12.50	20.00	44.00	90.00
1861 PV	—	12.50	20.00	44.00	90.00
1863 CE Error 1 for 1/2	—	15.00	25.00	49.50	100
1867 CE	—	12.50	20.00	44.00	90.00
1869 6/5 CE Error 1 for 1/2	—	12.50	20.00	44.00	90.00

KM# 370.3 1/2 REAL
1.6900 g., 0.9030 Silver 0.0491 oz. ASW **Obv:**
Facing eagle, snake in beak **Mint:** Durango **Note:**
Mint mark D, Do.

Date	Mintage	F	VF	XF	Unc
1832 RM	—	125	225	375	650
1832 RM/L	—	—	—	—	—
1833/2 RM/L	—	75.00	100	165	250
1833/1 RM/L	—	12.50	20.00	44.00	90.00
1833 RM	—	25.00	40.00	85.00	165
1834/1 RM	—	25.00	40.00	85.00	165
1834 RM	—	12.50	20.00	44.00	90.00
1837/1 RM	—	12.50	30.00	65.00	220
1837/4 RM	—	12.50	30.00	65.00	220
1837/6 RM	—	12.50	30.00	65.00	220
1841/33 RM	—	15.00	30.00	65.00	275
1842/32 RM	—	12.50	20.00	44.00	90.00
1842 RM	—	12.50	20.00	44.00	90.00
1842 RM 8R Error	—	12.50	20.00	44.00	90.00
1842 1/2 RM 8R Error	—	12.50	20.00	44.00	90.00
1843/33 RM	—	15.00	25.00	55.00	110
1843 RM	—	15.00	25.00	55.00	110
1845/31 RM	—	12.50	20.00	44.00	90.00
1845/34 RM	—	12.50	20.00	44.00	90.00
1845/35 RM	—	12.50	20.00	44.00	90.00
1845 RM	—	15.00	25.00	55.00	110
1846 RM	—	30.00	50.00	90.00	220
1848/5 RM	—	35.00	55.00	120	275
1848/36 RM	—	25.00	40.00	85.00	220
1849 JMR	—	25.00	40.00	85.00	220
1850 RM Rare	—	—	—	—	—
1850 JMR	—	25.00	40.00	85.00	220
1851 JMR	—	20.00	35.00	55.00	110
1852/1 JMR	—	65.00	125	275	650

Date	Mintage	F	VF	XF	Unc
1852 JMR	—	30.00	50.00	90.00	220
1853 CP	—	12.50	20.00	44.00	90.00
1854 CP	—	25.00	40.00	85.00	220
1855 CP	—	25.00	40.00	65.00	165
1856/5 CP	—	20.00	35.00	55.00	110
1857 CP	—	20.00	35.00	55.00	110
1858/7 CP	—	20.00	35.00	55.00	110
1859 CP	—	20.00	35.00	55.00	110
1860/59 CP	—	40.00	65.00	150	325
1861 CP	—	125	250	450	775
1862 CP	—	25.00	40.00	65.00	140
1864 LT	—	100	300	550	1,100
1869 CP	—	40.00	65.00	140	300

KM# 370.11 1/2 REAL
1.6900 g., 0.9030 Silver 0.0491 oz. ASW **Obv:**
Facing eagle, snake in beak **Mint:** Zacatecas **Note:**
Mint mark Z, Zs.

Date	Mintage	F	VF	XF	Unc
1826 AZ	—	5.00	10.00	22.50	65.00
1826 AO	—	5.00	10.00	22.50	65.00
1827 AO	—	5.00	10.00	22.50	65.00
1828/7 AO	—	5.00	10.00	22.50	65.00
1829 AO	—	5.00	10.00	22.50	65.00
1830 OV	—	5.00	10.00	22.50	65.00
1831 OV	—	25.00	50.00	85.00	165
1831 OM	—	5.00	10.00	22.50	65.00
1832 OM	—	5.00	10.00	22.50	65.00
1833 OM	—	5.00	10.00	22.50	65.00
1834 OM	—	5.00	10.00	22.50	65.00
1835/4 OM	—	5.00	10.00	22.50	65.00
1835 OM	—	5.00	10.00	22.50	65.00
1836 OM	—	5.00	10.00	22.50	65.00
1837 OM	—	10.00	20.00	44.00	90.00
1838 OM	—	5.00	10.00	22.50	65.00
1839 OM	—	7.50	15.00	33.00	70.00
1840 OM	—	10.00	25.00	49.50	100
1841 OM	—	10.00	25.00	49.50	100
1842/1 OM	—	5.00	10.00	22.50	65.00
1842 OM	—	5.00	10.00	22.50	65.00
1843 OM	—	40.00	75.00	125	275
1844 OM	—	5.00	10.00	22.50	65.00
1845 OM	—	5.00	10.00	22.50	65.00
1846 OM	—	7.50	15.00	33.00	70.00
1847 OM	—	5.00	10.00	22.50	55.00
1848 OM	—	5.00	10.00	22.50	55.00
1849 OM	—	5.00	10.00	22.50	55.00
1850 OM	—	5.00	10.00	22.50	55.00
1851 OM	—	5.00	10.00	22.50	55.00
1852 OM	—	5.00	10.00	22.50	55.00
1853 OM	—	5.00	10.00	22.50	55.00
1854/3 OM	—	5.00	10.00	22.50	55.00
1854 OM	—	5.00	10.00	22.50	55.00
1855/3 OM	—	7.50	15.00	33.00	70.00
1855 OM	—	5.00	10.00	22.50	55.00
1856 OM	—	5.00	10.00	22.50	55.00
1857 MO	—	5.00	10.00	22.50	55.00
1858 MO	—	5.00	10.00	22.50	55.00
1859 MO	—	6.00	8.50	19.00	38.50
1859 VL	—	6.00	8.50	19.00	44.00
1860/50 VL Inverted A for V	—	5.00	10.00	22.50	55.00
1860/59 VL Inverted A for V	—	5.00	10.00	22.50	55.00
1860 MO	—	5.00	10.00	22.50	55.00
1860 VL	—	7.50	15.00	33.00	70.00
1861/0 VL Inverted A for V	—	5.00	10.00	22.50	55.00
1861 VL Inverted A for V	—	5.00	10.00	22.50	55.00
1862 VL Inverted A for V	—	5.00	10.00	22.50	55.00
1863 VL Inverted A for V	—	5.00	10.00	22.50	55.00
1863/1 VL Inverted A for V	—	7.50	15.00	33.00	70.00
1869 YH	—	5.00	10.00	22.50	55.00

KM# 370.7 1/2 REAL
1.6900 g., 0.9030 Silver 0.0491 oz. ASW **Obv:**
Facing eagle, snake in beak **Mint:** Guanajuato **Note:**
Varieties exist.

Date	Mintage	F	VF	XF	Unc
1826Go MJ	—	125	250	450	1,100
1827/6Go MJ	—	7.50	15.00	33.00	85.00
1828/7Go MJ	—	7.50	15.00	33.00	85.00

FIRST REPUBLIC - FEDERAL

Date	Mintage	F	VF	XF	Unc
1828Go MJ	—	—	—	—	—
Note: Denomination 2/1					
1828Go JG	—	—	—	—	—
1828Go MR	—	50.00	100	165	275
1829/8Go MJ	—	5.00	10.00	27.50	55.00
1829Go MJ	—	5.00	10.00	27.50	55.00
1829Go MJ	—	5.00	10.00	27.50	55.00
Note: Reversed N in MEXICANA					
1830Go MJ	—	5.00	10.00	27.50	55.00
1831/29Go MJ	—	15.00	30.00	65.00	165
1831Go MJ	—	10.00	20.00	44.00	90.00
1832/1Go MJ	—	7.50	15.00	33.00	85.00
1832Go MJ	—	7.50	15.00	33.00	85.00
1833Go MJ Round top 3	—	10.00	20.00	44.00	90.00
1833Go MJ Flat top 3	—	10.00	20.00	44.00	90.00
1834Go PJ	—	5.00	10.00	27.50	55.00
1835Go PJ	—	5.00	10.00	27.50	55.00
1836/5Go PJ	—	7.50	15.00	33.00	85.00
1836Go PJ	—	5.00	10.00	27.50	55.00
1837Go PJ	—	5.00	10.00	27.50	55.00
1838/7Go PJ	—	5.00	10.00	27.50	55.00
1839Go PJ	—	5.00	10.00	27.50	55.00
1839Go PJ	—	5.00	10.00	27.50	55.00
Note: Error: REPUBLIGA					
1840/39Go PJ	—	7.50	10.00	27.50	85.00
1840Go PJ Straight J	—	5.00	10.00	27.50	55.00
1840Go PJ Curved J	—	5.00	10.00	27.50	55.00
1841/31Go PJ	—	5.00	10.00	27.50	55.00
1841Go PJ	—	5.00	10.00	27.50	55.00
1842/1Go PJ	—	5.00	10.00	27.50	55.00
1842/1Go PM	—	5.00	10.00	27.50	55.00
1842Go PM/J	—	5.00	10.00	27.50	55.00
1842Go PJ	—	5.00	10.00	27.50	55.00
1842Go PM	—	5.00	10.00	27.50	55.00
1843/33Go PM 1/2 over 8	—	5.00	10.00	27.50	55.00
1843Go PM	—	5.00	10.00	27.50	55.00
Note: Convex wings					
1843Go PM	—	5.00	10.00	27.50	55.00
Note: Concave wings					
1844/3Go PM	—	5.00	10.00	27.50	55.00
1844Go PM	—	10.00	20.00	44.00	100
1845/4Go PM	—	5.00	10.00	27.50	55.00
1845Go PM	—	5.00	10.00	27.50	55.00
1846/4Go PM	—	5.00	10.00	27.50	55.00
1846/5Go PM	—	5.00	10.00	27.50	55.00
1846Go PM	—	5.00	10.00	27.50	55.00
1847/6Go PM	—	7.50	15.00	33.00	65.00
1847Go PM	—	7.50	15.00	33.00	65.00
1848/35Go PM	—	5.00	10.00	27.50	55.00
1848Go PM	—	5.00	10.00	27.50	55.00
1848Go PF/M	—	5.00	10.00	27.50	55.00
1849/39Go PF	—	5.00	10.00	27.50	55.00
1849Go PF	—	5.00	10.00	27.50	55.00
1849Go PF	—	5.00	10.00	27.50	55.00
Note: Error: MEXCANA					
1850Go PF	—	5.00	10.00	27.50	55.00
1851Go PF	—	5.00	10.00	27.50	55.00
1852/1Go PF	—	5.00	10.00	27.50	55.00
1852Go PF	—	2.50	7.50	19.00	44.00
1853Go PF/R	—	5.00	10.00	27.50	55.00
1853Go PF	—	5.00	10.00	27.50	55.00
1854Go PF	—	5.00	10.00	27.50	55.00
1855Go PF	—	5.00	10.00	27.50	55.00
1856/4Go PF	—	5.00	10.00	27.50	55.00
1856/5Go PF	—	5.00	10.00	27.50	55.00
1856Go PF	—	5.00	10.00	27.50	55.00
1857/6Go PF	—	5.00	10.00	27.50	55.00
1857Go PF	—	5.00	10.00	27.50	55.00
1858/7Go PF	—	7.50	15.00	33.00	65.00
1858Go PF	—	5.00	10.00	27.50	55.00
1859Go PF	—	5.00	10.00	27.50	55.00
1860Go PF Small 1/2	—	5.00	10.00	27.50	55.00
1860Go PF Large 1/2	—	5.00	10.00	27.50	55.00
1860/59Go PF	—	5.00	10.00	27.50	55.00
1861Go PF Small 1/2	—	5.00	10.00	27.50	55.00
1861Go PF Large 1/2	—	5.00	10.00	27.50	55.00
1862/1Go YE	—	5.00	10.00	27.50	55.00
1862Go YE	—	2.50	7.50	19.00	44.00
1862Go YF	—	5.00	10.00	27.50	55.00

Date	Mintage	F	VF	XF	Unc
1867Go YF	—	2.50	7.50	19.00	44.00
1868Go YF	—	2.50	7.50	19.00	44.00

KM# 370.1 1/2 REAL
1.6900 g., 0.9030 Silver 0.0491 oz. ASW **Obv:** Facing eagle **Mint:** Chihuahua

Date	Mintage	F	VF	XF	Unc
1844Ca RG	—	75.00	125	195	325
1845Ca RG	—	75.00	125	165	300

KM# 370 1/2 REAL
1.6900 g., 0.9030 Silver 0.0491 oz. ASW **Obv:** Hooked-neck eagle **Mint:** Alamos

Date	Mintage	F	VF	XF	Unc
1862A PG Rare	—	—	—	—	—

KM# 370.4 1/2 REAL
1.6900 g., 0.9030 Silver 0.0491 oz. ASW **Obv:** Facing eagle, snake in beak **Mint:** Estado de Mexico

Date	Mintage	F	VF	XF	Unc
1829EoMo LF	—	175	300	550	1,650

KM# 372 REAL
3.3800 g., 0.9030 Silver 0.0981 oz. ASW **Obv:** Facing eagle, snake in beak **Mint:** Chihuahua

Date	Mintage	F	VF	XF	Unc
1844Ca RG	—	600	1,200	1,800	3,300
1845Ca RG	—	600	1,200	1,800	3,300
1855Ca RG	—	120	180	270	575

KM# 372.1 REAL
3.3800 g., 0.9030 Silver 0.0981 oz. ASW **Obv:** Facing eagle, snake in beak **Mint:** Culiacan

Date	Mintage	F	VF	XF	Unc
1846C CE	—	14.00	27.50	44.00	120
1848C CE	—	14.00	27.50	44.00	120
1850C CE	—	14.00	27.50	44.00	120
1851/0C CE	—	14.00	27.50	44.00	120
1852/1C CE	—	8.00	17.00	33.00	110
1853/2C CE	—	8.00	17.00	33.00	110
1854C CE	—	8.00	17.00	33.00	110
1856C CE	—	44.00	70.00	110	250
1857/4C CE	—	11.00	22.50	38.50	110
1857/6C CE	—	11.00	22.50	38.50	110
1858C CE	—	6.00	8.00	17.00	110
1859C CE	—	—	—	—	—
1860/9C PV/N	—	7.00	11.00	19.00	130
1860C PV	—	6.00	8.00	17.00	110
1861C PV	—	6.00	8.00	17.00	110
1863C CE	—	—	—	1,800	2,500
Note: 3 known					
1869C CE	—	6.00	8.00	17.00	110

KM# 372.2 REAL
3.3800 g., 0.9030 Silver 0.0981 oz. ASW **Obv:** Facing eagle, snake in beak **Mint:** Durango

Date	Mintage	F	VF	XF	Unc
1832/1Do RM	—	6.00	11.00	22.50	100
1832Do RM/RL	—	11.00	17.00	33.00	110
1832Do RM	—	6.00	11.00	22.50	110
1834/24Do RM/RL	—	17.00	27.50	55.00	165
1834/3Do RM/RL	—	17.00	27.50	55.00	165
1834Do RM	—	11.00	22.50	44.00	120
1836/4Do RM	—	6.00	8.00	17.00	110
1836Do RM	—	6.00	8.00	17.00	110
1837Do RM 3/2	—	14.00	22.50	44.00	120
1837Do RM	—	14.00	22.50	44.00	120
1841Do RM	—	8.00	17.00	33.00	110
1842/32Do RM	—	11.00	22.50	44.00	120
1842Do RM	—	8.00	17.00	33.00	110
1843/37Do RM	—	11.00	22.50	44.00	120
1843Do RM	—	6.00	8.00	17.00	110
1844/34Do RM	—	17.00	27.50	49.50	140
1845Do RM	—	6.00	8.00	17.00	110
1846Do RM	—	8.00	17.00	33.00	110
1847Do RM	—	11.00	17.00	38.50	110
1848/31Do RM	—	11.00	17.00	38.50	110
1848/33Do RM	—	11.00	17.00	38.50	110
1848/5Do RM	—	11.00	17.00	38.50	110
1848Do RM	—	8.00	14.00	22.50	110

FIRST REPUBLIC - FEDERAL

Date	Mintage	F	VF	XF	Unc
1849/8Do CM	—	11.00	17.00	33.00	110
1850Do JMR	—	22.50	44.00	85.00	195
1851Do JMR	—	22.50	44.00	85.00	195
1852Do JMR	—	22.50	44.00	85.00	195
1853Do CP	—	14.00	22.50	38.50	110
1854/1Do CP	—	11.00	17.00	27.50	110
1854Do CP	—	8.00	14.00	22.50	110
1855Do CP	—	11.00	17.00	27.50	110
1856Do CP	—	14.00	22.50	38.50	110
1857Do CP	—	14.00	22.50	38.50	110
1858Do CP	—	14.00	22.50	38.50	110
1859Do CP	—	8.00	14.00	22.50	110
1860/59Do CP	—	11.00	17.00	27.50	110
1861Do CP	—	17.00	27.50	44.00	120
1862/1Do CP	—	250	325	500	1,400
1864Do LT	—	17.00	27.50	44.00	120

KM# 372.4 REAL
3.3800 g., 0.9030 Silver 0.0981 oz. ASW **Obv:**
Facing eagle, snake in beak **Mint:** Guadalajara

Date	Mintage	F	VF	XF	Unc
1826Ga FS	—	17.00	33.00	55.00	140
1828/7Ga FS	—	17.00	33.00	55.00	140
1829/8/7Ga FS	—	—	—	—	—
1829Ga FS	—	17.00	33.00	55.00	140
1830Ga FS	—	275	475	650	—
1831Ga LP	—	17.00	33.00	55.00	140
1831Ga LP/FS	—	325	500	650	—
1832Ga FS	—	275	375	550	—
1833/2Ga G FS	—	110	165	300	600
1833Ga FS	—	85.00	140	250	550
1834/3Ga FS	—	85.00	140	250	550
1835Ga FS	—	—	—	—	—
1837/6Ga JG/FS	—	14.00	22.50	38.50	110
1838/7Ga JG/FS	—	110	220	450	—
1839Ga JG	—	275	375	550	—
1840Ga JG	—	14.00	22.50	38.50	110
1840Ga MC	—	8.00	14.00	27.50	75.00
1841Ga MC	—	55.00	85.00	140	275
1842/0Ga JG/MC	—	11.00	17.00	33.00	110
1842Ga JG	—	8.00	14.00	22.50	110
1843Ga JG	—	165	220	325	825
1843Ga MC	—	6.00	8.00	17.00	110
1844Ga MC	—	8.00	14.00	22.50	110
1845Ga MC	—	11.00	17.00	27.50	110
1845Ga JG	—	6.00	8.00	22.50	110
1846Ga JG	—	14.00	22.50	38.50	110
1847/6Ga JG	—	11.00	17.00	27.50	110
1847Ga JG	—	11.00	17.00	27.50	110
1848Ga JG	—	450	600	775	—
1849Ga JG	—	8.00	14.00	22.50	110
1850Ga JG	—	195	300	450	—
1851Ga JG	—	11.00	17.00	27.50	110
1852Ga JG	—	11.00	17.00	27.50	110
1853/2Ga JG	—	11.00	17.00	27.50	110
1854Ga JG	—	11.00	17.00	27.50	110
1855Ga JG	—	17.00	27.50	44.00	110
1856Ga JG	—	8.00	14.00	22.50	110
1857/6Ga JG	—	14.00	22.50	38.50	110
1858/7Ga JG	—	17.00	27.50	44.00	120
1859/8Ga JG	—	27.50	55.00	85.00	165
1860/59Ga JG	—	33.00	65.00	100	250
1861/0Ga JG	—	22.50	33.00	55.00	140
1861Ga JG	—	27.50	55.00	110	275
1862Ga JG	—	8.00	14.00	22.50	110

KM# 372.5 REAL
3.3800 g., 0.9030 Silver 0.0981 oz. ASW **Obv:**
Facing eagle, snake in beak **Obv. Legend:**

REPUBLICA MEXICANA Rev: Radiant cap **Mint:**
Guadalupe y Calvo

Date	Mintage	F	VF	XF	Unc
1844GC MP	—	40.00	60.00	110	325
1845GC MP	—	40.00	60.00	110	325
1846GC MP	—	40.00	60.00	110	325
1847GC MP	—	40.00	60.00	110	325
1848GC MP	—	40.00	60.00	110	325
1849/7GC MP	—	40.00	60.00	110	325
1849/8GC MP	—	40.00	60.00	110	325
1849GC MP	—	40.00	60.00	110	325
1850GC MP	—	40.00	60.00	110	325
1851GC MP	—	40.00	60.00	110	325

KM# 372.6 REAL
3.3800 g., 0.9030 Silver 0.0981 oz. ASW **Obv:**
Facing eagle, snake in beak **Mint:** Guanajuato

Date	Mintage	F	VF	XF	Unc
1826/5Go JJ	—	6.00	8.00	17.00	95.00
1826Go MJ	—	4.00	7.00	17.00	95.00
1827Go MJ	—	4.00	7.00	17.00	70.00
1827Go JM	—	11.00	17.00	27.50	85.00
1828/7Go MR	—	4.00	7.00	17.00	95.00
1828Go MJ	—	4.00	7.00	17.00	95.00
Note: Straight J, small 8					
1828Go MJ	—	4.00	7.00	17.00	95.00
Note: Full J, large 8					
1828/6G MR/JJ	—	4.00	7.00	17.00	95.00
1828G MR/JJ	—	4.00	7.00	17.00	95.00
1828Go MR	—	4.00	7.00	17.00	95.00
1829/8Go MG Small eagle	—	4.00	7.00	17.00	95.00
1829Go MJ Small eagle	—	4.00	7.00	17.00	95.00
1829Go MJ Large eagle	—	4.00	7.00	17.00	95.00
1830Go MJ Small initials	—	4.00	7.00	17.00	95.00
1830Go MJ Medium initials	—	4.00	7.00	17.00	95.00
1830Go MJ Large initials	—	4.00	7.00	17.00	95.00
1830Go MJ	—	4.00	7.00	17.00	95.00
Note: Reversed N in MEXICANA					
1830 MJ 3/2	—	4.00	7.00	17.00	95.00
1831/0Go MJ	—	4.00	7.00	17.00	95.00
Note: Reversed N in MEXICANA					
1831Go MJ	—	4.00	7.00	17.00	95.00
1832/1Go MJ	—	17.00	33.00	55.00	140
1832Go MJ	—	17.00	33.00	55.00	140
1833Go MJ Top of 3 round	—	4.00	7.00	17.00	95.00
1833Go MJ Top of 3 flat	—	4.00	7.00	17.00	95.00
1834Go PJ	—	4.00	7.00	17.00	95.00
1835Go PJ	—	8.00	14.00	22.50	95.00
1836Go PJ	—	4.00	7.00	17.00	95.00
1837Go PJ	—	17.00	33.00	55.00	140
1838/7Go PJ	—	11.00	22.50	38.50	95.00
1839Go PJ	—	4.00	7.00	17.00	95.00
1840/39Go PJ	—	4.00	7.00	17.00	95.00
1840Go PJ	—	4.00	7.00	17.00	95.00
1841/31Go PJ	—	11.00	22.50	38.50	95.00
1841Go PJ	—	4.00	7.00	17.00	95.00
1842Go PJ	—	4.00	7.00	17.00	95.00
1842Go PM	—	4.00	7.00	17.00	95.00
1843Go PM Convex wings	—	4.00	7.00	17.00	95.00
1843Go PM Concave wings	—	4.00	7.00	17.00	95.00
1844Go PM	—	4.00	7.00	17.00	95.00
1845/4Go PM	—	4.00	7.00	17.00	95.00
1845Go PM	—	4.00	7.00	17.00	95.00
1846/5Go PM	—	8.00	14.00	22.50	95.00
1846Go PM	—	4.00	7.00	17.00	95.00
1847/6Go PM	—	4.00	7.00	17.00	95.00
1847Go PM	—	4.00	7.00	17.00	95.00
1848Go PM	—	4.00	7.00	17.00	95.00
1849Go PF	—	11.00	22.50	38.50	95.00
1850Go PF	—	4.00	7.00	17.00	95.00
1851Go PF	—	11.00	22.50	38.50	110
1853/2Go PF	—	8.00	14.00	22.50	85.00
1853Go PF	—	4.00	7.00	17.00	85.00
1853Go PF/M 5/4	—	8.00	14.00	22.50	85.00
1854/3Go PF	—	4.00	7.00	17.00	85.00
1854Go PF Large eagle	—	4.00	7.00	17.00	85.00
1854Go PF Small eagle	—	4.00	7.00	17.00	85.00
1855/3Go PF	—	4.00	7.00	17.00	85.00
1855/4Go PF	—	4.00	7.00	17.00	85.00
1855Go PF	—	4.00	7.00	17.00	85.00

FIRST REPUBLIC - FEDERAL

Date	Mintage	F	VF	XF	Unc
1856/5Go PF	—	4.00	7.00	17.00	85.00
1856Go PF	—	4.00	7.00	17.00	85.00
1857/6Go PF	—	4.00	7.00	17.00	85.00
1857Go PF	—	4.00	7.00	17.00	85.00
1858Go PF	—	4.00	7.00	17.00	85.00
1859Go PF	—	4.00	7.00	17.00	85.00
1860/50Go PF	—	4.00	7.00	17.00	85.00
1860Go PF	—	4.00	7.00	17.00	85.00
1861Go PF	—	4.00	7.00	17.00	85.00
1862Go YE	—	4.00	7.00	17.00	85.00
1862/1Go YF	—	8.00	14.00	22.50	85.00
1862Go YF	—	4.00	7.00	17.00	85.00
1867Go YF	—	4.00	7.00	17.00	85.00
1868/7Go YF	—	4.00	7.00	17.00	85.00

KM# 372.7 REAL
3.3800 g., 0.9030 Silver 0.0981 oz. ASW **Obv:** Facing eagle, snake in beak **Mint:** Hermosillo

Date	Mintage	F	VF	XF	Unc
1867Ho PR	—	46.25	90.00	145	300
Note: Small 7/1					
1867Ho PR	—	46.25	90.00	145	300
Note: Large 7/ small 7					
1868Ho PR	—	46.25	90.00	145	300

KM# 372.8 REAL
3.3800 g., 0.9030 Silver 0.0981 oz. ASW **Obv:** Facing eagle, snake in beak **Mint:** Mexico City

Date	Mintage	F	VF	XF	Unc	BU
1825Mo JM	—	11.00	22.50	44.00	140	—
1826Mo JM	—	8.00	17.00	33.00	125	—
1827/6Mo JM	—	8.00	17.00	33.00	95.00	—
1827Mo JM	—	6.00	11.00	22.50	90.00	—
1828Mo JM	—	8.00	17.00	33.00	120	—
1830/29Mo JM	—	6.00	11.00	22.50	120	—
1830Mo JM	—	6.00	14.00	27.50	120	—
1831Mo JM	—	110	220	325	875	—
1832Mo JM	—	6.00	11.00	22.50	120	—
1833/2Mo MJ	—	6.00	11.00	22.50	120	—
1850Mo GC	—	6.00	11.00	22.50	120	—
1852Mo GC	—	300	475	625	—	—
1854Mo GC	—	11.00	22.50	44.00	120	—
1855Mo GF	—	6.00	11.00	22.50	100	—
1856Mo GF	—	110	220	450	1,100	—
1857Mo GF	—	6.00	11.00	22.50	100	—
1858Mo FH	—	6.00	11.00	22.50	100	—
1859Mo FH	—	6.00	11.00	22.50	100	—
1861Mo CH	—	6.00	11.00	22.50	100	—
1862Mo CH	—	6.00	11.00	22.50	100	—
1863/2Mo CH	—	8.00	14.00	27.50	100	—

KM# 372.9 REAL
3.3800 g., 0.9030 Silver 0.0981 oz. ASW **Obv:** Facing eagle, snake in beak **Mint:** San Luis Potosi

Date	Mintage	F	VF	XF	Unc	BU
1831Pi JS	—	6.00	11.00	22.50	140	—
1837Pi JS	—	650	825	1,100	—	—
1838/7Pi JS	—	275	325	425	—	—
1838Pi JS	—	22.50	38.50	65.00	140	—
1840/39Pi JS	—	8.00	17.00	33.00	140	—
1840Pi JS	—	8.00	17.00	33.00	140	—
1841Pi JS	—	8.00	17.00	33.00	140	—
1842Pi JS	—	17.00	33.00	60.00	165	—
1842Pi PS	—	6.00	11.00	22.50	140	—
1843Pi PS	—	14.00	22.50	38.50	140	—
1843Pi AM	—	44.00	65.00	90.00	165	—
1844Pi AM	—	44.00	65.00	90.00	165	—
1845Pi AM	—	8.00	17.00	33.00	140	—
1846/5Pi AM	—	8.00	17.00	33.00	140	—
1847/6Pi AM	—	8.00	17.00	33.00	140	—
1847Pi AM	—	8.00	17.00	33.00	140	—
1848/7Pi AM	—	8.00	17.00	33.00	140	—
1849Pi PS	—	8.00	17.00	33.00	140	—
1849/8Pi SP	—	65.00	110	165	—	—
1849Pi SP	—	17.00	27.50	44.00	140	—
1850Pi MC	—	6.00	11.00	22.50	140	—
1851/0Pi MC	—	8.00	17.00	33.00	140	—
1851Pi MC	—	8.00	17.00	33.00	140	—
1852/1/0Pi MC	—	11.00	22.50	38.50	140	—

Date	Mintage	F	VF	XF	Unc	BU
1852Pi MC	—	8.00	17.00	33.00	140	—
1853/1Pi MC	—	14.00	22.50	38.50	140	—
1853Pi MC	—	11.00	22.50	38.50	140	—
1854/2Pi MO	—	33.00	65.00	110	—	—
1854/3Pi MC	—	22.50	44.00	65.00	165	—
1855Pi MC	—	17.00	27.50	49.50	140	—
1855/4Pi MC	—	22.50	44.00	65.00	165	—
1856Pi MC	—	17.00	27.50	49.50	140	—
1857Pi PS	—	22.50	38.50	60.00	150	—
1857Pi MC	—	22.50	44.00	65.00	165	—
1858Pi MC	—	14.00	22.50	38.50	140	—
1859Pi PS	—	11.00	17.00	33.00	140	—
1860/59Pi PS	—	11.00	17.00	33.00	140	—
1861Pi PS	—	8.00	14.00	22.50	140	—
1861Pi RO	—	14.00	22.50	38.50	140	—
1862/1Pi RO	—	14.00	22.50	38.50	100	—
1862Pi RO	—	8.00	14.00	22.50	140	—

KM# 372.10 REAL
3.3800 g., 0.9030 Silver 0.0981 oz. ASW **Obv:** Facing eagle, snake in beak **Mint:** Zacatecas

Date	Mintage	F	VF	XF	Unc
1826Zs AZ	—	6.00	14.00	38.50	130
1826Zs AO	—	6.00	14.00	38.50	130
1827Zs AO	—	6.00	14.00	38.50	130
1828/7Zs AO	—	6.00	14.00	38.50	130
1828Zs AO	—	6.00	14.00	38.50	130
1828Zs AO Inverted V for A	—	6.00	14.00	38.50	130
1829Zs AO	—	6.00	14.00	38.50	130
1830Zs ZsOV	—	6.00	14.00	38.50	130
1830Zs ZOV	—	6.00	14.00	38.50	130
1831Zs OV	—	6.00	14.00	38.50	130
1831Zs OM	—	6.00	14.00	33.00	130
1832Zs OM	—	6.00	14.00	33.00	130
1833/2Zs OM	—	6.00	14.00	33.00	130
1833/2Zs OM/V	—	6.00	14.00	33.00	130
1833Zs OM	—	6.00	14.00	33.00	130
1834/3Zs OM	—	6.00	14.00	33.00	130
1834Zs OM	—	6.00	14.00	33.00	130
1835/4Zs OM	—	22.50	38.50	65.00	165
1835Zs OM	—	4.00	9.00	22.50	70.00
1836/5Zs OM	—	4.00	9.00	22.50	95.00
1836Zs OM	—	4.00	9.00	22.50	95.00
1837Zs OM	—	4.00	9.00	22.50	95.00
1838Zs OM	—	4.00	9.00	22.50	95.00
1839Zs OM	—	4.00	9.00	22.50	95.00
1840Zs OM	—	4.00	9.00	22.50	95.00
1841Zs OM	—	22.50	44.00	65.00	165
1842/1Zs OM	—	4.00	9.00	22.50	95.00
1842Zs OM	—	4.00	9.00	22.50	95.00
1843Zs OM	—	4.00	9.00	22.50	95.00
1844Zs OM	—	4.00	9.00	22.50	95.00
1845/4Zs OM	—	6.00	14.00	33.00	110
1845Zs OM	—	4.00	9.00	22.50	95.00
1846Zs OM	—	4.00	9.00	22.50	95.00
Note: Old font and obverse					
1846Zs OM	—	4.00	9.00	22.50	95.00
Note: New font and obverse					
1847Zs OM	—	4.00	9.00	22.50	95.00
1848Zs OM	—	4.00	9.00	22.50	95.00
1849Zs OM	—	11.00	27.50	55.00	140
1850Zs OM	—	4.00	7.00	17.00	95.00
1851Zs OM	—	4.00	7.00	17.00	95.00
1852Zs OM	—	4.00	7.00	17.00	95.00
1853Zs OM	—	4.00	7.00	17.00	95.00
1854/2Zs OM	—	4.00	7.00	17.00	95.00
1854/3Zs OM	—	4.00	7.00	17.00	95.00
1854Zs OM	—	4.00	7.00	17.00	95.00
1855/4Zs OM	—	4.00	7.00	17.00	95.00
1855Zs OM	—	4.00	7.00	17.00	95.00
1855Zs MO	—	4.00	7.00	17.00	95.00
1856Zs MO	—	4.00	7.00	17.00	95.00
1856Zs MO/OM	—	4.00	7.00	17.00	95.00
1857Zs MO	—	4.00	7.00	17.00	95.00
1858Zs MO	—	4.00	7.00	17.00	95.00
1859Zs MO	—	4.00	7.00	17.00	85.00
1860 MO	—	275	—	—	—
1860Zs VL	—	4.00	7.00	17.00	85.00
1860Zs VL Inverted A for V	—	4.00	7.00	17.00	85.00

FIRST REPUBLIC - FEDERAL

Date	Mintage	F	VF	XF	Unc
1861Zs VL	—	4.00	7.00	17.00	85.00
1861Zs VL Inverted A for V	—	4.00	7.00	17.00	85.00
1862Zs VL	—	6.00	14.00	33.00	110
1868Zs JS	—	27.50	49.50	100	195
1869Zs YH	—	4.00	9.00	22.50	85.00

KM# 372.3   REAL
3.3800 g., 0.9030 Silver 0.0981 oz. ASW **Obv:**
Facing eagle, snake in beak **Mint:** Estado de Mexico

Date	Mintage	F	VF	XF	Unc	BU
1828EoMo LF	—	240	350	550	1,900	—

KM# 374.2   2 REALES
6.7600 g., 0.9030 Silver 0.1962 oz. ASW **Obv:**
Facing eagle, snake in beak **Edge:** Reeded **Mint:**
Chihuahua

Date	Mintage	F	VF	XF	Unc
1832Ca MR	—	34.50	70.00	115	230
1833Ca MR	—	34.50	70.00	145	575
1834Ca MR	—	40.25	85.00	145	575
1834Ca AM	—	40.25	85.00	145	575
1835Ca AM	—	40.25	85.00	145	575
1836Ca AM	—	22.50	46.00	90.00	230
1844Ca AM Rare	—	—	—	—	—
1844Ca RG Unique	—	—	—	—	—
1845Ca RG	—	22.50	46.00	90.00	230
1855Ca RG	—	22.50	46.00	90.00	230

KM# 374.3   2 REALES
6.7600 g., 0.9030 Silver 0.1962 oz. ASW **Obv:**
Facing eagle, snake in beak **Edge:** Reeded **Mint:**
Culiacan

Date	Mintage	F	VF	XF	Unc	BU
1846/1146C CE	—	30.00	60.00	115	260	—
1847C CE	—	14.00	22.50	46.00	230	—
1848C CE	—	14.00	22.50	46.00	230	—
1850C CE	—	30.00	60.00	85.00	230	—
1851C CE	—	14.00	22.50	46.00	230	—
1852/1C CE	—	14.00	22.50	46.00	230	—
1853/2C CE	—	14.00	22.50	46.00	230	—
1854C CE	—	17.00	34.50	60.00	230	—
1856C CE	—	22.50	40.25	80.00	230	—
1857C CE	—	14.00	22.50	46.00	230	—
1860C PV	—	14.00	22.50	46.00	230	—
1861C PV	—	14.00	22.50	46.00	230	—
1869C CE	—	14.00	22.50	46.00	230	—

KM# 374.4   2 REALES
6.7600 g., 0.9030 Silver 0.1962 oz. ASW **Obv:**
Facing eagle, snake in beak **Edge:** Reeded **Mint:**
Durango

Date	Mintage	F	VF	XF	Unc	BU
1826Do RL	—	22.50	46.00	70.00	230	—
1832Do RM	—	22.50	46.00	70.00	230	—
Note: Style of pre-1832						
1832Do RM	—	22.50	46.00	70.00	230	—
Note: Style of post-1832						
1834/2Do RM	—	22.50	46.00	70.00	230	—
1834/3Do RM	—	22.50	46.00	70.00	230	—
1835/4Do RM/RL	—	230	350	575	—	—
1841/31Do RM	—	60.00	85.00	145	290	—
1841Do RM	—	60.00	85.00	145	290	—
1842/32Do RM	—	14.00	22.50	46.00	230	—
1843Do RM/RL	—	14.00	22.50	46.00	230	—
1844Do RM	—	40.25	60.00	90.00	230	—
1845/34Do RM/RL	—	14.00	22.50	46.00	230	—
1846/36Do RM	—	115	175	230	400	—
1848/36Do RM	—	14.00	22.50	46.00	230	—
1848/37Do RM	—	14.00	22.50	46.00	230	—
1848/7Do RM	—	14.00	22.50	46.00	230	—
1848Do RM	—	14.00	22.50	46.00	230	—
1849Do CM/RM	—	14.00	22.50	46.00	230	—
1849Do CM	—	14.00	22.50	46.00	230	—
1851Do JMR/RL	—	14.00	22.50	46.00	230	—
1852Do JMR	—	14.00	22.50	46.00	230	—
1854Do CP/CR	—	34.50	60.00	90.00	230	—
1855Do CP	—	290	400	575	—	—
1856Do CP	—	115	175	290	575	—
1858Do CP	—	14.00	22.50	46.00	230	—

Date	Mintage	F	VF	XF	Unc	BU
1859/8Do CP	—	14.00	22.50	46.00	230	—
1861Do CP	—	14.00	22.50	46.00	230	—

KM# 374.6   2 REALES
6.7600 g., 0.9030 Silver 0.1962 oz. ASW **Obv:**
Facing eagle, snake in beak **Edge:** Reeded **Mint:**
Guadalajara

Date	Mintage	F	VF	XF	Unc	BU
1825Ga FS	—	22.50	46.00	90.00	230	—
1826Ga FS	—	22.50	46.00	90.00	230	—
1828/7Ga FS	—	115	175	260	450	—
1829Ga FS Rare	—	—	—	—	—	—
1832/0Ga FS/LP	—	115	175	260	400	—
1832Ga FS	—	14.00	22.50	46.00	230	—
1833/2Ga FS/LP	—	14.00	22.50	46.00	230	—
1834/27Ga FS Rare	—	—	—	—	—	—
1834Ga FS	—	14.00	22.50	46.00	230	—
1835Ga FS	—	2,400	—	—	—	—
1837Ga JG	—	14.00	22.50	46.00	230	—
1838Ga JG	—	14.00	22.50	46.00	230	—
1840/30Ga MC	—	14.00	22.50	46.00	230	—
1841Ga MC	—	34.50	60.00	230	575	—
1842/32Ga JG/MC	—	40.25	60.00	115	230	—
1842Ga JG	—	22.50	46.00	90.00	230	—
1843Ga JG	—	14.00	22.50	46.00	230	—
1843Ga MC/JG	—	14.00	22.50	46.00	230	—
1844Ga MC	—	14.00	22.50	46.00	230	—
1845/3Ga MC/JG	—	14.00	22.50	46.00	230	—
1845/4Ga MC/JG	—	14.00	22.50	46.00	230	—
1845Ga JG	—	14.00	22.50	46.00	230	—
1846Ga JG	—	14.00	22.50	46.00	230	—
1847/6Ga JG	—	30.00	46.00	90.00	230	—
1848/7Ga JG	—	14.00	22.50	46.00	230	—
1849Ga JG	—	14.00	22.50	46.00	230	—
1850/40Ga JG	—	14.00	22.50	46.00	230	—
1851Ga JG	—	290	400	575	—	—
1852Ga JG	—	14.00	22.50	46.00	230	—
1853/1Ga JG	—	14.00	22.50	46.00	230	—
1854/3Ga JG	—	290	400	575	—	—
1855Ga JG	—	40.25	60.00	90.00	230	—
1856Ga JG	—	14.00	22.50	46.00	230	—
1857Ga JG	—	290	400	575	—	—
1859/8Ga JG	—	14.00	22.50	46.00	230	—
1859Ga JG	—	14.00	22.50	46.00	230	—
1862/1Ga JG	—	14.00	22.50	46.00	230	—

KM# 374.7   2 REALES
6.7600 g., 0.9030 Silver 0.1962 oz. ASW **Obv:**
Facing eagle, snake in beak **Edge:** Reeded **Mint:**
Guadalupe y Calvo

Date	Mintage	F	VF	XF	Unc	BU
1844GC MP	—	46.00	70.00	145	325	—
1845GC MP	—	46.00	70.00	145	325	—
1846GC MP	—	60.00	115	175	350	—
1847GC MP	—	40.25	60.00	115	290	—
1848GC MP	—	60.00	115	175	350	—
1849GC MP	—	60.00	115	175	350	—
1850GC MP	—	145	290	—	—	—
1851/0GC MP	—	60.00	115	175	350	—
1851GC MP	—	60.00	115	175	350	—

KM# 374.9   2 REALES
6.7600 g., 0.9030 Silver 0.1962 oz. ASW **Obv:**
Facing eagle, snake in beak **Edge:** Reeded **Mint:**
Hermosillo

Date	Mintage	F	VF	XF	Unc	BU
1861Ho FM	—	230	350	450	750	—
1862/52Ho FM/C. CE	—	290	400	625	—	—
1867/1Ho PR/FM	—	85.00	175	290	575	—

KM# 374.11   2 REALES
6.7600 g., 0.9030 Silver 0.1962 oz. ASW **Obv:**
Facing eagle, snake in beak **Edge:** Reeded **Mint:**
San Luis Potosi

Date	Mintage	F	VF	XF	Unc	BU
1829Pi JS	—	12.00	17.00	34.50	230	—
1830/20Pi JS	—	22.50	34.50	70.00	230	—
1837Pi JS	—	12.00	17.00	34.50	230	—
1841Pi JS	—	12.00	17.00	34.50	230	—

Date	Mintage	F	VF	XF	Unc	BU
1842/1Pi JS	—	12.00	17.00	34.50	230	—
1842Pi JS	—	12.00	17.00	34.50	230	—
1842Pi PS	—	22.50	40.25	70.00	230	—
1843Pi PS	—	14.00	22.50	46.00	230	—
1843Pi AM	—	12.00	17.00	34.50	230	—
1844Pi AM	—	12.00	17.00	34.50	230	—
1845Pi AM	—	12.00	17.00	34.50	230	—
1846Pi AM	—	12.00	17.00	34.50	230	—
1849Pi MC	—	12.00	17.00	34.50	230	—
1850Pi MC	—	12.00	17.00	34.50	230	—
1856Pi MC	—	46.00	70.00	145	290	—
1857Pi MC	—	—	—	—	—	—
1858Pi MC	—	14.00	22.50	46.00	230	—
1859Pi MC	—	60.00	80.00	115	230	—
1861Pi PS	—	12.00	17.00	34.50	230	—
1862Pi RO	—	14.00	22.50	46.00	230	—
1863Pi RO	—	115	290	400	575	—
1868Pi PS	—	12.00	17.00	34.50	230	—
1869/8Pi PS	—	12.00	17.00	34.50	230	—
1869Pi PS	—	12.00	17.00	34.50	230	—

KM# 374.8 2 REALES
6.7600 g., 0.9030 Silver 0.1962 oz. ASW **Obv:**
Facing eagle, snake in beak **Edge:** Reeded **Mint:**
Guanajuato **Note:** Varieties exist.

Date	Mintage	F	VF	XF	Unc	BU
1825Go JJ	—	9.00	17.00	34.50	175	—
1826/5Go JJ	—	9.00	17.00	34.50	175	—
1826Go JJ	—	9.00	12.00	30.00	175	—
1826Go MJ	—	9.00	12.00	30.00	175	—
1827/6Go MJ	—	9.00	12.00	30.00	175	—
1827Go MJ	—	9.00	12.00	30.00	175	—
1828/7Go MR	—	9.00	17.00	34.50	175	—
1828Go MJ	—	9.00	12.00	22.50	175	—
1828Go JM	—	9.00	12.00	22.50	175	—
1829Go MJ	—	9.00	12.00	22.50	175	—
1831Go MJ	—	9.00	12.00	22.50	175	—
1832Go MJ	—	9.00	12.00	22.50	175	—
1833Go MJ	—	9.00	12.00	22.50	175	—
1834Go PJ	—	9.00	12.00	22.50	175	—
1835/4Go PJ	—	9.00	17.00	34.50	175	—
1835Go PJ	—	9.00	12.00	22.50	175	—
1836Go PJ	—	9.00	12.00	22.50	175	—
1837/6Go PJ	—	9.00	12.00	22.50	175	—
1837Go PJ	—	9.00	12.00	22.50	175	—
1838/7Go PJ	—	9.00	12.00	22.50	175	—
1838Go PJ	—	9.00	12.00	22.50	175	—
1839/8Go PJ	—	9.00	17.00	34.50	175	—
1839Go PJ	—	9.00	12.00	22.50	175	—
1840Go PJ	—	9.00	12.00	22.50	175	—
1841Go PJ	—	9.00	12.00	22.50	175	—
1842Go PJ	—	9.00	12.00	22.50	175	—
1842Go PM/PJ	—	9.00	12.00	22.50	175	—
1842Go PM	—	9.00	12.00	22.50	175	—
1843/2Go PM	—	9.00	12.00	22.50	175	—

Note: Concave wings, thin rays, small letters

1843Go PM	—	9.00	12.00	22.50	175	—

Note: Convex wings, thick rays, large letters

1844Go PM	—	9.00	12.00	22.50	175	—
1845/4Go PM	—	9.00	12.00	22.50	175	—
1845Go PM	—	9.00	12.00	22.50	175	—
1846/5Go PM	—	12.00	17.00	40.25	175	—
1846Go PM	—	9.00	12.00	22.50	175	—
1847Go PM	—	9.00	12.00	22.50	175	—
1848/7Go PM	—	9.00	17.00	34.50	175	—
1848Go PM	—	9.00	17.00	34.50	175	—
1848Go PF	—	115	175	290	575	—
1849/8Go PF/PM	—	9.00	12.00	22.50	175	—
1849Go PF	—	9.00	12.00	22.50	175	—
1850/40Go PF	—	9.00	12.00	22.50	175	—
1850Go PF	—	9.00	12.00	22.50	175	—
1851Go PF	—	9.00	12.00	22.50	175	—
1852/1Go PF	—	9.00	12.00	22.50	175	—
1852Go PF	—	9.00	12.00	22.50	175	—
1853Go PF	—	9.00	12.00	22.50	175	—
1854/3Go PF	—	9.00	12.00	22.50	175	—
1854Go PF	—	9.00	12.00	22.50	175	—

Note: Old font and obverse

1854Go PF	—	9.00	12.00	22.50	175	—

Date	Mintage	F	VF	XF	Unc	BU
Note: New font and obverse						
1855Go PF	—	9.00	12.00	22.50	175	—
1855Go PF	—	9.00	12.00	22.50	175	—
Note: Star in G of mint mark						
1856/5Go PF	—	12.00	17.00	40.25	175	—
1856Go PF	—	12.00	17.00	30.00	175	—
1857/6Go PF	—	9.00	12.00	22.50	175	—
1857Go PF	—	9.00	12.00	22.50	175	—
1858/7Go PF	—	9.00	12.00	22.50	175	—
1858Go PF	—	9.00	12.00	22.50	175	—
1859/7Go PF	—	9.00	12.00	22.50	175	—
1859Go PF	—	9.00	12.00	22.50	175	—
1860/7Go PF	—	9.00	12.00	22.50	175	—
1860/50Go PF	—	9.00	12.00	22.50	175	—
1860/59Go PF	—	9.00	12.00	22.50	175	—
1860Go PF	—	9.00	12.00	22.50	175	—
1861/51Go PF	—	9.00	12.00	22.50	175	—
1861/57Go PF	—	9.00	12.00	22.50	175	—
1861/0Go PF	—	9.00	12.00	22.50	175	—
1861Go PF	—	9.00	12.00	22.50	175	—
1862/1Go YE	—	9.00	12.00	22.50	145	—
1862Go YE	—	9.00	12.00	22.50	145	—
1862/57Go YE	—	9.00	12.00	22.50	145	—
1862Go YE/PF	—	9.00	12.00	22.50	145	—
1862/57Go YF/E	—	9.00	12.00	22.50	145	—
1862/57Go YF	—	9.00	12.00	22.50	145	—
1862Go YF	—	9.00	12.00	22.50	145	—
1863/52Go YF/PE	—	9.00	12.00	22.50	145	—
1863/52Go YF	—	9.00	12.00	22.50	145	—
1863Go YF	—	9.00	12.00	22.50	145	—
1867/57Go YF	—	9.00	12.00	22.50	145	—
1868/57Go YF	—	12.00	17.00	30.00	145	—

KM# 374.10 2 REALES
6.7600 g., 0.9030 Silver 0.1962 oz. ASW **Obv:**
Facing eagle, snake in beak **Obv. Legend:**
REPUBLICA MEXICANA. **Rev:** Radiant cap **Edge:**
Reeded **Mint:** Mexico City **Note:** Varieties exist.

Date	Mintage	F	VF	XF	Unc
1825Mo JM	—	12.00	17.00	34.50	200
1826Mo JM	—	12.00	17.00	34.50	200
1827Mo JM	—	12.00	17.00	34.50	200
1828Mo JM	—	12.00	17.00	34.50	200
1829/8Mo JM	—	12.00	17.00	34.50	200
1829Mo JM	—	12.00	17.00	34.50	200
1830Mo JM	—	46.00	70.00	145	290
1831Mo JM	—	12.00	17.00	34.50	200
1832Mo JM	—	115	230	450	—
1833/2Mo MJ/JM	—	12.00	17.00	34.50	200
1834Mo ML	—	60.00	115	230	450
1836Mo MF	—	12.00	17.00	34.50	200
1837Mo ML	—	12.00	17.00	34.50	200
1840/7Mo ML	—	175	260	400	—
1840Mo ML	—	175	260	400	—
1841Mo ML	—	17.00	46.00	115	290
1842 ML Rare	—	—	—	—	—
1847Mo RC Narrow date	—	12.00	17.00	34.50	200
1847Mo RC Wide date	—	12.00	17.00	34.50	200
1848Mo GC	—	12.00	17.00	34.50	200
1849Mo GC	—	12.00	17.00	34.50	200
1850Mo GC	—	12.00	17.00	34.50	200
1851Mo GC	—	46.00	70.00	145	290
1852Mo GC	—	12.00	17.00	34.50	200
1853Mo GC	—	12.00	17.00	34.50	200
1854/44Mo GC	—	12.00	17.00	34.50	200
1855Mo GC	—	12.00	17.00	34.50	200
1855Mo GF/GC	—	12.00	17.00	34.50	200

FIRST REPUBLIC - FEDERAL

Date	Mintage	F	VF	XF	Unc
1855Mo GF	—	12.00	17.00	34.50	200
1856/5Mo GF/GC	—	12.00	17.00	34.50	200
1857Mo GF	—	12.00	17.00	34.50	200
1858Mo FH	—	9.00	14.00	30.00	175
1858Mo FH/GF	—	9.00	14.00	30.00	175
1859Mo FH	—	9.00	14.00	30.00	175
1860Mo FH	—	9.00	14.00	30.00	175
1860Mo TH	—	9.00	14.00	30.00	175
1861Mo CH	—	9.00	14.00	30.00	175
1862Mo CH	—	9.00	14.00	30.00	175
1863Mo CH	—	9.00	14.00	30.00	175
1863Mo TH	—	9.00	14.00	30.00	175
1867Mo CH	—	12.00	17.00	34.50	175
1868Mo CH	—	12.00	17.00	34.50	175
1868Mo PH	—	9.00	14.00	30.00	175

KM# 374.12 2 REALES
6.7600 g., 0.9030 Silver 0.1962 oz. ASW **Obv:** Facing eagle, snake in beak **Edge:** Reeded **Mint:** Zacatecas **Note:** Varieties exist.

Date	Mintage	F	VF	XF	Unc
1825Zs AZ	—	12.00	17.00	34.50	175
1826Zs AV	—	9.00	12.00	30.00	175
Note: A is inverted V					
1826Zs AZ	—	9.00	12.00	30.00	175
Note: A is inverted V					
1826Zs AO	—	12.00	17.00	34.50	175
1827Zs AO	—	7.00	9.00	14.00	175
Note: A is inverted V					
1827Zs AO	—	7.00	9.00	14.00	175
1828/7Zs AO	—	17.00	34.50	70.00	200
1828Zs AO	—	9.00	12.00	30.00	115
1828Zs AO	—	9.00	12.00	30.00	175
Note: A is inverted V					
1829Zs AO	—	9.00	12.00	30.00	175
1829Zs OV	—	9.00	12.00	30.00	175
1830Zs OV	—	9.00	12.00	30.00	175
1831Zs OV	—	9.00	12.00	30.00	175
1831Zs OM/OV	—	9.00	12.00	30.00	175
1831Zs OM	—	9.00	12.00	30.00	175
1832/1Zs OM	—	17.00	34.50	70.00	175
1832Zs OM	—	9.00	12.00	30.00	175
1833/27Zs OM	—	9.00	12.00	30.00	175
1833/2Zs OM	—	9.00	12.00	30.00	175
1833Zs OM	—	9.00	12.00	30.00	175
1834Zs OM	—	46.00	70.00	145	230
1835Zs OM	—	9.00	12.00	30.00	175
1836Zs OM	—	9.00	12.00	30.00	175
1837Zs OM	—	9.00	12.00	30.00	175
1838Zs OM	—	17.00	34.50	70.00	175
1839Zs OM	—	9.00	12.00	22.50	175
1840Zs OM	—	9.00	12.00	22.50	175
1841/0Zs OM	—	9.00	12.00	22.50	175
1841Zs OM	—	9.00	12.00	22.50	175
1842Zs OM Narrow date	—	9.00	12.00	22.50	175
1842Zs OM Wide date	—	9.00	12.00	22.50	175
1843Zs OM	—	9.00	12.00	22.50	175
1844Zs OM	—	9.00	12.00	22.50	175
1845Zs OM	—	9.00	12.00	22.50	175
Note: Small letters with leaves					
1845Zs OM	—	9.00	12.00	22.50	175
Note: Large letters with leaves					
1846Zs OM	—	9.00	12.00	22.50	175
1847Zs OM	—	9.00	12.00	22.50	175
1848Zs OM	—	9.00	12.00	22.50	175
1849Zs OM	—	9.00	12.00	22.50	175
1850Zs OM	—	9.00	12.00	22.50	175
1851Zs OM	—	9.00	12.00	22.50	175
1852Zs OM	—	9.00	12.00	22.50	175
1853Zs OM	—	9.00	12.00	22.50	175
1854/3Zs OM	—	9.00	12.00	22.50	175
1854Zs OM	—	9.00	12.00	22.50	175
1855/4Zs OM	—	9.00	12.00	22.50	175
1855Zs OM	—	9.00	12.00	22.50	175
1855Zs MO	—	9.00	12.00	22.50	175
1856/5Zs MO	—	9.00	12.00	22.50	175
1856Zs MO	—	9.00	12.00	22.50	175
1857Zs MO	—	9.00	12.00	22.50	175
1858Zs MO	—	9.00	12.00	22.50	175

Date	Mintage	F	VF	XF	Unc
1859Zs MO	—	9.00	12.00	22.50	175
1860/59Zs MO	—	9.00	12.00	22.50	175
1860Zs MO	—	9.00	12.00	22.50	115
1860Zs VL	—	9.00	12.00	22.50	175
1861Zs VL	—	9.00	12.00	22.50	175
1862Zs VL	—	9.00	12.00	22.50	115
1863Zs MO	—	14.00	22.50	46.00	175
1863Zs VL	—	9.00	12.00	22.50	175
1864Zs MO	—	9.00	12.00	22.50	175
1864Zs VL	—	9.00	12.00	22.50	175
1865Zs MO	—	9.00	12.00	22.50	175
1867Zs JS	—	9.00	12.00	22.50	175
1868Zs JS	—	12.00	17.00	40.25	175
1868Zs YH	—	9.00	12.00	22.50	175
1869Zs YH	—	9.00	12.00	22.50	175
1870Zs YH	—	9.00	12.00	22.50	175

KM# 374 2 REALES
6.7600 g., 0.9030 Silver 0.1962 oz. ASW **Obv:** Facing eagle, snake in beak **Edge:** Reeded **Mint:** Alamos

Date	Mintage	F	VF	XF	Unc	BU
1872A AM	15,000	70.00	145	290	700	—

KM# 374.1 2 REALES
6.7600 g., 0.9030 Silver 0.1962 oz. ASW **Obv:** Facing eagle, snake in beak **Edge:** Reeded **Mint:** Real de Catorce

Date	Mintage	F	VF	XF	Unc	BU
1863Ce ML	—	145	230	375	800	—

KM# 374.5 2 REALES
6.7600 g., 0.9030 Silver 0.1962 oz. ASW **Obv:** Facing eagle, snake in beak **Edge:** Reeded **Mint:** Estado de Mexico

Date	Mintage	F	VF	XF	Unc	BU
1828EoMo LF	—	375	600	1,050	2,900	—

KM# 375.1 4 REALES
13.5400 g., 0.9030 Silver 0.3931 oz. ASW **Obv:** Facing eagle, snake in beak **Mint:** Culiacan

Date	Mintage	F	VF	XF	Unc	BU
1846C CE	—	500	700	1,200	—	—
1850C CE	—	95.00	155	325	—	—
1852C CE	—	250	375	625	—	—
1857C CE Rare	—	—	—	—	—	—
1858C CE	—	125	250	450	—	—
1860C PV	—	31.25	65.00	155	—	—

KM# 375.2 4 REALES
13.5400 g., 0.9030 Silver 0.3931 oz. ASW **Obv:**
Facing eagle, snake in beak **Mint:** Guadalajara

Date	Mintage	F	VF	XF	Unc	BU
1843Ga MC	—	25.00	50.00	100	—	—
1844/3Ga MC	—	37.50	75.00	155	—	—
1844Ga MC	—	25.00	50.00	100	—	—
1845Ga MC	—	25.00	50.00	100	—	—
1845Ga JG	—	25.00	50.00	100	—	—
1846Ga JG	—	25.00	50.00	100	—	—
1847Ga JG	—	50.00	100	190	—	—
1848/7Ga JG	—	50.00	100	190	—	—
1849Ga JG	—	50.00	100	190	—	—
1850Ga JG	—	80.00	155	325	—	—
1852Ga JG Rare	—	—	—	—	—	—
1854Ga JG Rare	—	—	—	—	—	—
1855Ga JG	—	125	250	500	—	—
1856Ga JG Rare	—	—	—	—	—	—
1857/6Ga JG	—	80.00	155	325	—	—
1858Ga JG	—	155	325	575	—	—
1859/8Ga JG	—	155	325	575	—	—
1860Ga JG	—	1,050	1,800	—	—	—
1863/2Ga JG	—	190	375	1,550	—	—
1863Ga JG	—	190	375	1,550	—	—

KM# 375.3 4 REALES
13.5400 g., 0.9030 Silver 0.3931 oz. ASW **Obv:**
Facing eagle, snake in beak **Mint:** Guadalupe y
Calvo

Date	Mintage	F	VF	XF	Unc	BU
1844GC MP	—	3,750	6,300	—	—	—
1845GC MP	—	8,100	10,000	—	—	—
1846GC MP	—	2,150	3,500	—	—	—
1847GC MP	—	1,900	3,150	—	—	—
1849GC MP	—	3,750	5,000	—	—	—
1850GC MP	—	1,900	3,150	—	—	—

KM# 375.5 4 REALES
13.5400 g., 0.9030 Silver 0.3931 oz. ASW **Obv:**
Facing eagle, snake in beak **Mint:** Hermosillo

Date	Mintage	F	VF	XF	Unc	BU
1861Ho FM	—	250	450	625	—	—
1867/1Ho PR/FM	—	190	350	500	—	—

KM# 375.6 4 REALES
13.5400 g., 0.9030 Silver 0.3931 oz. ASW **Obv:**
Facing eagle, snake in beak **Mint:** Mexico City

Date	Mintage	F	VF	XF	Unc	BU
1827/6Mo JM	—	250	500	1,000	—	—
1850Mo GC Rare	—	—	—	—	—	—
1852Mo GC Rare	—	—	—	—	—	—
1854Mo GC Rare	—	—	—	—	—	—
1855Mo GF/GC	—	65.00	125	250	—	—

Date	Mintage	F	VF	XF	Unc	BU
1855Mo GF	—	125	250	450	—	—
1856Mo GF/GC	—	65.00	155	500	—	—
1856Mo GF Rare	—	—	—	—	—	—
1859Mo FH	—	25.00	65.00	190	—	—
1861Mo CH	—	19.00	43.75	155	—	—
1862Mo CH	—	25.00	65.00	190	—	—
1863/2Mo CH	—	25.00	65.00	190	—	—
1863Mo CH	—	95.00	190	375	—	—
1867Mo CH	—	25.00	65.00	190	—	—
1868Mo CH/PH	—	37.50	95.00	190	—	—
1868Mo CH	—	25.00	65.00	190	—	—
1868Mo PH	—	37.50	95.00	250	—	—

KM# 375.8 4 REALES
13.5400 g., 0.9030 Silver 0.3931 oz. ASW **Obv:**
Facing eagle, snake in beak **Mint:** San Luis Potosi

Date	Mintage	F	VF	XF	Unc	BU
1837Pi JS	—	250	450	—	—	—
1838Pi JS	—	190	325	500	—	—
1842Pi PS	—	65.00	125	250	—	—
1843/2Pi PS	—	65.00	125	250	—	—
1843/2Pi PS	—	65.00	125	250	—	—
Note: 3 cut from 8 punch						
1843Pi AM	—	37.50	95.00	190	—	—
1843Pi PS	—	65.00	125	250	—	—
1844Pi AM	—	37.50	95.00	190	—	—
1845/4Pi AM	—	25.00	65.00	125	—	—
1845Pi AM	—	25.00	65.00	125	—	—
1846Pi AM	—	25.00	65.00	125	—	—
1847Pi AM	—	95.00	190	325	—	—
1848Pi AM Rare	—	—	—	—	—	—
1849Pi MC/AM	—	25.00	65.00	125	—	—
1849Pi MC	—	25.00	65.00	125	—	—
1849Pi PS	—	25.00	65.00	125	—	—
1850Pi MC	—	25.00	65.00	125	—	—
1851Pi MC	—	25.00	65.00	125	—	—
1852Pi MC	—	25.00	65.00	125	—	—
1853Pi MC	—	25.00	65.00	125	—	—
1854Pi MC	—	125	250	500	—	—
1855Pi MC	—	220	375	950	—	—
1856Pi MC	—	325	500	875	—	—
1857Pi MC Rare	—	—	—	—	—	—
1857Pi PS Rare	—	—	—	—	—	—
1858Pi MC	—	125	250	500	—	—
1859Pi MC	—	2,500	3,750	—	—	—
1860Pi PS	—	375	575	875	—	—
1861Pi PS	—	190	375	750	—	—
1861/0Pi PS	—	375	750	—	—	—
1861Pi RO/PS	—	37.50	95.00	190	—	—
1861Pi RO	—	65.00	125	250	—	—
1862Pi RO	—	37.50	95.00	190	—	—
1863Pi RO	—	37.50	95.00	190	—	—
1864Pi RO	—	3,150	4,400	—	—	—
1868Pi PS	—	37.50	95.00	190	—	—
1869/8Pi PS	—	37.50	95.00	190	—	—
1869Pi PS	—	37.50	95.00	190	—	—

KM# 375.9 4 REALES
13.5400 g., 0.9030 Silver 0.3931 oz. ASW **Obv:**
Facing eagle, snake in beak **Mint:** Zacatecas

Date	Mintage	F	VF	XF	Unc
1830Zs OM	—	25.00	65.00	125	—
1831Zs OM	—	19.00	37.50	95.00	—
1832/1Zs OM	—	25.00	65.00	125	—
1832Zs OM	—	25.00	65.00	125	—
1833/2Zs OM	—	25.00	65.00	125	—
1833/27Zs OM	—	19.00	37.50	95.00	—
1833Zs OM	—	19.00	37.50	95.00	—
1834/3Zs OM	—	25.00	65.00	125	—
1834Zs OM	—	19.00	37.50	95.00	—
1835Zs OM	—	19.00	37.50	95.00	—
1836Zs OM	—	19.00	37.50	95.00	—
1837/5Zs OM	—	25.00	65.00	125	—
1837/6Zs OM	—	25.00	65.00	125	—
1837Zs OM	—	25.00	65.00	125	—
1838/7Zs OM	—	19.00	37.50	95.00	—
1839Zs OM	—	325	475	625	—
1840Zs OM	—	625	1,650	—	—
1841Zs OM	—	19.00	37.50	95.00	—

FIRST REPUBLIC - FEDERAL

Date	Mintage	F	VF	XF	Unc
1842Zs OM Small letters	—	19.00	50.00	105	—
1842Zs OM Large letters	—	19.00	37.50	95.00	—
1843Zs OM	—	19.00	37.50	95.00	—
1844Zs OM	—	25.00	65.00	125	—
1845Zs OM	—	25.00	65.00	125	—
1846/5Zs OM	—	31.25	75.00	155	—
1846Zs OM	—	25.00	65.00	125	—
1847Zs OM	—	19.00	37.50	95.00	—
1848/6Zs OM	—	65.00	95.00	155	—
1848Zs OM	—	25.00	65.00	125	—
1849Zs OM	—	25.00	65.00	125	—
1850Zs OM	—	25.00	65.00	125	—
1851Zs OM	—	19.00	37.50	95.00	—
1852Zs OM	—	19.00	37.50	95.00	—
1853Zs OM	—	25.00	65.00	125	—
1854/3Zs OM	—	37.50	95.00	190	—
1855/4Zs OM	—	25.00	65.00	125	—
1855Zs OM	—	19.00	37.50	95.00	—
1856Zs OM	—	19.00	37.50	95.00	—
1856Zs MO	—	25.00	65.00	125	—
1857/5Zs MO	—	25.00	65.00	125	—
1857Zs O/M	—	25.00	65.00	125	—
1857Zs MO	—	19.00	37.50	95.00	—
1858Zs MO	—	25.00	65.00	125	—
1859Zs MO	—	19.00	37.50	95.00	—
1860/59Zs MO	—	25.00	65.00	125	—
1860Zs MO	—	19.00	37.50	95.00	—
1860Zs VL	—	25.00	65.00	125	—
1861/0Zs VL	—	25.00	65.00	125	—
1861Zs VL	—	19.00	37.50	95.00	—
1861Zs VL 6/5	—	25.00	65.00	125	—
1862/1Zs VL	—	25.00	65.00	125	—
1862Zs VL	—	25.00	65.00	125	—
1863Zs VL	—	25.00	65.00	125	—
1863Zs MO	—	25.00	65.00	125	—
1864Zs VL	—	19.00	37.50	95.00	—
1868Zs JS	—	25.00	65.00	125	—
1868Zs YH	—	19.00	37.50	95.00	—
1869Zs YH	—	19.00	37.50	95.00	—
1870Zs YH	—	19.00	37.50	95.00	—

Date	Mintage	F	VF	XF	Unc	BU
1842Go PJ Rare	—	—	—	—	—	—
1842Go PM	—	19.00	37.50	95.00	—	—
1843/2Go PM	—	16.00	31.25	75.00	—	—
Note: Eagle with convex wings, thick rays						
1843Go PM	—	16.00	31.25	75.00	—	—
Note: Eagle with concave wings, thin rays						
1844/3Go PM	—	19.00	37.50	95.00	—	—
1844Go PM	—	25.00	65.00	125	—	—
1845/4Go PM	—	25.00	65.00	125	—	—
1845Go PM	—	25.00	65.00	125	—	—
1846/5Go PM	—	19.00	37.50	95.00	—	—
1846Go PM	—	19.00	37.50	95.00	—	—
1847/6Go PM	—	19.00	37.50	95.00	—	—
1847Go PM	—	19.00	37.50	95.00	—	—
1848/7Go PM	—	25.00	65.00	125	—	—
1848Go PM	—	25.00	65.00	125	—	—
1849Go PF	—	25.00	65.00	125	—	—
1850Go PF	—	16.00	31.25	75.00	—	—
1851Go PF	—	16.00	31.25	75.00	—	—
1852Go PF	—	19.00	37.50	95.00	—	—
1852Go PF 5/4	—	25.00	65.00	125	—	—
1853Go PF	—	19.00	37.50	95.00	—	—
1854Go PF	—	19.00	37.50	95.00	—	—
Note: Large eagle						
1854Go PF	—	19.00	37.50	95.00	—	—
Note: Small eagle						
1855/4Go PF	—	19.00	37.50	95.00	—	—
1855Go PF	—	16.00	31.25	75.00	—	—
1856Go PF	—	16.00	31.25	75.00	—	—
1857Go PF	—	25.00	65.00	125	—	—
1858Go PF	—	25.00	65.00	125	—	—
1859Go PF	—	25.00	65.00	125	—	—
1860/59Go PF	—	19.00	37.50	95.00	—	—
1860Go PF	—	19.00	37.50	95.00	—	—
1861/51Go PF	—	19.00	37.50	95.00	—	—
1861Go PF	—	25.00	65.00	125	—	—
1862/1Go YE	—	19.00	37.50	95.00	—	—
1862/1Go YF	—	19.00	37.50	95.00	—	—
1862Go YE/PF	—	19.00	37.50	95.00	—	—
1862Go YE	—	19.00	37.50	95.00	—	—
1862Go YF	—	19.00	37.50	95.00	—	—
1863/53Go YF	—	19.00	37.50	95.00	—	—
1863Go YF/PF	—	19.00	37.50	95.00	—	—
186/53Go YF	—	19.00	37.50	95.00	—	—
1863Go YF	—	19.00	37.50	95.00	—	—
1867/57Go YF/PF	—	19.00	37.50	95.00	—	—
1868/58Go YF/PF	—	19.00	37.50	95.00	—	—
1870Go FR	—	19.00	37.50	95.00	—	—

KM# 375.4   4 REALES
13.5400 g., 0.9030 Silver 0.3931 oz. ASW **Obv:** Facing eagle, snake in beak **Obv. Legend:** REPUBLICA MEXICANA **Rev:** Radiant cap **Mint:** Guanajuato **Note:** Varieties exist. Some 1862 dates appear to be 1869 because of weak dies.

Date	Mintage	F	VF	XF	Unc	BU
1835Go PJ	—	16.00	31.25	75.00	—	—
1836/5Go PJ	—	19.00	37.50	95.00	—	—
1836Go PJ	—	19.00	37.50	95.00	—	—
1837Go PJ	—	16.00	31.25	75.00	—	—
1838/7Go PJ	—	19.00	37.50	95.00	—	—
1838Go PJ	—	16.00	37.50	95.00	—	—
1839Go PJ	—	16.00	31.25	75.00	—	—
1840/30Go PJ	—	25.00	65.00	125	—	—
1840 PJ	—	25.00	65.00	125	—	—
1841/30 PJ	—	250	400	750	—	—
1841/31Go PJ	—	190	325	575	—	—

KM# 375   4 REALES
13.5400 g., 0.9030 Silver 0.3931 oz. ASW **Obv:** Facing eagle, snake in beak **Obv. Legend:** REPUBLICA MEXICANA. **Rev:** Radiant cap **Mint:** Real de Catorce

Date	Mintage	F	VF	XF	Unc	BU
1863Ce ML Large C	—	250	625	1,050	—	—
1863Ce ML Small C	—	280	825	1,900	—	—

FIRST REPUBLIC - FEDERAL

KM# 375.7 4 REALES

13.5400 g., 0.9030 Silver 0.3931 oz. ASW **Obv:**
Facing eagle, snake in beak **Obv. Legend:**
REPUBLICA MEXICANA. **Rev:** Radiant cap **Mint:**
Oaxaca

Date	Mintage	F	VF	XF	Unc	BU
1861O FR	—	280	575	950	—	—
Note: Ornamental edge						
1861O FR	—	375	700	1,050	—	—
Note: Herringbone edge						
1861O FR	—	250	500	875	—	—
Note: Obliquely reeded edge						

KM# 377.5 8 REALES

27.0700 g., 0.9030 Silver 0.7859 oz. ASW **Obv:**
Facing eagle, snake in beak **Rev:** Radiant cap **Mint:**
Estado de Mexico

Date	Mintage	F	VF	XF	Unc	BU
1828EoMo LF/LP	—	375	925	2,850	—	—
1828EoMo LF	—	375	925	2,850	9,600	—
1829EoMo LF	—	325	825	2,400	7,700	—
1830/20EoMo LF	—	1,400	3,050	5,900	—	—
1830EoMo LF	—	1,100	2,200	4,250	10,500	—

KM# 377.7 8 REALES

27.0700 g., 0.9030 Silver 0.7859 oz. ASW **Obv:**
Facing eagle, snake in beak **Obv. Legend:**
REPUBLICA MEXICANA. **Rev:** Radiant cap **Mint:**
Guadalupe y Calvo

Date	Mintage	F	VF	XF	Unc	BU
1844GC MP	—	425	600	1,450	3,850	—
1844GC MP	—	500	725	1,700	4,300	—
Note: Error, reversed S in Ds, Gs						
1845GC MP	—	155	240	450	1,350	—
Note: Eagle's tail square						
1845GC MP	—	215	425	950	2,300	—
Note: Eagle's tail round						
1846GC MP	—	215	425	1,050	3,200	—
Note: Eagle's tail square						
1846GC MP	—	155	240	500	1,450	—
Note: Eagle's tail round						
1847GC MP	—	180	300	575	1,500	—
1848GC MP	—	215	350	725	1,750	—
1849GC MP	—	215	350	750	1,900	—
1850GC MP	—	215	350	825	2,100	—
1851GC MP	—	350	600	1,300	3,050	—
1852GC MP	—	425	725	1,800	4,800	—

KM# 377 8 REALES

27.0700 g., 0.9030 Silver 0.7859 oz. ASW **Obv:**
Facing eagle, snake in beak **Obv. Legend:**
REPUBLICA MEXICANA. **Rev:** Radiant cap **Mint:**
Alamos **Note:** Mint mark A, As. Varieties exist.

FIRST REPUBLIC - FEDERAL

Date	Mintage	F	VF	XF	Unc
1864 PG	—	825	1,400	2,600	—
1865/4 PG Rare	—	—	—	—	—
1865 PG	—	550	825	1,300	—
1866/5 PG Rare	—	—	—	—	—
1866 PG	—	1,400	2,500	—	—
1866 DL Rare	—	—	—	—	—
1867 DL	—	1,250	2,350	—	—
1868 DL	—	65.00	110	210	650
1869/8 DL	—	65.00	110	210	—
1869 DL	—	65.00	100	170	650
1870 DL	—	45.00	75.00	170	650
1871 DL	—	33.00	49.50	110	450
1872 AM/DL	—	38.50	65.00	145	650
1872 AM	—	38.50	65.00	145	550
1873 AM	509,000	38.50	38.50	80.00	350
1874/3As DL	—	38.50	65.00	145	550
1874 DL	—	30.00	38.50	80.00	350
1875A DL 7/7	—	55.00	100	170	650
1875A DL	—	30.25	38.50	80.00	350
1875As DL	—	45.00	75.00	155	550
1876 DL	—	30.00	38.50	80.00	350
1877 DL	515,000	30.00	38.50	80.00	350
1878 DL	513,000	30.00	38.50	80.00	350
1879 DL	—	33.00	50.00	110	400
1879 ML	—	44.00	75.00	175	750
1880 ML	—	27.50	30.00	50.00	325
1881 ML	966,000	27.50	30.00	50.00	325
1882 ML	480,000	27.50	30.00	50.00	325
1883 ML	464,000	27.50	30.00	50.00	325
1884 ML	—	27.50	30.00	50.00	325
1885 ML	280,000	27.50	30.00	50.00	325
1886 ML	857,000	27.50	30.00	45.50	270
1886/0As/Cn ML/JD	Inc. above	30.00	33.00	60.00	350
1887 ML	650,000	27.50	30.00	45.50	270
1888/7 ML	508,000	44.00	75.00	145	850
1888 ML	Inc. above	27.50	30.00	45.50	270
1889 ML	427,000	27.50	30.00	45.50	270
1890 ML	450,000	27.50	30.00	45.50	270
1891 ML	533,000	27.50	30.00	45.50	270
1892/0 ML	—	33.00	44.00	90.00	350
1892 ML	465,000	27.50	30.00	45.50	270
1893 ML	734,000	27.50	30.00	42.50	230
1894 ML	725,000	27.50	30.00	42.50	230
1895 ML	477,000	27.50	30.00	42.50	230

Date	Mintage	F	VF	XF	Unc	BU
1846 CE	—	165	325	1,050	3,000	—
1846 CE	—	195	425	1,150	3,300	—
Note: Dot after G						
1846 CE	—	140	290	975	2,900	—
Note: No dot after G						
1847 CE	—	450	775	1,950	—	—
1848 CE	—	140	275	575	2,000	—
1849 CE C/G	—	85.00	140	260	800	—
1849 CE	—	85.00	140	260	800	—
1850 CE	—	85.00	140	260	800	—
1851 CE	—	140	275	575	2,000	—
1852/1 CE	—	110	165	325	1,000	—
1852 CE	—	110	220	400	1,200	—
1853/0 CE	—	220	375	900	2,600	—
1853/2/0	—	220	450	975	2,800	—
1853 CE	—	110	195	400	1,200	—
Note: Thick rays						
1853 CE	—	220	375	850	—	—
Note: Error: MEXIGANA						
1854 CE	—	825	1,400	—	—	—
1854 CE	—	195	375	975	2,400	—
Note: Large eagle and hat						
1855/6 CE	—	55.00	75.00	145	450	—
1855 CE	—	38.50	55.00	110	350	—
1856 CE	—	65.00	120	240	750	—
1857 CE	—	33.00	49.50	110	350	—
1858 CE	—	44.00	55.00	110	350	—
1859 CE	—	33.00	49.50	110	350	—
1860/9 PV/CV	—	65.00	90.00	145	450	—
1860/9 PV/E	—	65.00	90.00	145	450	—
1860 CE	—	38.50	55.00	110	350	—
1860/9 PV	—	55.00	75.00	130	400	—
1860 PV	—	55.00	75.00	130	400	—
1861/0 CE	—	65.00	100	170	550	—
1861 PV/CE	—	95.00	150	275	750	—
1861 CE	—	33.00	49.50	90.00	350	—
1862 CE	—	33.00	49.50	90.00	350	—
1863/2 CE	—	44.00	65.00	110	450	—
1863 CE	—	33.00	44.00	90.00	350	—
1864 CE	—	44.00	75.00	145	650	—
1865 CE	—	150	230	425	1,350	—
1866 CE	—	450	825	1,650	4,500	—
1867 CE	—	150	230	450	1,450	—
1868/7 CE	—	44.00	55.00	110	350	—
1868/8	—	65.00	120	210	650	—
1868 CE	—	44.00	55.00	110	350	—
1869 CE	—	44.00	55.00	110	400	—
1870 CE	—	65.00	120	210	750	—
1873 MP	—	65.00	120	210	650	—
1874/3 MP	—	44.00	55.00	110	350	—
1874C MP	—	33.00	44.00	70.00	290	—
1874CN MP	—	150	230	400	1,250	—
1875 MP	—	27.50	30.00	41.50	230	—
1876 GP	—	27.50	30.00	50.00	240	—
1876 CG	—	27.50	30.00	41.50	230	—
1877 CG	339,000	27.50	30.00	41.50	230	—
1877Gn CG Error	—	85.00	150	275	850	—
1877 JA	Inc. above	49.50	95.00	175	550	—
1878/7 CG	483,000	49.50	95.00	175	550	—
1878 CG	Inc. above	30.00	38.50	60.00	290	—
1878 JD/CG	—	38.50	49.50	80.00	350	—
1878 JD	Inc. above	30.00	35.00	50.00	290	—
1878 JD	Inc. above	33.00	44.00	65.00	350	—
Note: D over retrograde D						
1879 JD	—	27.50	30.00	50.00	300	—
1880/70 JD	—	30.00	35.00	50.00	240	—
1880 JD	—	27.50	30.00	41.50	280	—
1881/0 JD	1,032,000	30.25	33.00	50.00	240	—
1881C JD	Inc. above	27.50	30.00	41.50	230	—
1881Cn JD	Inc. above	55.00	75.00	130	350	—
1882 JD	397,000	27.50	30.00	41.50	230	—
1882 AM	Inc. above	27.50	30.00	41.50	230	—
1883 AM	333,000	27.50	30.00	41.50	290	—
1884 AM	—	27.50	30.00	41.50	230	—
1885/6 AM	227,000	33.00	44.00	70.00	290	—
1885C AM	Inc. above	49.50	90.00	210	750	—
1885Cn AM	Inc. above	27.50	30.00	41.50	230	—

KM# 377.3   8 REALES
27.0700 g., 0.9030 Silver 0.7859 oz. ASW **Obv:**
Facing eagle, snake in beak **Obv. Legend:**
REPUBLICA MEXICANA **Rev:** Radiant cap **Mint:**
Culiacan **Note:** Mint mark C, Cn. Varieties exist.

FIRST REPUBLIC - FEDERAL

Date	Mintage	F	VF	XF	Unc	BU
1885Gn AM Error	Inc. above	38.50	65.00	145	600	—
1886 AM	571,000	27.50	30.00	41.50	230	—
1887 AM	732,000	27.50	30.00	41.50	230	—
1888 AM	768,000	27.50	30.00	41.50	230	—
1889 AM	1,075,000	27.50	30.00	41.50	230	520
1890 AM	874,000	27.50	29.50	39.00	220	—
1891 AM	777,000	27.50	29.50	39.00	220	—
1892 AM	681,000	27.50	29.50	39.00	220	—
1893 AM	1,144,000	27.50	29.50	39.00	220	—
1894 AM	2,118,000	27.50	29.50	39.00	220	—
1895 AM	1,834,000	27.50	29.50	39.00	220	—
1896 AM	2,134,000	27.50	29.50	39.00	220	—
1897 AM	1,580,000	27.50	29.50	39.00	220	—

Date	Mintage	F	VF	XF	Unc
1887/6 AE	115,000	38.50	65.00	115	450
1887 AE	Inc. above	30.00	38.50	65.00	300
1888 AE	145,000	30.00	38.50	65.00	300
1889 AE	150,000	33.00	45.00	90.00	400
1890 AE	181,000	33.00	45.00	90.00	400
1891 EN	160,000	30.00	38.50	65.00	300
1892 EN	120,000	30.00	38.50	65.00	300
1893 EN	66,000	60.00	95.00	165	650

KM# 377.11 8 REALES
27.0700 g., 0.9030 Silver 0.7859 oz. ASW **Obv:** Facing eagle, snake in beak **Rev:** Radiant cap **Mint:** Oaxaca **Note:** Mint mark O, Oa. Varieties exist.

Date	Mintage	F	VF	XF	Unc
1858O AE	—	2,750	4,400	—	—
1858Oa AE Unique	—	—	—	—	—
1859 AE	—	550	1,000	2,300	—
Note: A in O of mint mark					
1860 AE	—	220	500	1,050	—
Note: A in O of mint mark					
1861O FR	—	140	275	725	2,700
1861Oa FR	—	165	375	975	—
1862O FR	—	55.00	100	275	800
1862Oa FR	—	85.00	150	350	950
1863O FR	—	45.00	75.00	145	550
1863O AE	—	45.00	75.00	145	550
1863Oa AE	—	120	175	350	950
Note: A in O of mint mark					
1863Oa AE	—	1,100	1,950	3,600	—
Note: A above O in mint mark					
1864 FR	—	38.50	65.00	110	450
1865 AE	—	2,050	3,300	—	—
1867 AE	—	55.00	100	210	850
1868 AE	—	55.00	100	210	850
1869 AE	—	45.00	75.00	145	550
1873 AE	—	220	325	725	2,700
1874 AE	142,000	32.00	44.00	80.00	450
1875/4 AE	131,000	38.50	65.00	110	450
1875 AE	Inc. above	32.00	44.00	65.00	300
1876 AE	140,000	33.00	49.50	85.00	450
1877 AE	139,000	33.00	44.00	80.00	450
1878 AE	125,000	33.00	44.00	80.00	450
1879 AE	153,000	33.00	44.00	80.00	450
1880 AE	143,000	32.00	44.00	70.00	350
1881 AE	134,000	33.00	49.50	90.00	350
1882 AE	100,000	33.00	49.50	90.00	350
1883 AE	122,000	32.00	44.00	70.00	350
1884 AE	142,000	32.00	44.00	80.00	350
1885 AE	158,000	30.00	38.50	65.00	300
1886 AE	120,000	32.00	44.00	70.00	350

KM# 377.4 8 REALES
27.0700 g., 0.9030 Silver 0.7859 oz. ASW **Obv:** Facing eagle, snake in beak **Mint:** Durango **Note:** Varieties exist.

Date	Mintage	F	VF	XF	Unc
1825Do RL	—	44.00	85.00	210	800
1826Do RL	—	55.00	105	275	1,000
1827/6Do RL	—	49.50	75.00	125	450
1827/8Do RL	—	175	325	650	—
1827Do RL	—	44.00	65.00	130	450
1828/7Do RL	—	49.50	75.00	130	450
1828Do RL	—	38.50	65.00	115	400
1829Do RL	—	38.50	65.00	115	400
1830Do RM	—	38.50	65.00	130	450
Note: B on eagle's claw					
1831Do RM	—	33.00	44.00	90.00	350
Note: B on eagle's claw					
1832Do RM	—	49.50	75.00	170	650
Note: Mexican dies, B on eagle's claw					
1832/1Do RM	—	38.50	49.50	110	375
Note: French dies, REPUB MEX spaced					
1833/2Do RM/RL	—	33.00	49.50	110	375
1833Do RM	—	30.00	44.00	90.00	350
1834/3/2Do RM/RL	—	33.00	49.50	110	375
1834Do RM	—	30.00	38.50	80.00	350
1835/4Do RM/RL	—	33.00	49.50	100	350
1835Do RM	—	33.00	49.50	100	350
Note: Mexican dies, REPUBMEX not spaced					
1836/1Do RM	—	33.00	49.50	100	350
1836/4Do RM	—	33.00	49.50	100	350
1836/5/4Do RM/RL	—	95.00	175	350	1,050
1836Do RM	—	33.00	44.00	85.00	350
1836Do RM	—	33.00	44.00	85.00	350
Note: M on snake					
1837/1Do RM	—	33.00	44.00	85.00	350
1837Do RM	—	33.00	44.00	85.00	350
1838/1Do RM	—	33.00	44.00	90.00	375
1838/7Do RM	—	33.00	44.00	90.00	375
1838Do RM	—	33.00	44.00	85.00	350
1839/1Do RM/RL	—	33.00	44.00	85.00	350
1839/1Do RM	—	33.00	44.00	85.00	350
1839Do RM	—	33.00	44.00	85.00	350
1840/38/31Do RM	—	33.00	44.00	85.00	350
1840/39Do RM	—	33.00	44.00	85.00	350
1840Do RM	—	33.00	44.00	85.00	350
1841/31Do RM	—	85.00	150	375	950
1841/39Do RM/L	—	38.50	65.00	125	450
1841/39Do RM	—	38.50	65.00	125	450
1842/31Do RM	—	150	285	525	1,550
Note: B below cactus					
1842/31Do RM	—	55.00	100	175	550
1842/32Do RM	—	55.00	100	175	550
1842Do RM	—	33.00	44.00	85.00	350
Note: Eagle of 1832-41					

FIRST REPUBLIC · FEDERAL

Date	Mintage	F	VF	XF	Unc
1842Do RM	—	33.00	44.00	85.00	350
Note: Pre-1832 eagle resumed					
1842Do RM	—	55.00	100	175	550
1843/33Do RM	—	65.00	110	210	550
1843Do RM	—	65.00	110	210	550
1844/34Do RM	—	120	230	400	1,050
1844/35Do RM	—	120	230	400	1,050
1844/43Do RM	—	75.00	145	300	900
1845/31Do RM	—	120	230	400	1,050
1845/34Do RM	—	49.50	95.00	175	550
1845/35Do RM	—	49.50	95.00	175	550
1845Do RM	—	33.00	44.00	85.00	350
1846/31Do RM	—	33.00	44.00	85.00	350
1846/36Do RM	—	33.00	44.00	85.00	350
1846Do RM	—	33.00	44.00	85.00	350
1847Do RM	—	38.50	65.00	115	400
1848/7Do RM	—	150	285	525	1,550
1848/7Do CM/RM	—	120	230	450	1,450
1848Do CM/RM	—	120	230	450	1,450
1848Do RM	—	120	230	400	1,250
1848Do CM	—	65.00	120	275	850
1849/39Do CM	—	120	230	450	1,450
1849Do CM	—	85.00	150	350	1,150
1849Do JMR/CM Oval 0	—	230	450	575	1,650
1849Do JMR Oval 0	—	230	350	575	1,650
1849Do JMR Round 0	—	230	450	775	2,000
1850Do JMR	—	120	175	350	1,050
1851/0Do JMR	—	85.00	150	300	1,000
1851Do JMR	—	120	175	350	1,050
1852Do CP/JMR	—	500	900	1,950	—
1852Do CP	—	825	1,350	2,950	—
1852Do JMR	—	205	285	500	1,350
1853Do CP/JMR	—	150	270	450	1,250
1853Do CP	—	230	375	775	2,400
1854Do CP	—	38.50	49.50	100	650
1855Do CP	—	65.00	120	240	750
Note: Eagle type of 1854					
1855Do CP	—	65.00	120	240	750
Note: Eagle type of 1856					
1856Do CP	—	65.00	120	240	750
1857Do CP	—	49.50	85.00	175	550
1858/7Do CP	—	38.50	49.50	105	375
1858Do CP	—	33.00	44.00	90.00	375
1859Do CP	—	33.00	44.00	90.00	375
1860/59Do CP	—	44.00	65.00	145	450
1860Do CP	—	33.00	44.00	90.00	375
1861/0Do CP	—	33.00	44.00	90.00	375
1861Do CP	—	33.00	44.00	80.00	290
1862/1Do CP	—	38.50	49.50	90.00	290
1862Do CP	—	33.00	44.00	90.00	400
1863/1Do CP	—	44.00	75.00	130	450
1863/2Do CP	—	38.50	65.00	110	400
1863/53Do CP	—	44.00	75.00	130	450
1863Do CP	—	38.50	65.00	110	400
1864Do CP	—	120	175	350	1,050
1864Do LT	—	38.50	55.00	115	400
1864Do LT/T	—	38.50	55.00	115	400
1864Do LT/CP	—	65.00	120	240	750
1865Do LT Rare	—	—	—	—	—
1866/4Do CM	—	3,050	6,100	—	—
1866Do CM	—	1,950	3,600	7,200	17,000
1867Do CM	—	3,850	—	—	—
1867/6Do CP	—	220	450	775	2,400
1867Do CP	—	195	325	650	2,000
1867Do CP/CM	—	140	275	525	1,800
1867Do CP/LT	—	220	450	850	2,500
1868Do CP	—	38.50	55.00	115	400
1869Do CP	—	33.00	44.00	80.00	300
1870/69Do CP	—	33.00	44.00	80.00	290
1870/9Do CP	—	33.00	44.00	80.00	290
1870Do CP	—	33.00	44.00	80.00	290
1873Do CP	—	150	260	425	1,250
1873Do CM	—	44.00	65.00	145	450
1874/3Do CM	—	27.50	30.00	45.50	290
1874Do CM	—	27.50	30.00	45.50	290
1874Do JH	—	1,250	1,950	3,600	—
1875Do CM	—	27.50	30.00	45.50	290
1875Do JH	—	100	175	350	950
1876Do CM	—	27.50	30.00	45.50	290

Date	Mintage	F	VF	XF	Unc
1877Do CM	431,000	1,600	2,750	—	—
1877Do CP	Inc. above	27.50	30.00	45.50	290
1877Do JMP	Inc. above	825	1,400	2,600	—
1878Do PE	409,000	30.00	38.50	65.00	290
1878Do TB	Inc. above	27.50	30.00	45.50	290
1879Do TB	—	27.50	30.00	45.50	290
1880/70Do TB	—	75.00	120	240	750
1880/70Do TB/JP	—	175	285	500	1,350
1880/70Do JP	—	30.00	38.50	65.00	290
1880Do TB	—	175	285	500	1,350
1880Do JP	—	27.50	30.00	45.50	290
1881Do JP	928,000	27.50	30.00	45.50	290
1882Do JP	414,000	27.50	30.00	45.50	290
1882Do MC/JP	Inc. above	44.00	75.00	145	450
1882Do MC	Inc. above	38.50	65.00	110	350
1883/73Do MC	452,000	30.00	38.50	65.00	290
1883Do MC	Inc. above	27.50	30.00	45.50	290
1884/3Do MC	—	30.00	38.50	65.00	290
1884Do MC	—	27.50	30.00	45.50	290
1885Do MC M/J	—	30.00	38.50	65.00	290
1885Do MC	547,000	27.50	29.50	41.50	290
1885Do JB	Inc. above	38.50	49.50	80.00	300
1886/5Do MC	—	30.00	38.50	65.00	240
1886/3Do MC	955,000	30.00	38.50	65.00	240
1886Do MC	Inc. above	27.50	29.50	41.50	220
1887Do MC	1,004,000	27.50	29.50	41.50	220
1888/7Do MC	—	85.00	150	350	950
1888Do MC	996,000	27.50	29.50	41.50	220
1889Do MC	874,000	27.50	29.50	41.50	220
1890Do MC	1,119,000	27.50	29.50	41.50	220
1890Do JP	Inc. above	27.50	29.50	41.50	220
1891Do JP	1,487,000	27.50	29.50	41.50	220
1892Do JP	1,597,000	27.50	29.50	41.50	220
1892Do ND	Inc. above	38.50	65.00	145	450
1893Do ND	1,617,000	27.50	29.50	41.50	220
1894Do ND	1,537,000	27.50	29.50	41.50	220
1895/3Do ND	761,000	30.00	38.50	65.00	240
1895Do ND	Inc. above	27.50	29.50	41.50	220
1895Do ND/P	—	30.00	38.50	65.00	240

KM# 377.6   8 REALES
27.0700 g., 0.9030 Silver 0.7859 oz. ASW **Obv:**
Facing eagle, snake in beak **Obv. Legend:**
REPUBLICA MEXICANA. **Rev:** Radiant cap **Mint:**
Guadalajara **Note:** Varieties exist.

Date	Mintage	F	VF	XF	Unc
1825Ga FS	—	165	300	625	2,000
1826/5Ga FS	—	140	275	575	2,000
1826Ga FS	—	140	275	575	2,000
1827/87Ga FS	—	140	275	575	2,000
1827Ga FS	—	140	275	575	2,000
1287Ga FS Error	—	9,400	10,500	—	—
1828Ga FS	—	220	425	725	2,400
1829/8Ga FS	—	220	425	725	2,400

Date	Mintage	F	VF	XF	Unc
1829Ga FS	—	195	350	625	1,900
1830/29Ga FS	—	110	195	400	1,200
1830Ga FS	—	110	195	400	1,200
1830Ga LP/FS	—	875	1,600	—	—

Note: The 1830 LP/FS is currently only known with a Philippine countermark

Date	Mintage	F	VF	XF	Unc
1831Ga LP	—	220	450	775	2,400
1831Ga FS/LP	—	325	550	975	3,000
1831Ga FS	—	140	300	525	—
1832/1Ga FS	—	65.00	120	240	650
1832/1Ga FS/LP	—	65.00	120	240	650
1832Ga FS/LP	—	95.00	175	375	1,150
1832Ga FS	—	38.50	65.00	145	500
1833/2/1Ga FS/LP	—	60.00	95.00	175	550
1833/2Ga FS	—	38.50	65.00	145	500
1834/2Ga FS	—	75.00	150	275	750
1834/3Ga FS	—	75.00	150	275	750
1834/0Ga FS	—	65.00	120	210	650
1834Ga FS	—	65.00	120	210	650
1835Ga FS	—	38.50	65.00	145	500
1836/5Ga FS	—	205	375	—	—
1836/1Ga JG/FS	—	55.00	100	175	550
1836Ga FS	—	325	500	975	—
1836Ga JG/FS	—	38.50	65.00	145	500
1836Ga JG	—	38.50	65.00	145	500
1837/6Ga JG/FS	—	65.00	120	240	650
1837/6Ga JG	—	60.00	110	220	600
1837Ga JG	—	55.00	100	175	550
1838/7Ga JG	—	120	205	400	1,150
1838Ga JG	—	120	175	375	1,050
1839Ga MC	—	120	230	450	1,250
1839Ga MC/JG	—	120	230	400	1,150
1839Ga JG	—	75.00	150	275	750
1840/30Ga MC	—	65.00	95.00	210	600
1840Ga MC	—	44.00	75.00	175	550
1841Ga MC	—	44.00	75.00	175	550
1842/1Ga JG/MG	—	120	175	350	950
1842/1Ga JG/MC	—	120	175	350	950
1842Ga JG	—	38.50	65.00	145	500
1842Ga JG/MG	—	38.50	65.00	145	500
1843/2Ga MC/JG	—	38.50	65.00	145	500
1843Ga MC/JG	—	38.50	65.00	145	500
1843Ga JG	—	450	650	1,150	3,600
1843Ga MC	—	65.00	120	210	650
1844Ga MC	—	65.00	120	210	650
1845Ga MC	—	95.00	175	400	1,450
1845Ga JG	—	550	925	1,650	3,700
1846Ga JG	—	55.00	100	210	650
1847Ga JG	—	120	175	300	850
1848/7Ga JG	—	70.00	105	175	550
1848Ga JG	—	65.00	95.00	145	500
1849Ga JG	—	110	150	240	700
1849/39Ga JG	—	275	550	—	—
1850Ga JG	—	65.00	120	210	650
1851Ga JG	—	140	220	450	1,300
1852Ga JG	—	110	165	325	900
1853/2Ga JG	—	140	195	325	950
1853Ga JG	—	110	150	240	650
1854/3Ga JG	—	85.00	110	175	550
1854Ga JG	—	65.00	95.00	155	500
1855/4Ga JG	—	65.00	120	210	600
1855Ga JG	—	38.50	65.00	145	500
1856/4Ga JG	—	75.00	150	240	650
1856/5Ga 56	—	75.00	150	240	650
1856Ga JG	—	65.00	120	210	600
1857Ga JG	—	65.00	120	300	950
1858Ga JG	—	120	175	400	1,050
1859/7Ga JG	—	38.50	65.00	155	500
1859/8Ga JG	—	38.50	65.00	145	450
1859Ga JG	—	33.00	55.00	115	400
1860Ga JG Without dot	—	375	825	1,550	4,500
1860Ga JG	—	2,200	3,600	5,900	—

Note: Dot in loop of snake's tail, base alloy

Date	Mintage	F	VF	XF	Unc
1861Ga JG	—	2,400	6,300	—	—
1862Ga JG	—	925	1,500	3,600	9,000
1863/52Ga JG	—	—	—	—	—
1863Ga JG	—	—	—	—	—
1863/59Ga JG	—	60.00	65.00	125	325
1863/2Ga JG	—	44.00	65.00	130	400
1863/4Ga JG	—	55.00	95.00	210	550

Date	Mintage	F	VF	XF	Unc
1863Ga JG	—	38.50	60.00	110	350
1863Ga FV Rare	—	—	—	—	—
1867Ga JM Rare	—	—	—	—	—
1868/7Ga JM	—	65.00	95.00	175	450
1868Ga JM	—	65.00	95.00	175	450
1869Ga JM	—	65.00	95.00	175	450
1869Ga IC	—	95.00	150	275	800
1870/60Ga IC	—	75.00	110	210	600
1870Ga IC	—	75.00	110	210	600
1873Ga IC	—	27.50	38.50	80.00	300
1874Ga IC	—	27.50	29.50	41.50	220
1874Ga MC	—	38.50	65.00	145	450
1875Ga IC	—	30.00	44.00	90.00	300
1875Ga MC	—	27.50	29.50	41.50	290
1876Ga IC	559,000	30.00	44.00	80.00	290
1876Ga MC	Inc. above	150	205	350	800
1877Ga IC	928,000	27.50	30.00	45.50	290
1877/6Ga JA	—	27.50	30.00	45.50	290
1877Ga JA	Inc. above	27.50	30.00	45.50	290
1878Ga JA	764,000	27.50	30.00	45.50	290
1879Ga JA	—	27.50	30.00	45.50	290
1880/70Ga FS	—	30.00	38.50	80.00	300
1880Ga JA	—	27.50	30.00	45.50	290
1880Ga FS	—	27.50	30.00	45.50	290
1881Ga FS	1,300,000	27.50	30.00	45.50	290
1882/1Ga FS	537,000	30.00	38.50	80.00	300
1882Ga FS	Inc. above	27.50	30.00	45.50	290
1882Ga TB/FS	Inc. above	65.00	120	240	650
1882Ga TB	Inc. above	65.00	120	240	650
1883Ga TB	561,000	30.00	38.50	65.00	300
1884Ga TB	—	27.50	29.50	41.50	290
1884Ga AH	—	27.50	29.50	41.50	290
1885Ga AH	443,000	27.50	29.50	41.50	290
1885Ga JS	Inc. above	27.50	29.50	145	450
1886Ga JS/H	—	27.50	29.50	41.50	290
1886Ga JS	1,038,999	27.50	29.50	41.50	290
1887Ga JS	878,000	27.50	29.50	41.50	290
1888Ga JS	1,159,000	27.50	29.50	41.50	290
1889Ga JS	1,583,000	27.50	29.50	41.50	290
1890Ga JS	1,658,000	27.50	29.50	41.50	260
1891Ga JS	1,507,000	27.50	29.50	41.50	260
1892/1Ga JS	1,627,000	30.00	38.50	80.00	290
1892Ga JS	Inc. above	27.50	29.50	41.50	260
1893Ga JS	1,952,000	27.50	29.50	41.50	260
1894Ga JS	2,045,999	27.50	29.50	41.50	260
1895/3Ga JS	—	27.50	33.00	60.00	270
1895Ga JS	1,146,000	27.50	29.50	41.50	260

KM# 377.8 8 REALES
27.0700 g., 0.9030 Silver 0.7859 oz. ASW **Obv:** Facing eagle, snake in beak **Obv. Legend:** REPUBLICA MEXICANA. **Rev:** Radiant cap **Mint:** Guanajuato **Note:** Varieties exist.

Date	Mintage	F	VF	XF	Unc
1825Go JJ	—	55.00	90.00	210	650
1825G JJ	—	1,400	1,800	—	—
Note: Error mint mark G					
1826Go JJ	—	55.00	100	240	750
Note: Straight J's					
1826Go JJ	—	44.00	75.00	175	550
Note: Full J's					
1826Go MJ	—	275	500	1,100	—
1827Go MJ	—	55.00	95.00	175	550
1827Go MJ/JJ	—	—	—	—	—
1827Go MR	—	120	230	450	1,250
1828Go MJ	—	—	—	—	—
Note: Error mint mark Goo					
1828Go MJ	—	44.00	75.00	175	550
1828/7Go MJ	—	165	325	775	2,400
1828Go MR	—	165	325	775	2,400
1829Go MJ	—	33.00	49.50	85.00	375
1830Go MJ	—	33.00	44.00	85.00	375
Note: Oblong beading and narrow J					
1830Go MJ	—	33.00	44.00	85.00	375
Note: Regular beading and wide J					
1831Go MJ	—	27.50	33.00	65.00	350
Note: Colon after date					
1831Go MJ	—	27.50	33.00	65.00	350
Note: 2 stars after date					
1832Go MJ	—	27.50	33.00	65.00	300
1832Go MJ	—	33.00	49.50	100	400
Note: 1 of date over inverted 1					
1833Go MJ/1	—	33.00	49.50	100	400
1833Go MJ	—	27.50	33.00	65.00	350
1833Go JM	—	450	825	1,650	5,000
1834Go PJ	—	27.50	33.00	65.00	350
1835Go PJ	—	27.50	33.00	65.00	350
Note: Star on cap					
1835Go PJ	—	27.50	33.00	65.00	350
Note: Dot on cap					
1836Go PJ	—	27.50	33.00	65.00	350
1837Go PJ	—	27.50	33.00	65.00	350
1838Go PJ	—	27.50	33.00	65.00	350
1839Go PJ/JJ	—	27.50	33.00	65.00	350
1839Go PJ	—	27.50	33.00	65.00	350
1840/30Go PJ	—	33.00	44.00	80.00	350
1840Go PJ	—	27.50	33.00	60.00	290
1841/31Go PJ	—	27.50	33.00	60.00	290
1841Go PJ	—	27.50	33.00	60.00	290
1842/1Go PM	—	33.00	44.00	80.00	290
1842/31Go PM/PJ	—	38.50	49.50	90.00	350
1842/1Go PJ	—	33.00	44.00	80.00	290
1842Go PJ	—	33.00	44.00	80.00	290
1842Go PM/PJ	—	27.50	33.00	60.00	290
1842Go PM	—	27.50	33.00	60.00	290
1843Go PM	—	27.50	33.00	60.00	290
Note: Dot after date					
1843Go PM	—	27.50	33.00	60.00	290
Note: Triangle of dots after date					
1844Go PM	—	27.50	33.00	60.00	290
1845Go PM	—	27.50	33.00	60.00	290
1846/5Go PM	—	33.00	44.00	80.00	350
Note: Eagle type of 1845					
1846Go PM	—	33.00	44.00	80.00	350
Note: Eagle type of 1845					
1846Go PM	—	30.25	38.50	65.00	300
Note: Eagle type of 1847					
1847Go PM Narrow date	—	27.50	33.00	60.00	290
1847Go PM Wide date	—	27.50	33.00	60.00	290
1848/7Go PM	—	27.50	49.50	100	350
1848Go PM	—	33.00	49.50	100	350
1848Go PF	—	27.50	33.00	60.00	290
1849Go PF	—	27.50	33.00	60.00	290
1850Go PF	—	27.50	33.00	60.00	290
1851/0Go PF	—	33.00	44.00	80.00	350
1851Go PF	—	27.50	33.00	60.00	290
1852/1Go PF	—	33.00	44.00	80.00	350
1852Go PF	—	27.50	33.00	60.00	290
1853/2Go PF	—	33.00	44.00	80.00	350
1853Go PF	—	27.50	33.00	60.00	290
1854Go PF	—	27.50	33.00	60.00	290
1855Go PF Large letters	—	27.50	33.00	60.00	290
1855Go PF Small letters	—	27.50	33.00	60.00	290
1856/5Go PF	—	33.00	44.00	80.00	350
1856Go PF	—	27.50	33.00	60.00	290
1857/5Go PF	—	33.00	44.00	80.00	350
1857/6Go PF	—	33.00	49.50	105	450
1857Go PF	—	27.50	30.00	41.50	220
1858/7Go PI Narrow date	—	27.50	33.00	60.00	290
1858Go PF Wide date	—	27.50	33.00	60.00	290
1859/7Go PF	—	27.50	33.00	60.00	290
1859/8Go PF	—	33.00	44.00	80.00	350
1859Go PF	—	27.50	33.00	60.00	290
1860/50Go PF	—	33.00	44.00	80.00	350
1860/59Go PF	—	27.50	30.00	45.50	230
1860Go PF	—	27.50	30.00	41.50	220
1861/51Go PF	—	27.50	33.00	50.00	240
Note: Narrow and wide dates exist					
1861/0Go PF	—	27.50	30.00	41.50	220
1861Go PF	—	27.50	30.00	41.50	220
186/52Go YE	—	30.00	33.00	50.00	240
1862Go YE/PF	—	30.00	33.00	50.00	240
186/52Go YF	—	30.00	33.00	50.00	240
1862Go YE	—	27.50	30.00	41.50	220
1862Go YF	—	27.50	30.00	41.50	220
1862Go YF/PF	—	27.50	30.00	41.50	220
1863/53Go YF	—	27.50	30.00	45.50	220
1863/54Go YF	—	30.00	33.00	50.00	240
1863Go YE Rare	—	—	—	—	—
1863Go YF	—	27.50	30.00	41.50	220
1867/57Go YF	—	30.00	33.00	50.00	240
1867Go YF	—	27.50	30.00	41.50	220
1868/58Go YF	—	30.00	33.00	50.00	240
1868/7Go YF	—	30.00	33.00	50.00	240
1868Go YF	—	27.50	30.00	41.50	220
1870/60Go FR	—	2,000	3,300	6,500	15,000
1870Go FR/YF	—	33.00	49.50	105	450
1870Go FR	—	27.50	30.00	41.50	220
1873Go FR	—	27.50	30.00	41.50	220
1874/3Go FR	—	30.00	33.00	50.00	230
1874Go FR	—	30.00	38.50	60.00	240
1875/3Go FR	—	30.00	33.00	50.00	230
1875/6Go FR	—	30.00	33.00	50.00	230
1875Go FR	—	27.50	30.00	41.50	220
Note: Small circle with dot on eagle					
1876/5Go FR	—	30.00	33.00	50.00	230
1876Go FR	—	27.50	30.00	41.50	220
1877Go FR Narrow date	—	27.50	30.00	41.50	220
1877Go FR Wide date	2,477,000	27.50	30.00	41.50	220
1878/7Go FR	2,273,000	30.00	33.00	50.00	220
1878/7Go SM, S/F	—	30.00	33.00	50.00	220
1878/7Go SM	—	30.00	33.00	50.00	220
1878Go FR	Inc. above	27.50	30.00	41.50	220
1878Go SM, S/F	—	30.25	33.00	45.50	220
1878Go SM	—	27.50	30.00	41.50	220
1879/7Go SM	—	30.00	33.00	50.00	220
1879/8Go SM	—	30.00	33.00	50.00	220
1879/8Go SM/FR	—	30.00	33.00	50.00	220
1879Go SM	—	27.50	30.00	41.50	220
1879Go SM/FR	—	30.00	33.00	50.00	220
1880/70Go SB	—	30.00	33.00	50.00	220
1880Go SB/SM	—	27.50	30.00	41.50	220
1880Go SB	—	27.50	30.00	41.50	220
1881/71Go SB	3,974,000	30.00	33.00	50.00	220
1881/0Go SB	Inc. above	30.00	33.00	50.00	220
1881Go SB	Inc. above	27.50	30.00	41.50	220
1882Go SB	2,015,000	27.50	30.00	41.50	220
1883Go SB	2,100,000	49.50	95.00	175	550
1883Go BR	Inc. above	27.50	30.00	41.50	220
1883Go BR/SR	—	27.50	30.00	41.50	220
1883Go BR/SB	Inc. above	27.50	30.00	41.50	220
1884/73Go BR	—	33.00	44.00	65.00	240
1884/74Go BR	—	33.00	44.00	65.00	240
1884/3Go BR	—	33.00	44.00	90.00	350
1884Go BR	—	27.50	30.00	41.50	220
1884/74Go RR	—	65.00	120	240	750
1884Go RR	—	38.50	65.00	145	550
1885/75Go RR/BR	—	30.00	33.00	400	220
1885/75Go RR	2,363,000	30.00	33.00	50.00	220
1885Go RR	Inc. above	27.50	30.00	41.50	220
1886/75Go RR/BR	—	30.00	33.00	45.50	220

Date	Mintage	F	VF	XF	Unc
1886/75Go RR	4,127,000	30.00	33.00	45.50	220
1886/76Go RR/BR	—	27.50	30.00	41.50	220
1886/76Go RR	Inc. above	27.50	30.00	41.50	220
1886/5Go RR/BR	Inc. above	27.50	30.00	41.50	220
1886Go RR	Inc. above	27.50	30.00	41.50	220
1887Go RR	4,205,000	27.50	30.00	41.50	220
1888Go RR	3,985,000	27.50	30.00	41.50	220
1889Go RR	3,646,000	27.50	30.00	41.50	220
1890Go RR	3,615,000	27.50	30.00	41.50	220
1891Go RS/R	—	27.50	30.00	41.50	220
1891Go RS	3,197,000	27.50	30.00	41.50	220
1892/0Go/A RS	—	27.50	30.00	41.50	220
1892/0Go RS	—	27.50	30.00	41.50	220
1892Go RS	3,672,000	27.50	30.00	41.50	220
1892Go/A RS	—	27.50	30.00	41.50	220
1893Go RS	3,854,000	27.50	30.00	41.50	220
1894Go RS	4,127,000	27.50	30.00	41.50	220
1895/1Go RS	3,768,000	30.00	33.00	41.50	220
1895/3Go RS	Inc. above	30.00	33.00	45.50	220
1895Go RS	Inc. above	27.50	30.00	41.50	220
1896/1Go/As RS/ML	5,229,000	30.00	33.00	45.50	220
1896/1Go RS	Inc. above	27.50	30.00	41.50	220
1896Go/Ga RS	Inc. above	—	—	—	—
1896Go RS	Inc. above	27.50	29.50	39.00	220
1897Go RS	4,344,000	27.50	29.50	39.00	220

Date	Mintage	F	VF	XF	Unc
1867Ho PR	—	110	195	350	1,000
1868Ho PR	—	33.00	49.50	100	400
1869Ho PR	—	55.00	75.00	175	550
1870Ho PR	—	120	205	375	1,150
1871/0Ho PR	—	65.00	95.00	175	550
1871Ho PR	—	44.00	65.00	130	450
1872/1Ho PR	—	49.50	75.00	130	450
1872Ho PR	—	44.00	65.00	110	400
1873Ho PR	351,000	44.00	65.00	125	350
1874Ho PR	—	30.00	35.00	65.00	290
1875Ho PR	—	30.00	35.00	65.00	290
1876Ho AF	—	30.00	35.00	65.00	290
1877Ho AF	410,000	33.00	44.00	80.00	350
1877Ho GR	Inc. above	120	175	300	850
1877Ho JA	Inc. above	38.50	65.00	125	400
1878Ho JA	451,000	30.00	35.00	65.00	280
1879Ho JA	—	30.00	35.00	65.00	280
1880Ho JA	—	30.00	35.00	65.00	280
1881Ho JA	586,000	30.00	35.00	65.00	280
1882Ho JA	240,000	38.50	55.00	100	290
Note: O above H					
1882Ho JA	Inc. above	38.50	55.00	100	290
Note: O after H					
1883/2Ho JA	204,000	230	400	675	2,050
1883/2Ho FM/JA	Inc. above	38.50	55.00	110	350
1883Ho FM/JA	—	40.00	60.00	125	375
1883Ho FM	Inc. above	33.00	44.00	90.00	290
1883Ho JA	Inc. above	325	500	1,050	3,050
1884/3Ho FM	—	33.00	38.50	80.00	290
1884Ho FM	—	30.00	35.00	65.00	280
1885Ho FM	132,000	30.00	35.00	65.00	280
1886Ho FM	225,000	33.00	44.00	70.00	290
1886Ho FG	Inc. above	33.00	44.00	70.00	290
1887/6Ho FG	—	33.00	49.50	100	350
1887Ho FG	150,000	33.00	49.50	100	350
1888Ho FG	364,000	27.50	33.00	50.00	260
1889Ho FG	490,000	27.50	33.00	50.00	260
1890Ho FG	565,000	27.50	33.00	50.00	260
1891Ho FG	738,000	27.50	33.00	50.00	260
1892Ho FG	643,000	27.50	33.00	50.00	260
1893Ho FG	518,000	27.50	33.00	50.00	260
1894Ho FG	504,000	27.50	33.00	50.00	260
1895Ho FG	320,000	27.50	33.00	50.00	260

KM# 377.9 8 REALES
27.0700 g., 0.9030 Silver 0.7859 oz. ASW **Obv:** Facing eagle, snake in beak **Rev:** Radiant cap **Mint:** Hermosillo **Note:** Varieties exist.

Date	Mintage	F	VF	XF	Unc
1835Ho PP Rare	—	—	—	—	—
1836Ho PP Rare	—	—	—	—	—
1839Ho PR Unique	—	—	—	—	—
1861Ho FM	—	4,950	8,300	—	—
Note: Reeded edge					
1862Ho FM Rare	—	—	—	—	—
Note: Plain edge, snakes tail left, long ray over *8R					
1862Ho FM	—	1,700	2,950	—	—
Note: Plain edge, snake's tail left					
1862Ho FM	—	1,800	3,050	—	—
Note: Reeded edge, snakes tail right					
1863Ho FM	—	165	325	1,050	—
1864Ho FM	—	925	1,800	3,600	—
1864Ho PR/FM	—	1,300	2,400	—	—
1864Ho PR	—	725	1,400	2,800	6,700
1865Ho FM	—	275	550	1,250	3,700
1866Ho FM	—	1,250	2,350	4,550	11,000
1866Ho MP	—	1,050	1,950	3,900	9,300

KM# 377.12 8 REALES
27.0700 g., 0.9030 Silver 0.7859 oz. ASW **Obv:** Facing eagle, snake in beak **Obv. Legend:** REPUBLICA MEXICANA **Rev:** Radiant cap **Mint:** San Luis Potosi **Note:** Varieties exist.

FIRST REPUBLIC · FEDERAL

FIRST REPUBLIC - FEDERAL

Date	Mintage	F	VF	XF	Unc
1827Pi JS	—	4,200	—	—	—
Note: Heritage World Coin Auction #3004, 1-09, MS63 realized $63,250					
1827Pi SA	—	6,600	9,900	—	—
1828/7Pi JS	—	300	475	850	2,700
1828Pi JS	—	250	425	725	2,400
1829Pi JS	—	49.50	85.00	175	550
1830Pi JS	—	44.00	65.00	145	450
Note: Varities with low cap or centered cap					
1831/0Pi JS	—	49.50	95.00	275	750
1831Pi JS	—	38.50	49.50	110	450
1832/22Pi JS	—	38.50	49.50	100	375
18/032Pi JS	—	55.00	100	240	650
1832Pi JS	—	38.50	49.50	100	375
1833/2Pi JS	—	44.00	60.00	115	550
1833Pi JS Narrow date	—	33.00	44.00	80.00	350
Note: Planchet diameter 37.5 mm					
1833Pi JS Wide date	—	33.00	44.00	80.00	350
Note: Planchet diameter 38.5 mm					
1834/3Pi JS	—	49.50	85.00	175	650
1834Pi JS	—	30.00	38.50	80.00	350
Note: Varieties with low cap or centered cap					
1835/4Pi JS	—	75.00	150	350	1,050
1835Pi JS	—	33.00	44.00	100	400
Note: Denomination as 8R					
1835Pi JS	—	30.00	38.50	80.00	350
Note: Denomination as 8Rs					
1836Pi JS	—	33.00	44.00	85.00	350
1837Pi JS	—	44.00	65.00	125	450
1838Pi JS	—	33.00	44.00	85.00	350
1839Pi JS	—	33.00	55.00	105	350
Note: Varieties with small low cap or large high cap					
1840Pi JS	—	33.00	44.00	90.00	350
184/31Pi JS	—	38.50	55.00	125	450
1841Pi JS	—	38.50	55.00	125	450
1841iP JS Error	—	230	400	725	—
1842/1Pi JS	—	55.00	85.00	175	650
1842/1Pi JS/PS	—	49.50	70.00	130	450
1842Pi JS	—	44.00	65.00	115	400
Note: Eagle type of 1843					
1842Pi PS	—	44.00	65.00	115	400
1842Pi PS/JS	—	44.00	65.00	115	400
Note: Eagle type of 1841					
1843/2Pi PS Round-top 3	—	65.00	95.00	210	650
1843Pi PS Flat-top 3	—	75.00	120	275	1,000
1843Pi AM Round-top 3	—	33.00	44.00	85.00	350
1843Pi AM Flat-top 3	—	33.00	44.00	85.00	350
1844Pi AM	—	33.00	44.00	85.00	350
1845/4Pi AM	—	49.50	70.00	170	550
1845Pi AM	—	38.50	65.00	145	500
1846/5Pi AM	—	55.00	85.00	175	650
1846Pi AM	—	30.00	38.50	80.00	350
1847Pi AM	—	44.00	65.00	125	400
1848/7Pi AM	—	44.00	75.00	145	450
1848Pi AM	—	44.00	65.00	125	400
1849/8Pi PS/AM	—	1,050	1,950	—	—
1849Pi PS	—	1,050	1,950	—	—
1849Pi MC/PS	—	75.00	150	350	1,050
1849Pi AM	—	2,050	3,600	6,500	—
1849Pi MC	—	75.00	150	350	1,050
1850Pi MC	—	55.00	100	210	650
185/41Pi MC	—	95.00	175	375	1,150
1851Pi MC	—	95.00	175	375	1,150
1852Pi MC	—	95.00	150	275	850
1853Pi MC	—	175	325	525	1,750
1854Pi MC	—	120	175	350	1,050
1855Pi MC	—	120	175	350	1,050
1856Pi MC	—	85.00	120	275	850
1857Pi MC	—	450	775	1,650	—
1857Pi PS/MC	—	165	275	575	2,000
1857Pi PS	—	140	220	450	1,300
1858Pi MC/PS	—	275	450	850	2,400
1858Pi MC	—	275	450	850	2,400
1858Pi PS	—	725	1,250	2,300	—
1859/8Pi MC/PS	—	4,000	6,300	—	—
1859Pi MC/PS	—	1,000	1,950	—	—
1859Pi MC	—	2,200	3,850	6,500	—
1859Pi PS/MC	—	875	1,650	3,250	—
1860Pi FC Rare	—	—	—	—	—

Date	Mintage	F	VF	XF	Unc
1860Pi FE Rare	—	—	—	—	—
1860Pi MC	—	1,950	3,050	7,800	—
1860Pi PS/FE	—	550	1,100	—	—
1860Pi RO Rare	—	—	—	—	—
Note: Spink America Gerber sale 6-96 cleaned VF or better realized $33,000					
1860Pi PS	—	450	650	1,150	3,500
1861Pi PS	—	44.00	75.00	130	400
1861Pi RO	—	38.50	49.50	85.00	300
1862/1Pi RO	—	33.00	38.50	80.00	300
1862Pi RO	—	30.00	35.00	70.00	280
Note: Round O/M					
1862Pi RO	—	30.00	35.00	70.00	280
Note: Oval O in RO					
1862Pi RO	—	33.00	44.00	80.00	300
Note: Round O in RO, 6 is an inverted 9					
1863Pi RO	—	38.50	49.50	100	350
1863Pi RO/MO/FC	—	33.00	44.00	80.00	350
1863/5Pi RO	—	33.00	38.50	70.00	350
1863Pi RO	—	30.25	33.00	65.00	300
1863	—	38.50	49.50	85.00	300
Note: 6 over inverted 6					
1863Pi FC	—	3,050	5,200	—	—
1864Pi RO Rare	—	—	—	—	—
1867Pi CA	—	325	550	—	—
1867Pi LR	—	275	450	850	—
1867Pi PS/CA	—	925	—	—	—
1867Pi PS	—	44.00	75.00	175	600
1868/7Pi PS	—	44.00	75.00	175	550
1868Pi PS	—	33.00	44.00	80.00	300
1869/8Pi PS	—	33.00	38.50	70.00	300
1869Pi PS	—	30.00	35.00	70.00	300
1870/69Pi PS	—	825	1,600	4,550	—
1870Pi PS	—	725	1,400	3,250	—
1873Pi MH	—	30.00	38.50	70.00	350
1874/3Pi MH	—	38.50	65.00	170	550
1874Pi MH	—	27.50	29.50	41.50	280
1875Pi MH	—	27.50	29.50	41.50	260
1876/5Pi MH	—	30.00	38.50	70.00	350
1876Pi MH	—	27.50	29.50	41.50	260
1877/6Pi MH	—	195	375	725	—
1877Pi MH	1,018,000	27.50	29.50	41.50	280
1878Pi MH	1,046,000	30.00	44.00	145	500
1879/8Pi MH	—	30.00	35.00	50.00	290
1879Pi MH	—	27.50	29.50	41.50	260
1879Pi BE	—	38.50	65.00	110	350
1879Pi MR	—	44.00	65.00	145	450
1880Pi MR	—	285	425	1,000	—
1880/70Pi MH/R	—	27.50	29.50	41.50	260
1880Pi MH/R	—	27.50	29.50	41.50	260
1880Pi MR	—	27.50	29.50	41.50	260
1881/71Pi MH/R	—	27.50	29.50	41.50	260
1881Pi MH/R	—	27.50	29.50	41.50	260
1881Pi MH	2,100,000	27.50	29.50	41.50	260
1882/1Pi MH	1,602,000	30.00	35.00	50.00	290
1882Pi MH	Inc. above	27.50	29.50	41.50	260
1883/2Pi MH	—	30.00	35.00	50.00	290
1883Pi MH	1,545,000	27.50	29.50	41.50	260
1884/3Pi MH	—	30.00	35.00	50.00	290
1884Pi MH/MM	—	27.50	30.00	41.50	230
1884Pi MH	—	27.50	29.50	39.00	220
1885/4Pi MH	1,736,000	30.00	35.00	50.00	290
1885/8Pi MH	Inc. above	30.00	35.00	50.00	290
1885Pi MH	Inc. above	27.50	29.50	39.00	220
1885Pi LC	Inc. above	30.00	33.00	45.50	260
1886Pi LC	3,347,000	27.50	29.50	39.00	220
1886Pi MR	Inc. above	27.50	29.50	39.00	220
1887Pi MR	2,922,000	27.50	29.50	39.00	220
1888/7Pi MR	—	30.00	35.00	50.00	290
1888Pi MR	2,438,000	27.50	29.50	39.00	220
1889Pi MR	2,103,000	27.50	29.50	39.00	220
1890Pi MR	1,562,000	27.50	29.50	39.00	220
1891Pi MR	1,184,000	27.50	29.50	39.00	220
1892Pi MR	1,336,000	27.50	29.50	39.00	220
1893Pi MR	530,000	27.50	29.50	39.00	220

KM# 377.13 8 REALES

27.0700 g., 0.9030 Silver 0.7859 oz. ASW **Obv:**
Facing eagle, snake in beak **Obv. Legend:**
REPUBLICA MEXICANA. **Rev:** Radiant cap **Mint:**
Zacatecas **Note:** Varieties exist.

Date	Mintage	F	VF	XF	Unc
1825Zs AZ	—	38.50	49.50	100	400
1826/5Zs AZ	—	38.50	60.00	125	450
1826Zs AZ	—	110	220	525	1,600
1826Zs AV	—	195	375	775	3,000
1826/5Zs AO/AZ	—	325	650	1,300	4,000
1826Zs AO	—	220	375	975	4,000
1827Zs AO/AZ	—	49.50	65.00	175	550
1827Zs AO	—	38.50	60.00	125	450
1828Zs AO	—	30.00	35.00	70.00	375

Note: Wide and narrow date varieties exist

Date	Mintage	F	VF	XF	Unc
1829Zs AO	—	30.00	35.00	70.00	375
1829Zs OV	—	65.00	110	210	650
1830Zs OM	—	—	—	—	—
1830Zs OV	—	30.00	35.00	70.00	375
1831Zs OV	—	38.50	65.00	130	450
1831Zs OM	—	30.00	38.50	85.00	375
1832/1Zs OM	—	33.00	38.50	70.00	375
1832Zs OM	—	30.00	35.00	65.00	350
1833/2Zs OM	—	33.00	44.00	70.00	375
1833Zs OM/MM	—	30.00	38.50	65.00	350
1833Zs OM	—	30.00	35.00	60.00	350
1834Zs OM	—	30.00	35.00	60.00	350

Note: Known with large, medium and small "34" in date

Date	Mintage	F	VF	XF	Unc
1835Zs OM	—	30.00	35.00	65.00	350
1836/4Zs OM	—	33.00	44.00	80.00	375
1836/5Zs OM	—	33.00	44.00	80.00	375
1836Zs OM	—	30.00	35.00	60.00	350
1837Zs OM	—	30.00	35.00	60.00	350
1838/7Zs OM	—	33.00	44.00	70.00	375
1838Zs OM	—	30.00	35.00	60.00	350
1839Zs OM	—	30.00	35.00	60.00	350
1840Zs OM	—	30.00	35.00	60.00	350
1841Zs OM	—	30.00	35.00	60.00	350
1842Zs OM	—	30.00	35.00	60.00	350

Note: Eagle type of 1841

Date	Mintage	F	VF	XF	Unc
1842Zs OM	—	30.00	35.00	60.00	350

Note: Eagle type of 1843

Date	Mintage	F	VF	XF	Unc
1843Zs OM	—	30.00	35.00	60.00	350
1844Zs OM	—	30.00	35.00	60.00	350
1845Zs OM	—	30.00	35.00	60.00	350
1846Zs OM	—	30.00	35.00	60.00	350
1847Zs OM	—	30.00	35.00	60.00	350
1848/7Zs OM	—	33.00	44.00	70.00	375
1848Zs OM	—	30.00	35.00	60.00	350
1849Zs OM	—	30.00	35.00	60.00	350
1850Zs OM	—	30.00	35.00	60.00	350
1851Zs OM	—	30.00	35.00	60.00	350

Date	Mintage	F	VF	XF	Unc
1852Zs OM	—	30.00	35.00	60.00	350
1853Zs OM	—	44.00	60.00	110	450
1854/3Zs OM	—	33.00	44.00	90.00	400
1854Zs OM	—	30.00	38.50	70.00	375
1855Zs OM	—	33.00	44.00	90.00	400
1855Zs MO	—	44.00	75.00	130	450
1856/5Zs MO	—	33.00	44.00	70.00	375
1856Zs MO	—	30.00	35.00	60.00	350
1857/5Zs MO	—	33.00	44.00	70.00	375
1857Zs MO	—	30.00	35.00	60.00	350
1858/7Zs MO	—	30.00	35.00	60.00	350
1858Zs MO	—	30.00	35.00	60.00	350
1859/8Zs MO	—	30.00	35.00	60.00	350
1859Zs MO	—	30.00	35.00	60.00	350
1859Zs VL/MO	—	38.50	65.00	110	400
1859Zs VL	—	33.00	55.00	90.00	375
1860/50Zs MO	—	27.50	29.50	41.50	220
1860/59Zs MO	—	27.50	29.50	41.50	220
1860Zs MO	—	27.50	29.50	41.50	220
1860Zs VL/MO	—	27.50	29.50	41.50	220
1860Zs VL	—	27.50	29.50	41.50	220
1861Zs VL	—	27.50	29.50	41.50	220
1861/0Zs VL/MO	—	27.50	29.50	41.50	220
1861/0Zs VL	—	27.50	29.50	41.50	220
1862/1Zs VL	—	27.50	29.50	60.00	260
1862Zs VL	—	27.50	29.50	41.50	220
1863Zs VL	—	27.50	29.50	41.50	220
1863Zs MO	—	27.50	29.50	41.50	220
1864/3Zs VL	—	27.50	29.50	60.00	260
1864Zs VL	—	27.50	29.50	41.50	220
1864Zs MO	—	27.50	35.00	60.00	260
1865/4Zs MO	—	220	500	1,050	3,100
1865Zs MO	—	165	325	775	2,500
1866Zs VL	—	—	—	—	—

Note: Contemporary counterfeit

Date	Mintage	F	VF	XF	Unc
1867Zs JS Rare	—	—	—	—	—
1868Zs JS	—	27.50	29.50	41.50	220
1868Zs YH	—	27.50	29.50	41.50	220
1869Zs YH	—	27.50	29.50	41.50	220
1870Zs YH Rare	—	—	—	—	—
1873Zs YH	—	27.50	29.50	41.50	220
1874Zs YH	—	27.50	29.50	41.50	220
1874Zs JA/YA	—	27.50	29.50	41.50	220
1874Zs JA	—	27.50	29.50	41.50	220
1875Zs JA	—	27.50	29.50	41.50	220
1876Zs JA	—	27.50	29.50	41.50	220
1876Zs JS	—	27.50	29.50	41.50	220
1877Zs JS	2,700,000	27.50	29.50	41.50	220
1878Zs JS	2,310,000	27.50	29.50	41.50	220
1879/8Zs JS	—	30.00	35.00	60.00	260
1879Zs JS	—	27.50	29.50	41.50	220
1880Zs JS	—	27.50	29.50	41.50	220
1881Zs JS	5,592,000	27.50	29.50	41.50	220
1882/1Zs JS	2,485,000	30.00	35.00	60.00	260
1882Zs JS Straight J	Inc. above	27.50	29.50	41.50	220
1882Zs JS Full J	Inc. above	27.50	29.50	41.50	220
1883/2Zs JS	2,563,000	30.00	35.00	60.00	260
1883Zs JS	Inc. above	27.50	29.50	41.50	220
1884Zs JS	—	27.50	29.50	41.50	220
1885Zs JS	2,252,000	27.50	29.50	41.50	220
1886/5Zs JS	5,303,000	30.00	35.00	60.00	260
1886/8Zs JS	Inc. above	30.00	35.00	60.00	260
1886Zs JS	Inc. above	27.50	29.50	41.50	220
1886Zs FZ	Inc. above	27.50	29.50	41.50	220
1887Zs FZ	4,733,000	27.50	29.50	41.50	220
1887Z FZ	Inc. above	33.00	44.00	80.00	260
1888/7Zs FZ	5,132,000	27.50	30.00	45.50	230
1888Zs FZ	Inc. above	27.50	29.50	41.50	220
1889Zs FZ	4,344,000	27.50	29.50	41.50	220
1890Zs FZ	3,887,000	27.50	29.50	41.50	220
1891Zs FZ	4,114,000	27.50	29.50	41.50	220
1892/1Zs FZ	4,238,000	27.50	30.00	45.50	230
1892Zs FZ Narrow date	Inc. above	27.50	29.50	41.50	220
1892Zs FZ Wide date	—	27.50	29.50	41.50	220
1893Zs FZ	3,872,000	27.50	29.50	41.50	220
1894Zs FZ	3,081,000	27.50	29.50	41.50	220
1895Zs FZ	4,718,000	27.50	29.50	41.50	220
1896Zs FZ	4,226,000	27.50	29.50	41.50	220
1897Zs FZ	4,877,000	27.50	29.50	41.50	220

KM# 377.10   8 REALES

27.0700 g., 0.9030 Silver 0.7859 oz. ASW **Obv:** Facing eagle, snake in beak **Obv. Legend:** REPUBLICA MEXICANA. **Rev:** Radiant cap **Mint:** Mexico City **Note:** Varieties exist. 1874 CP is a die struck counterfeit.

Date	Mintage	F	VF	XF	Unc
1824Mo JM Round tail	—	95.00	150	350	1,050
1824Mo JM Square tail	—	95.00	150	350	1,050
1825Mo JM	—	38.50	55.00	110	450
1826/5Mo JM	—	38.50	55.00	110	450
1826Mo JM	—	33.00	44.00	85.00	375
1827Mo JM	—	38.50	49.50	90.00	400
Note: Medal alignment					
1827Mo JM	—	38.50	49.50	90.00	400
Note: Coin alignment					
1828Mo JM	—	44.00	75.00	145	550
1829Mo JM	—	33.00	45.00	130	475
1830/20Mo JM	—	49.50	85.00	210	650
1830Mo JM	—	44.00	65.00	130	475
1831Mo JM	—	44.00	65.00	145	525
1832/1Mo JM	—	38.50	55.00	100	400
1832Mo JM	—	33.00	44.00	85.00	375
1833Mo MJ	—	38.50	55.00	115	450
1833Mo ML	—	500	725	1,250	4,000
1834/3Mo ML	—	38.50	49.50	90.00	400
1834Mo ML	—	33.00	44.00	85.00	375
1835Mo ML Narrow date	—	33.00	44.00	85.00	375
1835Mo ML Wide date	—	33.00	44.00	85.00	375
1836Mo ML	—	65.00	120	210	700
1836Mo ML/MF	—	65.00	120	210	700
1836Mo MF	—	44.00	65.00	130	475
1836Mo MF/ML	—	49.50	75.00	145	525
1837/6Mo ML	—	44.00	65.00	115	450
1837/6Mo MM	—	44.00	65.00	115	450
1837/6Mo MM/ML	—	44.00	65.00	115	450
1837/6Mo MM/MF	—	44.00	65.00	115	450
1837Mo ML	—	44.00	65.00	115	450
1837Mo MM	—	95.00	150	240	700
1838Mo MM	—	44.00	65.00	115	450
1838Mo ML	—	33.00	49.50	90.00	400
1838Mo ML/MM	—	33.00	49.50	90.00	400
1839Mo ML Narow date	—	30.00	38.50	80.00	375
1839Mo ML Wide date	—	30.00	38.50	80.00	375
1840Mo ML	—	30.00	38.50	80.00	375
1841Mo ML	—	30.00	38.50	70.00	350
1842Mo ML	—	30.00	38.50	70.00	350
1842Mo MM	—	30.00	38.50	70.00	350
1843Mo MM	—	30.00	38.50	70.00	350
1844Mo MF/MM	—	—	—	—	—
1844Mo MF	—	30.00	38.50	70.00	350
1845/4Mo MF	—	30.00	38.50	70.00	350
1845Mo MF	—	30.00	38.50	70.00	350
1846/5Mo MF	—	30.00	38.50	80.00	375

Date	Mintage	F	VF	XF	Unc
1846Mo MF	—	30.00	38.50	80.00	375
1847/6Mo MF	—	2,200	3,900	—	—
1847Mo MF	—	1,650	3,050	6,500	15,000
1847Mo RC	—	33.00	44.00	85.00	375
1847Mo RC/MF	—	30.00	38.50	70.00	350
1848Mo GC	—	30.00	38.50	70.00	350
1849/8Mo GC	—	33.00	49.50	90.00	400
1849Mo GC	—	30.00	38.50	70.00	350
1850/40Mo GC	—	38.50	65.00	145	525
1850/49Mo GC	—	38.50	65.00	145	525
1850Mo GC	—	33.00	55.00	110	450
1851Mo GC	—	33.00	55.00	90.00	400
1852Mo GC	—	33.00	55.00	110	450
1853Mo GC	—	30.00	38.50	80.00	350
1854Mo GC	—	27.50	30.00	50.00	290
1855Mo GC	—	33.00	49.50	100	400
1855Mo GF	—	27.50	30.00	50.00	290
1855Mo GF/GC	—	27.50	30.00	50.00	290
1856/4Mo GF	—	30.00	38.50	70.00	325
1856/5Mo GF	—	30.00	38.50	70.00	325
1856Mo GF	—	27.50	30.00	50.00	290
1857Mo GF	—	27.50	30.00	50.00	290
1858Mo FH Narrow date	—	27.50	30.00	50.00	290
1858/7Mo FH/GF	—	27.50	30.00	50.00	290
1858Mo FH Wide date	—	27.50	30.00	50.00	290
1859Mo FH	—	27.50	30.00	50.00	290
1859/8Mo FH	—	38.50	65.00	145	525
1860/59Mo FH	—	30.00	33.00	50.00	290
1860Mo FH	—	27.50	30.00	50.00	290
1860Mo TH	—	27.50	30.00	65.00	325
1861Mo TH	—	27.50	30.00	65.00	325
1861Mo CH	—	27.50	30.00	41.50	220
1862Mo CH	—	27.50	30.00	41.50	220
1863Mo CH	—	27.50	30.00	41.50	220
1863Mo CH/TH	—	27.50	30.00	41.50	220
1863Mo TH	—	27.50	30.00	41.50	220
1867Mo CH	—	27.50	30.00	41.50	220
1867Mo CH/TH	—	33.00	60.00	105	400
1868Mo CH	—	27.50	30.00	41.50	220
1868Mo PH	—	27.50	30.00	41.50	220
1868Mo CH/PH	—	27.50	30.00	41.50	220
1868Mo PH Narrow date	—	27.50	30.00	41.50	220
1868Mo PH Wide date	—	27.50	30.00	41.50	220
1869Mo CH	—	27.50	30.00	41.50	220
1873Mo MH	—	27.50	30.00	41.50	220
1873Mo MH/HH	—	27.50	30.00	45.50	230
1874/69Mo MH	—	33.00	60.00	105	400
1874Mo MH	—	27.50	30.00	45.50	230
1874Mo BH/MH	—	27.50	30.00	45.50	230
1874Mo BH	—	27.50	30.00	45.50	230
1875Mo BH	—	27.50	30.00	41.50	220
1876/4Mo BH	—	27.50	30.00	45.50	230
1876/5Mo BH	—	27.50	30.00	45.50	230
1876Mo BH	—	27.50	30.00	41.50	220
1877Mo MH	898,000	27.50	30.00	41.50	220
1877Mo MH/BH	Inc. above	27.50	30.00	45.50	230
1878Mo MH	2,154,000	27.50	30.00	41.50	220
1879/8Mo MH	—	27.50	30.00	41.50	230
1879Mo MH	—	27.50	30.00	41.50	220
1880/79Mo MH	—	30.00	33.00	50.00	240
1880Mo MH	—	27.50	30.00	41.50	220
1881Mo MH	5,712,000	27.50	30.00	41.50	220
1882/1Mo MH	2,746,000	27.50	30.00	41.50	220
1882Mo MH	Inc. above	27.50	30.00	41.50	220
1883/2Mo MH	2,726,000	27.50	30.00	45.50	230
1883Mo MH Narrow date	Inc. above	27.50	30.00	41.50	220
1883Mo MH Wide date	—	27.50	30.00	41.50	220
1884/3Mo MH	—	30.00	33.00	50.00	240
1884Mo MH	—	27.50	30.00	41.50	220
1885Mo MH	3,649,000	27.50	30.00	41.50	220
1886Mo MH	7,558,000	27.50	29.50	39.00	220
1887Mo MH	7,681,000	27.50	29.50	39.00	220
1888Mo MH Narrow date	7,179,000	27.50	29.50	39.00	220
1888Mo MH Wide date	—	27.50	29.50	39.00	220
1889Mo MH	7,332,000	27.50	30.00	41.50	220
1890Mo MH Narrow date	7,412,000	27.50	29.50	39.00	220
1890Mo AM Wide date	—	27.50	29.50	39.00	220

Date	Mintage	F	VF	XF	Unc
1890Mo AM	Inc. above	27.50	29.50	39.00	220
1891Mo AM	8,076,000	27.50	29.50	39.00	220
1892Mo AM	9,392,000	27.50	29.50	39.00	220
1893Mo AM	10,773,000	27.50	29.50	39.00	220
1894Mo AM	12,394,000	27.50	29.50	39.00	220
1895Mo AM	10,474,000	27.50	29.50	39.00	220
1895Mo AB	Inc. above	27.50	29.50	39.00	220
1896Mo AB	9,327,000	27.50	29.50	39.00	220
1896Mo AM	Inc. above	27.50	29.50	39.00	220
1897Mo AM	8,621,000	27.50	29.50	39.00	220

KM# 377.1   8 REALES

27.0700 g., 0.9030 Silver 0.7859 oz. ASW **Obv:** Facing eagle, snake in beak **Obv. Legend:** REPUBLICA MEXICANA. **Rev:** Radiant cap **Mint:** Real de Catorce

Date	Mintage	F	VF	XF	Unc
1863Ce ME	—	575	975	2,200	7,500
1863Ce /PI ML/MC	—	575	1,050	2,450	8,000

KM# 377.2   8 REALES

27.0700 g., 0.9030 Silver 0.7859 oz. ASW **Obv:** Facing eagle, snake in beak **Obv. Legend:** REPUBLICA MEXICANA. **Rev:** Radiant cap **Mint:** Chihuahua **Note:** Varieties exist.

Date	Mintage	F	VF	XF	Unc	BU
1831Ca MR	—	1,100	1,950	2,950	6,500	—
1832Ca MR	—	140	220	400	1,200	—
1833Ca MR	—	275	600	1,300	—	—
1834Ca MR	—	325	650	1,500	—	—
1834Ca AM	—	375	550	900	—	—
1835Ca AM	—	165	275	625	1,800	—

Date	Mintage	F	VF	XF	Unc	BU
1836Ca AM	—	110	220	400	1,200	—
1837Ca AM	—	600	1,250	—	—	—
1838Ca AM	—	110	220	400	1,200	—
1839Ca RG	—	825	1,400	3,250	—	—
1840Ca RG	—	325	550	1,050	3,000	—
Note: 1 dot after date						
1840Ca RG	—	325	550	1,050	3,000	—
Note: 3 dots after date						
1841Ca RG	—	65.00	120	210	650	—
1842Ca RG	—	38.50	55.00	110	350	—
1843Ca RG	—	55.00	100	175	550	—
1844/1Ca RG	—	49.50	90.00	145	450	—
1844Ca RG	—	38.50	55.00	110	350	—
1845Ca RG	—	38.50	55.00	110	350	—
1846Ca RG	—	44.00	75.00	145	550	—
1847Ca RG	—	55.00	100	175	550	—
1848Ca RG	—	49.50	90.00	175	550	—
1849Ca RG	—	44.00	75.00	145	450	—
1850/40Ca RG	—	55.00	100	175	550	—
1850Ca RG	—	44.00	75.00	145	450	—
1851/41Ca RG	—	120	230	400	1,050	—
1851Ca RG	—	175	285	525	1,550	—
1852/42Ca RG	—	175	285	525	1,550	—
1852Ca RG	—	175	285	525	1,550	—
1853/43Ca RG	—	175	285	525	1,550	—
1853Ca RG	—	175	285	450	1,450	—
1854/44Ca RG	—	120	230	400	1,050	—
1854Ca RG	—	65.00	120	210	650	—
1855/45Ca RG	—	120	230	450	1,350	—
1855Ca RG	—	65.00	120	210	650	—
1856/45Ca RG	—	325	500	975	2,500	—
1856/5Ca RG	—	450	775	1,950	7,000	—
1857Ca JC/RG	—	55.00	100	175	550	—
1857Ca JC	—	65.00	120	210	550	—
1858Ca JC	—	49.50	90.00	175	550	—
1858Ca BA	—	2,200	3,850	—	—	—
1859Ca JC	—	55.00	100	175	550	—
1860Ca JC	—	33.00	55.00	130	400	—
1861Ca JC	—	30.00	38.50	85.00	300	—
1862Ca JC	—	30.00	38.50	85.00	300	—
1863Ca JC	—	33.00	49.50	110	350	—
1864Ca JC	—	33.00	49.50	110	350	—
1865Ca JC	—	120	230	450	1,250	—
1865Ca FP	—	1,400	2,350	4,250	—	—
1866Ca JC	—	825	1,250	2,950	—	—
1866Ca FP	—	1,100	2,200	4,250	10,000	—
1866Ca JG	—	925	1,800	3,600	8,500	—
1867Ca JG	—	110	220	450	1,200	—
1868Ca JG	—	85.00	165	325	800	—
1868Ca MM	—	70.00	140	260	700	—
1869Ca MM	—	33.00	49.50	100	325	—
1870Ca MM	—	33.00	49.50	100	325	—
1871/0Ca MM	—	30.00	38.50	85.00	300	—
1871Ca MM	—	30.00	38.50	85.00	300	—
1871Ca MM	—	33.00	49.50	100	325	—
Note: Known with first M over inverted M and second M over inverted M						
1873/5Ca MM	—	33.00	49.50	100	325	—
1873Ca MM	—	33.00	49.50	100	325	—
1873Ca MM/T	—	30.00	38.50	85.00	300	—
1874Ca MM	—	27.50	30.00	50.00	260	—
1875Ca MM	—	27.50	30.00	50.00	260	—
1876Ca MM	—	27.50	30.00	50.00	260	—
1877Ca EA E/G	—	33.00	55.00	125	450	—
1877Ca EA	472,000	33.00	55.00	125	450	—
1877Ca GR	Inc. above	38.50	60.00	100	350	—
1877Ca JM	Inc. above	27.50	30.00	50.00	260	—
1877Ca AV	Inc. above	120	230	450	1,550	—
1878Ca AV	439,000	27.50	30.00	45.50	220	—
1879Ca AV	—	27.50	30.00	45.50	220	—
1880Ca AV	—	220	375	775	2,500	—
1880Ca PM	—	550	875	1,650	5,000	—
1880Ca MG	—	27.50	30.00	45.50	260	—
Note: Normal initials						
1880Ca MG	—	27.50	30.00	45.50	260	—
Note: Tall initials						
1880Ca MG	—	27.50	30.00	45.50	260	—
1881Ca MG	1,085,000	27.50	29.50	41.50	220	—
1882Ca MG	779,000	27.50	29.50	41.50	220	—

FIRST REPUBLIC - FEDERAL

Date	Mintage	F	VF	XF	Unc	BU
1882Ca MM	Inc. above	27.50	29.50	41.50	220	—
1882Ca MM	Inc. above	33.00	60.00	145	400	—
Note: Second M over sideways M						
1883Ca MM	818,000	—	—	—	—	—
Note: Sideways M						
1883/2Ca MM/G		27.50	30.00	50.00	230	—
1883Ca MM	Inc. above	27.50	29.50	41.50	220	—
1884/3Ca MM	—	27.50	30.00	50.00	220	—
1884Ca MM	—	27.50	29.50	41.50	220	—
1885/4Ca MM	1,345,000	30.00	38.50	85.00	300	—
1885/6Ca MM	Inc. above	30.00	38.50	85.00	300	—
1885Ca MM	Inc. above	27.50	29.50	41.50	220	—
1886Ca MM	2,483,000	27.50	29.50	41.50	220	—
1887Ca MM	2,625,000	27.50	29.50	41.50	220	—
1888/7Ca MM	2,434,000	30.00	38.50	100	325	—
1888Ca MM	Inc. above	27.50	29.50	41.50	220	—
1889Ca MM	2,681,000	27.50	29.50	41.50	220	—
1890/89Ca MM	—	30.00	38.50	85.00	300	—
1890Ca MM	2,137,000	27.50	29.50	41.50	220	—
1891/0Ca MM	2,268,000	30.00	38.50	85.00	300	—
1891Ca MM	Inc. above	27.50	29.50	41.50	230	—
1892Ca MM	2,527,000	27.50	29.50	41.50	220	—
1893Ca MM	2,632,000	27.50	29.50	41.50	220	—
1894Ca MM	2,642,000	27.50	29.50	41.50	220	—
1895Ca MM	1,112,000	27.50	29.50	41.50	220	—

KM# 378.2   1/2 ESCUDO
1.6900 g., 0.8750 Gold 0.0475 oz. AGW **Obv:** Facing eagle, snake in beak **Obv. Legend:** REPUBLICA MEXICANA **Rev:** Hand holding cap on stick, open book **Rev. Legend:** LIBERTAD... **Mint:** Guadalajara

Date	Mintage	VG	F	VF	XF	Unc
1825Ga FS	—	90.00	105	155	245	600
1829Ga FS	—	90.00	105	155	245	—
1831Ga FS	—	90.00	105	155	245	—
1834Ga FS	—	100	125	200	450	2,500
1835Ga FS	—	90.00	105	155	245	—
1837Ga JG	—	90.00	105	155	245	—
1838Ga JG	—	90.00	105	155	245	—
1839Ga JG	—	—	—	—	—	—
1840Ga MC Unique						
Note: Ponterio & Associates Sale 157, 1-11, AU realized $12,000						
1842Ga JG	—	—	—	—	—	—
1847Ga JG	—	90.00	105	155	245	—
1850Ga JG	—	90.00	115	185	300	—
1852Ga JG	—	85.00	115	125	215	—
1859Ga JG	—	90.00	105	155	245	—
1861Ga JG	—	85.00	100	125	215	600

KM# 378.3   1/2 ESCUDO
1.6900 g., 0.8750 Gold 0.0475 oz. AGW **Obv:** Facing eagle, snake in beak **Obv. Legend:** REPUBLICA MEXICANA. **Rev:** Hand holding cap on stick, open book **Rev. Legend:** LIBERTAD... **Mint:** Guadalupe y Calvo

Date	Mintage	VG	F	VF	XF	Unc
1846GC MP	—	95.00	125	155	245	—
1847GC MP	—	95.00	125	155	245	600
1848/7GC MP	—	95.00	125	155	275	800
1850GC MP	—	95.00	125	155	245	—
1851GC MP	—	95.00	125	155	245	—
Revised eagle						

KM# 378.4   1/2 ESCUDO
1.6900 g., 0.8750 Gold 0.0475 oz. AGW **Obv:** Facing eagle, snake in beak **Rev:** Hand holding cap on stick, open book **Mint:** Guanajuato

Date	Mintage	F	VF	XF	Unc
1845Go PM	—	75.00	90.00	115	185	—
1849Go PF	—	75.00	95.00	145	245	775
1851/41Go PF	—	75.00	90.00	115	185	—
1851Go PF	—	75.00	90.00	115	185	—
1852Go PF/FF	—	—	—	—	—	—
1852Go PF	—	75.00	90.00	115	185	—
1853Go PF	—	75.00	95.00	130	215	—
1855Go PF	—	75.00	90.00	115	185	—
1857Go PF	—	75.00	90.00	115	185	—
1858/7Go PF	—	75.00	90.00	115	185	—
1859Go PF	—	75.00	90.00	115	185	450
1860Go PF	—	75.00	90.00	115	185	—
1861Go PF	—	75.00	90.00	115	185	—
1862/1Go YE	—	75.00	90.00	150	220	—
1863Go PF	—	75.00	95.00	130	215	—
1863Go YF	—	75.00	90.00	115	185	—

KM# 378.5   1/2 ESCUDO
1.6900 g., 0.8750 Gold 0.0475 oz. AGW **Obv:** Facing eagle, snake in beak **Obv. Legend:** REPUBLICA MEXICANA. **Rev:** Hand holding cap on stick, open book **Rev. Legend:** LIBERTAD... **Mint:** Mexico City

Date	Mintage	VG	F	VF	XF	Unc
1825/1Mo JM	—	90.00	120	180	270	—
1825/4Mo JM	—	90.00	120	180	270	—
1825Mo JM	—	75.00	90.00	125	210	450
1827/6Mo JM	—	75.00	90.00	125	210	—
1827Mo JM	—	75.00	90.00	125	210	450
1829Mo JM	—	75.00	90.00	125	210	—
1831/0Mo JM	—	75.00	90.00	125	210	—
1831Mo JM	—	75.00	85.00	110	180	—
1832Mo	—	75.00	85.00	110	180	—
1833Mo MJ	—	75.00	90.00	140	240	575
Note: Olive and oak branches reversed						
1834Mo ML	—	75.00	85.00	120	210	500
1835Mo ML	—	75.00	85.00	125	210	500
1838Mo ML	—	70.00	90.00	140	240	—
1839Mo ML	—	75.00	90.00	140	240	—
1840Mo ML	—	75.00	85.00	110	180	—
1841Mo ML	—	75.00	85.00	110	180	—
1842Mo ML	—	75.00	85.00	125	210	—
1842Mo MM	—	75.00	85.00	125	210	—
1843Mo MM	—	75.00	85.00	110	180	400
1844Mo MF	—	75.00	85.00	110	180	325
1845Mo MF	—	75.00	85.00	110	180	350
1846/5Mo MF	—	75.00	85.00	110	180	—
1846Mo MF	—	75.00	85.00	110	180	—
1848Mo GC	—	75.00	90.00	140	240	575
1850Mo GC	—	75.00	85.00	110	180	—
1851Mo GC	—	75.00	85.00	110	180	—
1852Mo GC	—	75.00	85.00	110	180	350
1853Mo GC	—	80.00	100	150	270	800
1854Mo GC	—	75.00	85.00	110	180	600
1855Mo GF	—	75.00	85.00	120	210	450
1856/4Mo GF	—	75.00	85.00	110	180	350
1857Mo GF	—	75.00	85.00	110	180	—
1858/7Mo FH/GF	—	75.00	90.00	120	210	—
1858Mo FH	—	75.00	85.00	110	180	—
1859Mo FH	—	75.00	85.00	110	180	—
1860/59Mo FH	—	75.00	85.00	110	180	325
1861Mo CH/FH	—	75.00	85.00	125	210	—
1862Mo CH	—	75.00	85.00	110	180	270
1863/57Mo CH/GF	—	75.00	85.00	110	180	325
1868/58Mo PH	—	75.00	85.00	125	210	—
1869/59Mo CH	—	75.00	85.00	125	210	—

KM# 378.6   1/2 ESCUDO
1.6900 g., 0.8750 Gold 0.0475 oz. AGW **Obv:** Facing eagle, snake in beak **Obv. Legend:** REPUBLICA MEXICANA. **Rev:** Hand holding cap on stick, open book **Rev. Legend:** LIBERTAD... **Mint:** Zacatecas

Date	Mintage	VG	F	VF	XF	Unc
1860Zs VL	—	85.00	95.00	125	215	350
1862/1Zs VL	—	85.00	95.00	125	215	350
1862Zs VL	—	75.00	90.00	115	185	325

KM# 378   1/2 ESCUDO
1.6900 g., 0.8750 Gold 0.0475 oz. AGW **Obv:** Facing eagle, snake in beak **Obv. Legend:** REPUBLICA MEXICANA **Rev:** Hand holding cap on stick, open book **Rev. Legend:** LIBERTAD... **Mint:** Culiacan

Date	Mintage	VG	F	VF	XF	Unc
1848C CE	—	85.00	95.00	125	215	375
1853C CE	—	85.00	95.00	125	215	—
1854C CE Revised eagle	—	85.00	95.00	125	215	—

Note: Dates 1854-1870 of this type display the revised eagle

1856C CE	—	95.00	155	215	325	—
1857C CE	—	85.00	95.00	125	215	300
1859C CE	—	85.00	95.00	125	215	—
1860C CE	—	85.00	95.00	125	215	300
1862C CE	—	85.00	95.00	125	185	—
1863C CE	—	85.00	95.00	125	185	375
1866C CE	—	85.00	95.00	125	185	—
1867C CE	—	85.00	95.00	125	185	325
1870C CE	—	125	215	350	575	1,850

KM# 378.1   1/2 ESCUDO
1.6900 g., 0.8750 Gold 0.0475 oz. AGW **Obv:** Facing eagle, snake in beak **Rev:** Hand holding cap on stick, open book **Mint:** Durango

Date	Mintage	VG	F	VF	XF	Unc
1833Do RM/RL	—	85.00	95.00	125	215	—
1834/1Do RM	—	85.00	95.00	125	215	900
1834/3Do RM	—	85.00	95.00	125	215	—
1835/2Do RM	—	85.00	95.00	125	215	—
1835/3Do RM	—	85.00	95.00	125	215	—
1835/4Do RM	—	85.00	95.00	125	215	—
1836/5/4Do RM/L	—	90.00	105	155	245	575
1836/4Do RM	—	85.00	95.00	125	215	—
1837Do RM	—	85.00	95.00	125	215	—
1838Do RM	—	90.00	105	155	245	—
1843Do RM	—	90.00	105	155	245	—
1844/33Do RM	—	90.00	105	155	245	—
1844/33Do R,/RL	—	115	185	350	575	—
1845Do CM	—	90.00	105	155	245	—
1846Do RM	—	90.00	105	155	245	—
1848Do RM	—	90.00	105	155	245	—
1850/33Do JMR	—	90.00	105	155	245	600
1851Do JMR	—	90.00	105	155	275	—
1852Do JMR	—	90.00	105	155	245	—
1853/33Do CP	—	125	215	375	625	—
1853Do CP	—	95.00	120	215	325	675
1854Do CP	—	85.00	95.00	125	215	—
1855Do CP	—	85.00	95.00	125	215	—
1859Do CP	—	85.00	95.00	125	215	—
1861Do CP	—	85.00	95.00	125	215	—
1862Do CP	—	85.00	95.00	125	215	—
1864Do LT	—	125	185	325	500	—

KM# 379   ESCUDO
3.3800 g., 0.8750 Gold 0.0951 oz. AGW **Obv:** Facing eagle, snake in beak **Rev:** Hand holding cap on stick, open book **Mint:** Culiacan

Date	Mintage	VG	F	VF	XF	Unc
1846C CE	—	170	190	290	475	—
1847C CE	—	150	160	200	260	—
1848C CE	—	150	160	200	260	850
1849/8C CE	—	155	190	230	325	—
1850C CE	—	150	160	200	260	—
1851C CE	—	155	190	230	325	—
1853/1C CE	—	155	190	230	325	—
1854C CE	—	150	160	200	260	—
1856/5/4C CE	—	155	190	230	325	—
1856C CE	—	150	160	200	260	—
1857/1C CE	—	155	190	230	325	—
1857C CE	—	150	160	200	260	—
1861C PV	—	150	160	200	260	—
1862C CE	—	150	160	200	260	—
1863C CE	—	150	160	200	260	—
1866C CE	—	150	160	200	260	—
1870C CE	—	150	160	200	260	—

KM# 379.1   ESCUDO
3.3800 g., 0.8750 Gold 0.0951 oz. AGW **Obv:** Facing eagle, snake in beak **Obv. Legend:** REPUBLICA MEXICANA. **Rev:** Hand holding cap on stick, open book **Rev. Legend:** LIBERTAD... **Mint:** Durango

Date	Mintage	VG	F	VF	XF
1832Do R.L.	—	—	—	—	—
1833/2Do RM/R.L.	—	170	220	290	400
1834Do RM	—	155	190	230	350
1835Do RM	—	—	—	—	—
1836Do RM/RL	—	155	190	230	350
1838Do RM	—	155	190	230	350
1846/38Do RM	—	170	220	290	400
1850Do JMR	—	170	220	260	375
1851/31Do JMR	—	170	220	290	400
1851Do JMR	—	170	220	260	375
1853Do CP	—	170	220	260	375
1854/34Do CP	—	170	220	260	375
1854/44Do CP/RP	—	170	220	260	375
1855Do CP	—	170	220	260	375
1859Do CP	—	170	220	260	375
1861Do CP	—	170	220	260	375
1864Do LT/CP Rare	—	—	—	—	—

KM# 379.2   ESCUDO
3.3800 g., 0.8750 Gold 0.0951 oz. AGW **Obv:** Facing eagle, snake in beak **Obv. Legend:** REPUBLICA MEXICANA. **Rev:** Hand holding cap on stick, open book **Mint:** Guadalajara

Date	Mintage	VG	F	VF	XF	Unc
1825Ga FS	—	155	180	200	290	—
1826Ga FS	—	155	180	200	290	—

FIRST REPUBLIC · FEDERAL

Date	Mintage	VG	F	VF	XF	Unc
1829Ga FS	—	—	—	—	—	—
1831Ga FS	—	155	180	200	290	—
1834Ga FS	—	155	180	200	290	—
1835Ga JG	—	155	180	200	290	—
1842Ga JG/MC	—	155	180	200	290	—
1843Ga MC	—	155	180	200	290	—
1847Ga JG	—	155	180	200	290	—
1848/7Ga JG	—	155	180	200	290	—
1849Ga JG	—	155	180	200	290	—
1850/40Ga JG	—	160	220	325	450	—
1850Ga JG	—	155	180	200	290	—
1852/1Ga JG	—	155	180	200	290	1,150
1856Ga JG	—	155	180	200	290	—
1857Ga JG	—	155	180	200	290	—
1859/7Ga JG	—	155	180	200	290	—
1860/59Ga JG	—	160	190	260	375	—
1860Ga	—	155	180	200	290	—

Date	Mintage	VG	F	VF	XF	Unc
1843Mo MM	—	150	160	200	260	1,050
1845Mo MF	—	150	155	170	230	—
1846/5Mo MF	—	150	155	170	230	—
1848Mo GC	—	150	160	200	260	—
1850Mo GC	—	150	160	200	260	—
1856/4Mo GF	—	150	155	170	230	—
1856/5Mo GF	—	150	155	170	230	—
1856Mo GF	—	150	155	170	230	—
1858Mo FH	—	150	160	200	260	—
1859Mo FH	—	150	160	200	260	900
1860Mo TH	—	150	160	200	260	—
1861Mo CH	—	150	160	200	260	1,200
1862Mo CH	—	150	160	200	260	—
1863Mo TH	—	150	155	170	230	475
1869Mo CH	—	150	160	200	260	775

KM# 379.3 ESCUDO
3.3800 g., 0.8750 Gold 0.0951 oz. AGW **Obv:** Facing eagle, snake in beak **Obv. Legend:** REPUBLICA MEXICANA. **Rev:** Hand holding cap on stick, open book **Mint:** Guadalupe y Calvo

Date	Mintage	VG	F	VF	XF	Unc
1844GC MP	—	170	190	260	350	—
1845GC MP	—	170	190	260	350	—
1846GC MP	—	170	190	260	350	—
1847GC MP	—	170	190	260	350	—
1848GC MP	—	170	190	260	350	—
1849GC MP	—	170	190	260	350	—
1850GC MP	—	200	250	350	650	2,400
1851GC MP	—	170	190	260	350	—
Revised eagle						

KM# 379.4 ESCUDO
3.3800 g., 0.8750 Gold 0.0951 oz. AGW **Obv:** Facing eagle, snake in beak **Rev:** Hand holding cap on stick, open book **Mint:** Guanajuato

Date	Mintage	VG	F	VF	XF	Unc
1845Go PM	—	155	165	200	290	—
1849Go PF	—	155	165	200	290	—
1851Go PF	—	155	165	200	290	—
1853Go PF	—	155	165	200	290	—
1860Go PF	—	170	220	290	400	—
1862Go YE	—	155	165	200	290	725

KM# 379.5 ESCUDO
3.3800 g., 0.8750 Gold 0.0951 oz. AGW **Obv:** Facing eagle, snake in beak **Obv. Legend:** REPUBLICA MEXICANA. **Rev:** Hand holding cap on stick, open book **Mint:** Mexico City

Date	Mintage	VG	F	VF	XF	Unc
1825Mo JM/FM	—	150	155	170	230	475
1825Mo JM	—	150	155	170	230	—
1827/6Mo JM	—	150	155	170	230	—
1827Mo JM	—	150	155	170	230	—
1830/29Mo JM	—	150	155	170	230	—
1831Mo JM	—	150	160	200	260	650
1832Mo JM	—	150	160	200	260	—
1833Mo MJ	—	150	155	170	230	—
1834Mo ML	—	150	160	200	260	—
1841Mo ML	—	150	160	200	260	—

KM# 379.6 ESCUDO
3.3800 g., 0.8750 Gold 0.0951 oz. AGW **Obv:** Facing eagle, snake in beak **Rev:** Hand holding cap on stick, open book **Mint:** Zacatecas **Note:** Struck at Zacatecas Mint, mint mark Zs.

Date	Mintage	VG	F	VF	XF
1853Zs OM	—	200	220	290	400
1860/59Zs VL V is inverted A	—	170	190	290	475
1860Zs VL	—	170	190	230	290
1862Zs VL	—	170	190	230	290

KM# 380.3 2 ESCUDOS
6.7700 g., 0.8750 Gold 0.1904 oz. AGW **Obv:** Facing eagle, snake in beak **Obv. Legend:** REPUBLICA MEXICANA. **Rev:** Hand holding cap on stick, open book **Rev. Legend:** LIBERTAD... **Mint:** Guadalajara

Date	Mintage	VG	F	VF	XF	Unc
1835Ga FS	—	325	350	400	525	—
1836/5Ga JG	—	350	400	600	725	—
1839/5Ga JG	—	—	—	—	—	—
1839Ga JG	—	325	325	375	475	—
1840Ga MC	—	325	325	375	475	—
1841Ga MC	—	325	350	425	600	—
1847/6Ga JG	—	325	350	400	475	—
1848/7Ga JG	—	325	350	400	475	—
1850/40Ga JG	—	325	325	375	475	—
1851Ga JG	—	325	325	375	475	—
1852Ga JG	—	325	325	400	525	—
1853Ga JG	—	325	325	375	475	—
1854/2Ga JG	—	—	—	—	—	—
1858Ga JG	—	325	325	375	475	—
1859/8Ga JG	—	325	350	400	475	—
1859Ga JG	—	325	350	400	475	—
1860/50Ga JG	—	325	350	400	475	—
1860Ga JG	—	325	350	400	475	950
1861/59Ga JG	—	325	325	375	475	—
1861/0Ga JG	—	325	325	375	475	—
1863/2Ga JG	—	325	350	400	475	975
1863/1Ga JG	—	325	325	375	475	—
1870Ga IC	—	325	325	375	475	—

FIRST REPUBLIC - FEDERAL

KM# 380.4   2 ESCUDOS
6.7700 g., 0.8750 Gold 0.1904 oz. AGW   **Obv:** Facing eagle, snake in beak **Rev:** Hand holding cap on stick, open book **Mint:** Guadalupe y Calvo

Date	Mintage	VG	F	VF	XF	Unc
1844GC MP	—	450	700	1,300	2,500	—
1845GC MP	—	1,050	1,650	2,500	3,700	—
1846GC MP	—	1,050	1,650	2,500	3,700	—
1847GC MP	—	750	1,350	2,500	3,700	—
1848GC MP	—	350	400	575	825	—
1849GC MP	—	1,050	1,650	—	—	—
1850GC MP	—	450	700	1,300	2,500	—

KM# 380.5   2 ESCUDOS
6.7700 g., 0.8750 Gold 0.1904 oz. AGW   **Obv:** Facing eagle, snake in beak **Rev:** Hand holding cap on stick, open book **Mint:** Guanajuato

Date	Mintage	VG	F	VF	XF	Unc
1845Go PM	—	325	350	425	600	—
1849Go PF	—	325	350	425	600	—
1853Go PF	—	350	500	900	1,350	—
1856Go PF	—	—	—	—	—	—
1859Go PF	—	350	500	900	1,350	—
1860/59Go PF	—	—	—	—	—	—
1860Go PF	—	325	350	425	600	—
1862Go YE	—	325	350	425	600	—

KM# 380   2 ESCUDOS
6.7700 g., 0.8750 Gold 0.1904 oz. AGW   **Obv:** Facing eagle, snake in beak **Obv. Legend:** REPUBLICA MEXICANA. **Rev:** Hand holding cap on stick, open book **Mint:** Culiacan

Date	Mintage	VG	F	VF	XF	Unc
1846C CE	—	325	350	400	525	—
1847C CE	—	325	350	400	525	—
1848C CE	—	325	350	400	525	—
1852C CE	—	325	350	400	525	—
1854C CE	—	325	350	425	575	—
1856/4C CE	—	325	350	425	575	—
1857C CE	—	325	350	400	525	—

KM# 380.1   2 ESCUDOS
6.7700 g., 0.8750 Gold 0.1904 oz. AGW   **Obv:** Facing eagle, snake in beak **Obv. Legend:** REPUBLICA MEXICANA. **Rev:** Hand holding cap on stick, open book **Rev. Legend:** LIBERTAD... **Mint:** Durango

Date	Mintage	VG	F	VF	XF	Unc
1833Do RM	—	550	700	975	1,600	—
1837/4Do RM	—	—	—	—	—	—
1837Do RM	—	—	—	—	—	—
1844Do RM	—	500	625	850	1,350	—

KM# 380.7   2 ESCUDOS
6.7700 g., 0.8750 Gold 0.1904 oz. AGW   **Obv:** Facing eagle, snake in beak **Obv. Legend:** REPUBLICA MEXICANA **Rev:** Hand holding cap on stick, open book **Rev. Legend:** LIBERTAD... **Mint:** Mexico City

Date	Mintage	VG	F	VF	XF	Unc
1825Mo JM	—	315	325	375	475	—
1827/6Mo JM	—	315	325	375	475	—
1827Mo JM	—	315	325	375	475	—
1830/29Mo JM	—	315	325	375	475	—
1831Mo JM	—	315	325	375	475	—
1833Mo ML	—	315	325	375	475	—
1841Mo ML	—	315	325	375	475	—
1844Mo MF	—	315	325	375	475	—
1845Mo MF	—	315	325	375	475	—
1846Mo MF	—	315	400	600	850	—
1848Mo GC	—	315	325	375	475	—
1850Mo GC	—	315	325	375	475	—
1856/5Mo GF	—	315	325	375	475	—
1856Mo GF	—	315	325	375	475	—
1858Mo FH	—	315	325	375	475	—
1859Mo FH	—	315	325	375	475	—
1861Mo TH	—	315	325	375	475	—
1861Mo CH	—	315	325	375	475	—
1862Mo CH	—	315	325	375	475	—
1863Mo TH	—	315	325	375	475	950
1868Mo PH	—	315	325	375	475	—
1869Mo CH	—	315	325	375	475	—

KM# 380.8   2 ESCUDOS
6.7700 g., 0.8750 Gold 0.1904 oz. AGW   **Obv:** Facing eagle, snake in beak **Obv. Legend:** REPUBLICA MEXICANA. **Rev:** Hand holding cap on stick, open book **Rev. Legend:** LA LIBERTAD... **Mint:** Zacatecas

Date	Mintage	VG	F	VF	XF	Unc
1860Zs VL	—	350	500	850	1,600	—
1862Zs VL	—	475	750	1,100	1,600	—
1864Zs MO	—	350	500	850	1,600	—

KM# 380.2   2 ESCUDOS
6.7700 g., 0.8750 Gold 0.1904 oz. AGW   **Obv:** Facing eagle, snake in beak **Obv. Legend:**

FIRST REPUBLIC - FEDERAL

REPUBLICA MEXICANA. **Rev:** Hand holding cap on stick, open book **Rev. Legend:** LIBERTAD... **Mint:** Estado de Mexico

Date	Mintage	VG	F	VF	XF	Unc
1828EoMo LF	—	1,000	1,350	2,200	3,700	—

KM# 380.6   2 ESCUDOS
6.7700 g., 0.8750 Gold 0.1904 oz. AGW **Obv:** Facing eagle, snake in beak **Rev:** Hand holding cap on stick, open book **Mint:** Hermosillo

Date	Mintage	VG	F	VF	XF	Unc
1861Ho FM	—	750	1,350	1,950	2,800	—

KM# 381   4 ESCUDOS
13.5400 g., 0.8750 Gold 0.3809 oz. AGW **Obv:** Facing eagle, snake in beak **Obv. Legend:** REPUBLICA MEXICANA. **Rev:** Hand holding cap on stick, open book **Rev. Legend:** LA LIBERTAD... **Mint:** Culiacan

Date	Mintage	VG	F	VF	XF	Unc
1846C CE	—	1,650	2,350	—	—	—
1847C CE	—	750	1,050	1,250	2,050	—
1848C CE	—	900	1,300	1,700	2,650	—

KM# 381.1   4 ESCUDOS
13.5400 g., 0.8750 Gold 0.3809 oz. AGW **Obv:** Facing eagle, snake in beak **Obv. Legend:** REPUBLICA MEXICANA. **Rev:** Hand holding cap on stick, open book **Rev. Legend:** LA LIBERTAD.... **Mint:** Durango

Date	Mintage	VG	F	VF	XF
1832Do RM/LR Rare	—	—	—	—	—
1832Do RM	—	900	1,300	1,700	2,650
1833Do RM/RL Rare	—	—	—	—	—
1852Do JMR Rare	—	—	—	—	—

KM# 381.3   4 ESCUDOS
13.5400 g., 0.8750 Gold 0.3809 oz. AGW **Obv:** Facing eagle, snake in beak **Obv. Legend:** REPUBLICA MEXICANA **Rev:** Hand holding cap on

stick, open book **Rev. Legend:** LA LIBERTAD... **Mint:** Guadalupe y Calvo

Date	Mintage	VG	F	VF	XF	Unc
1844GC MP	—	750	1,050	1,250	1,850	—
1845GC MP	—	700	875	1,100	1,450	—
1846GC MP	—	750	1,050	1,250	1,850	—
1848GC MP	—	750	1,050	1,250	1,850	—
1850GC MP	—	825	1,100	1,450	2,150	—

KM# 381.4   4 ESCUDOS
13.5400 g., 0.8750 Gold 0.3809 oz. AGW **Obv:** Facing eagle, snake in beak **Obv. Legend:** REPUBLICA MEXICANA. **Rev:** Hand holding cap on stick, open book **Rev. Legend:** LA LIBERTAD... **Mint:** Guanajuato

Date	Mintage	VG	F	VF	XF	Unc
1829/8Go MJ	—	625	700	800	1,250	—
1829Go JM	—	625	700	800	1,250	—
1829Go MJ	—	625	700	800	1,250	—
1831Go MJ	—	625	700	800	1,250	—
1832Go MJ	—	625	700	800	1,250	—
1833Go MJ	—	625	725	850	1,350	—
1834Go PJ	—	650	900	1,050	1,450	—
1835Go PJ	—	650	900	1,050	1,450	—
1836Go PJ	—	625	725	850	1,350	—
1837Go PJ	—	625	725	850	1,350	3,500
1838Go PJ	—	625	725	850	1,350	—
1839Go PJ	—	650	900	1,050	1,450	—
1840Go PJ	—	625	725	900	1,450	—
1841Go PJ	—	650	900	1,050	1,450	—
1845Go PM	—	625	725	850	1,350	—
1847/5Go YE	—	650	900	1,050	1,450	—
1847Go PM	—	650	900	1,050	1,450	—
1849Go PF	—	650	900	1,050	1,450	—
1851Go PF	—	650	900	1,050	1,450	—
1852Go PF	—	625	725	850	1,350	—
1855Go PF	—	625	725	850	1,350	—
1857/5Go PF	—	625	725	850	1,350	—
1858/7Go PF	—	625	725	850	1,350	—
1858Go PF	—	625	725	850	1,350	—
1859/7Go PF	—	650	900	1,050	1,450	—
1860Go PF	—	650	950	1,150	1,700	—
1862Go YE	—	625	725	850	1,350	—
1863Go YF	—	625	725	850	1,350	—

KM# 381.6   4 ESCUDOS
13.5400 g., 0.8750 Gold 0.3809 oz. AGW **Obv:** Facing eagle, snake in beak **Obv. Legend:** REPUBLICA MEXICANA. **Rev:** Hand holding cap on stick, open book **Rev. Legend:** LA LIBERTAD... **Mint:** Mexico City

FIRST REPUBLIC · FEDERAL

Date	Mintage	VG	F	VF	XF	Unc
1825Mo JM	—	625	725	875	1,400	—
1827/6Mo JM	—	625	725	850	1,350	—
1829Mo JM	—	625	775	1,050	1,450	—
1831Mo JM	—	625	775	1,050	1,450	—
1832Mo JM	—	650	950	1,150	1,700	—
1844Mo MF	—	625	775	1,050	1,450	—
1850Mo GC	—	625	775	1,050	1,450	—
1856Mo GF	—	625	725	850	1,350	—
1857/6Mo GF	—	625	725	850	1,350	—
1857Mo GF	—	625	725	850	1,350	—
1858Mo FH	—	625	775	1,050	1,450	—
1859/8Mo FH	—	625	775	1,050	1,450	—
1861Mo CH	—	750	1,300	1,650	2,300	—
1863Mo CH	—	625	775	1,050	1,450	2,500
1868Mo PH	—	625	725	850	1,350	—
1869Mo CH	—	625	725	850	1,350	1,950

KM# 381.8   4 ESCUDOS
13.5400 g., 0.8750 Gold 0.3809 oz. AGW   **Obv:**
Facing eagle, snake in beak **Obv. Legend:**
REPUBLICA MEXICANA. **Rev:** Hand holding cap on
stick, open book **Rev. Legend:** LA LIBERTAD...
Mint: Zacatecas

Date	Mintage	VG	F	VF	XF	Unc
1860Zs VL Rare	—	—	—	—	—	—
1862Zs VL	—	1,000	1,650	2,850	4,800	—

Note: American Numismatic Rarities Eliasberg sale 4-05,
MS-64 realized $18,400.

KM# 381.2   4 ESCUDOS
13.5400 g., 0.8750 Gold 0.3809 oz. AGW   **Obv:**
Facing eagle, snake in beak **Obv. Legend:**
REPUBLICA MEXICANA. **Rev:** Hand holding cap on
stick, open book **Rev. Legend:** LA LIBERTAD...
Mint: Guadalajara

Date	Mintage	VG	F	VF	XF	Unc
1844Ga MC	—	875	1,200	1,450	2,150	—
1844Ga JG	—	750	1,050	1,250	1,850	—

KM# 381.5   4 ESCUDOS
13.5400 g., 0.8750 Gold 0.3809 oz. AGW   **Obv:**
Facing eagle, snake in beak **Rev:** Hand holding cap
on stick, open book **Mint:** Hermosillo

Date	Mintage	VG	F	VF	XF	Unc
1861Ho FM	—	1,400	2,000	3,250	5,000	—

KM# 381.7   4 ESCUDOS
13.5400 g., 0.8750 Gold 0.3809 oz. AGW   **Obv:**
Facing eagle, snake in beak **Obv. Legend:**
REPUBLICA MEXICANA. **Rev:** Hand holding cap on
stick, open book **Rev. Legend:** LA LIBERTAD EN
LA LEY... **Mint:** Oaxaca **Note:** Mint mark O, Oa.

Date	Mintage	VG	F	VF	XF	Unc
1861O FR	—	2,000	3,250	5,000	9,000	—

KM# 383   8 ESCUDOS
27.0700 g., 0.8750 Gold 0.7615 oz. AGW   **Obv:**
Facing eagle, snake in beak **Obv. Legend:**
REPUBLICA MEXICANA **Rev:** Hand holding cap on
stick, open book **Rev. Legend:** LA LIBERTAD...
Mint: Alamos

Date	Mintage	F	VF	XF	Unc	BU
1864A PG	—	1,400	2,050	3,000	—	—
1866A DL	—	—	—	9,000	—	—
1868/7A DL	—	2,500	4,400	6,600	—	—
1869A DL	—	—	5,000	7,200	—	—
1870A DL	—	—	3,150	6,000	—	—
1872A AM Rare	—	—	—	—	—	—

KM# 383.1   8 ESCUDOS
27.0700 g., 0.8750 Gold 0.7615 oz. AGW   **Obv:**
Facing eagle, snake in beak **Obv. Legend:**
REPUBLICA MEXICANA **Rev:** Hand holding cap on
stick, open book **Rev. Legend:** LA LIBERTAD....
Mint: Chihuahua

Date	Mintage	F	VF	XF	Unc
1841Ca RG	—	1,300	1,600	1,950	2,700
1842Ca RG	—	1,250	1,400	1,650	2,350
1843Ca RG	—	1,250	1,400	1,650	2,350
1844Ca RG	—	1,250	1,400	1,650	2,350

FIRST REPUBLIC · FEDERAL

Date	Mintage	F	VF	XF	Unc
1845Ca RG	—	1,250	1,400	1,650	2,350
1846Ca RG	—	1,450	2,300	2,300	3,000
1847Ca RG	—	1,950	4,150	—	—
1848Ca RG	—	1,250	1,400	1,650	2,350
1849Ca RG	—	1,250	1,400	1,650	2,350
1850/40Ca RG	—	1,250	1,400	1,650	2,350
1851/41Ca RG	—	1,250	1,400	1,650	2,350
1852/42Ca RG	—	1,250	1,400	1,650	2,350
1853/43Ca RG	—	1,250	1,400	1,650	2,350
1854/44Ca RG	—	1,250	1,400	1,650	2,350
1855/43Ca RG	—	1,250	1,400	1,650	2,350
1856/46Ca RG	—	1,250	1,450	1,950	2,700
1857Ca JC/RG	—	1,250	1,300	1,400	2,050
1858Ca JC	—	1,250	1,300	1,400	2,050
1858Ca BA/RG	—	1,250	1,300	1,400	2,050
1859Ca JC/RG	—	1,250	1,300	1,400	2,050
1860Ca JC/RG	—	1,250	1,400	1,650	2,350
1861Ca JC	—	1,250	1,300	1,400	2,050
1862Ca JC	—	1,250	1,300	1,400	2,050
1863Ca JC	—	1,400	1,950	2,600	3,350
1864Ca JC	—	1,300	1,600	1,950	2,700
1865Ca JC	—	1,600	2,700	3,550	4,950
1866Ca JC	—	1,250	1,300	1,650	2,350
1866Ca FP	—	1,450	2,300	2,900	3,650
1866Ca JG	—	1,250	1,400	1,650	2,350
1867Ca JG	—	1,250	1,300	1,400	2,050
1868Ca JG Concave wings	—	1,250	1,300	1,400	2,050
1869Ca MM Regular eagle	—	1,250	1,300	1,400	2,050
1870/60Ca MM	—	1,250	1,300	1,400	2,050
1871/61Ca MM	—	1,250	1,300	1,400	2,050

KM# 383.2 8 ESCUDOS
27.0700 g., 0.8750 Gold 0.7615 oz. AGW **Obv:**
Facing eagle, snake in beak **Obv. Legend:**
REPUBLICA MEXICANA. **Rev:** Hand holding cap on
stick, open book **Rev. Legend:** LA LIBERTAD...
Mint: Culiacan

Date	Mintage	F	VF	XF	Unc	BU
1846C CE	—	1,250	1,400	1,650	2,700	—
1847C CE	—	1,250	1,300	1,400	2,050	—
1848C CE	—	1,250	1,400	1,650	2,700	—
1849C CE	—	1,250	1,300	1,400	2,050	—
1850C CE	—	1,250	1,300	1,400	2,050	—
1851C CE	—	1,250	1,300	1,400	2,050	—
1852C CE	—	1,250	1,300	1,400	2,050	—
1853/1C CE	—	1,250	1,300	1,350	1,950	—
1854C CE	—	1,250	1,300	1,350	1,950	—
1855/4C CE	—	1,250	1,250	1,650	2,700	—
1855C CE	—	1,250	1,300	1,400	2,050	—
1856C CE	—	1,250	1,300	1,350	1,950	—
1857C CE	—	1,250	1,300	1,350	1,950	—
1857C CE	—	—	—	—	—	—
Note: Without periods after C's						
1858C CE	—	1,250	1,300	1,350	1,950	—
1859C CE	—	1,250	1,300	1,350	1,950	—
1860/58C CE	—	1,250	1,300	1,400	2,050	—
1860C CE	—	1,250	1,300	1,400	2,050	—
1860C PV	—	1,250	1,300	1,350	1,950	—
1861C PV	—	1,250	1,300	1,400	2,050	—
1861C CE	—	1,250	1,300	1,400	2,050	—
1862C CE	—	1,250	1,300	1,400	2,050	—
1863C CE	—	1,250	1,300	1,400	2,050	—

Date	Mintage	F	VF	XF	Unc	BU
1864C CE	—	1,250	1,300	1,350	1,950	—
1865C CE	—	1,250	1,300	1,350	1,950	—
1866/5C CE	—	1,250	1,300	1,350	1,950	—
1866C CE	—	1,250	1,300	1,350	1,950	—
1867C CB Error	—	1,250	1,300	1,350	1,950	—
1867C CE/CB	—	1,250	1,300	1,350	1,950	—
1868C CB Error	—	1,250	1,300	1,350	1,950	—
1869C CE	—	1,250	1,300	1,350	1,950	—
1870C CE	—	1,250	1,300	1,400	2,050	—

KM# 383.3 8 ESCUDOS
27.0700 g., 0.8750 Gold 0.7615 oz. AGW **Obv:**
Facing eagle, snake in beak **Obv. Legend:**
REPUBLICA MEXICANA **Rev:** Hand holding cap on
stick, open book **Rev. Legend:** LA LIBERTAD....
Mint: Durango

Date	Mintage	F	VF	XF	Unc	BU
1832Do RM	—	1,250	1,300	2,900	4,300	—
1833Do RM/RL	—	1,250	1,300	1,400	2,050	—
1834Do RM	—	1,250	1,300	1,400	2,050	—
1835Do RM	—	1,250	1,300	1,400	2,050	—
1836Do RM/RL	—	1,250	1,300	1,400	2,050	—
1836Do RM	—	1,250	1,300	1,400	2,050	—
Note: M on snake						
1837Do RM	—	1,250	1,300	1,400	2,050	—
1838/6Do RM	—	1,250	1,300	1,400	2,050	—
1838Do RM	—	1,250	1,300	1,400	2,050	—
1839Do RM	—	1,250	1,300	1,400	2,050	2,600
1840/30Do RM/RL	—	1,250	1,450	1,650	2,700	—
1841/0Do RM	—	1,250	1,300	1,350	2,050	—
1841/30Do RM	—	1,300	1,600	1,400	3,000	—
1841/31Do RM	—	1,250	1,300	1,400	2,050	—
1841/34Do RM	—	1,250	1,300	1,400	2,050	—
1841Do RM/RL	—	1,250	1,300	1,400	2,050	—
1842/32Do RM	—	1,250	1,300	1,400	2,050	—
1843/33Do RM	—	1,300	1,600	1,950	3,000	—
1843/1Do RM	—	1,250	1,300	1,400	2,050	—
1843Do RM	—	1,250	1,300	1,400	2,050	—
1844/34Do RM/RL	—	1,400	1,950	2,300	3,650	—
1844Do RM	—	1,300	1,650	1,950	3,000	—
1845/36Do RM	—	1,250	1,450	1,650	2,700	—
1845Do RM	—	1,250	1,450	1,650	2,700	—
1846Do RM	—	1,250	1,300	1,400	2,050	—
1847/37Do RM	—	1,250	1,300	1,400	2,050	—
1848/37Do RM	—	—	—	—	—	—
1848/38Do CM	—	1,250	1,300	1,400	2,050	—
1849/39Do CM	—	1,250	1,300	1,400	2,050	—
1849Do J.M.R. Rare	—	—	—	—	—	—
1850Do .JMR.	—	1,250	1,600	1,950	3,000	—
1851Do JMR	—	1,250	1,600	1,950	3,000	—
1852/1Do JMR	—	1,250	1,650	1,950	3,000	—
1852Do CP	—	1,250	1,650	1,950	3,000	—
1853Do CP	—	1,250	1,650	1,950	3,000	—
1854Do CP	—	1,250	1,450	1,650	2,700	—
1855/4Do CP	—	1,250	1,300	1,400	2,050	—
1855Do CP	—	1,250	1,300	1,400	2,050	—
1856Do CP	—	1,250	1,400	1,550	2,550	—
1857Do CP	—	1,250	1,300	1,400	2,050	—
Note: French style eagle, 1832-57						
1857Do CP	—	1,250	1,300	1,400	2,050	—
Note: Mexican style eagle						
1858Do CP	—	1,250	1,400	1,550	2,550	—
1859Do CP	—	1,250	1,300	1,400	2,050	—

Date	Mintage	F	VF	XF	Unc	BU
1860/59Do CP	—	1,250	1,600	1,950	3,250	—
1861/0Do CP	—	1,250	1,450	1,650	2,700	—
1862/52Do CP	—	1,250	1,300	1,400	2,050	—
1862/1Do CP	—	1,250	1,300	1,400	2,050	—
1862Do CP	—	1,250	1,300	1,400	2,050	—
1863/53Do CP	—	1,250	1,300	1,400	2,050	—
1864Do LT	—	1,250	1,300	1,400	2,050	3,000
1865/4Do LT	—	1,400	1,950	2,450	4,000	—
1866/4Do CM	—	2,300	3,400	3,550	—	—
1866Do CM	—	1,250	1,450	1,650	2,700	—
1867/56Do CP	—	1,250	1,450	1,650	2,700	—
1867/4Do CP	—	1,250	1,300	1,400	2,050	—
1868/4Do CP/LT	—	—	—	—	—	—
1869Do CP	—	1,450	2,300	2,600	4,000	—
1870Do CP	—	1,250	1,450	1,650	2,700	—

Date	Mintage	F	VF	XF	Unc	BU
1825Ga FS	—	1,400	1,800	1,950	2,700	—
1826Ga FS	—	1,400	1,800	1,950	2,700	—
1830Ga FS	—	1,400	1,800	1,950	2,700	—
1836Ga FS	—	1,600	2,700	2,900	4,300	—
1836Ga JG	—	1,950	4,150	4,800	—	—
1837Ga JG	—	1,950	4,150	4,800	—	—
1840Ga MC Rare	—	—	—	—	—	—
1841/31Ga MC	—	1,950	4,150	—	—	—
1841Ga MC	—	1,750	2,900	3,100	—	—
1842Ga JG Rare	—	—	4,850	6,900	—	—
1843Ga MC	—	—	4,150	8,900	—	—
1845Ga MC Rare	—	—	—	—	—	—
1847Ga JG	—	3,250	—	—	—	—
1849Ga JG	—	1,400	1,800	1,950	2,700	—
1850Ga JG	—	1,300	1,700	1,800	2,550	—
1851Ga JG	—	1,950	4,150	4,800	—	—
1852/1Ga JG	—	1,400	1,800	1,950	2,700	—
1855Ga JG	—	1,950	4,150	4,800	—	—
1856Ga JG	—	1,300	1,700	1,800	2,550	—
1857Ga JG	—	1,300	1,700	1,800	2,550	—
1861/0Ga JG	—	1,400	1,800	1,950	2,700	—
1861Ga JG	—	1,250	1,500	1,900	2,700	—
1863/1Ga JG	—	1,400	1,800	1,950	2,700	—
1866Ga JG	—	1,300	1,700	1,800	2,550	—

KM# 383.4 8 ESCUDOS
27.0700 g., 0.8750 Gold 0.7615 oz. AGW **Obv:**
Facing eagle, snake in beak **Obv. Legend:**
REPUBLICA MEXICANA **Rev:** Hand holding cap on
stick, open book **Rev. Legend:** LA LIBERTAD...
Mint: Estado de Mexico

Date	Mintage	F	VF	XF	Unc
1828EoMo LF Rare	—	—	—	—	—
1829EoMo LF	—	4,850	7,600	11,500	—

KM# 383.6 8 ESCUDOS
27.0700 g., 0.8750 Gold 0.7615 oz. AGW **Obv:**
Facing eagle, snake in beak **Obv. Legend:**
REPUBLICA MEXICANA **Rev:** Hand holding cap on
stick, open book **Rev. Legend:** LA LIBERTAD...
Mint: Guadalupe y Calvo

Date	Mintage	F	VF	XF	Unc	BU
1844GC MP	—	1,300	1,600	1,950	3,000	—
1845GC MP	—	1,300	1,600	1,950	3,000	—
Note: Eagle's tail square						
1845GC MP	—	1,300	1,600	1,950	3,000	—
Note: Eagle's tail round						
1846GC MP	—	1,250	1,450	1,650	2,700	—
Note: Eagle's tail square						
1846GC MP	—	1,250	1,450	1,650	2,700	—
Note: Eagle's tail round						
1847GC MP	—	1,250	1,450	1,650	2,700	—
1848GC MP	—	1,300	1,600	1,950	3,000	—
1849GC MP	—	1,300	1,600	1,950	3,000	—
1850GC MP	—	1,250	1,450	1,650	2,700	—
1851GC MP	—	1,250	1,450	1,650	2,700	—
1852GC MP	—	1,300	1,600	1,950	3,000	—

KM# 383.5 8 ESCUDOS
27.0700 g., 0.8750 Gold 0.7615 oz. AGW **Obv:**
Facing eagle, snake in beak **Obv. Legend:**
REPUBLICA MEXICANA **Rev:** Hand holding cap on
stick, open book **Rev. Legend:** LA LIBERTAD...
Mint: Guadalajara

FIRST REPUBLIC - FEDERAL

KM# 383.7   8 ESCUDOS
27.0700 g., 0.8750 Gold 0.7615 oz. AGW **Obv:**
Facing eagle, snake in beak **Obv. Legend:**
REPUBLICA MEXICANA **Rev:** Hand holding cap on
stick, open book **Rev. Legend:** LA LIBERTAD...
Mint: Guanajuato

Date	Mintage	F	VF	XF	Unc	BU
1828Go MJ	—	1,600	3,050	3,200	4,300	—
1829Go MJ	—	1,450	2,700	2,900	4,000	—
1830Go MJ	—	1,250	1,300	1,350	1,700	—
1831Go MJ	—	1,450	2,700	2,900	4,000	—
1832Go MJ	—	1,300	1,950	2,300	3,650	—
1833Go MJ	—	1,250	1,300	1,350	1,700	—
1834Go PJ	—	1,250	1,300	1,350	1,700	—
1835Go PJ	—	1,250	1,300	1,350	1,700	—
1836Go PJ	—	1,250	1,450	1,550	2,050	—
1837Go PJ	—	1,250	1,450	1,550	2,050	—
1838/7Go PJ	—	1,250	1,300	1,350	1,700	—
1838Go PJ	—	1,250	1,300	1,400	1,950	—
1839/8Go PJ	—	1,250	1,300	1,350	1,700	—
1839Go PJ	—	1,250	1,300	1,400	1,950	—
Note: Regular eagle						
1840Go PJ	—	1,250	1,300	1,350	1,700	—
Note: Concave wings						
1841Go PJ	—	1,250	1,300	1,350	1,700	—
1842Go PJ	—	1,250	1,300	1,350	1,550	—
1842Go PM	—	1,250	1,300	1,350	1,700	—
1843Go PM	—	1,250	1,300	1,350	1,700	—
Note: Small eagle						
1844/3Go PM	—	1,250	1,450	1,550	2,050	—
1844Go PM	—	1,250	1,300	1,350	1,700	—
1845Go PM	—	1,250	1,300	1,350	1,700	—
1846/5Go PM	—	1,250	1,300	1,400	1,950	—
1846Go PM	—	1,250	1,300	1,350	1,700	—
1847Go PM	—	1,250	1,450	1,550	2,050	—
1848/7Go PM	—	1,250	1,300	1,350	1,700	—
1848Go PM	—	1,250	1,300	1,350	1,700	—
1848Go PF	—	1,250	1,300	1,350	1,700	—
1849Go PF	—	1,250	1,300	1,350	1,650	—
1850Go PF	—	1,250	1,300	1,350	1,650	—
1851Go PF	—	1,250	1,300	1,350	1,700	—
1852Go PF	—	1,250	1,300	1,350	1,700	—
1853Go PF	—	1,250	1,300	1,350	1,700	—
1854Go PF	—	1,250	1,300	1,350	1,700	—
Note: Eagle of 1853						
1854Go PF	—	1,250	1,300	1,350	1,700	—
Note: Eagle of 1855						
1855/4Go PF	—	1,250	1,300	1,350	1,700	—
1855Go PF	—	1,250	1,300	1,350	1,700	—
1856Go PF	—	1,250	1,300	1,350	1,700	—
1857Go PF	—	1,250	1,300	1,350	1,700	—
1858Go PF	—	1,250	1,300	1,350	1,700	—
1859Go PF	—	1,250	1,300	1,350	1,550	—
1860/50Go PF	—	1,250	1,300	1,350	1,550	—
1860/59Go PF	—	1,250	1,300	1,350	1,850	—
1860Go PF	—	1,250	1,300	1,350	1,850	—
1861/0Go PF	—	1,250	1,300	1,350	1,500	—
1861Go PF	—	1,250	1,300	1,350	1,500	—
1862/1Go YE	—	1,250	1,300	1,350	1,700	—
1862Go YE	—	1,250	1,300	1,350	1,650	—
1862Go YF	—					
1863/53Go YF	—	1,250	1,300	1,350	1,700	3,650
1863Go PF	—	1,250	1,300	1,350	1,700	—

Date	Mintage	F	VF	XF	Unc	BU
1867/57Go YF/PF	—	1,250	1,300	1,350	1,700	—
1867Go YF	—	1,250	1,300	1,350	1,650	—
1868/58Go YF	—	1,250	1,300	1,350	1,700	2,700
1870Go FR	—	1,250	1,300	1,350	1,550	—

KM# 383.8   8 ESCUDOS
27.0700 g., 0.8750 Gold 0.7615 oz. AGW **Obv:**
Facing eagle, snake in beak **Obv. Legend:**
REPUBLICA MEXICANA. **Rev:** Hand holding cap on
stick, open book **Rev. Legend:** LA LIBERTAD...
Mint: Hermosillo

Date	Mintage	F	VF	XF	Unc	BU
1863Ho FM	—	1,300	1,500	1,650	3,000	—
1864Ho FM	—	1,450	2,300	2,600	4,000	—
1864Ho PR/FM	—	1,300	1,500	1,650	3,000	—
1865Ho FM/PR	—	1,400	1,650	1,950	3,650	—
1867/57Ho PR	—	1,300	1,500	1,650	3,000	—
1868Ho PR	—	1,400	1,650	1,950	3,650	—
1868Ho PR/FM	—	1,400	1,650	1,950	3,650	—
1869Ho PR/FM	—	1,300	1,500	1,650	3,000	—
1869Ho PR	—	1,300	1,500	1,650	3,000	—
1870Ho PR	—	1,400	1,650	1,950	4,000	7,600
1871/0Ho PR	—	1,400	1,650	1,950	3,650	—
1871Ho PR	—	1,400	1,650	1,950	3,650	—
1872/1Ho PR	—	1,450	2,300	2,600	4,000	—
1873Ho PR	—	1,300	1,500	1,650	3,000	—

KM# 383.10   8 ESCUDOS
27.0700 g., 0.8750 Gold 0.7615 oz. AGW **Obv:**
Facing eagle, snake in beak **Obv. Legend:**
REPUBLICA MEXICANA **Rev:** Hand holding cap on
stick, open book **Rev. Legend:** LA LIBERTAD...
Mint: Oaxaca

Date	Mintage	F	VF	XF	Unc	BU
1858Oa AE	—	3,200	4,800	5,500	8,600	—
1859O AE	—	1,950	4,150	5,100	7,600	—
1860O AE	—	1,950	4,150	5,100	7,600	—
1861O FR	—	1,400	1,750	1,950	4,000	—
1862O FR	—	1,400	1,750	1,950	4,000	—
1863O FR	—	1,400	1,750	1,950	4,000	—
1864O FR	—	1,400	1,750	1,950	4,000	—
1867O AE	—	1,400	1,750	1,950	4,000	—
1868O AE	—	1,400	1,750	1,950	4,000	—
1869O AE	—	1,400	1,750	1,950	4,000	—

KM# 383.11 8 ESCUDOS
27.0700 g., 0.8750 Gold 0.7615 oz. AGW **Obv:**
Facing eagle, snake in beak **Obv. Legend:**
REPUBLICA MEXICANA **Rev:** Hand holding cap on
stick, open book **Rev. Legend:** LA LIBERTAD...
Mint: Zacatecas

Date	Mintage	F	VF	XF	Unc	BU
1858Zs MO	—	1,300	1,600	1,650	3,000	—
1859Zs MO	—	1,250	1,300	1,350	1,700	—
1860/59Zs VL/MO	—	3,200	4,800	5,500	—	—
1860/9Zs MO	—	1,300	1,600	1,650	3,000	—
1860Zs MO	—	1,250	1,300	1,400	1,850	—
1861/0Zs VL	—	1,250	1,300	1,400	1,850	—
1861Zs VL	—	1,250	1,300	1,400	1,850	4,300
1862Zs VL	—	1,250	1,300	1,400	1,900	—
1863Zs VL	—	1,250	1,300	1,400	1,950	—
1863Zs MO	—	1,250	1,300	1,400	1,850	—
1864Zs MO	—	1,600	1,950	2,300	4,950	—
1865Zs MO	—	1,600	1,950	2,400	5,300	—
1868Zs JS	—	1,250	1,400	1,550	2,050	—
1868Zs YH	—	1,250	1,400	1,550	2,050	—
1869Zs YH	—	1,250	1,400	1,550	2,050	—
1870Zs YH	—	1,250	1,400	1,550	2,050	—
1871Zs YH	—	1,250	1,400	1,550	2,050	—

KM# 383.9 8 ESCUDOS
27.0700 g., 0.8750 Gold 0.7615 oz. AGW **Obv:**
Facing eagle, snake in beak **Obv. Legend:**
REPUBLICA MEXICANA **Rev:** Hand holding cap on
stick, open book **Rev. Legend:** LA LIBERTAD...
Mint: Mexico City **Note:** Formerly reported 1825/3
JM is merely a reworked 5.

Date	Mintage	F	VF	XF	Unc	BU
1824Mo JM	—	1,400	1,750	1,950	3,000	—
Note: Large book reverse						
1825Mo JM	—	1,250	1,300	1,350	1,700	3,000
Note: Small book reverse						
1826/5Mo JM	—	1,600	2,850	3,200	4,300	—
1827/6Mo JM	—	1,250	1,300	1,350	1,700	—
1827Mo JM	—	1,250	1,300	1,350	1,700	—
1828Mo JM	—	1,250	1,300	1,350	1,700	—
1829Mo JM	—	1,250	1,300	1,350	1,700	—
1830Mo JM	—	1,250	1,300	1,350	1,700	—
1831Mo JM	—	1,250	1,300	1,350	1,700	—
1832/1Mo JM	—	1,250	1,300	1,350	1,700	—

Date	Mintage	F	VF	XF	Unc	BU
1832Mo JM	—	1,250	1,300	1,350	1,700	—
1833Mo MJ	—	1,300	1,600	1,700	2,350	—
1833Mo ML	—	1,250	1,300	1,350	1,700	—
1834Mo ML	—	1,300	1,600	1,700	2,350	—
1835/4Mo ML	—	1,400	1,750	1,950	3,000	—
1836Mo ML	—	1,250	1,300	1,250	1,700	—
1836Mo MF	—	1,300	1,600	1,900	3,000	—
1837/6Mo ML	—	1,250	1,300	1,350	1,700	—
1838Mo ML	—	1,250	1,300	1,350	1,700	—
1839Mo ML	—	1,250	1,300	1,350	1,700	—
1840Mo ML	—	1,250	1,300	1,350	1,700	—
1841Mo ML	—	1,250	1,300	1,350	1,700	—
1842/1Mo ML	—	—	—	—	—	—
1842Mo ML	—	1,250	1,300	1,350	1,700	—
1842Mo MM	—	—	—	—	—	—
1843Mo MM	—	1,250	1,300	1,350	1,700	—
1844Mo MF	—	1,250	1,300	1,350	1,700	—
1845Mo MF	—	1,250	1,300	1,350	1,700	—
1846Mo MF	—	1,400	1,750	1,950	3,000	—
1847Mo MF	—	1,950	3,750	—	—	—
1847Mo RC	—	1,250	1,400	1,550	2,050	—
1848Mo GC	—	1,250	1,300	1,350	1,700	—
1849Mo GC	—	1,250	1,300	1,350	1,700	—
1850Mo GC	—	1,250	1,300	1,350	1,700	3,000
1851Mo GC	—	1,250	1,300	1,350	1,700	—
1852Mo GC	—	1,250	1,300	1,350	1,700	—
1853Mo GC	—	1,250	1,300	1,350	1,700	—
1854/44Mo GC	—	1,250	1,300	1,350	1,700	—
1854/3Mo GC	—	1,250	1,300	1,350	1,700	—
1855Mo GF	—	1,250	1,300	1,350	1,700	—
1856/5Mo GF	—	1,250	1,300	1,350	1,650	—
1856Mo GF	—	1,250	1,300	1,350	1,650	—
1857Mo GF	—	1,250	1,300	1,350	1,650	—
1858Mo FH	—	1,250	1,300	1,350	1,650	—
1859Mo FH	—	1,300	1,600	1,700	2,350	—
1860Mo FH	—	1,250	1,300	1,350	1,650	—
1860Mo TH	—	1,250	1,300	1,350	1,650	—
1861/51Mo CH	—	1,250	1,300	1,350	1,650	—
1862Mo CH	—	1,250	1,300	1,350	1,650	—
1863/53Mo CH	—	1,250	1,300	1,350	1,650	6,600
1863/53Mo TH	—	1,250	1,300	1,350	1,650	—
1867Mo CH	—	1,250	1,300	1,350	1,650	—
1868Mo CH	—	1,250	1,300	1,350	1,650	—
1868Mo PH	—	1,250	1,300	1,350	1,650	—
1869Mo CH	—	1,250	1,300	1,350	1,650	—

EMPIRE OF MAXIMILIAN

RULER
Maximilian, Emperor, 1864-1867
MINT MARKS
Refer To Republic Coinage
MONETARY SYSTEM
100 Centavos = 1 Peso (8 Reales)

MILLED COINAGE

KM# 384 CENTAVO
Copper **Ruler:** Maximilian **Obv:** Crowned facing
eagle, snake in beak **Obv. Legend:** IMPERIO
MEXICANO **Rev:** Value and date within wreath
Edge: Coarsely reeded **Mint:** Mexico City

Date	Mintage	F	VF	XF	Unc	BU
1864M	—	50.00	100	250	1,250	1,850

EMPIRE OF MAXIMILIAN

KM# 385   5 CENTAVOS
1.3537 g., 0.9030 Silver 0.0393 oz. ASW **Ruler:**
Maximilian **Mint:** Guanajuato

Date	Mintage	F	VF	XF	Unc	BU
1864G	90,000	17.50	35.00	85.00	320	—
1865G	—	20.00	30.00	65.00	300	—
1866G	—	75.00	150	300	2,000	—

KM# 385.1   5 CENTAVOS
1.3537 g., 0.9030 Silver 0.0393 oz. ASW **Ruler:**
Maximilian **Mint:** Mexico City

Date	Mintage	F	VF	XF	Unc	BU
1864M	—	12.50	20.00	55.00	300	—
1866/4M	—	25.00	40.00	75.00	425	—
1866M	—	20.00	35.00	65.00	400	—

KM# 385.2   5 CENTAVOS
1.3537 g., 0.9030 Silver 0.0393 oz. ASW **Ruler:**
Maximilian **Mint:** San Luis Potosi

Date	Mintage	F	VF	XF	Unc	BU
1864P	—	150	400	1,500	2,500	—

KM# 385.3   5 CENTAVOS
1.3537 g., 0.9030 Silver 0.0393 oz. ASW **Ruler:**
Maximilian **Obv:** Crowned facing eagle, snake in
beak **Obv. Legend:** IMPERIO MEXICANO **Rev:**
Value and date within wreath **Mint:** Zacatecas

Date	Mintage	F	VF	XF	Unc	BU
1865Z	—	25.00	45.00	150	450	650

KM# 386   10 CENTAVOS
2.7073 g., 0.9030 Silver 0.0786 oz. ASW **Ruler:**
Maximilian **Obv:** Crowned facing eagle, snake in
beak **Obv. Legend:** IMPERIO MEXICANO **Rev:**
Value and date within wreath **Mint:** Guanajuato

Date	Mintage	F	VF	XF	Unc	BU
1864G	45,000	20.00	45.00	90.00	325	—
1865G	—	30.00	60.00	110	375	—

KM# 386.1   10 CENTAVOS
2.7073 g., 0.9030 Silver 0.0786 oz. ASW **Ruler:**
Maximilian **Obv:** Crowned facing eagle, snake in
beak **Obv. Legend:** IMPERIO MEXICANO **Rev:**
Value and date within wreath **Mint:** Mexico City **Note:**
Struck at Mexico City Mint, mint mark M.

Date	Mintage	F	VF	XF	Unc	BU
1864M	—	15.00	25.00	55.00	285	—
1866/4M	—	25.00	35.00	70.00	320	—
1866/5M	—	25.00	40.00	85.00	375	—
1866M	—	25.00	35.00	75.00	375	—

KM# 386.2   10 CENTAVOS
2.7073 g., 0.9030 Silver 0.0786 oz. ASW **Ruler:**
Maximilian **Mint:** San Luis Potosi

Date	Mintage	F	VF	XF	Unc	BU
1864P	—	70.00	150	300	700	—

KM# 386.3   10 CENTAVOS
2.7073 g., 0.9030 Silver 0.0786 oz. ASW **Ruler:**
Maximilian **Mint:** Zacatecas

Date	Mintage	F	VF	XF	Unc	BU
1865Z	—	22.50	55.00	165	525	750

KM# 387   50 CENTAVOS
13.5365 g., 0.9030 Silver 0.3930 oz. ASW **Ruler:**
Maximilian **Obv:** Head right, with beard **Obv.**
Legend: MAXIMILIANO EMPERADOR **Rev:**
Crowned oval shield **Rev. Legend:** IMPERIO
MEXICANO **Mint:** Mexico City **Designer:** S. Navalon

Date	Mintage	F	VF	XF	Unc	BU
1866Mo	31,000	40.00	95.00	225	850	2,250

KM# 388   PESO
27.0700 g., 0.9030 Silver 0.7859 oz. ASW **Ruler:**

Maximilian **Obv:** Head right, with beard **Obv.**
Legend: MAXIMILIANO EMPERADOR **Rev:**
Crowned arms with supporters **Rev. Legend:**
IMPERIO MEXICANO **Mint:** Guanajuato **Designer:**
S. Navalon

Date	Mintage	F	VF	XF	Unc	BU
1866Go	—	375	575	1,200	3,750	—

KM# 388.1   PESO
27.0700 g., 0.9030 Silver 0.7859 oz. ASW **Ruler:**
Maximilian **Obv:** Head right, with beard **Obv.**
Legend: MAXIMILIANO EMPERADOR **Rev:**
Crowned arms with supporters **Rev. Legend:**
IMPERIO MEXICANO **Mint:** Mexico City **Designer:**
S. Navalon

Date	Mintage	F	VF	XF	Unc	BU
1866Mo	2,148,000	36.00	55.00	175	400	—
1867Mo	1,238,000	48.00	80.00	240	450	—

KM# 388.2   PESO
27.0700 g., 0.9030 Silver 0.7859 oz. ASW **Ruler:**
Maximilian **Obv:** Head right, with beard **Obv.**
Legend: MAXIMILIANO EMPERADOR **Rev:**
Crowned arms with supporters **Rev. Legend:**
IMPERIO MEXICANO **Mint:** San Luis Potosi
Designer: S. Navalon

Date	Mintage	F	VF	XF	Unc	BU
1866Pi	—	55.00	110	350	800	—

KM# 389   20 PESOS
33.8400 g., 0.8750 Gold 0.9519 oz. AGW **Ruler:**
Maximilian **Obv:** Head right, with beard **Obv.**
Legend: MAXIMILIANO EMPERADOR **Rev:**

Crowned arms with supporters **Rev. Legend:**
IMPERIO MEXICANO **Mint:** Mexico City **Designer:**
S. Navalon

Date	Mintage	F	VF	XF	Unc	BU
1866Mo	8,274	1,650	2,000	3,200	5,000	—

REPUBLIC
Second

DECIMAL COINAGE
100 CENTAVOS = 1 PESO

KM# 390   CENTAVO
Copper, 25 mm. **Obv:** Seated Liberty **Rev:** Thick
wreath. **Mint:** Mexico City

Date	Mintage	F	VF	XF	Unc	BU
1863Mo	—	10.00	30.00	70.00	500	—
Note: Flat-top 3, reeded edge						
1863Mo	—	13.50	32.50	75.00	500	—
Note: Round-top 3, plain edge						
1863Mo	—	13.50	32.50	75.00	500	—
Note: Round-top 3, reeded edge						

KM# 390.1   CENTAVO
Copper, 26.5 mm. **Obv:** Seated liberty **Obv.**
Legend: LIBERTAD V REFORMA. **Rev:** Value and
date within wreath **Mint:** San Luis Potosi

Date	Mintage	F	VF	XF	Unc	BU
1863SLP	1,024,999	15.00	32.50	75.00	425	—

KM# 391   CENTAVO
Copper **Obv:** Facing eagle, snake in beak **Rev:**
Value and date within wreath **Edge:** Reeded. **Mint:**
Alamos

Date	Mintage	F	VF	XF	Unc	BU
1875As Rare	—	—	—	—	—	—
1876As	50,000	100	200	300	650	—
1880As	—	25.00	50.00	200	500	—
1881As	—	30.00	60.00	125	350	—

KM# 391.1   CENTAVO
Copper **Obv:** Facing eagle, snake in beak **Obv.**
Legend: REPUBLICA MEXICANA **Rev:** Value and
date within wreath **Edge:** Plain **Mint:** Culiacan

Date	Mintage	F	VF	XF	Unc	BU
1874Cn	266,000	12.50	17.50	35.00	250	—
1875/4Cn	153,000	15.00	20.00	45.00	250	—
1875Cn	Inc. above	10.00	15.00	25.00	250	—
1876Cn	154,000	5.00	8.00	15.00	200	—
1877/6Cn	993,000	7.50	11.50	17.50	200	—
1877Cn	Inc. above	6.00	9.00	15.00	200	—
1880Cn	142,000	7.50	10.00	12.50	200	—

SECOND REPUBLIC

Date	Mintage	F	VF	XF	Unc	BU
1881Cn	167,000	7.50	10.00	25.00	200	—
1897Cn	300,000	2.50	5.00	12.00	50.00	—

Note: Large N in mint mark

Date	Mintage	F	VF	XF	Unc	BU
1897Cn	Inc. above	2.50	5.00	9.00	45.00	—

Note: Small N in mint mark

KM# 391.2 CENTAVO
Copper **Obv:** Facing eagle, snake in beak **Rev:** Value and date within wreath **Mint:** Durango

Date	Mintage	F	VF	XF	Unc	BU
1879Do	110,000	10.00	35.00	60.00	200	—
1880Do	69,000	40.00	90.00	175	500	—
1891Do	—	8.00	25.00	50.00	200	—
1891Do/Mo	—	8.00	25.00	50.00	200	—

KM# 391.3 CENTAVO
Copper **Obv:** Facing eagle, snake in beak **Obv. Legend:** REPUBLICA MEXICANA **Rev:** Value and date within wreath **Mint:** Guadalajara

Date	Mintage	F	VF	XF	Unc	BU
1872Ga	263,000	15.00	30.00	60.00	225	—
1873Ga	333,000	6.00	9.00	25.00	200	—
1874Ga	76,000	15.00	25.00	50.00	200	—
1875Ga	—	10.00	15.00	30.00	200	—
1876Ga	303,000	3.00	6.00	17.50	200	—
1877Ga	108,000	4.00	6.00	20.00	200	—
1878Ga	543,000	4.00	6.00	15.00	200	—
1881/71Ga	975,000	7.00	9.00	20.00	—	—
1881Ga	Inc. above	7.00	9.00	20.00	200	—
1889Ga/Mo	—	3.50	5.00	25.00	200	—
1890Ga	—	4.00	7.50	20.00	200	—

KM# 391.4 CENTAVO
Copper **Obv:** Facing eagle, snake in beak **Rev:** Value and date within wreath **Mint:** Guanajuato

Date	Mintage	F	VF	XF	Unc	BU
1874Go	—	20.00	40.00	80.00	250	—
1875Go	190,000	11.50	20.00	60.00	200	—
1876Go	—	125	200	350	750	—
1877Go Rare	—	—	—	—	—	—
1878Go	576,000	8.00	11.00	30.00	200	—
1880Go	890,000	6.00	10.00	25.00	200	—

KM# 391.5 CENTAVO
Copper **Obv:** Facing eagle, snake in beak **Obv. Inscription:** REPUBLICA MEXICANA **Rev:** Value and date within wreath **Mint:** Hermosillo

Date	Mintage	F	VF	XF	Unc
1875Ho	3,500	450	—	—	—
1876Ho	8,508	50.00	100	225	500
1880Ho Short H, round O	102,000	7.50	15.00	50.00	200
1880Ho Tall H, oval O	Inc. above	7.50	15.00	50.00	200
1881Ho	459,000	5.00	10.00	50.00	200

KM# 391.7 CENTAVO
Copper **Obv:** Facing eagle, snake in beak **Obv. Legend:** REPUBLICA MEXICANA **Rev:** Value and date within wreath **Mint:** Oaxaca

Date	Mintage	F	VF	XF	Unc	BU
1872Oa	16,000	300	500	1,200	—	—
1873Oa	11,000	350	600	—	—	—
1874Oa	4,835	450	—	—	—	—
1875Oa	2,860	500	—	—	—	—

KM# 391.8 CENTAVO
Copper **Obv:** Facing eagle, snake in beak **Obv. Legend:** REPUBLICA MEXICANA **Rev:** Value and date within wreath **Mint:** San Luis Potosi

Date	Mintage	F	VF	XF	Unc	BU
1871Pi Rare	—	—	—	—	—	—
1877Pi	249,000	15.00	50.00	200	—	—
1878Pi	751,000	12.50	25.00	50.00	200	—
1878	—	—	—	—	—	—

Note: Pp error mintmark - rare

Date	Mintage	F	VF	XF	Unc	BU
1891Pi/Mo	—	10.00	50.00	150	300	—
1891Pi	—	8.00	25.00	125	250	—

KM# 391.9 CENTAVO
Copper **Obv:** Facing eagle, snake in beak **Rev:** Value and date within wreath **Mint:** Zacatecas **Note:** Struck at Zacatecas Mint, mint mark Zs.

Date	Mintage	F	VF	XF	Unc	BU
1872Zs	55,000	22.50	30.00	100	300	—
1873Zs	1,460,000	4.00	8.00	25.00	150	—
1874/3Zs	685,000	5.50	11.00	30.00	250	—
1874Zs	Inc. above	4.00	8.00	25.00	200	—
1875/4Zs	200,000	8.50	17.00	45.00	250	—
1875Zs	Inc. above	7.00	14.00	35.00	200	—
1876Zs	—	5.00	10.00	25.00	200	—
1877Zs	—	50.00	125	300	750	—
1878Zs	—	4.50	9.00	25.00	200	—
1880Zs	100,000	5.00	10.00	30.00	200	—
1881Zs	1,200,000	4.25	8.00	25.00	150	—

KM# 391.6 CENTAVO
7.4000 g., Copper **Obv:** Facing eagle, snake in beak **Obv. Legend:** REPUBLICA MEXICANA **Rev:** Value and date within wreath **Mint:** Mexico City **Note:** Varieties exist.

Date	Mintage	F	VF	XF	Unc	BU
1869Mo	1,874,000	7.50	25.00	60.00	200	—
1870/69Mo	1,200,000	10.00	25.00	60.00	225	—
1870Mo	Inc. above	8.00	20.00	50.00	200	—
1871Mo	918,000	8.00	15.00	40.00	200	—
1872/1Mo	1,625,000	6.50	10.00	30.00	200	—
1872Mo	Inc. above	6.00	9.00	25.00	200	—
1873Mo	1,605,000	4.00	7.50	20.00	200	—
1874/3Mo	1,700,000	5.00	7.00	15.00	100	—
1874Mo	Inc. above	3.00	5.50	15.00	100	—
1874Mo	Inc. above	5.00	10.00	25.00	200	—
1875Mo	1,495,000	6.00	8.00	30.00	100	—
1876Mo	1,600,000	3.00	5.50	12.50	100	—
1877Mo	1,270,000	3.00	5.50	13.50	100	—
1878/5Mo	1,900,000	7.50	11.00	22.50	125	—
1878/6Mo	Inc. above	7.50	11.00	22.50	125	—
1878/7Mo	Inc. above	7.50	11.00	20.00	125	—
1878Mo	Inc. above	6.00	9.00	13.50	100	—
1879/8Mo	1,505,000	4.50	6.50	13.50	100	—
1879Mo	Inc. above	3.00	5.50	12.50	75.00	—
1880/70Mo	1,130,000	5.50	7.50	15.00	100	—
1880/72Mo	Inc. above	20.00	50.00	100	250	—
1880/79Mo	Inc. above	15.00	35.00	75.00	175	—
1880Mo	Inc. above	4.25	6.00	12.50	75.00	—
1881Mo	1,060,000	4.50	7.00	15.00	75.00	—
1886Mo	12,687,000	1.50	2.00	10.00	40.00	—
1887Mo	7,292,000	1.50	2.00	10.00	35.00	—
1888/78Mo	9,984,000	2.50	3.00	10.00	30.00	—
1888/7Mo	Inc. above	2.50	3.00	10.00	30.00	—
1888Mo	Inc. above	1.50	2.00	10.00	30.00	—
1889Mo	19,970,000	2.00	3.00	10.00	30.00	—
1890/89Mo	18,726,000	2.50	3.00	12.00	40.00	—
1890/990Mo	Inc. above	2.50	3.00	12.00	40.00	—
1890Mo	Inc. above	1.50	2.00	10.00	30.00	—
1891Mo	14,544,000	1.50	2.00	10.00	30.00	—
1892Mo	12,908,000	1.50	2.00	10.00	30.00	—
1893/2Mo	5,078,000	2.50	3.00	12.00	35.00	—
1893Mo	Inc. above	1.50	2.00	10.00	30.00	—
1894/3Mo	1,896,000	3.00	6.00	15.00	50.00	—
1894Mo	Inc. above	2.00	3.00	12.00	35.00	—
1895/3Mo	3,453,000	3.00	4.50	12.50	35.00	—
1895/85Mo	Inc. above	3.00	6.00	15.00	50.00	—
1895Mo	Inc. above	2.00	3.00	10.00	30.00	—
1896Mo	3,075,000	2.00	3.00	10.00	30.00	—
1897Mo	4,150,000	1.50	2.00	10.00	30.00	—

KM# 392 CENTAVO
Copper-Nickel **Obv:** Crossed bow and quiver above date **Obv. Legend:** REPUBLICA MEXICANA **Rev:** Value within wreath **Mint:** Mexico City

Date	Mintage	F	VF	XF	Unc	BU
1882Mo	99,955,000	7.50	12.50	17.50	35.00	—
1883Mo	Inc. above	0.50	0.75	1.00	1.50	—

KM# 393 CENTAVO
Copper **Obv:** Facing eagle, snake in beak **Obv. Legend:** REPUBLICA MEXICANA **Rev:** Value and date within wreath **Mint:** Mexico City **Note:** Varieties exist.

Date	Mintage	F	VF	XF	Unc	BU
1898Mo	1,529,000	4.00	6.00	15.00	50.00	—

KM# 394.1 CENTAVO
2.6100 g., Copper **Obv:** Facing eagle, snake in beak **Obv. Legend:** REPUBLICA MEXICANA **Rev:** Value below date within wreath **Mint:** Mexico City **Note:** Reduced size. Varieties exist.

Date	Mintage	F	VF	XF	Unc	BU
1899M	51,000	150	175	300	800	—
1900M Wide date	4,010,000	2.50	4.00	8.00	28.00	—
1900M Narrow date	Inc. above	2.50	4.00	8.00	28.00	—
1901M	1,494,000	3.00	8.00	25.00	100	—
1902/899M	2,090,000	30.00	60.00	150	500	—
1902M	Inc. above	2.25	4.00	10.00	40.00	—
1903M	8,400,000	1.50	3.00	7.00	20.00	—
1904/3M	10,250,000	1.50	10.00	20.00	55.00	—
1904M	Inc. above	1.50	3.00	8.00	25.00	—
1905M	3,643,000	2.25	4.00	10.00	40.00	—

KM# 394 CENTAVO
Copper **Obv:** National arms **Rev:** Value below date within wreath **Mint:** Culiacan **Note:** Reduced size. Varieties exist.

Date	Mintage	F	VF	XF	Unc	BU
1901C	220,000	15.00	22.50	60.00	150	—
1902C	320,000	15.00	22.50	50.00	90.00	—
1903C	536,000	7.50	12.50	20.00	50.00	—
1904/3C	148,000	35.00	50.00	100	350	—
1905C	110,000	100	150	300	600	—

KM# 395 2 CENTAVOS
Copper-Nickel **Obv:** Crossed bow and quiver above date **Obv. Legend:** REPUBLICA MEXICANA **Rev:** Value within wreath **Mint:** Mexico City

Date	Mintage	F	VF	XF	Unc	BU
1882	50,023,000	2.00	3.00	7.50	15.00	—
1883/2	Inc. above	2.00	3.00	7.50	15.00	—
1883	Inc. above	0.50	0.75	1.00	2.50	—

KM# 396.1 5 CENTAVOS
1.3530 g., 0.9030 Silver 0.0393 oz. ASW **Obv:** Facing eagle, snake in beak **Rev:** Value within wreath **Mint:** San Luis Potosi

Date	Mintage	F	VF	XF	Unc	BU
1863SLP	—	37.50	135	350	1,200	—

KM# 397 5 CENTAVOS
1.3530 g., 0.9030 Silver 0.0393 oz. ASW **Obv:**

SECOND REPUBLIC

Facing eagle, snake in beak **Obv. Legend:**
REPUBLICA MEXICANA **Rev:** Radiant cap **Mint:**
Mexico City **Note:** Varieties exist.

Date	Mintage	F	VF	XF	Unc	BU
1867Mo	—	20.00	45.00	110	400	—
1867/3Mo	—	22.50	50.00	125	425	—
1868/7Mo	—	22.50	50.00	150	500	—
1868Mo	—	18.50	42.50	100	400	—

KM# 397.1   5 CENTAVOS
1.3530 g., 0.9030 Silver 0.0393 oz. ASW   **Obv:**
Facing eagle, snake in beak **Rev:** Radiant cap **Mint:**
San Luis Potosi

Date	Mintage	F	VF	XF	Unc	BU
1868P	Inc. above	20.00	45.00	100	400	—
1868/7P	34,000	25.00	50.00	125	450	—
1869P	14,000	150	300	600	—	—

KM# 396   5 CENTAVOS
1.3530 g., 0.9030 Silver 0.0393 oz. ASW   **Obv:**
Facing eagle, snake in beak **Obv. Legend:**
REPUBLICA MEXICANA **Rev:** Value within wreath
Mint: Chihuahua

Date	Mintage	F	VF	XF	Unc	BU
1868Ca	—	40.00	65.00	125	450	—
1869Ca	30,000	25.00	40.00	100	400	—
1870/69Ca	—	35.00	55.00	120	425	—
1870Ca	35,000	30.00	50.00	100	400	—

KM# 398.7   5 CENTAVOS
1.3530 g., 0.9030 Silver 0.0393 oz. ASW   **Obv:**
Facing eagle, snake in beak **Obv. Legend:**
REPUBLICA MEXICANA **Rev:** Value within 1/2
wreath **Mint:** Mexico City **Note:** Mint mark Mo.
Varieties exist.

Date	Mintage	F	VF	XF	Unc	BU
1869/8Mo C	40,000	8.00	15.00	40.00	120	—
1870Mo C	140,000	4.00	7.00	20.00	60.00	—
1871Mo C	103,000	9.00	20.00	40.00	100	—
1871Mo M	Inc. above	7.50	12.50	25.00	60.00	—
1872Mo M	266,000	5.00	8.00	20.00	55.00	—
1873Mo M	20,000	40.00	60.00	100	225	—
1874/69Mo M	—	7.50	15.00	30.00	75.00	—
1874Mo M	—	4.00	7.00	17.50	50.00	—
1874/3Mo B	—	5.00	8.00	22.50	55.00	—
1874Mo B	—	5.00	8.00	22.50	55.00	—
1875Mo B	—	4.00	7.00	15.00	50.00	—
1875Mo B/M	—	6.00	9.00	17.50	60.00	—
1876/5Mo B	—	4.00	7.00	15.00	50.00	—
1876Mo B	—	4.00	7.00	12.50	50.00	—
1877/6Mo M	80,000	4.00	7.00	15.00	60.00	—
1877Mo M	Inc. above	4.00	7.00	12.50	60.00	—
1878/7Mo M	100,000	4.00	7.00	15.00	55.00	—
1878Mo M	Inc. above	2.50	5.00	12.50	45.00	—
1879/8Mo M	—	8.00	12.50	22.50	55.00	—
1879Mo M	—	4.50	7.00	15.00	50.00	—
1879Mo M 9/ inverted 9	—	10.00	15.00	25.00	75.00	—
1880/76Mo M/B	—	5.00	7.50	15.00	50.00	—
1880/76Mo M	—	5.00	7.50	15.00	50.00	—
1880Mo M	—	4.00	6.00	12.00	40.00	—
1881/0Mo M	180,000	4.00	6.00	10.00	35.00	—
1881Mo M	Inc. above	3.00	4.50	9.00	35.00	—
1886/0Mo M	398,000	2.00	2.75	7.50	25.00	—
1886/1Mo M	Inc. above	2.00	2.75	7.50	25.00	—
1886Mo M	Inc. above	1.75	2.25	6.00	20.00	—

Date	Mintage	F	VF	XF	Unc	BU
1887Mo m	720,000	1.75	2.00	5.00	20.00	—
1887Mo M/m	Inc. above	1.75	2.00	6.00	20.00	—
1888/7Mo M	1,360,000	2.25	2.50	6.00	20.00	—
1888Mo M	Inc. above	1.75	2.00	5.00	20.00	—
1889/8Mo M	1,242,000	2.25	2.50	6.00	20.00	—
1889Mo M	Inc. above	1.75	2.00	5.00	20.00	—
1890/00Mo M	1,694,000	1.75	2.75	6.00	20.00	—
1890Mo M	Inc. above	1.50	2.00	5.00	20.00	—
1891Mo M	1,030,000	1.75	2.00	5.00	20.00	—
1892Mo M	1,400,000	1.75	2.00	5.00	20.00	—
1892Mo M 9/ inverted 9	Inc. above	2.00	2.75	7.50	20.00	—
1893Mo M	220,000	1.75	2.00	5.00	15.00	—
1894Mo M	320,000	1.75	2.00	5.00	15.00	—
1895Mo B	78,000	3.00	5.00	8.00	25.00	—
1896Mo B	80,000	1.75	2.00	5.00	20.00	—
1897Mo B	160,000	1.75	2.00	5.00	15.00	—

KM# 398.1   5 CENTAVOS
1.3530 g., 0.9030 Silver 0.0393 oz. ASW   **Obv:**
Facing eagle, snake in beak **Rev:** Value within 1/2
wreath **Mint:** Chihuahua **Note:** Mint mark: *Ca or
Ch*.

Date	Mintage	F	VF	XF	Unc
1871* M	14,000	20.00	40.00	100	250
1873* M Crude date	—	100	150	250	500
1874* M Crude date	—	25.00	50.00	75.00	150
1886* M	25,000	7.50	15.00	30.00	100
1887* M	37,000	7.50	15.00	30.00	100
1887* Ca/MoM	Inc. above	10.00	20.00	40.00	125
1888* M	145,000	1.50	3.00	6.00	25.00
1889* M	44,000	5.00	10.00	20.00	50.00
1890* M	102,000	1.50	3.00	6.00	25.00
1891* M	164,000	1.50	3.00	6.00	25.00
1892* M	85,000	1.50	3.00	6.00	25.00
1892* M/U	—	2.00	4.00	7.50	30.00
1892* M 9/inverted 9	Inc. above	2.00	4.00	7.50	30.00
1893* M	133,000	1.50	3.00	6.00	25.00
1894* M	108,000	1.50	3.00	6.00	25.00
1895* M	74,000	2.00	4.00	7.50	30.00

KM# 398   5 CENTAVOS
1.3530 g., 0.9030 Silver 0.0393 oz. ASW   **Obv:**
Facing eagle, snake in beak **Rev:** Value within 1/2
wreath **Mint:** Alamos

Date	Mintage	F	VF	XF	Unc	BU
1874As DL	—	10.00	20.00	40.00	150	—
1875As DL	—	10.00	20.00	40.00	150	—
1876As L	—	22.00	45.00	70.00	160	—
1878As L	—	250	350	650	950	—
Note: Mule, gold peso reverse						
1879As L	—	40.00	65.00	120	275	—
Note: Mule, gold peso obverse						
1880As L	12,000	55.00	85.00	165	325	—
Note: Mule, gold peso obverse						
1886As L	43,000	12.00	25.00	50.00	165	—
1886As L	Inc. above	55.00	85.00	165	300	—
Note: Mule, gold peso obverse						
1887As L	20,000	25.00	50.00	75.00	165	—
1888As L	32,000	12.00	25.00	50.00	125	—
1889As L	16,000	25.00	50.00	100	200	—
1890As L	30,000	25.00	50.00	85.00	175	—
1891As L	8,000	65.00	125	200	400	—
1892As L	13,000	20.00	40.00	60.00	125	—
1893As L	24,000	10.00	20.00	45.00	90.00	—
1895As L	20,000	10.00	20.00	45.00	90.00	—

KM# 398.2   5 CENTAVOS
1.3530 g., 0.9030 Silver 0.0393 oz. ASW   **Obv:**
Facing eagle, snake in beak **Rev:** Value within 1/2
wreath **Mint:** Culiacan

Date	Mintage	F	VF	XF	Unc	BU
1871Cn P	—	125	200	350	—	—
1873Cn P	4,992	50.00	100	200	400	—
1874Cn P	—	25.00	50.00	100	200	—
1875Cn P Rare	—	—	—	—	—	—
1876Cn P	—	25.00	50.00	100	200	—
1886Cn M	10,000	25.00	50.00	100	200	—
1887Cn M	10,000	25.00	50.00	100	200	—

Date	Mintage	F	VF	XF	Unc	BU
1888Cn M	119,000	1.50	3.00	6.00	30.00	—
1889Cn M	66,000	4.00	7.50	15.00	50.00	—
189/80Cn M	—	2.00	4.00	8.00	40.00	—
1890Cn M	180,000	1.50	3.00	6.00	25.00	—
1890/9Cn M	—	2.00	4.00	8.00	40.00	—
1890Cn D Error	Inc. above	175	275	400	—	—
1891Cn M	87,000	2.00	4.00	7.50	25.00	—
1894Cn M	24,000	4.00	7.50	15.00	40.00	—
1896Cn M	16,000	7.50	12.50	25.00	75.00	—
1897Cn M	223,000	1.50	2.50	5.00	20.00	—

KM# 398.3 5 CENTAVOS
1.3530 g., 0.9030 Silver 0.0393 oz. ASW **Obv:** Facing eagle, snake in beak **Rev:** Value within 1/2 wreath **Mint:** Durango

Date	Mintage	F	VF	XF	Unc	BU
1874Do M	—	100	150	225	500	—
1877Do P	4,795	75.00	125	225	450	—
1878/7Do E/P	4,300	200	300	450	—	—
1879Do B	—	125	200	350	—	—
1880Do B Rare	—	—	—	—	—	—
1881Do P	3,020	300	500	800	—	—
1887Do C	42,000	5.00	8.00	17.50	60.00	—
1888/9Do C	91,000	6.00	10.00	20.00	70.00	—
1888Do C	Inc. above	4.00	7.50	15.00	55.00	125
1889Do C	49,000	3.50	6.00	12.50	50.00	—
1890Do C	136,000	4.00	7.50	15.00	55.00	—
1890Do P	Inc. above	5.00	8.00	17.50	60.00	—
1891/0Do P	48,000	3.50	6.00	12.50	50.00	—
1891Do P	Inc. above	3.00	5.00	10.00	45.00	—
1894Do D	38,000	3.50	6.00	12.50	50.00	—

KM# 398.4 5 CENTAVOS
1.3530 g., 0.9030 Silver 0.0393 oz. ASW **Obv:** Facing eagle, snake in beak **Rev:** Value within 1/2 wreath **Mint:** Guadalajara

Date	Mintage	F	VF	XF	Unc
1877Ga A	—	15.00	30.00	60.00	150
1881Ga S	156,000	4.00	7.50	15.00	60.00
1886Ga S	87,000	2.00	4.00	7.50	25.00
1888Ga S Large G	262,000	2.00	4.00	10.00	30.00
1888Ga S Small G	Inc. above	2.00	4.00	10.00	30.00
1889Ga S	178,000	1.50	3.00	7.50	25.00
1890Ga S	68,000	4.00	7.50	12.50	35.00
1891Ga S	50,000	4.00	6.50	10.00	35.00
1892Ga S	78,000	2.00	4.00	7.50	25.00
1893Ga S	44,000	4.00	7.50	15.00	45.00

KM# 398.5 5 CENTAVOS
1.3530 g., 0.9030 Silver 0.0393 oz. ASW **Obv:** Facing eagle, snake in beak **Obv. Legend:** REPUBLICA MEXICANA **Rev:** Value within 1/2 wreath **Mint:** Guanajuato

Date	Mintage	F	VF	XF	Unc	BU
1869Go S	80,000	15.00	30.00	75.00	175	—
1871Go S	100,000	5.00	10.00	25.00	75.00	—
1872Go S	30,000	30.00	60.00	125	250	—
1873Go S	40,000	30.00	60.00	125	250	—
1874Go S	—	7.00	12.00	25.00	75.00	—
1875Go S	—	8.00	15.00	30.00	75.00	—
1876Go S	—	8.00	15.00	30.00	75.00	—
1877Go S	—	7.00	12.00	20.00	75.00	—

Date	Mintage	F	VF	XF	Unc	BU
1878/7Go S	20,000	8.00	15.00	25.00	75.00	—
1879Go S	—	8.00	15.00	25.00	75.00	—
1880Go S	55,000	15.00	30.00	60.00	200	—
1881/0Go S	160,000	5.00	8.00	17.50	60.00	150
1881Go S	Inc. above	4.00	6.00	12.00	45.00	110
1886Go R	230,000	1.50	3.00	6.00	30.00	75.00
1887Go R/S	—	1.50	3.00	6.00	30.00	75.00
1887Go R	230,000	1.50	2.50	5.00	30.00	75.00
1888Go R	320,000	1.50	2.50	5.00	20.00	60.00
1889Go R/S	—	4.00	6.00	12.00	45.00	110
1889Go R	60,000	4.00	6.00	12.00	45.00	110
1890/5Go R/S	—	1.50	3.00	6.00	30.00	75.00
1890Go R	250,000	1.50	2.50	5.00	20.00	60.00
1891/0Go R	168,000	1.80	3.00	6.00	30.00	75.00
1891Go R	Inc. above	1.50	2.50	5.00	20.00	60.00
1892Go R	138,000	1.50	3.00	6.00	25.00	65.00
1893Go R	200,000	1.25	2.50	5.00	20.00	60.00
1894Go R	200,000	1.25	2.50	5.00	20.00	60.00
1896Go R	525,000	1.25	2.00	4.00	15.00	50.00
1896Go R/S	—	1.50	3.00	6.00	25.00	65.00
1897Go R	596,000	1.50	2.00	4.00	15.00	50.00
1898Go R	—	—	—	—	—	—

KM# 398.6 5 CENTAVOS
1.3530 g., 0.9030 Silver 0.0393 oz. ASW **Obv:** Facing eagle, snake in beak **Rev:** Value within 1/2 wreath **Mint:** Hermosillo

Date	Mintage	F	VF	XF	Unc
1874/69Ho R	—	125	225	350	—
1874Ho R	—	100	200	325	—
1878/7Ho A Rare	22,000	—	—	—	—
1878Ho A	Inc. above	20.00	40.00	80.00	175
1878Ho A	Inc. above	40.00	80.00	150	300

Note: Mule, gold peso obverse

Date	Mintage	F	VF	XF	Unc
1880Ho A	43,000	7.50	15.00	30.00	75.00
1886Ho G	44,000	5.00	10.00	20.00	75.00
1887Ho G	20,000	5.00	10.00	20.00	75.00
1888Ho G	12,000	7.50	15.00	30.00	85.00
1889Ho G	67,000	3.00	6.00	12.50	40.00
1890Ho G	50,000	3.00	6.00	12.50	40.00
1891Ho G	46,000	3.00	6.00	12.50	40.00
1893Ho G	84,000	2.50	5.00	10.00	30.00
1894Ho G	68,000	2.00	4.00	10.00	30.00

KM# 398.9 5 CENTAVOS
1.3530 g., 0.9030 Silver 0.0393 oz. ASW **Obv:** Facing eagle, snake in beak **Rev:** Value within 1/2 wreath **Mint:** San Luis Potosi **Note:** Varieties exist.

Date	Mintage	F	VF	XF	Unc	BU
1869Pi S	—	375	500	625	—	—
1870Pi S/MoC	20,000	190	325	500	—	—
1870Pi O	Inc. above	250	375	575	—	—
1871Pi O Rare	5,400	—	—	—	—	—
1872Pi O	—	75.00	100	175	400	—
1873Pi Rare	5,000	—	—	—	—	—
1874Pi H	—	30.00	50.00	100	225	—
1875Pi H	—	7.50	12.50	30.00	75.00	—
1876Pi H	—	10.00	20.00	45.00	100	—
1877Pi H	—	7.50	12.50	20.00	60.00	—
1878/7Pi H Rare	—	—	—	—	—	—
1878Pi H	—	60.00	90.00	150	300	—
1879 H	—	200	400	—	—	—
1880Pi H Rare	6,200	—	—	—	—	—
1881Pi H Rare	4,500	—	—	—	—	—
1886Pi R	33,000	12.50	25.00	50.00	125	—
1887/0Pi R	169,000	4.00	7.50	15.00	45.00	—
1887Pi R	Inc. above	3.00	5.00	10.00	32.00	—
1888Pi R	210,000	2.00	4.00	9.00	30.00	—
1889/7Pi R	197,000	2.50	5.00	10.00	32.00	—
1889Pi R	Inc. above	2.00	4.00	9.00	30.00	—
1890Pi R	221,000	2.00	3.00	6.00	25.00	—
1891/89Pi R/B	176,000	2.00	4.00	8.00	25.00	—
1891/0Pi R/B	—	2.00	4.00	8.00	25.00	—
1891Pi R	Inc. above	2.00	3.00	6.00	20.00	—
1892/89Pi R	182,000	2.00	4.00	8.00	25.00	—
1892/0Pi R	Inc. above	2.00	4.00	8.00	25.00	—
1892Pi R	Inc. above	2.00	3.00	6.00	20.00	—
1893Pi R	41,000	5.00	10.00	20.00	60.00	—

SECOND REPUBLIC

KM# 398.10 5 CENTAVOS
1.3530 g., 0.9030 Silver 0.0393 oz. ASW **Obv:** Facing eagle, snake in beak **Rev:** Value within 1/2 wreath **Mint:** Zacatecas

Date	Mintage	F	VF	XF	Unc
1870Zs H	40,000	12.50	25.00	50.00	125
1871Zs H	40,000	12.50	25.00	50.00	125
1872Zs H	40,000	12.50	25.00	50.00	125
1873/2Zs H	20,000	35.00	65.00	125	275
1873Zs H	Inc. above	25.00	50.00	100	250
1874Zs H	—	7.50	12.50	25.00	75.00
1874Zs A	—	40.00	75.00	150	300
1875Zs A	—	7.50	12.50	25.00	75.00
1876Zs A	—	50.00	75.00	150	500
1876/5Zs S	—	15.00	30.00	60.00	150
1876Zs S	—	12.50	25.00	50.00	125
1877Zs S	—	3.00	6.00	12.00	40.00
1878Zs S	60,000	3.00	6.00	12.00	40.00
1879/8Zs S	—	3.00	6.00	15.00	50.00
1879Zs S	—	3.00	6.00	12.00	40.00
1880/79Zs S	130,000	6.00	10.00	20.00	60.00
1880Zs S	Inc. above	5.00	8.00	16.00	45.00
1881Zs S	210,000	2.50	5.00	10.00	35.00
1886/4Zs S	360,000	6.00	10.00	20.00	60.00
1886Zs S	Inc. above	2.00	3.00	6.00	20.00
1886Zs Z	Inc. above	5.00	10.00	25.00	65.00
1887Zs Z	400,000	2.00	3.00	6.00	25.00
1888/7Zs Z	500,000	2.00	3.00	6.00	25.00
1888Zs Z	Inc. above	2.00	3.00	6.00	25.00
1889Zs Z	520,000	2.00	3.00	6.00	25.00
1889Zs Z 9/inverted 9	Inc. above	2.00	3.00	6.00	25.00
1889Zs Z/MoM	Inc. above	2.00	3.00	6.00	25.00
1890Zs Z	580,000	1.75	2.50	5.00	20.00
1890Zs Z/MoM	Inc. above	2.00	3.00	6.00	25.00
1890Zs ZsZ 9/8	—	2.00	3.00	6.00	25.00
1890Zs ZsZ 0/9 Z/M	—	2.00	3.00	6.00	25.00
1891Zs Z	420,000	1.75	2.50	5.00	20.00
1892Zs Z	346,000	1.75	2.50	5.00	20.00
1893Zs Z	258,000	1.75	2.50	5.00	20.00
1894Zs Z	228,000	1.75	2.50	5.00	20.00
1894Zs ZoZ Error	Inc. above	2.00	4.00	8.00	30.00
1895Zs Z	260,000	1.75	2.50	5.00	20.00
1895/4Zs ZsZ	—	2.00	3.00	6.00	25.00
1896Zs Z	200,000	1.75	2.50	5.00	20.00
1896Zs 6/inverted 6	Inc. above	2.00	3.00	6.00	25.00
1897/6Zs Z	200,000	2.00	3.00	6.00	25.00
1897Zs Z	Inc. above	1.75	2.50	5.00	20.00

KM# 398.8 5 CENTAVOS
1.3530 g., 0.9030 Silver 0.0393 oz. ASW **Obv:** Facing eagle, snake in beak **Obv. Legend:** REPUBLICA MEXICANA **Rev:** Value within 1/2 wreath **Mint:** Oaxaca

Date	Mintage	F	VF	XF	Unc	BU
1890Oa E Rare	48,000	—	—	—	—	—
1890Oa N	Inc. above	65.00	125	200	350	—

KM# 399 5 CENTAVOS
Copper-Nickel **Obv:** Crossed bow and quiver above date **Obv. Legend:** REPUBLICA MEXICANA **Rev:** Value within wreath **Mint:** Mexico City

Date	Mintage	F	VF	XF	Unc	BU
1882	Inc. above	0.50	1.00	2.50	7.50	—
1883	Inc. above	25.00	50.00	80.00	250	—

KM# 400.2 5 CENTAVOS
1.3530 g., 0.9027 Silver 0.0393 oz. ASW, 15 mm. **Obv:** Facing eagle, snake in beak **Rev:** Value within 1/2 wreath **Edge:** Reeded **Mint:** Mexico City

Date	Mintage	F	VF	XF	Unc	BU
1898Mo M	80,000	2.50	5.00	8.00	30.00	—
1899Mo M	168,000	2.00	3.00	5.00	18.00	—
1900/800Mo M	300,000	5.00	8.00	12.00	36.00	—
1900Mo M	Inc. above	2.00	3.00	5.00	18.00	—
1901Mo M	100,000	2.00	3.00	8.00	25.00	—
1902Mo M	144,000	1.50	2.50	5.00	14.00	18.00
1902/1Mo MoM	—	2.00	4.00	8.00	20.00	22.50
1903Mo M	500,000	1.50	2.50	5.00	14.00	18.00
1904/804Mo M	1,090,000	2.00	4.00	10.00	20.00	22.50
1904/94Mo M	Inc. above	2.00	5.00	11.00	20.00	22.50
1904Mo M	Inc. above	2.00	4.00	7.00	18.00	20.00
1905Mo M	344,000	2.00	4.00	8.00	20.00	22.50

KM# 400.3 5 CENTAVOS
1.3530 g., 0.9027 Silver 0.0393 oz. ASW **Obv:** Facing eagle, snake in beak **Rev:** Value within 1/2 wreath **Mint:** Zacatecas

Date	Mintage	F	VF	XF	Unc	BU
1898Zs Z	100,000	2.00	2.75	5.00	15.00	—
1899Zs Z	50,000	2.50	4.00	8.00	25.00	—
1900Zs Z	55,000	2.00	3.00	6.00	20.00	—
1901Zs Z	40,000	2.50	5.00	11.00	30.00	—
1902/1Zs Z	34,000	2.50	5.00	11.00	27.50	30.00
1902Zs Z	Inc. above	2.00	5.00	9.00	22.50	27.50
1903Zs Z	217,000	1.50	2.50	6.00	15.00	19.00
1904Zs Z	191,000	2.00	3.00	6.00	15.00	19.00
1904Zs M	Inc. above	2.00	3.00	7.00	20.00	22.50
1905Zs M	46,000	2.50	5.00	11.00	27.50	30.00
1905Zs M	Inc. above	—	—	—	—	—
Repullica; Rare						

KM# 400 5 CENTAVOS
1.3530 g., 0.9027 Silver 0.0393 oz. ASW, 14 mm. **Obv:** Facing eagle, snake in beak **Obv. Legend:** REPUBLICA MEXICANA **Rev:** Value within 1/2 wreath **Mint:** Culiacan **Note:** Varieties exist.

Date	Mintage	F	VF	XF	Unc	BU
1898Cn M	44,000	2.00	5.00	10.00	25.00	—
1899Cn M	111,000	7.00	10.00	25.00	60.00	—
1899Cn Q	Inc. above	2.00	3.00	5.00	18.00	—
1900/800Cn Q	239,000	4.00	6.00	15.00	36.00	—
1900Cn Q	Inc. above	2.00	4.00	7.00	20.00	—
Note: Round Q, single tail						
1900Cn Q	Inc. above	2.00	4.00	7.00	20.00	—
Note: Narrow C, oval Q						
1900Cn Q	Inc. above	2.00	4.00	7.00	20.00	—
Note: Wide C, oval Q						
1901Cn Q	148,000	2.00	4.00	7.00	25.00	35.00
1902Cn Q	262,000	2.00	4.00	7.00	20.00	25.00
Note: Narrow C, heavy serifs						
1902Cn Q	Inc. above	2.00	4.00	7.00	20.00	25.00
Note: Wide C, light serifs						
1903/1Cn Q	331,000	2.50	4.00	7.00	20.00	25.00
1903Cn Q	Inc. above	2.00	3.00	5.00	18.00	22.50
1903/1898Cn V	Inc. above	4.00	5.00	11.00	27.50	27.50
1903Cn V	Inc. above	2.00	3.00	5.00	18.00	22.50
1904Cn H	352,000	2.00	2.75	6.00	20.00	25.00
1904Cn H/C	—	2.00	3.00	6.00	20.00	25.00
1904Cn H 0/9	—	2.00	3.00	6.00	20.00	25.00

SECOND REPUBLIC

KM# 400.1   5 CENTAVOS
1.3530 g., 0.9027 Silver 0.0393 oz. ASW **Obv:**
Facing eagle, snake in beak **Rev:** Value within 1/2
wreath **Mint:** Guanajuato **Note:** Varieties exist.

Date	Mintage	F	VF	XF	Unc	BU
1898Go R	180,000	7.50	15.00	30.00	75.00	—
Note: Mule, gold peso obverse						
1899Go R	260,000	1.75	2.50	4.50	15.00	—
1900Go R	200,000	1.75	2.50	4.50	15.00	—

KM# 402   10 CENTAVOS
2.7070 g., 0.9030 Silver 0.0786 oz. ASW **Obv:**
Facing eagle, snake in beak **Rev:** Radiant cap **Mint:**
Mexico City

Date	Mintage	F	VF	XF	Unc	BU
1867/3Mo	—	50.00	100	200	550	—
1867Mo	—	20.00	50.00	150	450	—
1868/7Mo	—	20.00	50.00	175	500	—
1868Mo	—	20.00	55.00	175	500	—

KM# 402.1   10 CENTAVOS
2.7070 g., 0.9030 Silver 0.0786 oz. ASW **Obv:**
Facing eagle, snake in beak **Obv. Legend:**
REPUBLICA MEXICANA **Rev:** Radiant cap **Mint:**
San Luis Potosi

Date	Mintage	F	VF	XF	Unc	BU
1868/7P	38,000	50.00	95.00	200	675	—
1868P	Inc. above	25.00	45.00	125	575	—
1869/7P	4,900	60.00	130	275	825	—

KM# 401.1   10 CENTAVOS
2.7070 g., 0.9030 Silver 0.0786 oz. ASW **Obv:**
Facing eagle, snake in beak **Rev:** Value within wreath
Mint: Chihuahua **Note:** Previous KM#401.

Date	Mintage	F	VF	XF	Unc	BU
1868/7Ca	—	30.00	60.00	150	550	—
1868Ca	—	30.00	60.00	150	550	—
1869Ca	15,000	25.00	50.00	125	600	—
1870Ca	17,000	22.50	45.00	100	550	—

KM# 401.2   10 CENTAVOS
2.7070 g., 0.9030 Silver 0.0786 oz. ASW **Obv:**
Facing eagle, snake in beak **Obv. Legend:**
REPUBLICA MEXICANA **Rev:** Value and date within
wreath **Mint:** San Luis Potosi

Date	Mintage	F	VF	XF	Unc	BU
1863SLP	—	75.00	150	275	900	—

KM# 403   10 CENTAVOS
2.7070 g., 0.9030 Silver 0.0786 oz. ASW **Obv:**
Facing eagle, snake in beak **Rev:** Value within 1/2
wreath **Mint:** Alamos **Note:** Varieties exist.

Date	Mintage	F	VF	XF	Unc	BU
1874As DL	—	20.00	40.00	80.00	175	—
1875As L	—	5.00	10.00	25.00	90.00	—
1876As L	—	10.00	18.00	40.00	110	—
1878As L	—	5.00	10.00	30.00	100	—
1878/7As L	—	10.00	18.00	45.00	120	—
1879As L	—	10.00	18.00	40.00	110	—
1880As L	13,000	10.00	18.00	40.00	110	—
1882As L	22,000	10.00	18.00	40.00	110	—
1883As L	8,520	25.00	50.00	100	225	—
1884As L	—	7.50	12.50	35.00	100	—

Date	Mintage	F	VF	XF	Unc	BU
1885As L	15,000	7.50	12.50	35.00	100	—
1886As L	45,000	7.50	12.50	35.00	100	—
1887As L	15,000	7.50	12.50	35.00	100	—
1888As L	38,000	7.50	12.50	35.00	100	—
1889As L	20,000	7.50	12.50	35.00	100	—
1890As L	40,000	7.50	12.50	35.00	100	—
1891As L	38,000	7.50	12.50	35.00	100	—
1892As L	57,000	5.00	10.00	25.00	90.00	—
1893As L	70,000	10.00	18.00	40.00	110	—

Note: An 1891 As L over 1889 HoG exists which was evi-
dently produced at the Alamos Mint using dies sent from the
Hermosillo Mint

KM# 403.4   10 CENTAVOS
2.7070 g., 0.9030 Silver 0.0786 oz. ASW **Obv:**
Facing eagle, snake in beak **Rev:** Value within 1/2
wreath **Mint:** Guadalajara **Note:** Varieties exist.

Date	Mintage	F	VF	XF	Unc
1871Ga C	4,734	75.00	125	200	500
1873/1Ga C	25,000	10.00	15.00	35.00	150
1873Ga C	Inc. above	10.00	15.00	35.00	150
1874Ga C	—	10.00	15.00	35.00	150
1877Ga A	—	10.00	15.00	30.00	150
1881Ga S	115,000	6.00	11.00	27.50	150
1883Ga B	90,000	5.00	9.00	17.00	90.00
1884Ga H	—	4.00	6.00	12.00	90.00
1884Ga B	—	6.00	11.00	22.50	90.00
1884Ga B/S	—	7.00	14.00	27.50	90.00
1885Ga H	93,000	4.00	6.00	12.00	90.00
1886Ga S	151,000	4.00	5.00	11.00	90.00
1887Ga S	162,000	2.50	4.00	8.00	90.00
1888Ga GaS/HoG	Inc. above	2.50	4.00	8.00	90.00
1888Ga S	225,000	2.50	4.00	8.00	90.00
1889Ga S	310,000	2.50	4.00	8.00	40.00
1890Ga S	303,000	2.50	4.00	8.00	40.00
1891Ga S	199,000	6.00	11.00	22.50	45.00
1892Ga S	329,000	2.50	4.00	8.00	40.00
1893Ga S	225,000	2.50	4.00	8.00	40.00
1894Ga S	243,000	4.00	7.00	14.00	40.00
1895Ga S	80,000	2.50	4.00	8.00	40.00

KM# 403.5   10 CENTAVOS
2.7070 g., 0.9030 Silver 0.0786 oz. ASW **Obv:**
Facing eagle, snake in beak **Rev:** Value within 1/2
wreath **Mint:** Guanajuato **Note:** Varieties exist.

Date	Mintage	F	VF	XF	Unc
1869Go S	7,000	20.00	40.00	80.00	200
1871/0Go S	60,000	15.00	25.00	50.00	125
1872Go S	60,000	15.00	25.00	50.00	125
1873Go S	50,000	15.00	25.00	50.00	125
1874Go S	—	15.00	25.00	50.00	125
1875Go S	—	250	350	500	800
1876Go S	—	10.00	20.00	40.00	100
1877Go S	—	80.00	120	200	400
1878/7Go S	10,000	10.00	20.00	45.00	110
1878Go S	Inc. above	7.50	12.00	20.00	75.00
1879Go S	—	7.50	12.00	20.00	75.00
1880Go S	—	100	200	300	450
1881/71Go S	100,000	4.00	6.00	12.00	75.00
1881/0Go S	Inc. above	5.00	6.00	12.00	75.00
1881Go S	Inc. above	4.00	6.00	12.00	75.00
1882/1Go S	40,000	4.00	7.00	14.00	75.00
1883Go B	—	4.00	6.00	12.00	75.00
1884Go B	—	2.50	4.00	8.00	75.00
1884Go S	—	7.00	14.00	27.50	90.00
1885Go R	100,000	2.50	4.00	8.00	75.00
1886Go R	95,000	4.00	6.00	12.00	75.00
1887Go R	330,000	4.00	6.00	12.00	75.00
1888Go R	270,000	2.50	4.00	8.00	75.00
1889Go R	205,000	3.00	5.00	10.00	75.00
1889Go GoR/HoG	Inc. above	4.00	6.00	12.00	75.00
1890Go R	270,000	2.50	4.00	8.00	35.00
1890Go GoR/Cn M	Inc. above	2.50	4.00	8.00	35.00
1891Go R	523,000	2.50	4.00	8.00	35.00
1891Go R/G	—	2.50	4.00	8.00	35.00
1891Go GoR/HoG	Inc. above	2.50	4.00	8.00	35.00
1892Go R	440,000	2.50	4.00	8.00	35.00
1893/1Go R	389,000	4.00	6.00	12.00	35.00
1893Go R	Inc. above	2.50	4.00	8.00	35.00

SECOND REPUBLIC

Date	Mintage	F	VF	XF	Unc
1894Go R	400,000	2.50	4.00	7.00	35.00
1895Go R	355,000	2.50	4.00	7.00	35.00
1896Go R	190,000	2.50	4.00	7.00	35.00
1897Go R	205,000	2.50	4.00	7.00	35.00

KM# 403.7 10 CENTAVOS

2.7070 g., 0.9020 Silver 0.0785 oz. ASW **Obv:** Facing eagle, snake in beak **Obv. Legend:** REPUBLICA MEXICANA **Rev:** Value within 1/2 wreath **Mint:** Mexico City **Note:** Varieties exist.

Date	Mintage	F	VF	XF	Unc
1869/8Mo C	30,000	10.00	20.00	40.00	100
1869Mo C	Inc. above	8.00	17.50	35.00	90.00
1870Mo C	110,000	5.00	9.00	17.00	50.00
1871Mo C	84,000	50.00	75.00	125	250
1871Mo M	Inc. above	12.00	17.50	45.00	125
1872/69Mo M	198,000	10.00	20.00	35.00	100
1872Mo M	Inc. above	5.00	9.00	17.00	65.00
1873Mo M	40,000	10.00	15.00	30.00	75.00
1874Mo M	—	6.00	11.00	22.50	65.00
1874Mo M/C	—	6.00	11.00	22.50	65.00
1874/64Mo B	—	6.00	11.00	22.50	65.00
1874Mo B/M	—	20.00	40.00	60.00	125
1874Mo B	—	6.00	11.00	17.00	65.00
1875Mo B	—	20.00	40.00	60.00	125
1876/5Mo B	—	5.00	7.00	12.00	65.00
1876/5Mo B/M	—	5.00	7.00	12.00	65.00
1877/6Mo M	—	5.00	7.00	12.00	65.00
1877/6Mo M/B	—	5.00	7.00	12.00	65.00
1877Mo M	—	5.00	7.00	12.00	65.00
1878/7Mo M	100,000	5.00	7.00	12.00	65.00
1878Mo M	Inc. above	5.00	7.00	12.00	65.00
1879/69Mo M	—	5.00	7.00	12.00	65.00
1879Mo M/C	—	5.00	7.00	12.00	65.00
1880/79Mo M	—	5.00	7.00	12.00	65.00
1881/0Mo M	510,000	5.00	7.00	12.00	35.00
1881Mo M	Inc. above	5.00	7.00	12.00	35.00
1882/1Mo M	550,000	5.00	7.00	12.00	35.00
1882Mo M	Inc. above	5.00	7.00	12.00	35.00
1883/2Mo M	250,000	5.00	7.00	12.00	35.00
1884Mo M	—	5.00	7.00	12.00	35.00
1885Mo M	470,000	5.00	7.00	12.00	35.00
1886Mo M	603,000	5.00	7.00	12.00	35.00
1887/6Mo M	—	5.00	7.00	12.00	35.00
1887Mo M	580,000	5.00	7.00	12.00	35.00
1888/7Mo MoM	710,000	5.00	7.00	12.00	35.00
1888Mo MoM	Inc. above	5.00	7.00	12.00	35.00
1888Mo MOM	Inc. above	5.00	7.00	12.00	35.00
1889/8Mo M	622,000	5.00	7.00	12.00	35.00
1889Mo M	Inc. above	5.00	7.00	12.00	35.00
1890/89Mo M	815,000	5.00	7.00	12.00	35.00
1890Mo M	Inc. above	5.00	7.00	12.00	35.00
1891Mo M	859,000	3.00	5.00	10.00	25.00
1892Mo M	1,030,000	3.00	5.00	10.00	25.00
1893Mo M	310,000	3.00	5.00	10.00	25.00
1893Mo M/C	Inc. above	3.00	5.00	10.00	25.00
1893Mo Mo/Ho M/G	—	3.00	5.00	10.00	25.00
1894/3Mo M	—	6.00	11.00	22.50	60.00
1894Mo M	350,000	6.00	11.00	22.50	60.00
1895Mo M	320,000	3.00	5.00	10.00	25.00
1896Mo B/G	340,000	3.00	5.00	10.00	25.00
1896Mo M	Inc. above	35.00	70.00	100	150
1897Mo M	170,000	3.00	5.00	8.00	22.00

KM# 403.9 10 CENTAVOS

2.7070 g., 0.9030 Silver 0.0786 oz. ASW **Obv:** Facing eagle, snake in beak **Rev:** Value within 1/2 wreath **Mint:** San Luis Potosi **Note:** Varieties exist.

Date	Mintage	F	VF	XF	Unc	BU
1869/8Pi S Rare	4,000	—	—	—	—	—

Date	Mintage	F	VF	XF	Unc	BU
1870/69Pi O Rare	18,000	—	—	—	—	—
1870Pi G	Inc. above	125	200	325	600	—
1871Pi O	21,000	50.00	100	150	300	—
1872Pi O	16,000	150	225	350	650	—
1873Pi O Rare	4,750	—	—	—	—	—
1874Pi H	—	25.00	50.00	100	200	—
1875Pi H	—	75.00	125	200	400	—
1876Pi H	—	75.00	125	200	400	—
1877Pi H	—	75.00	125	200	400	—
1878Pi H	—	250	500	750	—	—
1879Pi H	—	—	—	—	—	—
1880Pi H	—	150	250	350	—	—
1881Pi H	7,600	250	350	500	—	—
1882Pi H Rare	4,000	—	—	—	—	—
1883Pi H	—	125	200	300	500	—
1884Pi H	—	25.00	50.00	100	200	—
1885Pi H	51,000	25.00	50.00	100	200	—
1885Pi C Rare	Inc. above	—	—	—	—	—
1886Pi C	52,000	15.00	30.00	60.00	150	—
1886Pi R	Inc. above	6.00	11.00	22.50	65.00	—
1887Pi R	118,000	4.00	7.00	14.00	50.00	—
1888Pi R	136,000	4.00	7.00	14.00	50.00	—
1889/8Pi R/G	—	9.00	14.00	22.50	60.00	—
1889/7Pi R	131,000	9.00	14.00	22.50	60.00	—
1890Pi R/G	—	4.00	6.00	12.00	40.00	—
1890Pi R	204,000	3.00	5.00	11.00	40.00	—
1891/89Pi R	163,000	4.00	7.00	14.00	40.00	—
1891Pi R	Inc. above	3.00	6.00	10.00	30.00	—
1892/0Pi R/G	—	4.00	6.00	12.00	40.00	—
1892/0Pi R	200,000	4.00	6.00	12.00	40.00	—
1892Pi R	Inc. above	3.00	4.00	7.00	40.00	—
1892Pi R/G	—	4.00	6.00	12.00	40.00	—
1893Pi R/G	—	3.00	11.00	20.00	60.00	—
1893Pi R	48,000	9.00	11.00	20.00	60.00	—

KM# 403.2 10 CENTAVOS

2.7070 g., 0.9030 Silver 0.0786 oz. ASW **Obv:** Facing eagle, snake in beak **Rev:** Value within 1/2 wreath **Mint:** Culiacan

Date	Mintage	F	VF	XF	Unc	BU
1871Cn P Rare	—	—	—	—	—	—
1873Cn P	8,732	20.00	50.00	100	225	—
1881Cn D	9,440	75.00	175	325	500	—
1882Cn D	12,000	75.00	125	200	400	—
1885Cn M	18,000	25.00	50.00	100	200	—
Note: Mule, gold 2-1/2 peso obverse						
1886Cn M	13,000	50.00	100	150	300	—
Note: Mule, gold 2-1/2 peso obverse						
1887Cn M	11,000	20.00	40.00	75.00	175	—
1888Cn M	56,000	5.00	10.00	25.00	125	—
1889Cn M	42,000	5.00	10.00	20.00	75.00	—
1890Cn M	132,000	4.00	6.00	12.00	75.00	—
1891Cn M	84,000	5.00	10.00	20.00	75.00	—
1892/1Cn M	37,000	5.00	9.00	17.00	75.00	—
1892Cn M	Inc. above	4.00	7.00	14.00	75.00	—
1894Cn M	43,000	4.00	7.00	14.00	75.00	—
1895Cn M	23,000	4.00	7.00	14.00	60.00	—
1896Cn M	121,000	3.00	5.00	9.00	50.00	—

KM# 403.3 10 CENTAVOS

2.7070 g., 0.9030 Silver 0.0786 oz. ASW **Obv:** Facing eagle, snake in beak **Rev:** Value within 1/2 wreath **Mint:** Durango

Date	Mintage	F	VF	XF	Unc
1878Do E	2,500	100	175	300	600
1879Do B Rare	—	—	—	—	—
1880/70Do B Rare	—	—	—	—	—
1880/79Do B Rare	—	—	—	—	—
1884Do C	—	30.00	60.00	100	225
1886Do C	13,000	75.00	150	300	500
1887Do C	81,000	5.00	9.00	17.00	100
1888Do C	31,000	7.00	13.00	32.00	100
1889Do C	55,000	5.00	9.00	17.00	100
1890Do C	50,000	5.00	9.00	17.00	100
1891Do P	139,000	3.00	5.00	10.00	80.00
1892Do P	212,000	3.00	5.00	10.00	80.00
1892Do D	Inc. above	3.00	5.00	10.00	80.00
1893Do D	258,000	3.00	5.00	10.00	80.00

SECOND REPUBLIC

Date	Mintage	F	VF	XF	Unc
1893Do D/C	Inc. above	4.00	6.00	12.00	80.00
1894Do D	184,000	2.50	4.00	8.00	80.00
1894Do D/C	Inc. above	3.00	5.00	10.00	80.00
1895Do D	142,000	2.50	4.00	8.00	80.00

KM# 403.6 10 CENTAVOS
2.7070 g., 0.9030 Silver 0.0786 oz. ASW **Obv:** Facing eagle, snake in beak **Rev:** Value within 1/2 wreath **Mint:** Hermosillo

Date	Mintage	F	VF	XF	Unc	BU
1874Ho R	—	30.00	60.00	100	200	—
1876Ho F	3,140	200	300	450	750	—
1878Ho A	—	6.00	11.00	17.00	85.00	—
1879Ho A	—	25.00	50.00	90.00	175	—
1880Ho A	—	5.00	8.00	16.00	85.00	—
1881Ho A	28,000	5.00	9.00	19.00	85.00	—
1882/1Ho A	25,000	6.00	11.00	22.50	85.00	—
1882/1Ho a	Inc. above	7.00	14.00	27.50	85.00	—
1882Ho A	Inc. above	5.00	9.00	19.00	85.00	—
1883Ho	7,000	65.00	100	200	400	—
1884/3Ho M	—	10.00	20.00	40.00	90.00	—
1884Ho A	—	35.00	75.00	150	300	—
1884/3Ho M	—	7.50	15.00	30.00	85.00	—
1884Ho M	—	7.50	15.00	30.00	85.00	—
1885Ho M	21,000	12.50	25.00	50.00	100	—
1886Ho M Rare	10,000	—	—	—	—	—
1886Ho G	Inc. above	7.50	12.50	25.00	85.00	—
1887Ho G	—	25.00	50.00	75.00	150	—
1888Ho G	25,000	7.00	14.00	27.50	85.00	—
1889Ho G	42,000	5.00	8.00	14.00	85.00	—
1890Ho G	48,000	5.00	8.00	14.00	85.00	—
1891/80Ho G	136,000	5.00	8.00	14.00	85.00	—
1891/0Ho G	Inc. above	5.00	8.00	14.00	85.00	—
1891Ho G	Inc. above	5.00	8.00	14.00	85.00	—
1892Ho G	67,000	5.00	8.00	14.00	85.00	—
1893Ho G	67,000	5.00	8.00	14.00	85.00	—

KM# 403.8 10 CENTAVOS
2.7070 g., 0.9030 Silver 0.0786 oz. ASW **Obv:** Facing eagle, snake in beak **Rev:** Value within 1/2 wreath **Mint:** Oaxaca

Date	Mintage	F	VF	XF	Unc	BU
1889Oa E	21,000	225	425	650	—	—
1890Oa E	31,000	125	175	275	550	—
1890Oa N Rare	Inc. above	—	—	—	—	—

KM# 403.10 10 CENTAVOS
2.7070 g., 0.9030 Silver 0.0786 oz. ASW **Obv:** Facing eagle, snake in beak **Obv. Legend:** REPUBLICA MEXICANA **Rev:** Value within 1/2 wreath **Mint:** Zacatecas **Note:** Varieties exist.

Date	Mintage	F	VF	XF	Unc
1870Zs H	20,000	100	150	200	400
1871Zs H	Inc. above	—	—	—	—
1871/0Zs H	10,000	—	—	—	—
1872Zs H	10,000	150	200	275	500
1873Zs H	10,000	250	350	600	—
1874Zs A	—	200	300	500	—
1874/3Zs H	—	50.00	75.00	150	300
1875Zs A	—	6.00	11.00	27.50	100
1876Zs A	—	6.00	11.00	27.50	100
1876Zs S	—	100	200	300	500
1877Zs S Small S	—	7.50	12.50	25.00	100
1877Zs Regular S over small S	—	7.50	12.50	25.00	100
1877Zs S Regular S	—	7.50	12.50	25.00	100
1878Zs S	Inc. above	6.00	11.00	22.50	80.00
1878/7Zs S	30,000	6.00	11.00	22.50	80.00
1879Zs S	—	6.00	11.00	22.50	80.00
1880Zs S	—	6.00	11.00	22.50	80.00
1881Zs S	Inc. above	5.00	8.00	15.00	50.00

Date	Mintage	F	VF	XF	Unc
1881/0Zs S	120,000	5.00	8.00	15.00	50.00
1882Zs S	Inc. above	12.50	25.00	50.00	125
1882/1Zs S	64,000	12.50	25.00	50.00	125
1883Zs S	Inc. above	4.00	6.00	12.00	50.00
1883/73Zs S	102,000	4.00	6.00	12.00	50.00
1884Zs S	—	4.00	6.00	12.00	50.00
1884/3Zs S	—	4.00	6.00	12.00	50.00
1885Zs S	297,000	3.00	5.00	9.00	50.00
1885Zs Z	Inc. above	5.00	10.00	19.00	65.00
Note: Without assayers initials, error					
1885Zs S Small S in mint mark	Inc. above	4.00	6.00	12.00	50.00
1886Zs S	274,000	3.00	5.00	9.00	30.00
1886Zs Z	Inc. above	12.50	25.00	50.00	125
1887Zs ZsZ	233,000	3.00	5.00	9.00	30.00
1887Zs Z Z Error	Inc. above	5.00	11.00	27.50	100
1888Zs ZsZ	270,000	3.00	5.00	9.00	30.00
1888Zs Z Z Error	Inc. above	5.00	11.00	27.50	100
1889/7Zs Z/S	240,000	6.00	9.00	15.00	40.00
1889Zs ZS	Inc. above	5.00	6.00	12.00	30.00
1889Zs Z/G	—	3.00	6.00	12.00	30.00
1892Zs Z	Inc. above	3.00	5.00	9.00	30.00
1890Zs ZsZ	410,000	3.00	5.00	9.00	30.00
1890Zs Z Z Error	Inc. above	5.00	11.00	27.50	100
1891Zs Z	1,105,000	3.00	5.00	9.00	30.00
1891Zs ZsZ Double s	Inc. above	4.00	6.00	11.00	30.00
1892Zs Z	1,102,000	3.00	5.00	9.00	30.00
1892Zs Z/G	—	4.00	6.00	11.00	30.00
1893/2Zs Z	—	4.00	6.00	12.00	40.00
1893Zs Z	1,010,999	3.00	5.00	9.00	25.00
1894Zs Z	892,000	3.00	5.00	9.00	30.00
1895Zs Z	920,000	3.00	5.00	9.00	30.00
1895Zs Z 9/5	—	4.00	6.00	12.00	30.00
1896/5Z S/O Z/G	—	4.00	6.00	12.00	30.00
1896/5Zs Z/G	—	3.00	5.00	9.00	30.00
1896Zs Z/G	—	3.00	5.00	9.00	30.00
1896/5Zs ZsZ	700,000	3.00	5.00	9.00	30.00
1896Zs ZsZ	Inc. above	3.00	5.00	9.00	30.00
1896Zs Z Z Error	Inc. above	5.00	11.00	27.50	100
1897Zs Z	Inc. above	3.00	5.00	9.00	30.00
1897/6Zs ZsZ	900,000	4.00	7.00	12.00	30.00
1897/6Zs Z Z Error	Inc. above	5.00	11.00	27.50	100

KM# 403.1 10 CENTAVOS
2.7070 g., 0.9030 Silver 0.0786 oz. ASW **Obv:** Facing eagle, snake in beak **Rev:** Value within 1/2 wreath **Mint:** Chihuahua **Note:** Mint mark CH, Ca. Varieties exist.

Date	Mintage	F	VF	XF	Unc	BU
1871 M	8,150	15.00	30.00	60.00	150	—
1873 M Crude date	—	35.00	75.00	125	175	—
1874 M	—	10.00	17.50	35.00	100	—
1880 G/g	Inc. above	15.00	25.00	50.00	125	—
1880/70 G	7,620	20.00	40.00	80.00	175	—
1881 Rare	340	—	—	—	—	—
1883 M	9,000	10.00	20.00	40.00	125	—
1884/73	—	5.00	30.00	60.00	150	—
1884 M	—	10.00	20.00	40.00	125	—
1886 M	45,000	7.50	12.50	30.00	100	—
1887/3 M/G	96,000	5.00	10.00	20.00	75.00	—
1887 M/G	—	4.00	6.00	12.00	75.00	—
1887 M	Inc. above	4.00	6.00	12.00	75.00	—
1888 M/G	—	4.00	6.00	12.00	75.00	—
1888 M	299,000	3.00	5.00	9.00	75.00	—
1888 Ca/Mo	Inc. above	3.00	5.00	9.00	75.00	—
1889 M	Inc. above	4.00	6.00	12.00	75.00	—
Note: Small 89 (5 Centavo font)						
1889/8 M	115,000	4.00	6.00	12.00	75.00	—
1890 M	Inc. above	3.00	5.00	11.00	75.00	—
1890/80 M	140,000	4.00	6.00	12.00	75.00	—
1890/89 M	Inc. above	4.00	6.00	12.00	75.00	—
1891 M	163,000	3.00	5.00	11.00	75.00	—
1892 M	169,000	3.00	5.00	11.00	75.00	—
1892 M 9/ inverted 9	Inc. above	4.00	6.00	12.00	75.00	—
1893 M	246,000	3.00	5.00	11.00	75.00	—
1894 M	163,000	3.00	5.00	11.00	75.00	—
1895 M	127,000	3.00	5.00	11.00	75.00	—

SECOND REPUBLIC

KM# 404   10 CENTAVOS
2.7070 g., 0.9030 Silver 0.0786 oz. ASW **Obv:**
Facing eagle, snake in beak **Obv. Legend:**
REPUBLICA MEXICANA **Rev:** Value within 1/2
wreath **Mint:** Culiacan **Note:** Varieties exist.

Date	Mintage	F	VF	XF	Unc	BU
1898Cn M	9,870	50.00	100	200	500	—
1899Cn Q Oval Q, double tail	Inc. above	5.00	7.50	25.00	100	—
1899Cn Q Round Q, single tail	80,000	5.00	7.50	25.00	100	—
1900Cn Q	160,000	3.75	4.25	9.50	30.00	—
1901Cn Q	235,000	2.75	3.25	7.00	25.00	30.00
1902Cn Q	186,000	2.75	3.25	7.00	27.50	30.00
1903Cn V	Inc. above	2.75	3.25	7.00	20.00	30.00
1903Cn Q	256,000	2.75	3.25	8.00	27.50	22.50
1904Cn H	307,000	2.75	3.25	7.00	20.00	22.50

KM# 404.1   10 CENTAVOS
2.7070 g., 0.9030 Silver 0.0786 oz. ASW **Obv:**
Facing eagle, snake in beak **Rev:** Value within 1/2
wreath **Mint:** Guanajuato

Date	Mintage	F	VF	XF	Unc	BU
1898Go R	435,000	3.00	4.50	9.00	20.00	—
1899Go R	270,000	3.00	4.50	9.00	25.00	—
1900Go R	130,000	7.50	12.50	25.00	60.00	—

KM# 404.2   10 CENTAVOS
2.7070 g., 0.9030 Silver 0.0786 oz. ASW **Obv:**
Facing eagle, snake in beak **Obv. Legend:**
REPUBLICA MEXICANA **Rev:** Value within 1/2
wreath **Mint:** Mexico City

Date	Mintage	F	VF	XF	Unc	BU
1898Mo M	130,000	3.75	6.00	10.00	27.50	—
1899Mo M	190,000	3.75	6.00	10.00	27.50	—
1900Mo M	311,000	3.75	6.00	10.00	27.50	—
1901Mo M	80,000	2.75	3.50	8.00	27.50	30.00
1902Mo M	181,000	2.75	3.50	8.00	27.50	30.00
1903Mo M	581,000	2.75	3.50	8.00	27.50	30.00
1904Mo M	1,266,000	2.75	3.50	6.00	25.00	27.50
1904Mo MM (Error)	Inc. above	3.00	7.00	14.00	33.75	37.75
1905Mo M	266,000	3.00	5.00	10.00	27.50	30.00

KM# 404.3   10 CENTAVOS
2.7070 g., 0.9020 Silver 0.0785 oz. ASW **Obv:**
Facing eagle, snake in beak **Rev:** Value within 1/2
wreath **Mint:** Zacatecas

Date	Mintage	F	VF	XF	Unc	BU
1898Zs Z	240,000	3.75	6.00	15.00	30.00	—
1899Zs Z	105,000	3.75	6.00	18.00	35.00	—
1900Zs Z	219,000	10.00	14.00	27.50	60.00	—
1901Zs Z	70,000	3.00	7.00	18.00	50.00	75.00
1902Zs Z	120,000	3.00	7.00	14.00	33.75	37.75
1903Zs Z	228,000	2.75	4.00	12.00	25.00	27.50
1904Zs Z	368,000	2.75	4.00	12.00	25.00	27.50
1904Zs M	Inc. above	2.75	4.00	12.00	30.00	33.75
1905Zs M	66,000	10.00	27.50	70.00	270	—

KM# 405   20 CENTAVOS
5.4150 g., 0.9030 Silver 0.1572 oz. ASW **Obv:**
Facing eagle, snake in beak **Rev:** Value within 1/2
wreath **Mint:** Culiacan

Date	Mintage	F	VF	XF	Unc	BU
1898Cn M	114,000	5.50	11.50	36.00	145	—
1899Cn M	44,000	12.00	20.00	45.00	225	—
1899Cn Q	Inc. above	20.00	35.00	100	250	—
1900Cn Q	68,000	6.50	12.50	35.00	140	—
1901Cn Q	185,000	7.00	12.50	25.00	145	—
1902/802Cn Q	98,000	7.00	12.50	36.00	145	—

Date	Mintage	F	VF	XF	Unc	BU
1902Cn Q	Inc. above	5.50	11.50	36.00	145	—
1903Cn Q	93,000	5.50	11.50	36.00	145	—
1904/3Cn H	258,000	—	—	—	—	—
1904Cn H	Inc. above	6.00	12.00	36.00	145	—

KM# 405.1   20 CENTAVOS
5.4150 g., 0.9027 Silver 0.1572 oz. ASW **Obv:**
Facing eagle, snake in beak **Obv. Legend:**
REPUBLICA MEXICANA **Rev:** Value within 1/2
wreath **Mint:** Guanajuato

Date	Mintage	F	VF	XF	Unc	BU
1898Go R	135,000	7.00	12.00	25.00	115	—
1899Go R	215,000	7.00	12.00	25.00	115	—
1900/800Go R	38,000	12.00	22.00	65.00	265	—

KM# 405.3   20 CENTAVOS
5.4150 g., 0.9027 Silver 0.1572 oz. ASW **Obv:**
Facing eagle, snake in beak **Obv. Legend:**
REPUBLICA MEXICANA **Rev:** Value within 1/2
wreath **Mint:** Zacatecas

Date	Mintage	F	VF	XF	Unc	BU
1898Zs Z	195,000	8.00	14.00	30.00	115	—
1899Zs Z	210,000	8.00	14.00	30.00	115	—
1900/800Zs Z	97,000	8.00	14.00	50.00	215	—
1901Zs Z	Inc. above	6.00	12.00	25.00	120	—
1901/0Zs Z	130,000	50.00	75.00	125	400	—
1902Zs Z	105,000	6.00	12.00	25.00	120	—
1903Zs Z	143,000	6.00	12.00	25.00	120	—
1904Zs Z	246,000	6.00	12.00	25.00	120	—
1904Zs M	Inc. above	6.00	12.00	60.00	350	—
1904/804Zs	—	30.00	50.00	125	300	—
1905Zs M	59,000	12.00	85.00	100	900	—

KM# 405.2   20 CENTAVOS
5.4150 g., 0.9030 Silver 0.1572 oz. ASW **Obv:**
Facing eagle, snake in beak **Rev:** Value within 1/2
wreath **Mint:** Mexico City **Note:** Varieties exist.

Date	Mintage	F	VF	XF	Unc	BU
1898Mo M	150,000	7.50	12.00	25.00	140	—
1899Mo M	425,000	7.50	12.00	25.00	140	—
1900/800Mo M	295,000	7.50	12.00	25.00	140	—
1901Mo M	110,000	5.50	10.00	25.00	110	—
1902Mo M	120,000	5.50	10.00	25.00	110	—
1903Mo M	213,000	5.50	10.00	25.00	110	—
1904Mo M	276,000	5.50	10.00	25.00	110	—
1905Mo M	117,000	5.50	25.00	60.00	180	—

KM# 406.2   25 CENTAVOS
6.7680 g., 0.9030 Silver 0.1965 oz. ASW **Obv:**
Facing eagle, snake in beak **Rev:** Radiant cap above
scales **Mint:** Culiacan

Date	Mintage	F	VF	XF	Unc
1871Cn P	—	250	500	750	—
1872Cn P	2,780	300	550	800	—
1873Cn P	20,000	100	150	250	500
1874Cn P	—	20.00	50.00	125	250
1875Cn P	—	250	500	750	—
1876Cn P Rare	—	—	—	—	—

SECOND REPUBLIC

Date	Mintage	F	VF	XF	Unc
1878Cn Cn/Go D/S	—	100	150	250	500
1878/7Cn D/S	—	100	150	250	500
1878Cn D	—	100	150	250	500
1879Cn D	—	15.00	35.00	70.00	175
1880Cn D	—	250	500	750	—
1881/0Cn D	18,000	15.00	30.00	60.00	175
1882Cn D	—	200	350	600	—
1882Cn M Rare	—	—	—	—	—
1883Cn M	15,000	50.00	100	150	300
1884Cn M	—	20.00	40.00	80.00	175
1885/4Cn M	19,000	20.00	40.00	80.00	175
1886Cn M	22,000	12.50	20.00	50.00	175
1887Cn M	32,000	12.50	20.00	50.00	175
1888Cn M Cn/Mo	—	—	—	—	—
1888Cn M	86,000	8.00	15.00	30.00	175
1889Cn M	50,000	10.00	25.00	50.00	175
1890Cn M 9/8	—	9.00	17.50	40.00	175
1890Cn M	91,000	9.00	17.50	40.00	175
1892/0Cn M	16,000	20.00	40.00	80.00	200
1892Cn M	Inc. above	20.00	40.00	80.00	200

KM# 406.3 25 CENTAVOS
6.7680 g., 0.9030 Silver 0.1965 oz. ASW **Obv:**
Facing eagle, snake in beak **Rev:** Radiant cap above
scales **Mint:** Durango

Date	Mintage	F	VF	XF	Unc	BU
1873Do P Rare	892	—	—	—	—	—
1877Do P	—	25.00	50.00	100	200	—
1878/7Do E	—	250	500	750	—	—
1878Do B Rare	—	—	—	—	—	—
1879Do B	—	50.00	75.00	125	250	—
1880Do B Rare	—	—	—	—	—	—
1882Do C	17,000	25.00	50.00	100	225	—
1884/3Do C	—	25.00	50.00	100	200	—
1885Do C	15,000	20.00	40.00	80.00	200	—
1885Do C/S	—	20.00	40.00	80.00	200	—
1886Do C	33,000	15.00	30.00	60.00	200	—
1887Do C	27,000	10.00	20.00	50.00	200	—
1888Do C	25,000	10.00	20.00	50.00	200	—
1889Do C	29,000	10.00	20.00	50.00	200	—
1890Do C	68,000	8.00	15.00	40.00	200	—

KM# 406.4 25 CENTAVOS
6.7680 g., 0.9030 Silver 0.1965 oz. ASW **Obv:**
Facing eagle, snake in beak **Rev:** Radiant cap above
scales **Mint:** Guadalajara

Date	Mintage	F	VF	XF	Unc	BU
1880Ga A	38,000	25.00	50.00	100	200	—
1881/0Ga S	39,000	25.00	50.00	100	200	—
1881Ga S	Inc. above	25.00	50.00	100	200	—
1882Ga S	18,000	25.00	50.00	100	200	—
1883/2Ga B/S	—	50.00	100	150	300	—
1884Ga B	—	20.00	40.00	80.00	150	—
1889Ga S	30,000	20.00	40.00	80.00	150	—

KM# 406 25 CENTAVOS
6.7680 g., 0.9030 Silver 0.1965 oz. ASW **Obv:**
Facing eagle, snake in beak **Rev:** Radiant cap above
scales **Mint:** Alamos **Note:** Mint mark A, As.

Date	Mintage	F	VF	XF	Unc	BU
1874 L	—	20.00	40.00	90.00	200	—
1875 L	—	15.00	30.00	70.00	200	—
1876 L	—	30.00	50.00	100	200	—
1877 L	11,000	200	300	500	—	—
1877.	Inc. above	10.00	25.00	60.00	200	—
1878 L	25,000	10.00	25.00	60.00	200	—
1879 L	—	10.00	25.00	60.00	200	—
1880 L	—	10.00	25.00	60.00	200	—

Date	Mintage	F	VF	XF	Unc	BU
1880. L	—	10.00	25.00	60.00	200	—
1881 L	8,800	500	700		200	—
1882 L	7,777	15.00	35.00	80.00	200	—
1883 L	28,000	10.00	25.00	60.00	200	—
1884 L	—	10.00	25.00	60.00	200	—
1885 L	—	20.00	40.00	90.00	200	—
1886 L	46,000	15.00	30.00	70.00	200	—
1887 L	12,000	12.50	27.50	65.00	200	—
1888 L	20,000	12.50	27.50	65.00	200	—
1889 L	14,000	12.50	27.50	65.00	200	—
1890 L	23,000	10.00	25.00	60.00	200	—

KM# 406.1 25 CENTAVOS
6.7680 g., 0.9030 Silver 0.1965 oz. ASW **Obv:**
Facing eagle, snake in beak **Rev:** Radiant cap above
scales **Mint:** Chihuahua **Note:** Mint mark CA, CH, Ca.

Date	Mintage	F	VF	XF	Unc
1871 M	18,000	25.00	50.00	100	200
1872 M Very crude date	24,000	50.00	100	150	300
1883 M	12,000	10.00	25.00	50.00	175
1885/3 M	35,000	10.00	25.00	50.00	175
1885 M	Inc. above	10.00	25.00	50.00	175
1886 M	22,000	10.00	25.00	50.00	175
1887/6 M	26,000	10.00	15.00	30.00	175
1887 M	Inc. above	10.00	25.00	50.00	175
1888 M	14,000	10.00	25.00	50.00	175
1889 M	50,000	10.00	15.00	30.00	175

KM# 406.5 25 CENTAVOS
6.7680 g., 0.9030 Silver 0.1965 oz. ASW **Obv:**
Facing eagle, snake in beak **Rev:** Radiant cap above
scales **Mint:** Guanajuato **Note:** Varieties exist.

Date	Mintage	F	VF	XF	Unc
1870Go S	128,000	10.00	20.00	50.00	125
1871Go S	172,000	10.00	20.00	50.00	125
1872/1Go S	178,000	10.00	20.00	50.00	125
1872Go S	Inc. above	10.00	20.00	50.00	125
1873Go S	120,000	10.00	20.00	50.00	125
1874Go S	—	15.00	30.00	60.00	150
1875/4Go S	—	15.00	30.00	60.00	150
1875Go S	—	10.00	20.00	50.00	125
1876Go S	—	20.00	40.00	80.00	175
1877Go S	124,000	10.00	20.00	50.00	125
1878Go S	146,000	10.00	20.00	50.00	125
1879Go S	—	10.00	20.00	50.00	125
1880Go S	—	20.00	40.00	80.00	175
1881Go S	408,000	9.00	17.50	45.00	125
1882Go S	204,000	9.00	17.50	45.00	125
1883Go B	168,000	9.00	17.50	45.00	125
1884/69Go B	—	9.00	17.50	45.00	125
1884/3Go B	—	9.00	17.50	45.00	125
1884/3Go B/R	—	9.00	17.50	45.00	125
1884Go B	—	9.00	17.50	45.00	125
1885/65Go R	300,000	9.00	17.50	45.00	125
1885/69Go R	Inc. above	9.00	17.50	45.00	125
1885Go R	Inc. above	9.00	17.50	45.00	125
1886/65Go R	—	9.00	17.50	45.00	125
1886/66Go R	322,000	9.00	17.50	45.00	125
1886/69Go R/S	Inc. above	9.00	17.50	45.00	125
1886/5/69Go R	Inc. above	9.00	15.00	45.00	125
1886Go R	Inc. above	9.00	15.00	45.00	125
1887Go R	254,000	9.00	15.00	45.00	125
1887Go/Cn R/D	Inc. above	9.00	15.00	45.00	125
1888Go R	312,000	8.00	15.00	45.00	125
1889/8Go R RS inverted B	—	—	—	—	—
1889/8Go R	304,000	8.00	15.00	45.00	125
1889/8Go/Cn R/D	Inc. above	8.00	15.00	45.00	125
1889Go R	Inc. above	8.00	15.00	45.00	125
1890Go R	236,000	8.00	15.00	45.00	125

KM# 406.6 25 CENTAVOS
6.7680 g., 0.9030 Silver 0.1965 oz. ASW **Obv:**
Facing eagle, snake in beak **Rev:** Radiant cap above
scales **Mint:** Hermosillo **Note:** Varieties exist.

Date	Mintage	F	VF	XF	Unc	BU
1874/64Ho R	Inc. above	10.00	20.00	40.00	125	—
1874/69Ho R	—	10.00	20.00	40.00	125	—
1874Ho R	23,000	10.00	20.00	40.00	125	—
1875Ho R Rare	—	—	—	—	—	—

SECOND REPUBLIC

Date	Mintage	F	VF	XF	Unc	BU
1876/4Ho F/R	34,000	10.00	20.00	50.00	150	—
1876Ho F/R	Inc. above	10.00	25.00	60.00	150	—
1876Ho F	Inc. above	10.00	25.00	55.00	135	—
1877Ho F	—	10.00	20.00	50.00	125	—
1878Ho A	23,000	10.00	20.00	50.00	125	—
1879Ho A	—	10.00	20.00	50.00	125	—
1880Ho A	—	15.00	30.00	60.00	125	—
1881Ho A	19,000	15.00	30.00	60.00	125	—
1882Ho A	8,120	20.00	40.00	80.00	150	—
1883Ho M	2,000	100	200	300	600	—
1884Ho M	—	12.50	25.00	50.00	150	—
1885Ho M	—	10.00	20.00	50.00	125	—
1886Ho G	6,400	30.00	60.00	125	250	—
1887Ho G	12,000	10.00	20.00	40.00	125	—
1888Ho G	20,000	10.00	20.00	40.00	125	—
1889Ho G	28,000	10.00	20.00	40.00	125	—
1890/80Ho G	18,000	25.00	50.00	100	125	—
1890Ho G	Inc. above	25.00	50.00	100	125	—

KM# 406.7 25 CENTAVOS
6.7680 g., 0.9027 Silver 0.1964 oz. ASW **Obv:** Facing eagle, snake in beak **Obv. Legend:** REPUBLICA MEXICANA **Rev:** Radiant cap above scales **Mint:** Mexico City **Note:** Varieties exist.

Date	Mintage	F	VF	XF	Unc	BU
1869Mo C	76,000	10.00	25.00	50.00	125	—
1870/69Mo C	—	6.50	12.00	30.00	125	—
1870/9Mo C	136,000	6.50	12.00	30.00	125	—
1870Mo C	Inc. above	6.50	12.00	30.00	125	—
1871Mo M	138,000	6.50	12.00	30.00	125	—
1872Mo M	220,000	6.50	12.00	30.00	125	—
1873/1Mo M	48,000	10.00	25.00	50.00	125	—
1873Mo M	Inc. above	10.00	25.00	50.00	125	—
1874/69Mo B/M	—	10.00	25.00	50.00	125	—
1874/3Mo M	—	10.00	25.00	50.00	125	—
1874/3Mo B	—	10.00	25.00	50.00	125	—
1874/3Mo B/M	—	10.00	25.00	50.00	125	—
1874Mo M	—	6.50	12.00	30.00	125	—
1874Mo B/M	—	10.00	25.00	50.00	125	—
1875Mo B	—	6.50	12.00	30.00	125	—
1876/5Mo B	—	8.00	15.00	40.00	125	—
1876Mo B	—	6.50	12.00	30.00	125	—
1877Mo M	56,000	10.00	25.00	50.00	125	—
1878/1Mo M	120,000	10.00	25.00	50.00	125	—
1878/7Mo M	Inc. above	10.00	25.00	50.00	125	—
1878Mo M	Inc. above	6.50	12.00	30.00	125	—
1879Mo M	—	10.00	20.00	40.00	125	—
1880Mo M	—	8.00	15.00	35.00	125	—
1881/0Mo M	300,000	10.00	25.00	50.00	125	—
1881Mo M	Inc. above	10.00	25.00	50.00	125	—
1882Mo M	212,000	8.00	15.00	35.00	125	—
1883Mo M	108,000	8.00	15.00	35.00	125	—
1884/3Mo M	—	10.00	25.00	50.00	125	—
1884Mo M	—	10.00	20.00	40.00	125	—
1885Mo M	216,000	10.00	20.00	40.00	125	—
1886/5Mo M	436,000	8.00	15.00	35.00	125	—
1886Mo M	Inc. above	8.00	15.00	35.00	125	—
1887Mo M	376,000	8.00	15.00	35.00	125	—
1888Mo M	192,000	8.00	15.00	35.00	125	—
1889Mo M	132,000	8.00	15.00	35.00	125	—
1890Mo M	60,000	10.00	20.00	40.00	125	—

KM# 406.8 25 CENTAVOS
6.7680 g., 0.9030 Silver 0.1965 oz. ASW **Obv:** Facing eagle, snake in beak **Rev:** Radiant cap above scales **Mint:** San Luis Potosi **Note:** Varieties exist.

Date	Mintage	F	VF	XF	Unc
1869Pi S	—	25.00	75.00	150	300

Date	Mintage	F	VF	XF	Unc
1870Pi G	50,000	10.00	30.00	75.00	150
1870Pi O	Inc. above	15.00	35.00	85.00	175
1871Pi O	30,000	10.00	30.00	75.00	150
1872Pi O	46,000	10.00	30.00	75.00	150
1873Pi O	13,000	15.00	40.00	90.00	175
1874Pi H	—	15.00	40.00	90.00	200
1875Pi H	—	10.00	20.00	60.00	150
1876/5Pi H	—	15.00	30.00	80.00	175
1876Pi H	—	10.00	25.00	65.00	150
1877Pi H	19,000	10.00	25.00	65.00	150
1878Pi H	—	15.00	30.00	60.00	150
1879/8Pi H	—	10.00	25.00	60.00	150
1879Pi H	—	10.00	25.00	60.00	150
1879Pi E	—	100	200	300	600
1880Pi H	—	20.00	40.00	100	200
1880Pi H/M	—	20.00	40.00	100	200
1881Pi H	50,000	20.00	40.00	80.00	175
1881Pi E Rare	Inc. above	—	—	—	—
1882Pi H	20,000	10.00	20.00	60.00	150
1883Pi H	17,000	10.00	25.00	65.00	150
1884Pi H	—	10.00	25.00	65.00	150
1885/4Pi H	—	10.00	20.00	60.00	150
1885Pi H	43,000	10.00	20.00	60.00	150
1886Pi C	78,000	10.00	25.00	65.00	150
1886Pi R	Inc. above	9.00	20.00	50.00	150
1886Pi R 6/inverted 6	Inc. above	9.00	20.00	50.00	150
1887Pi/ZsR	92,000	9.00	20.00	50.00	150
1887Pi/ZsB	Inc. above	100	150	300	500
1887Pi R	—	9.00	20.00	50.00	150
1888Pi R	106,000	9.00	20.00	50.00	150
1888Pi/ZsR	Inc. above	10.00	20.00	50.00	150
1888Pi R/B	Inc. above	10.00	20.00	50.00	150
1889Pi R	115,000	8.00	15.00	40.00	150
1889Pi/ZsR	Inc. above	10.00	20.00	50.00	150
1889Pi R/B	Inc. above	10.00	20.00	50.00	150
1890Pi R	64,000	10.00	20.00	50.00	150
1890Pi/ZsR/B	Inc. above	8.00	15.00	40.00	150
1890Pi R/B	Inc. above	10.00	20.00	50.00	150

KM# 406.9 25 CENTAVOS
6.7680 g., 0.9030 Silver 0.1965 oz. ASW **Obv:** Facing eagle, snake in beak **Rev:** Radiant cap above scales **Mint:** Zacatecas **Note:** Varieties exist.

Date	Mintage	F	VF	XF	Unc	BU
1870Zs H	152,000	8.00	15.00	50.00	125	—
1871Zs H	250,000	8.00	15.00	50.00	125	—
1872Zs H	260,000	8.00	15.00	50.00	125	—
1872Zs/Cn H	—	—	—	—	—	—
1872Zs H	—	—	—	—	—	—
1873Zs H	132,000	8.00	15.00	50.00	125	—
1874Zs H	—	10.00	20.00	60.00	125	—
1874Zs A	—	10.00	20.00	60.00	125	—
1875Zs A	—	9.00	20.00	60.00	125	—
1876Zs A	—	8.00	15.00	50.00	125	—
1876Zs S	—	8.00	15.00	50.00	125	—
1877Zs S	350,000	8.00	15.00	50.00	125	—
1878Zs S	252,000	8.00	15.00	50.00	125	—
1878/1Zs S	—	9.00	20.00	60.00	125	—
1878/7Zs S	—	9.00	20.00	60.00	125	—
1879Zs S	—	8.00	15.00	50.00	125	—
1880Zs S	—	8.00	15.00	50.00	125	—
1881/0Zs S	570,000	8.00	15.00	50.00	125	—
1881Zs S	Inc. above	8.00	15.00	50.00	125	—
1882/1Zs S	300,000	10.00	17.50	55.00	125	—
1882Zs S	Inc. above	8.00	15.00	50.00	125	—
1883/2Zs S	193,000	10.00	17.50	55.00	125	—
1883Zs S	Inc. above	8.00	15.00	50.00	125	—
1884/3Zs S	—	10.00	17.50	55.00	125	—
1884Zs S	—	8.00	15.00	50.00	125	—
1885Zs S	309,000	8.00	15.00	50.00	125	—
1886/2Zs S	—	10.00	17.50	50.00	125	—
1886/5Zs S	613,000	8.00	15.00	50.00	125	—
1886Zs S	Inc. above	8.00	15.00	50.00	125	—
1886Zs Z	Inc. above	8.00	15.00	55.00	125	—
1887Zs Z	389,000	8.00	15.00	50.00	125	—
1888Zs Z	408,000	8.00	15.00	50.00	125	—
1889Zs Z	400,000	8.00	15.00	50.00	125	—
1890Zs Z	269,000	8.00	15.00	50.00	125	—

SECOND REPUBLIC

KM# 407.7 50 CENTAVOS
13.5360 g., 0.9030 Silver 0.3930 oz. ASW **Obv:** Facing eagle, snake in beak **Rev:** Radiant cap above scales **Mint:** San Luis Potosi

Date	Mintage	F	VF	XF	Unc	BU
1870Pi G	Inc. above	22.50	42.00	105	450	—
1870/780Pi G	50,000	27.50	47.00	115	500	—
1870Pi O	Inc. above	22.50	42.00	105	450	—
1871Pi O	—	17.00	32.00	85.00	400	—
1871Pi O/G	64,000	17.00	32.00	85.00	400	—
1872Pi O	52,000	17.00	32.00	85.00	400	—
1872Pi O/G	Inc. above	17.00	32.00	85.00	400	—
1873Pi O	32,000	22.50	42.00	105	450	—
1873Pi H	Inc. above	27.50	52.00	130	550	—
1874Pi H/O	—	17.00	32.00	85.00	400	—
1875/3Pi H	—	17.00	32.00	85.00	400	—
1875Pi H	—	17.00	32.00	85.00	400	—
1876Pi H	—	32.00	62.00	155	700	—
1877Pi H	34,000	22.50	42.00	105	450	—
1878Pi H	9,700	22.50	42.00	105	450	—
1879Pi H	—	17.00	37.00	95.00	400	—
1879/7Pi H	—	17.00	37.00	95.00	450	—
1880Pi H	—	22.50	42.00	105	450	—
1881Pi H	28,000	22.50	42.00	105	450	—
1882Pi H	22,000	17.00	32.00	85.00	400	—
1883Pi H	Inc. above	17.00	32.00	85.00	400	—
1883Pi H 8/8	29,000	50.00	100	200	750	—
1884Pi H	—	50.00	100	175	600	—
1885/3Pi H	—	22.50	42.00	105	450	—
1885/0Pi H	45,000	22.50	42.00	105	450	—
1885/4Pi H	Inc. above	22.50	42.00	105	450	—
1885Pi H	Inc. above	27.50	52.00	130	450	—
1885Pi C	Inc. above	17.00	32.00	85.00	400	—
1886/1Pi R	92,000	50.00	100	175	600	—
1886/1Pi C	—	27.50	42.00	105	450	—
1886Pi C	Inc. above	17.00	32.00	85.00	400	—
1886Pi R	Inc. above	17.00	32.00	85.00	400	—
1887Pi R	32,000	17.00	32.00	95.00	450	—

KM# 407 50 CENTAVOS
13.5360 g., 0.9030 Silver 0.3930 oz. ASW **Obv:** Facing eagle, snake in beak **Rev:** Radiant cap above scales **Mint:** Alamos **Note:** Mint mark A, As.

Date	Mintage	F	VF	XF	Unc	BU
1875 L	—	14.00	27.50	75.00	400	—
1876/5 L	—	27.50	50.00	125	450	—
1876 L	—	14.00	27.50	75.00	400	—
1876. L	—	14.00	27.50	75.00	400	—
1877 L	26,000	17.00	32.00	90.00	450	—
1878 L	—	14.00	27.50	75.00	400	—
1879 L	—	27.50	52.00	125	450	—
1880 L	57,000	14.00	27.50	75.00	400	—
1881 L	18,000	17.00	32.00	85.00	450	—
1884 L	6,286	65.00	120	250	650	—
1885As/HoL	21,000	17.00	37.00	95.00	450	—
1888 L	—	4,000	5,000	7,000	—	—

KM# 407.1 50 CENTAVOS
13.5360 g., 0.9030 Silver 0.3930 oz. ASW **Obv:** Facing eagle, snake in beak **Rev:** Radiant cap above scales **Mint:** Chihuahua **Note:** Mint mark Ca, CHa.

Date	Mintage	F	VF	XF	Unc	BU
1883 M	12,000	32.00	62.00	130	500	—
1884 M	—	27.50	52.00	130	500	—
1885 M	13,000	17.00	37.00	95.00	400	—
1886 M	18,000	22.50	42.00	105	450	—
1887 M	26,000	27.50	67.00	155	500	—

KM# 407.4 50 CENTAVOS
13.5360 g., 0.9030 Silver 0.3930 oz. ASW **Obv:** Facing eagle, snake in beak **Rev:** Radiant cap above scales **Mint:** Guanajuato **Note:** Struck at Guanajuato Mint, mitn mark Go. Varieties exist.

Date	Mintage	F	VF	XF	Unc
1869Go S	—	17.00	37.00	80.00	550
1870Go S	166,000	14.00	27.50	55.00	450
1871Go S	148,000	14.00	27.50	55.00	450
1872/1Go S	144,000	17.00	32.00	65.00	500
1872Go S	Inc. above	14.00	27.50	55.00	450

Date	Mintage	F	VF	XF	Unc
1873Go S	50,000	14.00	27.50	55.00	450
1874Go S	—	14.00	27.50	55.00	450
1875Go S	—	17.00	37.00	80.00	450
1876/5Go S	—	14.00	27.50	55.00	450
1877Go S	76,000	14.00	27.50	65.00	450
1878Go S	37,000	17.00	32.00	80.00	550
1879/8Go S	—	17.00	32.00	65.00	500
1879Go S	—	14.00	27.50	55.00	450
1880Go S	—	14.00	27.50	55.00	450
1881/79Go S	32,000	17.00	32.00	65.00	500
1881Go S	Inc. above	14.00	27.50	55.00	450
1882Go S	18,000	14.00	27.50	55.00	450
1883/2Go B/S	—	17.00	32.00	65.00	500
1883Go B	—	14.00	27.50	55.00	450
1883Go S Rare	—	—	—	—	—
1884Go B/S	—	17.00	32.00	65.00	500
1885/4Go R/B	—	17.00	32.00	65.00	500
1885Go R	53,000	14.00	27.50	55.00	450
1886/5Go R/B	59,000	17.00	32.00	65.00	500
1886/5Go R/S	Inc. above	22.50	42.00	80.00	500
1886Go R	Inc. above	22.50	42.00	80.00	450
1887Go R	18,000	22.50	42.00	80.00	550
1888Go R 1 known; Rare	—	—	—	—	—

KM# 407.8 50 CENTAVOS
13.5360 g., 0.9030 Silver 0.3930 oz. ASW **Obv:** Facing eagle, snake in beak **Rev:** Radiant cap above scales **Mint:** Zacatecas **Note:** Varieties exist.

Date	Mintage	F	VF	XF	Unc	BU
1870Zs H	86,000	14.00	27.50	65.00	450	—
1871Zs H	146,000	14.00	27.50	55.00	400	—
1872Zs H	132,000	14.00	27.50	55.00	400	—
1873Zs H	56,000	14.00	27.50	55.00	400	—
1874Zs H	—	14.00	27.50	55.00	400	—
1874Zs A Rare	—	—	—	—	—	—
1875Zs A	—	14.00	27.50	55.00	400	—
1876Zs A	—	14.00	27.50	55.00	400	—
1876Zs S	—	17.00	32.00	65.00	450	—
1876/5Zs A	—	100	200	350	750	—
1877Zs S	100,000	14.00	27.50	55.00	400	—
1878Zs S	Inc. above	17.00	32.00	65.00	400	—
1878/7Zs S	254,000	17.00	32.00	65.00	400	—
1879Zs S	—	14.00	27.50	55.00	400	—
1880Zs S	—	14.00	27.50	55.00	400	—
1881Zs S	201,000	14.00	27.50	55.00	400	—
1882Zs S	Inc. above	60.00	110	260	660	—
1882/1Zs S	2,000	60.00	110	260	660	—
1883Zs S	Inc. above	27.50	52.00	105	450	—
1883Zs/Za S	31,000	32.00	62.00	105	450	—
1884Zs S	—	14.00	27.50	55.00	400	—
1884/3Zs S	—	17.00	32.00	65.00	450	—
1885Zs S	Inc. above	27.50	52.00	130	450	—
1885/4Zs S	2,000	27.50	52.00	130	450	—
1886Zs Z	2,000	150	275	400	1,000	—
1887Zs Z	63,000	32.00	62.00	130	450	—

KM# 407.5 50 CENTAVOS
13.5360 g., 0.9030 Silver 0.3930 oz. ASW **Obv:** Facing eagle, snake in beak **Rev:** Radiant cap above scales **Mint:** Hermosillo **Note:** With and without dot after 50 of denomination, in medal and coin alignment.

Date	Mintage	F	VF	XF	Unc	BU
1874Ho R	—	22.50	42.00	110	600	—
1875/4Ho R	—	22.50	52.00	135	600	—

SECOND REPUBLIC

Date	Mintage	F	VF	XF	Unc	BU
1875Ho R	—	22.50	52.00	135	600	—
1876/5Ho F/R	—	17.00	37.00	110	550	—
1876Ho F	—	17.00	37.00	110	550	—
1877Ho F	—	52.00	77.00	160	650	—
1880/70Ho A	—	17.00	37.00	110	550	—
1880Ho A	—	17.00	37.00	110	550	—
1881Ho A	13,000	17.00	37.00	110	550	—
1882Ho A	—	75.00	150	250	750	—
1888Ho G	—	2,000	3,000	6,000	—	—
1894Ho G	59,000	17.00	32.00	110	450	—
1895Ho G	8,000	250	350	700	1,500	—

Date	Mintage	F	VF	XF	Unc	BU
1871Do P Rare	591	—	—	—	—	—
1873Do P	4,010	150	250	500	1,250	—
1873Do M/P	Inc. above	150	250	500	1,250	—
1874Do M	—	22.50	42.00	180	750	—
1875Do M	—	22.50	42.00	85.00	350	—
1875Do H	—	150	250	450	1,000	—
1876/5Do M	—	37.00	72.00	155	500	—
1876Do M	—	37.00	72.00	155	500	—
1877Do P	2,000	32.00	47.00	155	1,250	—
1878Do B Rare	—	—	—	—	—	—
1879Do B Rare	—	—	—	—	—	—
1880Do P	—	32.00	62.00	130	500	—
1881Do P	10,000	42.00	82.00	155	550	—
1882Do C	8,957	32.00	77.00	205	800	—
1884/2Do C	—	22.50	52.00	130	600	—
1884Do C	—	—	—	—	—	—
1885Do B	—	17.00	42.00	110	500	—
1885Do B/P	—	17.00	42.00	110	500	—
1886Do C	16,000	17.00	42.00	110	500	—
1887Do C	—	17.00	42.00	110	500	—
1887Do/Mo C	28,000	17.00	42.00	110	500	—

KM# 407.2 50 CENTAVOS
13.5360 g., 0.9030 Silver 0.3930 oz. ASW **Obv:** Facing eagle, snake in beak **Obv. Legend:** REPUBLICA MEXICANA **Rev:** Radiant cap above scales **Mint:** Culiacan

Date	Mintage	F	VF	XF	Unc	BU
1871Cn P	—	400	550	750	1,500	—
1873Cn P	—	400	550	750	1,500	—
1874Cn P	—	200	300	500	1,000	—
1875/4Cn P	—	22.50	42.00	80.00	450	—
1875Cn P	—	14.00	27.50	55.00	450	—
1876Cn P	—	17.00	32.00	65.00	450	—
1877/6Cn G	—	17.00	32.00	65.00	450	—
1877Cn G	—	14.00	27.50	55.00	450	—
1878Cn G	18,000	22.50	42.00	80.00	450	—
1878Cn/Mo D	Inc. above	32.00	62.00	105	450	—
1878Cn D	Inc. above	17.00	37.00	80.00	450	—
1879Cn D	—	14.00	27.50	55.00	450	—
1879Cn D/G	—	14.00	27.50	55.00	450	—
1880/8Cn D	—	17.00	32.00	65.00	450	—
1880Cn D	—	17.00	32.00	65.00	450	—
1881/0Cn D	188,000	17.00	32.00	65.00	450	—
1881Cn D	Inc. above	17.00	32.00	65.00	450	—
1881Cn G	Inc. above	125	175	275	550	—
1882Cn D	—	175	300	500	2,000	—
1882Gn G	—	100	250	300	1,000	—
1883 D	19,000	27.50	82.00	110	500	—
1885Cn M/M/G	—	32.00	62.00	110	500	—
1885/3Cn M/H	9,254	32.00	62.00	110	500	—
1886Cn M/G	7,030	50.00	100	300	1,500	—
1886Cn M	Inc. above	42.00	82.00	160	800	—
1887Cn M	76,000	22.50	42.00	110	450	—
1888Cn M	—	4,000	6,000	—	—	—
1892Cn M	8,200	42.00	82.00	155	650	—

KM# 407.6 50 CENTAVOS
13.5360 g., 0.9027 Silver 0.3928 oz. ASW **Obv:** Facing eagle, snake in beak **Obv. Legend:** REPUBLICA MEXICANA **Rev:** Radiant cap above scales **Mint:** Mexico City

Date	Mintage	F	VF	XF	Unc	BU
1869Mo C	46,000	17.00	37.00	100	600	—
1870Mo C	52,000	17.00	32.00	95.00	550	—
1871Mo M/C	Inc. above	37.00	77.00	155	600	—
1871Mo C	14,000	42.00	77.00	155	650	—
1872Mo M	60,000	37.00	77.00	155	550	—
1872/1Mo M	60,000	37.00	77.00	155	550	—
1873Mo M	6,000	37.00	77.00	155	600	—
1874/3Mo M	—	200	400	600	1,250	—
1874/2Mo B	—	17.00	32.00	80.00	500	—
1874/2Mo B/M	—	17.00	32.00	80.00	500	—
1874/3Mo B/M	—	17.00	32.00	80.00	500	—
1874Mo B	—	17.00	32.00	80.00	500	—
1875Mo B	—	17.00	32.00	80.00	550	—
1876Mo B	—	14.00	27.50	80.00	500	—
1876/5Mo B	—	17.00	32.00	80.00	500	—
1877Mo M	—	17.00	32.00	95.00	500	—
1877/2Mo M	—	22.50	42.00	105	550	—
1878Mo M	Inc. above	17.00	37.00	105	550	—
1878/7Mo M	8,000	27.50	52.00	130	600	—
1879Mo M	—	27.50	52.00	130	550	—
1880Mo M	—	100	150	250	750	—
1881Mo M	16,000	27.50	52.00	130	600	—
1881/0Mo M	—	32.00	52.00	130	600	—
1882/1Mo M	2,000	32.00	62.00	155	750	—
1883/2Mo M	4,000	150	225	350	1,000	—
1884Mo M	—	150	225	350	1,000	—
1885Mo M	12,000	32.00	62.00	155	600	—
1886Mo M	Inc. above	14.00	27.50	80.00	450	—
1886/5Mo M	66,000	17.00	37.00	95.00	475	—
1887Mo M	—	17.00	37.00	80.00	475	—
1887/6Mo M	88,000	17.00	37.00	95.00	475	—
1888Mo M	—	3,000	4,000	6,000	—	—

KM# 407.3 50 CENTAVOS
13.5360 g., 0.9030 Silver 0.3930 oz. ASW **Obv:** Facing eagle, snake in beak **Obv. Legend:** REPUBLICA MEXICANA **Rev:** Radiant cap above scales **Mint:** Durango

SECOND REPUBLIC

KM# 408 PESO

27.0730 g., 0.9030 Silver 0.7860 oz. ASW **Obv:** Facing eagle, snake in beak **Rev:** Radiant cap above scales **Mint:** Chihuahua

Date	Mintage	F	VF	XF	Unc	BU
1872CH P/M	747,000	750	1,500	3,500	—	—
1872CH P	Inc. above	350	700	1,500	—	—
1872/1CH M	Inc. above	35.00	55.00	100	525	—
1872CH M	Inc. above	27.50	38.50	70.00	325	—
1873CH M	320,000	30.00	44.00	85.00	350	—
1873CH M/P	Inc. above	35.00	55.00	100	450	—

KM# 408.1 PESO

27.0730 g., 0.9030 Silver 0.7860 oz. ASW **Obv:** Facing eagle, snake in beak **Rev:** Radiant cap above scales **Mint:** Culiacan

Date	Mintage	F	VF	XF	Unc
1870Cn E	—	49.50	95.00	185	650
1871Cn P	Inc. above	27.50	49.50	95.00	400
1871/11Cn P	478,000	33.00	55.00	125	575
1872/1Cn P	—	27.50	49.50	95.00	400
1872Cn P	209,000	27.50	49.50	95.00	400
1873Cn P Narrow date	527,000	27.50	49.50	95.00	400
1873Cn P Wide date	Inc. above	27.50	49.50	95.00	400

KM# 408.2 PESO

27.0730 g., 0.9027 Silver 0.7857 oz. ASW **Obv:** Facing eagle, snake in beak **Obv. Legend:** REPUBLICA MEXICANA **Rev:** Radiant cap above scales **Mint:** Durango

Date	Mintage	F	VF	XF	Unc	BU
1870Do P	—	60.00	115	215	575	—
1871Do P	427,000	35.00	65.00	100	400	—
1872Do P	296,000	30.00	50.00	100	450	—
1872Do PT	Inc. above	110	195	300	1,100	—
1873Do P	203,000	35.00	60.00	115	450	—

KM# 408.3 PESO

27.0730 g., 0.9030 Silver 0.7860 oz. ASW **Obv:** Facing eagle, snake in beak **Obv. Legend:** REPUBLICA MEXICANA **Rev:** Radiant cap above scales **Mint:** Guadalajara

Date	Mintage	F	VF	XF	Unc	BU
1870Ga C	—	850	1,100	—	—	—
1871Ga C	829,000	37.00	85.00	175	775	—
1872Ga C	485,000	50.00	110	220	850	—
1873/2Ga C	277,000	50.00	110	220	900	—
1873Ga C	Inc. above	37.00	85.00	175	775	—

KM# 408.4 PESO

27.0730 g., 0.9027 Silver 0.7857 oz. ASW **Obv:** Facing eagle, snake in beak **Obv. Legend:** REPUBLICA MEXICANA **Rev:** Radiant cap above scales **Mint:** Guanajuato

Date	Mintage	F	VF	XF	Unc	BU
1871/0Go S	3,946,000	35.00	60.00	115	450	—
1871/3Go S	Inc. above	26.00	44.00	90.00	350	—
1871Go S	Inc. above	BV	27.50	55.00	285	—
1872Go S	4,067,000	BV	27.50	55.00	325	—
1873/2Go S	1,560,000	26.00	33.00	65.00	325	—
1873Go S	Inc. above	BV	27.50	60.00	325	—
1873Go/Mo/S/M	Inc. above	BV	27.50	60.00	325	—

KM# 408.5 PESO

27.0730 g., 0.9030 Silver 0.7860 oz. ASW **Obv:** Facing eagle, snake in beak **Rev:** Radiant cap above scales **Mint:** Mexico City

Date	Mintage	F	VF	XF	Unc	BU
1869Mo C	—	50.00	90.00	180	775	—
1870Mo C	Inc. above	26.00	36.00	65.00	325	—
1870Mo M	Inc. above	30.00	47.25	100	400	—
1870Mo M/C	Inc. above	30.00	47.25	100	400	—
1870/69Mo C	5,115,000	27.50	42.00	85.00	350	—
1871Mo M	Inc. above	26.00	36.00	65.00	325	—
1871/0Mo M	6,974,000	27.50	42.00	85.00	350	—
1872/1Mo M	—	27.50	41.50	80.00	350	—
1872/1Mo M/C	4,801,000	27.50	41.50	80.00	350	—
1872Mo M	Inc. above	26.00	36.00	65.00	325	—
1873Mo M	1,765,000	26.00	36.00	65.00	325	—

Note: The 1869 C with large LEY on the scroll is a pattern

Date	Mintage	F	VF	XF	Unc	BU
1903Cn FV	Inc. above	40.00	80.00	175	425	—
1904Cn MH	1,554,000	28.00	30.00	44.00	145	—
1904Cn RP	Inc. above	80.00	160	265	650	—
1905Cn RP	598,000	40.00	80.00	175	475	—

KM# 410.2 PESO
1.6920 g., 0.8750 Gold 0.0476 oz. AGW **Obv:** Facing eagle, snake in beak **Obv. Legend:** REPUBLICA MEXICANA **Rev:** Value within 1/2 wreath **Mint:** Culiacan

Date	Mintage	F	VF	XF	Unc	BU
1873Cn P	1,221	105	125	165	250	—
1875Cn P	—	115	150	165	250	—
1878Cn G	248	130	200	240	500	—
1879Cn D	—	130	175	215	475	—
1881/0Cn D	338	130	175	215	475	—
1882Cn D	340	130	175	215	475	—
1883Cn D	—	130	175	215	475	—
1884Cn M	—	130	175	215	475	—
1886/4Cn M	277	130	175	240	500	—
1888/7Cn M	2,586	130	175	215	450	—
1888Cn M	Inc. above	95.00	125	165	265	—
1889Cn M Rare	—	—	—	—	—	—
1891/89Cn M	969	105	125	165	275	—
1892Cn M	780	105	125	165	275	—
1893Cn M	498	115	150	165	275	—
1894Cn M	493	110	150	165	275	—
1895Cn M	1,143	95.00	125	165	250	350
1896/5Cn M	1,028	95.00	125	165	250	350
1897Cn M	785	95.00	125	165	250	350
1898Cn M	3,521	95.00	125	165	225	325
1898Cn/MoM	Inc. above	95.00	125	165	250	350
1899Cn Q	2,000	95.00	125	165	225	325
1901Cn Q	Inc. above	90.00	110	150	225	325
1901/0Cn Q	2,350	90.00	110	150	225	325
1902Cn Q	2,480	90.00	110	150	225	325
1902Cn/MoQ/C	Inc. above	90.00	110	150	225	325
1904Cn H	3,614	90.00	110	150	225	325
1904Cn/Mo/ H	Inc. above	90.00	110	150	250	350
1905Cn P	1,000	—	—	—	—	—

Note: Reported, not confirmed

KM# 410.3 PESO
1.6920 g., 0.8750 Gold 0.0476 oz. AGW **Obv:** Facing eagle, snake in beak **Obv. Legend:** REPUBLICA MEXICANA **Rev:** Value within 1/2 wreath **Mint:** Guanajuato

Date	Mintage	F	VF	XF	Unc	BU
1870Go S	—	130	150	165	265	—
1871Go S	500	130	200	240	475	—
1888Go R	210	165	225	265	550	—
1890Go R	1,916	100	125	165	265	—
1892Go R	533	130	175	190	350	—
1894Go R	180	195	225	265	550	—
1895Go R	676	130	175	190	325	—
1896/5Go R	4,671	85.00	125	165	250	—
1897/6Go R	4,280	85.00	125	165	250	—
1897Go R	Inc. above	85.00	125	165	250	—
1898Go R	5,193	85.00	125	165	250	750
Note: Regular obverse						
1898Go R	Inc. above	100	125	165	250	750
Note: Mule, 5 Centavos obverse, normal reverse						
1899Go R	2,748	85.00	125	165	250	—
1900/800Go R	864	100	150	165	285	—

KM# 408.6 PESO
27.0730 g., 0.9030 Silver 0.7860 oz. ASW **Obv:** Facing eagle, snake in beak **Obv. Legend:** REPUBLICA MEXICANA **Rev:** Radiant cap above scales **Mint:** Oaxaca

Date	Mintage	F	VF	XF	Unc	BU
1869Oa E	—	300	450	725	2,600	—
1870Oa E Small A	Inc. above	26.00	44.00	100	525	—
1870OA E Large A	Inc. above	110	165	350	1,150	—
1871/69Oa E	140,000	42.00	65.00	160	725	—
1871Oa E Small A	Inc. above	27.50	44.00	85.00	400	—
1871Oa E Large A	Inc. above	27.50	44.00	100	525	—
1872Oa E Small A	180,000	27.50	44.00	100	525	—
1872Oa E Large A	Inc. above	60.00	110	240	575	—
1873Oa E	105,000	27.50	44.00	100	450	—

KM# 409 PESO
27.0730 g., 0.9030 Silver 0.7860 oz. ASW, 39 mm. **Obv:** Facing eagle, snake in beak **Rev:** Radiant cap **Mint:** Culiacan

Date	Mintage	F	VF	XF	Unc	BU
1898Cn/MoAM	Inc. above	28.00	40.00	110	185	—
1898Cn AM	1,720,000	28.00	30.00	55.00	120	—
1899Cn AM	1,722,000	32.50	55.00	110	215	—
1899Cn JQ	Inc. above	28.00	30.00	70.00	155	—
1900Cn JQ	1,804,000	28.00	30.00	55.00	120	—
1901Cn JQ	1,473,000	28.00	30.00	65.00	160	—
1902Cn JQ	1,194,000	28.00	30.00	75.00	240	—
1903Cn JQ	1,514,000	28.00	30.00	55.00	160	—

SECOND REPUBLIC

KM# 410.4 PESO
1.6920 g., 0.8750 Gold 0.0476 oz. AGW **Obv:**
Facing eagle, snake in beak **Obv. Legend:**
REPUBLICA MEXICANA **Rev:** Value within 1/2
wreath **Mint:** Hermosillo

Date	Mintage	F	VF	XF	Unc
1875Ho R Rare	310	—	—	—	—
1876Ho F Rare		—	—	—	—
1888Ho G/MoM Rare		—	—	—	—

KM# 410.5 PESO
1.6920 g., 0.8750 Gold 0.0476 oz. AGW **Obv:**
Facing eagle, snake in beak **Obv. Legend:**
REPUBLICA MEXICANA **Rev:** Value within 1/2
wreath **Mint:** Mexico City

Date	Mintage	F	VF	XF	Unc	BU
1870Mo C	2,540	85.00	95.00	110	185	250
1871Mo M/C	1,000	95.00	120	165	250	250
1872Mo M/C	3,000	85.00	95.00	110	185	300
1873/1Mo M	2,900	85.00	95.00	115	200	250
1873Mo M	Inc. above	85.00	95.00	110	185	250
1874Mo M	—	85.00	95.00	110	185	250
1875Mo B/M	—	85.00	95.00	110	185	250
1876/5Mo B/M	—	85.00	95.00	110	185	250
1877Mo M	—	85.00	95.00	110	185	250
1878Mo M	2,000	85.00	95.00	110	185	250
1879Mo M	—	85.00	95.00	110	185	250
1880/70Mo M	—	85.00	95.00	110	185	250
1881/71Mo M	1,000	85.00	95.00	110	185	250
1882/72Mo M	—	85.00	95.00	110	185	250
1883/72Mo M	1,000	85.00	95.00	110	185	250
1884Mo M	—	85.00	95.00	110	185	250
1885/71Mo M	—	85.00	95.00	110	185	250
1885Mo M	—	85.00	95.00	110	185	250
1886Mo M	1,700	85.00	95.00	110	185	250
1887Mo M	2,200	85.00	95.00	110	185	250
1888Mo M	1,000	85.00	95.00	110	185	250
1889Mo M	500	125	170	215	285	—
1890Mo M	570	125	170	215	285	—
1891Mo M	746	125	170	215	285	—
1892/0Mo M	2,895	85.00	95.00	110	185	250
1893Mo M	5,917	85.00	95.00	110	185	250
1894/3MMo	—	85.00	95.00	110	185	250
1894Mo M	6,244	85.00	95.00	110	185	250
1895Mo M	8,994	85.00	95.00	110	185	250
1895Mo B	Inc. above	85.00	95.00	110	185	250
1896Mo B	7,166	85.00	95.00	110	185	250
1896Mo M	Inc. above	85.00	95.00	110	185	250
1897Mo M	5,131	85.00	95.00	110	185	250
1898/7Mo M	5,368	85.00	95.00	110	185	250
1899Mo M	9,515	85.00	95.00	110	185	250
1900/800Mo M	9,301	85.00	95.00	110	185	250
1900/880Mo M	Inc. above	85.00	95.00	110	185	250
1900/890Mo M	Inc. above	85.00	95.00	110	185	250
1900Mo M	Inc. above	85.00	95.00	110	185	250
1901Mo M Small date	Inc. above	90.00	100	115	205	270
1901/801Mo M Large date	8,293	90.00	100	115	205	270
1902Mo M Large date	11,000	90.00	100	115	205	270
1902Mo M Small date	Inc. above	90.00	100	115	205	270
1903Mo M Large date	10,000	90.00	100	115	205	270
1903Mo M Small date	Inc. above	90.00	100	145	220	325

Date	Mintage	F	VF	XF	Unc	BU
1904Mo M	9,845	90.00	100	115	205	270
1905Mo M	3,429	90.00	100	115	205	270

KM# 410.6 PESO
1.6920 g., 0.8750 Gold 0.0476 oz. AGW **Obv:**
Facing eagle, snake in beak **Obv. Legend:**
REPUBLICA MEXICANA **Rev:** Value within 1/2
wreath **Mint:** Zacatecas

Date	Mintage	F	VF	XF	Unc	BU
1872Zs H	2,024	155	175	190	295	—
1875/3Zs A	—	155	175	215	350	—
1878Zs S	—	155	175	190	295	—
1888Zs Z	280	205	250	350	725	—
1889Zs Z	492	180	200	240	475	—
1890Zs Z	738	180	200	240	475	—

KM# 409.3 PESO
27.0730 g., 0.9030 Silver 0.7860 oz. ASW, 39 mm.
Obv: Facing eagle, snake in beak **Rev:** Radiant cap
Mint: Zacatecas **Note:** Mint mark Zs. Varieties exist.

Date	Mintage	F	VF	XF	Unc	BU
1898Zs FZ	5,714,000	27.50	32.50	49.50	130	—
1899Zs FZ	5,618,000	27.50	32.50	49.50	140	—
1900Zs FZ	5,357,000	27.50	32.50	49.50	140	—
1901Zs FZ	Inc. above	28.00	30.00	36.00	110	—
1901Zs AZ	5,706,000	4,000	6,000	11,000	—	—
1902Zs FZ	7,134,000	28.00	30.00	36.00	110	—
1903/2Zs FZ	3,080,000	28.00	30.00	90.00	240	—
1903Zs FZ	Inc. above	28.00	30.00	37.00	125	—
1904Zs FZ	2,423,000	28.00	30.00	50.00	160	—
1904Zs FM	Inc. above	28.00	30.00	45.00	145	—
1905Zs FM	995,000	32.00	65.00	110	290	—

KM# 408.7 PESO
27.0730 g., 0.9030 Silver 0.7860 oz. ASW **Obv:**
Facing eagle, snake in beak **Rev:** Radiant cap above
scales **Mint:** San Luis Potosi **Note:** Varieties exist.

Date	Mintage	F	VF	XF	Unc	BU
1870Pi S	1,967,000	220	375	600	1,300	—
1870Pi S/A	Inc. above	220	375	650	1,550	—
1870Pi G	Inc. above	37.00	55.00	100	725	—
1870Pi H	Inc. above	—	—	—	—	—
Note: Contemporary counterfeits						
1870Pi O/G	Inc. above	37.00	55.00	100	725	—
1870Pi O	Inc. above	30.00	44.00	130	525	—
1871Pi O	—	27.50	44.00	85.00	650	—
1871Pi O/G	Inc. above	27.50	44.00	85.00	650	—
1871/69Pi O	2,103,000	90.00	120	265	650	—
1872Pi O	1,873,000	27.50	44.00	85.00	650	—
1873Pi H	Inc. above	27.50	44.00	85.00	650	—
1873Pi O	893,000	27.50	44.00	85.00	650	—

SECOND REPUBLIC

KM# 408.8 PESO
27.0730 g., 0.9030 Silver 0.7860 oz. ASW **Obv:** Facing eagle, snake in beak **Rev:** Radiant cap above scales **Mint:** Zacatecas **Note:** Varieties exist.

Date	Mintage	F	VF	XF	Unc	BU
1870Zs H	4,519,000	27.00	47.00	65.00	285	—
1871Zs H	4,459,000	26.00	36.00	65.00	285	—
1872Zs H	4,039,000	26.00	36.00	65.00	285	—
1873/1Zs H	Inc. above	26.00	36.00	65.00	285	—
1873Zs H	1,782,000	26.00	36.00	65.00	285	—

KM# 409.1 PESO
27.0730 g., 0.9030 Silver 0.7860 oz. ASW, 39 mm. **Obv:** Facing eagle, snake in beak **Rev:** Radiant cap **Mint:** Guanajuato **Note:** Varieties exist.

Date	Mintage	F	VF	XF	Unc	BU
1898Go/MoRS	Inc. above	27.50	35.00	70.00	150	—
1898Go RS	4,256,000	BV	26.00	47.00	100	—
1899Go RS	3,207,000	BV	26.00	42.00	95.00	—
1900Go RS	1,489,000	32.50	55.00	120	300	—

KM# 409.2 PESO
27.0730 g., 0.9027 Silver 0.7857 oz. ASW, 39 mm. **Obv:** Facing eagle, snake in beak **Obv. Legend:** REPUBLICA MEXICANA **Rev:** Radiant cap **Mint:** Mexico City **Note:** Varieties exist.

Date	Mintage	F	VF	XF	Unc	BU
1898Mo AM	10,250,000	28.00	30.00	35.00	75.00	—
Note: Restrike (1949) - reverse with 134 beads						
1898Mo AM	10,156,000	28.00	30.00	35.00	85.00	—
Note: Original strike - reverse with 139 beads						
1899Mo AM	7,930,000	28.00	30.00	37.00	95.00	—
1900Mo AM	8,226,000	28.00	30.00	37.00	95.00	—
1901Mo AM	14,505,000	28.00	30.00	37.00	80.00	—
1902/1Mo AM	16,224,000	240	475	875	1,800	—
1902Mo AM	Inc. above	28.00	30.00	37.00	130	—
1903Mo AM	22,396,000	28.00	30.00	37.00	130	—
1903Mo MA (Error)	Inc. above	1,500	2,500	3,850	9,000	—
1904Mo AM	14,935,000	28.00	30.00	37.00	130	—
1905Mo AM	3,557,000	28.00	40.00	100	240	—
1908Mo AM	7,575,000	28.00	30.00	37.00	115	—
1908Mo GV	Inc. above	28.00	30.00	37.00	80.00	—
1909Mo GV	2,924,000	28.00	30.00	37.00	80.00	—

KM# 410 PESO
1.6920 g., 0.8750 Gold 0.0476 oz. AGW **Obv:** Facing eagle, snake in beak **Obv. Legend:**

REPUBLICA MEXICANA **Rev:** Value within 1/2 wreath **Mint:** Alamos

Date	Mintage	F	VF	XF	Unc
1888AsL/MoM Rare	—	—	—	—	—
1888As L Rare	—	—	—	—	—

KM# 410.1 PESO
1.6920 g., 0.8750 Gold 0.0476 oz. AGW **Obv:** Facing eagle, snake in beak **Obv. Legend:** REPUBLICA MEXICANA **Rev:** Value within 1/2 wreath **Mint:** Chihuahua

Date	Mintage	F	VF	XF	Unc	BU
1888Ca/MoM Rare	104	—	—	—	—	—

KM# 411.3 2-1/2 PESOS
4.2300 g., 0.8750 Gold 0.1190 oz. AGW **Obv:** Facing eagle, snake in beak **Obv. Legend:** REPUBLICA MEXICANA **Rev:** Value within 1/2 wreath **Mint:** Guanajuato

Date	Mintage	F	VF	XF	Unc	BU
1871Go S	600	1,250	2,000	2,500	3,250	—
1888Go/MoR	110	1,750	2,250	2,750	3,500	—

KM# 411.4 2-1/2 PESOS
4.2300 g., 0.8750 Gold 0.1190 oz. AGW **Obv:** Facing eagle, snake in beak **Obv. Legend:** REPUBLICA MEXICANA **Rev:** Value within 1/2 wreath **Mint:** Hermosillo

Date	Mintage	F	VF	XF	Unc	BU
1874Ho R Rare	—	—	—	—	—	—
1888Ho G Rare	—	—	—	—	—	—

KM# 411.5 2-1/2 PESOS
4.2300 g., 0.8750 Gold 0.1190 oz. AGW **Obv:** Facing eagle, snake in beak **Rev:** Value within 1/2 wreath **Mint:** Mexico City

Date	Mintage	F	VF	XF	Unc	BU
1870Mo C	820	215	300	400	800	—
1872Mo M/C	800	215	300	400	800	—
1873/2Mo M	—	250	400	800	1,400	—
1874Mo M	—	250	400	800	1,400	—
1874Mo B/M	—	250	400	800	1,400	—
1875Mo B	—	250	400	800	1,400	—
1876Mo B	—	300	550	1,050	1,900	—
1877Mo M	—	250	400	800	1,400	—
1878Mo M	400	250	400	800	1,400	—
1879Mo M	—	250	400	800	1,400	—
1880/79Mo M	—	250	400	800	1,400	—
1881Mo M	400	250	400	800	1,400	—

SECOND REPUBLIC

Date	Mintage	F	VF	XF	Unc	BU
1882Mo M	—	275	450	900	1,550	2,000
1883/73Mo M	400	250	400	800	1,400	—
1884Mo M	—	300	550	1,050	1,650	—
1885Mo M	—	450	900	1,800	3,050	—
1886Mo M	400	250	400	800	1,400	—
1887Mo M	400	250	400	800	1,400	—
1888Mo M	540	250	400	800	1,400	—
1889Mo M	240	200	350	575	1,000	—
1890Mo M	420	250	400	800	1,400	—
1891Mo M	188	250	400	800	1,400	—
1892Mo M	240	250	400	800	1,400	—

KM# 411.6 2-1/2 PESOS
4.2300 g., 0.8750 Gold 0.1190 oz. AGW **Obv:**
Facing eagle, snake in beak **Obv. Legend:**
REPUBLICA MEXICANA **Rev:** Value within 1/2
wreath **Mint:** Zacatecas

Date	Mintage	F	VF	XF	Unc	BU
1872Zs H	1,300	250	400	550	1,250	—
1873Zs H	—	225	375	525	950	—
1875/3Zs A	—	250	400	800	1,400	—
1877Zs S	—	250	400	800	1,400	—
1878Zs S	300	250	400	800	1,400	—
1888Zs/MoS	80	350	550	1,050	1,850	—
1889Zs/Mo Z	184	300	500	1,000	1,650	—
1890Zs Z	326	250	400	800	1,400	—

KM# 411 2-1/2 PESOS
4.2300 g., 0.8750 Gold 0.1190 oz. AGW **Obv:**
Facing eagle, snake in beak **Obv. Legend:**
REPUBLICA MEXICANA **Rev:** Value within 1/2
wreath **Mint:** Alamos

Date	Mintage	F	VF	XF	Unc
1888As/MoL Rare	—	—	—	—	—

KM# 411.1 2-1/2 PESOS
4.2300 g., 0.8750 Gold 0.1190 oz. AGW **Obv:**
Facing eagle, snake in beak **Rev:** Value within 1/2
wreath **Mint:** Culiacan

Date	Mintage	F	VF	XF	Unc	BU
1893Cn M	141	1,500	2,000	2,500	3,500	—

KM# 411.2 2-1/2 PESOS
4.2300 g., 0.8750 Gold 0.1190 oz. AGW **Obv:**
Facing eagle, snake in beak **Rev:** Value within 1/2
wreath **Mint:** Durango

Date	Mintage	F	VF	XF	Unc	BU
1888Do C Rare	—	—	—	—	—	—

KM# 412.2 5 PESOS
8.4600 g., 0.8750 Gold 0.2380 oz. AGW **Obv:**
Facing eagle, snake in beak **Obv. Legend:**

REPUBLICA MEXICANA **Rev:** Radiant cap above
scales **Mint:** Culiacan

Date	Mintage	F	VF	XF	Unc	BU
1873Cn P	—	450	750	1,200	2,200	—
1874Cn P	—	—	—	—	—	—
1875Cn P	—	450	650	1,000	1,950	—
1876Cn P	—	450	650	1,000	1,950	—
1877Cn G	—	450	650	1,000	1,950	—
1882Cn Rare	174	—	—	—	—	—
1888Cn M	—	650	1,150	1,450	2,200	—
1890Cn M	435	475	650	950	1,800	—
1891Cn M	1,390	450	550	750	1,200	—
1894Cn M	484	475	650	950	1,800	—
1895Cn M	142	650	900	1,500	2,700	—
1900Cn Q	1,536	450	500	675	1,100	—
1903Cn Q	1,000	450	475	550	1,000	—

KM# 412.3 5 PESOS
8.4600 g., 0.8750 Gold 0.2380 oz. AGW **Obv:**
Facing eagle, snake in beak **Obv. Legend:**
REPUBLICA MEXICANA **Rev:** Radiant cap above
scales **Mint:** Durango

Date	Mintage	F	VF	XF	Unc	BU
1873/2Do P	—	750	1,250	1,850	3,000	—
1877Do P	—	750	1,250	1,850	3,000	—
1878Do E	—	750	1,250	1,850	3,000	—
1879Do B	—	750	1,250	1,850	3,000	—
1879/7Do B	—	750	1,250	1,850	3,000	—

KM# 412.4 5 PESOS
8.4600 g., 0.8750 Gold 0.2380 oz. AGW **Obv:**
Facing eagle, snake in beak **Obv. Legend:**
REPUBLICA MEXICANA **Rev:** Radiant cap above
scales **Mint:** Guanajuato

Date	Mintage	F	VF	XF	Unc	BU
1871Go S	1,600	550	950	1,450	2,450	—
1887Go R	140	750	1,350	1,750	3,200	—
1888Go R Rare	65	—	—	—	—	—
1893Go R Rare	16	—	—	—	—	—

KM# 412 5 PESOS
8.4600 g., 0.8750 Gold 0.2380 oz. AGW **Obv:**
Facing eagle, snake in beak **Obv. Legend:**
REPUBLICA MEXICANA **Rev:** Radiant cap above
scales **Mint:** Alamos

Date	Mintage	F	VF	XF	Unc	BU
1875As L	—	—	—	—	—	—
1878As L	383	900	1,700	3,000	4,500	—

SECOND REPUBLIC

KM# 412.6 5 PESOS
8.4600 g., 0.8750 Gold 0.2380 oz. AGW **Obv:**
Facing eagle, snake in beak **Obv. Legend:**
REPUBLICA MEXICANA **Rev:** Radiant cap above
scales **Mint:** Mexico City

Date	Mintage	F	VF	XF	Unc	BU
1870Mo C	550	475	550	750	1,650	—
1871/69Mo M	1,600	475	525	600	850	—
1871Mo M	Inc. above	475	525	600	850	—
1872Mo M	1,600	475	525	600	850	—
1873/2Mo M	—	475	550	700	1,000	—
1874Mo M	—	475	550	700	1,000	—
1875/3Mo B/M	—	475	550	700	1,100	—
1875Mo B	—	475	550	700	1,100	—
1876/5Mo B/M	—	475	550	700	1,150	—
1877Mo M	—	475	600	900	1,800	—
1878/7Mo M	400	475	550	700	1,400	—
1878Mo M	Inc. above	475	550	700	1,400	—
1879/8Mo M	—	475	550	700	1,400	—
1880Mo M	—	475	550	700	1,400	—
1881Mo M	—	475	550	700	1,400	—
1882Mo M	200	475	600	900	1,800	—
1883Mo M	200	475	600	900	1,800	—
1884Mo M	—	475	600	900	1,800	—
1886Mo M	200	475	600	900	1,800	—
1887Mo M	200	475	600	900	1,800	—
1888Mo M	250	475	550	700	1,800	—
1889Mo M	190	475	600	900	1,800	—
1890Mo M	149	475	600	900	1,800	—
1891Mo M	156	475	600	900	1,800	—
1892Mo M	214	475	600	900	1,800	—
1893Mo M	1,058	450	550	650	950	—
1897Mo M	370	475	550	700	1,150	—
1898Mo M	376	475	550	700	1,150	—
1900Mo M	1,014	450	475	500	850	1,200
1901Mo M	1,071	450	475	500	850	1,300
1902Mo M	1,478	450	475	500	850	1,300
1903Mo M	1,162	450	475	500	850	1,300
1904Mo M	1,415	450	475	500	850	1,300
1905Mo M	563	450	500	600	1,550	2,050

KM# 412.7 5 PESOS
8.4600 g., 0.8750 Gold 0.2380 oz. AGW **Obv:**
Facing eagle, snake in beak **Obv. Legend:**
REPUBLICA MEXICANA **Rev:** Radiant cap above
scales **Mint:** Zacatecas

Date	Mintage	F	VF	XF	Unc	BU
1874Zs A	—	475	650	900	1,650	—
1875Zs A	—	450	550	650	1,150	—
1877Zs S/A	—	450	550	700	1,150	—
1878/7Zs S/A	—	450	550	700	1,150	—
1883Zs S	—	425	450	600	900	—
1888Zs Z	70	1,150	1,650	2,150	3,150	—
1889Zs Z	373	425	450	650	1,000	—
1892Zs Z	1,229	425	450	600	900	1,400

KM# 412.1 5 PESOS
8.4600 g., 0.8750 Gold 0.2380 oz. AGW **Obv:**
Facing eagle, snake in beak **Obv. Legend:**
REPUBLICA MEXICANA **Rev:** Radiant cap above
scales **Mint:** Chihuahua

Date	Mintage	F	VF	XF	Unc	BU
1888Ca M Rare	120	—	—	—	—	—

KM# 412.5 5 PESOS
8.4600 g., 0.8750 Gold 0.2380 oz. AGW **Obv:**
Facing eagle, snake in beak **Obv. Legend:**
REPUBLICA MEXICANA **Rev:** Radiant cap above
scales **Mint:** Hermosillo

Date	Mintage	F	VF	XF	Unc	BU
1874Ho R	—	1,950	2,700	3,200	4,700	—
1877Ho A	Inc. above	700	1,350	1,950	2,950	—
1877Ho R	990	800	1,150	1,800	2,800	—
1888Ho G Rare	—	—	—	—	—	—

KM# 413.2 10 PESOS
16.9200 g., 0.8750 Gold 0.4760 oz. AGW **Obv:**
Facing eagle, snake in beak **Obv. Legend:**
REPUBLICA MEXICANA **Rev:** Radiant cap above
scales **Mint:** Culiacan

Date	Mintage	F	VF	XF	Unc	BU
1881Cn D	—	875	900	1,300	2,050	—
1882Cn D	874	875	900	1,300	2,050	—
1882Cn E	Inc. above	875	900	1,300	2,050	—
1883Cn D	221	—	—	—	—	—
1883Cn D	Inc. above	875	900	1,300	2,050	—
1884Cn D	—	875	900	1,300	2,050	—
1884Cn M	—	875	900	1,300	2,050	—
1885Cn M	1,235	875	900	1,300	2,050	—
1886Cn M	981	875	900	1,300	2,050	—
1887Cn M	2,289	875	900	1,300	2,050	—
1888Cn M	767	875	900	1,300	2,050	—
1889Cn M	859	875	900	1,300	2,050	—
1890Cn M	1,427	875	900	1,300	2,050	—
1891Cn M	670	875	900	1,300	2,050	—
1892Cn M	379	875	900	1,300	2,050	—
1893Cn M	1,806	875	900	1,300	2,050	—
1895Cn M	179	900	1,300	1,800	2,800	—
1903Cn Q	774	875	950	1,100	2,100	—

SECOND REPUBLIC

KM# 413.3 10 PESOS
16.9200 g., 0.8750 Gold 0.4760 oz. AGW **Obv:**
Facing eagle, snake in beak **Obv. Legend:**
REPUBLICA MEXICANA **Rev:** Radiant cap above
scales **Mint:** Durango

Date	Mintage	F	VF	XF	Unc	BU
1872Do P	1,755	875	950	1,100	1,550	—
1873/2Do P	1,091	875	950	1,150	1,650	—
1873/2Do M/P	Inc. above	875	950	1,200	1,750	—
1874Do M	—	875	950	1,200	1,750	—
1875Do M	—	875	950	1,200	1,750	—
1876Do M	—	900	1,050	1,550	2,300	—
1877Do P	—	875	950	1,200	1,750	—
1878Do E	582	875	950	1,200	1,750	—
1879/8Do B	—	875	950	1,200	1,750	—
1879Do B	—	875	950	1,200	1,750	—
1880Do P	2,030	875	950	1,200	1,750	4,050
1881/79Do P	2,617	875	950	1,200	1,750	—
1882Do P Rare	1,528	—	—	—	—	—
1882Do C	Inc. above	875	950	1,200	1,750	—
1883Do C	793	900	1,050	1,550	2,300	—
1884Do C	108	900	1,050	1,550	2,300	—

KM# 413.4 10 PESOS
16.9200 g., 0.8750 Gold 0.4760 oz. AGW **Obv:**
Facing eagle, snake in beak **Obv. Legend:**
REPUBLICA MEXICANA **Rev:** Radiant cap above
scales **Mint:** Guadalajara

Date	Mintage	F	VF	XF	Unc	BU
1870Ga C	490	875	1,100	1,250	2,100	—
1871Ga C	1,910	875	1,100	1,500	2,600	—
1872Ga C	780	900	1,250	2,250	2,850	—
1873Ga C	422	900	1,250	2,250	3,350	—
1874/3Ga C	477	900	1,250	2,250	3,350	—
1875Ga C	710	900	1,250	2,250	3,350	—
1878Ga A	183	925	1,450	2,750	3,850	—
1879Ga A	200	925	1,450	2,750	3,850	—
1880Ga S	404	900	1,250	2,250	3,350	—
1881Ga S	239	925	1,450	2,750	3,850	—
1891Ga S	196	925	1,450	2,750	3,850	—

KM# 413.5 10 PESOS
16.9200 g., 0.8750 Gold 0.4760 oz. AGW **Obv:**
Facing eagle, snake in beak **Obv. Legend:**

Date	Mintage	F	VF	XF	Unc	BU
1872Go S	1,400	2,000	4,000	6,500	10,000	—
1887Go R Rare	80	—	—	—	—	—

Note: Stack's Rio Grande Sale 6-93, P/L AU realized,
$12,650

1888Go R Rare	68	—	—	—	—	—

KM# 413.6 10 PESOS
16.9200 g., 0.8750 Gold 0.4760 oz. AGW **Obv:**
Facing eagle, snake in beak **Obv. Legend:**
REPUBLICA MEXICANA **Rev:** Radiant cap above
scales **Mint:** Hermosillo

Date	Mintage	F	VF	XF	Unc	BU
1874Ho R Rare	—	—	—	—	—	—
1876Ho F Rare	357	—	—	—	—	—
1878Ho A	814	1,750	3,000	3,500	5,500	—
1879Ho A	—	1,000	2,000	2,500	4,000	—
1880Ho A	—	1,000	2,000	2,500	4,000	—
1881Ho A Rare	—	—	—	—	—	—

Note: American Numismatic Rarities Eliasberg sale 4-05,
MS-62 realized $34,500.

KM# 413.7 10 PESOS
16.9200 g., 0.8750 Gold 0.4760 oz. AGW **Obv:**
Facing eagle, snake in beak **Obv. Legend:**
REPUBLICA MEXICANA **Rev:** Radiant cap above
scales **Mint:** Mexico City

Date	Mintage	F	VF	XF	Unc	BU
1870Mo C	480	875	1,200	1,500	2,300	—
1872/1Mo M/C	2,100	875	900	1,200	1,650	—
1873Mo M	—	875	900	1,250	1,750	—
1874/3Mo M	—	875	900	1,250	1,750	—
1875Mo B/M	—	875	900	1,250	1,750	—
1876Mo B Rare	—	—	—	—	—	—
1878Mo M	300	875	900	1,250	1,750	—
1879Mo M	—	—	—	—	—	—
1881Mo M	100	900	1,300	1,900	2,800	—
1882Mo M	—	875	900	1,250	1,750	—
1883Mo M	100	900	1,300	1,900	2,800	—
1884Mo M	—	900	1,300	1,900	2,800	—
1885Mo M	—	875	900	1,250	1,750	—
1886Mo M	100	900	1,300	1,900	2,800	—
1887Mo M	100	900	1,300	1,950	3,050	—
1888Mo M	144	875	1,050	1,500	2,300	—
1889Mo M	88	900	1,300	1,900	2,800	—
1890Mo M	137	900	1,300	1,900	2,800	—
1891Mo M	133	900	1,300	1,900	2,800	—
1892Mo M	45	900	1,300	1,900	2,800	—
1893Mo M	1,361	875	900	1,200	1,650	—
1897Mo M	239	875	900	1,250	1,750	—
1898/7Mo M	244	875	925	1,300	2,050	—
1900Mo M	733	875	900	1,250	1,750	—
1901Mo M	562	875	900	950	1,600	—
1902Mo M	719	875	900	950	1,600	2,600
1903Mo M	713	875	900	950	1,600	2,600

Date	Mintage	F	VF	XF	Unc	BU
1904Mo M	694	875	900	950	1,600	—
1905Mo M	401	875	900	1,100	1,800	—

Date	Mintage	F	VF	XF	Unc	BU
1888Zs Z	4,810	875	925	1,250	1,750	—
1889Zs Z	6,154	850	875	1,050	1,550	—
1890Zs Z	1,321	850	925	1,250	1,750	—
1891Zs Z	1,930	850	925	1,250	1,750	3,550
1892Zs Z	1,882	850	925	1,250	1,750	—
1893Zs Z	2,899	850	925	1,250	1,750	—
1894Zs Z	2,501	850	925	1,250	1,750	—
1895Zs Z	1,217	850	925	1,250	1,750	—

KM# 413.8   10 PESOS
16.9200 g., 0.8750 Gold 0.4760 oz. AGW **Obv:**
Facing eagle, snake in beak **Obv. Legend:**
REPUBLICA MEXICANA **Rev:** Radiant cap above
scales **Mint:** Oaxaca

Date	Mintage	F	VF	XF	Unc	BU
1870Oa E	4,614	850	900	1,200	1,900	—
1871Oa E	2,705	850	900	1,250	1,950	—
1872Oa E	5,897	850	900	1,150	1,800	—
1873Oa E	3,537	850	900	1,150	1,800	—
1874Oa E	2,205	875	950	1,500	2,150	—
1875Oa E	312	875	1,050	1,700	2,550	—
1876Oa E	766	875	1,050	1,700	2,550	—
1877Oa E	463	875	1,050	1,700	2,550	—
1878Oa E	229	875	1,050	1,700	2,550	—
1879Oa E	210	875	1,050	1,700	2,550	—
1880Oa E	238	875	1,050	1,700	2,550	—
1881Oa E	961	875	950	1,500	2,300	—
1882Oa E	170	900	1,300	1,800	2,800	—
1883Oa E	111	900	1,300	1,800	2,800	—
1884Oa E	325	875	1,050	1,700	2,550	—
1885Oa E	370	875	1,050	1,700	2,550	—
1886Oa E	400	875	1,050	1,700	2,550	—
1887Oa E	—	1,000	1,550	2,550	4,300	—
1888Oa E	—	—	—	—	—	—

KM# 413   10 PESOS
16.9200 g., 0.8750 Gold 0.4760 oz. AGW **Obv:**
Facing eagle, snake in beak **Obv. Legend:**
REPUBLICA MEXICANA **Rev:** Radiant cap above
scales **Mint:** Alamos

Date	Mintage	F	VF	XF	Unc	BU
1874As DL Rare	—	—	—	—	—	—
1875As L	642	950	1,500	2,750	3,850	—
1878As L	977	900	1,250	2,250	3,350	—
1879As L	1,078	900	1,250	2,250	3,350	—
1880As L	2,629	900	1,250	2,250	3,350	—
1881As L	2,574	900	1,250	2,250	3,350	—
1882As L	3,403	900	1,250	2,250	3,350	—
1883As L	3,597	900	1,250	2,250	3,350	—
1884As L Rare	—	—	—	—	—	—
1885As L	4,562	900	1,250	2,250	3,350	—
1886As L	4,643	900	1,250	2,250	3,350	—
1887As L	3,667	900	1,250	2,250	3,350	—
1888As L	4,521	900	1,250	2,250	3,350	—
1889As L	5,615	900	1,250	2,250	3,350	—
1890As L	4,920	900	1,250	2,250	3,350	—
1891As L	568	900	1,250	2,250	3,350	—
1892As L	—	—	—	—	—	—
1893As L	817	900	1,250	2,250	3,350	—
1894/3As L	1,658	—	—	—	—	—
1894As L	Inc. above	900	1,250	2,250	3,350	—
1895As L	1,237	900	1,250	2,250	3,350	—

KM# 413.9   10 PESOS
16.9200 g., 0.8750 Gold 0.4760 oz. AGW **Obv:**
Facing eagle, snake in beak **Obv. Legend:**
REPUBLICA MEXICANA **Rev:** Radiant cap above
scales **Mint:** Zacatecas

Date	Mintage	F	VF	XF	Unc	BU
1871Zs H	2,000	850	900	1,100	1,550	—
1872Zs H	3,092	850	900	1,050	1,450	—
1873Zs H	936	875	925	1,250	1,750	—
1874Zs H	—	875	925	1,250	1,750	—
1875/3Zs A	—	875	950	1,300	2,050	—
1876/5Zs S	—	875	950	1,300	2,050	—
1877Zs S/H	506	875	950	1,300	2,050	—
1878Zs S	711	875	950	1,300	2,050	—
1879/8Zs S	—	900	1,050	1,700	2,550	—
1879Zs S	—	900	1,050	1,700	2,550	—
1880Zs S	2,089	875	925	1,250	1,750	—
1881Zs S	736	875	950	1,300	2,050	—
1882/1Zs Z	—	875	950	1,300	2,050	2,800
1882Zs S	1,599	875	925	1,250	1,750	—
1883/2Zs S	256	875	950	1,300	2,050	—
1884/3Zs S	—	875	925	1,250	1,900	—
1884Zs S	—	875	925	1,250	1,900	—
1885Zs S	1,588	875	925	1,250	1,750	—
1886Zs S	5,364	875	925	1,250	1,750	—
1887Zs Z	2,330	875	925	1,250	1,750	—

KM# 413.1   10 PESOS
16.9200 g., 0.8750 Gold 0.4760 oz. AGW **Obv:**
Facing eagle, snake in beak **Obv. Legend:**
REPUBLICA MEXICANA **Rev:** Radiant cap above
scales **Mint:** Chihuahua

Date	Mintage	F	VF	XF	Unc	BU
1888Ca M	175	—	—	7,500	—	—

KM# 414   20 PESOS
33.8400 g., 0.8750 Gold 0.9519 oz. AGW **Obv:**
Facing eagle, snake in beak **Rev:** Radiant cap above
scales **Mint:** Alamos

Date	Mintage	F	VF	XF	Unc	BU
1876As L Rare	276	—	—	—	—	—
1877As L Rare	166	—	—	—	—	—
1878As L	—	—	—	—	—	—
1888As L Rare	—	—	—	—	—	—

SECOND REPUBLIC

KM# 414.2 20 PESOS
33.8400 g., 0.8750 Gold 0.9519 oz. AGW **Obv:** Facing eagle, snake in beak **Obv. Legend:** REPUBLICA MEXICANA **Rev:** Radiant cap above scales **Mint:** Culiacan

Date	Mintage	F	VF	XF	Unc	BU
1870Cn E	3,749	BV	1,750	1,850	2,950	—
1871Cn P	3,046	BV	1,750	1,850	2,950	—
1872Cn P	972	BV	1,750	1,850	2,950	—
1873Cn P	1,317	BV	1,750	1,850	2,950	—
1874Cn P	—	BV	1,750	1,850	2,950	—
1875Cn P	—	1,750	2,000	2,750	3,500	—
1876Cn P	—	BV	1,750	1,850	2,950	—
1876Cn G	—	BV	1,750	1,850	2,950	—
1877Cn G	167	1,750	1,850	2,200	3,200	—
1878Cn Rare	842	—	—	—	—	—
1881/0Cn D	2,039	—	—	—	—	—
1881Cn D	Inc. above	BV	1,750	1,850	2,950	—
1882/1Cn D	736	BV	1,750	1,850	2,950	—
1883Cn M	1,836	BV	1,750	1,850	2,950	—
1884Cn M	—	BV	1,750	1,850	2,950	—
1885Cn M	544	BV	1,750	1,850	2,950	—
1886Cn M	882	BV	1,750	1,850	2,950	—
1887Cn M	837	BV	1,750	1,850	2,950	—
1888Cn M	473	BV	1,750	1,850	2,950	—
1889Cn M	1,376	BV	1,750	1,850	2,950	—
1890Cn M	—	1,750	2,450	4,600	11,500	—
1891Cn M	237	BV	1,800	2,000	3,200	—
1892Cn M	526	BV	1,750	1,850	2,950	—
1893Cn M	2,062	BV	1,750	1,850	2,950	—
1894Cn M	4,516	BV	1,750	1,850	2,950	—
1895Cn M	3,193	BV	1,750	1,850	2,950	—
1896Cn M	4,072	BV	1,750	1,850	2,950	—
1897/6Cn M	959	BV	1,750	1,850	2,950	—
1897Cn M	Inc. above	BV	1,750	1,850	2,950	—
1898Cn M	1,660	BV	1,750	1,850	2,950	—
1899Cn M	1,243	BV	1,750	1,850	2,950	—
1899Cn Q	Inc. above	BV	1,800	2,000	3,200	—
1900Cn Q	1,558	BV	1,750	1,850	2,950	—
1901Cn Q	1,496	BV	1,750	1,850	2,950	—
1901/0Cn Q	Inc. above	—	—	—	—	—
1902Cn Q	1,059	BV	1,750	1,850	2,950	—
1903Cn Q	1,121	BV	1,750	1,850	2,950	—
1904Cn H	4,646	BV	1,750	1,700	2,950	—
1905Cn P	1,738	BV	1,750	1,850	3,150	—

KM# 414.3 20 PESOS
33.8400 g., 0.8750 Gold 0.9519 oz. AGW **Obv:** Facing eagle, snake in beak **Obv. Legend:**

REPUBLICA MEXICANA **Rev:** Radiant cap above scales **Mint:** Durango

Date	Mintage	F	VF	XF	Unc	BU
1870Do P	416	1,800	2,100	2,950	3,600	—
1871Do P	Inc. above	1,800	2,100	2,950	3,600	—
1871/0Do P	1,073	1,800	2,400	3,250	3,900	—
1872/1Do PT	—	2,000	3,750	6,100	9,300	—
1876Do M	—	1,800	2,100	2,950	3,600	—
1877Do P	94	2,000	2,950	3,900	4,500	—
1878Do Rare	258	—	—	—	—	—

KM# 414.4 20 PESOS
33.8400 g., 0.8750 Gold 0.9519 oz. AGW **Obv:** Facing eagle, snake in beak **Obv. Legend:** REPUBLICA MEXICANA **Rev:** Radiant cap above scales **Mint:** Guanajuato

Date	Mintage	F	VF	XF	Unc	BU
1870Go S	3,250	BV	1,700	1,750	2,300	—
1871Go S	20,000	BV	1,700	1,750	2,300	2,950
1872Go S	18,000	BV	1,700	1,750	2,300	—
1873Go S	7,000	BV	1,700	1,750	2,300	—
1874Go S	—	BV	1,700	1,750	2,300	—
1875Go S	—	BV	1,700	1,750	2,300	—
1876Go S	—	BV	1,700	1,750	2,300	—
1876Go M/S	—	—	—	—	—	—
1877Go M/S Rare	15,000	—	—	—	—	—
1877Go R	Inc. above	BV	1,700	1,750	2,300	—
1877Go S Rare	Inc. above	—	—	—	—	—
1878/7Go M/S	13,000	1,500	2,150	2,900	3,900	—
1878Go M	Inc. above	1,500	2,150	2,900	3,900	—
1878Go S	Inc. above	BV	1,700	1,750	2,300	—
1879Go S	8,202	BV	1,700	1,750	3,300	—
1880Go S	7,375	BV	1,700	1,750	2,300	—
1881Go S	4,909	BV	1,700	1,750	2,300	—
1882Go S	4,020	BV	1,700	1,750	2,300	—
1883/2Go B	3,705	BV	1,700	1,950	3,200	—
1883Go B	Inc. above	BV	1,700	1,750	2,300	—
1884Go B	1,798	BV	1,700	1,750	2,300	—
1885Go R	2,660	BV	1,700	1,750	2,300	—
1886Go R	1,090	1,500	1,750	1,950	3,550	—
1887Go R	1,009	1,500	1,750	1,950	3,550	—
1888Go R	1,011	1,500	1,750	1,950	3,550	—
1889Go R	956	1,500	1,750	1,950	3,550	—
1890Go R	879	1,500	1,750	1,950	3,550	—
1891Go R	818	1,500	1,750	1,950	3,550	—
1892Go R	730	1,500	1,750	1,950	3,550	—
1893Go R	3,343	BV	1,700	1,850	2,700	—
1894/3Go R	6,734	BV	1,700	1,750	2,300	—
1894Go R	Inc. above	BV	1,700	1,750	2,300	—
1895/3Go R	7,118	BV	1,700	1,750	2,300	—
1895Go R	Inc. above	BV	1,700	1,750	2,300	—
1896Go R	9,219	BV	1,700	1,750	2,300	7,200
1897/6Go R	6,781	BV	1,700	1,750	2,300	—
1897Go R	Inc. above	BV	1,700	1,750	2,300	—
1898Go R	7,710	BV	1,700	1,750	2,300	—
1899Go R	8,527	BV	1,700	1,750	2,300	—
1900Go R	4,512	BV	1,750	1,950	3,350	—

SECOND REPUBLIC

KM# 414.5 20 PESOS
33.8400 g., 0.8750 Gold 0.9519 oz. AGW **Obv:**
Facing eagle, snake in beak **Obv. Legend:**
REPUBLICA MEXICANA **Rev:** Radiant cap above
scales **Mint:** Hermosillo

Date	Mintage	F	VF	XF	Unc	BU
1874Ho R Rare	—	—	—	—	—	—
Note: Stack's Bowers & Ponterio Sale 161, 8-11, AU55 realized $6,500.						
1875Ho R Rare	—	—	—	—	—	—
1876Ho F Rare	—	—	—	—	—	—
1888Ho g Rare	—	—	—	—	—	—

KM# 414.6 20 PESOS
33.8400 g., 0.8750 Gold 0.9519 oz. AGW **Obv:**
Facing eagle, snake in beak **Obv. Legend:**
REPUBLICA MEXICANA **Rev:** Radiant cap above
scales **Mint:** Mexico City

Date	Mintage	F	VF	XF	Unc	BU
1870Mo C	14,000	BV	1,750	1,850	2,450	—
1871Mo M	21,000	BV	1,750	1,850	2,450	—
1872/1Mo M	11,000	BV	1,750	1,850	2,550	—
1872Mo M	Inc. above	BV	1,750	1,850	2,450	—
1873Mo M	5,600	BV	1,750	1,850	2,450	—
1874/2Mo M	—	BV	1,750	1,850	2,450	—
1874/2Mo B	—	BV	1,750	1,950	2,550	—
1875Mo B	—	BV	1,750	1,950	2,500	—
1876Mo B	—	BV	1,750	1,950	2,500	—
1876Mo M	—	—	—	—	—	—
Note: Reported, not confirmed						
1877Mo M	2,000	BV	1,800	2,200	3,000	—
1878Mo M	7,000	BV	1,750	1,850	2,500	—
1879Mo M	—	BV	1,750	1,850	2,700	—
1880Mo M	—	BV	1,750	1,850	2,700	—
1881/0Mo M	11,000	BV	1,750	1,850	2,450	—
1881Mo M	Inc. above	BV	1,750	1,850	2,450	—
1882/1Mo M	5,800	BV	1,750	1,850	2,450	—
1882Mo M	Inc. above	BV	1,750	1,850	2,450	—
1883/1Mo M	4,000	BV	1,750	1,850	2,450	—
1883Mo M	Inc. above	BV	1,750	1,850	2,450	—
1884/3Mo M	—	BV	1,750	1,850	2,500	—
1884Mo M	—	BV	1,750	1,850	2,500	—
1885Mo M	6,000	BV	1,750	1,850	2,700	—
1886Mo M	10,000	BV	1,750	1,850	2,450	—
1887Mo M	12,000	BV	1,800	2,600	3,500	—
1888Mo M	7,300	BV	1,750	1,850	2,450	—
1889Mo M	6,477	BV	1,800	2,750	5,000	—
1890Mo M	7,852	BV	1,750	1,850	2,500	—
1891/0Mo M	8,725	BV	1,750	1,850	2,500	—

Date	Mintage	F	VF	XF	Unc	BU
1891Mo M	Inc. above	BV	1,750	1,850	2,500	—
1892Mo M	11,000	BV	1,750	1,850	2,450	—
1893Mo M	15,000	BV	1,750	1,850	2,450	—
1894Mo M	14,000	BV	1,750	1,850	2,450	—
1895Mo M	13,000	BV	1,750	1,850	2,450	—
1896Mo B	14,000	BV	1,750	1,850	2,450	—
1897/6Mo M	12,000	BV	1,750	1,850	2,450	—
1897Mo M	Inc. above	BV	1,750	1,850	2,450	—
1898Mo M	20,000	BV	1,750	1,850	2,450	—
1899Mo M	23,000	BV	1,750	1,850	2,450	—
1900Mo M	21,000	BV	1,750	1,850	2,450	—
1901Mo M	29,000	BV	1,750	1,850	2,450	—
1902Mo M	38,000	BV	1,750	1,850	2,450	—
1903/2Mo M	31,000	BV	1,750	1,850	2,450	—
1903Mo M	Inc. above	BV	1,750	1,850	2,450	—
1904Mo M	52,000	BV	1,750	1,850	2,450	—
1905Mo M	9,757	BV	1,750	1,850	2,450	—

KM# 414.7 20 PESOS
33.8400 g., 0.8750 Gold 0.9519 oz. AGW **Obv:**
Facing eagle, snake in beak **Obv. Legend:**
REPUBLICA MEXICANA **Rev:** Radiant cap above
scales **Mint:** Oaxaca

Date	Mintage	F	VF	XF	Unc	BU
1870Oa E	1,131	1,800	2,500	3,600	6,800	—
1871Oa E	1,591	1,800	2,500	3,600	6,800	—
1872Oa E	255	1,800	2,200	4,200	9,300	—
1888Oa E	170	2,450	3,950	6,800	—	—

KM# 414.8 20 PESOS
33.8400 g., 0.8750 Gold 0.9519 oz. AGW **Obv:**
Facing eagle, snake in beak **Rev:** Radiant cap above
scales **Mint:** Zacatecas

Date	Mintage	F	VF	XF	Unc	BU
1871Zs H	1,000	3,850	6,900	9,200	12,000	—
1875Zs A	—	4,350	6,400	9,800	12,500	—
1878Zs S	441	4,350	6,400	9,800	12,500	—
1888Zs Z Rare	50	—	—	—	—	—
1889Zs Z	640	3,900	5,900	9,200	12,000	—

KM# 414.1 20 PESOS
33.8400 g., 0.8750 Gold 0.9519 oz. AGW **Obv:**
Facing eagle, snake in beak **Rev:** Radiant cap above
scales **Mint:** Chihuahua **Note:** Mint mark CH, Ca.

Date	Mintage	F	VF	XF	Unc	BU
1872CH M	995	BV	1,750	1,850	3,500	—
1873CH M	950	BV	1,750	1,850	3,500	—
1874CH M	1,116	BV	1,750	1,850	3,500	—
1875CH M	750	BV	1,750	1,850	3,500	—
1876CH M	600	BV	1,800	2,000	3,750	—
1877CH Rare	55	—	—	—	—	—
1882CH M	1,758	BV	1,750	1,850	3,500	—
1883CH M	161	1,750	1,850	2,500	4,000	—
1884CH M	496	BV	1,750	1,850	3,500	—
1885CH M	122	1,750	1,850	2,500	4,000	—
1887Ca M	550	BV	1,750	1,850	3,500	—
1888Ca M	351	BV	1,750	1,850	3,500	—
1889Ca M	464	BV	1,750	1,850	3,500	—
1890Ca M	1,209	BV	1,750	1,850	3,500	—
1891Ca M	2,004	BV	1,750	1,800	3,250	—
1893Ca M	418	BV	1,750	1,850	3,500	—
1895Ca M	133	1,750	1,850	2,500	4,000	—

ESTADOS UNIDOS

DECIMAL COINAGE

100 CENTAVOS = 1 PESO

KM# 415   CENTAVO
3.0000 g., Bronze, 20 mm. **Obv:** National arms **Rev:** Value below date within wreath **Mint:** Mexico City **Note:** Mint mark Mo.

Date	Mintage	F	VF	XF	Unc	BU
1905 Narrow date	6,040,000	4.00	6.50	14.00	90.00	—
1905 Wide date	—	4.00	6.50	14.00	90.00	—
1906 Narrow date	Est. 67,505,000	0.50	0.75	1.25	14.00	25.00

Note: 50,000,000 pcs. were struck at the Birmingham Mint

Date	Mintage	F	VF	XF	Unc	BU
1906 Wide date	Inc. above	0.75	1.50	2.50	22.00	—
1910 Narrow date	8,700,000	2.00	3.00	6.50	85.00	100
1910 Wide date	—	2.00	3.00	6.50	85.00	100
1911 Narrow date	16,450,000	0.60	1.00	2.75	22.50	—
1911 Wide date	Inc. above	0.75	1.00	4.00	35.00	—
1912	12,650,000	1.00	1.35	3.25	35.00	—
1913	12,850,000	0.75	1.25	3.00	35.00	—
1914 Narrow date	17,350,000	0.75	1.00	3.00	15.00	20.00
1914 Wide date	Inc. above	0.75	1.00	3.00	15.00	20.00
1915	2,277,000	11.00	25.00	67.50	250	—
1916	500,000	45.00	80.00	170	1,200	—
1920	1,433,000	22.00	50.00	115	400	—
1921	3,470,000	5.50	15.50	47.00	275	—
1922	1,880,000	9.00	17.00	50.00	250	—
1923	4,800,000	0.75	1.25	1.75	13.50	—
1924/3	2,000,000	65.00	170	275	525	—
1924	Inc. above	4.50	11.00	22.00	250	300
1925	1,550,000	4.50	10.00	25.00	220	—
1926	5,000,000	1.00	2.00	4.00	20.00	28.00
1927/6	6,000,000	30.00	45.00	70.00	175	—
1927	Inc. above	0.75	1.25	4.50	32.00	45.00
1928	5,000,000	0.75	1.00	3.25	16.50	25.00
1929	4,500,000	0.75	1.00	1.75	17.00	25.00
1930	7,000,000	0.75	1.00	2.50	20.00	—
1933	10,000,000	0.25	0.35	1.75	16.50	22.00
1934	7,500,000	0.25	0.95	3.25	40.00	—
1935	12,400,000	0.15	0.25	0.40	11.50	15.00
1936	20,100,000	0.15	0.20	0.30	9.00	—
1937	20,000,000	0.15	0.25	0.35	4.00	6.00
1938	10,000,000	0.10	0.15	0.30	2.00	3.00
1939	30,000,000	0.10	0.20	0.30	1.00	2.50
1940	10,000,000	0.20	0.30	0.60	5.50	8.50
1941	15,800,000	0.15	0.25	0.35	2.00	3.00
1942	30,400,000	0.15	0.20	0.30	1.25	2.00
1943	4,310,000	0.30	0.50	0.75	9.00	12.50
1944	5,645,000	0.15	0.25	0.50	6.00	8.50
1945	26,375,000	0.10	0.15	0.25	1.00	1.75
1946	42,135,000	—	0.15	0.20	0.60	1.50
1947	13,445,000	—	0.10	0.15	0.80	1.50
1948	20,040,000	0.10	0.15	0.30	1.10	2.25
1949	6,235,000	0.10	0.15	0.30	1.25	3.00

Note: Varieties exist

KM# 416   CENTAVO
1.5000 g., Bronze, 16 mm. **Obv:** National arms **Rev:** Value below date within wreath **Mint:** Mexico City **Note:** Zapata issue. Struck at Mexico City Mint, mint mark Mo. Reduced size. Weight varies 1.39-1.5g.

Date	Mintage	F	VF	XF	Unc	BU
1915	179,000	18.00	30.00	60.00	85.00	—

KM# 417   CENTAVO
2.0000 g., Brass, 16 mm. **Obv:** National arms, eagle left **Rev:** Oat sprigs **Mint:** Mexico City **Note:** Mint mark Mo.

Date	Mintage	F	VF	XF	Unc	BU
1950	12,815,000	—	0.15	0.35	1.65	2.25
1951	25,740,000	—	0.15	0.35	0.65	1.25
1952	24,610,000	—	0.10	0.25	0.40	0.85
1953	21,160,000	—	0.10	0.25	0.40	0.85
1954	25,675,000	—	0.10	0.15	0.85	1.50
1955	9,820,000	—	0.15	0.25	0.85	1.75
1956	11,285,000	—	0.15	0.25	0.80	1.75
1957	9,805,000	—	0.15	0.25	0.85	1.50
1958	12,155,000	—	0.10	0.25	0.45	0.75
1959	11,875,000	—	0.10	0.25	0.75	1.50
1960	10,360,000	—	0.10	0.15	0.40	0.65
1961	6,385,000	—	0.10	0.15	0.45	0.85
1962	4,850,000	—	0.10	0.15	0.55	0.90
1963	7,775,000	—	0.10	0.15	0.25	0.45
1964	4,280,000	—	0.10	0.15	0.20	0.30
1965	2,255,000	—	0.10	0.15	0.25	0.40
1966	1,760,000	—	0.10	0.25	0.60	1.00
1967	1,290,000	—	0.10	0.15	0.40	0.75
1968	1,000,000	—	0.10	0.20	0.85	1.45
1969	1,000,000	—	0.10	0.15	0.65	0.85

KM# 418   CENTAVO
1.5000 g., Brass, 13 mm. **Obv:** National arms, eagle left **Rev:** Oat sprigs **Mint:** Mexico City **Note:** Reduced size.

Date	Mintage	F	VF	XF	Unc	BU
1970Mo	1,000,000	—	0.20	0.40	1.45	2.25
1972Mo	1,000,000	—	0.20	0.45	2.50	4.00
1972/2Mo	—	—	0.50	1.25	3.50	5.00
1973Mo	1,000,000	—	1.65	2.75	9.00	17.50

KM# 419   2 CENTAVOS
6.0000 g., Bronze, 25 mm. **Obv:** National arms **Rev:** Value below date within wreath **Mint:** Mexico City **Note:** Mint mark Mo.

ESTADOS UNIDOS MEXICANOS

Date	Mintage	F	VF	XF	Unc	BU
1905	50,000	150	300	500	1,200	1,350
1906 Inverted 6	9,998,000	30.00	55.00	120	375	—
1906 Wide date	Inc. above	5.00	11.00	28.00	95.00	110
1906 Narrow date	Inc. above	6.50	14.00	30.00	95.00	—

Note: 5,000,000 pieces were struck at the Birmingham Mint

1920	1,325,000	6.50	17.50	75.00	350	—
1921	4,275,000	2.50	4.75	15.00	100	—
1922	—	225	550	1,750	5,500	—
1924	750,000	8.50	27.50	75.00	450	—
1925	3,650,000	2.50	3.50	7.50	35.00	40.00
1926	4,750,000	1.00	2.25	5.50	40.00	—
1927	7,250,000	0.60	1.00	4.50	22.00	35.00
1928	3,250,000	0.75	1.50	4.75	25.00	35.00
1929	250,000	85.00	225	550	1,200	—
1935	1,250,000	4.25	9.25	65.00	225	275
1939	5,000,000	0.60	0.90	2.25	20.00	30.00
1941	3,550,000	0.45	0.60	1.25	18.00	28.00

KM# 420 2 CENTAVOS
3.0000 g., Bronze, 20 mm. **Obv:** National arms **Rev:**
Value below date within wreath **Mint:** Mexico City
Note: Zapata issue. Mint mark Mo. Reduced size.
Weight varies 3-3.03g.

Date	Mintage	F	VF	XF	Unc	BU
1915	487,000	7.50	9.00	17.50	75.00	—

KM# 421 5 CENTAVOS
5.0000 g., Nickel, 20 mm. **Obv:** National arms **Rev:**
Value and date within beaded circle **Mint:** Mexico
City **Note:** Mint mark Mo. Varieties exist.

Date	Mintage	F	VF	XF	Unc	BU
1905	1,420,000	7.00	10.00	28.00	325	375
1906/5	10,615,000	13.00	30.00	70.00	375	—
1906	Inc. above	0.75	1.35	3.25	55.00	75.00
1907	4,000,000	1.25	4.00	35.00	350	450
1909	2,052,000	3.25	10.00	50.00	360	—
1910	6,181,000	1.30	3.50	9.00	85.00	125
1911 Narrow date	4,487,000	1.00	3.00	7.00	95.00	135
1911 Wide date	Inc. above	2.50	5.00	9.00	110	170
1912 Small mint mark	420,000	90.00	100	230	725	—
1912 Large mint mark	Inc. above	70.00	95.00	200	575	—
1913	2,035,000	1.75	4.25	30.00	200	300

Note: Wide and narrow dates exist for 1913

1914	2,000,000	1.00	2.00	5.00	75.00	110

Note: 5,000,000 pieces appear to have been struck at the
Birmingham Mint in 1914 and all of 1909-1911. The Mexican
Mint report does not mention receiving the 1914 dated coins

KM# 422 5 CENTAVOS
9.0000 g., Bronze, 28 mm. **Obv:** National arms **Rev:**
Value below date within wreath **Mint:** Mexico City

Date	Mintage	F	VF	XF	Unc	BU
1914Mo	2,500,000	10.00	23.00	65.00	300	—
1915Mo	11,424,000	3.00	5.00	35.00	165	265
1916Mo	2,860,000	15.00	35.00	175	650	—
1917Mo	800,000	75.00	225	400	900	—
1918Mo	1,332,000	35.00	90.00	250	675	—
1919Mo	400,000	115	225	360	950	—
1920Mo	5,920,000	3.00	8.00	45.00	265	350
1921Mo	2,080,000	10.00	24.00	75.00	275	—
1924Mo	780,000	40.00	95.00	275	700	—
1925Mo	4,040,000	5.50	11.00	47.50	225	—
1926Mo	3,160,000	5.50	11.00	48.00	325	—
1927Mo	3,600,000	4.00	7.00	35.00	250	350
1928Mo Large date	1,740,000	11.00	18.00	65.00	250	325
1928Mo Small date	Inc. above	30.00	45.00	100	385	—
1929Mo	2,400,000	5.50	12.00	50.00	200	—
1930Mo	2,600,000	5.00	8.00	27.50	225	—

Note: Large oval O in date

1930Mo	Inc. above	65.00	125	250	565	—

Note: Small square O in date

1931Mo	—	475	750	1,450	4,000	—
1933Mo	8,000,000	1.50	2.25	3.50	27.50	45.00
1934Mo	10,000,000	1.25	1.75	2.75	25.00	50.00
1935Mo	21,980,000	0.75	1.20	2.50	22.50	40.00

KM# 423 5 CENTAVOS
4.0000 g., Copper-Nickel, 20.5 mm. **Obv:** National
arms, eagle left **Rev:** Value and date within circle
Mint: Mexico City

Date	Mintage	F	VF	XF	Unc	BU
1936M	46,700,000	—	0.65	1.25	7.50	8.50
1937M	49,060,000	—	0.50	1.00	7.00	8.00
1938M	3,340,000	—	4.00	10.00	80.00	200
1940M	22,800,000	—	0.75	1.25	8.00	10.00
1942M	7,100,000	—	1.50	3.00	35.00	50.00

ESTADOS UNIDOS MEXICANOS

KM# 424 5 CENTAVOS
6.5000 g., Bronze, 25.5 mm. **Obv:** National arms, eagle left **Rev:** Head left **Mint:** Mexico City

Date	Mintage	F	VF	XF	Unc	BU
1942Mo	900,000	—	25.00	75.00	375	550
1943Mo	54,660,000	—	0.50	0.75	2.50	3.50
1944Mo	53,463,000	—	0.25	0.35	0.75	1.00
1945Mo	44,262,000	—	0.25	0.35	0.75	1.25
1946Mo	49,054,000	—	0.50	1.00	2.00	3.00
1951Mo	50,758,000	—	0.75	0.90	3.00	5.00
1952Mo	17,674,000	—	1.50	2.50	9.50	11.50
1953Mo	31,568,000	—	1.25	2.00	6.00	9.00
1954Mo	58,680,000	—	0.40	1.00	2.75	4.00
1955Mo	31,114,000	—	2.00	3.00	11.00	14.00

KM# 425 5 CENTAVOS
4.0000 g., Copper-Nickel, 20.5 mm. **Obv:** National arms, eagle left **Rev:** Bust right flanked by date and value **Mint:** Mexico City

Date	Mintage	F	VF	XF	Unc	BU
1950Mo	5,700,000	—	0.75	1.50	6.00	7.00

Note: 5,600,000 pieces struck at Connecticut melted

KM# 426 5 CENTAVOS
4.0000 g., Brass, 20.4 mm. **Obv:** National arms, eagle left **Rev:** Bust right **Mint:** Mexico City

Date	Mintage	F	VF	XF	Unc	BU
1954Mo Dot	—	—	10.00	50.00	300	375
1954Mo Without dot	—	—	15.00	35.00	275	325
1955Mo	12,136,000	—	0.75	1.50	9.00	12.50
1956Mo	60,216,000	—	0.20	0.30	0.75	1.25
1957Mo	55,288,000	—	0.15	0.20	0.90	1.50
1958Mo	104,624,000	—	0.15	0.20	0.60	1.00
1959Mo	106,000,000	—	0.15	0.25	0.75	1.25
1960Mo	99,144,000	—	0.10	0.15	0.50	0.75
1961Mo	61,136,000	—	0.10	0.15	0.50	0.75
1962Mo	47,232,000	—	0.10	0.15	0.25	0.35
1963Mo	156,680,000	—	—	0.15	0.25	0.40
1964Mo	71,168,000	—	—	0.15	0.20	0.40
1965Mo	155,720,000	—	—	0.15	0.25	0.35
1966Mo	124,944,000	—	—	0.15	0.40	0.65
1967Mo	118,816,000	—	—	0.15	0.25	0.40
1968Mo	189,588,000	—	—	0.15	0.50	0.75
1969Mo	210,492,000	—	—	0.15	0.55	0.80

KM# 426a 5 CENTAVOS
Copper-Nickel, 20.5 mm. **Obv:** National arms, eagle left **Rev:** Bust right **Mint:** Mexico City

Date	Mintage	F	VF	XF	Unc	BU
1960Mo	—	—	250	300	375	—
1962Mo	19	—	250	300	375	—
1965Mo	—	—	250	300	375	—

KM# 427 5 CENTAVOS
2.7500 g., Brass, 18 mm. **Obv:** National arms, eagle left **Rev:** Bust right **Note:** Due to some minor alloy variations this type is often encountered with a bronze-color toning. Reduced size.

Date	Mintage	F	VF	XF	Unc	BU
1970Mo	163,368,000	—	0.10	0.15	0.35	0.45
1971Mo	198,844,000	—	0.10	0.15	0.25	0.30
1972Mo	225,000,000	—	0.10	0.15	0.25	0.30
1973Mo Flat top 3	595,070,000	—	0.10	0.15	0.25	0.40
1973Mo Round top 3	Inc. above	—	0.10	0.15	0.20	0.30
1974Mo	401,584,000	—	0.10	0.15	0.30	0.40
1975Mo	342,308,000	—	0.10	0.15	0.25	0.35
1976Mo	367,524,000	—	0.10	0.15	0.40	0.60

KM# 428 10 CENTAVOS
2.5000 g., 0.8000 Silver 0.0643 oz. ASW, 18 mm. **Obv:** National arms **Rev:** Value and date within 3/4 wreath with Liberty cap above **Mint:** Mexico City **Note:** Mint mark Mo.

Date	Mintage	F	VF	XF	Unc	BU
1905	3,920,000	2.50	6.00	8.00	40.00	50.00
1906	8,410,000	2.50	5.50	7.50	27.00	40.00
1907/6	5,950,000	15.00	50.00	135	325	375
1907	Inc. above	2.50	5.50	6.25	35.00	50.00
1909	2,620,000	2.75	8.50	13.00	80.00	110
1910/00	3,450,000	3.00	10.00	40.00	75.00	85.00
1910	Inc. above	2.50	7.00	15.00	25.00	40.00
1911 Narrow date	2,550,000	3.00	11.00	17.00	88.00	125
1911 Wide date	Inc. above	2.50	7.50	10.00	45.00	65.00
1912	1,350,000	3.00	10.00	18.00	130	175
1912 Low 2	Inc. above	3.00	10.00	18.00	115	155
1913/2	1,990,000	3.00	10.00	25.00	40.00	70.00
1913	Inc. above	2.50	7.00	10.00	33.00	45.00
1914	3,110,000	2.50	5.50	7.00	15.00	25.00

Note: Wide and narrow dates exist for 1914

KM# 429 10 CENTAVOS
1.8125 g., 0.8000 Silver 0.0466 oz. ASW, 15 mm. **Obv:** National arms **Rev:** Value and date within 3/4 wreath with Liberty cap above **Mint:** Mexico City **Note:** Mint mark Mo. Reduced size.

Date	Mintage	F	VF	XF	Unc	BU
1919	8,360,000	3.00	10.00	15.00	95.00	125

ESTADOS UNIDOS MEXICANOS

KM# 430   10 CENTAVOS

12.0000 g., Bronze, 30.5 mm. **Obv:** National arms **Rev:** Value below date within wreath **Mint:** Mexico City **Note:** Mint mark Mo.

Date	Mintage	F	VF	XF	Unc	BU
1919	1,232,000	7.00	25.00	85.00	475	550
1920	6,612,000	5.00	15.00	50.00	400	475
1921	2,255,000	10.00	35.00	95.00	650	800
1935	5,970,000	4.50	14.00	35.00	125	200

KM# 431   10 CENTAVOS

1.6600 g., 0.7200 Silver 0.0384 oz. ASW, 15 mm. **Obv:** National arms **Rev:** Value and date within wreath with Liberty cap above **Mint:** Mexico City **Note:** Mint mark Mo.

Date	Mintage	F	VF	XF	Unc	BU
1925/15	5,350,000	10.00	30.00	75.00	125	175
1925/3	Inc. above	8.00	20.00	40.00	125	175
1925	Inc. above	BV	2.00	5.00	40.00	50.00
1926/16	2,650,000	10.00	30.00	75.00	125	175
1926	Inc. above	1.80	3.50	7.50	65.00	95.00
1927	2,810,000	BV	2.25	3.00	17.50	25.00
1928	5,270,000	BV	2.00	2.75	13.50	20.00
1930	2,000,000	1.75	3.75	5.00	18.75	28.00
1933	5,000,000	BV	1.50	3.00	10.00	17.00
1934	8,000,000	BV	1.75	2.50	8.00	16.00
1935	3,500,000	1.50	2.75	5.00	11.00	18.00

KM# 432   10 CENTAVOS

5.5000 g., Copper-Nickel, 23.5 mm. **Obv:** National arms, eagle left **Rev:** Value and date within circle **Mint:** Mexico City **Note:** Mint mark Mo.

Date	Mintage	F	VF	XF	Unc	BU
1936	33,030,000	—	0.75	2.50	10.00	12.00
1937	3,000,000	2.00	10.00	50.00	215	250
1938	3,650,000	1.25	2.00	7.00	70.00	85.00
1939	6,920,000	—	1.00	3.50	27.50	35.00
1940	12,300,000	—	0.40	1.25	5.00	7.00
1942	14,380,000	—	0.60	1.50	7.00	10.00
1945	9,558,000	—	0.40	0.70	3.50	5.00
1946	46,230,000	—	0.40	0.60	2.50	4.00

KM# 433   10 CENTAVOS

5.5000 g., Bronze, 23.5 mm. **Obv:** National arms, eagle left **Rev:** Bust left **Mint:** Mexico City **Note:** Mint mark Mo.

Date	Mintage	F	VF	XF	Unc	BU
1955	1,818,000	—	0.75	3.25	23.00	35.00
1956	5,255,000	—	0.75	3.25	23.00	32.00
1957	11,925,000	—	0.20	0.40	5.50	9.00
1959	26,140,000	—	0.30	0.45	0.75	1.25
1966	5,873,000	—	0.15	0.25	0.60	1.75
1967	32,318,000	—	0.10	0.15	0.30	0.40

Sharp stem

KM# 434.1   10 CENTAVOS

1.5000 g., Copper-Nickel **Obv:** National arms, eagle left **Rev:** Upright ear of corn **Edge:** Reeded **Mint:** Mexico City **Note:** Variety I- Sharp stem and wide date

Date	Mintage	F	VF	XF	Unc	BU
1974Mo	6,000,000	—	—	0.35	0.75	1.00
1975Mo	5,550,000	—	0.10	0.35	0.75	1.00
1976Mo	7,680,000	—	0.10	0.20	0.30	0.40
1977Mo	144,650,000	—	1.25	2.25	3.50	5.50
1978Mo	271,870,000	—	—	1.00	1.50	2.25
1979Mo	375,660,000	—	—	0.50	1.00	1.75
1980/79Mo	21,290,000	—	2.45	3.75	7.00	9.00
1980Mo	Inc. above	—	1.50	2.00	4.50	6.50

Blunt stem

KM# 434.2   10 CENTAVOS

1.5000 g., Copper-Nickel **Obv:** National arms, eagle left **Rev:** Upright ear of corn **Edge:** Reeded **Mint:** Mexico City **Note:** Variety II- Blunt stem and narrow date

Date	Mintage	F	VF	XF	Unc	BU
1974Mo	Inc. above	—	—	0.10	0.20	0.30
1977Mo	Inc. above	—	0.15	0.50	1.25	2.25
1978Mo	Inc. above	—	—	0.10	0.30	0.40
1979Mo	Inc. above	—	0.15	0.35	0.85	1.50
1980Mo	Inc. above	—	—	0.10	0.20	0.30

KM# 434.4   10 CENTAVOS

1.5000 g., Copper-Nickel **Obv:** National arms, eagle left **Rev:** Upright ear of corn **Edge:** Reeded **Mint:** Mexico City **Note:** Variety IV- Sharp stem and narrow date

Date	Mintage	F	VF	XF	Unc	BU
1974Mo	—	—	—	—	1.50	2.50
1979Mo	—	—	—	—	1.50	2.50

ESTADOS UNIDOS MEXICANOS

KM# 434.3 10 CENTAVOS

1.5000 g., Copper-Nickel **Obv:** National arms, eagle left **Rev:** Upright ear of corn **Edge:** Reeded **Mint:** Mexico City **Note:** Variety III- Blunt stem and wide date

Date	Mintage	F	VF	XF	Unc	BU
1980/79Mo	—	—	—	2.50	7.00	9.00

KM# 435 20 CENTAVOS

5.0000 g., 0.8000 Silver 0.1286 oz. ASW, 22 mm. **Obv:** National arms **Rev:** Value and date within wreath with Liberty cap above **Mint:** Mexico City **Note:** Mint mark Mo.

Date	Mintage	F	VF	XF	Unc	BU
1905	2,565,000	5.00	12.00	25.00	175	195
1906	6,860,000	4.75	9.00	16.50	60.00	85.00
1907 Straight 7	4,000,000	5.00	11.50	22.00	75.00	125
1907 Curved 7	5,435,000	4.50	7.50	15.00	70.00	120
1908	350,000	50.00	95.00	250	1,800	—
1910	1,135,000	5.00	11.00	16.00	90.00	110
1911	1,150,000	12.00	15.00	40.00	145	175
1912	625,000	20.00	40.00	70.00	350	400
1913	1,000,000	5.00	14.50	30.00	100	125
1914	1,500,000	5.00	10.00	22.50	65.00	80.00

KM# 436 20 CENTAVOS

3.6250 g., 0.8000 Silver 0.0932 oz. ASW, 19 mm. **Obv:** National arms **Rev:** Value and date within wreath with Liberty cap above **Mint:** Mexico City **Note:** Mint mark Mo. Reduced size.

Date	Mintage	F	VF	XF	Unc	BU
1919	4,155,000	10.00	30.00	65.00	200	275

KM# 437 20 CENTAVOS

15.0000 g., Bronze, 32.5 mm. **Obv:** National arms **Rev:** Value below date within wreath **Mint:** Mexico City **Note:** Mint mark Mo.

Date	Mintage	F	VF	XF	Unc	BU
1920	4,835,000	12.00	45.00	155	650	775
1935	20,000,000	2.00	6.00	10.00	95.00	145

KM# 438 20 CENTAVOS

3.3333 g., 0.7200 Silver 0.0772 oz. ASW, 19 mm. **Obv:** National arms **Rev:** Value and date within wreath with Liberty cap above **Mint:** Mexico City **Note:** Mint mark Mo.

Date	Mintage	F	VF	XF	Unc	BU
1920	3,710,000	3.00	9.00	20.00	175	220
1921	6,160,000	3.00	7.00	14.00	100	150
1925	1,450,000	4.00	12.00	20.00	155	165
1926/5	1,465,000	7.00	20.00	70.00	350	375
1926	Inc. above	2.75	5.00	11.00	90.00	110
1927	1,405,000	2.75	5.00	12.00	95.00	115
1928	3,630,000	2.75	6.00	8.00	19.00	27.50
1930	1,000,000	2.75	8.00	12.00	30.00	42.00
1933	2,500,000	2.75	3.00	5.00	12.00	16.00
1934	2,500,000	2.75	3.00	6.00	13.00	20.00
1935	2,460,000	2.75	3.00	6.00	13.00	20.00
1937	10,000,000	BV	2.75	3.00	6.00	9.00
1939	8,800,000	BV	2.75	3.00	6.00	9.00
1940	3,000,000	BV	2.75	3.00	5.00	9.00
1941	5,740,000	BV	2.25	3.00	5.00	8.00
1942	12,460,000	BV	2.25	3.00	5.00	8.00
1943	3,955,000	BV	3.00	4.00	5.00	9.00

KM# 439 20 CENTAVOS

10.0000 g., Bronze, 28.5 mm. **Obv:** National arms, eagle left **Rev:** Liberty cap divides value above Pyramid of the Sun at Teotihuacán, volcanos Ixtaccihuatl and Popocatepet in background **Edge:** Plain **Mint:** Mexico City **Note:** Mint mark Mo.

Date	Mintage	F	VF	XF	Unc	BU
1943	46,350,000	—	1.25	3.00	20.00	28.00
1944	83,650,000	—	0.40	0.65	8.00	12.00
1945	26,801,000	—	1.25	3.50	9.50	15.00
1946	25,695,000	—	1.10	2.25	6.00	9.00
1951	11,385,000	0.50	3.00	8.75	100	120
1952	6,560,000	0.50	5.00	25.00	35.00	
1953	26,948,000	—	0.35	0.80	9.00	15.00
1954	40,108,000	—	0.35	0.80	9.00	15.00
1955	16,950,000	0.50	2.75	7.00	60.00	75.00

KM# 440 20 CENTAVOS

10.0000 g., Bronze, 28.5 mm. **Obv:** National arms, eagle left **Rev:** Liberty cap divides value above Pyramid of the Sun at Teotihuacán, volcanos

Ixtaccihuatl and Popocatepet in background **Edge:**
Plain **Mint:** Mexico City **Note:** Mint mark Mo.

Date	Mintage	F	VF	XF	Unc	BU
1955 Inc. KM#439	Inc. above	—	0.75	1.75	17.00	22.00
1956	22,431,000	—	0.30	0.35	3.00	5.00
1957	13,455,000	—	0.45	1.25	9.00	13.00
1959	6,017,000	0.75	4.50	9.00	75.00	100
1960	39,756,000	—	0.15	0.25	0.75	1.00
1963	14,869,000	—	0.25	0.35	0.80	1.00
1964	28,654,000	—	0.25	0.40	0.90	1.25
1965	74,162,000	—	0.20	0.35	0.80	1.00
1966	43,745,000	—	0.15	0.25	0.75	1.00
1967	46,487,000	—	0.20	0.50	1.00	1.25
1968	15,477,000	—	0.30	0.55	1.35	1.65
1969	63,647,000	—	0.20	0.35	0.80	1.00
1970	76,287,000	—	0.15	0.20	0.90	1.30
1971	49,892,000	—	0.30	0.50	1.25	2.00

KM# 441   20 CENTAVOS
10.0000 g., Bronze, 28.5 mm. **Obv:** National arms,
eagle left **Rev:** Liberty cap divides value above
Pyramid of the Sun at Teotihuacán, volcanos
Ixtaccihuatl and Popocatepet in background **Edge:**
Plain **Mint:** Mexico City

Date	Mintage	F	VF	XF	Unc	BU
1971Mo Inc. KM#440	Inc. above	—	0.20	0.35	1.85	2.50
1973Mo	78,398,000	—	0.25	0.35	0.95	1.65
1974Mo	34,200,000	—	0.20	0.35	1.25	2.00

KM# 442   20 CENTAVOS
3.0000 g., Copper-Nickel, 20 mm. **Obv:** National
arms, eagle left **Rev:** Bust 3/4 facing flanked by value
and date **Edge:** Reeded **Mint:** Mexico City

Date	Mintage	F	VF	XF	Unc	BU
1974Mo	112,000,000	—	0.10	0.15	0.25	0.30
1975Mo	611,000,000	—	0.10	0.15	0.30	0.35
1976Mo	394,000,000	—	0.10	0.15	0.35	0.45
1977Mo	394,350,000	—	0.10	0.15	0.40	0.45
1978Mo	527,950,000	—	0.10	0.15	0.25	0.30
1979Mo	524,615,000	—	0.10	0.15	0.25	0.30
1979Mo	—	—	1.25	2.00	4.00	8.00

Note: Doubled die obv. small letters

1979Mo	—	—	1.25	2.00	4.00	8.00

Note: Doubled die obv. large letters

1980Mo	326,500,000	—	0.15	0.20	0.30	0.40
1981Mo Open 8	106,205,000	—	0.30	0.50	1.00	2.00
1981Mo Closed 8, high date	248,500,000	—	0.30	0.50	1.00	2.00
1981Mo Closed 8, low date	—	—	1.00	1.50	3.50	4.25
1981/1982Mo	—	10.00	40.00	75.00	175	195

Note: The 1981/1982 overdate is often mistaken as 1982/1981

1982Mo	286,855,000	—	0.40	0.60	0.90	1.10
1983Mo Round top 3	100,930,000	—	0.25	0.40	1.75	2.25

Date	Mintage	F	VF	XF	Unc	BU
1983Mo Flat top 3	Inc. above	—	0.25	0.50	1.25	1.75
1983Mo Proof	998	Value: 45.00				

KM# 491   20 CENTAVOS
3.0000 g., Bronze, 20 mm. **Subject:** Olmec Culture
Obv: National arms, eagle left **Rev:** Mask 3/4 right
with value below **Mint:** Mexico City

Date	Mintage	F	VF	XF	Unc	BU
1983Mo	260,000,000	—	0.20	0.25	1.25	1.75
1983Mo Proof	53	Value: 185				
1984Mo	180,320,000	—	0.20	0.35	1.85	2.25

KM# 443   25 CENTAVOS
3.3330 g., 0.3000 Silver 0.0321 oz. ASW, 21.5 mm.
Obv: National arms, eagle left **Rev:** Scale below
Liberty cap **Edge:** Reeded **Mint:** Mexico City **Note:**
Mint mark Mo.

Date	Mintage	F	VF	XF	Unc	BU
1950	77,060,000	—	1.25	1.50	2.00	2.50
1951	41,172,000	—	1.25	1.50	2.00	2.50
1952	29,264,000	—	1.25	1.50	2.25	2.75
1953	38,144,000	—	1.25	1.25	2.00	2.50

KM# 444   25 CENTAVOS
5.5000 g., Copper-Nickel, 23 mm. **Obv:** National
arms, eagle left **Rev:** Bust 3/4 facing **Edge:** Reeded
Mint: Mexico City

Date	Mintage	VF	XF	Unc	BU
1964Mo	20,686,000	—	0.15	0.20	0.30
1966Mo Closed beak	180,000	0.75	1.25	3.00	4.50
1966Mo Open beak	Inc. above	2.00	4.00	12.00	15.00

KM# 445   50 CENTAVOS
12.5000 g., 0.8000 Silver 0.3215 oz. ASW, 30 mm.
Obv: National arms **Rev:** Value and date within 3/4
wreath with Liberty cap above **Mint:** Mexico City
Note: Mint mark Mo.

Date	Mintage	F	VF	XF	Unc	BU
1905	2,446,000	12.50	20.00	35.00	175	250
1906 Open 9	16,966,000	BV	12.00	15.00	55.00	85.00
1906 Closed 9	Inc. above	BV	11.50	14.00	48.00	70.00
1907 Straight 7	18,920,000	BV	11.50	14.00	36.00	42.00
1907 Curved 7	14,841,000	BV	11.50	14.00	36.00	45.50

ESTADOS UNIDOS MEXICANOS

Date	Mintage	F	VF	XF	Unc	BU
1908	488,000	25.00	80.00	190	550	675
1912	3,736,000	12.00	22.50	20.00	55.00	85.00
1913/07	10,510,000	15.00	40.00	90.00	250	300
1913/2	Inc. above	12.00	20.00	27.50	75.00	100
1913	Inc. above	BV	11.50	13.00	33.00	42.00
1914	7,710,000	BV	14.00	20.00	42.00	65.00
1916 Narrow date	480,000	20.00	60.00	85.00	250	350
1916 Wide date	Inc. above	20.00	60.00	85.00	250	350
1917	37,112,000	BV	12.00	14.00	27.50	33.00
1918	1,320,000	20.00	70.00	135	300	400

KM# 446 50 CENTAVOS
9.0625 g., 0.8000 Silver 0.2331 oz. ASW, 27 mm.
Obv: National arms **Rev:** Value and date within 3/4 wreath with Liberty cap above **Mint:** Mexico City
Note: Mint mark Mo. Reduced size.

Date	Mintage	F	VF	XF	Unc	BU
1918/7	2,760,000	175	525	700	1,450	—
1918	Inc. above	9.00	20.00	70.00	350	450
1919	29,670,000	BV	12.00	25.00	150	180

KM# 447 50 CENTAVOS
8.3333 g., 0.7200 Silver 0.1929 oz. ASW, 27 mm.
Obv: National arms **Rev:** Value and date within 3/4 wreath with Liberty cap above **Edge Lettering:** INDEPENDENCIA Y LIBERTAD **Mint:** Mexico City
Note: Mint mark Mo.

Date	Mintage	F	VF	XF	Unc	BU
1919	10,200,000	BV	12.00	22.00	100	130
1920	27,166,000	BV	9.00	17.00	75.00	90.00
1921	21,864,000	BV	9.00	17.00	95.00	120
1925	3,280,000	7.00	17.50	35.00	145	185
1937	20,000,000	BV	7.00	9.00	13.00	18.00
1938	100,000	15.00	50.00	95.00	245	350
1939	10,440,000	BV	7.00	9.00	16.00	25.00
1942	800,000	BV	7.00	10.00	18.00	22.00
1943	41,512,000	BV	7.00	9.00	12.00	15.00
1944	55,806,000	BV	7.00	9.00	12.00	15.00
1945	56,766,000	BV	7.00	9.00	12.00	15.00

KM# 448 50 CENTAVOS
7.9730 g., 0.4200 Silver 0.1077 oz. ASW, 27 mm.
Obv: National arms **Rev:** Value and date within 3/4 wreath with Liberty cap above **Mint:** Mexico City
Note: Mint mark Mo.

Date	Mintage	F	VF	XF	Unc	BU
1935	70,800,000	4.00	4.25	5.00	9.00	12.00

KM# 449 50 CENTAVOS
6.6600 g., 0.3000 Silver 0.0642 oz. ASW, 26 mm.
Obv: National arms, eagle left **Rev:** Head with head covering right **Mint:** Mexico City **Note:** Mint mark Mo.

Date	Mintage	F	VF	XF	Unc	BU
1950	13,570,000	—	2.50	2.75	5.00	8.00
1951	3,650,000	—	3.00	4.00	6.00	9.00

KM# 450 50 CENTAVOS
14.0000 g., Bronze, 33 mm. **Obv:** National arms, eagle left **Rev:** Head with headdress left **Edge:** Reeded **Mint:** Mexico City **Note:** Mint mark Mo.

Date	Mintage	F	VF	XF	Unc	BU
1955	3,502,000	—	1.50	3.00	8.00	4.00
1956	34,643,000	—	0.75	1.50	9.00	7.00
1957	9,675,000	—	1.00	2.00	8.00	6.50
1959	4,540,000	—	0.50	0.75	3.50	2.00

KM# 451 50 CENTAVOS
6.5000 g., Copper-Nickel, 25 mm. **Obv:** National arms, eagle left **Rev:** Head with headdress left **Edge:** Reeded **Mint:** Mexico City

Date	Mintage	F	VF	XF	Unc	BU
1964Mo	43,806,000	—	0.15	0.20	0.40	0.60
1965Mo	14,326,000	—	0.20	0.25	0.45	0.65
1966Mo	1,726,000	—	0.20	0.40	1.50	2.00
1967Mo	55,144,000	—	0.20	0.30	0.75	1.25
1968Mo	80,438,000	—	0.15	0.30	0.65	1.00
1969Mo	87,640,000	—	0.20	0.35	0.80	1.25

KM# 452 50 CENTAVOS
6.5000 g., Copper-Nickel, 25 mm. **Obv:** National

ESTADOS UNIDOS MEXICANOS

arms, eagle left **Rev:** Head with headdress left **Edge:** Reeded **Mint:** Mexico City **Note:** Coins dated 1975 and 1976 exist with and without dots in centers of three circles on plumage on reverse. Edge varieties exist.

Date	Mintage	VF	XF	Unc	BU
1970Mo	76,236,000	0.15	0.20	0.80	1.35
1971Mo	125,288,000	0.15	0.20	0.90	1.45
1972Mo	16,000,000	1.25	2.00	3.50	5.50
1975Mo Dots	177,958,000	0.65	1.75	3.50	6.00
1975Mo No dots	Inc. above	0.15	0.20	0.75	1.25
1976Mo Dots	37,480,000	0.75	1.50	5.00	7.00
1976Mo No dots	Inc. above	0.15	0.20	0.50	0.90
1977Mo	12,410,000	6.50	10.00	32.50	45.00
1978Mo	85,400,000	0.15	0.25	0.50	1.20
1979Mo Round 2nd 9 in date	229,000,000	0.15	0.25	0.50	1.00
1979Mo Square 9's in date	Inc. above	0.20	0.40	1.60	2.25
1980Mo Narrow date, square 9	89,978,000	0.45	0.75	1.75	2.50
1980Mo Wide date, round 9	178,188,000	0.20	0.25	1.00	2.25
1981Mo Rectangular 9, narrow date	142,212,000	0.50	0.75	1.75	2.50
1981Mo Round 9, wide date	Inc. above	0.30	0.50	1.25	1.75
1982Mo	45,474,000	0.20	0.40	1.95	1.75
1983Mo	90,318,000	0.50	0.75	1.75	2.50
1983Mo Proof	998	Value: 45.00			

KM# 492   50 CENTAVOS
4.4000 g., Stainless Steel, 22 mm. **Subject:** Palenque Culture **Obv:** National arms, eagle left **Rev:** Head with headdress 3/4 left **Mint:** Mexico City

Date	Mintage	F	VF	XF	Unc	BU
1983Mo	99,540,000	—	—	0.30	1.50	2.50
1983Mo Proof	53	Value: 195				

KM# 453   PESO
27.0700 g., 0.9030 Silver 0.7859 oz. ASW, 39 mm. **Subject:** Caballito **Obv:** National arms **Rev:** Horse and rider facing left among sun rays **Mint:** Mexico City **Designer:** Charles Pillet **Note:** Mint mark Mo.

Date	Mintage	F	VF	XF	Unc	BU
1910	3,814,000	BV	45.00	50.00	200	275
1911	1,227,000	BV	45.00	75.00	200	300

Note: Long lower left ray on reverse

1911	Inc. above	50.00	145	250	750	950

Note: Short lower left ray on reverse

1912	322,000	35.00	100	210	365	500
1913/2	2,880,000	BV	45.00	75.00	300	450
1913	Inc. above	BV	45.00	70.00	200	300

Note: 1913 coins exist with even and unevenly spaced date

1914	120,000	300	700	1,200	4,000	—

KM# 454   PESO
18.1300 g., 0.8000 Silver 0.4663 oz. ASW, 34 mm.
Obv: National arms **Rev:** Value and date within 3/4 wreath with Liberty cap above **Mint:** Mexico City **Note:** Mint mark Mo.

Date	Mintage	F	VF	XF	Unc	BU
1918/7	—	250	350	—	—	—
1918	3,050,000	20.00	45.00	150	1,350	2,500
1919	6,151,000	18.00	30.00	125	950	1,750

KM# 455   PESO
16.6600 g., 0.7200 Silver 0.3856 oz. ASW, 34 mm.
Obv: National arms **Rev:** Value and date within 3/4 wreath with Liberty cap above **Edge Lettering:** INDEPENDENCIA Y LIBERTAD **Mint:** Mexico City **Note:** Mint mark Mo.

Date	Mintage	F	VF	XF	Unc	BU
1920/10	8,830,000	18.00	50.00	90.00	325	—
1920	Inc. above	BV	15.00	35.00	195	350
1921	5,480,000	BV	15.00	35.00	195	275
1922	33,620,000	—	BV	15.00	20.00	35.00
1923	35,280,000	—	BV	15.00	20.00	35.00
1924	33,060,000	—	BV	15.00	20.00	35.00
1925	9,160,000	—	BV	15.00	60.00	85.00
1926	28,840,000	—	BV	15.00	25.00	40.00
1927	5,060,000	BV	15.00	16.00	70.00	90.00
1932 Open 9	50,770,000	—	—	BV	14.00	16.00
1932 Closed 9	Inc. above	—	—	BV	14.00	16.00
1933/2	43,920,000	15.00	20.00	35.00	100	—
1933	Inc. above	—	BV	15.00	16.50	18.00
1934	22,070,000	—	—	BV	15.00	22.00
1935	8,050,000	—	BV	15.00	16.00	24.00
1938	30,000,000	—	—	BV	15.00	16.50
1940	20,000,000	—	—	BV	15.00	16.50
1943	47,662,000	—	—	BV	15.00	16.50
1944	39,522,000	—	—	BV	15.00	16.50
1945	37,300,000	—	—	BV	15.00	16.50

KM# 456 PESO
14.0000 g., 0.5000 Silver 0.2250 oz. ASW, 32 mm.
Obv: National arms, eagle left **Rev:** Head with
headcovering right **Edge:** Reeded **Mint:** Mexico City
Note: Mint mark Mo.

Date	Mintage	F	VF	XF	Unc	BU
1947	61,460,000	—	—	BV	8.00	10.00
1948	22,915,000	—	—	BV	8.00	10.00
1949	4,000,000	300	600	1,200	1,600	2,500

Note: Not released for circulation
1949 Proof   — Value: 4,000

KM# 457 PESO
13.3300 g., 0.3000 Silver 0.1286 oz. ASW, 32 mm.
Obv: National arms, eagle left **Rev:** Armored bust 3/
4 left **Mint:** Mexico City **Note:** Mint mark Mo.

Date	Mintage	F	VF	XF	Unc	BU
1950	3,287,000	—	5.00	6.00	10.00	15.00

KM# 458 PESO
16.0000 g., 0.1000 Silver 0.0514 oz. ASW, 34.5 mm.
Subject: 100th Anniversary of Constitution **Obv:**
National arms, eagle left within wreath **Obv.**
Designer: Manuel L. Negrete **Rev:** Head left **Edge
Lettering:** INDEPENDENCIA Y LIBERTAD **Mint:**
Mexico City **Note:** Mint mark Mo.

Date	Mintage	F	VF	XF	Unc	BU
1957	500,000	—	4.00	6.00	12.50	16.50

KM# 459 PESO
16.0000 g., 0.1000 Silver 0.0514 oz. ASW, 34.5 mm.
Obv: National arms, eagle left within wreath **Rev:**
Armored bust right within wreath **Edge Lettering:**
INDEPENDENCIA Y LIBERTAD **Mint:** Mexico City
Note: Mint mark Mo.

Date	Mintage	F	VF	XF	Unc	BU
1957	28,273,000	—	BV	2.00	3.00	10.00
1958	41,899,000	—	—	BV	2.00	3.00
1959	27,369,000	—	BV	2.00	5.50	8.00
1960	26,259,000	—	BV	2.00	3.50	6.00
1961	52,601,000	—	—	BV	2.50	5.00
1962	61,094,000	—	—	BV	2.00	4.00
1963	26,394,000	—	—	BV	2.00	2.50
1964	15,615,000	—	—	BV	2.00	2.50
1965	5,004,000	—	—	BV	2.00	2.50
1966	30,998,000	—	—	BV	2.00	2.25
1967	9,308,000	—	—	BV	2.75	4.50

Tall date   Short date

KM# 460 PESO
9.0000 g., Copper-Nickel, 29 mm. **Obv:** National
arms, eagle left **Rev:** Head left **Edge:** Reeded **Mint:**
Mexico City

Date	Mintage	VF	XF	Unc	BU
1970Mo Narrow date	102,715,000	0.25	0.35	0.65	0.80
1970Mo Wide date	Inc. above	1.25	2.50	7.50	10.00
1971Mo	426,222,000	0.20	0.25	0.55	0.75
1972Mo	120,000,000	0.20	0.25	0.40	0.65
1974Mo	63,700,000	0.20	0.25	0.65	0.90
1975Mo Tall narrow date	205,979,000	0.25	0.45	1.00	1.35
1975Mo Short wide date	Inc. above	0.30	0.40	0.75	1.00
1976Mo	94,489,000	0.15	0.20	0.50	0.75
1977Mo Thick date close to rim	94,364,000	0.25	0.45	1.00	1.25
1977Mo Thin date, space between sideburns and collar	Inc. above	1.00	2.50	8.50	16.50
1978Mo Closed 8	208,300,000	0.20	0.30	1.00	1.50
1978Mo Open 8	55,140,000	1.00	2.50	14.00	20.00
1979Mo Thin date	117,884,000	0.20	0.30	1.15	1.50
1979Mo Thick date	Inc. above	0.20	0.30	1.25	1.75
1980Mo Closed 8	318,800,000	0.25	0.35	1.00	1.25
1980Mo Open 8	23,865,000	0.75	1.50	8.00	15.00
1981Mo Closed 8	413,349,000	0.20	0.30	0.75	0.90
1981Mo Open 8	58,616,000	0.50	1.25	6.50	9.00

ESTADOS UNIDOS MEXICANOS

Date	Mintage	VF	XF	Unc	BU
1982Mo Closed 8	235,000,000	0.25	0.75	2.25	2.50
1982Mo Open 8	—	0.75	1.50	8.00	15.00
1983Mo Wide date	100,000,000	0.30	0.45	3.00	3.50
1983Mo Narrow date	Inc. above	0.30	0.45	3.00	4.50
1983Mo Proof	1,051,000	Value: 38.00			

KM# 496   PESO
5.7000 g., Stainless Steel, 24.5 mm. **Obv:** National arms, eagle left **Rev:** Armored bust right **Mint:** Mexico City

Date	Mintage	F	VF	XF	Unc	BU
1984Mo	722,802,000	—	0.10	0.25	0.65	1.45
1985Mo	985,000,000	—	0.10	0.25	0.50	1.25
1986Mo	740,000,000	—	0.10	0.25	0.50	1.25
1987Mo	250,000,000	—	0.10	0.25	0.50	1.25
1987Mo Proof; 2 known	—	Value: 1,000				

KM# 461   2 PESOS
1.6666 g., 0.9000 Gold 0.0482 oz. AGW, 13 mm. **Obv:** National arms **Rev:** Date above value within wreath **Mint:** Mexico City **Note:** Mint mark Mo.

Date	Mintage	F	VF	XF	Unc
1919	1,670,000	—	BV	100	110
1920/10	—	BV	100	105	145
1920	4,282,000	—	BV	100	105
1944	10,000	BV	100	110	130
1945	Est. 140,000	—	—	—	BV+20%
1946	168,000	BV	100	110	165
1947	25,000	BV	100	110	145
1948 No specimens known	45,000	—	—	—	—

Note: During 1951-1972 a total of 4,590,493 pieces were restruck, most likely dated 1945. In 1996 matte restrikes were produced. An additional 260,000 pieces dated 1945 were struck during 2000-2011

KM# 462   2 PESOS
26.6667 g., 0.9000 Silver 0.7716 oz. ASW, 39 mm.

Subject: Centennial of Independence **Obv:** National arms, eagle left within wreath **Rev:** Winged Victory **Mint:** Mexico City **Designer:** Emilio del Moral **Note:** Mint mark Mo.

Date	Mintage	F	VF	XF	Unc	BU
1921	1,278,000	30.00	45.00	75.00	450	700

KM# 463   2-1/2 PESOS
2.0833 g., 0.9000 Gold 0.0603 oz. AGW, 15.5 mm. **Obv:** National arms **Rev:** Miguel Hidalgo y Costilla **Mint:** Mexico City **Note:** Mint mark Mo.

Date	Mintage	F	VF	XF	Unc
1918	1,704,000	—	BV	110	130
1919	984,000	—	BV	110	130
1920/10	607,000	—	BV	110	180
1920	Inc. above	—	BV	110	125
1944	20,000	—	BV	115	145
1945	Est. 180,000	—	—	—	BV+18%
1946	163,000	—	BV	115	145
1947	24,000	230	300	425	750
1948	63,000	—	BV	115	145

Note: During 1951-1972 a total of 5,025,087 pieces were restruck, most likely dated 1945. In 1996 matte restrikes were produced. An additional 539,000 pieces dated 1945 were struck during 2000-2011

KM# 464   5 PESOS
4.1666 g., 0.9000 Gold 0.1206 oz. AGW, 19 mm. **Obv:** National arms **Rev:** Miguel Hidalgo y Costilla **Mint:** Mexico City **Note:** Mint mark Mo.

Date	Mintage	F	VF	XF	Unc	BU
1905	18,000	220	230	325	700	—
1906	4,638,000	—	—	BV	220	—
1907/6	—	—	—	—	—	—
1907	1,088,000	—	—	BV	220	—
1910	100,000	—	—	BV	220	—
1918/7	609,000	—	—	BV	255	—
1918	Inc. above	—	—	BV	220	—
1919	506,000	—	—	BV	220	—
1920	2,385,000	—	—	BV	220	—
1955	Est. 48,000	—	—	—	BV+12%	—

Note: During 1955-1972 a total of 1,767,645 pieces were restruck, most likely dated 1955. In 1996 matte restrikes were produced. An additional 94,000 pieces dated 1955 were struck during 2000-2011

KM# 465   5 PESOS
30.0000 g., 0.9000 Silver 0.8680 oz. ASW, 40 mm.

Obv: National arms, eagle left **Rev:** Head with headdress left **Edge:** Reeded **Mint:** Mexico City
Note: Mint mark Mo.

Date	Mintage	F	VF	XF	Unc	BU
1947	5,110,000	—	—	BV	32.50	35.00
1948	26,740,000	—	—	BV	32.50	35.00

KM# 468 5 PESOS
27.7800 g., 0.7200 Silver 0.6430 oz. ASW, 40 mm.
Subject: Bicentennial of Hidalgo's Birth **Obv:** National arms, eagle left **Rev:** Half-length figure facing to right of building and dates **Edge Lettering:** COMERCIO - AGRICULTURA - INDUSTRIA **Mint:** Mexico City **Designer:** Manuel L. Negrete **Note:** Mint mark Mo.

Date	Mintage	F	VF	XF	Unc	BU
1953	1,000,000	—	—	BV	23.00	25.00

KM# 466 5 PESOS
27.7800 g., 0.7200 Silver 0.6430 oz. ASW, 40 mm.
Subject: Opening of Southern Railroad **Obv:** National arms, eagle left **Rev:** Radiant sun flanked by palm trees above train **Edge Lettering:** COMERCIO - AGRICULTURA - INDUSTRIA **Mint:** Mexico City **Designer:** Manuel L. Negrete **Note:** Mint mark Mo.

Date	Mintage	F	VF	XF	Unc	BU
1950	200,000	—	27.50	45.00	65.00	75.00

Note: It is recorded that 100,000 pieces were melted to be used for the 1968 Mexican Olympic 25 Pesos

KM# 469 5 PESOS
18.0500 g., 0.7200 Silver 0.4178 oz. ASW, 36 mm.
Obv: National arms, eagle left **Rev:** Head left **Mint:** Mexico City **Note:** Mint mark Mo.

Date	Mintage	F	VF	XF	Unc	BU
1955	4,271,000	—	—	BV	15.00	16.50
1956	4,596,000	—	—	BV	15.00	16.50
1957	3,464,000	—	—	BV	15.00	16.50

KM# 467 5 PESOS
27.7800 g., 0.7200 Silver 0.6430 oz. ASW, 40 mm.
Obv: National arms, eagle left **Rev:** Head left within wreath **Edge Lettering:** COMERCIO - AGRICULTURA - INDUSTRIA **Mint:** Mexico City
Note: Mint mark Mo.

Date	Mintage	F	VF	XF	Unc	BU
1951	4,958,000	—	—	BV	22.50	25.00
1952	9,595,000	—	—	BV	22.50	25.00
1953	20,376,000	—	—	BV	22.50	25.00
1954	30,000	—	30.00	60.00	70.00	85.00

KM# 470 5 PESOS
18.0500 g., 0.7200 Silver 0.4178 oz. ASW, 36 mm.
Subject: 100th Anniversary of Constitution **Obv:** National arms, eagle left **Rev:** Head left **Edge Lettering:** INDEPENDENCIA Y LIBERTAD **Mint:** Mexico City **Designer:** Manuel L. Negrete **Note:** Mint mark Mo.

Date	Mintage	F	VF	XF	Unc	BU
1957	200,000	—	BV	15.00	16.00	18.00

ESTADOS UNIDOS MEXICANOS

KM# 471 5 PESOS

18.0500 g., 0.7200 Silver 0.4178 oz. ASW, 36 mm.
Subject: Centennial of Carranza's Birth **Obv:**
National arms, eagle left **Rev:** Head left **Edge:** Plain
Mint: Mexico City **Designer:** Manuel L. Negrete
Note: Mint mark Mo.

Date	Mintage	F	VF	XF	Unc	BU
1959	1,000,000	—	—	BV	15.00	16.50

Small date   Large date

KM# 472 5 PESOS

14.0000 g., Copper-Nickel, 33 mm. **Obv:** National
arms, eagle left **Rev:** Armored bust right **Edge
Lettering:** INDEPENDENCIA Y LIBERTAD **Mint:**
Mexico City **Note:** Small date, large date varieties.

Date	Mintage	VF	XF	Unc	BU
1971Mo	28,457,000	0.50	0.95	2.50	3.25
1972Mo	75,000,000	0.60	1.25	2.00	2.50
1973Mo	19,405,000	1.25	2.00	4.50	5.50
1974Mo	34,500,000	0.50	0.80	1.75	2.25
1976Mo Small date	26,121,000	0.75	1.45	3.25	4.00
1976Mo Large date	121,550,000	0.35	0.50	1.50	1.75
1977Mo	102,000,000	0.35	0.50	1.50	1.75
1978Mo	25,700,000	1.00	1.50	4.50	6.25

KM# 485 5 PESOS

10.2000 g., Copper-Nickel, 27 mm. **Subject:**
Quetzalcoatl **Obv:** National arms, eagle left **Rev:**

Native sculpture to lower right of value and dollar sign
Edge Lettering: LIBERTAD Y INDEPENDENCIA
Mint: Mexico City **Note:** Inverted and normal edge
legend varieties exist for the 1980 and 1981 dates.

Date	Mintage	VF	XF	Unc	BU
1980Mo	266,899,999	0.25	0.50	1.75	2.25
1981Mo	30,500,000	0.45	0.65	2.75	3.25
1982Mo	20,000,000	1.50	2.35	4.25	5.25
1982Mo Proof	1,051	Value: 50.00			
1983Mo Proof; 7 known	—	Value: 1,200			
1984Mo	16,300,000	1.25	2.00	4.75	6.00
1985Mo	76,900,000	2.00	3.25	4.25	5.00

KM# 502 5 PESOS

3.1000 g., Brass, 17 mm. **Obv:** National arms, eagle
left **Rev:** Date and value **Edge:** Reeded **Mint:** Mexico
City

Date	Mintage	F	VF	XF	Unc	BU
1985Mo	30,000,000	—	—	0.15	0.35	0.50
1987Mo	81,900,000	2.00	8.00	9.50	12.50	16.50
1988Mo	76,600,000	—	—	0.10	0.25	0.35
1988Mo Proof; 2 known	—	Value: 600				

KM# 473 10 PESOS

8.3333 g., 0.9000 Gold 0.2411 oz. AGW, 22.5 mm.
Obv: National arms **Rev:** Miguel Hidalgo y Costilla
Mint: Mexico City **Note:** Mint mark Mo.

Date	Mintage	F	VF	XF	Unc	BU
1905	39,000	—	BV	450	475	500
1906	2,949,000	—	BV	450	475	500
1907	1,589,000	—	BV	450	475	500
1908	890,000	—	BV	450	475	500
1910	451,000	—	BV	450	475	500
1916	26,000	—	BV	475	500	525
1917	1,967,000	—	BV	450	475	500
1919	266,000	—	BV	450	475	500
1920	12,000	—	BV	550	925	1,000
1959	Est. 50,000	—	—	—	BV+7%	—

Note: *During 1961-1972 a total of 954,983 pieces were
restruck, most likely dated 1959. In 1996 matte restrikes
were produced. An additional 61,500 pieces dated 1959
were struck during 2000-2011

KM# 474 10 PESOS

28.8880 g., 0.9000 Silver 0.8359 oz. ASW, 40 mm.

Obv: National arms **Rev:** Head left **Edge:** Reeded
Mint: Mexico City **Note:** Mint mark Mo.

Date	Mintage	F	VF	XF	Unc	BU
1955	585,000	—	—	BV	32.00	35.00
1956	3,535,000	—	—	BV	32.00	33.00

KM# 475   10 PESOS
28.8800 g., 0.9000 Silver 0.8356 oz. ASW, 40 mm.
Subject: 100th Anniversary of Constitution **Obv:**
National arms, eagle left **Rev:** Head left **Edge
Lettering:** INDEPENDENCIA Y LIBERTAD **Mint:**
Mexico City **Designer:** Manuel L. Negrete **Note:** Mint
mark Mo.

Date	Mintage	F	VF	XF	Unc	BU
1957	100,000	BV	32.00	40.00	55.00	60.00

KM# 476   10 PESOS
28.8880 g., 0.9000 Silver 0.8359 oz. ASW, 40 mm.
Subject: 150th Anniversary - War of Independence
Obv: National arms, eagle left **Rev:** Conjoined busts
facing flanked by dates **Edge:** Reeded **Mint:** Mexico
City **Designer:** Manuel L. Negrete **Note:** Mint mark Mo.

Date	Mintage	F	VF	XF	Unc	BU
1960	1,000,000	—	—	BV	32.00	34.00

KM# 477.1   10 PESOS
10.0000 g., Copper-Nickel, 30.5 mm. **Subject:**

Miguel Hidalgo y Costilla **Obv:** National arms, eagle
left **Rev:** Head left **Shape:** 7-sided **Mint:** Mexico City
Note: Thin flan - 1.6mm

Date	Mintage	F	VF	XF	Unc	BU
1974Mo	3,900,000	—	0.50	1.00	3.00	4.50
1974Mo Proof	—	Value: 650				
1975Mo	1,000,000	—	2.25	3.25	7.50	8.50
1976Mo	74,500,000	—	0.25	0.75	1.75	2.75
1977Mo	79,620,000	—	0.50	1.00	2.00	3.00

KM# 477.2   10 PESOS
11.5000 g., Copper-Nickel, 30.5 mm. **Subject:**
Miguel Hidalgo y Costilla **Obv:** National arms, eagle
left **Rev:** Head left **Shape:** 7-sided **Mint:** Mexico City
Note: Thick flan - 2.3mm

Date	Mintage	F	VF	XF	Unc	BU
1978Mo	124,850,000	—	0.50	0.75	2.50	2.75
1979Mo	57,200,000	—	0.50	0.75	2.50	2.75
1980Mo	55,200,000	—	0.50	0.75	2.50	3.75
1981Mo	222,768,000	—	0.40	0.60	2.25	2.75
1982Mo	151,770,000	—	0.50	0.80	2.50	3.50
1982Mo Proof	1,051	Value: 45.00				
1983Mo Proof; 3 known	—	Value: 1,800				
1985Mo	58,000,000	—	1.25	1.75	5.75	8.00

KM# 512   10 PESOS
3.8400 g., Stainless Steel, 19 mm. **Obv:** National
arms, eagle left **Rev:** Head facing with diagonal value
at left **Mint:** Mexico City **Note:** Date varieties exist.

Date	Mintage	F	VF	XF	Unc	BU
1985Mo	257,000,000	—	—	0.15	0.50	0.75
1986Mo	392,000,000	—	—	0.15	0.50	1.50
1987Mo	305,000,000	—	—	0.15	0.35	0.50
1988Mo	500,300,000	—	—	0.15	0.25	0.35
1989Mo	336,900,000	—	0.20	0.25	0.75	1.50
1990Mo	101,000,000	—	—	0.25	0.75	1.25
1990Mo Proof; 2 known	—	Value: 550				

KM# 478   20 PESOS
16.6666 g., 0.9000 Gold 0.4822 oz. AGW, 27.5 mm.
Obv: National arms, eagle left **Rev:** Aztec Sunstone
with denomination below **Edge:** Lettered **Edge
Lettering:** INDEPEDENCIA Y LIBERTAD **Mint:**
Mexico City **Note:** Mint mark Mo.

Date	Mintage	F	VF	XF	Unc	BU
1917	852,000	—	—	BV	910	—
1918	2,831,000	—	—	BV	910	—
1919	1,094,000	—	—	BV	910	—
1920/10	462,000	—	—	BV	910	—
1920	Inc. above	—	—	BV	925	—
1921/11	922,000	—	—	BV	910	—
1921/10	—	—	—	—	—	—
1921	Inc. above	—	—	BV	925	—
1959	Est. 13,000	—	—	—	BV+4%	—

Note: During 1960-1971 a total of 1,158,414 pieces were
restruck, most likely dated 1959. In 1996 matte restrikes
were produced. An additional 92,000 pieces dated 1959
were struck in 2000-2011

ESTADOS UNIDOS MEXICANOS

KM# 486   20 PESOS
15.2000 g., Copper-Nickel, 32 mm. **Obv:** National
arms, eagle left **Rev:** Figure with headdress facing
left within circle **Edge Lettering:** INDEPENDENCIA
Y LIBERTAD **Mint:** Mexico City

Date	Mintage	F	VF	XF	Unc	BU
1980Mo	84,900,000	—	0.50	0.85	2.25	3.25
1981Mo	250,573,000	—	0.60	0.80	2.25	3.25
1982Mo	236,892,000	—	1.00	1.75	2.50	3.75
1982Mo Proof	1,051	Value: 50.00				
1983Mo Proof; 3 known	—	Value: 575				
1984Mo	55,000,000	—	1.00	1.50	2.50	4.75

KM# 508   20 PESOS
6.0000 g., Brass, 21 mm. **Obv:** National arms, eagle
left **Rev:** Bust facing with diagonal value at left **Edge:**
Reeded **Mint:** Mexico City

Date	Mintage	VF	XF	Unc	BU
1985Mo Wide date	25,000,000	0.10	0.20	1.00	1.50
1985Mo Narrow date	Inc. above	0.10	0.25	1.50	2.25
1986Mo	10,000,000	1.00	1.75	5.00	6.00
1988Mo	355,200,000	0.10	0.20	0.45	0.75
1989Mo	289,100,000	0.15	0.30	1.50	2.00
1990Mo	126,550,000	0.15	0.30	1.50	2.50
1990Mo Proof; 3 known	—	Value: 600			

Snake's tongue straight

KM# 479.1   25 PESOS
22.5000 g., 0.7200 Silver 0.5208 oz. ASW, 38 mm.
Obv: National arms, eagle left **Rev:** Olympic rings
below dancing native left, numeral design in
background **Designer:** Lorenzo Rafael **Note:** Type
I, Rings aligned.

Date	Mintage	F	VF	XF	Unc	BU
1968Mo	27,182,000	—	—	BV	19.00	21.00

KM# 479.2   25 PESOS
22.5000 g., 0.7200 Silver 0.5208 oz. ASW, 38 mm.
Subject: Summer Olympics - Mexico City **Obv:**
National arms, eagle left **Rev:** Olympic rings below
dancing native left, numeral design in background
Mint: Mexico City **Note:** Type II, center ring low.

Date	Mintage	F	VF	XF	Unc	BU
1968Mo	Inc. above	—	BV	19.00	20.00	21.00

Snake's tongue curved

KM# 479.3   25 PESOS
22.5000 g., 0.7200 Silver 0.5208 oz. ASW, 38 mm.
Subject: Summer Olympics - Mexico City **Obv:**
National arms, eagle left **Rev:** Olympic rings below
dancing native left, numeral design in background
Mint: Mexico City **Note:** Snake with long curved or
normal tongue. Type III, center rings low.

Date	Mintage	F	VF	XF	Unc	BU
1968Mo	Inc. above	—	BV	19.00	20.00	22.50

KM# 480   25 PESOS
22.5000 g., 0.7200 Silver 0.5208 oz. ASW, 38 mm.
Obv: National arms, eagle left **Rev:** Bust facing **Mint:**
Mexico City

Date	Mintage	F	VF	XF	Unc	BU
1972Mo	2,000,000	—	BV	19.00	20.00	21.00

ESTADOS UNIDOS MEXICANOS

KM# 497 25 PESOS
7.7760 g., 0.7200 Silver 0.1800 oz. ASW **Subject:**
1986 World Cup Soccer Games **Obv:** National arms,
eagle left **Rev:** Value above soccer ball with date
below **Mint:** Mexico City

Date	Mintage	F	VF	XF	Unc	BU
1985Mo	354,000	—	—	—	—	10.00

KM# 503 25 PESOS
8.4060 g., 0.9250 Silver 0.2500 oz. ASW **Subject:**
1986 World Cup Soccer Games **Obv:** National arms,
eagle left **Rev:** Pre-Columbian hieroglyphs, ojo de
buey, and soccer ball **Mint:** Mexico City

Date	Mintage	F	VF	XF	Unc	BU
1985Mo Proof	277,000	Value: 15.00				

KM# 514 25 PESOS
8.4060 g., 0.9250 Silver 0.2500 oz. ASW **Subject:**
1986 World Cup Soccer Games **Obv:** National arms,
eagle left **Rev:** Value above soccer ball **Mint:** Mexico
City

Date	Mintage	F	VF	XF	Unc	BU
1985Mo Proof	234,000	Value: 15.00				

KM# 519 25 PESOS
8.4060 g., 0.9250 Silver 0.2500 oz. ASW **Subject:**
1986 World Cup Soccer Games **Obv:** National arms,
eagle left **Rev:** Soccer ball within net, date and value
to left **Mint:** Mexico City

Date	Mintage	F	VF	XF	Unc	BU
1986Mo Proof	—	Value: 15.00				

KM# 497a 25 PESOS
8.4060 g., 0.9250 Silver 0.2500 oz. ASW **Subject:**
1986 World Cup Soccer Games **Obv:** National arms,
eagle left **Rev:** Value above soccerball with date
below **Mint:** Mexico City **Note:** Without finess
statement- reverse description

Date	Mintage	F	VF	XF	Unc	BU
1986Mo Proof	—	Value: 15.00				

KM# 481 50 PESOS
41.6666 g., 0.9000 Gold 1.2056 oz. AGW, 37 mm.
Subject: Centennial of Independence **Obv:** National
arms **Rev:** Winged Victory **Edge:** Reeded **Mint:**
Mexico City **Designer:** Emilio del Moral **Note:** During
1949-1972 a total of 3,975,654 pieces were restruck,
most likely dated 1947 and an additional 342,000
pieces dated 1947 were struck during 2000-2011. In
1996 matte restrikes were produced. Mint mark Mo.

Date	Mintage	F	VF	XF	Unc	BU
1921	180,000	—	—	BV	2,300	3,300
1922	463,000	—	—	BV	2,200	2,400
1923	432,000	—	—	BV	2,200	2,400
1924	439,000	—	—	BV	2,200	2,400
1925	716,000	—	—	BV	2,200	2,400
1926	600,000	—	—	BV	2,200	2,400
1927	606,000	—	—	BV	2,200	2,400
1928	538,000	—	—	BV	2,200	2,400
1929	458,000	—	—	BV	2,200	2,400
1930	372,000	—	—	BV	2,200	2,400
1931	137,000	—	—	BV	2,250	2,500
1944	593,000	—	—	BV	2,200	2,300
1945	1,012,000	—	—	BV	2,200	2,300
1946	1,588,000	—	—	BV	2,200	2,300
1947	309,000	—	—	— BV+3%	—	
1947 Specimen	—	—	—	—	—	—

Note: Value, $6,500

KM# 482 50 PESOS
41.6666 g., 0.9000 Gold 1.2056 oz. AGW, 37 mm.
Obv: National arms **Rev:** Winged Victory

Date	Mintage	F	VF	XF	Unc	BU
1943Mo	89,000	—	—	—	BV	2,300

KM# 481a   50 PESOS
Platinum APW   **Subject:** Centennial of
Independence **Obv:** National arms **Rev:** Winged
Victory **Edge:** Reeded **Mint:** Mexico City

Date	Mintage	F	VF	XF	Unc	BU
1947Mo	Est. 5	—	—	—	—	13,500

KM# 490   50 PESOS
19.8400 g., Copper-Nickel, 39 mm.   **Subject:**
Coyolxauhqui **Obv:** National arms, eagle left **Rev:**
Value to right of artistic designs **Edge:** Reeded **Mint:**
Mexico City **Note:** Doubled die examples of 1982
and 1983 dates exist.

Date	Mintage	VF	XF	Unc	BU
1982Mo	222,890,000	1.00	2.50	5.00	6.50
1983Mo	45,000,000	1.50	3.00	6.00	7.00
1983Mo Proof	1,051	Value: 55.00			
1984Mo	73,537,000	1.00	1.35	3.50	4.50
1984Mo Proof; 4 known	—	Value: 750			

KM# 495   50 PESOS
8.6000 g., Copper-Nickel, 23.5 mm.   **Subject:**
Benito Juarez **Obv:** National arms, eagle left **Rev:**
Bust 1/4 left with diagonal value at left **Edge:** Reeded
Mint: Mexico City

Date	Mintage	F	VF	XF	Unc	BU
1984Mo	94,216,000	—	0.65	1.25	2.70	3.25
1985Mo	296,000,000	—	0.25	0.45	1.25	2.25
1986Mo	50,000,000	—	6.00	10.00	12.00	14.00
1987Mo	210,000,000	—	0.25	0.45	1.00	1.25
1988Mo	80,200,000	—	6.25	9.00	13.50	16.00

KM# 495a   50 PESOS
7.1000 g., Stainless Steel, 23.5 mm.   **Subject:**
Benito Juarez **Obv:** National arms, eagle left **Rev:**
Bust 1/4 left with diagonal value at left **Edge:** Plain
Mint: Mexico City

Date	Mintage	F	VF	XF	Unc	BU
1988Mo	353,300,000	—	—	0.20	1.25	1.75
1989Mo	20,000	10.00	12.00	15.00	25.00	30.00
Note: Reported not confirmed.						
1990Mo	180,000,000	—	—	0.30	1.00	2.00
1992Mo	84,520,000	—	—	0.25	1.00	2.75

KM# 504   50 PESOS
16.8310 g., 0.9250 Silver 0.5005 oz. ASW **Subject:**
1986 World Cup Soccer Games **Obv:** National arms,
eagle left **Rev:** Stylized athlete as soccer forerunner
Mint: Mexico City

Date	Mintage	F	VF	XF	Unc	BU
1985Mo Proof	347,000	Value: 25.00				

KM# 515   50 PESOS
16.8310 g., 0.9250 Silver 0.5005 oz. ASW **Subject:**
1986 World Cup Soccer Games **Obv:** National arms,
eagle left **Rev:** Value to right of soccer player **Mint:**
Mexico City

Date	Mintage	F	VF	XF	Unc	BU
1985Mo Proof	234,000	Value: 25.00				

KM# 498   50 PESOS
15.5520 g., 0.7200 Silver 0.3600 oz. ASW **Subject:**
1986 World Cup Soccer Games **Obv:** National arms,
eagle left **Rev:** Pair of feet and soccer ball **Mint:**
Mexico City

Date	Mintage	F	VF	XF	Unc	BU
1985Mo	347,000	—	—	—	—	16.50

ESTADOS UNIDOS MEXICANOS

KM# 523   50 PESOS
16.8310 g., 0.9250 Silver 0.5005 oz. ASW **Subject:**
1986 World Cup Soccer Games **Obv:** National arms,
eagle left **Rev:** Value to left of soccer balls **Mint:**
Mexico City

Date	Mintage	F	VF	XF	Unc	BU
1986Mo Proof	190,000	Value: 25.00				

KM# 498a   50 PESOS
16.8310 g., 0.9250 Silver 0.5005 oz. ASW **Subject:**
1986 World Cup Soccer Games **Obv:** National arms,
eagle left **Rev:** Without fineness statement **Mint:**
Mexico City

Date	Mintage	F	VF	XF	Unc	BU
1986Mo Proof	10,000	Value: 25.00				

KM# 532   50 PESOS
15.5500 g., 0.9990 Silver 0.4994 oz. ASW **Subject:**
50th Anniversary - Nationalization of Oil Industry
Obv: National arms, eagle left **Rev:** Monument **Mint:**
Mexico City

Date	Mintage	F	VF	XF	Unc	BU
ND(1988)Mo	20,000	—	—	—	22.50	25.00

Low 7's

KM# 483.1   100 PESOS
27.7700 g., 0.7200 Silver 0.6428 oz. ASW, 39 mm.
Obv: National arms, eagle left **Rev:** Bust facing,
sloping right shoulder, round left shoulder with no
clothing folds **Edge:** Reeded **Mint:** Mexico City

Date	Mintage	VF	XF	Unc	BU
1977Mo Low 7's	5,225,000	—	BV	23.00	25.00
1977Mo High 7's	Inc. above	—	BV	23.00	25.00

High 7's

KM# 483.2   100 PESOS
27.7700 g., 0.7200 Silver 0.6428 oz. ASW, 39 mm.
Obv: National arms, eagle left **Rev:** Bust facing,
higher right shoulder, left shoulder with clothing folds.
Mint: Mexico City **Note:** Mintage inc. KM#483.1

Date	Mintage	VF	XF	Unc	BU
1977Mo Date in line	—	—	BV	23.00	25.00
1978Mo	9,879,000	—	BV	23.00	25.00
1979Mo	784,000	—	BV	23.00	25.00
1979Mo Proof	—	Value: 650			

KM# 493   100 PESOS
11.7000 g., Aluminum-Bronze, 26.5 mm. **Obv:**
National arms, eagle left **Rev:** Head 1/4 right with
diagonal value at right **Edge:** Segmented reeding
Mint: Mexico City

Date	Mintage	F	VF	XF	Unc	BU
1984Mo	227,809,000	—	0.45	0.60	2.50	4.00
1985Mo	377,423,000	—	0.30	0.50	2.00	3.00
1986Mo	43,000,000	—	1.00	2.50	4.75	7.50
1987Mo	165,000,000	—	0.60	1.25	2.25	3.00
1988Mo	433,100,000	—	0.30	0.50	2.00	2.75
1989Mo	135,630,000	—	0.35	0.65	2.00	2.75
1990Mo	248,350,000	—	0.15	0.40	1.50	2.50
1990Mo Proof; 1 known	—	Value: 650				
1991Mo	189,900,000	—	0.15	0.25	1.00	2.50
1992Mo	277,310,000	—	0.30	0.75	1.75	3.00

ESTADOS UNIDOS MEXICANOS

KM# 499   100 PESOS
31.1030 g., 0.7200 Silver 0.7200 oz. ASW **Subject:**
1986 World Cup Soccer Games **Obv:** National arms,
eagle left **Rev:** Value above artistic designs and
soccer ball **Mint:** Mexico City

Date	Mintage	F	VF	XF	Unc	BU
1985Mo	302,000	—	—	—	—	30.00

KM# 521   100 PESOS
32.6250 g., 0.9250 Silver 0.9702 oz. ASW **Subject:**
1986 World Cup Soccer Games **Obv:** National arms,
eagle left **Rev:** Without fineness statement **Mint:**
Mexico City

Date	Mintage	F	VF	XF	Unc	BU
1986Mo Proof	208,000	Value: 55.00				

KM# 499a   100 PESOS
32.6250 g., 0.9250 Silver 0.9702 oz. ASW **Subject:**
1986 World Cup Soccer Games **Obv:** National arms,
eagle left **Rev:** Without fineness statement **Mint:**
Mexico City

Date	Mintage	F	VF	XF	Unc	BU
1985Mo Proof	9,006	Value: 55.00				

KM# 524   100 PESOS
32.6250 g., 0.9250 Silver 0.9702 oz. ASW **Subject:**
1986 World Cup Soccer Games **Obv:** National arms,
eagle left **Rev:** Without fineness statement **Mint:**
Mexico City

Date	Mintage	F	VF	XF	Unc	BU
1986Mo Proof	190,000	Value: 55.00				

KM# 505   100 PESOS
32.6250 g., 0.9250 Silver 0.9702 oz. ASW, 38 mm.
Subject: 1986 World Cup Soccer Games **Obv:**
National arms, eagle left **Rev:** Without fineness
statement **Mint:** Mexico City

Date	Mintage	F	VF	XF	Unc	BU
1985Mo Proof	9,006	Value: 50.00				

KM# 537   100 PESOS
32.6250 g., 0.7200 Silver 0.7552 oz. ASW **Subject:**
World Wildlife Fund **Obv:** National arms, eagle left
Rev: Monarch butterflies **Mint:** Mexico City

Date	Mintage	F	VF	XF	Unc	BU
1987Mo Proof	28,500	Value: 65.00				

ESTADOS UNIDOS MEXICANOS

KM# 533   100 PESOS
31.1030 g., 0.9990 Silver 0.9989 oz. ASW **Subject:**
50th Anniversary - Nationalization of Oil Industry
Obv: National arms, eagle left **Rev:** Bust facing
above sprigs and dates **Mint:** Mexico City

Date	Mintage	F	VF	XF	Unc	BU
1988Mo	20,000	—	—	—	40.00	55.00

KM# 566   100 PESOS
31.1035 g., 0.9990 Silver 0.9990 oz. ASW **Subject:**
Save the Vaquita Porpoise **Obv:** National arms,
eagle left **Rev:** Swimming vaquita porpoise **Mint:**
Mexico City

Date	Mintage	F	VF	XF	Unc	BU
1992Mo Proof	28,007	Value: 60.00				

KM# 539   100 PESOS
33.6250 g., 0.9250 Silver 0.9999 oz. ASW **Subject:**
Save the Children **Obv:** National arms, eagle left
Rev: Child flying kite, two others sitting and playing
Mint: Mexico City

Date	Mintage	F	VF	XF	Unc	BU
1991Mo Proof	11,000	Value: 50.00				

KM# 509   200 PESOS
Copper-Nickel, 29.5 mm. **Subject:** 175th
Anniversary of Independence **Obv:** National arms,
eagle left **Rev:** Conjoined busts left **Mint:** Mexico City

Date	Mintage	F	VF	XF	Unc	BU
1985Mo	75,000,000	—	—	2.00	3.50	5.50

KM# 510   200 PESOS
Copper-Nickel, 29.5 mm. **Subject:** 75th
Anniversary of 1910 Revolution **Obv:** National arms,
eagle left **Rev:** Conjoined heads left below building
Mint: Mexico City

Date	Mintage	F	VF	XF	Unc	BU
1985Mo	98,590,000	—	—	2.00	4.00	6.00

KM# 540   100 PESOS
27.0000 g., 0.9250 Silver 0.8029 oz. ASW, 40 mm.
Series: Ibero - America **Obv:** National arms, eagle
left within center of assorted arms **Rev:** Maps within
circles flanked by pillars above sailboats **Mint:**
Mexico City

Date	Mintage	F	VF	XF	Unc	BU
1991Mo Proof	30,000	Value: 85.00				
1992Mo Proof	20,000	Value: 80.00				

ESTADOS UNIDOS MEXICANOS

KM# 525   200 PESOS
Copper-Nickel, 29.5 mm. **Subject:** 1986 World Cup
Soccer Games **Obv:** National arms, eagle left **Rev:**
Soccer players **Edge:** Reeded **Mint:** Mexico City

Date	Mintage	F	VF	XF	Unc	BU
1986Mo	50,000,000	—	—	2.50	4.00	6.00

KM# 526   200 PESOS
62.2060 g., 0.9990 Silver 1.9979 oz. ASW **Subject:**
1986 World Cup Soccer Games **Obv:** National arms,
eagle left **Rev:** Value above 3 soccer balls **Mint:**
Mexico City

Date	Mintage	F	VF	XF	Unc	BU
1986Mo	50,000	—	—	—	80.00	90.00

KM# 500.1   250 PESOS
8.6400 g., 0.9000 Gold 0.2500 oz. AGW **Subject:**
1986 World Cup Soccer Games **Obv:** National arms,
eagle left **Rev:** Soccer ball within top 1/2 of design
with value, date, and state below **Mint:** Mexico City

Date	Mintage	F	VF	XF	Unc	BU
1985Mo	100,000	—	—	—	—	475
1986Mo	—	—	—	—	—	475

KM# 500.2   250 PESOS
8.6400 g., 0.9000 Gold 0.2500 oz. AGW **Subject:**
1986 World Cup Soccer Games **Obv:** National arms,
eagle left **Rev:** Without fineness statement **Mint:**
Mexico City

Date	Mintage	F	VF	XF	Unc	BU
1985Mo Proof	4,506	Value: 500				
1986Mo Proof	—	Value: 500				

KM# 506.1   250 PESOS
8.6400 g., 0.9000 Gold 0.2500 oz. AGW **Subject:**
1986 World Cup Soccer Games **Obv:** National arms,
eagle left **Rev:** Equestrian left within circle **Mint:**
Mexico City

Date	Mintage	F	VF	XF	Unc	BU
1985Mo	88,000	—	—	—	—	475

KM# 506.2   250 PESOS
8.6400 g., 0.9000 Gold 0.2500 oz. AGW **Subject:**
1986 World Cup Soccer Games **Obv:** National arms,
eagle left **Rev:** Without fineness statement **Mint:**
Mexico City

Date	Mintage	F	VF	XF	Unc	BU
1985Mo Proof	Est. 80,000	Value: 475				

KM# 501.1   500 PESOS
17.2800 g., 0.9000 Gold 0.5000 oz. AGW **Subject:**
1986 World Cup Soccer Games **Obv:** National arms,
eagle left **Rev:** Soccer player to right within emblem
Mint: Mexico City

Date	Mintage	F	VF	XF	Unc	BU
1985Mo	102,000	—	—	—	—	950
1986Mo	—	—	—	—	—	950

KM# 501.2   500 PESOS
17.2800 g., 0.9000 Gold 0.5000 oz. AGW **Subject:**
1986 World Cup Soccer Games **Obv:** National arms,
eagle left **Rev:** Without fineness statement **Mint:**
Mexico City

Date	Mintage	F	VF	XF	Unc	BU
1985Mo Proof	5,506	Value: 950				
1986Mo Proof	—	Value: 950				

KM# 507.1   500 PESOS
17.2800 g., 0.9000 Gold 0.5000 oz. AGW **Subject:**
1986 World Cup Soccer Games **Obv:** National arms,
eagle left **Rev:** Soccer ball within emblem flanked by
value and date **Mint:** Mexico City

Date	Mintage	F	VF	XF	Unc	BU
1985Mo	—	—	—	—	—	950

KM# 507.2   500 PESOS
17.2800 g., 0.9000 Gold 0.5000 oz. AGW **Subject:**

1986 World Cup Soccer Games **Obv:** National arms, eagle left **Rev:** Without fineness statement **Mint:** Mexico City

Date	Mintage	F	VF	XF	Unc	BU
1985Mo Proof	—	Value: 950				

KM# 511   500 PESOS

33.4500 g., 0.9250 Silver 0.9947 oz. ASW **Subject:** 75th Anniversary of 1910 Revolution **Obv:** National arms, eagle left **Rev:** Conjoined heads left below building **Mint:** Mexico City

Date	Mintage	F	VF	XF	Unc	BU
1985Mo Proof	40,002	Value: 65.00				

KM# 529   500 PESOS

12.6000 g., Copper-Nickel, 28.5 mm. **Obv:** National arms, eagle left **Rev:** Head 1/4 right **Edge:** Reeded **Mint:** Mexico City

Date	Mintage	F	VF	XF	Unc	BU
1986Mo	20,000,000	—	—	1.00	3.25	4.00
1987Mo	180,000,000	—	—	0.75	2.25	3.00
1988Mo	230,000,000	—	—	0.50	2.25	3.00
1988Mo Proof; 2 known	—	Value: 650				
1989Mo	40,000,000	—	—	0.75	2.25	3.50
1992Mo	20,000,000	—	—	1.00	2.25	4.00

KM# 534   500 PESOS

17.2800 g., 0.9000 Gold 0.5000 oz. AGW **Subject:** 50th Anniversary - Nationalization of Oil Industry **Obv:** National arms, eagle left **Rev:** Monument **Mint:** Mexico City **Note:** Similar to 5000 Pesos, KM#531.

Date	Mintage	F	VF	XF	Unc	BU
1988Mo	611	—	—	—	—	1,000

KM# 513   1000 PESOS

17.2800 g., 0.9000 Gold 0.5000 oz. AGW **Subject:** 175th Anniversary of Independence **Obv:** National

arms, eagle left **Rev:** Conjoined heads left below value **Mint:** Mexico City

Date	Mintage	F	VF	XF	Unc	BU
1985Mo Proof	3,721	Value: 950				

KM# 527   1000 PESOS

31.1050 g., 0.9990 Gold 0.9990 oz. AGW **Subject:** 1986 World Cup Soccer Games **Obv:** National arms, eagle left **Rev:** Value above soccer ball and two hemispheres **Mint:** Mexico City

Date	Mintage	F	VF	XF	Unc	BU
1986Mo	1,279	—	—	—	—	2,000

KM# 536   1000 PESOS

15.0000 g., Aluminum-Bronze, 30.5 mm. **Subject:** Juana de Asbaje **Obv:** National arms, eagle left **Rev:** Bust 1/4 left with diagonal value at left **Edge:** Reeded **Mint:** Mexico City

Date	Mintage	F	VF	XF	Unc	BU
1988Mo	229,300,000	—	0.85	2.00	4.25	5.75
1989Mo	215,716,000	—	0.85	2.00	4.25	5.75
1990Mo	41,291,000	—	0.85	2.00	4.00	5.50
1990Mo Proof; 2 known	—	Value: 550				
1991Mo	42,468,000	—	1.00	2.00	3.00	7.00
1992Mo	84,725,000	—	1.00	2.00	3.50	7.50

KM# 535   1000 PESOS

34.5590 g., 0.9000 Gold 0.9999 oz. AGW **Subject:** 50th Anniversary - Nationalization of Oil Industry **Obv:** National arms, eagle left **Rev:** Portrait of Cardenas **Mint:** Mexico City **Note:** Similar to 5000 Pesos, KM#531.

Date	Mintage	F	VF	XF	Unc	BU
1988Mo Proof	657	Value: 2,000				

KM# 643   1000 PESOS

31.1030 g., 0.9990 Silver 0.9989 oz. ASW **Rev:** Emiliano Zapata **Mint:** Mexico City **Note:** Unissued type due to currency reform.

Date	Mintage	F	VF	XF	Unc	BU
1990Mo Proof	—	Value: 1,600				

ESTADOS UNIDOS MEXICANOS

KM# 528   2000 PESOS
62.2000 g., 0.9990 Gold 1.9977 oz. AGW **Subject:**
1986 World Cup Soccer Games **Obv:** National arms,
eagle left **Rev:** Value above soccer ball and two
hemispheres **Mint:** Mexico City

Date	Mintage	F	VF	XF	Unc	BU
1986Mo	964	—	—	—	—	4,000

KM# 531   5000 PESOS
Copper-Nickel, 33.5 mm.   **Subject:** 50th
Anniversary - Nationalization of Oil Industry **Obv:**
National arms, eagle left **Rev:** Monument above
dates with diagonal value at left **Mint:** Mexico City

Date	Mintage	F	VF	XF	Unc	BU
ND(1988)Mo	50,000,000	—	—	4.75	7.75	10.00

REFORM COINAGE
**1 New Peso = 1000 Old Pesos;
100 centavos = 1 New Peso;
100 Centavos = 1 Peso**

KM# 546   5 CENTAVOS
1.5800 g., Stainless Steel, 15.5 mm.   **Obv:** National
arms **Rev:** Large value **Edge:** Plain **Mint:** Mexico City

Date	Mintage	F	VF	XF	Unc	BU
1992Mo	136,800,000	—	—	0.15	0.20	0.50
1993Mo	234,000,000	—	—	0.15	0.20	0.50
1994Mo	125,000,000	—	—	0.15	0.20	0.50
1995Mo	195,000,000	—	—	0.15	0.20	0.50
1995Mo Proof	6,981	Value: 2.00				
1996Mo	104,831,000	—	—	0.15	0.20	0.50
1997Mo	153,675,000	—	—	0.15	0.20	0.50
1998Mo	64,417,000	—	—	0.15	0.20	0.50
1999Mo	9,949,000	—	—	0.20	0.75	1.00
2000Mo	10,871,000	—	—	0.20	0.75	1.00
2001Mo	34,811,000	—	—	0.15	0.20	0.50
2002Mo	14,901,000	—	—	0.20	0.75	1.00

KM# 547   10 CENTAVOS
2.0800 g., Stainless Steel, 17 mm.   **Obv:** National
arms, eagle left **Rev:** Large value **Mint:** Mexico City

Date	Mintage	F	VF	XF	Unc	BU
1992Mo	121,250,000	Value: 0.75				
1993Mo	755,000,000	—	—	0.20	0.25	6.00
1994Mo	557,000,000	—	—	0.20	0.25	0.60
1995Mo	560,000,000	—	—	0.20	0.25	0.60
1995Mo Proof	6,981	Value: 2.00				
1996Mo	594,216,000	—	—	0.20	0.25	0.60
1997Mo	581,622,000	—	—	0.20	0.25	0.60
1998Mo	602,667,000	—	—	0.20	0.25	0.60
1999Mo	488,346,000	—	—	0.20	0.25	0.60
2000Mo	577,546,000	—	—	0.20	0.30	0.75
2001Mo	618,061,000	—	—	0.20	0.25	0.30
2002Mo	463,968,000	—	—	0.20	0.25	0.30
2003Mo	378,938,000	—	—	0.20	0.25	0.30
2004Mo	393,705,000	—	—	0.20	0.25	0.30
2005Mo	488,594,000	—	—	0.20	0.25	0.30
2006Mo	473,261,000	—	—	0.20	0.25	0.30
2007Mo	498,735,000	—	—	0.20	0.25	0.30
2008Mo	433,951,000	—	—	0.20	0.25	0.30
2009Mo	90,968,000	—	—	0.20	0.25	0.30

KM# 934   10 CENTAVOS
1.7500 g., Stainless Steel, 14 mm.   **Obv:** National
arms **Rev:** Large value **Edge:** Grooved **Mint:** Mexico
City

Date	Mintage	F	VF	XF	Unc	BU
2009Mo	343,772,000	—	—	—	0.10	0.25

KM# 548   20 CENTAVOS
3.0400 g., Aluminum-Bronze, 19.5 mm.   **Obv:**
National arms, eagle left **Rev:** Value and date within
3/4 wreath **Shape:** 12-sided **Mint:** Mexico City

Date	Mintage	F	VF	XF	Unc	BU
1992Mo	95,000,000	—	—	0.25	0.35	1.00
1993Mo	95,000,000	—	—	0.25	0.35	1.00
1994Mo	105,000,000	—	—	0.25	0.35	11.00
1995Mo	180,000,000	—	—	0.25	0.35	1.00
1995Mo Proof	6,981	Value: 3.00				
1996Mo	54,896,000	—	—	0.25	0.35	1.00
1997Mo	178,807,000	—	—	0.25	0.35	1.00
1998Mo	223,847,000	—	—	0.25	0.35	1.00
1999Mo	233,753,000	—	—	0.25	0.35	1.00
2000Mo	223,973,000	—	—	0.25	0.35	1.00
2001Mo	234,360,000	—	—	0.25	0.35	0.40
2002Mo	229,256,000	—	—	0.25	0.35	0.40
2003Mo	149,518,000	—	—	0.25	0.35	0.40
2004Mo	174,351,000	—	—	0.25	0.35	0.40
2005Mo	204,426,000	—	—	0.25	0.35	0.40
2006Mo	234,263,000	—	—	0.25	0.35	0.40
2007Mo	234,301,000	—	—	0.25	0.35	0.40
2008Mo	214,313,000	—	—	0.25	0.35	0.40
2009Mo	41,167,000	—	—	0.25	0.35	0.40

ESTADOS UNIDOS MEXICANOS

KM# 935 20 CENTAVOS
2.2580 g., Stainless Steel, 15.3 mm. **Obv:** National arms **Rev:** Value and date within wreath **Edge:** Segmented reeding **Mint:** Mexico City

Date	Mintage	F	VF	XF	Unc	BU
2009Mo	164,362,000	—	—	—	0.25	0.35

KM# 549 50 CENTAVOS
4.3900 g., Aluminum-Bronze, 22 mm. **Obv:** National arms, eagle left **Rev:** Value and date within 1/2 designed wreath **Shape:** 12-sided **Mint:** Mexico City

Date	Mintage	F	VF	XF	Unc	BU
1992Mo	120,150,000	—	—	0.45	0.85	1.75
1993Mo	330,000,000	—	—	0.45	0.75	1.50
1994Mo	100,000,000	—	—	0.45	0.75	1.50
1995Mo	60,000,000	—	—	0.45	0.75	1.50
1995Mo Proof	6,981	Value: 5.00				
1996Mo	69,956,000	—	—	0.45	0.75	1.50
1997Mo	129,029,000	—	—	0.45	0.75	1.50
1998Mo	223,605,000	—	—	0.45	0.75	1.50
1999Mo	89,516,000	—	—	0.45	0.75	1.50
2000Mo	135,112,000	—	—	0.45	0.75	1.50
2001Mo	199,006,000	—	—	0.45	0.75	1.00
2002Mo	94,552,000	—	—	0.45	0.75	1.00
2003Mo	124,522,000	—	—	0.45	0.75	1.00
2004Mo	154,434,000	—	—	0.45	0.75	1.00
2005Mo	179,296,000	—	—	0.45	0.75	1.00
2006Mo	234,142,000	—	—	0.45	0.75	1.00
2007Mo	253,634,000	—	—	0.45	0.75	1.00
2008Mo	249,279,000	—	—	0.45	0.75	1.00
2009Mo	90,602,000	—	—	0.45	0.75	1.00

KM# 936 50 CENTAVOS
3.1030 g., Stainless Steel, 17 mm. **Obv:** National arms **Rev:** Value and date within wreath **Edge:** Reeded **Mint:** Mexico City

Date	Mintage	F	VF	XF	Unc	BU
2009Mo	19,910,000	—	—	—	0.75	1.00

KM# 550 NUEVO PESO
3.9500 g., Bi-Metallic Aluminum-Bronze center in Stainless Steel ring, 21 mm. **Obv:** National arms, eagle left **Rev:** Value **Mint:** Mexico City

Date	Mintage	VF	XF	Unc	BU
1992Mo	144,000,000	—	0.60	1.50	2.75
1993Mo	329,860,000	—	0.60	1.50	2.75
1994Mo	221,000,000	—	0.60	1.50	2.75
1995Mo Small date	125,000,000	—	0.60	1.50	2.75
1995Mo Large date	Inc. above	—	0.60	1.50	2.75
1995Mo Proof	6,981	Value: 6.00			

KM# 603 PESO
3.9500 g., Bi-Metallic Aluminum-Bronze center in Stainless Steel ring, 21 mm. **Obv:** National arms, eagle left within circle **Rev:** Value and date within circle **Mint:** Mexico City **Note:** Similar to KM#550 but without N.

Date	Mintage	F	VF	XF	Unc	BU
1996Mo	169,510,000	—	—	—	1.25	2.25
1997Mo	222,870,000	—	—	—	1.25	2.25
1998Mo	261,942,000	—	—	—	1.25	2.25
1999Mo	99,168,000	—	—	—	1.25	2.25
2000Mo	158,379,000	—	—	—	1.25	2.25
2001Mo	208,576,000	—	—	—	1.25	2.75
2002Mo	119,514,000	—	—	—	1.25	2.75
2003Mo	169,320,000	—	—	—	1.25	2.75
2004Mo	208,611,000	—	—	—	1.25	2.75
2005Mo	253,923,000	—	—	—	1.25	2.75
2006Mo	289,834,000	—	—	—	1.25	2.75
2007Mo	368,408,000	—	—	—	1.25	2.75
2008Mo	363,878,000	—	—	—	1.25	2.75
2009Mo	239,229,000	—	—	—	1.25	2.75

KM# 551 2 NUEVO PESOS
5.1900 g., Bi-Metallic Aluminum-Bronze center in Stainless Steel ring, 23 mm. **Obv:** National arms, eagle left within circle **Rev:** Value and date within circle with assorted emblems around border **Mint:** Mexico City

Date	Mintage	F	VF	XF	Unc	BU
1992Mo	60,000,000	—	—	1.00	2.50	4.00
1993Mo	77,000,000	—	—	1.00	2.50	4.00
1994Mo	44,000,000	—	—	1.00	2.50	4.00
1995Mo	20,000,000	—	—	1.00	2.50	4.00
1995Mo Proof	6,981	Value: 6.00				

KM# 604 2 PESOS
5.1900 g., Bi-Metallic Aluminum-Bronze center in Stainless Steel ring, 23 mm. **Obv:** National arms, eagle left within circle **Rev:** Value and date within center circle of assorted emblems **Mint:** Mexico City **Note:** Similar to KM#551, but denomination without N.

Date	Mintage	F	VF	XF	Unc	BU
1996Mo	24,902,000	—	—	—	2.50	4.00
1997Mo	34,560,000	—	—	—	2.50	4.00
1998Mo	104,138,000	—	—	—	2.50	4.00
1999Mo	34,713,000	—	—	—	2.50	4.00
2000Mo	69,322,000	—	—	—	2.50	4.00
2001Mo	74,563,000	—	—	—	2.35	4.00
2002Mo	74,547,000	—	—	—	2.35	4.00
2003Mo	39,814,000	—	—	—	2.35	4.00
2004Mo	89,496,000	—	—	—	2.35	4.00
2005Mo	94,532,000	—	—	—	2.35	4.00
2006Mo	144,123,000	—	—	—	2.35	4.00
2007Mo	129,422,000	—	—	—	2.35	4.00
2008Mo	134,235,000	—	—	—	2.35	4.00
2009Mo	64,650,000	—	—	—	2.35	4.00

KM# 552   5 NUEVO PESOS
7.0700 g., Bi-Metallic Aluminum-Bronze center in Stainless Steel ring, 25.5 mm. **Obv:** National arms, eagle left within circle **Rev:** Value and date within circle with bow below **Mint:** Mexico City

Date	Mintage	F	VF	XF	Unc	BU
1992Mo	70,000,000	—	—	2.00	6.00	8.50
1993Mo	168,240,000	—	—	2.00	6.00	8.50
1994Mo	58,000,000	—	—	2.00	6.00	8.50
1995Mo Proof	6,981	Value: 25.00				

KM# 588   5 NUEVO PESOS
27.0000 g., 0.9250 Silver 0.8029 oz. ASW **Series:** Ibero-America **Subject:** Environmental Protection **Obv:** National arms, eagle left within center of past and present arms **Rev:** Pacific Ridley Sea Turtle

Date	Mintage	F	VF	XF	Unc	BU
1994Mo Proof	11,005	Value: 50.00				

KM# 627   5 PESOS
31.1035 g., 0.9990 Silver 0.9990 oz. ASW **Subject:** World Wildlife Fund **Obv:** National arms, eagle left **Rev:** Wolf with pup

Date	Mintage	F	VF	XF	Unc	BU
1997Mo	—	—	—	—	—	—
1998Mo Proof	13,004	Value: 95.00				

KM# 629   5 PESOS
27.0000 g., 0.9250 Silver 0.8029 oz. ASW, 40 mm. **Series:** Ibero-America **Subject:** Jarabe Tapatio **Obv:** National arms, eagle left within center of assorted arms **Rev:** Mexican dancers

Date	Mintage	F	VF	XF	Unc	BU
1997Mo Proof	8,011	Value: 350				
1998Mo Proof	3,000	Value: 350				

KM# 605   5 PESOS
7.0700 g., Bi-Metallic Aluminum-Bronze center in Stainless Steel ring, 25.5 mm. **Obv:** National arms, eagle left within circle **Rev:** Value within circle **Mint:** Mexico City **Note:** Similar to KM#552 but denomination without N.

Date	Mintage	F	VF	XF	Unc	BU
1997Mo	39,468,000	—	—	2.00	4.00	7.00
1998Mo	103,729,000	—	—	2.00	4.00	7.00
1999Mo	59,427,000	—	—	2.00	4.00	7.00
2000Mo	20,869,000	—	—	2.00	4.50	7.00
2001Mo	79,169,000	—	—	2.00	3.50	8.00
2002Mo	34,754,000	—	—	2.00	3.50	6.00
2003Mo	54,676,000	—	—	2.00	3.50	6.00
2004Mo	89,518,000	—	—	2.00	3.50	6.00
2005Mo	94,482,000	—	—	2.00	3.50	6.00
2006Mo	89,447,000	—	—	2.00	3.50	6.00
2007Mo	123,382,000	—	—	2.00	3.50	6.00
2008Mo	9,939,000	—	—	2.50	4.00	6.00
2009Mo	9,898,000	—	—	2.50	4.00	6.00

KM# 630   5 PESOS
31.1800 g., 0.9990 Silver 1.0014 oz. ASW **Subject:** Millennium Series **Obv:** National arms, eagle left within center of past and present arms **Rev:** Butterfly flanked by sprigs above hands **Rev. Designer:** Francisco Ortega Romero

Date	Mintage	F	VF	XF	Unc	BU
1999-2000Mo Proof	47,435	Value: 60.00				

KM# 631   5 PESOS
31.1800 g., 0.9990 Silver 1.0014 oz. ASW **Subject:**

ESTADOS UNIDOS MEXICANOS

Millennium Series **Obv:** National arms, eagle left within center of past and present arms **Rev:** Stylized dove as hand of peace **Rev. Designer:** Omar Jiminez Torres

Date	Mintage	F	VF	XF	Unc	BU
1999-2000Mo Proof	47,389	Value: 55.00				

KM# 632 5 PESOS
31.1800 g., 0.9990 Silver 1.0014 oz. ASW **Subject:** Millennium Series **Obv:** National arms, eagle left within center of past and present arms **Rev:** Aztec bird design and value

Date	Mintage	F	VF	XF	Unc	BU
1999-2000Mo Proof	48,080	Value: 55.00				

KM# 635 5 PESOS
19.6000 g., 0.9250 Silver 0.5829 oz. ASW **Subject:** Millennium Series **Obv:** National arms, eagle left **Rev:** Naval training ship Cuauhtemoc sailing into world globe

Date	Mintage	F	VF	XF	Unc	BU
1999Mo Proof	15,504	Value: 45.00				

KM# 640 5 PESOS
31.1030 g., 0.9990 Silver 0.9989 oz. ASW, 40 mm. **Subject:** UNICEF **Obv:** National arms, eagle left **Rev:** Two children flying kite **Edge:** Reeded **Mint:** Mexico City

Date	Mintage	F	VF	XF	Unc	BU
1999Mo Proof	4,010	Value: 60.00				

KM# 655 5 PESOS
31.1710 g., 0.9990 Silver 1.0011 oz. ASW, 40 mm. **Series:** Endangered Wildlife **Subject:** Cocodrilo de Rio **Obv:** National arms, eagle left within center of past and present arms **Rev:** American Crocodile, value and date

Date	Mintage	F	VF	XF	Unc	BU
2000Mo	30,000	—	—	—	45.00	55.00

KM# 656 5 PESOS
31.1710 g., 0.9990 Silver 1.0011 oz. ASW, 40 mm. **Series:** Endangered Wildlife **Subject:** Nutria de Rio **Obv:** National arms, eagle left within center of past and present arms **Rev:** Neotropical River Otter, value and date

Date	Mintage	F	VF	XF	Unc	BU
2000Mo	30,000	—	—	—	45.00	55.00

KM# 657 5 PESOS
31.1710 g., 0.9990 Silver 1.0011 oz. ASW, 40 mm. **Series:** Endangered Wildlife - American Antelope **Obv:** National arms, eagle left within center of past and present arms **Rev:** Peninsular Pronghorn, giant cardon cactus in back, value and date

Date	Mintage	F	VF	XF	Unc	BU
2000Mo	30,000	—	—	—	45.00	55.00

KM# 652 5 PESOS
31.1710 g., 0.9990 Silver 1.0011 oz. ASW, 40 mm. **Series:** Endangered Wildlife **Subject:** Aguila Real **Obv:** National arms, eagle left within center of past and present arms **Rev:** Golden Eagle on branch, value and date

Date	Mintage	F	VF	XF	Unc	BU
2000Mo	30,000	—	—	—	45.00	55.00

KM# 670 5 PESOS
27.0000 g., 0.9250 Silver 0.8029 oz. ASW, 40 mm. **Series:** Ibero-America **Obv:** National arms, eagle left within center of past and present arms **Rev:** Cowboy trick riding two horses **Edge:** Reeded **Mint:** Mexico City

Date	Mintage	F	VF	XF	Unc	BU
2000Mo Proof	9,000	Value: 85.00				

KM# 653 5 PESOS
31.1710 g., 0.9990 Silver 1.0011 oz. ASW, 40 mm. **Series:** Endangered Wildlife **Subject:** Harpy Eagle (Aguila Arpia) **Obv:** National arms in center of past and present arms **Rev:** Crowned Harpy Eagle perched on branch, value and date

Date	Mintage	F	VF	XF	Unc	BU
2001Mo	30,000	—	—	—	40.00	50.00

KM# 654 5 PESOS
31.1710 g., 0.9990 Silver 1.0011 oz. ASW, 40 mm. **Series:** Endangered Wildlife **Subject:** Black Bear (Oso Negro) **Obv:** National arms in center of past and present arms **Rev:** Black bear, value and date

Date	Mintage	F	VF	XF	Unc	BU
2001Mo	30,000	—	—	—	40.00	50.00

ESTADOS UNIDOS MEXICANOS

KM# 658   5 PESOS
31.1710 g., 0.9990 Silver 1.0011 oz. ASW, 40 mm.
Series: Endangered Wildlife - Jaguar **Obv:** National arms in center of past and present arms **Rev:** Jaguar, value and date

Date	Mintage	F	VF	XF	Unc	BU
2001Mo	30,000	—	—	—	40.00	50.00

KM# 659   5 PESOS
31.1710 g., 0.9990 Silver 1.0011 oz. ASW, 40 mm.
Series: Endangered Wildlife - Prairie Dog **Obv:** National arms in center of past and present arms **Rev:** Prairie dog, value and date

Date	Mintage	F	VF	XF	Unc	BU
2001Mo	30,000	—	—	—	40.00	50.00

KM# 660   5 PESOS
31.1710 g., 0.9990 Silver 1.0011 oz. ASW, 40 mm.
Series: Endangered Wildlife - Volcano Rabbit **Obv:** National arms in center of past and present arms **Rev:** Volcano rabbit, value and date

Date	Mintage	F	VF	XF	Unc	BU
2001Mo	30,000	—	—	—	40.00	50.00

KM# 651   5 PESOS
31.1710 g., 0.9990 Silver 1.0011 oz. ASW, 40 mm.
Series: Endangered Wildlife - Nanatee **Obv:** National arms in center of past and present arms **Rev:** Manatee, value and date **Edge:** Reeded **Mint:** Mexico City

Date	Mintage	F	VF	XF	Unc	BU
2001Mo	30,000	—	—	—	40.00	50.00

KM# 678   5 PESOS
27.0000 g., 0.9250 Silver 0.8029 oz. ASW, 40 mm.
Series: Ibero-America **Subject:** Acapulco Galleon **Obv:** National arms in center of past and present arms **Rev:** Spanish galleon with Pacific Ocean background and trading scene in foreground **Edge:** Reeded **Mint:** Mexico City

Date	Mintage	F	VF	XF	Unc	BU
2003Mo Proof	17,015	Value: 90.00				

KM# 765   5 PESOS
31.1035 g., 0.9250 Silver 0.9250 oz. ASW, 40 mm.
Series: Ibero-America **Subject:** Palacio de Bellas Artes **Obv:** Mexican Eagle and Snake **Rev:** Palace of Fine Arts **Edge:** Reeded **Mint:** Mexico City

Date	Mintage	F	VF	XF	Unc	BU
2005Mo Proof	8,005	Value: 90.00				

KM# 769   5 PESOS
15.5518 g., 0.9990 Silver 0.4995 oz. ASW, 33 mm.
Subject: Monetary Reform of 1905 **Obv:** Mexican Eagle and Snake **Rev:** Cap and rays coin design **Mint:** Mexico City

Date	Mintage	F	VF	XF	Unc	BU
2005Mo Proof	1,505	Value: 60.00				

KM# 770   5 PESOS
31.1035 g., 0.9990 Silver 0.9990 oz. ASW, 40 mm.
Subject: World Cup Soccer **Obv:** Mexican Eagle and

Snake **Rev:** Mayan Pelota player and soccer ball **Mint:** Mexico City

Date	Mintage	F	VF	XF	Unc	BU
2006Mo Proof	40,005	Value: 90.00				

KM# 805   5 PESOS
31.1050 g., 0.9250 Silver 0.9250 oz. ASW, 40 mm.
Series: Ibero-America **Obv:** Eagle on cactus within shields **Rev:** Mayan ball game

Date	Mintage	F	VF	XF	Unc	BU
2008Mo Proof	8,013	Value: 75.00				

KM# 900.2   5 PESOS
7.0700 g., 0.9990 Bi-Metallic Aluminum-Bronze center in Stainless Steel ring 0.2271 oz., 25.5 mm.
Series: Mexican Independence 200th Anniversary **Subject:** Francisco Primode Verdad y Ramos **Obv:** National arms - Eagle left **Rev:** Francisco Primode Verdad y Ramos bust right **Mint:** Mexico City **Note:** No pellets at 4 and 7 o'clock in legend.

Date	Mintage	F	VF	XF	Unc	BU
2008Mo	Inc. above	—	—	—	—	—

KM# 894   5 PESOS
7.0700 g., Bi-Metallic Aluminum-bronze center in stainless steel ring, 25.5 mm.   **Series:** Mexican Independence, 200th Anniversary **Subject:** Ignacio Rayon **Obv:** National Arms - Eagle left **Rev:** Ignacio Rayon bust left **Mint:** Mexico City

Date	Mintage	F	VF	XF	Unc	BU
2008Mo	9,934,397	—	—	0.75	1.50	—
2008Mo Prooflike	4,267	—	—	—	—	7.50

KM# 895   5 PESOS
7.0700 g., Bi-Metallic Aluminum-bronze center in stainless steel ring, 25.5 mm.   **Series:** Mexican Revolution 100th Anniversary **Subject:** Alvaro Obregon **Obv:** National Arms - Eagle left **Rev:** Alvaro Obregon bust 3/4 facing left **Mint:** Mexico City

Date	Mintage	F	VF	XF	Unc	BU
2008Mo	9,948,722	—	—	0.75	1.50	—
2008Mo Prooflike	4,727	—	—	—	—	7.50

KM# 896   5 PESOS
7.0700 g., Bi-Metallic Aluninum-bronze center in stainless steel ring, 25.5 mm.   **Series:** Mexican

ESTADOS UNIDOS MEXICANOS

Independence 200th Anniversary **Subject:** Carlos
Maria de Bustamante **Obv:** National Arms - Eagle
left **Rev:** Carlos Maria de Bustamante bust left **Mint:**
Mexico City

Date	Mintage	F	VF	XF	Unc	BU
2008Mo	9,941,302	—	—	0.75	1.50	—
2008Mo Prooflike	4,852	—	—	—	—	7.50

KM# 897 5 PESOS
7.0700 g., Bi-Metallic Aluminum-bronze center in
stainless steel ring, 25.5 mm. **Series:** Mexican
Revolution 100th Anniversary **Subject:** Jose
Vasconcelos **Obv:** National Arms - Eagle left **Rev:**
Jose Vasconcelos bust left **Mint:** Mexico City

Date	Mintage	F	VF	XF	Unc	BU
2008Mo	9,939,839	—	—	0.75	1.50	—
2008Mo Prooflike	4,767	—	—	—	—	7.50

KM# 898 5 PESOS
7.0700 g., Bi-Metallic Aluminum-bronze center in
stainless steel ring, 25.5 mm. **Series:** Mexican
Independence 200th Anniversary **Subject:**
Francisco Xavier Mina **Obv:** National Arms - Eagle
left **Rev:** Francisco Mina bust 3/4 facing left **Mint:**
Mexico City

Date	Mintage	F	VF	XF	Unc	BU
2008Mo	9,914,938	—	—	0.75	1.50	—
2008Mo Prooflike	4,523	—	—	—	—	7.50

KM# 899 5 PESOS
7.0700 g., Bi-Metallic Aluminum-bronze center in
stainless steel ring, 25.5 mm. **Series:** Mexican
Revolution 100th Anniversary **Subject:** Francisco
Villa **Obv:** National Arms - Eagle left **Rev:** Francisco
Villa on horseback left **Mint:** Mexico City

Date	Mintage	F	VF	XF	Unc	BU
2008Mo	9,917,084	—	—	0.75	1.50	—
2008Mo Prooflike	4,866	—	—	—	—	7.50

KM# 900.1 5 PESOS
7.0700 g., Bi-Metallic Aluminum-Bronze center in
Stainless Steel ring, 25.5 mm. **Series:** Mexican
Independence 200th Anniversary **Subject:**
Francisco Primo de Verdad y Ramos **Obv:** National
Arms - Eagle left **Rev:** Francisco Primode Verdad y
Ramos bust right **Mint:** Mexico City **Note:** Pellets at
4 and 7 o'clock in legend.

Date	Mintage	F	VF	XF	Unc	BU
2008Mo	9,937,000	—	—	0.75	1.50	—
2008Mo Prooflike	4,279	—	—	—	—	7.50

KM# 901 5 PESOS
7.0700 g., Bi-Metallic Aluminum-Bronze center in
Stainless Steel ring, 25.5 mm. **Series:** Mexican
Revolution 100th Anniversary **Subject:** Heriberto
Jara **Obv:** National Arms - Eagle left **Rev:** Heriberto
Jara bust 3/4 left **Mint:** Mexico City

Date	Mintage	F	VF	XF	Unc	BU
2008Mo	9,936,333	—	—	0.75	1.50	—
2008Mo Prooflike	4,870	—	—	—	—	7.50

KM# 902 5 PESOS
7.0700 g., Bi-Metallic Aluminum-Bronze center in
Stainless Steel ring, 25.5 mm. **Series:** Mexican
Independence 200th Anniversary **Subject:** Mariano
Matamoros **Obv:** National Arms - Eagle left **Rev:**
Mariano Matamoros bust 3/4 facing right **Mint:**
Mexico City

Date	Mintage	F	VF	XF	Unc	BU
2008Mo	9,947,802	—	—	0.75	1.50	—
2008Mo Prooflike	4,820	—	—	—	—	7.50

KM# 903 5 PESOS
7.0700 g., Bi-Metallic Aluminum-Bronze center in

ESTADOS UNIDOS MEXICANOS

Stainless Steel ring, 25.5 mm. **Series:** Mexican
Revolution 100th Anniversary **Subject:** Ricardo
Magon **Obv:** National Arms - Eagle left **Rev:** Ricardo
Magon bust right **Mint:** Mexico City

Date	Mintage	F	VF	XF	Unc	BU
2008Mo	9,940,278	—	—	0.75	1.50	—
2008Mo Prooflike	4,690	—	—	—	—	7.50

KM# 904   5 PESOS
7.0700 g., Bi-Metallic Aluminum-Bronze center in
Stainless Steel ring, 25.5 mm. **Series:** Mexican
Independence 200th Anniversary **Subject:** Miguel
Ramos Arizpe **Obv:** National Arms - Eagle left **Rev:**
Miguel Ramos Arizpe bust right **Mint:** Mexico City

Date	Mintage	F	VF	XF	Unc	BU
2008Mo	9,927,433	—	—	0.75	1.50	—
2008Mo Prooflike	4,863	—	—	—	—	7.50

KM# 905   5 PESOS
7.0700 g., Bi-Metallic Aluminum-Bronze center in
Stainless Steel ring, 25.5 mm. **Series:** Mexican
Revolution 100th Anniversary **Subject:** Francisco J.
Mugica **Obv:** National arms, eagle left **Rev:** Francisco
J. Mugica bust 3/4 facing left **Mint:** Mexico City

Date	Mintage	F	VF	XF	Unc	BU
2008Mo	9,926,537	—	—	0.75	1.50	—
2008Mo Prooflike	4,588	—	—	—	—	7.50

KM# 906   5 PESOS
7.0700 g., Bi-Metallic Aluminum-Bronze center in
Stainless Steel ring, 25.5 mm. **Series:** Mexican
Independence 200th Anniversary **Subject:**
Hermenegildo Galeana **Obv:** National Arms, eagle
left **Rev:** Hermenegildo Galeana bust 3/4 facing left
Mint: Mexico City

Date	Mintage	F	VF	XF	Unc	BU
2008Mo	9,935,901	—	—	0.75	1.50	—
2008Mo Prooflike	4,966	—	—	—	—	7.50

KM# 907   5 PESOS
7.0700 g., Bi-Metallic Aluminum-Bronze center in
Stainless Steel ring, 25.5 mm. **Series:** Mexican
Revolution, 100th Anniversary **Subject:** Filomeno
Mata **Obv:** National arms, eagle left **Rev:** Filomeno
Mata bust facing left. **Mint:** Mexico City

Date	Mintage	F	VF	XF	Unc	BU
2009Mo	9,935,689	—	—	0.75	1.50	—
2009Mo Prooflike	4,920	—	—	—	—	7.50

KM# 908   5 PESOS
7.0700 g., Bi-Metallic Aluminum-Bronze cetner in
Stainless Steel ring, 25.5 mm. **Series:** Mexican
Independence 200th Anniversary **Subject:** Jose
Maria Cos **Obv:** National arms, eagle left. **Rev:** Jose
Maria Cos bust right **Mint:** Mexico City

Date	Mintage	F	VF	XF	Unc	BU
2009Mo	9,935,040	—	—	0.75	1.50	—
2009Mo Prooflike	4,950	—	—	—	—	7.50

KM# 909   5 PESOS
7.0700 g., Bi-Metallic Aluminum-Bronze center in
Stainless Steel ring, 25.5 mm. **Series:** Mexican
Revolution 100th Anniversary **Subject:** Carmen
Serdan **Obv:** National Amrs, Eagle left **Rev:** Carmen
Serdan bust facing slightly right **Mint:** Mexico City

Date	Mintage	F	VF	XF	Unc	BU
2009Mo	7,160,841	—	—	0.75	1.50	—
2009Mo Prooflike	4,787	—	—	—	—	7.50

KM# 910   5 PESOS
7.0700 g., Bi-Metallic Aluminum-Bronze center in
Stainless Steel ring, 25.5 mm. **Series:** Mexican
Independence, 200th Anniversary **Subject:** Pedro

ESTADOS UNIDOS MEXICANOS

Moreno **Obv:** National arms, eagle left **Rev:** Pedro Moreno bust 3/4 right **Mint:** Mexico City

Date	Mintage	F	VF	XF	Unc	BU
2009Mo	6,942,480	—	—	0.75	1.50	—
2009Mo Prooflike	4,940	—	—	—	—	7.50

KM# 911   5 PESOS

7.0700 g., Bi-Metallic Aluminum-Bronze center in Stainless Steel ring, 25.5 mm. **Series:** Mexican Revolution 100th Anniversary **Subject:** Andres Molina Enriquez **Obv:** National arms, eagle left **Rev:** Andres Molina Enriquez, bust 3/4 right **Mint:** Mexico City

Date	Mintage	F	VF	XF	Unc	BU
2009Mo	6,942,763	—	—	0.75	1.50	—
2009Mo Prooflike	4,666	—	—	—	—	7.50

KM# 912   5 PESOS

7.0700 g., Bi-Metallic Aluminum-Bronze center in Stainless Steel ring, 25.5 mm. **Series:** Mexican Independence, 200th Anniversary **Subject:** Agustin de Iturbide **Obv:** National arms, eagle left **Rev:** Agustin de Iturbide bust left **Mint:** Mexico City

Date	Mintage	F	VF	XF	Unc	BU
2009Mo	6,944,222	—	—	0.75	1.50	—
2009Mo Prooflike	4,838	—	—	—	—	7.50

KM# 913   5 PESOS

7.0700 g., Bi-Metallic Aluminumn-Bronze center in Stainless Steel ring, 25.5 mm. **Series:** Mexican Revolution 100th Anniversary **Subject:** Luis Cabrera **Obv:** National Arms, eagle left **Rev:** Luis Cabrera bust 3/4 facing left **Mint:** Mexico City

Date	Mintage	F	VF	XF	Unc	BU
2009Mo	6,902,593	—	—	0.75	1.50	—
2009Mo Prooflike	4,656	—	—	—	—	7.50

KM# 914   5 PESOS

7.0700 g., Bi-Metallic Aluminum-Bronze center Stainless Steel ring, 25.5 mm. **Series:** Mexican Independence 200th Anniversary **Subject:** Nicolas Bravo **Obv:** National Arms, Eagle left **Rev:** Nicolas Bravo bust 3/4 facing left **Mint:** Mexico City

Date	Mintage	F	VF	XF	Unc	BU
2009Mo	6,930,174	—	—	0.75	0.50	—
2009Mo Prooflike	4,780	—	—	—	—	7.50

KM# 915   5 PESOS

7.0700 g., Bi-Metallic Aluminum-bronze center in Stainless steel ring, 25.5 mm. **Series:** Mexican Revolution 100th Anniversary **Subject:** Eulalio Gutierrez **Obv:** National Arms, eagle left **Rev:** Eulalio Gutierrez bust 3/4 right **Mint:** Mexico City

Date	Mintage	F	VF	XF	Unc	BU
2009Mo	6,908,760	—	—	0.75	1.50	—
2009Mo Prooflike	4,862	—	—	—	—	7.50

KM# 916   5 PESOS

7.0700 g., Bi-Metallic Aluminum-Bronze center in Stainless Steel ring, 25.5 mm. **Series:** Mexican Independence 200th Anniversary **Subject:** Servando Teresa de Mier **Obv:** National Arms, eagle left **Rev:** Servando Teresa de Mier bust left **Mint:** Mexico City

Date	Mintage	F	VF	XF	Unc	BU
2009Mo	6,937,421	—	—	0.75	1.50	—
2009Mo Prooflike	4,675	—	—	—	—	7.50

KM# 917   5 PESOS

7.0700 g., Bi-Metallic Aluminum-Bronze center in Stainless Steel ring, 25.5 mm. **Series:** Mexican Revolution 100th Anniversary **Subject:** Otilio Montano **Obv:** National Arms, eagle left **Rev:** Otilio Montano bust left **Mint:** Mexico City

Date	Mintage	F	VF	XF	Unc	BU
2009Mo	6,890,052	—	—	0.75	1.50	—
2009Mo Prooflike	4,923	—	—	—	—	7.50

ESTADOS UNIDOS MEXICANOS

Date	Mintage	F	VF	XF	Unc	BU
2004Mo	74,739,000	—	—	2.50	4.00	8.00
2005Mo	64,616,000	—	—	2.50	4.00	8.00
2006Mo	84,575,000	—	—	2.50	4.00	8.00
2007Mo	89,678,000	—	—	2.50	4.00	8.00
2008Mo	64,744,000	—	—	2.50	4.00	8.00
2009Mo	54,812,000	—	—	2.00	3.00	6.00

KM# 918   5 PESOS
7.0700 g., Bi-Metallic Aluminum-Bronze center in Stainless Steel ring, 25.5 mm. **Series:** Mexican Revolution 100th Anniversary **Subject:** Belisario Dominguez **Obv:** National Arms, eagle left **Rev:** Belisario Dominguez bust 3/4 left **Mint:** Mexico City

Date	Mintage	F	VF	XF	Unc	BU
2009Mo	6,926,606	—	—	0.75	1.50	—
2009Mo Prooflike	4,773	—	—	—	—	7.50

KM# 919   5 PESOS
7.0700 g., Bi-Metallic Aluminum-Bronze center in Stainless Steel ring, 25.5 mm. **Series:** Mexican Independence 200th Anniversary **Subject:** Leona Vicario **Obv:** National Arms, eagle left **Rev:** Leona Vicario bust left **Mint:** Mexico City

Date	Mintage	F	VF	XF	Unc	BU
2009Mo	6,937,872	—	—	0.75	1.50	—
2009Mo Prooflike	4,730	—	—	—	—	7.50

KM# 553   10 NUEVO PESOS
11.1800 g., Bi-Metallic 0.925 Silver center, .1667 oz. ASW within Aluminum-Bronze ring, 28 mm. **Obv:** National arms **Obv. Legend:** Estados Unidos Mexicanos **Rev:** Assorted shields within circle **Edge:** Groved **Mint:** Mexico City

Date	Mintage	F	VF	XF	Unc	BU
1992Mo	20,000,000	—	—	7.00	10.00	14.00
1993Mo	47,981,000	—	—	7.00	10.00	14.00
1994Mo	15,000,000	—	—	7.00	10.00	14.00
1995Mo	15,000,000	—	—	7.00	10.00	14.00
1995Mo Proof	6,981	Value: 20.00				

KM# 616   10 PESOS
10.3300 g., Bi-Metallic Copper-Nickel-Zinc center in Aluminum-Bronze ring, 28 mm. **Obv:** National arms **Obv. Legend:** ESTADOS UNIDOS MEXICANOS **Rev:** Aztec design of Tonatiuh with the Fire Mask **Mint:** Mexico City

Date	Mintage	F	VF	XF	Unc	BU
1997Mo	44,837,000	—	—	2.50	4.00	8.00
1998Mo	203,735,000	—	—	2.50	4.00	8.00
1999Mo	29,842,000	—	—	2.50	4.00	8.00
2002Mo	44,721,000	—	—	2.50	4.00	8.00

KM# 633   10 PESOS
62.0300 g., 0.9990 Silver 1.9922 oz. ASW **Subject:** Millennium Series **Obv:** National arms, eagle left within center of past and present arms **Rev:** Ancient and modern buildings within circle

Date	Mintage	F	VF	XF	Unc	BU
1999-2000Mo Proof	47,641	Value: 80.00				

KM# 636   10 PESOS
10.3300 g., Bi-Metallic Copper-Nickel-Zinc center in Aluminum-Bronze ring, 28 mm. **Series:** Millennium **Obv:** National arms **Obv. Legend:** ESTADOS UNIDOS MEXICANOS **Rev:** Aztec carving **Edge Lettering:** ANO (year) repeated 3 times **Mint:** Mexico City

Date	Mintage	F	VF	XF	Unc	BU
2000Mo	24,839,000	—	—	3.50	4.50	8.50
2001Mo	44,768,000	—	—	3.00	4.00	8.00

ESTADOS UNIDOS MEXICANOS

KM# 679 10 PESOS
31.1040 g., 0.9990 Silver 0.9990 oz. ASW, 39.9 mm.
Series: First **Subject:** 180th Anniversary of
Federation **Obv:** National arms **Obv. Legend:**
ESTADOS UNIDOS MEXICANOS **Rev:** State Arms
Rev. Legend: ESTADO DE ZACATECAS **Edge:**
Reeded **Mint:** Mexico City

Date	Mintage	F	VF	XF	Unc	BU
2003Mo Proof	10,000	Value: 70.00				

KM# 680 10 PESOS
31.1040 g., 0.9990 Silver 0.9990 oz. ASW, 39.9 mm.
Series: First **Subject:** 180th Anniversary of
Federation **Obv:** National arms **Obv. Legend:**
ESTADOS UNIDOS MEXICANOS **Rev:** State arms
Rev. Legend: ESTADO DE YUCATÁN **Edge:**
Reeded **Mint:** Mexico City

Date	Mintage	F	VF	XF	Unc	BU
2003Mo Proof	10,000	Value: 70.00				

KM# 681 10 PESOS
31.1040 g., 0.9990 Silver 0.9990 oz. ASW, 39.9 mm.
Series: First **Subject:** 180th Anniversary of
Federation **Obv:** National arms **Obv. Legend:**
ESTADOS UNIDOS MEXICANOS **Rev:** State arms
Rev. Legend: ESTADO DE VERACRUZ-LLAVE
Edge: Reeded **Mint:** Mexico City

Date	Mintage	F	VF	XF	Unc	BU
2003Mo Proof	10,000	Value: 70.00				

KM# 682 10 PESOS
31.1040 g., 0.9990 Silver 0.9990 oz. ASW, 39.9 mm.
Series: First **Subject:** 180th Anniversary of
Frederation **Obv:** National arms **Obv. Legend:**
ESTADOS UNIDOS MEXICANOS **Rev:** State arms
Rev. Legend: ESTADO DE TLAXCALA **Edge:**
Reeded **Mint:** Mexico City

Date	Mintage	F	VF	XF	Unc	BU
2003Mo Proof	10,000	Value: 70.00				

KM# 683 10 PESOS
31.1040 g., 0.9990 Silver 0.9990 oz. ASW, 39.9 mm.
Series: First **Subject:** 180th Anniversary of
Federation **Obv:** National arms **Obv. Legend:**
ESTADOS UNIDOS MEXICANOS **Rev:** State arms
Rev. Legend: ESTADO DE TAMAULIPAS **Edge:**
Reeded **Mint:** Mexico City

Date	Mintage	F	VF	XF	Unc	BU
2004Mo Proof	10,000	Value: 70.00				

KM# 684 10 PESOS
31.1040 g., 0.9990 Silver 0.9990 oz. ASW, 39.9 mm.
Series: First **Subject:** 180th Anniversary of
Federation **Obv:** National arms **Obv. Legend:**
ESTADOS UNIDOS DE MEXICANOS **Rev:** State

arms **Rev. Legend:** ESTADO DE TABASCO **Edge:**
Reeded **Mint:** Mexico City

Date	Mintage	F	VF	XF	Unc	BU
2004Mo Proof	10,000	Value: 70.00				

KM# 685   10 PESOS
31.1040 g., 0.9990 Silver 0.9990 oz. ASW, 39.9 mm.
Series: First **Subject:** 180th Anniversary of
Federation **Obv:** National arms **Obv. Legend:**
ESTADOS UNIDOS MEXICANOS **Rev:** State arms
Rev. Legend: ESTADO DE SONORA **Edge:**
Reeded **Mint:** Mexico City **Note:** Mexican States:
Sonora

Date	Mintage	F	VF	XF	Unc	BU
2004Mo Proof	10,000	Value: 70.00				

KM# 686   10 PESOS
31.1040 g., 0.9990 Silver 0.9990 oz. ASW, 39.9 mm.
Series: First **Subject:** 180th Anniversary of
Federation **Obv:** National arms **Obv. Legend:**
ESTADOS UNIDOS DE MEXICANOS **Rev:** State
arms **Rev. Legend:** ESTADO DE SINALOA **Edge:**
Reeded **Mint:** Mexico City **Note:** Mexican States:
Sinaloa

Date	Mintage	F	VF	XF	Unc	BU
2004Mo Proof	10,000	Value: 70.00				

KM# 687   10 PESOS
31.1040 g., 0.9990 Silver 0.9990 oz. ASW, 39.9 mm.
Series: First **Subject:** 180th Anniversary of
Federation **Obv:** National arms **Obv. Legend:**
ESTADOS UNIDOS MEXICANOS **Rev:** State arms
Rev. Legend: ESTADO DE SAN LUIS POTOSÍ
Edge: Reeded **Mint:** Mexico City

Date	Mintage	F	VF	XF	Unc	BU
2004Mo Proof	10,000	Value: 70.00				

KM# 735   10 PESOS
31.1040 g., 0.9990 Silver 0.9990 oz. ASW, 39.9 mm.
Series: First **Subject:** 180th Anniversary of
Federation **Obv:** National arms **Obv. Legend:**
ESTADOS UNIDOS MEXICANOS **Rev:** State arms
Rev. Legend: ESTADO DE QUINTANA ROO

Date	Mintage	F	VF	XF	Unc	BU
2004Mo Proof	10,000	Value: 70.00				

KM# 733   10 PESOS
31.1040 g., 0.9990 Silver 0.9990 oz. ASW, 39.9 mm.
Series: First **Subject:** 180th Anniversary of
Federation **Obv:** National arms **Obv. Legend:**
ESTADOS UNIDOS MEXICANOS **Rev:** State arms
Rev. Legend: ESTADO DE QUERÉTARO
ARTEAGA **Edge:** Reeded

Date	Mintage	F	VF	XF	Unc	BU
2004Mo Proof	10,000	Value: 70.00				

ESTADOS UNIDOS MEXICANOS

KM# 737 10 PESOS
31.1040 g., 0.9990 Silver 0.9990 oz. ASW, 39.9 mm.
Series: First **Subject:** 180th Anniversary of
Federation **Obv:** National arms **Obv. Legend:**
ESTADOS UNIDOS MEXICANOS **Rev:** State arms
Rev. Legend: ESTADO DE PUEBLA **Edge:** Reeded
Mint: Mexico City

Date	Mintage	F	VF	XF	Unc	BU
2004Mo Proof	10,000	Value: 70.00				

KM# 739 10 PESOS
31.1040 g., 0.9990 Bi-Metallic 0.9990 oz., 39.9 mm.
Series: First **Subject:** 180th Anniversary of
Federation **Obv:** National arms **Obv. Legend:**
ESTADOS UNIDOS MEXICANOS **Rev:** State arms
Rev. Legend: ESTADO DE OAXACA **Edge:**
Reeded **Mint:** Mexico City

Date	Mintage	F	VF	XF	Unc	BU
2004Mo Proof	10,000	Value: 70.00				

KM# 741 10 PESOS
31.1040 g., 0.9990 Silver 0.9990 oz. ASW, 39.9 mm.
Series: First **Subject:** 180th Anniversary of
Federation **Obv:** National arms **Obv. Legend:**
ESTADOS UNIDOS MEXICANOS **Rev:** State arms

Rev. Legend: ESTADO DE NUEVO LEÓN **Edge:**
Reeded **Mint:** Mexico City

Date	Mintage	F	VF	XF	Unc	BU
2004Mo Proof	10,000	Value: 70.00				

KM# 743 10 PESOS
31.1040 g., 0.9990 Silver 0.9990 oz. ASW, 39.9 mm.
Series: First **Subject:** 180th Anniversary of
Federation **Obv:** National arms **Obv. Legend:**
ESTADOS UNIDOS MEXICANOS **Rev:** State arms
Rev. Legend: ESTADO DE NAYARIT **Edge:**
Reeded **Mint:** Mexico City

Date	Mintage	F	VF	XF	Unc	BU
2004Mo Proof	10,000	Value: 70.00				

KM# 745 10 PESOS
31.1040 g., 0.9990 Silver 0.9990 oz. ASW, 39.9 mm.
Series: First **Subject:** 180th Anniversary of
Federation **Obv:** National arms **Obv. Legend:**
ESTADOS UNIDOS MEXICANOS **Rev:** State arms
Rev. Legend: ESTADO DE MORELOS **Edge:**
Reeded **Mint:** Mexico City

Date	Mintage	F	VF	XF	Unc	BU
2004Mo Proof	10,000	Value: 70.00				

KM# 796 10 PESOS
31.1040 g., 0.9990 Silver 0.9990 oz. ASW, 39.9 mm.

ESTADOS UNIDOS MEXICANOS

Series: First **Subject:** 180th Anniversary of
Federation **Obv:** National arms **Obv. Legend:**
ESTADOS UNIDOS MEXICANOS **Rev:** State arms
Rev. Legend: ESTADO DE MICHOACÁN DE
OCAMPO **Edge:** Reeded **Mint:** Mexico City

Date	Mintage	F	VF	XF	Unc	BU
2004Mo Proof	10,000	Value: 70.00				

KM# 747   10 PESOS
31.1040 g., 0.9990 Silver 0.9990 oz. ASW, 39.9 mm.
Series: First **Subject:** 180th Anniversary of
Federation **Obv:** National arms **Obv. Legend:**
ESTADOS UNIDOS MEXICANOS **Rev:** State arms
Rev. Legend: ESTADO DE MÉXICO **Edge:** Reeded
Mint: Mexico City

Date	Mintage	F	VF	XF	Unc	BU
2004Mo Proof	10,000	Value: 70.00				

KM# 749   10 PESOS
31.1040 g., 0.9990 Silver 0.9990 oz. ASW, 39.9 mm.
Series: First **Subject:** 180th Anniversary of
Federation **Obv:** National arms **Obv. Legend:**
ESTADOS UNIDOS MEXICANOS **Rev:** State arms
Rev. Legend: ESTADO DE JALISCO **Edge:**
Reeded **Mint:** Mexico City

Date	Mintage	F	VF	XF	Unc	BU
2004Mo Proof	10,000	Value: 70.00				

KM# 766   10 PESOS
31.1035 g., 0.9990 Silver 0.9990 oz. ASW, 40 mm.
Subject: Cervantes Festival **Obv:** Mexican Eagle
and Snake **Rev:** Don Quixote **Edge:** Reeded **Mint:**
Mexico City

Date	Mintage	F	VF	XF	Unc	BU
2005Mo Proof	1,205	Value: 75.00				

KM# 768   10 PESOS
31.1035 g., 0.9990 Silver 0.9990 oz. ASW, 40 mm.
Subject: 470th Anniversary - Mexico City Mint **Obv:**
Mexican Eagle and Snake **Rev:** Antique coin press
Mint: Mexico City

Date	Mintage	F	VF	XF	Unc	BU
2005Mo Proof	2,005	Value: 65.00				

KM# 711   10 PESOS
31.1040 g., 0.9990 Silver 0.9990 oz. ASW, 39.9 mm.
Series: First **Subject:** 180th Anniversary of
Federation **Obv:** National arms **Obv. Legend:**
ESTADOS UNIDOS MEXICANOS **Rev:** State arms
Rev. Legend: ESTADO DE HIDALGO **Edge:**
Reeded **Mint:** Mexico City

Date	Mintage	F	VF	XF	Unc	BU
2005Mo Proof	10,000	Value: 70.00				

KM# 710   10 PESOS
31.1040 g., 0.9990 Silver 0.9990 oz. ASW, 39.9 mm.
Series: First **Subject:** 180th Anniversary of
Federation **Obv:** National arms **Obv. Legend:**
ESTADOS UNIDOS MEXICANOS **Rev:** State arms
Rev. Legend: ESTADO DE GUERRERO **Edge:**
Reeded **Mint:** Mexico City

Date	Mintage	F	VF	XF	Unc	BU
2005Mo Proof	10,000	Value: 70.00				

KM# 709   10 PESOS
31.1040 g., 0.9990 Silver 0.9990 oz. ASW, 39.9 mm.
Series: First **Subject:** 180th Anniversary of
Federation **Obv:** National arms **Obv. Legend:**
ESTADOS UNIDOS MEXICANOS **Rev:** State arms

Rev. Legend: ESTADO DE GUANAJUATO Edge: Reeded Mint: Mexico City

Date	Mintage	F	VF	XF	Unc	BU
2005Mo Proof	10,000	Value: 70.00				

KM# 708   10 PESOS

31.1040 g., 0.9990 Silver 0.9990 oz. ASW, 39.9 mm. Series: First Subject: 180th Anniversary of Federation Obv: National arms Obv. Legend: ESTADOS UNIDOS MEXICANOS Rev: State arms Rev. Legend: ESTADO DE DURANGO Edge: Reeded Mint: Mexico City

Date	Mintage	F	VF	XF	Unc	BU
2005Mo Proof	10,000	Value: 70.00				

KM# 707   10 PESOS

31.1040 g., 0.9990 Silver 0.9990 oz. ASW, 39.9 mm. Series: First Subject: 180th Anniversary of Federation Obv: National arms Obv. Legend: ESTADOS UNIDOS MEXICANOS Rev: Federal District arms Rev. Legend: DISTRITO FEDERAL Edge: Reeded Mint: Mexico City

Date	Mintage	F	VF	XF	Unc	BU
2005Mo Proof	10,000	Value: 70.00				

KM# 753   10 PESOS

31.1040 g., 0.9990 Silver 0.9990 oz. ASW, 39.9 mm.

Series: First Subject: 180th Anniversary of Federation Obv: National arms Obv. Legend: ESTADOS UNIDOS MEXICANOS Rev: State arms Rev. Legend: ESTADO DE CHIHUAHUA Edge: Reeded Mint: Mexico City

Date	Mintage	F	VF	XF	Unc	BU
2005Mo Proof	10,000	Value: 70.00				

KM# 706   10 PESOS

31.1040 g., 0.9990 Silver 0.9990 oz. ASW, 39.9 mm. Series: First Subject: 180th Anniversary of Federation Obv: National arms Obv. Legend: ESTADOS UNIDOS MEXICANOS Rev: State arms Rev. Legend: ESTADO DE CHIAPAS Edge: Reeded Mint: Mexico City

Date	Mintage	F	VF	XF	Unc	BU
2005Mo Proof	10,000	Value: 70.00				

KM# 728   10 PESOS

31.1040 g., 0.9990 Silver 0.9990 oz. ASW, 39.9 mm. Series: First Subject: 180th Anniversary of Federation Obv: National arms Obv. Legend: ESTADOS UNIDOS MEXICANOS Rev: State arms Rev. Legend: ESTADO DE COLIMA Edge: Reeded Mint: Mexico City

Date	Mintage	F	VF	XF	Unc	BU
2005Mo Proof	10,000	Value: 70.00				

ESTADOS UNIDOS MEXICANOS

KM# 751   10 PESOS
31.1040 g., 0.9990 Silver 0.9990 oz. ASW, 39.9 mm.
Series: First **Subject:** 180th Anniversary of
Federation **Obv:** National arms **Obv. Legend:**
ESTADOS UNIDOS MEXICANOS **Rev:** State arms
Rev. Legend: ESTADO DE COAHUILA DE
ZARAGOZA **Edge:** Reeded **Mint:** Mexico City

Date	Mintage	F	VF	XF	Unc	BU
2005Mo Proof	10,000	Value: 70.00				

KM# 726   10 PESOS
31.1040 g., 0.9990 Silver 0.9990 oz. ASW, 39.9 mm.
Series: First **Subject:** 180th Anniversary of
Federation **Obv:** National arms **Obv. Legend:**
ESTADOS UNIDOS MEXICANOS **Rev:** State arms
Rev. Legend: ESTADO DE CAMPECHE **Edge:**
Reeded **Mint:** Mexico City

Date	Mintage	F	VF	XF	Unc	BU
2005Mo Proof	10,000	Value: 70.00				

KM# 724   10 PESOS
31.1040 g., 0.9990 Silver 0.9990 oz. ASW, 39.9 mm.
Series: First **Subject:** 180th Anniversary of
Federation **Obv:** National arms **Obv. Legend:**
ESTADOS UNIDOS MEXICANOS **Rev:** State arms

Rev. Legend: ESTADO DE BAJA CALIFORNIA
SUR **Edge:** Reeded **Mint:** Mexico City

Date	Mintage	F	VF	XF	Unc	BU
2005Mo Proof	10,000	Value: 70.00				

KM# 722   10 PESOS
31.1040 g., 0.9990 Silver 0.9990 oz. ASW, 39.9 mm.
Series: First **Subject:** 180th Anniversary of
Federation **Obv:** National arms **Obv. Legend:**
ESTADOS UNIDOS MEXICANOS **Rev:** State arms
Rev. Legend: ESTADO DE BAJA CALIFORNIA
Edge: Reeded **Mint:** Mexico City

Date	Mintage	F	VF	XF	Unc	BU
2005Mo Proof	10,000	Value: 70.00				

KM# 720   10 PESOS
31.1040 g., 0.9990 Silver 0.9990 oz. ASW, 39.9 mm.
Series: First **Subject:** 180th Anniversary of
Federation **Obv:** National arms **Obv. Legend:**
ESTADOS UNIDOS MEXICANOS **Rev:** State arms
Rev. Legend: ESTADO DE AGUASCALIENTES
Edge: Reeded **Mint:** Mexico City

Date	Mintage	F	VF	XF	Unc	BU
2005Mo Proof	10,000	Value: 70.00				

KM# 718   10 PESOS
31.1040 g., 0.9990 Silver 0.9990 oz. ASW, 40 mm.

Series: Second **Obv:** National arms **Obv. Legend:** ESTADOS UNIDOS MEXICANOS **Rev:** Facade of the San Marcos garden above sculpture of national emblem at left, San Antonio Temple at right **Rev. Legend:** AGUASCALIENTES **Edge:** Reeded **Mint:** Mexico City

Date	Mintage	F	VF	XF	Unc	BU
2005Mo Proof	6,000	Value: 65.00				

KM# 757   10 PESOS

31.1040 g., 0.9990 Silver 0.9990 oz. ASW, 40 mm. **Series:** Second **Obv:** National arms **Obv. Legend:** ESTADOS UNIDOS MEXICANOS **Rev:** Rams head, mountain outline in background **Rev. Legend:** BAJA CALIFORNIA - GOBIERNO DEL ESTADO **Edge:** Reeded **Mint:** Mexico City

Date	Mintage	F	VF	XF	Unc	BU
2005Mo Proof	6,000	Value: 65.00				

KM# 755   10 PESOS

31.1040 g., 0.9990 Silver 0.9990 oz. ASW, 40 mm. **Obv:** National arms **Rev:** Baja California del Norte arms

Date	Mintage	F	VF	XF	Unc	BU
2005Mo Proof	—	Value: 75.00				

KM# 763   10 PESOS

31.1040 g., 0.9990 Silver 0.9990 oz. ASW, 40 mm. **Obv:** National arms **Rev:** Benito Juarez **Edge:** Reeded **Mint:** Mexico City

Date	Mintage	F	VF	XF	Unc	BU
2006Mo Proof	—	Value: 75.00				

KM# 761   10 PESOS

31.1040 g., 0.9990 Silver 0.9990 oz. ASW, 40 mm. **Series:** Second **Obv:** National arms **Obv. Legend:** ESTADOS UNIDOS MEXICANOS **Rev:** Outlined map of peninsula at center, cave painting of deer behind, cactus at right **Rev. Legend:** ESTADO DE BAJA CALIFORNIA SUR **Edge:** Reeded **Mint:** Mexico City

Date	Mintage	F	VF	XF	Unc	BU
2006Mo Proof	6,000	Value: 65.00				

KM# 759   10 PESOS

31.1040 g., 0.9990 Silver 0.9990 oz. ASW, 40 mm. **Series:** Second **Obv:** National arms **Obv. Legend:** ESTADOS UNIDOS MEXICANOS **Rev:** Jade mask - Calakmul, Campeche **Rev. Legend:** ESTADO DE CAMPECHE **Edge:** Reeded **Mint:** Mexico City

Date	Mintage	F	VF	XF	Unc	BU
2006Mo Proof	6,000	Value: 65.00				

KM# 780   10 PESOS

31.1040 g., 0.9990 Silver 0.9990 oz. ASW, 40 mm. **Series:** Second **Obv:** National arms **Obv. Legend:** ESTADOS UNIDOS MEXICANOS **Rev:** Outlined map with turtle, mine cart above grapes at center, Friendship dam above Christ of the Nodas at left, chimneys above crucibles and bell tower of Santiago's cathedral at right **Rev. Inscription:** COAHUILA DE ZARAGOZA **Edge:** Reeded **Mint:** Mexico City

Date	Mintage	F	VF	XF	Unc	BU
2006Mo Proof	6,000	Value: 65.00				

KM# 776   10 PESOS

31.1040 g., 0.9990 Silver 0.9990 oz. ASW, 40 mm. **Series:** Second **Obv:** National arms **Obv. Legend:** ESTADOS UNIDOS MEXICANOS **Rev:** State arms at lower center, Nevado de Colima and Volcan de

Fuego volcanos in background **Rev. Legend:**
Colima **Rev. Inscription:** *GENEROSO* **Edge:**
Reeded **Mint:** Mexico City

Date	Mintage	F	VF	XF	Unc	BU
2006Mo Proof	6,000	Value: 65.00				

KM# 772   10 PESOS
31.1040 g., 0.9990 Silver 0.9990 oz. ASW, 40 mm.
Series: Second **Obv:** National arms **Obv. Legend:**
ESTADOS UNIDOS MEXICANOS **Rev:** Head of
Pakal, ancient Mayan king, Palenque **Rev. Legend:**
ESTADO DE CHIAPAS - CABEZA MAYA DEL REY
PAKAL, PALENQUE **Edge:** Reeded **Mint:** Mexico City

Date	Mintage	F	VF	XF	Unc	BU
2006Mo Proof	6,000	Value: 65.00				

KM# 774   10 PESOS
31.1040 g., 0.9990 Silver 0.9990 oz. ASW, 40 mm.
Series: Second **Obv:** National arms **Obv. Legend:**
ESTADOS UNIDOS MEXICANOS **Rev:** Angel of
Liberty **Rev. Legend:** MÉXICO - ANGEL DE LA
LIBERTAD, CHIHUAHUA **Edge:** Reeded **Mint:**
Mexico City

Date	Mintage	F	VF	XF	Unc	BU
2006Mo Proof	6,000	Value: 65.00				

KM# 778   10 PESOS
31.1040 g., 0.9990 Silver 0.9990 oz. ASW, 40 mm.
Series: Second **Obv:** National arms **Obv. Legend:**
ESTADOS UNIDOS MEXICANOS **Rev:** National
Palace **Rev. Legend:** DISTRITO FEDERAL -
ANTIGUO AYUNTAMIENTO **Edge:** Reeded **Mint:**
Mexico City

Date	Mintage	F	VF	XF	Unc	BU
2006Mo Proof	6,000	Value: 65.00				

KM# 786   10 PESOS
31.1040 g., 0.9990 Silver 0.9990 oz. ASW, 40 mm.
Series: Second **Obv:** National arms **Obv. Legend:**
ESTADOS UNIDOS MEXICANOS **Rev:** Tree **Rev.
Legend:** PRIMERA RESERVA NACIONAL
FORESTAL - DURANGO **Edge:** Reeded **Mint:**
Mexico City

Date	Mintage	F	VF	XF	Unc	BU
2006Mo Proof	6,000	Value: 65.00				

KM# 788   10 PESOS
31.1040 g., 0.9990 Silver 0.9990 oz. ASW, 40 mm.
Series: Second **Obv:** National arms **Obv. Legend:**
ESTADOS UNIDOS MEXICANOS **Rev:** State arms
at center, statue of Miguel Hidalgo at left, monument
to Pípila at lower right **Rev. Inscription:** *Guanajuato*
Edge: Reeded **Mint:** Mexico City

Date	Mintage	F	VF	XF	Unc	BU
2006Mo Proof	6,000	Value: 65.00				

ESTADOS UNIDOS MEXICANOS

KM# 790   10 PESOS
31.1040 g., 0.9990 Silver 0.9990 oz. ASW, 40 mm.
Series: Second **Obv:** National arms **Obv. Legend:**
ESTADOS UNIDOS MEXICANOS **Rev:** Stylized
portrait of Vicente Guerrero at left, church of Taxco
at upper center, Acapulco's la Quebrada with diver
above Christmas Eve flower and mask **Rev. Legend:**
GUERRERO **Edge:** Reeded **Mint:** Mexico City

Date	Mintage	F	VF	XF	Unc	BU
2006Mo Proof	6,000	Value: 65.00				

KM# 792   10 PESOS
31.1040 g., 0.9990 Silver 0.9990 oz. ASW, 40 mm.
Series: Second **Obv:** National arms **Obv. Legend:**
ESTADOS UNIDOS MEXICANOS **Rev:** Monument
of Pachuca Hidalgo **Rev. Inscription:** *RELOJ /
MONUMENTAL / DE / PACHUCA / HIDALGO - La
/ Bella / Airosa* **Edge:** Reeded **Mint:** Mexico City

Date	Mintage	F	VF	XF	Unc	BU
2006Mo Proof	6,000	Value: 65.00				

KM# 794   10 PESOS
31.1040 g., 0.9990 Silver 0.9990 oz. ASW, 40 mm.
Series: Second **Obv:** National arms **Obv. Legend:**
ESTADOS UNIDOS MEXICANOS **Rev:** Hospicio

Cabañas orphanage **Rev. Legend:** ESTADO DE
JALISCCO **Edge:** Reeded **Mint:** Mexico City

Date	Mintage	F	VF	XF	Unc	BU
2006Mo Proof	6,000	Value: 65.00				

KM# 830   10 PESOS
31.1040 g., 0.9990 Silver 0.9990 oz. ASW, 40 mm.
Series: Second **Obv:** National arms **Obv. Legend:**
ESTADOS UNIDOS MEXICANOS **Rev:** Pyramid de
la Loona (Moon) **Rev. Legend:** ESTADO DE
MÉXICO **Edge:** Reeded **Mint:** Mexico City

Date	Mintage	F	VF	XF	Unc	BU
2006Mo Proof	6,000	Value: 65.00				

KM# 831   10 PESOS
31.1040 g., 0.9990 Silver 0.9990 oz. ASW, 40 mm.
Series: Second **Obv:** National arms **Obv. Legend:**
ESTADOS UNIDOS MEXICANOS **Rev:** Four
Monarch butterflies **Rev. Legend:** ESTADO DE
MICHOACÁN **Edge:** Reeded **Mint:** Mexico City

Date	Mintage	F	VF	XF	Unc	BU
2006Mo Proof	6,000	Value: 65.00				

KM# 832   10 PESOS
31.1040 g., 0.9990 Silver 0.9990 oz. ASW, 40 mm.
Series: Second **Obv:** National arms **Obv. Legend:**
ESTADOS UNIDOS MEXICANOS **Rev:** 1/2 length

ESTADOS UNIDOS MEXICANOS

figure of Chinelo (local dancer) at right, Palacio de
Cortes in background **Rev. Inscription:** ESTADO
DE / MORELOS **Edge:** Reeded **Mint:** Mexico City

Date	Mintage	F	VF	XF	Unc	BU
2006Mo Proof	6,000	Value: 65.00				

KM# 833   10 PESOS
31.1040 g., 0.9990 Silver 0.9990 oz. ASW, 40 mm.
Series: Second **Obv:** National arms **Obv. Legend:**
ESTADOS UNIDOS MEXICANOS **Rev:** Isle de
Mexcaltitlán **Rev. Legend:** ESTADO DE NAYARIT
Edge: Reeded **Mint:** Mexico City

Date	Mintage	F	VF	XF	Unc	BU
2007Mo Proof	6,000	Value: 65.00				

KM# 834   10 PESOS
31.1040 g., 0.9990 Silver 0.9990 oz. ASW, 40 mm.
Series: Second **Obv:** National arms **Obv. Legend:**
ESTADOS UNIDOS MEXICANOS **Rev:** Old foundry
in Pargue Fundidora (public park) at right, Cerro de
la Silla (Saddle Hill) in background **Rev. Legend:**
ESTADO DE NUEVO LEÓN **Edge:** Reeded **Mint:**
Mexico City

Date	Mintage	F	VF	XF	Unc	BU
2007Mo Proof	6,000	Value: 65.00				

KM# 835   10 PESOS
31.1040 g., 0.9990 Silver 0.9990 oz. ASW, 40 mm.
Series: Second **Obv:** National arms **Obv. Legend:**
ESTADOS UNIDOS MEXICANOS **Rev:** Teatro
Macedonio Alcala (theater) **Rev. Legend:** OAXACA
Edge: Reeded **Mint:** Mexico City

Date	Mintage	F	VF	XF	Unc	BU
2007Mo Proof	6,000	Value: 65.00				

KM# 836   10 PESOS
31.1040 g., 0.9990 Silver 0.9990 oz. ASW, 40 mm.
Series: Second **Obv:** National arms **Obv. Legend:**
ESTADOS UNIDOS MEXICANOS **Rev:** Talavera
porcelain dish **Rev. Legend:** ESTADO DE PUEBLA
Edge: Reeded **Mint:** Mexico City

Date	Mintage	F	VF	XF	Unc	BU
2007Mo Proof	6,000	Value: 65.00				

KM# 837   10 PESOS
31.1040 g., 0.9990 Silver 0.9990 oz. ASW, 40 mm.
Series: Second **Obv:** National arms **Obv. Legend:**
ESTADOS UNIDOS MEXICANOS **Rev:** Mask at left,
rays above state arms at center, Mayan ruins at right
Rev. Legend: QUINTANA ROO **Edge:** Reeded
Mint: Mexico City

Date	Mintage	F	VF	XF	Unc	BU
2007Mo Proof	6,000	Value: 65.00				

ESTADOS UNIDOS MEXICANOS

KM# 838   10 PESOS
31.1040 g., 0.9990 Silver 0.9990 oz. ASW, 40 mm.
Series: Second **Obv:** National arms **Obv. Legend:**
ESTADOS UNIDOS MEXICANOS **Rev:** Acqueduct
of Querétaro at left, church of Santa Rosa de Viterbo
at right **Rev. Legend:** ESTADO DE QUERÉTARO
ARTEAGA **Edge:** Reeded **Mint:** Mexico City

Date	Mintage	F	VF	XF	Unc	BU
2007Mo Proof	6,000	Value: 65.00				

KM# 839   10 PESOS
31.1040 g., Silver, 40 mm.   **Series:** Second **Obv:**
National arms **Obv. Legend:** ESTADOS UNIDOS
MEXICANOS **Rev:** Facade of Caja Real **Rev. Legend:**
• SAN LUIS POTOSÍ • **Edge:** Reeded **Mint:** Mexico City

Date	Mintage	F	VF	XF	Unc	BU
2007Mo Proof	6,000	Value: 65.00				

KM# 840   10 PESOS
31.1040 g., 0.9990 Silver 0.9990 oz. ASW, 40 mm.
Series: Second **Obv:** National arms **Obv. Legend:**
ESTADOS UNIDOS MEXICANOS **Rev:** Shield on
pile of cactus fruits **Rev. Legend:** ESTADO DE
SINALOA - LUGAR DE PITAHAYAS **Edge:** Reeded
Mint: Mexico City

Date	Mintage	F	VF	XF	Unc	BU
2007Mo Proof	6,000	Value: 65.00				

KM# 841   10 PESOS
31.1040 g., 0.9990 Silver 0.9990 oz. ASW, 40 mm.
Series: Second **Obv:** National arms **Obv. Legend:**
ESTADOS UNIDOS MEXICANOS **Rev:** Local in
Dance of the Deer at left, cactus at right, mountains
in background **Rev. Legend:** ESTADO DE SONORA
Edge: Reeded **Mint:** Mexico City

Date	Mintage	F	VF	XF	Unc	BU
2007Mo Proof	6,000	Value: 65.00				

KM# 842   10 PESOS
31.1040 g., 0.9990 Silver 0.9990 oz. ASW, 40 mm.
Series: Second **Obv:** National arms **Obv. Legend:**
ESTADOS UNIDOS MEXICANOS **Rev:** Fuente de los
Pescadores (fisherman fountain) at lower left, giant
head from the Olmec-pre-Hispanic culture at right,
Planetario Tabasco in background **Rev. Legend:**
TABASCO **Edge:** Reeded **Mint:** Mexico City

Date	Mintage	F	VF	XF	Unc	BU
2007Mo Proof	6,000	Value: 65.00				

KM# 843   10 PESOS
31.1040 g., 0.9990 Silver 0.9990 oz. ASW, 40 mm.
Series: Second **Obv:** National arms **Obv. Legend:**
ESTADOS UNIDOS MEXICANOS **Rev:** Ridge -

ESTADOS UNIDOS MEXICANOS

Cerro Del Bernal, Gonzáles **Rev. Legend:**
TAMAULIPAS **Edge:** Reeded **Mint:** Mexico City

Date	Mintage	F	VF	XF	Unc	BU
2007Mo Proof	6,000	Value: 65.00				

KM# 844   10 PESOS
31.1040 g., 0.9990 Silver 0.9990 oz. ASW, 40 mm.
Series: Second **Obv:** National arms **Obv. Legend:**
ESTADOS UNIDOS MEXICANOS **Rev:** Basilica de
Ocotlán at left, state arms above Capilla Abierta,
Plaza de Toros Ranchero Aguilar below, Exconvento
de San Francisco at right **Rev. Legend:** ESTADO
DE TLAXCALA **Edge:** Reeded **Mint:** Mexico City

Date	Mintage	F	VF	XF	Unc	BU
2007Mo Proof	6,000	Value: 65.00				

KM# 845   10 PESOS
31.1040 g., 0.9990 Silver 0.9990 oz. ASW, 40 mm.
Series: Second **Obv:** National arms **Obv. Legend:**
ESTADOS UNIDOS MEXICANOS **Rev:** Pyramid of
El Tajín **Rev. Legend:** • VERACRUZ • • • DE
IGNACIO DE LA LLAVE • **Edge:** Reeded **Mint:**
Mexico City

Date	Mintage	F	VF	XF	Unc	BU
2007Mo Proof	6,000	Value: 65.00				

KM# 846   10 PESOS
31.1030 g., 0.9990 Silver 0.9989 oz. ASW, 40 mm.

Series: Second **Obv:** National arms **Obv. Legend:**
ESTADOS UNIDOS MEXICANOS **Rev:** Stylized
pyramid of Chichén-Itzá **Rev. Legend:** Castillo de
Chichén Itzá **Rev. Inscription:** YUCATÁN **Edge:**
Reeded **Mint:** Mexico City

Date	Mintage	F	VF	XF	Unc	BU
2007Mo Proof	6,000	Value: 65.00				

KM# 847   10 PESOS
31.1040 g., 0.9990 Silver 0.9990 oz. ASW, 40 mm.
Series: Second **Obv:** National arms **Obv. Legend:**
ESTADOS UNIDOS MEXICANOS **Rev:** Cable car
above Monumento al Minero at left, Cathedral de
Zacatecas at center right **Rev. Legend:** Zacatecas
Edge: Reeded **Mint:** Mexico City

Date	Mintage	F	VF	XF	Unc	BU
2007Mo Proof	6,000	Value: 65.00				

KM# 561   20 NUEVO PESOS
16.9200 g., Bi-Metallic 0.925 Silver (.2500 oz. ASW)
center within Aluminum-Bronze ring, 31.86 mm.
Obv: National arms **Obv. Legend:** ESTADOS
UNIDOS MEXICANOS **Rev:** Head of Hidalgo left
within wreath **Edge:** Reeded **Mint:** Mexico City

Date	Mintage	F	VF	XF	Unc	BU
1993Mo	25,000,000	—	—	10.00	12.00	15.00
1994Mo	5,000,000	—	—	10.00	12.00	15.00
1995Mo	5,000,000	—	—	10.00	12.00	15.00

KM# 641   20 PESOS
6.2210 g., 0.9990 Gold 0.1998 oz. AGW, 21.9 mm.
Subject: UNICEF **Obv:** National arms, eagle left
Rev: Child playing with lasso **Edge:** Reeded **Mint:**
Mexico City

Date	Mintage	F	VF	XF	Unc	BU
1999Mo Proof	1,510	Value: 375				

Date	Mintage	F	VF	XF	Unc	BU
2005Mo	—	—	—	—	—	80.00
2005Mo Proof	3,005	Value: 90.00				

KM# 637   20 PESOS
Bi-Metallic Copper-Nickel center within Brass ring, 32 mm. **Subject:** Xiuhtecuhtli **Obv:** National arms, eagle left within circle **Rev:** Aztec with torch within spiked circle

Date	Mintage	F	VF	XF	Unc	BU
2000Mo	14,850,000	—	—	2.50	15.00	18.50
2001Mo	2,478,000	—	—	2.50	16.00	18.00

KM# 638   20 PESOS
Bi-Metallic Copper-Nickel center within Brass ring, 32 mm. **Subject:** Octavio Paz **Obv:** National arms, eagle left within circle **Rev:** Head 1/4 right within circle

Date	Mintage	F	VF	XF	Unc	BU
2000Mo	14,943,000	—	2.50	3.50	15.00	18.50
2001Mo	2,515,000	—	2.50	3.50	16.00	18.50

KM# 571   50 NUEVO PESOS
34.1100 g., Bi-Metallic 0.925 Silver .5000 ASW center within Brass ring, 38.87 mm. **Subject:** Nino Heroes **Obv:** National arms **Obv. Legend:** ESTADOS UNIDOS MEXICANOS **Rev:** Six heads facing with date at upper right, all within circle and 1/2 wreath **Edge:** Reeded **Mint:** Mexico City

Date	Mintage	F	VF	XF	Unc	BU
1993Mo	2,000,000	—	—	18.00	25.00	32.50
1994Mo	1,500,000	—	—	18.00	25.00	32.50
1995Mo	1,500,000	—	—	18.00	25.00	32.50

KM# 704   20 PESOS
62.4000 g., 0.9990 Silver 2.0041 oz. ASW, 48.1 mm. **Subject:** 400th Anniversary of Don Quijote de la Manchia **Obv:** National arms **Rev:** Skeletal figure horseback with spear galloping right **Edge:** Plain **Mint:** Mexico City

Date	Mintage	F	VF	XF	Unc	BU
ND(2005)Mo Proof	3,605	Value: 85.00				

KM# 767   20 PESOS
62.4000 g., 0.9990 Silver 2.0041 oz. ASW, 48 mm. **Subject:** 80th Anniversary - Bank of Mexico **Obv:** National arms **Rev:** 100 Peso banknote design of 1925 **Mint:** Mexico City

KM# 688   100 PESOS
33.9400 g., Bi-Metallic .925 Silver 16.812g center in Aluminum-Bronze ring, 39.04 mm. **Series:** First **Subject:** 180th Anniversary of Federation **Obv:** National arms **Obv. Legend:** ESTADOS UNIDOS MEXICANOS **Rev:** State arms **Rev. Legend:** ESTADO DE ZACATECAS **Edge:** Segmented reeding **Mint:** Mexico City

Date	Mintage	F	VF	XF	Unc	BU
2003Mo	244,900	—	—	—	40.00	50.00

KM# 696   100 PESOS
29.1690 g., Bi-Metallic .999 Gold 17.154g center in .999 Silver 12.015g ring, 34.5 mm. **Series:** First **Subject:** 180th Anniversary of Federation **Obv:** National arms **Obv. Legend:** ESTADOS UNIDOS MEXICANOS **Rev:** State arms **Rev. Legend:** ESTADO DE ZACATECAS **Edge:** Segmented reeding **Mint:** Mexico City

Date	Mintage	F	VF	XF	Unc	BU
2003Mo Proof	1,000	Value: 1,200				

ESTADOS UNIDOS MEXICANOS

KM# 689   100 PESOS
33.9400 g., Bi-Metallic .925 Silver 16.812g center in
Aluminum-Bronze ring, 39.04 mm. **Series:** First
Subject: 180th Anniversary of Federation **Obv:**
National arms **Obv. Legend:** ESTADOS UNIDOS
MEXICANOS **Rev:** State arms **Rev. Legend:**
ESTADO DE YUCATÁN **Edge:** Segmented reeding
Mint: Mexico City

Date	Mintage	F	VF	XF	Unc	BU
2003Mo	235,763	—	—	—	40.00	50.00

KM# 697   100 PESOS
29.1690 g., Bi-Metallic .999 Gold 17.154g center in
.999 Silver 12.015g ring, 34.5 mm. **Series:** First
Subject: 180th Anniversary of Federation **Obv:**
National arms **Obv. Legend:** ESTADOS UNIDOS
MEXICANOS **Rev:** State arms **Rev. Legend:**
ESTADO DE YUCATÁN **Edge:** Segmented reeding
Mint: Mexico City

Date	Mintage	F	VF	XF	Unc	BU
2003Mo Proof	1,000	Value: 1,200				

KM# 691   100 PESOS
33.9400 g., Bi-Metallic .925 Silver 16.812g center in
Aluminum-Bronze ring, 39.9 mm. **Series:** First
Subject: 180th Anniversary of Federation **Obv:**
National arms **Obv. Legend:** ESTADOS UNIDOS
MEXICANOS **Rev:** State arms **Rev. Legend:**
ESTADO DE TLAXCALA **Edge:** Segmented reeding
Mint: Mexico City

Date	Mintage	F	VF	XF	Unc	BU
2003Mo	248,976	—	—	—	35.00	40.00

KM# 699   100 PESOS
29.1690 g., Bi-Metallic .999 Gold 17.154g center in
.999 Silver 12.015g ring, 34.5 mm. **Series:** First
Subject: 180th Anniversary of Federation **Obv:**
National arms **Obv. Legend:** ESTADOS UNIDOS
MEXICANOS **Rev:** State arms **Rev. Legend:**
ESTADO DE TLAXCALA **Edge:** Segmented reeding
Mint: Mexico City

Date	Mintage	F	VF	XF	Unc	BU
2003Mo Proof	1,000	Value: 1,200				

KM# 690   100 PESOS
33.9400 g., Bi-Metallic .925 Silver 16.812g center in
Aluminum-Bronze ring, 39.04 mm. **Series:** First
Subject: 180th Anniversary of Federation **Obv:**
National arms **Obv. Legend:** ESTADOS UNIDOS
MEXICANOS **Rev:** State arms **Rev. Legend:**
ESTADO DE VERACRUZ-LLAVE **Edge:**
Segmented reeding **Mint:** Mexico City

Date	Mintage	F	VF	XF	Unc	BU
2003Mo	248,810	—	—	—	40.00	50.00

KM# 698   100 PESOS
29.1690 g., Bi-Metallic .999 Gold 17.154g center in
.999 Silver 12.015g ring, 34.5 mm. **Series:** First
Subject: 180th Anniversary of Federation **Obv:**
National arms **Obv. Legend:** ESTADOS UNIDOS
MEXICANOS **Rev:** State arms **Rev. Legend:**
ESTADO DE VERACRUZ-LLAVE **Edge:**
Segmented reeding **Mint:** Mexico City

Date	Mintage	F	VF	XF	Unc	BU
2003Mo Proof	1,000	Value: 1,200				

KM# 692   100 PESOS
33.9400 g., Bi-Metallic .925 Silver 16.812g center in
Aluminum-Bronze ring, 39.04 mm. **Series:** First
Subject: 180th Anniversay of Federation **Obv:**
National arms **Obv. Legend:** ESTADOS UNIDOS
MEXICANOS **Rev:** State arms **Rev. Legend:**
ESTADO DE TAMAULIPAS **Edge:** Segmented
reeding **Mint:** Mexico City

Date	Mintage	F	VF	XF	Unc	BU
2004Mo	249,398	—	—	—	35.00	40.00

KM# 700   100 PESOS
29.1690 g., Bi-Metallic .999 Gold 17.154g center in
.999 Silver 12.015g ring, 34.5 mm. **Series:** First
Subject: 180th Anniversary of Federation **Obv:**
National arms **Obv. Legend:** ESTADOS UNIDOS
MEXICANOS **Rev:** State arms **Rev. Legend:**
ESTADO DE TAMAULIPAS **Edge:** Segmented
reeding **Mint:** Mexico City

Date	Mintage	F	VF	XF	Unc	BU
2004Mo Proof	1,000	Value: 1,200				

KM# 693   100 PESOS
33.9400 g., Bi-Metallic .925 Silver 16.812g center in
Aluminum-Bronze ring, 39.04 mm.   **Series:** First
Subject: 180th Anniversary of Federation **Obv:**
National arms **Obv. Legend:** ESTADOS UNIDOS
MEXICANOS **Rev:** State arms **Rev. Legend:**
ESTADO DE TABASCO **Edge:** Segmented reeding
Mint: Mexico City

Date	Mintage	F	VF	XF	Unc	BU
2004Mo	249,318	—	—	—	35.00	40.00

KM# 701   100 PESOS
29.1690 g., Bi-Metallic .999 Gold 17.154g center in
.999 Silver 12.015g ring, 34.5 mm.   **Series:** First
Subject: 180th Anniversary of Federation **Obv:**
National arms **Obv. Legend:** ESTADOS UNIDOS
MEXICANOS **Rev:** State arms **Rev. Legend:**
ESTADO DE TABASCO **Edge:** Segmented reeding
Mint: Mexico City

Date	Mintage	F	VF	XF	Unc	BU
2004Mo Proof	1,000	Value: 1,200				

KM# 695   100 PESOS
33.9400 g., Bi-Metallic .925 Silver 16.812g center in
Aluminum-Bronze ring, 39.04 mm.   **Series:** First
Subject: 180th Anniversary of Federation **Obv:**
National arms **Obv. Legend:** ESTADOS UNIDOS
MEXICANOS **Rev:** State arms **Rev. Legend:**
ESTADO DE SINALOA **Edge:** Segmented reeding
Mint: Mexico City

Date	Mintage	F	VF	XF	Unc	BU
2004Mo	244,722	—	—	—	35.00	40.00

KM# 703   100 PESOS
29.1690 g., Bi-Metallic .999 Gold 17.154g center in
.999 Silver 12.015g ring, 34.5 mm.   **Series:** First
Subject: 180th Anniversary of Federation **Obv:**
National arms **Obv. Legend:** ESTADOS UNIDOS
MEXICANOS **Rev:** State arms **Rev. Legend:**
ESTADO DE SINALOA **Edge:** Segmented reeding
Mint: Mexico City

Date	Mintage	F	VF	XF	Unc	BU
2004Mo Proof	1,000	Value: 1,200				

KM# 694   100 PESOS
33.9400 g., Bi-Metallic .925 Silver 16.812g center in
Aluminum-Bronze ring, 39.04 mm.   **Series:** First
Subject: 180th Anniversary of Federation **Obv:**
National arms **Obv. Legend:** ESTADOS UNIDOS
MEXICANOS **Rev:** State arms **Rev. Legend:**
ESTADO DE SONORA **Edge:** Segmented reeding
Mint: Mexico City

Date	Mintage	F	VF	XF	Unc	BU
2004Mo	249,300	—	—	—	35.00	40.00

KM# 702   100 PESOS
29.1690 g., Bi-Metallic .999 Gold 17.154g center in
.999 Silver 12.015g ring, 34.5 mm.   **Series:** First
Subject: 180th Anniversary of Federation **Obv:**
National arms **Obv. Legend:** ESTADOS UNIDOS
MEXICANOS **Rev:** State arms **Rev. Legend:**
ESTADO DE SONORA **Edge:** Segmented reeding
Mint: Mexico City

Date	Mintage	F	VF	XF	Unc	BU
2004Mo Proof	1,000	Value: 1,200				

KM# 803   100 PESOS
33.9400 g., Bi-Metallic .925 Silver 16.812g center in
Aluminum-Bronze ring, 39.04 mm.   **Series:** First
Subject: 180th Anniversary of Federation **Obv:**
National arms **Obv. Legend:** ESTADOS UNIDOS
MEXICANOS **Rev:** State arms **Rev. Legend:**
ESTADO DE SAN LUIS POTOSÍ **Edge:** Segmented
reeding **Mint:** Mexico City

Date	Mintage	F	VF	XF	Unc	BU
2004Mo	249,662	—	—	—	35.00	40.00

KM# 806   100 PESOS
29.1690 g., Bi-Metallic .999 Gold 17.154g center in
.999 silver 12.015 ring, 34.5 mm.   **Series:** First
Subject: 180th Anniversary of Federation **Obv:**
National arms **Obv. Legend:** ESTADOS UNIDOS
MEXICANOS **Rev:** State arms **Rev. Legend:**
ESTADO DE SAN LUIS POTOSÍ **Edge:** Segmented
reeding **Mint:** Mexico City

Date	Mintage	F	VF	XF	Unc	BU
2004Mo Proof	1,000	Value: 1,200				

ESTADOS UNIDOS MEXICANOS

KM# 736   100 PESOS
33.9400 g., Bi-Metallic .925 Silver 16.812g center in Aluminum-Bronze ring, 39.04 mm. **Series:** First **Subject:** 180th Anniversary of Federation **Obv:** National arms **Obv. Legend:** ESTADOS UNIDOS MEXICANOS **Rev:** State arms **Rev. Legend:** ESTADO DE QUINTANA ROO **Edge:** Segmented reeding **Mint:** Mexico City

Date	Mintage	F	VF	XF	Unc	BU
2004Mo	249,134	—	—	—	35.00	40.00

KM# 807   100 PESOS
29.1690 g., Bi-Metallic .999 Gold 17.154g center in .999 Silver 12.015g ring, 34.5 mm. **Series:** First **Subject:** 180th Anniversary of Federation **Obv:** National arms **Obv. Legend:** ESTADOS UNIDOS MEXICANOS **Rev:** State arms **Rev. Legend:** ESTADO DE QUINTANA ROO **Edge:** Segmented reeding **Mint:** Mexico City

Date	Mintage	F	VF	XF	Unc	BU
2004Mo Proof	1,000	Value: 1,200				

KM# 738   100 PESOS
33.9400 g., Bi-Metallic .925 Silver 16.812g center in Aluminum-Bronze ring, 39.04 mm. **Series:** First **Subject:** 180th Anniversary of Federation **Obv:** National arms **Obv. Legend:** ESTADOS UNIDOS MEXICANOS **Rev:** State arms **Rev. Legend:** ESTADO DE PUEBLA **Edge:** Segmented reeding **Mint:** Mexico City

Date	Mintage	F	VF	XF	Unc	BU
2004Mo	248,850	—	—	—	35.00	40.00

KM# 809   100 PESOS
Bi-Metallic .999 Gold 17.154g center in .999 Silver 12.015g ring, 34.5 mm. **Series:** First **Subject:** 180th Anniversary of Federation **Obv:** National arms **Obv. Legend:** ESTADOS UNIDOS MEXICANOS **Rev:** State arms **Rev. Legend:** ESTADO DE PUEBLA **Edge:** Segmented reeding **Mint:** Mexico City

Date	Mintage	F	VF	XF	Unc	BU
2004Mo Proof	1,000	Value: 1,200				

KM# 734   100 PESOS
33.9400 g., Bi-Metallic .925 Silver 16.812g center in Aluminum-Bronze ring, 39.04 mm. **Series:** First **Subject:** 180th Anniversary of Federation **Obv:** National arms **Obv. Legend:** ESTADOS UNIDOS MEXICANOS **Rev:** State arms **Rev. Legend:** ESTADO DE QUERÉTARO ARTEAGA **Edge:** Segmented reeding **Mint:** Mexico City

Date	Mintage	F	VF	XF	Unc	BU
2004Mo	249,263	—	—	—	35.00	40.00

KM# 808   100 PESOS
29.1690 g., Bi-Metallic .999 Gold 17.154g center in .999 Silver 12.015g ring, 34.5 mm. **Series:** First **Subject:** 180th Anniversary of Federation **Obv:** National arms **Obv. Legend:** ESTADOS UNIDOS MEXICANOS **Rev:** State arms **Rev. Legend:** ESTADO DE QUERÉTARO ARTEAGA **Edge:** Segmented reeding **Mint:** Mexico City

Date	Mintage	F	VF	XF	Unc	BU
2004Mo Proof	1,000	Value: 1,200				

KM# 740   100 PESOS
33.9400 g., Bi-Metallic .925 Silver 16.812g center in Aluminum-Bronze ring, 39.04 mm. **Series:** First **Subject:** 180th Anniversary of Federation **Obv:** National arms **Obv. Legend:** ESTADOS UNIDOS MEXICANOS **Rev:** State arms **Rev. Legend:** ESTADO DE OAXACA **Edge:** Segmented reeding **Mint:** Mexico City

Date	Mintage	F	VF	XF	Unc	BU
2004Mo	249,589	—	—	—	35.00	40.00

KM# 810   100 PESOS
29.1690 g., Bi-Metallic .999 Gold 17.154g center in .999 Silver 12.015g ring, 34.5 mm. **Series:** First **Subject:** 180th Anniversary of Federation **Obv:** National arms **Obv. Legend:** ESTADOS UNIDOS MEXICANOS **Rev:** State arms **Rev. Legend:** ESTADO DE OAXACA **Edge:** Segmented reeding **Mint:** Mexico City

Date	Mintage	F	VF	XF	Unc	BU
2004Mo Proof	1,000	Value: 1,200				

KM# 742 100 PESOS
33.9400 g., Bi-Metallic .925 Silver 16.812g center in
Aluminum-Bronze ring, 39.04 mm. **Series:** First
Subject: 180th Anniversary of Federation **Obv:**
National arms **Obv. Legend:** ESTADOS UNIDOS
MEXICANOS **Rev:** State arms **Rev. Legend:**
ESTADO DE NUEVO LEÓN **Edge:** Segmented
reeding **Mint:** Mexico City

Date	Mintage	F	VF	XF	Unc	BU
2004Mo	249,199	—	—	—	35.00	40.00

KM# 811 100 PESOS
29.1690 g., Bi-Metallic .999 Gold 17.154g center in
.999 Silver 12.015g ring, 34.5 mm. **Series:** First
Subject: 180th Anniversary of Federation **Obv:**
National arms **Obv. Legend:** ESTADOS UNIDOS
MEXICANOS **Rev:** State arms **Rev. Legend:**
ESTADO DE NUEVO LEÓN **Edge:** Segmented
reeding **Mint:** Mexico City

Date	Mintage	F	VF	XF	Unc	BU
2004Mo Proof	1,000	Value: 1,200				

KM# 746 100 PESOS
33.9400 g., Bi-Metallic .925 Silver 16.812g center in
Aluminum-Bronze ring, 39.04 mm. **Series:** First
Subject: 180th Anniversary of Federation **Obv:**
National arms **Obv. Legend:** ESTADOS UNIDOS
MEXICANOS **Rev:** State arms **Rev. Legend:**
ESTADO DE MORELOS **Edge:** Segmented reeding
Mint: Mexico City

Date	Mintage	F	VF	XF	Unc	BU
2004Mo	249,260	—	—	—	35.00	40.00

KM# 813 100 PESOS
29.1690 g., Bi-Metallic .999 Gold 17.154g center in
.999 Silver 12.015g ring, 34.5 mm. **Series:** First
Subject: 180th Anniversary of Federation **Obv:**
National arms **Obv. Legend:** ESTADOS UNIDOS
MEXICANOS **Rev:** State arms **Rev. Legend:**
ESTADO DE MORELOS **Edge:** Segmented reeding
Mint: Mexico City

Date	Mintage	F	VF	XF	Unc	BU
2004Mo Proof	1,000	Value: 1,200				

KM# 744 100 PESOS
33.9400 g., Bi-Metallic .925 Silver 16.812g center in
Aluminum-Bronze ring, 39.04 mm. **Series:** First
Subject: 180th Anniversary of Federation **Obv:**
National arms **Obv. Legend:** ESTADOS UNIDOS
MEXICANOS **Rev:** State arms **Rev. Legend:**
ESTADO DE NAYARIT **Edge:** Segmented reeding
Mint: Mexico City

Date	Mintage	F	VF	XF	Unc	BU
2004Mo	248,305	—	—	—	35.00	40.00

KM# 812 100 PESOS
29.1690 g., Bi-Metallic .999 Gold 17.154g center in
.999 Silver 12.015g ring, 34.5 mm. **Series:** First
Subject: 180th Anniversary of Federation **Obv:**
National arms **Obv. Legend:** ESTADOS UNIDOS
MEXICANOS **Rev:** State arms **Rev. Legend:**
ESTADO DE NAYARIT **Edge:** Segmented reeding
Mint: Mexico City

Date	Mintage	F	VF	XF	Unc	BU
2004Mo Proof	1,000	Value: 1,200				

KM# 804 100 PESOS
33.9400 g., Bi-Metallic .925 Silver 16.812g center in
Aluminum-Bronze ring, 39.04 mm. **Series:** First
Subject: 180th Anniversary of Federation **Obv:**
National arms **Obv. Legend:** ESTADOS UNIDOS
MEXICANOS **Rev:** State arms **Rev. Legend:**
ESTADO DE MICHOACÁN DE OCAMPO **Edge:**
Segmented reeding **Mint:** Mexico City

Date	Mintage	F	VF	XF	Unc	BU
2004Mo	249,492	—	—	—	35.00	40.00

KM# 814 100 PESOS
29.1690 g., Bi-Metallic .999 Gold 17.154g center in
.999 12.015g ring, 34.5 mm. **Series:** First **Subject:**
180th Anniversary of Federation **Obv:** National arms
Obv. Legend: ESTADOS UNIDOS MEXICANOS
Rev: State arms **Rev. Legend:** ESTADO DE
MICHOACÁN DE OCAMPO **Edge:** Segmented
reeding **Mint:** Mexico City

Date	Mintage	F	VF	XF	Unc	BU
2004Mo Proof	1,000	Value: 1,200				

KM# 748   100 PESOS
33.9400 g., Bi-Metallic .925 Silver 16.812g center in Aluminum-Bronze ring, 39.04 mm.   **Series:** First **Subject:** 180th Anniversary of Federation **Obv:** National arms **Obv. Legend:** ESTADOS UNIDOS MEXICANOS **Rev:** State arms **Rev. Legend:** ESTADO DE MÉXICO **Edge:** Segmented reeding **Mint:** Mexico City

Date	Mintage	F	VF	XF	Unc	BU
2004Mo	249,800	—	—	—	35.00	40.00

KM# 815   100 PESOS
29.1690 g., Bi-Metallic .999 Gold 17.154 center in .999 Silver 12.015 ring, 34.5 mm.   **Series:** First **Subject:** 180th Anniversary of Federation **Obv:** National arms **Obv. Legend:** ESTADOS UNIDOS MEXICANOS **Rev:** State arms **Rev. Legend:** ESTADO DE MÉXICO **Edge:** Segmented reeding **Mint:** Mexico City

Date	Mintage	F	VF	XF	Unc	BU
2004Mo Proof	1,000	Value: 1,200				

KM# 750   100 PESOS
33.9400 g., Bi-Metallic .925 Silver 16.812g center in Aluminum-Bronze ring, 39.04 mm.   **Series:** First **Subject:** 180th Anniversary of Federation **Obv:** National arms **Obv. Legend:** ESTADOS UNIDOS MEXICANOS **Rev:** State arms **Rev. Legend:** ESTADO DE JALISCO **Edge:** Segmented reeding **Mint:** Mexico City

Date	Mintage	F	VF	XF	Unc	BU
2004Mo	249,115	—	—	—	35.00	40.00

KM# 816   100 PESOS
29.1690 g., Bi-Metallic .999 Gold 17.154g center in .999 Silver 12.015g ring, 34.5 mm.   **Series:** First **Subject:** 180th Anniversary of Federation **Obv:** National arms **Obv. Legend:** ESTADOS UNIDOS MEXICANOS **Rev:** State arms **Rev. Legend:** ESTADO DE JALISCO **Edge:** Segmented reeding **Mint:** Mexico City

Date	Mintage	F	VF	XF	Unc	BU
2004Mo Proof	1,000	Value: 1,200				

KM# 705   100 PESOS
33.7400 g., Bi-Metallic .925 16.812g Silver center in Aluminum-Bronze ring, 39 mm.   **Subject:** 400th Anniversary of Don Quijote de la Manchia **Obv:** National arms **Obv. Legend:** ESTADOS UNIDOS MEXICANOS **Rev:** Skeletal figure on horseback with spear galloping right **Edge:** Segmented reeding **Mint:** Mexico City

Date	Mintage	F	VF	XF	Unc	BU
2005Mo	726,833	—	—	—	25.00	32.00
2005Mo Prooflike	3,761	—	—	—	—	75.00
2006Mo Proof	5,201	Value: 60.00				

KM# 730   100 PESOS
33.8250 g., Bi-Metallic .925 Silver 16.812g center in Aluminum-Bronze ring, 39.9 mm.   **Subject:** Monetary Reform Centennial **Obv:** National arms **Rev:** Radiant Liberty Cap divides date above value within circle **Edge:** Segmented reeding **Mint:** Mexico City

Date	Mintage	F	VF	XF	Unc	BU
2005Mo	49,716	—	—	—	40.00	45.00
2005Mo Proof	—	Value: 75.00				

KM# 731   100 PESOS
33.8250 g., Bi-Metallic .925 Silver 16.812g center in Aluminum-Bronze ring, 39.9 mm.   **Subject:** Mexico City Mint's 470th Anniversary **Obv:** National arms

ESTADOS UNIDOS MEXICANOS

Rev: Screw press, value and date within circle **Edge:** Segmented reeding **Mint:** Mexico City

Date	Mintage	F	VF	XF	Unc	BU
2005Mo	49,895	—	—	—	40.00	45.00
2005Mo Proof	—	Value: 95.00				

KM# 732 100 PESOS

33.8250 g., Bi-Metallic .925 Silver 16.812g center in Aluminum-Bronze ring, 39.9 mm. **Subject:** Bank of Mexico's 80th Anniversary **Obv:** National arms **Rev:** Back design of the 1925 hundred peso note **Edge:** Segmented reeding **Mint:** Mexico City

Date	Mintage	F	VF	XF	Unc	BU
2005Mo	49,712	—	—	—	40.00	45.00
2005Mo Proof	—	Value: 95.00				

KM# 717 100 PESOS

33.9400 g., Bi-Metallic .925 Silver 16.812g center in Brass ring, 39.04 mm. **Series:** First **Subject:** 180th Anniversary of Federation **Obv:** National arms **Obv. Legend:** ESTADOS UNIDOS MEXICANOS **Rev:** State arms **Rev. Legend:** ESTADO DE HIDALGO **Edge:** Segmented reeding **Mint:** Mexico City

Date	Mintage	F	VF	XF	Unc	BU
2005Mo	249,820	—	—	—	35.00	40.00

KM# 817 100 PESOS

29.1690 g., Bi-Metallic .999 Gold 17.154g center in .999 Silver 12.015g ring, 34.5 mm. **Series:** First **Subject:** 180th Anniversary of Federation **Obv:** National arms **Obv. Legend:** ESTADOS UNIDOS MEXICANOS **Rev:** State arms **Rev. Legend:** ESTADO DE HIDALGO **Edge:** Segmented reeding **Mint:** Mexico City

Date	Mintage	F	VF	XF	Unc	BU
2005Mo Proof	1,000	Value: 1,200				

KM# 716 100 PESOS

33.9400 g., Bi-Metallic .925 Silver 16.812g center in Brass ring, 39.04 mm. **Series:** First **Subject:** 180th Anniversary of Federation **Obv:** National arms **Obv. Legend:** ESTADOS UNIDOS MEXICANOS **Rev:** State arms **Rev. Legend:** ESTADO DE GUERRERO **Edge:** Segmented reeding **Mint:** Mexico City

Date	Mintage	F	VF	XF	Unc	BU
2005Mo	248,850	—	—	—	35.00	40.00

KM# 818 100 PESOS

29.1690 g., Bi-Metallic .999 Gold 17.154g center in .999 Silver 12.015g ring, 34.5 mm. **Series:** First **Subject:** 180th Anniversary of Federation **Obv:** National arms **Obv. Legend:** ESTADOS UNIDOS MEXICANOS **Rev:** State arms **Rev. Legend:** ESTADO DE GUERRERO **Edge:** Segmented reeding **Mint:** Mexico City

Date	Mintage	F	VF	XF	Unc	BU
2005Mo Proof	1,000	Value: 1,200				

KM# 715 100 PESOS

33.9400 g., Bi-Metallic .925 Silver 16.812g center in Brass ring, 39.04 mm. **Series:** First **Subject:** 180th Anniversary of Federation **Obv:** National arms **Obv. Legend:** ESTADOS UNIDOS MEXICANOS **Rev:** State arms **Rev. Legend:** ESTADO DE GUANAJUATO **Edge:** Segmented reeding **Mint:** Mexico City

Date	Mintage	F	VF	XF	Unc	BU
2005Mo	249,489	—	—	—	35.00	40.00

KM# 819 100 PESOS

29.1690 g., Bi-Metallic .999 Gold 17.154g center in .999 Silver 12.015g ring, 34.5 mm. **Series:** First **Subject:** 180th Anniversary of Federation **Obv:** National arms **Obv. Legend:** ESTADOS UNIDOS MEXICANOS **Rev:** State arms **Rev. Legend:** ESTADO DE GUANAJUATO **Edge:** Segmented reeding **Mint:** Mexico City

Date	Mintage	F	VF	XF	Unc	BU
2005Mo Proof	1,000	Value: 1,200				

ESTADOS UNIDOS MEXICANOS

ESTADOS UNIDOS MEXICANOS

KM# 714   100 PESOS
33.9400 g., Bi-Metallic .925 Silver 16.812g center in
Brass ring, 39.04 mm. **Series:** First **Subject:** 180th
Anniversary of Federation **Obv:** National arms **Obv.**
Legend: ESTADOS UNIDOS MEXICANOS **Rev:**
State arms **Rev. Legend:** ESTADO DE DURANGO
Edge: Segmented reeding **Mint:** Mexico City

Date	Mintage	F	VF	XF	Unc	BU
2005Mo	249,774	—	—	—	35.00	40.00

KM# 820   100 PESOS
29.1690 g., Bi-Metallic .999 Gold 17.154g center in
.999 silver 12.015g ring, 34.5 mm. **Series:** First
Subject: 180th Anniversary of Federation **Obv:**
National arms **Obv. Legend:** ESTADOS UNIDOS
MEXICANOS **Rev:** State arms **Rev. Legend:**
ESTADO DE DURANGO **Edge:** Segmented reeding
Mint: Mexico City

Date	Mintage	F	VF	XF	Unc	BU
2005Mo Proof	1,000	Value: 1,200				

KM# 754   100 PESOS
33.9400 g., Bi-Metallic .925 Silver 16.812g center in
Aluminum-Bronze ring, 39.04 mm. **Series:** First
Subject: 180th Anniversary of Federation **Obv:**
National arms **Obv. Legend:** ESTADOS UNIDOS
MEXICANOS **Rev:** State arms **Rev. Legend:**
ESTADO DE CHIHUAHUA **Edge:** Segmented
reeding **Mint:** Mexico City

Date	Mintage	F	VF	XF	Unc	BU
2005Mo	249,102	—	—	—	35.00	40.00

KM# 822   100 PESOS
29.1690 g., Bi-Metallic .999 Gold 17.154g center in
.999 Silver 12.015g ring, 34.5 mm. **Series:** First
Subject: 180th Anniversary of Federation **Obv:**
National arms **Obv. Legend:** ESTADOS UNIDOS
MEXICANOS **Rev:** State arms **Rev. Legend:**
ESTADO DE CHIHUAHUA **Edge:** Segmented
reeding **Mint:** Mexico City

Date	Mintage	F	VF	XF	Unc	BU
2005Mo Proof	1,000	Value: 1,200				

KM# 713   100 PESOS
33.9400 g., Bi-Metallic .925 Silver 16.812g center
in Brass ring, 39.04 mm. **Series:** First **Subject:**
180th Anniversary of Federation **Obv:** National
arms **Obv. Legend:** ESTADOS UNIDOS
MEXICANOS **Rev:** Federal District arms **Rev.**
Legend: DISTRITO FEDERAL **Edge:** Segmented
reeding **Mint:** Mexico City

Date	Mintage	F	VF	XF	Unc	BU
2005Mo	249,461	—	—	—	35.00	40.00

KM# 821   100 PESOS
29.1690 g., Bi-Metallic .999 Gold 17.154g center in
.999 Silver 12.015g ring, 34.5 mm. **Series:** First
Subject: 180th Anniversary of Federation **Obv:**
National arms **Obv. Legend:** ESTADOS UNIDOS
MEXICANOS **Rev:** Federal District arms **Rev.**
Legend: DISTRITO FEDERAL **Edge:** Segmented
reeding **Mint:** Mexico City

Date	Mintage	F	VF	XF	Unc	BU
2005Mo Proof	1,000	Value: 1,200				

KM# 712   100 PESOS
33.9400 g., Bi-Metallic .925 Silver 16.812g center in
Brass ring, 39.04 mm. **Series:** First **Subject:** 180th
Anniversary of Federation **Obv:** National arms **Obv.**
Legend: ESTADOS UNIDOS MEXICANOS **Rev:**
State arms **Rev. Legend:** ESTADO DE CHIAPAS
Edge: Segmented reeding **Mint:** Mexico City

Date	Mintage	F	VF	XF	Unc	BU
2005Mo	249,417	—	—	—	35.00	40.00

KM# 823   100 PESOS
29.1690 g., Bi-Metallic .999 Gold 17.154g center in
.999 Silver 12.015g ring, 34.5 mm. **Series:** First
Subject: 180th Anniversary of Federation **Obv:**
National arms **Obv. Legend:** ESTADOS UNIDOS
MEXICANOS **Rev:** State arms **Rev. Legend:**
ESTADO DE CHIAPAS **Edge:** Segmented reeding
Mint: Mexico City

Date	Mintage	F	VF	XF	Unc	BU
2005Mo Proof	1,000	Value: 1,200				

KM# 729 100 PESOS
33.8250 g., Bi-Metallic .925 Silver 16.812g center in
Aluminum-Bronze ring, 39.04 mm. **Series:** First
Subject: 180th Anniversary of Federation **Obv:**
National arms **Obv. Legend:** ESTADOS UNIDOS
MEXICANOS **Rev:** State arms **Rev. Legend:**
ESTADO DE COLIMA **Edge:** Segmented reeding
Mint: Mexico City

Date	Mintage	F	VF	XF	Unc	BU
2005Mo	248,850	—	—	—	35.00	40.00

KM# 824 100 PESOS
29.1690 g., Bi-Metallic .999 Gold 17.154g center in
.999 Silver 12.015g ring, 34.5 mm. **Series:** First
Subject: 180th Anniversary of Federation **Obv:**
National arms **Obv. Legend:** ESTADOS UNIDOS
MEXICANOS **Rev:** State arms **Rev. Legend:**
ESTADO DE COLIMA **Edge:** Segmented reeding
Mint: Mexico City

Date	Mintage	F	VF	XF	Unc	BU
2005Mo Proof	1,000	Value: 1,200				

KM# 727 100 PESOS
33.9400 g., Bi-Metallic .925 Silver 16.812g center in
Aluminum-Bronze ring, 39.04 mm. **Series:** First
Subject: 180th Anniversary of Federation **Obv:**
National arms **Obv. Legend:** ESTADOS UNIDOS
MEXICANOS **Rev:** State arms **Rev. Legend:**
ESTADO DE CAMPECHE **Edge:** Segmented
reeding **Mint:** Mexico City

Date	Mintage	F	VF	XF	Unc	BU
2005Mo	249,040	—	—	—	35.00	40.00

KM# 826 100 PESOS
29.1690 g., Bi-Metallic .999 Gold 17.154g center in
.999 Silver 12.015g ring, 34.5 mm. **Series:** First
Subject: 180th Anniversary of Federation **Obv:**
National arms **Obv. Legend:** ESTADOS UNIDOS
MEXICANOS **Rev:** State arms **Rev. Legend:**
ESTADO DE CAMPECHE **Edge:** Segmented
reeding **Mint:** Mexico City

Date	Mintage	F	VF	XF	Unc	BU
2005Mo Proof	1,000	Value: 1,200				

KM# 752 100 PESOS
33.9400 g., Bi-Metallic .925 Silver 16.812g center in
Aluminum-Bronze ring, 39.04 mm. **Series:** First
Subject: 180th Anniversary of Federation **Obv:**
National arms **Obv. Legend:** ESTADOS UNIDOS
MEXICANOS **Rev:** State arms **Rev. Legend:**
ESTADO DE COAHUILA DE ZARAGOZA **Edge:**
Segmented reeding **Mint:** Mexico City

Date	Mintage	F	VF	XF	Unc	BU
2005Mo	247,991	—	—	—	35.00	40.00

KM# 825 100 PESOS
29.1690 g., Bi-Metallic .999 Gold 17.154g center in
.999 Silver 12.015g ring, 34.5 mm. **Series:** First
Subject: 180th Anniversary of Federation **Obv:**
National arms **Obv. Legend:** ESTADOS UNIDOS
MEXICANOS **Rev:** State arms **Rev. Legend:**
ESTADO DE COAHUILA DE ZARAGOZA **Edge:**
Segmented reeding **Mint:** Mexico City

Date	Mintage	F	VF	XF	Unc	BU
2005Mo Proof	1,000	Value: 1,200				

KM# 725 100 PESOS
33.9400 g., Bi-Metallic .925 Silver 16.812g center in
Aluminum-Bronze ring, 39.04 mm. **Series:** First
Subject: 180th Anniversary of Federation **Obv:**
National arms **Obv. Legend:** ESTADOS UNIDOS
MEXICANOS **Rev:** State arms **Rev. Legend:**
ESTADO DE BAJA CALIFORNIA SUR **Edge:**
Segmented reeding **Mint:** Mexico City

Date	Mintage	F	VF	XF	Unc	BU
2005Mo	249,585	—	—	—	35.00	40.00

KM# 827 100 PESOS
29.1690 g., Bi-Metallic .999 Gold 17.154g center in
.999 Silver 12.015g ring, 34.5 mm. **Series:** First
Subject: 180th Anniversary of Federation **Obv:**
National arms **Obv. Legend:** ESTADOS UNIDOS
MEXICANOS **Rev:** State arms **Rev. Legend:**
ESTADO DE BAJA CALIFORNIA SUR **Edge:**
Segmented reeding **Mint:** Mexico City

Date	Mintage	F	VF	XF	Unc	BU
2005Mo Proof	1,000	Value: 1,200				

KM# 723   100 PESOS
33.9400 g., Bi-Metallic .925 Silver 16.812g center in
Aluminum-Bronze ring, 39.04 mm. **Series:** First
Subject: 180th Anniversary of Federation **Obv:**
National arms **Obv. Legend:** ESTADOS UNIDOS
MEXICANOS **Rev:** State arms **Rev. Legend:**
ESTADO DE BAJA CALIFORNIA **Edge:** Segmented
reeding **Mint:** Mexico City

Date	Mintage	F	VF	XF	Unc	BU
2005Mo	249,263	—	—	—	35.00	40.00

KM# 828   100 PESOS
29.1690 g., Bi-Metallic .999 Gold 17.154g center in
.999 Silver 12.015g ring, 34.5 mm. **Series:** First
Subject: 180th Anniversary of Federation **Obv:**
National arms **Obv. Legend:** ESTADOS UNIDOS
MEXICANOS **Rev:** State arms **Rev. Legend:**
ESTADO DE BAJA CALIFORNIA **Edge:** Segmented
reeding **Mint:** Mexico City

Date	Mintage	F	VF	XF	Unc	BU
2005Mo Proof	1,000	Value: 1,200				

KM# 721   100 PESOS
33.9400 g., Bi-Metallic .925 Silver 16.812g center in
Aluminum-Bronze ring, 39.04 mm. **Series:** First
Subject: 180th Anniversary of Federation **Obv:**
National arms **Obv. Legend:** ESTADOS UNIDOS
MEXICANOS **Rev:** Estados de Aguascalientes state
arms **Rev. Legend:** ESTADO DE
AGUASCALIENTES **Edge:** Segmented reeding
Mint: Mexico City

Date	Mintage	F	VF	XF	Unc	BU
2005Mo	248,410	—	—	—	35.00	40.00

KM# 829   100 PESOS
29.1690 g., Bi-Metallic .999 Gold 17.154g center in
.999 Silver 12.015g ring, 34.5 mm. **Series:** First
Subject: 180th Anniversary of Federation **Obv:**
National arms **Obv. Legend:** ESTADOS UNIDOS
MEXICANOS **Rev:** State arms **Rev. Legend:**

ESTADO DE AGUASCALIENTES **Edge:**
Segmented reeding **Mint:** Mexico City

Date	Mintage	F	VF	XF	Unc	BU
2005Mo Proof	1,000	Value: 1,200				

KM# 719   100 PESOS
33.8250 g., Bi-Metallic .925 Silver 16.812g center in
Aluminum-Bronze ring, 39.04 mm. **Series:** Second
Obv: National arms **Obv. Legend:** ESTADOS
UNIDOS MEXICANOS **Rev:** Facade of the San
Marcos garden above sculpture of national emblem
at left, San Antonio Temple at right **Rev. Legend:**
AGUASCALIENTES **Edge:** Segmented reeding
Mint: Mexico City

Date	Mintage	F	VF	XF	Unc	BU
2005Mo	149,705	—	—	—	25.00	30.00

KM# 862   100 PESOS
29.1690 g., Bi-Metallic .999 Gold 17.154g center in
.999 Silver 12.015g ring, 34.5 mm. **Series:** Second
Obv: National arms **Obv. Legend:** ESTADOS
UNIDOS MEXICANOS **Rev:** Facade of the San
Marcos garden above sculpture of national emblem
at left, San Antonio temple at right **Rev. Legend:**
AGUASCALIENTES **Edge:** Segmented reeding
Mint: Mexico City

Date	Mintage	F	VF	XF	Unc	BU
2005Mo Proof	600	Value: 1,200				

KM# 758   100 PESOS
33.9400 g., Bi-Metallic .925 Silver 16.812g center in
Aluminum-Bronze ring, 39.04 mm. **Series:** Second
Obv: National arms **Obv. Legend:** ESTADOS
UNIDOS MEXICANOS **Rev:** Ram's head and value
within circle **Rev. Legend:** BAJA CALIFORNIA -
GOBIERNO DEL ESTADO **Edge:** Segmented
reeding **Mint:** Mexico City

Date	Mintage	F	VF	XF	Unc	BU
2005Mo	149,771	—	—	—	25.00	30.00

KM# 863   100 PESOS
29.1690 g., Bi-Metallic .999 Gold 17.154g center in
.999 Silver 12.015g ring, 34.5 mm. **Series:** Second
Obv: National arms **Obv. Legend:** ESTTADOS

The following appears at the top of the right column:

Date	Mintage	F	VF	XF	Unc	BU
2005Mo Proof	1,000	Value: 1,200				

ESTADOS UNIDOS MEXICANOS

UNIDOS MEXICANOS **Rev:** Ram's head, mountain
outline in background **Rev. Legend:** BAJA
CALIFORNIA - GOBIERNO DEL ESTADO **Edge:**
Segmented reeding **Mint:** Mexico City

Date	Mintage	F	VF	XF	Unc	BU
2005Mo Proof	600	Value: 1,200				

KM# 762   100 PESOS
33.9400 g., Bi-Metallic .925 Silver 16.812g center in
Aluminum-Bronze ring, 39.04 mm. **Series:** Second
Obv: National arms **Obv. Legend:** ESTADOS
UNIDOS MEXICANOS **Rev:** Outlined map of
peninsula at center, cave painting of deer behind,
cactus at right **Rev. Legend:** ESTADO DE BAJA
CALIFORNIA SUR **Edge:** Segmented reeding **Mint:**
Mexico City

Date	Mintage	F	VF	XF	Unc	BU
2005Mo	149,152	—	—	—	25.00	30.00

KM# 764   100 PESOS
33.7000 g., Bi-Metallic .925 Silver 16.812g center in
Aluminum-Bronze ring **Subject:** 200th Anniversary
Birth of Benito Juarez Garcia **Obv:** National arms
Rev: Bust 1/4 left within circle **Mint:** Mexico City

Date	Mintage	F	VF	XF	Unc	BU
2006Mo	49,913	—	—	—	40.00	45.00

KM# 864   100 PESOS
29.1690 g., Bi-Metallic .999 Gold 17.154g center in
.999 Silver 12.015g ring, 34.5 mm. **Series:** Second
Obv: National arms **Obv. Legend:** ESTADOS
UNIDOS MEXICANOS **Rev:** Outlined map of
peninsula at center, cave painting of deer behind,
cactus at right **Rev. Legend:** ESTADO DE BAJA
CALIFORNIA SUR **Edge:** Segmented reeding **Mint:**
Mexico City

Date	Mintage	F	VF	XF	Unc	BU
2006Mo Proof	600	Value: 1,200				

KM# 760   100 PESOS
33.9400 g., Bi-Metallic .925 Silver 16.812g center in
Aluminum-Bronze ring, 39.04 mm. **Series:** Second
Subject: Estado de Campeche **Obv:** National arms
Obv. Legend: ESTADOS UNIDOS MEXICANOS
Rev: Jade mask - Calakmul, Campeche **Rev.
Legend:** ESTADO DE CAMPECHE **Edge:**
Segmented reeding **Mint:** Mexico City

Date	Mintage	F	VF	XF	Unc	BU
2006Mo	149,803	—	—	—	25.00	30.00

KM# 865   100 PESOS
29.1690 g., Bi-Metallic .999 Gold 17.154g center in
.999 Silver 12.015g ring, 34.5 mm. **Series:** Second
Obv: National arms **Obv. Legend:** ESTADOS
UNIDOS MEXICANOS **Rev:** Jade mask - Calakmul,
Campeche **Rev. Legend:** ESTADO DE CAMPECHE
Edge: Segmented reeding **Mint:** Mexico City

Date	Mintage	F	VF	XF	Unc	BU
2006Mo Proof	600	Value: 1,200				

KM# 781   100 PESOS
33.7000 g., Bi-Metallic .925 Silver 16.812g center in
Aluminum-Bronze ring, 39.04 mm. **Series:** Second
Obv: National arms **Obv. Legend:** ESTADOS
UNIDOS MEXICANOS **Rev:** Outlined map with
turtle, mine cart above grapes at center, Friendship
Dam above Christ of the Nodas at left, chimneys
above crucibles and bell tower of Santiago's
cathedral at right **Rev. Legend:** COAHUILA DE
ZARAGOZA **Edge:** Segmented reeding **Mint:**
Mexico City

Date	Mintage	F	VF	XF	Unc	BU
2006Mo	149,560	—	—	—	25.00	30.00

KM# 866   100 PESOS
29.1690 g., Bi-Metallic .999 Gold 17.154g center in
.999 Silver 12.015g ring, 34.5 mm. **Series:** Second
Obv: National arms **Obv. Legend:** ESTADOS
UNIDOS MEXICANOS **Rev:** Outlined map with
turtle, mine cart above grapes at center, Friendship
dam above Christ of the Nodas at left, chimneys

ESTADOS UNIDOS MEXICANOS

above crucibles and bell tower of Santiago's cathedral at right **Rev. Inscription:** COAHUILA DE ZARAGOZA **Edge:** Segmented reeding **Mint:** Mexico City

Date	Mintage	F	VF	XF	Unc	BU
2006Mo Proof	600	Value: 1,200				

KM# 777   100 PESOS
33.9400 g., Bi-Metallic .925 Silver 16.812g center in Aluminum-Bronze ring, 39.04 mm. **Series:** Second **Obv:** National arms **Obv. Legend:** ESTADOS UNIDOS MEXICANOS **Rev:** State arms at lower center, Nevado de Colima and Volcan de Fuego volcanos in background **Rev. Legend:** *Colima* **Rev. Inscription:** GENEROSO **Edge:** Segmented reeding **Mint:** Mexico City

Date	Mintage	F	VF	XF	Unc	BU
2006Mo	149,041	—	—	—	25.00	30.00

KM# 867   100 PESOS
29.1690 g., Bi-Metallic .999 Gold 17.154g center in .999 Silver 12.015 ring, 34.5 mm. **Series:** Second **Obv:** National arms **Obv. Legend:** ESTADOS UNIDOS MEXICANOS **Rev:** State arms at lower center, Nevado de Colima and Volcan de Fuego volcanos in background **Rev. Legend:** *Colima* **Rev. Inscription:** GENEROSO **Edge:** Segmented reeding **Mint:** Mexico City

Date	Mintage	F	VF	XF	Unc	BU
2006Mo Proof	600	Value: 1,200				

KM# 773   100 PESOS
33.9400 g., Bi-Metallic .925 Silver 16.812g center in Aluminum-Bronze ring, 39.04 mm. **Series:** Second **Obv:** National arms **Obv. Legend:** ESTADOS UNIDOS MEXICANOS **Rev:** Head of Pakal, ancient Mayan king, Palenque **Rev. Legend:** ESTADO DE CHIAPAS - CABEZA MAYA DEL REY PAKAL, PALENQUE **Edge:** Segmented reeding **Mint:** Mexico City

Date	Mintage	F	VF	XF	Unc	BU
2006Mo	149,491	—	—	—	25.00	30.00

KM# 868   100 PESOS
29.1690 g., Bi-Metallic .999 Gold 17.154g center in .999 Silver 12.015g ring, 34.5 mm. **Series:** Second **Obv:** National arms **Obv. Legend:** ESTADOS UNIDOS MEXICANOS **Rev:** Head of Pakal, ancient Mayan king, Palenque **Rev. Legend:** ESTADO DE CHIAPAS - CABEZA MAYA DEL REY PAKAL, PALENQUE **Edge:** Segmented reeding **Mint:** Mexico City

Date	Mintage	F	VF	XF	Unc	BU
2006Mo Proof	600	Value: 1,200				

KM# 775   100 PESOS
33.9400 g., Bi-Metallic .925 Silver 16.812g center in Aluminum-Bronze ring, 39.04 mm. **Series:** Second **Obv:** National arms **Obv. Legend:** ESTADOS UNIDOS MEXICANOS **Rev:** Angel of Liberty **Rev. Legend:** MÉXICO - ANGEL DE LA LIBERTAD, CHIHUAHUA **Edge:** Segmented reeding **Mint:** Mexico City

Date	Mintage	F	VF	XF	Unc	BU
2006Mo	149,557	—	—	—	25.00	30.00

KM# 869   100 PESOS
29.1690 g., Bi-Metallic .999 Gold 17.154g center in .999 Silver 12.015g ring, 34.5 mm. **Series:** Second **Obv:** National arms **Obv. Legend:** ESTADOS UNIDOS MEXICANOS **Rev:** Angel of Liberty **Rev. Legend:** MÉXICO - ANGEL DE LA LIBERTAD, CHIHUAHUA **Edge:** Segmented reeding **Mint:** Mexico City

Date	Mintage	F	VF	XF	Unc	BU
2006Mo Proof	600	Value: 1,200				

KM# 779   100 PESOS
33.9400 g., Bi-Metallic .925 Silver 16.812g center in Aluminum-Bronze ring, 39.04 mm. **Series:** Second **Obv:** National arms **Obv. Legend:** ESTADOS UNIDOS MEXICANOS **Rev:** National Palace **Rev. Legend:** DISTRITO FEDERAL - ANTIGUO AYUNTAMIENTO **Edge:** Segmented reeding **Mint:** Mexico City

Date	Mintage	F	VF	XF	Unc	BU
2006Mo	149,525	—	—	—	25.00	30.00

KM# 870   100 PESOS
29.1690 g., Bi-Metallic .999 Gold 17.154g center in .999 Silver 12.015g ring, 34.5 mm.   **Series:** Second **Obv:** National arms **Obv. Legend:** ESTADOS UNIDOS MEXICANOS **Rev:** National palace **Rev. Legend:** DISTRITO FEDERAL - ANTIGUO AYUNTAMIENTO **Edge:** Segmented reeding **Mint:** Mexico City

Date	Mintage	F	VF	XF	Unc	BU
2006Mo Proof	600	Value: 1,200				

KM# 872   100 PESOS
29.1690 g., Bi-Metallic .999 Gold 17.154g center in .999 Silver 12.015g ring, 34.50 mm.   **Series:** Second **Obv:** National arms **Obv. Legend:** ESTADOS UNIDOS MEXICANOS **Rev:** State arms at lower center, statue of Miguel Hidalgo at left, monument to Pipila at lower right **Rev. Inscription:** *Guanajauto* **Edge:** Segmented reeding **Mint:** Mexico City

Date	Mintage	F	VF	XF	Unc	BU
2006Mo Proof	600	Value: 1,200				

KM# 787   100 PESOS
33.9400 g., Bi-Metallic .925 Silver 16.812g center in Brass ring, 39.04 mm.   **Series:** Second **Obv:** National arms **Obv. Legend:** ESTADOS UNIDOS MEXICANOS **Rev:** Tree **Rev. Legend:** PRIMERA RESERVA NACIONAL FORESTAL - DURANGO **Edge:** Segmented reeding **Mint:** Mexico City

Date	Mintage	F	VF	XF	Unc	BU
2006Mo	149,034	—	—	—	25.00	30.00

KM# 871   100 PESOS
29.1690 g., Bi-Metallic .999 Gold 17.154g center in .999 Silver 12.015g ring, 34.5 mm.   **Series:** Second **Obv:** National arms **Obv. Legend:** ESYADOS UNIDOS MEXICANOS **Rev:** Tree **Rev. Legend:** PRIMERA RESERVA NACIONAL RORESTAL - DURANGO **Edge:** Segmented reeding **Mint:** Mexico City

Date	Mintage	F	VF	XF	Unc	BU
2006Mo Proof	600	Value: 1,200				

KM# 791   100 PESOS
33.9400 g., Bi-Metallic .925 Silver 16.812g center in Brass ring, 39.04 mm.   **Series:** Second **Obv:** National arms **Obv. Legend:** ESTADOS UNIDOS MEXICANOS **Rev:** Stylized portrait of Vicente Guerrero at left, church of Taxco at upper center, Acapulco's la Quebrada with diver above Christmas Eve flower and mask **Rev. Legend:** GUERRERO **Edge:** Segmented reeding **Mint:** Mexico City

Date	Mintage	F	VF	XF	Unc	BU
2006Mo	149,675	—	—	—	25.00	30.00

KM# 873   100 PESOS
29.1690 g., Bi-Metallic .999 Gold 17.154g center in .999 Silver 12.015g ring, 34.5 mm.   **Series:** Second **Obv:** National arms **Obv. Legend:** ESTADOS UNIDOS MEXICANOS **Rev:** Stylized portrait of Vicente Guerrero at left, church of Taxco at upper center, Acapulco's la Quebrada with diver over Christmas Eve flower and mask **Rev. Legend:** GUERRERO **Edge:** Segmented reeding **Mint:** Mexico City

Date	Mintage	F	VF	XF	Unc	BU
2006Mo Proof	600	Value: 1,200				

KM# 789   100 PESOS
33.9400 g., Bi-Metallic .925 Silver 16.812g center in Brass ring, 39.04 mm.   **Series:** Second **Obv:** National arms **Obv. Legend:** ESTADOS UNIDOS MEXICANOS **Rev:** State arms at center, statue of Miguel Hidalgo at left, monument to Pipila at lower right **Rev. Inscription:** *Guanajuato* **Edge:** Segmented reeding **Mint:** Mexico City

Date	Mintage	F	VF	XF	Unc	BU
2006Mo	149,921	—	—	—	25.00	30.00

KM# 793   100 PESOS
33.9400 g., Bi-Metallic .925 Silver 16.812g center in Aluminum-Bronze ring, 39.04 mm.   **Series:** Second **Obv:** National arms **Obv. Legend:** ESTADOS UNIDOS MEXICANOS **Rev:** Monument of Pachuca Hidalgo **Rev. Inscription:** *RELOJ / MONUMENTAL*

ESTADOS UNIDOS MEXICANOS

/ DE / PACHUCA / HIDALGO - La / Bella / Airosa
Edge: Segmented reeding **Mint:** Mexico City

Date	Mintage	F	VF	XF	Unc	BU
2006Mo	149,273	—			25.00	30.00

KM# 874   100 PESOS
29.1690 g., Bi-Metallic .999 Gold 17.154g center in
.999 Silver 12.015g ring, 34.5 mm. **Series:** Second
Obv: National arms **Obv. Legend:** ESTADOS
UNIDOS MEXICANOS **Rev:** Monument of Pachuca
Hidalgo **Rev. Inscription:** *RELOJ / MONUMENTAL
/ DE / PACHUCA / HIDALGO* **Edge:** Segmented
reeding **Mint:** Mexico City

Date	Mintage	F	VF	XF	Unc	BU
2006Mo Proof	600	Value: 1,200				

KM# 795   100 PESOS
33.9400 g., Bi-Metallic .925 Silver 16.812g center in
Brass ring, 39.04 mm. **Series:** Second **Obv:**
National arms **Obv. Legend:** ESTADOS UNIDOS
MEXICANOS **Rev:** Hospicio Cabañas orphanage
Rev. Legend: ESTADO DE JALISCO **Edge:**
Segmented reeding **Mint:** Mexico City

Date	Mintage	F	VF	XF	Unc	BU
2006Mo	149,750	—	—	—	25.00	30.00

KM# 875   100 PESOS
29.1690 g., Bi-Metallic .999 Gold 17.154g center in
.999 Silver 12.015g ring, 34.5 mm. **Series:** Second
Obv: National arms **Obv. Legend:** ESTADOS
UNIDOS MEXICANOS **Rev:** Hospicio Cabañas
orphanage **Rev. Legend:** ESTADO DE JALISCO
Edge: Segmented reeding **Mint:** Mexico City

Date	Mintage	F	VF	XF	Unc	BU
2006Mo Proof	600	Value: 1,200				

KM# 802   100 PESOS
33.9400 g., Bi-Metallic .925 Silver 16.812g center in
Aluminum-Bronze ring, 39.04 mm. **Series:** Second
Obv: National arms **Obv. Legend:** ESTADOS
UNIDOS MEXICANOS **Rev:** Pyramid de la Loona
(moon) **Rev. Legend:** ESTADO DE MÉXICO **Edge:**
Segmented reeding **Mint:** Mexico City

Date	Mintage	F	VF	XF	Unc	BU
2006Mo	149,377	—	—	—	25.00	30.00

KM# 876   100 PESOS
29.1690 g., Bi-Metallic .999 Gold 17.154g center in
.999 Silver 12.015g ring, 34.5 mm. **Series:** Second
Obv: National arms **Obv. Legend:** ESTADOS
UNIDOS MEXICANOS **Rev:** Pyramid de la Looona
(moon) **Rev. Legend:** ESTADO DE MÉXICO **Edge:**
Segmented reeding **Mint:** Mexico City

Date	Mintage	F	VF	XF	Unc	BU
2006Mo Proof	600	Value: 1,200				

KM# 785   100 PESOS
33.9400 g., Bi-Metallic .925 Silver 16.812g center in
Aluminum-Bronze ring, 39.04 mm. **Series:** Second
Obv: National arms **Obv. Legend:** ESTADOS
UNIDOS MEXICANOS **Rev:** Four Monarch
butterflies **Rev. Legend:** ESTADO DE MICHOACÁN
Edge: Segmented reeding **Mint:** Mexico City

Date	Mintage	F	VF	XF	Unc	BU
2006Mo	149,730	—	—	—	25.00	30.00

KM# 877   100 PESOS
29.1690 g., Bi-Metallic .999 Gold 17.154g center in
.999 Silver 12.015g ring, 34.5 mm. **Series:** Second
Obv: National arms **Obv. Legend:** ESTADOS
UNIDOS MEXICANOS **Rev:** Four Monarch
butterflies **Rev. Legend:** ESTADO DE MICHOACÁN
Edge: Segmented reeding **Mint:** Mexico City

Date	Mintage	F	VF	XF	Unc	BU
2006Mo Proof	600	Value: 1,200				

KM# 800   100 PESOS
33.9400 g., Bi-Metallic .925 Silver 16.812g center
in Aluminum-Bronze ring, 39.04 mm. **Series:**
Second **Obv:** National arms **Obv. Legend:**
ESTADOS UNIDOS MEXICANOS **Rev:** 1/2 length
figure of Chinelo (local dancer) at right, Palacio de
Cortes in background **Rev. Inscription:** ESTADO
DE / MORELOS **Edge:** Segmented reeding **Mint:**
Mexico City

Date	Mintage	F	VF	XF	Unc	BU
2006Mo	149,648	—	—	—	25.00	30.00

KM# 878   100 PESOS
29.1690 g., Bi-Metallic .999 Gold 17.154g center in
.999 Silver 12.015g ring, 34.5 mm. **Series:** Second
Obv: National arms **Obv. Legend:** ESTADOS
UNIDOS MEXICANOS **Rev:** 1/2 length figure of
Chinelo (local dancer) at right, Palacio de Cortes in
background **Rev. Inscription:** ESTADO DE /
MORELOS **Edge:** Segmented reeding **Mint:**
Mexico City

Date	Mintage	F	VF	XF	Unc	BU
2006Mo Proof	600	Value: 1,200				

ESTADOS UNIDOS MEXICANOS

KM# 798   100 PESOS
33.9400 g., 33.8250 Bi-Metallic .925 Silver 16.812g center in Aluminum-Bronze ring 36.908 oz., 39.04 mm. **Series:** Second **Obv:** National arms **Obv. Legend:** ESTADOS UNIDOS MEXICANOS **Rev:** Isle de Mexcaltitlán **Rev. Legend:** ESTADO DE NAYARIT **Edge:** Segmented reeding **Mint:** Mexico City

Date	Mintage	F	VF	XF	Unc	BU
2007Mo	149,560	—	—	—	25.00	30.00

KM# 879   100 PESOS
29.1690 g., Bi-Metallic .999 Gold 17.154g center in .999 12.015g ring, 34.5 mm. **Series:** Second **Obv:** National arms **Obv. Legend:** ESTADOS UNIDOS MEXICANOS **Rev:** Isle de Mexcaltitlán **Rev. Legend:** ESTADO DE NAYARIT **Edge:** Segmented reeding **Mint:** Mexico City

Date	Mintage	F	VF	XF	Unc	BU
2007Mo Proof	600	Value: 1,200				

KM# 849   100 PESOS
33.9400 g., Bi-Metallic .925 Silver 20.1753g center in Aluminum-Bronze ring, 39.04 mm. **Series:** Second **Obv:** National arms **Obv. Legend:** ESTADOS UNIDOS MEXICANOS **Rev:** Teatro Macedonio Alcala (theater) **Rev. Legend:** OAXACA **Edge:** Segmented reeding **Mint:** Mexico City

Date	Mintage	F	VF	XF	Unc	BU
2007Mo	149,892	—	—	—	25.00	30.00

KM# 881   100 PESOS
29.1690 g., Bi-Metallic .999 Gold 17.154g center in .999 Silver 12.015g ring, 34.50 mm. **Series:** Second **Obv:** National arms **Obv. Legend:** ESTADOS UNIDOS MEXICANOS **Rev:** Teatro Macedonio Alcala (theater) **Rev. Legend:** OAXACA **Edge:** Segmented reeding **Mint:** Mexico City

Date	Mintage	F	VF	XF	Unc	BU
2007Mo Proof	600	Value: 1,200				

KM# 848   100 PESOS
33.9400 g., Bi-Metallic .925 Silver 20.1753 center in Aluminum-Bronze ring, 39.04 mm. **Series:** Second **Obv:** National arms **Obv. Legend:** ESTADOS UNIDOS MEXICANOE **Rev:** Old foundry in Parque Fundidora (public park) at right, Cerro de la Silla (Saddle Hill) in background **Rev. Legend:** ESTADO DE NUEVO LÉON **Edge:** Segmented reeding **Mint:** Mexico City

Date	Mintage	F	VF	XF	Unc	BU
2007Mo	149,425	—	—	—	25.00	30.00

KM# 880   100 PESOS
29.1690 g., Bi-Metallic .999 Gold 17.154g center in .999 Silver 12.015g ring, 34.5 mm. **Series:** Second **Obv:** National arms **Obv. Legend:** ESTADOS UNIDOS MEXICANOS **Rev:** Old foundry in Parque Fundidora (public park) at right, Cerro de la Silla (Saddle hill) in background **Rev. Legend:** ESTADO DE NUEVO LEÓN **Edge:** Segmented reeding **Mint:** Mexico City

Date	Mintage	F	VF	XF	Unc	BU
2007Mo Proof	600	Value: 1,200				

KM# 850   100 PESOS
33.9400 g., Bi-Metallic .925 Silver 20.1753g center in Aluminum-Bronze ring, 39.04 mm. **Series:** Second **Obv:** National arms **Obv. Legend:** ESTADOS UNIDOS MEXICANOS **Rev:** Talavera porcelain dish **Rev. Legend:** ESTADO DE PUEBLA **Edge:** Segmented reeding **Mint:** Mexico City

Date	Mintage	F	VF	XF	Unc	BU
2007Mo	149,474	—	—	—	25.00	30.00

KM# 882   100 PESOS
29.1690 g., Bi-Metallic .999 Gold 17.154g center in .999 Silver 12.015g ring, 34.5 mm. **Series:** Second **Obv:** National arms **Obv. Legend:** ESTADOS UNIDOS MEXICANOS **Rev:** Talavera porcelain dish **Rev. Legend:** ESTADO DE PUEBLA **Edge:** Segmented reeding **Mint:** Mexico City

Date	Mintage	F	VF	XF	Unc	BU
2007Mo Proof	600	Value: 1,200				

ESTADOS UNIDOS MEXICANOS

KM# 851   100 PESOS
33.9400 g., Bi-Metallic .925 Silver 20.1753g center in Aluminum-Bronze ring, 39.04 mm.   **Series:** Second **Obv:** National arms **Obv. Legend:** ESTADOS UNIDOS MEXICANOS **Rev:** Mask at left, rays above state arms at center, Mayan ruins at right **Rev. Legend:** QUINTANA ROO **Edge:** Segmented reeding **Mint:** Mexico City

Date	Mintage	F	VF	XF	Unc	BU
2007Mo	149,582	—	—	—	25.00	30.00

KM# 883   100 PESOS
29.1690 g., Bi-Metallic .999 Gold 17.154g center in .999 Silver 12.015g ring, 34.5 mm.   **Series:** Second **Obv:** National arms **Obv. Legend:** ESTADOS UNIDOS MEXICANOS **Rev:** Mask at left, rays above state arms at center, Mayan ruins at right **Rev. Legend:** QUINTANA ROO **Edge:** Segmented reeding **Mint:** Mexico City

Date	Mintage	F	VF	XF	Unc	BU
2007Mo Proof	600	Value: 1,200				

KM# 853   100 PESOS
33.9400 g., Bi-Metallic .925 Silver 20.1753g center in Aluminum-Bronze ring, 39.04 mm.   **Series:** Second **Obv:** National arms **Obv. Legend:** ESTADOS UNIDOS MEXICANOS **Rev:** Facade of Caja Real **Rev. Legend:** • SAN LUIS POTOSÍ • **Edge:** Segmented reeding **Mint:** Mexico City

Date	Mintage	F	VF	XF	Unc	BU
2007Mo	148,750	—	—	—	25.00	30.00

KM# 885   100 PESOS
29.1690 g., Bi-Metallic .999 Gold 17.154g center in .999 Silver 12.015 ring, 34.5 mm.   **Series:** Second **Obv:** National arms **Obv. Legend:** ESTADOS UNIDOS MEXICANOS **Rev:** Facade of Caja Real **Rev. Legend:** • SAN LUIS POTOSÍ • **Edge:** Segmented reeding **Mint:** Mexico City

Date	Mintage	F	VF	XF	Unc	BU
2007Mo Proof	600	Value: 1,200				

KM# 852   100 PESOS
33.9400 g., Bi-Metallic .925 Silver 20.1753 center in Aluminum-Bronze ring, 39.04 mm.   **Series:** Second **Obv:** National arms **Obv. Legend:** ESTADOS UNIDOS MEXICANOS **Rev:** Aqueduct of Querétaro at left, church of Santa Rosa de Viterbo at right **Rev. Legend:** ESTADO DE QUERÉTARO ARTEAGA **Edge:** Segmented reeding **Mint:** Mexico City

Date	Mintage	F	VF	XF	Unc	BU
2007Mo	149,127	—	—	—	25.00	30.00

KM# 884   100 PESOS
29.1690 g., Bi-Metallic .999 Gold 17.154g center in .999 Silver 12.015g ring, 34.5 mm.   **Series:** Second **Obv:** National arms **Obv. Legend:** ESTADOS UNIDOS MEXICANOS **Rev:** Aqueduct of Querétaro at left, church of Santa Rosa de Viterbo at right **Rev. Legend:** ESTADO DE QUERÉTARO ARTEAGA **Edge:** Segmented reeding **Mint:** Mexico City

Date	Mintage	F	VF	XF	Unc	BU
2007Mo Proof	600	Value: 1,200				

KM# 854   100 PESOS
33.9400 g., Bi-Metallic .925 Silver 20.1753g center in Aluminum-Bronze ring, 39.04 mm.   **Series:** Second **Obv:** National arms **Obv. Legend:** ESTADOS UNIDOS MEXICANOS **Rev:** Shield on pile of cactus fruits **Rev. Legend:** ESTADO DE SINALOA - LUGAR DE PITAHAYAS **Edge:** Segmented reeding **Mint:** Mexico City

Date	Mintage	F	VF	XF	Unc	BU
2007Mo	149,032	—	—	—	25.00	30.00

KM# 886   100 PESOS
29.1690 g., Bi-Metallic .999 Gold 17.154 center in .999 Silver 12.015g ring, 34.5 mm.   **Series:** Second **Obv:** National arms **Obv. Legend:** ESTADOS UNIDOS MEXICANOS **Rev:** Shield on pile of cactus fruits **Rev. Legend:** ESTADO DE SINALOA - LUGAR DE PITAHAYES **Edge:** Segmented reeding **Mint:** Mexico City

Date	Mintage	F	VF	XF	Unc	BU
2007Mo Proof	600	Value: 1,200				

KM# 855   100 PESOS
33.9400 g., Bi-Metallic .925 Silver 20.1753g center in Aluminum-Bronze ring, 39.04 mm. **Series:** Second **Obv:** National arms **Obv. Legend:** ESTADOS UNIDOS MEXICANOS **Rev:** Local in Dance of the Deer at left, cactus at right, mountains in background **Rev. Legend:** ESTADO DE SONORA **Edge:** Segmented reeding **Mint:** Mexico City

Date	Mintage	F	VF	XF	Unc	BU
2007Mo	149,891	—	—	—	25.00	30.00

KM# 887   100 PESOS
29.1690 g., Bi-Metallic .999 Gold 17.154g center in .999 Silver 12.015g ring, 34.5 mm. **Series:** Second **Obv:** National arms **Obv. Legend:** ESTADOS UNIDOS MEXICANOS **Rev:** Local in Dance of the Deer at left, cactus at right, mountains in background **Rev. Legend:** ESTADO DE SONORA **Edge:** Segmented reeding **Mint:** Mexico City

Date	Mintage	F	VF	XF	Unc	BU
2007Mo Proof	600	Value: 1,200				

KM# 856   100 PESOS
33.9400 g., Bi-Metallic .925 Silver 20.1753 center in Aluminum-Bronze ring, 39.04 mm. **Series:** Second **Obv:** National arms **Obv. Legend:** ESTADOS UNIDOS MEXICANOS **Rev:** Fuente de los Pescadores (fisherman fountain) at lower left, giant head from the Olmec-pre-Hispanic culture at right, Planetario Tabasco in background **Rev. Legend:** TABASCO **Edge:** Segmented reeding **Mint:** Mexico City

Date	Mintage	F	VF	XF	Unc	BU
2007Mo	149,715	—	—	—	25.00	30.00

KM# 888   100 PESOS
29.1690 g., Bi-Metallic .999 Gold 17.154g center in .999 Silver 12.015g ring, 34.5 mm. **Series:** Second **Obv:** National arms **Obv. Legend:** ESTADOS UNIDOS MEXICANOS **Rev:** Fuente de los Pescadores (fisherman fountain) at lower left, giant head from the Olmec-pre-Hispanic culture at right, Planetario Tabasco in background **Rev.**

Legend: TABASCO **Edge:** Segmented reeding **Mint:** Mexico City

Date	Mintage	F	VF	XF	Unc	BU
2007Mo Proof	600	Value: 1,200				

KM# 857   100 PESOS
33.9400 g., Bi-Metallic .925 Silver 20.1753g center in Aluminum-Bronze ring, 39.04 mm. **Series:** Second **Obv:** National arms **Obv. Legend:** ESTADOS UNIDOS MEXICANOS **Rev:** Ridge - Cerro Del Bermal, Gonzáles **Rev. Legend:** TAMAULIPAS **Edge:** Segmented reeding **Mint:** Mexico City

Date	Mintage	F	VF	XF	Unc	BU
2007Mo	149,776	—	—	—	25.00	30.00

KM# 889   100 PESOS
29.1690 g., Bi-Metallic .999 Gold 17.154g center in .999 Silver 12.015g ring, 34.5 mm. **Series:** Second **Obv:** National arms **Obv. Legend:** ESTADOS DE MEXICANOS **Rev:** Ridge - Cerro Del Bermal, Gonzáles **Rev. Legend:** TAMAULIPAS **Edge:** Segmented reeding **Mint:** Mexico City

Date	Mintage	F	VF	XF	Unc	BU
2007Mo Proof	600	Value: 1,200				

KM# 858   100 PESOS
33.9400 g., Bi-Metallic .925 Silver 20.1753g center in Aluminum-Bronze ring, 39.04 mm. **Series:** Second **Obv:** National arms **Obv. Legend:** ESTADOS UNIDOS MEXICANOS **Rev:** Basilica de Ocotlán at left, state arms above Capilla Abierta, Plaza de Toros Ranchero Aguilar below, Exconvento de San Francisco at right **Rev. Legend:** ESTADO DE TLAXCALA **Edge:** Segmented reeding **Mint:** Mexico City

Date	Mintage	F	VF	XF	Unc	BU
2007Mo	149,465	—	—	—	25.00	30.00

KM# 890   100 PESOS
29.1690 g., Bi-Metallic .999 Gold 17.154g center in .999 Silver 12.015g ring, 34.5 mm. **Series:** Second **Obv:** National arms **Obv. Legend:** ESTADOS UNIDOS

Legend: TABASCO **Edge:** Segmented reeding
Mint: Mexico City

Date	Mintage	F	VF	XF	Unc	BU
2007Mo Proof	600	Value: 1,200				

ESTADOS UNIDOS MEXICANOS

MEXICANOS **Rev:** Basilica de Ocotlán at left, state arms above Capilla Abierta, Plaza de Toros Ranchero Aguilar below, Exconvento de San Francisco at right **Rev. Legend:** ESTADO DE TLAXCALA **Edge:** Segmented reeding **Mint:** Mexico City

Date	Mintage	F	VF	XF	Unc	BU
2007Mo Proof	600	Value: 1,200				

KM# 859   100 PESOS
33.9400 g., Bi-Metallic .912 Silver 20.1753g center in Aluminum-Bronze ring, 39.04 mm.   **Series:** Second **Obv:** National arms **Obv. Legend:** ESTADOS UNIDOS MEXICANOS **Rev:** Pyramid of El Tajín **Rev. Legend:** • VERACRUZ • - • DE IGNACIO DE LA LLAVE • **Edge:** Segmented reeding **Mint:** Mexico City

Date	Mintage	F	VF	XF	Unc	BU
2007Mo	149,703	—	—	—	25.00	30.00

KM# 891   100 PESOS
29.1690 g., Bi-Metallic .999 Gold 17.154g center in .999 Silver 12.015g ring, 34.5 mm.   **Series:** Second **Obv:** National arms **Obv. Legend:** ESTADOS UNIDOS MEXICANOS **Rev:** Pyramid of El Tajín **Rev. Legend:** • VERACRUZ • - • DE IGNACIO DE LA LLAVE • **Edge:** Segmented reeding **Mint:** Mexico City

Date	Mintage	F	VF	XF	Unc	BU
2007Mo Proof	600	Value: 1,200				

KM# 860   100 PESOS
33.9400 g., Bi-Metallic .925 Silver 20.1753 center in Aluminum-Bronze ring, 39.04 mm.   **Series:** Second **Obv:** National arms **Obv. Legend:** ESTADOS UNIDOS MEXICANOS **Rev:** Stylized pyramid of Chichén Itzá **Rev. Legend:** Castillo de Chichén Itzá **Edge:** Segmented reeding **Mint:** Mexico City

Date	Mintage	F	VF	XF	Unc	BU
2007Mo	149,579	—	—	—	25.00	30.00

KM# 892   100 PESOS
29.1690 g., Bi-Metallic .999 Gold 17.154g center in .999 Silver 12.015g ring, 34.5 mm.   **Series:** Second **Obv:** National arms **Obv. Legend:** ESTADOS UNIDOS MEXICANOS **Rev:** Stylized pyramid of

Chichén-Itzá **Rev. Inscription:** YUCATÁN **Edge:** Segmented reeding **Mint:** Mexico City

Date	Mintage	F	VF	XF	Unc	BU
2007Mo Proof	600	Value: 1,200				

KM# 861   100 PESOS
33.9400 g., Bi-Metallic .925 Silver 20.1753g center in Aluminum-Bronze ring, 39.04 mm.   **Series:** Second **Obv:** National arms **Obv. Legend:** ESTADOS UNIDOS MEXICANOS **Rev:** Cable car above Monumento al Minero at left, Cathedral de Zacatecas at center right **Rev. Legend:** ZACATECAS **Edge:** Segmented reeding **Mint:** Mexico City

Date	Mintage	F	VF	XF	Unc	BU
2007Mo	148,833	—	—	—	25.00	30.00

KM# 893   100 PESOS
29.1690 g., Bi-Metallic .999 Gold 17.154g center in .999 Silver 12.015g ring, 34.5 mm.   **Series:** Second **Obv:** National arms **Obv. Legend:** ESTADOS UNIDOS MEXICANOS **Rev:** Cable car above Monumento al Minero at left, Cathedral de Zacatecas at center right **Rev. Legend:** Zacatecas **Edge:** Segmented reeding **Mint:** Mexico City

Date	Mintage	F	VF	XF	Unc	BU
2007Mo Proof	600	Value: 1,200				

KM# 771   50000 PESOS
7.7700 g., 0.9990 Gold 0.2496 oz. AGW, 23 mm. **Subject:** World Cup Soccer **Obv:** Mexican Eagle and Snake **Rev:** Kneeling Mayan Pelota player and soccer ball **Mint:** Mexico City

Date	Mintage	F	VF	XF	Unc	BU
2006Mo Proof	9,505	Value: 600				

SILVER BULLION COINAGE

LIBERTAD SERIES

KM# 921   100 PESOS
1000.0000 g., 0.9990 Silver 32.117 oz. ASW   **Obv:** National arms in center of past and present arms **Rev:** Aztec Calendar **Edge:** Plain **Mint:** Mexico City

Date	Mintage	F	VF	XF	Unc	BU
2007Mo Prooflike	303	—	—	—	—	2,000
2008Mo Prooflike	1,000	—	—	—	—	2,000
2009Mo Prooflike	1,500	—	—	—	—	2,000

KM# 542   1/20 ONZA (1/20 Troy Ounce of Silver)
1.5551 g., 0.9990 Silver 0.0499 oz. ASW, 16 mm. **Obv:** National arms, eagle left **Rev:** Winged Victory **Mint:** Mexico City

Date	Mintage	F	VF	XF	Unc	BU
1991Mo	50,017	—	—	—	—	5.50
1992Mo	295,783	—	—	—	—	4.50
1992Mo Proof	5,000	Value: 10.00				
1993Mo	100,000	—	—	—	—	4.50
1993Mo Proof	5,002	Value: 10.00				
1994Mo	90,100	—	—	—	—	4.50
1994Mo Proof	5,002	Value: 10.00				
1995Mo	50,000	—	—	—	—	5.50
1995Mo Proof	2,000	Value: 12.00				

KM# 609 1/20 ONZA (1/20 Troy Ounce of Silver)
1.5551 g., 0.9990 Silver 0.0499 oz. ASW, 16 mm.
Obv: National arms, eagle left **Rev:** Winged Victory
Mint: Mexico City

Date	Mintage	F	VF	XF	Unc	BU
1996Mo	50,000	—	—	—	—	20.00
1996Mo Proof	1,000	Value: 30.00				
1997Mo	20,000	—	—	—	—	20.00
1997Mo Proof	800	Value: 30.00				
1998Mo	6,400	—	—	—	—	30.00
1998Mo Proof	300	Value: 37.00				
1999Mo	8,001	—	—	—	—	25.00
1999Mo Proof	600	Value: 33.00				
2000Mo	57,500	—	—	—	—	25.00
2000Mo Proof	900	Value: 33.00				
2001Mo	4,500	—	—	—	—	25.00
2001Mo Proof	1,500	Value: 30.00				
2002Mo	50,000	—	—	—	—	16.00
2002Mo Proof	2,800	Value: 25.00				
2003Mo	30,000	—	—	—	—	16.00
2003Mo Proof	4,400	Value: 25.00				
2004Mo	30,000	—	—	—	—	16.00
2004Mo Proof	2,700	Value: 25.00				
2005Mo	15,000	—	—	—	—	16.00
2005Mo Proof	2,600	Value: 25.00				
2006Mo	20,000	—	—	—	—	16.00
2006Mo Proof	3,300	Value: 25.00				
2007Mo	3,500	—	—	—	—	16.00
2007Mo Proof	4,000	Value: 25.00				
2008Mo	7,000	—	—	—	—	16.00
2008Mo Proof	3,300	Value: 25.00				
2009Mo	10,000	—	—	—	—	16.00
2009Mo Proof	5,000	Value: 25.00				

KM# 543 1/10 ONZA (1/10 Troy Ounce of Silver)
3.1103 g., 0.9990 Silver 0.0999 oz. ASW **Obv:**
National arms, eagle left **Rev:** Winged Victory **Mint:**
Mexico City

Date	Mintage	F	VF	XF	Unc	BU
1991Mo	50,017	—	—	—	—	7.50
1992Mo	299,983	—	—	—	—	6.50
1992Mo Proof	5,000	Value: 12.00				
1993Mo	100,000	—	—	—	—	6.50
1993Mo Proof	5,002	Value: 12.00				
1994Mo	90,100	—	—	—	—	6.50
1994Mo Proof	5,002	Value: 12.00				
1995Mo	50,000	—	—	—	—	7.50
1995Mo Proof	2,000	Value: 13.50				

KM# 610 1/10 ONZA (1/10 Troy Ounce of Silver)
3.1103 g., 0.9990 Silver 0.0999 oz. ASW, 20 mm.
Obv: National arms, eagle left **Rev:** Winged Victory
Mint: Mexico City

Date	Mintage	F	VF	XF	Unc	BU
1996Mo	50,000	—	—	—	—	25.00
1996Mo Proof	1,000	Value: 35.00				
1997Mo	20,000	—	—	—	—	25.00
1997Mo Proof	800	Value: 35.00				
1998Mo	6,400	—	—	—	—	33.00
1998Mo Proof	300	Value: 45.00				
1999Mo	8,000	—	—	—	—	27.50
1999Mo Proof	600	Value: 40.00				
2000Mo	27,500	—	—	—	—	27.50
2000Mo Proof	1,000	Value: 40.00				
2001Mo	25,000	—	—	—	—	27.50
2001Mo Proof	1,500	Value: 36.00				
2002Mo	35,000	—	—	—	—	20.00
2002Mo Proof	2,800	Value: 30.00				
2003Mo	20,000	—	—	—	—	20.00
2003Mo Proof	4,900	Value: 30.00				
2004Mo	15,000	—	—	—	—	20.00
2004Mo Proof	2,500	Value: 30.00				
2005Mo	9,277	—	—	—	—	20.00
2005Mo Proof	3,000	Value: 27.50				
2006Mo	15,000	—	—	—	—	20.00
2006Mo Proof	3,000	Value: 27.50				
2007Mo	3,500	—	—	—	—	20.00
2007Mo Proof	4,000	Value: 27.50				
2008Mo	10,000	—	—	—	—	20.00
2008Mo Proof	5,000	Value: 27.50				
2009Mo	10,000	—	—	—	—	20.00
2009Mo Proof	5,000	Value: 27.50				

KM# 544 1/4 ONZA (1/4 Troy Ounce of Silver)
7.7758 g., 0.9990 Silver 0.2497 oz. ASW, 25 mm.
Obv: National arms, eagle left **Rev:** Winged Victory
Mint: Mexico City

Date	Mintage	F	VF	XF	Unc	BU
1991Mo	50,017	—	—	—	—	11.50
1992Mo	104,000	—	—	—	—	10.00
1992Mo Proof	5,000	Value: 16.50				
1993Mo	90,500	—	—	—	—	10.00
1993Mo Proof	5,002	Value: 16.50				
1994Mo	90,100	—	—	—	—	10.00
1994Mo Proof	5,002	Value: 16.50				
1995Mo	50,000	—	—	—	—	11.50
1995Mo Proof	2,000	Value: 17.50				

BULLION LIBERTAD

KM# 611   1/4 ONZA (1/4 Troy Ounce of Silver)
7.7758 g., 0.9990 Silver 0.2497 oz. ASW, 27 mm.
Obv: National arms, eagle left **Rev:** Winged Victory
Mint: Mexico City

Date	Mintage	F	VF	XF	Unc	BU
1996Mo	50,000	—	—	—	—	32.00
1996Mo Proof	1,000	Value: 40.00				
1997Mo	20,000	—	—	—	—	32.00
1997Mo Proof	800	Value: 40.00				
1998Mo	6,400	—	—	—	—	40.00
1998Mo Proof	300	Value: 65.00				
1999Mo	7,000	—	—	—	—	36.00
1999Mo Proof	600	Value: 50.00				
2000Mo	21,000	—	—	—	—	36.00
2000Mo Proof	700	Value: 50.00				
2001Mo	25,000	—	—	—	—	36.00
2001Mo Proof	1,000	Value: 44.00				
2002Mo	35,000	—	—	—	—	27.50
2002Mo Proof	2,800	Value: 40.00				
2003Mo	22,000	—	—	—	—	27.50
2003Mo Proof	3,900	Value: 40.00				
2004Mo	15,000	—	—	—	—	27.50
2004Mo Proof	2,500	Value: 40.00				
2005Mo	15,000	—	—	—	—	27.50
2005Mo Proof	2,400	Value: 37.00				
2006Mo	15,000	—	—	—	—	25.00
2006Mo Proof	2,900	Value: 37.00				
2007Mo	3,500	—	—	—	—	25.00
2007Mo Proof	3,000	Value: 37.00				
2008Mo	9,000	—	—	—	—	25.00
2008Mo Proof	2,900	Value: 37.00				
2009Mo	10,000	—	—	—	—	25.00
2009Mo Proof	3,000	Value: 37.00				

KM# 545   1/2 ONZA (1/2 Troy Ounce of Silver)
15.5517 g., 0.9990 Silver 0.4995 oz. ASW, 30 mm.
Obv: National arms, eagle left **Rev:** Winged Victory
Mint: Mexico City

Date	Mintage	F	VF	XF	Unc	BU
1991Mo	50,618	—	—	—	—	24.00
1992Mo	119,000	—	—	—	—	22.00
1992Mo Proof	5,000	Value: 27.00				
1993Mo	90,500	—	—	—	—	22.00
1993Mo Proof	5,002	Value: 27.00				
1994Mo	90,100	—	—	—	—	22.00
1994Mo Proof	5,002	Value: 27.00				
1995Mo	50,000	—	—	—	—	22.00
1995Mo Proof	2,000	Value: 28.00				

KM# 612   1/2 ONZA (1/2 Troy Ounce of Silver)
15.5517 g., 0.9990 Silver 0.4995 oz. ASW, 30 mm.
Obv: National arms, eagle left **Rev:** Winged Victory
Mint: Mexico City

Date	Mintage	F	VF	XF	Unc	BU
1996Mo	50,000	—	—	—	—	40.00
1996Mo Proof	1,000	Value: 60.00				
1997Mo	20,000	—	—	—	—	40.00
1997Mo Proof	800	Value: 60.00				
1998Mo	6,400	—	—	—	—	60.00
1998Mo Proof	2,500	Value: 90.00				
1999Mo	2,000	—	—	—	—	45.00
1999Mo Proof	7,000	Value: 70.00				
2000Mo	20,000	—	—	—	—	45.00
2000Mo Proof	700	Value: 70.00				
2001Mo	20,000	—	—	—	—	45.00
2001Mo Proof	1,000	Value: 60.00				
2002Mo	35,000	—	—	—	—	37.00
2002Mo Proof	2,800	Value: 50.00				
2003Mo	28,000	—	—	—	—	37.00
2003Mo Proof	3,400	Value: 50.00				
2004Mo	20,000	—	—	—	—	37.00
2004Mo Proof	2,500	Value: 50.00				
2005Mo	10,000	—	—	—	—	37.00
2005Mo Proof	2,800	Value: 44.00				
2006Mo	15,000	—	—	—	—	37.00
2006Mo Proof	2,900	Value: 44.00				
2007Mo	3,500	—	—	—	—	37.00
2007Mo Proof	1,500	Value: 44.00				
2008Mo	9,000	—	—	—	—	37.00
2008Mo Proof	2,500	Value: 44.00				
2009Mo	10,000	—	—	—	—	37.00
2009Mo Proof	3,000	Value: 44.00				

KM# 494.1   ONZA (Troy Ounce of Silver)
31.1000 g., 0.9990 Silver 0.9988 oz. ASW, 36 mm.
Subject: Libertad **Obv:** National arms, eagle left
Rev: Winged Victory **Edge:** Plain **Mint:** Mexico City

Date	Mintage	F	VF	XF	Unc	BU
1982Mo	1,049,680	—	—	—	BV	38.00
1983Mo	1,001,768	—	—	—	BV	47.00
1983Mo Proof	998	Value: 600				
1984Mo	1,014,000	—	—	—	BV	38.00
1985Mo	2,017,000	—	—	—	BV	38.00
1986Mo	1,699,426	—	—	—	BV	38.00
1986Mo Proof	30,006	Value: 45.00				
1987Mo	500,000	—	—	—	BV	60.00
1987Mo Doubled die	Inc. above	—	—	—	—	80.00
1987Mo Proof	12,000	Value: 60.00				
1988Mo	1,500,500	—	—	—	BV	65.00
1989Mo	1,396,500	—	—	—	BV	45.00
1989Mo Proof	10,000	Value: 95.00				

KM# 494.2   ONZA (Troy Ounce of Silver)
31.1000 g., 0.9990 Silver 0.9988 oz. ASW, 36 mm.
Obv: National arms, eagle left **Rev:** Winged Victory
Edge: Reeded **Mint:** Mexico City

Date	Mintage	F	VF	XF	Unc	BU
1988Mo Proof	10,000	Value: 105				
1990Mo	1,200,000	—	—	—	BV	38.00
1990Mo Proof	10,000	Value: 90.00				
1991Mo	1,650,518	—	—	—	BV	52.00

BULLION LIBERTAD

KM# 494.5   ONZA (Troy Ounce of Silver)
31.1000 g., 0.9990 Silver 0.9988 oz. ASW **Subject:**
Libertad **Obv:** National arms, eagle left, KM#494.3
Rev: Winged Victory, KM#494.2 **Edge:** Reeded
Mint: Mexico City **Note:** Mule

Date	Mintage	F	VF	XF	Unc	BU
1991Mo Proof	10,000	Value: 85.00				

KM# 494.3   ONZA (Troy Ounce of Silver)
31.1000 g., 0.9990 Silver 0.9988 oz. ASW, 36 mm.
Subject: Libertad **Obv:** National arms, eight dots below
eagle's left talons **Rev:** Winged Victory with revised
design and lettering **Edge:** Reeded **Mint:** Mexico City

Date	Mintage	F	VF	XF	Unc	BU
1991Mo	Inc. above	—	—	—	BV	55.00
1991Mo Proof	10,000	Value: 85.00				
1992Mo	2,458,000	—	—	—	BV	50.00
1992Mo Proof	10,000	Value: 85.00				

KM# 494.4   ONZA (Troy Ounce of Silver)
31.1000 g., 0.9990 Silver 0.9988 oz. ASW, 36 mm.
Subject: Libertad **Obv:** National arms, Seven dots
below eagle's left talon, dull claws on right talon, thick
lettering **Rev:** Winged Victory with revised design
and lettering **Edge:** Reeded **Mint:** Mexico City

Date	Mintage	F	VF	XF	Unc	BU
1993Mo	1,000,000	—	—	—	BV	40.00
1993Mo Proof	5,002	Value: 90.00				
1994Mo	400,000	—	—	—	BV	45.00
1994Mo Proof	5,002	Value: 85.00				
1995Mo	500,000	—	—	—	BV	45.00
1995Mo Proof	2,000	Value: 85.00				

KM# 613   ONZA (Troy Ounce of Silver)
31.1050 g., 0.9990 Silver 0.9990 oz. ASW, 40 mm.
Obv: National arms, eagle left **Rev:** Winged Victory
Mint: Mexico City

Date	Mintage	F	VF	XF	Unc	BU
1996Mo	300,000	—	—	—	—	48.00
1996Mo Proof	2,000	Value: 90.00				
1997Mo	100,000	—	—	—	—	58.00
1997Mo Proof	1,500	Value: 70.00				
1998Mo	67,000	—	—	—	—	135
1998Mo Proof	500	Value: 205				
1999Mo	95,000	—	—	—	—	50.00
1999Mo Proof	600	Value: 95.00				

KM# 639   ONZA (Troy Ounce of Silver)
31.1000 g., 0.9990 Silver 0.9988 oz. ASW, 40 mm.
Subject: Libertad **Obv:** National arms, eagle left
within center of past and present arms **Rev:** Winged
Victory **Edge:** Reeded **Mint:** Mexico City

Date	Mintage	F	VF	XF	Unc	BU
2000Mo	340,000	—	—	—	—	80.00
2000Mo Proof	1,600	Value: 140				
2001Mo	725,000	—	—	—	—	60.00
2001Mo Proof	2,000	Value: 140				
2002Mo	854,000	—	—	—	—	55.00
2002Mo Proof	3,800	Value: 150				
2003Mo	805,000	—	—	—	—	55.00
2003Mo Proof	5,400	Value: 130				
2004Mo	450,000	—	—	—	—	75.00
2004Mo Proof	3,000	Value: 130				
2005Mo	698,281	—	—	—	—	90.00
2005Mo Proof	3,300	Value: 150				
2006Mo	300,000	—	—	—	—	55.00
2006Mo Proof	4,000	Value: 140				
2007Mo	200,000	—	—	—	—	95.00
2007Mo Proof	5,800	Value: 150				
2008Mo	950,000	—	—	—	—	65.00
2008Mo Proof	11,000	Value: 150				
2009Mo	1,650,000	—	—	—	—	50.00
2009Mo Proof	10,000	Value: 150				

KM# 614   2 ONZAS (2 Troy Ounces of Silver)
62.2070 g., 0.9990 Silver 1.9979 oz. ASW, 48 mm.

Subject: Libertad **Obv:** National arms, eagle left within center of past and present arms **Rev:** Winged Victory **Edge:** Reeded **Mint:** Mexico City

Date	Mintage	F	VF	XF	Unc	BU
1996Mo	50,000	—	—	—	—	120
1996Mo Proof	1,200	Value: 180				
1997Mo	15,000	—			—	120
1997Mo Proof	1,300	Value: 150				
1998Mo	7,000	—			—	110
1998Mo Proof	400	Value: 450				
1999Mo	5,000	—			—	130
1999Mo Proof	280	Value: 7,100				
2000Mo	7,500	—			—	130
2000Mo Proof	500	Value: 300				
2001Mo	6,700	—			—	120
2001Mo Proof	500	Value: 300				
2002Mo	8,700	—			—	110
2002Mo Proof	1,000	Value: 225				
2003Mo	9,500	—			—	110
2003Mo Proof	800	Value: 225				
2004Mo	8,000	—			—	100
2004Mo Proof	1,000	Value: 175				
2005Mo	3,549	—			—	100
2005Mo Proof	600	Value: 500				
2006Mo	5,800	—			—	100
2006Mo Proof	1,100	Value: 175				
2007Mo	8,000	—			—	100
2007Mo Proof	500	Value: 250				
2008Mo	17,000	—			—	110
2008Mo Proof	1,000	Value: 170				
2009Mo	46,000	—			—	110
2009Mo Proof	6,200	Value: 150				

KM# 615   5 ONZAS (5 Troy Ounces of Silver)
155.5175 g., 0.9990 Silver 4.9948 oz. ASW, 65 mm.
Subject: Libertad **Obv:** National arms, eagle left within center of past and present arms **Rev:** Winged Victory **Edge:** Reeded **Mint:** Mexico City **Note:** Illustration reduced.

Date	Mintage	F	VF	XF	Unc	BU
1996Mo	20,000	—	—	—	—	265
1996Mo Proof	1,200	Value: 295				
1997Mo	10,000	—			—	265
1997Mo Proof	1,300	Value: 295				
1998Mo	3,500	—			—	325
1998Mo Proof	400	Value: 1,000				
1999Mo	2,800	—			—	255
1999Mo Proof	100	Value: 1,250				
2000Mo	4,000	—			—	255
2000Mo Proof	500	Value: 375				

Date	Mintage	F	VF	XF	Unc	BU
2001Mo	4,000	—	—	—	—	190
2001Mo Proof	600	Value: 325				
2002Mo	5,200	—			—	190
2002Mo Proof	1,000	Value: 325				
2003Mo	6,000	—			—	180
2003Mo Proof	1,500	Value: 250				
2004Mo	3,923	—			—	180
2004Mo Proof	800	Value: 225				
2005Mo	2,401	—			—	205
2005Mo Proof	1,000	Value: 225				
2006Mo	3,000	—			—	180
2006Mo Proof	700	Value: 265				
2007Mo	3,000	—			—	180
2007Mo Proof	500	Value: 205				
2008Mo	9,000	—			—	205
2008Mo Proof	900	Value: 270				
2009Mo	21,000	—			—	225
2009Mo Proof	5,000	Value: 270				

KM# 677   KILO (32.15 Troy Ounces of Silver)
999.9775 g., 0.9990 Silver 32.116 oz. ASW, 110 mm. **Subject:** Collector Bullion **Obv:** National arms in center of past and present arms **Rev:** Winged Victory **Edge:** Reeded **Mint:** Mexico City

Date	Mintage	F	VF	XF	Unc	BU
2001Mo Prooflike	—	—	—	—	—	2,200
2002Mo Prooflike	1,820	—	—	—	—	1,750
2003Mo Prooflike	1,514	—	—	—	—	1,650
2004Mo Prooflike	1,501	—	—	—	—	1,800
2005Mo Prooflike	500	—	—	—	—	1,750
2006Mo Prooflike	874	—	—	—	—	1,650
2007Mo Prooflike	700	—	—	—	—	1,650
2008Mo	2,003	—	—	—	—	1,400
2008Mo Prooflike	1,700	—	—	—	—	1,650
2009Mo	4,000	—	—	—	—	
2009Mo Prooflike	1,700	—	—	—	—	1,650

GOLD BULLION COINAGE

KM# 530   1/20 ONZA (1/20 Ounce of Pure Gold)
1.7500 g., 0.9000 Gold 0.0506 oz. AGW **Obv:** Winged Victory **Rev:** Calendar stone **Mint:** Mexico City

Date	Mintage	F	VF	XF	Unc	BU
1987Mo	—	—	—	—	—	275
1988Mo	—	—	—	—	—	

KM# 589   1/20 ONZA (1/20 Ounce of Pure Gold)
1.5551 g., 0.9990 Gold 0.0499 oz. AGW, 13 mm. **Obv:** Winged Victory **Rev:** National arms, eagle left **Mint:** Mexico City

Date	Mintage	F	VF	XF	Unc	BU
1991Mo	10,000	—	—	—	—	BV+30%
1992Mo	65,225	—	—	—	—	BV+30%

Note: According to Mexican mint records combined mintages of 1991 and 1992 BU and proof coins are 73,858.

Date	Mintage	F	VF	XF	Unc	BU
1993Mo	10,000	—	—	—	—	BV+30%
1994Mo	10,000	—	—	—	—	BV+30%

KM# 642   1/20 ONZA (1/20 Ounce of Pure Gold)
1.5551 g., 0.9990 Gold 0.0499 oz. AGW **Obv:** National arms, eagle left **Rev:** Native working **Mint:** Mexico City

Date	Mintage	F	VF	XF	Unc	BU
2000Mo Proof	—	Value: 95.00				

KM# 671   1/20 ONZA (1/20 Ounce of Pure Gold)
1.5551 g., 0.9990 Gold 0.0499 oz. AGW, 13 mm. **Obv:** National arms, eagle left **Rev:** Winged Victory **Edge:** Reeded **Mint:** Mexico City **Note:** Design similar to KM#609. Value estimates do not include the high taxes and surcharges added to the issue prices by the Mexican Government.

Date	Mintage	F	VF	XF	Unc	BU
2000Mo	5,300	—	—	—	—	BV+30%
2002Mo	5,000	—	—	—	—	BV+30%
2003Mo	800	—	—	—	—	BV+32%

BULLION LIBERTAD

Date	Mintage	F	VF	XF	Unc	BU
2004Mo	4,000	—	—	—	—BV+30%	
2005Mo	3,200	—	—	—	—BV+30%	
2005Mo Proof	400	BV+35%				
2006Mo	3,000	—	—	—	—BV+30%	
2006Mo Proof	520	BV+35%				
2007Mo	1,200	—	—	—	—BV+30%	
2007Mo Proof	500	BV+35%				
2008Mo	800	—	—	—	—BV+30%	
2008Mo Proof	500	BV+35%				
2009Mo	2,000	—	—	—	—BV+30%	
2009Mo Proof	600	BV+35%				

KM# 628 1/15 ONZA (1/15 Ounce of Pure Gold)
0.9990 Gold **Obv:** Winged Victory above legend **Rev:** National arms, eagle left within circle **Mint:** Mexico City

Date	Mintage	F	VF	XF	Unc	BU
1987Mo	—	—	—	—	—	275

KM# 541 1/10 ONZA (1/10 Ounce of Pure Gold)
3.1103 g., 0.9990 Gold 0.0999 oz. AGW, 16 mm. **Obv:** National arms, eagle left **Rev:** Winged Victory **Mint:** Mexico City

Date	Mintage	F	VF	XF	Unc	BU
1991Mo	10,000	—	—	—	—BV+20%	
1992Mo	50,777	—	—	—	—BV+20%	
1993Mo	10,000	—	—	—	—BV+20%	
1994Mo	10,000	—	—	—	—BV+20%	

Note: According to Mexican mint records combined mintages of 1991 and 1992 coins are 60,592.

KM# 672 1/10 ONZA (1/10 Ounce of Pure Gold)
3.1103 g., 0.9990 Gold 0.0999 oz. AGW, 16 mm. **Obv:** National arms, eagle left **Rev:** Winged Victory **Edge:** Reeded **Mint:** Mexico City **Note:** Design similar to KM#610. Value estimates do not include the high taxes and surcharges added to the issue prices by the Mexican Government.

Date	Mintage	F	VF	XF	Unc	BU
2000Mo	3,500	—	—	—	— BV+20%	
2002Mo	5,000	—	—	—	— BV+20%	
2003Mo	300	—	—	—	— BV+22%	
2004Mo	2,000	—	—	—	— BV+20%	
2005Mo	500	—	—	—	— BV+20%	
2005Mo Proof	400	BV+22%				
2006Mo	2,500	—	—	—	— BV+20%	
2006Mo Proof	520	BV+22%				
2007Mo	1,200	—	—	—	— BV+20%	
2007Mo Proof	500	BV+22%				
2008Mo	2,500	—	—	—	— BV+20%	
2008Mo Proof	500	BV+22%				
2009Mo	9,000	—	—	—	— BV+20%	
2009Mo Proof	600	BV+22%				

KM# 487 1/4 ONZA (1/4 Ounce of Pure Gold)
8.6396 g., 0.9000 Gold 0.2500 oz. AGW. **Obv:** National arms, eagle left **Rev:** Winged Victory **Mint:** Mexico City **Note:** Similar to KM#488.

Date	Mintage	F	VF	XF	Unc	BU
1981Mo	313,000	—	—	—	— BV+11%	
1982Mo		—	—	—	— BV+11%	

KM# 590 1/4 ONZA (1/4 Ounce of Pure Gold)
7.7758 g., 0.9990 Gold 0.2497 oz. AGW, 23 mm. **Obv:** Winged Victory above legend **Rev:** National arms, eagle left **Mint:** Mexico City

Date	Mintage	F	VF	XF	Unc	BU
1991Mo	10,000	—	—	—	—BV+11%	
1992Mo	28,106	—	—	—	—BV+11%	
1993Mo	2,500	—	—	—	—BV+11%	
1994Mo	2,500	—	—	—	—BV+11%	

Note: According to Mexican mint records, combined mintages of 1991 and 1992 are 37,321.

KM# 673 1/4 ONZA (1/4 Ounce of Pure Gold)
7.7758 g., 0.9990 Gold 0.2497 oz. AGW, 23 mm. **Obv:** National arms, eagle left **Rev:** Winged Victory **Edge:** Reeded **Mint:** Mexico City **Note:** Design similar to KM#611. Value estimates do not include the high taxes and surcharges added to the issue prices by the Mexican Government.

Date	Mintage	F	VF	XF	Unc	BU
2000Mo	2,500	—	—	—	—BV+12%	
2002Mo	5,000	—	—	—	—BV+12%	
2003Mo	300	—	—	—	—BV+14%	
2004Mo	1,500	—	—	—	—BV+12%	
2004Mo Proof	1,000	BV+15%				
2005Mo	500	—	—	—	—BV+14%	
2005Mo Proof	2,600	BV+15%				
2006Mo	1,500	—	—	—	—BV+12%	
2006Mo Proof	2,120	BV+15%				
2007Mo	500	—	—	—	—BV+14%	
2007Mo Proof	1,500	BV+15%				
2008Mo	800	—	—	—	—BV+14%	
2008Mo Proof	800	BV+15%				
2009Mo	3,000	—	—	—	—BV+12%	
2009Mo Proof	1,700	BV+15%				

KM# 488 1/2 ONZA (1/2 Ounce of Pure Gold)
17.2792 g., 0.9000 Gold 0.5000 oz. AGW **Obv:** National arms, eagle left **Rev:** Winged Victory **Mint:** Mexico City

Date	Mintage	F	VF	XF	Unc	BU
1981Mo	193,000	—	—	—	— BV+8%	
1982Mo		—	—	—	— BV+8%	
1989Mo Proof	704	Value: 850				

KM# 591 1/2 ONZA (1/2 Ounce of Pure Gold)
15.5517 g., 0.9990 Gold 0.4995 oz. AGW, 29 mm. **Obv:** Winged Victory above legend **Rev:** National arms, eagle left **Mint:** Mexico City

Date	Mintage	F	VF	XF	Unc	BU
1991Mo	10,000	—	—	—	— BV+8%	
1992Mo	25,220	—	—	—	— BV+8%	
1993Mo	2,500	—	—	—	— BV+8%	
1994Mo	2,500	—	—	—	— BV+8%	

Note: According to Mexican mint records, combined mintages of 1981-1992 BU and proof coins are 35,047.

KM# 674 1/2 ONZA (1/2 Ounce of Pure Gold)
15.5517 g., 0.9990 Gold 0.4995 oz. AGW, 29 mm. **Obv:** National arms, eagle left **Rev:** Winged Victory **Edge:** Reeded **Mint:** Mexico City **Note:** Design similar to KM#612. Value estimates do not include the high taxes and surcharges added to the issue prices by the Mexican Government.

Date	Mintage	F	VF	XF	Unc	BU
2000Mo	1,500	—	—	—	— BV+8%	
2002Mo	5,000	—	—	—	— BV+8%	

BULLION LIBERTAD

Date	Mintage	F	VF	XF	Unc	BU
2003Mo	300	—	—	—		—BV+10%
2004Mo	500	—	—	—		—BV+8%
2005Mo	500	—	—	—		—BV+10%
2005Mo Proof	400	BV+12%				
2006Mo	500	—	—	—		—BV+10%
2006Mo Proof	520	BV+12%				
2007Mo	500	—	—	—		—BV+10%
2007Mo Proof	500	BV+12%				
2008Mo	300	—	—	—		—BV+10%
2008Mo Proof	500	BV+12%				
2009Mo	3,000	—	—	—		—BV+8%
2009Mo Proof	600	BV+12%				

KM# 489 ONZA (Ounce of Pure Gold)
34.5585 g., 0.9000 Gold 0.9999 oz. AGW **Obv:** National arms, eagle left **Rev:** Winged Victory **Mint:** Mexico City **Note:** Similar to KM#488.

Date	Mintage	F	VF	XF	Unc	BU
1981Mo	596,000	—	—	—		—BV+3%
1985Mo		—	—	—		—BV+3%
1988Mo		—	—	—		—BV+3%

KM# 592 ONZA (Ounce of Pure Gold)
31.1035 g., 0.9990 Gold 0.9990 oz. AGW, 34.5 mm. **Obv:** Winged Victory above legend **Rev:** National arms, eagle left **Mint:** Mexico City

Date	Mintage	F	VF	XF	Unc	BU
1991Mo	109,193	—	—	—		—BV+3%
1992Mo	46,281	—	—	—		—BV+3%
1993Mo	73,881	—	—	—		—BV+3%
1994Mo	1,000	—	—	—		—BV+5%

Note: According to Mexican mint redords, combined mint-ages of 1981-1992 BU and proof coins are 90,384.

KM# 675 ONZA (Ounce of Pure Gold)
31.1035 g., 0.9990 Gold 0.9990 oz. AGW, 34.5 mm. **Obv:** National arms, eagle left **Rev:** Winged Victory **Edge:** Reeded **Mint:** Mexico City **Note:** Design similar to KM#639. Value estimates do not include the high taxes and surcharges added to the issue prices by the Mexican Government.

Date	Mintage	F	VF	XF	Unc	BU
2000Mo	2,370	—	—	—		—BV+3%
2002Mo	15,000	—	—	—		—BV+3%
2003Mo	500	—	—	—		—BV+4%
2004Mo	3,000	—	—	—		—BV+3%
2005Mo	3,000	—	—	—		—BV+3%
2005Mo Proof	250	BV+5%				
2006Mo	4,000	—	—	—		—BV+3%
2006Mo Proof	520	BV+5%				
2007Mo	2,500	—	—	—		—BV+3%
2007Mo Proof	500	BV+5%				
2008Mo	800	—	—	—		—BV+3%
2008Mo Proof	500	BV+5%				
2009Mo	6,200	—	—	—		—BV+3%
2009Mo Proof	600	BV+5%				

PLATINUM BULLION COINAGE

KM# 538 1/4 ONZA (1/4 Ounce)
7.7775 g., 0.9990 Platinum 0.2498 oz. APW **Obv:** National arms, eagle left **Rev:** Winged Victory **Mint:** Mexico City

Date	Mintage	F	VF	XF	Unc	BU
1989Mo Proof	3,500	Value: 550				

BULLION LIBERTAD

BULLION COINAGE AZTEC SERIES

KM# 644 NUEVO PESO
7.7700 g., 0.9990 Silver 0.2496 oz. ASW, 26.8 mm. **Subject:** Eagle Warrior **Obv:** National arms, eagle left within D-shaped circle and dotted border **Rev:** Eagle warrior within D-shaped circle and dotted border **Edge:** Reeded **Mint:** Mexico City

Date	Mintage	F	VF	XF	Unc	BU
1993Mo	1,500	—	—	—	—	18.00
1993 Proof	900	Value: 30.00				

KM# 645 2 NUEVO PESOS
15.4200 g., 0.9990 Silver 0.4952 oz. ASW, 32.9 mm. **Subject:** Eagle Warrior **Obv:** National arms, eagle left **Rev:** Eagle warrior **Edge:** Reeded **Mint:** Mexico City

Date	Mintage	F	VF	XF	Unc	BU
1993Mo	1,500	—	—	—	—	20.00
1993 Proof	800	Value: 40.00				

KM# 646 5 NUEVO PESOS
31.0500 g., 0.9990 Silver 0.9972 oz. ASW, 40 mm. **Subject:** Eagle Warrior **Obv:** National arms, eagle left **Rev:** Eagle warrior **Edge:** Reeded **Mint:** Mexico City

Date	Mintage	F	VF	XF	Unc	BU
1993	2,000	—	—	—	—	35.00
1993 Proof	1,000	Value: 70.00				

KM# 647 5 NUEVO PESOS
31.0000 g., 0.9990 Silver 0.9956 oz. ASW, 40 mm. **Subject:** Xochipilli **Obv:** National arms, eagle left within D-shaped circle and flower blossom border **Rev:** Seated figure sculpture within D-shaped circle and flower blossom border **Edge:** Reeded **Mint:** Mexico City

Date	Mintage	F	VF	XF	Unc	BU
1993	2,000	—	—	—	—	35.00
1993 Proof	800	Value: 75.00				

KM# 649 5 NUEVO PESOS
31.0000 g., 0.9990 Silver 0.9956 oz. ASW, 40 mm. **Subject:** Huchucteotl **Obv:** National arms, eagle left within D-shaped circle and designed border **Rev:** Aztec sculpture within D-shaped circle and designed border **Edge:** Reeded

Date	Mintage	F	VF	XF	Unc	BU
1993	5,000	—	—	—	—	35.00
1993 Proof	800	Value: 75.00				

KM# 648 5 NUEVO PESOS
31.0000 g., 0.9990 Silver 0.9956 oz. ASW, 40 mm. **Subject:** Brasco Efigie **Obv:** National arms, eagle left within D-shaped circle and designed border **Rev:** Sculpture within D-shaped circle and designed border **Edge:** Reeded

Date	Mintage	F	VF	XF	Unc	BU
1993	2,000	—	—	—	—	50.00
1993 Proof	500	Value: 75.00				

KM# 650 10 NUEVO PESOS
155.3100 g., 0.9990 Silver 4.9881 oz. ASW, 65 mm. **Subject:** Piedra de Tizoc **Obv:** National arms, eagle left **Rev:** Warrior capturing woman **Edge:** Reeded

Mint: Mexico City **Note:** Illustration reduced, similar to 100 Pesos, KM# 557

Date	Mintage	F	VF	XF	Unc	BU
1992 Proof	—	Value: 300				
1993	1,000	—	—	—	—	175
1993 Proof	1,000	Value: 200				

KM# 554 25 PESOS
7.7758 g., 0.9990 Silver 0.2497 oz. ASW **Obv:**
National arms, eagle left within D-shaped circle and designed border **Rev:** Eagle warrior right within D-shaped circle and a designed border **Mint:** Mexico City

Date	Mintage	F	VF	XF	Unc	BU
1992	50,000	—	—	—	18.00	—
1992 Proof	3,000	Value: 30.00				

Note: Combined mintages of KM#554 and 644 through 2011 is 54,505 Unc. and 2,700 Proof.

KM# 555 50 PESOS
15.5517 g., 0.9990 Silver 0.4995 oz. ASW **Obv:**
National arms, eagle left within D-shaped circle designed border **Rev:** Eagle warrior right within D-shaped circle and designed border **Mint:** Mexico City

Date	Mintage	F	VF	XF	Unc	BU
1992	50,000	—	—	—	25.00	—
1992 Proof	3,000	Value: 40.00				

Note: Combined mintages for KM#555 and #645 through 2011 is 52,000 Unc. and 4,300 Proof.

KM# 556 100 PESOS
31.1035 g., 0.9990 Silver 0.9990 oz. ASW **Obv:**
National arms, eagle left **Rev:** Eagle warrior **Mint:**
Mexico City

Date	Mintage	F	VF	XF	Unc	BU
1992	205,000	—	—	—	37.50	47.50

Date	Mintage	F	VF	XF	Unc	BU
1992	4,000	Value: 75.00				

Note: Combined mintages of KM#556 and #646 through 2011 is 208,300 Unc and 6,800 Proof.

KM# 562 100 PESOS
31.1035 g., 0.9990 Silver 0.9990 oz. ASW **Obv:**
National arms, eagle left within D-shaped circle and designed border **Rev:** Seated figure sculpture within D-shaped circle and designed border **Mint:** Mexico City

Date	Mintage	F	VF	XF	Unc	BU
1992Mo Proof	4,000	Value: 90.00				

Note: KM#562 and #647 thru 2011 have a combined mintage of 3,311 Unc and 6,200 Proof.

KM# 563 100 PESOS
31.1035 g., 0.9990 Silver 0.9990 oz. ASW **Obv:**
National arms, eagle left within D-shaped circle and designed border **Rev:** Brasero Efigie - The God of Rain within D-shaped circle and designed border **Mint:** Mexico City

Date	Mintage	F	VF	XF	Unc	BU
1992Mo Proof	4,000	Value: 75.00				

Note: KM#563 and #648 have a combined mintage thru 2011 of 4,180 Unc. and 6,300 Proof.

KM# 564 100 PESOS
31.1035 g., 0.9990 Silver 0.9990 oz. ASW **Obv:**

BULLION PRE-COLUMBIAN

National arms, eagle left within D-shaped circle and designed border **Rev:** Huehueteotl - The God of Fire within D-shaped circle and designed border **Mint:** Mexico City

Date	Mintage	F	VF	XF	Unc	BU
1992Mo Proof	4,000	Value: 70.00				

Note: KM#564 and #649 have a combined mintage thru 2011 of 6,005 Unc. and 6,200 Proofs.

KM# 558   250 PESOS
7.7758 g., 0.9990 Gold 0.2497 oz. AGW **Subject:** Native Culture **Obv:** National arms, eagle left within D-shaped circle and designed border **Rev:** Sculpture of Jaguar head within D-shaped circle and designed border **Mint:** Mexico City

Date	Mintage	F	VF	XF	Unc	BU
1992Mo	12,000	—	—	—	—	475
1992Mo Proof	2,000	Value: 450				

KM# 559   500 PESOS
15.5517 g., 0.9990 Gold 0.4995 oz. AGW **Subject:** Native Culture **Obv:** National arms, eagle left within D-shaped circle and designed border **Rev:** Sculpture of Jaguar head within D-shaped circle and designed border **Mint:** Mexico City

Date	Mintage	F	VF	XF	Unc	BU
1992Mo	12,000	—	—	—	—	900
1992Mo Proof	2,000	Value: 925				

KM# 560   1000 PESOS
31.1035 g., 0.9990 Gold 0.9990 oz. AGW **Subject:** Native Culture **Obv:** National arms, eagle left within D-shaped circle and designed border **Rev:** Sculpture of Jaguar head within D-shaped circle and designed border **Mint:** Mexico City

Date	Mintage	F	VF	XF	Unc	BU
1992Mo	19,850	—	—	—	—	1,750
1992Mo Proof	2,000	Value: 1,800				

KM# 557   10000 PESOS
155.5175 g., 0.9990 Silver 4.9948 oz. ASW, 64 mm. **Subject:** Pieora De Tizoc **Obv:** National arms, eagle left within D-shaped circle and designed border **Rev:** Native warriors within D-shaped circle and designed border **Mint:** Mexico City **Note:** Similar to 10 Nuevo Pesos, KM#650

Date	Mintage	F	VF	XF	Unc	BU
1992Mo	51,900	—	—	—	—	175
1992Mo Proof	3,300	Value: 275				

Note: KM#557 and #650 have a combined mintage thru 2011 of 54,305 Unc. and 5,400 Proof.

CENTRAL VERACRUZ SERIES

KM# 567   NUEVO PESO
7.7601 g., 0.9990 Silver 0.2492 oz. ASW, 27 mm. **Subject:** Bajo relieve de el Tajin **Obv:** National arms, eagle left within D-shaped circle and designed border **Rev:** Design within D-shaped circle and designed border **Mint:** Mexico City

Date	Mintage	F	VF	XF	Unc	BU
1993Mo	100,005	—	—	—	—	20.00
1993Mo Proof	4,005	Value: 35.00				

KM# 568   2 NUEVO PESOS
15.5516 g., 0.9990 Silver 0.4995 oz. ASW, 33 mm. **Subject:** Bajo relieve de el Tajin **Obv:** National arms, eagle left within D-shaped circle and designed border **Rev:** Design within D-shaped circle and designed border **Mint:** Mexico City

Date	Mintage	F	VF	XF	Unc	BU
1993Mo	100,005	—	—	—	—	25.00
1993Mo Proof	3,005	Value: 35.00				

KM# 569   5 NUEVO PESOS
31.1035 g., 0.9990 Silver 0.9990 oz. ASW, 40 mm. **Subject:** Bajo relieve de el Tajin **Obv:** National arms, eagle left within D-shaped circle and designed border **Rev:** Design within D-shaped circle and designed border **Mint:** Mexico City

BULLION PRE-COLUMBIAN

Date	Mintage	F	VF	XF	Unc	BU
1993Mo	100,005	—	—	—	—	37.50
1993Mo Proof	3,905	Value: 70.00				

KM# 582 5 NUEVO PESOS
31.1035 g., 0.9990 Silver 0.9990 oz. ASW, 40 mm.
Subject: Palma Con Cocodrilo **Obv:** National arms, eagle left within D-shaped circle and designed border **Rev:** Aerial view of crocodile within D-shaped circle and designed border **Mint:** Mexico City

Date	Mintage	F	VF	XF	Unc	BU
1993Mo	4,605	—	—	—	—	37.50
1993Mo Proof	3,555	Value: 75.00				

KM# 583 5 NUEVO PESOS
31.1035 g., 0.9990 Silver 0.9990 oz. ASW, 40 mm.
Subject: Anciano Con Brasero **Obv:** National arms, eagle left within D-shaped circle and designed border **Rev:** Kneeling figure sculpture within D-shaped circle and designed border **Mint:** Mexico City

Date	Mintage	F	VF	XF	Unc	BU
1993Mo	3,200	—	—	—	—	37.50
1993Mo Proof	3,660	Value: 75.00				

KM# 584 5 NUEVO PESOS
31.1035 g., 0.9990 Silver 0.9990 oz. ASW, 40 mm.
Subject: Carita Sonriente **Obv:** National arms, eagle left **Rev:** Sculptured head **Mint:** Mexico City

Date	Mintage	F	VF	XF	Unc	BU
1993Mo	4,605	—	—	—	—	37.50
1993Mo Proof	4,205	Value: 75.00				

KM# 570 10 NUEVO PESOS
155.5175 g., 0.9990 Silver 4.9948 oz. ASW, 65 mm.
Subject: Piramide Del El Tajin **Obv:** National arms, eagle left within flat shaped circle and designed border **Rev:** Pyramid within flat shaped circle and designed border **Note:** Illustration reduced.

Date	Mintage	F	VF	XF	Unc	BU
1993Mo	50,405	—	—	—	—	175
1993Mo Proof	3,948	Value: 190				

KM# 585 25 NUEVO PESOS
7.7758 g., 0.9990 Gold 0.2497 oz. AGW **Subject:** Hacha Ceremonial **Obv:** National arms, eagle left **Rev:** Mask left **Note:** Similar to 100 New Pesos, KM#587.

Date	Mintage	F	VF	XF	Unc	BU
1993Mo	15,508	—	—	—	—	475
1993Mo Proof	802	Value: 500				

KM# 586 50 NUEVO PESOS
15.5517 g., 0.9990 Gold 0.4995 oz. AGW **Subject:** Hacha Ceremonial **Obv:** National arms, eagle left **Rev:** Mask left **Note:** Similar to 100 New Pesos, KM#587.

Date	Mintage	F	VF	XF	Unc	BU
1993Mo	15,508	—	—	—	—	900
1993Mo Proof	802	Value: 925				

KM# 587 100 NUEVO PESOS
31.1035 g., 0.9990 Gold 0.9990 oz. AGW **Subject:** Hacha Ceremonial **Obv:** National arms, eagle left **Rev:** Mask left

Date	Mintage	F	VF	XF	Unc	BU
1993Mo	7,160	—	—	—	—	1,800
1993Mo Proof	500	Value: 1,850				

MAYAN SERIES

KM# 572 NUEVO PESO
7.7601 g., 0.9990 Silver 0.2492 oz. ASW **Subject:** Chaac Mool **Obv:** National arms, eagle left within six sided shield and designed border **Rev:** Reclining figure within six sided shield and designed border **Mint:** Mexico City

Date	Mintage	F	VF	XF	Unc	BU
1994 Matte	30,000	—	—	—	—	20.00
1994 Proof	2,500	Value: 35.00				

KM# 573 2 NUEVO PESOS
15.5516 g., 0.9990 Silver 0.4995 oz. ASW **Subject:** Chaac Mool **Obv:** National arms, eagle left within six sided shield and designed border **Rev:** Reclining figure within six sided shield and designed border **Mint:** Mexico City

Date	Mintage	F	VF	XF	Unc	BU
1994Mo Matte	30,000	—	—	—	—	25.00
1994Mo Proof	2,500	Value: 35.00				

KM# 574 5 NUEVO PESOS
31.1035 g., 0.9990 Silver 0.9990 oz. ASW **Subject:** Chaac Mool **Obv:** National arms, eagle left within six sided shield and designed border **Rev:** Reclining figure within six sided shield and designed border **Mint:** Mexico City

Date	Mintage	F	VF	XF	Unc	BU
1994Mo Matte	50,000	—	—	—	—	37.00
1994Mo Proof	3,000	Value: 70.00				

KM# 575 5 NUEVO PESOS
31.1035 g., 0.9990 Silver 0.9990 oz. ASW **Subject:** Chaac Mool **Obv:** National arms, eagle left within six sided shield and designed border **Rev:** Tomb of Palenque Memorial Stone within six sided shield and designed border **Mint:** Mexico City

Date	Mintage	F	VF	XF	Unc	BU
1994Mo	4,500	—	—	—	—	37.00
1994Mo Proof	2,800	Value: 70.00				

KM# 577 5 NUEVO PESOS
31.1035 g., 0.9990 Silver 0.9990 oz. ASW **Subject:** Mascaron Del Dios Chaac **Rev:** Elaborately carved wall segment **Mint:** Mexico City

Date	Mintage	F	VF	XF	Unc	BU
1994Mo	4,500	—	—	—	—	37.00
1994Mo Proof	2,500	Value: 70.00				

KM# 578 5 NUEVO PESOS
31.1035 g., 0.9990 Silver 0.9990 oz. ASW **Subject:** Dintel 26 **Obv:** National arms, eagle left within six sided shield and designed border **Rev:** Two seated figures wall carving within six sided shield and designed border

Date	Mintage	F	VF	XF	Unc	BU
1994Mo	4,500	—	—	—	—	45.00
1994Mo Proof	2,600	Value: 75.00				

KM# 676 10 NUEVO PESOS
155.5175 g., 0.9990 Silver 4.9948 oz. ASW, 65 mm.
Subject: Piramide Del Castillo **Obv:** National arms, eagle left above metal content statement **Rev:** Pyramid above two-line inscription **Rev. Inscription:** PIRAMIDE DEL CASTILLO / CHICHEN-ITZA **Edge:** Reeded **Mint:** Mexico City

Date	Mintage	F	VF	XF	Unc	BU
1993Mo Proof	—	Value: 650				

KM# 576 10 NUEVO PESOS
155.7000 g., 0.9990 Silver 5.0007 oz. ASW, 64 mm.
Subject: Piramide del Castillo **Obv:** National arms, eagle left **Rev:** Pyramid **Note:** Illustration reduced.

Date	Mintage	F	VF	XF	Unc	BU
1994Mo	20,000	—	—	—	—	175
1994Mo Proof	2,100	Value: 225				

BULLION PRE-COLUMBIAN

KM# 579   25 NUEVO PESOS
7.7758 g., 0.9990 Gold 0.2497 oz. AGW **Subject:** Personaje de Jaina **Rev:** Seated figure

Date	Mintage	F	VF	XF	Unc	BU
1994Mo	2,000	—	—	—	—	475
1994Mo Proof	501	Value: 500				

KM# 580   50 NUEVO PESOS
15.5517 g., 0.9990 Gold 0.4995 oz. AGW **Subject:** Personaje de Jaina **Rev:** Seated figure

Date	Mintage	F	VF	XF	Unc	BU
1994Mo	1,000	—	—	—	—	900
1994Mo Proof	501	Value: 925				

KM# 581   100 NUEVO PESOS
31.1035 g., 0.9990 Gold 0.9990 oz. AGW **Subject:** Personaje de Jaina **Obv:** National arms, eagle left within six sided shield and designed border **Rev:** Seated figure within six sided shield and designed border

Date	Mintage	F	VF	XF	Unc	BU
1994Mo	1,000	—	—	—	—	1,800
1994Mo Proof	501	Value: 1,850				

OLMEC SERIES

KM# 593   PESO
7.7750 g., 0.9990 Silver 0.2497 oz. ASW **Subject:** Senor De Las Limas **Obv:** National arms, eagle left within square and designed border **Rev:** Sitting figure facing within square and designed border **Mint:** Mexico City **Note:** Similar to 5 Pesos, KM#595.

Date	Mintage	F	VF	XF	Unc	BU
1996Mo	6,400	—	—	—	—	20.00
1996Mo Proof	3,700	Value: 35.00				
1998Mo Matte	2,400	—	—	—	—	22.00

$2

KM# 594   2 PESOS
15.5517 g., 0.9990 Silver 0.4995 oz. ASW **Subject:** Senor De Las Limas **Obv:** National arms, eagle left within square and designed border **Rev:** Sitting figure facing within square and designed border **Mint:** Mexico City **Note:** Similar to 5 Pesos, KM#595.

Date	Mintage	F	VF	XF	Unc	BU
1996Mo	6,400	—	—	—	—	25.00
1996Mo Proof	2,200	Value: 35.00				
1998Mo Matte	2,400	—	—	—	—	28.00

$5

KM# 596   5 PESOS
31.1035 g., 0.9990 Silver 0.9990 oz. ASW **Subject:** Hombre Jaguar **Obv:** National arms, eagle left within square and designed border **Rev:** Statue facing within square and designed border

Date	Mintage	F	VF	XF	Unc	BU
1996Mo	5,300	—	—	—	—	90.00
1996Mo Proof	4,000	Value: 70.00				
1998Mo Matte	6,000	—	—	—	—	37.50
1998Mo Proof	4,800	Value: 75.00				

$5

KM# 595   5 PESOS
31.1035 g., 0.9990 Silver 0.9990 oz. ASW **Subject:** Senor De Las Limas **Obv:** National arms, eagle left within square and designed border **Rev:** Seated figure facing within square and designed border

Date	Mintage	F	VF	XF	Unc	BU
1996Mo	8,700	—	—	—	—	37.50
1996Mo Proof	3,800	Value: 70.00				
1998 Matte	3,400	—	—	—	—	40.00

KM# 597   5 PESOS
31.1035 g., 0.9990 Silver 0.9990 oz. ASW **Subject:** El Luchador **Obv:** National arms, eagle left **Rev:** El Luchador

Date	Mintage	F	VF	XF	Unc	BU
1996Mo	6,600	—	—	—	—	37.50
1996Mo Proof	3,600	Value: 70.00				
1998 Matte	2,000	—	—	—	—	40.00

$5

KM# 598   5 PESOS
31.1035 g., 0.9990 Silver 0.9990 oz. ASW **Subject:** Hacha Ceremonial **Obv:** National arms, eagle left within square and designed border **Rev:** Statue within square and designed border

Date	Mintage	F	VF	XF	Unc	BU
1996Mo	7,000	—	—	—	—	37.50
1996Mo Proof	3,500	Value: 70.00				
1998 Matte	2,000	—	—	—	—	40.00

BULLION PRE-COLUMBIAN

KM# 599   10 PESOS
155.5175 g., 0.9990 Silver 4.9948 oz. ASW, 64 mm.
Subject: Cabeza Olmeca **Obv:** National arms, eagle
left **Rev:** Native mask **Note:** Illustration reduced.

Date	Mintage	F	VF	XF	Unc	BU
1996Mo	5,060	—	—	—	—	180
1996Mo Proof	3,550	Value: 190				
1998 Matte	2,150	—	—	—	—	180

KM# 600   25 PESOS
7.7758 g., 0.9990 Gold 0.2497 oz. AGW **Subject:**
Sacerdote **Obv:** National arms, eagle left **Rev:**
Sculpture **Note:** Similar to 100 Pesos, KM#602.

Date	Mintage	F	VF	XF	Unc	BU
1996Mo	500	—	—	—	—	475
1996Mo Proof	750	Value: 500				

KM# 601   50 PESOS
15.5517 g., 0.9990 Gold 0.4995 oz. AGW **Subject:**
Sacerdote **Obv:** National arms, eagle left **Rev:**
Sculpture **Note:** Similar to 100 Pesos, KM#602.

Date	Mintage	F	VF	XF	Unc	BU
1996Mo	500	—	—	—	—	900
1996Mo Proof	500	Value: 925				

KM# 602   100 PESOS
31.1035 g., 0.9990 Gold 0.9990 oz. AGW **Subject:**
Sacerdote **Obv:** National arms, eagle left within
square and designed border **Rev:** Sculpture within
square and designed border

Date	Mintage	F	VF	XF	Unc	BU
1996Mo	500	—	—	—	—	1,800
1996Mo Proof	500	Value: 1,850				

TEOTIHUACAN SERIES

KM# 617   PESO
7.7759 g., 0.9990 Silver 0.2497 oz. ASW **Subject:**
Disco De La Muerte **Obv:** National arms, eagle left
within oblong circle and designed border **Rev:**
Sculpture within oblong circle and designed border
Mint: Mexico City

Date	Mintage	F	VF	XF	Unc	BU
1997Mo	3,000	—	—	—	—	20.00
1997Mo Proof	1,600	Value: 35.00				
1998Mo Matte	2,400	—	—	—	—	25.00
1998Mo Proof	500	Value: 45.00				

KM# 618   2 PESOS
15.5517 g., 0.9990 Silver 0.4995 oz. ASW **Subject:**
Disco De La Muerte **Obv:** National arms, eagle left
within oblong circle and designed border **Rev:**
Sculpture within oblong circle and designed border
Mint: Mexico City

Date	Mintage	F	VF	XF	Unc	BU
1997Mo	3,000	—	—	—	—	25.00
1997Mo Proof	1,600	Value: 35.00				
1998Mo	2,400	—	—	—	—	30.00
1998Mo Proof	500	Value: 50.00				

KM# 621   5 PESOS
31.1035 g., 0.9990 Silver 0.9990 oz. ASW **Subject:**
Teotihuacan - Vasija **Obv:** National arms, eagle left
within oval and designed border **Rev:** Seated woman
joined to pottery vase within oval and designed border

Date	Mintage	F	VF	XF	Unc	BU
1997Mo	4,500	—	—	—	—	42.00
1997Mo Proof	Est. 1,800	Value: 75.00				
1998Mo Matte	2,000	—	—	—	—	42.00
1998Mo Proof	500	Value: 150				

BULLION PRE-COLUMBIAN

KM# 622 5 PESOS
31.1035 g., 0.9990 Silver 0.9990 oz. ASW **Subject:** Teotihuacan - Jugador de Pelota **Obv:** National arms, eagle left

Date	Mintage	F	VF	XF	Unc	BU
1997	4,500	—	—	—	—	37.50
1997 Proof	Est. 1,800	Value: 75.00				
1998 Matte	2,000	—	—	—	—	40.00
1998 Proof	500	Value: 150				

KM# 619 5 PESOS
31.1035 g., 0.9990 Silver 0.9990 oz. ASW **Subject:** Teotihuacan - Disco de la Muerte **Obv:** National arms, eagle left within oblong circle and designed border **Rev:** Sculpture within oblong circle and designed border

Date	Mintage	F	VF	XF	Unc	BU
1997Mo	3,500	—	—	—	—	37.50
1997Mo Proof	Est. 1,800	Value: 75.00				
1998Mo	3,400	—	—	—	—	40.00
1998Mo Proof	500	Value: 150				

KM# 620 5 PESOS
31.1035 g., 0.9990 Silver 0.9990 oz. ASW **Subject:** Teotihuacan - Mascara **Obv:** National arms, eagle left within oblong circle and designed border **Rev:** Face sculpture within oblong circle and designed border

Date	Mintage	F	VF	XF	Unc	BU
1997Mo	4,500	—	—	—	—	37.50
1997Mo Proof	Est. 1,800	Value: 75.00				
1998Mo	2,000	—	—	—	—	40.00
1998Mo Proof	500	Value: 150				

KM# 623 10 PESOS
155.5175 g., 0.9990 Silver 4.9948 oz. ASW, 64 mm. **Subject:** Piramide Del Sol **Obv:** National arms, eagle left within oblong circle and designed border **Rev:** Pyramid within oblong circle and designed border **Note:** Illustration reduced.

Date	Mintage	F	VF	XF	Unc	BU
1997Mo	1,500	—	—	—	—	200
1997Mo Proof	2,100	Value: 225				
1998Mo Matte	2,150	—	—	—	—	200

KM# 624 25 PESOS
7.7758 g., 0.9990 Gold 0.2497 oz. AGW **Subject:** Serpiente Emplumada **Obv:** National arms, eagle left **Note:** Similar to 100 Pesos, KM#626.

Date	Mintage	F	VF	XF	Unc	BU
1997Mo	500	—	—	—	—	475
1997Mo Proof	206	Value: 525				

KM# 625 50 PESOS
15.5517 g., 0.9990 Gold 0.4995 oz. AGW **Subject:** Serpiente Emplumada **Obv:** National arms, eagle left **Note:** Similar to 100 Pesos, KM#626.

Date	Mintage	F	VF	XF	Unc	BU
1997Mo	500	—	—	—	—	925
1997Mo Proof	206	Value: 950				

KM# 626 100 PESOS
31.1035 g., 0.9990 Gold 0.9990 oz. AGW **Subject:** Teotihuacan - Serpiente Emplumada **Obv:** National arms, eagle left

Date	Mintage	F	VF	XF	Unc	BU
1997Mo	500	—	—	—	—	1,850
1997Mo Proof	206	Value: 1,900				

TOLTECA SERIES

KM# 661 PESO
7.7759 g., 0.9990 Silver 0.2497 oz. ASW, 27 mm. **Subject:** Jaguar **Obv:** National arms, eagle left **Rev:** Jaguar carving **Edge:** Reeded **Mint:** Mexico City

Date	Mintage	F	VF	XF	Unc	BU
1998Mo	6,400	—	—	—	—	20.00
1998Mo Proof	3,700	Value: 30.00				

KM# 662 2 PESOS
15.5517 g., 0.9990 Silver 0.4995 oz. ASW, 33 mm. **Subject:** Jaguar **Obv:** National arms, eagle left **Rev:** Jaguar carving **Edge:** Reeded **Mint:** Mexico City

Date	Mintage	F	VF	XF	Unc	BU
1998Mo	6,400	—	—	—	—	25.00
1998Mo Proof	2,200	Value: 35.00				

BULLION PRE-COLUMBIAN

Subject: Serpiente con Craneo **Obv:** National arms, eagle left **Rev:** Large sculpture **Edge:** Reeded **Mint:** Mexico City

Date	Mintage	F	VF	XF	Unc	BU
1998Mo	8,700	—	—	—	—	37.50
1998Mo Proof	3,800	Value: 75.00				

KM# 663   5 PESOS
31.1035 g., 0.9990 Silver 0.9990 oz. ASW, 40 mm.
Subject: Jaguar **Obv:** National arms, eagle left within shield and designed border **Rev:** Jaguar carving within shield and designed border **Edge:** Reeded **Mint:** Mexico City

Date	Mintage	F	VF	XF	Unc	BU
1998Mo	5,300	—	—	—	—	37.50
1998Mo Proof	4,000	Value: 75.00				

KM# 665   5 PESOS
31.1035 g., 0.9990 Silver 0.9990 oz. ASW, 40 mm.
Subject: Quetzalcoatl **Obv:** National arms, eagle left **Rev:** Quetzalcoatl sculpture **Edge:** Reeded **Mint:** Mexico City

Date	Mintage	F	VF	XF	Unc	BU
1998Mo	6,600	—	—	—	—	37.50
1998Mo Proof	3,600	Value: 75.00				

KM# 664   5 PESOS
31.1035 g., 0.9990 Silver 0.9990 oz. ASW, 40 mm.
Obv: National arms, eagle left **Rev:** Sacerdote sculpture **Edge:** Reeded **Mint:** Mexico City

Date	Mintage	F	VF	XF	Unc	BU
1998Mo	7,000	—	—	—	—	37.50
1998Mo Proof	3,500	Value: 75.00				

KM# 634   10 PESOS
155.7300 g., 0.9990 Silver 5.0016 oz. ASW
Subject: Atlantes **Obv:** National arms, eagle left within shield and designed border **Rev:** Three carved statues within shield and designed border

Date	Mintage	F	VF	XF	Unc	BU
1998Mo	5,060	—	—	—	—	180
1998Mo Proof	3,550	Value: 200				

KM# 667   25 PESOS
7.7759 g., 0.9990 Gold 0.2497 oz. AGW, 23 mm.
Subject: Aguila **Obv:** National arms, eagle left **Rev:** Eagle sculpture **Edge:** Reeded **Mint:** Mexico City

Date	Mintage	F	VF	XF	Unc	BU
1998Mo	303	—	—	—	—	500
1998Mo Proof	303	Value: 525				

KM# 668   50 PESOS
15.5517 g., 0.9990 Gold 0.4995 oz. AGW, 29 mm.
Subject: Aguila **Obv:** National arms, eagle left **Rev:** Eagle sculpture **Edge:** Reeded **Mint:** Mexico City

Date	Mintage	F	VF	XF	Unc	BU
1998Mo	303	—	—	—	—	925
1998Mo Proof	303	Value: 950				

KM# 666   5 PESOS
31.1035 g., 0.9990 Silver 0.9990 oz. ASW, 40 mm.

BULLION PRE-COLUMBIAN

KM# 669   100 PESOS
31.1035 g., 0.9990 Gold 0.9990 oz. AGW, 34.5 mm.
Subject: Aguila **Obv:** National arms, eagle left within designed shield **Rev:** Eagle sculpture within designed shield **Edge:** Reeded **Mint:** Mexico City

Date	Mintage	F	VF	XF	Unc	BU
1998Mo	303	—	—	—	—	1,850
1998Mo Proof	303	Value: 1,900				

MEDALLIC SILVER BULLION COINAGE

KM# M49a   ONZA
33.6250 g., 0.9250 Silver 0.9999 oz. ASW, 41 mm.
Obv: Mint mark above coin press

Date	Mintage	F	VF	XF	Unc	BU
1949	1,000,000	BV	36.50	40.00	45.00	60.00

KM# M49b.1   ONZA
33.6250 g., 0.9250 Silver 0.9999 oz. ASW, 41 mm.
Obv: Wide spacing between DE MONEDA **Rev:** Mint mark below balance scale **Mint:** Mexico City **Note:** Type I

Date	Mintage	F	VF	XF	Unc	BU
1978Mo	280,000	—	—	BV	37.50	45.00

KM# M49b.2   ONZA
33.6250 g., 0.9250 Silver 0.9999 oz. ASW, 41 mm.
Obv: Close spacing between DE MONEDA **Rev:** Mint mark below balance scale **Mint:** Mexico City **Note:** Type II

Date	Mintage	F	VF	XF	Unc	BU
1978Mo	Inc. above	—	—	BV	38.50	48.00

KM# M49b.3   ONZA
33.6250 g., 0.9250 Silver 0.9999 oz. ASW, 41 mm.
Obv: Close spacing between DE MONEDA **Rev:** Left scale pan points to U in UNA **Mint:** Mexico City **Note:** Type III

Date	Mintage	F	VF	XF	Unc	BU
1979Mo	4,508,000	—	—	BV	37.50	42.00

KM# M49b.4   ONZA
33.6250 g., 0.9250 Silver 0.9999 oz. ASW, 41 mm.
Obv: Close spacing between DE MONEDA **Rev:** Left scale pan points between U and N of UNA **Mint:** Mexico City **Note:** Type IV

Date	Mintage	F	VF	XF	Unc	BU
1979Mo	Inc. above	—	—	BV	37.50	42.00

BULLION PRE-COLUMBIAN

KM# M49b.5 ONZA
33.6250 g., 0.9250 Silver 0.9999 oz. ASW, 41 mm.
Obv: Close spacing between DE MONEDA **Rev:** Left
scale pan points between U and N of UNA **Mint:**
Mexico City **Note:** Type V

Date	Mintage	F	VF	XF	Unc	BU
1980Mo	6,104,000	—	—	BV	37.50	42.00
1980/70Mo	Inc. above	—	—	BV	38.50	46.00

MEDALLIC GOLD COINAGE

KM# M91a 10 PESOS
8.3333 g., 0.9000 Gold 0.2411 oz. AGW **Subject:**
200th Anniversary - Birth of Hidalgo

Date	Mintage	F	VF	XF	Unc	BU
1953	—	—	—	—	BV	450

KM# M123a 10 PESOS
8.3333 g., 0.9000 Gold 0.2411 oz. AGW **Subject:**
Centennial of Constitution

Date	Mintage	F	VF	XF	Unc	BU
1957	Est. 73,000	—	—	—	BV	450

Note: Mintage includes #M122a

KM# M92a 20 PESOS
16.6666 g., 0.9000 Gold 0.4822 oz. AGW **Subject:**
200th Anniversary - Birth of Hidalgo

Date	Mintage	F	VF	XF	Unc	BU
1953	—	—	—	—	BV	850

KM# M122a 50 PESOS
41.6666 g., 0.9000 Gold 1.2056 oz. AGW **Subject:**
Centennial of Constitution

Date	Mintage	F	VF	XF	Unc	BU
1957	—	—	—	—	BV	2,150

Note: Mintage included in total for KM#M123a

REVOLUTIONARY

AGUASCALIENTES

Aguascalientes is a state in central Mexico. Its coin
issues, struck by authority of Pancho Villa, represent his
deepest penetration into the Mexican heartland. Lack of silver made it necessary to make all denominations in copper.

FRANCISCO PANCHO VILLA

REVOLUTIONARY COINAGE

KM# 601 CENTAVO
3.5500 g., Copper, 17 mm. **Obv:** Liberty cap **Rev:**
Value within 3/4 wreath below date **Note:** Large date
weight 3.55g.

Date	Mintage	VG	F	VF	XF	Unc
1915	—	250	350	450	—	—
Note: Large date, plain edge						
1915	—	30.00	60.00	100	300	—
Note: Large date, reeded edge						
1915	—	30.00	60.00	100	300	—
Note: Small date, plain edge						
1915	—	30.00	60.00	80.00	250	—
Note: Small date, reeded edge						

KM# 602.1 2 CENTAVOS
4.2800 g., Copper **Obv:** Liberty cap **Rev:** Value
within 3/4 wreath below date

Date	Mintage	VG	F	VF	XF	Unc
1915	—	40.00	100	300	450	—
Note: Round front 2, plain edge						

MEXICO - REVOLUTIONARY

KM# 602.2 2 CENTAVOS
3.3500 g., Copper, 19 mm. **Obv:** Liberty cap **Rev:**
Value within 1/2 wreath below date

Date	Mintage	VG	F	VF	XF	Unc
1915	—	35.00	60.00	85.00	300	—
Note: Square front 2, reeded edge
1915 Plain edge	—	50.00	90.00	200	500	—
Note: Square front 2

KM# 603 5 CENTAVOS
Copper, 25 mm. **Obv:** National arms **Rev:** Liberty
cap and value above sprigs

Date	Mintage	VG	F	VF	XF
1915 Plain edge; Rare	—	—	—	—	—
1915 Reeded edge	—	10.00	20.00	30.00	75.00

KM# 604.1 5 CENTAVOS
7.1300 g., Copper, 25 mm. **Obv:** National arms
Rev: Vertically shaded 5 within sprigs

Date	Mintage	VG	F	VF	XF	Unc
1915	—	100	150	225	400	—
Note: Plain edge
1915	—	20.00	40.00	50.00	175	—
Note: Reeded edge

KM# 604.2 5 CENTAVOS
Copper, 25 mm. **Obv:** National arms **Rev:**
Horizontally shaded 5 within sprigs

Date	Mintage	VG	F	VF	XF	Unc
1915	—	30.00	50.00	80.00	175	—
Note: Plain edge
1915	—	25.00	40.00	65.00	150	—
Note: Reeded edge

KM# 606 20 CENTAVOS
Copper, 29 mm. **Obv:** National arms **Rev:** Value

below Liberty cap within sprigs

Date	Mintage	VG	F	VF	XF	Unc
1915 Reeded edge	—	10.00	20.00	60.00	100	—

KM# 605 20 CENTAVOS
Copper, 29 mm. **Obv:** National arms **Rev:** Value
below Liberty cap within sprigs

Date	Mintage	VG	F	VF	XF	Unc
1915 Reeded edge	—	10.00	20.00	75.00	100	—

KM# 600 20 CENTAVOS
Copper **Obv:** National arms **Rev:** Value below
Liberty cap within sprigs **Edge:** Reeded

Date	Mintage	VG	F	VF	XF	Unc
1915	—	15.00	20.00	50.00	100	—
Note: Varieties exist with both plain and milled edges and many variations in the shading of the numerals

CHIHUAHUA

Chihuahua is a northern state of Mexico bordering the
U.S. It was the arena that introduced Pancho Villa to the
world. Villa, an outlaw, was given a title when asked by Madero to participate in maintaining order during Madero's pres-
idency. After Madero's death in February 1913, Villa became
a persuasive leader. Chihuahua was where he made his first
coins - the Parral series. The *Army of the North* pesos also
came from this state. This coin helped Villa recruit soldiers
because of his ability to pay in silver while others were paying in worthless paper money.

ARMY OF THE NORTH
Ejercito Del Norte

REVOLUTIONARY COINAGE

KM# 619   PESO
29.2700 g., Silver   **Obv:** National arms **Rev:** Liberty cap

Date	Mintage	VG	F	VF	XF	Unc
1915	—	25.00	40.00	75.00	200	500

KM# 619a   PESO
Copper   **Obv:** National arms **Rev:** Liberty cap

Date	Mintage	VG	F	VF	XF	Unc
1915	—	500	1,000	1,500	2,500	—

KM# 619b   PESO
Brass   **Obv:** National arms **Rev:** Liberty cap **Note:** Uniface obverse

Date	Mintage	VG	F	VF	XF	Unc
1915 Rare	—	—	—	—	—	—

CONSTITUTIONALIST ARMY
Ejercito Constitucionalista

REVOLUTIONARY COINAGE

KM# 612   5 CENTAVOS
Copper   **Obv:** Liberty cap **Rev:** Value above date

Date	Mintage	VG	F	VF	XF	Unc
1914	—	25.00	45.00	100	250	—

KM# 613   5 CENTAVOS
6.6000 g., Copper, 25 mm.   **Obv:** Liberty cap **Rev:** Value above date **Note:** Numerous varieties exist. Weight varies 6.3-6.93g.

Date	Mintage	VG	F	VF	XF	Unc
1914	—	1.00	2.50	4.00	10.00	—
1915	—	1.00	2.50	4.00	10.00	—

KM# 613a   5 CENTAVOS
Brass   **Obv:** Liberty cap **Rev:** Value above date **Note:** Numerous varieties exist.

Date	Mintage	VG	F	VF	XF	Unc
1914	—	2.00	3.00	8.00	10.00	—
1915	—	2.00	3.00	8.00	10.00	—

KM# 613b   5 CENTAVOS
Cast Copper   **Obv:** Liberty cap **Rev:** Value above date

Date	Mintage	VG	F	VF	XF	Unc
1914	—	75.00	200	300	450	—

KM# 614a   5 CENTAVOS
Copper   **Obv:** National arms **Rev:** Value below date within sprigs with solid V

Date	Mintage	VG	F	VF	XF	Unc
1915 Rare	—	—	—	—	—	—

KM# 614b   5 CENTAVOS
Copper   **Obv:** National arms **Rev:** Value above date **Note:** Mule.

Date	Mintage	VG	F	VF	XF	Unc
1915	—	—	500	—	—	—

KM# 614c   5 CENTAVOS
Copper   **Obv:** National arms **Rev:** Liberty cap **Note:** Mule.

Date	Mintage	VG	F	VF	XF	Unc
1915 Rare	—	—	—	—	—	—

KM# 614   5 CENTAVOS
Copper   **Obv:** National arms **Rev:** Value below date within sprigs with double-lined V

Date	Mintage	VG	F	VF	XF	Unc
1915 SS Unique	—	—	—	—	—	—

KM# 615   10 CENTAVOS
8.7900 g., Copper, 27.5 mm.   **Obv:** Liberty cap **Rev:** Value above date

Date	Mintage	VG	F	VF	XF	Unc
1915	—	1.25	2.50	3.50	8.00	20.00

KM# 615a   10 CENTAVOS
8.8900 g., Brass, 27.5 mm.   **Obv:** Liberty cap **Rev:** Value above date

Date	Mintage	VG	F	VF	XF	Unc
1915	—	5.00	10.00	30.00	50.00	—

Note: Many varieties exist

HIDALGO DEL PARRAL
Fuerzas Constitucionalistas

REVOLUTIONARY COINAGE

MEXICO · REVOLUTIONARY

KM# 607   2 CENTAVOS
6.8500 g., Copper, 25 mm. **Obv:** Liberty cap within circle flanked by sprigs **Rev:** Value flanked by sprigs within circle

Date	Mintage	VG	F	VF	XF	Unc
1913	—	5.00	10.00	25.00	50.00	—

KM# 607a   2 CENTAVOS
Brass **Obv:** Liberty cap within circle flanked by sprigs **Rev:** Value flanked by sprigs within circle

Date	Mintage	VG	F	VF	XF	Unc
1913	—	95.00	150	200	400	—

KM# 608   50 CENTAVOS
12.6500 g., Silver **Obv:** Liberty cap **Rev:** Value flanked by sprigs below Liberty cap **Edge:** Reeded

Date	Mintage	VG	F	VF	XF	Unc
1913	—	18.00	40.00	80.00	150	—

KM# 609   50 CENTAVOS
12.1700 g., Silver, 30 mm. **Edge:** Plain

Date	Mintage	VG	F	VF	XF	Unc
1913	—	50.00	70.00	125	250	—

KM# 609a   50 CENTAVOS
Copper **Edge:** Plain

Date	Mintage	VG	F	VF	XF	Unc
1913 rare	—	200	500	800	1,000	—

KM# 610   PESO
30.0000 g., Silver **Obv:** Inscription **Rev:** 1 through PESO and small circle above sprigs **Note:** Weight varies 29.18-30.9g.

Date	Mintage	VG	F	VF	XF	Unc
1913	—	1,200	2,000	3,000	6,500	14,000

KM# 611   PESO
Silver, 38 mm. **Obv:** Inscription **Rev:** Value above sprigs **Note:** Well struck counterfeits of this coin exist with the dot at the end of the word Peso even with the bottom of the O. On legitimate pieces the dot is slightly higher. Weight varies 27.3-28.85g.

Date	Mintage	VG	F	VF	XF	Unc
1913	—	35.00	45.00	125	275	475

DURANGO

A state in north central Mexico. Another area of operation for Pancho Villa. The *Muera Huerta* peso originates in this state. The coins were made in Cuencame under the orders of Generals Cemceros and Contreras.

CUENCAME
Muera Huerta (Death to Huerta)

REVOLUTIONARY COINAGE

KM# 620   PESO
Silver, 38 mm. **Obv:** National arms **Rev:** Liberty cap with written value flanked by stars

Date	Mintage	VG	F	VF	XF	Unc
1914	—	1,000	2,000	4,000	8,000	12,000

MEXICO · REVOLUTIONARY

ESTADO DE DURANGO

KM# 625 CENTAVO
3.2900 g., Copper, 20 mm. **Obv:** Large date in center **Rev:** Value within wreath

Date	Mintage	VG	F	VF	XF	Unc
1914	—	2.00	4.00	10.00	15.00	—

KM# 625a CENTAVO
Brass **Obv:** Large date in center **Rev:** Value within wreath

Date	Mintage	VG	F	VF	XF	Unc
1914	—	75.00	200	400	500	—

KM# 625b CENTAVO
Lead **Obv:** Large date in center **Rev:** Value within wreath

Date	Mintage	VG	F	VF	XF	Unc
1914	—	20.00	40.00	65.00	90.00	—

KM# 625c CENTAVO
Copper **Obv:** Large date in center **Rev:** Value within wreath

Date	Mintage	VG	F	VF	XF	Unc
1914	—	25.00	50.00	80.00	125	—

KM# 626a CENTAVO
Brass **Obv:** Date **Rev:** Value within wreath

Date	Mintage	VG	F	VF	XF	Unc
1914	—	75.00	100	300	500	—

KM# 626b CENTAVO
Lead **Obv:** Date **Rev:** Value within wreath

Date	Mintage	VG	F	VF	XF	Unc
1914	—	20.00	40.00	70.00	125	—

Note: Varieties in size exist

KM# 621 PESO
23.2000 g., Silver, 39 mm. **Obv:** National arms with continuous border **Rev:** Liberty cap with continuous border

Date	Mintage	VG	F	VF	XF	Unc
1914	—	75.00	150	300	700	1,200

KM# 621a PESO
Copper **Obv:** National arms with continuous border **Rev:** Liberty cap with continuous border **Note:** Varieties exist.

Date	Mintage	VG	F	VF	XF	Unc
1914	—	400	600	2,000	3,000	—

KM# 621b PESO
Brass **Obv:** National arms **Rev:** Liberty cap

Date	Mintage	VG	F	VF	XF	Unc
1914	—	—	2,000	3,000	4,000	—

KM# 627 CENTAVO
Copper, 20 mm. **Obv:** Stars below date **Rev:** Value with retrograde N

Date	Mintage	VG	F	VF	XF	Unc
1914	—	6.00	12.00	30.00	45.00	—

KM# 627a CENTAVO
Lead, 20 mm. **Obv:** Stars below date **Rev:** Value with retrograde N

Date	Mintage	VG	F	VF	XF	Unc
1914	—	20.00	40.00	60.00	125	—

KM# 622 PESO
23.4000 g., Silver, 38.5 mm. **Obv:** National arms with dot and dash border **Rev:** Liberty cap with continuous border **Note:** The so-called 20 Pesos gold Muera Huerta pieces are modern fantasies. Refer to Unusual World Coins, 4th edition, ©2005, KP Books, Inc.

Date	Mintage	VG	F	VF	XF	Unc
1914	—	65.00	120	300	600	1,100

KM# 628 CENTAVO
Aluminum **Obv:** National arms within sprigs **Rev:** Value

Date	Mintage	VG	F	VF	XF	Unc
1914	—	0.65	1.00	2.00	4.00	12.00

KM# 624   CENTAVO
Lead **Obv:** Date **Rev:** Value within wreath **Note:** Cast.

Date	Mintage	VG	F	VF	XF	Unc
1914	—	45.00	75.00	100	200	—

KM# 626   CENTAVO
2.8000 g., Copper, 20 mm. **Obv:** Date **Rev:** Value within wreath **Note:** Weight varies 2.46-2.78g.

Date	Mintage	VG	F	VF	XF	Unc
1914	—	15.00	20.00	40.00	50.00	—

KM# 634b   5 CENTAVOS
6.8900 g., Copper-Nickel, 25.53 mm. **Obv:** National arms above sprigs **Obv. Legend:** REPUBLICA MEXICANA **Rev:** Value **Rev. Legend:** ESTADO DE DURANGO **Edge:** Plain

Date	Mintage	F	VF	XF	Unc	BU
1914	—	25.00	50.00	85.00	135	200

KM# 629   5 CENTAVOS
6.2000 g., Copper, 24 mm. **Obv:** Date above sprigs **Obv. Legend:** ESTADO DE DURANGO **Rev:** Value within designed wreath

Date	Mintage	VG	F	VF	XF	Unc
1914	—	2.00	3.00	8.00	15.00	—

KM# 630   5 CENTAVOS
Copper **Obv:** Date above sprigs **Obv. Legend:** E. DE DURANGO **Rev:** Value within designed wreath

Date	Mintage	VG	F	VF	XF	Unc
1914	—	125	275	450	700	—

KM# 631   5 CENTAVOS
5.0500 g., Copper, 23.5 mm. **Obv:** Date above sprigs **Obv. Legend:** E. DE DURANGO **Rev:** Value within designed wreath

Date	Mintage	VG	F	VF	XF	Unc
1914	—	1.25	3.00	6.00	15.00	—

KM# 631a   5 CENTAVOS
Brass **Obv:** Date above sprigs **Obv. Legend:** E. DE DURANGO **Rev:** Value within designed wreath

Date	Mintage	VG	F	VF	XF	Unc
1914	—	30.00	40.00	70.00	100	—

KM# 631b   5 CENTAVOS
Lead **Obv:** Date above sprigs **Obv. Legend:** E. DE DURANGO **Rev:** Value within designed wreath

Date	Mintage	VG	F	VF	XF	Unc
1914	—	45.00	70.00	100	180	—

KM# 632   5 CENTAVOS
4.6100 g., Copper, 23.5 mm. **Obv:** Date above sprigs **Obv. Legend:** E. DE DURANGO **Rev:** Roman numeral value

Date	Mintage	VG	F	VF	XF	Unc
1914	—	4.00	8.00	20.00	50.00	—

KM# 632a   5 CENTAVOS
Lead **Obv:** Date above sprigs **Obv. Legend:** E. DE DURANGO **Rev:** Roman numeral value

Date	Mintage	VG	F	VF	XF	Unc
1914	—	50.00	75.00	100	150	—

KM# 634   5 CENTAVOS
Brass **Obv:** National arms above sprigs **Obv. Legend:** REPUBLICA MEXICANA **Rev:** Value **Rev. Legend:** ESTADO DE DURANGO

Date	Mintage	VG	F	VF	XF	Unc
1914	—	0.50	1.00	2.50	6.00	10.00

KM# 633   5 CENTAVOS
Lead **Obv:** Three stars below 1914 **Rev:** 5 CVS **Note:** Counterfeits are prevalent in the market

Date	Mintage	VG	F	VF	XF	Unc
1914	—	—	600	2,000	—	—

MEXICO • REVOLUTIONARY

KM# 634a 5 CENTAVOS
Copper **Obv:** National arms above sprigs **Obv.**
Legend: REPUBLICA MEXICANA **Rev:** Value **Rev.**
Legend: ESTADO DE DURANGO **Note:** There are
numerous varieties of these general types of the
Durango 1 and 5 Centavo pieces.

Date	Mintage	VG	F	VF	XF	Unc
1914	—	75.00	125	175	250	—

GUERRERO

Guerrero is a state on the southwestern coast of Mexico. It was one of the areas of operation of Zapata and his
forces in the south of Mexico. The Zapata forces operated
seven different mints in this state. The date ranges were
from 1914 to 1917 and denominations from 2 Centavos to 2
Pesos. Some were cast but most were struck and the rarest
coin of the group is the Suriana 1915 2 Pesos.

EMILIANO ZAPATA
(General Salgado)

REVOLUTIONARY COINAGE

KM# 638 2 CENTAVOS
6.0000 g., Copper, 22 mm. **Obv:** National arms
Obv. Legend: REPUBLICA H MEXICANA **Rev:**
Value within wreath **Note:** Weight varies 5.4-6.03g.

Date	Mintage	VG	F	VF	XF	Unc
1915	—	75.00	125	175	250	—

KM# 635 3 CENTAVOS
Copper, 25 mm. **Obv:** National arms **Obv. Legend:**
REPUBLICA MEXICANA **Rev:** Value within wreath
Note: Weight varies 4.63-6.87g.

Date	Mintage	VG	F	VF	XF	Unc
1915	—	500	1,500	2,000	3,000	—

KM# 636 5 CENTAVOS
Copper, 26 mm. **Obv:** National arms **Rev:** Value
within wreath

Date	Mintage	VG	F	VF	XF	Unc
1915GRO	—	800	1,200	2,000	3,000	—

KM# 637.1 10 CENTAVOS
Copper, 27-28.5 mm. **Obv:** National arms, snake
head ends at L in REPUBLICA **Obv. Legend:**
REPUBLICA MEXICANA **Rev:** Date and value within
wreath **Note:** Size varies.

Date	Mintage	VG	F	VF	XF	Unc
1915GRO	—	600	1,000	1,500	2,000	—

KM# 637.2 10 CENTAVOS
Copper, 27-28.5 mm. **Obv:** National arms, snake
head ends at C in REPUBLICA **Obv. Legend:**
REPUBLICA MEXICANA **Rev:** Value within wreath
Note: Size varies.

Date	Mintage	VG	F	VF	XF	Unc
1915GRO	—	3.00	5.00	8.00	15.00	—

KM# 637.2a 10 CENTAVOS
8.2300 g., Brass, 26 mm. **Obv:** National arms,
snake head ends at C in REPUBLICA **Obv. Legend:**
REPUBLICA MEXICANA **Rev:** Value within wreath

Date	Mintage	VG	F	VF	XF	Unc
1915GRO	—	8.00	15.00	25.00	50.00	—

KM# 637.2b 10 CENTAVOS
Lead **Obv:** National arms, snake head ends at C in
REPUBLICA **Obv. Legend:** REPUBLICA
MEXICANA **Rev:** Value within wreath

Date	Mintage	VG	F	VF	XF	Unc
1915GRO	—	50.00	75.00	175	275	—

KM# 637.3 10 CENTAVOS
Copper **Obv:** National arms, snake head ends
before A in REPUBLICA **Obv. Legend:** REPUBLICA
MEXICANA **Rev:** Date and value within wreath

Date	Mintage	VG	F	VF	XF	Unc
1915.GRO	—	3.00	5.00	8.00	15.00	—

KM# 637.3a 10 CENTAVOS
Brass **Obv:** National arms, snake head ends before
A in REPUBLICA **Obv. Legend:** REPUBLICA
MEXICANA **Rev:** Value and date within wreath

Date	Mintage	VG	F	VF	XF	Unc
1915.GRO	—	12.00	20.00	50.00	100	—

MEXICO - REVOLUTIONARY

KM# 639   25 CENTAVOS
7.5000 g., Silver, 25 mm.   **Obv:** Liberty cap **Obv.**
Legend: Mexicana REPUbLICA **Rev:** Value above
date **Note:** Weight varies 7.41-7.5g.

Date	Mintage	VG	F	VF	XF	Unc
1915	—	125	300	500	900	—

KM# 642   PESO (UN)
Gold With Silver, 30.5-31 mm.   **Obv:** National arms
Obv. Legend: REPUBLICA MEXICANA - H UN
PESO H **Rev:** Liberty cap and rays within sprigs **Rev.**
Legend: "REFORMA.LIBERTAD.JUSTICIA Y LEY"
Rev. Inscription: Oro:0,300 **Note:** Weight varies
12.93-14.66g. Coin is 0.300g fine Gold.

Date	Mintage	VG	F	VF	XF	Unc
1914GRO	—	50.00	75.00	100	180	—
1915GRO	—	600	1,000	1,500	1,850	—

KM# 640   50 CENTAVOS
14.8000 g., Silver, 34 mm.   **Obv:** Liberty cap **Rev:**
Date and value within beaded border **Note:** Weight
varies 14.5-14.8g.

Date	Mintage	VG	F	VF	XF	Unc
1915	—	1,000	2,000	4,500	8,000	—

KM# 641a   PESO (UN)
Copper **Obv:** National arms **Obv. Legend:**
REPUBLICA MEXICANA - H UN PESO **Rev:** Liberty
cap and rays within sprigs **Rev. Legend:** "REFORMA
LIBERTAD JUSTICIA Y LEY"

Date	Mintage	Good	VG	F	VF	XF
1914GRO	—	32.00	80.00	200	500	1,500

KM# 643   2 PESOS (Dos)
Gold With Silver, 38.25-39.6 mm.   **Obv:** National
arms **Obv. Legend:** REPUBLICA MEXICANA **Rev:**
Radiant sun face above high mountain peaks **Rev.**
Legend: "REFORMA LIBERTAD, JUSTICIA Y LEY",
Rev. Inscription: Oro:0,595 **Note:** Many varieties
exist. Coin is 0.595g fine Gold.

Date	Mintage	VG	F	VF	XF	Unc
1914GRO	—	25.00	45.00	125	200	425

KM# 643a   2 PESOS (Dos)
Copper, 38-38.5 mm.   **Obv:** National arms **Obv.**
Legend: REPUBLICA MEXICANA **Rev:** Radiant sun
face above high mountain peaks **Rev. Legend:**
"REFORMA, LIBERTAD, JUSTICIA Y LEY" **Note:**
Size varies.

Date	Mintage	Good	VG	F	VF	XF
1914GRO	—	—	—	1,400	1,800	4,000

KM# 641   PESO (UN)
Gold With Silver, 29-31 mm.   **Obv:** National arms
Obv. Legend: REPUBLICA MEXICANA - H UN
PESO **Rev:** Liberty cap and rays within sprigs **Rev.**
Legend: "REFORMA LIBERTAD JUSTICIA Y LEY"
Rev. Inscription: Oro:0,300 **Note:** Many die
varieties exist. Size varies. Weight varies 10.28-
14.84g. Coin is 0.30g fine Gold.

Date	Mintage	VG	F	VF	XF	Unc
1914GRO	—	20.00	30.00	40.00	85.00	—

KM# 644a   2 PESOS (Dos)
Copper **Obv:** National arms **Obv. Legend:**
REPUBLICA MEXICANA **Rev:** Radiant sun face
above high and low mountain peaks **Rev. Legend:**
"REFORMA, LIBERTAD, JUSTICIA Y LEY"

Date	Mintage	VG	F	VF	XF	Unc
1915GRO	—	400	1,000	1,500	2,500	—

MEXICO · REVOLUTIONARY

KM# 644 2 PESOS (Dos)

Gold With Silver, 39-40 mm. **Obv:** National arms **Obv. Legend:** REPUBLICA MEXICANA **Rev:** Radiant sun face above high and low mountain peaks **Rev. Legend:** "REFORMA, LIBERTAD, JUSTICIA Y LEY" **Rev. Inscription:** Oro:0,595 **Note:** Weight varies 21.71-26.54g. Coin is 0.595g fine Gold.

Date	Mintage	VG	F	VF	XF	Unc
1915GRO	—	65.00	85.00	160	250	550

ATLIXTAC

REVOLUTIONARY COINAGE

KM# 645 10 CENTAVOS

Copper, 27.5-28 mm. **Obv:** National arms **Obv. Legend:** REPUBLICA MEXICANA **Rev:** Value within sprigs **Note:** Size varies. Weight varies 4.76-9.74g.

Date	Mintage	VG	F	VF	XF	Unc
1915	—	3.00	5.00	8.00	15.00	—

KM# 646 10 CENTAVOS

Copper, 27.55-28 mm. **Obv:** National arms **Obv. Legend:** REPUBLICA H MEXICANA **Rev:** Value within sprigs **Note:** Size varies. Weight varies 6.13-7.94g.

Date	Mintage	VG	F	VF	XF	Unc
1915	—	3.00	5.00	8.00	15.00	—

CACAHUATEPEC

REVOLUTIONARY COINAGE

KM# 648 5 CENTAVOS

12.1900 g., Copper, 28 mm. **Obv:** National arms

Obv. Legend: ESTADOS UNIDOS MEXICANOS **Rev:** Value within wreath

Date	Mintage	VG	F	VF	XF	Unc
1917	—	12.00	25.00	40.00	75.00	—

KM# 649 20 CENTAVOS

Silver, 21-23.8 mm. **Obv:** National arms **Obv. Legend:** ESTADOS UNIDOS MEXICANOS **Rev:** Value within sprigs below liberty cap and rays **Note:** Size varies. Weight varies 3.99-6.2g.

Date	Mintage	VG	F	VF	XF	Unc
1917	—	100	200	350	400	—

KM# 650 50 CENTAVOS

13.8000 g., Silver, 30-30.3 mm. **Obv:** National arms **Obv. Legend:** ESTADOS UNIDOS MEXICANOS **Rev:** Value and date within sprigs below Liberty cap **Note:** Size varies. Weight varies 13.45-13.78g.

Date	Mintage	VG	F	VF	XF	Unc
1917	—	25.00	65.00	150	375	—

KM# 651 PESO (UN)

Silver, 38 mm. **Obv:** National arms **Rev:** Liberty cap **Note:** Weight varies 26.81-32.05g.

Date	Mintage	VG	F	VF	XF	Unc
1917 L.V. Go	—	2,000	4,000	8,000	10,000	—

CACALOTEPEC

REVOLUTIONARY COINAGE

KM# 652 20 CENTAVOS
Silver, 22.5 mm. **Obv:** National arms **Obv. Legend:**
ESTADOS UNIDOS MEXICANOS **Rev:** Date and
value within sprigs below Liberty cap and rays **Note:**
Weight varies 3.89-5.73g.

Date	Mintage	VG	F	VF	XF	Unc
1917	—	1,000	1,800	4,000	8,000	—

CAMPO MORADO

REVOLUTIONARY COINAGE

KM# 653 5 CENTAVOS
4.3700 g., Copper, 23.5-24 mm. **Obv:** National
arms **Rev:** Value within wreath **Note:** Size varies.

Date	Mintage	VG	F	VF	XF	Unc
1915 C.M.	—	9.00	15.00	22.50	50.00	—

KM# 654 10 CENTAVOS
Copper, 25.25-26 mm. **Obv:** National arms **Rev:**
Value and date within wreath **Note:** Size varies.
Weight varies. 4.48-8.77g.

Date	Mintage	VG	F	VF	XF	Unc
1915 C.M. GRO	—	6.00	10.00	20.00	30.00	—

KM# 655 20 CENTAVOS
Copper, 28 mm. **Obv:** National arms **Rev:** Date
above star and value within wreath **Note:** Weight
varies 4.48-9g.

Date	Mintage	VG	F	VF	XF	Unc
1915 C.M. GRO	—	15.00	25.00	35.00	50.00	—

KM# 657a 50 CENTAVOS
Billon **Obv:** National arms **Rev:** Date and value
within wreath **Note:** Regular obverse.

Date	Mintage	VG	F	VF	XF	Unc
1915 C.M. GRO	—	200	300	500	1,000	—

KM# 657 50 CENTAVOS
Copper, 30-31 mm. **Obv:** National arms **Rev:** Date
and value within wreath **Note:** Regular obverse. Size
varies. Weight varies 6.49-13.19g.

Date	Mintage	VG	F	VF	XF	Unc
1915 C.M. GRO	—	6.00	10.00	15.00	50.00	—

KM# 656 50 CENTAVOS
Copper, 29-31 mm. **Obv:** National arms **Rev:** Date
and value within wreath **Note:** Size varies. Weight
varies 9.81-16.77g.

Date	Mintage	VG	F	VF	XF	Unc
1915 C.M. GRO	—	12.00	20.00	30.00	60.00	—

KM# 658a PESO (UN)
Brass **Obv:** National arms **Rev:** Liberty cap

Date	Mintage	VG	F	VF	XF
1914 Co Mo Gro Unique	—	—	—	—	10,000

KM# 659 PESO (UN)
Gold With Silver, 30-31 mm. **Obv:** National arms
Rev: Liberty cap within sprigs **Rev. Inscription:**
Oro:0,300 **Note:** Weight varies 12.26-15.81g. Coin
is 0.300g fine Gold.

Date	Mintage	VG	F	VF	XF	Unc
1914 CAMPO Mo	—	20.00	35.00	50.00	85.00	—

MEXICO · REVOLUTIONARY

KM# 658   PESO (UN)
Gold With Silver, 32-32.5 mm. **Obv:** National arms **Rev:** Liberty cap **Rev. Inscription:** Oro:0,300 **Note:** Weight varies 12.42-16.5g. Coin is 0.300g fine Gold.

Date	Mintage	VG	F	VF	XF	Unc
1914 Co Mo Gro	—	500	600	1,000	1,200	—

KM# 660a   2 PESOS (Dos)
Copper   **Obv:** National arms **Rev:** Sun over mountains

Date	Mintage	VG	F	VF	XF	Unc
1915 Co. Mo.	—	—	800	1,000	1,200	—

KM# 662a.1   2 PESOS (Dos)
Copper   **Obv:** National arms **Rev:** Liberty cap

Date	Mintage	VG	F	VF	XF	Unc
1915 C. M. GRO	—	—	—	—	1,200	—

KM# 662a.2   2 PESOS (Dos)
Copper   **Obv:** National arms **Rev:** Liberty cap

Date	Mintage	VG	F	VF	XF
1915 C. M. GRO Unique	—	—	—	—	—

KM# 662   2 PESOS (Dos)
0.5950 g., 1.0000 Gold With Silver 0.0191 oz., 34.5-35 mm. **Obv:** National arms **Rev:** Liberty cap **Note:** Size varies. Weight varies 18.27-20.08g.

Date	Mintage	VG	F	VF	XF	Unc
1915 C. M. GRO	—	25.00	35.00	65.00	125	—

KM# 660   2 PESOS (Dos)
Gold With Silver, 38.9-39 mm. **Obv:** National arms **Rev:** Sun over mountains **Rev. Inscription:** Oro:0,595 **Note:** Weight varies 20.6-26.02g. Coin is 0.595g fine Gold.

Date	Mintage	VG	F	VF	XF	Unc
1915 Co. Mo.	—	18.00	22.00	40.00	85.00	425

CHILPANCINGO

REVOLUTIONARY COINAGE

KM# 663   10 CENTAVOS
2.5200 g., Cast Silver, 18 mm. **Obv:** National arms **Rev:** Sun above value and sprigs

Date	Mintage	VG	F	VF	XF	Unc
1914	—	700	1,000	1,200	1,500	—

Note: Many counterfeits exist

KM# 661   2 PESOS (Dos)
29.4400 g., Gold With Silver, 39 mm. **Obv:** National arms **Rev:** Sun and mountains **Rev. Inscription:** Oro:0,595 **Note:** Coin is 0.595g fine Gold.

Date	Mintage	VG	F	VF	XF	Unc
1915 Co. Mo.	—	2,500	5,000	9,000	15,000	—

KM# 664   20 CENTAVOS
4.9400 g., Cast Silver, 21.5 mm. **Obv:** National arms **Rev:** Sun above value and sprigs

Date	Mintage	VG	F	VF	XF	Unc
1914	—	700	1,000	1,200	1,500	—

Note: Many counterfeits exist

MEXICO - REVOLUTIONARY

SURIANA

REVOLUTIONARY COINAGE

KM# 665   2 PESOS (Dos)
22.9300 g., Gold With Silver, 39 mm. **Obv:** National arms **Rev:** Sun over mountains **Rev. Inscription:** Oro:0,595 **Note:** Coin is 0.595g fine Gold.

Date	Mintage	VG	F	VF	XF	Unc
1915 Rare	—	—	—	20,000	35,000	—

Note: Ira & Larry Goldberg - Millenia sale, 5-08 AU-55 replica. Ponterio & Associates sale, 4-09 VF realized $17,000. Spink America Gerber sale part 2, 6-96 VF realized $16,500

TAXCO

REVOLUTIONARY COINAGE

KM# 667   2 CENTAVOS
Copper, 25.25-26 mm. **Obv:** National arms **Obv. Legend:** EDO.DE.GRO **Rev:** Value within sprigs **Note:** Size varies. Weight varies 6.81-8.55g.

Date	Mintage	VG	F	VF	XF	Unc
1915 O/T	—	25.00	40.00	60.00	90.00	—

KM# 668   5 CENTAVOS
Copper **Obv:** National arms **Obv. Legend:** REPUBLICA H MEXICANA **Rev:** Value within sprigs **Note:** Weight varies 7.13-7.39g.

Date	Mintage	VG	F	VF	XF	Unc
1915	—	10.00	20.00	40.00	80.00	—

KM# 669   10 CENTAVOS
Copper, 27-28 mm. **Obv:** National arms **Obv. Legend:** REPUBLICA H MEXICANA **Rev:** Date and value within sprigs **Note:** Size varies. Weight varies 7.51-8.67g.

Date	Mintage	VG	F	VF	XF	Unc
1915	—	9.00	20.00	35.00	50.00	—

KM# 670   50 CENTAVOS
5.4500 g., Copper, 27-28 mm. **Obv:** National arms with legend in large letters **Rev:** Value within sprigs **Note:** Size varies.

Date	Mintage	VG	F	VF	XF	Unc
1915	—	15.00	25.00	50.00	65.00	—

KM# 671   50 CENTAVOS
Silver, 27.6-28 mm. **Obv:** National arms **Rev:** Sun above value and sprigs **Note:** Size varies. Weight varies 8.95-10.85g.

Date	Mintage	VG	F	VF	XF	Unc
1915	—	25.00	40.00	80.00	150	—

KM# 672a   PESO (UN)
Brass **Obv:** National arms **Rev:** Liberty cap within sprigs

Date	Mintage	VG	F	VF	XF	Unc
1915	—	200	400	600	800	—

KM# 672b   PESO (UN)
Lead **Obv:** National arms **Rev:** Liberty cap within sprigs

Date	Mintage	VG	F	VF	XF	Unc
1915	—	50.00	200	300	500	—

MEXICO · REVOLUTIONARY

KM# 672c PESO (UN)
Copper **Obv:** National arms **Rev:** Liberty cap within sprigs

Date	Mintage	VG	F	VF	XF	Unc
1915	—	200	300	400	650	—

KM# 673 PESO (UN)
11.6000 g., Gold With Silver, 30 mm. **Obv:** National arms **Rev:** Liberty cap within sprigs **Rev. Inscription:** Oro:0,300 **Note:** Coin is 0.300g fine Gold.

Date	Mintage	VG	F	VF	XF	Unc
1915	—	250	500	800	1,000	—

KM# 674 PESO (UN)
Gold With Silver, 30 mm. **Obv:** National arms **Rev:** Liberty cap within sprigs **Rev. Inscription:** Oro:0,300 **Note:** Weight varies 10.51-12.79g. Coin is 0.300g fine Gold.

Date	Mintage	VG	F	VF	XF	Unc
1915	—	100	200	300	550	—

KM# 672 PESO (UN)
Gold With Silver, 30-31 mm. **Obv:** National arms **Rev:** Liberty cap within sprigs **Rev. Inscription:** Oro:0,300 **Note:** Weight varies 30-31g. Coin is 0.300g fine Gold.

Date	Mintage	VG	F	VF	XF	Unc
1915	—	18.00	22.00	50.00	90.00	—

JALISCO

Jalisco is a state on the west coast of Mexico. The few coins made for this state show that the *Army of the North* did not restrict their operations to the northern border states. The coins were made in Guadalajara under the watchful eye of General Dieguez, commander of this segment of Villa's forces.

GUADALAJARA

REVOLUTIONARY COINAGE

KM# 675 CENTAVO
Copper **Obv:** Liberty cap **Rev:** Value

Date	Mintage	VG	F	VF	XF	Unc
1915	—	9.50	15.00	20.00	30.00	—

KM# 675a CENTAVO
Brass **Obv:** Liberty cap **Rev:** Value

Date	Mintage	VG	F	VF	XF	Unc
1915	—	—	—	400	550	—

KM# A676 CENTAVO
Copper **Obv:** Liberty cap **Rev:** Retrograde value **Note:** Varieties exist.

Date	Mintage	VG	F	VF	XF	Unc
1915	—	100	300	600	1,000	—

KM# 676.1 2 CENTAVOS
Copper, 20 mm. **Obv:** Liberty cap **Rev:** Value

Date	Mintage	VG	F	VF	XF	Unc
1915	—	10.00	18.00	20.00	35.00	—

Note: Varieties exist.

KM# 676.2 2 CENTAVOS
Copper **Obv:** Sm. Liberty cap **Rev:** Value

Date	Mintage	VG	F	VF	XF	Unc
1915	—	200	300	500	800	—

KM# 677 5 CENTAVOS
Copper, 24 mm. **Obv:** Liberty cap **Rev:** Value

Date	Mintage	VG	F	VF	XF	Unc
1915	—	6.50	12.00	20.00	40.00	—

MEXICO · REVOLUTIONARY

KM# 677a   5 CENTAVOS
Brass **Obv:** Liberty cap **Rev:** Value

Date	Mintage	VG	F	VF	XF	Unc
1915 rare	—	—	—	—	—	—

KM# 678   10 CENTAVOS
Copper **Obv:** Liberty cap above value and date **Rev:** Crowned shield

Date	Mintage	VG	F	VF	XF	Unc
1915	—	—	—	4,000	8,000	—

KM# A678   PESO
Copper **Obv:** Liberty cap above value and date **Rev:** Crowned shield

Date	Mintage	VG	F	VF	XF	Unc
1915	—	—	—	—	20,000	—

MEXICO, ESTADO DE

Estado de Mexico is a state in central Mexico that surrounds the Federal District on three sides. The issues by the Zapata forces in this state have two distinctions – the Amecameca pieces are the crudest and the Toluca cardboard piece is the most unusual. General Tenorio authorized the crude incuse Amecameca pieces.

AMECAMECA

REVOLUTIONARY COINAGE

KM# 679   5 CENTAVOS
12.5500 g., Brass, 24.5 mm. **Obv:** Legend **Obv. Legend:** EJERCITO CONVENCIONISTA **Rev:** Value above cent sign

Date	Mintage	VG	F	VF	XF	Unc
ND unique	—	—	—	—	—	—

KM# 680   5 CENTAVOS
12.7700 g., Brass, 24.6 mm. **Obv:** National arms above RM **Rev:** Value above cent sign **Note:** Hand stamped.

Date	Mintage	VG	F	VF	XF	Unc
ND	—	300	400	600	800	—

KM# 681a   10 CENTAVOS
Copper **Obv:** National arms above RM **Rev:** Value above cent sign **Note:** Hand stamped.

Date	Mintage	VG	F	VF	XF	Unc
ND	—	75.00	125	225	350	—

KM# 681   10 CENTAVOS
15.0000 g., Brass, 24.5-24.8 mm. **Obv:** National arms above RM **Rev:** Value above cent sign **Note:** Hand stamped. Varieties exist. Size varies.

Date	Mintage	VG	F	VF	XF	Unc
ND	—	60.00	90.00	150	200	—

KM# 682   20 CENTAVOS
Brass, 24-25 mm. **Obv:** National arms above RM **Rev:** Value above cent sign **Note:** Hand stamped. Varieties exist. Size varies. Weight varies 11.34-12.86g.

Date	Mintage	VG	F	VF	XF	Unc
ND	—	15.00	22.50	35.00	60.00	—

KM# 682a   20 CENTAVOS
Copper **Obv:** National arms above RM **Rev:** Value above cent sign **Note:** Hand stamped.

Date	Mintage	VG	F	VF	XF	Unc
ND	—	25.00	50.00	175	250	—

KM# 683   20 CENTAVOS
Copper, 19-20 mm. **Obv:** National arms above A. D. J. **Rev:** Value **Note:** Size varies. Weight varies 3.99-5.35g.

Date	Mintage	VG	F	VF	XF	Unc
ND	—	7.50	12.50	20.00	35.00	—

KM# 683a   20 CENTAVOS
Brass **Obv:** National arms above A. D. J. **Rev:** Value

Date	Mintage	VG	F	VF	XF	Unc
ND	—	—	—	300	500	—

KM# 684   25 CENTAVOS
Brass **Obv:** Legend **Obv. Legend:** EJERCITO

MEXICO - REVOLUTIONARY

CONVENCIONISTA **Rev:** Value above cent sign

Date	Mintage	VG	F	VF	XF	Unc
ND unique	—	—	—	—	—	—

KM# 685 25 CENTAVOS
Copper, 25 mm. **Obv:** National arms above sprigs
Rev: Large numeral value **Note:** Hand stamped.
Many modern counterfeits exist in all metals. Weight
varies 6.32-6.99g.

Date	Mintage	VG	F	VF	XF	Unc
ND	—	15.00	20.00	30.00	40.00	—

KM# 685a 25 CENTAVOS
7.9200 g., Brass, 25 mm. **Obv:** National arms above
sprigs **Rev:** Large numeral value **Note:** Hand stamped.

Date	Mintage	VG	F	VF	XF	Unc
ND	—	—	—	100	300	—

KM# 685b 25 CENTAVOS
Silver **Obv:** National arms above sprigs **Rev:** Large
numeral value **Note:** Hand stamped.

Date	Mintage	VG	F	VF	XF	Unc
ND	—	—	—	300	500	—

KM# 687 50 CENTAVOS
Copper, 23.5-29 mm. **Obv:** National arms above
sprigs **Rev:** Large numeral value **Note:**
Contemporary counterfeit, hand engraved. Size
varies. Weight varies 8.8-10.8g.

Date	Mintage	VG	F	VF	XF	Unc
ND	—	12.00	30.00	50.00	80.00	—

Note: "¢" clears top of 5

KM# 686a 50 CENTAVOS
16.0400 g., Brass, 28.5 mm. **Obv:** National arms

above sprigs **Rev:** Large numeral value **Note:** Hand
stamped.

Date	Mintage	VG	F	VF	XF	Unc
ND	—	100	200	300	400	—

Note: Stem of "¢" above the 5

KM# 686 50 CENTAVOS
Copper, 28-28.5 mm. **Obv:** Eagle over sprays **Note:**
Hand stamped. Size varies.

Date	Mintage	VG	F	VF	XF	Unc
ND	—	8.00	10.00	18.00	30.00	—

TENANCINGO, TOWN
(Distrito Federal Mexico)

REVOLUTIONARY COINAGE

KM# 688.1 2 CENTAVOS
Copper **Obv:** National arms **Rev:** Value within
wreath without TM below value

Date	Mintage	VG	F	VF	XF	Unc
1915	—	—	400	1,000	5,000	—

KM# 688.2 2 CENTAVOS
Copper **Obv:** National arms **Rev:** Value within
wreath with TM below value

Date	Mintage	VG	F	VF	XF	Unc
1915	—	—	400	1,000	5,000	—

KM# 689.1 5 CENTAVOS
Copper, 19 mm. **Obv:** National arms **Rev:** Numeral
value over lined C within wreath **Note:** Weight varies
2.83-2.84g.

Date	Mintage	VG	F	VF	XF	Unc
1915	—	10.00	20.00	40.00	60.00	—

MEXICO · REVOLUTIONARY

KM# 689.2   5 CENTAVOS
Copper, 19 mm.   **Obv:** National arms **Rev:** Numeral
value over solid C within wreath **Note:** Weight varies
2.83-2.84g.

Date	Mintage	VG	F	VF	XF	Unc
1915	—	200	400	800	1,200	—

KM# 690.1   10 CENTAVOS
Copper, 25.25 mm.   **Obv:** National arms **Rev:** Value
over lined C within wreath below date **Note:** Weight
varies 4.27-5.64g.

Date	Mintage	VG	F	VF	XF	Unc
1916	—	10.00	20.00	40.00	80.00	—

KM# 690.2   10 CENTAVOS
Copper, 25.25 mm.   **Obv:** National arms **Rev:** Value
over lined C within wreath **Note:** Weight varies 4.27-
5.64g.

Date	Mintage	VG	F	VF	XF	Unc
1916	—	100	300	500	800	—

KM# 691   20 CENTAVOS
Copper, 27.5-28 mm.   **Obv:** National arms **Rev:**
Value and date above sprigs **Note:** Size varies.
Weight varies 8.51-11.39g.

Date	Mintage	VG	F	VF	XF	Unc
1915	—	25.00	40.00	55.00	85.00	—

TOLUCA CITY
(Distrito Federal Mexico)

REVOLUTIONARY COINAGE

KM# 692.1   5 CENTAVOS
Cardboard grey in color, 27-28 mm.   **Obv:** Crowned
shield within sprigs **Rev:** Banner accross large numeral
value **Note:** Size varies. Weight varies 1.04-1.16g.

Date	Mintage	VG	F	VF	XF	Unc
1915	—	15.00	30.00	50.00	100	—

KM# 692.2   5 CENTAVOS
Cardboard grey in color, 27-28 mm.   **Obv:** Crowned
shield within sprigs **Rev:** Banner accross large numeral
value **Note:** Size varies. Weight varies 1.04-1.16g.

Date	Mintage	VG	F	VF	XF	Unc
1915	—	15.00	30.00	50.00	100	—

COUNTERMARKED COINAGE

KM# 693.1   20 CENTAVOS
Copper, 20 mm.   **Countermark:** 20 within C **Obv:**
National arms **Rev:** Numeral 20 within C and inner
circle within sprigs **Note:** Countermark on 1 Centavo,
KM#415. Varieties exist. Weight varies 2.65-2.95g.

CM Date	Host Date	Good	VG	F	VF	XF
ND(1915)	ND	—	20.00	40.00	55.00	95.00

KM# 693.2   20 CENTAVOS
Copper, 20 mm.   **Countermark:** 20 within C **Obv:**
National arms **Rev:** Numeral 20 within C and inner
circle within 3/4 wreath **Note:** Countermark on 1
Centavo, KM#394.1. Weight varies 2.65-2.95g.

CM Date	Host Date	Good	VG	F	VF	XF
ND(1915)	1904	—	30.00	50.00	90.00	165

MEXICO - REVOLUTIONARY

KM# 694   40 CENTAVOS
5.8600 g., Copper, 24.75-25 mm. **Countermark:**
40 within C **Obv:** National arms **Rev:** Numeral 40
within C and inner circle within wreath **Note:**
Countermark on 2 Centavos, KM#419. Varieties
exist. Size varies.

CM Date	Host Date	Good	VG	F	VF	XF
ND(1915)	ND	—	25.00	60.00	80.00	150

MORELOS

Morelos is a state in south central Mexico, adjoining
the federal district on the south. It was the headquarters of
Emiliano Zapata. His personal quarters were at Tlatizapan
in Morelos. The Morelos coins from 2 Centavos to 1 Peso
were all copper except one type of 1 Peso in silver. The two
operating Zapatista mints in Morelos were Atlihuayan and
Tlaltizapan.

EMILIANO ZAPATA
(Zapatista)

REVOLUTIONARY COINAGE

KM# 695   2 CENTAVOS
Copper, 23 mm. **Obv:** National arms **Obv. Legend:**
E.L. DE MORELOS **Rev:** Value within wreath

Date	Mintage	VG	F	VF	XF	Unc
1915	—	1,000	1,400	1,800	2,750	—

KM# 696   5 CENTAVOS
9.0000 g., Copper, 25.9 mm. **Obv:** National arms
Rev: Value within 3/4 wreath **Rev. Legend:** E. DE
MOR. 1915

Date	Mintage	VG	F	VF	XF	Unc
1915	—	300	500	1,000	3,500	—

KM# 697   10 CENTAVOS
8.6900 g., Copper, 24 mm. **Obv:** National arms
Rev: Value within lined C and wreath

Date	Mintage	VG	F	VF	XF	Unc
1915	—	12.00	20.00	30.00	40.00	—

KM# 699   10 CENTAVOS
Copper **Obv:** National arms **Rev:** Date and value
within wreath **Rev. Legend:** E. DE MOR

Date	Mintage	VG	F	VF	XF	Unc
1915	—	1,000	2,000	3,000	5,000	—

KM# 698   10 CENTAVOS
Copper, 24-24.5 mm. **Obv:** National arms **Rev:**
Value within lined C and wreath with date effaced
from die **Note:** Size varies. Weight varies 4.83-6.8g.

Date	Mintage	VG	F	VF	XF	Unc
ND	—	12.00	20.00	35.00	55.00	—

KM# 700   10 CENTAVOS
Copper, 28 mm. **Obv:** National arms **Rev:** Date and
value within wreath **Rev. Legend:** MOR **Note:**
Weight varies 5.56-8.36g.

Date	Mintage	VG	F	VF	XF	Unc
1916	—	5.00	20.00	40.00	60.00	—

MEXICO · REVOLUTIONARY

KM# 701   20 CENTAVOS
Copper, 23.75-24.75 mm. **Obv:** National arms **Rev:**
Value within lined C and 3/4 wreath **Note:** Size varies.
Weight varies 3.88-4.15g.

Date	Mintage	VG	F	VF	XF	Unc
1915	—	9.00	15.00	25.00	35.00	—

KM# 702   50 CENTAVOS
Copper, 28.8 mm. **Obv:** National arms with MOR
beneath eagle **Rev:** 50C monogram

Date	Mintage	VG	F	VF	XF	Unc
1915	—	300	500	900	1,450	—

KM# 703a   50 CENTAVOS
Brass **Obv:** National arms above sprigs **Rev:** 50C
monogram

Date	Mintage	VG	F	VF	XF	Unc
1915	—	100	200	400	600	—

KM# 706   50 CENTAVOS
Copper, 28 mm. **Obv:** National arms **Rev:** Date
above large numeral value **Rev. Legend:**
REFORMA LIBERTAD JUSTICIA Y LEY

Date	Mintage	VG	F	VF	XF	Unc
1915	—	350	500	950	1,500	—

KM# 703   50 CENTAVOS
Copper, 28-29.5 mm. **Obv:** National arms **Rev:**
Numeral value within lined C and 1/2 wreath **Note:**
This coin exists with a silver and also a brass wash.
Size varies. Weight varies 5.73-13.77g.

Date	Mintage	VG	F	VF	XF	Unc
1915	—	12.50	17.50	30.00	50.00	—

KM# 704   50 CENTAVOS
Copper, 29-30 mm. **Obv:** National arms with
Morelos written below **Rev:** Value within wreath
Note: Size varies. Weight varies 8.56-11.47g.

Date	Mintage	VG	F	VF	XF	Unc
1916	—	12.50	20.00	40.00	60.00	—

KM# 708   PESO (UN)
Silver **Obv:** National arms **Rev:** Liberty cap within
wreath

Date	Mintage	VG	F	VF	XF	Unc
1916	—	450	750	1,150	1,850	—

KM# 708a   PESO (UN)
10.0000 g., Copper, 30 mm. **Obv:** National arms
Rev: Liberty cap within wreath

Date	Mintage	VG	F	VF	XF	Unc
1916	—	500	1,000	1,200	2,300	—

OAXACA

Oaxaca is one of the southern states in Mexico. The
coins issued in this state represent the most prolific series of
the Revolution. Most of the coins bear the portrait of Benito
Juarez, have corded or plain edges and were issued by a
provisional government in the state. The exceptions are the
rectangular 1 and 3 Centavos pieces that begin the series.

PROVISIONAL GOVERNMENT

REVOLUTIONARY COINAGE

KM# 709   CENTAVO (UN)
Copper, 19 mm. **Obv:** Legend within beaded
rectangle **Rev:** Legend within beaded rectangle
Note: Rectangular flan.

Date	Mintage	VG	F	VF	XF	Unc
1915	—	90.00	125	400	650	—

MEXICO · REVOLUTIONARY

KM# 710 CENTAVO (UN)
Copper, 18 mm. **Obv:** Bust left with date flanked by stars below **Rev:** Value within lined C and 1/2 wreath

Date	Mintage	VG	F	VF	XF	Unc
1915	—	12.00	17.50	25.00	40.00	—

KM# 710a CENTAVO (UN)
Brass **Obv:** Head left with date flanked by stars below **Rev:** Value within lined C and 1/2 wreath

Date	Mintage	VG	F	VF	XF	Unc
1915	—	50.00	100	200	350	—

KM# 711 3 CENTAVOS (Tres)
Copper, 24 mm. **Obv:** Legend within rectangle with date below, stars in corners **Rev:** Legend within rectangle with stars in corners **Rev. Legend:** PROVISIO... **Note:** Rectangular flan.

Date	Mintage	VG	F	VF	XF	Unc
1915	—	100	200	400	600	—

KM# 712 3 CENTAVOS (Tres)
Copper **Obv:** Legend within rectangle with date below, stars in corners **Rev:** Legend within rectangle with stars in corners **Rev. Legend:** PROVISI... **Note:** Rectangular flan.

Date	Mintage	VG	F	VF	XF	Unc
1915	—	1,000	3,000	5,000	9,000	—

KM# 713.1 3 CENTAVOS (Tres)
2.2500 g., Copper, 20 mm. **Obv:** Bust left flanked by stars below **Rev:** Value above sprigs **Note:** Without TM below value

Date	Mintage	VG	F	VF	XF	Unc
1915	—	3.00	5.00	12.00	25.00	—

KM# 713.2 3 CENTAVOS (Tres)
2.2500 g., Copper, 20 mm. **Obv:** Bust left flanked by stars below **Rev:** Value above sprigs **Edge:** Plain **Note:** Without TM below value

Date	Mintage	VG	F	VF	XF	Unc
1915	—	—	—	70.00	100	—

KM# 713.3 3 CENTAVOS (Tres)
2.2500 g., Copper, 20 mm. **Obv:** Bust left flanked by stars below **Rev:** Value above sprigs **Note:** With TM below value

Date	Mintage	VG	F	VF	XF	Unc
1915	—	100	200	500	600	—

KM# 714 3 CENTAVOS (Tres)
Copper, 20 mm. **Obv:** Bust left **Rev:** Value above sprigs **Note:** Small 3

Date	Mintage	VG	F	VF	XF	Unc
1915	—	6.00	10.00	15.00	30.00	—

KM# 715 5 CENTAVOS
Copper **Note:** JAN. 15 1915. incuse lettering

Date	Mintage	VG	F	VF	XF	Unc
1915 Rare	—	—	—	—	—	—

KM# 716 5 CENTAVOS
Copper **Obv:** Bust facing within circle **Rev:** Value above sprigs

Date	Mintage	VG	F	VF	XF	Unc
1915	—	—	—	—	8,000	—

KM# 717 5 CENTAVOS
Copper, 22 mm. **Obv:** Low relief bust left with date flanked by stars below **Rev:** Value above sprigs **Note:** Low relief with long, pointed truncation

Date	Mintage	VG	F	VF	XF	Unc
1915	—	1.50	3.00	4.50	12.00	—

KM# 718 5 CENTAVOS
Copper, 22 mm. **Obv:** Raised bust left with date

MEXICO · REVOLUTIONARY

MEXICO - REVOLUTIONARY

flanked by stars below **Rev:** Value above sprigs
Note: Heavy with short unfinished lapels

Date	Mintage	VG	F	VF	XF	Unc
1915	—	1.50	2.50	4.00	12.00	—

KM# 719   5 CENTAVOS
Copper, 22 mm.   **Obv:** Raised bust left with date
flanked by stars below **Rev:** Value above sprigs
Note: Curved bottom

Date	Mintage	VG	F	VF	XF	Unc
1915	—	1.50	2.50	4.00	12.00	—

KM# 720   5 CENTAVOS
Copper, 22 mm.   **Obv:** Bust left with date flanked by
stars below **Rev:** Value above sprigs **Note:** Short
truncation with closed lapels

Date	Mintage	VG	F	VF	XF	Unc
1915	—	1.50	3.00	4.50	12.00	—

KM# 721   5 CENTAVOS
Copper, 22 mm.   **Obv:** Bust left with date flanked by
stars below **Rev:** Value above sprigs **Note:** Short
curved truncation

Date	Mintage	VG	F	VF	XF	Unc
1915	—	1.50	2.50	5.00	12.00	—

KM# 722   10 CENTAVOS
Copper **Obv:** Low relief bust left with date flanked
by stars below **Rev:** Value above sprigs **Note:** Low
relief with long pointed truncation

Date	Mintage	VG	F	VF	XF	Unc
1915	—	1.50	2.50	5.00	12.00	—

KM# 723   10 CENTAVOS
Copper **Obv:** Bust left with date flanked by stars
below **Rev:** Value above sprigs **Note:** Obverse and
reverse legend retrograde.

Date	Mintage	VG	F	VF	XF	Unc
1915 Rare	—	—	—	—	—	—

KM# 724   10 CENTAVOS
Copper, 26.5 mm.   **Obv:** Raised bust left with date
flanked by stars below **Rev:** Value above sprigs
Note: Bold and unfinished truncation using 1 peso
obverse die of km#740

Date	Mintage	VG	F	VF	XF	Unc
1915	—	3.00	5.00	8.00	12.00	—

KM# 725   10 CENTAVOS
Copper, 26.5 mm.   **Obv:** Bust left with date flanked
by stars below **Rev:** Value above sprigs **Note:** Heavy
with short unfinished lapels centered high

Date	Mintage	VG	F	VF	XF	Unc
1915	—	1.50	2.50	4.00	12.00	—

KM# 726   10 CENTAVOS
Copper **Obv:** Raised bust left with date flanked by
stars below **Rev:** Value above sprigs **Note:** Curved
bottom

Date	Mintage	VG	F	VF	XF	Unc
1915	—	1.50	2.50	4.00	12.00	—

KM# 727.1   10 CENTAVOS
Copper **Obv:** Raised bust left with date flanked by
stars below **Rev:** Value above sprigs **Note:** Short
truncation with closed lapels

Date	Mintage	VG	F	VF	XF	Unc
1915	—	1.50	2.50	4.00	12.00	—

KM# 727.2   10 CENTAVOS
Copper **Obv:** Bust left with date flanked by stars
below **Rev:** Value above sprigs **Note:** At present,
only four pieces of this type are known. All are VF or
better; T below bow with M below first leaf

Date	Mintage	VG	F	VF	XF	Unc
1915	—	—	—	500	700	—

KM# 727.3 10 CENTAVOS
Copper **Obv:** Raised bust left flanked by letters GV with date flanked by stars below **Rev:** Value above sprigs **Note:** This counterstamp appears on several different type host 10 cent coins.

Date	Mintage	VG	F	VF	XF	Unc
1915	—	100	200	400	500	—

Note: Letters GV correspond to General Garcia Vigil

KM# 730 20 CENTAVOS
Copper **Obv:** Bust left with date flanked by stars below **Rev:** Value above sprigs **Note:** 5th bust, heavy with short unfinished lapels using 20 Pesos obverse die

Date	Mintage	VG	F	VF	XF	Unc
1915	—	5.00	7.00	10.00	15.00	—

KM# 729.2 20 CENTAVOS
Copper **Counterstamp:** Liberty cap **Obv:** Bust left with date flanked by stars below **Rev:** Value above sprigs **Note:** Counterstamp: Liberty cap and rays with bold unfinished truncation using 1 peso obverse die

Date	Mintage	VG	F	VF	XF	Unc
1915	—	100	150	300	375	—

KM# 728 20 CENTAVOS
Silver, 19 mm. **Obv:** Low relief bust left with date flanked by stars below **Rev:** Value above sprigs **Note:** Low relief with long pointed truncation

Date	Mintage	VG	F	VF	XF	Unc
1915	—	800	2,000	4,000	6,000	—

KM# 728a 20 CENTAVOS
Copper, 19 mm. **Obv:** Bust left with date flanked by stars below **Rev:** Value above sprigs **Note:** Low relief with long pointed truncation

Date	Mintage	VG	F	VF	XF	Unc
1915 Rare	—	—	—	—	—	—

KM# 729.1 20 CENTAVOS
Copper **Obv:** Raised bust left with date flanked by stars below **Rev:** Value above sprigs **Note:** Unfinished truncation using 1 peso obverse die

Date	Mintage	VG	F	VF	XF	Unc
1915	—	1.50	3.00	4.50	12.00	—

KM# 731.1 20 CENTAVOS
Copper, 31 mm. **Obv:** Raised bust left with date flanked by stars below **Rev:** Value above sprigs **Note:** Curved bottom

Date	Mintage	VG	F	VF	XF	Unc
1915	—	1.50	2.50	5.00	12.00	—

KM# 731.2 20 CENTAVOS
Copper **Obv:** Raised bust left with date flanked by stars below **Rev:** Value above sprigs **Note:** Similar to KM#731.1 but with fourth bust.

Date	Mintage	VG	F	VF	XF	Unc
1915 Unique	—	—	—	—	—	—

KM# 732 20 CENTAVOS
Copper **Obv:** Raised bust left with date flanked by stars below **Rev:** Value above sprigs

Date	Mintage	VG	F	VF	XF	Unc
1915	—	1.50	2.50	4.00	12.00	—

MEXICO • REVOLUTIONARY

KM# 733   20 CENTAVOS

Copper **Obv:** Bust left with date flanked by stars below **Rev:** Value above sprigs **Note:** 7th bust, short truncation with closed lapels

Date	Mintage	VG	F	VF	XF	Unc
1915	—	1.50	3.00	4.50	12.00	—

KM# 735   50 CENTAVOS

Silver, 22 mm. **Obv:** Raised bust left with date flanked by stars below **Rev:** Value above sprigs **Note:** Curved bottom

Date	Mintage	VG	F	VF	XF	Unc
1915	—	8.00	15.00	30.00	75.00	—

KM# 734   50 CENTAVOS

4.0700 g., Silver, 22 mm. **Obv:** Raised bust left with date flanked by stars below **Rev:** Value above sprigs **Note:** Heavy with short unfinished lapels

Date	Mintage	VG	F	VF	XF	Unc
1915	—	10.00	20.00	50.00	100	—

KM# 739   50 CENTAVOS

Billon, 28 mm. **Obv:** Raised bust left with date flanked by stars below **Rev:** Value above sprigs **Note:** Ninth bust, high nearly straight truncation

Date	Mintage	VG	F	VF	XF	Unc
1915	—	—	—	—	6,000	—

KM# 739a   50 CENTAVOS

Copper, 28 mm. **Obv:** Raised bust left with date flanked by stars below **Rev:** Value above sprigs **Note:** Ninth bust, high nearly straight truncation

Date	Mintage	VG	F	VF	XF	Unc
1915	—	—	—	—	—	—

KM# 736   50 CENTAVOS

Silver **Obv:** Bust left with date flanked by stars below

Rev: Value above sprigs **Note:** Short truncation with closed lapels

Date	Mintage	VG	F	VF	XF	Unc
1915	—	8.00	15.00	30.00	50.00	—

KM# 737   50 CENTAVOS

4.5400 g., Silver, 22 mm. **Obv:** Bust left with date flanked by stars below **Rev:** Value above sprigs **Note:** Short truncation with pronounced curve

Date	Mintage	VG	F	VF	XF	Unc
1915	—	10.00	15.00	25.00	50.00	—

KM# 741   PESO (UN)

Silver **Obv:** Raised bust with date flanked by stars below **Rev:** Value above sprigs **Note:** Fifth bust, heavy with short unfinished lapels, centered high

Date	Mintage	VG	F	VF	XF	Unc
1915	—	8.00	10.00	35.00	45.00	—

KM# 740.1   PESO (UN)

Silver, 26 mm. **Obv:** Raised bust left with date flanked by stars below **Rev:** Written value above sprigs **Note:** Fourth bust with heavy unfinished truncation

Date	Mintage	VG	F	VF	XF	Unc
1915	—	7.00	12.00	30.00	50.00	—

KM# 740.2   PESO (UN)

Silver, 26 mm. **Obv:** Raised bust left with date flanked by stars below **Rev:** Written value above sprigs **Note:** Fourth bust with heavy unfinished truncation w/TM.

Date	Mintage	VG	F	VF	XF	Unc
1915	—	150	300	400	650	—

KM# 743   PESO (UN)

Silver **Obv:** Low relief bust left with date flanked by stars below **Rev:** Value above sprigs **Note:** Seventh bust, short truncation with closed lapels

Date	Mintage	VG	F	VF	XF	Unc
1915	—	10.00	20.00	30.00	50.00	—

KM# 743a   PESO (UN)
Silver **Obv:** Low relief bust left with date flanked by stars below **Rev:** Value above sprigs **Note:** Seventh bust, short truncation with closed lapels

Date	Mintage	VG	F	VF	XF	Unc
1915	—	35.00	75.00	150	200	—

KM# 742   PESO (UN)
Silver **Obv:** Low relief bust left with date flanked by stars below **Rev:** Value above sprigs **Note:** Sixth bust; Curved bottom line

Date	Mintage	VG	F	VF	XF	Unc
1915	—	10.00	15.00	30.00	50.00	—

KM# 742a   PESO (UN)
Copper **Obv:** Low relief bust left with date flanked by stars below **Rev:** Value above sprigs **Note:** Sixth bust; Curved bottom line

Date	Mintage	VG	F	VF	XF	Unc
1915	—	—	—	—	600	—

KM# 744   2 PESOS (Dos)
Silver, 30 mm. **Obv:** Raised bust left with date flanked by stars below **Rev:** Value above sprigs **Note:** Fourth bust, using 1 peso obverse die

Date	Mintage	VG	F	VF	XF	Unc
1915	—	18.00	28.00	45.00	75.00	—

KM# 744a   2 PESOS (Dos)
Copper **Obv:** Raised bust left with date flanked by stars below **Rev:** Value above sprigs **Note:** Fourth bust, using 1 peso obverse die

Date	Mintage	VG	F	VF	XF	Unc
1915 Rare	—	—	—	—	—	—

KM# 745   2 PESOS (Dos)
Gold With Silver, 22 mm. **Obv:** Low relief bust left with date flanked by stars below **Rev:** Value above sprigs **Note:** 0.9020 Silver, 0.0100 Gold. Fifth bust, curved bottom 2 over pesos

Date	Mintage	VG	F	VF	XF	Unc
1915	—	15.00	25.00	50.00	90.00	—

KM# 745a   2 PESOS (Dos)
Copper **Obv:** Low relief bust left with date flanked by stars below **Rev:** Value above sprigs **Note:** Fifth bust, curved bottom 2 over pesos

Date	Mintage	VG	F	VF	XF	Unc
1915	—	75.00	100	200	400	—

KM# A746   2 PESOS (Dos)
Copper **Obv:** Raised bust left with date flanked by stars below **Rev:** Balance scale below liberty cap **Note:** Seventh bust, short truncation with closed lapels

Date	Mintage	VG	F	VF	XF	Unc
1915 Unique	—	—	—	—	—	—

KM# 746   2 PESOS (Dos)
Silver **Obv:** Raised bust left with date flanked by stars below **Rev:** Balance scale below liberty cap

Date	Mintage	VG	F	VF	XF	Unc
1915	—	22.00	28.00	50.00	75.00	—

KM# A747   2 PESOS (Dos)
Silver **Obv:** Bust left with date flanked by stars below **Rev:** Balance scale below liberty cap **Note:** Obverse die is free hand engraved.

Date	Mintage	VG	F	VF	XF	Unc
1915	—	—	—	185	275	—

KM# 746a   2 PESOS (Dos)
Copper **Obv:** Bust left with date flanked by stars below **Rev:** Balance scale below liberty cap

Date	Mintage	Good	VG	F	VF	XF
1915	—	—	150	200	600	1,000

MEXICO · REVOLUTIONARY

KM# 747.1   2 PESOS (Dos)
13.4400 g., Silver, 33 mm.   **Obv:** Bust left with date flanked by stars below **Rev:** Balance scale below liberty cap

Date	Mintage	VG	F	VF	XF	Unc
1915	—	20.00	25.00	55.00	95.00	—

KM# 747.2   2 PESOS (Dos)
13.4400 g., Silver, 33 mm.   **Obv:** Bust left with date flanked by stars below **Rev:** Balance scale below liberty cap

Date	Mintage	VG	F	VF	XF	Unc
1915	—	22.00	28.00	60.00	100	—

KM# 747.3   2 PESOS (Dos)
13.4400 g., Silver, 33 mm.   **Obv:** Bust left with date flanked by stars below **Rev:** Balance scale below liberty cap

Date	Mintage	VG	F	VF	XF	Unc
1915	—	20.00	30.00	60.00	100	—

KM# 748   2 PESOS (Dos)
0.9020 Silver, 22 mm.   **Obv:** Bust left with date flanked by stars below **Rev:** Value above sprigs

Date	Mintage	VG	F	VF	XF	Unc
1915	—	20.00	30.00	60.00	100	—

KM# 749   2 PESOS (Dos)
Silver   **Obv:** Head left with date flanked by stars below **Rev:** Value above sprigs

Date	Mintage	VG	F	VF	XF	Unc
1915 Unique	—	—	—	—	3,000	—

KM# 751   5 PESOS
16.7700 g., Silver, 30 mm.   **Obv:** Low relief bust left with date flanked by stars below **Rev:** Value above sprigs **Note:** Seventh bust, short truncation with closed lapels

Date	Mintage	VG	F	VF	XF	Unc
1915	—	50.00	80.00	175	275	—

KM# 751a   5 PESOS
Copper   **Obv:** Low relief bust left with date flanked by stars below **Rev:** Value above sprigs **Note:** Seventh bust, short truncation with closed lapels

Date	Mintage	VG	F	VF	XF	Unc
1915	—	125	200	300	800	—

KM# 750   5 PESOS
0.1750 Gold, 19 mm.   **Obv:** Bust left **Rev:** Value above sprigs **Note:** Third bust, heavy, with short unfinished lapels

Date	Mintage	VG	F	VF	XF	Unc
1915	—	175	225	350	550	900

KM# 750a   5 PESOS
Copper   **Obv:** Bust left **Rev:** Value above sprigs **Note:** Third bust, heavy, with short unfinished lapels

Date	Mintage	VG	F	VF	XF	Unc
1915 Unique	—	—	—	—	—	—

KM# A752   10 PESOS
0.1500 Gold   **Obv:** Bust left with date flanked by stars below **Rev:** Value above sprigs

Date	Mintage	VG	F	VF	XF	Unc
1915 Rare	—	—	—	—	—	—

KM# 752   10 PESOS
0.1750 Gold, 23 mm.   **Obv:** Bust left with date flanked by stars below **Rev:** Value above sprigs

Date	Mintage	VG	F	VF	XF	Unc
1915	—	225	350	450	650	1,000

KM# 752a   10 PESOS
Copper   **Obv:** Bust left with date flanked by stars below **Rev:** Value above sprigs

Date	Mintage	VG	F	VF	XF	Unc
1915	—	800	1,500	2,000	4,000	—

KM# 753   20 PESOS
0.1750 Gold   **Obv:** Bust left with date flanked by

stars below **Rev:** Value above sprigs

Date	Mintage	VG	F	VF	XF	Unc
1915	—	400	500	800	1,000	1,500

KM# 754 20 PESOS
0.1750 Gold, 27 mm. **Obv:** Bust left with date flanked by stars below **Rev:** Value above sprigs

Date	Mintage	VG	F	VF	XF	Unc
1915	—	250	450	650	950	1,700

KM# A753 20 PESOS
0.1500 Gold **Obv:** Bust left with date flanked by stars below **Rev:** Value above sprigs **Note:** Fourth bust

Date	Mintage	VG	F	VF	XF	Unc
1915 Unique	—	—	—	—	—	—

KM# 755 60 PESOS
50.0000 g., 0.8590 Gold 1.3808 oz. AGW **Obv:** Head left within 3/4 wreath **Rev:** Balance scale below liberty cap **Edge:** Reeded

Date	Mintage	F	VF	XF	Unc	BU
1916 Rare	—	—	10,000	20,000	28,000	—

KM# 755a 60 PESOS
Silver **Obv:** Head left within 3/4 wreath **Rev:** Balance scales below liberty cap **Edge:** Reeded

Date	Mintage	F	VF	XF	Unc	BU
1916	—	—	—	—	15,000	—

KM# 755b 60 PESOS
Copper **Obv:** Head left within 3/4 wreath **Rev:** Balance scales below liberty cap **Edge:** Plain

Date	Mintage	F	VF	XF	Unc	BU
1916	—	—	—	2,000	3,000	—

PUEBLA

A state of central Mexico. Puebla was a state that occasionally saw Zapata forces active within its boundaries. Also active, and an issuer of coins, was the Madero brigade who issued coins with their name two years after Madero's death. The state issue of 2, 5, 10 and 20 Centavos saw limited circulation and recent hoards have been found of some values.

CHICONCUAUTLA
Madero Brigade

REVOLUTIONARY COINAGE

KM# 756 10 CENTAVOS
6.7300 g., Copper, 27 mm. **Obv:** Date below national arms **Rev:** Letters X and C entwined

Date	Mintage	VG	F	VF	XF	Unc
1915	—	7.50	12.50	17.50	25.00	—

KM# 758 20 CENTAVOS
Copper, 28 mm. **Obv:** Date below national arms **Rev:** Value

Date	Mintage	VG	F	VF	XF	Unc
1915	—	2.50	4.00	6.50	12.00	—

KM# 757 20 CENTAVOS
Copper, 28 mm. **Obv:** Date below national arms **Rev:** Value **Note:** Varieties exist.

Date	Mintage	VG	F	VF	XF	Unc
1915	—	2.50	4.00	6.50	12.00	—

TETELA DEL ORO Y OCAMPO

REVOLUTIONARY COINAGE

KM# 759   2 CENTAVOS
Copper, 16 mm. **Obv:** National arms above date
Rev: Value

Date	Mintage	VG	F	VF	XF	Unc
1915	—	12.50	20.00	28.00	45.00	—
1915 Restrikes	—	—	1.00	1.50	2.00	—

KM# 760   2 CENTAVOS
Copper, 20 mm. **Obv:** National arms within beaded circle **Rev:** Value within beaded circle **Rev. Legend:** E. DE PU.

Date	Mintage	VG	F	VF	XF	Unc
1915	—	15.00	25.00	35.00	75.00	—

KM# 761   2 CENTAVOS
Copper, 20 mm. **Obv:** National arms within beaded circle **Rev:** Value within beaded circle **Rev. Legend:** E. DE PUE.

Date	Mintage	VG	F	VF	XF	Unc
1915	—	9.00	20.00	25.00	50.00	—

KM# 762   5 CENTAVOS
Copper, 21 mm. **Obv:** National arms within beaded circle **Rev:** Value within beaded circle

Date	Mintage	VG	F	VF	XF	Unc
1915	—	100	200	300	400	—

KM# 764   20 CENTAVOS
Copper, 24 mm. **Obv:** National arms **Rev:** Value above sprigs

Date	Mintage	VG	F	VF	XF	Unc
1915	—	50.00	100	150	225	—

SINALOA

A state along the west coast of Mexico. The cast pieces of this state have been attributed to two people - Generals Rafael Buelna and Juan Carrasco. The cap and rays 8 Reales is usually attributed to General Buelna and the rest of the series to Carrasco. Because of their crude nature it is questionable whether separate series or mints can be determined.

BUELNA / CARRASCO

CAST COINAGE

REVOLUTIONARY

KM# 766   50 CENTAVOS
Cast Silver, 29-31 mm. **Obv:** National arms **Rev:** Numeral value within wreath **Note:** Sand molded using regular 50 Centavos, KM#445. Size varies. Weight varies 12.81-14.8g.

Date	Mintage	Good	VG	F	VF	XF
ND(1905-1918)	—	200	300	—	—	—

COUNTERMARKED COINAGE

REVOLUTIONARY

These are all crude sand cast coins using regular coins to prepare the mold. Prices below give a range for how much of the original coin from which the mold was prepared is visible.

KM# 765   20 CENTAVOS
Cast Silver **Obv:** National arms within beaded circle

MEXICO · REVOLUTIONARY

Rev: Value within beaded circle **Note:** Sand molded using regular 20 Centavos.

CM Date	Host Date	Good	VG	F	VF
ND(ca.1915)	ND(1898-1905)	200	300	—	—

KM# 767 50 CENTAVOS
Cast Silver **Countermark:** G.C. **Obv:** National arms with additional countermark **Rev:** Value and date within wreath with liberty cap above **Note:** Sand molded using regular 50 Centavos, KM#445.

CM Date	Host Date	Good	VG	F	VF	XF
ND	ND(1905-1918)	100	150	200	300	—

KM# 768.1 PESO
Cast Silver, 38.8-39 mm. **Note:** Sand molded using regular 8 Reales, KM#377. Size varies. Weight varies 26-33.67g.

CM Date	Host Date	Good	VG	F	VF
ND(ca.1915)	ND(1824-97)	20.00	35.00	45.00	60.00

KM# 768.2 PESO
Cast Silver, 38.5-39 mm. **Countermark:** G.C. **Obv:** With additional countermark **Note:** Sand molded using regular 8 Reales, KM#377. Size varies. Weight varies 26-33.67g.

CM Date	Host Date	Good	VG	F	VF
ND(ca.1915)	ND(1824-97)	25.00	45.00	100	150

KM# 770 PESO
Cast Silver, 38.5 mm. **Countermark:** G.C **Obv:** National arms with additional countermark **Rev:** Liberty cap with additional countermark **Note:** Sand molded using regular Peso, KM#409.

CM Date	Host Date	Good	VG	F	VF
ND(ca.1915)	ND(1898-1909)	35.00	65.00	150	185

KM# 769 PESO
Cast Silver **Note:** Sand molded using regular Peso, KM#409.

CM Date	Host Date	Good	VG	F	VF
	ND(1898-1909)	15.00	25.00	40.00	55.00

THE HOBBY LEADER IN THE WORLD OF NUMISMATICS

KRAUSE PUBLICATIONS

MAGAZINES

Our veteran editors bring you such respected publications as Numismatic News, World Coin News, Bank Note Reporter and Coins Magazine.

BOOKS

Our expert price analysts publish must-have reference books like the Standard Catalog line of world coin and paper money books, as well as U.S. Coin Digest and North American Coins & Prices.

DIGITAL PRODUCTS

Our latest products allow you to enjoy price guides as never before, with greater portability, photo enlargement, and individual page printing capabilities.

ONLINE

NumisMaster.com and NumismaticNews.com bring you the most up-to-date industry news and pricing, and our weekly email newsletters are must-reads.

SHOWS

Our Chicago Paper Money Expo and Chicago International Coin Fair make Chicago a must-stop for dealers and collectors.

A wealth of information awaits you at NumisMaster.com and ShopNumisMaster.com

Krause Publications, 700 E. State St, Iola, WI 54990-0001 • 855-842-5272 • ShopNumisMaster.com